CONTENTS

Buckland-Tout-Saints, Devon

Cover Picture: Buckland Manor, Worcestershire** **(see page 141)

HILDON
NATURAL MINERAL WATER
ESTABLISHED
1989
WELL... DE GUSTIBUS
NON EST DISPUTANDUM
HILDON
AN ENGLISH
NATURAL MINERAL WATER
OF EXCEPTIONAL TASTE
DELIGHTFULLY STILL
Composition in accordance with the results of the officially
recognized analysis 26 March 1992.
Hildon Ltd., Broughton, Hampshire SO20 8DG, ☎ 01794-301 747
WELL... DE GUSTIBUS
NON EST DISPUTANDUM
AN ENGLISH
GENTLY CARBONATED
recognized analysis 26 March 1992.
Hildon Ltd., Broughton, Hampshire SO20 8DG, ☎ 01794 - 301 747

Key to Symbols / Signification des Symboles / Zeichenerklärung

13	Total number of rooms	Nombre de chambres	Anzahl der Zimmer
MasterCard	MasterCard accepted	MasterCard accepté	MasterCard akzeptiert
VISA	Visa accepted	Visa accepté	Visa akzeptiert
American Express	American Express accepted	American Express accepté	American Express akzeptiert
	Diners Club accepted	Diners Club accepté	Diners Club akzeptiert
	Quiet location	Lieu tranquille	Ruhige Lage
	Access for wheelchairs to at least one bedroom and public rooms	Accès handicapé dans au moins une chambre et salles communes	Zugang für Behinderte (in mind. einem Zimmer und Aufenthaltsräumen)

(The 'Access for wheelchairs' symbol ( ) does not necessarily indicate that the property fulfils National Accessible Scheme grading)

	Chef-patron	Chef-patron	Chef-patron
M 20	Meeting/conference facilities with maximum number of delegates	Salle(s) de conférences – capacité maximale	Seminar- und Tagungsräumlichkeiten – max. Kapazität
8	Children welcome, with minimum age where applicable	Enfants bienvenus (âge minimum indiqué)	Kinder willkommen – Mindestalter in Klammern
	Dogs accommodated in rooms or kennels	Chiens autorisés	Hunde erlaubt
	At least one room has a four-poster bed	Lit à baldaquin dans au moins 1 chambre	Mindestens 1 Zimmer mit Himmelbett
	Cable/satellite TV in all bedrooms	TV câblée/satellite dans toutes les chambres	Kabel-/Satellitenfernsehen in allen Zimmern
	CD player in bedrooms	Lecteur CD dans toutes les chambres	CD-Player in bedrooms
VCR	Video players in bedrooms	Lecteur video dans toutes les chambres	Videogerät in allen Zimmern
	ISDN/Modem point in all bedrooms	Ligne ISDN/point modem dans toutes les chambres	ISDN-/Modemanschluss in allen Zimmern
	At least one non-smoking bedroom	Au moins une chambre non-fumeur	Mindestens 1 Zimmer für Nichtraucher
	Lift available for guests' use	Ascenseur	Fahrstuhl
	Indoor swimming pool	Piscine couverte	Hallenbad
	Outdoor swimming pool	Piscine en plein air	Freibad
	Tennis court at hotel	Tennis à l'hôtel	Hoteleigener Tennisplatz
	Croquet lawn at hotel	Croquet à l'hôtel	Krocketrasen
	Fishing can be arranged	Pêche peut être organisé	Angeln möglich
	Golf course on site or nearby, which has an arrangement with the hotel allowing guests to play	Golf sur site ou à proximité (Arrangement avec l'hôtel)	Hoteleigener oder nahegelegener Golfplatz (Arrangement mit Hotel)
	Shooting can be arranged	Tir peut être organisé	Schiessen möglich
	Riding can be arranged	Équitation possible	Reiten möglich
H	Hotel has a helicopter landing pad	Hélipad	Hubschrauberlandeplatz
	Licensed for wedding ceremonies	Licencé pour cérémonies de mariage	Konzession für Eheschliessungen

ATLANTIC
OCEAN
SCOTLAND
Page 424
NORTH
SEA
NORTHERN
IRELAND
Page 398
IRISH
SEA
REPUBLIC
OF
IRELAND
Page 398
ENGLAND
Pages 71-74
WALES
Page 466
London
Page 16
CELTIC
SEA
THE CHANNEL ISLANDS
Page 62
ALDERNEY
GUERNSEY
SARK
JERSEY

FOREWORD

Lainston House Hotel, Hampshire

We are pleased to present you with our latest Recommendations for this, the 20th edition of **'Johansens Recommended Hotels – Great Britain & Ireland'**.

Since Derek Johansen published the first edition in 1983, our Guide to the British Isles and Ireland has continued to grow in quality rather than in volume. Today, we are pleased to be able to recommend 459 fine hotels, some of which have been with us from the beginning, but all of which have changed or even reinvented themselves to meet your needs as a guest in the 21st century. The facilities available at each hotel continue to expand; they are represented by the symbols on each entry page for easy reference.

The word 'Recommendation' in the title of our Guides reflects the critical contribution made each year by our team of inspectors. Many of them have worked with us for over ten years, and all have a wealth of experience from which you can benefit when you choose to stay at a Johansens Recommendation. This year we are delighted to welcome some exciting new hotels to the Johansens family as well as many more traditional favourites, but constant selectivity inevitably means that others are no longer included for recommendation in this edition.

If you have any comments regarding your stay at any of our Recommendations, please use the Guest Survey Reports provided at the back of this Guide. More information about our Recommendations can be obtained by using the Brochure Request Service, and if you would like to receive more copies of our Guides for yourself or as a gift, Order Forms are also provided.

We hope that you enjoy the wonderful hotels recommended in this edition; they have all been chosen for their ability to offer a unique experience. Remember to mention Johansens when you make your reservation and again when you arrive – you will be made to feel most welcome.

Andrew Warren
Managing Director

Published by
Johansens Limited, Therese House, Glasshouse Yard, London EC1A 4JN
Tel: +44 (0)20 7566 9700 Fax: +44 (0)20 7490 2538
Find Johansens on the Internet at: **www.johansens.com**
E-Mail: info@johansens.com

Publishing Director: Stuart Johnson
P.A. to Publishing Director: Laura Kerry
Regional Inspectors: Jean Branham, Geraldine Bromley, Robert Bromley, Julie Dunkley, Pat Gillson, Martin Greaves, Joan Henderson, Marie Iversen, Pauline Mason, John O'Neill, Mary O'Neill, Fiona Patrick, John Sloggie, David Wilkinson
Production Director: Daniel Barnett
Production Controller: Kevin Bradbrook
Senior Designer: Michael Tompsett
Editorial Manager: Stephanie Cook
Copywriters: Norman Flack, Debra Giles, Rozanne Paragon, Leonora Sandwell
Sales and Marketing Director: Tim Sinclair
Marketing Executive: Adam Crabtree
Sales Administrator: Susan Butterworth
Internet Executive: Tamsin Appleton
P.A. to Managing Director : Joanne Jones

Managing Director: Andrew Warren

Johansens is a subsidiary of the Daily Mail & General Trust plc

ISBN 1 903665 01 9

Printed in England by St Ives plc
Colour origination by Graphic Facilities

Distributed in the UK and Europe by Solo Communications UK) Ltd, Sandwich & Portfolio, Greenford (bookstores). In North America by Hobsons DMI, Cincinnati (direct sales) and Hunter Publishing, New Jersey (bookstores). In Australia and New Zealand by Bookwise International, Wingfield, South Australia. In Southern Africa by Liquid Amber Distributions, Gillitts, South Africa.

HOW TO USE THIS GUIDE

If you want to identify a Hotel whose name you already know, look for it in the Regional Indexes on pages 509–518.

If you want to find a Hotel in a particular area you can

- Turn to the Maps on pages 4, 16, 62, 71–74, 398, 424 and 466.
- Search the Indexes on pages 511–520.
- Look for the Town or Village where you wish to stay in the main body of the Guide. This is divided into Countries. Place names in each Country appear at the head of the pages in alphabetical order.

The Indexes list the Hotels by Countries and by Counties, they also show those with amenities such as wheelchair access, conference facilities, swimming, golf, etc. (Please note some recent Local Government Boundary changes).

The Maps cover all regions including London. Each Hotel symbol (a blue circle) relates to a Hotel in this guide situated in or near the location shown.

If you cannot find a suitable hotel near where you wish to stay, you may decide to choose one of Johansens Recommended Country Houses, Small Hotels or Traditional Inns as an alternative. These smaller establishments are all listed by place names on pages 493–498.

Properties which did not feature in our last (2001) edition are identified with a "NEW" symbol at the top of the page.

Rates are correct at the time of going to press but always should be checked with the hotel before you make your reservation.

We occasionally receive letters from guests who have been charged for accommodation booked in advance but later cancelled. Readers should be aware that by making a reservation with a hotel, either by telephone, e-mail or in writing, they are entering into a legal contract. A hotelier under certain circumstances is entitled to make a charge for accommodation when guests fail to arrive, even if notice of the cancellation is given.

All guides are obtainable from bookshops or by Johansens Freephone 0800 269397 or by using the order coupons on pages 523.

JOHANSENS AWARDS FOR EXCELLENCE 2001

The Winners of the 2001 Awards for Excellence at The Dorchester

The Johansens 2001 Awards for Excellence were presented at the Johansens Annual Dinner held at The Dorchester on November 13th, 2000.

Johansens Most Excellent Country Hotel Award:
Ashford Castle – Cong, Ireland

Johansens Most Excellent City Hotel Award:
The Howard – Edinburgh, Scotland

Johansens Most Excellent Country House Award:
Bibury Court – Bibury, Gloucestershire, England

Johansens Most Excellent Traditional Inn Award:
Boar's Head Hotel – Ripley Castle, Ireland

Johansens Most Excellent London Hotel Award:
The Milestone

Johansens Most Excellent Value for Money Award:
White Vine House – Rye, West Sussex, England

Johansens Most Excellent Service Award:
The Old Rectory – Thorpe St Andrew, Norfolk, England

Johansens Most Excellent Restaurant Award:
Fischer's – Baslow, Derbyshire, England

Johansens – Europe: The Most Excellent City Hotel:
Hotel Hoffmeister – Prague, Czech Republic

Johansens – Europe: The Most Excellent Country Hotel:
La Posada del Torcal – Málaga, Spain

Johansens – Europe: The Most Excellent Waterside Resort:
Quinta da Bela Vista – Madeira, Portugal

Johansens – North America: Most Excellent Hotel:
Vanderbilt Hall – Newport, Rhode Island, USA

Johansens – North America: Most Excellent Inn:
Gingerbread Mansion Inn – Ferndale, California, USA

Johansens Special Award for Excellence:
Mago Estate Hotel – St Lucia, West Indies

Knight Frank Award for Outstanding Excellence and Innovation:
Giuseppe Pecorelli

Barrels & Bottles Wine List of the Year Award:
Recommended Hotels Great Britain & Ireland:
The Cottage in the Wood – Malvern Wells, Worcestershire, England

Recommended Country Houses & Small Hotels Great Britain & Ireland:
The Pend – Dunkeld, Perthshire, Scotland

Recommended Traditional Inns, Hotels & Restaurants Great Britain:
Fence Gate Inn – Burnley, Lancashire, England

AWARD WINNER 2001

Ashford Castle, Cong, Ireland
Winner of the 2001 Johansens Most Excellent Country Hotel Award

As one of the world's greatest resort properties, it was with pride that we accepted the Johansens Award for the Most Excellent Country Hotel 2001. To be acknowledged in this way is a tribute to the dedication of everyone working at Ashford Castle to exceed on the expectations of our guests. We would therefore like to extend a warm thank you to those involved in the decision making process.

We have been members of Johansens for many years, and like most who control marketing budgets, I monitor all memberships to determine their benefits to the Castle. Consistently, our clients refer to the Johansens book and therefore we know it delivers on its promise, particularly from the UK market place. Ashford Castle has become a partner in success with Johansens, and this award can only help deliver even more clients than in the past.

Why were we chosen from some of those other outstanding properties featured in the guide? Perhaps it was because we are an all-inclusive 350-acre estate dating from 1228, offering a wide range of sporting activities which include fishing, golfing, tennis, archery, clay-pigeon shooting and Ireland's only school of falconry? Perhaps it was our international reputation for excellent food? Perhaps it was our health and leisure facilities or beauty treatments? Or nightly entertainment through dinner, followed by our Irish-style evenings in the Dungeon Bar? While our impressive guest list will reveal Kings, Queens, captains of industry, international film stars and other such celebrities, we believe that Ashford Castle extends the same warmth of welcome to all our guests, and provides a "stress free" zone, which makes the destination unique, and this is probably one of the main reasons why Johansens chose to honour Ashford Castle with this award.

Whatever the reason, we will continue to support the Johansens brand because it has proven to be the best of all the rest.

Paula Carroll
Director of Sales and Marketing

For full entry, please turn to page 402.

AWARD 2001 J WINNER

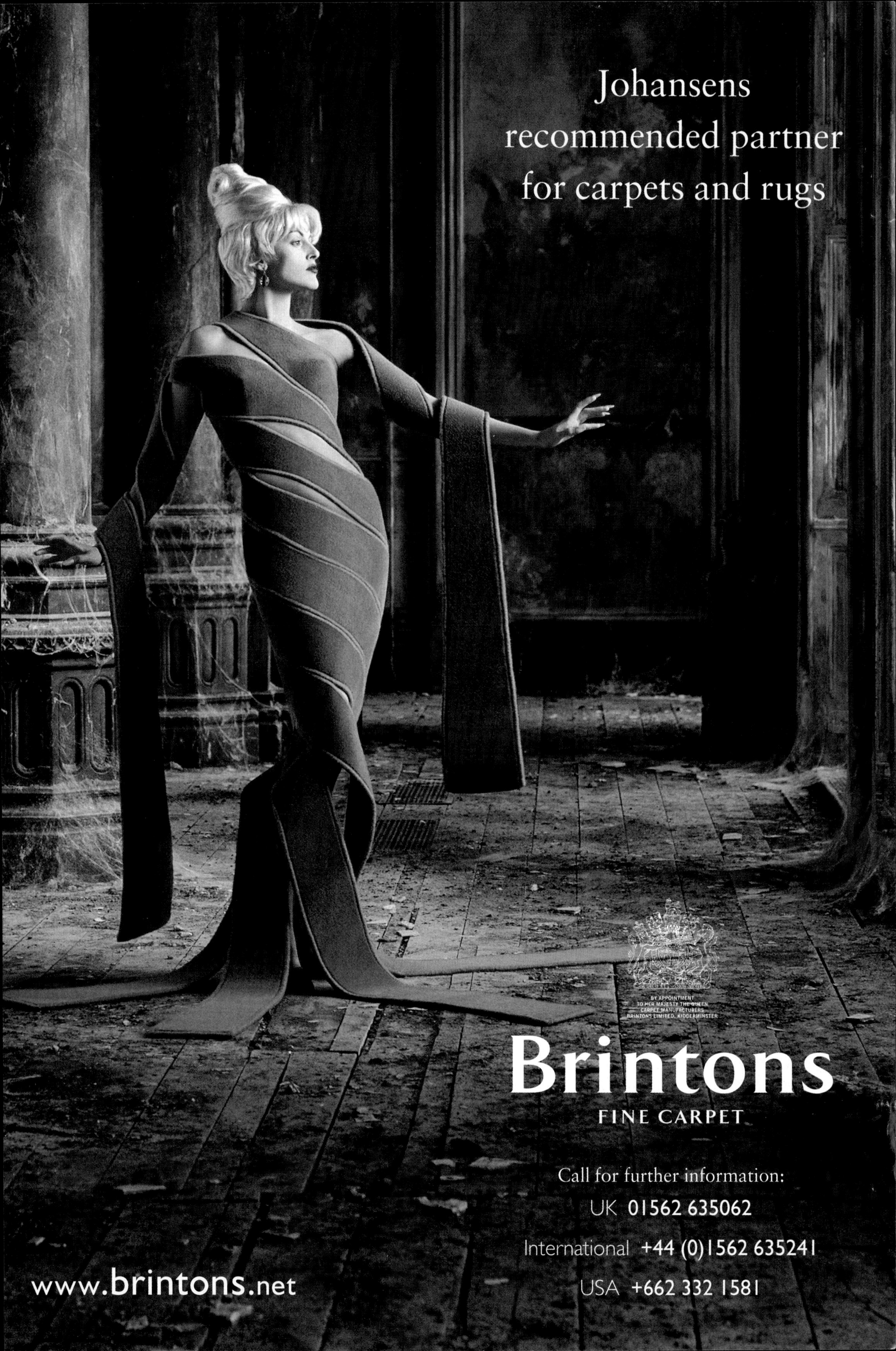
Johansens
recommended partner
for carpets and rugs
BY APPOINTMENT
TO HER MAJESTY THE QUEEN
CARPET MANUFACTURERS
BRINTONS LIMITED, KIDDERMINSTER
Brintons
FINE CARPET
Call for further information:
UK 01562 635062
International +44 (0)1562 635241
USA +662 332 1581
www.brintons.net

AWARD WINNER 2001

The Howard, Edinburgh
Winner of the 2001 Johansens Most Excellent City Hotel Award

The Howard celebrates a successful 2001 with the addition of three new individually designed first-class suites and a clutch of awards to add to our credentials. The 2001 Johansens' Most Excellent City Hotel Award is one that I am particularly proud of as it is judged on a UK-wide platform. There are so many terrific city hotels across the UK; it's wonderful to know that our hotel in Great King Street has been recognised as the most excellent.

Together with our red stars rating, a first for any hotel in Edinburgh, The Howard is poised to deliver a level of service in Edinburgh that is unmatched. Our approach is founded on first-class service in a homely environment. Our team of staff at The Howard work together as a family to ensure a discreet approach to our guests in peaceful and private surroundings.

This year at The Howard, we have also introduced a 24-hour butler service. It furthers the ambience of The Howard as a private home with a unique, individual feel. The intimacy of the surroundings, personal attention and privacy is what we find our guests love. It's the allure of being at home which keeps our guests coming back. The Howard really is a gem of a small hotel.

Shaune Ayers
General Manager

For full entry, please turn to page 440.

AWARD WINNER 2001

Fischer's, Baslow, Derbyshire
Winner of the 2001 Johansens Most Excellent Restaurant Award

In 1998 Max and I bought this beautiful small manor house as a fitting setting for our Restaurant-with-Rooms. Now 14 years later, with the opening of our five new 'Garden House' bedrooms we have reached the final stage of our long term plans for the house and its grounds.

The heart of this home of course lies in the kitchen. Attention to detail is evident in all aspects of the dining experience starting with the initial sourcing of organic meat from Derbyshire farmers right through to the last coat of tempered chocolate on the post-dinner petit fours. Max is, after all, a classically trained chef, who flatly refuses to cut corners. Menu descriptions are brief and to the point, listing only the key ingredients and leaving the originality of the dish to the brigade. As you would expect, he cooks with the seasons, making use of Derbyshire spring lamb, Chatsworth venison and Yorkshire forced rhubarb. Presentation is appropriate to the style of the dish, ranging from rustic simplicity to exquisite artistry.

An atmosphere of comfort and character pervades the dining room, which retains the elegance of bygone days when Baslow Hall was a private residence. Staff are trained to be technically correct without being regimented or stuffy.

Johansens Guides have a huge and loyal following throughout the UK and the world. We are extremely flattered by the 'Most Excellent Restaurant' award confirming as it does our belief that we really do offer something special here. Whether you come to stay as an overnight guests or visit us in search of quality food in beautiful surroundings, you will be most welcome.

Max & Susan Fischer

For full entry, please turn to page 102.

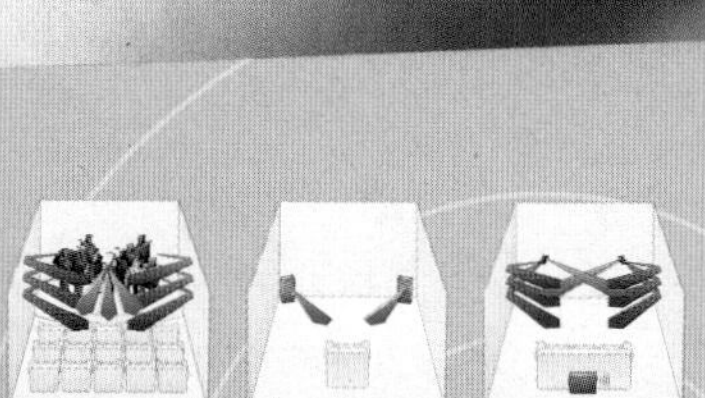

AWARD WINNER 2001

The Milestone, Kensington
Winner of the 2001 Johansens Most Excellent London Hotel Award

We are honoured and delighted to have received the 2001 Award for the Johansens Most Excellent London Hotel. I truly believe that it is only through the commitment, enthusiasm, professionalism and effort from each and every team member that The Milestone Hotel and Apartments is able to be merited with this prestigious accolade. Our philosophy is that "people should be enriched by the experience of hospitality" and it is wholly rewarding to read the very, very many complimentary guest comments on the high levels of personal service that the staff delivers every day of the year.

As a hotel, we are also blessed to have Mrs Beatrice Tollman, our Founder and President, who is the creative driving force behind The Milestone and the Red Carnation Hotel Collection. Mrs Tollman's exceptional design, flair and talent, incredible attention to detail and real understanding of what a guest wants has pushed The Milestone to new limits in luxury and comfort. As an example, our extensive evening turn-down service includes a hot water bottle, a personal book light, a little book of quotes, a foot mat with flower petals, a floating votive candle, a bottle of mineral water, nougat, plush bathrobe and slippers, weather forecast card and TV guide with remote control. We really do specialise in personal touches and we send each guest a preference form prior to arrival so we can anticipate needs. A few other guest favourites are a welcome drink upon arrival, a soap selection delivered to their suite and delicious, freshly made canapés also delivered to suites each evening. All this and a great deal more ensures The Milestone is living up to its growing reputation as 'one of the best hotels in the world' – as quoted in Architectural Digest.

2002 is set to be an exciting year for us all at The Milestone, and our goal is to carry on reaching new heights in the 'art of hospitality' and delivering exceptional service levels amidst the highest luxury surroundings. Our aim is to remain 'London's Most Excellent Hotel', officially or un-officially, and we look forward to welcoming back Johansens customers as well as extending a friendly greeting to many new readers at The Milestone throughout the year.

Caroline King
General Manager

For full entry, please turn to page 49.

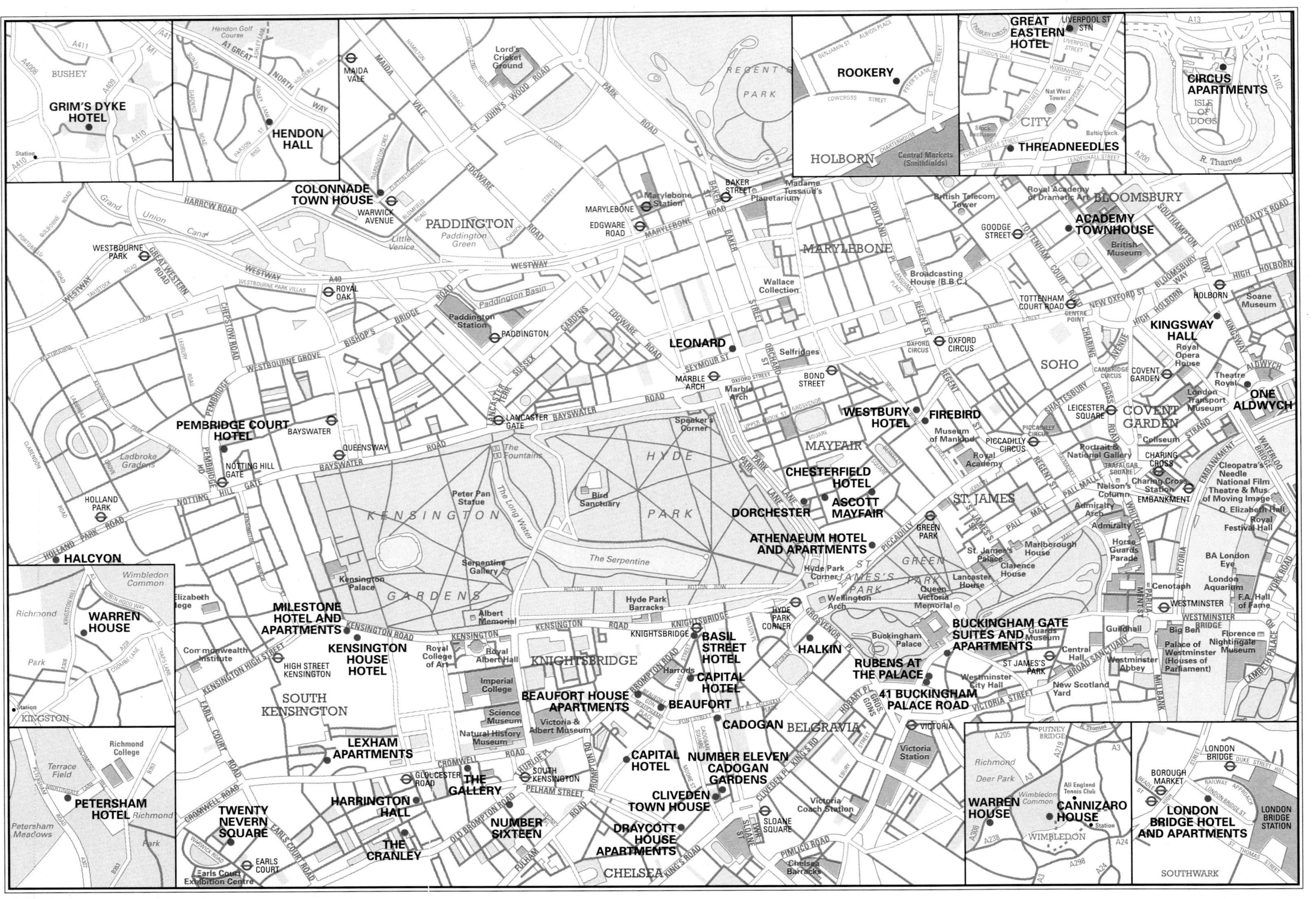

GREAT EASTERN HOTEL
ROOKERY
CIRCUS APARTMENTS
ISLE OF DOGS
THREADNEEDLES
CITY
HOLBORN
BLOOMSBURY
ACADEMY TOWNHOUSE
GRIM'S DYKE HOTEL
BUSHEY
HENDON HALL
COLONNADE TOWN HOUSE
PADDINGTON
MARYLEBONE
LEONARD
KINGSWAY HALL
SOHO
ONE ALDWYCH
COVENT GARDEN
WESTBURY HOTEL
FIREBIRD
MAYFAIR
CHESTERFIELD HOTEL
ASCOTT MAYFAIR
DORCHESTER
ST. JAMES
ATHENAEUM HOTEL AND APARTMENTS
PEMBRIDGE COURT HOTEL
HYDE PARK
KENSINGTON GARDENS
HALCYON
WARREN HOUSE
MILESTONE HOTEL AND APARTMENTS
KENSINGTON HOUSE HOTEL
SOUTH KENSINGTON
BASIL STREET HOTEL
CAPITAL HOTEL
HALKIN
BUCKINGHAM GATE SUITES AND APARTMENTS
RUBENS AT THE PALACE
41 BUCKINGHAM PALACE ROAD
KNIGHTSBRIDGE
BEAUFORT HOUSE APARTMENTS
BEAUFORT
CADOGAN
BELGRAVIA
LEXHAM APARTMENTS
HARRINGTON HALL
THE CRANLEY
THE GALLERY
NUMBER SIXTEEN
CAPITAL HOTEL
NUMBER ELEVEN CADOGAN GARDENS
CLIVEDEN TOWN HOUSE
DRAYCOTT HOUSE APARTMENTS
CHELSEA
PETERSHAM HOTEL
TWENTY NEVERN SQUARE
WARREN HOUSE
CANNIZARO HOUSE
WIMBLEDON
LONDON BRIDGE HOTEL AND APARTMENTS
SOUTHWARK

Johansens Recommended Hotels

London

London by night (©www.britainonview.com)

With its variety of cultural and historical attractions and colourful mix of people, London is one of the most fascinating cities in the world. Alongside cutting edge fashion and art and the trendiest restaurants and markets, this vibrant metropolis still retains its old traditions and the flair of a bygone era.

Attractions include old favourites such as The Tower of London, Buckingham Palace, Hampton Court and Windsor Castle. London's museums and galleries are a must for every visitor – the capital has more than 300 to choose from! The British Museum houses fascinating collections and exhibitions. Situated along the river near the Houses of Parliament in Millbank, Tate Britain holds the greatest collection of British art in the world including works by Constable, Gainsborough, Gilbert and George, Hockney, Hodgin, Hogarth, Moore, Rossetti and Turner. Tate Modern, housed in the spectacularly transformed Bankside Power Station, is the new British showcase for international modern art dating from 1900 to the present day. The collections are displayed within the grand Turbine Hall on the ground floor as well as in the other three floors, and feature work by artists such as Picasso and Dalí. The stunning view from the seventh floor is not to be missed.

London's major new attractions include the British Airways London Eye, which celebrated its first birthday on 8th March 2001. Standing 135m above the ground, this is the world's highest observation wheel. It is situated at County Hall, on London's South Bank, and offers spectacular views across London during a 30-minute "flight". Shakespeare's Globe Exhibition is also worth a visit. The world's largest exhibition dedicated to Shakespeare and his workplace opened at the Globe in 2000. Located beneath the theatre, it focuses on the actors involved in staging Shakespeare's plays, the architecture of the playhouses and the audiences attending the performances. Tennis enthusiasts may want to venture a bit further out to visit Wimbledon Lawn Tennis Museum. Tours are available to the public around the All England Lawn Tennis and Croquet Club, and include privileged access to areas of the site such as the International Box in Centre Court, Number 1 Court and the BBC Television Studio.

London's great annual events are also very popular. One of the classics is the Chelsea Flower Show, which never fails to attract large crowds both from the UK and overseas. Visitors can expect to see beautiful themed displays in the attractive setting of the Royal Hospital Chelsea. Held from 1st to 31st May 2002. If you visit London in June, don't miss the Queen's Birthday Parade; this traditional event on Horse Guards Parade will give you the opportunity to experience British ancestry and culture at its best. A highlight for music lovers is the BBC Proms, a magnificent music festival comprising a series of concerts, held from July to September in the Royal Albert Hall.

For further information on London please contact:

London Tourist Board
Glen House, Stag Place
London SW1E 5LT
Tel: +44 (0)20 7932 2000 or 2041
Internet: www.londontouristboard.com

41

41 BUCKINGHAM PALACE ROAD, LONDON SW1W 0PS
TEL: 020 7300 0041 US TOLL FREE: 1 877 955 1515 FAX: 020 7300 0141 E-MAIL: book41@rchmail.com

London's first all-inclusive luxury boutique hotel is quietly situated, overlooking the Royal Mews and Buckingham Palace gardens. Adjacent also to St James's Park it is perfectly positioned for access to the City and West End. The hotel reflects a remarkable attention to detail, from its discreet and secluded guest entrance and magnificent architectural features to the beautiful furniture and club-like qualities of its superb day-rooms. The 16 de luxe bedrooms and 4 split-level suites are furnished with traditional mahogany and black leather décor. The room tariff encompasses an unparalleled list of luxury amenities from a personal butler to premium brand cocktails and an all-day light buffet and à la carte dining offered in the Club Lounge. "41" has the world's most comfortable, hand-made English mattresses and pure wool carpets throughout; bathrooms are in marble with bespoke bath and beauty products. Every room features an interactive audio-visual station with DVD/CD players and full Internet/E-mail facilities. A state-of-the-art boardroom offers ISDN teleconferencing; secretarial support, chauffeur driven cars, chef services and private dining are also available. Trafalgar Square, the Houses of Parliament and West End Theatres are all nearby. **Directions:** Victoria Station and Underground links are within minutes' walk; Gatwick Express 30 minutes; Heathrow 40 minutes. Price Guide: Single £382; suite £617.

20 MasterCard VISA AMERICAN EXPRESS M 10 VCR

51 Buckingham Gate

51 BUCKINGHAM GATE, WESTMINSTER, LONDON SW1E 6AF
TEL: 020 7769 7766 FAX: 020 7828 5909 E-MAIL: info@51-buckinghamgate.co.uk

Close to Buckingham Palace, St James's Park and the Houses of Parliament, 51 Buckingham Gate is contemporary style and luxury on a grand scale. This attractive Victorian town house offers everything the discerning guest could wish for: privacy, relaxation and superb service delivered by multilingual staff which includes a team of Ivor Spencer trained butlers. Guests have a choice of dining options: Quilon, offering southern coastal Indian cuisine, Bank Westminster and Zander Bar, winner of the Evening Standard's London Bar award and The Library Bar. There are 82 suites and apartments, ranging from junior suites to the five-bedroom Prime Minister's Suite, which combine contemporary interior design with luxury facilities. Deluxe suites offer award-winning bathrooms, whilst designated Ivor Spencer Suites have 16-hour personal butler service, limousine pick-up and an exclusive range of special amenities. Each suite provides sophisticated technology including two-line speaker telephones, voicemail, dataport, fax/copier/printer, CD and DVD player. Fully equipped kitchens as well as 24-hour room service are available. A team of talented chefs is also at hand to prepare private dinners. Guests can enjoy treatments at the exclusive Shiseido Qi Salon and a fully equipped gymnasium at the Club at St James's Court. Directions: Nearest underground stations are St James's Park and Victoria. Price Guide: Suites £295–£975.

THE ACADEMY, THE BLOOMSBURY TOWN HOUSE

21 GOWER STREET, LONDON WC1E 6HG

TEL: 020 7631 4115 FAX: 020 7636 3442 E-MAIL: res_academy@etontownhouse.com

Set in a superb location within London's leafy Bloomsbury district with its many garden squares, The Academy is just a few minutes' walk from the West End, Oxford Street and Covent Garden and very convenient for The British Museum. This charming collection of 5 Georgian Town Houses which hides away 2 private patio gardens, offers an oasis of style and tranquility that belies its prime location amongst the city hustle and bustle. In 2000 the hotel underwent a complete refurbishment programme, the result of which is a unique blend of contemporary style and period charm creating a wonderfully comfortable ambience. Each of the 49 guestrooms is beautifully designed, retaining many of the original Georgian features, with elegant drapes, Regency striped wallpaper and free standing baths. The Garden Suite even has its own private courtyard garden – a real luxury in the heart of London. The Boardroom leads directly to the Conservatory Lounge and Garden, and with facilities for up to 16 delegates makes it an ideal small meeting venue, and perfect for intimate cocktail or wedding parties. The Alchemy breakfast room and Bar also lend themselves to functions. **Directions:** Nearest tube Goodge Street or Tottenham Court Road. Euston and King's Cross stations are within a mile. Price Guide: (excl. VAT): Single £130; double/twin £152; suites £205–£225.

www.johansens.com/academytownhouse

The Ascott Mayfair

49 HILL STREET, LONDON W1J 5NB
TEL: 020 7499 6868 FAX: 020 7499 0705 E-MAIL: martin.king@the–ascott.com

This, the latest concept in city centre accommodation, offers all the benefits of a hotel and yet also privacy and space in what the brochure describes as "residences", with one, two or three bedrooms, in a spectacular art deco building. The apartments have a 24 hour concierge for security and assistance. A maid will be assigned to you for the full duration of your stay. A complimentary Continental breakfast is served in The Terrace, overlooking the private gardens. There is an Honour Bar in The Club where guests can mingle or entertain. The Hothouse offers a gym, sauna, steam room and solarium. The Business Service includes the use of a private boardroom. A marvellous kitchen is provided in each apartment with everything necessary for entertaining in the versatile lounge. The study area has fax and computer links. The sitting room is extremely comfortable and beautifully decorated. It has satellite television, a music system and video. The luxurious bedrooms have amazing en suite bathrooms, full of soft white towels. The Ascott is in the heart of London – Mayfair being close to all the major shopping centres and best restaurants, theatre-land and sightseeing. **Directions:** Hill Street is off Berkeley Square, near Green Park Underground Station. Price Guide: Studio £200 daily, £1340 weekly; 1 bed £295 daily, £1,950 weekly; 2 beds £428 daily, £2,800 weekly. (All rates are subject to VAT).

56 MasterCard VISA AMERICAN EXPRESS M 30 VCR

THE ATHENAEUM HOTEL & APARTMENTS

116 PICCADILLY, LONDON W1J 7BJ

TEL: 020 7499 3464 FAX: 020 7493 1860 E-MAIL: info@athenaeumhotel.com

Set in a superb location, the stylish Athenaeum Hotel & Apartments is extremely welcoming with friendly staff and highly personalised service. Comfortable and luxurious décor adorns the cosy, secluded Windsor Lounge and the public areas. Lovely airy and bright bedrooms, some with views over Green Park, have fresh colour schemes, double, twin or king-size beds and all the modern conveniences to create a contemporary yet traditional ambience. Housed in Edwardian town houses adjacent to the hotel, the spacious and elegantly furnished one and two-bedroom apartments have a private entrance and kitchenette facilities. Modern British cuisine using the finest seasonal ingredients is served in the highly acclaimed Bullochs restaurant who's warm and intimate surroundings feature a floor of imported Jerusalem stone. For the energetic or those wishing to be pampered, the Spa offers a well-equipped gym, Jacuzzi, steam room, sauna, beauty therapy and massage. With its central location, the Athenaeum is ideal for business, leisure and shopping. Buckingham Palace, Hyde Park, Bond Street and the theatre district are a short walk away; Harrods, Covent Garden, Westminster, Kensington Palace and Soho are only a few minutes by taxi or underground. **Directions:** Nearest underground station is Green Park. Price Guide: (excl. VAT) Single from £265; double/twin from £295; suite/apartment from £415.

157 MasterCard VISA AMERICAN EXPRESS M 55 VCR

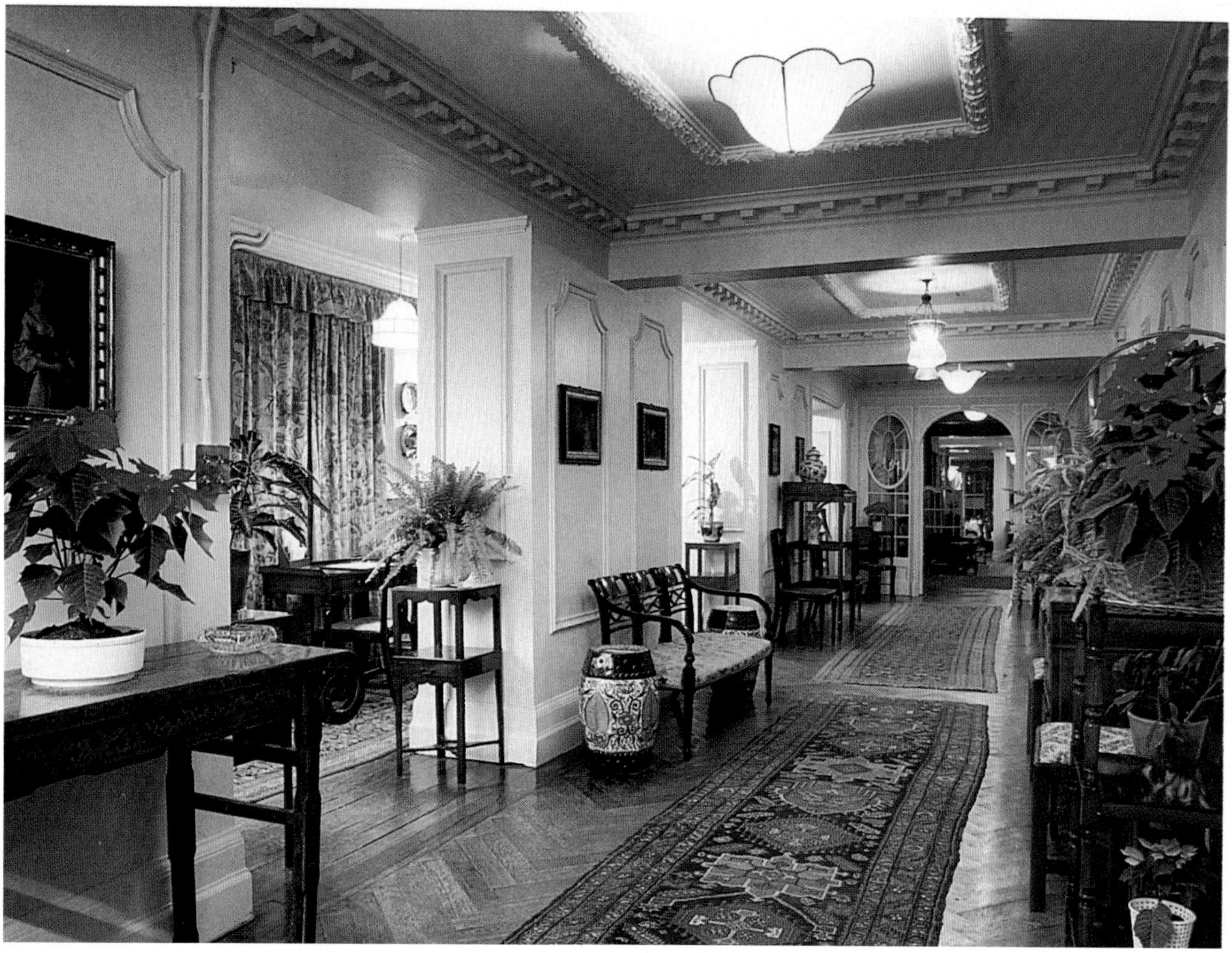

BASIL STREET HOTEL

BASIL STREET, LONDON SW3 1AH

TEL: 020 7581 3311 FAX: 020 7581 3693 FROM USA TOLL FREE: UTELL 1 800 448 8355 E-MAIL: info@thebasil.com

The Basil with its traditional and caring service feels more like an English home than a hotel. Privately owned by the same family for three generations, this traditional Edwardian hotel is situated in a quiet corner of Knightsbridge, in the midst of London's most exclusive residential and shopping area. Harrods, Harvey Nichols and other famous stores are only minutes away. It is also close to museums and theatres. The spacious public rooms are furnished with antiques, paintings, mirrors and objets d'art. All the bedrooms are individually furnished and vary in size, style and décor. The Hotel's Dining Room is an ideal venue either for unhurried, civilised lunch or dinner by candlelight with piano music whilst the Parrot Club, a lounge for the exclusive use of ladies, is a haven of rest in delightful surroundings. There are also a number of smaller intimate rooms available for private dining and meetings. The Basil ideally suits the leisure guest but with its own business centre and modem points in all bedrooms, equally meets the needs of international business travellers. There is a discount scheme for regular guests, for weekends and stays of five nights or more. Garage parking space available on request **Directions:** Close to Pavilion Road car park. Basil Street runs off Sloane Street in the direction of Harrods. Near Knightsbridge Underground and bus routes. Price Guide: Single from £138; double/twin from £198; family room from £275. (excluding VAT).

THE BEAUFORT

33 BEAUFORT GARDENS, KNIGHTSBRIDGE, LONDON SW3 1PP
TEL: 020 7584 5252 FAX: 020 7589 2834 E-MAIL: enquiries@thebeaufort.co.uk

The Beaufort offers the sophisticated traveller all the style and comfort of home – combining warm, contemporary colourings with the highest possible personal attention. The Beaufort is situated in a quiet, tree-lined square only 100 yards from Harrods. On arrival, guests are greeted at the front door and given their own door key to come and go as they please. The closed front door gives added security and completes that feeling of home. All bedrooms are individually decorated, with air conditioning, twice daily maid service and many extras such as shortbread, Belgium chocolates and fruit cup. The hotel owns a video and cassette library and is hometo a magnificent collection of original English floral watercolours. Breakfast comprises hot rolls and croissants, freshly squeezed orange juice and home-made preserves, tea and coffee. Complimentary offerings include champagne and all drinks from the bar, an English cream tea plus membership of a top London Health Club. A private car to or from the airport is available if staying in a Junior Suite. Open all year. **Directions:** From Harrods exit at Knightsbridge underground station take third left. Price Guide: (excl. VAT): Single from £155; double/twin from £180; junior suite £295.

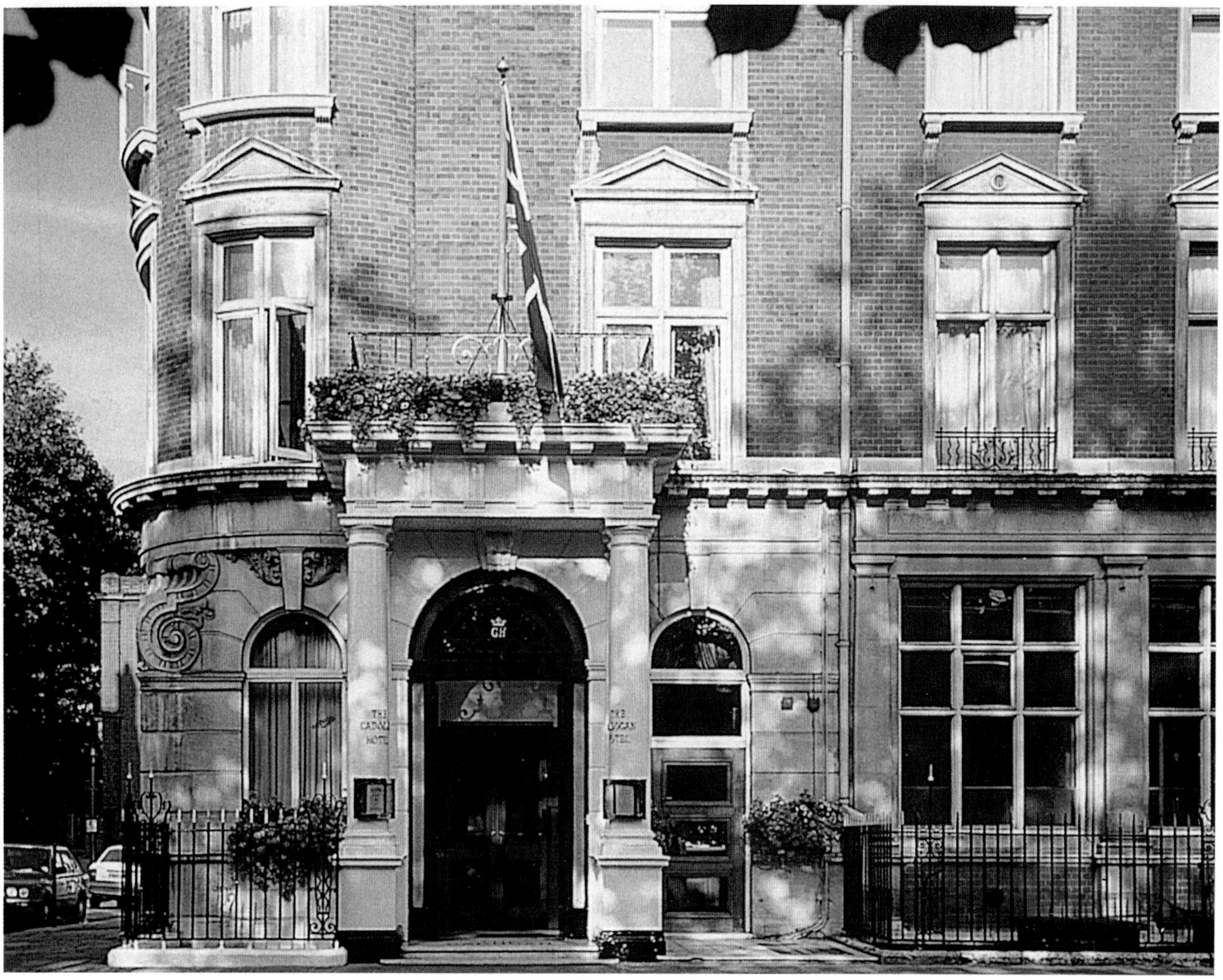

THE CADOGAN

SLOANE STREET, LONDON SW1X 9SG
TEL: 020 7235 7141 FAX: 020 7245 0994 E-MAIL: info@cadogan.com

The Cadogan is an imposing late-Victorian building in terracotta brick situated in a desirable location in Sloane Street, Knightsbridge. It is well-known for its association with Lillie Langtry, the 'Jersey Lily', actress and friend of King Edward VII. Her house in Pont Street now forms part of the hotel. Playwright Oscar Wilde was a regular guest here and was arrested in the hotel in 1895. The Cadogan's elegant drawing room is popular for afternoon tea, and the meals served in the air-conditioned restaurant, which has 2 AA Rosettes, combine imaginative cuisine with value for money. The hotel has 65 comfortable, air-conditioned bedrooms and suites equipped to the highest standards. The Langtry Rooms on the ground floor, once the famous actress's drawing room, make a delightful setting for small meetings, private parties and wedding receptions. The hotel also has a wedding licence. The Cadogan, close to Harrods and Harvey Nichols, is an excellent base for shopping trips. Business visitors will find its central position and easy access make it a fine place to stay when visiting London. Directions: The hotel is halfway along Sloane Street at junction with Pont Street. Close to Knightsbridge and Sloane Square tubes. Price Guide: Single £185–£310; double/twin £260–£325; studio/suite £360–£460 (incl. continental breakfast and VAT).

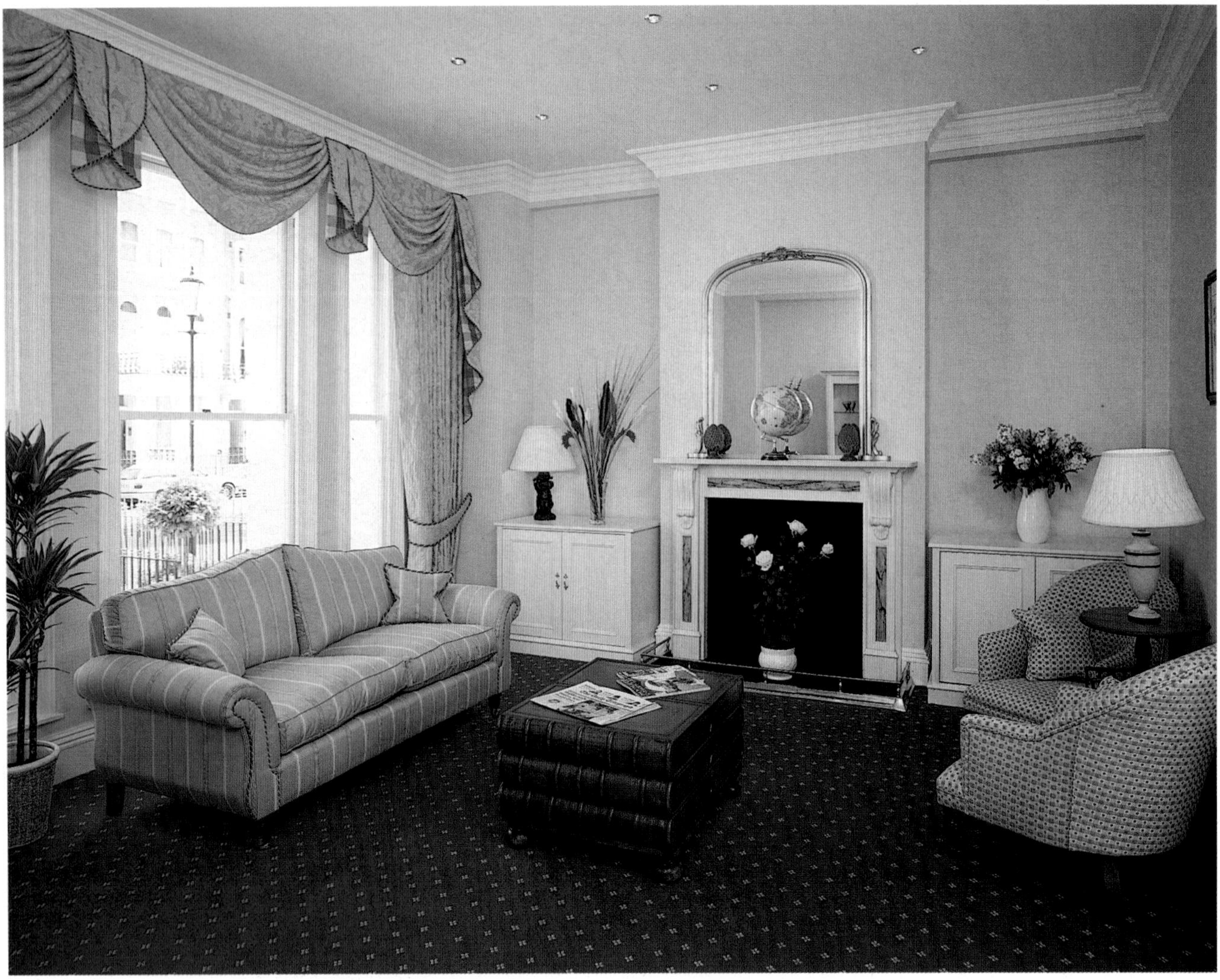

Beaufort House

45 BEAUFORT GARDENS, KNIGHTSBRIDGE, LONDON SW3 1PN
TEL: 020 7584 2600 FAX: 020 7584 6532 US TOLL FREE: 1 800 23 5463 E-MAIL: info@beauforthouse.co.uk

Situated in Beaufort Gardens, a quiet tree-lined Regency cul-de-sac in the heart of Knightsbridge, 250 yards from Harrods, Beaufort House is an exclusive establishment comprising 21 self-contained fully serviced luxury apartments. All the comforts of a first-class hotel are combined with the privacy, discretion and relaxed atmosphere of home. Accommodation ranges in size from an intimate one bedroom to a spacious four-bedroomed apartment. Each apartment has been individually and traditionally decorated to the highest standard. All apartments have direct dial telephones with voice mail, personal safes, satellite television and DVD players. Some apartments benefit from balconies or patios. The fully equipped kitchens include washer/dryers and many have dishwashers. A daily maid service is included at no additional charge. Full laundry/dry cleaning services are available. A dedicated Guests Services team provides 24 hours coverage and will be happy to organise tours, theatre tickets, restaurant bookings, taxis or chauffeur driven limousines and other services. Complimentary membership at Champney's Health Club in Piccadilly is offered to all guests during their stay. Awarded five stars by the English Tourism Council. **Directions:** Beaufort Gardens leads off Brompton road near Knightsbridge underground station. 24hr car park nearby. Price Guide: (excl. VAT) £230–£650.

21 MasterCard VISA AMERICAN EXPRESS VCR

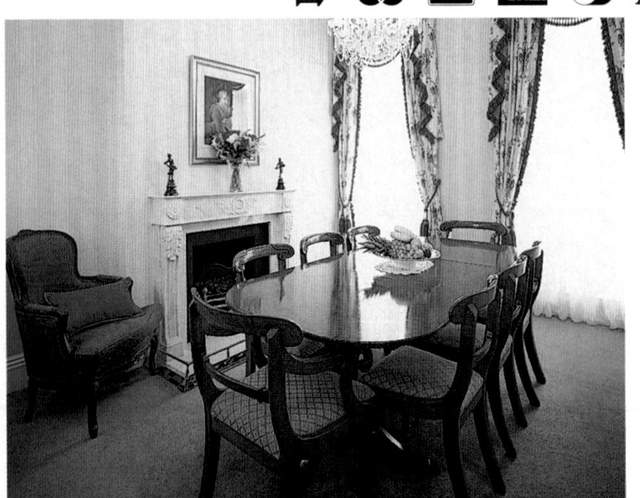

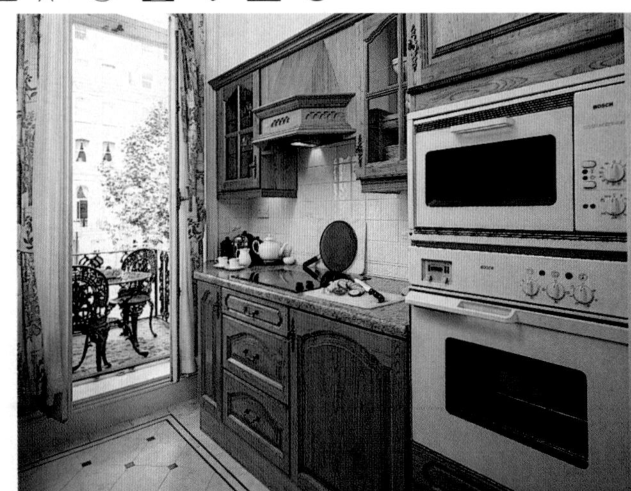

CANNIZARO HOUSE

WEST SIDE, WIMBLEDON COMMON, LONDON SW19 4UE
TEL: 0870 333 9124 FAX: 020 8970 2753 E-MAIL: cannizaro.house@thistle.co.uk

Cannizaro House, an elegant Georgian country house, occupies a tranquil position on the edge of Wimbledon Common, yet is only 18 minutes by train from London Waterloo and the Eurostar terminal. Cannizaro House restored as a superb hotel has, throughout its history, welcomed Royalty and celebrities such as George III, Oscar Wilde and William Pitt. The 18th century is reflected in the ornate fireplaces and mouldings, gilded mirrors and many antiques. All the hotel's 45 bedrooms are individually designed, with many overlooking beautiful Cannizaro Park. All of the 17 executive rooms have air-conditioning. Several intimate rooms are available for meetings and private dining, including the elegant Queen Elizabeth Room – a popular venue for wedding ceremonies. The Viscount Melville Suite offers air-conditioned comfort for up to 100 guests. There is a spacious south facing summer terrace as ideal for afternoon tea and receptions as it is for evening cocktails. The award-winning kitchen, under the leadership of Jeff Hammerschlag, produces the finest modern and classical cuisine, complemented by an impressive list of wines. **Directions:** The nearest tube and British Rail station is Wimbledon. Price Guide: (room only): Double/twin from £221; suite from £243. Special weekend rates (for example riding and golf) and celebratory and incentive packages available.

THE CAPITAL HOTEL

22-24 BASIL STREET, KNIGHTSBRIDGE, LONDON SW3 1AT
TEL: 020 7589 5171 FAX: 020 7225 0011 E-MAIL: reservations@capitalhotel.co.uk

This lovely little town house hotel is one of the capital's secrets, tucked away in a quiet street just a short walk from Harrods, Sloane Street, Hyde Park and the West End. Guests are welcomed in winter by an open fire and in summer by vases of flowers and cool air conditioning. The luxurious Capital was created by its Scottish proprietor, David Levin, more than 30 years ago and is still family-owned and run. Each of the comfortable bedrooms has its own specially selected fabrics, wallpapers and original paintings, and offers lavish marble bathrooms. Radio and television are controlled from bedside consoles and the beds – some super king-size – have hand-made mattresses. The hotel's small restaurant attracts a discriminating clientele who enjoy French inspired cuisine prepared by Michelin star chef Eric Chavot. An attractive bar is a favourite pre and after dinner venue. Afternoon tea can be enjoyed in a snug sitting room whilst light meals can be had throughout the day at the exclusive Le Metro café just two doors away. Guests have access to an exclusive private members gym and pool nearby. The concierge can arrange theatre tickets and limousines, book flights or provide a bellboy to accompany guests on shopping trips. Car parking facilities are on site. **Directions:** Next to Harrods, between Sloane Street and Beauchamp Place. Nearest underground station: Knightsbridge. Price Guide: Single £190; double/twin £245–£315; suite £375.

48 MasterCard VISA AMERICAN EXPRESS M 22

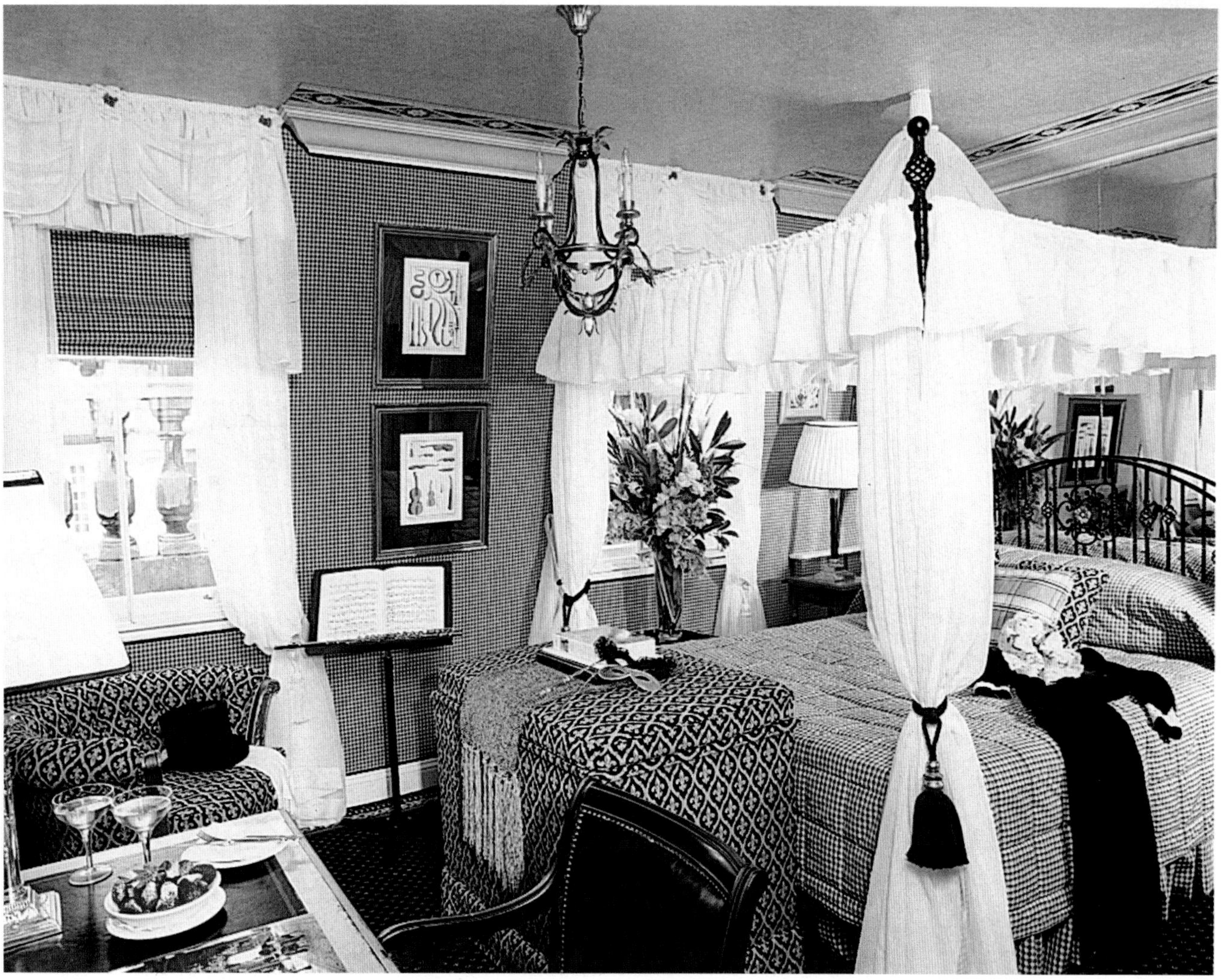

THE CHESTERFIELD MAYFAIR

35 CHARLES STREET, MAYFAIR, LONDON W1J 5EB

TEL: 020 7491 2622 US TOLL FREE: 1 877 955 1515 FAX: 020 7491 4793 E-MAIL: bookch@rchmail.com

Set in the heart of Mayfair, this charming hotel has recently undergone a £3-million transformation. Its Georgian elegance combines with up-to-date facilities and an excellent, truly personal service. All rooms and public areas are air-conditioned, and the surroundings provide the perfect ambience in which to dine or relax. Guests can enjoy the tranquil 'al fresco' atmosphere of The Conservatory, catch up on reading and correspondence in the wood-panelled Library, or unwind with a drink to the sound of a gentle piano in the club-style Bar. There is a range of themed rooms including the Music Room and Theatre Room. The AA Rosette Restaurant serves the finest in British and international cuisine, complemented by superb wines which can be sampled in the wine room. Bedrooms are beautifully furnished and include many thoughtful extras such as bathrobes, complimentary bottled water, and deluxe toiletries. The business traveller has also been considered, and can take advantage of full secretarial support, voicemail, fax and modem lines and essential office supplies. All events, from meetings to conferences and banquets can be held at The Chesterfield, and the Hotel is licensed for wedding ceremonies. Bond Street with its shops is close by, as are numerous museums and theatres and the City. **Directions:** Nearest underground station is Green Park. Price Guide: (Excl. VAT) Single £195; double/twin £265; suite from £365.

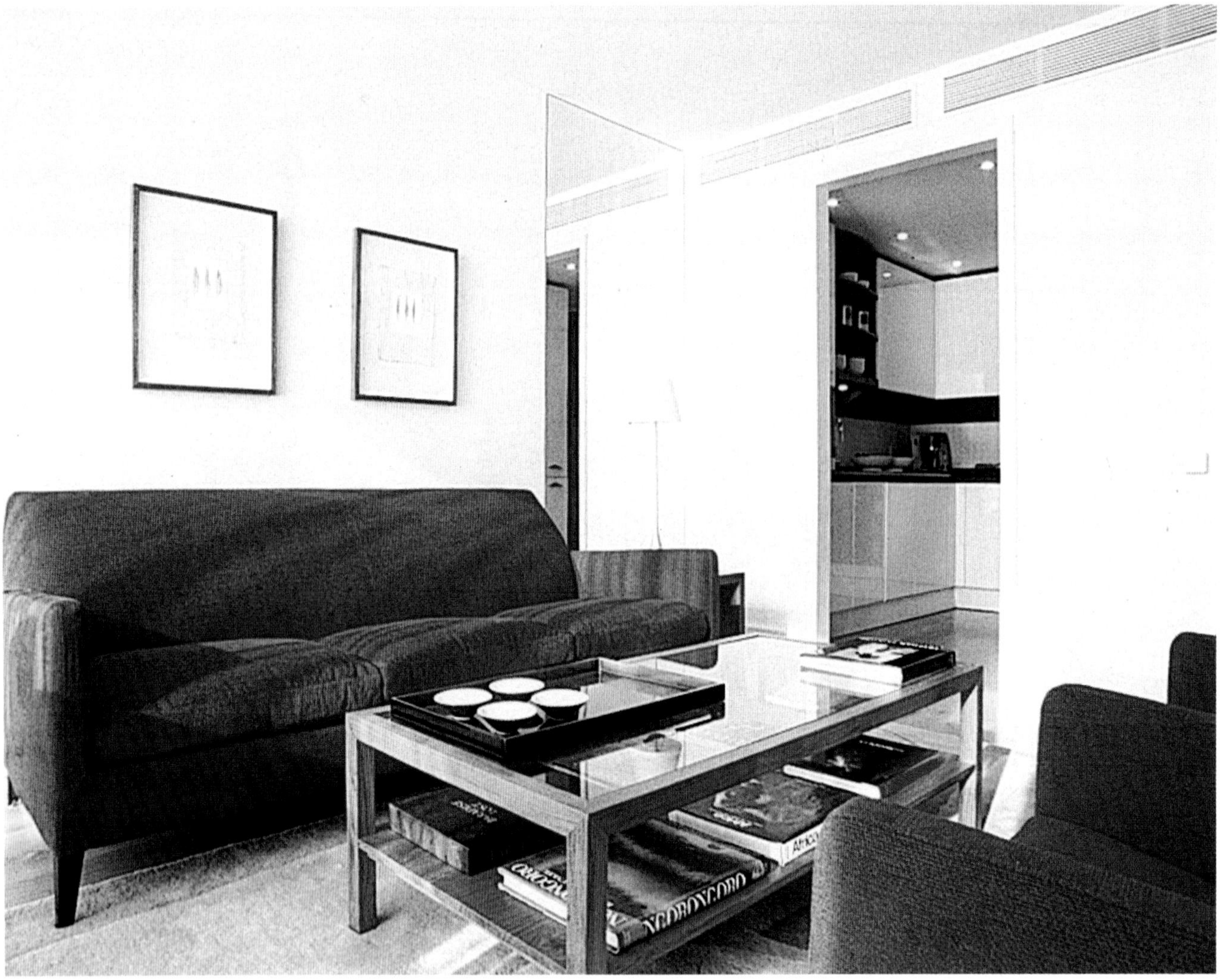

CIRCUS APARTMENTS

39 WESTFERRY CIRCUS, CANARY WHARF, LONDON E14 8RW
TEL: 020 7719 7000 FAX: 020 7719 7001 E-MAIL: res@circusapartments.co.uk

These modern and stylish serviced apartments are situated in the heart of London's latest cosmopolitan and dynamic business district and provide convenient surroundings for a private or business visit. The Square Mile lies a short distance to the West of the apartments, City Airport is a 10-minute drive away, the West End 15 minutes by underground. Around and about is a chic enclave teeming with bars and some of the best eateries in the capital, all inhabited by high-flying, design-conscious customers. Circus Apartments provide an exclusive retreat with all the comforts of a first-class hotel combined with the privacy and relaxed atmosphere of home. Each luxury one or two-bedroom apartment is spacious, individually designed to the highest standard, with every modern facility catered for. Huge floor-to-ceiling windows offer superb views; cavernous baths provide total relaxation after a busy day. Nearby Holmes Place health club with its extensive gymnasium and riverside swimming pool is available for guests' use during their stay. For the travelling executive and corporate meeting organiser, Circus has its own meetings area and fully equipped, high-tech business centre. **Directions:** Nearest underground station is Canary Wharf. Price Guide: (excluding VAT)1-bed apartments £225 (daily) £1498 (weekly); 2-bed apartments £275 (daily) £1790 (weekly).

The Cliveden Town House

26 CADOGAN GARDENS, LONDON SW3 2RP

TEL: 020 7730 6466 FAX: 020 7730 0236 FROM USA TOLL FREE 1 800 747 4942 E-MAIL: reservations@clivedentownhouse.co.uk

The award-winning Cliveden Town House offers the perfect balance of luxury, service, privacy and location. Tucked away in a tranquil, tree-lined garden square between Harrods and the Kings Road, it is at the centre of fashionable London and epitomises style and elegance. Like its gracious country cousin at Cliveden, one of England's most famous stately homes, it combines the grandeur of the past with the conveniences of today, offering guests the exclusive ambience of a grand private residence. All 35 rooms are individually decorated reflecting the Edwardian period and combine 24-hour room service with all that today's discerning traveller requires. Nine of the opulent suites can be arranged to create the atmosphere of a private home with a fully-equipped kitchen and/or separate sitting room. The beautifully panelled boardroom overlooking the private residents' garden provides the perfect venue for small meetings and private parties. The shops and restaurants of Knightsbridge, Chelsea and Belgravia, West End theatres and the City are within easy reach, and a chauffeur is available for airport transfers and personalised tours. Enjoy complimentary afternoon tea or a glass of champagne in the Drawing Room. **Directions:** Nearest underground station is Sloane Square. Price Guide: (excl. VAT) Single from £140; Queen double from £220; deluxe double/twin from £250; suites from £320. Weekend rates from £190.

The Colonnade, The Little Venice Town House

2 WARRINGTON CRESCENT, LONDON W9 1ER
TEL: 020 7286 1052 FAX: 020 7286 1057 E-MAIL: res_colonnade@etontownhouse.com

This tall, elegant Victorian town house is delightfully situated in the smart and sophisticated residential area of Little Venice which embodies the tranquil Regents Canal. It is a beautifully furnished residence offering all the comforts of a luxury hotel and is conveniently within reach of London's many sights, restaurants, theatres and business areas. The Colonnade was originally built as two private homes in 1865 and later converted into a girl's boarding school and a hospital for ladies until opening as a hotel in 1935. The House has recently been completely refurbished and has an innovative, boutique style interior. Sumptuous fabrics and lavish antiques have been carefully selected to create a unique style and ambience in each of the 43 guest rooms and suites, many of them with a terrace and four poster bed. All are individually decorated and feature every modern facility. The relaxing drawing room is ideal for guests to have pre dinner drinks or a night cap. The renowned Town House breakfast is served in the stylish breakfast room and is second to none. Car parking and airport transfers can be arranged. **Directions:** Warwick Avenue underground station and taxi rank are close by. Paddington station with its direct Heathrow link is one stop away or a quick taxi ride. Price Guide: (excl. VAT): Single £126; suites £245. From March 2002.

THE CRANLEY

10-12 BINA GARDENS, SOUTH KENSINGTON, LONDON SW5 0LA
TEL: 020 7373 0123 FAX: 020 7373 9497 E-MAIL: info@thecranley.com

Standing in a quiet, tree-lined street in the heart of Kensington, this charming and sophisticated Victorian town house is an ideal city venue for the leisure and business visitor alike, blending traditional style and service with 21st-century technology. Furnished with beautiful antiques and hand-embroidered linen fabrics The Cranley has an understated elegance. Striking colour combinations and stone used throughout the bedrooms and reception areas are derived from the original floor in the entrance hall. Recently completely refurbished, the Cranley's bedrooms are now among some of the most comfortable in the capital. All are delightfully decorated and have king-size four-poster or half-tester canopied beds. Each room is light, air-conditioned and has facilities ranging from antique desk, two direct dial telephone lines and voicemail to interactive television with Internet access. The luxury bathrooms have traditional Victorian-style fittings combined with a lavish use of warm limestone. Guests can enjoy copious Continental breakfasts, complimentary English afternoon tea and an evening help-yourself apéritif with canapés. Many of London's attractions are within easy walking distance, including the shops and restaurants of Knightsbridge and the Kings Road. **Directions:** Nearest underground stations are Gloucester Road and South Kensington. Price Guide: Single £182.12; double/twin £211.50; suite £246.75 Continental Breakfast £9.95.

38 MasterCard VISA AMERICAN EXPRESS

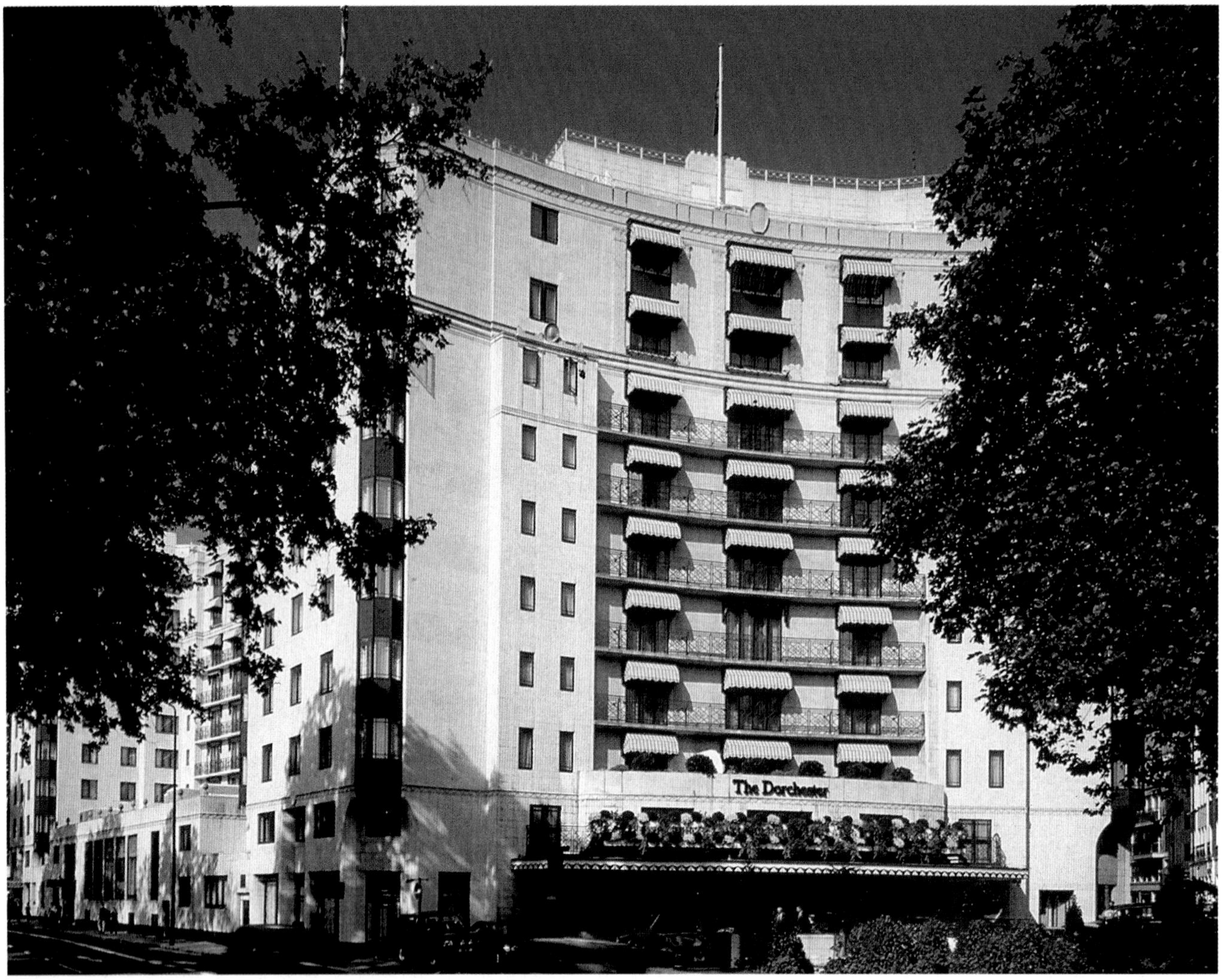

THE DORCHESTER

PARK LANE, MAYFAIR, LONDON W1A 2HJ

TEL: 020 7629 8888 FAX: 020 7409 0114 E-MAIL: reservations@dorchesterhotel.com

The Dorchester first opened its doors in 1931, offering a unique experience which almost instantly became legendary. Constant updating and refurbishing over the years, using the cream of international designers, has ensured that it has remained at the top as one of the world's finest hotels. Its history has been consistently glamorous; from the early days a host of outstanding figures has been welcomed, including monarchs, statesmen and celebrities. The architectural features have been restored to their original splendour and remain at the heart of The Dorchester's heritage. The 195 bedrooms and 55 suites have been luxuriously designed in a variety of materials, furnishings and lay-outs. All bedrooms are fully air-conditioned and have spectacular Italian marble bathrooms. In addition to The Grill Room, there is the Oriental Restaurant where the accent is on Cantonese cuisine. Specialised health and beauty treatments are offered in the Dorchester Spa with its statues, Lalique-style glass and water fountain. The Bar, a classic, is the venue for some of the best live traditional jazz in London. A series of meeting rooms, with full support services, is available for business clientèle. Personalised care is a pillar of The Dorchester's fine reputation. **Directions:** Towards Hyde Park Corner/Piccadilly end of Park Lane. Price Guide: (excluding VAT): Single £295–£315; double/twin £330–£360; suite £485–£2,100. Year round special packages are available.

DRAYCOTT HOUSE APARTMENTS

10 DRAYCOTT AVENUE, CHELSEA, LONDON SW3 3AA
TEL: 020 7584 4659 FAX: 020 7225 3694 E-MAIL: sales@draycotthouse.co.uk

Draycott House stands in a quiet, tree-lined avenue in the heart of Chelsea. Housed in an attractive period building, the apartments have been designed in traditional styles to provide the ideal surroundings for a private or business visit, combining comfort, privacy and security with a convenient location. All are spacious, luxury, serviced apartments, with three, two or one bedrooms. Some have private balconies, a roof terrace and overlook the private courtyard garden. Each apartment is fully equipped with all home comforts; cable television, video, CD/hi-fi, private direct lines for telephone/fax/answer machine/data. Complimentary provisions on arrival, newspapers delivered daily. Maid service Monday to Friday. In-house laundry room and covered garage parking. Additional services, laundry and dry cleaning services. On request cars, airport transfers, catering, travel and theatre arrangements, child-minders etc and complimentary membership to an exclusive nearby health club. The West End is within easy reach. Knightsbridge within walking distance. **Directions:** Draycott House is situated on the corner of Draycott Avenue and Draycott Place, close to Sloane Square. Price Guide: from £1173–£2863 +VAT per week: £184–£450 +VAT per night. Long term reservations may attract preferential terms. Contact: Jane Renton, General Manager.

13 MasterCard VISA AMERICAN EXPRESS VCR

FIREBIRD

23 CONDUIT STREET, MAYFAIR, LONDON W1S 2XS
TEL: 020 7493 7000 FAX: 020 7493 7088

Just a few steps from Oxford Street, in the heart of Mayfair, the exterior of this elegant town house belies the unique restaurant within. Upon entering FireBird – named after the beautiful bird of Russian folklore – it is as if one has been transported to an aristocratic house in pre-revolutionary Russia. There are four floors of dining rooms, and furnishings include William Morris wallpaper, antique Russian blue crystal chandeliers, sumptuous drapes, and china and collectibles from owner J William Holt's family collection. On the ground floor a piano bar leads into the China Room and the Library; the Blue and White Rooms can be found on the first floor. There are two further floors of private dining rooms. Seating 10 people, the Room of Luxury is a recreation of an Orient-Express carriage and features a mural depicting the journey from London to Istanbul, whilst the Fabergé Room boasts a collection of the world-famous eggs and pictures from the designer's photograph album. Menus are overseen by Benjamin Bowen, formerly of The Savoy and Claridge's, and Executive Head Chef Koenraad Inghelram, and are styled on the period when Catherine the Great used her love of France and its food to influence Russian cuisine. Offering an unparalleled culinary and aesthetic experience, FireBird is considered to be one of the world's finest Tsarist Franco-Russian restaurants. **Directions:** Nearest underground stations are Oxford Circus and Green Park.

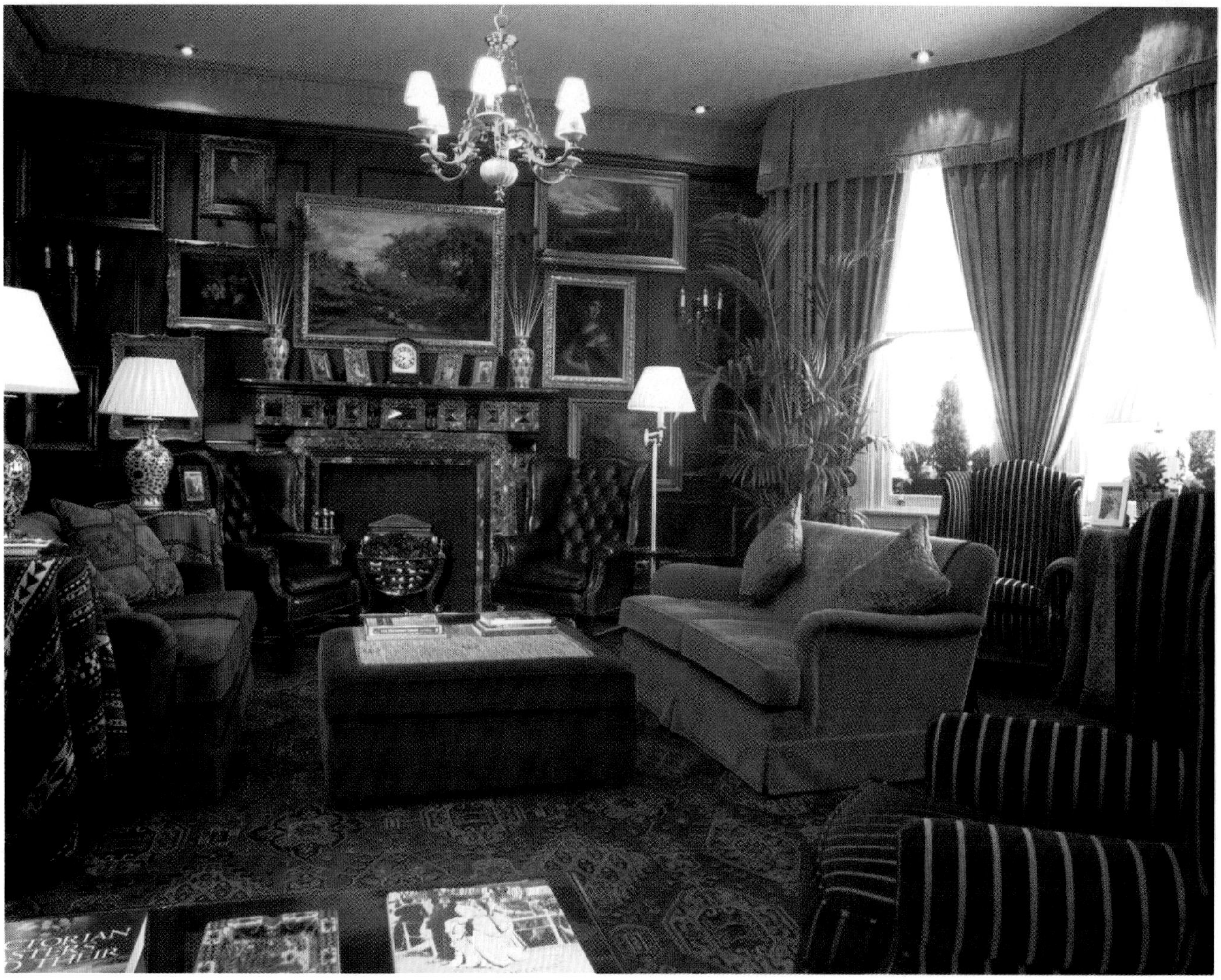

THE GALLERY

8-10, QUEENSBERRY PLACE, SOUTH KENSINGTON, LONDON SW7 2EA
TEL: 020 7915 0000 FAX: 020 7915 4400 E-MAIL: reservations@eeh.co.uk

A unique experience awaits guests at this elegant Victorian house where the highest standards of comfort and amenities can be enjoyed. The Gallery's atmosphere is one of quiet refinement and, true to its name, the hotel displays original art in every room. The welcoming mahogany panelled reception area and lounge features an imposing Jacobean Revival chimney piece, plump sofas and discrete bar. Old kilims adorn side tables, an Ottoman theme is repeated in the rich pile carpeting. Everything from Oriental porcelain in the lobby to the furniture and décor of the Morris Room has been expertly selected. This beautiful drawing room evokes the arts and crafts style popularised by the famed Victorian painter and designer – arbutus wallpaper, tulip and lily carpet, an oak-cased Manxman piano and an antique bar billiards table. The 34 individually decorated guest rooms offer every facility including two direct dial telephones with data port. Two master suites, Rossetti and Leighton, are furnished with the refinement befitting their names; each has its own roof terrace, Jacuzzi, CD and DVD players. Light snacks are available. The Gallery's location is ideal – close to Harrods, fashionable Knightsbridge, bohemian Chelsea and numerous museums. **Directions:** Three minutes' walk from South Kensington underground station, just off Cromwell Road. Price Guide: (not incl. VAT) Single £120; double/twin £145; suites £250.

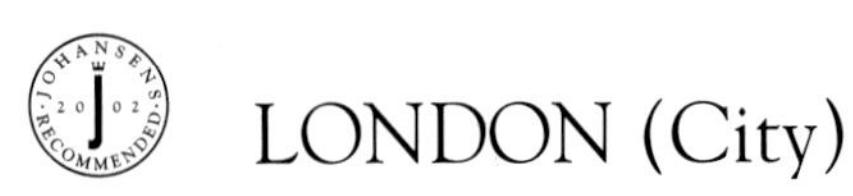

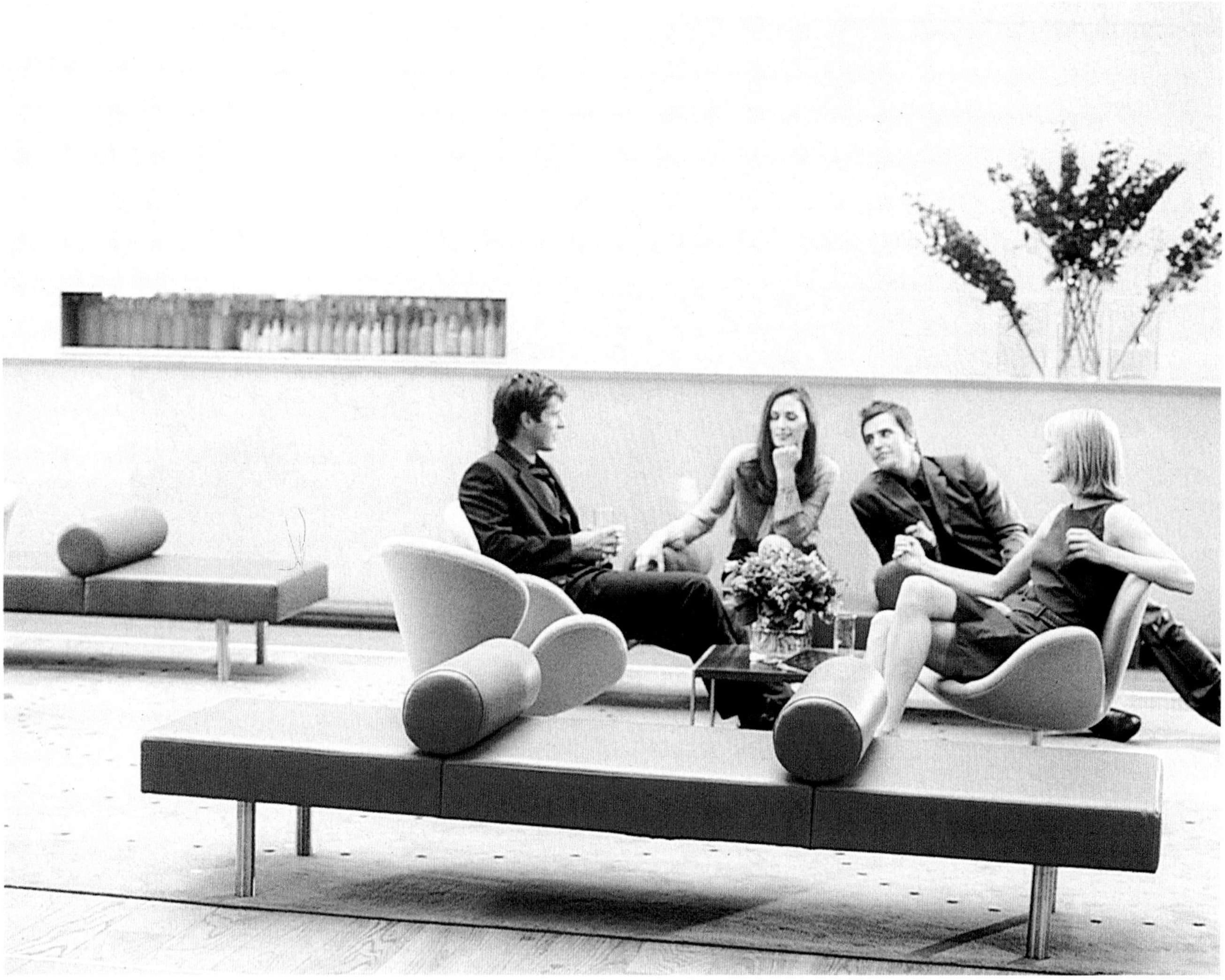

GREAT EASTERN HOTEL

LIVERPOOL STREET, LONDON EC2M 7QN
TEL: 020 7618 5000 FAX: 020 7618 5001 E-MAIL: sales@great-eastern-hotel.co.uk

From the moment visitors enter the hotel lobby or the imposing, high-rise atrium they realise that this is an especially exciting hotel. It reopened with 246 bedrooms and 21 suites, four restaurants, three bars, gym, treatment rooms and 12 private dining rooms in 2000 after extensive refurbishment. Grade II listed and situated on the eastern edges of the City of London, the Great Eastern originally opened in two phases, in 1884 and 1901. The refurbishment beautifully revives the splendour of those eras, combined with 21st century modernity and facilities. No two bedrooms are alike. Those on the fifth and sixth floors have a light and airy 'loft' feel; those below have higher ceilings and period features. Rooms in the east wing are detailed with ornate late Victorian features; those in the west wing are more restrained. All have every home comfort and high-tech business facilities. Each of the hotel's restaurants and bars has its own distinctive identity. Terminus re-interprets the classic railway buffet-brasserie, Fishmarket is sea green beneath plaster cherubs, Aurora is grand and beautiful and George is Tudor style oak-panelled. The food is equally distinctive, from classically inspired dishes to sushi and sashimi to fish and crustacea. London's major tourist attractions and theatreland are within easy reach **Directions:** Adjacent to Liverpool Street rail and tube station on the corner of Bishopgate. Price Guide: Queen Double from £240.

267 MasterCard VISA AMERICAN EXPRESS M 300 VCR

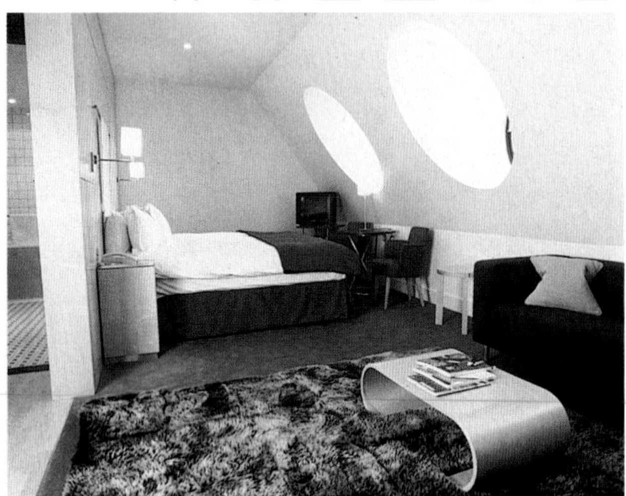

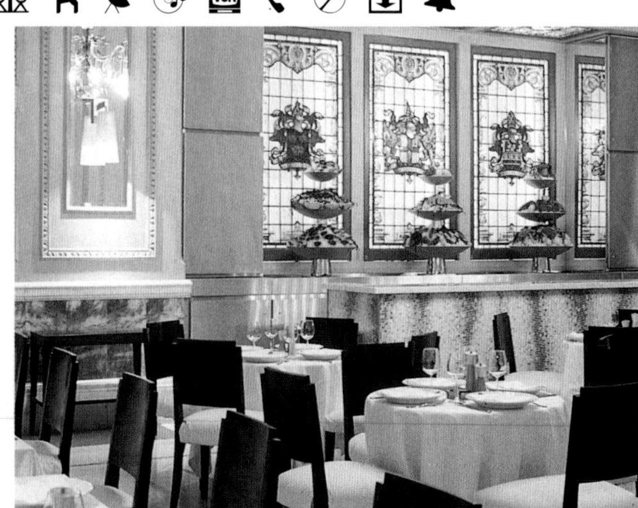

GRIM'S DYKE HOTEL

OLD REDDING, HARROW WEALD, MIDDLESEX HA3 6SH
TEL: 020 8385 3100 FAX: 020 8954 4560 E-MAIL: enquiries@grimsdyke.com

Steeped in history, the Grim's Dyke Hotel is surrounded by 40 acres of gardens and woodlands. This Grade II listed building derives its name from an ancient defensive earthwork that runs through the grounds from Pinner Hill to Bentley Priory and was also the home of the musician, Sir William Gilbert, from the famous Gilbert & Sullivan opera writing partnership. High ceilings and rustic staircases combined with period details create a delightful atmosphere. The 44 bedrooms and suites, 35 of which are situated in the adjacent garden lodge, are elegant and decorated with rich fabrics. Delicious meals using fresh ingredients are served in the Music Room, the largest and most ornate room in the house dominated by a beautiful alabaster fireplace that stretches from floor to ceiling. A pianist entertains diners on Fridays, Saturdays and Sundays. Tea and drinks can be taken on the terrace overlooking the croquet lawn or guests may enjoy a quiet moment to read or relax in the Morning Room, which has stunning views over the sunken rose garden. Leisure activities include croquet, horse riding and walking in the hotel grounds. Gilbert and Sullivan evenings, Murder Mystery evenings and gardening weekends can be arranged. The hotel caters for weddings and corporate occasions. **Directions:** M25 Jct23, M1 Jct5, 25 minutes by car from central London. Price Guide: Single £123; double/twin £149; suites £165–£295.

The Halcyon

81 HOLLAND PARK, LONDON W11 3RZ

TEL: 020 7727 7288 FAX: 020 7229 8516 E-MAIL: reservations@thehalcyon.com

Strolling down the leafy broad avenue of Holland Park, just a couple of minutes' walk from bohemian Portobello Market and Notting Hill, you will find The Halcyon Hotel an oasis of calm away from the bustle of the capital city. Set on the cusp of London's most captivating park with its woodlands and formal gardens. The hotel provides 42 large and individually designed suites and bedrooms offering comfort and luxury in a classic and elegant setting. Your choice of room can range from the Egyptian Suite with its Bedouin tent canopy to sleeping under the moon and stars in the Blue Room. You will find the flair of Provence in the Restaurant where chef Nigel Davis cooks with consummate skill and a delicate touch. With flagstone flooring and garden terrace, the Restaurant has a sunny character. Service is warm and caring. The hideaway bar is the perfect place to sip a cocktail with a few friends or simply relax with a cappuccino and your favourite newspaper. The Halcyon offers highly personalised service and discretion ensuring guests have a comfortable, private and secure stay. Secretarial, Internet and fax facilities are all available. **Directions:** From Holland Park tube station turn right; the Halcyon is on the left after the second set of traffic lights. Price Guide: Single from £173; double/twin from £213; Suites from £270.

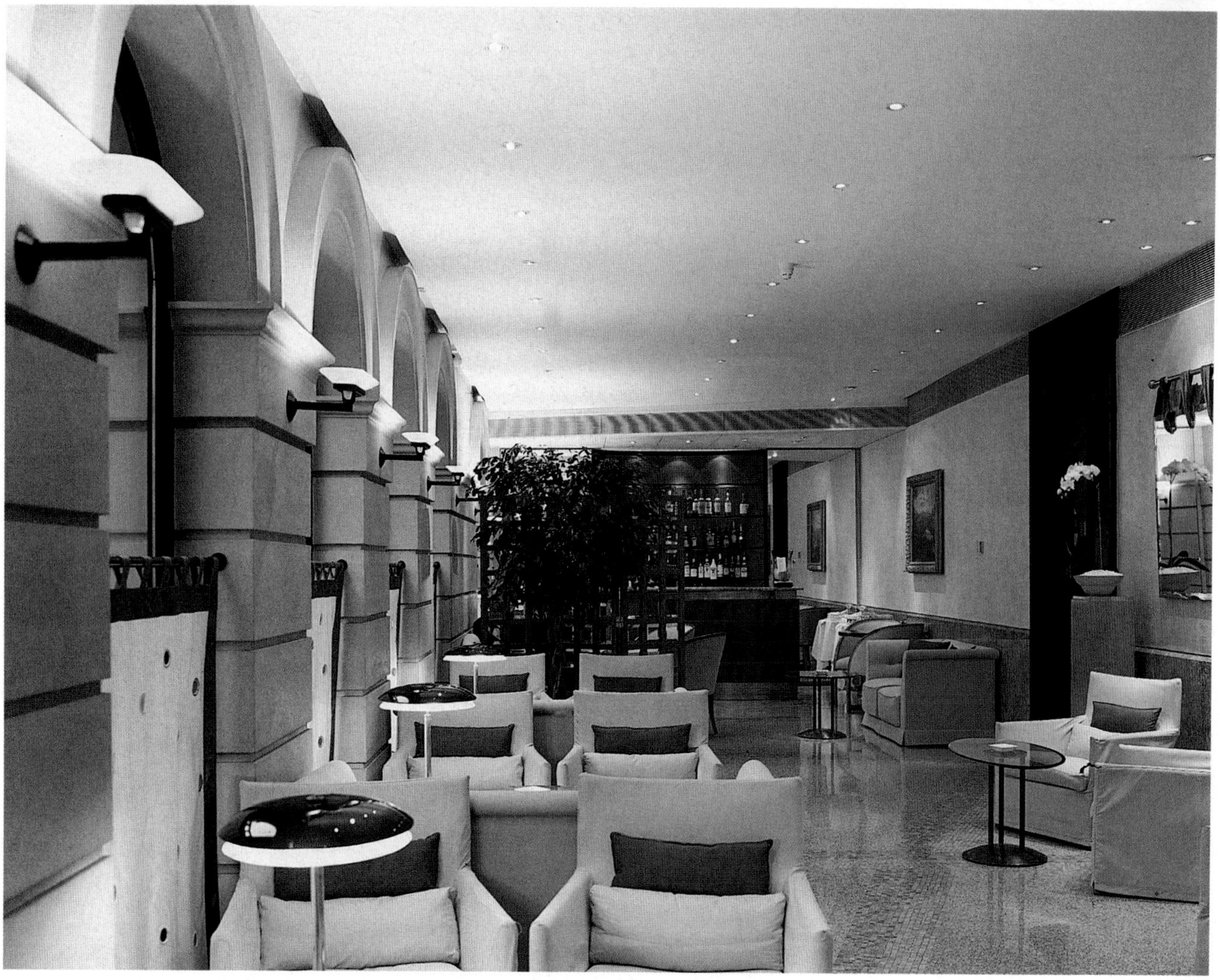

THE HALKIN

5 HALKIN STREET, BELGRAVIA, LONDON SW1X 7DJ

TEL: 020 7333 1000 FAX: 020 7333 1100 E-MAIL: sales@halkin.co.uk

Quality of service, luxury, opulence and style are the very essence of The Halkin, an elegant and tranquil haven in the very heart of fashionable Belgravia just minutes from Knightsbridge's exclusive shopping and dining. Room design, décor, furniture, furnishings and facilities are magnificently modernistic, clear and refreshing, giving the hotel a very special feel that has guests returning time and again. Each of 41 spacious and luxurious air-conditioned rooms and suites have individual harmonious colour themes and combine the comforts of home with personal, 24-hour service. Facilities include superb all-marble bathroom, direct number fax, dual line telephone with voice mail, cable and CNN television, VCR and CD player and a high security key system. Valet and butler services are also available together with a concierge who handle entertainment, travel and sightseeing. The Halkin is renowned for its creative and innovative cuisine presented in the light and delightful restaurant overlooking a charming private garden. Excellent and imaginative menus are complemented by an extensive wine list in keeping with the hotel's high standards. Pre and post dinner drinks can be enjoyed in a comfortable bar and lounge. **Directions:** The nearest tube station is Hyde Park Corner. Price Guide: Room £285; suite £625.

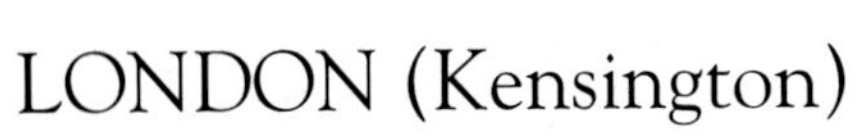

HARRINGTON HALL

5-25 HARRINGTON GARDENS, LONDON SW7 4JW

TEL: 020 7396 9696 FAX: 020 7396 9090 E-MAIL: harringtonsales@compuserve.com

The original façade of late Victorian houses cleverly conceals a privately owned hotel of substantial proportions and contemporary comfort. Harrington Hall offers 200 air-conditioned spacious bedrooms which have all been most pleasantly furnished and equipped with an extensive array of facilities. 125 of the rooms feature king-size beds. A marble fireplace dominates the comfortable and relaxing Lounge Bar, where guests can enjoy a drink in pleasant surroundings. Serving a varied international menu, the restaurant is a delightful setting for all diners from large luncheon parties to those enjoying intimate evening meals. A choice of buffet or à la carte menu is available, both offering a tempting selection of dishes. Nine fully air-conditioned conference and banqueting suites, with walls panelled in rich lacewood and solid cherry, provide a sophisticated venue for conferences, exhibitions or corporate hospitality. Harrington Hall also has a Business Centre for the exclusive use of its guests, along with a private new equipped Fitness Centre with saunas and showers **Directions:** Harrington Hall is situated in the Royal Borough of Kensington and Chelsea, in Harrington Gardens south of the Cromwell Road, close to Gloucester Road underground station, two stops from Knightsbridge and Harrods. Price Guide: Single from £180; double £180; suites £220 (including VAT & service).

200 MasterCard VISA AMERICAN EXPRESS M 260

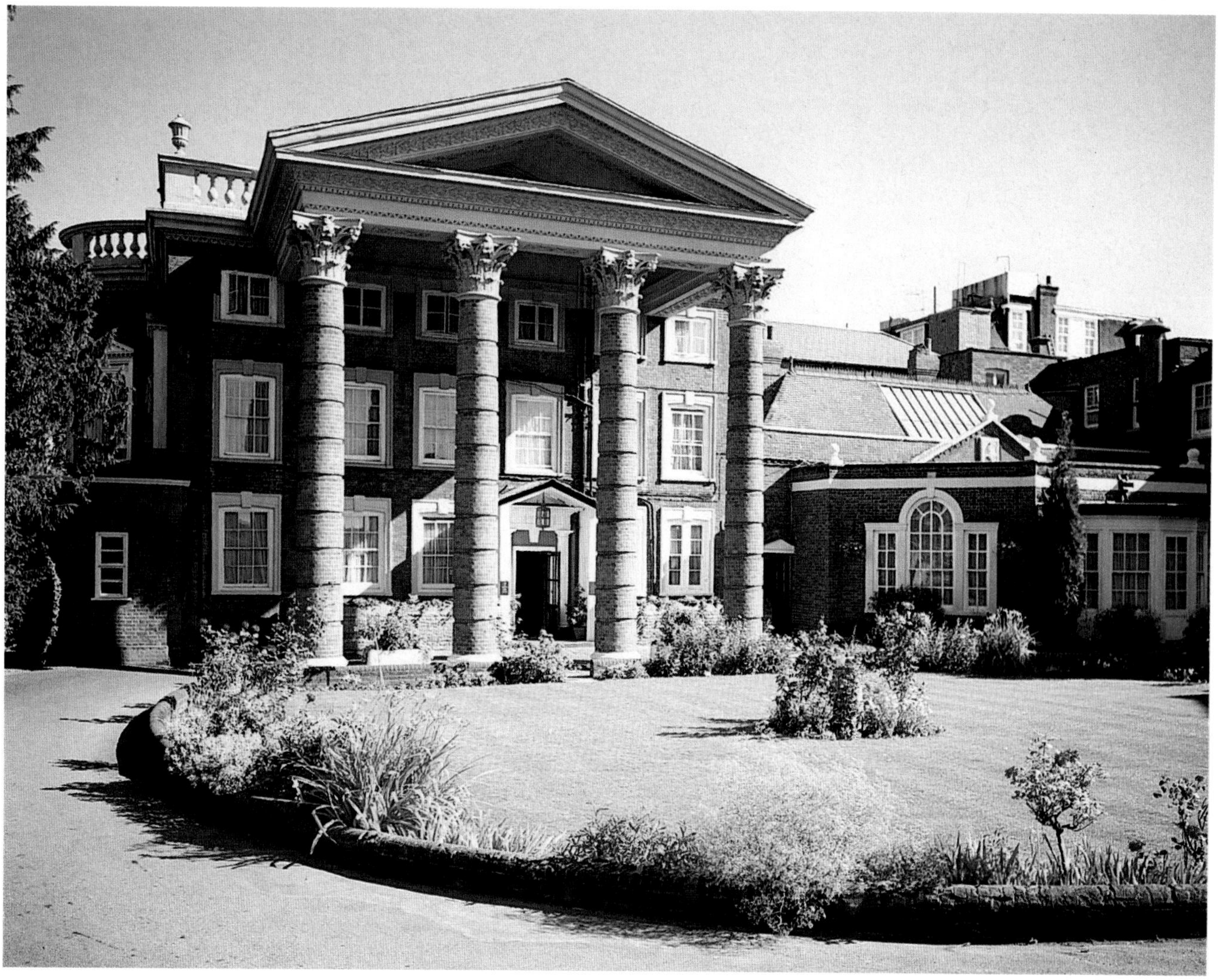

HENDON HALL

ASHLEY LANE, HENDON, LONDON NW4 1HF

TEL: 020 8203 3341 FAX: 020 8203 9709 E-MAIL: Hendon.Hall@Thistle.co.uk

Hendon Hall stands at the head of a sweeping drive encircling a manicured lawn. Its white entrance way is framed by four massive pillars soaring up to a rooftop encased with an attractive ornamental parapet. An elegant Georgian building with award-winning gardens, it is situated in a residential area seven miles from the heart of London and a two minute drive from the M1, which offers easy access to many attractions. It was originally known as Hendon Manor and dates back to the 16th century. King Henry's son, Edward, gave the manor to the Earl of Pembroke in return for 'good and faithful service' and he gave it to his son, Edward, as a wedding present in 1569. Behind its classical façade it has been extensively refurbished to provide spacious and stylish accommodation with many original features retained. All bedrooms and suites are tastefully decorated and equipped with air-conditioning, modem points and dual adapters. Visitors can relax in a cosy cocktail bar before enjoying the tasty Pavillion Restaurant cuisine created by their executive chef. Meeting, conference, banqueting and wedding facilities are also available. **Directions:** From M1, exit at junction 2 signposted North Circular East (A406) and The City A1. At first set of traffic lights turn right into Parson Street. Turn right into Ashley Lane and Hendon Hall is on the right. Nearest underground station is Hendon Central (Northern line) Price Guide: Double/twin from £189; suite from £244.

KENSINGTON HOUSE HOTEL

15-16 PRINCE OF WALES TERRACE, KENSINGTON, LONDON W8 5PQ
TEL: 020 7937 2345 FAX: 020 7368 6700 E-MAIL: reservations@kenhouse.com

This attractive hotel with its architecturally splendid tall, ornate windows and pillared entrance stands grandly on a 19th-century site long associated with style and elegance. Just off Kensington High Street, this charming town house is an ideal base from which to explore London's attractions. Views cover delightful mews houses, leafy streets and out across city rooftops. The emphasis is on providing informal, professional service in an atmosphere of relaxation and comfort. Each of the 41 intimate bedrooms offers en suite facilities. Rooms are bright and airy with modern furniture and fittings adding to the fresh, contemporary treatment of a classic design. Home-from-home comforts include crisp linen, duvets and bathrobe. Other features are courtesy tray, ceiling fan, voicemail, modem connection and in-room safe. The two junior suites can convert into a family room. The stylish Tiger Bar is a popular venue for coffee or cocktails prior to enjoying a delicious dinner, with a menu that draws on a range of influences offering both traditional and modern dishes. The serenity of Kensington Gardens is just a gentle stroll away, and some of the capital's most fashionable shops, restaurants and cultural attractions are within walking distance. **Directions:** Nearest underground station is High Street Kensington. Price Guide: Single £145; double/twin £170; junior suites £210.

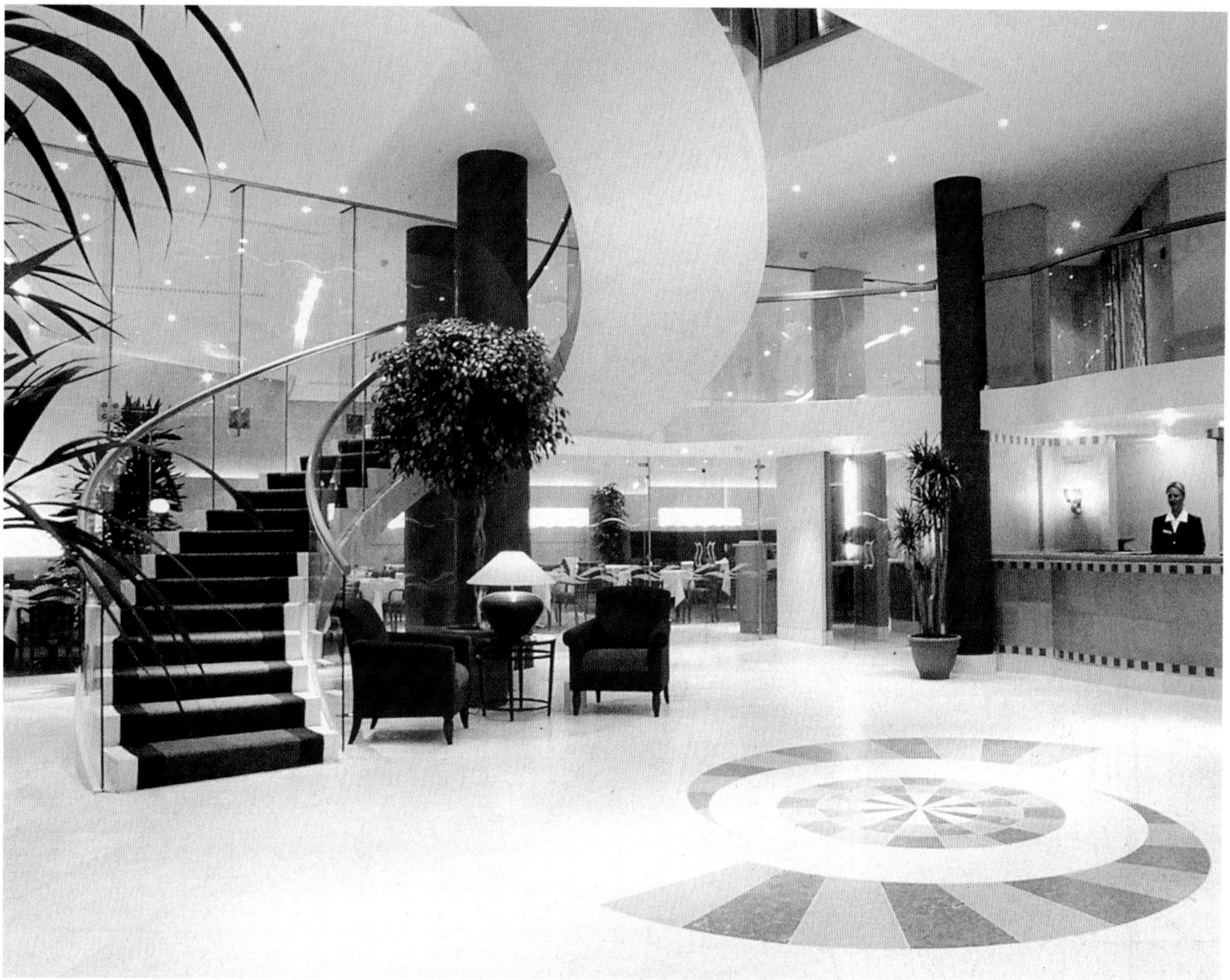

Kingsway Hall

GREAT QUEEN STREET, LONDON WC2B 5BX
TEL: 020 7309 0909 FAX: 020 7309 9696 E-MAIL: kingswayhall@compuserve.com

Situated in the heart of London's cosmopolitan Covent Garden, Kingsway Hall, opened in September 1999 is ideal for both the business and leisure visitor to London. One of the few remaining privately-owned hotels, this luxury 170-bedroom, fully air-conditioned hotel is convenient for theatreland and the City. Behind its classical façade is a spacious and dramatic foyer of modern glass and warm textured walls, leading to an elegant Lounge Bar with comfortable traditional furnishings, an ideal rendezvous for business or pleasure, especially pre- or post-theatre. Exquisite modern cuisine in the restaurant is matched by an oak-timbered and marble floor set against softly-lit, painted walls under a gently undulating ceiling – dramatic in concept and colours. Facilities in all the 170 bedrooms include satellite and interactive TV, mini-bar, in-room safe and four ISDN lines. There are non-smoking floors, same-day laundry and dry cleaning and 24-hour room service. Excellent service is provided both for the individual guest and business meetings for ten up to 150 delegates. The convivial location offers a plethora of shops, bars, restaurants and theatres to explore; the Royal Opera House is close by, and easily accessible are the British Museum and Oxford Street. Directions: Kingsway Hall is just a five minute walk from either Covent Garden or Holborn tube stations. Price Guide: Single from £230; double/twin from £240; suite from £325.

THE LEONARD

15 SEYMOUR STREET, LONDON W1H 7JW
TEL: 020 7935 2010 FAX: 020 7935 67000 E-MAIL: the.leonard@dial.pipex.com

Four late 18th-century Georgian town houses set the character of this relaxing Johansens award-winning property. Superbly located off Portman Square, and celebrating its 6th anniversary in 2002, The Leonard has become popular very quickly with discerning travellers and celebrities alike. Imaginative reconstruction has created nine rooms and 20 suites decorated individually to a very high standard, with a further 12 rooms and a small roof garden due for completion in December 2001. All rooms are fully air-conditioned and include private safe, mini-bar, hi-fi system and provision for fax/modem. Bathrooms are finished in marble, and some of the larger suites have a butler's pantry or fully-fitted kitchen. The first-floor Grand suites are particularly impressive, and the Café Bar offers breakfast and light meals throughout the day. For physical fitness and stress reduction there is a compact exercise room. With professional, friendly 'Can-do' staff, The Leonard is the epitome of casual luxury in the heart of London's West End. Available opposite, also part of the hotel, The Leonard residence offers five serviced apartments which are available for longer stays. **Directions:** The Leonard is north of Marble Arch off Portman Square and just around the corner from Oxford Street and Selfridges. Parking in Bryanston Street. Price Guide: (excl. VAT) Double from £220; suites £280– £550.

THE LEXHAM APARTMENTS

32-38 LEXHAM GARDENS, KENSINGTON, LONDON W8 5JE
TEL: 020 7559 4444 FAX: 020 7559 4400 E-MAIL: reservations@lexham.com

The Lexham has been created from four of the elegant and gracious early Victorian houses surrounding a quiet, tree-lined garden square in the heart of one of the most fashionable areas of London. The luxury one and two bedroom apartments have been stylishly furnished to provide the ideal surroundings for a family or business visit, combining comfort, flexibility, privacy and security with a convenient location. All are spacious, light and airy and equipped with all home comforts, including cable television, safe, voice mail and private phone and fax lines. Each has a full-sized, well-appointed kitchen including a washing machine/tumble dryer and a dishwasher. Many feature extra comforts such as an additional sofa bed. There is daily maid service on weekdays and 24-hour porterage. Reservations for a restaurant, theatre, car or nearby health club/swimming pool can be arranged. The Lexham has a spacious landscaped garden at the rear in which guests can relax on warmer days and evenings. The fashionable shops and restaurants of Kensington, Knightsbridge and Chelsea as well as West End theatres and the capital's tourist attractions are within easy reach. Minimum stay at the Lexham is seven days. **Directions:** Nearest underground stations are Gloucester Road and High Street Kensington. Price Guide: (excl VAT): 1-bed apartment £1,292 per week; 2-bed apartment £1,622 per week. Additional days pro rata.

31

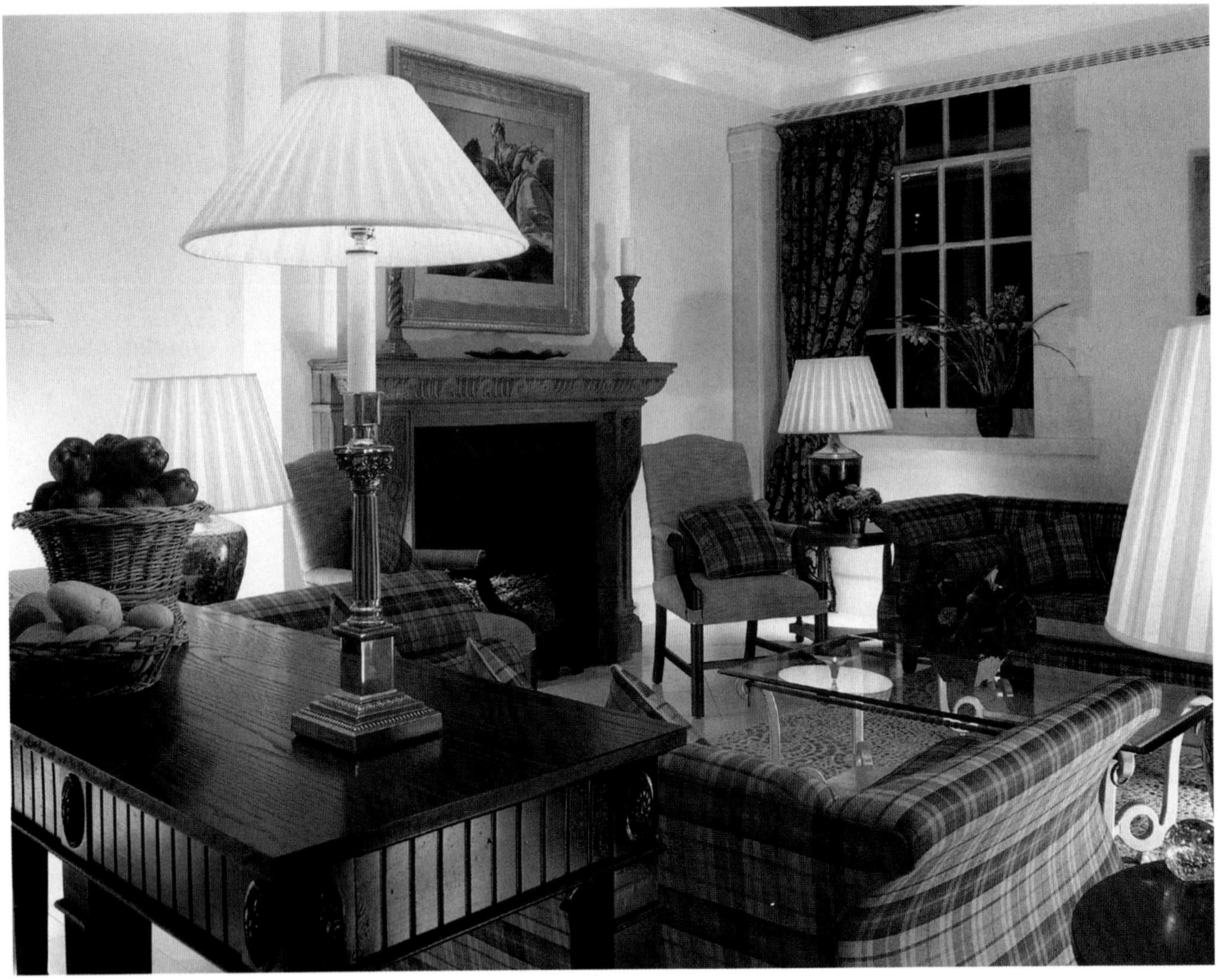

LONDON BRIDGE HOTEL & APARTMENTS

8–18 LONDON BRIDGE STREET, LONDON SE1 9SG
TEL: 020 7855 2200 FAX: 020 7855 2233 E-MAIL: sales@london–bridge–hotel.co.uk

This elegant 4-star hotel is as ideal for the leisure visitor seeking to enjoy the cultural delights of London as it is for the business executive. It stands on the edge of the City with easy access to the Docklands, London City Airport and the West End. Local attractions include Tate Modern, Shakespeare's Globe, the London Eye and Vinopolis city of wine. Its heritage dates back to Roman times; archaeological finds are in the Museum of London. All 138 en suite bedrooms and suites are air-conditioned and have a blend of modern and classic furnishings with up-to-date facilities. There are also six rooms specially designed for the less mobile guest, two non-smoking floors and an executive wing. The three apartments, each with two bedrooms, are extremely spacious and comfortable and available for short and long term stays. There are five conference rooms complete with the latest audiovisual equipment. Hitchcock's city bar is a convenient venue for an informal chat over drinks or a snack. London Bridge is home to one of the famed Simply Nico restaurants, which provides a popular and sophisticated setting in which to enjoy excellent and imaginative cuisine with a modern French flavour. Guests have free use of Curzons state-of-the-art gymnasium. **Directions:** Opposite London Bridge tube/rail station. Price Guide: (room only): Standard rooms from £185; studio suites £260– £470. Weekend rates available.

138 MasterCard VISA AMERICAN EXPRESS M 100

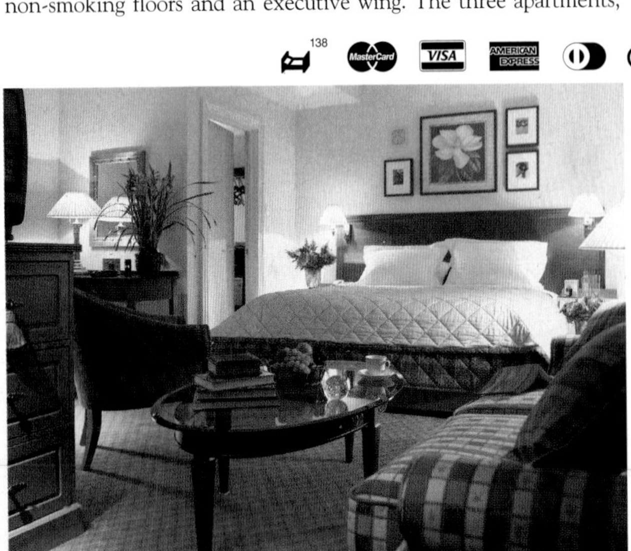

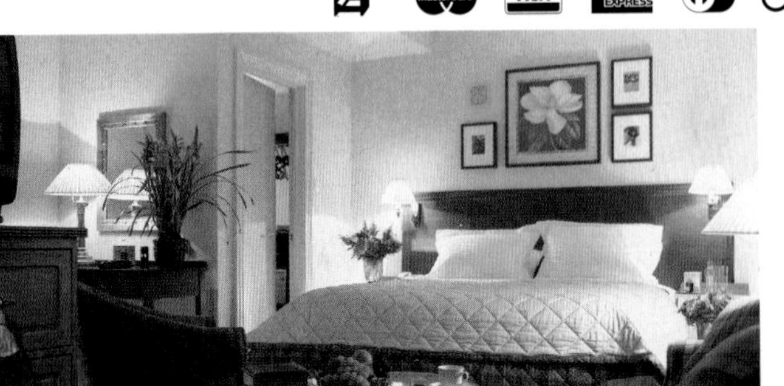

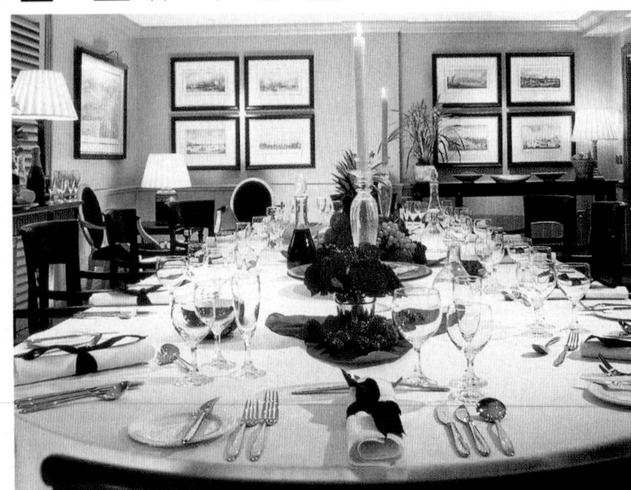

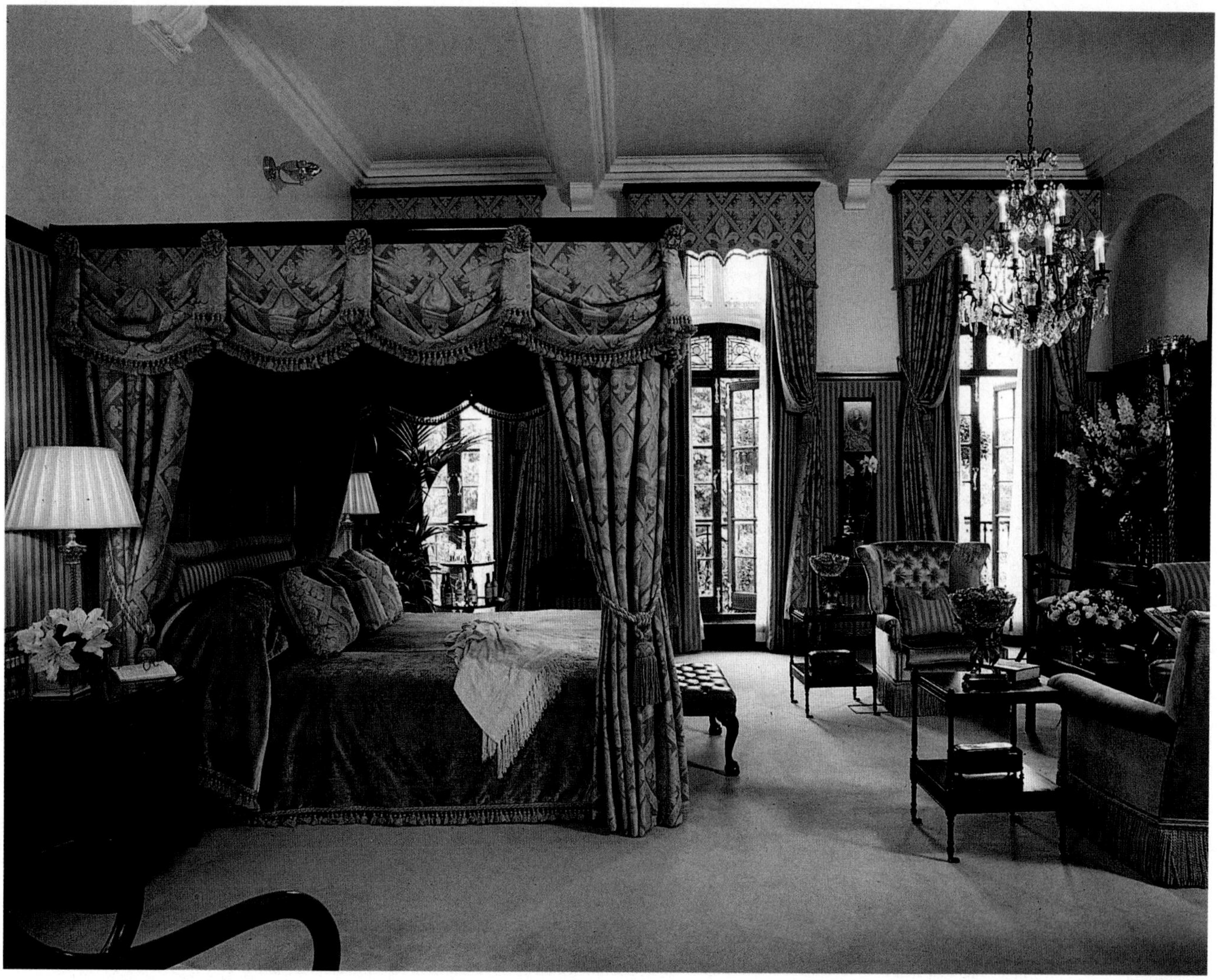

The Milestone Hotel & Apartments

1 KENSINGTON COURT, LONDON W8 5DL

TEL: 020 7917 1000 FAX: 020 7917 1010 FROM USA TOLL FREE: 1 877 955 1515 E-MAIL: bookms@rchmail.com

The beautifully appointed Johansens award winning Milestone Hotel is situated opposite Kensington Palace with views over Kensington Gardens and the Royal parklands. A Victorian showpiece, this unique hotel has been carefully restored to its original splendour whilst incorporating every modern facility. The 57 bedrooms include 12 suites and six apartments; all are individually designed with antiques, elegant furnishings and some have private balconies. Guests may relax in the comfortable, panelled Park Lounge which, in company with all other rooms, provides a 24-hour service. The hotel's restaurant, Cheneston's, the early spelling of Kensington, has an elaborately carved ceiling, original fireplace and ornate windows. The Windsor Suite is a versatile function room, perfect for private dining and corporate meetings. The health and fitness centre offers guests the use of a Jacuzzi, sauna and gymnasium. The traditional bar, Stables, on the ground floor as well as the bright and airy conservatory are ideal for meeting and entertaining friends. The Milestone is within walking distance of some of the finest shopping in Kensington and in Knightsbridge such as Harrods and is a short taxi ride to the West End, the heart of London's Theatreland. The Royal Albert Hall and all the museums in Exhibition Road are nearby. **Directions:** At the end of Kensington High Street, at the junction with Princes Gate. Price Guide: Single from £250; double/twin £270; suites from £430.

Number Eleven Cadogan Gardens

11 CADOGAN GARDENS, SLOANE SQUARE, KNIGHTSBRIDGE, LONDON SW3 2RJ
TEL: 020 7730 7000 FAX: 020 7730 5217 E-MAIL: reservations@number–eleven.co.uk

In a quiet tree-lined square between Harrods and the Kings Road, Number Eleven Cadogan Gardens is an elegant town house hotel with a reputation for first class service. The hotel remains traditional yet stylish; no reception desk, no endless signing of bills, total privacy and security. The 60 bedrooms are well-appointed and furnished with antiques and oriental rugs. The Garden Suite, with its large double bedroom, has a particularly spacious drawing room overlooking the attractive gardens. Pre-dinner drinks and canapés are served every evening in the Drawing Room, whilst a varied menu is available throughout the day in the Dining Room; room service operates around the clock. The Library is one of three private rooms available where small parties and business meetings can be held. Sauna and massage facilities are available or for a more strenuous work out, a personal trainer is on call in the in-house gymnasium. The fashionable shops and restaurants of Knightsbridge and Chelsea are within easy walking distance whilst the chauffeured Mercedes is available for airport and Eurostar connections. Theatre tickets, restaurant bookings and travel arrangements are all part of our unique personal service. **Directions:** Off Sloane Street. Nearest underground is Sloane Square Price Guide: (excl. VAT) Single from £140; double/twin from £180; suite from £260.

60 MasterCard VISA AMERICAN EXPRESS M 15 VCR

NUMBER SIXTEEN

16 SUMNER PLACE, LONDON SW7 3EG

TEL: 020 7589 5232 US TOLL FREE: 1 800 553 6674 FAX: 020 7584 8615 E-MAIL: reservations@numbersixteenhotel.co.uk

Freshly refurbished behind an immaculate pillared façade, Number Sixteen, situated in the heart of South Kensington, is surrounded by some of London's best restaurants, bars, shops and museums. Harrods, Knightsbridge shopping, Hyde Park and the Victoria & Albert Museum are all just a short walk away. Although the area has a buzzy, cosmopolitan character, the hotel is a haven of calm and seclusion. In winter an open fire and honesty bar in the drawing room entices with its warmth, whilst in summer the conservatory opens onto an award-winning private garden. The library is ideal for greeting friends or holding an informal business meeting. The 39 bedrooms are individually designed and decorated in a traditional English style complete with crisp Frette bedlinen and white, hand-embroidered bedspreads. Each is appointed with facilities expected by the modern traveller, including mini-bar, personal safe and direct dial telephone with voice mail and modem point. A light breakfast is served in the comfort of your room. Staff are friendly and attentive ensuring that guests are looked after almost as if they were staying in a private home. South Kensington underground station is just a two-minute walk away, providing easy access to the West End and the City and a direct link to Heathrow airport. **Directions:** Sumner Place is off the old Brompton Road near Onslow Square. Price Guide: Single from £85; double/twin from £145; junior suite from £195; apartment from £220.

39 MasterCard VISA AMERICAN EXPRESS

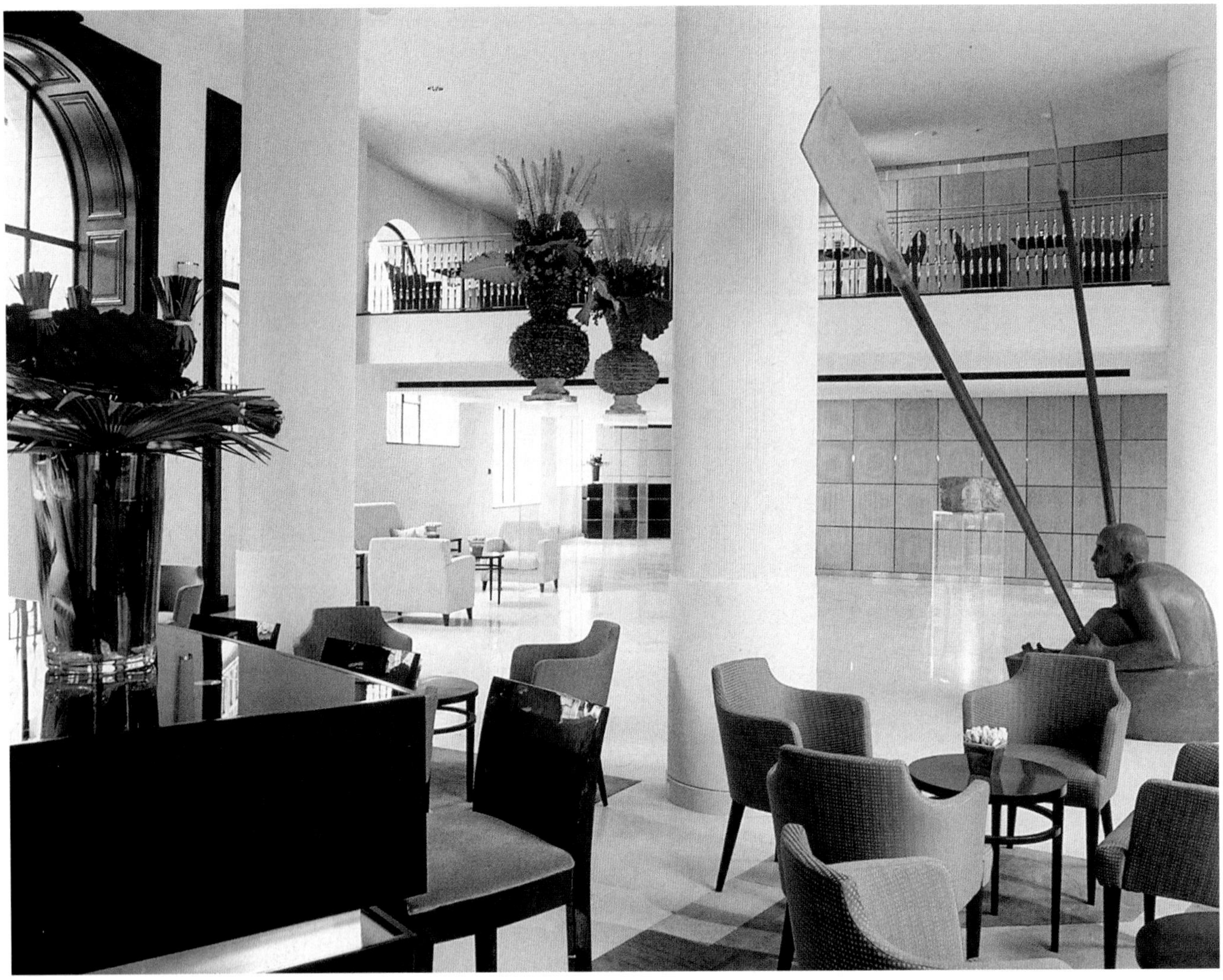

One Aldwych

ONE ALDWYCH, LONDON WC2B 4RH

TEL: 020 7300 1000 FAX: 020 7300 1001 E-MAIL: reservations@onealdwych.com

Brilliant contemporary interiors, two fabulous restaurants, the happening Lobby Bar, friendly professional service, an original art collection, cutting-edge technology and a great location in the middle of Covent Garden – just some of the reasons to stay at the award-winning One Aldwych. All rooms and suites offer the same high standards of luxury and technology and are superbly equipped with ISDN lines, European and US sockets, CD players and CD library, fibre optic reading lights, on-command movies and mini televisions in every bathroom. Thoughtful, luxurious touches include fresh fruit and flowers delivered daily, crisp white Frette linen, feather and down duvets and bespoke furniture. Guests have the choice of two of London's busiest and most fashionable restaurants, Axis and Indigo. Both are within walking distance of 15 West End theatres, making them ideal for pre or post-theatre supper. Fitness facilities include a large gymnasium with Rebok and Cybex equipment, an 18-metre lap swimming pool with underwater music, personal trainers, sauna, steamroom and beauty/therapy treatments. **Directions:** Located at the point where the Strand meets Aldwych, opposite Waterloo Bridge on the edge of Covent Garden. Price Guide: (excl. VAT) Single £285–£345; double/twin £305–£365. Weekend programmes available from £280 (double) incl. VAT and breakfast.

PEMBRIDGE COURT HOTEL

34 PEMBRIDGE GARDENS, LONDON W2 4DX

TEL: 020 7229 9977 FAX: 020 7727 4982 E-MAIL: reservations@pemct.co.uk

This gracious Victorian town house has been lovingly restored to its former glory whilst providing all the modern facilities demanded by today's discerning traveller. The 20 rooms all of which have air conditioning and are individually decorated with pretty fabrics and the walls adorned with an unusual collection of framed fans and Victoriana. The charming and tranquil sitting room is as ideal for a quiet drink as it is for a small informal meeting. The Pembridge Court is renowned for the devotion and humour with which it is run. Its long serving staff and its two famous cats "Spencer" and "Churchill" assure you of an immensely warm welcome and the very best in friendly, personal service. Over the years the hotel has built up a loyal following amongst its guests, many of whom regard it as their genuine 'home from home' in London. The Pembridge is situated in quiet tree-lined gardens just off Notting Hill Gate, an area described by Travel & Leisure magazine as 'one of the liveliest, most prosperous corners of the city'. "The Gate" as it is affectionately known, is certainly lively, colourful and full of life with lots of great pubs and restaurants and the biggest antiques market in the world at nearby Portobello Road. Directions: Pembridge Gardens is a small turning off Notting Hill Gate/Bayswater Road, just 2 minutes from Portobello Road Antiques Market Price Guide: Single £125–£165; double/twin £190–£200 (inclusive of both English breakfast & VAT).

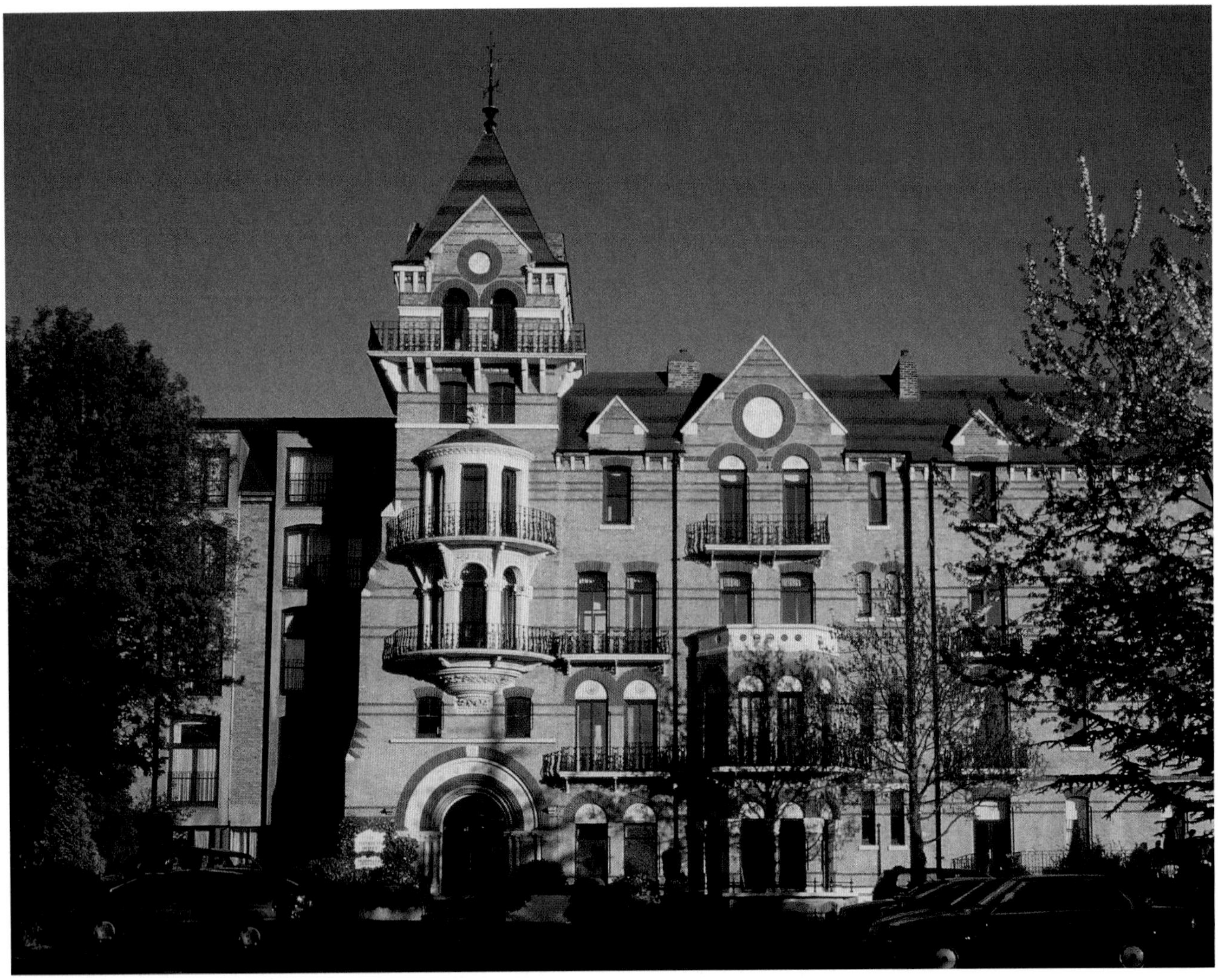

THE PETERSHAM

NIGHTINGALE LANE, RICHMOND-UPON-THAMES, SURREY TW10 6UZ
TEL: 020 8940 7471 FAX: 020 8939 1098 E-MAIL: enq@petershamhotel.co.uk

With its curves, columns and arches, tall slim windows, elaborate carvings, wrought-iron balcony railings and a majestic peaked tower this luxurious Victorian hotel impresses its visitors again and again. Beautifully situated in 'the London countryside', it is just 8 miles from the capital's centre. It stands high on Richmond Hill with views over one of the most attractive stretches of the River Thames. Built in 1865, the hotel's character emanates from its architecture which, as well as the landmark tower, features the longest unsupported Portland Stone staircase in England. Overhead are superb restored ceiling paintings. The classically styled en suite bedrooms and suites combine every modern comfort with the elegance and grandeur of the past. The Petersham Penthouse is particularly sumptuous and extremely good value. Many of the guest rooms offer panoramic Thamesside views. Exceptional and imaginative cuisine, complemented by an extensive wine list, is prepared by talented chef Andy Johns and served with aplomb in the sophisticated Nightingales restaurant. Apart from large Richmond Park with its herds of deer there are many visitor attractions nearby, including Hampton Court Palace, Syon Park, Ham House and the Royal Botanic Gardens at Kew. **Directions:** From the M25, exit at junctions 8, 9, 12 or 15. From London via Cromwell Road and the A316. Price Guide: Single £135–£160; double/twin £170–£230; suite £295.

61 MasterCard VISA AMERICAN EXPRESS M 40

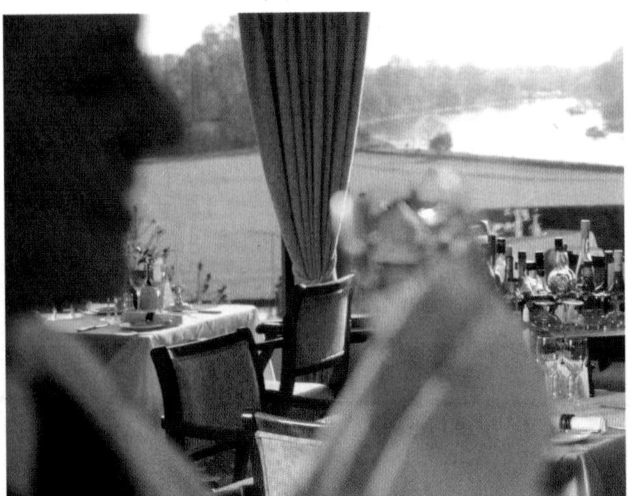

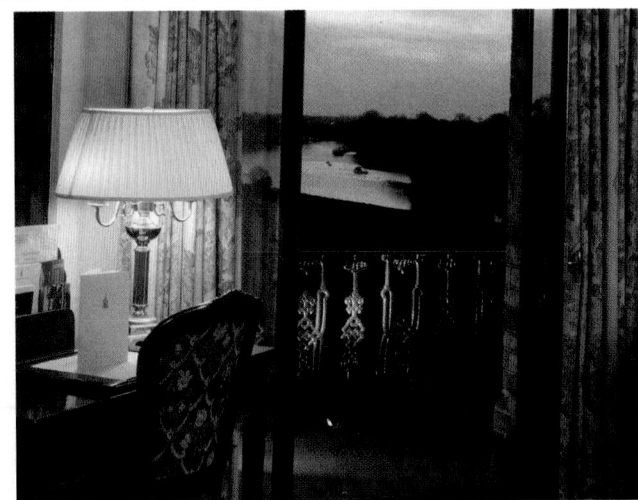

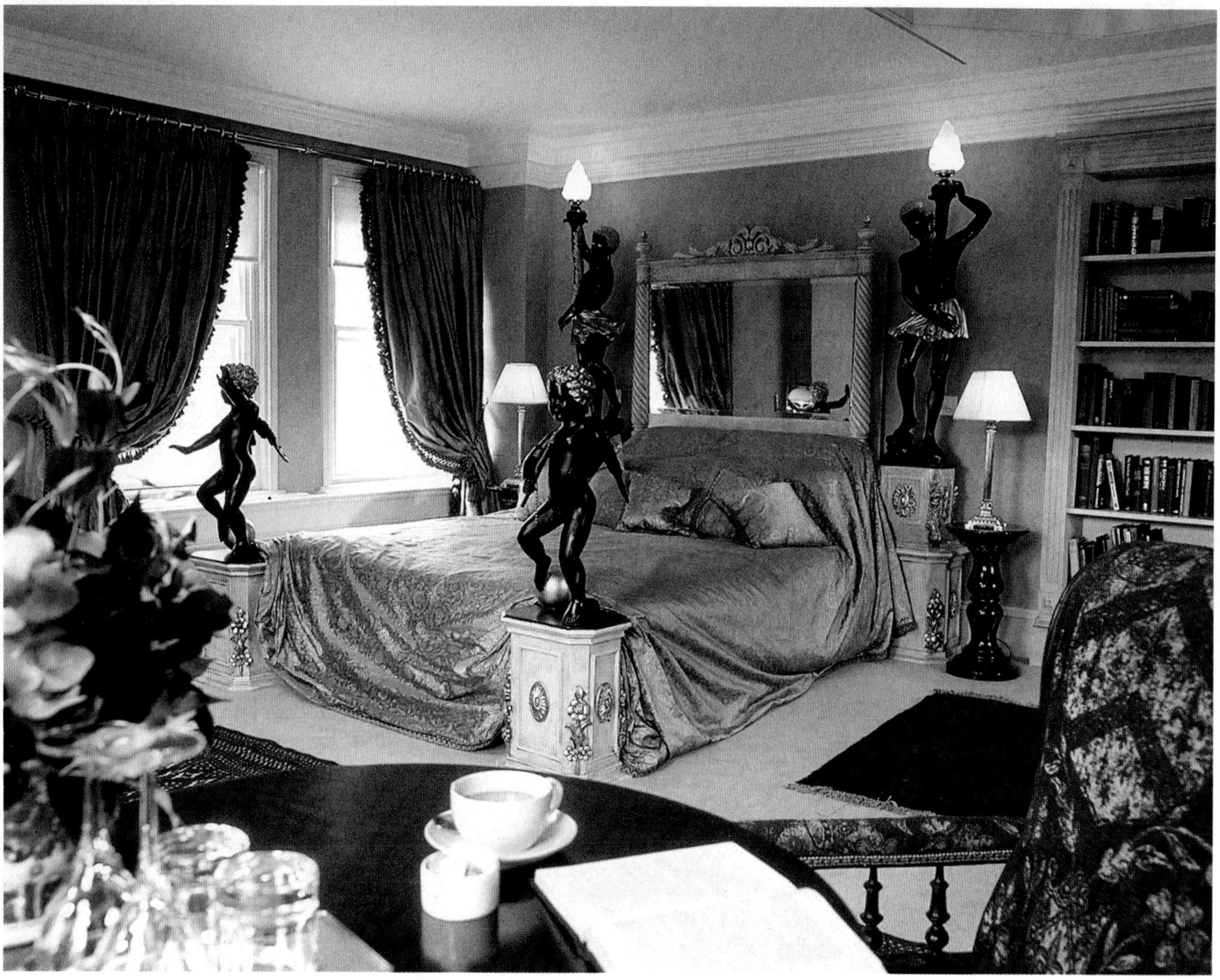

THE ROOKERY

PETER'S LANE, COWCROSS STREET, LONDON EC1M 6DS
TEL: 020 7336 0931 FAX: 020 7336 0932 E-MAIL: reservations@rookery.co.uk

Tucked away in the fashionable streets of London's Clerkenwell, this 18th century hotel is a wonderful find, full of history and style. A secret place for those in the know, it takes its name from that of the particularly lawless areas which once upon a time attracted all manner of villains including, reputedly, Charles Dickens' immortal rascal Fagin. Nowadays it glories in a stunning restoration, which reflects its rich heritage. Amazing attention to detail is found in each of the 33 different bedrooms, most of which are named after people who used to live there. Many of the beautiful antique furnishings were found in the stately homes of England, whilst specialist craftsmen have cleverly adapted Victorian plumbing techniques for modern use. Guests can relax in the welcoming atmosphere of the drawing room and conservatory overlooking a garden, itself a unique feature in a City location. The Rookery is a popular venue for business meetings, with visitors attracted by its oak-panelled library and stone-flagged floors, although it is said to be populated by ghosts! Clerkenwell is full of exuberant architecture and lively street life, with a deliciously raffish air. There are many excellent restaurants, and the wealth of the City of London is at your door, with nearby attractions including St Paul's Cathedral, Old Bailey and the Bank of England. **Directions:** Nearest station is Farringdon tube. Price Guide: (Room only excl. VAT): Single £175–£190; double/twin from £205; suites £265–£475.

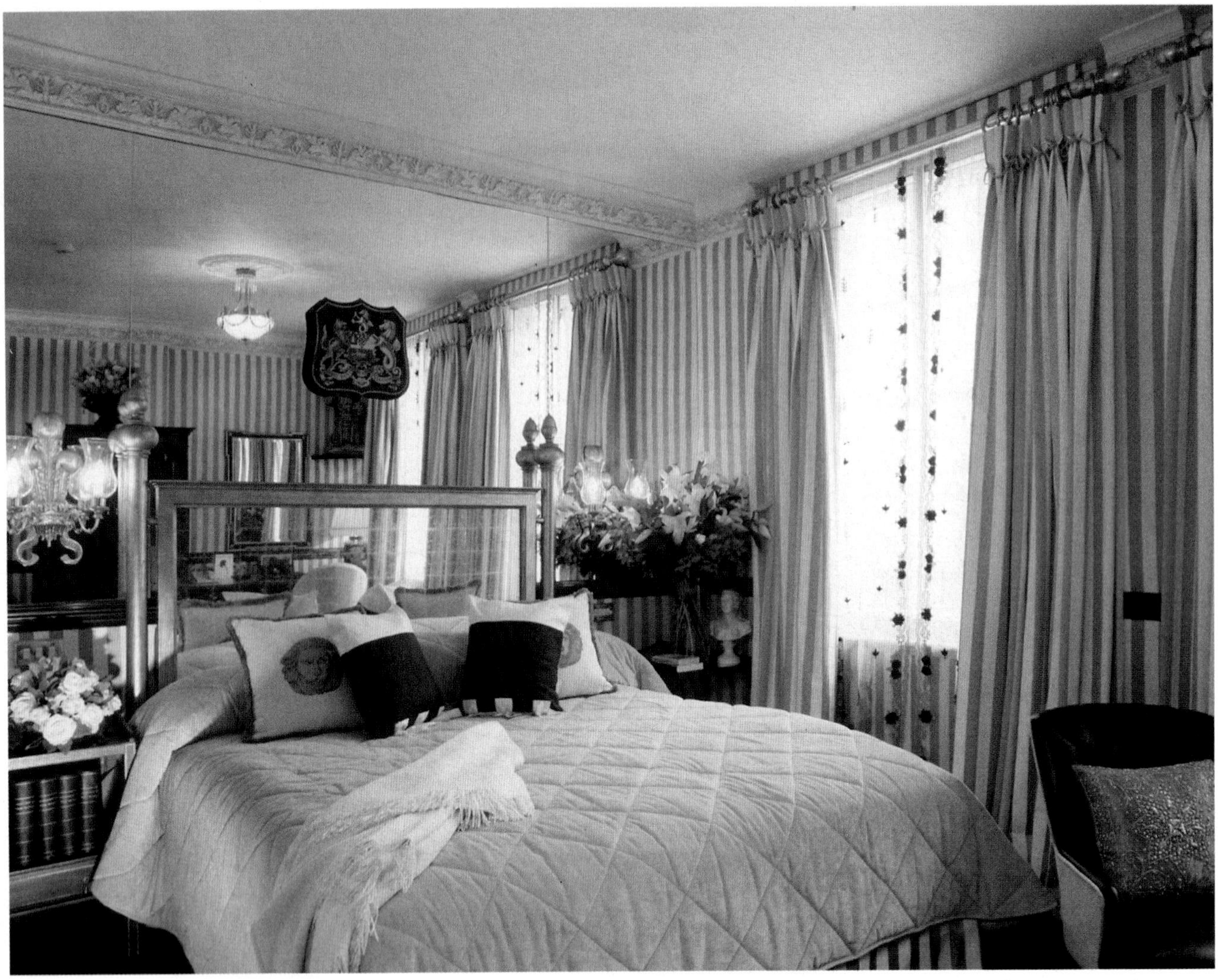

The Rubens At The Palace

39 BUCKINGHAM PALACE ROAD, LONDON SW1W 0PS

TEL: 020 7834 6600 US TOLL FREE: 1 877 955 FAX: 020 7828 5401 E-MAIL: bookrb@rchmail.com

Excellently placed for the leisure visitor as well as the corporate customer, the Rubens has completed refurbishment of the highest order to meet the demands of the modern traveller including an exclusive Royal Wing. Located opposite Buckingham Palace, just a short stroll from St James's Park and Green Park. Providing guests with outstanding personal service and comfort, it is exquisitely furnished with attention to detail. In the Cavalry Bar, with its traditional English theme, there is discreet service and live piano music every evening, whilst the Palace Lounge overlooking the Royal Mews is an ideal venue for afternoon tea. In addition to the Carvery, the 2 AA rosette Library Restaurant provides an intimate and luxurious atmosphere for fine dining. Guest bedrooms offer ultimate luxury in traditional surroundings. Facilities include satellite TV and movies, fax/modem lines, complimentary beverages and 24-hour room service. The 13 air-conditioned Signature Suites and 8 Royal Rooms, in addition to the above, offer CD systems, personal safes, mini-bars and fax machines. The Rubens also has five well appointed air-conditioned meeting and conference rooms, the largest accommodating up to 90 delegates. The Palace, Westminster Abbey and Parliament are all close by. **Directions:** 3 minutes' walk from Victoria Station, for Gatwick Express rail connection, and 10 minutes' taxi ride to Heathrow Express line Price Guide: (room only excl. VAT): Single from £150; double/twin from £160.

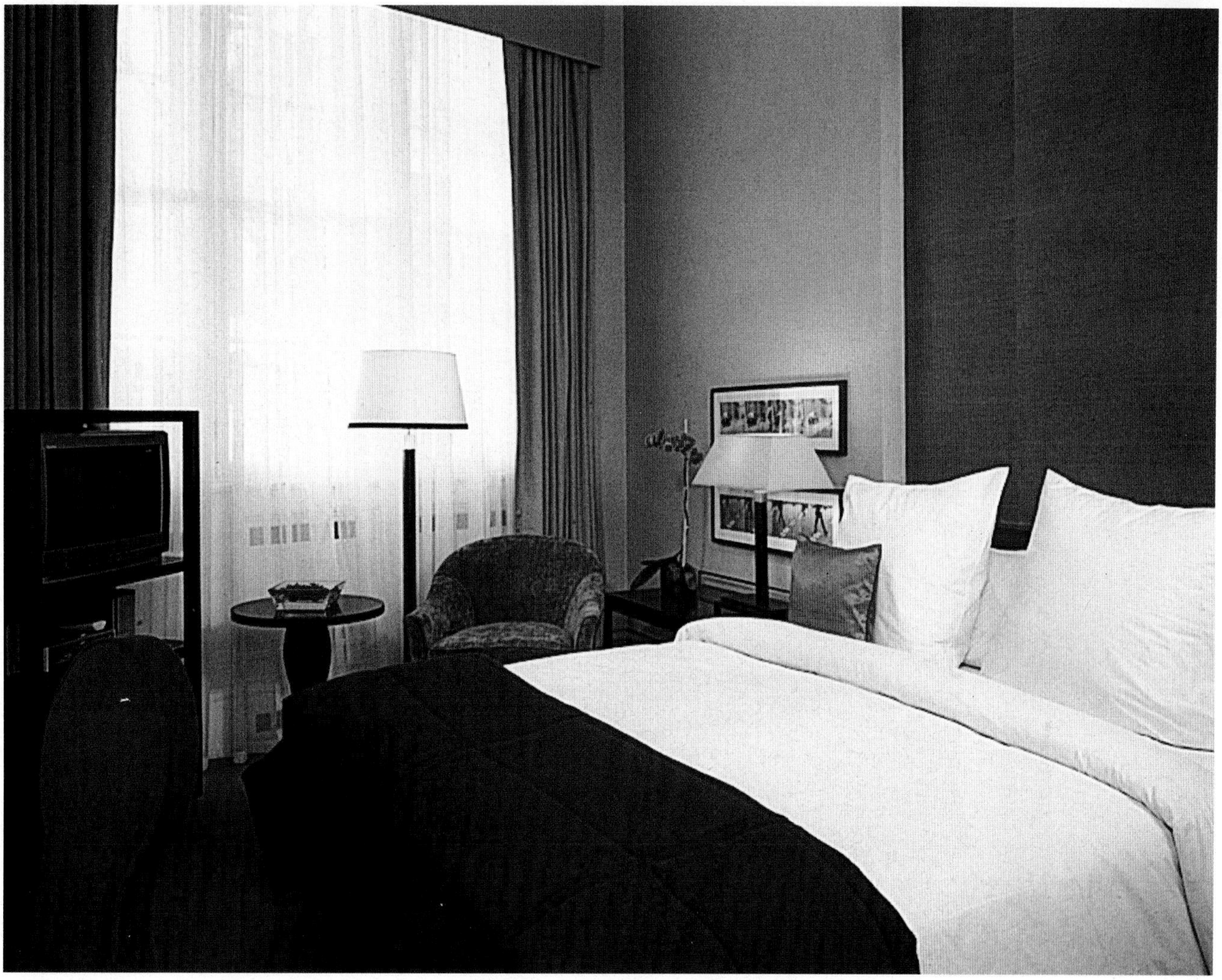

THREADNEEDLES - THE CITY'S BOUTIQUE HOTEL

5 THREADNEEDLE STREET, LONDON EC2R 8BD
TEL: 020 7657 8080 E-MAIL: res_threadneedles@etontownhouse.com

One of London's newest boutique hotels situated in the heart of the City, Threadneedles is within minutes of The Strand and Thames water taxis that link the capital's bustling business area with the bright lights of the West End. It is a sympathetically converted mid-19th-century banking hall with an interior of understated luxury that features solid oak doors, rich mahogany panelling, impressive marble columns and a beautiful hand painted glass dome. Soft tones and innovative lighting create a relaxed environment in the guest rooms, complemented by luxurious en suite bathrooms featuring stylish chrome and glass accessories. The ultimate indulgence for visitors is the Penthouse with its unique interior and private balcony. Discreet modern facilities and the latest technology ensure every comfort. Bonds the restaurant & bar, with leather seating and plush fabrics, exudes style, whilst the restaurant, serving modern European cuisine, combines classic sophistication with City chic. Private rooms can be arranged for more intimate dining. A fully equipped fitness club is available. Threadneedles has excellent corporate event facilities with three state-of-the-art meeting rooms seating up to 30 theatre style. City airport, Canary Wharf, Tate Modern, the Tower and St Paul's Cathedral are within close proximity. **Directions:** Nearest underground stations are Bank and Liverpool Street. Price Guide: (room only, excl. VAT) Single from £265; double/twin £265–£310; suite £395–£2370.

TWENTY NEVERN SQUARE

LONDON SW5 9PD

TEL: 020 7565 9555 FAX: 020 7565 9444 E-MAIL: hotel@twentynevernsquare.co.uk

A unique experience in hospitality awaits guests at this elegant 4-star town house hotel. Sumptuously restored, the emphasis is on natural materials and beautiful hand-carved beds and furniture. The hotel overlooks a tranquil garden square and has its own delightful restaurant, Café Twenty, which is also available for small dinner & cocktail parties. Each of the 20 intimate bedrooms provides white marble, compact en suite facilities, and is individually designed echoing both Asian and European influences. You can choose the delicate silks of the Chinese Room or a touch of opulence in the Rococo Room. The grandeur of the Pasha Suite, complete with four-poster bed and balcony, makes an ideal setting for a special occasion. All rooms have full modern facilities including wide-screen digital TV, CD player, private safe and a separate telephone and internet/fax connection. Gym facilities are available by arrangement. The location is ideal – close to Earl's Court and Olympia exhibition centres and the tube. The Piccadilly Line brings guests arriving at Heathrow in just over 30 minutes. Guests are a mere 10 minutes from London's most fashionable shopping areas, restaurants, theatres and cultural attractions such as the V&A and Science Museums. **Directions:** Two minutes from Earls Court station. Price Guide: Single £110–£140; double/twin £140–£195; suite £275. Price includes service, VAT and luxury buffet breakfast.

20 MasterCard VISA AMERICAN EXPRESS

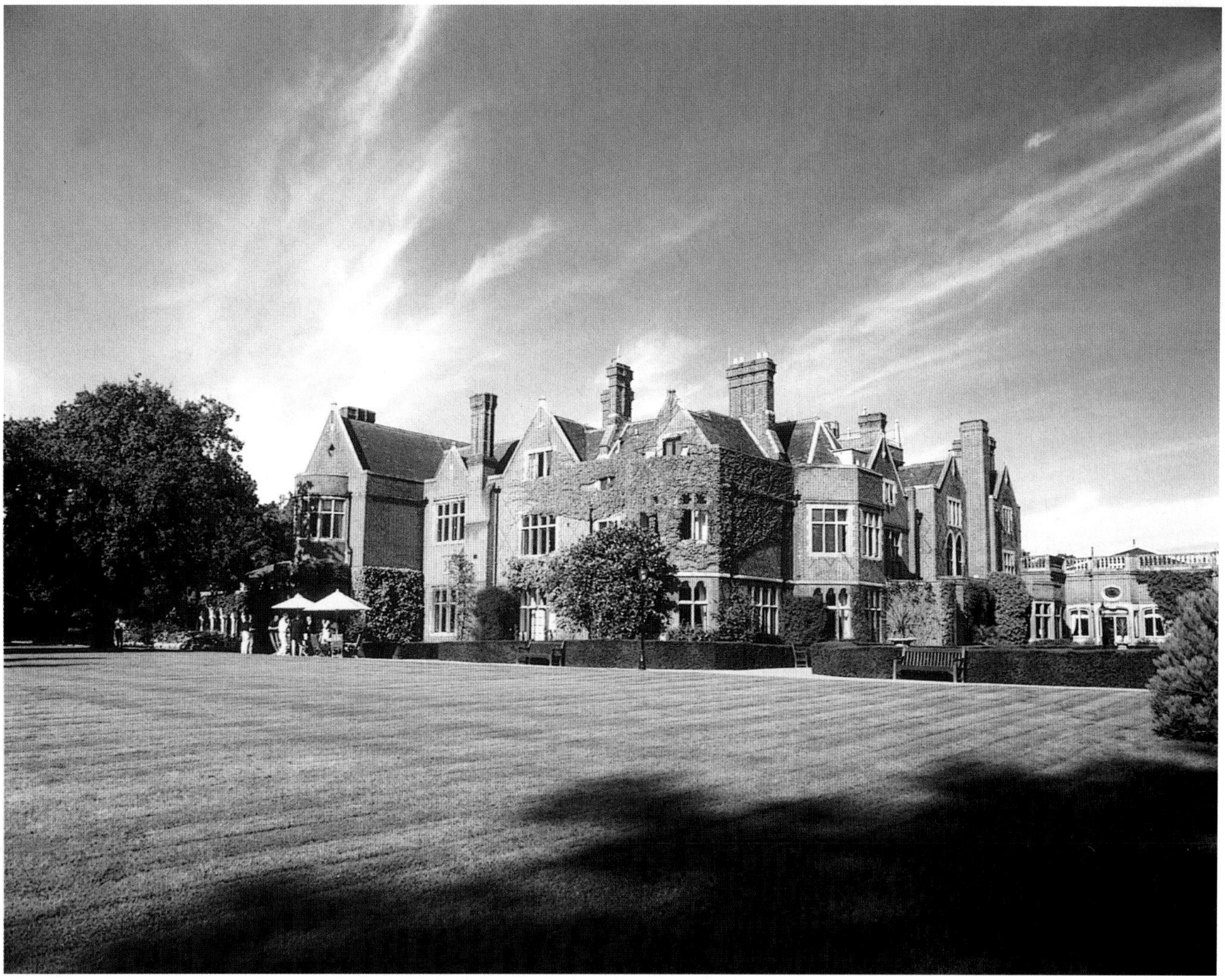

WARREN HOUSE

WARREN ROAD, COOMBE, KINGSTON-UPON-THAMES, SURREY KT2 7HY
TEL: 020 8547 1777 FAX: 020 8547 1175 E-MAIL: carolyn@warrenhouse.com

This impressive 19th-century redbrick house with its York stone door surrounds, balustrades and tall chimneys stands in four acres of landscaped gardens. It is ideally situated for both the leisure and business visitor, just five miles from Central London, within easy reach of Heathrow and Gatwick airports and on the doorstep of Surrey's sweeping countryside and attractions. For some years Warren House has been a dedicated business venue, but under new ownership is widening its appeal. Built in 1884, the house has been sensitively restored to its original style with the addition of 21st-century facilities. The en suite bedrooms and suites are individually designed, tastefully decorated and furnished to the highest standard, including desk, television, direct dial telephone and modem connection. Chef Paul Bellingham prides himself on his international cuisine, attentively served in an elegant restaurant featuring an Oriental tiled fireplace. There is a spacious lounge, well-stocked library and excellent leisure facilities including a heated swimming pool and gymnasium. Richmond Park and two golf courses are close by with Hampton Court, Wisley Gardens, Windsor, Sandown Park, Epsom and Kempton racecourses within easy reach. **Directions:** From M25 Jct 10 follow A3 north to Robin Hood roundabout. Turn left onto A308 to Kingston Hill. At the top turn left after 2nd zebra crossing into Warren Lane. Price Guide: Single from £155; double/twin from £195.

WESTBURY HOTEL

BOND STREET, MAYFAIR, LONDON W1S 2YF
TEL: 020 7629 7755 FAX: 020 7495 1163 E-MAIL: westburyhotel@compuserve.com

Situated in the heart of Mayfair, the Westbury Hotel is surrounded by fashionable neighbours such as Versace, Tiffany's, Armani and Sotheby's and the attractions of the major stores of Knightsbridge, Oxford Street and Regent Street. Rising tall and imposingly it has an architecturally splendid exterior and a luxurious interior with an atmosphere that arriving guests find instantly calming. The spacious public rooms are light and airy with soft lighting, wood panelling, delicate fabrics and tasteful furnishings. Individually decorated, all Westbury's en suite guest rooms and 26 suites offer every comfort from air-conditioning, satellite television and hi-tech facilities, to a bar and use of a newly fitted gym. Guests when staying in certain suites, can enjoy breakfast or a chat over a drink on their private balcony while absorbing a rooftop view over the capital. The Polo Bar has been a favourite meeting place for four decades and is a delightful venue for cocktails prior to dining on modern British cuisine in a charming restaurant decorated with contemporary art and looking out onto a flower garden. Light meals and afternoon tea are also served in the Polo Lounge. Major tourist attractions and theatreland are within walking distance with St James' and Hyde Park just minutes away. **Directions:** Close to Bond Street/Oxford Street underground stations. Price Guide: Single £230; double/twin £240; suites £330–£650 (Excluding VAT).

254 MasterCard VISA AMERICAN EXPRESS M 150

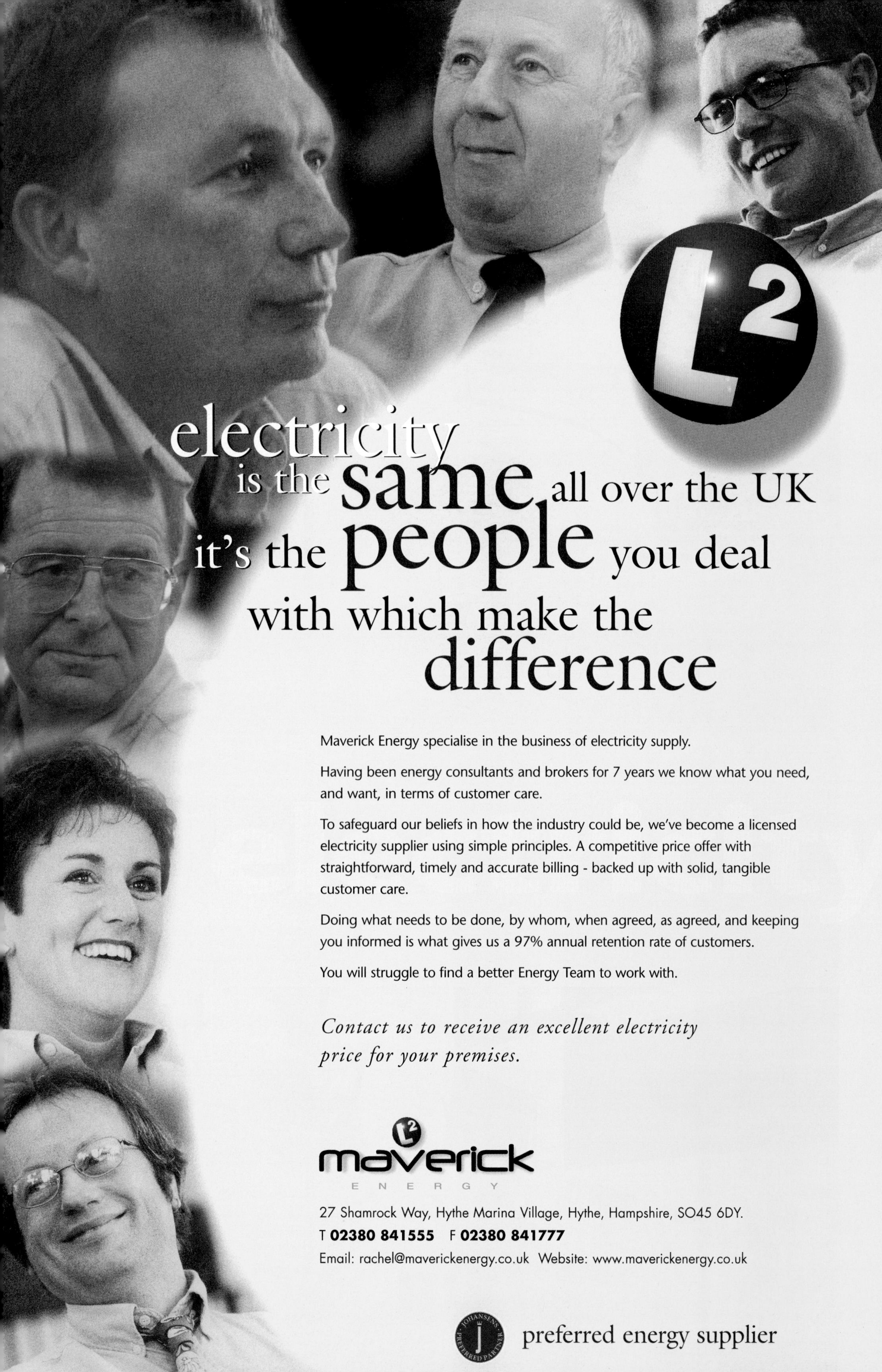

electricity is the same all over the UK
it's the people you deal with which make the difference
Maverick Energy specialise in the business of electricity supply.
Having been energy consultants and brokers for 7 years we know what you need, and want, in terms of customer care.
To safeguard our beliefs in how the industry could be, we've become a licensed electricity supplier using simple principles. A competitive price offer with straightforward, timely and accurate billing - backed up with solid, tangible customer care.
Doing what needs to be done, by whom, when agreed, as agreed, and keeping you informed is what gives us a 97% annual retention rate of customers.
You will struggle to find a better Energy Team to work with.
Contact us to receive an excellent electricity price for your premises.
maverick
ENERGY
27 Shamrock Way, Hythe Marina Village, Hythe, Hampshire, SO45 6DY.
T 02380 841555 F 02380 841777
Email: rachel@maverickenergy.co.uk Website: www.maverickenergy.co.uk
JOHANSENS PREFERRED PARTNER
preferred energy supplier
• CUSTOMER ORIENTATED • RELIABLE • INNOVATIVE • EFFICIENT • FRIENDLY • ENERGETIC • ACCURATE •

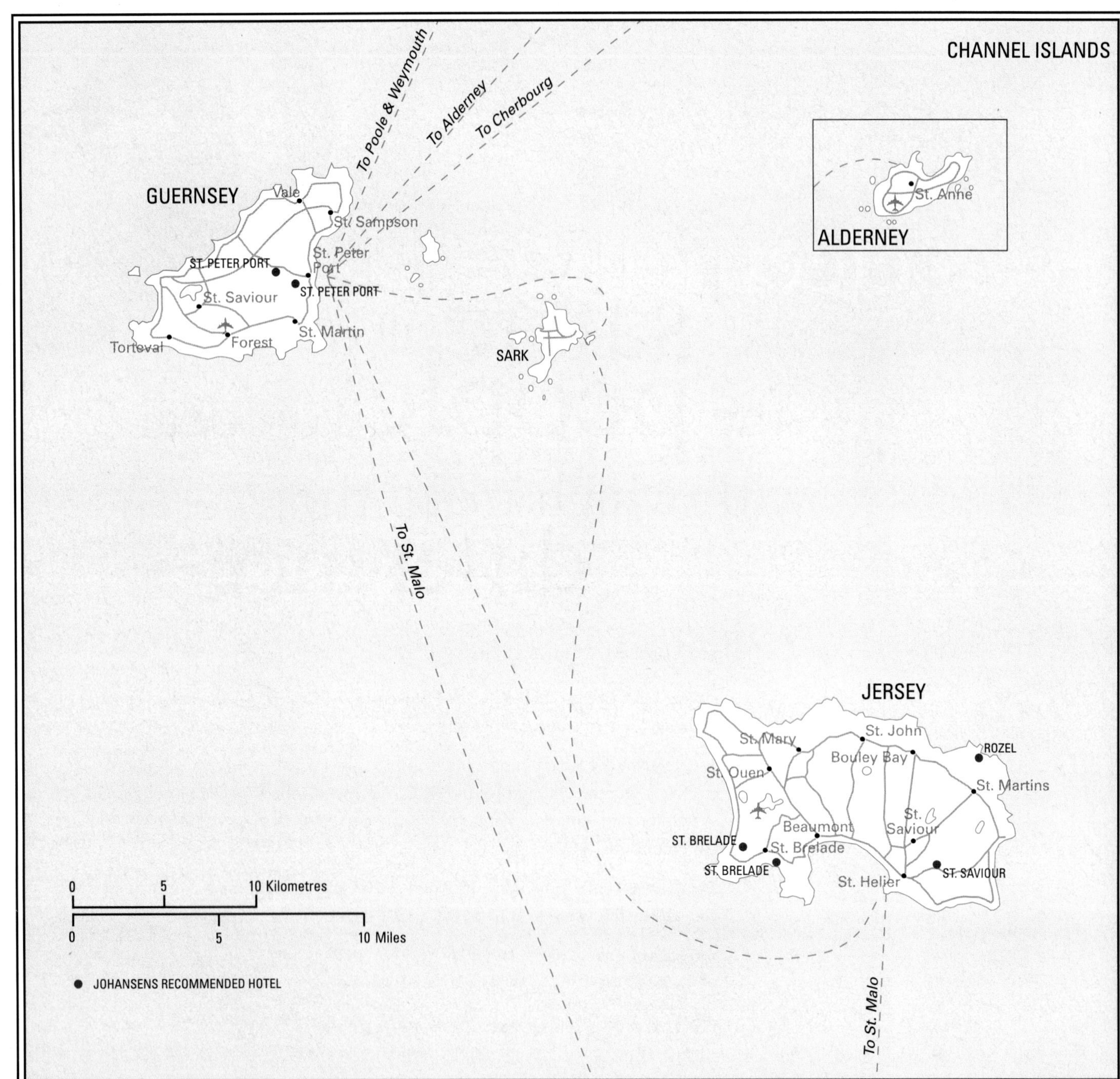
CHANNEL ISLANDS
GUERNSEY
Vale
St. Sampson
St. Peter Port
ST. PETER PORT
ST. PETER PORT
St. Saviour
St. Martin
Torteval
Forest
SARK
To Poole & Weymouth
To Alderney
To Cherbourg
ALDERNEY
St. Anne
To St. Malo
JERSEY
St. Mary
St. John
Bouley Bay
ROZEL
St. Ouen
St. Martins
St. Saviour
Beaumont
ST. BRELADE
St. Brelade
ST. BRELADE
St. Helier
ST. SAVIOUR
To St. Malo
0 5 10 Kilometres
0 5 10 Miles
● JOHANSENS RECOMMENDED HOTEL

Johansens Recommended Hotels

Channel Islands

Grande Grève, Sark

With their wonderful scenery, magnificent coastlines, historic buildings, natural and man-made attractions and mouthwatering local produce, the Channel Islands provide a memorable destination that is charmingly different. These islands are the last remnants of the mediaeval Dukedom of Normandy, which held sway both in France and in England. The islands were the only British soil to be occupied in World War II, and were liberated on May 9, 1945.

The capital of Guernsey is Saint Peter Port, which boasts a large deepwater harbour, providing excellent facilities for the numerous boats that crowd its quaysides. Inland, the visitor may be surprised to find that there are still some speakers of the islands' Norman French dialect. A host of cultural events throughout the year include the Floral Festival Week in June, which offers a range of activities for gardening enthusiasts and horticulturists.

The island of Jersey hold various musical events in April, when the Jazz Festival takes place. The Jersey International Food Festival, held in May, gives visitors the chance to taste finest local produce and experience the skills of top Jersey Chefs. The Battle of Flowers parade in August features floats covered in flowers, musicians, dancers and carnival queens.

Sark, the fourth smallest of the Channel Islands, is situated just six miles from Guernsey, reached by regular ferries. Jersey is further away, but linked to Sark by daily boats in summer. The island is unique, the last feudal state in the western world. There are no cars on Sark; transport is by bicycle or horse and carriage. Visitors can tour the island at a leisurely pace in a carriage and enjoy the wealth of wild flowers, birds and butterflies. Sark's spell is cast as soon as the visitor travels up the harbour hill to the plateau, high above the sea. The narrow lanes, flower-studded fields and ever present birdsong delight the eye and enchant the ear. Magnificent cliffs sheltering sandy beaches promise idyllic days by the sea, and artists find something to paint wherever they look.

Herm, only 20 minutes by fast ferry from Guernsey, is a castaway's dream, only 1½ miles long and ½ mile wide. There are no cars and your hotel room will not include TV. It is all pure escapism – 500 acres of wildlife, dramatic cliffs, golden beaches and secluded coves, puffins, cypress trees and clear blue waters lapping along a pine-fringed coastline.

For further information on the Channel Islands please contact:

Guernsey Tourist Board
PO Box 23, St Peter Port, Guernsey GY1 3AN
Tel: +44 (0)1481 723552
Internet: www.guernseytouristboard.com

Jersey Tourism
Liberation Square, St Helier, Jersey JE1 1BB
Tel: +44 (0)1534 500777
Internet: www.jtourism.com

Sark Tourism
Harbour Hill, Sark, Channel Islands GY9 0SB
Tel: +44 (0)1481 832345
Internet: www.sark-tourism.com

Herm
The White House Hotel, Herm Island via Guernsey GY1 3HR
Tel: +44 (0)1481 722159
Internet: www.herm-island.com

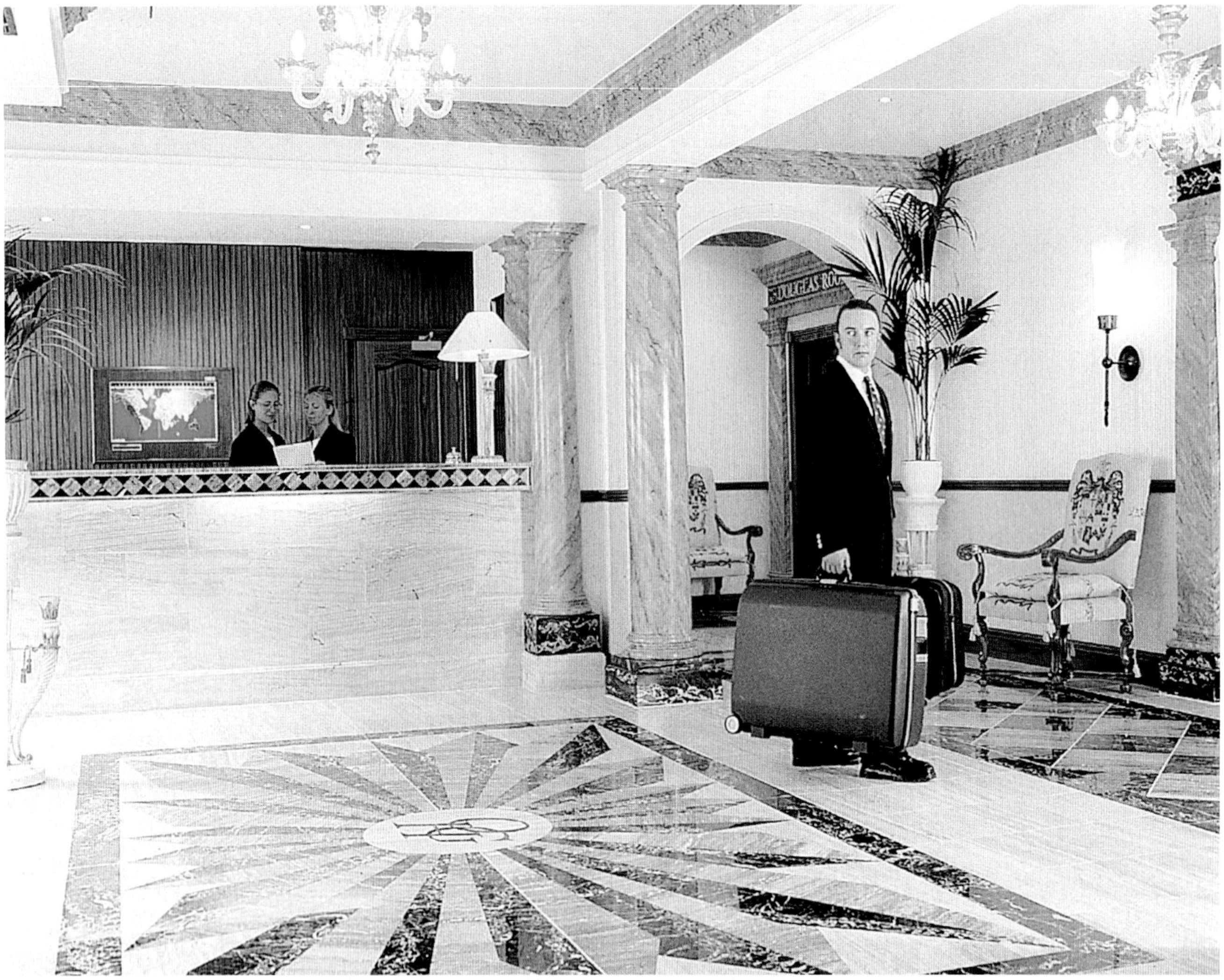

The Old Government House Hotel

ANN'S PLACE, ST PETER PORT, GUERNSEY, CHANNEL ISLANDS GY1 4AZ
TEL: 01481 724921 FAX: 01481 724429 E-MAIL: ogh@guernsey.net

Originally built in the 18th century for the Governors of the island, The Old Government House is a definite part of Guernsey's history. Currently with 68 bedrooms, the Old Government House has undergone a refurbishment programme to restore the building to its former glory and take it into the 21st century. Additionally, a recently approved significant development programme will provide further expansion including a superb health club facility to supplement the existing heated and sheltered outdoor pool. The project is a triumph with no stone being left unturned to ensure the hotel remains one of the finest on the island, and deserving of its prime location within minutes of the town centre. The bedrooms are light and spacious and elegantly appointed, whilst the marble bathrooms boast every modern amenity. The award-winning Regency Restaurant, with its graceful windows, has panoramic views over the neighbouring islands and offers a range of fine cuisine including locally selected seafood. A ferry port just minutes from the hotel can link guests to the other islands, and a day on Sark or Herm is a must for any visitor, as is the wealth of duty free shops and boutiques. **Directions:** In the heart of St Peter Port, the hotel is best accessed off St Julian's Avenue which heads inland from the roundabout at St Julian's Place. Price Guide: Single from £105; double/twin £115–£210, suites £220–£410.

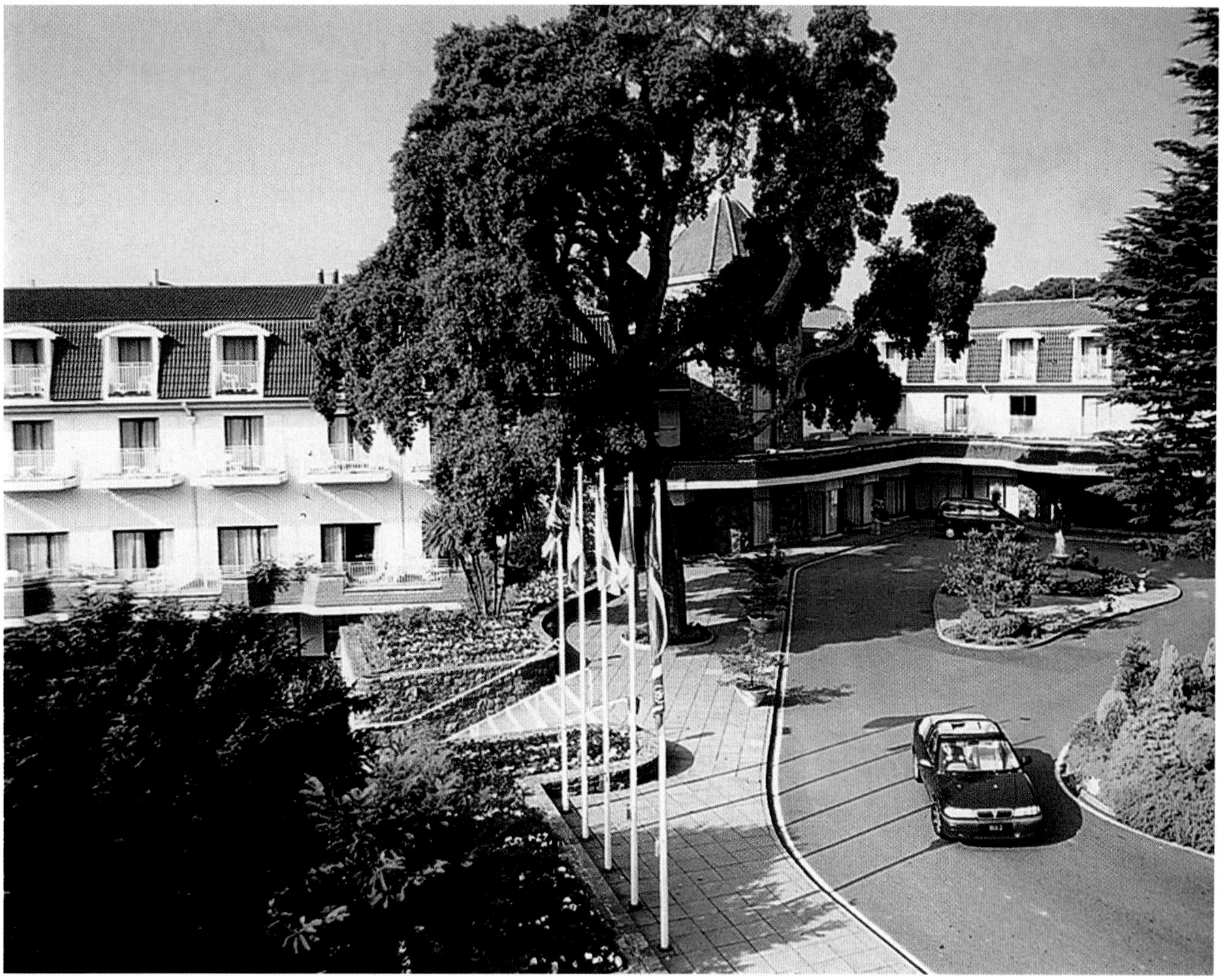

ST PIERRE PARK HOTEL

ROHAIS, ST PETER PORT, GUERNSEY, CHANNEL ISLANDS GY1 1FD
TEL: 01481 728282 FAX: 01481 712041 E-MAIL: enquiries@stpierrepark.co.uk

Conveniently situated only minutes away from the airport and St Peter Port, this 5 Crown hotel is an ideal choice for a business function, short break, sporting or family holiday. Nestling in 45 acres of glorious parkland, the estate has its own lake, fountain, driving range and a challenging 9-hole golf course, designed by Tony Jacklin. Following extensive refurbishment, the en suite bedrooms offer comfortable accommodation and many of the latest amenities. Specialising in delicate seafood recipes, the Victor Hugo is one of Guernsey's finest restaurants and uses the freshest local produce. A more informal ambience may be found in the Café Renoir, where guests savour brasserie-style snacks and refreshments. Fitness enthusiasts will be pleased with the extensive leisure facilities at the hotel's Le Mirage Health Suite, including an indoor swimming pool and individual saunas and steam rooms. Golf, tennis, croquet and other sports may also be practised on site. With its French influence and varied coastline, Guernsey has so much to offer. Guests may explore the delightful harbour town of St Peter Port and enjoy exclusive VAT free shopping. **Directions:** The hotel is centrally situated, only 10 minutes from the airport and 5 minutes from St Peter Port, Guernsey's main town. Take the Rohais road westbound out of St Peter Port. Price Guide: Single from £125; double/twin from £165; suite from £320.

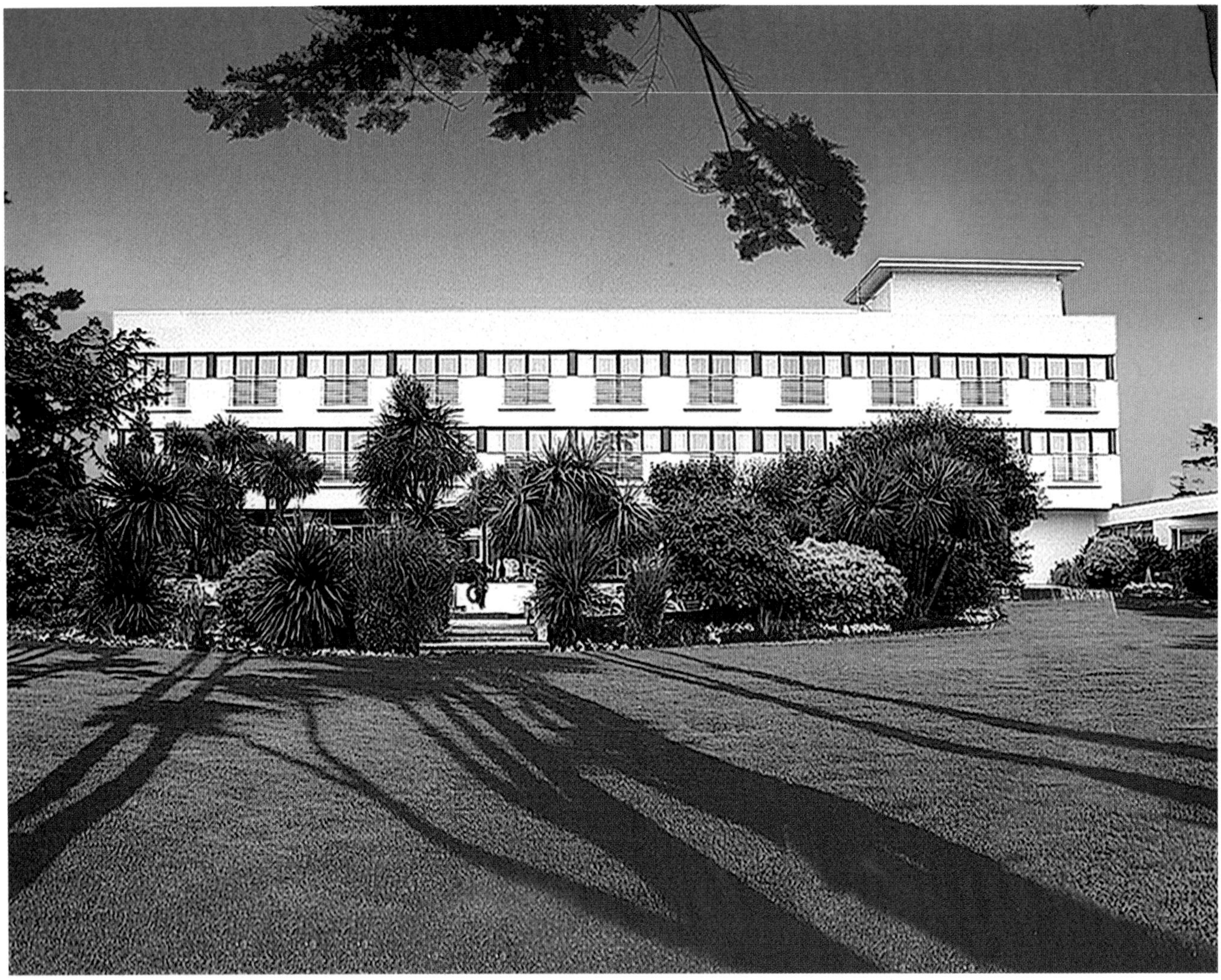

The Atlantic Hotel

LE MONT DE LA PULENTE, ST BRELADE, JERSEY JE3 8HE
TEL: 01534 744101 FAX: 01534 744102 E-MAIL: info@theatlantichotel.com

This is a stunning luxury hotel that offers elegance, grace, comfort, exquisite cuisine and impeccable service. It is excellent in every way, from majestic interior pillars and magnificent wood panelling to sumptuous furnishings, warm décor and perfect location. The Atlantic stands regally in 3 acres of private grounds alongside the La Moye Golf Course overlooking the 5-mile sweep of St Ouen's Bay. A multi-million pound refurbishment of the hotel including the enlargement of bedrooms and remodelling of the building's exterior to give a 'marine' flavour, has resulted in even more venue quality and the hotel's elevation to 5-Sun status by Jersey Tourism. No expense has been spared in refurnishing the bedrooms, suites and garden studios. Tastefully decorated, they offer occupants the highest standard of facilities and comfort together with splendid views of the sea or the golf course. Most prestigious and stylish is the spacious Atlantic Suite with its own entrance hall, living room, guest cloakroom and service pantry in addition to the en suite master bedroom. The delightful, award-winning restaurant overlooks the open-air swimming pool and sun terrace. Head Chef Ken Healy specialises in modern British cooking and produces excellent and imaginative menus. **Directions:** Off a private drive off the A13 at La Pulente, 2 miles from the airport. Price Guide: Single £135–£175; double/twin £175–£280; suite £370–£400.

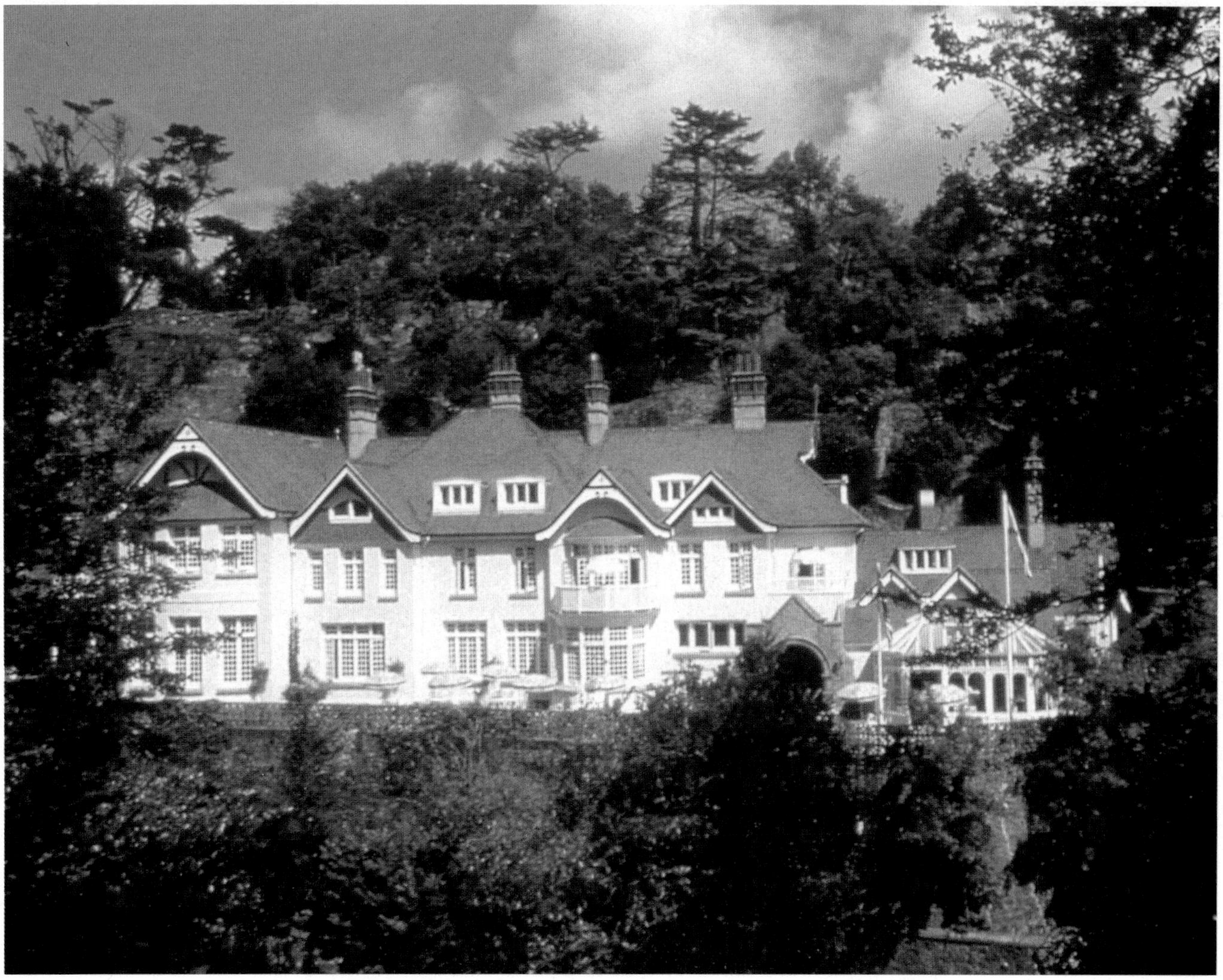

CHATEAU LA CHAIRE

ROZEL BAY, JERSEY JE3 6AJ
TEL: 01534 863354 FAX: 01534 865137 E-MAIL: res@chateau-la-chaire.co.uk

Nestling on the Rozel Valley's sunny slopes is Château La Chaire, an elegantly proportioned Victorian house surrounded by terraced gardens. Built in 1843, the Château has been enhanced and transformed into a luxurious hotel providing its guests with a superb blend of superior comfort, service and cuisine. Each of the bedrooms has been furnished to the highest standards and offers an impressive array of personal comforts; many en suite bathrooms feature Jacuzzis. The same attention to detail is evident in the public rooms, such as the splendid rococo lounge. Exceptional personal service is acknowledged by the RAC Gold Ribbon award. Both adventurous and traditional dishes can be enjoyed in the oak panelled setting of La Chaire restaurant. Seafood is a speciality, but there is plenty of choice to cater for all tastes. Awarded 3AA Red Stars and 2 AA Rosettes. A few minutes from the hotel is the picturesque Rozel Bay, a bustling fishing harbour with safe beaches close by. The island's capital, St Helier, is just six miles away. Local tours, golf, fishing and riding are among the many leisure activities that the hotel's staff will be happy to arrange for guests. **Directions:** The hotel is signposted off the main coastal road to Rozel Bay, six miles north east of St Helier Price Guide: Single from £90; double/twin from £120; suites from £210.

Hotel L'Horizon

ST BRELADE'S BAY, JERSEY, JE3 8EF, CHANNEL ISLANDS
TEL: 01534 743101 FAX: 01534 746269 E-MAIL: lhorizon@hotellhorizon.com

A premier hotel in the Channel Islands, L'Horizon is situated on Jersey's lovely St Brelade's Bay. Its south facing position ensures that the hotel enjoys many hours of sunshine. A variety of reception areas provides guests with a choice of environments in which to sit and relax. Comfortable and spacious bedrooms offer every modern amenity and many enjoy a wonderful view across the bay. All sea facing bedrooms have balconies. There are three restaurants, each noted for its individual style, the traditional and elegant Crystal Room, fine dining in the intimate Grill Room and the relaxed atmosphere of the pool side Brasserie. L'Horizon has won many international accolades and its menus are compiled from the best fresh Jersey produce and from speciality ingredients from the world's top markets. In summer, relax and sip your favourite cocktails enjoying the panoramic views from the terrace. Guests are invited to take advantage of the superb facilities of the Club L'Horizon, which include a mini gym, large swimming pool, steam room, and sauna. Activities available nearby are swimming, walking and golf. There are three 18-hole golf courses on the island. Seafarers can go on boat trips round the island or across to Guernsey, Alderney, Herm, Sark, even France. **Directions:** In the heart of St Brelade's Bay, ten minutes from the airport. Price guide Price Guide: Rooms £130–£200; suite from £340. Special breaks available.

107 200

LONGUEVILLE MANOR

ST SAVIOUR, JERSEY JE2 7WF

TEL: 01534 725501 **FAX:** 01534 731613 **E-MAIL:** longman@itl.net

Three generations of the Lewis family have welcomed guests to this 13th-century Manor, which is today a very fine and prestigious hotel. Ever attentive staff, superb public rooms, exquisite bedrooms and sumptuous cuisine, which in 2001 earned the Manor's restaurant its 8th consecutive Michelin star, suggest the standards you may expect. Guests dine in either the elegant oak-panelled room or the spacious garden room. Many of the fruits, vegetables and herbs for the kitchen are grown in the hotel's walled garden or the traditional greenhouse which provides fresh produce throughout the seasons - it even has a banana tree! The wine list offers a selection by Longueville's Master Sommelier, and includes gems from the New World, great vintages from the best of the French chateaux and superb champagnes. Continued upgrading has seen the introduction of delightful new suites, both in the main house and in the restored garden cottage, along with a small meeting and private dining facility. The large heated pool has an adjoining bar, where guests may enjoy a light alfresco meal during the summer. Tennis can be played on the synthetic grass court whilst the lawn is ideal for croquet. Guests may stroll through the magnificent garden with its picturesque lake, home to a black swan and mandarin ducks. **Directions:** On A3, 1 m from St Helier. Price Guide: Single from £156; double/twin £180–£270; suite £340–£370.

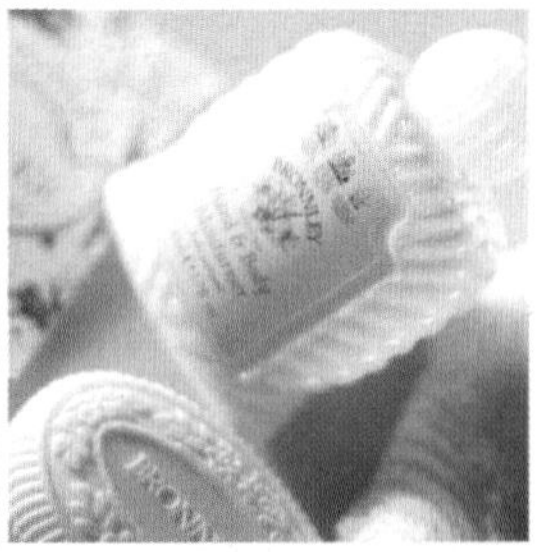

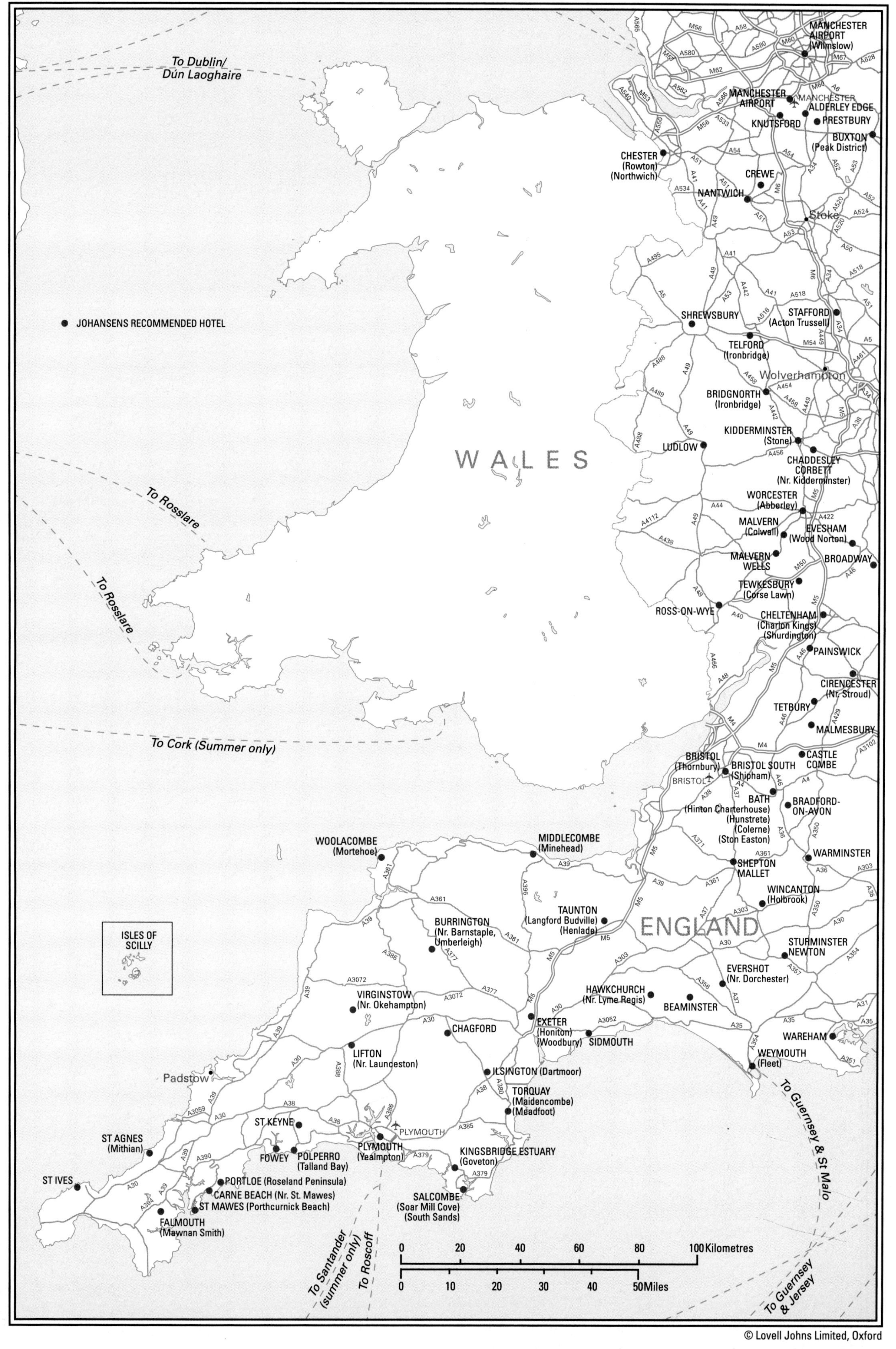

To Dublin/
Dún Laoghaire
JOHANSENS RECOMMENDED HOTEL
To Rosslare
To Rosslare
To Cork (Summer only)
WALES
ENGLAND
MANCHESTER AIRPORT
(Wilmslow)
MANCHESTER AIRPORT
MANCHESTER
ALDERLEY EDGE
PRESTBURY
KNUTSFORD
BUXTON
(Peak District)
CHESTER
(Rowton)
(Northwich)
CREWE
NANTWICH
Stoke
SHREWSBURY
STAFFORD
(Acton Trussell)
TELFORD
(Ironbridge)
Wolverhampton
BRIDGNORTH
(Ironbridge)
KIDDERMINSTER
(Stone)
LUDLOW
CHADDESLEY CORBETT
(Nr. Kidderminster)
WORCESTER
(Abberley)
MALVERN
(Colwall)
EVESHAM
(Wood Norton)
MALVERN WELLS
BROADWAY
TEWKESBURY
(Corse Lawn)
ROSS-ON-WYE
CHELTENHAM
(Charlton Kings)
(Shurdington)
PAINSWICK
CIRENCESTER
(Nr. Stroud)
TETBURY
MALMESBURY
BRISTOL
(Thornbury)
BRISTOL SOUTH
(Shipham)
CASTLE COMBE
BRISTOL
BATH
(Hinton Charterhouse)
(Hunstrete)
(Colerne)
(Ston Easton)
BRADFORD-ON-AVON
WARMINSTER
WOOLACOMBE
(Mortehoe)
MIDDLECOMBE
(Minehead)
SHEPTON MALLET
WINCANTON
(Holbrook)
ISLES OF SCILLY
BURRINGTON
(Nr. Barnstaple,
Umberleigh)
TAUNTON
(Langford Budville)
(Henlade)
STURMINSTER NEWTON
EVERSHOT
(Nr. Dorchester)
VIRGINSTOW
(Nr. Okehampton)
HAWKCHURCH
(Nr. Lyme Regis)
BEAMINSTER
CHAGFORD
EXETER
(Honiton)
(Woodbury)
SIDMOUTH
WAREHAM
LIFTON
(Nr. Launceston)
WEYMOUTH
(Fleet)
Padstow
ILSINGTON (Dartmoor)
TORQUAY
(Maidencombe)
(Meadfoot)
To Guernsey & St Malo
ST KEYNE
PLYMOUTH
ST AGNES
(Mithian)
FOWEY
POLPERRO
(Talland Bay)
PLYMOUTH
(Yealmpton)
KINGSBRIDGE ESTUARY
(Goveton)
ST IVES
PORTLOE (Roseland Peninsula)
CARNE BEACH (Nr. St. Mawes)
ST MAWES (Porthcurnick Beach)
SALCOMBE
(Soar Mill Cove)
(South Sands)
FALMOUTH
(Mawnan Smith)
To Santander
(summer only)
To Roscoff
0 20 40 60 80 100 Kilometres
0 10 20 30 40 50 Miles
To Guernsey
& Jersey

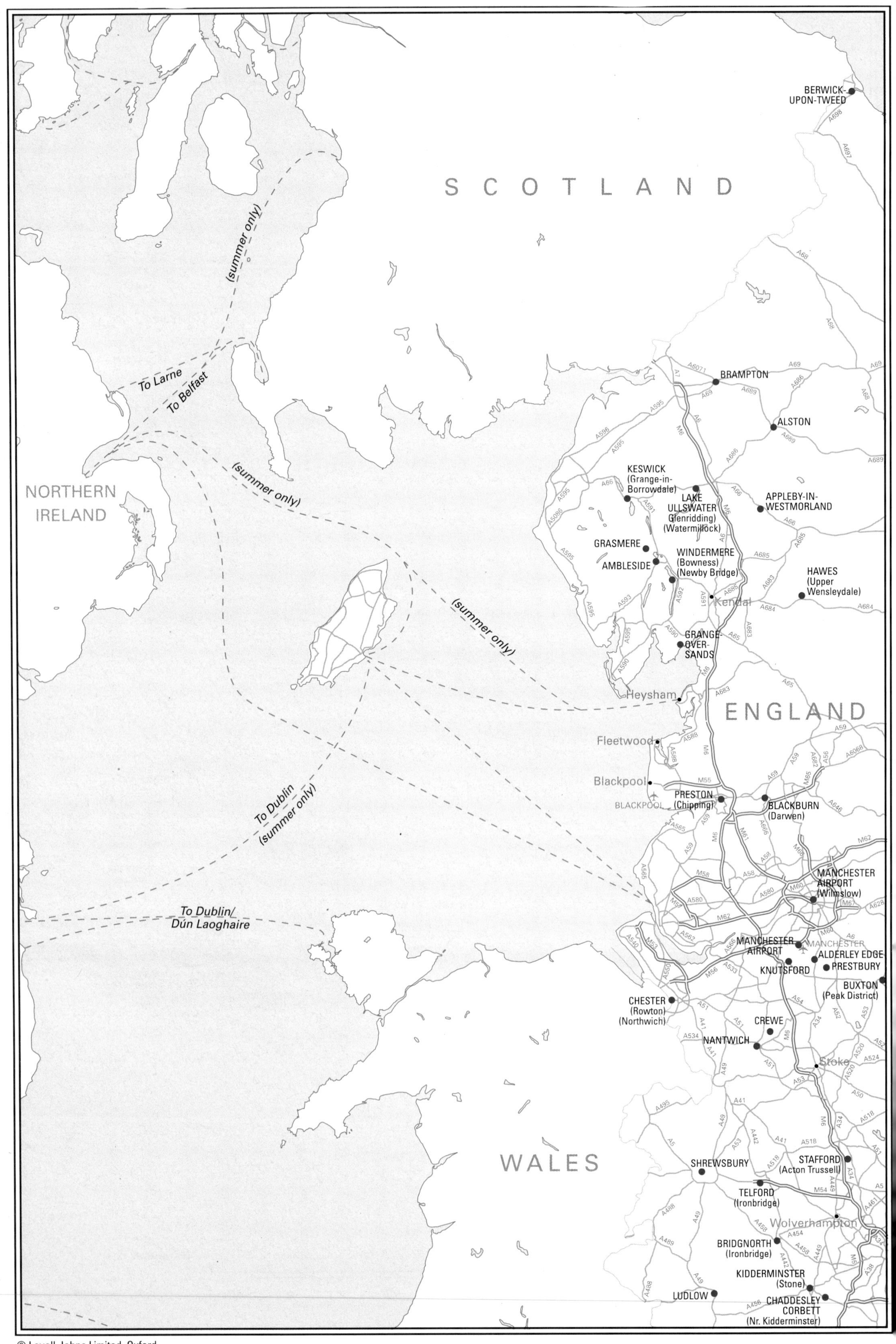

SCOTLAND
NORTHERN IRELAND
ENGLAND
WALES
BERWICK-UPON-TWEED
BRAMPTON
ALSTON
KESWICK (Grange-in-Borrowdale)
LAKE ULLSWATER (Glenridding) (Watermillock)
APPLEBY-IN-WESTMORLAND
GRASMERE
AMBLESIDE
WINDERMERE (Bowness) (Newby Bridge)
HAWES (Upper Wensleydale)
Kendal
GRANGE-OVER-SANDS
Heysham
Fleetwood
Blackpool
BLACKPOOL
PRESTON (Chipping)
BLACKBURN (Darwen)
MANCHESTER AIRPORT (Wilmslow)
MANCHESTER AIRPORT
MANCHESTER
KNUTSFORD
ALDERLEY EDGE
PRESTBURY
BUXTON (Peak District)
CHESTER (Rowton) (Northwich)
CREWE
NANTWICH
Stoke
SHREWSBURY
STAFFORD (Acton Trussell)
TELFORD (Ironbridge)
Wolverhampton
BRIDGNORTH (Ironbridge)
KIDDERMINSTER (Stone)
CHADDESLEY CORBETT (Nr. Kidderminster)
LUDLOW
To Larne
To Belfast
(summer only)
(summer only)
(summer only)
To Dublin (summer only)
To Dublin/ Dún Laoghaire

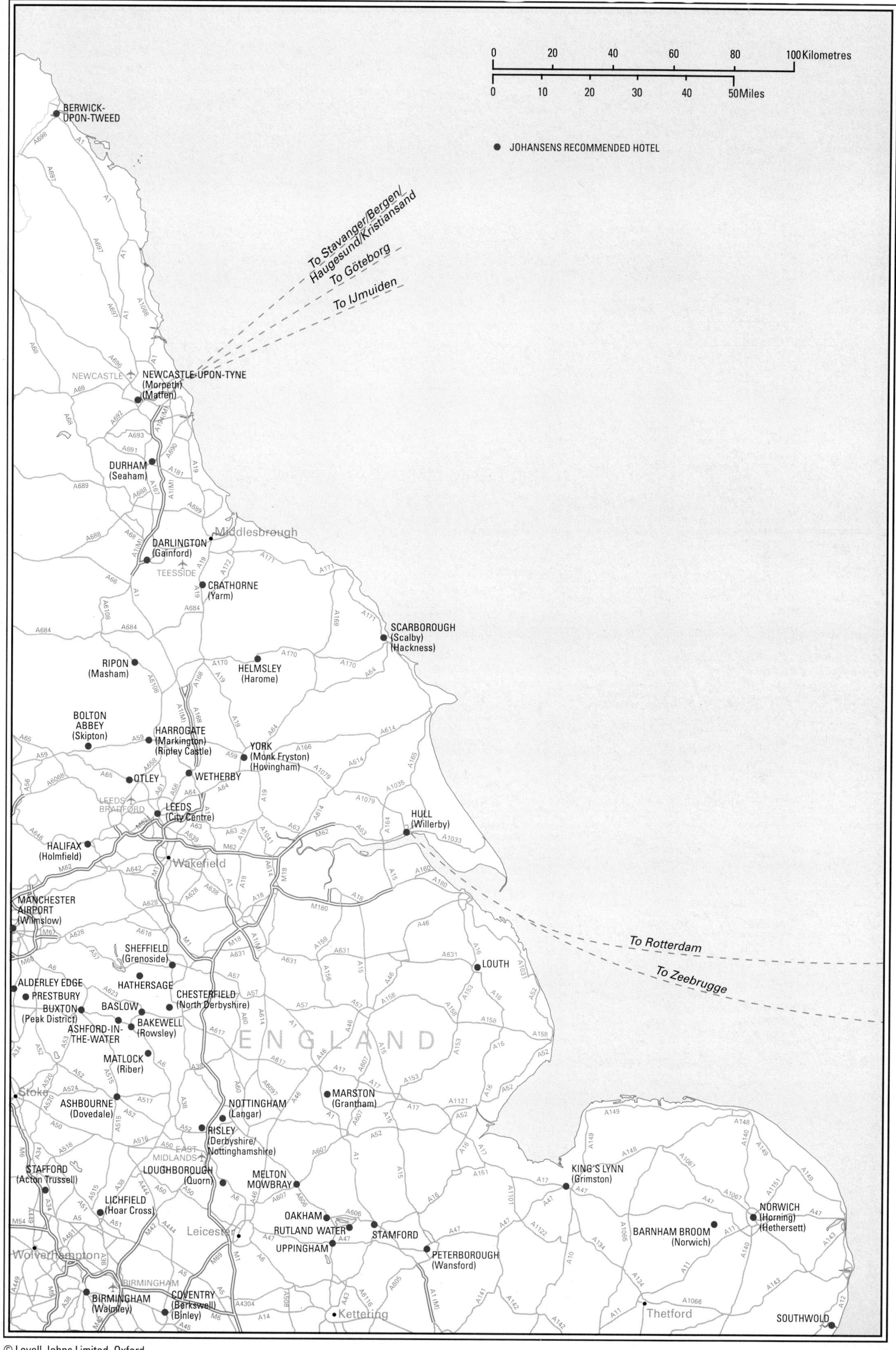

0 20 40 60 80 100 Kilometres
0 10 20 30 40 50 Miles
JOHANSENS RECOMMENDED HOTEL
To Stavanger/Bergen/Haugesund/Kristiansand
To Göteborg
To IJmuiden
To Rotterdam
To Zeebrugge
BERWICK-UPON-TWEED
NEWCASTLE
NEWCASTLE-UPON-TYNE (Morpeth) (Matfen)
DURHAM (Seaham)
Middlesbrough
DARLINGTON (Gainford)
TEESSIDE
CRATHORNE (Yarm)
SCARBOROUGH (Scalby) (Hackness)
RIPON (Masham)
HELMSLEY (Harome)
BOLTON ABBEY (Skipton)
HARROGATE (Markington) (Ripley Castle)
YORK (Monk Fryston) (Hovingham)
OTLEY
WETHERBY
LEEDS BRADFORD
LEEDS (City Centre)
HULL (Willerby)
HALIFAX (Holmfield)
Wakefield
MANCHESTER AIRPORT (Wilmslow)
SHEFFIELD (Grenoside)
LOUTH
HATHERSAGE
ALDERLEY EDGE
PRESTBURY
CHESTERFIELD (North Derbyshire)
BUXTON (Peak District)
BASLOW
BAKEWELL (Rowsley)
ASHFORD-IN-THE-WATER
ENGLAND
MATLOCK (Riber)
Stoke
MARSTON (Grantham)
ASHBOURNE (Dovedale)
NOTTINGHAM (Langar)
RISLEY (Derbyshire/Nottinghamshire)
EAST MIDLANDS
STAFFORD (Acton Trussell)
LOUGHBOROUGH (Quorn)
MELTON MOWBRAY
KING'S LYNN (Grimston)
NORWICH (Horning) (Hethersett)
LICHFIELD (Hoar Cross)
OAKHAM
RUTLAND WATER
STAMFORD
BARNHAM BROOM (Norwich)
Leicester
UPPINGHAM
Wolverhampton
PETERBOROUGH (Wansford)
BIRMINGHAM
BIRMINGHAM (Walmley)
COVENTRY (Berkswell) (Binley)
Kettering
Thetford
SOUTHWOLD

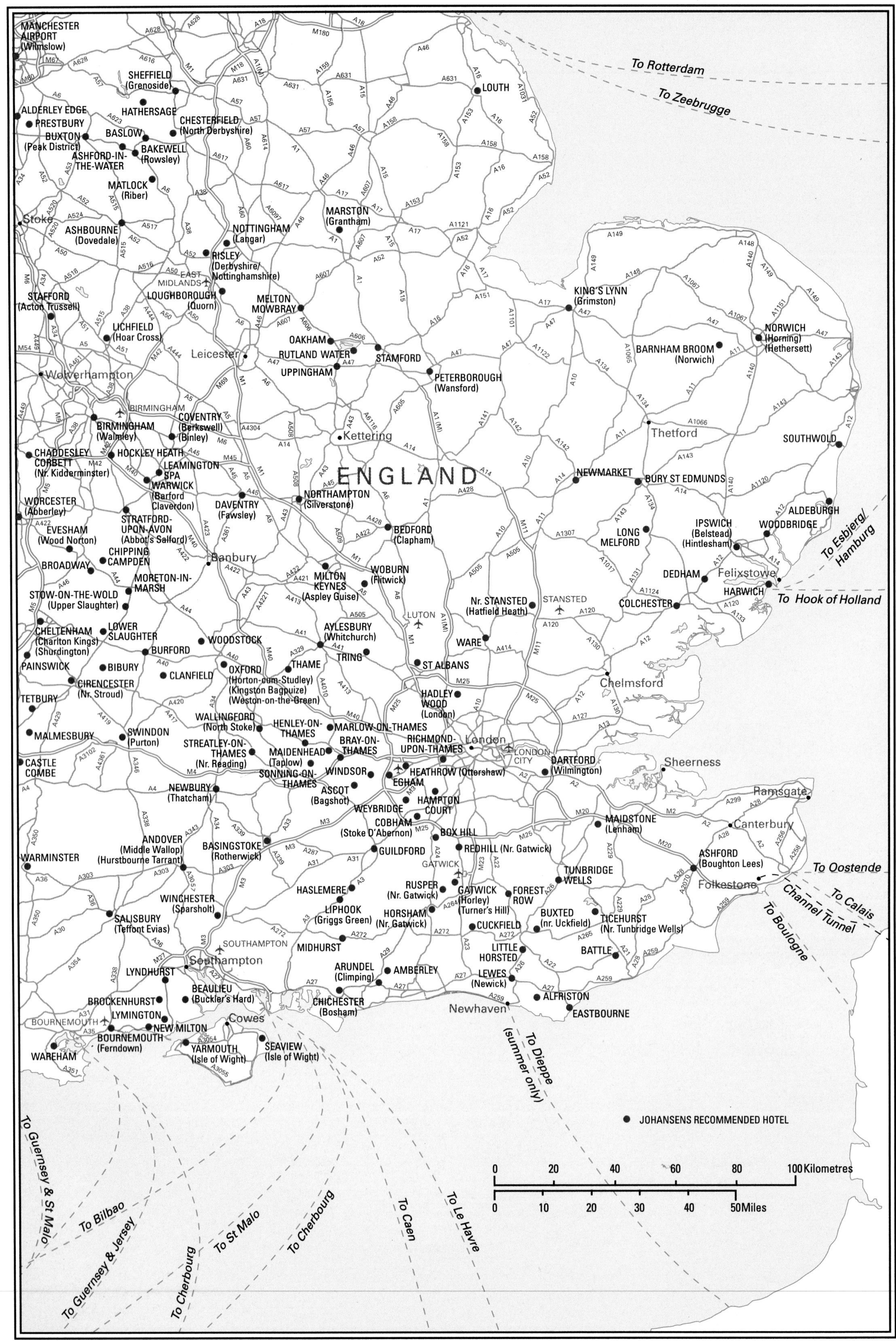

ENGLAND
To Rotterdam
To Zeebrugge
To Esbjerg/ Hamburg
To Hook of Holland
To Oostende
To Calais
Channel Tunnel
To Boulogne
To Dieppe (summer only)
To Le Havre
To Caen
To Cherbourg
To St Malo
To Cherbourg
To Guernsey & Jersey
To Bilbao
To Guernsey & St Malo
MANCHESTER AIRPORT (Wilmslow)
SHEFFIELD (Grenoside)
HATHERSAGE
ALDERLEY EDGE
PRESTBURY
CHESTERFIELD (North Derbyshire)
BASLOW
BUXTON (Peak District)
ASHFORD-IN-THE-WATER
BAKEWELL (Rowsley)
MATLOCK (Riber)
Stoke
ASHBOURNE (Dovedale)
NOTTINGHAM (Langar)
RISLEY (Derbyshire/ Nottinghamshire)
EAST MIDLANDS
STAFFORD (Acton Trussell)
LOUGHBOROUGH (Quorn)
MELTON MOWBRAY
MARSTON (Grantham)
LOUTH
KING'S LYNN (Grimston)
NORWICH (Horning) (Hethersett)
BARNHAM BROOM (Norwich)
LICHFIELD (Hoar Cross)
OAKHAM
RUTLAND WATER
STAMFORD
Leicester
UPPINGHAM
PETERBOROUGH (Wansford)
Wolverhampton
BIRMINGHAM
BIRMINGHAM (Walmley)
COVENTRY (Berkswell) (Binley)
Kettering
Thetford
SOUTHWOLD
CHADDESLEY CORBETT (Nr. Kidderminster)
HOCKLEY HEATH
LEAMINGTON SPA
WARWICK (Barford Claverdon)
NEWMARKET
BURY ST EDMUNDS
WORCESTER (Abberley)
DAVENTRY (Fawsley)
NORTHAMPTON (Silverstone)
ALDEBURGH
WOODBRIDGE
IPSWICH (Belstead) (Hintlesham)
EVESHAM (Wood Norton)
STRATFORD-UPON-AVON (Abbot's Salford)
BEDFORD (Clapham)
LONG MELFORD
CHIPPING CAMPDEN
BROADWAY
Banbury
MILTON KEYNES (Aspley Guise)
WOBURN (Flitwick)
DEDHAM
Felixstowe
HARWICH
MORETON-IN-MARSH
STOW-ON-THE-WOLD (Upper Slaughter)
Nr. STANSTED (Hatfield Heath)
STANSTED
COLCHESTER
LUTON
CHELTENHAM (Charlton Kings) (Shurdington)
LOWER SLAUGHTER
AYLESBURY (Whitchurch)
WARE
BURFORD
WOODSTOCK
TRING
PAINSWICK
BIBURY
CLANFIELD
OXFORD (Horton-cum-Studley) (Kingston Bagpuize) (Weston-on-the-Green)
THAME
ST ALBANS
CIRENCESTER (Nr. Stroud)
Chelmsford
TETBURY
HADLEY WOOD (London)
WALLINGFORD (North Stoke)
HENLEY-ON-THAMES
MARLOW-ON-THAMES
MALMESBURY
SWINDON (Purton)
STREATLEY-ON-THAMES (Nr. Reading)
MAIDENHEAD (Taplow)
BRAY-ON-THAMES
RICHMOND-UPON-THAMES
London
LONDON CITY
DARTFORD (Wilmington)
Sheerness
CASTLE COMBE
SONNING-ON-THAMES
WINDSOR
HEATHROW (Ottershaw)
EGHAM
NEWBURY (Thatcham)
ASCOT (Bagshot)
HAMPTON COURT
Ramsgate
WEYBRIDGE
COBHAM (Stoke D'Abernon)
MAIDSTONE (Lenham)
Canterbury
ANDOVER (Middle Wallop) (Hurstbourne Tarrant)
BASINGSTOKE (Rotherwick)
BOX HILL
GUILDFORD
REDHILL (Nr. Gatwick)
WARMINSTER
GATWICK
ASHFORD (Boughton Lees)
TUNBRIDGE WELLS
HASLEMERE
RUSPER (Nr. Gatwick)
GATWICK (Horley) (Turner's Hill)
FOREST ROW
Folkestone
WINCHESTER (Sparsholt)
LIPHOOK (Griggs Green)
HORSHAM (Nr. Gatwick)
BUXTED (nr. Uckfield)
TICEHURST (Nr. Tunbridge Wells)
SALISBURY (Teffont Evias)
CUCKFIELD
SOUTHAMPTON
MIDHURST
LITTLE HORSTED
BATTLE
Southampton
LYNDHURST
ARUNDEL (Climping)
AMBERLEY
LEWES (Newick)
BEAULIEU (Buckler's Hard)
BROCKENHURST
CHICHESTER (Bosham)
ALFRISTON
Newhaven
EASTBOURNE
LYMINGTON
BOURNEMOUTH
Cowes
NEW MILTON
BOURNEMOUTH (Ferndown)
WAREHAM
YARMOUTH (Isle of Wight)
SEAVIEW (Isle of Wight)
JOHANSENS RECOMMENDED HOTEL
0 20 40 60 80 100 Kilometres
0 10 20 30 40 50 Miles

England

View from Miller Howe, Windermere

Regional Tourist Boards

Cumbria Tourist Board
Ashleigh, Holly Road
Windermere, Cumbria LA23 2AQ
Tel: +44 (0)15394 44444
Internet: www.cumbria-the-lake-district.co.uk
England's most beautiful lakes and tallest mountains reach out from the Lake District National Park to a landscape of spectacular coasts, hills and dales.

East of England Tourist Board
Toppesfield Hall
Hadleigh, Suffolk IP7 5DN
Tel: +44 (0)1473 822922
Internet: www.eastofenglandtouristboard.com
Cambridgeshire, Essex, Hertfordshire, Bedfordshire, Norfolk and Suffolk.

Heart of England Tourist Board
Woodside, Larkhill Road
Worcester, Worcestershire WR5 2EZ
Tel: +44 (0)1905 761100
Internet: www.visitheartofengland.com
Lincolnshire, Gloucestershire, Hereford & Worcester, Shropshire, Staffordshire, Warwickshire, West Midlands, Derbyshire, Leicestershire, Northamptonshire, Nottinghamshire & Rutland. Districts of Cherwell & West Oxfordshire in the county of Oxfordshire.

Northumbria Tourist Board
Aykley Heads
Durham DH1 5UX
Tel: +44 (0)191 375 3028
Internet: www.visitnorthumbria.com
The Tees Valley, Durham, Northumberland, Tyne & Wear.

North West Tourist Board
Swan House, Swan Meadow Road
Wigan Pier, Wigan, Lancashire WN3 5BB
Tel: +44 (0)1942 821 222
Internet: www.visitnorthwest.com
Cheshire, Greater Manchester, Lancashire, Merseyside & the High Peak District of Derbyshire.

South East England Tourist Board
The Old Brew House, Warwick Park
Tunbridge Wells, Kent TN2 5TU
Tel: +44 (0)1892 540766
Internet: www.seetb.org.uk
East & West Sussex, Kent & Surrey

Southern Tourist Board
40 Chamberlayne Road
Eastleigh, Hampshire SO50 5JH
Tel: +44 (0)1703 620006
Internet: www.southerntb.co.uk
East & North Dorset, Hampshire, Isle of Wight, Berkshire, Buckinghamshire & Oxfordshire.

South West Tourist Board
Woodwater Park
Exeter, Devon EX2 5WT
Tel: +44 (0)870 442 0830
Internet: www.westcountrynow.com
Bath & NE Somerset, Bristol, Cornwall, Isles of Scilly, Devon, Dorset (Western), North Somerset & Wiltshire.

Yorkshire Tourist Board
312 Tadcaster Road
York, YorkshireYO2 2HF
Tel: +44 (0)1904 707961
Internet: www.ytb.org.uk
Yorkshire and North & North East Lincolnshire.

Further Information:

English Heritage
Customer Services Department
PO Box 569, Swindon SN2 2YP
Tel: +44 (0) 870 333 1181
Internet: www.english-heritage.org.uk
Offers an unrivalled choice of properties to visit.

Historic Houses Association
2 Chester Street
London SW1X 7BB
Tel: +44 (0)20 7259 5688
Internet: www.hha.org.uk
Ensures the survival of historic houses and gardens in private ownership in Great Britain

The National Trust
36 Queen Anne's Gate
London SW1H 9AS
Tel: +44 (0)20 7222 9251
Internet: www.nationaltrust.org.uk
Cares for more than 590,000 acres of countryside and over 400 historic buildings.

Wentworth Hotel

WENTWORTH ROAD, ALDEBURGH, SUFFOLK IP15 5BD
TEL: 01728 452312 FAX: 01728 454343 E-MAIL: stay@wentworth–aldeburgh.co.uk

The Wentworth Hotel is ideally situated opposite the beach at Aldeburgh on Suffolk's unspoilt coast. Aldeburgh has maritime traditions dating back to the 15th century which are still maintained today by the longshore fishermen who launch their boats from the shore. It has also become a centre for music lovers: every June the Aldeburgh International Festival of Music, founded by the late Benjamin Britten, is held at Snape Maltings. Privately owned by the Pritt family since 1920, the Wentworth has established a reputation for comfort and service, good food and wine, for which many guests return year after year. Relax in front of an open fire in one of the hotel lounges, or sample a pint of the famous local Adnam's ales in the bar, which also serves meals. Many of the 37 elegantly furnished en suite bedrooms have sea views. The restaurant offers an extensive menu for both lunch and dinner and there is a comprehensive wine list. The garden terrace is the perfect venue for a light lunch alfresco. Nearby, the Minsmere Bird Sanctuary will be of interest to nature enthusiasts, while for the keen golfer, two of Britain's most challenging courses are within easy reach of the hotel at Aldeburgh and Thorpeness. Closed from December 27 to early new year. **Directions:** Aldeburgh is on A1094 just 7 miles from the A12 between Ipswich and Lowestoft. Price Guide: Single £63-£73; double/twin £106-£130.

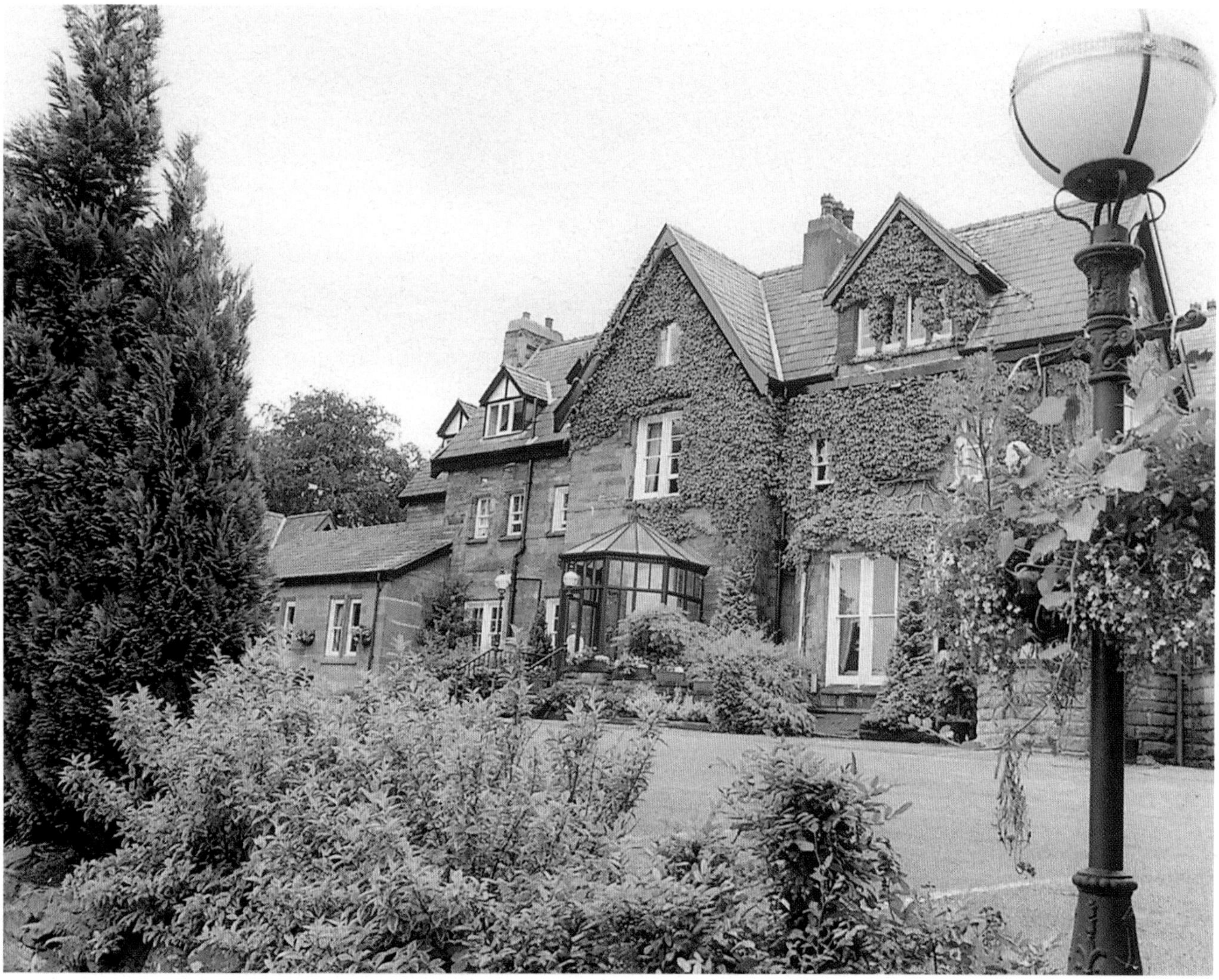

THE ALDERLEY EDGE HOTEL

MACCLESFIELD ROAD, ALDERLEY EDGE, CHESHIRE SK9 7BJ
TEL: 01625 583033 FAX: 01625 586343 E-MAIL: sales@alderley–edge–hotel.co.uk

This privately owned award-winning hotel has 31 executive bedrooms, 11 superior rooms and 4 suites including the Presidential and Bridal Suites offering a high standard of decor. The restaurant is in the sumptuous conservatory with exceptional views and attention is given to the highest standards of cooking; fresh produce, including fish delivered daily, is provided by local suppliers. Specialities include hot and cold seafood dishes, puddings served piping hot from the oven and a daily selection of unusual and delicious breads, baked each morning in the hotel bakery. The wine list features 100 champagnes and 600 wines. Special wine and champagne dinners are held quarterly. In addition to the main conference room there is a suite of meeting and private dining rooms. The famous Edge walks are nearby, as are Tatton and Lyme Parks, Quarry Bank Mill and Dunham Massey. Manchester's thriving city centre is 15 miles away and the airport is a 20-minute drive. **Directions:** Follow M6 to M56 Stockport. Exit junction 6, take A538 to Wilmslow. Follow signs 1½ miles through to Alderley Edge. Turn left at the end of the main shopping area on to Macclesfield Road (B5087) and the hotel is situated 200 yards on the right. From M6 take junction 18 and follow signs for Holmes Chapel and Alderley Edge. Price Guide: Single £45–£145; double £90–£150; suites from £200.

White Lodge Country House Hotel

SLOE LANE, ALFRISTON, EAST SUSSEX BN26 5UR

TEL: 01323 870265 FAX: 01323 870284 E-MAIL: sales@whitelodge–hotel.com

Nestled in five acres of landscaped grounds in the heart of the Cuckmere Valley, the White Lodge Country House Hotel offers a friendly welcome and excellent service in relaxed and peaceful surroundings. This recently refurbished hotel has individually and tastefully decorated bedrooms with full private facilities, colour television, direct dial telephone and tea and coffee making facilities. Guests can enjoy romantic, candlelit dinners in the Orchid Restaurant, which serves a wide range of mouthwatering menus featuring traditional dishes, home-made soups and desserts using only the freshest of ingredients. Snooker or board games are available in the games room and guests may relax in the cosy lounges which feature open fireplaces with real log fires in the winter. Murder and Mystery evenings are held at the hotel on a regular basis. Outdoor activities might include a leisurely walk to the sea or a more challenging but very beautiful walk to the internationally known Seven Sisters, There are a wide range of high quality shops, the "Clergy House" and "the Cathedral of the Downs" in Alfriston as well as many castles and heritage sites in the area. **Directions:** Alfriston is on the B2108 between the A27/A259. The hotel is well signed from the village centre. Price Guide: Single from £50; double/twin from £100; suite from £130.

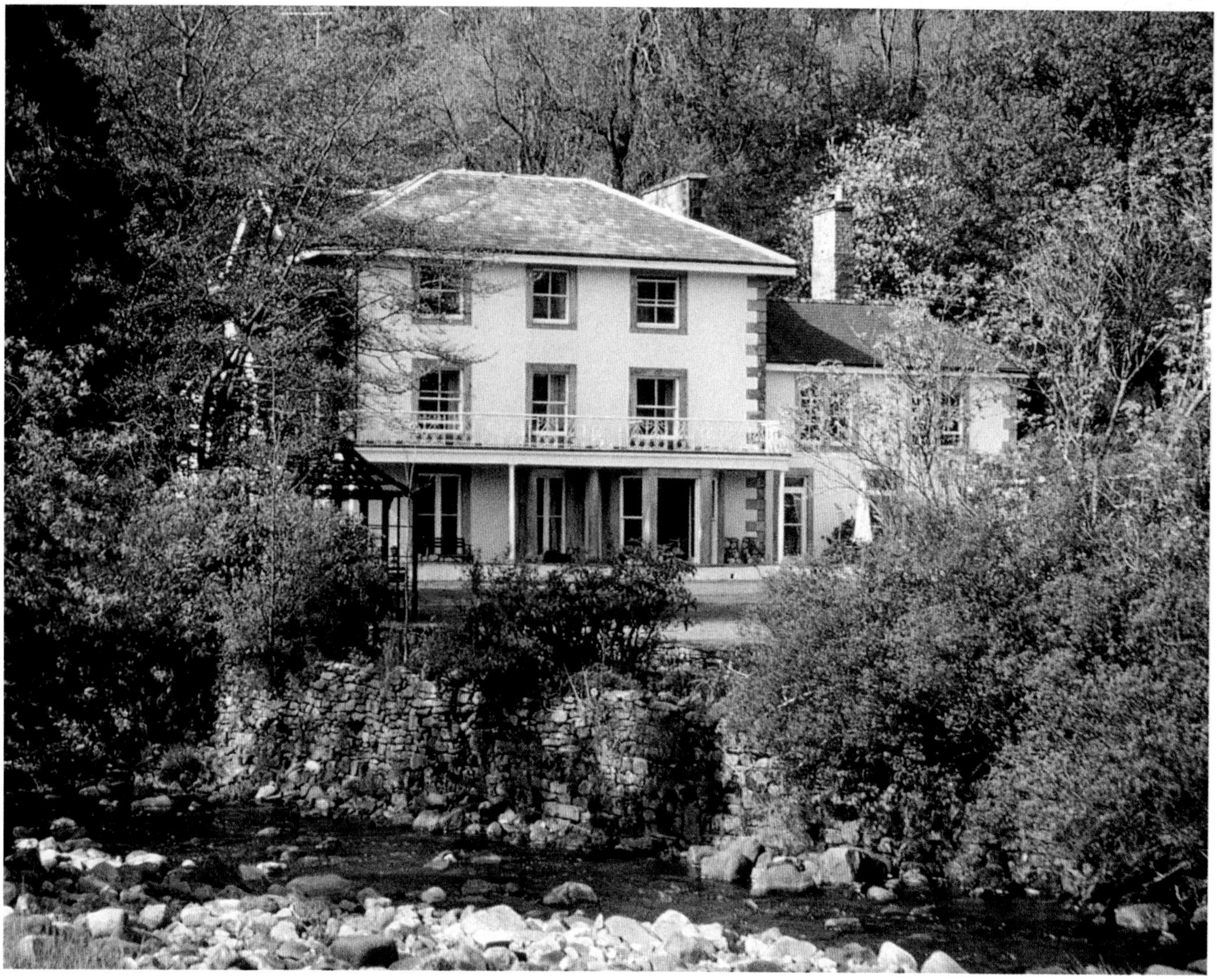

LOVELADY SHIELD COUNTRY HOUSE HOTEL

NENTHEAD ROAD, ALSTON, CUMBRIA CA9 3LF

TEL: 01434 381203 FAX: 01434 381515 E-MAIL: enquiries@lovelady.co.uk

Reached by the A646, one of the worlds ten best drives and two-and-a-half miles from Alston, England's highest market town, Lovelady Shield, nestles in three acres of secluded riverside gardens. Bright log fires in the library and drawing room enhance the hotel's welcoming atmosphere. Owners Peter and Marie Haynes take great care to create a peaceful and tranquil haven where guests can relax and unwind. The five-course dinners created by master chef Barrie Garton, rounded off by home-made puddings and a selection of English farmhouse cheeses, have won the hotel 2 AA Rosettes for food. Many guests first discover Lovelady Shield en route to Scotland. They then return to explore this beautiful and unspoiled part of England and experience the comforts of the hotel. Golf, fishing, shooting, pony-trekking and riding can be arranged locally. The Pennine Way, Hadrian's Wall and the Lake District are within easy reach. Facilities for small conferences and boardroom meetings are available. Open all year, Special Christmas, New Year, and short breaks are offered with special rates for 2 and 3 day stays. **Directions:** The hotel's driveway is by the junction of the B6294 and the A689, 2¼ miles east of Alston. Price Guide: : Single £70–£90; double/twin £140–£180.

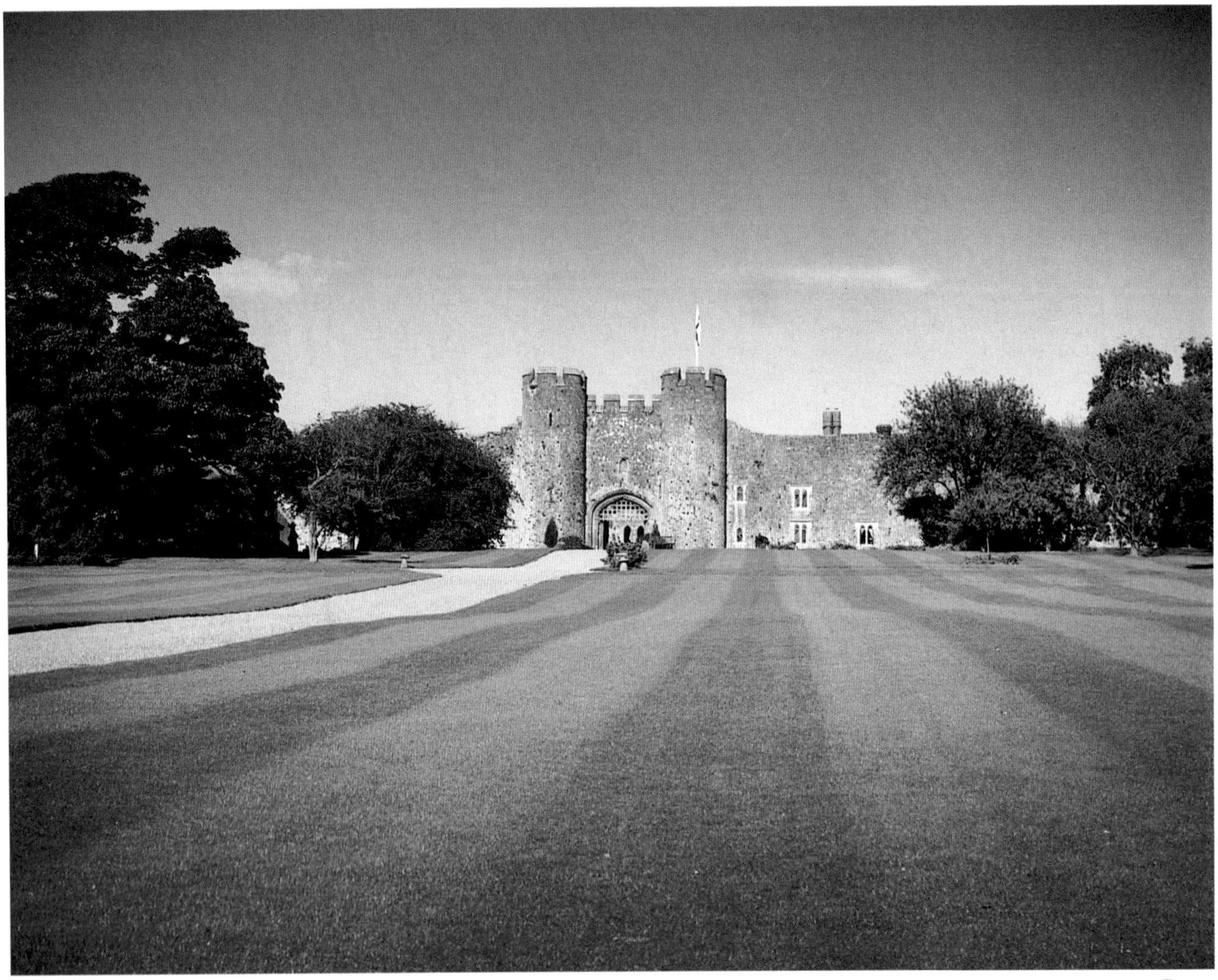

AMBERLEY CASTLE

AMBERLEY, NR ARUNDEL, WEST SUSSEX BN18 9ND
TEL: 01798 831992 FAX: 01798 831998 E-MAIL: info@amberleycastle.co.uk

Winner of the Johansens 1995 Country Hotel Award, Amberley Castle is over 900 years old and is set between the rolling South Downs and the peaceful expanse of the Amberley Wildbrooks. Its towering battlements give breathtaking views while its massive, 14th-century curtain walls and mighty portcullis bear silent testimony to its fascinating history. Resident proprietors, Joy and Martin Cummings, have transformed this medieval fortress into a unique country castle hotel. They offer a warm, personal welcome and their hotel provides the ultimate in contemporary luxury, while retaining an atmosphere of timelessness. Five distinctive new suites were added last year in the Bishopric by the main gateway. Each room is individually designed and has its own Jacuzzi bath. The exquisite 12th-century Queen's Room is the perfect setting for the creative cuisine of head chef James Peyton and his team. Amberley Castle is a natural first choice for romantic or cultural weekends, sporting breaks or confidential executive meetings. Roman ruins, antiques, stately homes, castle gardens, horse racing and history 'everywhere' you look, all within a short distance. It is easily accessible from London and the major air and channel ports. **Directions:** Amberley Castle is on the B2139, off the A29 between Fontwell and Bury. Price Guide: (Room only) Double/twin £145–£300; suite £275–£325.

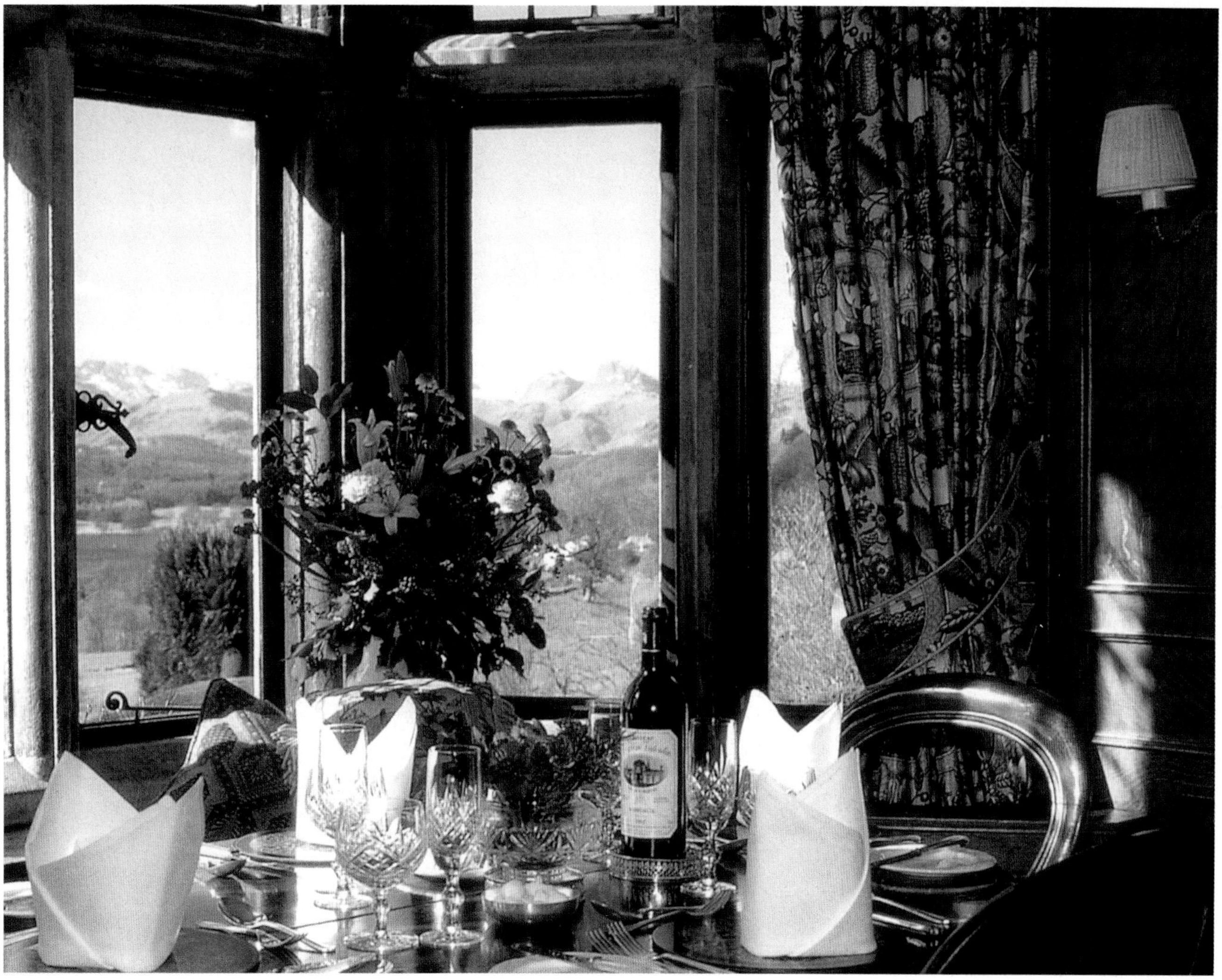

HOLBECK GHYLL COUNTRY HOUSE HOTEL

HOLBECK LANE, WINDERMERE, CUMBRIA LA23 1LU
TEL: 015394 32375 FAX: 015394 34743 E-MAIL: stay@holbeckghyll.com

The saying goes that all the best sites for building a house in England were taken long before the days of the motor car. Holbeck Ghyll has one such prime position. It was built in the early days of the 19th century and is superbly located overlooking Lake Windermere and the Langdale Fells. Today this luxury hotel has an outstanding reputation and is managed personally and expertly by its proprietors, David and Patricia Nicholson. As well as being awarded the RAC Gold Ribbon and 3 AA Red Stars they are among an élite who have won an AA Courtesy and Care Award, Holbeck Ghyll was 2000 Cumbria Tourist Board Hotel of the Year. The majority of bedrooms are large and have spectacular and breathtaking views. All are recently refurbished to a very high standard and include decanters of sherry, fresh flowers, fluffy bathrobes and much more. There are six new suites in the lodge. The oak-panelled restaurant, awarded a coveted Michelin star and 3 AA Rosettes, is a delightful setting for memorable dining and the meals are classically prepared, with the focus on flavours and presentation, while an extensive wine list reflects quality and variety. The hotel has an all-weather tennis court and a health spa with gym, sauna and treatment facilities. **Directions:** From Windermere, pass Brockhole Visitors Centre, then after ½ mile turn right into Holbeck Lane. Hotel is ½ mile on left Price Guide: (inc. dinner): Single from £95; double/twin £150–£320; suite £200–£320.

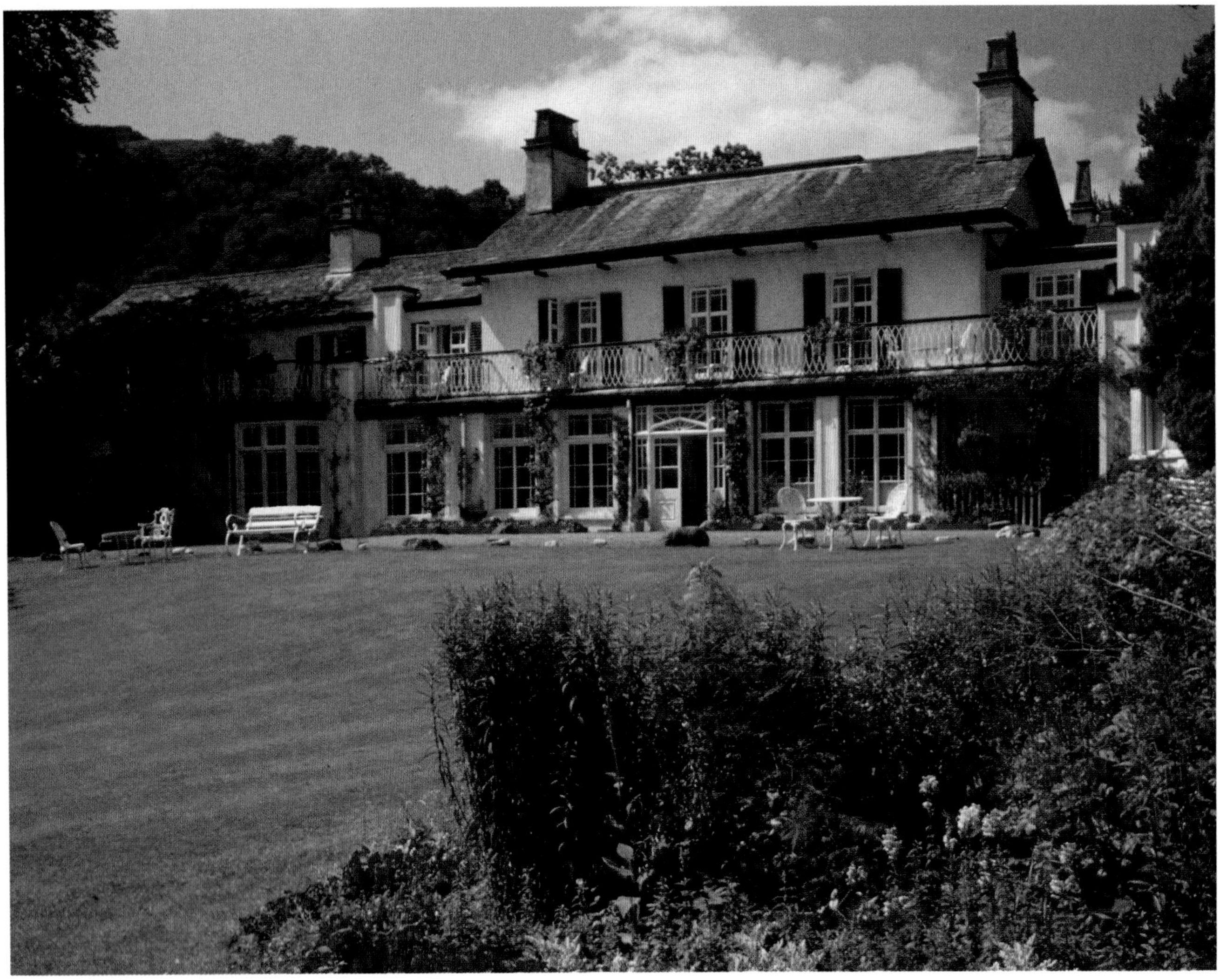

ROTHAY MANOR

ROTHAY BRIDGE, AMBLESIDE, CUMBRIA LA22 0EH
TEL: 015394 33605 FAX: 015394 33607 E-MAIL: hotel@rothaymanor.co.uk

Situated just a ¼ mile from Lake Windermere and a short walk from Ambleside, this elegant Regency country house stands in its own landscaped gardens. The individually designed bedrooms include 3 beautifully furnished suites close to the manor which afford space and privacy. Two can easily accommodate up to 5 people, while one suite and a ground floor bedroom have been designed with particular attention to the comfort of guests with disabilities. Care and consideration are evident throughout. The menu is varied and meals are prepared with flair and imagination to high standards, complemented by a comprehensive wine list. For health and fitness, residents have free use of the nearby Low Wood Leisure Club, with swimming pool, sauna, steam room, Jacuzzi, squash, sunbeds and a health and beauty salon. Cycling, sailing, horseriding, fishing (permits available) and golf can be arranged locally, or guests can take a cruise on Lake Windermere or a trip on a steam railway. Small functions and conferences can be catered for. A full programme of special-interest holidays is offered, including antiques, painting, bridge, walking, gardening, photography and music. Closed 3 January to 8 February. Represented in the USA by Josephine Barr: 800 323 5463. **Directions:** ¼ mile from Ambleside on the A593 to Coniston. Price Guide: Single £70–£80; double/twin £115–£145; suite £160–£185.

18 MasterCard VISA AMERICAN EXPRESS M 20

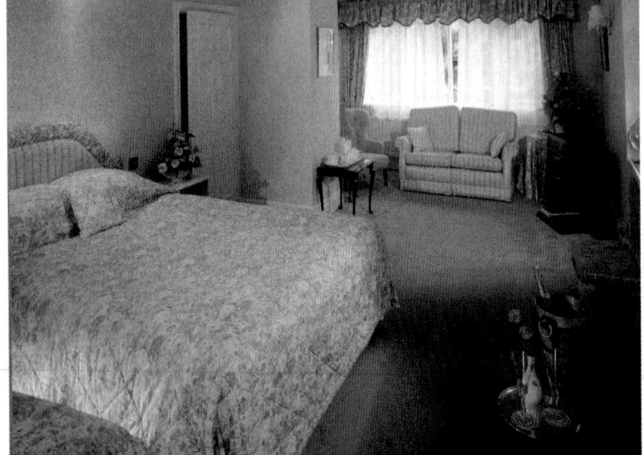

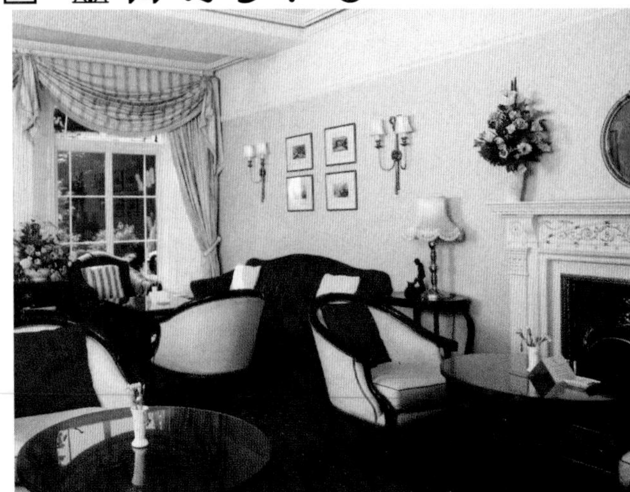

THE SAMLING

AMBLESIDE ROAD, WINDERMERE, CUMBRIA LA23 1LR
TEL: 015394 31922 FAX: 015394 30400 E-MAIL: info@thesamling.com

Not so much a country house hotel as a house in the country, The Samling is the epitome of unpretentious luxury. In ancient Cumbria, a samling was a gathering, and here on the north eastern shore of Lake Windermere gatherings of up to 20 can enjoy this unique hideaway, tucked amongst 67 acres of woodlands and gardens. Built in the early 1780s, the house has numerous literary connections; William Wordsworth once paid his rent to the master of The Samling, and many other writers and poets have stayed or lived within its grounds. The drawing room with its comfortable armchairs is the natural centre of the house, whilst each of the ten individually decorated beautiful suites has its own sitting room, open fire, and spectacular views across the lake. Only the very finest, freshest local ingredients are used for the imaginative dishes prepared by the chef, and accompanied by fine wines from the extensive list. Friendly, discreet staff are on hand to cater to every whim. The Dutch Barn is available for wedding celebrations or conferences for up to 60 business delegates. One of the most popular meeting points at the hotel is the outdoor hot tub. **Directions:** Leave M6 at Jct36 and take A590/A591 past Windermere towards Ambleside. The Samling is up a long drive, 100 yards past the Low Wood Hotel. Price Guide: Single £110–£265; double/twin £120–£275.

ESSEBORNE MANOR

HURSTBOURNE TARRANT, ANDOVER, HAMPSHIRE SP11 0ER
TEL: 01264 736444 FAX: 01264 736725 E-MAIL: esseborne–manor@cs.com

Esseborne Manor is small and unpretentious, yet stylish. The present house was built at the end of the 19th century and carries the name used to record details of the local village in the Domesday Book. It is set in a pleasing garden amid the rich farmland of the North Wessex Downs in a designated area of outstanding natural beauty. Ian and Lucilla Hamilton, who manage the house, have established the restful atmosphere of a private country home where guests can unwind and relax. There are just 15 comfortable bedrooms, some reached via a courtyard. Two doubles and a delightful suite are in converted cottages with their own patio overlooking the main gardens. The pretty sitting room and cosy library are comfortable areas in which to relax. Scott Foy's fine 2 Rosette cooking is set off to advantage in the new dining room and adjoining bar. There is now a spacious meeting and function facility. In the grounds there is a herb garden, an all-weather tennis court, a croquet lawn and plenty of good walking beyond. Nearby Newbury racecourse has a busy programme of steeple-chasing and flat racing. Places to visit include Highclere Castle, Stonehenge, Salisbury, Winchester and Oxford **Directions:** Midway between Newbury and Andover on the A343, 1½ miles north of Hurstbourne Tarrant. Price guide Price Guide: Single £95–£130; double/twin £100–£180.

FIFEHEAD MANOR

MIDDLE WALLOP, STOCKBRIDGE. HAMPSHIRE SO20 8EG
TEL: 01264 781565 FAX: 01264 781400

The foundations of this lovely Manor House date from the 11th century when it was owned by the wife of the Saxon Earl of Godwin whose son, King Harold, was killed at the Battle of Hastings. Today, Fifehead Manor offers all the comfort of a country house hotel but, with its barns and stables surrounded by acres of gardens, the historic atmosphere lingers. The beamed dining room with its lead-paned windows and huge open fireplace has a unique atmosphere illuminated by the light of flickering candles and a warmth generated by centuries of hospitality. Substantial changes have brought about vast improvements to this fine hotel. The award-winning cuisine is outstanding and the restaurant is featured in major guides throughout Europe. All 17 en suite bedrooms are individually furnished and have every amenity, 9 are located in the garden wing. Fifehead Manor is ideally situated for visiting Salisbury, Winchester, Stonehenge, Romsey Abbey, Broadlands and Wilton House. Golf, fishing, riding and motor racing at Thruxton are nearby. **Directions:** From M3, exit at junction 8 onto A303 to Andover. Then take A343 south for 6 miles to Middle Wallop. Price Guide: Single £70–£90; double/twin £110–£150.

17 MasterCard VISA AMERICAN EXPRESS M 40

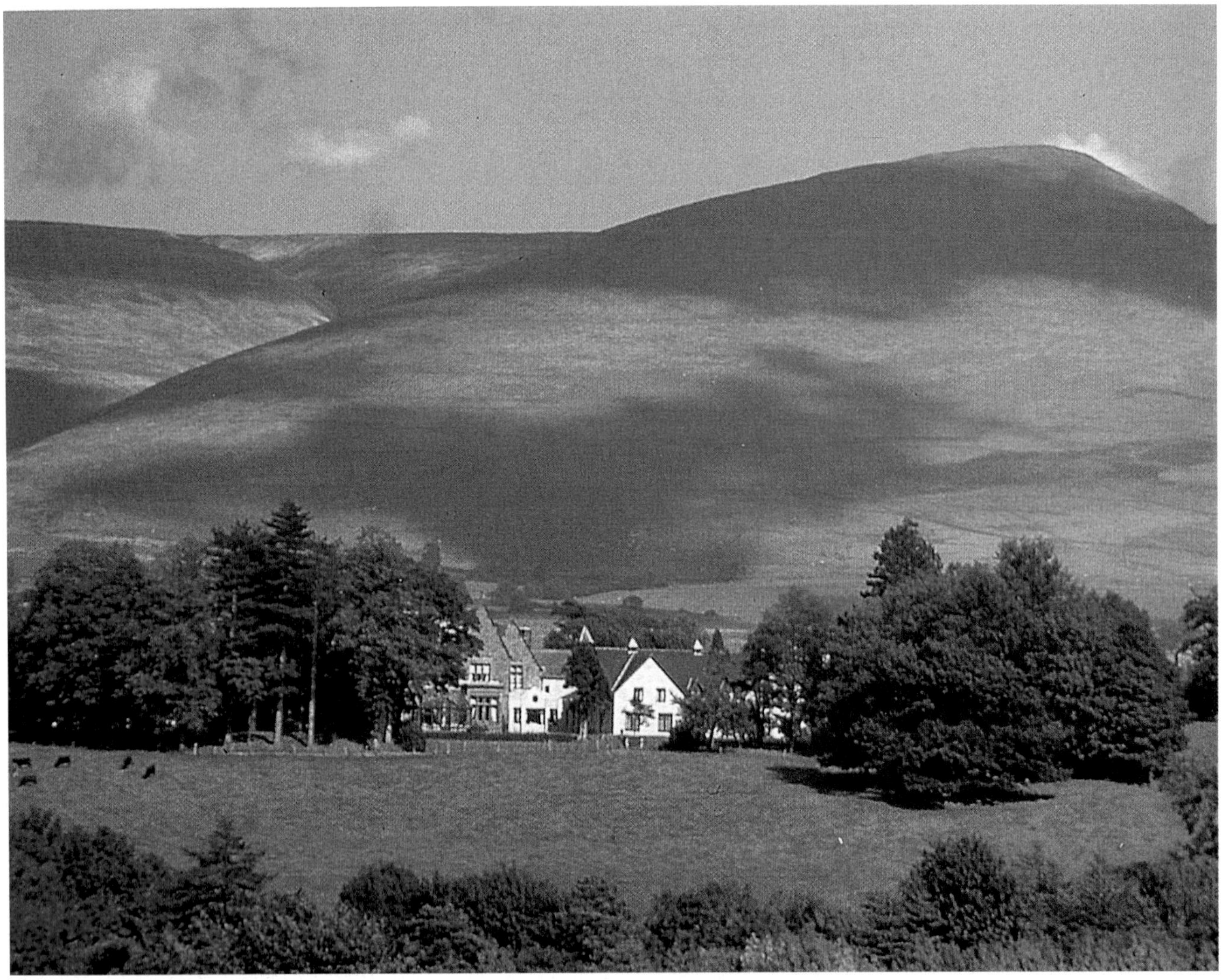

APPLEBY MANOR COUNTRY HOUSE HOTEL

ROMAN ROAD, APPLEBY-IN-WESTMORLAND, CUMBRIA CA16 6JB
TEL: 017683 51571 FAX: 017683 52888 E-MAIL: reception@applebymanor.co.uk

Surrounded by half a million acres of some of the most beautiful landscapes in England, sheltered by the mountains and fells of the Lake District, by the North Pennine Hills and Yorkshire Dales, in an area aptly known as Eden stands Appleby Manor, a friendly and relaxing hotel owned and run by the Swinscoe family. The high quality, spotlessly clean, bedrooms induce peaceful, undisturbed sleep. (Dogs are welcome in The Coach House accommodation). The public areas are also restfully comfortable – the inviting lounges nicely warmed by log fires on cooler days, the cocktail bar and sunny conservatory luring guests with a choice of more than 70 malt whiskies and the restaurant offering an imaginative selection of tasty dishes and fine wines. The hotel pool, sauna, steam room, Jacuzzi, solarium and games room keep indoor athletes happy. Locally there are outdoor sports: fishing, golf, riding, squash and for the more venturesome, rambling on the fells. Appleby is an ideal base from which to visit the Lake District and an attractive stopover on journeys north-south. **Directions:** From the South take junction 38 of the M6 and then the B6260 to Appleby (13 miles). Drive through the town to a T-junction, turn left, first right and follow road for two-thirds of a mile. Price Guide: Single £72–£91; double/twin £104–£142.

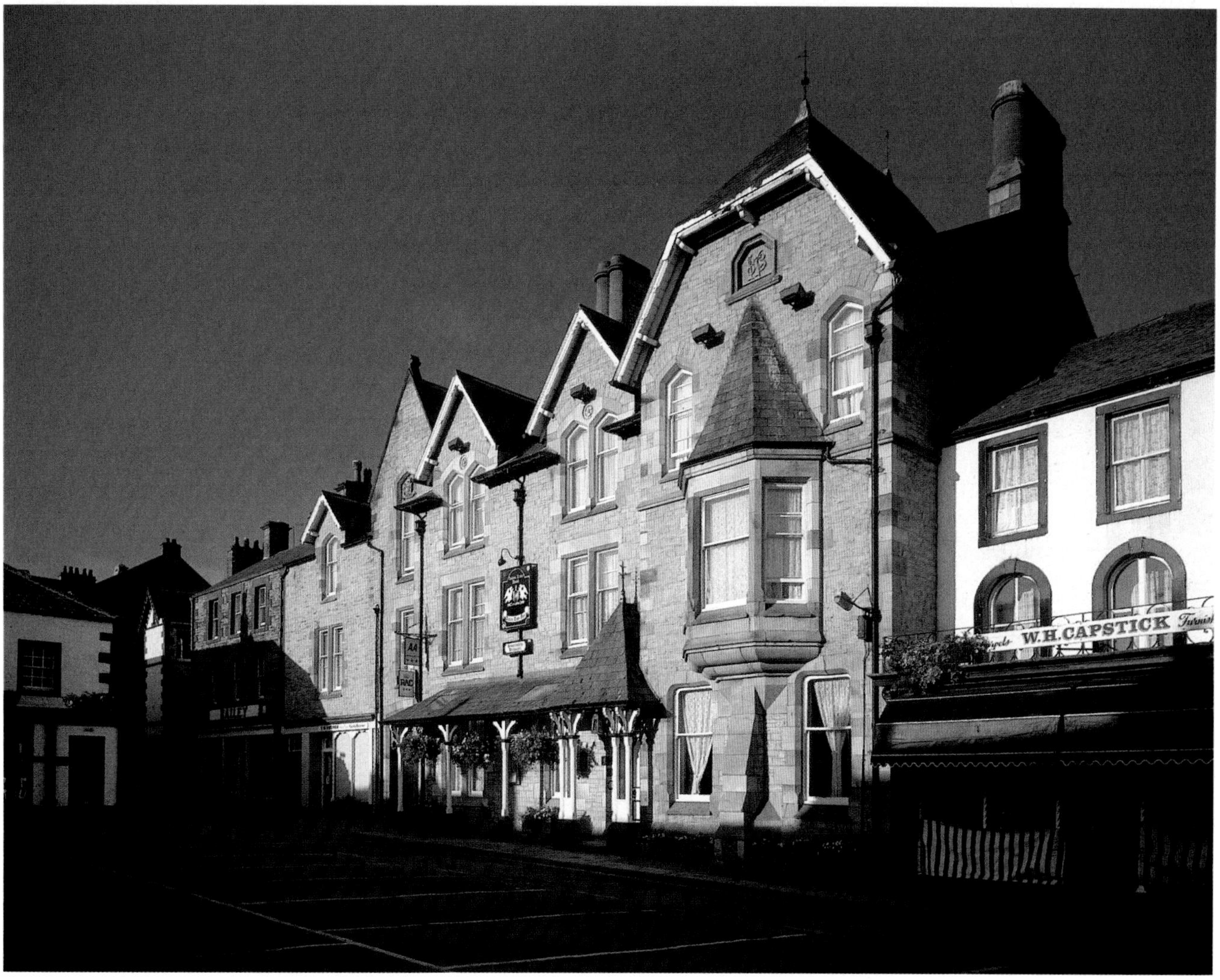

TUFTON ARMS HOTEL

MARKET SQUARE, APPLEBY-IN-WESTMORLAND, CUMBRIA CA16 6XA
TEL: 017683 51593 FAX: 017683 52761 E-MAIL: info@tuftonarmshotel.co.uk

This distinguished Victorian coaching inn, owned and run by the Milsom family, has been refurbished to provide a high standard of comfort. The bedrooms evoke the style of the 19th century, when the Tufton Arms became one of the premier hotels in Victorian England. The kitchen is run under the auspices of David Milsom, who spoils guests for choice with a gourmet dinner menu as well as a grill menu. The AA Rosette awarded restaurant is renowned for its fish dishes. Complementing the cuisine is an extensive wine list. There are conference and meeting rooms including the air conditioned Hothfield Suite which can accommodate up to 100 people. Appleby, the historic county town of Westmorland, stands in splendid countryside and is ideal for touring the Lakes, Yorkshire Dales and Pennines. It is also a convenient stop-over en route to Scotland. Members of the Milsom family also run The Royal Hotel in Comrie. Superb fishing for wild brown trout on a 24-mile stretch of the main River Eden, salmon fishing can be arranged on the lower reaches of the river. Shooting parties for grouse, duck and pheasant are a speciality. Appleby has an 18-hole moorland golf course. **Directions:** In centre of Appleby (bypassed by the A66), 38 miles west of Scotch Corner, 13 miles east of Penrith (M6 junction 40), 12 miles from M6 junction 38. Price Guide: Single £65–£100; double/twin £90–£135; suite £150.

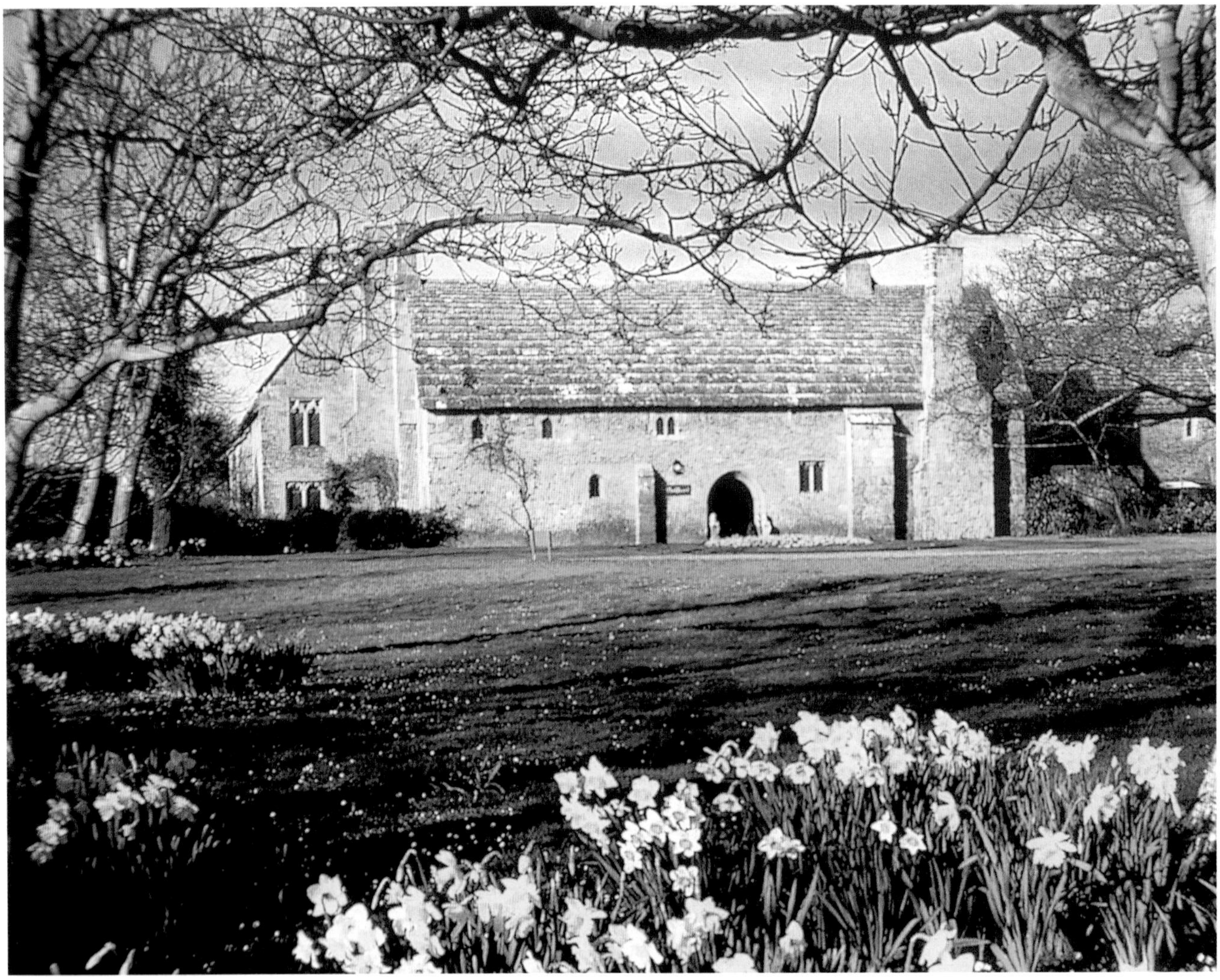

BAILIFFSCOURT

CLIMPING, WEST SUSSEX BN17 5RW

TEL: 01903 723511 FAX: 01903 723107 E-MAIL: bailiffscourt@hshotels.co.uk

Bailiffscourt is a perfectly preserved 'medieval' house, built in the 1930s using authentic material salvaged from historic old buildings. Gnarled 15th century beams and gothic mullioned windows combine to recreate a home from the Middle Ages. Set in 30 acres of beautiful pastures and walled gardens, it provides guests with a wonderful sanctuary in which to relax or work. The bedrooms are all individually decorated and luxuriously furnished, with many offering four poster beds, open log fires and beautiful views over the surrounding countryside. The restaurant offers a varied menu and summer lunches can be taken alfresco in a rose-clad courtyard or the walled garden. A good list of well-priced wines accompanies meals. Private dining rooms are available for weddings, conferences and meetings and companies can hire the hotel as their 'country house' for 2 or 3 days. Bailiffscourt, which is AA two Rosettes and AA Courtesy & Care Award 1997 accredited, is surrounded by tranquil parkland with a golf practice area, heated outdoor pool and tennis courts. Climping Beach, 100 yards away, is ideal for windsurfing. Nearby are Arundel with its castle, Chichester and Goodwood. **Directions:** Three miles south of Arundel, off the A259. Price Guide: Single from £135; double from £150.

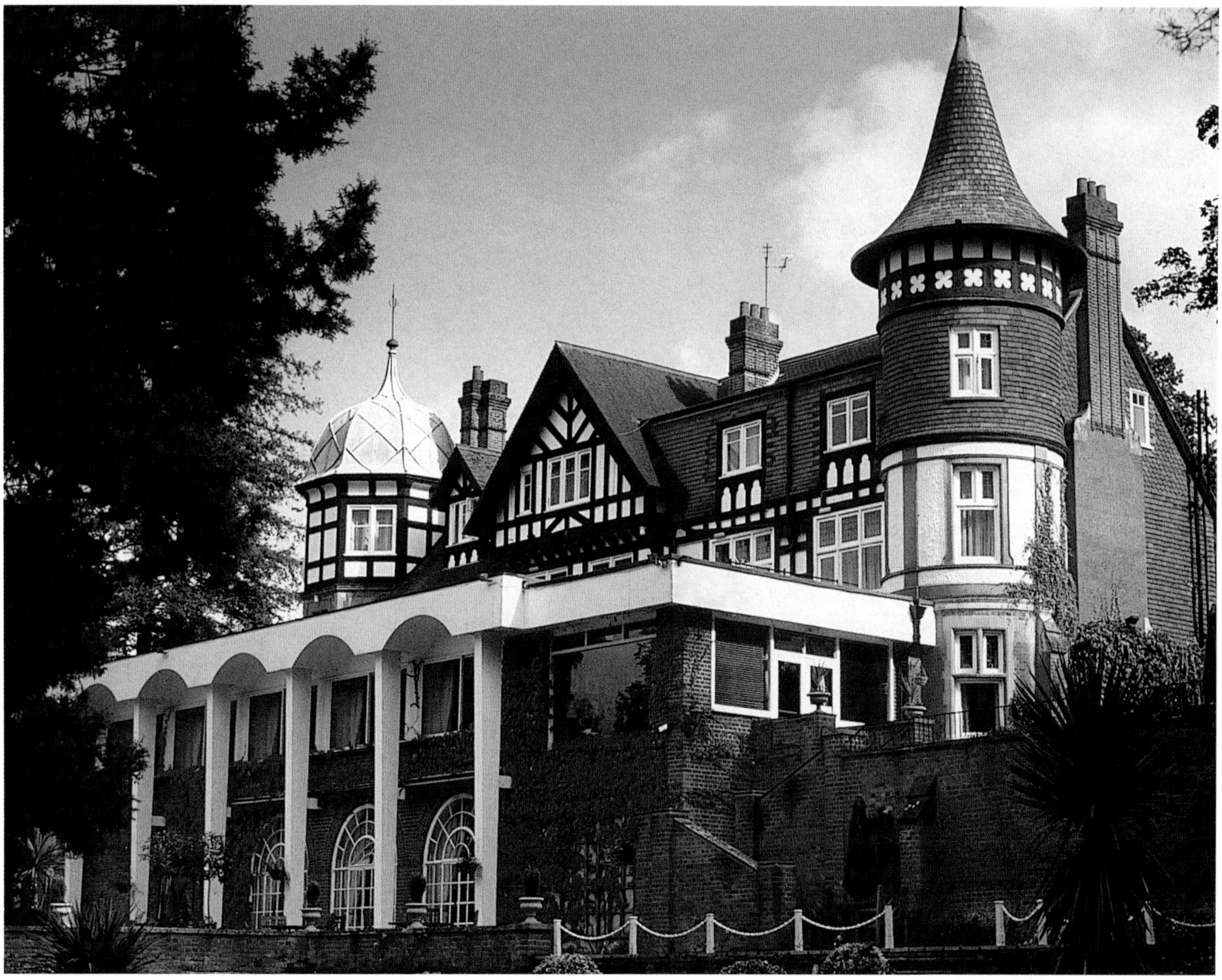

The Berystede

BAGSHOT ROAD, SUNNINGHILL, ASCOT, BERKSHIRE SL5 9JH
TEL: 0870 400 8111 FAX: 01344 872301 E-MAIL: heritagehotels_ascot.berystede@forte–hotels.com

Standing regally in 9 acres of landscaped gardens and woodlands this former country house is a unique and attractive blend of Gothic, Tudor and modern styles. It is a peaceful and comfortable holiday retreat and particularly convenient for golf, horseracing or polo enthusiasts. Close by is the famed Wentworth Golf Course, much favoured by showbusiness and golfing celebrities, Ascot Racecourse and the Guards Polo Ground at Windsor. The hotel's range of leisure facilities include an outdoor swimming pool, croquet lawn, putting lawn and nearby there is an ice rink, 10-pin bowling and a dry ski slope. The Berystede's spacious interiors are delightfully decorated in keeping with its country house character; the Diadem Bar is fashioned after a traditional gentleman's club smoking room – a comfortable haven of relaxation, as is the quiet Library Lounge with its open fire in winter. All bedrooms, which include six family rooms, three four-posters and four suites, are individually furnished and equipped with every modern facility. Many enjoy splendid views over the grounds. The handsome Hyperion Restaurant has a diverse menu of award-winning cuisine prepared with meticulous attention to presentation. Excellent business and conference facilities are available. **Directions:** Exit M3 at junction 3, take Bagshot Road for 3 miles. Or join B3020 from A329. Price Guide: Single £175; double/twin £195–£225; suite £225.

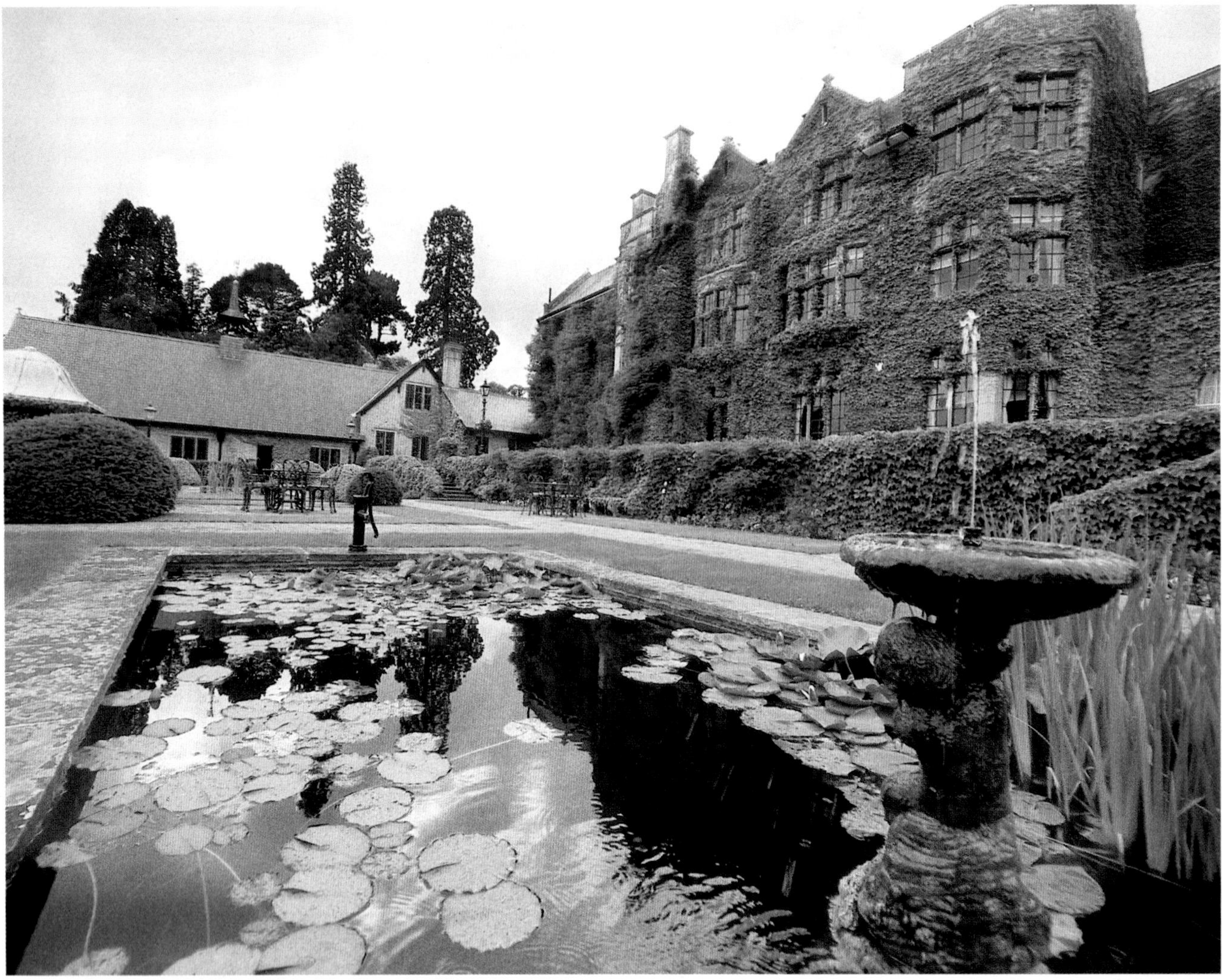

PENNYHILL PARK HOTEL AND COUNTRY CLUB

LONDON ROAD, BAGSHOT, SURREY GU19 5EU
TEL: 01276 471774 FAX: 01276 473217 E-MAIL: enquiries@pennyhillpark.co.uk

Bagshot has been a centre of hospitality since the early Stuart sovereigns James I and Charles I had a hunting lodge there. Pennyhill Park Hotel continues to uphold that tradition. Built in 1849, this elegant mansion reflects its journey through Victorian and Edwardian times while providing every modern amenity. The bedrooms are outstanding: no two are identical, and infinite care has been invested in creating practical rooms with distinctive features. Impeccable service is to be expected, as staff are trained to classical, Edwardian standards. Haute cuisine and a listing of fine wines is offered in the wonderful oak panelled Latymer Room or less formal eating is available in the sparkling new St James Restaurant. Recreational facilities are available within the grounds, which span 120 acres and include landscaped gardens, a 9-hole golf course, a swimming pool, a three acre lake, gym, rugby/football pitch, archery, jogging and walking path. Pennyhill Park is conveniently located only 27 miles from central London and not far from Heathrow, Windsor Castle, Ascot, Wentworth and Sunningdale. **Directions:** From the M3, exit 3, take A322 towards Bracknell. Turn left on to A30 signposted to Camberley. ¾ mile after Bagshot; turn right 50 yards past the Texaco garage Price Guide: Single from £176.25; double/twin from £193.88; suite from £352.50; apartments from £411.25.

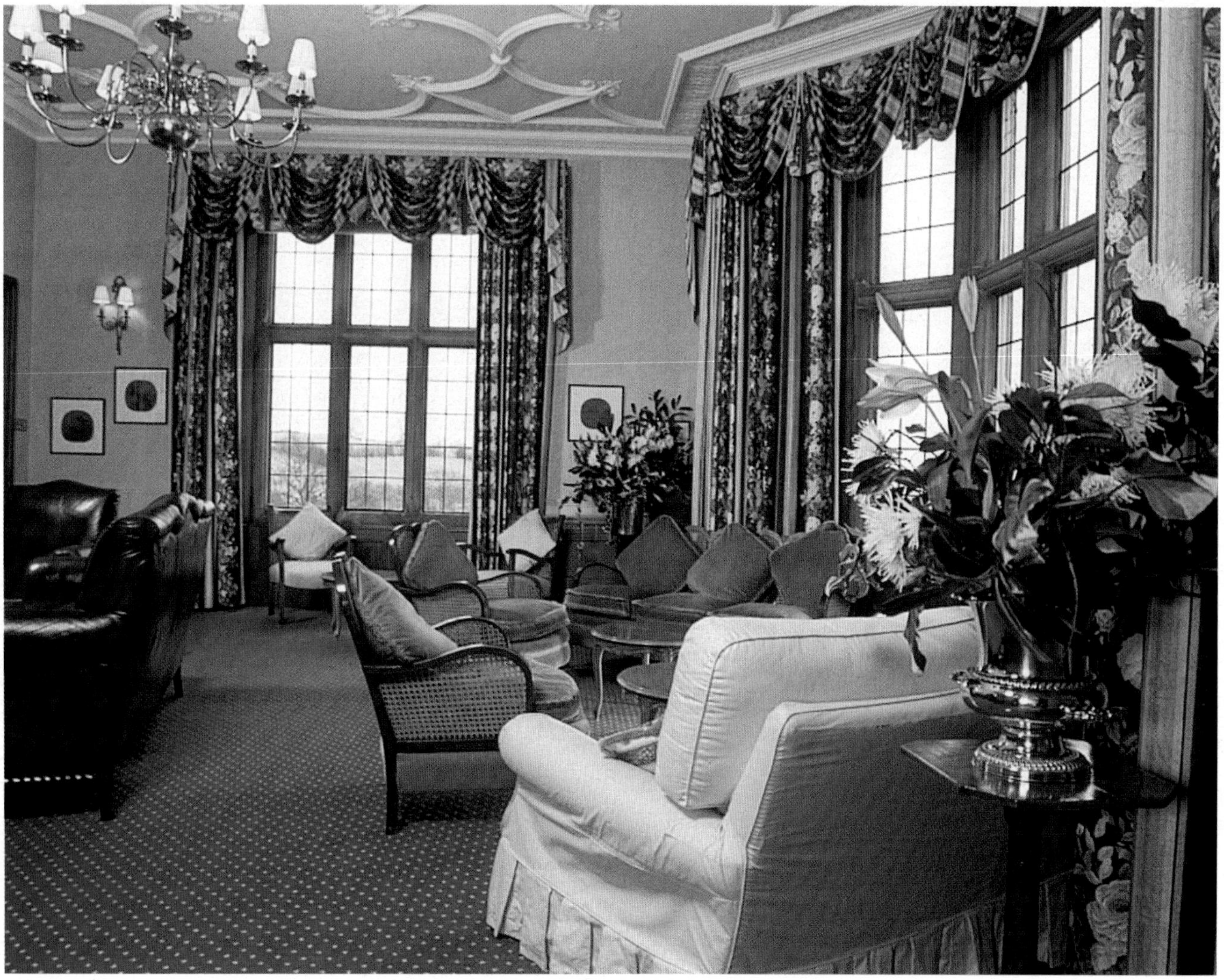

CALLOW HALL

MAPPLETON ROAD, ASHBOURNE, DERBYSHIRE DE6 2AA
TEL: 01335 300900 FAX: 01335 300512 E-MAIL: stay@callowhall.co.uk

The approach to Callow Hall is up a tree-lined drive through the 44-acre grounds. On arrival visitors can take in the splendid views from the hotel's elevated position, overlooking the valleys of Bentley Brook and the River Dove. The majestic building and Victorian gardens have been restored by resident proprietors, David, Dorothy and their son, Anthony Spencer, who represent the fifth and sixth generations of hoteliers in the Spencer family. The famous local Ashbourne mineral water and home-made biscuits greet guests in the spacious period bedrooms. Fresh local produce is selected daily for use in the kitchen, where the term 'home-made' comes into its own. Home-cured bacon, sausages, fresh bread, traditional English puddings and melt-in-the-mouth pastries are among the items prepared on the premises. Visiting anglers can enjoy a rare opportunity to fish for trout and grayling along a mile-long private stretch of the Bentley Brook, which is mentioned in Izaak Walton's The Compleat Angler. Callow Hall is ideally located for some of England's finest stately homes. Closed at Christmas. **Directions:** Take the A515 through Ashbourne towards Buxton. At the Bowling Green Inn on the brow of a steep hill, turn left, then take the first right, signposted Mappleton and the hotel is over the bridge on the right. Price Guide: Single £85–£110; double/twin £130–£165; suite £190.

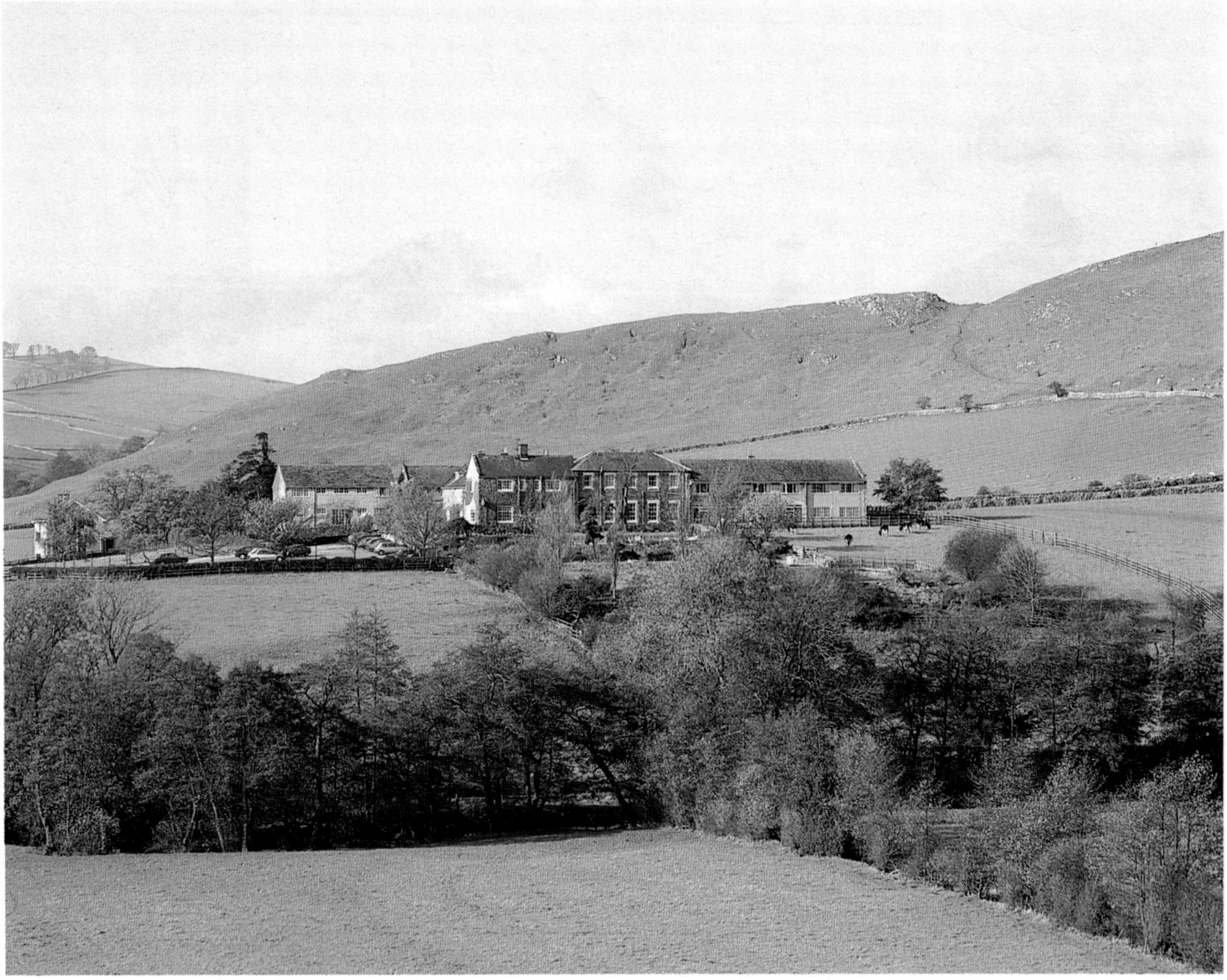

THE IZAAK WALTON HOTEL

DOVEDALE, NEAR ASHBOURNE, DERBYSHIRE DE6 2AY

TEL: 01335 350555 FAX: 01335 350539 E-MAIL: reception@izaakwalton-hotel.com

This converted 17th-century farmhouse hotel, named after the renowned author of 'The Compleat Angler', enjoys glorious views of the surrounding Derbyshire Peaks. The River Dove runs in the valley below. The Izaak Walton is ideal for guests wishing to indulge in a warm welcome and a relaxing ambience. The 30 en suite bedrooms are diverse in their designs; some have four-poster beds whilst others are located in the old farmhouse building and still retain their old oak beams and décor. All the bedrooms are beautifully furnished and offer television, radio, hairdryer, direct dial telephone and several other amenities.The Haddon Restaurant has a diverse menu of creative yet traditional cuisine. Informal meals and light snacks may be enjoyed in the Dovedale Bar. Leisure pursuits include rambling, fishing, mountain biking and hand-gliding. As the hotel has corporate membership at a private leisure club in Ashbourne, guests have full use of their gym facilities free of charge. Places of interest nearby include the Peak District, Alton Towers, the Staffordshire Potteries and fine properties such as Haddon Hall and Chatsworth. **Directions:** Dovedale is 2 miles north-west of Ashbourne between A515 and A52. Price Guide: Single £85; double/twin £112–£152.

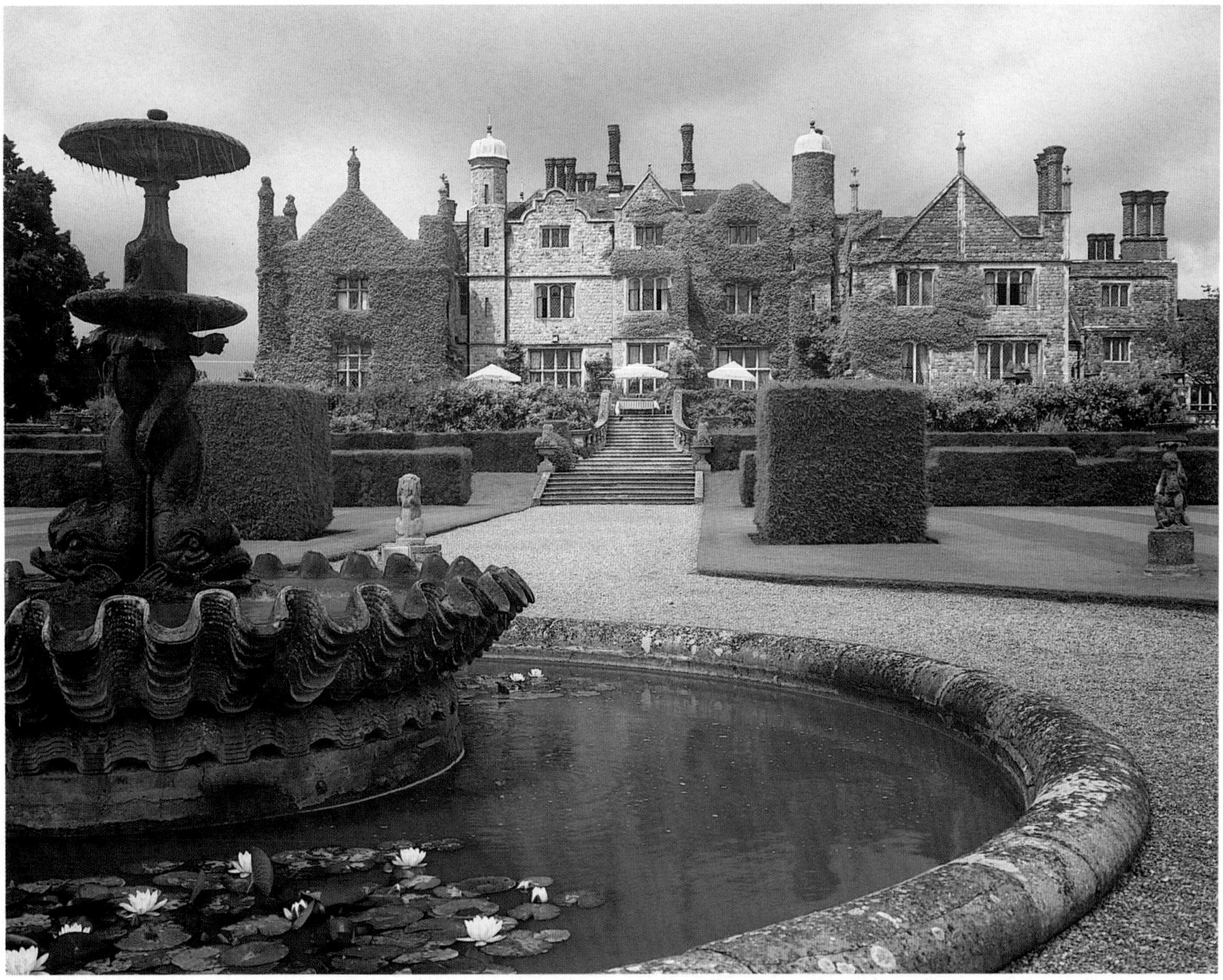

EASTWELL MANOR

BOUGHTON LEES, NR ASHFORD, KENT TN25 4HR
TEL: 01233 213000 FAX: 01233 635530 E-MAIL: eastwell@btinternet.com

Set in the 'Garden of England', Eastwell Manor has a past steeped in history dating back to the 16th century when Richard Plantagenet, son of Richard III, lived on the estate. Surrounded by impressive grounds it encompasses a formal Italian garden, scented rose gardens and attractive lawns and parkland. The magnificent exterior is matched with the splendour of the interior. Exquisite plasterwork and carved oak panelling adorn the public rooms whilst throughout the Manor interesting antique pieces abound. The individually furnished bedrooms and suites, some with fine views across the gardens, feature every possible comfort. There are 19 courtyard apartments giving 39 more bedrooms, all with en suite facilities. The new health & fitness spa features an indoor and outdoor heated 20m pool, hydrotherapy pool, sauna, steam room, Technogym gymnasium, 14 beauty treatment rooms and a hairdressing salon. Guests can enjoy a choice of dining experiences, fine British cuisine in the Manor Restaurant, and a similar standard of food at the less formal Brasserie. Nearby attractions include the cathedral city of Canterbury, Leeds Castle and several charming market towns. Situated near Ashford Eurostar station, Eastwell is perfect for trips to Paris and Brussels. **Directions:** M20 Jct 9. A28 towards Canterbury, then A251 signed Faversham. Hotel is 3 miles north of Ashford in Boughton Lees Price Guide: Single From £170; double/twin £200–£245; suites £265–£355.

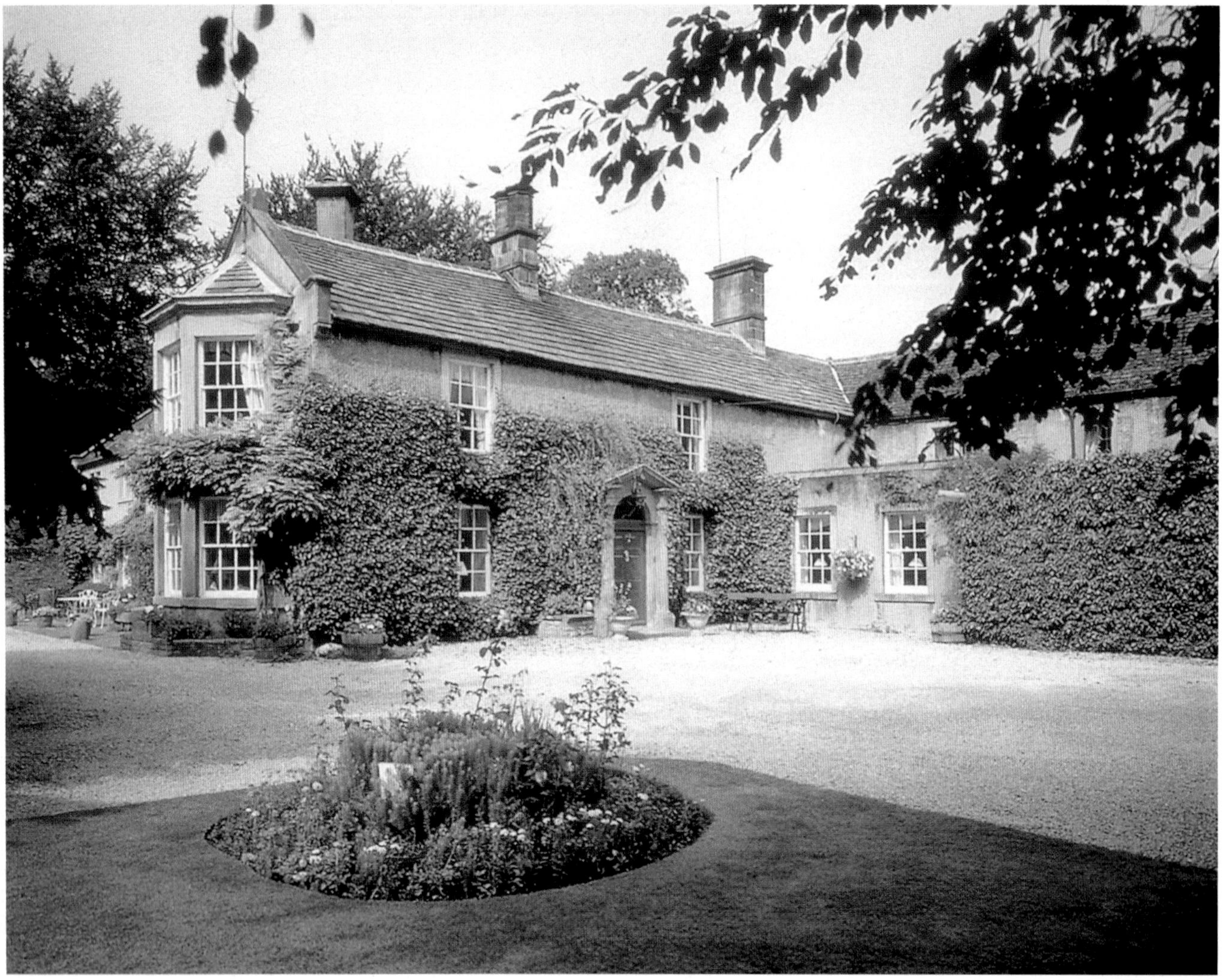

RIVERSIDE HOUSE

ASHFORD-IN-THE-WATER, NR BAKEWELL, DERBYSHIRE DE45 1QF
TEL: 01629 814275 FAX: 01629 812873 E-MAIL: riversidehouse@enta.net

Nestling in one of the Peak District's most picturesque villages, the Riverside House is an intimate country hotel in the finest traditions of classic hospitality. The small ivy-clad Georgian mansion sits in secluded grounds with the tranquil river Wye flowing past landscaped gardens and lawns. The individually designed bedrooms with rich fabrics and antique pieces and the elegant yet cosy public rooms combine with a warmth of welcome and a sense of informality to create an atmosphere of complete relaxation. The 2 AA Rosetted restaurant, with its distinctive fusion of modern English, international and local cuisine, is enhanced by the use of fresh and seasonal ingredients. Conveniently situated for some of the National Park's leading attractions such as Chatsworth and Haddon Hall, the hotel is also an ideal touring base for those wishing to explore the Derbyshire Dales, Lathkill and Dovedale. **Directions:** 1½ miles north of Bakewell on the A6 heading towards Buxton. Ashford-in-the-Water lies on the right side of the river. The hotel is at the end of the village main street next to the Sheepwash Bridge Price Guide: Single £85–£120; double/twin £115–£150.

HARTWELL HOUSE HOTEL, RESTAURANT & SPA

OXFORD ROAD, NR AYLESBURY, BUCKINGHAMSHIRE HP17 8NL

TEL: 01296 747444 FAX: 01296 747450 FROM USA FAX FREE: 1 800 260 8338 E-MAIL: info@hartwell-house.com

Standing in 90 acres of gardens and parkland landscaped by a contemporary of 'Capability' Brown, Hartwell House has both Jacobean and Georgian façades. This beautiful house, brilliantly restored by Historic House Hotels, was the residence in exile of King Louis XVIII of France from 1809 to 1814. The large ground floor reception rooms, with oak panelling and decorated ceilings, have antique furniture and fine paintings which evoke the elegance of the 18th century. There are 46 individually designed bedrooms and suites, some in the house and some in Hartwell Court, the restored 18th-century stables. The dining room at Hartwell is the setting for excellent food awarded 3 AA Rosettes. (Gentlemen are requested to wear a jacket and tie for dinner). The Old Rectory, Hartwell with its two acres of gardens, tennis court and swimming pool, provides beautiful accommodation and offers great comfort and privacy. The Hartwell Spa adjacent to the hotel includes an indoor pool, whirlpool spa bath, steam room, saunas, gymnasium and beauty salons. Situated in the Vale of Aylesbury, the hotel, which is a member of Relais & Châteaux, is only an hour from London and 20 miles from Oxford. Blenheim Palace, Waddesdon Manor and Woburn Abbey are nearby. Dogs are permitted only in Hartwell Court bedrooms. **Directions:** On the A418 Oxford Road, 2 miles from Aylesbury Price Guide: (room only): Single £140–£185; double/twin £225–£395; suites £325–£700

THE PRIORY HOTEL

HIGH STREET, WHITCHURCH, AYLESBURY, BUCKINGHAMSHIRE HP22 4JS
TEL: 01296 641239 FAX: 01296 641793

The Priory Hotel is a beautifully preserved, timber-framed house dating back to 1360. It is set in the picturesque conservation village of Whitchurch, which is about 5 miles north of Aylesbury. With its exposed timbers, leaded windows and open fires, it retains all its traditional character and charm – a refreshing alternative to the all-too-familiar chain hotels of today. All ten bedrooms are individually furnished and many of them have four-poster beds. At the heart of the hotel is La Boiserie Restaurant, where classical French cuisine is served in intimate surroundings. An imaginative à la carte fixed-price menu is offered, including a range of seasonal dishes. Start, for example, with a rich terrine of partridge, wild mushrooms and pistachios, then perhaps choose marinated saddle of venison in Cognac butter sauce and garnished with truffles. Specialities include fresh lobster and flambé dishes. The self-contained conference suite can be used for private lunches, dinners and receptions. Among the places to visit locally are Waddesdon Manor, Claydon House, Stowe, Silverstone motor circuit and Oxford. Closed between Christmas and New Year's Eve; the restaurant, not the hotel, also closes on Sunday evenings. **Directions:** Situated on the A413 4 miles north of Aylesbury Price Guide: Single £70–£85; double £110–£130; suite from £115.

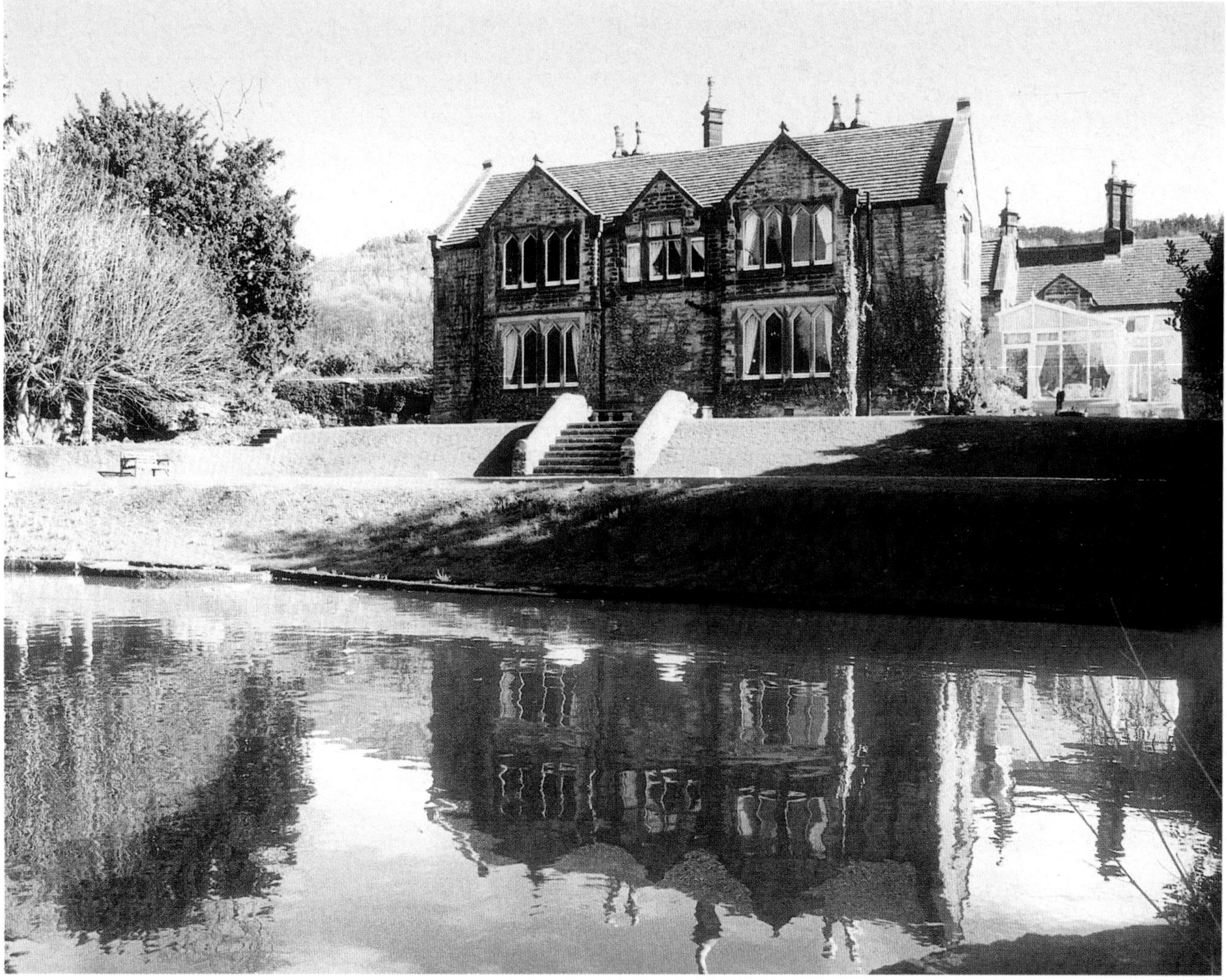

EAST LODGE COUNTRY HOUSE HOTEL

ROWSLEY, NR MATLOCK, DERBYSHIRE DE4 2EF
TEL: 01629 734474 FAX: 01629 733949 E-MAIL: info@eastlodge.com

This graceful 17th century lodge on the edge of the Peak District was originally built as the East Lodge to Haddon Hall, the Derbyshire seat of the Duke of Rutland. Converted to a hotel in the 1980's, East Lodge is now owned and run by Joan and David Hardman and their attentive staff. The lodge has won many accolades including AA 3 star 74%. The attractive conservatory, charming restaurant and spacious hall offers high levels of comfort combined with a warm and relaxed atmosphere. The 15 en suite bedrooms are tastefully furnished, each having its own distinctive character. Imaginative lunches and dinners are served daily in the excellent AA Rosetted restaurant with lighter meals available in the conservatory. A wide selection of fine wines is on offer. Set in 10 acres of attractive gardens and surrounded by rolling Derbyshire countryside, East Lodge provides a tranquil setting for relaxing breaks, conferences and corporate activity/team building events. The nearby Peak District National Park, boasts some of the country's most spectacular walks. The famous stately homes, Chatsworth House and Haddon Hall, are within 2 miles. Bakewell, Buxton, Matlock and Crich are a short drive away. **Directions:** Set back from the A6 in Rowsley village, 3 miles from Bakewell. The hotel entrance is adjacent to the B6012 junction to Sheffield/Chatsworth. Price Guide: Single £75; double/twin from £95.

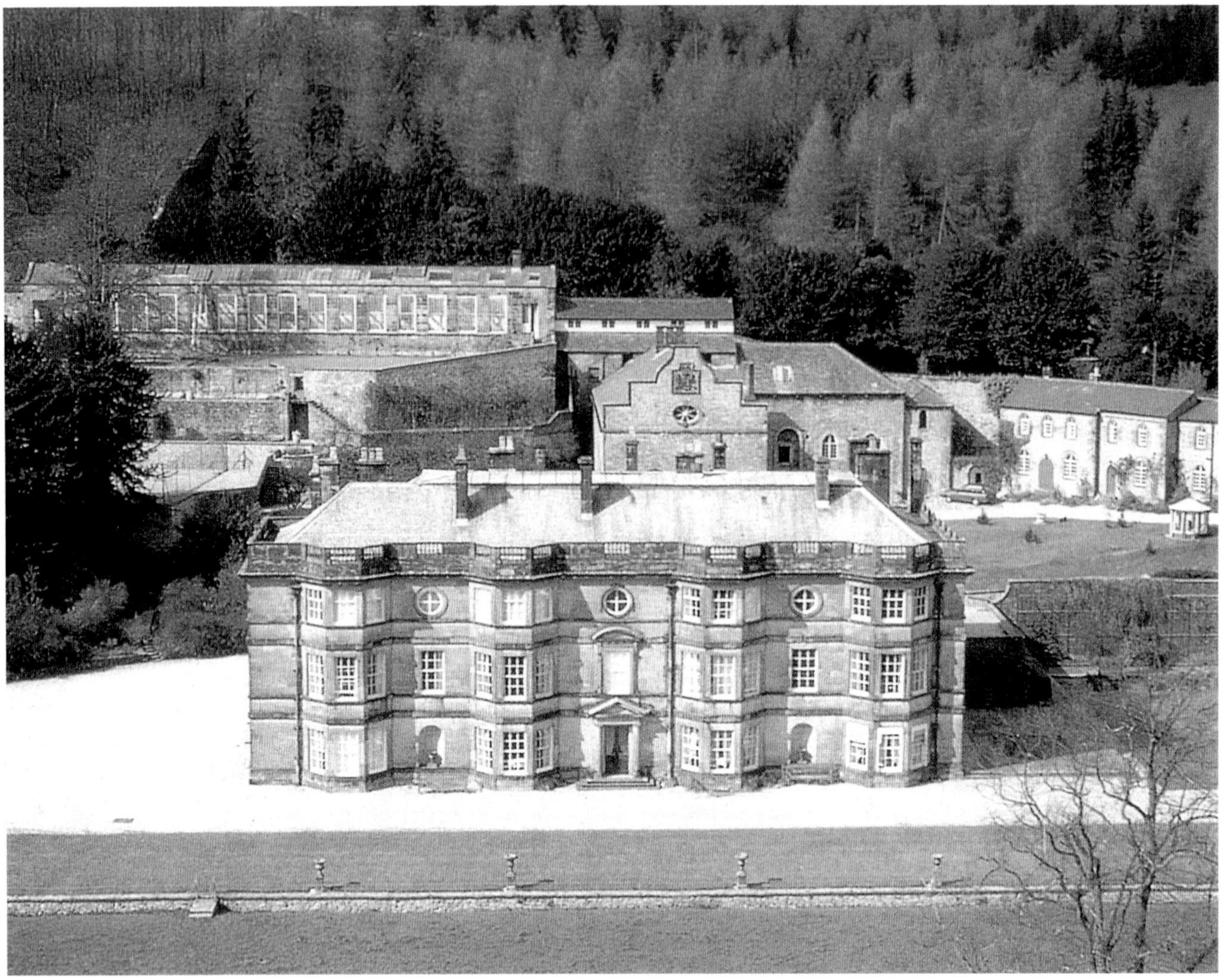

HASSOP HALL

HASSOP, NR BAKEWELL, DERBYSHIRE DE45 1NS
TEL: 01629 640488 FAX: 01629 640577 E-MAIL: hassophallhotel@btinternet.com

The recorded history of Hassop Hall reaches back 900 years to the Domesday Book, to a time when the political scene in England was still dominated by the power struggle between the barons and the King, when the only sure access to that power was through possession of land. By 1643, when the Civil War was raging, the Hall was under the ownership of Rowland Eyre, who turned it into a Royalist garrison. It was the scene of several skirmishes before it was recaptured after the Parliamentary victory. Since purchasing Hassop Hall in 1975, Thomas Chapman has determinedly pursued the preservation of its outstanding heritage. Guests can enjoy the beautifully maintained gardens as well as the splendid countryside of the surrounding area. The bedrooms, some of which are particularly spacious, are well furnished and comfortable. A four-poster bedroom is available for romantic occasions. A comprehensive dinner menu offers a wide and varied selection of dishes, with catering for most tastes. As well as the glories of the Peak District, places to visit include Chatsworth House, Haddon Hall and Buxton Opera House. Christmas opening – details on application. **Directions:** From M1 exit 29 (Chesterfield), take A619 to Baslow, then A623 to Calver; left at lights to B6001 Hassop Hall is 2 miles on right. Price Guide: (excluding breakfast) Double/twin £79–£149. Inclusive rates available on request.

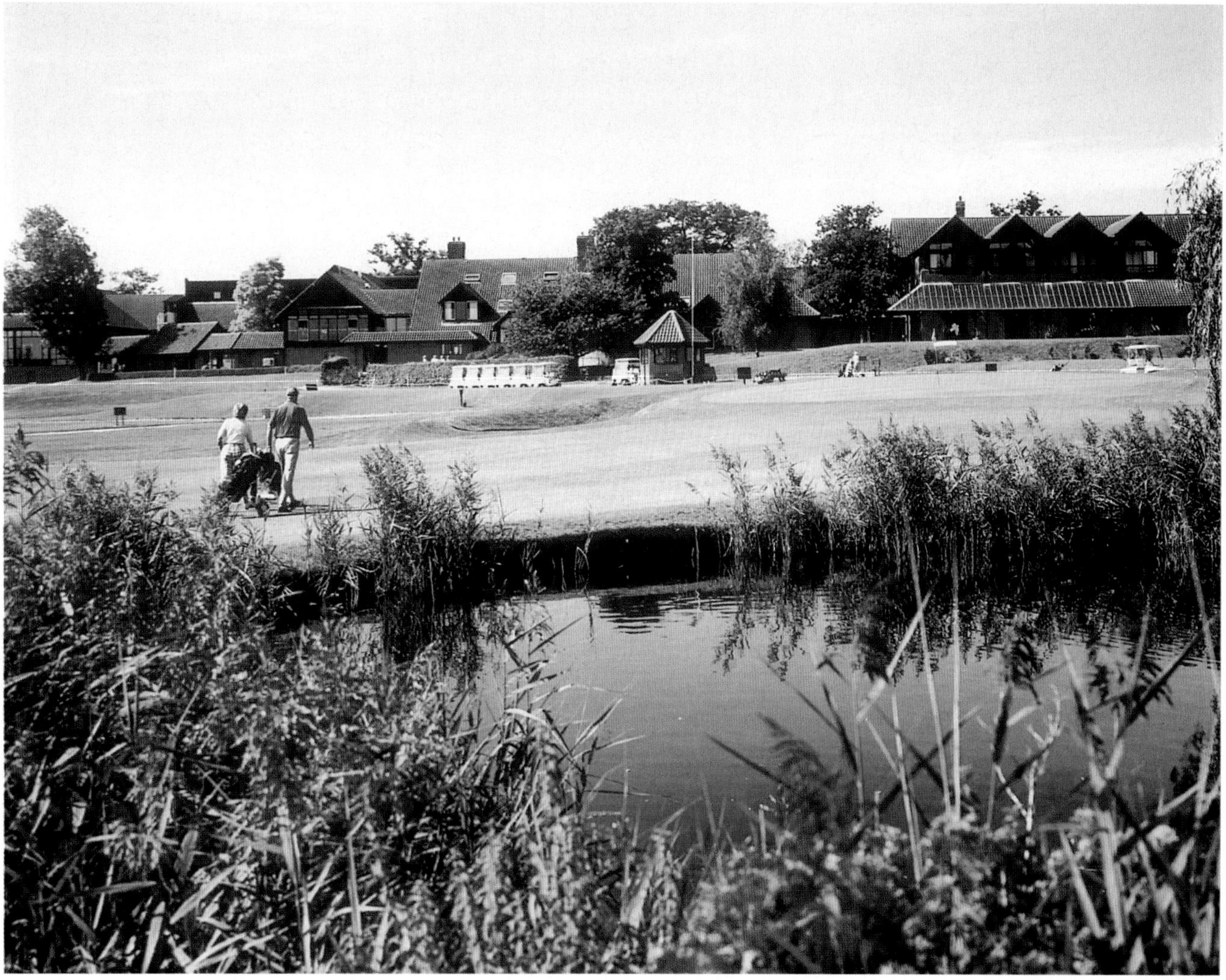

BARNHAM BROOM

NORWICH, NORFOLK NR9 4DD

TEL: 01603 759393 FAX: 01603 758224 E-MAIL: enquiry@barnhambroomhotel.co.uk

Barnham Broom is a golfers' paradise. Situated in 250 acres of the beautiful River Yare Valley 10 miles from the cathedral city of Norwich, it offers everything for the sporting enthusiast, and tranquillity for leisure seekers. The complex has two 18-hole golf courses of character and quality. The par 72 Valley course, dominated by water features and mature trees, was designed by Frank Pennink, one of Europe's most respected course architects, and is one of the finest in Norfolk. The par 71 Hill, designed by Pennink's protégé, Donald Steel, offers fine views of the surrounding countryside with the main challenge being the constant breezes and the many bunkers guarding the greens. In addition, there are excellent practice facilities, including 3 full-length academy holes, PGA professional tuition by the Peter Ballingall Golf School. Hotel guests enjoy a choice of 52 tastefully decorated en suite bedrooms with every comfort. The main restaurant, Flints, offers full à la carte and table d'hôte menus. Lighter meals and beverages are available all day at the Sports Bar and Café with 6ft satellite TV screen. A superb, newly equipped leisure centre features an indoor pool, spa bath, sauna, steam room, solarium and gym. Conference and banqueting suites. **Directions:** Signposted from A47 in the East Midlands and A11 from London. Price Guide: Single from £90; double/twin from £110 suite from £120.

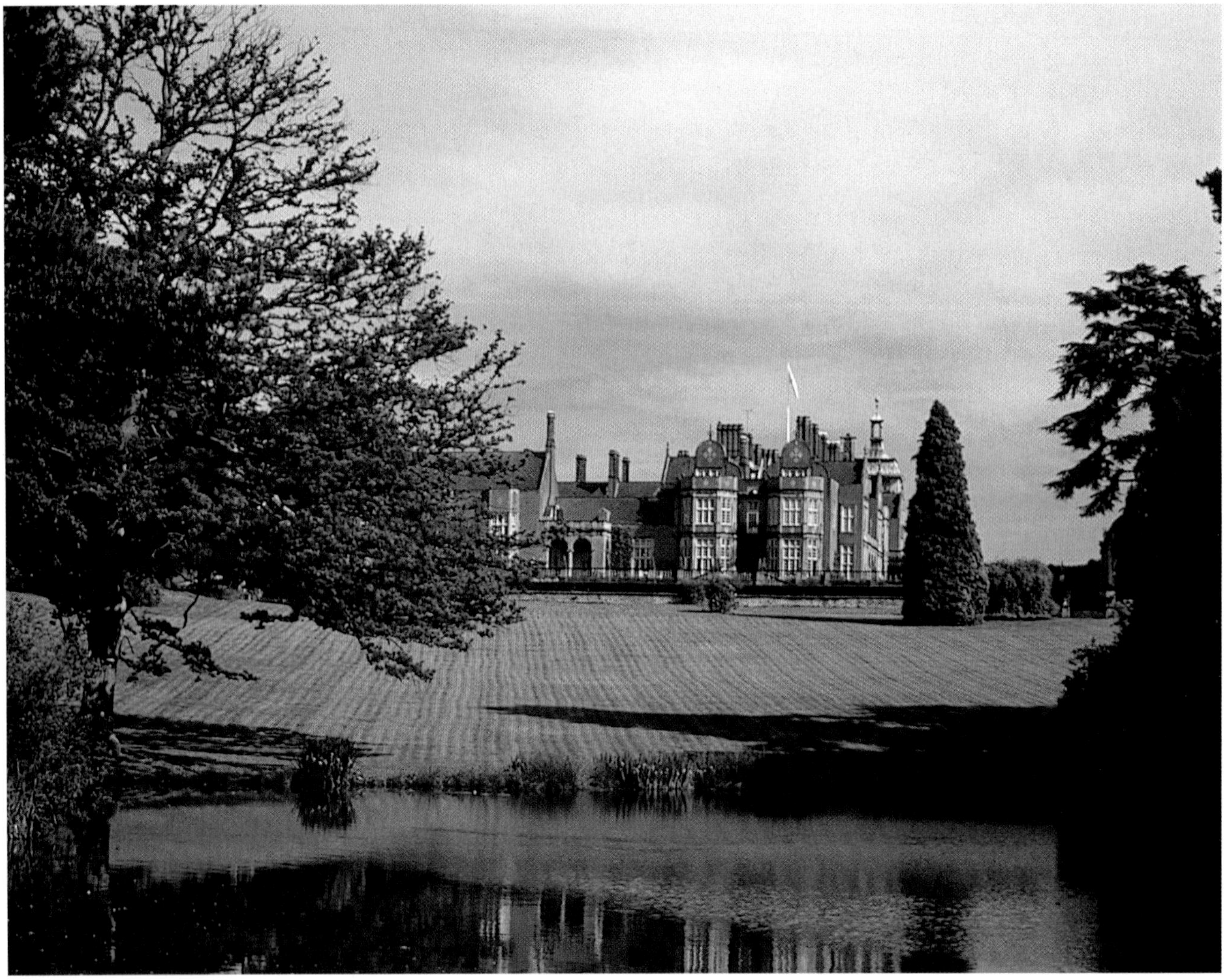

TYLNEY HALL

ROTHERWICK, HOOK, HAMPSHIRE RG27 9AZ

TEL: 01256 764881 FAX: 01256 768141 E-MAIL: reservations@tylneyhall.com

Arriving at this hotel in the evening with its floodlit exterior and forecourt fountain, you can imagine arriving for a party in a private stately home. Grade II listed and set in 66 acres of ornamental gardens and parkland, Tylney Hall typifies the great houses of the past. Apéritifs are taken in the wood-panelled library bar; haute cuisine is served in the glass-domed Oak Room restaurant. The hotel holds RAC and AA food awards also AA 4 Red Stars and RAC Gold Ribbon. Extensive leisure facilities include indoor and outdoor heated swimming pools, multi-gym, sauna, tennis, croquet and snooker, while hot-air ballooning, archery, clay pigeon shooting, golf and riding can be arranged. Surrounding the hotel are wooded trails ideal for rambling or jogging. Functions for up to 100 people are catered for in the Tylney Suite or Chestnut Suite; more intimate gatherings are held in one of the other ten private banqueting rooms. Tylney Hall is licensed to hold wedding ceremonies on site. The cathedral city of Winchester and Stratfield Saye House are nearby. Legoland and Windsor Castle are a 40-minute drive away. **Directions:** M4, Jct11, towards Hook and Rotherwick, follow signs to hotel. M3, Jct5, A287 towards Newnham, over A30 into Old School Road. Left for Newnham and right onto Ridge Lane. Hotel is on the left after 1 m. Price Guide: Single £130–£330; double/twin £165–£280; suite £280–£430.

Cavendish Hotel

BASLOW, DERBYSHIRE DE45 1SP

TEL: 01246 582311 **FAX:** 01246 582312 **E-MAIL:** info@cavendish–hotel.net

This enchanting hotel offers travellers an opportunity to stay on the famous Chatsworth Estate, close to one of England's greatest stately houses, the home of the Duke and Duchess of Devonshire. The hotel has a long history of its own – once known as the Peacock Inn on the turnpike road to Buxton Spa. When it became The Cavendish in 1975, the Duchess personally supervised the transformation, providing some of the furnishings from Chatsworth and her design talents are evident throughout. Guests have a warm welcome before they are conducted to the luxurious bedrooms, all of which overlook the Estate. Harmonious colours, gorgeous fabrics and immense comfort prevail. Every imaginable extra is provided, from library books to bathrobes. Breakfast is served until lunchtime – no rising at cockcrow – and informal meals are served from morning until bed-time in The Garden Room. Sit at the kitchen table and watch super food being prepared as you dine. At dusk you can sample cocktails and fine wines in the bar before dining in the handsome restaurant with its imaginative menu and extensive list of carefully selected wines. Climbing The Peak, exploring The Dales, fishing, golf and Sheffield's Crucible Theatre are among the many leisure pursuits nearby. **Directions:** M1/J29, A617 to Chesterfield then A619 west to Baslow. Price Guide (excluding breakfast): Single from £95; double/twin from £125.

FISCHER'S

BASLOW HALL, CALVER ROAD, BASLOW, DERBYSHIRE DE45 1RR
TEL: 01246 583259 FAX: 01246 583818

Situated on the edge of the magnificent Chatsworth Estate, Baslow Hall enjoys an enviable location surrounded by some of the country's finest stately homes and within easy reach of the Peak District's many cultural and historical attractions. Standing at the end of a winding chestnut tree-lined driveway, this fine Derbyshire manor house was tastefully converted by Max and Susan Fischer into an award winning country house hotel in 1989. Since opening, Fischer's has consistently maintained its position as one of the finest establishments in the Derbyshire/ South Yorkshire regions earning the prestigious Johansens 'Most Excellent UK Restaurant' award in 2001. Whether you are staying in the area for private or business reasons, it is a welcome change to find a place that feels less like a hotel and more like a home, combining comfort and character with an eating experience which is a delight to the palate. Max presides in the kitchen. Guests can choose from the more formal Michelin–starred gourmet menu or the Café-Max menu, where the emphasis is on more informal eating and modern tastes. Baslow Hall offers facilities for small conferences or private functions. **Directions:** Baslow is within 12 miles of the M1 motorway, Chesterfield and Sheffield. Fischer's is on the A623 in Baslow. Price Guide: Single £80–£100; double/twin £150; suite £150.

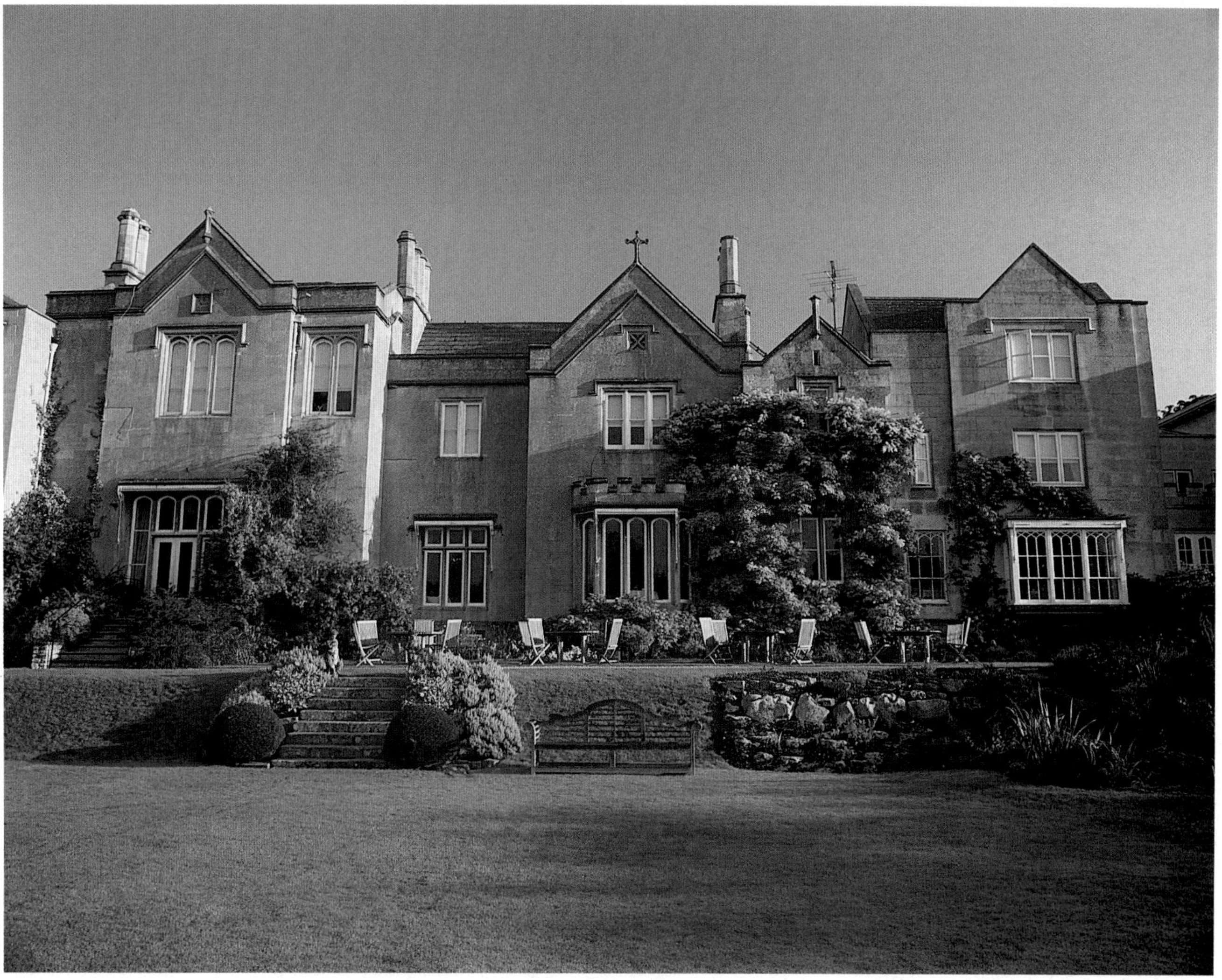

THE BATH PRIORY HOTEL AND RESTAURANT

WESTON ROAD, BATH, SOMERSET BA1 2XT
TEL: 01225 331922 FAX: 01225 448276 E-MAIL: bathprioryhotel@compuserve.com

Standing in four acres of gardens, The Bath Priory Hotel is close to some of England's most famous and finest architecture. Within walking distance of Bath city centre, this Gothic-style mellow stone building dates from 1835, when it formed part of a row of fashionable residences on the west side of the city. Visitors will sense the luxury as they enter the hotel: antique furniture, many superb oil paintings and objets d'art add interest to the two spacious reception rooms and the elegant drawing room. Well-defined colour schemes lend an uplifting brightness throughout, particularly in the tastefully appointed bedrooms. Michelin – starred Head Chef, Robert Clayton's classical style is the primary inspiration for the cuisine, served in three interconnecting dining rooms which overlook the garden. An especially good selection of wines can be recommended to accompany meals. Private functions can be accommodated both in the terrace, pavilion and the Orangery. The Roman Baths, Theatre Royal, Museum of Costume and a host of bijou shops offer plenty for visitors to see. The Garden Spa consists of a fitness suite, swimming pool, sauna, steam room and health & beauty spa. **Directions:** One mile west of the centre of Bath. Please contact the hotel for precise directions. Price Guide: Double/twin from £230 including full English breakfast.

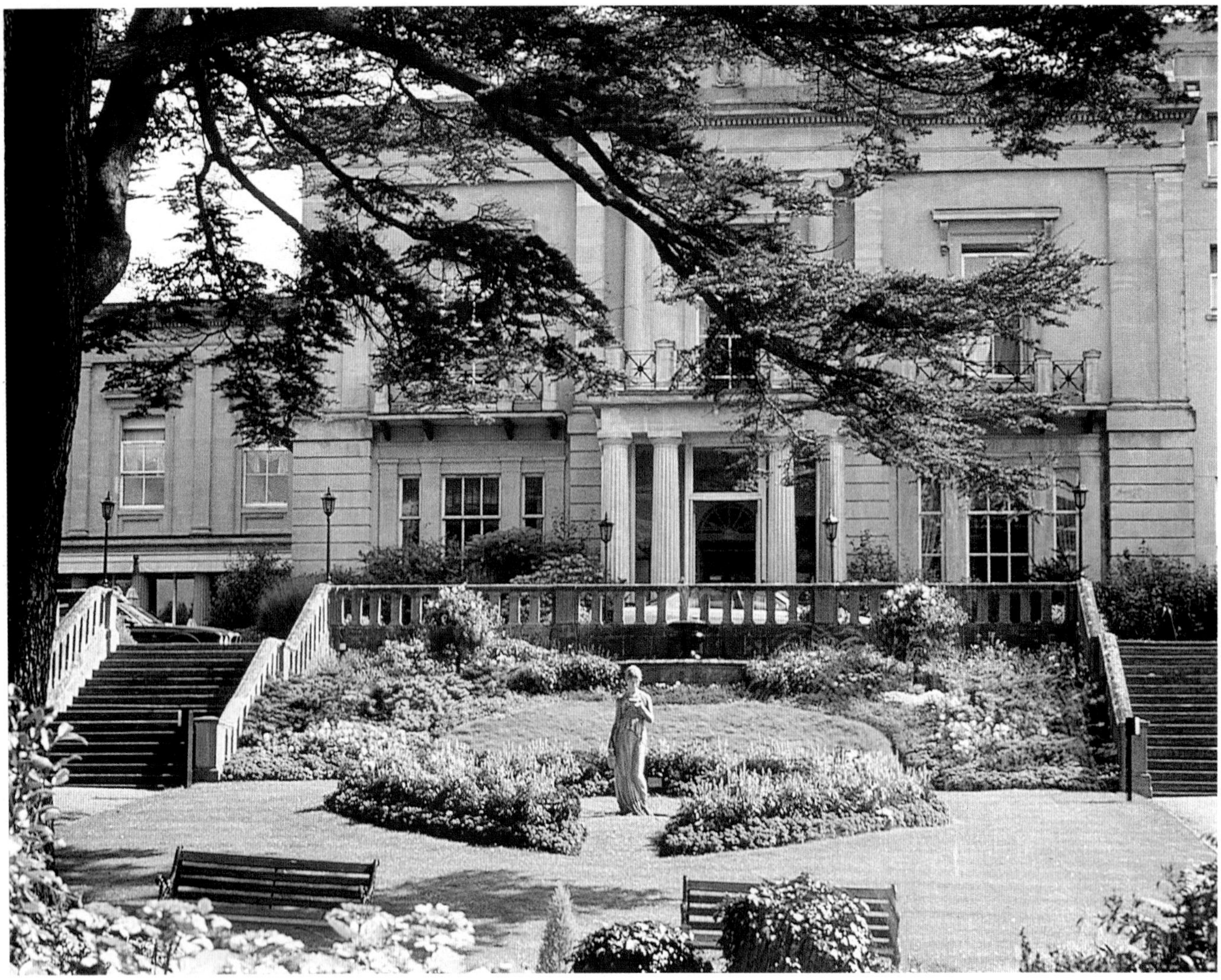

THE BATH SPA HOTEL

SYDNEY ROAD, BATH, SOMERSET BA2 6JF
TEL: 0870 400 8222 FAX: 01225 444006 E-MAIL: fivestar@bathspa.u–net.com

Nestling in seven acres of mature grounds dotted with ancient cedars, formal gardens, ponds and fountains, The Bath Spa Hotel's elegant Georgian façade can only hint at the warmth, style, comfort and attentive personal service. It is a handsome building in a handsome setting with antique furniture, richly coloured carpeting and well defined colour schemes lending an uplifting brightness throughout. The bedrooms are elegantly decorated; the bathrooms are luxuriously appointed in mahogany and marble. The Bath Spa offers all amenities that guests would expect of a Five Star Hotel while retaining the character of a homely country house. Chef Andrew Hamer's imaginative, contemporary style is the primary inspiration for the award-winning cuisine served in the two restaurants. For relaxation there is a fully equipped health and leisure spa which includes an indoor swimming pool, gymnasium, sauna, Jacuzzi, three treatment rooms, hair salon, tennis court and croquet lawn. Apart from the delights of Bath, there is motor racing at Castle Combe and hot air ballooning nearby. **Directions:** Exit the M4 at jct18 onto the A46 follow signs to Bath for 8miles until the major roundabout. Turn right onto A4 follow City Centre signs for one mile, at the first major set of lights turn left toward the A36. At mini roundabout turn right then next left after Holburne Museum into Sydney Place. The hotel is 200 yards up the hill on the right. Price Guide: Double/twin £180; 4-poster £280; suite £330.

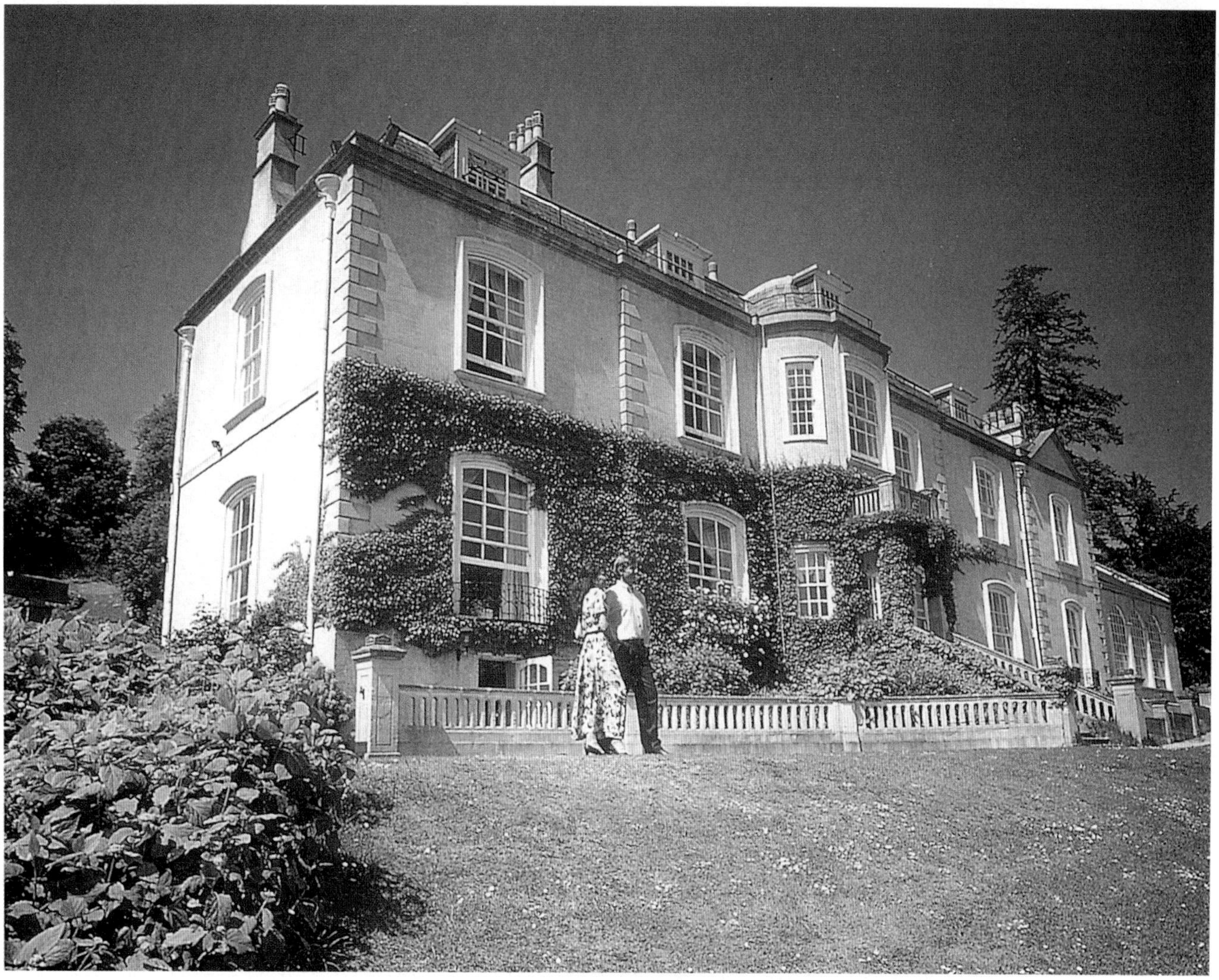

Combe Grove Manor Hotel & Country Club

BRASSKNOCKER HILL, MONKTON COMBE, BATH, SOMERSET BA2 7HS
TEL: 01225 834644 FAX: 01225 834961 E-MAIL: reservations@combegrovemanor.com

This is an exclusive 18th-century country house hotel situated two miles from the beautiful city of Bath. Built on the hillside site of a Roman settlement, Combe Grove Manor is set in 69 acres of private gardens and woodland, with magnificent views over the Limpley Stoke Valley. In addition to the Georgian Restaurant, which boasts an exciting varied menu, there is the more informal Manor Vaults Bar and Bistro with a terrace garden. After dinner guests may relax with drinks in the elegant drawing room or library. The bedrooms are lavishly furnished, all individually designed with en suite facilities, three of which have Jacuzzi baths. Within the grounds are some of the finest leisure facilities in the South West, including indoor and outdoor heated pools, hydrospa beds and steam room, four all-weather tennis courts, a 5-hole par 3 golf course and a two-tiered driving range. Guests may use the Life Fitness gym, aerobics studio, saunas and solaria or relax in the Clarins beauty rooms where a full range of treatments are offered. Separate from the Manor House is the Garden Lodge which provides 31 rooms, with spectacular views and some have a private terrace. **Directions:** Set south-east of Bath off the A36 near the University. Map can be supplied on request Price Guide: Single from £110; double/twin from £110; suite from £225.

DUKE'S HOTEL

GREAT PULTENEY STREET, BATH, SOMERSET BA2 4DN
TEL: 01225 787960 FAX: 01225 787961 E-MAIL: info@dukesbath.co.uk

With its grand exterior and tall windows this former palladian-style mansion blends in beautifully with Bath's famed architectural splendours. A homely hotel with townhouse characteristics, it is situated in a prestigious street which established itself as one of the country's most chic addresses. The Holburne Museum is at one end of the quiet street, the famous Pulteney Bridge at the other and Bath's shops and principal landmarks just a few minutes' walk away. Visitors enter a world of genteel elegance enhanced by the welcoming private owners and staff who provide extremely efficient service. Duke's has been completely refurbished and restored to its original Georgian splendour and style, combined with lavish comfort and 21st-century amenities. Most of the high-ceiling, spacious bedrooms incorporate unique features including original plasterwork and enormous sash windows which offer splendid views over Great Pulteney Street. Each room is named after a Duke and has a design inspired by Georgian influences. Award-winning cuisine is served in the highly acclaimed brasserie-style Martin Blunos at Fitzroys, which is operated by the 2 Michelin Star chef, and complemented by a comfortable bar overlooking a delightful walled garden. Private dining rooms are available for family occasions and small functions. **Directions:** Great Pulteney Street is in the centre of Bath. Price Guide: Single £115; double/twin £145–£185; suite £215–£235.

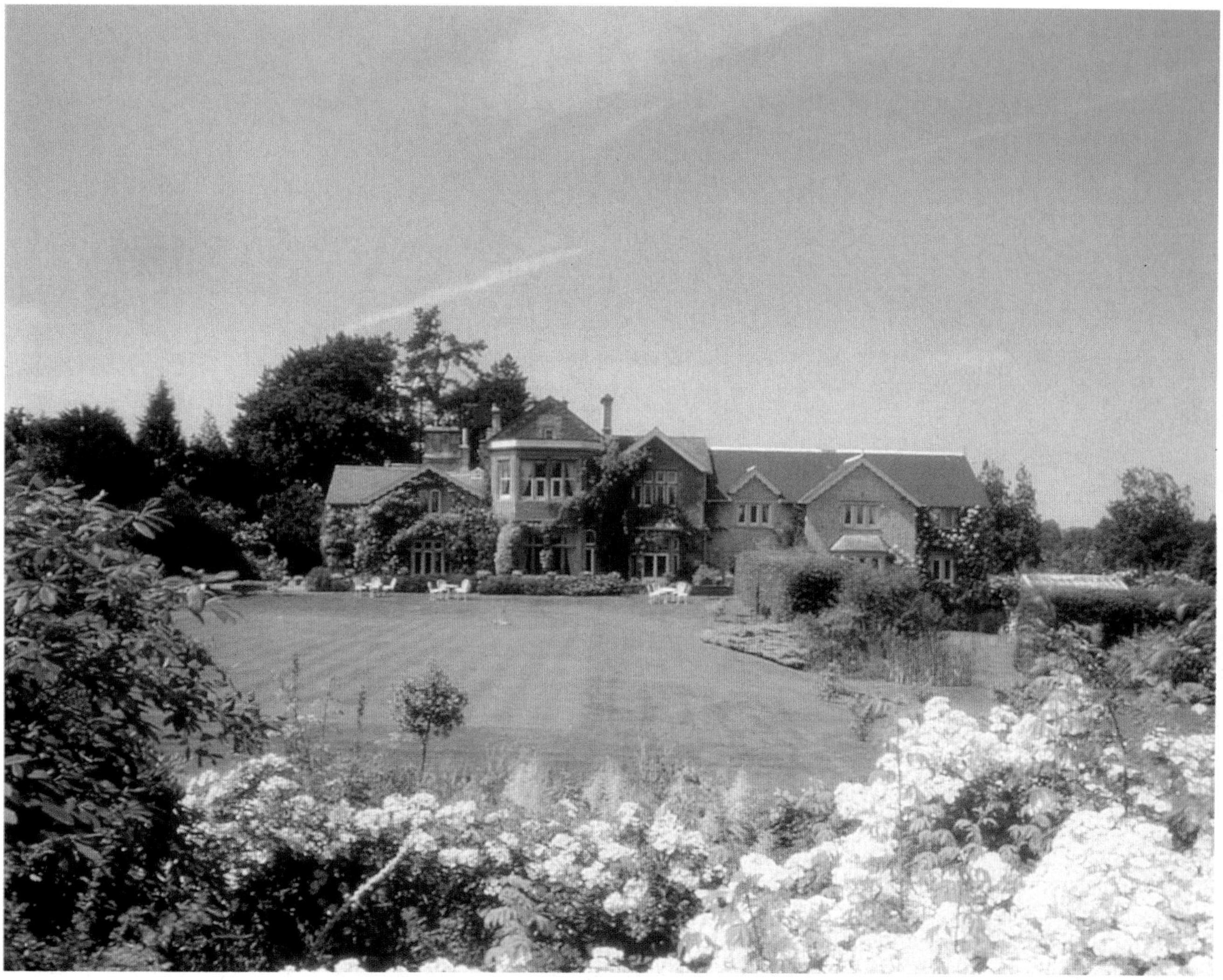

HOMEWOOD PARK

HINTON CHARTERHOUSE, BATH, SOMERSET BA2 7TB
TEL: 01225 723731 FAX: 01225 723820 E-MAIL: res@homewoodpark.com

Standing amid 10 acres of beautiful grounds and woodland on the edge of Limpley Stoke Valley, a designated area of natural beauty is Homewood Park, one of Britain's finest privately-owned smaller country house hotels. This lovely 19th century building has an elegant interior, adorned with beautiful fabrics, antiques, oriental rugs and original oil paintings. Lavishly furnished bedrooms offer the best in comfort, style and privacy. Each of them has a charm and character of its own and most have good views over the Victorian garden. The outstanding cuisine overseen by chef Nigel Godwin has won the hotel an excellent reputation. The à la carte menu uses wherever possible produce from local suppliers. A range of carefully selected wines, stored in the hotel's original medieval cellars, lies patiently waiting to augment lunch and dinner. Before or after a meal guests can enjoy a drink in the comfortable bar or drawing rooms, both of which have a log fire during the cooler months. The hotel is well placed for guests to enjoy the varied attractions of the wonderful city of Bath with its unique hot springs, Roman remains, superb Georgian architecture and American Museum. Further afield but within reach are Stonehenge and Cheddar caves. **Directions:** On the A36 six miles from Bath towards Warminster. Price Guide: Single from £114; double/twin from £144; suites from £255

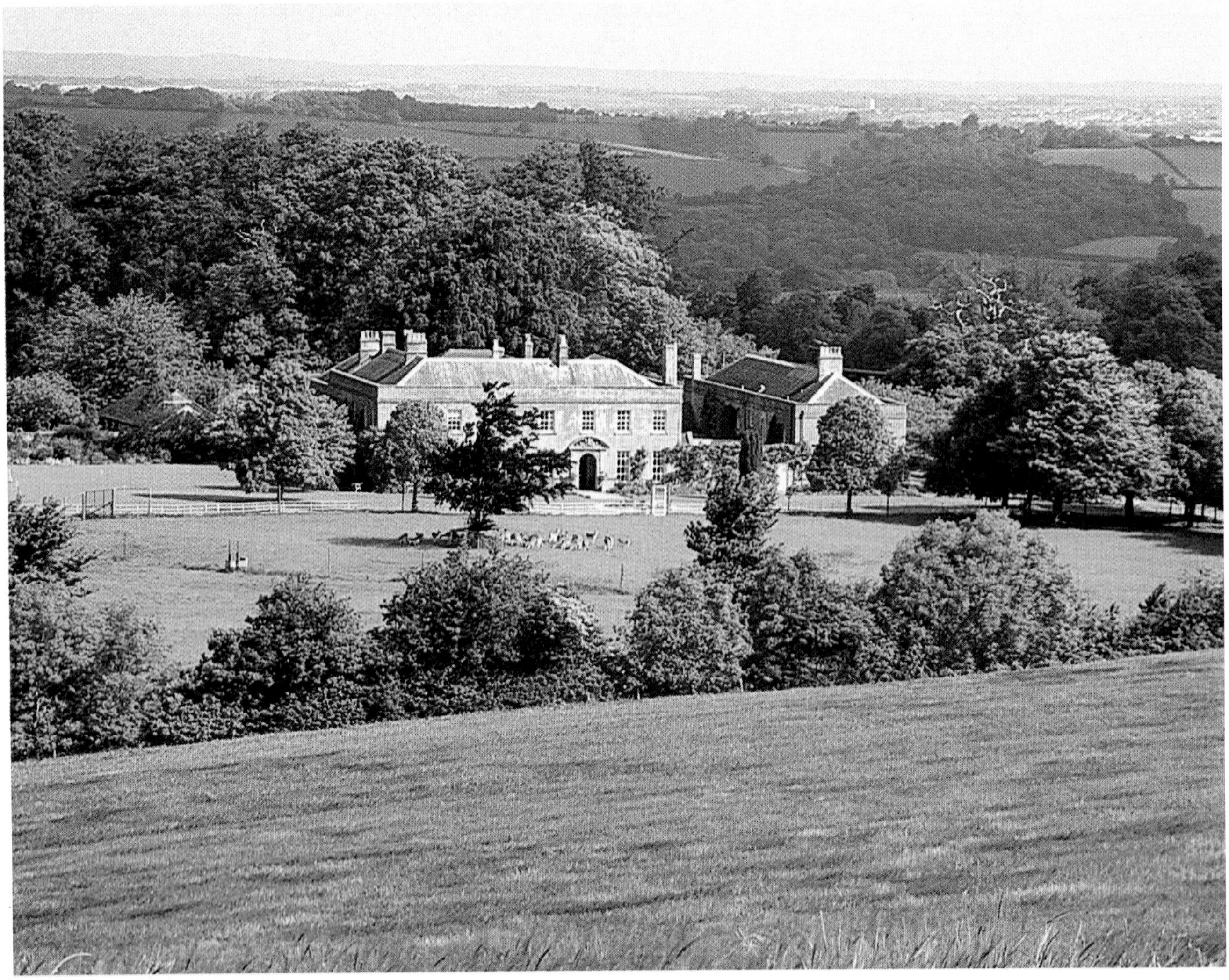

HUNSTRETE HOUSE

HUNSTRETE, NR BATH, SOMERSET BS39 4NS

TEL: 01761 490490 FAX: 01761 490732 E-MAIL: reservations@hunstretehouse.co.uk

In a classical English landscape on the edge of the Mendip Hills stands Hunstrete House. This unique hotel, surrounded by lovely gardens, is largely 18th century, although the history of the estate goes back to 963ad. Each of the bedrooms is individually decorated and furnished to a high standard, combining the benefits of a hotel room with the atmosphere of a charming private country house. Many offer uninterrupted views over undulating fields and woodlands. The reception areas exhibit warmth and elegance and are liberally furnished with beautiful antiques. Log fires burn in the hall, library and drawing room through the winter and on cooler summer evenings. The Terrace dining room looks out on to an Italianate, flower filled courtyard. A highly skilled head chef offers light, elegant dishes using produce from the extensive garden, including substantial use of organic meat and vegetables. The menu changes regularly and the hotel has an excellent reputation for the quality and interest of its wine list. In a sheltered corner of the walled garden there is a heated swimming pool for guests to enjoy. For the energetic, the all weather tennis court provides another diversion and there are riding stables in Hunstrete village, a five minute walk away. **Directions:** From Bath take the A4 towards Bristol and then the A368 to Wells. Price Guide: Single from £145; double/twin from £165; suite from £265.

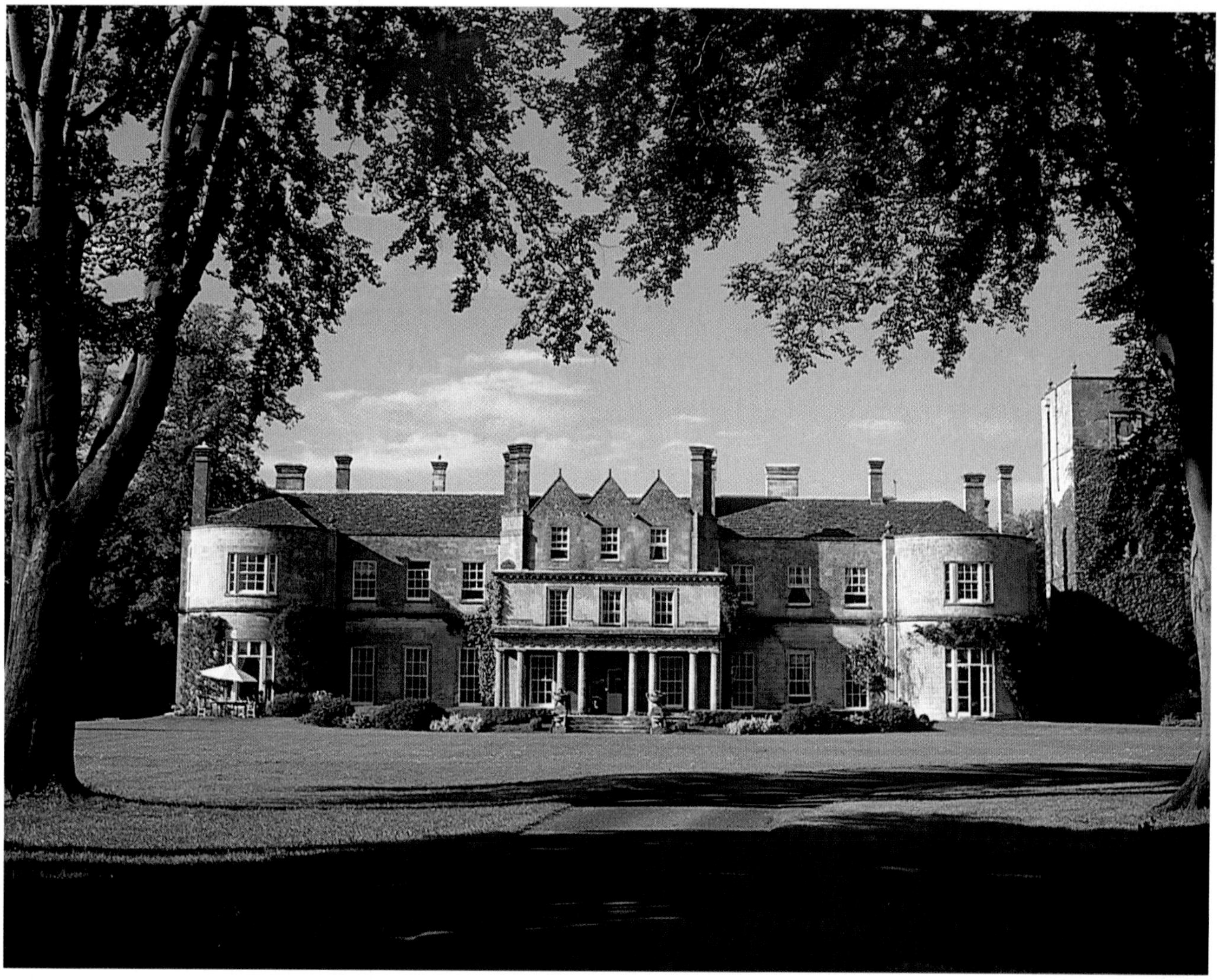

LUCKNAM PARK

COLERNE, CHIPPENHAM, WILTSHIRE SN14 8AZ
TEL: 01225 742777 FAX: 01225 743536 E-MAIL: reservations@lucknampark.co.uk

For over 250 years Lucknam Park has been a focus of fine society and aristocratic living, something guests will sense immediately upon their approach along the mile-long avenue lined with beech trees. Built in 1720, this magnificent Palladian mansion is situated just six miles from Bath on the southern edge of the Cotswolds. The delicate aura of historical context is reflected in fine art and antiques dating from the late Georgian and early Victorian periods. Award winning food can be savoured in the elegant restaurant, at tables laid with exquisite porcelain, silver and glassware, accompanied with wines from an extensive cellar. Set within the walled gardens of the hotel is the Leisure Spa, comprising an indoor pool, sauna, solarium, steam room, whirlpool spa, gymnasium, beauty salon and snooker room. Numerous activities can be arranged on request, including hot-air ballooning, golf and archery. The Lucknam Park Equestrian Centre, which is situated on the estate, welcomes complete beginners and experienced riders and takes liveries. Bowood House, Corsham Court and Castle Combe are all nearby. Lucknam Park is now a member of Relais et Châteaux. **Directions:** 15 minutes from M4, junctions 17 and 18, located between A420 and A4 near the village of Colerne. Price Guide: (room only): Single from £155; double/twin from £195; suite from £425.

The Queensberry

RUSSEL STREET, BATH, SOMERSET BA1 2QF

TEL: 01225 447928 FAX: 01225 446065 E-MAIL: enquiries@bathqueensberry.com

When the Marquis of Queensberry commissioned John Wood to build this house in Russel Street in 1772, little did he know that 200 years hence guests would still be being entertained in these elegant surroundings. An intimate town house hotel, The Queensberry is in a quiet residential street just a few minutes' walk from Wood's other splendours – the Royal Crescent, Circus and Assembly Rooms. Bath is one of England's most beautiful cities. Regency stucco ceilings, ornate cornices and panelling combined with enchanting interior décor complement the strong architectural style. However, the standards of hotel-keeping have far outpaced the traditional surroundings, with high quality en suite bedrooms, room service and up-to-date office support for executives. The Olive Tree Restaurant is one of the leading restaurants in the Bath area. Proprietors Stephen and Penny Ross are thoroughly versed in offering hospitality and a warm welcome. Represented in America by Josephine Barr. The hotel is closed for one week at Christmas. **Directions:** From junction 18 of M4, enter Bath along A4 London Road. Turn sharp right up Lansdown Road, left into Bennett Street, then right into Russel Street opposite the Assembly Rooms Price Guide: Single £90–£140; double/twin £120–£220.

THE ROYAL CRESCENT HOTEL

16 ROYAL CRESCENT, BATH, SOMERSET BA1 2LS
TEL: 01225 823333 FAX: 01225 339401 E-MAIL: reservations@royalcrescent.co.uk

The Royal Crescent Hotel is a Grade I listed building of the greatest historical and architectural importance, situated in the centre of one of Europe's finest masterpieces. A sweep of 30 houses with identical façades stretch in a 500ft curve, built in 1775. The Royal Crescent Hotel was completely refurbished in 1998 and the work undertaken has restored many of the classical Georgian features with all the additional modern comforts. Each of the 45 bedrooms is equipped with air conditioning, the Cliveden bed, video/compact disc player and personal facsimile machine. Pimpernel's restaurant offers a relaxed and informal dining atmosphere, presenting a contemporary menu, including subtle flavours from the Far East. Comprehensively equipped, the two secure private boardrooms provide self-contained business meeting facilities. Exclusive use of the hotel can be arranged for a special occasion or corporate event. Magnificent views of Bath and the surrounding countryside may be enjoyed from the hotel's vintage river launch and hot air balloon. The Bath House is a unique spa, in which to enjoy both complementary therapies and holistic massage. Adjacent to this tranquil setting is the gym & studio comprising seventeen pieces of cardio-vascular and resistance equipment. **Directions:** Detailed directions are available from the hotel on booking : Price Guide: (room only) Double/twin from £220; suites from £420.

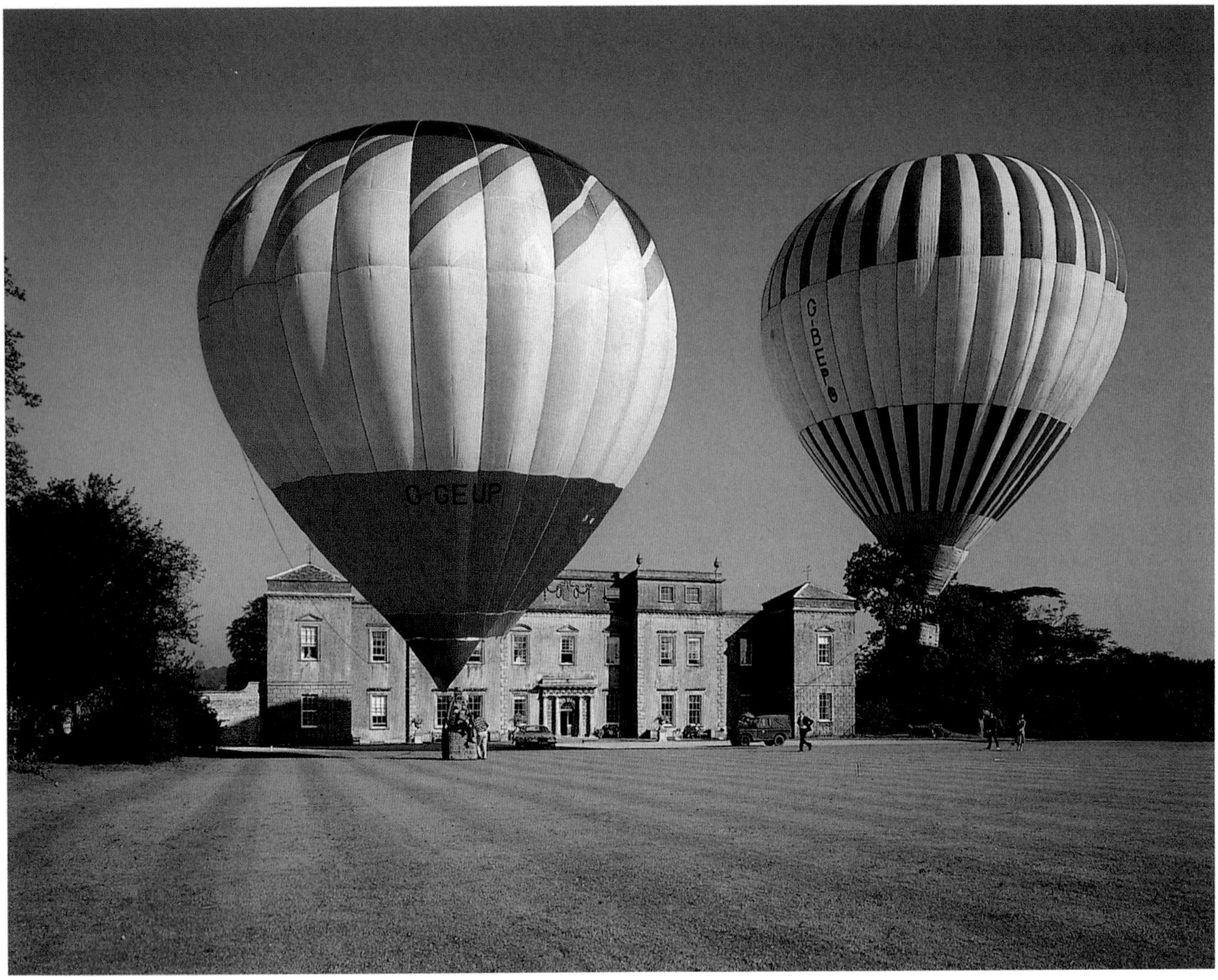

STON EASTON PARK

STON EASTON, BATH, SOMERSET BA3 4DF
TEL: 01761 241631 FAX: 01761 241377 E-MAIL: stoneastonpark@stoneaston.co.uk

The internationally renowned hotel at Ston Easton Park is a Grade I Palladian mansion of notable distinction. A showpiece for some exceptional architectural and decorative features of its period, it dates from 1739 and has recently undergone extensive restoration, offering a unique opportunity to enjoy the opulent splendour of the 18th century. A high priority is given to the provision of friendly and unobtrusive service. The hotel has won innumerable awards for its décor, service and food. Jean Monro, an acknowledged expert on 18th century decoration, supervised the design and furnishing of the interiors, complementing the original features with choice antiques, paintings and objets d'art. Fresh, quality produce, delivered from all parts of Britain, is combined with herbs and vegetables from the Victorian kitchen garden to create English and French dishes. To accompany the meal, a wide selection of rare wines and old vintages is stocked in the house cellars. The grounds, landscaped by Humphry Repton in 1793, consist of romantic gardens and parkland. The 17th century Gardener's Cottage, close to the main house on the wooded banks of the River Norr, provides private suite accommodation. **Directions:** 11 miles south of Bath on the A37 between Bath and Wells. Price Guide: Single £155; double/twin £185–£320; four-poster £320–£405.

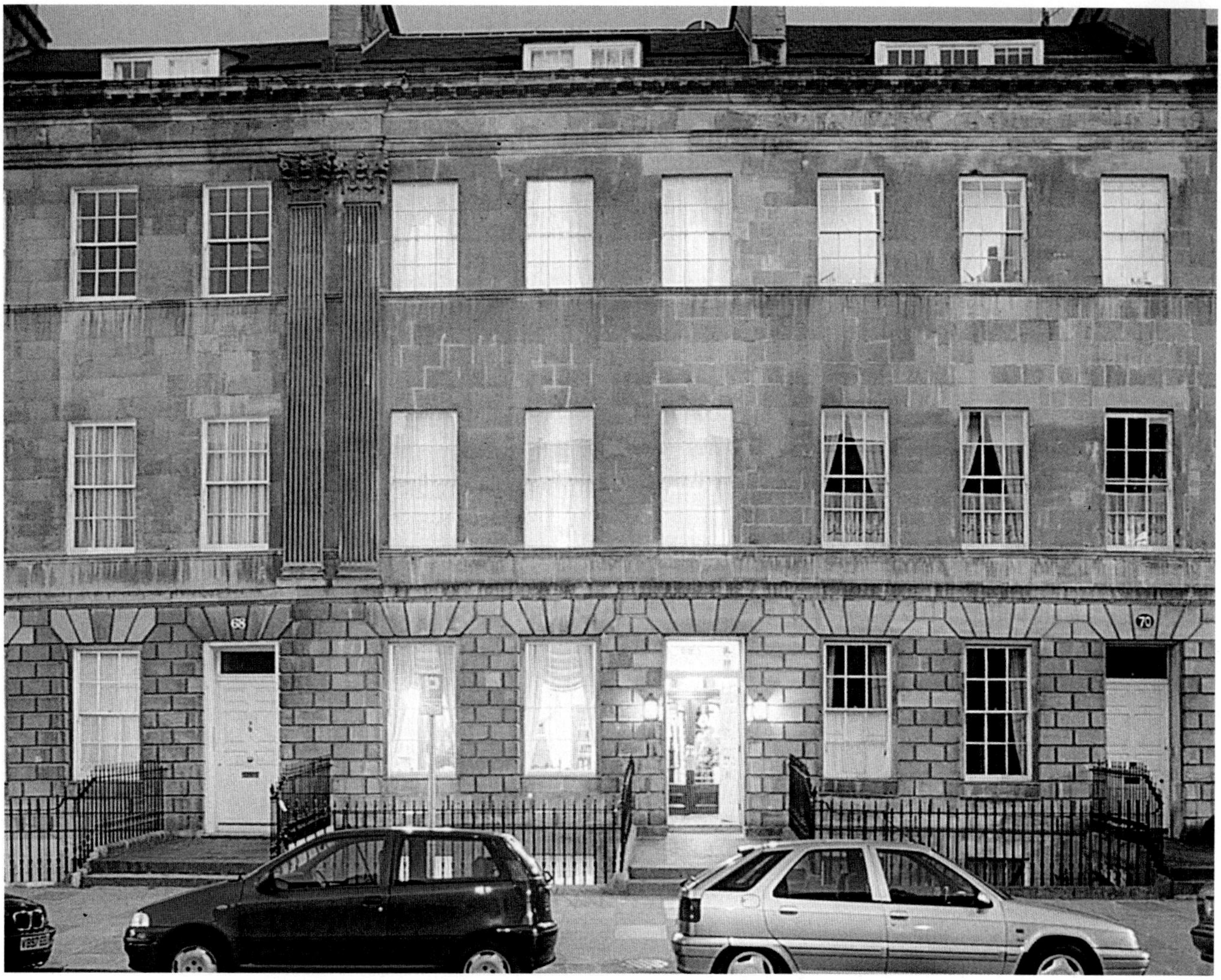

THE WINDSOR HOTEL

69 GREAT PULTENEY STREET, BATH BA2 4DL

Tel: 01225 422100 Fax: 01225 422550 E-Mail: sales@bathwindsorhotel.com

Elegant wrought-iron railings front this attractive town house situated in the heart of the best-preserved Georgian city in Britain. Grade I listed and refurbished to the highest standards, The Windsor Hotel stands on one of the finest boulevards in Europe just a short stroll from the Royal Crescent, Circus, Assembly Rooms and Roman Baths. The hotel's tall front windows look across Georgian façades inspired by Palladio, whilst rooms at the back have views of the rolling hills beyond. Enchanting interior décor complements the strong and pleasing architectural style, and fine furniture and fabrics abound. Each individually designed en suite bedroom and suite is the essence of high quality and comfort. Afternoon tea or after dinner drinks can be enjoyed in an exquisite drawing room while memorable menus are served in a small Japanese restaurant which overlooks its own special garden. Great Pulteney Street leads onto Pulteney Bridge and the city's tempting boutiques, antique shops and award-winning restaurants. Within easy reach are Longleat Estate, Ilford Manor, the American Museum and Limpley Stoke Valley. Limited car parking is available and can be arranged upon reservation. **Directions:** From Jct18 off M4, enter Bath along A4 London Road. Turn left into Bathwick Street, then right into Sydney Place and right again into Great Pulteney Street. Price Guide: Single £85-£115; double/twin £135-£195; suite £275.

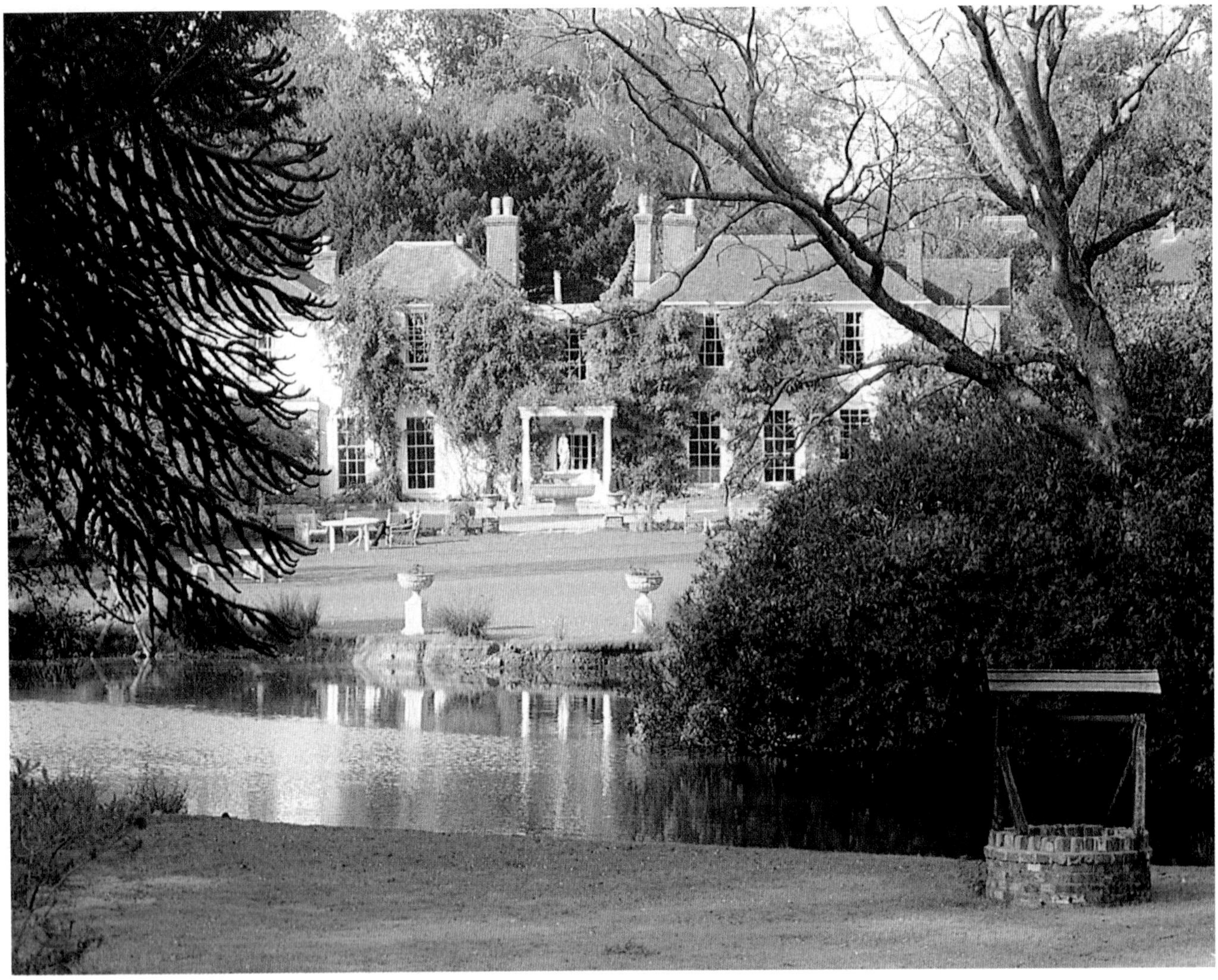

POWDERMILLS HOTEL

POWDERMILL LANE, BATTLE, EAST SUSSEX TN33 0SP
TEL: 01424 775511 FAX: 01424 774540 E-MAIL: powdc@aol.com

Situated outside the historic Sussex town famous for the 1066 battle, PowderMills is an 18th century listed country house which has been skilfully converted into an elegant hotel. Nestling in 150 acres of parks and woodland, the beautiful and tranquil grounds feature a 7-acre specimen fishing lake. Wild geese, swans, ducks, kingfishers and herons abound. Privately owned and run by Douglas and Julie Cowpland, the hotel has been carefully furnished with locally acquired antiques. On cooler days, log fires burn in the entrance hall and drawing room. The bedrooms – ten with four-posters – are all individually furnished and decorated. The Orangery Restaurant offers fine classical cooking by chef Daniel Ayton. Guests may dine on the terrace in summer, looking out over the swimming pool and grounds. Light meals and snacks are available in the library. The location an is ideal base from which to explore the beautiful Sussex and Kent countryside and there are many villages and small towns in the area. **Directions:** From centre of Battle take the Hastings road south. After ¼ mile turn right into Powdermill Lane. After a sharp bend, the entrance is on the right; cross over the bridge and lakes to reach the hotel. Price Guide: Single from £75; double/twin £99–£170.

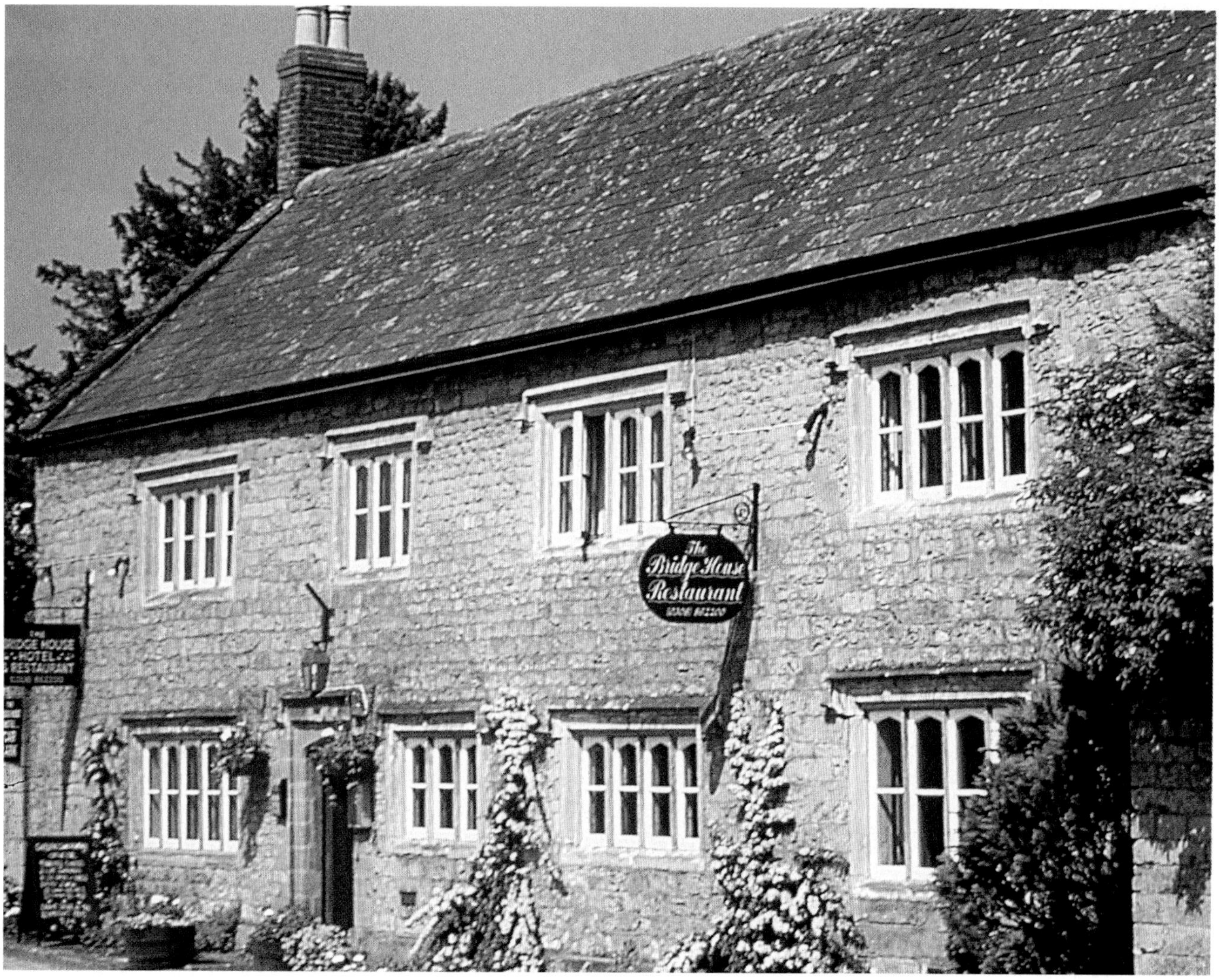

BRIDGE HOUSE HOTEL

BEAMINSTER, DORSET DT8 3AY
TEL: 01308 862200 FAX: 01308 863700 E-MAIL: enquiries@bridge–house.co.uk

This country town hotel, built of mellow stone, was once a priest's house and dates back to the 13th century. It is set in the heart of Beaminster, an old market town. In this charming hotel, enclosed by a beautiful walled garden, emphasis is placed on creating a relaxing atmosphere for guests and providing them with the highest standards of comfort without sacrificing the character of the surroundings. The warm stone, beams and large fireplaces combine with every modern day amenity to provide a pleasant environment which visitors will remember. Attractively decorated and furnished bedrooms include a colour television and tea and coffee making facilities. Four of them are on the ground floor and offer easy access. The pride of the house is its food, where attention to detail is evident. In the candlelit Georgian dining room an imaginative menu offers dishes that make use of fresh produce from the local farms and fishing ports. Beaminster is convenient for touring, walking and exploring the magnificent Dorset countryside. Places of interest nearby include many fine houses and gardens. Several golf courses, fresh and salt water fishing, riding, sailing and swimming in the sea are all within reach. **Directions:** From M3 take A303 Crewkerne exit then A356 through Crewkerne, then A3066 to Beaminster. Hotel is 100 yds from town centre car park, on the left. Price Guide: Single £68–£91; twin/double £94–£128.

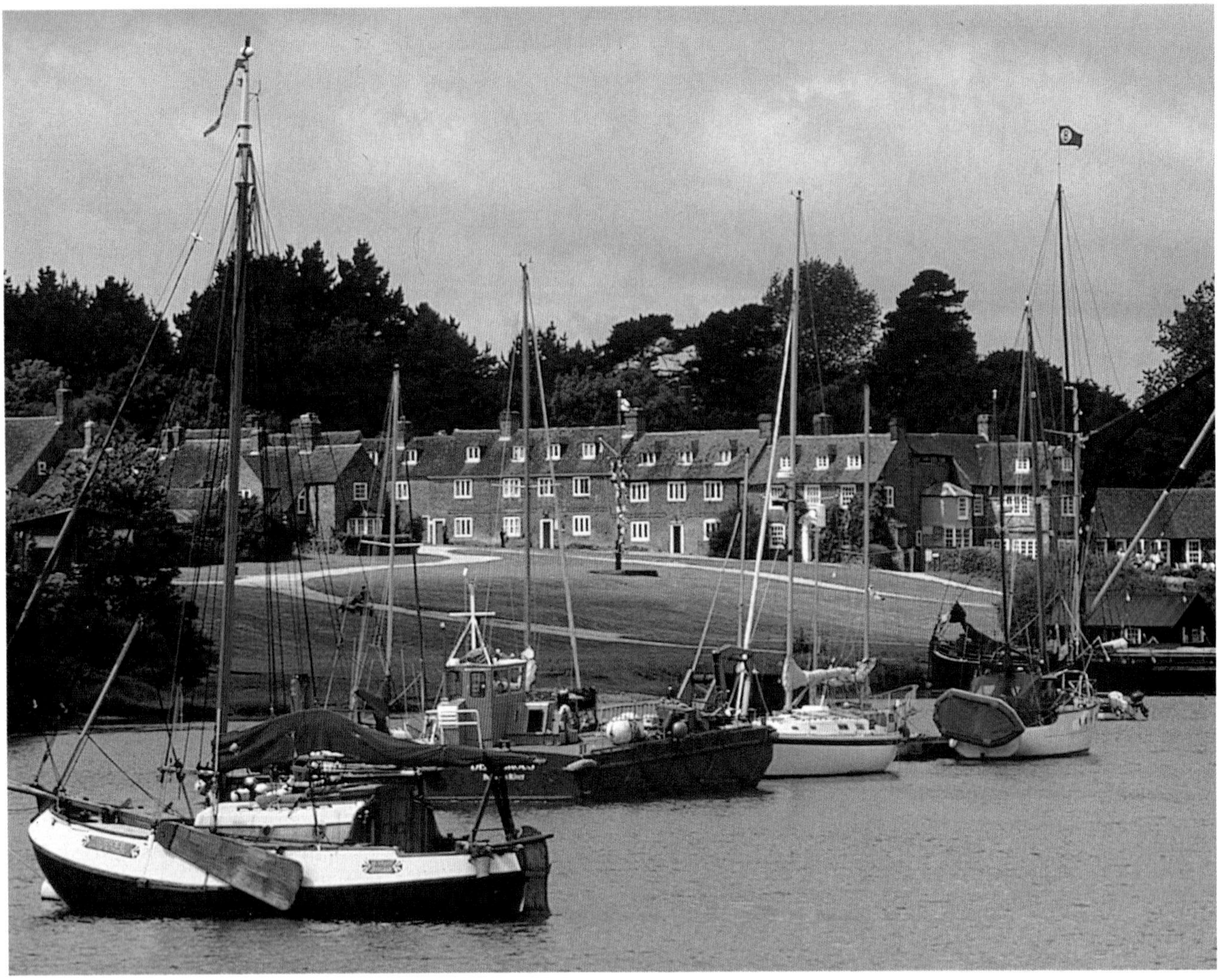

THE MASTER BUILDER'S HOUSE

BUCKLER'S HARD, BEAULIEU, NEW FOREST, HAMPSHIRE SO42 7XB
TEL: 01590 616253 FAX: 01590 616297 E-MAIL: res@themasterbuilders.co.uk

A careful and extensive refurbishment of the hotel has transformed The Master Builder's House into a top quality 3 star property, set in a magnificent location with beautiful views across the Beaulieu river. The heart of the estate was originally home to the Master shipbuilder Henry Adams who built Nelson's favourite, the Agamemnon. The 25 en suite bedrooms are beautifully appointed, offering every modern facility and a range of thoughtful extras. The public rooms are charming with Inglenook fireplaces and comfortable furnishings. A hearty full English breakfast is served in the morning whilst the restaurant, awarded 2 AA Rosettes, specialises in traditional cuisine comprising classic recipes and local produce. The beaches at Barton-on-Sea and Milford-on-Sea, the National Motor Museum and the Georgian town of Lymington are all worth a visit. The more adventurous may wish to explore the New Forest with its wildlife and picturesque villages. Sports such as golfing, sailing, fishing, salt-water angling, riding, trekking and wagon-riding may be practised close by. **Directions:** Leave the M27 at junction 1, then take the A337 to Lyndhurst and then the B3056 to Beaulieu. Follow signs to Buckler's Hard. Price Guide: Single from £115; double/twin from £155.

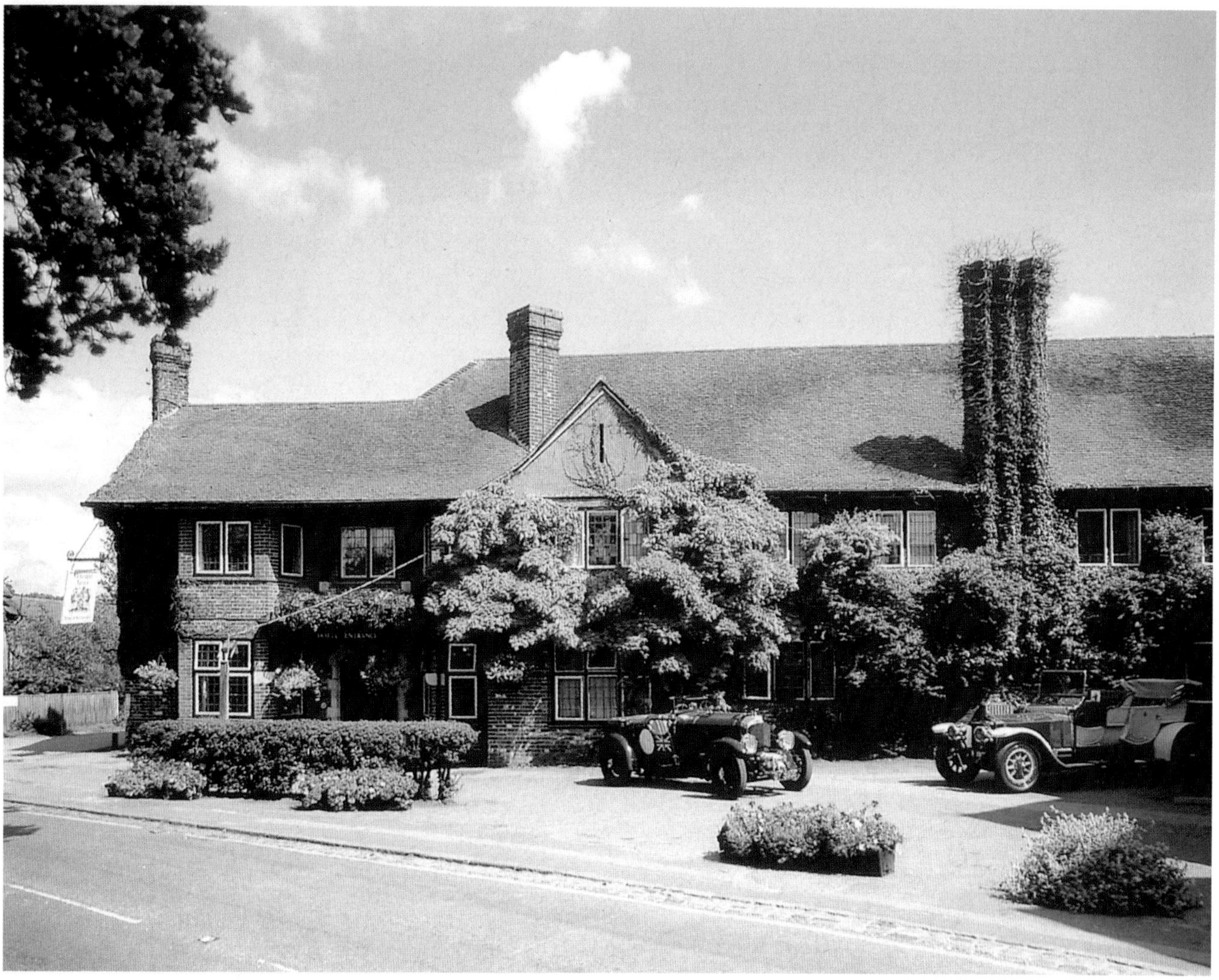

The Montagu Arms Hotel

BEAULIEU, NEW FOREST, HAMPSHIRE S042 7ZL

TEL: 01590 612324 FAX: 01590 612188 E-MAIL: enquiries@montagu–arms.co.uk

Situated at the head of the River Beaulieu in the heart of the New Forest, The Montagu Arms Hotel carries on a tradition of hospitality started 700 years ago. As well as being a good place for a holiday, the hotel is an ideal venue for small conferences. Each of the 24 bedrooms has been individually styled and many are furnished with four-poster beds. Dine in the oak-panelled restaurant overlooking the garden, where you can enjoy cuisine prepared by award-winning chef Steven Hurst. The menu is supported by an outstanding wine list. Alternatively dine less formally in Monty's Bar Brasserie now delightfully presented in keeping with the building. It offers homemade fare together with real ales and a good choice of wine.

The hotel offers complimentary membership of an exclusive health club 6 miles away. Facilities there include a supervised gymnasium, large indoor ozone pool, Jacuzzi, steam room, sauna and beauty therapist. With much to see and do around Beaulieu why not hire a mountain bike? Visit the National Motor Museum, Exbury Gardens or Bucklers Hard, or walk for miles through the beautiful New Forest. Special tariffs are available throughout the year. **Directions:** The village of Beaulieu is well-signposted and the hotel commands an impressive position at the foot of the main street. Price Guide: Single £85; double/twin £130–£140; suites £155–£200. Inclusive terms available.

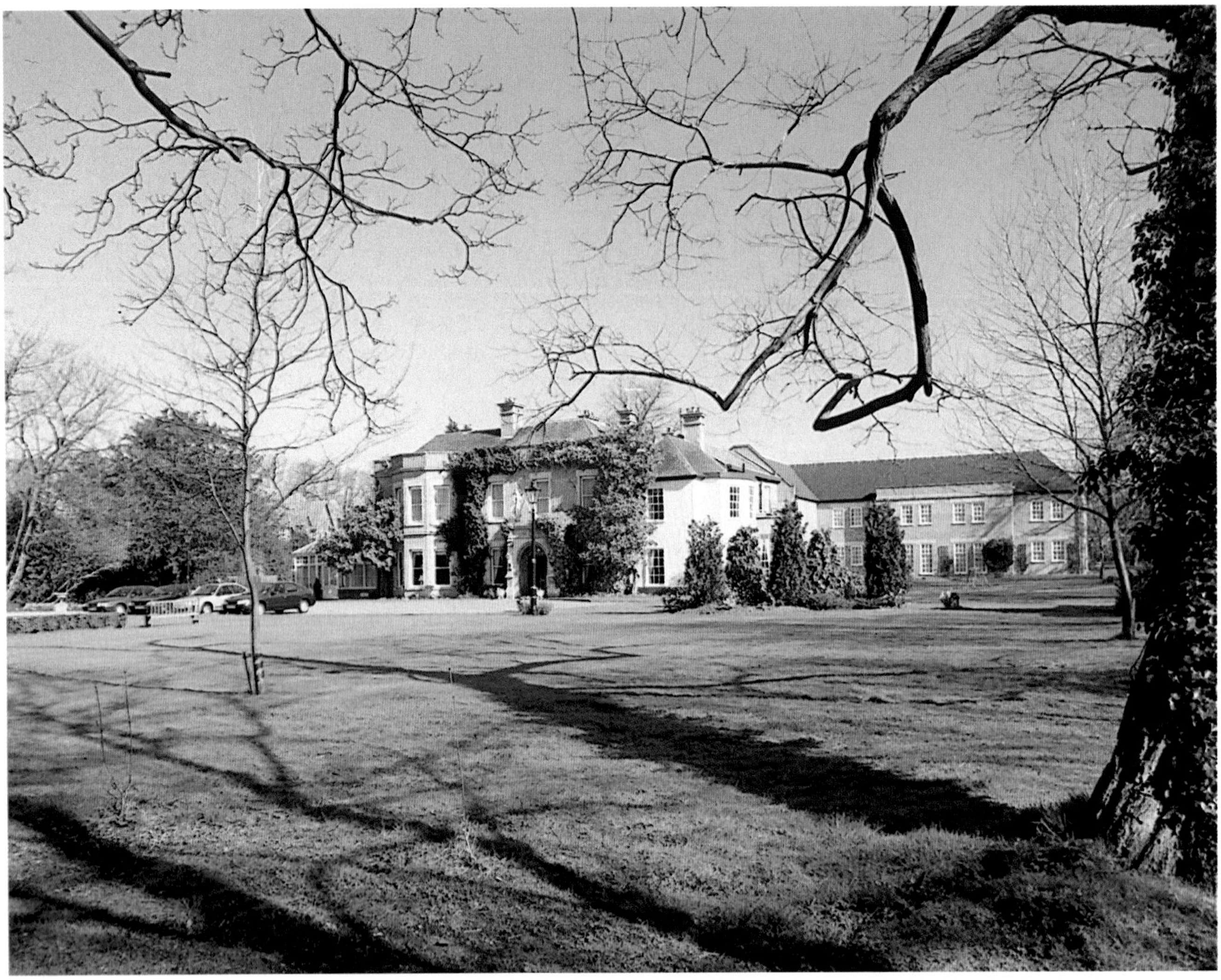

WOODLANDS MANOR

GREEN LANE, CLAPHAM, BEDFORD, BEDFORDSHIRE MK41 6EP
TEL: 01234 363281 FAX: 01234 272390 E-MAIL: woodlands.manor@pageant.co.uk

Woodlands Manor is a secluded period manor house, set in acres of wooded grounds and gardens, only two miles from the centre of Bedford. The hotel is privately owned and a personal welcome is assured. In the public rooms, stylish yet unpretentious furnishings preserve the feel of a country house, with open fires in winter. The en suite bedrooms are beautifully decorated and have extensive personal facilities. All have views of the gardens and surrounding countryside. The elegantly proportioned restaurant, once the house's main reception room, provides an agreeable venue for dining. The menus balance English tradition with the French flair for fresh, light flavours, complemented by wines from well-stocked cellars. The private library and conservatory are well suited to business meetings with video conferencing available, launches and intimate dinner parties. Woodlands Manor is conveniently located for touring: the historic centres of Ely, Cambridge and Oxford, all within easy reach and stately homes such as Woburn Abbey and Warwick Castle are not far away. The hotel is two miles from the county town of Bedford, with its riverside park and the Bunyan Museum. Other places of interest nearby include the RSPB at Sandy and the Shuttleworth Collection of aircraft at Biggleswade. **Directions:** Clapham village is two miles north of the centre of Bedford. Price Guide: Single £65–£85; double/twin £85–£97.50; suite £150.

MARSHALL MEADOWS COUNTRY HOUSE HOTEL

BERWICK-UPON-TWEED, NORTHUMBERLAND TD15 1UT
TEL: 01289 331133 FAX: 01289 331438 E-MAIL: stay@marshallmeadows.co.uk

Marshall Meadows can truly boast that it is England's most northerly hotel, just a quarter of a mile from the Scottish border, an ideal base for those exploring the rugged beauty of Northumberland. A magnificent Georgian mansion standing in 15 acres of woodland and formal gardens, Marshall Meadows today is a luxurious retreat, with a country house ambience – welcoming and elegant. It has a burn and small waterfall with attractive woodland walks. This is not a large hotel, there are just nineteen bedrooms, each individually designed. Restful harmonious colour schemes, comfortable beds and the tranquillity of its surroundings ensure a good night's sleep! The lounge is delightful, with traditional easy chairs and sofas, overlooking the patio. Ideal for summer afternoon tea. The congenial "Duck & Grouse Bar" stocks forty whiskies and real ale. Marshall Meadows has a galleried restaurant where diners enjoy local game, fresh seafood and good wine. Private dining facilities are also available. Excellent golf and historic Berwick-on-Tweed are nearby. **Directions:** A1 heading North, take Berwick by-pass and at Meadow House roundabout, head towards Edinburgh. After 300 yards, turn right, indicated by white sign – hotel is at end of small side road. Price Guide: Single £75; double/twin from £85; suite £100.

TILLMOUTH PARK

CORNHILL-ON-TWEED, NEAR BERWICK-UPON-TWEED, NORTHUMBERLAND TD12 4UU
TEL: 01890 882255 FAX: 01890 882540 E-MAIL: reception@tillmouthpark.f9.co.uk

This magnificent mansion house, built in 1882 using stones from nearby Twizel Castle, offers the same warm welcome to visitors today as when it was an exclusive private house. Tillmouth Park is situated in 15 acres of mature parkland gardens above the river Till. The generously sized bedrooms are individually designed with period and antique furniture, and are fully appointed with bathrobes, toiletries, hairdryer and trouser press. Most bedrooms offer spectacular views of the surrounding countryside. The wood-panelled restaurant serves fine à la carte and table d'hôte menus offering contemporary British cuisine, while the Bistro is less formal. A well-chosen wine list and a vast selection of malt whiskies complement the cuisine. The elegant, galleried main hall offers comfort and there are open log fires throughout the house. Tillmouth Park is ideally situated for country pursuits, with fishing on the Tweed and Till and clay shooting available on the grounds. The area also abounds in fine golf courses. Coldstream and Kelso are within easy reach; the Northumbrian coast and Berwick are 15 minutes away, and Flodden Field, Lindisfarne and Holy Island are nearby. There are many stately homes to visit in the area including Floors, Alnwick, Manderston and Paxton **Directions:** Tillmouth Park is on the A698 Coldstream to Berwick-upon-Tweed road. Price Guide: Single £90–£155; twin/double £130–£180.

14 MasterCard VISA AMERICAN EXPRESS M 50

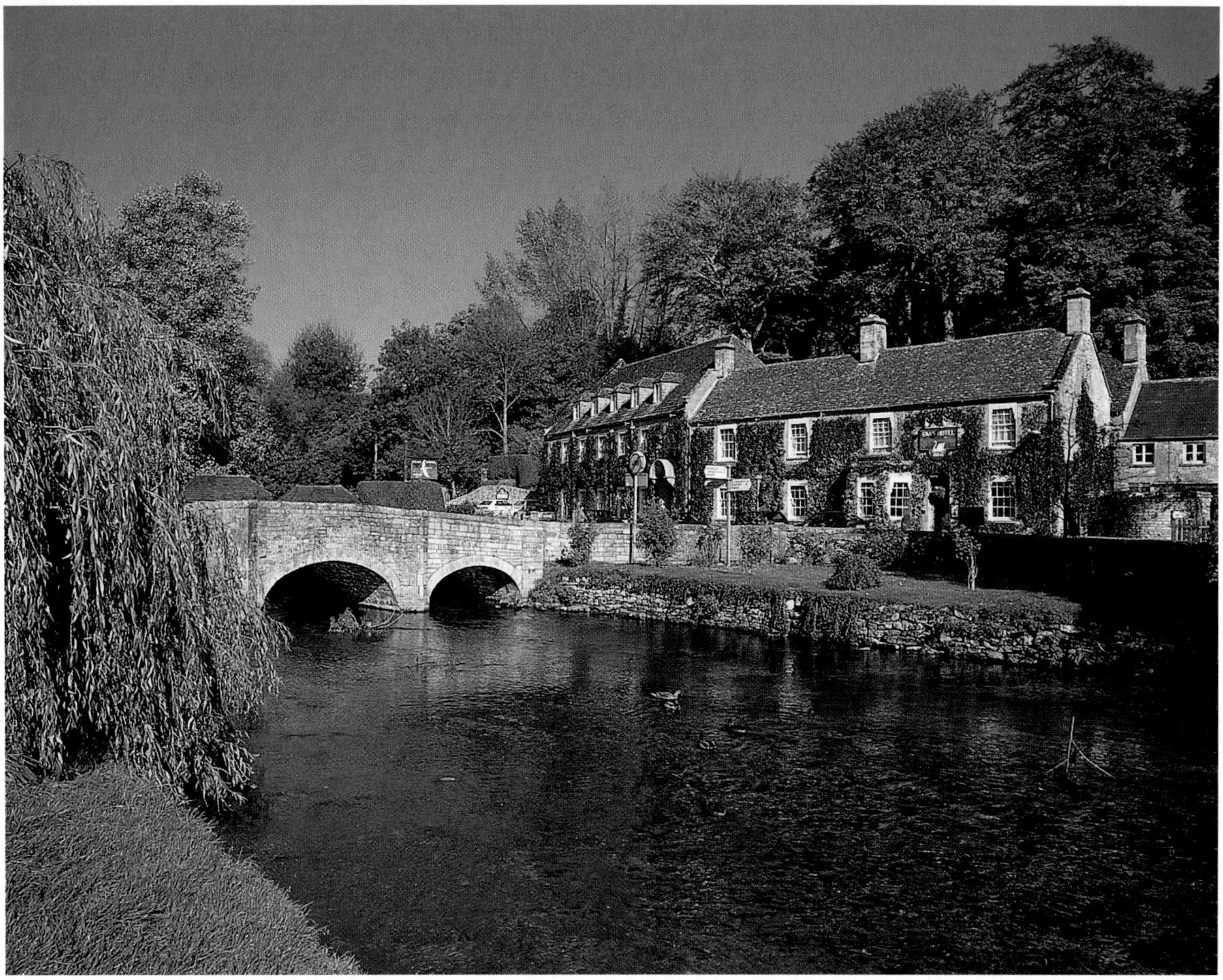

The Swan Hotel At Bibury

BIBURY, GLOUCESTERSHIRE GL7 5NW
TEL: 01285 740695 FAX: 01285 740473 E-MAIL: swanhotl@swanhotel-cotswold.co.uk

The Swan Hotel at Bibury in the South Cotswolds, a 17th century coaching inn, is a perfect base for both leisurely and active holidays which will appeal especially to motorists, fishermen and walkers. The hotel has its own fishing rights and a moated ornamental garden encircled by its own crystalline stream. Bibury itself is a delightful village, with its honey-coloured stonework, picturesque ponds, the trout filled River Coln and its utter lack of modern eyesores. The beautiful Arlington Row and its cottages are a vision of old England. When Liz Rose acquired The Swan, she had the clear intention of creating a distinctive hotel in the English countryside which would acknowledge the needs of the modern day sophisticated traveller. A programme of refurbishment and upgrading of the hotel and its services began with the accent on unpretentious comfort. Oak-panelling, plush carpets and sumptuous fabrics create the background for the fine paintings and antiques that grace the interiors. The 20 bedrooms are superbly appointed with luxury bathrooms and comfortable furnishings. Guests may dine in either the restaurant or the brasserie which serves meals all day during the summer months. **Directions:** Bibury is signposted off A40 Oxford–Cheltenham road, on the left-hand side. Secure free parking now available next to the hotel. Midweek saver rates available. Price Guide: Single £99–£155; double/twin £180–£260.

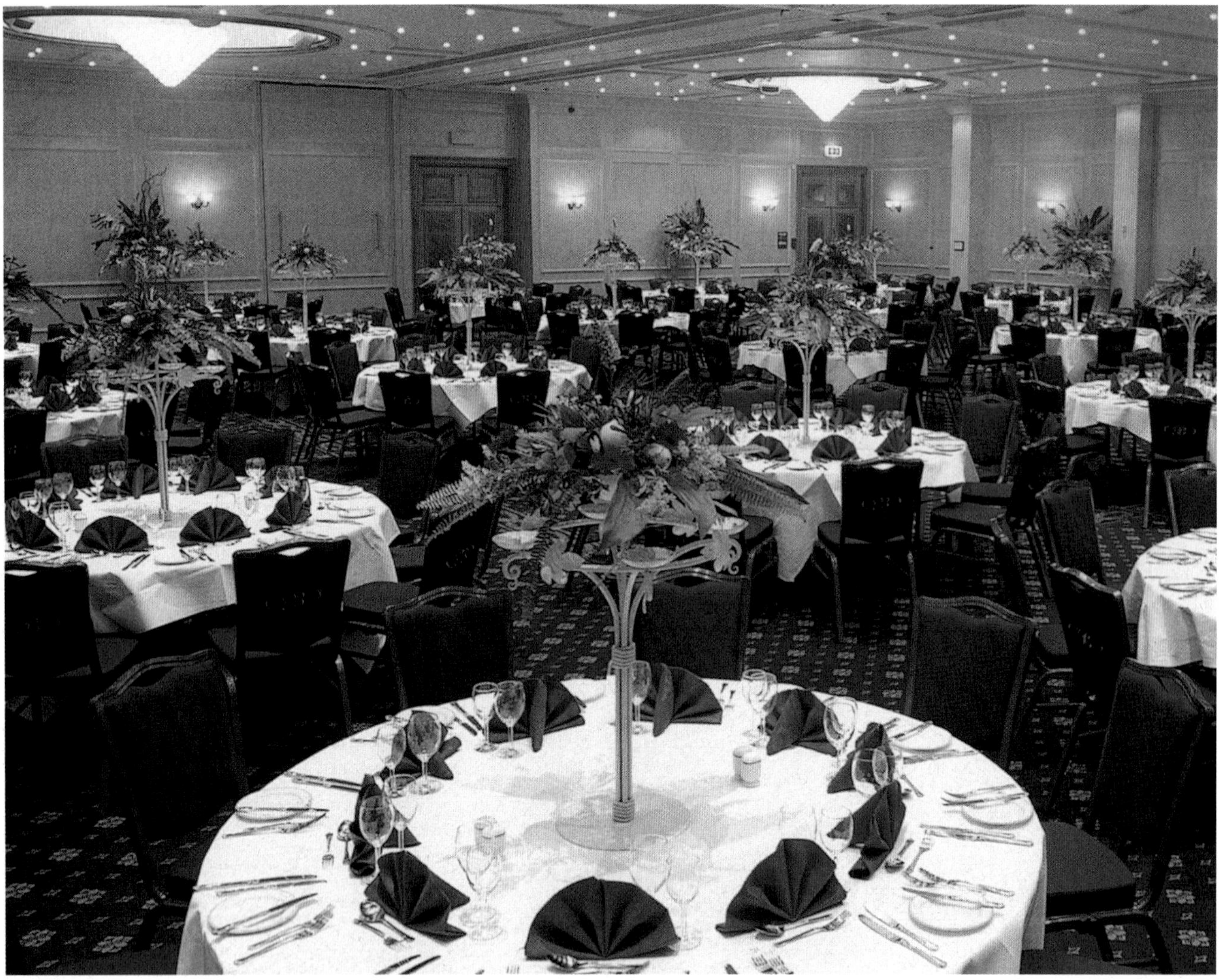

THE BURLINGTON HOTEL

BURLINGTON ARCADE, 126 NEW STREET, BIRMINGHAM, WEST MIDLANDS B2 4JQ
TEL: 0121 643 9191 FAX: 0121 643 5075 E-MAIL: mail@burlingtonhotel.com

The Burlington is a hotel embodying the legendary old Midland Hotel which had played such an important role since its opening in 1871. The original handsome Victorian façade has not been destroyed, only embellished, while skilful restoration has retained much of the historic charm within. The hotel is in Birmingham's pedestrianised City Centre, approached through an attractive arcade. It is focused on the commercial arena, with a strong emphasis on facilities for conferences and corporate activities. All bedrooms are pleasantly furnished, spacious, well-equipped and comfortable, with the extras expected by today's traveller, including fax and modem links, electronic voice mail box and satellite television. The bathrooms are well designed. On the first floor, guests will find the delightful lounge – a peaceful retreat – the traditional bar and the splendid Victorian restaurant with its swathed windows, chandeliers and moulded ceilings. The fifth floor houses the leisure centre. The main function area is self-contained, with its own entrance and foyer. Other rooms are ideal for seminars or board meetings. The Burlington is well placed for shopping, the Symphony Hall and just 15 minutes drive from the NEC. **Directions:** Close to New Street Station, 10 minutes from the airport, accessible from the M5, M6, M42. NCP parking. Price Guide: (room only): Single £135; double/twin £157; suite £310.

112 MasterCard VISA AMERICAN EXPRESS M 400

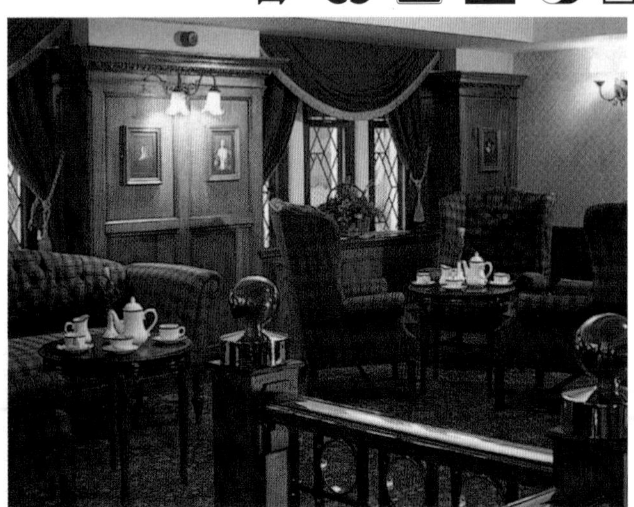

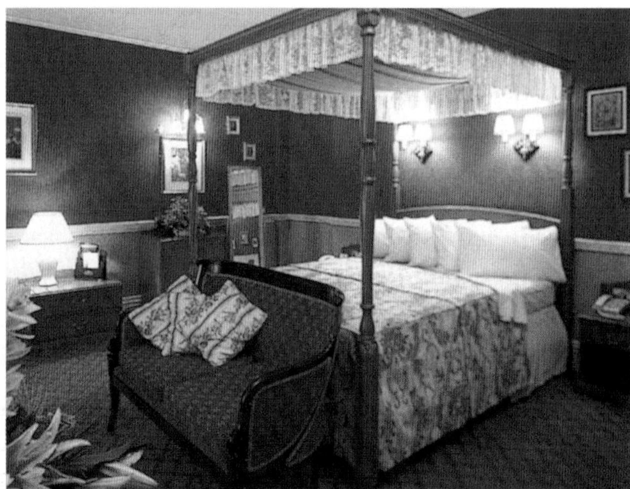

NEW HALL

WALMLEY ROAD, ROYAL SUTTON COLDFIELD, WEST MIDLANDS B76 1QX
TEL: 0121 378 2442 FAX: 0121 378 4637

Cocooned by a lily filled moat and surrounded by 26 acres of beautiful gardens and parkland, New Hall dates from the 12th century and is reputedly the oldest fully moated manor house in England. This prestigious hotel is full of warmth and luxury and exudes a friendly, welcoming atmosphere. New Hall proudly holds the coveted RAC Gold Ribbon Award, and AA Inspectors' Hotel of the Year for England 1994. The cocktail bar and adjoining drawing room overlook the terrace from which a bridge leads to the yew topiary, orchards and sunlit glades. The superbly appointed bedrooms and individually designed suites offer every modern comfort and amenity and have glorious views over the gardens and moat. A 9-hole par 3 golf course and floodlit tennis court are available for guests' use, as are a heated indoor pool, Jacuzzi, sauna, steam room and gymnasium. For those wishing to revitalise mind, body and soul, New Hall offers a superb range of beauty treatments. Surrounded by a rich cultural heritage, New Hall is convenient for Lichfield Cathedral, Warwick Castle, Stratford-upon-Avon, the NEC and the ICC in Birmingham. The Belfry Golf Centre is also nearby. **Directions:** From exit 9 of the M42, follow A4097 (ignoring signs to A38 Sutton Coldfield). At B4148 turn right at the traffic lights. New Hall is 1 mile on the left Price Guide: Single from £166; double/twin from £200; suite from £230.

58 MasterCard VISA AMERICAN EXPRESS M 50

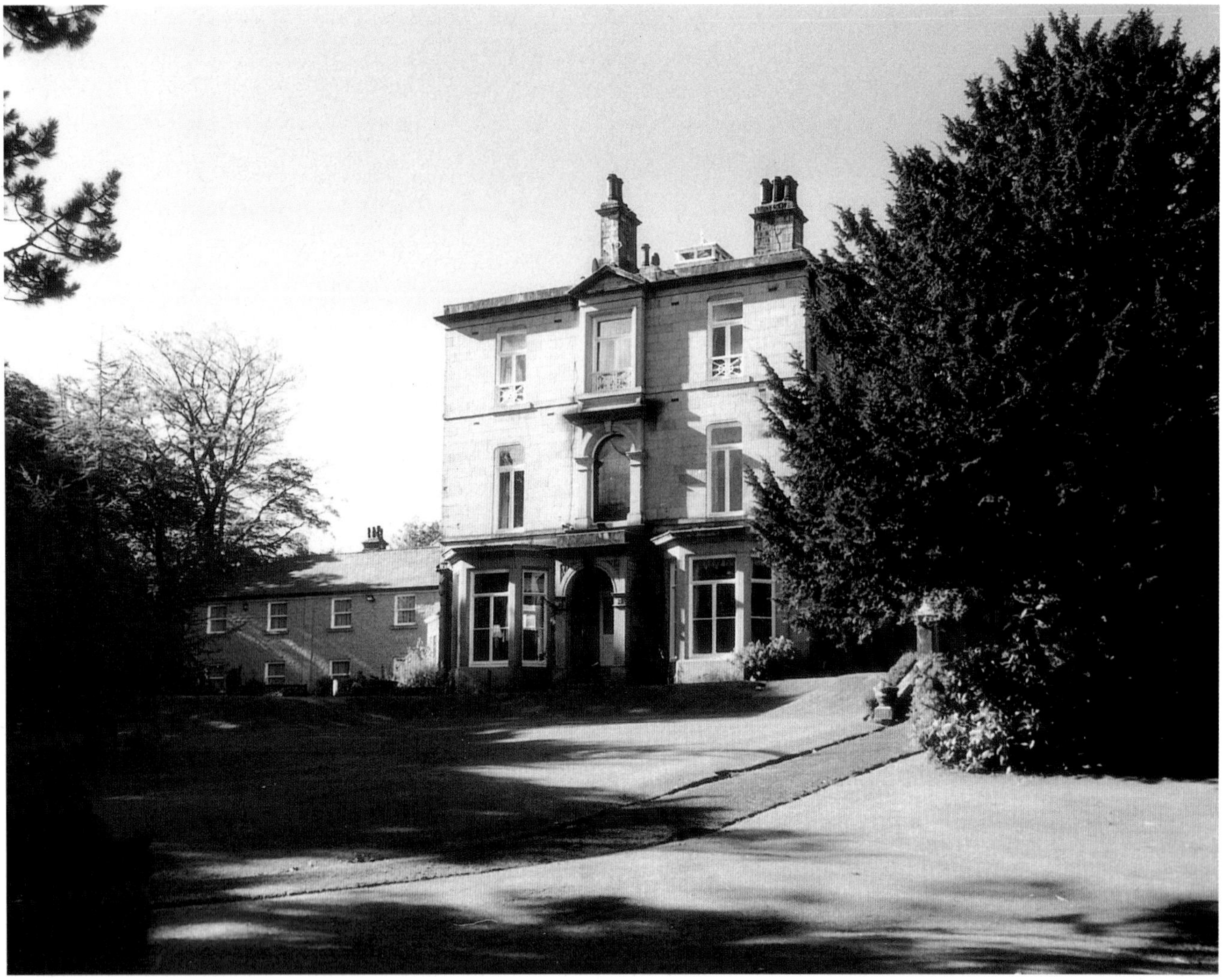

Astley Bank Hotel & Conference Centre

BOLTON ROAD, DARWEN, LANCASHIRE BB3 2QB

TEL: 01254 777700 FAX: 01254 777707 E-MAIL: sales@astleybank.co.uk

Astley Bank stands high and impressive overlooking six acres of magnificent grounds and flower-filled gardens adjacent to the peaceful West Pennine Moors midway between Blackburn and Bolton. Built in the early 19th century it was, over the years, home to some of Lancashire's leading dignitaries. Today it is a stylish, comfortable country retreat with a character and ambience reflecting its mansion house era combined with all modern facilities demanded by today's discerning visitor. The public rooms are spacious and elegant and the en suite bedrooms are decorated and furnished to the highest standard. Most of them enjoy superb views over the garden and the four-poster and executive bedrooms provide additional luxury. In the attractive garden restaurant chef James Andrew produces tasty à la carte and table d'hôte menus which are complemented by an extensive selection of wines. Being within easy reach of the motorway network and Manchester Airport, Astley Bank is a popular venue with meetings organisers. There are three conference rooms supported by six purpose built syndicate rooms. All have natural daylight and are fitted with a variety of audiovisual equipment. **Directions:** From Blackburn take the M65 east. Exit at junction 4 and take the A666 south towards Bolton. After approximately two miles pass through Darwen. The hotel is on the right. Price Guide: Single £78–£100; double/twin £98–£130.

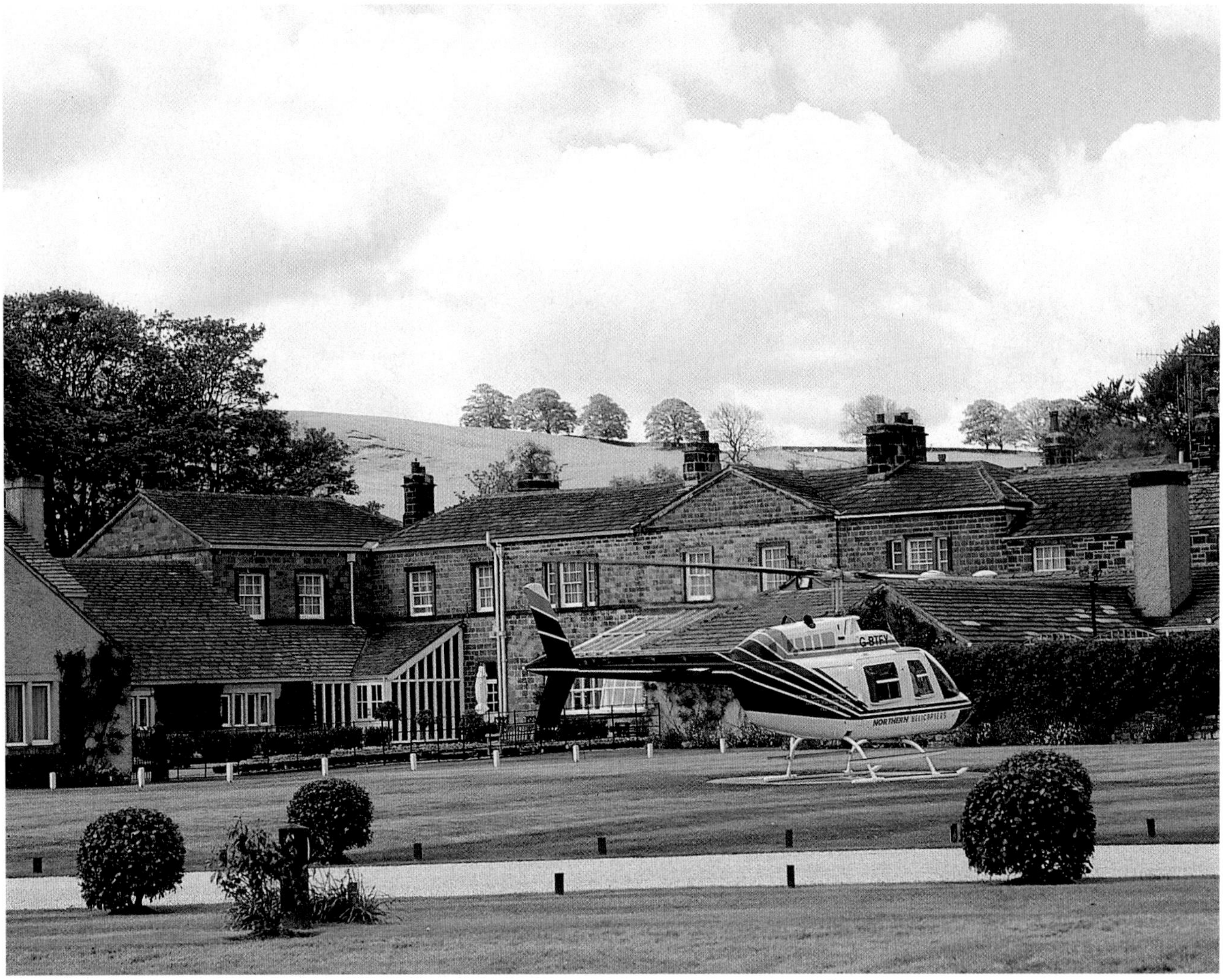

THE DEVONSHIRE ARMS COUNTRY HOUSE HOTEL

BOLTON ABBEY, SKIPTON, NORTH YORKSHIRE BD23 6AJ
TEL: 01756 710441 FAX: 01756 710564 E-MAIL: sales@thedevonshirearms.co.uk

The Devonshire reflects its charming setting in the Yorkshire Dales: a welcome escape from a busy and crowded world, peace and quiet, beautiful countryside – the perfect place in which to relax. The hotel is owned by the Duke and Duchess of Devonshire and is set in 12 acres of parkland on their Bolton Abbey Estate in the Yorkshire Dales National Park. Many antiques and paintings from Chatsworth in the public rooms and bedrooms (several of which are themed) add to the country house atmosphere, which is complemented by excellent service. Guests enjoy elegant and fine dining together with an impressive wine list in the award-winning Burlington Restaurant plus there is the less formal and brightly furnished Brasserie. In addition to the wide choice of outdoor activities including themed and activity breaks, The Devonshire Club offers a full range of leisure, health and beauty therapy facilities. Managing Director, Jeremy Rata, together with Stuart Procter lead an enthusiastic team committed to providing a high standard of service and hospitality. Three AA Red Stars, Good Food Guide 7/10, RAC Blue Ribbon and RAC four dining awards out of five. **Directions:** Off the A59 Skipton–Harrogate road at junction with the B6160. Price Guide: Single £135–£265; double/twin £175–£285; suite £350.

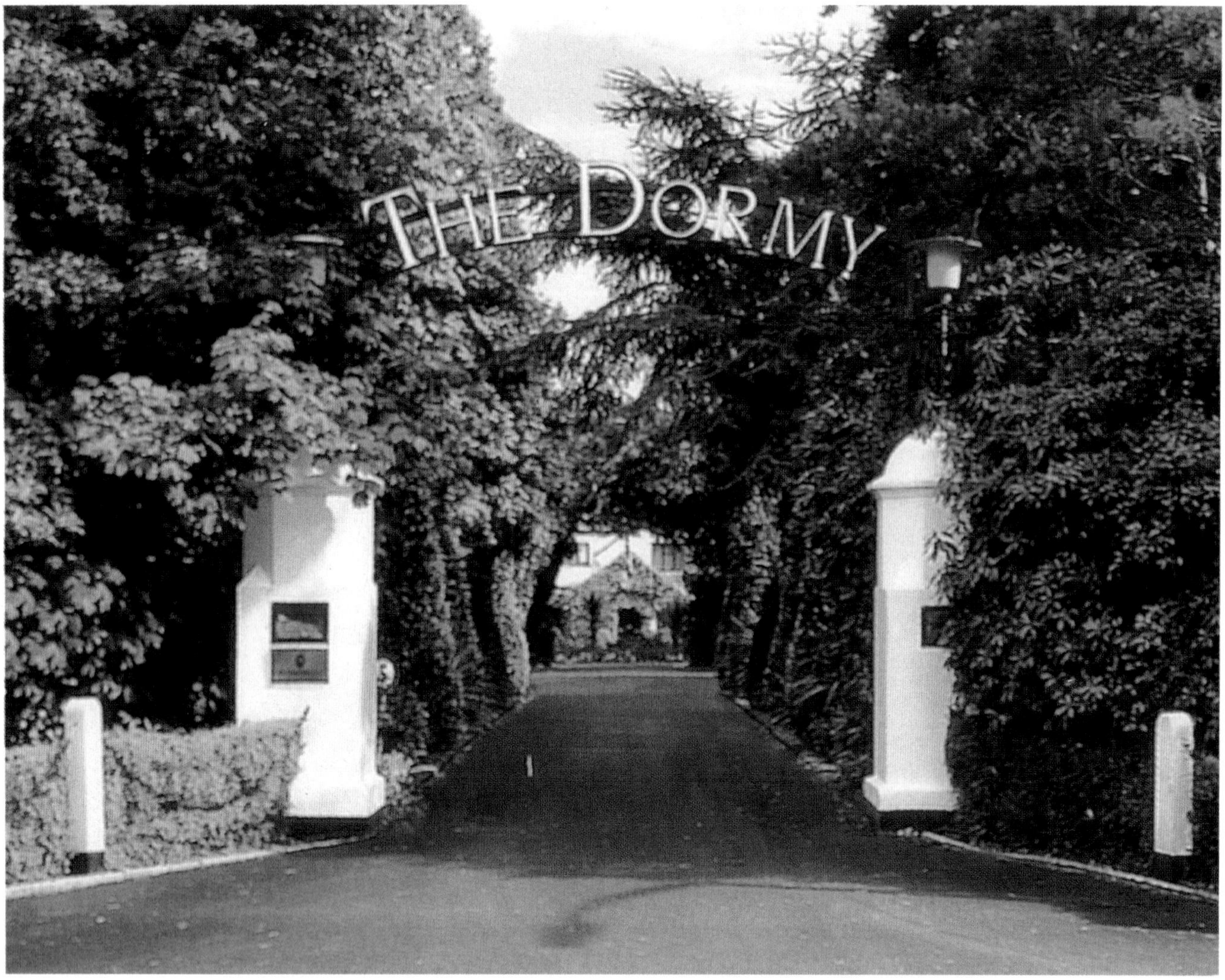

THE DORMY

NEW ROAD, FERNDOWN, NEAR BOURNEMOUTH, DORSET BH22 8ES
TEL: 01202 872121 FAX: 01202 895388 E-MAIL: devere.dormy@airtime.co.uk

Situated on the edge of the picturesque New Forest, The Dormy is the essence of comfort. This country style hotel, with its log fires and oak-panelled lounges, is surrounded by 12 acres of magnificent landscaped gardens. All bedrooms are furnished in either a traditional or a more modern fashion and include all the latest amenities such as satellite television, radio, telephone and hospitality tray. Guests can relax in the Dormy Bar and the golf themed Alliss Bar. Recently awarded two AA Rosettes, the elegant Hennessys Restaurant, situated in the hotel grounds, offers the finest contemporary cuisine. The Garden Restaurant continues to build upon its reputation and a third, more relaxed, option is the Pavillion Brasserie. The Leisure Club comprises of a large indoor pool and various other facilities such as sauna, spa bath and solaria. Fitness fanatics may exercise in the well-equipped gymnasium, toning suite and aerobics studio or make use of the squash and tennis courts. The Dormy lies adjacent to the Ferndown Golf Club, renowned for its championship 18-hole and 9-hole president's course. Activities nearby include quad biking, clay pigeon shooting and riding in the New Forest. Directions: Nearest motorway is M27 to Ringwood, then A31 to Ferndown, then left at the traffic lights onto A347. The hotel is just 1 m on the left hand side. Price Guide: Single from £110; double/twin £145–£200; suite £225–£255.

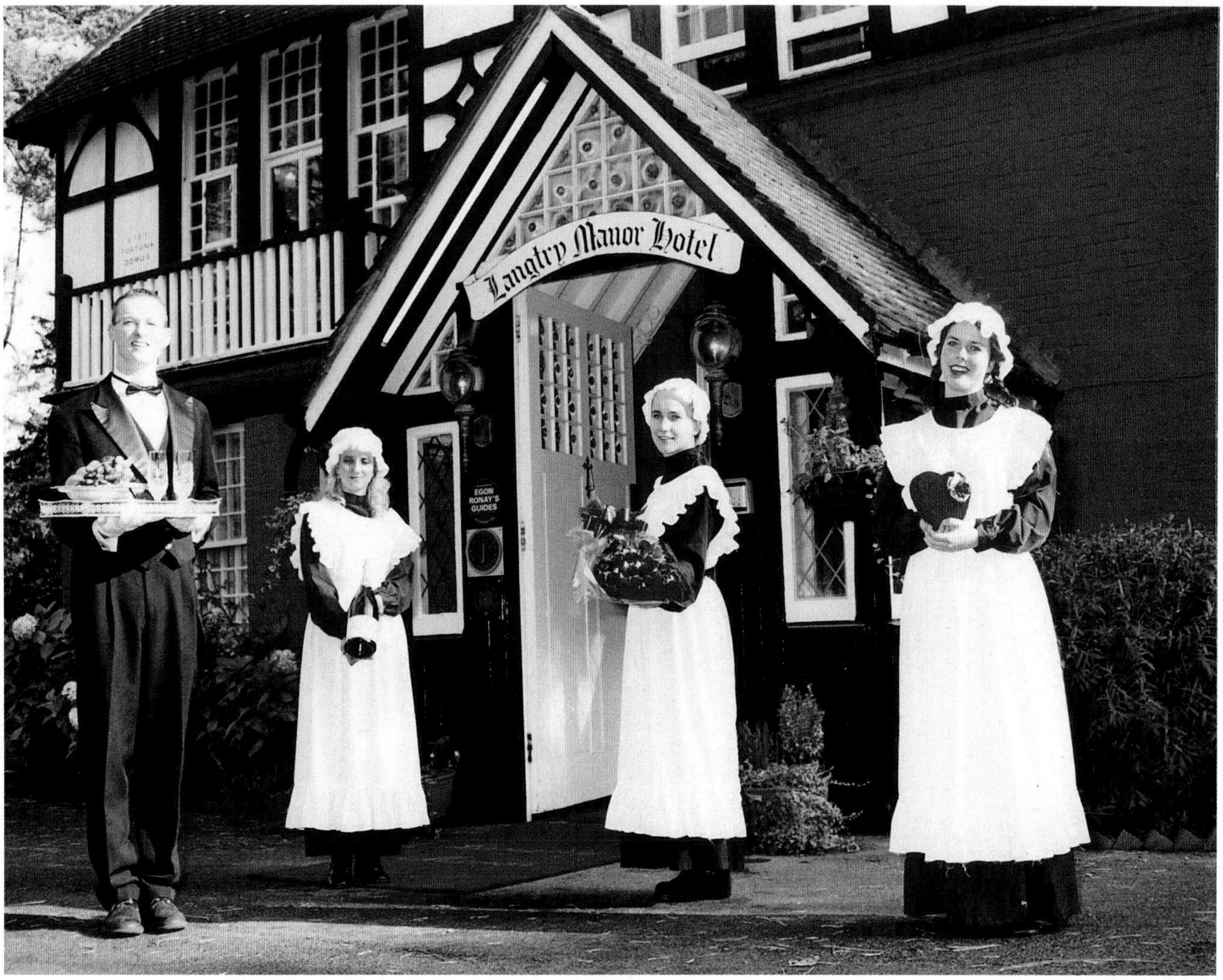

LANGTRY MANOR - LOVENEST OF A KING

DERBY ROAD, EAST CLIFF, BOURNEMOUTH, DORSET BH1 3QB
TEL: 01202 553887 FAX: 01202 290115 E-MAIL: lillie@langtrymanor.com

Known originally as The Red House, this fine house was built in 1877 by Edward VII (then Prince of Wales) as a love nest for his mistress. The concept of a themed small hotel was created by the present owners around the famous Lillie Langtry story exactly a hundred years later. The Edward VII suite is a fine spacious room which retains two original floral wall paintings and features a grand Jacobean four-poster bed. Other feature rooms have four-posters, corner spa baths and are all designed to engender a romantic ambience. This was the first hotel in Dorset to be licensed for civil marriages; it is a popular wedding venue – and a natural for honeymoons, anniversaries and birthdays. Saturday night guests are invited to take part in a delicious 6 course Edwardian Banquet – which features an interlude of words and music based on the life of the 'Jersey Lily' – served in the quite splendid Dining Hall with its minstrels gallery and stained glass windows. Some of the bedrooms offered are close by in The Lodge – once the home of Lord Derby. Guests can enjoy complementary use of a state of the art leisure club just 2 minutes away. Sandy beaches, Hardy Country, the New Forest, art galleries, theatres and gardens. **Directions:** Take A338 Wessex Way to the station. First exit at roundabout, over next roundabout, first left into Knyveton Road, second right into Derby Road. Price Guide: (minimum stay 2 nights)Double/twin £139.50

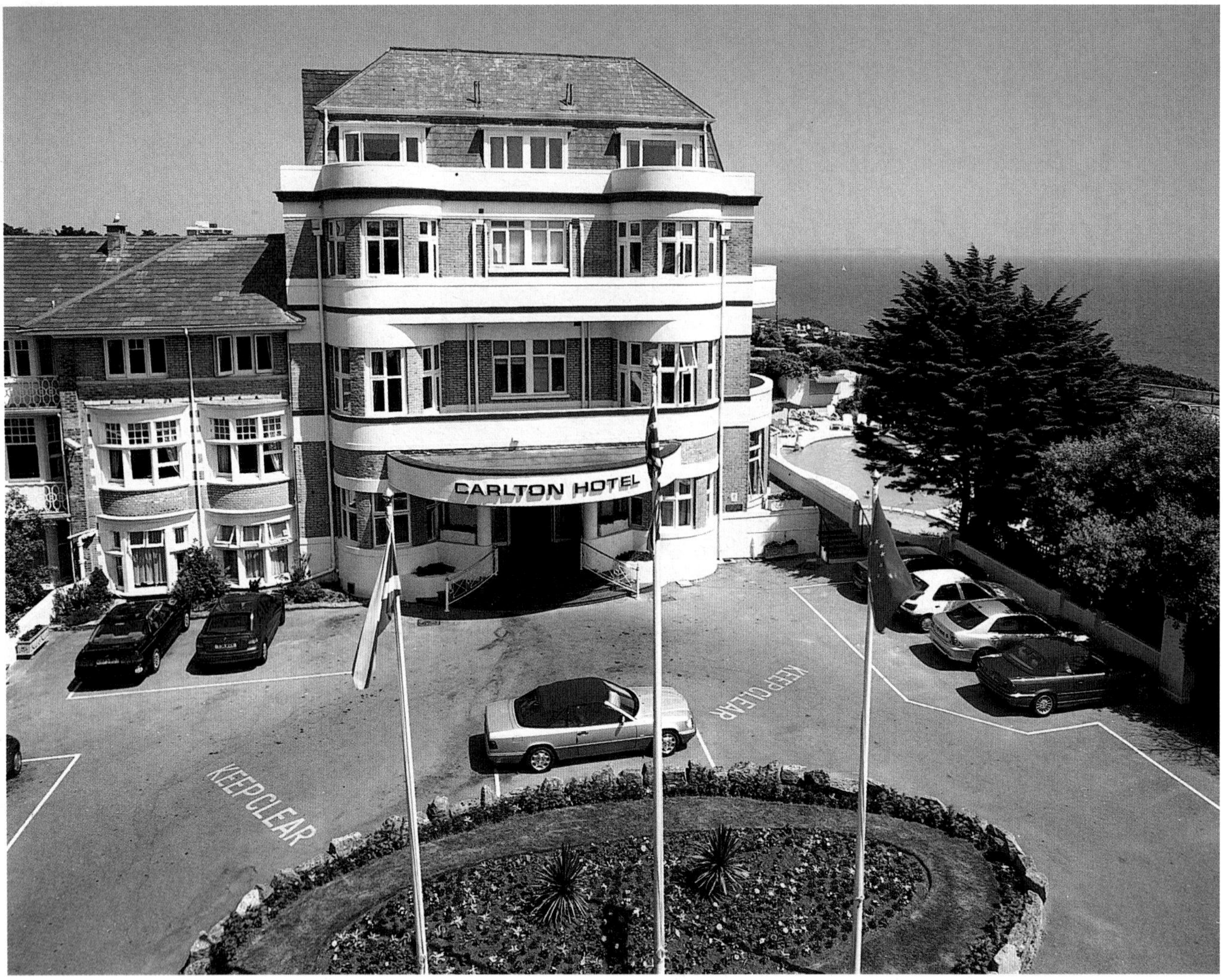

The Menzies Carlton Hotel

EAST OVERCLIFF, BOURNEMOUTH, DORSET BH1 3DN
TEL: 01202 552011 FAX: 01202 299573 E-MAIL: info@menzies-hotels.co.uk

The Menzies Carlton has provided hospitality to Royalty, Heads of State and Ministers of the Crown for generations. Positioned on the town's much favoured East Cliff, with miles of golden sands below, it has a touch of former seaside hotel grandeur. The welcoming Cocktail Bar is an ideal venue to enjoy pre-dinner drinks before sampling the very best of English and international cuisine in the award-winning Frederick's restaurant. Two new executive boardrooms, each accommodating up to 16 delegates, have recently been added to the extensive conference facilities, whilst the versatile Meyrick Suite is suitable for banquets, wedding receptions, conferences or promotional events. The bedrooms, all with excellent bathrooms, range from generous suites to more intimate rooms on the upper floors. 18 luxurious timeshare apartments, many of which have wonderful coastal views, are situated in the east wing. An outdoor heated pool is set in the hotel's sheltered sun-trap garden, and there is a superb leisure complex including indoor pool, up-to-date fitness equipment and a hair and beauty salon. 40 million pounds have been spent to provide magnificent new attractions, and Bournemouth has recently been awarded Resort of the Year. The New Forest, Poole Harbour and Beaulieu are all close by.
Directions: The Menzies Carlton is at the corner of Meyrick Road and East Overcliff Drive. Follow signs for seafront. Price Guide: Standard room from £120; superior/sea view from £160.

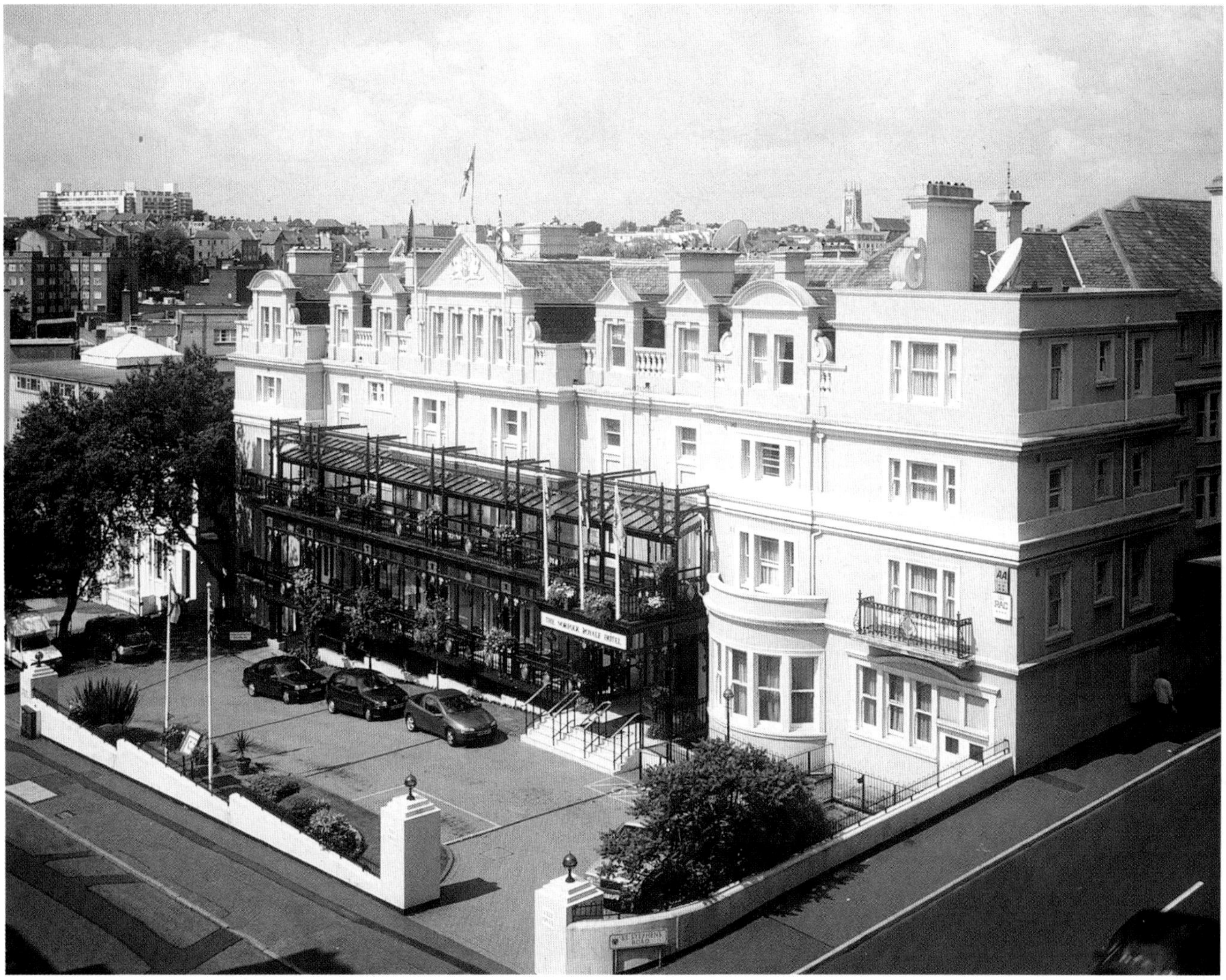

Norfolk Royale Hotel

RICHMOND HILL, BOURNEMOUTH, DORSET BH2 6EN
TEL: 01202 551521 FAX: 01202 299729 E-MAIL: norfolkroyale@englishrosehotels.co.uk

Bournemouth has long been a popular seaside resort and has not lost its unique character – The Norfolk Royale is a fine example of the elegant buildings that grace the town. It is a splendid Edwardian house, once the holiday home of the Duke of Norfolk, after whom it is named. Extensive restoration work throughout the hotel, while enhancing its comfort, has not eliminated the echoes of the past and new arrivals are impressed by the elegant furnishings and courtesy of the staff. The designs of the spacious bedrooms reflect consideration for lady travellers, busy business executives, non-smokers and the disabled. The rich fabrics of the delightful colour schemes contribute to their luxurious ambience. Guests relax in the lounge or attractive club bar, in summer enjoying the gardens or patio – all with waiter service – and delicious breakfasts, lunches and candle-lit dinners are served in the Orangery Restaurant, which has an excellent wine list. The good life includes the pleasures of a pool and spa while Bournemouth offers golf courses, tennis, water sports, a casino and theatre. It has a large conference and exhibition centre. Poole Harbour, The New Forest, Thomas Hardy country and long sandy beaches are nearby. **Directions:** From the M27, A31 & A338 find the hotel on the right, halfway down Richmond Hill approaching the town centre Price Guide: Single from £75; double/twin £105–£175; suite £185–£350.

BURFORD BRIDGE HOTEL

MICKLEHAM, AT THE FOOT OF BOX HILL, DORKING, SURREY RH6 6BX
TEL: 0870 400 8283 FAX: 0306 800386 E-MAIL: heritagehotels_box_hill.burford_bridge@forte–hotels.com

Every mellow brick of this historic hotel nestling at the foot of the 563ft high Box Hill beauty spot glows with history. Lord Nelson finally separated from Emma Hamilton here in 1800, Keats completed 'Endymion' at the hotel in 1818. Queen Victoria, Queen Alexandra, Robert Louise Stevenson, Keats, Wordsworth, Southey, Moore and Sheridan have all been visitors. There has been an inn on the site since the 13th century. Today, The Burford Bridge is a striking combination of ancient and modern and as popular with visitors as in the early 19th century when nearby Epsom was an ultra fashionable venue. Each of the 57 en suite bedrooms is delightfully decorated and offers every facility and home comfort. Superb cream teas can be enjoyed in the comfortable lounge and the elegant restaurant is renowned for its award-winning cuisine. A heated pool is a feature of the hotel's lovely gardens which run down to a stretch of the River Mole and from where guests can embark on a stroll up and around Box Hill. Places of interest nearby include the 19th century Regency house of Polesden Lacey, the Palladian villa and impressive grounds of Clandon Park and 18th century Hatchlands Park which houses the world's largest collection of keyboard instruments. **Directions:** Exit M25 at junction 9 and take the A24 south towards Dorking. Price Guide: Single from £75; double/twin from £120.

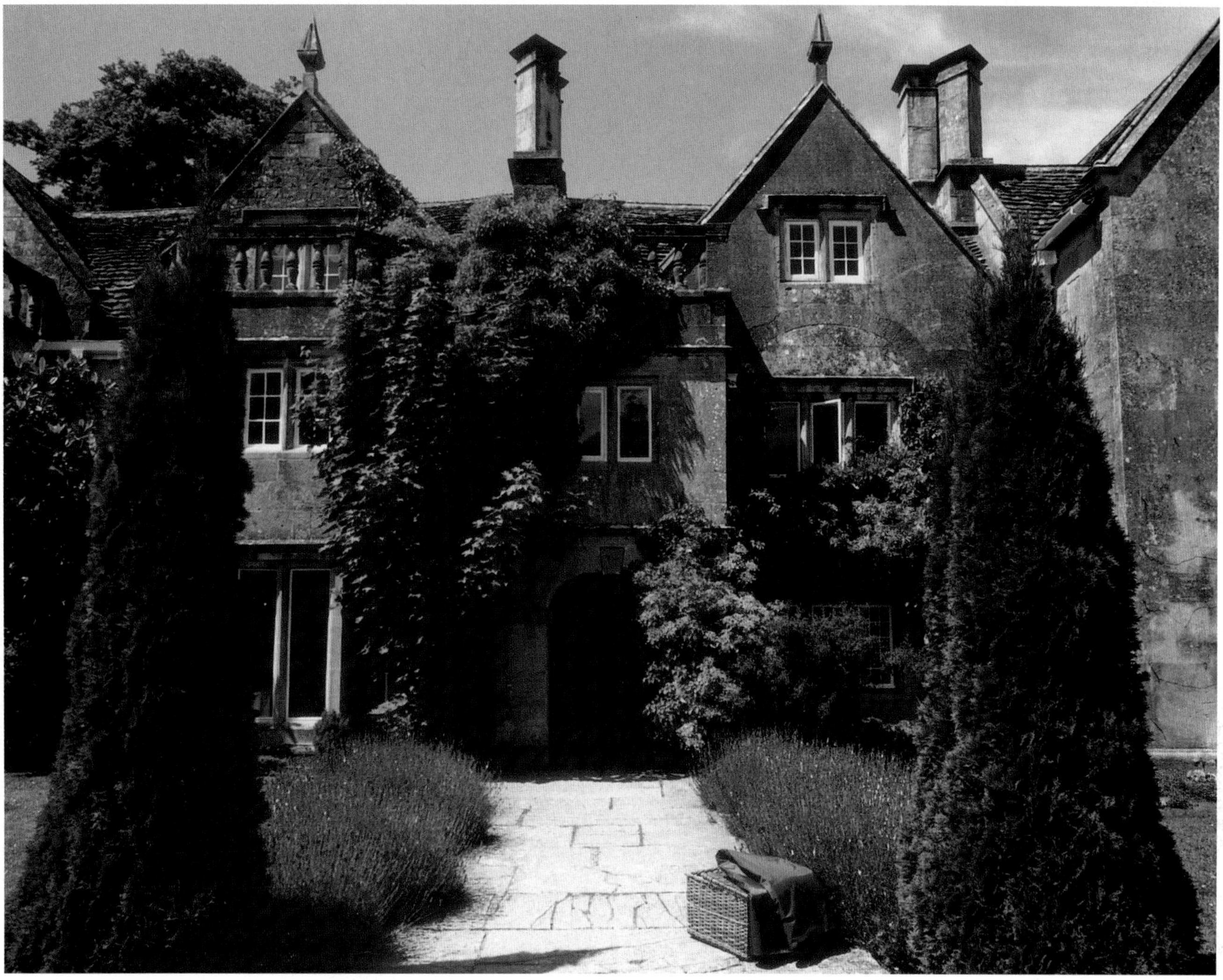

WOOLLEY GRANGE

WOOLLEY GREEN, BRADFORD-ON-AVON, WILTSHIRE BA15 1TX
TEL: 01225 864705 FAX: 01225 864059 E-MAIL: info@woolleygrange.com

Woolley Grange is a 17th-century Jacobean stone manor house set in 14 acres of formal gardens and paddocks. Standing on high ground, it affords southerly views of the White Horse at Westbury and beyond. Furnished with flair and an air of eccentricity, the interior décor and paintings echo the taste of owners Nigel and Heather Chapman. Woolley Grange has gained a reputation for outstanding cuisine. Using local farm produce and organically grown fruit and vegetables from the Victorian kitchen gardens, the chef has created a sophisticated style of country house food which aims to revive the focus on flavours. Children are particularly welcome; the owners have four of their own and they do not expect their young visitors to be 'seen but not heard'. In the Victorian coach house there is a huge games room and a well-equipped nursery with a full-time nanny available to look after guests' children 10–6pm every day. A children's lunch and tea are provided daily. Nearby attractions include medieval Bradford-on-Avon, Georgian Bath, Longleat and prehistoric Stonehenge. Riding can be arranged. **Directions:** From Bath on A363, fork left at Frankleigh House after town sign. From Chippenham, A4 to Bath, fork left on B3109; turn left after town sign. Price Guide: Single £95; double/twin £105–£200; suite from £175–£270.

FARLAM HALL HOTEL

BRAMPTON, CUMBRIA CA8 2NG

TEL: 016977 46234 FAX: 016977 46683 E-MAIL: farlamhall@dial.pipex.com

Farlam Hall was opened in 1975 by the Quinion and Stevenson families who over the years have managed to achieve and maintain consistently high standards of food, service and comfort. These standards have been recognised and rewarded by all the major guides and membership of Relais et Châteaux. This old border house, dating in parts from the 17th century, is set in mature gardens which can be seen from the elegant lounges and dining room, creating a relaxing and pleasing environment. The fine silver and crystal in the dining room complement the quality of the English country house cooking produced by Barry Quinion and his team of chefs. There are 12 individually decorated bedrooms varying in size and shape, some having Jacuzzi baths, one an antique four-poster bed and there are two ground floor bedrooms. This area offers many different attractions: miles of unspoiled countryside for walking, eight golf courses within 30 minutes of the hotel, Hadrian's Wall, Lanercost Priory and Carlisle with its castle, cathedral and museum. The Lake District, Scottish Borders and Yorkshire Dales each make an ideal day's touring. Winter and spring breaks are offered. Closed Christmas. **Directions:** Farlam Hall is 2½ miles east of Brampton on the A689, not in Farlam village. Price Guide: (including dinner): Single £125–£140; double/twin £230–£270.

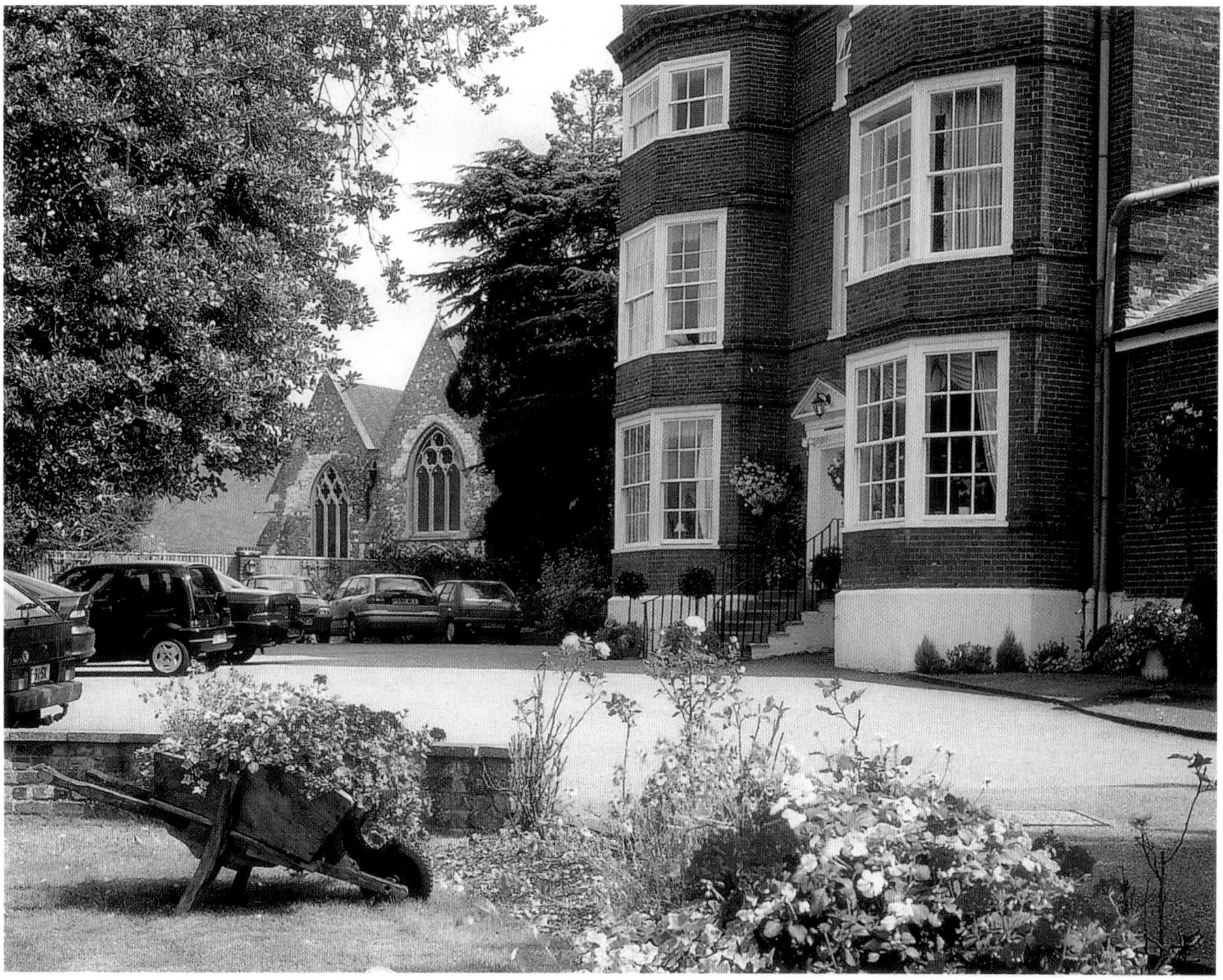

CHAUNTRY HOUSE HOTEL AND RESTAURANT

HIGH STREET, BRAY, BERKSHIRE SL6 2AB
TEL: 01628 673991 FAX: 01628 773089 E-MAIL: res@chauntryhouse.com

Tucked between the local church and cricket club in the small, delightful Thames-side village of Bray, and a minutes walk to the famous Roux's Waterside Inn, Chauntry House is comfortable, friendly and has a plentiful supply of charm and character. With a spacious and secluded garden in which to lounge it is a fine example of an early 18th century country house: an ideal place to relax. The 15 en suite bedrooms are individually appointed in the best English designs and all have cable television, radio, direct dial telephones and tea and coffee making facilities. The public rooms offer comfort in the traditional country house manner and the welcoming drawing room, with an open fire for the winter months, is an ideal and comfortable environment in which to enjoy a pre-dinner aperitif. Modern English and European specialities served in the stylish restaurant. The hotel can accommodate conferences and meetings in the Dower House for up to 20 delegates, boardroom style. Maidenhead, Royal Windsor, Eton, Henley, Ascot, Marlow, London and Heathrow Airport are within easy reach. River cruises, golf, fishing, riding and tennis can be arranged locally. **Directions:** From M4, exit at junction 8/9 and take A 308 (M) towards Maidenhead and Windsor. Then join B3028 to Bray village, just before M4 overhead bridge. Price Guide: Single £115–£125; double/twin £150–£175.

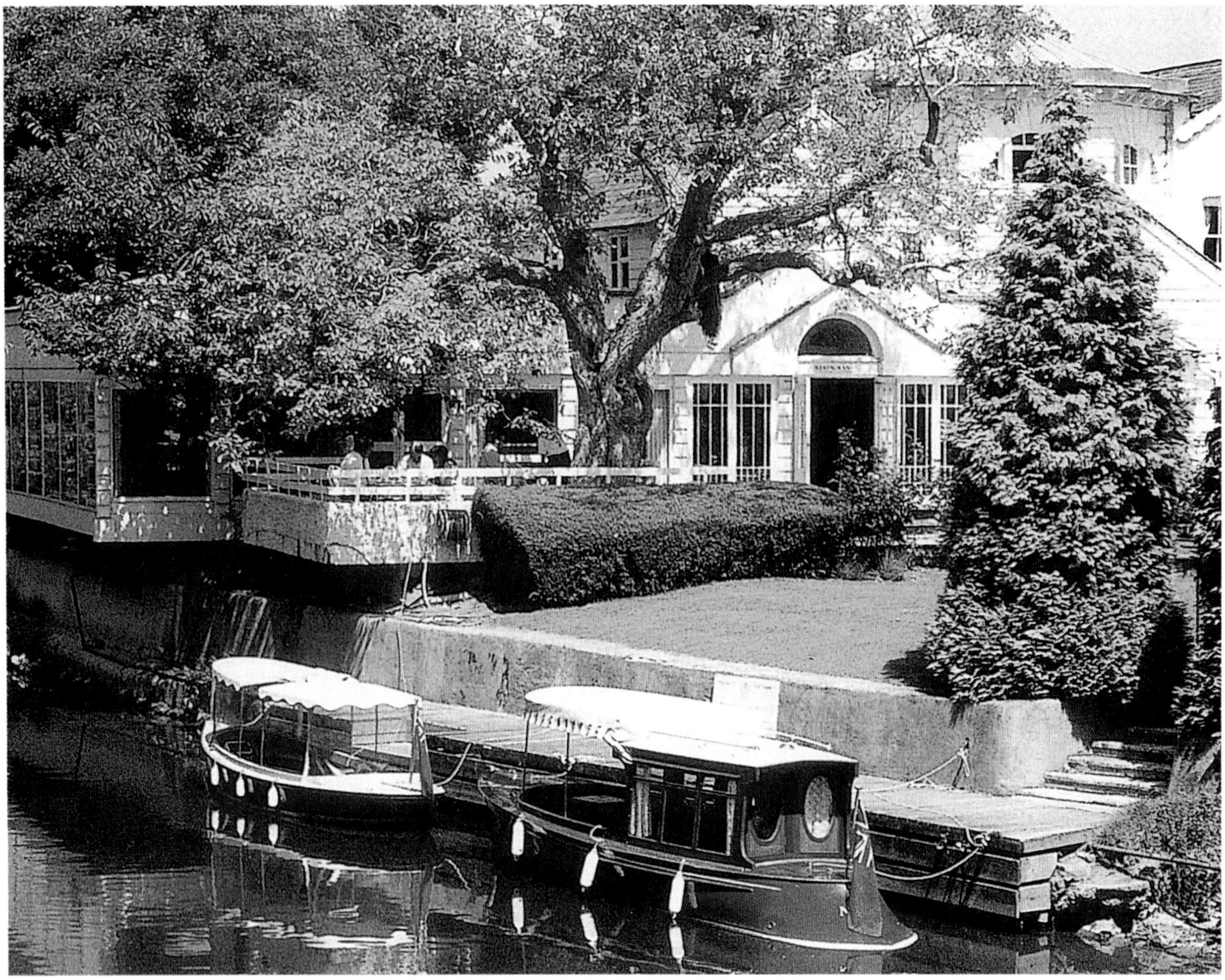

MONKEY ISLAND HOTEL

BRAY-ON-THAMES, MAIDENHEAD, BERKSHIRE SL6 2EE
TEL: 01628 623400 FAX: 01628 784732 E-MAIL: monkeyisland@btconnect.com

The name Monkey Island derives from the medieval Monk's Eyot. Circa 1723 the island was purchased by Charles Spencer, the third Duke of Marlborough, who built the fishing lodge now known as the Pavilion and the fishing temple, both of which are Grade I listed buildings. The Pavilion's Terrace Bar, overlooking acres of riverside lawn, is an ideal spot for a relaxing cocktail and the award winning Pavilion Restaurant, perched on the island's narrowest tip with fine views upstream, boasts fine English cuisine, an award-winning cellar and friendly service. The River Room is suitable for weddings or other large functions, while the Regency-style boardroom is perfect for smaller parties. It is even possible to arrange exclusive use of the whole island for a truly memorable occasion. The Temple houses 26 comfortable bedrooms and suites, the Wedgwood Room, with its splendid ceiling in high-relief plaster and octagonal Temple Room. Monkey Island is one mile downstream from Maidenhead, within easy reach of Royal Windsor, Eton, Henley and London. Weekend and boating breaks from £105 p.p. **Directions:** Take A308 from Maidenhead towards Windsor; turn left following signposts to Bray. Entering Bray, go right along Old Mill Lane, which goes over M4; the hotel is on the left. Price Guide: Single from £130; double/twin £190–£235; suite £295.

THE OLD VICARAGE HOTEL

WORFIELD, BRIDGNORTH, SHROPSHIRE WV15 5JZ

TEL: 01746 716497 FAX: 01746 716552 E-MAIL: admin@the-old-vicarage.demon.co.uk

Privately owned The Old Vicarage Stands in two acres of mature grounds, this Edwardian parsonage has hardly been altered since its days as a turn-of-the-century Parsonage. Extensive, subtle refurbishment has created an exceptional Country House Hotel offering guests a peaceful retreat in countryside of outstanding beauty. The spacious bedrooms are furnished in Victorian and Edwardian styles to complement the period features of the house. Four Coach House rooms offer complete luxury and comfort, and the Leighton suite has been specially designed with the disabled guest in mind. The property provides superb Grade 2 disabled facilities throughout. Award-winning imaginative menus include fresh and organic produce carefully sourced from local suppliers and small farmers. Award winning wine List. The Ironbridge Gorge Museum Complex and The Severn Valley Railway are just two of the many visitor attractions within easy reach of the hotel as well as the splendour of the border towns and villages nearby. Two-day breaks are available from £75 per person per day. The hotel's many accolades and awards include AA 3 Red Star and AA 3 Rosettes. **Directions:** 8 miles west of Wolverhampton, 1 mile off A454, 8 miles south of junction 4 of M54. Price Guide: £75–£110; double/twin £115–£175; suites £150–£175.

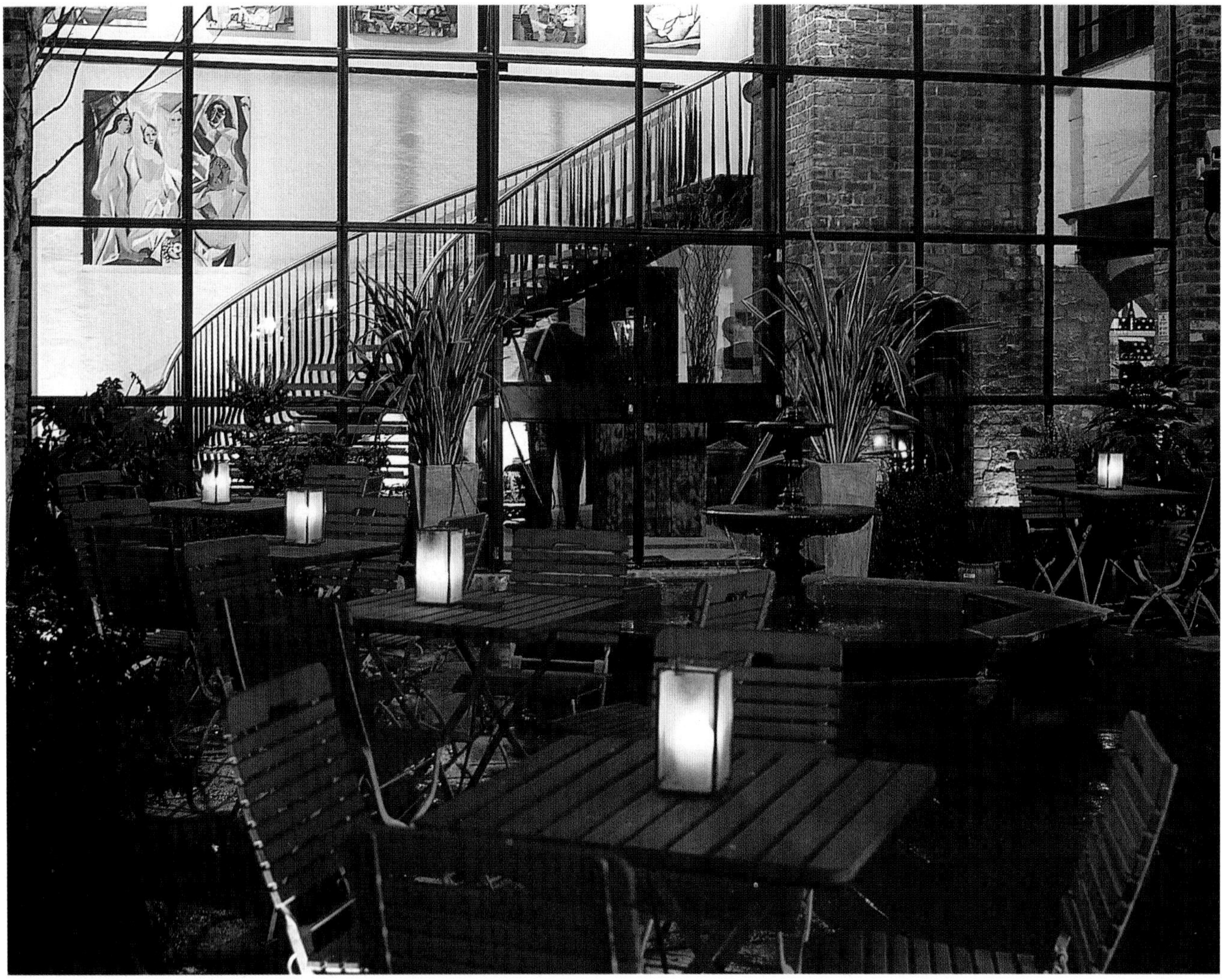

Hotel Du Vin & Bistro

THE SUGAR HOUSE, NARROW LEWINS MEAD, BRISTOL BS1 2NU
TEL: 0117 925 5577 FAX: 0117 925 1199 E-MAIL: info@bristol.hotelduvin.com

Set around a courtyard dating from the 1700's, this hotel comprises six listed warehouses that have been used for a number of industrial purposes over the centuries. The imposing 100ft chimney is a lasting testimony to the buildings' impressive past and other distinctive vestiges relating to this period feature inside. The individually named bedrooms are decorated with fine fabrics such as Egyptian linen and offer a good range of facilities including oversized baths and power showers. Guests may relax in the convivial Cocktail bar with its walk-in Cigar humidor or enjoy a glass of wine from the well-stocked cellar before dining in the Bistro. The traditional menu has been created using the freshest local ingredients and is complemented by an excellent wine list. Throughout the property the cool, understated elegance is evident as is the owners attention to even the smallest detail. The hotel has a selection of specially designed rooms for private meetings or dinner parties. Do not expect stuffy formality at the Hotel du Vin! **Directions:** Follow the M32 to the end and then follow signs for the City Centre. Go past House of Fraser on your left, and approximately 500 yards further on you will approach the War Memorial in the centre. Turn right and get onto the opposite side of the carriageway. The hotel is located about 400 yards further down on your left, offset from the main road. Price Guide: Single £109–£130; double/twin £109–£130; suite £160–£225.

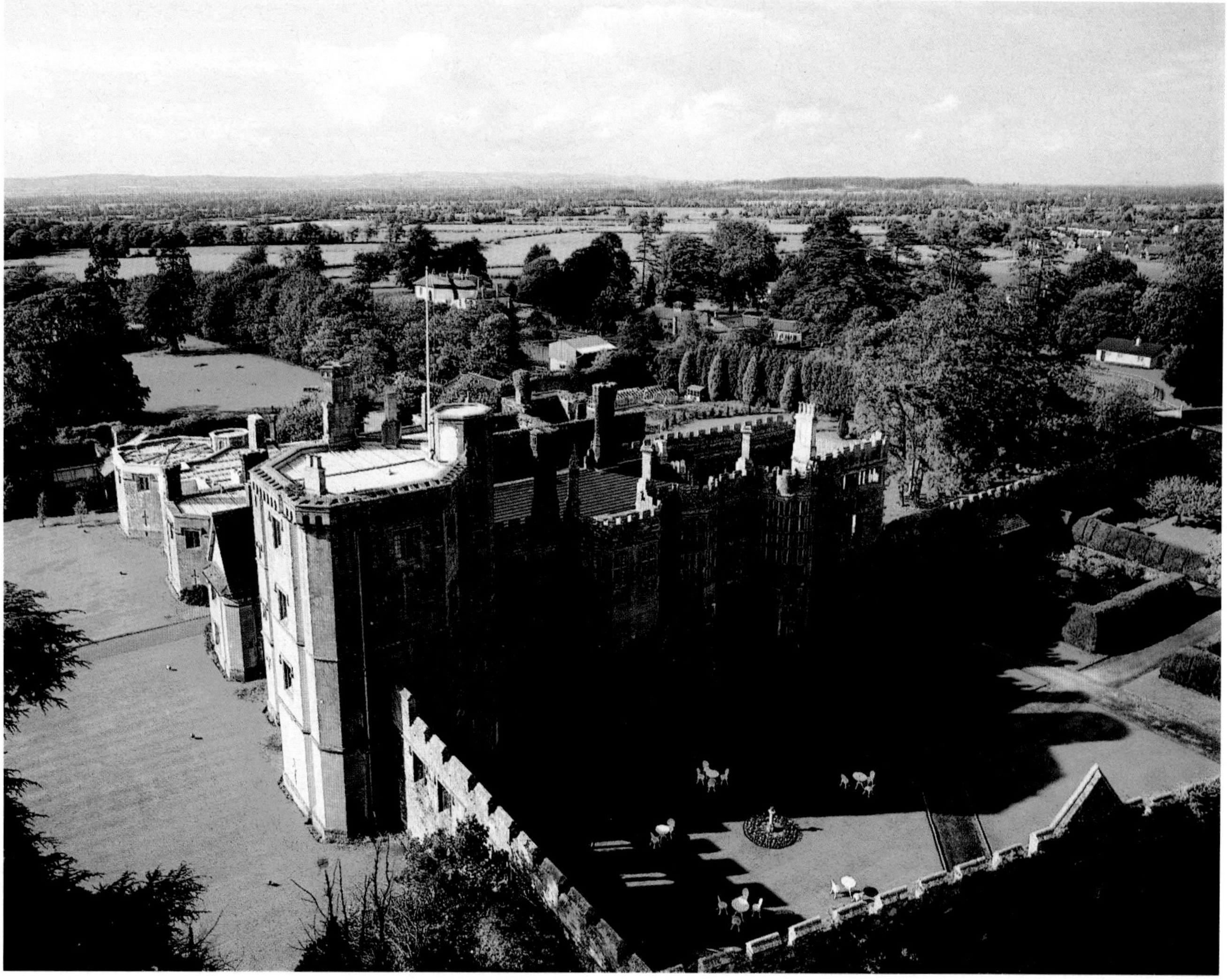

THORNBURY CASTLE

THORNBURY, SOUTH GLOUCESTERSHIRE BS35 1HH
TEL: 01454 281182 FAX: 01454 416188 E-MAIL: thornburycastle@compuserve.com

Built in 1511 by Edward Stafford, third Duke of Buckingham, Thornbury Castle was later owned by Henry VIII, who stayed here in 1535 with Anne Boleyn. Today it stands in 15 acres of regal splendour with its vineyard, high walls and the oldest Tudor garden in England. Rich furnishings are displayed against the handsome interior features, including ornate oriel windows, panelled walls and large open fireplaces. The 25 carefully restored bedchambers retain many period details. Thornbury Castle has received many accolades for its luxurious accommodation and excellent cuisine, which includes delights such as Marinated Field Mushrooms glazed with Goat Cheese, Carpaccio of Blue Fin Tuna or Glazed Barbary Duck Breast with Carrot Mousse. The Castle also provides peaceful and secluded meeting facilities. Thornbury is an ideal base from which to explore Bath, Wales and the Cotswolds. Personally guided tours are available to introduce guests to the little-known as well as the famous places which are unique to the area. In addition, clay pigeon shooting, archery and golf may be enjoyed locally. Closed for two days in January. **Directions:** The entrance to the Castle is left of the Parish Church at the lower end of Castle Street. Price guide Price Guide: Single from £110; double/twin from £135; suite from £270.

Tortworth Court Four Pillars Hotel

TORTWORTH, WOTTON-UNDER-EDGE, SOUTH GLOUCESTERSHIRE GL12 8HH
TEL: 01454 263000 FAX: 01454 263001 E-MAIL: bristol@four-pillars.co.uk

Recently refurbished to a high standard using architecturally sensitive period features, this impressive Grade II listed Victorian mansion is set within a prestigious arboretum, planted by Henry John Moreton in the mid-19th century, and boasts hundreds of trees and some rare specimens. An atmosphere of grandeur pervades with a towering gothic wooden staircase and panelled ceilings. Rooms all enjoy fine views, some over the beautiful gardens, and are elegantly decorated with splendid fabrics and superior furnishings. Delicious culinary feasts are created in the hotel's three unique restaurants: high ceilings and chandeliers set the scene in the ornate library, now the main restaurant. Fine dining can be experienced in the impressive Orangery or lighter meals in the glass-covered Atrium. The large heated indoor pool, sauna and steam room, gym and beauty rooms are perfect for relaxation. Friendly staff provide excellent fitness programmes and a range of beauty therapies. Corporate services with business facilities are also offered. Leisure activities include a self-guided tree walk around the arboretum and grounds of Tortworth Court. Guests can explore the charming, untouched Cotswold villages and surrounding countryside or visit nearby Bath and Bristol. **Directions:** Leave M5 at Jct14, travel for 1 mile and follow signs. Price Guide: Single £139–£189; double/twin £169–£219; suites £189–£219.

189 MasterCard VISA AMERICAN EXPRESS M 400

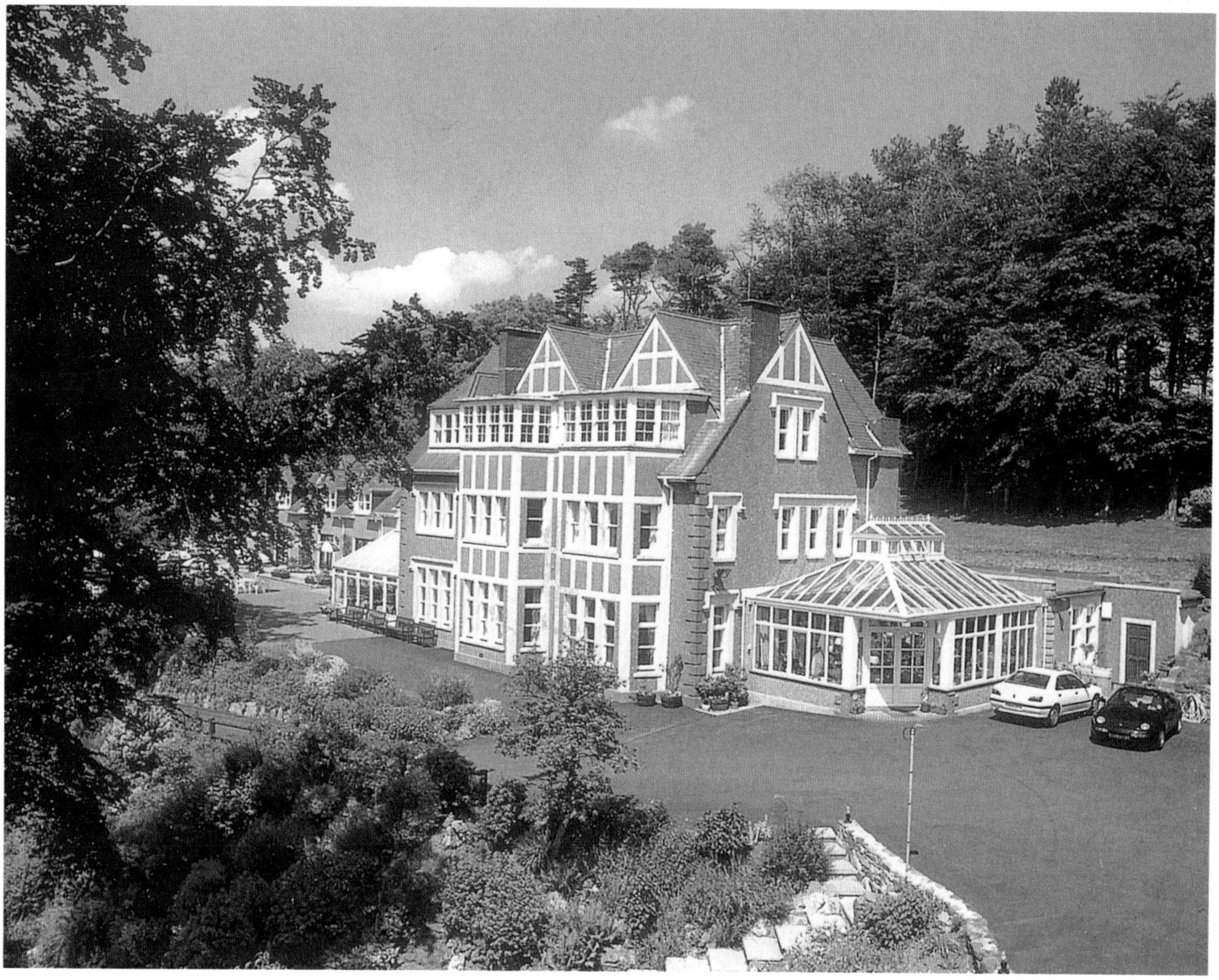

DANESWOOD HOUSE HOTEL

CUCK HILL, SHIPHAM, NR WINSCOMBE, SOMERSET BS25 1RD
TEL: 01934 843145 FAX: 01934 843824 E-MAIL: info@daneswoodhotel.co.uk

This tall, pebble-dashed Edwardian house nestles on the slopes of the Mendip Hills commanding spectacular views over the Somerset countryside towards the Bristol Channel and South Wales. Originally a homeopathic health hydro, it is now a hotel of distinction which has been in the enthusiastic ownership of David and Elise Hodges for almost 25 years. They have created a homely, welcoming and relaxing atmosphere and their continual pursuit of excellence has earned the hotel a reputation for comfort, culinary delights and service. The generous en suite bedrooms are individually designed, delightfully furnished and have every facility from colour TV to direct dial telephone. The Honeymoon Suite boasts a 7ft King-size bed while the Victorian Room has a Queen Anne four-poster. 5 recently added bedrooms open out onto the five acres of grounds and have private patios. Great emphasis is placed on using fresh produce and local meat and poultry for the superb dishes served in the period dining room, which has been awarded 2 AA Rosettes. Breakfast is in the sunny conservatory. Conference facilities. The hotel grounds offer direct access to the Mendip Walkway. Nearby are 5 18-hole golf courses, trout fishing, riding and several National Trust houses **Directions:** Shipham is signposted from the A38 Bristol-Bridgwater road. Go through the village towards Cheddar and the hotel is on the left. Price Guide: Single £89.50–£99.50; double/twin £105–£150; suites £150.

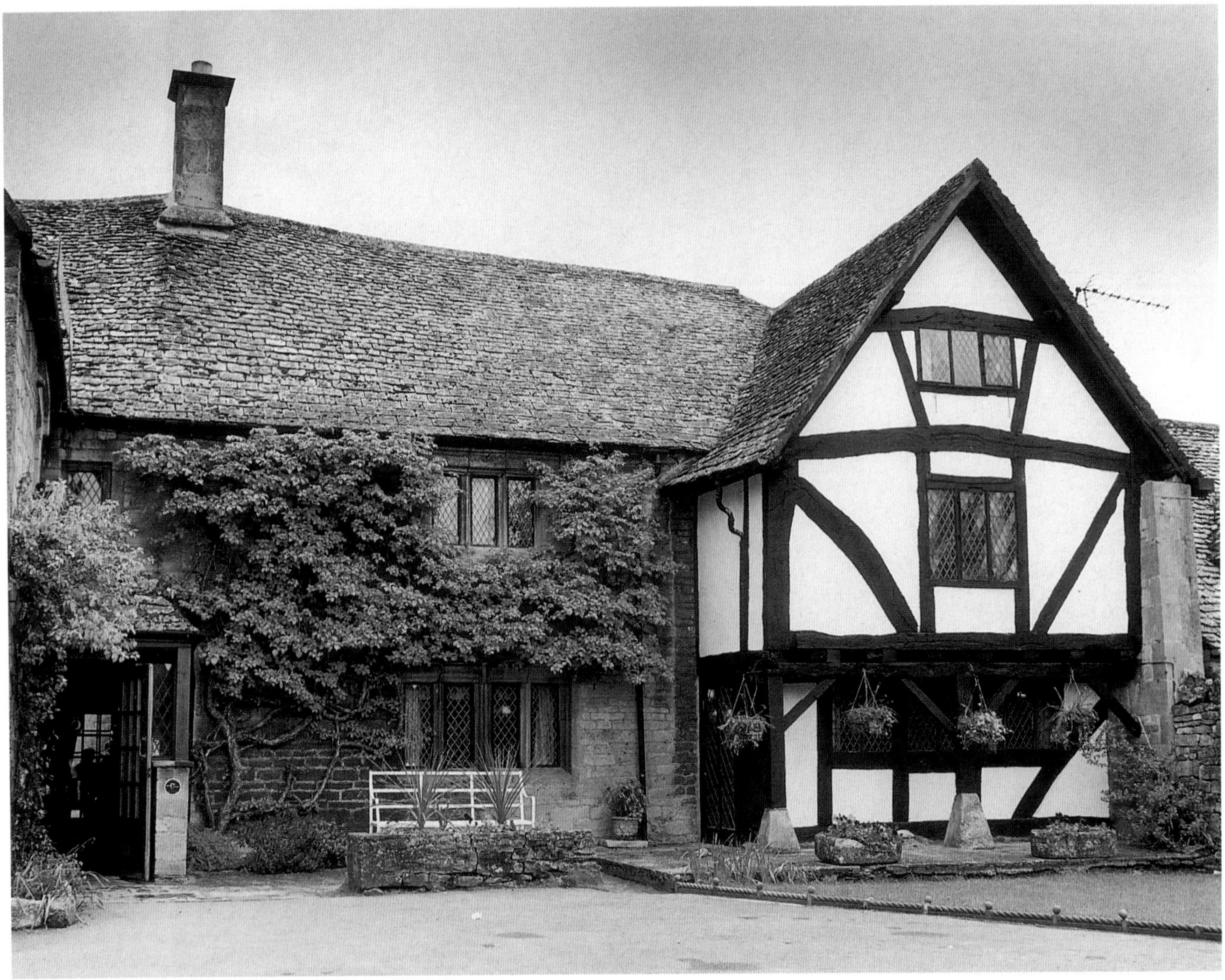

THE BROADWAY HOTEL

THE GREEN, BROADWAY, WORCESTERSHIRE WR12 7AA
TEL: 01386 852401 FAX: 01386 853879 E-MAIL: bookings@cotswold–inns–hotels.co.uk

The Broadway Hotel stands proudly in the centre of the picturesque Cotswold village of Broadway where every stone evokes memories of Elizabethan England. Once used by the Abbots of Pershore, the hotel was formerly a 16th-century house, as can be seen by its architecture which combines the half timbers of the Vale of Evesham with the distinctive honey-coloured and grey stone of the Cotswolds. It epitomises a true combination of old world charm and modern day amenities with friendly, efficient service. All bedrooms provide television, telephone and tea and coffee making facilities. Traditional English dishes and a peaceful ambience are offered in the beamed Courtyard Restaurant. There is an impressive variety of à la carte dishes complemented by good wines. The congenial Jockey Club bar is a pleasant place to enjoy a drink. The inn overlooks the village green at the bottom of the main street where guests can browse through shops offering an array of fine antiques. On a clear day, 13 counties of England and Wales can be viewed from Broadway Tower. Snowhill, Burford, Chipping Campden, Bourton-on-the-Water, Stow-on-the-Wold and Winchcombe as well as larger Cheltenham, Worcester and Stratford are within easy reach. **Directions:** From London M40 to Oxford, A40 to Burford, A429 through Stow-on-the-Wold, then A44 to Broadway. Price Guide: Single £72.50; double £115–£135.

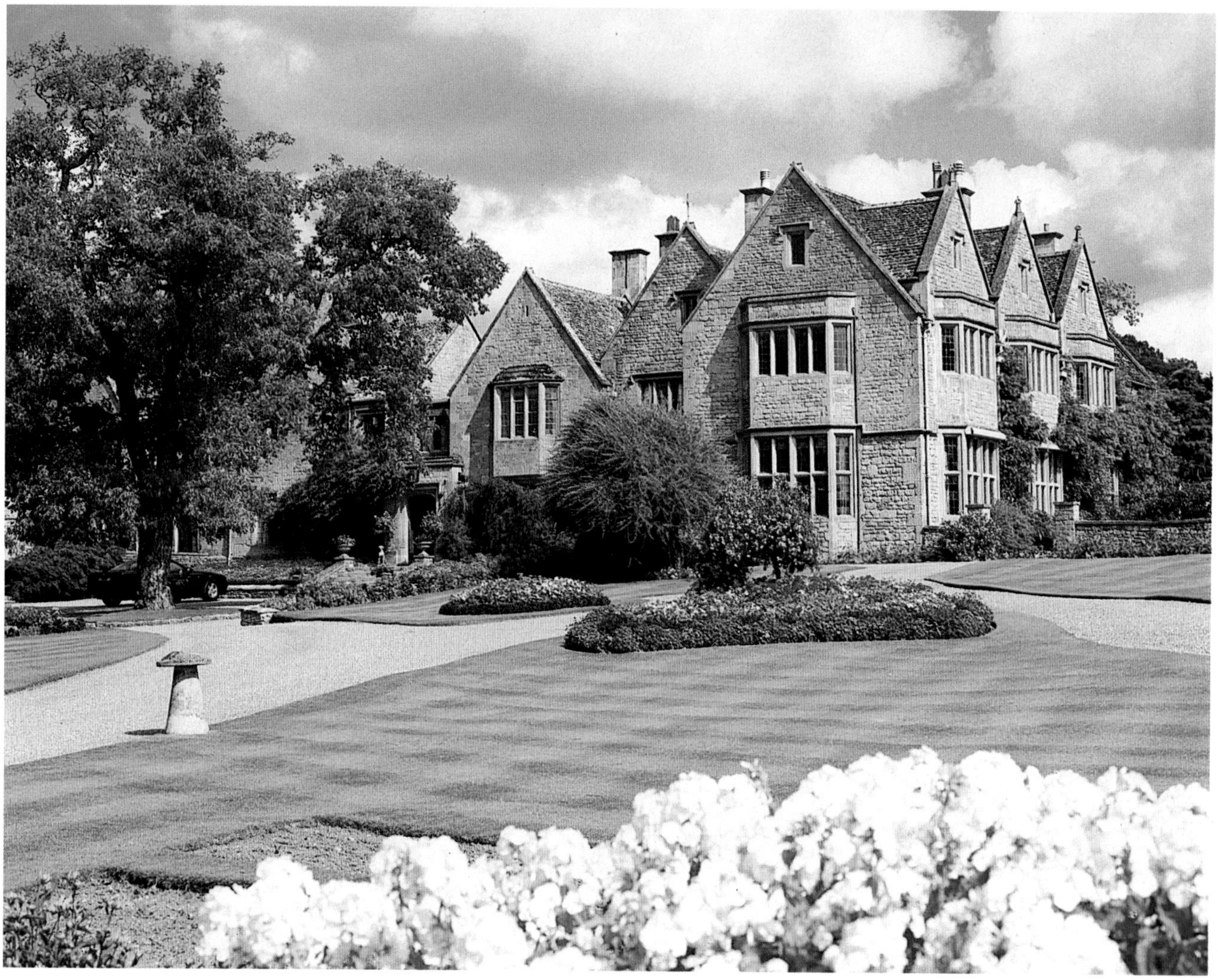

BUCKLAND MANOR HOTEL

NR BROADWAY, WORCESTERSHIRE WR12 7LY
TEL: 01386 852626 FAX: 01386 853557 E-MAIL: enquire@bucklandmanor.com

The warm glow of Buckland Manor's golden Cotswold stone exterior blends beautifully with the colourful flowers and green shades of the glorious grounds, serving as an appetiser to visitors of the tranquil luxury and history inside those weather-beaten walls. A manor house on the site was first mentioned in the records of Gloucester Abbey in 600AD when the Abbot received it as a gift from Kynred, ruler of Mercier and chief king of the seven kingdoms of England. Managed by Nigel Power, Buckland retains gracious living and tradition, with the addition of all modern comforts and best service. Guests can relax before log fires in two delightfully decorated lounges, one with lovely panelling and a beamed ceiling. The 13 excellently decorated en suite bedrooms are furnished with luxury fittings and accessories. Some have four-poster beds and fireplaces and all bathrooms use water drawn from the Manor's own spring. Views over the grounds with their small waterfalls, heated pool, tennis courts, putting green and croquet lawns are spectacular. The dining room is an oasis of calm, and chef Ken Wilson prepares delicious, award-winning cuisine. Broadway Golf Club, Cheltenham race course, Stratford, Stow-on-the-Wold, Warwick and Blenheim are nearby. **Directions:** From M40, exit at Jct8. Take A40 to Burford, A424 to Broadway and then B4632 signposted Winchcombe to Buckland. Price Guide: Single from £205; double/twin from £215; suite £350.

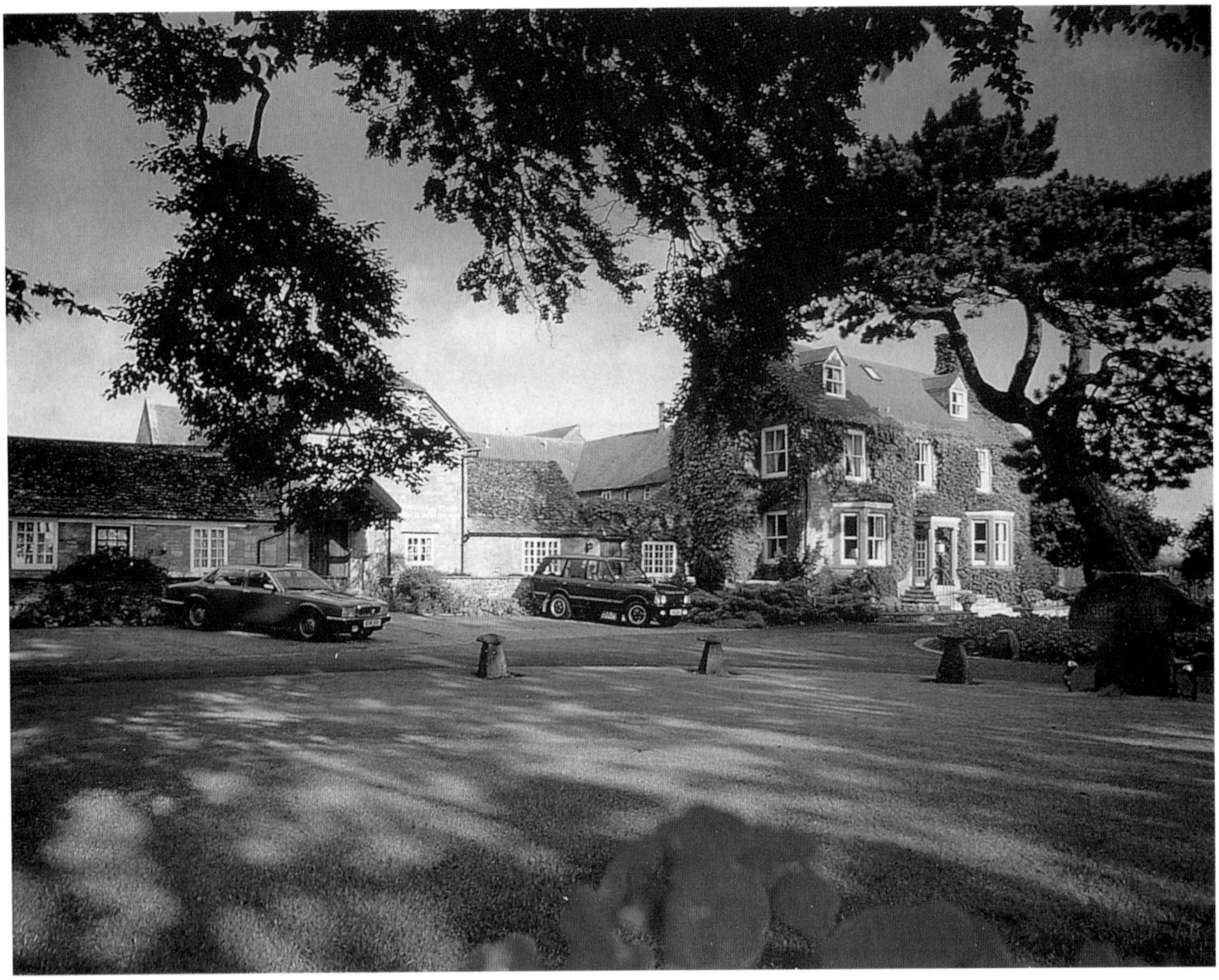

DORMY HOUSE

WILLERSEY HILL, BROADWAY, WORCESTERSHIRE WR12 7LF
TEL: 01386 852711 FAX: 01386 858636 E-MAIL: reservations@dormyhouse.co.uk

This former 17th century farmhouse has been beautifully converted into a delightful hotel which retains much of its original character. With its oak beams, stone-flagged floors and honey-coloured local stone walls it imparts warmth and tranquillity. Dormy House provides a wealth of comforts for the most discerning guest. Each bedroom is individually decorated – some are furnished with four-poster beds – and suites are available. Head Chef, Alan Cutler, prepares a superb choice of menus and Tapestries Restaurant offers an extensive wine list with a diverse range of half bottles. The versatile Dormy Suite is an ideal venue for conferences, meetings or private functions – professionally arranged to individual requirements. The hotel has its own leisure facilities which include a games room, gym, sauna/steam room, croquet lawn and putting green. Mountain bikes are available for hire. Broadway Golf Club is adjacent. The locality is idyllic for walkers. Stratford-upon-Avon, Cheltenham Spa, Hidcote Manor Garden and Sudeley Castle are all within easy reach. USA representative: Josephine Barr, 1-800-323-5463. Closed 2 days at Christmas. **Directions:** Hotel is ½ mile off A44 between Moreton-in-Marsh and Broadway. Taking the turning signposted Saintbury, the hotel is first on left past picnic area Price Guide: Single £108; double/twin £156–£196; suite £196

49 MasterCard VISA AMERICAN EXPRESS M 170

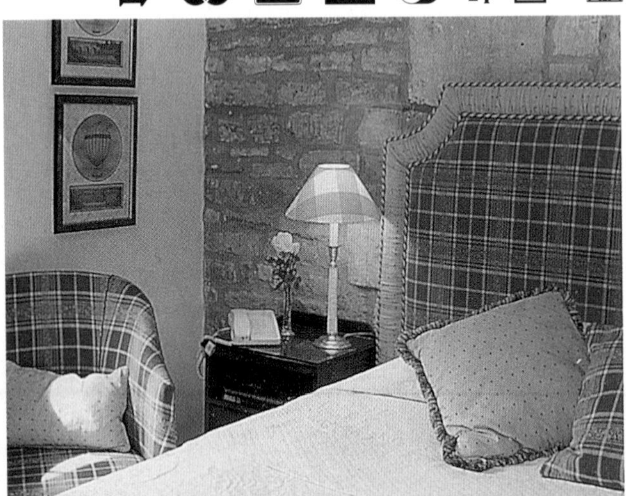

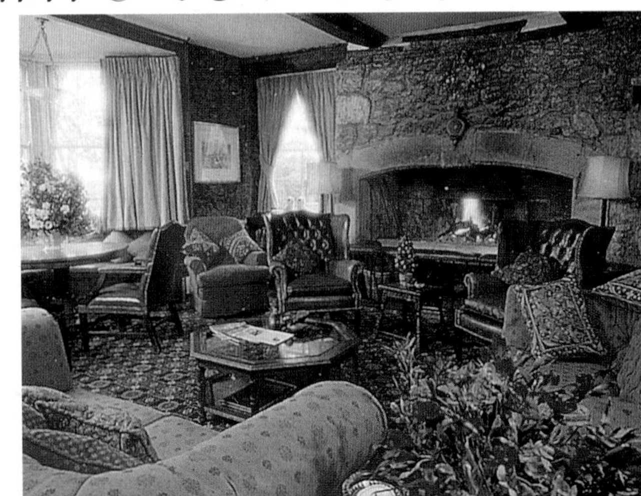

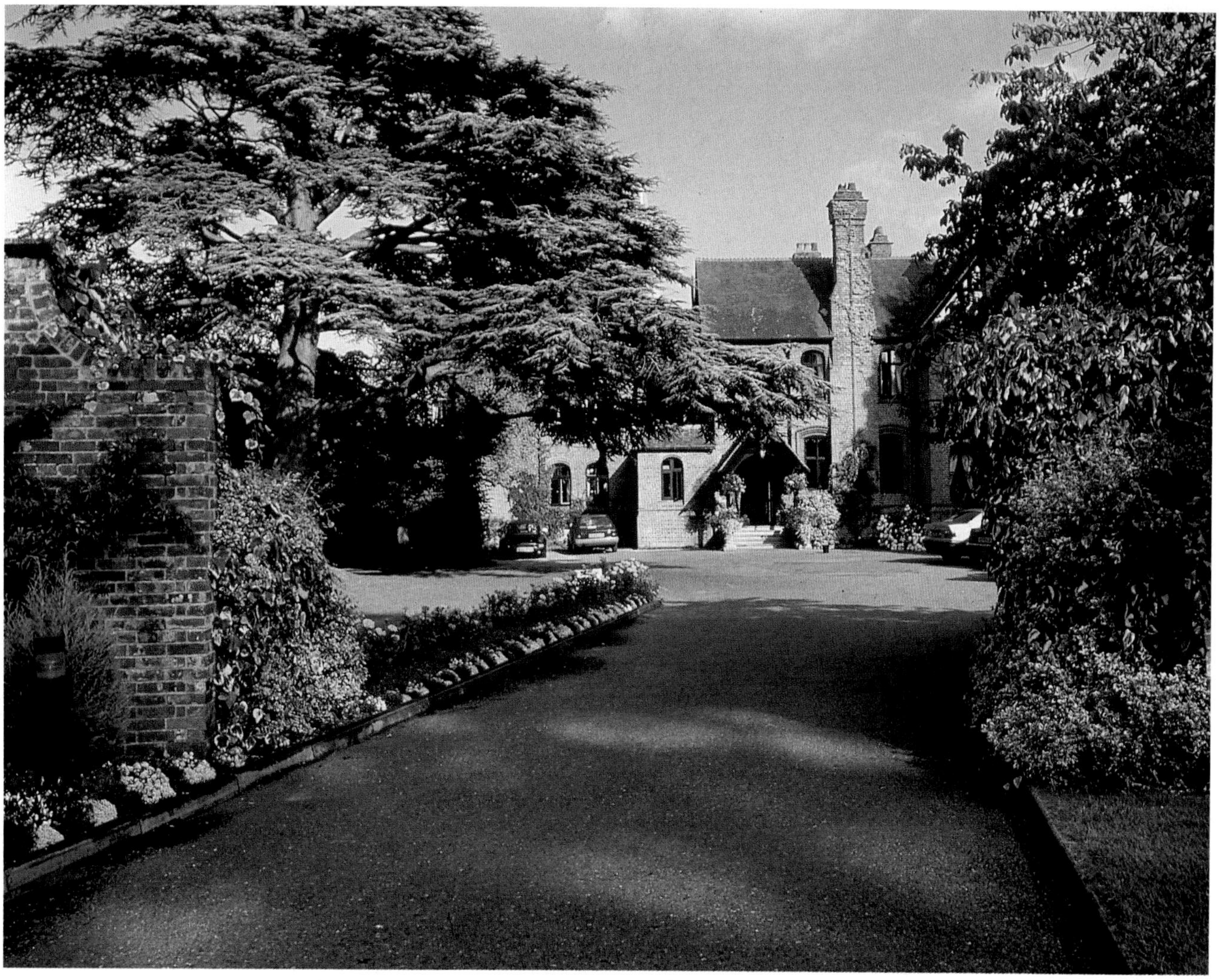

CAREYS MANOR HOTEL

BROCKENHURST, NEW FOREST, HAMPSHIRE SO42 7RH
TEL: 01590 623551 FAX: 01590 622799 E-MAIL: info@careysmanor.com

Careys Manor, dates from 1888 and is built on the site of a royal hunting lodge used by Charles II. Situated in landscaped grounds and close to the glorious New Forest countryside, the hotel is proud of the personal welcome and care it extends to its visitors. The comfortably furnished bedrooms are well-appointed. In the Garden Wing, there is a choice of bedrooms, some opening directly onto the lawns and others with a balcony overlooking the pretty gardens. The restaurant offers fine English and French cuisine. A prestigious sports complex comprises a large indoor swimming pool with Jacuzzi, sauna and a Turkish steam room. In addition, guests can work out in the professionally supervised fitness suite, where there are also rooms for massage, sports injury and beauty treatments. Windsurfing, riding and sailing can all be enjoyed locally, while Stonehenge, Beaulieu, Broadlands, Salisbury and Winchester are a short distance away. Business interests can be catered for – there are comprehensive self-contained conference facilities. **Directions:** From M27 junction 1, follow A337 signed to Lymington. Careys Manor is on the left after 30 mph sign at Brockenhurst Price Guide: Single from £89; double/twin £129–£179; suite £199.

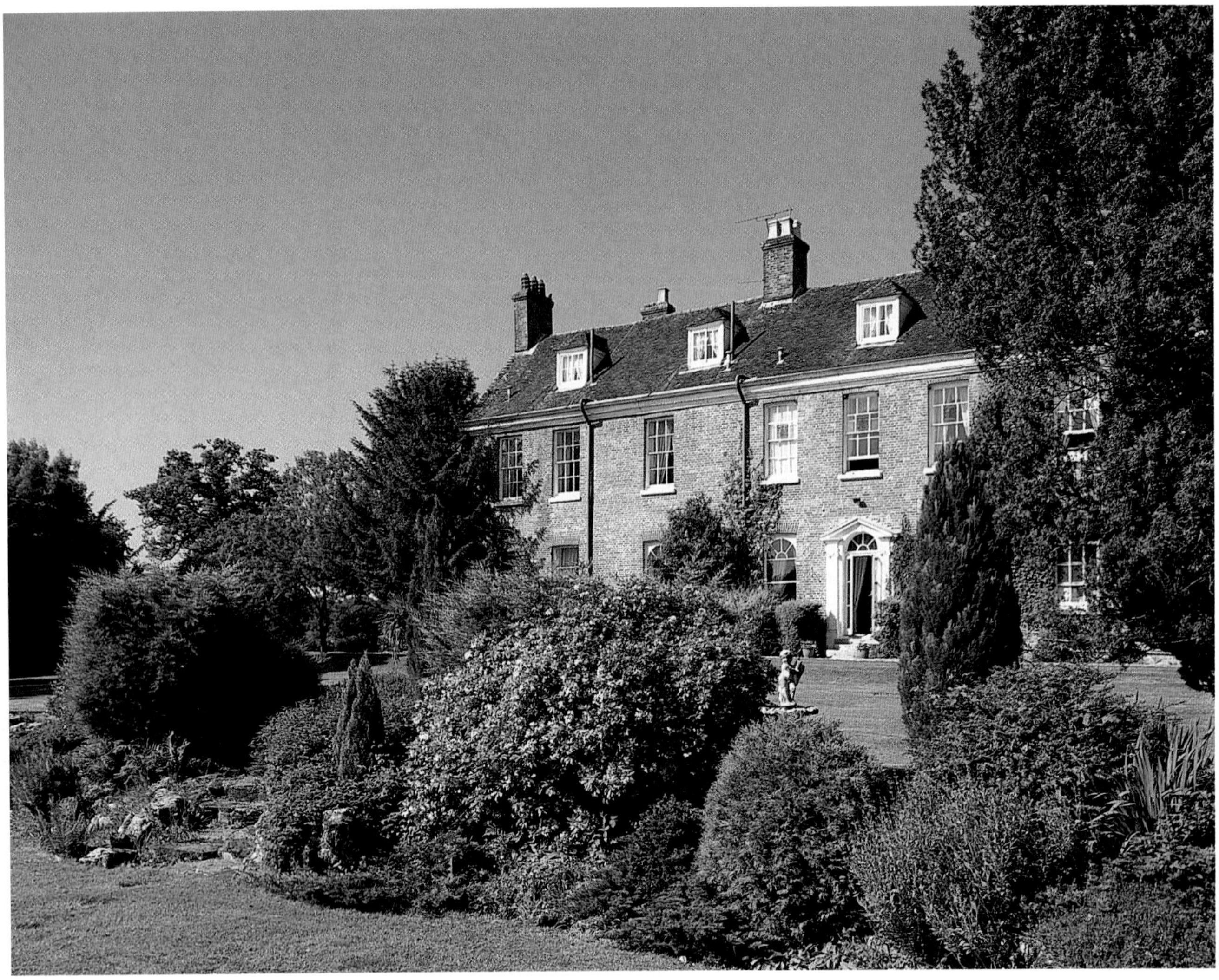

NEW PARK MANOR

LYNDHURST ROAD, BROCKENHURST, NEW FOREST, HAMPSHIRE SO42 7QH
TEL: 01590 623467 FAX: 01590 622268 E-MAIL: enquiries@newparkmanorhotel.co.uk

Escape from the crowds to one of the New Forest's finest country house hotels. A former hunting lodge of Charles II, the building is grade II listed and dates back to the 16th century. It stands in a very fine position a good distance from the road to Lyndhurst, the capital of the New Forest, where "Alice in Wonderland's" grave, and Rufus Stone are curiosities to be visited. The en suite bedrooms are all individually decorated, keeping in mind the style and grandeur of the old manor; most offer superb views over the surrounding parklands with its wandering ponies and deer. Enjoy a romantic evening with fine wines and French influenced cuisine in the Restaurant or relax with a good book from the library in front of the open log fire in the historic Rufus Bar. The New Forest suite creates a wonderful setting for all types of functions – tailor-made to suit your personal requirements. For the more energetic, New Park Manor offers riding from its own equestrian centre with BHS trained stable crew and a tennis court. **Directions:** New Park Manor is ½ mile off the A337 between Lyndhurst and Brockenhurst easily reached from M27 junction 1 Price Guide: Single from £85; double/twin £110–£190.

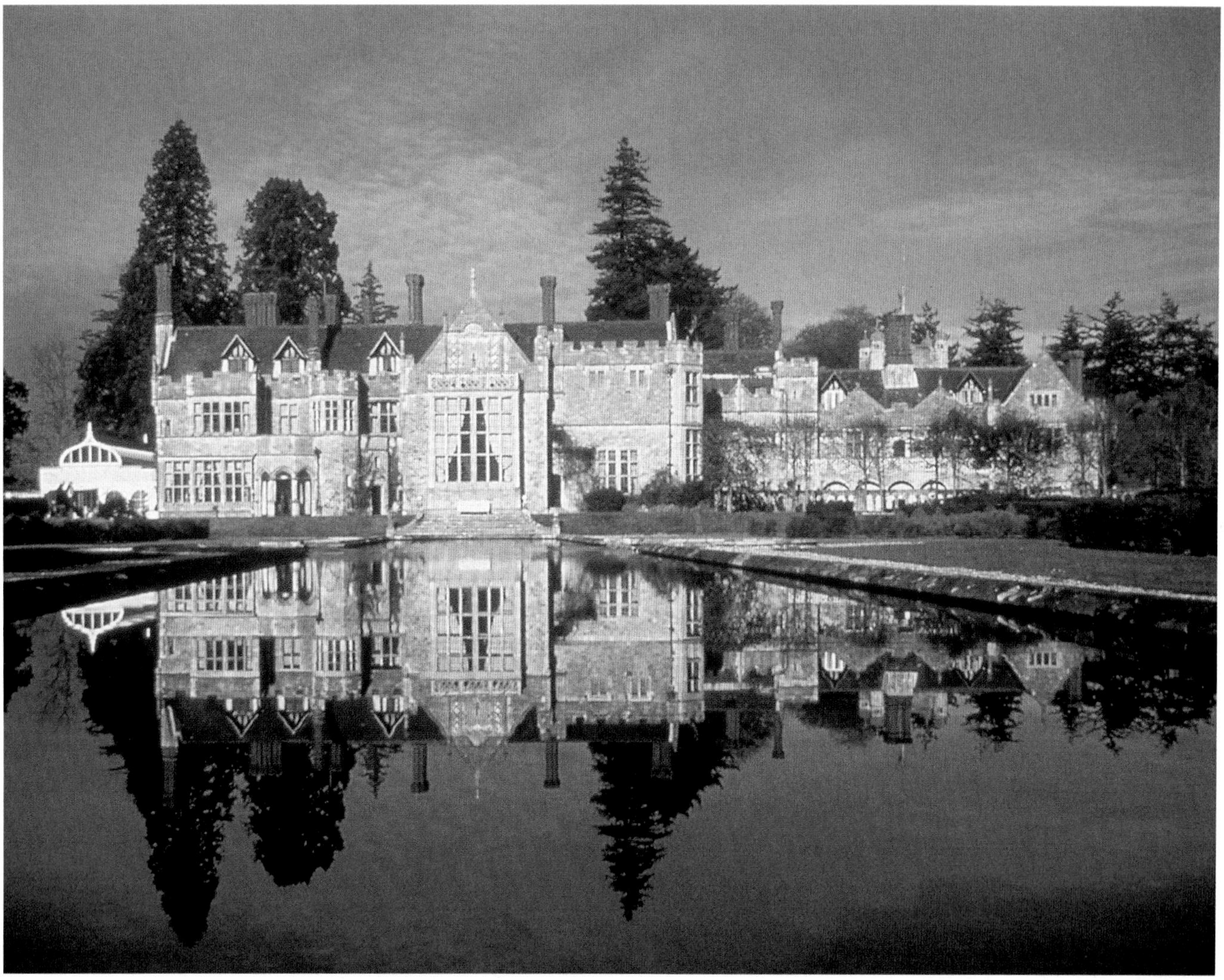

Rhinefield House Hotel

RHINEFIELD ROAD, BROCKENHURST, NEW FOREST, HAMPSHIRE SO42 7QB
TEL: 01590 622922 FAX: 01590 622800

Known locally as the 'jewel in the forest', at first sight the sheer grandeur of Rhinefield House surpasses all expectations. A hint of Italian Renaissance sweeps across ornamental gardens, with canals reflecting the mellow stonework. Lovingly restored to their original 1890s design, over 5,000 yew trees form the maze and formal parterres where a grass amphitheatre has been carved out of the western slopes for summer evening concerts. The interiors are equally impressive, the journey through the rooms is a voyage of discovery. Authentically created in the style of a Moorish Palace, the Alhambra Room has Islamic inscriptions, onyx pillars and mosaic flooring. Fine cuisine is served in the elegant Armada Restaurant – so called after its splendid carving depicting the Spanish Armada. An airy sunlit conservatory and attractive bedrooms appointed in accordance with the style of the house all add to Rhinefield's appeal. The Grand Hall is a model replica of Westminster Hall – an ideal setting for balls, society weddings and stylish banquets. A wide range of conference rooms and equipment is available for business events. Guests may unwind in the Atlantis Leisure Club with its plunge pool, sauna, steam room and small gymnasium. **Directions:** A35 West from Lyndhurst the hotel is signed in about 3 mile Price Guide: Single from £100; double/twin from £130; suite from £175

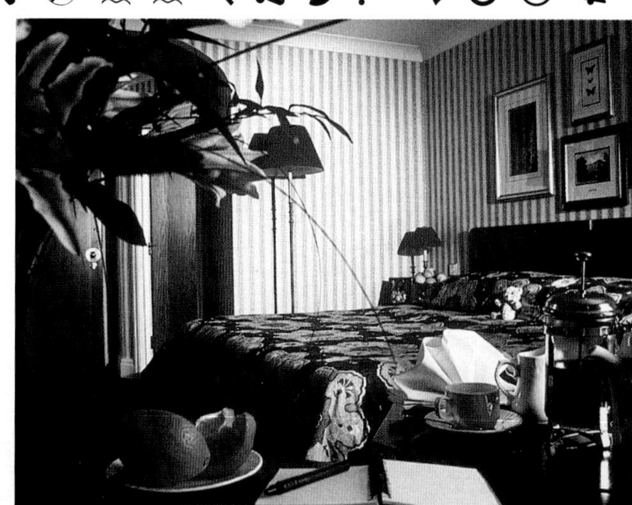

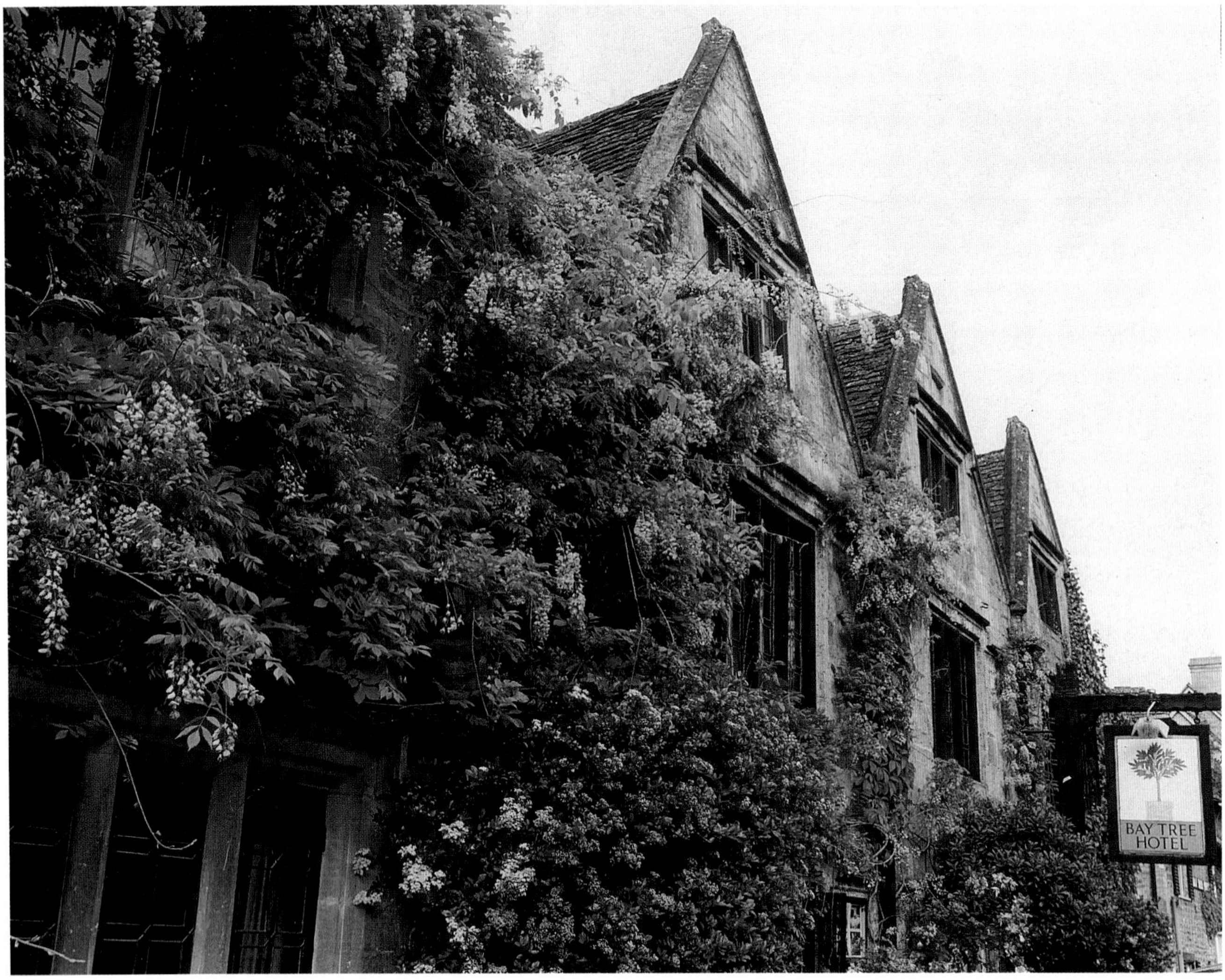

THE BAY TREE HOTEL

SHEEP STREET, BURFORD, OXON OX18 4LW
TEL: 01993 822791 FAX: 01993 823008 E-MAIL: bookings@cotswold–inns–hotels.co.uk

The Bay Tree has been expertly refurbished so that it retains all its Tudor splendour while offering every modern facility. The oak-panelled rooms have huge stone fireplaces and a galleried staircase leads upstairs from the raftered hall. All the bedrooms are en suite, three of them furnished with four-poster beds and two of the five suites have half-tester beds. In the summer, guests can enjoy the delightful walled gardens, featuring landscaped terraces of lawn and flower beds. A relaxing atmosphere is enhanced by the staff's attentive service in the flagstoned dining room where the head chef's creative cuisine is complemented by a comprehensive selection of fine wines. Light meals are served in a country-style bar. Burford, often described as the gateway to the Cotswolds, is renowned for its assortment of antique shops and the Tolsey Museum of local history. The Bay Tree Hotel makes a convenient base for day trips to Stratford-upon-Avon, Stow-on-the-Wold and Blenheim Palace. Golf, clay pigeon shooting and riding can be arranged locally. Directions: Burford is on the A40 between Oxford and Cheltenham. Proceed halfway down the hill into Burford, turn left into Sheep Street and The Bay Tree Hotel is 30 yards on your right. Price Guide: Single £99; double/twin £145–£220.

21 MasterCard VISA AMERICAN EXPRESS M 20

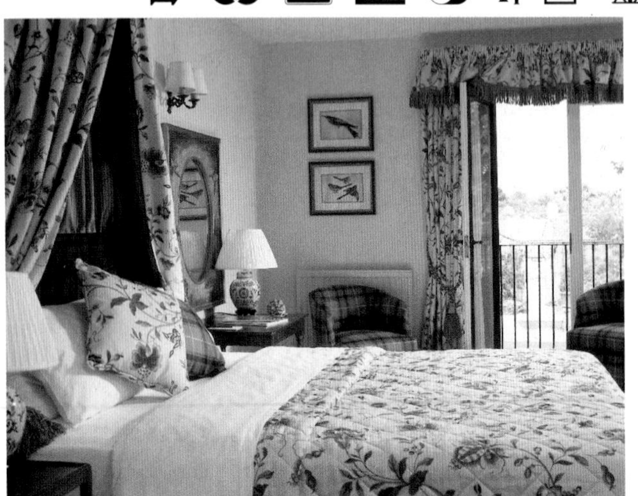

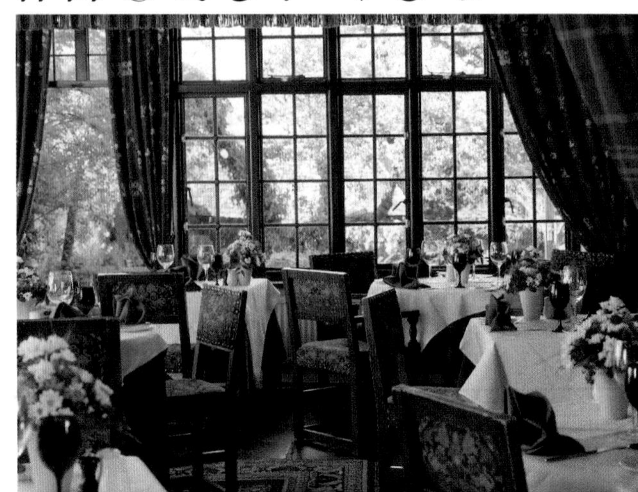

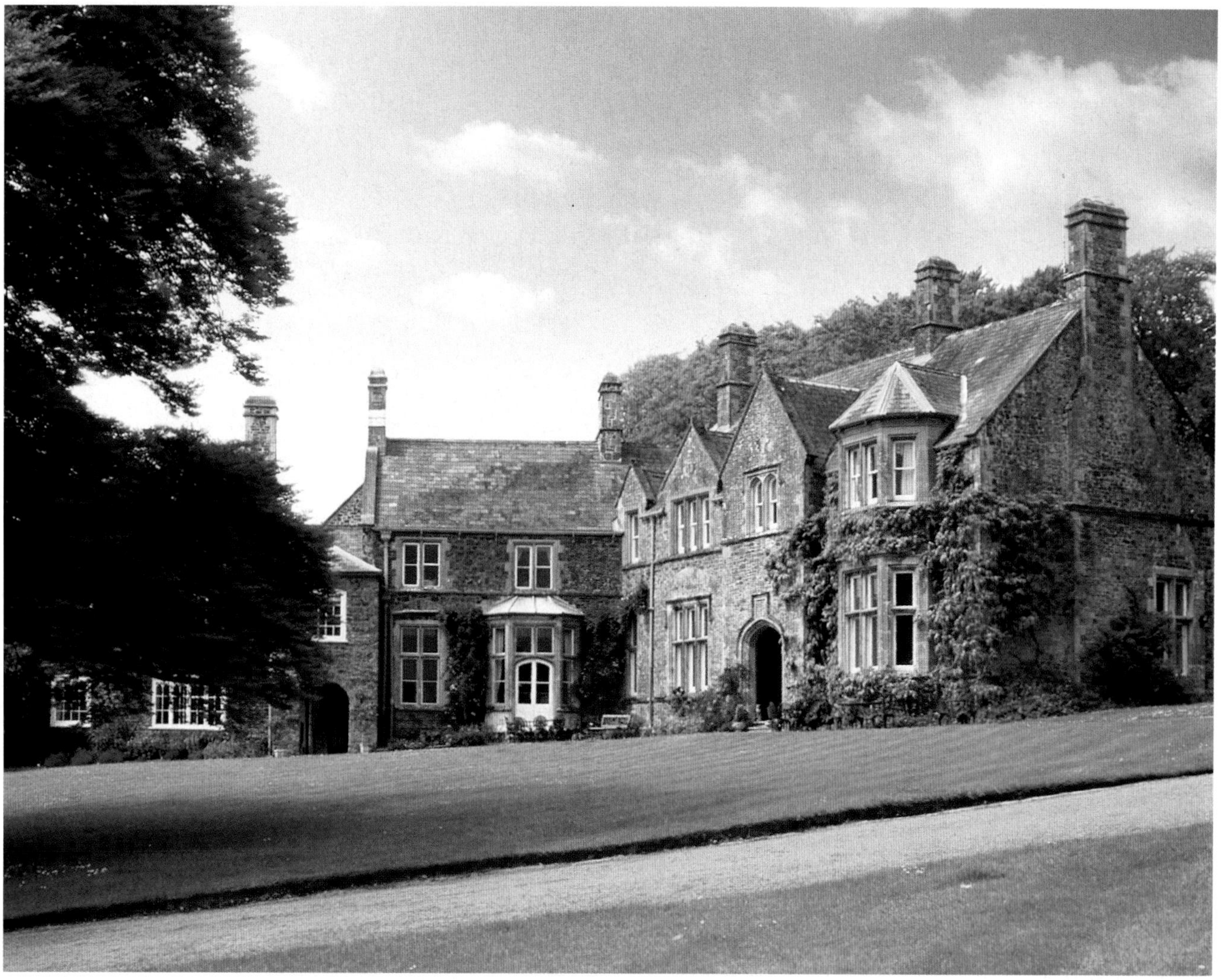

NORTHCOTE MANOR COUNTRY HOUSE HOTEL

BURRINGTON, UMBERLEIGH, DEVON EX37 9LZ
TEL: 01769 560501 FAX: 01769 560770 E-MAIL: rest@northcotemanor.co.uk

This 18th-century manor and the grounds high above the Taw River Valley combine to offer an ambience of timeless tranquillity. Situated in the peaceful Devonshire countryside, Northcote Manor offers complete relaxation and refreshment. Extensive refurbishment has created 11 luxury bedrooms and suites, resulting in a total redesign of the décor of the spacious sitting rooms, hall and restaurant. This has brought a series of accolades, including AA Three Red Stars in 2002, and, in 2001, the RAC Blue Ribbon Award, The Which? Hotel Guide, Tourist Board Silver Award, Michelin 2 Red Turrets Award, RAC Cooking Award level 3, and AA 2 Rosettes. The proprietors are planning to undertake extensive work in the 20-acre grounds to complete their vision of creating the West Country's leading country house hotel. North Devon is a delight to explore; Exmoor and Dartmoor are within easy reach, and guests may visit RHS Rosemoor and the many National Trust properties nearby. A challenging 18-hole golf course is next door, whilst outstanding fishing from the Taw at the bottom of the drive can be arranged with the Gillie. The area also hosts some of the best shoots in the country. A tennis court and croquet lawn are on site. Special breaks available. **Directions:** 25 miles from Exeter on A377 to Barnstaple. Private drive opposite the Portsmouth Arms pub/railway station. Price Guide: (incl. dinner) Single £122.50–£182.50; double/twin £185–£225; suite £265.

The Angel Hotel

BURY ST EDMUNDS, SUFFOLK IP33 1LT
TEL: 01284 714000 FAX: 01284 714001 E-MAIL: sales@angel.co.uk

Immortalised by Charles Dickens as the hostelry where Mr Pickwick enjoyed an excellent roast dinner, The Angel Hotel has recently added 23 air-conditioned bedrooms and a guest lift and is renowned for its first-class service, continuing the tradition since first becoming an inn in 1452. Visitors have the immediate impression of a hotel that is loved and nurtured by its owners. In the public rooms, guests will appreciate the carefully chosen ornaments and pictures, fresh flowers and log fires. Bedrooms are individually furnished and decorated and all have en suite bathrooms. The elegant dining room has been awarded 2 Rosettes by the AA for excellent food and service. Overlooking the ancient abbey, the restaurant serves classic English cuisine, including local speciality dishes and succulent roasts. The Angel can offer a wide range of quality conference and banqueting facilities catering for private dinners, meetings and weddings from 10–60 persons. The hotel is within an hour of the east coast ferry ports and 45 minutes from Stansted Airport. Nearby there is racing at Newmarket and several golf courses within easy reach. Bury St Edmunds is an interesting and historic market town and an excellent centre for touring East Anglia. **Directions:** Follow signs to Historic Centre. Price Guide: Single from £68; double/twin from £86; suite from £111. Weekend rates £53 per person bed and breakfast.

66 MasterCard VISA AMERICAN EXPRESS M 80

Ravenwood Hall

ROUGHAM, BURY ST EDMUNDS, SUFFOLK IP30 9JA
TEL: 01359 270345 FAX: 01359 270788 E-MAIL: enquiries@ravenwoodhall.co.uk

Nestling within 7 acres of lovely lawns and woodlands deep in the heart of Suffolk lies Ravenwood Hall. Now an excellent country house hotel, this fine Tudor building dates back to 1530 and retains many of its original features. The restaurant, still boasting the carved timbers and huge inglenook from Tudor times, creates a delightfully intimate atmosphere in which to enjoy imaginative cuisine. The menu is a combination of adventurous and classical dishes, featuring some long forgotten English recipes. The Hall's extensive cellars are stocked with some of the finest vintages, along with a selection of rare ports and brandies. A cosy bar offers a less formal setting in which to enjoy some unusual meals. Comfortable bedrooms are furnished with antiques, reflecting the historic tradition of the Hall, although each is equipped with every modern facility. A wide range of leisure facilities is available for guests, including a hard tennis court, a croquet lawn and heated swimming pool. There are golf courses and woodland walks to enjoy locally; hunting and shooting can be arranged. Places of interest nearby include the famous medieval wool towns of Lavenham and Long Melford; the historic cities of Norwich and Cambridge are within easy reach **Directions:** 2 miles East of Bury St. Edmunds off the A14 Price Guide: Single £71–£95; double/twin: £93–£129.

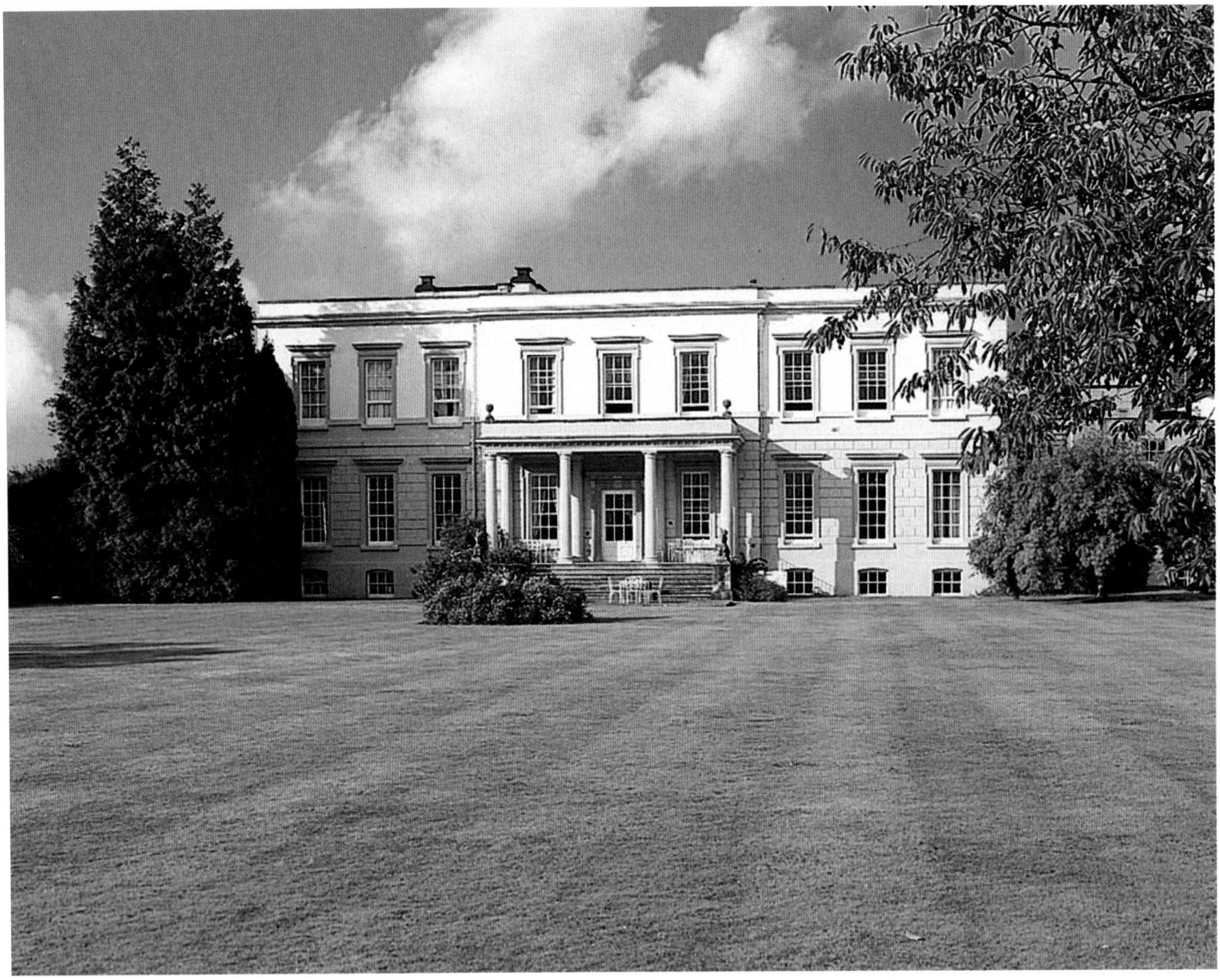

BUXTED PARK COUNTRY HOUSE HOTEL

BUXTED, NR UCKFIELD, EAST SUSSEX TN22 4AY
TEL: 01825 732711 FAX: 01825 732770

Few settings are more tranquil than Buxted Park's rural location, close to Ashdown Forest. Built in 1725, the attractive Georgian Mansion has been sympathetically restored to its former glory of time gone by, when Queen Victoria and Queen Mary were both regular visitors. Set in 312 acres of stunning gardens and parkland, the hotel also boasts extensive trout lakes, with fly-fishing available. There are 44 spacious bedrooms, most with delightful views of the gardens and estate, which is home to herds of fallow deer. The Orangery Restaurant situated in the restored Victorian conservatory provides rare and elegant surroundings in which to enjoy the excellent food and wines. There are several impressive and comfortable lounges to choose from as well as the magnificent ballroom, which opens out into the Coat of Arms Lounge. The hotel is justifiably proud of its health club, which has a well-equipped gym, saunas, steam rooms and Jacuzzi and a fabulous outdoor heated pool for the summer. **Directions:** The entrance to the hotel is located on the A272, east of its junction with the A22 Price Guide: Single from £80; double/twin from £95; suites from £135. Two night leisure breaks are available from £70 per person per night.

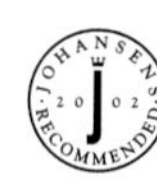

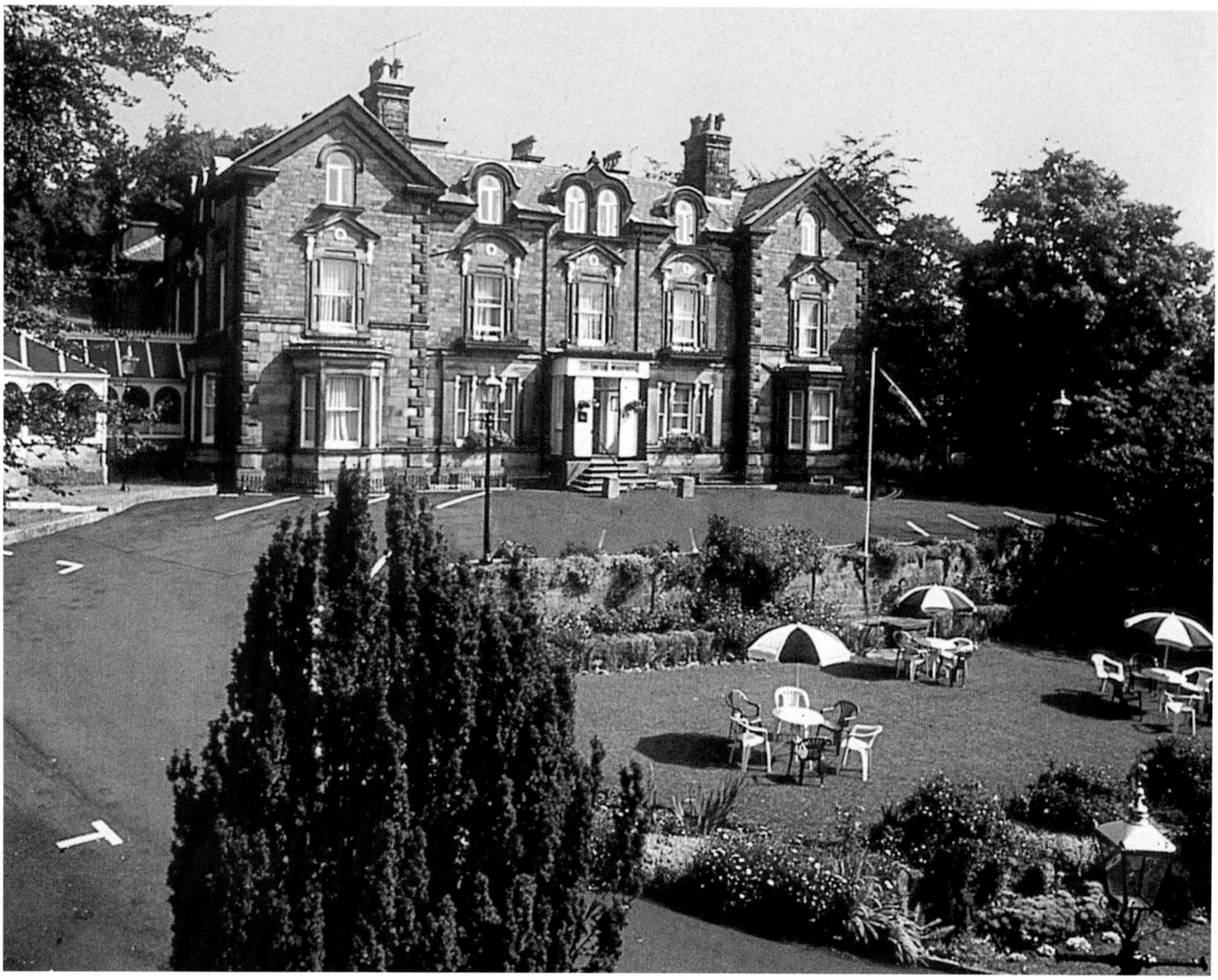

THE LEE WOOD HOTEL & RESTAURANT

THE PARK, BUXTON, DERBYSHIRE SK17 6TQ
TEL: 01298 23002 FAX: 01298 23228 E-MAIL: leewoodhotel@btinternet.com

This elegant Georgian hotel is full of charm, character and warmth. Situated close to the centre of the historic spa town of Buxton, it is set amidst mature lawned grounds with heather-filled borders. In the background are wooded sheltering hills and the rugged and lushly pastured Peak District. The Lee Wood has everything a visitor could expect from a family-owned, three-star hotel. Each of the 40 en suite bedrooms has been tastefully and stylishly decorated and refurbished to provide every comfort and facility. A number of executive and non-smoking bedrooms have views over the famous Pooles Cavern and Country Park. The hotel has achieved 2 AA Red Rosettes for the quality of its traditional and international à la carte and table d'hôte cuisine served with panache in the sunny Garden Restaurant. There are several golf courses, sailing and pony trekking nearby. Chatsworth House (pictured below) and Haddon Hall are among some of the many stately homes within easy driving distance. Other attractions include Alton Towers, Crich Tramway and Buxton Opera House. **Directions:** From the north: M1 Jct29 Chesterfield–Baslow–Buxton. M6 Jct19 A537 Knutsford–Macclesfield–Buxton. M56/M60 and M62 Stockport A6 to Buxton. From the south: M1 Jct23A/24; take A50 for approx. 19 miles then Ashbourne A515 to Buxton. M6 Jct14 Stone A53 to Leek/Buxton. Price Guide: Single £80; double/twin £90.

40 MasterCard VISA AMERICAN EXPRESS M 120

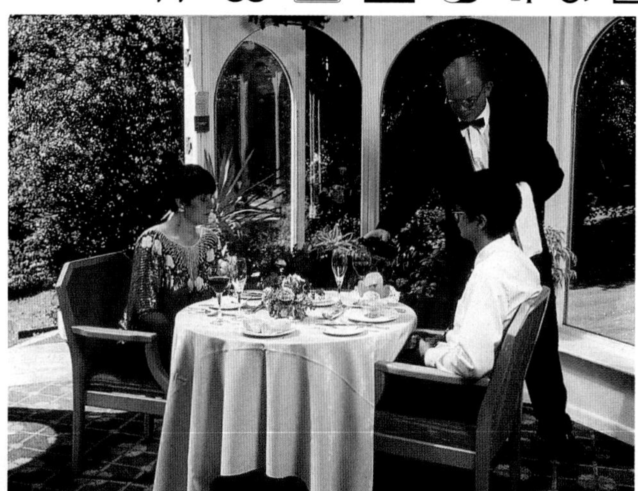

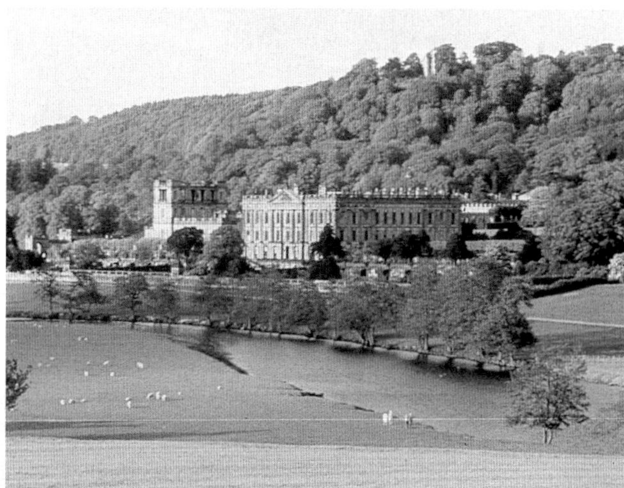

THE NARE HOTEL

CARNE BEACH, VERYAN-IN-ROSELAND, TRURO, CORNWALL TR2 5PF
TEL: 01872 501111 FAX: 01872 501856 E-MAIL: office@narehotel.co.uk

Peace, tranquillity and stunning sea views are what makes The Nare such a find. The hotel is superbly positioned overlooking the fine sandy beach of Gerrans Bay, facing south and sheltered by The Nare and St Mawes headlands. In recent years extensive refurbishments have ensured comfort and elegance without detracting from the country house charm of this friendly family-run hotel. All bedrooms are close to the sea, many with patios and balconies to take advantage of the spectacular outlook. While dining in the restaurant guests can enjoy the sea views from three sides of the room. Local seafood such as lobster and delicious home-made puddings, served with Cornish cream, are specialities, complemented by an interesting range of wines. The Nare remains the highest rated AA 4 star hotel in the South West with two Rosettes for its food. Surrounded by subtropical gardens and National Trust land, the hotel's peaceful seclusion is ideal for lazing or for exploring the coastline and villages of the glorious Roseland Peninsula. It is also central for many of Cornwall's beautiful houses and gardens including the famous Heligan. Guests arriving by train are met by prior arrangement at Truro. Christmas and New Year house parties **Directions:** Follow road to St Mawes; 2 miles after Tregony Bridge turn left for Veryan. The hotel is 1 mile beyond Veryan Price Guide: Single £76-£158; double/twin £152-£286; suite £280-£470.

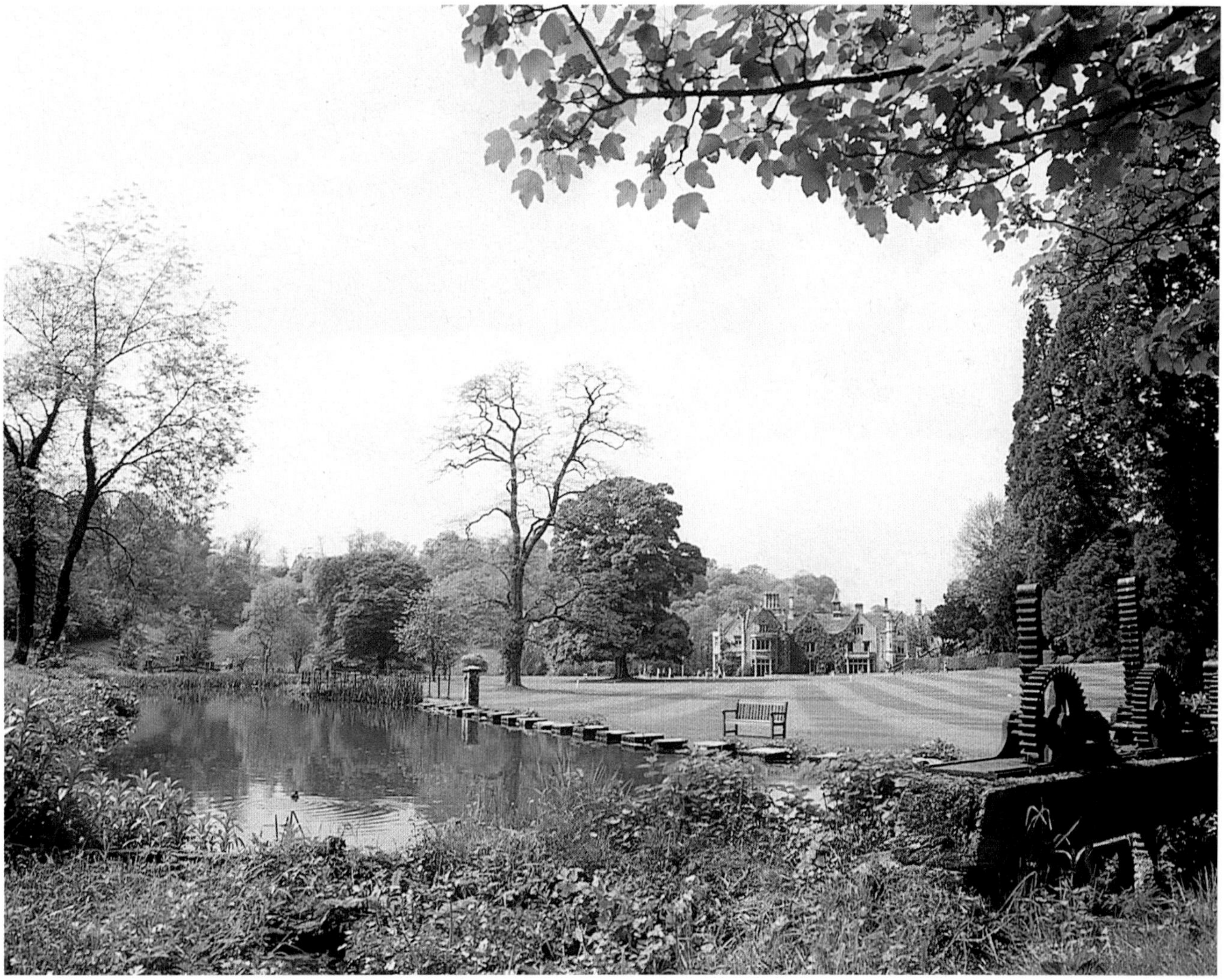

THE MANOR HOUSE HOTEL & GOLF CLUB

CASTLE COMBE, CHIPPENHAM, WILTSHIRE SN14 7HR

TEL: 01249 782206 FAX: 01249 782159 E-MAIL: enquiries@manor-house.co.uk

Nestling in the heart of one of England's prettiest villages deep in the Southern Cotswolds, the 14th-century Manor House at Castle Combe is one of Britain's most architecturally beautiful and idyllically set country house hotels. Ivy-clad stone walls and mullioned windows, oak panelling, log fires and antique furniture blend sympathetically with the individually designed bedrooms, many of which feature four poster beds, original beams and exposed walls. Set in the 300-acre estate of wooded valley and downland is the Peter Allis and Clive Clark 6340 yard, par 73, championship golf course, one of the most spectacular and challenging courses in the South of England. Delightful walks in the surrounding countryside or a stroll through the estate, unchanged for almost 200 years, are a magical experience. With its enchanting gardens and parkland, a gently flowing trout stream and the romance of a terraced Italian garden, the Manor House provides peace and tranquillity, together with a friendly atmosphere and award-winning cuisine and hospitality. **Directions:** A 15-minute drive from junctions 17 & 18 of the M4, or 20 minutes from the M5/M4 intersection. 12 miles from the beautiful Georgian city of Bath and only 2 hours drive from central London. Approached directly from A420 and B4039. Price Guide: Single/double/twin from £145; suite £265–£500.

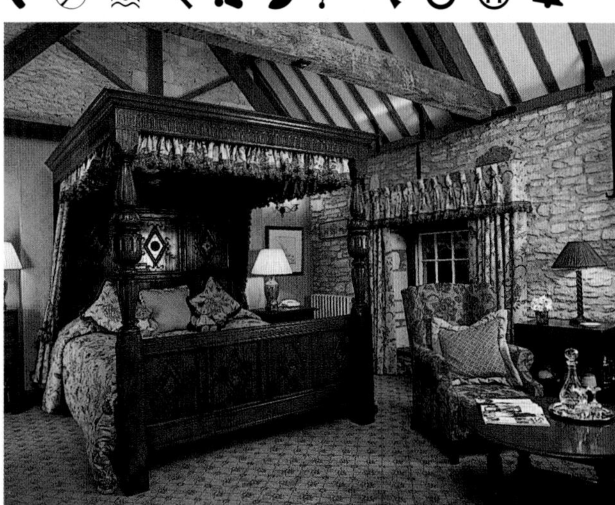

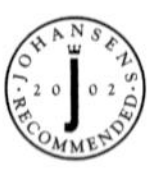

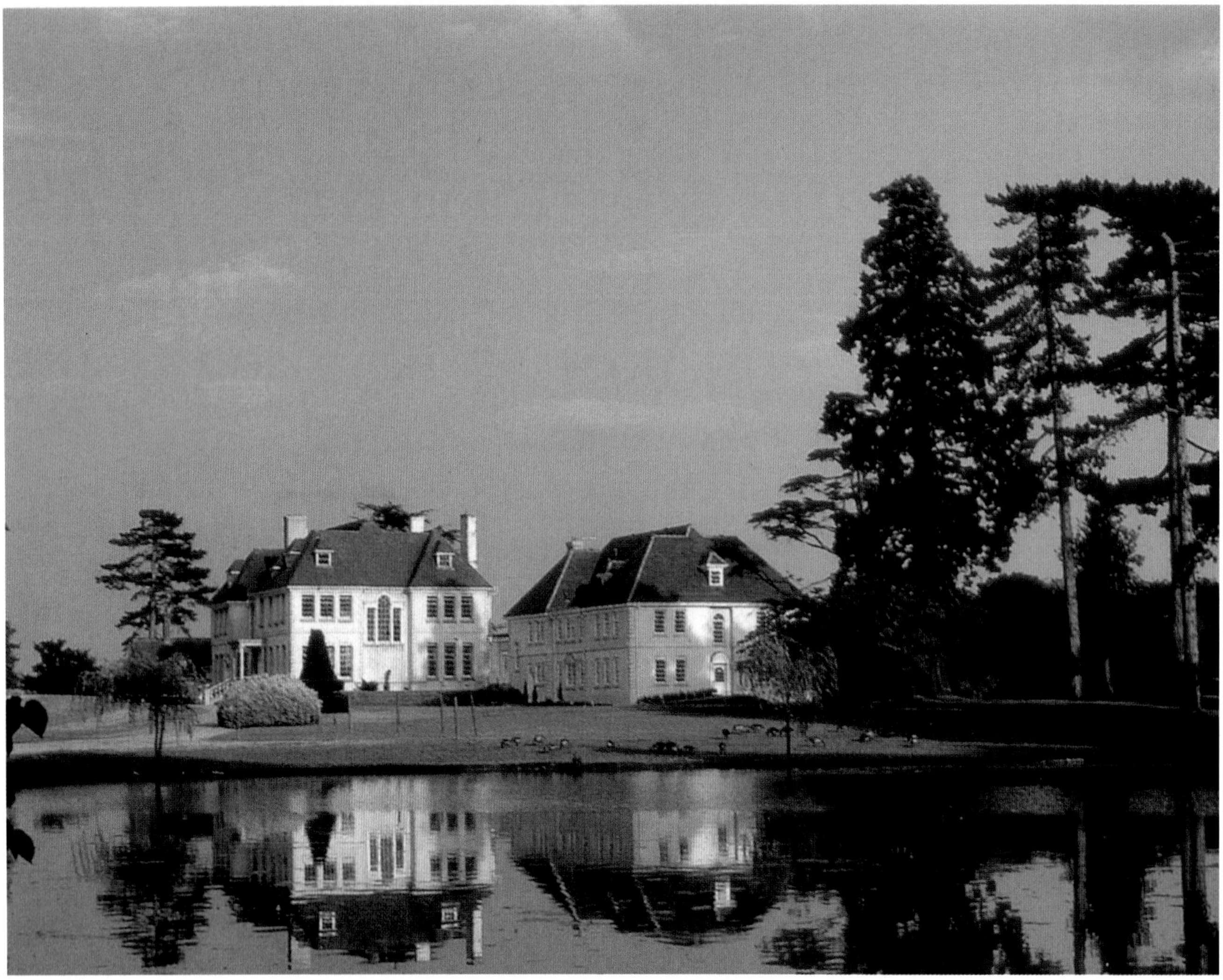

BROCKENCOTE HALL

CHADDESLEY CORBETT, NR KIDDERMINSTER, WORCESTERSHIRE DY10 4PY
TEL: 01562 777876 FAX: 01562 777872 E-MAIL: info@brockencotehall.com

The Brockencote estate consists of 70 acres of landscaped grounds surrounding a magnificent hall. There is a gatehouse, half-timbered dovecote, lake, some fine European and North American trees and an elegant conservatory. The estate dates back over three centuries and the style of the building reflects the changes which have taken place in fashion and taste. The hotel has been awarded 3 AA Red Stars and is Heart of England Tourist Board Midlands Hotel of the Year 1998. At present, the interior combines classical architectural features with contemporary creature comforts. As in most country houses, each of the bedrooms is different: all have their own character, complemented by tasteful furnishings and décor. The friendly staff provide a splendid service under the supervision of owners Alison and Joseph Petitjean. The Hall specialises in traditional French cuisine with occasional regional and seasonal specialities. Brockencote Hall is an ideal setting for those seeking peace and quiet in an unspoilt corner of the English countryside. Located a few miles south of Birmingham, it is convenient for business people and sightseers alike and makes a fine base for touring historic Worcestershire. **Directions:** Exit 4 from M5 or exit 1 from M42. Brockencote Hall is set back from A448 at Chaddesley Corbett between Bromsgrove and Kidderminster. Price Guide: Single £110–130; double/twin £135–£170.

17 MasterCard VISA AMERICAN EXPRESS M 20

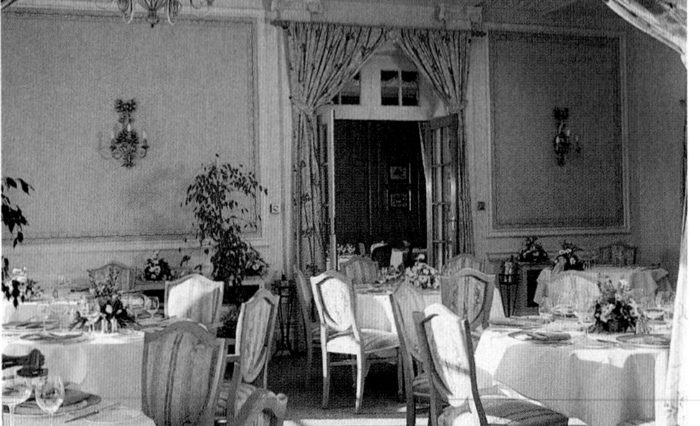

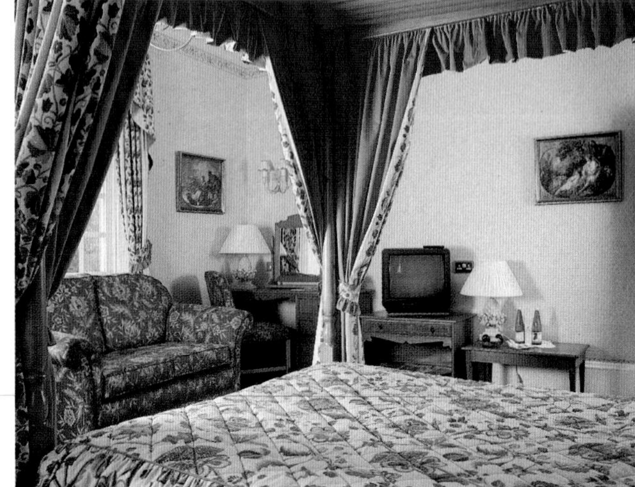

GIDLEIGH PARK

CHAGFORD, DEVON TQ13 8HH
TEL: 01647 432367 FAX: 01647 432574 E-MAIL: gidleighpark@gidleigh.co.uk

Gidleigh Park enjoys an outstanding international reputation among connoisseurs for its comfort and gastronomy. It has collected a clutch of top culinary awards including 2 Michelin stars for its imaginative cuisine and the Gidleigh Park wine list is one of the best in Britain. Service throughout the hotel is faultless. The en suite bedrooms – two of them in a converted chapel – are luxuriously furnished with antiques. The public rooms are elegantly appointed and during the cooler months, a fire burns merrily in the lounge's impressive fireplace. Set amid 45 secluded acres in the Teign Valley, Gidleigh Park is 11/2 miles from the nearest public road. Two croquet lawns, an all-weather tennis court, a bowling lawn and a splendid water garden can be found in the grounds. A 360 yard long, par 52 putting course designed by Peter Alliss was opened in 1995. Guests can swim in the river or explore Dartmoor on foot or in the saddle. There are 14 miles of trout, sea trout and salmon fishing, as well as golf facilities nearby. Gidleigh Park is a Relais et Châteaux member **Directions:** Approach from Chagford: go along Mill Street from Chagford Square. Fork right after 150 yards, cross into Holy Street at factory crossroads and follow lane for two miles Price Guide: (including dinner): Single £340–£440; double/twin £400–£500.

MILL END

DARTMOOR NATIONAL PARK, CHAGFORD, DEVON TQ13 8JN
TEL: 01647 432282 FAX: 01647 433106 E-MAIL: millendhotel@talk21.com

Gleaming white under slate grey roof tiles and with windows and doors opening onto a beautiful English country garden, Mill End is an idyllic hideaway in Dartmoor's National Park. The lawned garden with its wide, deeply shrubbed and colourful borders runs down to the languid waters of the River Teign where a water wheel slowly turns to the enjoyment of bankside loungers. Built in the mid 1700s the hotel was a former flour mill, and inside there are numerous little corner nooks, paintings and old photographs that imbue a feeling of seclusion, enhanced by the smell of wood smoke and polished wood. The delightful en suite bedrooms have undergone major refurbishment incorporating excellent décor, lovely fabrics and attractive local hand-crafted furniture. Plus, of course, every facility one would expect. The elegance of the dining room is matched by the delicious award-winning cuisine of chef Alan Lane. His dinner menus are full and varied; one shouldn't miss, for example, wild boar and duck terrine with apricot chutney followed by steamed fillet of turbot scented with elderflower and a chocolate and hazelnut praline truffle finished with 'Baileys' sauce. An 18-hole golf course is nearby and pony trekking and shooting can be arranged. **Directions:** From the M5 exit at junction 31 towards Okehampton. Take the A382 at Merrymount roundabout towards Moretonhampstead. Mill End is one the right. Price Guide: Single £56–£80; double/twin £75–£110.

THE CHELTENHAM PARK HOTEL

CIRENCESTER ROAD, CHARLTON KINGS, CHELTENHAM, GLOUCESTERSHIRE GL53 8EA
TEL: 01242 222021 FAX: 01242 254880 E-MAIL: cheltenhampark@paramount–hotels.co.uk

Set against the picturesque background of the rolling Cotswold hills, this elegant Georgian hotel rises high and majestically from beautifully lawned and flower-filled gardens ensconcing a tranquil lake. Whilst retaining echoes of its early heritage, The Cheltenham Park Hotel combines a relaxing and welcoming ambience with all the comforts expected by today's discerning visitor. The 144 en suite bedrooms are individually styled, tastefully furnished and have every facility to help occupants enjoy a comfortable and restful stay. Premium rooms have splendid views over the gardens and beyond to Lilley Brook Golf Course. Similar views are enjoyed by diners in the intimate Lakeside Restaurant where the best local produce is prepared with imagination and flair to create cuisine of international appeal. For relaxation there is a well equipped leisure club complete with heated swimming pool, gym, sauna, spa bath, steam room, solarium and health & beauty rooms . Fishing, quad biking, clay and air-rifle shooting can be arranged. Cheltenham, with its Regency architecture, attractive promenade, exclusive shops and famous racecourse is just a short drive away. Directions: Exit the M5 at junction 11a and follow the A417, the A436 and the A435 to Cheltenham. The hotel is on the left two miles south of the town. Price Guide: Single £103; double/twin from £131; suite £205.

144 MasterCard VISA AMERICAN EXPRESS M 350

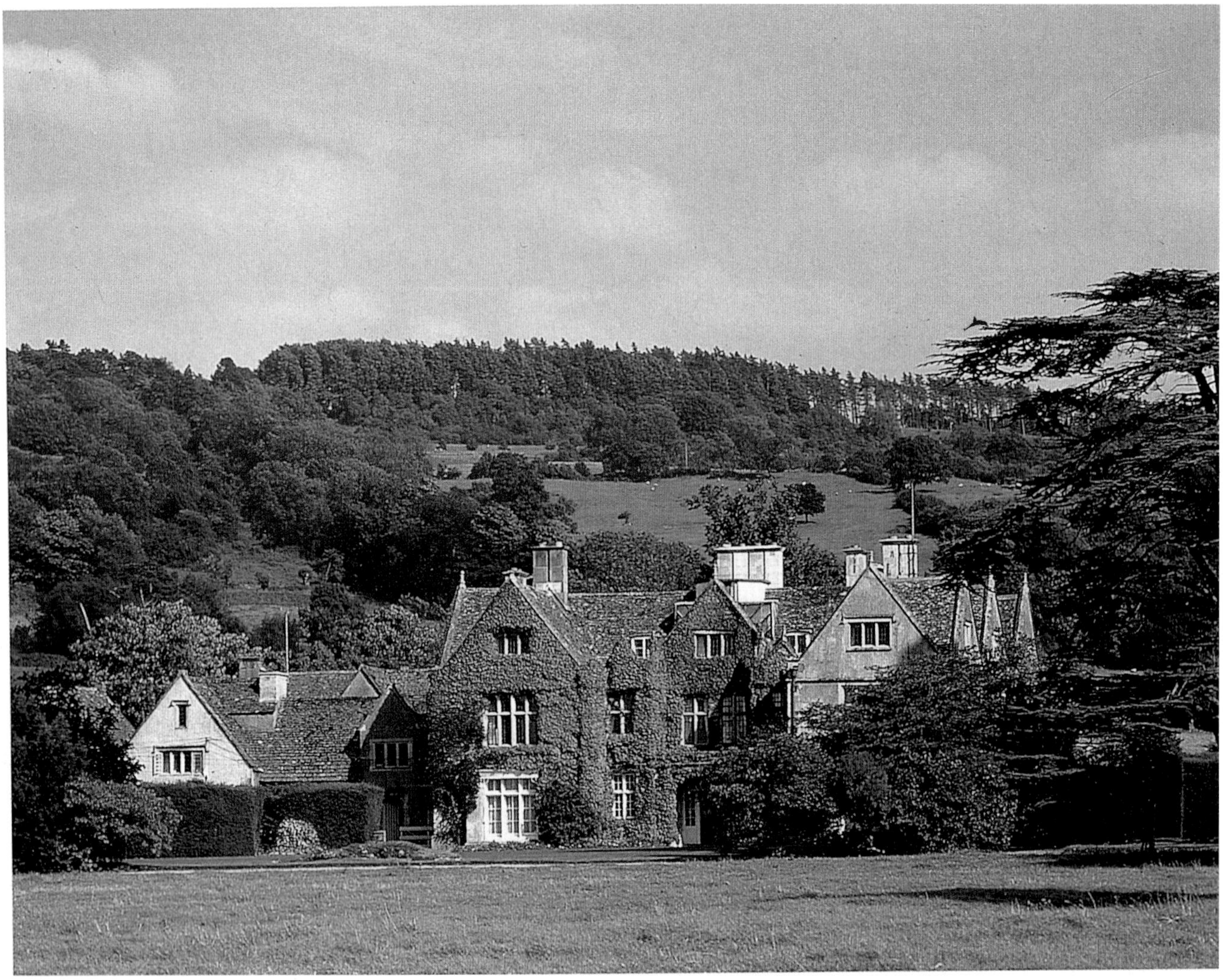

THE GREENWAY

SHURDINGTON, CHELTENHAM, GLOUCESTERSHIRE GL51 5UG
TEL: 01242 862352 FAX: 01242 862780 E-MAIL: greenway@btconnect.com

Set amidst gentle parkland with the rolling Cotswold hills beyond, The Greenway is an Elizabethan country house with a style that is uniquely its own – very individual and very special. Renowned for the warmth of its welcome, its friendly atmosphere and its immaculate personal service, The Greenway is the ideal place for total relaxation. The public rooms with their antique furniture and fresh flowers are elegant and spacious yet comfortable, with roaring log fires in winter and access to the formal gardens in summer. The 21 bedrooms all have private bathrooms and are individually decorated with co-ordinated colour schemes. Eleven of the rooms are located in the main house with a further ten rooms in the converted Georgian coach house immediately adjacent to the main building. The award-winning conservatory dining room overlooks the sunken garden and lily pond, providing the perfect backdrop to superb cuisine of international appeal complemented by an outstanding selection of wines. Situated in one of Britain's most charming areas, The Greenway is well placed for visiting the spa town of Cheltenham, the Cotswold villages and Shakespeare country. **Directions:** On the outskirts of Cheltenham off the A46 Cheltenham–Stroud road, 21/2 miles from the town centre. Price Guide: Single from £99; double/twin £150–£240.

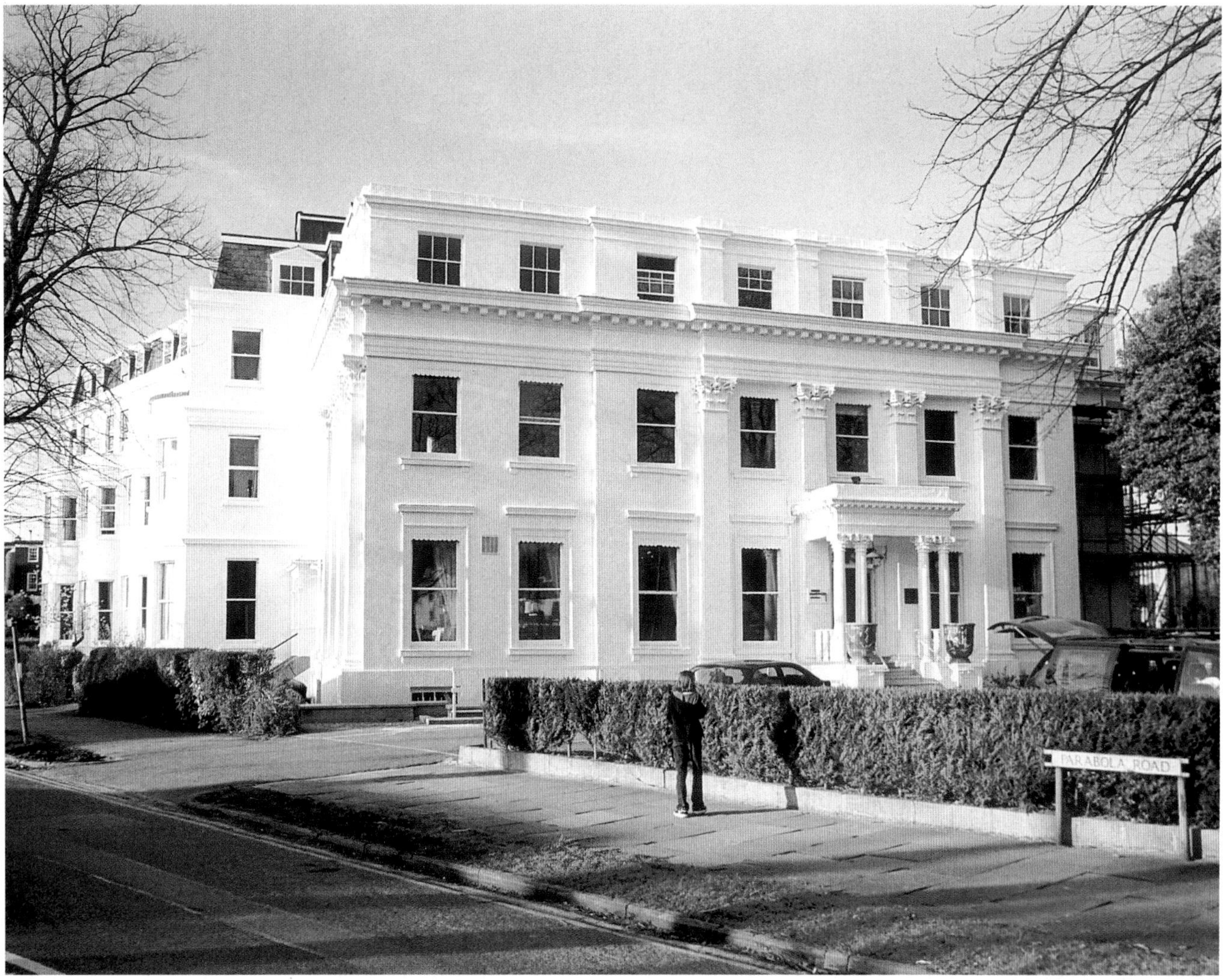

HOTEL KANDINSKY

BAYSHILL ROAD, MONTPELLIER, CHELTENHAM, GLOUCESTERSHIRE GL50 3AS
TEL: 01242 527788 FAX: 01242 226412 E-MAIL: info@hotelkandinsky.com

This smart Regency building houses the latest addition to Montpellier's hotel stock. With a contemporary approach to hotelkeeping, the Kandinsky provides a young feel to appeal to the young at heart. Aimed at both business and leisure guests it is a fun, stylish and comfortable place to stay. With slight tongue in cheek, the public areas are both buzzy and clubby with log fires providing that welcoming touch for those who simply wish to watch the world go by. A feature of the informal Cafe Paradiso is the brushwood oven in which Neapolitan pizzas are cooked to order, while salads from freshest organic produce are prepared at the table. The U-Bahn Club offering 50s style, music and exclusive membership free to hotel guests, is a perfect night venue. The bedrooms, unusual in their contemporary design, are comfortable and stylish with internationally inspired furnishings; many have six-foot beds. Bathrooms are sparkling and modern. Telephones with dataport facilities include a magic eye facility linked to the nightclub. Cheltenham, with its fine shopping and celebrated Racecourse stands at the gateway to the Cotswolds with excellent rail links from London and the West Country. **Directions:** From M5 J11 take A40 into town centre. From Lansdown Road, past Lansdown Crescent, follow left for Parabola Road: the hotel is on the corner. Price Guide: Single £75; double/twin £89; suite £99– £120.

Hotel On The Park

EVESHAM ROAD, CHELTENHAM, GLOUCESTERSHIRE GL52 2AH
TEL: 01242 518898 FAX: 01242 511526 E-MAIL: stay@hotelonthepark.co.uk

Set in the Regency town of Cheltenham, Hotel on the Park is an attractive town house hotel which combines the attentive service of bygone times with an excellent standard of accommodation. The impressive façade, dominated by the grand pillared doorway, hints at the splendour that lies inside. Each of the 12 bedrooms are individually styled and decorated with interesting antiques and exquisite fabrics. Every possible comfort has been provided. Throughout the property the theme of understated elegance prevails and this is truly evident in The Bacchanalian Restaurant, with its high ceilings and beautiful hand-detailed cornice work. Guests may enjoy the glorious views of Pittville Park whilst sampling the inspired creations from the extensive menu along with a selection from the detailed wine list. The well-appointed Library is an ideal venue for board meetings or seminars. Special occasions including private banquets or wedding receptions can be arranged. Synonymous with National Hunt Racing, the spa town of Cheltenham is particularly popular during the racing season and hosts the Gold Cup. The town is also renowned for its Regency architecture, attractive promenade and exclusive boutiques. Historic properties, museums and theatres abound whilst other activities include golf, horse-riding, rambling and exploring the Cotswolds.

Directions: Opposite Pittville Park, 5 mins walk from town centre.

Price Guide: Single from £84.75; double/twin from £111.

12 MasterCard VISA AMERICAN EXPRESS M 18 8

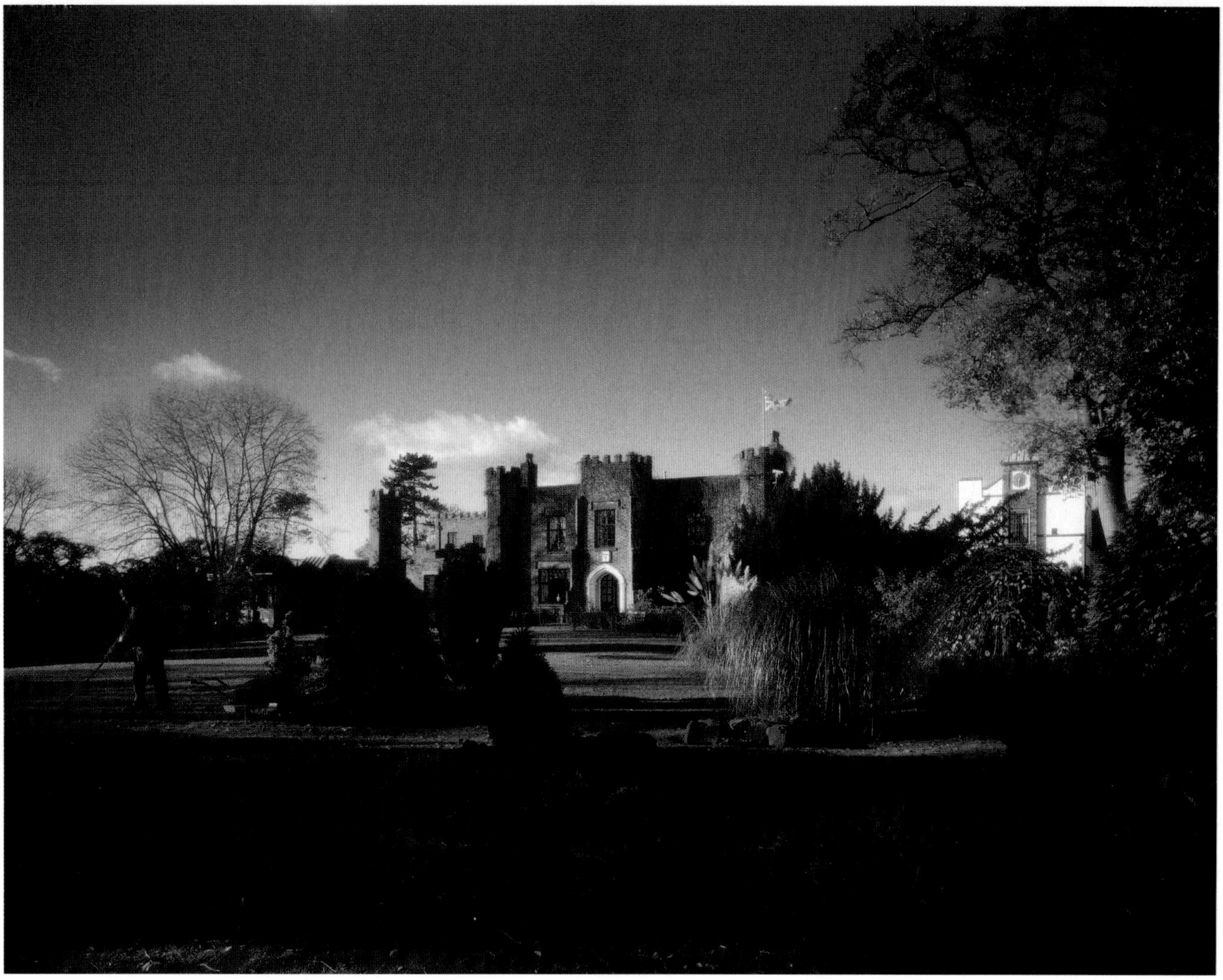

THE CHESTER CRABWALL MANOR

PARKGATE ROAD, MOLLINGTON, CHESTER, CHESHIRE CH1 6NE
TEL: 01244 851666 FAX: 01244 851400 E-MAIL: crabwallmanor@marstonhotels.com

Crabwall Manor can be traced back to Saxon England, prior to the Norman Conquest. Set in 11 acres of mature woodland on the outskirts of Chester, this Grade II listed manor house has a relaxed ambience, which is enhanced by staff who combine attentive service with friendliness and care. The interior boasts elegant drapes complemented by pastel shades which lend a freshness to the décor of the spacious lounge and reception areas, while the log fires in the inglenook fireplaces adds warmth. The hotel has won several awards for their renowned cuisine, complemented by an excellent selection of fine wines and outstanding levels of accommodation. Four meeting suites and a further ten syndicate rooms are available. The Refections leisure club features a 17 metre pool, gymnasium, dance studio, sauna, spa pool, juice bar. Those wishing to be pampered will enjoy the three beauty treatment rooms. 100 yards from the hotel guests have reduced green fees at Mollington Grange 18 hole championship golf course. The ancient city of Chester with its many attractions is only 1½ miles away **Directions:** Go to end of M56, ignoring signs to Chester. Follow signs to Queensferry and North Wales, taking A5117 to next roundabout. Left onto A540, towards Chester for 2 miles. Crabwall Manor is on the right. Price Guide: Single from £125; double/twin from £135–£150; suite from £160–£250. Weekend breaks available.

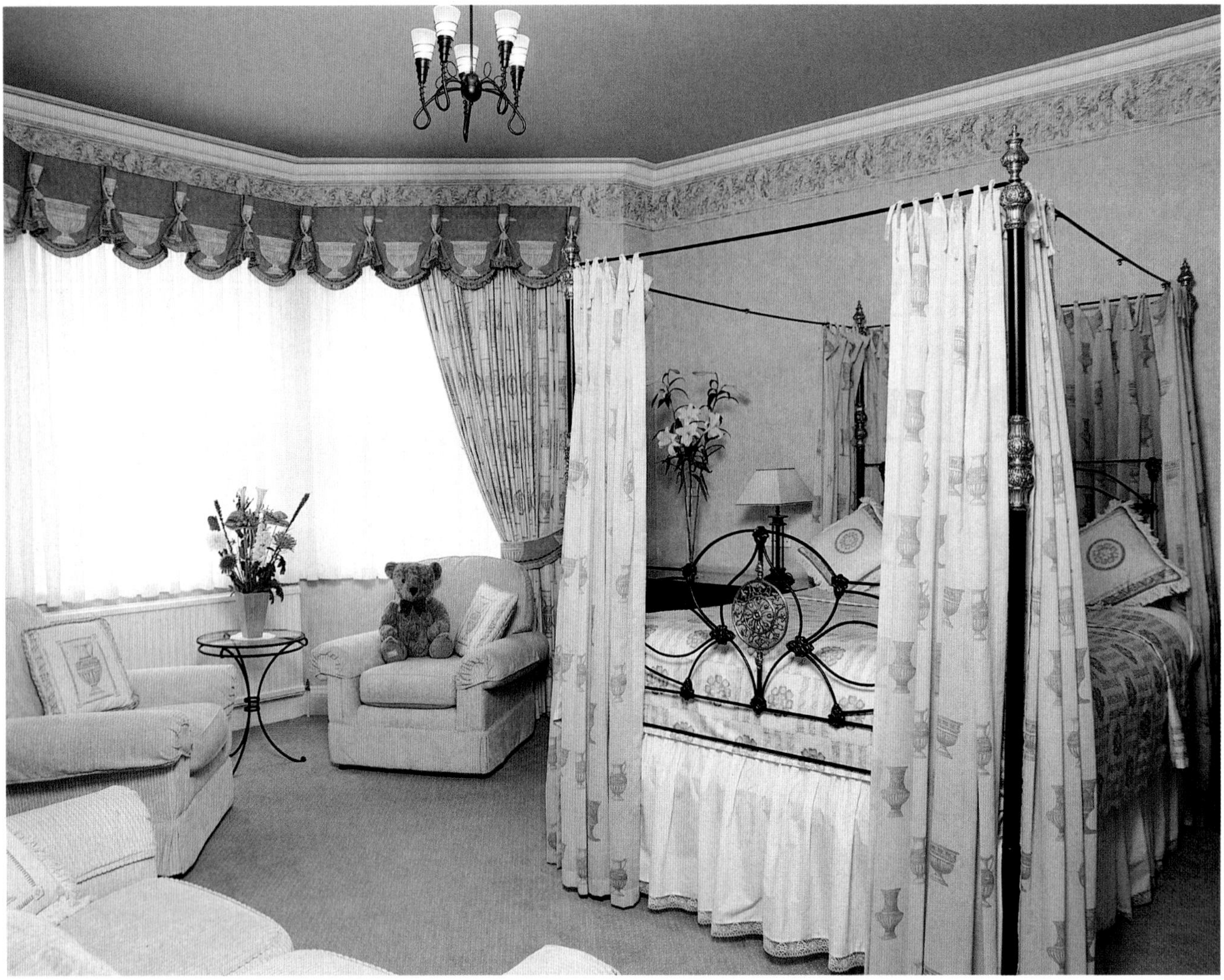

GREEN BOUGH HOTEL

60 HOOLE ROAD, CHESTER, CHESHIRE CH2 3NL
TEL: 01244 326241 FAX: 01244 326265 E-MAIL: greenboughhotel@cwcom.net

A late Victorian town house, the Green Bough Hotel is conveniently situated in the ancient city of Chester. Bought by Philip and Janice Martin in 1997, the hotel has been completely refurbished and redecorated; a Roman theme is evident throughout. This totally non-smoking hotel perfectly combines the convenience of modern facilities with the charm of period features and furnishings. Most bedrooms have antique beds, whilst many of the original architectural features of the building and the adjoining Victorian Lodge bedroom wing remain intact. The Olive Tree restaurant is presided over by Philip Martin who trained at the Savoy Hotel, working with the renowned Maître Chef de Cuisine Silvino S Trompetto. The menu, is complemented by a wine list of a range and quality that belies the relatively small size of the hotel. The Green Bough provides an excellent base for exploring the city of Chester and hires bicycles for this purpose. It is also ideal for those venturing further afield into the beautiful Cheshire countryside and Snowdonia. Places of interest in Chester include the cathedral, river, race course, and the Blue Planet Aquarium and Chester Zoo. **Directions:** Leave M53 at Jct12. Take A56 into Chester for 1 mile. The Green Bough Hotel is on the right. Price Guide: Single £75–£105; double/twin £95–£135; suites £150.

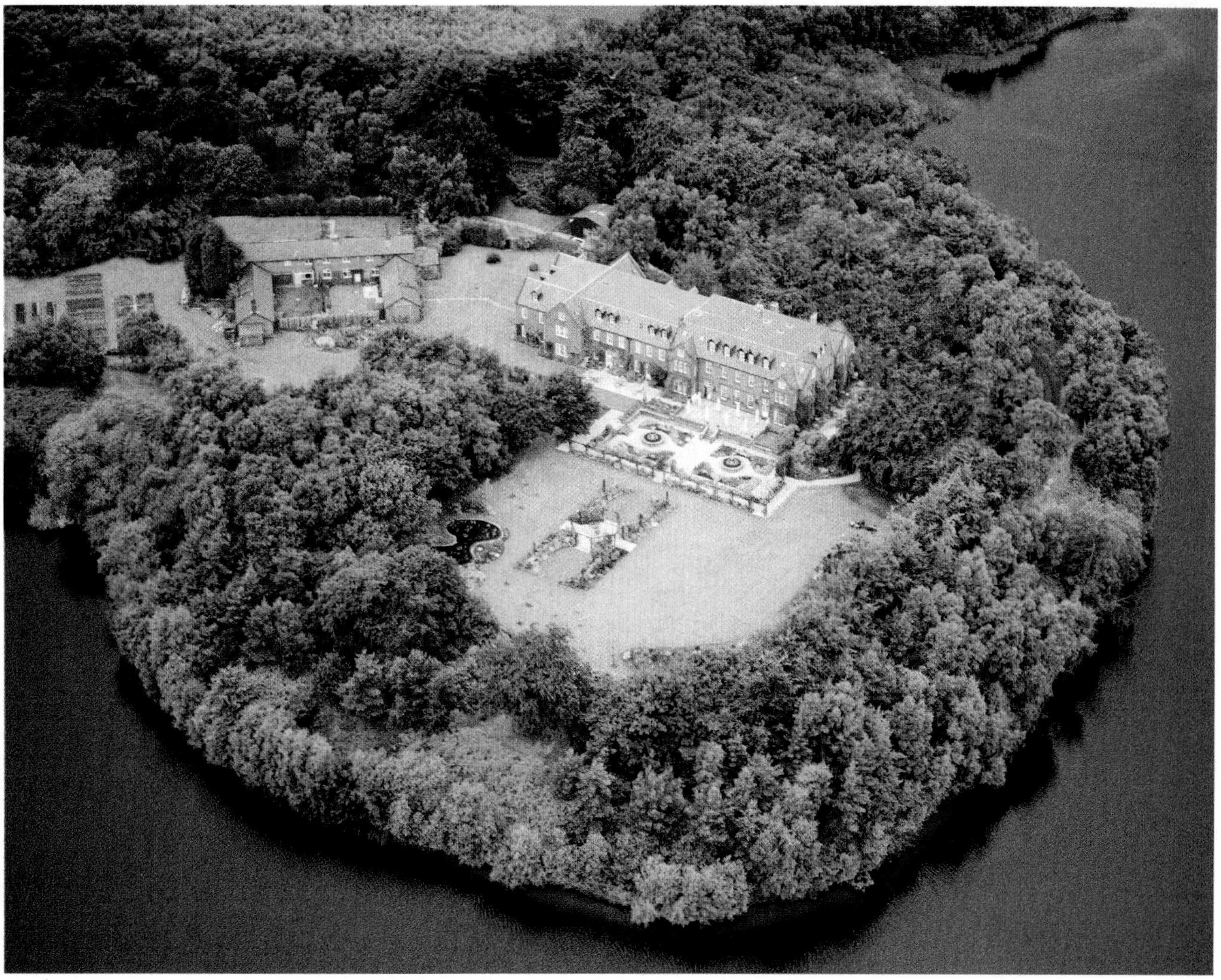

Nunsmere Hall

TARPORLEY ROAD, OAKMERE, NORTHWICH, CHESHIRE CW8 2ES
TEL: 01606 889100 FAX: 01606 889055 E-MAIL: reservations@nunsmere.co.uk

Set in peaceful Cheshire countryside and surrounded on three sides by a lake, Nunsmere Hall epitomises the elegant country manor where superior standards of hospitality still exist. Wood panelling, antique furniture, exclusive fabrics, Chinese lamps and magnificent chandeliers evoke an air of luxury. The 30 bedrooms and 6 suites most with spectacular views of the lake and gardens, are beautifully appointed with king-size beds, comfortable breakfast seating and marbled bathrooms containing soft bathrobes and toiletries. The Brocklebank, Delamere and Oakmere business suites are air-conditioned, soundproofed and offer excellent facilities for boardroom meetings, private dining and seminars. The Restaurant has a reputation for fine food and uses only fresh seasonal produce. Twice County Restaurant of the Year in the Good Food Guide. A snooker room is available and there are several championship golf courses nearby. Oulton Park racing circuit and the Cheshire Polo Club are next door. Golf pitch and putt is available in the grounds. Archery and air rifle shooting by arrangement. Although secluded, Nunsmere is convenient for major towns and routes. AA 3 Red Star and Two Rosettes. **Directions:** Leave M6 at junction 19, take A556 to Chester (approximately 12 miles). Turn left onto A49. Hotel is 1 mile on left Price Guide: Single £100–£160; double/twin £160–£240; suite from £250.

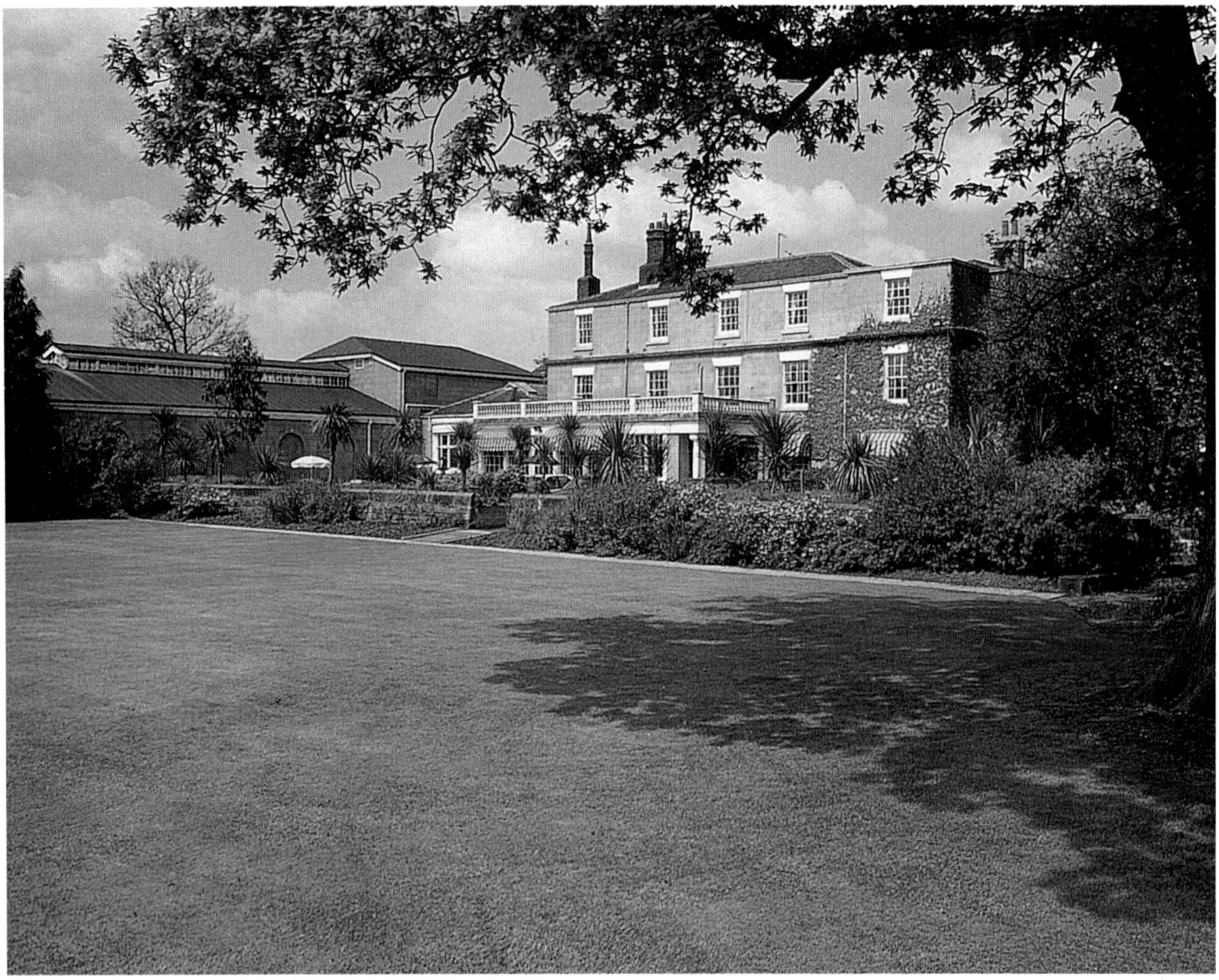

ROWTON HALL HOTEL

WHITCHURCH ROAD, ROWTON, CHESTER, CHESHIRE CH3 6AD
TEL: 01244 335262 FAX: 01244 335464 E-MAIL: rowtonhall@rowtonhall.co.uk

Set in over 8 acres of award-winning gardens, Rowton Hall is located at the end of a leafy lane, only 3 miles from Chester city centre. Built as a private residence in 1779, it retains many of its original features, including extensive oak panelling, a self-supporting hand-carved staircase, an original Inglenook fireplace and an elegant Robert Adam fireplace. Each luxury bedroom is individually and tastefully decorated with attention to detail, and is equipped with every modern amenity, including private bathroom, satellite television, direct dial telephone with modem points, personal safe, luxury bathrobes, trouser press and hostess tray. Dining in the oak-panelled Langdale Restaurant is a delight; every dish is carefully created by Executive Chef, Anthony O'Hare, who uses the finest ingredients from local markets and the Hall's gardens to produce exquisite cuisine. Guests can enjoy the indoor Health Club and relax in the Jacuzzi, steam room or sauna. For the more energetic, a workout in the well-equipped gymnasium and dance studio is available and 2 floodlit all-weather tennis courts are within the grounds. Four main conference and banqueting suites make the Hall an ideal venue for meetings, weddings, private dining or conferences and corporate events for up to 200 guests Marquee events can be arranged in the gardens. **Directions:** From the centre of Chester, take A41 towards Whitchurch. After 3 miles, turn right to Rowton village. The hotel is in the centre of the village Price Guide: Single £92–£140; double/twin £114–£175; suites £224.

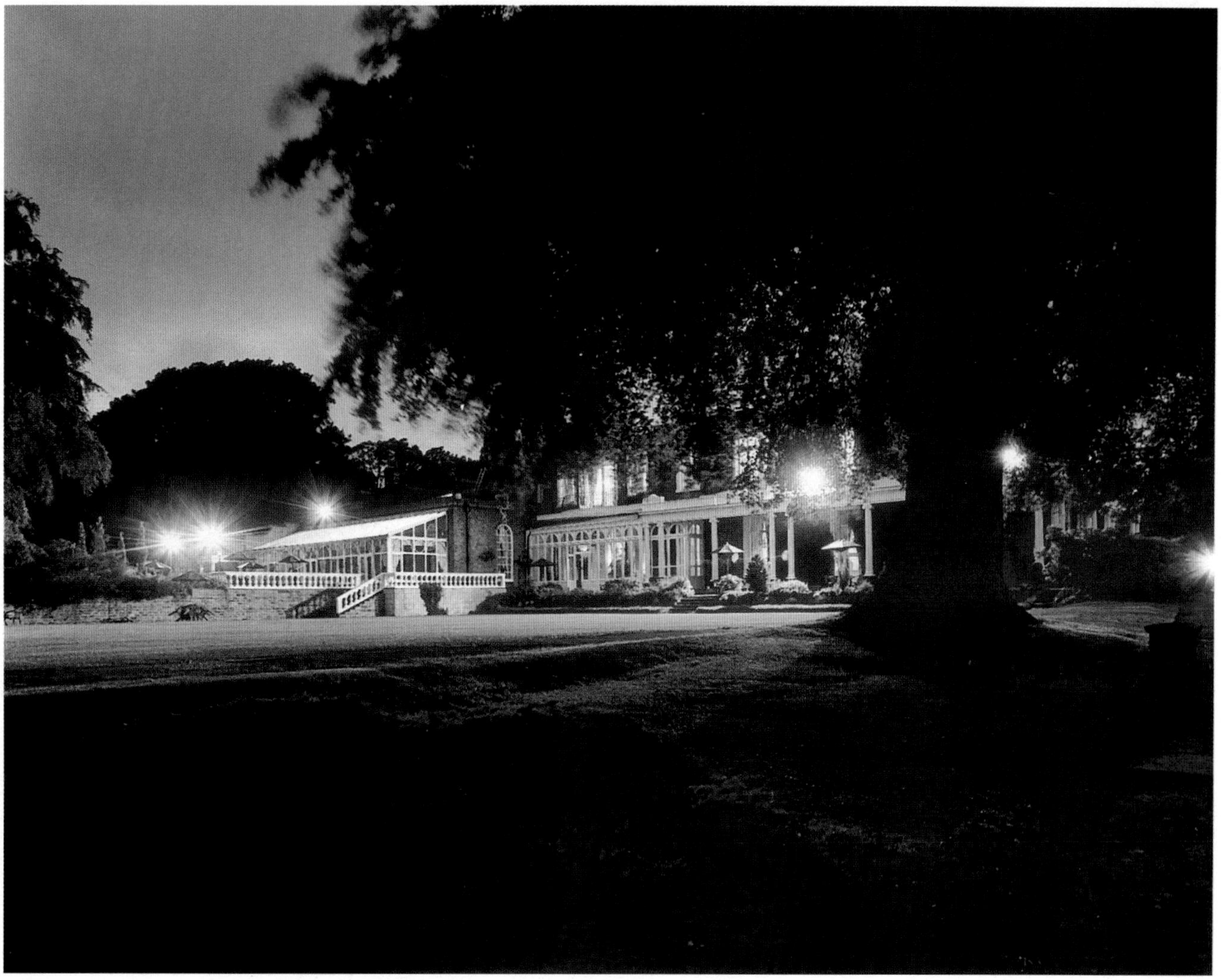

Ringwood Hall Hotel

RINGWOOD ROAD, BRIMINGTON, CHESTERFIELD, DERBYSHIRE S43 1DQ
TEL: 01246 280077 FAX: 01246 472241

Since its purchase by Lyric Hotels in November 1999, the Ringwood Hall Hotel has undergone major refurbishment. Sensitive and tasteful, the transformation has created one of the finest country house hotels in North East Derbyshire. The charm and character of the Grade II exterior is continued inside with an impressive reception area featuring intricate plaster frieze work, a galleried landing and glazed dome ceiling. 29 acres of gardens and parkland provide a magnificent backdrop, and even the original Victorian gardens are being carefully restored and replanted to provide vegetables and herbs for the hotel kitchen. Finest local produce is used for the extensive menus in the "Expressions" Restaurant. The hotel offers numerous conference packages and provides a wonderful setting for wedding receptions and civil ceremonies. Staff are on hand to assist in planning events. Ringwood Hall sits on the brink of the Peak District, and offers plenty of opportunities to explore the surrounding area. Families can enjoy trips to theme parks such as Alton Towers and The Wind in the Willows Exhibition, while those with an interest in history can soak up the past at the Chesterfield Museum, Hardwick Hall and Bolsover Castle. An impressive array of local events such as the Chatsworth Country Fair take place through the year **Directions:** From Jct 30 M1 take the A619 towards Chesterfield, passing through Mastin Moor and Staveley. Continue on A619 and rising out of the valley the hotel is set back on the left. Price Guide: Single from £60; double/twin from £70; suite from £98.

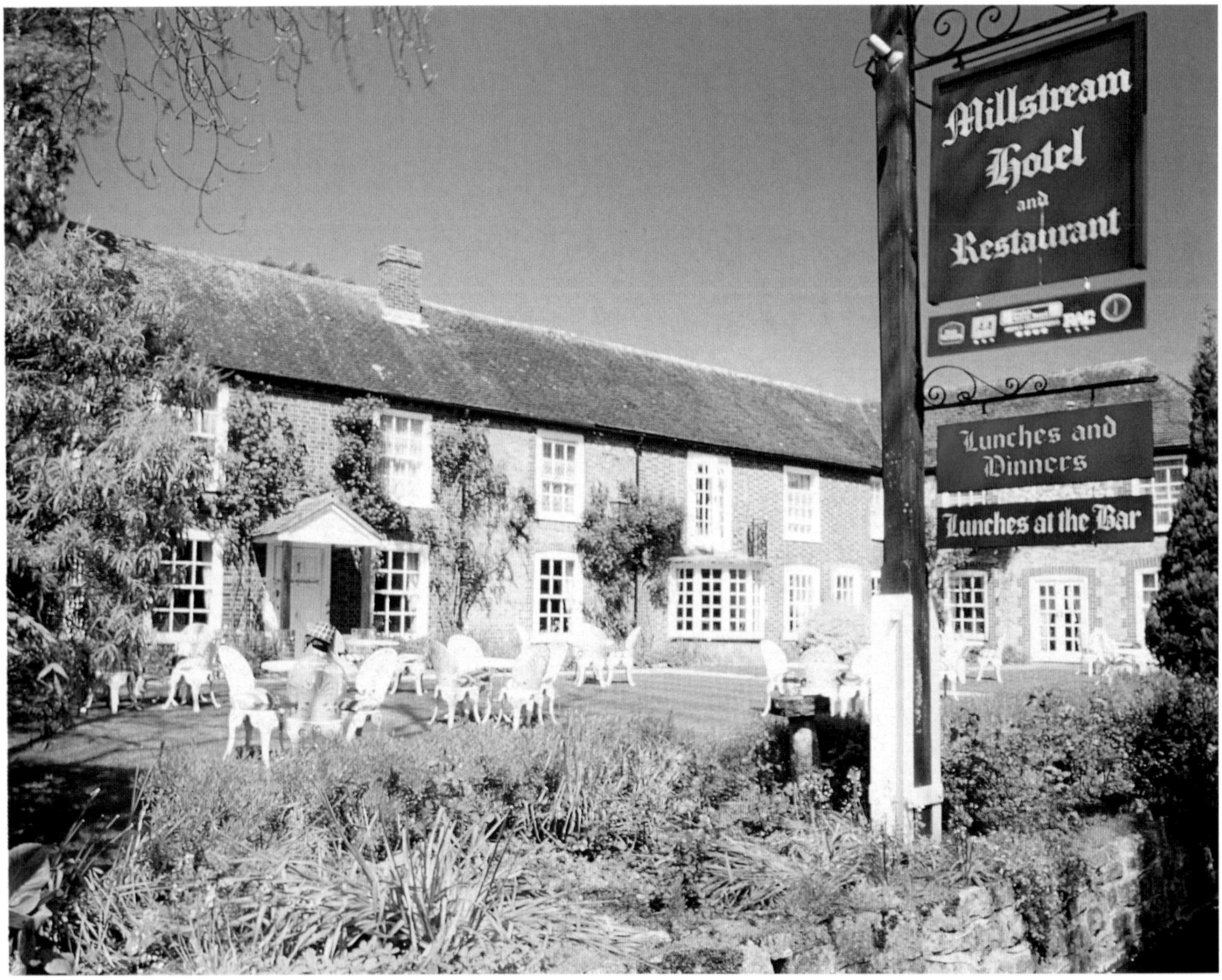

The Millstream Hotel

BOSHAM, NR CHICHESTER, WEST SUSSEX PO18 8HL
TEL: 01243 573234 FAX: 01243 573459 E-MAIL: info@millstream–hotel.co.uk

A village rich in heritage, Bosham is depicted in the Bayeux Tapestry and is associated with King Canute, whose daughter is buried in the local Saxon church. Moreover, sailors from the world over navigate their way to Bosham, which is a yachtsman's idyll on the banks of Chichester Harbour. The Millstream consists of a restored 18th-century malthouse and adjoining cottages linked to The Grange, a small English manor house. Individually furnished bedrooms are complemented by chintz fabrics and pastel décor. Period furniture, a grand piano and bowls of freshly cut flowers feature in the drawing room. A stream meanders past the front of the beautiful gardens. Cross the bridge to the two delightful new suites in "Waterside" the thatched cottage. Whatever the season, care is taken to ensure that the composition and presentation of the dishes reflect high standards. An appetising luncheon menu is offered and includes local seafood specialities such as: dressed Selsey crab, the Millstream's own home-smoked salmon and grilled fresh fillets of sea bass. During the winter, good-value 'Hibernation Breaks' are available. **Directions:** South of the A259 between Chichester and Havant. Price Guide: Single £80; double/twin £125; suite £165.

35 MasterCard VISA AMERICAN EXPRESS M 20

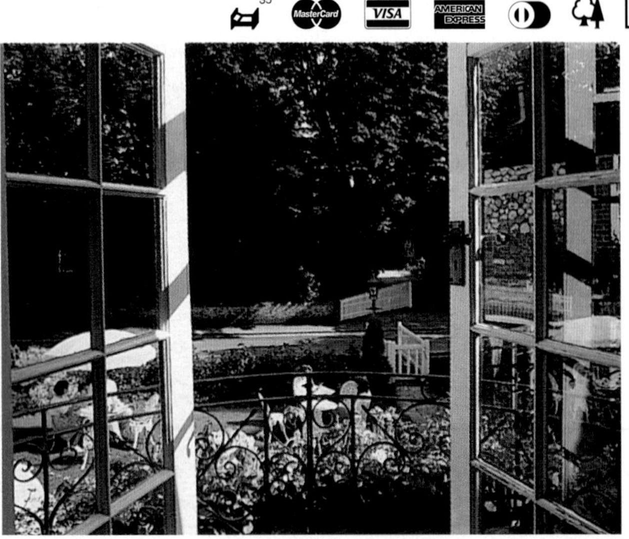

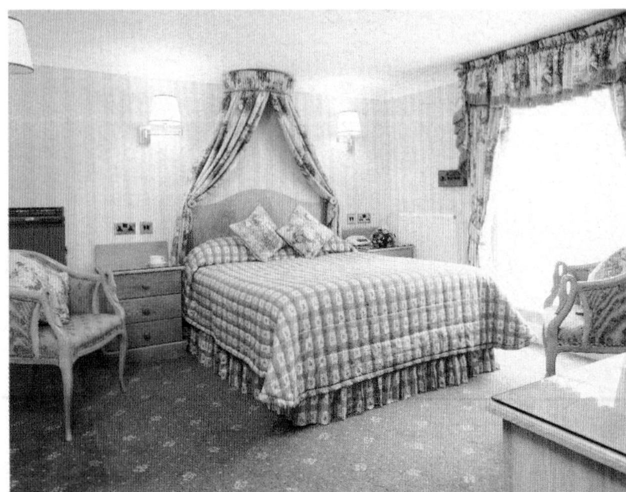

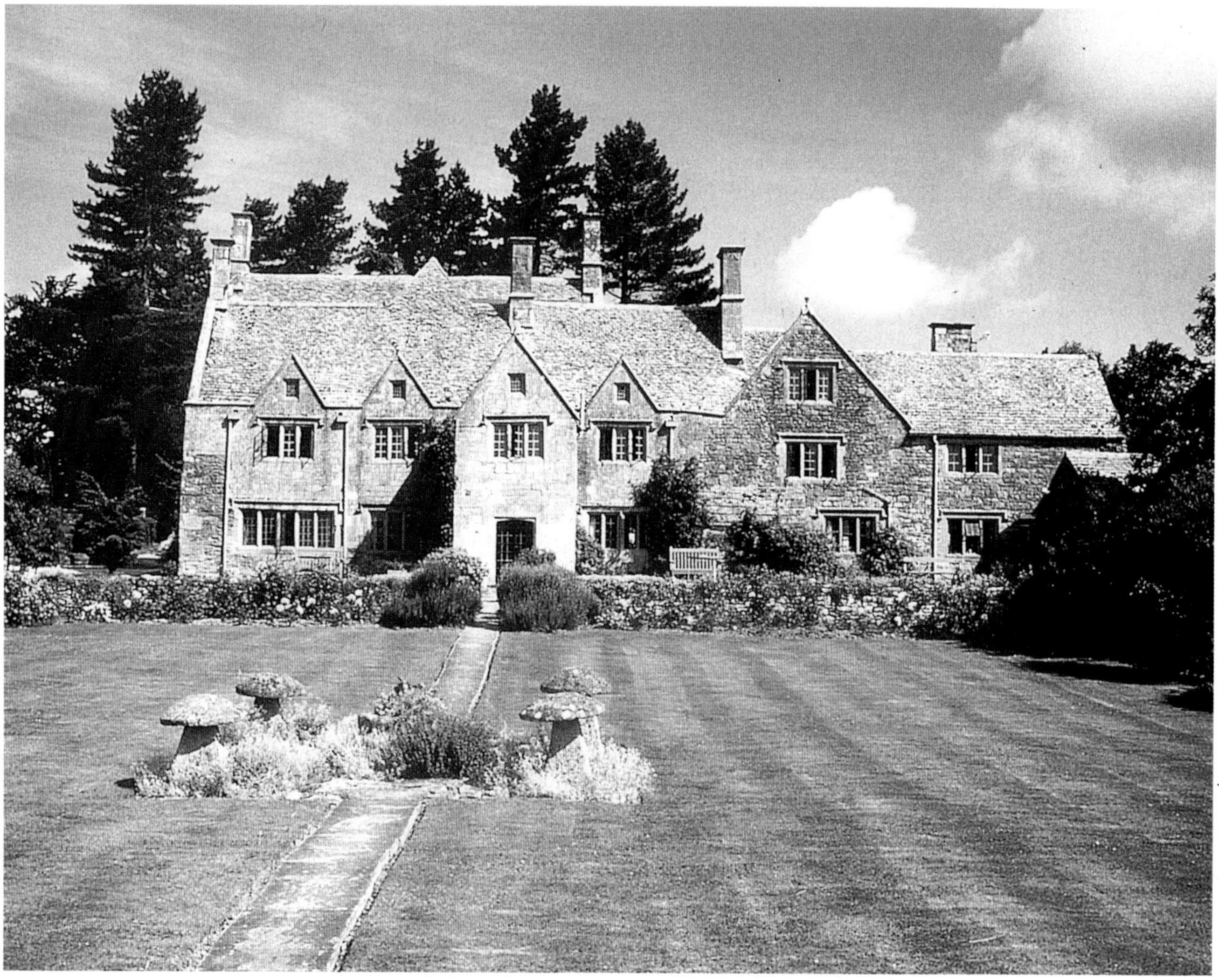

Charingworth Manor

NR CHIPPING CAMPDEN, GLOUCESTERSHIRE GL55 6NS
TEL: 01386 593555 FAX: 01386 593353 E-MAIL: charingworthmanor@englishrosehotels.co.uk

The ancient manor of Charingworth lies amid the gently rolling Cotswold countryside, just a few miles from the historic towns of Chipping Campden and Broadway. Beautiful old stone buildings everywhere recall the flourishing wool trade that gave the area its wealth. The 14th century manor house overlooks its own 50 acre grounds and offers peace and enthralling views. Inside, Charingworth is a historic patchwork of intimate public rooms with log fires burning during the colder months. There are 26 individually designed bedrooms, all furnished with antiques and fine fabrics. Outstanding cuisine is regarded as being of great importance and guests at Charingworth are assured of imaginative dishes. Great emphasis is placed on using only the finest produce and the AA has awarded the cuisine a Rosette. There is an all-weather tennis court within the grounds, while inside, a beautiful swimming pool, sauna, steam room, solarium and gym are available, allowing guests to relax and unwind. Warwick Castle, Hidcote Manor Gardens, Batsford Arboretum, Stratford-upon-Avon, Oxford and Cheltenham are all within easy reach. Short break rates are available on request. **Directions:** Charingworth Manor is on the B4035 between Chipping Campden and Shipston-on-Stour. Price Guide: (including full breakfast) Single from £105; double/twin from £170.

Cotswold House

HIGH STREET, CHIPPING CAMPDEN, GLOUCESTERSHIRE GL55 6AN
TEL: 01386 840330 FAX: 01386 840310 E-MAIL: reception@cotswoldhouse.com

Chipping Campden is a nostalgic Cotswold town, unspoilt by the twentieth century, and Cotswold House is a splendid 17th century mansion facing the town square, impressive with colonnades flanking the front door and built in the lovely soft local stone. The interior has been sensitively decorated and modernised so there is no distraction from the graceful pillared archway and staircase. Lovely antiques, fine paintings and fabrics reminiscent of the Regency era blend easily with comfortable sofas in the elegant drawing room. The bedrooms are very individual, with memorabilia appropriate to their theme, but all are peaceful, decorated in harmonious colours and have 'country house' style furnishings. Cotswold House is deservedly proud of its kitchen, which has won many accolades. The attractive Garden Room Restaurant has a splendid menu and a cellar book of 150 wines. Informal meals are in Hicks' Brasserie. Private functions and small conferences can be held in the secluded Courtyard Room. Guests enjoy exploring Chipping Campden's intriguing shops and alleyways. The hotel is a superb base for Stratford-on-Avon, Oxford **Directions:** Chipping Campden is 2 miles north-east of A44, on the B4081. The hotel has parking facilities. Price Guide: Single from £85; double/twin from £140; four poster from £190.

15 MasterCard VISA AMERICAN EXPRESS M 40 6

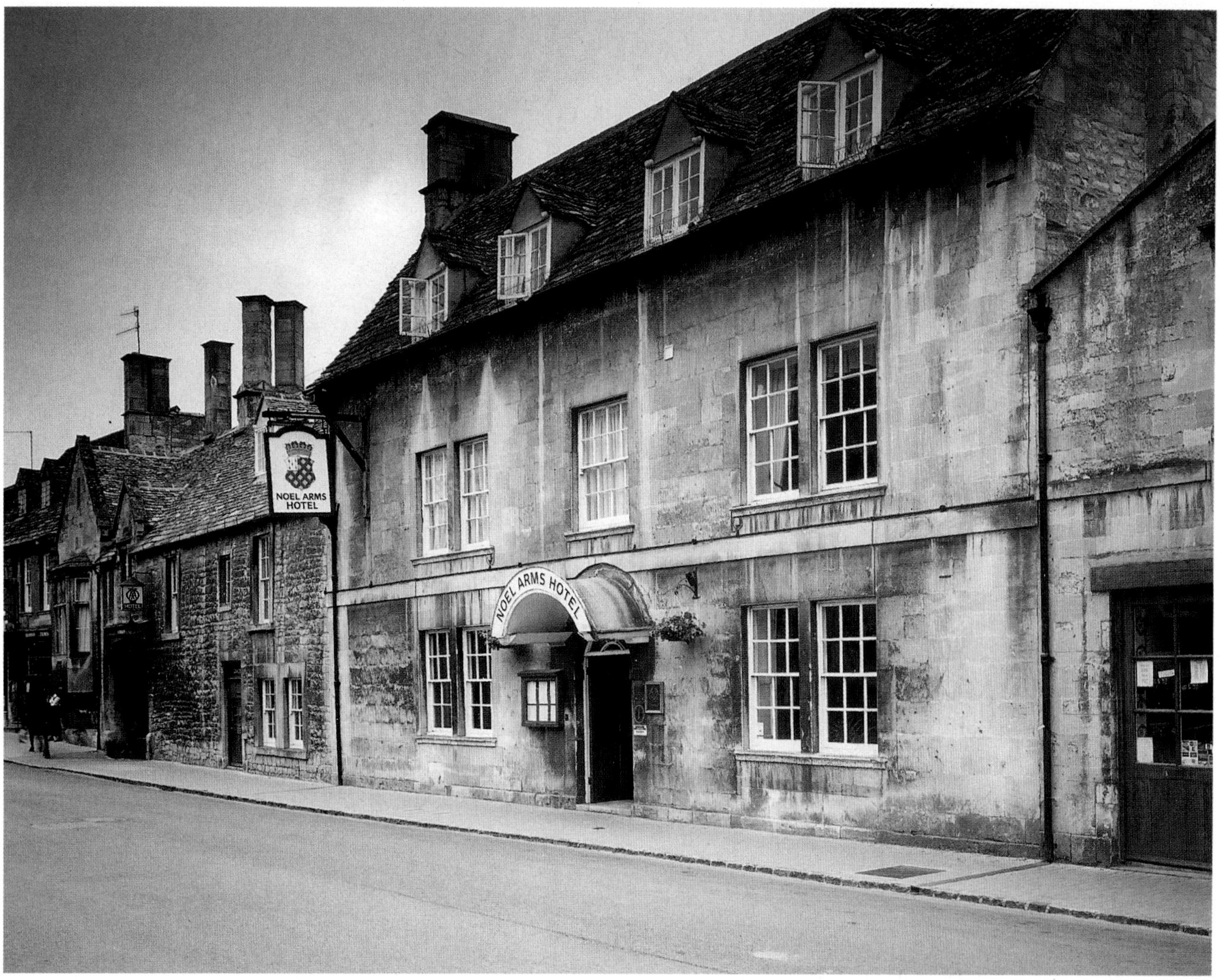

THE NOEL ARMS HOTEL

HIGH STREET, CHIPPING CAMPDEN, GLOUCESTERSHIRE GL55 6AT
TEL: 01386 840317 FAX: 01386 841136 E-MAIL: bookings@cotswold-inns-hotels.co.uk

A long tradition of hospitality awaits you at the Noel Arms Hotel. In 1651 the future Charles II rested here after his Scottish army was defeated by Cromwell at the battle of Worcester and for centuries the hotel has entertained visitors to the ancient and unspoilt, picturesque Cotswold Village of Chipping Campden. Many reminders of the past; fine antique furniture, swords, shields and other mementoes can be found around the hotel. There are 26 en suite bedrooms in either the main house or in the tastefully constructed new wing, some of which boast luxurious antique four-poster beds and all offering the standards you expect from a country hotel. The impressive oak panelled, restaurant, awarded 2 AA Rosettes, offers an excellent menu including a seasonal selection of fresh local produce. You may be tempted to choose from the extensive range of bar snacks available in the conservatory or Dovers Bar. The fine selection of wines from around the world are delicious accompaniments to any meal. Try some of the traditional cask ales and keg beers. Browse around the delightful array of shops in Chipping Campden or many of the enchanting honey-coloured Cotswold Villages, Hidcote Manor Gardens, Cheltenham Spa, Worcester, Oxford and Stratford-upon-Avon which are all close by. **Directions:** The Noel Arms is in the centre of Chipping Campden, which is on the B4081, 2 miles east of the A44 Price Guide: Single £75; double £115–£135.

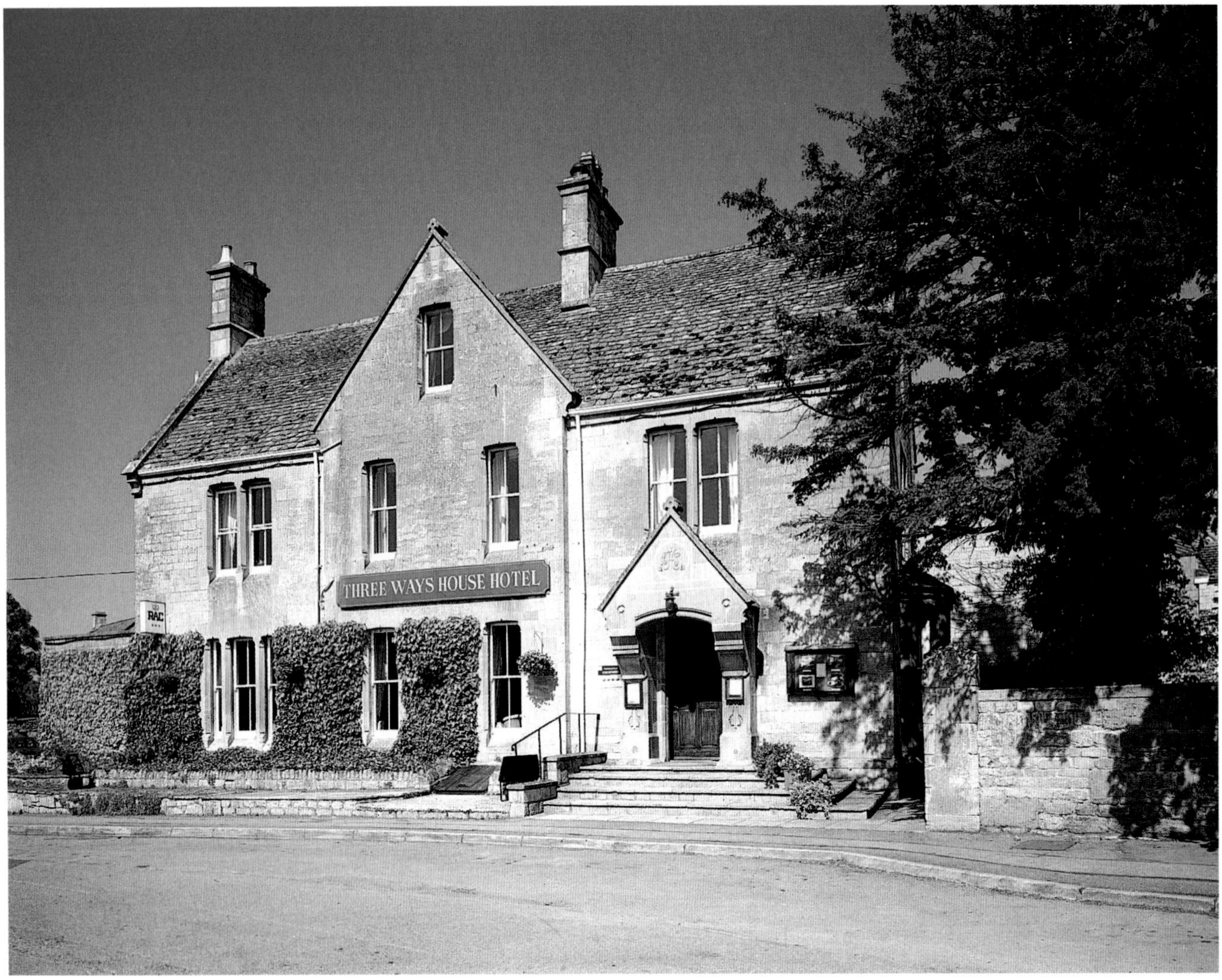

THREE WAYS HOUSE HOTEL

CHIPPING CAMPDEN, GLOUCESTERSHIRE GL55 6SB

TEL: 01386 438429 FAX: 01386 438118 E-MAIL: threeways@puddingclub.com

Set in the quaint village of Mickleton amidst picturesque Cotswolds countryside, Three Ways House was constructed in 1870 and opened as a hotel in the early 1900s. Many vestiges of the past are evident throughout the interior and when combined with modern additions, the result is a most charming property. The pleasant owners and their attentive staff provide a friendly, unobtrusive service. The 41 bedrooms, all of which offer en suite facilities, are well-appointed and feature a range of modern facilities. There is a good choice of accommodation including interlinked rooms designed for family use and rooms suitable for those with mobility problems. The house is the 'Home of the Pudding Club', and features some unique pudding-themed bedrooms such as the Spotted Dick and Custard Bedroom (as featured below). Gastronomic delights, of course, include mouthwatering traditional puddings such as syrup sponge and spotted dick or the more unusual Lord Randalls pudding. Those without a sweet tooth are also well-catered for at the Randalls Bar Brasserie. With its enchanting fire and Victorian tile floor, the ambience is intimate yet informal. Fresh produce from the Vale of Evesham, the village butcher's home-made sausages and Cotswold yoghurt are some of the many delights to be savoured here. **Directions:** Three Ways House is located on the B4632. Price Guide: Single £75; double/twin £105; theme room £125.

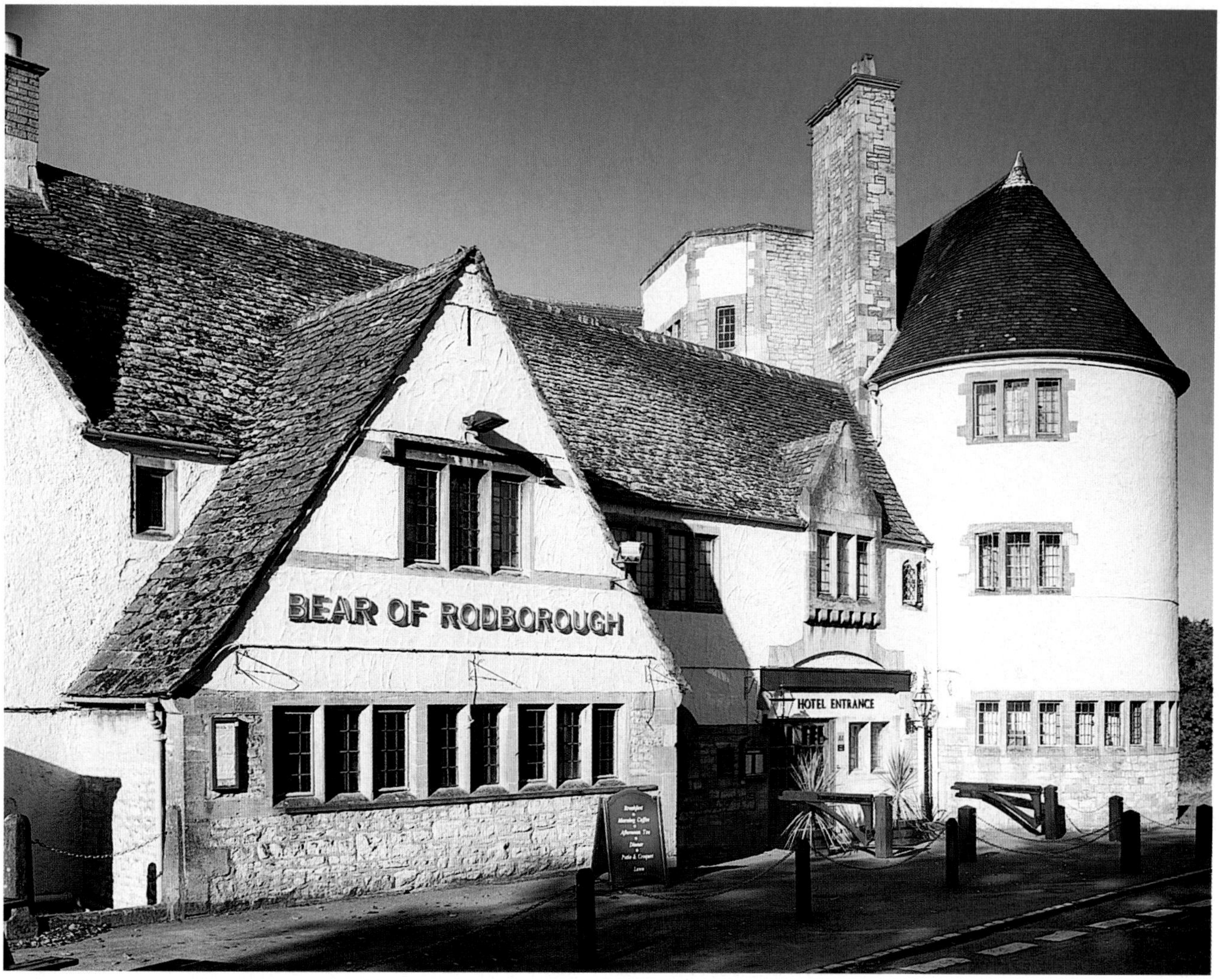

The Bear Of Rodborough

RODBOROUGH COMMON, STROUD, NR CIRENCESTER, GLOUCESTERSHIRE GL5 5DE
TEL: 01453 878522 FAX: 01453 872523 E-MAIL: bookings@cotswold-inns-hotels.co.uk

This 17th century former Ale House offers comfortable accommodation in an area of outstanding beauty. Nestling on the top of a steep hill, The Bear of Rodborough is situated in the verdant landscape of the western Cotswolds, described by the author, Laurie Lee, as "vegetative virginity". The inn has recently undergone a careful and precise restoration, at the request of the new owners, yet many of its past features such as the original archway entrance have been retained. The refurbished bedrooms are exquisite, adorned with plush carpets and beautiful fabrics. All have en suite facilities and several thoughtful extras. The superb bar, popular with the locals, is renowned for its large selection of traditional beers. Elegantly furnished, the restaurant is enhanced by the ceiling beams with a 'running bear' design. Specialities include the full English breakfast, made with fresh local produce, whilst the light luncheons and sumptuous dinners must also be savoured. Special breaks include the charming two day 'Cider with Rosie' breaks, based on the famous novel by Laurie Lee. Badger breaks designed for those with a passion for wildlife give an insight into the behavioural patterns of these fascinating creatures. **Directions:** The nearest motorway is the M5, junction 13. Price Guide: Single £75–£95; double/twin £120; suite £160.

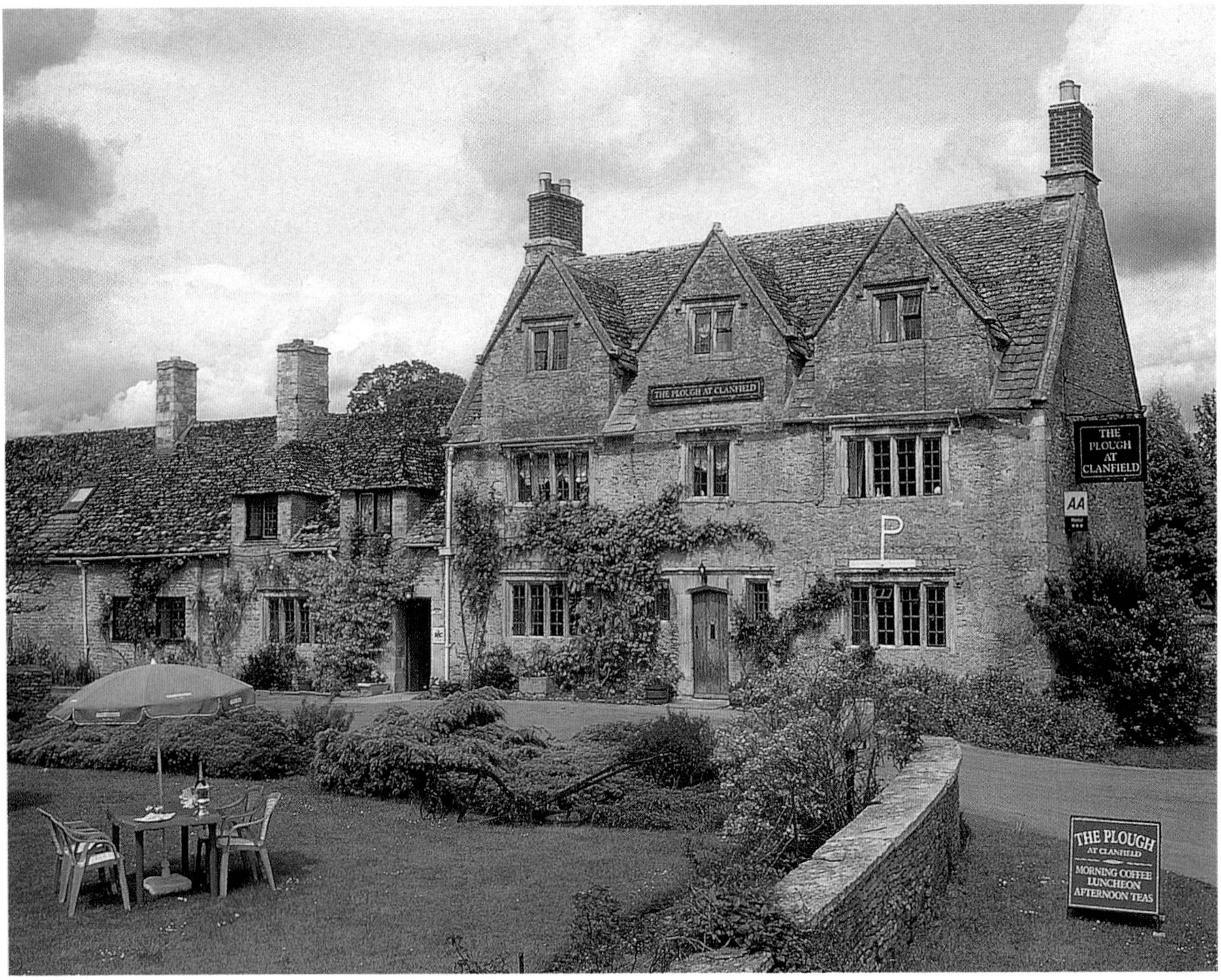

THE PLOUGH AT CLANFIELD

BOURTON ROAD, CLANFIELD, OXFORDSHIRE OX18 2RB

TEL: 01367 81022 FAX: 01367 810596 E-MAIL: ploughatclanfield@hotmail.com

The Plough at Clanfield is an idyllic hideaway for the romantic at heart. Set on the edge of the village of Clanfield, typical of the Oxfordshire Cotswolds, The Plough dates from 1560 and is a fine example of well-preserved Elizabethan architecture. The hotel is owned and personally run by John and Rosemary Hodges, who have taken great care to preserve the charm and character of this historic building. As there are only 12 bedrooms, guests can enjoy an intimate atmosphere and attentive, personal service. All the bedrooms are beautifully appointed to the highest standard and all have en suite bathrooms. At the heart of the hotel is the two AA Rosette Shires Restaurant, regarded as one of the finest in the area. The cuisine is superbly prepared and impeccably served, with an interesting selection of wines. Two additional dining rooms are available for private entertaining. The hotel is an ideal base from which to explore the Cotswolds or the Thames Valley. There are many historic houses and gardens in the area, as well as racing at Newbury and Cheltenham. Hotel closed 24th December to 7th January. **Directions:** The hotel is located on the edge of the village of Clanfield, at the junction of the A4095 and B4020, between the towns of Witney and Faringdon, some 15 miles to the west of the city of Oxford. Price Guide: Single £85; Double £115–£135.

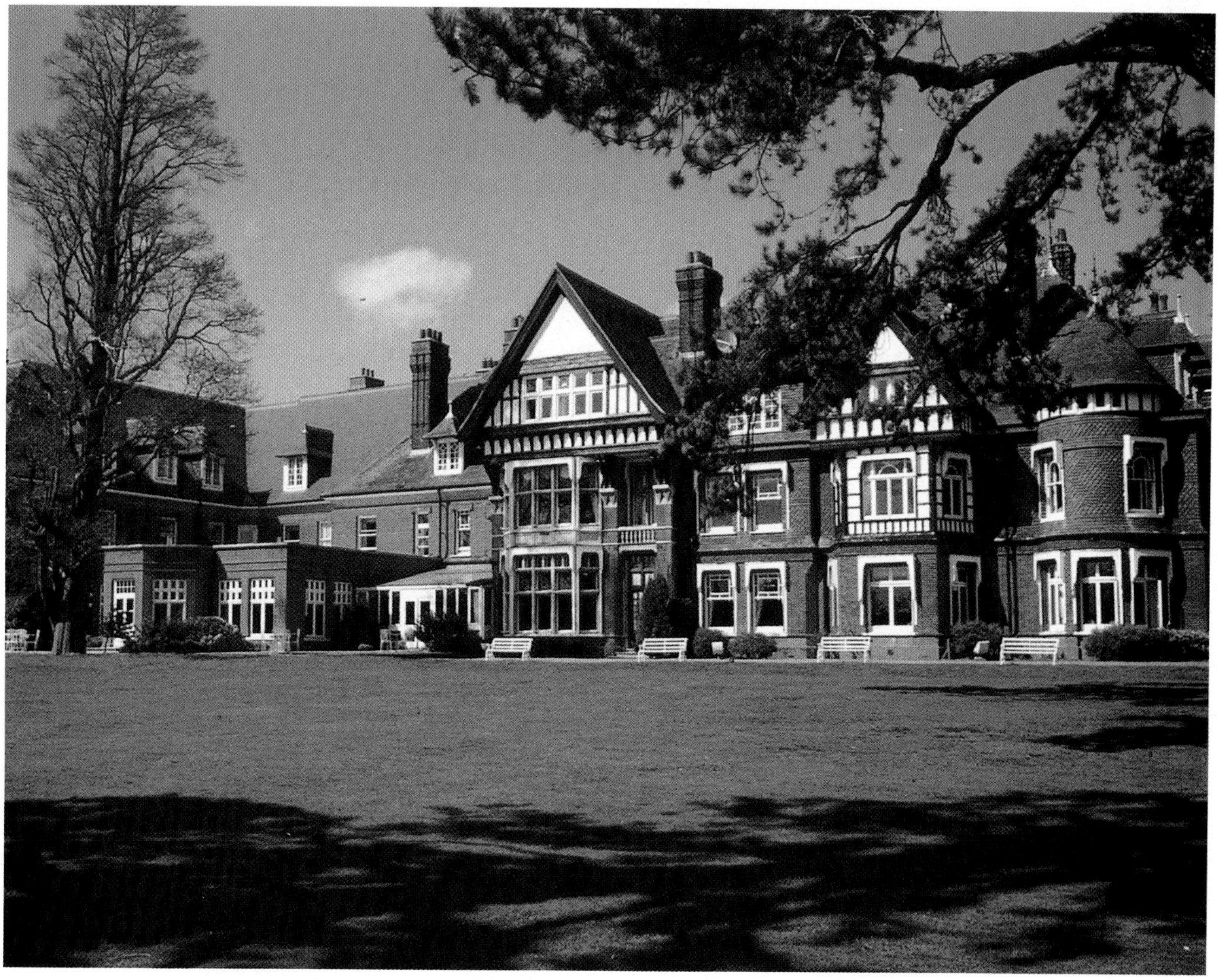

Woodlands Park Hotel

WOODLANDS LANE, STOKE D'ABERNON, COBHAM, SURREY KT11 3QB
TEL: 01372 843933 FAX: 01372 842704 E-MAIL: info@woodlandspark.co.uk

Set in 15 acres of wooded lawns, Woodlands Park Hotel is an ideal location for touring the surrounding Surrey and Berkshire countryside or for those seeking a base on the edge of Greater London. At the turn of the century, the then Prince of Wales and the famous actress Lillie Langtry were frequent visitors to this splendid Victorian mansion. Well-equipped en suite bedrooms retain an appealing Victorian theme and ambience, despite having been refurbished to the highest modern standards. Each offers its guests luxury, comfort and every up-to-date amenity. The Oak Room Restaurant, awarded 2 AA Rosettes, serves English and French cuisine in elegant surroundings, whilst in the newly refurbished Quotes Brasserie you will discover a wide selection of dishes from the speciality menu, designed for those who prefer less formal dining. Small meeting rooms can be reached from the Grand Hall and can accommodate between 10 and 60 for private dinners or meetings, while the modern Prince of Wales Suite seats up to 280. Nearby are Wisley Gardens, Hampton Court and Brooklands Museum. Kempton Park, Epsom and Sandown are within a short distance for those who enjoy racing. **Directions:** On the M25, take junction 9 or 10. The hotel is east of Cobham at Stoke d'Abernon on the A245. Price Guide: (Room only) Single £130–£160; twin/double £140–£230; suites £270–£460.

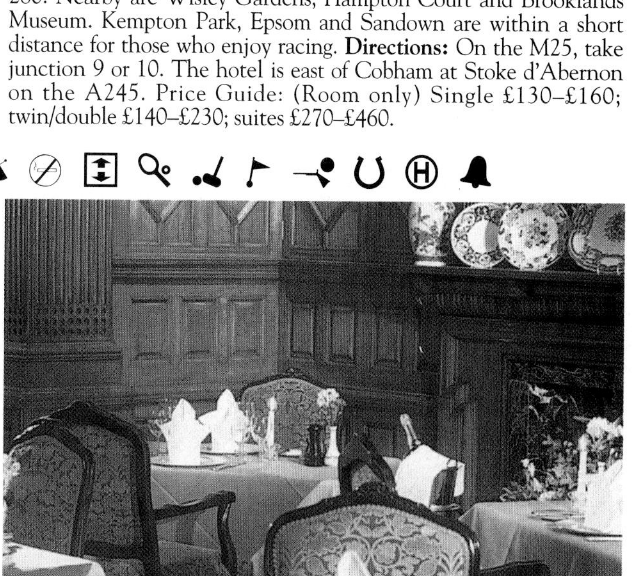

FIVE LAKES HOTEL, GOLF, COUNTRY CLUB & SPA

COLCHESTER ROAD, TOLLESHUNT KNIGHTS, MALDON, ESSEX CM9 8HX
TEL: 01621 868888 FAX: 01621 869696 E-MAIL: enquiries@fivelakes.co.uk

Set in 320 acres, Five Lakes is a superb hotel which combines the latest in sporting, leisure and health activities with state-of-the-art conference, meeting and banqueting facilities. The 114 bedrooms are furnished to a high standard and offer every comfort and convenience. With its two 18-hole golf courses – one of them, the Lakes Course, designed by Neil Coles MBE and used annually by the PGA European Tour – the hotel is already recognised as one of East Anglia's leading golf venues. Guests are also invited to take advantage of the championship standard indoor tennis courts; outdoor tennis; squash; indoor pool with Jacuzzi, steam and sauna; gymnasium; jogging trail; snooker and Viverano's Health and Beauty spa. There is a choice of restaurants, where good food is complemented by excellent service. Lounges and cocktail bars provide a comfortable environment in which to relax and enjoy a drink. Extensive facilities for conferences, meetings, exhibitions and functions include 18 meeting rooms and a 2,500 sqm exhibition hall, suitable for over 2,000 people. All meeting rooms are air-conditioned or comfort-cooled, with 16 rooms having natural daylight. **Directions:** A12 from north, the brown signs are at Feering and Kelvedon or A12 from south, brown signs at Silver End and Rivenhall and then brown signs all the way Price Guide: (room only) Single £105; double/twin £148; suites £198.

114 MasterCard VISA AMERICAN EXPRESS M 2000

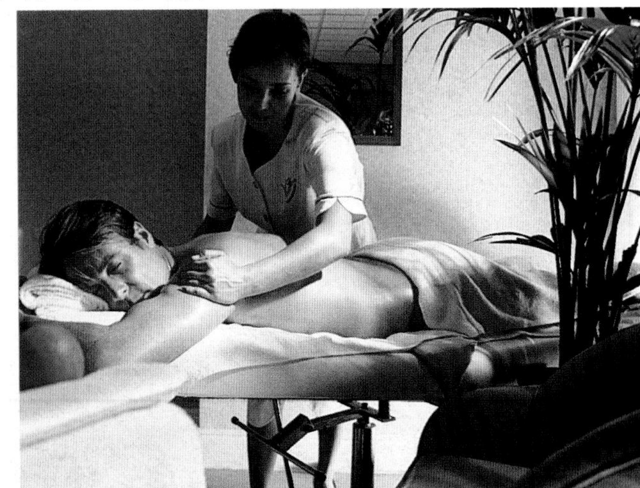

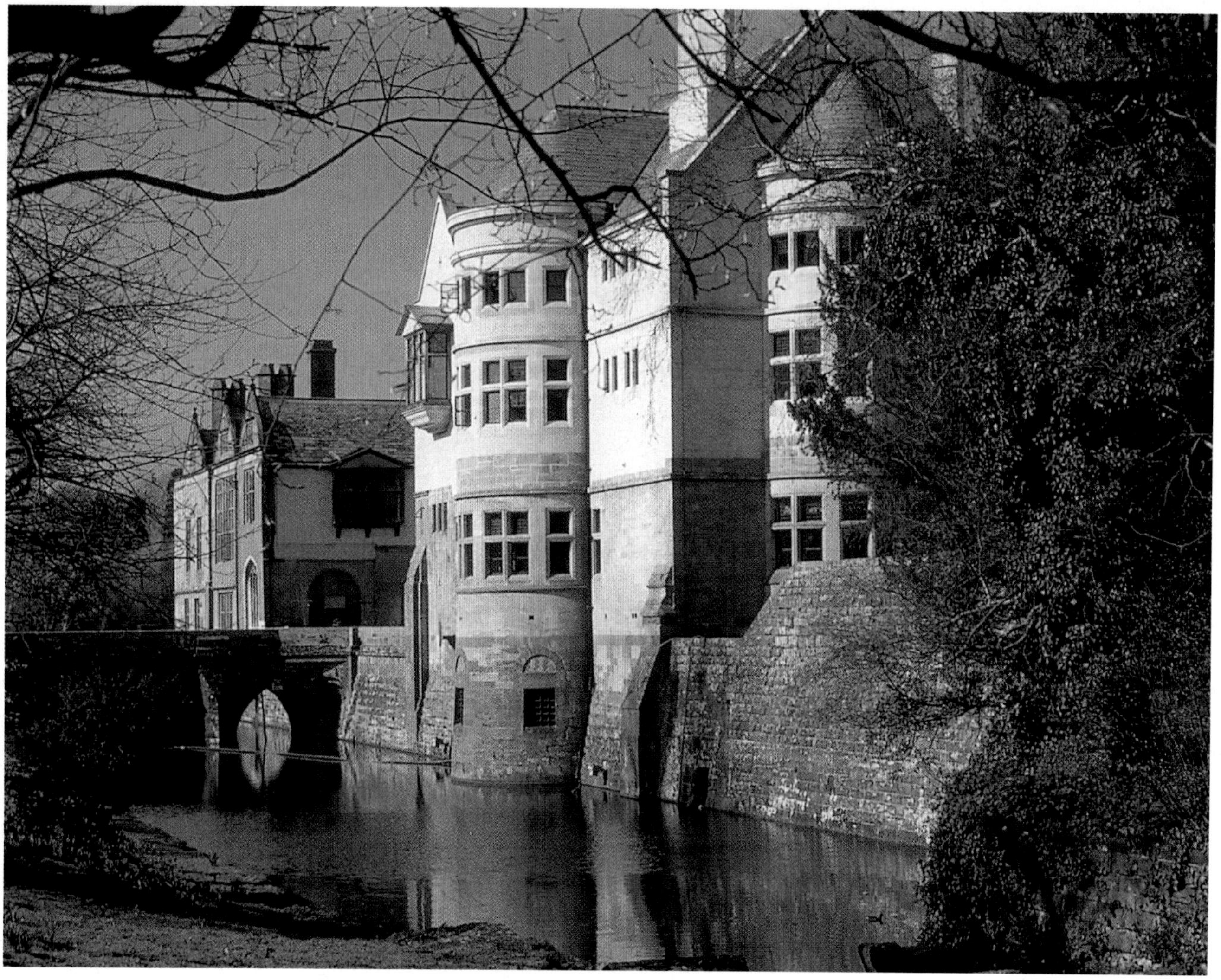

COOMBE ABBEY

BRINKLOW ROAD, BINLEY, WARWICKSHIRE CV3 2AB
TEL: 02476 450450 FAX: 02476 635101

Coombe Abbey is approached by travelling along a lovely avenue of lime trees and chestnuts, crossing a moat and passing through a cloistered entrance. Originally a Cistercian Abbey dating back to the 11th century, this hotel lies in the heart of 500 acres of parkland and formal gardens. Deep colours, carefully selected fabrics and antique furnishing and lighting are all features of its restful bedrooms. Room designs, often eccentric or mischievous, include hidden bathrooms, four poster beds and the occasional hand-painted Victorian bath in the centre of the room. Many bedrooms overlook the grounds with their splendid 80 acre lake. The restaurants and private dining rooms each have their individual charm and offer a variety of settings suitable for all occasions. Sophisticated and creative menus provide a good choice of delightful dishes and the service is attentive but never intrusive. The hotel is an ideal venue for conferences and weddings. Among the local attractions are Warwick Castle and Stratford and the surrounding area is excellent for walking and bird-watching. **Directions:** Leave the M40 at junction 15 and take the A46 towards Binley. Coombe Abbey is on the B4027. Price Guide: (Room only): Single £125; double/twin £140; feature double £170; grand feature £250–£365; suite £350. Special weekend rates available.

NAILCOTE HALL

NAILCOTE LANE, BERKSWELL, NR SOLIHULL, WARWICKSHIRE CV7 7DE
TEL: 02476 466174 FAX: 02476 470720 E-MAIL: info@nailcotehall.co.uk

Nailcote Hall is a charming Elizabethan country house hotel set in 15 acres of gardens and surrounded by Warwickshire countryside. Built in 1640, the house was used by Cromwell during the Civil War and was damaged by his troops prior to the assault on Kenilworth Castle. Ideally located in the heart of England, Nailcote Hall is within 15 minutes' drive of the castle towns of Kenilworth and Warwick, Coventry Cathedral, Birmingham International Airport/Station and the NEC. Situated at the centre of the Midlands motorway network, Birmingham city centre, the ICC and Stratford-upon-Avon are less than 30 minutes away. Leisure facilities include indoor swimming pool, gymnasium, solarium and sauna. Outside there are all-weather tennis courts, pétanque, croquet, a challenging 9-hole par-3 golf course and putting green (host to the British Championship Professional Short Course Championship). In the intimate Tudor surroundings of the Oak Room restaurant, the chef will delight you with superb cuisine, while the cellar boasts an extensive choice of international wines. En suite bedrooms offer luxury accommodation and elegant facilities are available for conferences, private dining and corporate hospitality **Directions:** Situated 6 miles south of Birmingham International Airport/ NEC on the B4101 Balsall Common–Coventry road. Price Guide: Single £150; double/twin £160; suite £195–£275.

CRATHORNE HALL

CRATHORNE, NR YARM, NORTH YORKSHIRE TS15 0AR
TEL: 01642 700398 FAX: 01642 700814 E-MAIL: enquiries@crathornehall.com

Crathorne Hall was the last great stately home built in the Edwardian era. Now a splendid country house hotel, it is set in 15 acres of woodland overlooking the River Leven and the Cleveland Hills. True to their original fashion, the interiors have elegant antique furnishings complementing the grand architectural style. There is no traffic to wake up to here: just the dawn chorus, all the comforts of a luxury hotel and if desired, a champagne breakfast in bed. From a simple main course to a gastronomic dinner, the food is of the highest quality, complemented by a comprehensive wine list. Whether catering for conferences, product launches, wedding receptions or a quiet weekend for two, professional, courteous service is guaranteed. In the grounds, guests can play croquet, follow the jogging trail or try clay-pigeon shooting with a tutor on a layout designed to entertain the beginner and test the expert. Leisure activities such as clay shooting, golf, ballooning and racing circuit driving can be arranged. The Yorkshire Dales, Durham and York are nearby.
Directions: From A19 Thirsk–Teesside road, turn to Yarm and Crathorne. Follow signs to Crathorne village; hotel is on left. Teesside Airport and Darlington rail station are both seven miles; a courtesy collection service is available. Price Guide: Single £70–£125; double/twin £130–£245. Special rates available.

37 MasterCard VISA AMERICAN EXPRESS M 150

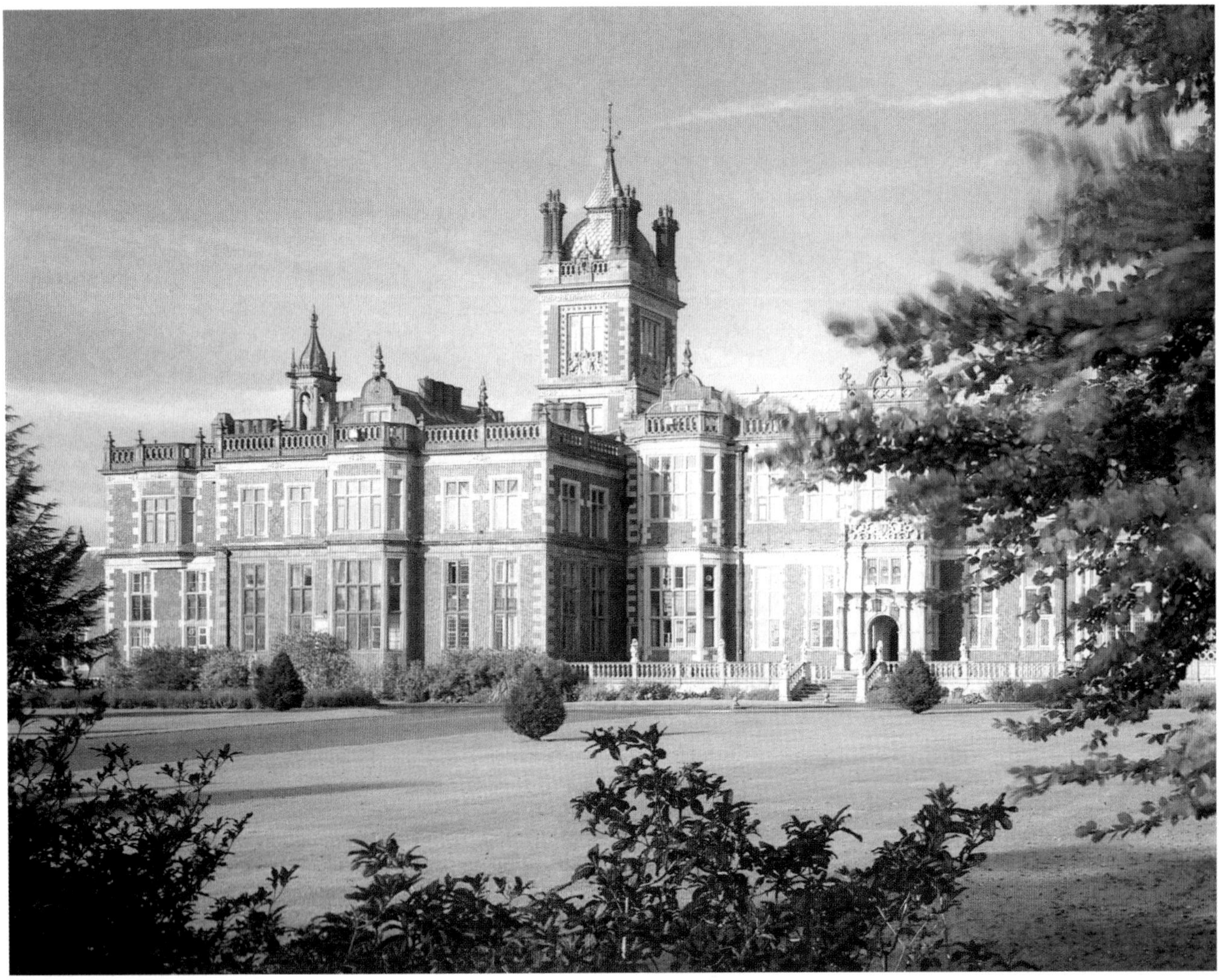

CREWE HALL

WESTON ROAD, CREWE, CHESHIRE CW1 6UZ
TEL: 01270 253333 FAX: 01270 253322 E-MAIL: info@crewehall.com

Magnificent and imposing Crewe Hall, seat of the Earls of Crewe from 1616 to 1922, was owned until 1998 by the Queen as part of the Estate of the Duchy of Lancaster. It is the jewel of Cheshire, a stately home of splendour where guests are transported back to a luxurious age when quality and service were imperative. The Hall stands in vast grounds and guests cannot but be impressed on driving up to the lavish main entrance which is surmounted by exquisite Jacobean stone carving. The ornamentation is reflected over the whole exterior, from the balustraded terraces to the tip of the tall West Wing tower. The Hall's beautiful interior is testament to a time when, for some, money was no constraint to imagination. There is magnificent panelling and marble, huge stone fireplaces, intricate carvings, ornate plasterwork, stained glass, antique furniture and furnishings – even a private chapel. The staircase in the East Hall is regarded as one of the finest specimens of Elizabethan architecture. It is a credit to the owners that the Hall has been handsomely returned to its former glory while being discreetly updated. The eleven public rooms are delightfully relaxing, the bedrooms are supreme and the cuisine in the dining room an experience to savour. **Directions:** From M6, exit at junction 16 and follow the A500 towards Crewe. At the roundabout take the A5020 signposted Crewe Hall. Price Guide: Single £125–£170; double/twin £150–£195; suite £250–£375.

50 MasterCard VISA AMERICAN EXPRESS M 250

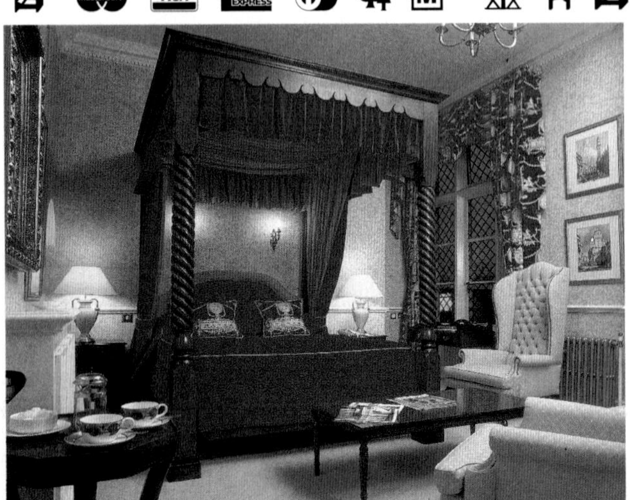

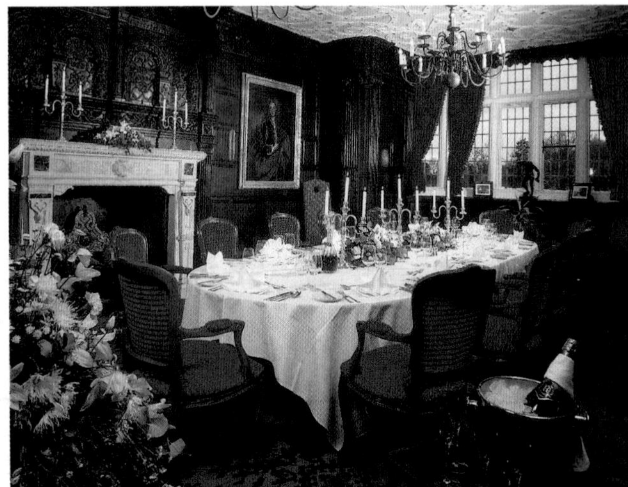

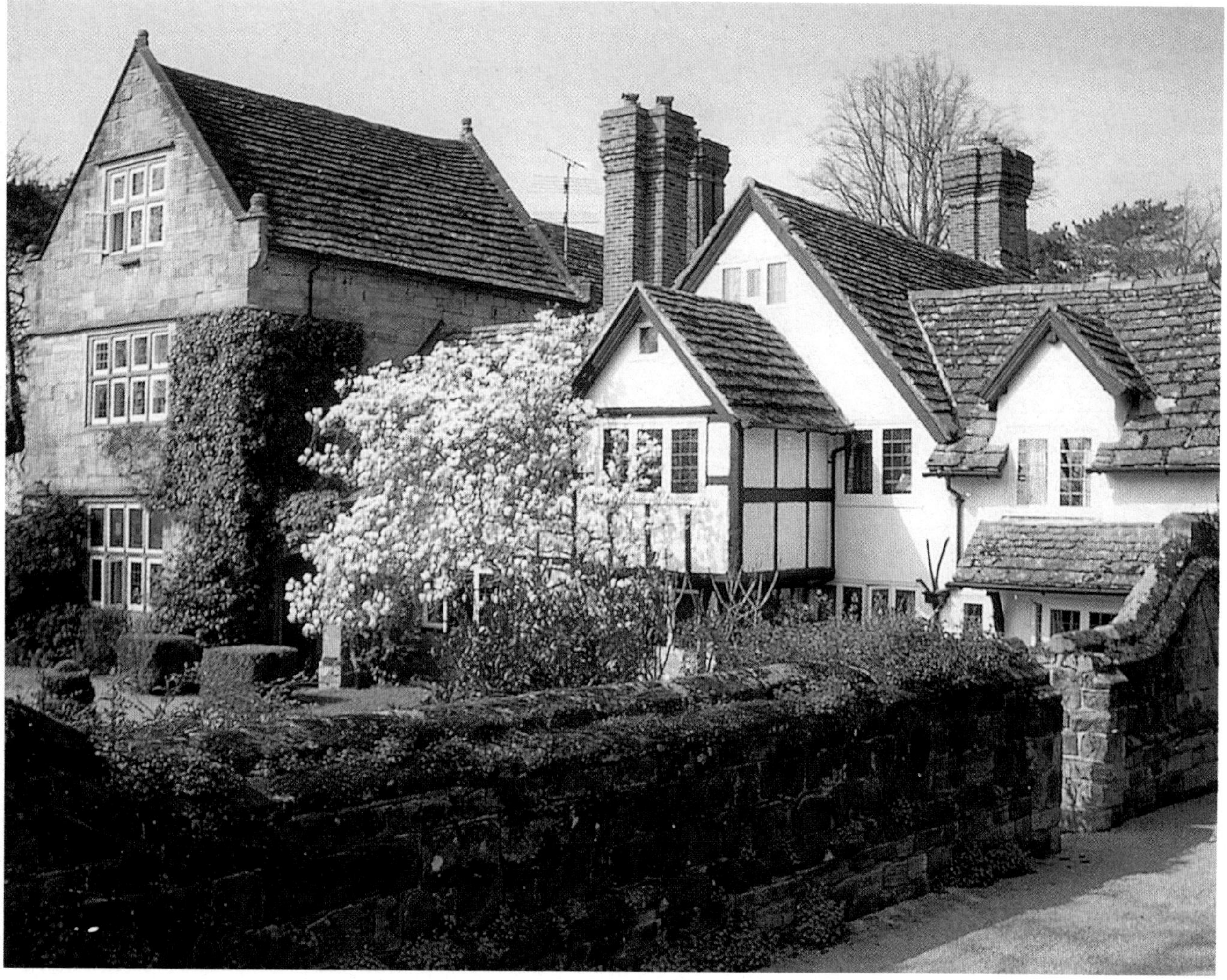

Ockenden Manor

OCKENDEN LANE, CUCKFIELD, WEST SUSSEX RH17 5LD
TEL: 01444 416111 FAX: 01444 415549 E-MAIL: ockenden@hshotels.co.uk

Set in 9 acres of gardens in the centre of the Tudor village of Cuckfield on the Southern Forest Ridge, this hotel is an ideal base from which to discover Sussex and Kent, the Garden of England. First recorded in 1520, Ockenden Manor has become a hotel of great charm and character. The bedrooms all have their own individual identity: climb your private staircase to Thomas or Elizabeth, look out across the glorious Sussex countryside from Victoria's bay window or choose Charles, with its handsome four-poster bed. The restaurant with its beautiful handpainted ceiling is the perfect setting in which to enjoy the chef's cuisine, which has been awarded the most prestigious awards. An outstanding, extensive wine list offers, for example, a splendid choice of first-growth clarets. Spacious and elegantly furnished, the Ockenden Suite welcomes private lunch and dinner parties. A superb conservatory is part of the Ockenden Suite, this opens on to the lawns, where marquees can be set up for summer celebrations. The gardens of Nymans, Wakehurst Place and Leonardslee are nearby, as is the opera at Glyndebourne. **Directions:** In the centre of Cuckfield on the A272. Less than 3 miles east of the A23. Price Guide: Single from £99; double/twin from £132; suite from £240.

Headlam Hall

HEADLAM, NR GAINFORD, DARLINGTON, COUNTY DURHAM DL2 3HA
TEL: 01325 730238 FAX: 01325 730790 E-MAIL: admin@headlamhall.co.uk

This magnificent 17th century Jacobean mansion stands in four acres of formal walled gardens. The grand main lawn, ancient beach hedges and flowing waters evoke an air of tranquillity. Located in the picturesque hamlet of Headlam and surrounded by over 200 acres of its own rolling farmland, Headlam Hall offers guests a special ambience of seclusion and opulence. The traditional bedrooms are all en suite and furnished to a high standard, many with period furniture. The restaurant offers the very best of classic English and Continental cuisine with the kitchen team enjoying a fine reputation for their dishes. An extensive well-chosen wine list highlights the dining experience. Guests may dine in the tasteful surroundings of either the Panelled room, the Victorian room, the Patio room or Conservatory. The main hall features huge stone pillars and the superb original carved oak fireplace, which has dominated the room for over 300 years. The elegant Georgian drawing room opens on to a stepped terrace overlooking the main lawn. The hotel also offers extensive conference facilities and a fine ballroom, the Edwardian Suite with its oak floor and glass ceiling, suitable for up to 150 people. The vast range of leisure facilities include an indoor pool, sauna, gym, tennis court, croquet lawn, course fishery and a snooker room. There are also eight golf courses within a 20 minute drive. **Directions:** Headlam is 2 miles N of Gainford off A67 Darlington–Barnard Castle road. Price Guide: Single £69–£84; double/twin £84–£99; suite £99–£114.

36 MasterCard VISA AMERICAN EXPRESS M 150

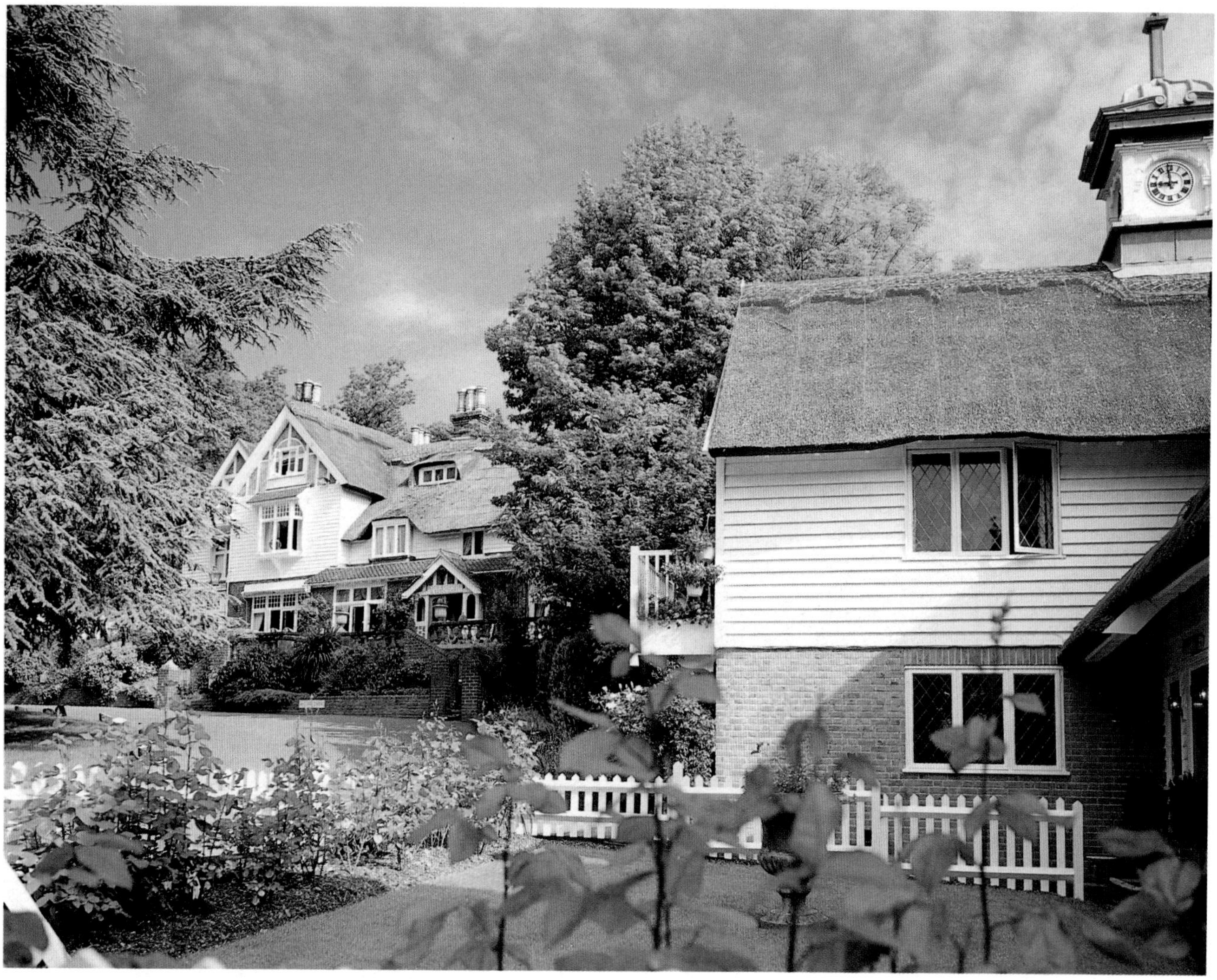

ROWHILL GRANGE HOTEL AND SPA

WILMINGTON, DARTFORD, KENT DA2 7QH
TEL: 01322 615136 FAX: 01322 615137 E-MAIL: admin@rowhillgrange.com

An unexpected find on the outer edge of London bordering on the Kent countryside, Rowhill Grange nestles in nine acres of woodlands and mature gardens descending to a picturesque lake. A combination of top service and friendliness makes Rowhill Grange the perfect venue for everything from weekend breaks to special occasions such as weddings and anniversaries. All the luxurious named bedrooms boast individual character and decoration, with a full range of facilities available to ensure maximum comfort and convenience for guests. The à la carte Restaurant is supplemented with the delightful Brasserie. From late spring and through the summer months guests may take dinner on the terrace, sharing a scenic view with the swans and ducks. For special occasions, business meetings or dinners. Private dining rooms are available. The Clockhouse Suite is a self contained functions annexe with a dining/dancing area, comfortable lounge and a bar. The Utopia Health and Leisure Spa is outstanding with all the latest equipment for women and for men including the UK's first therapy pool of its kind. **Directions:** M20 junction 1/M25 junction 3. Take the B2173 into Swanley and B258 north at Superstore roundabout. After Hextable Green the entrance is almost immediately on the left. Price Guide: (room only): Single £135–£165; double/twin £159–£189; suite £189–£259.

FAWSLEY HALL

FAWSLEY, NR DAVENTRY, NORTHAMPTONSHIRE NN11 3BA
TEL: 01327 892000 FAX: 01327 892001 E-MAIL: reservations@fawsleyhall.com

Set in the beautiful Northamptonshire countryside and surrounded by acres of rolling parkland with lakes landscaped by Capability Brown, Fawsley Hall combines the charm and character of a gracious manor with the facilities and comforts of a modern hotel. The original Tudor Manor house opened as a hotel in 1998 but many traces of its illustrious past have been retained such as the vaulted hall and Queen Elizabeth I chamber. The hotel accommodation comprises 30 wonderfully decorated rooms offering an extraordinary range of Tudor, Georgian and Victorian styles, many of which include four-poster beds. The former Tudor kitchen has been transformed into a restaurant that has established a reputation as the finest in Northamptonshire. There are seven conference and syndicate rooms that can accommodate up to 80 delegates and the attractive Salvin Suite can seat up to 140 for a private banquet or wedding reception. The surrounding countryside offers a host of activities for both the energetic and the more relaxed visitor, whilst places of historic interest abound: Sulgrave Manor, ancestral home of George Washington, Althorp, Canons Ashby, an Elizabethan manor house and Warwick Castle. Oxford, Stratford-upon-Avon and Blenheim Palace are nearby as are Silverstone and Towcester Racecourse. **Directions:** Motorways are M40, Jct11 or M1, Jct16: both 10 miles from Fawsley Hall. Price Guide: Single from £135; double/twin from £175; suite from £255.

30 MasterCard VISA AMERICAN EXPRESS M 80

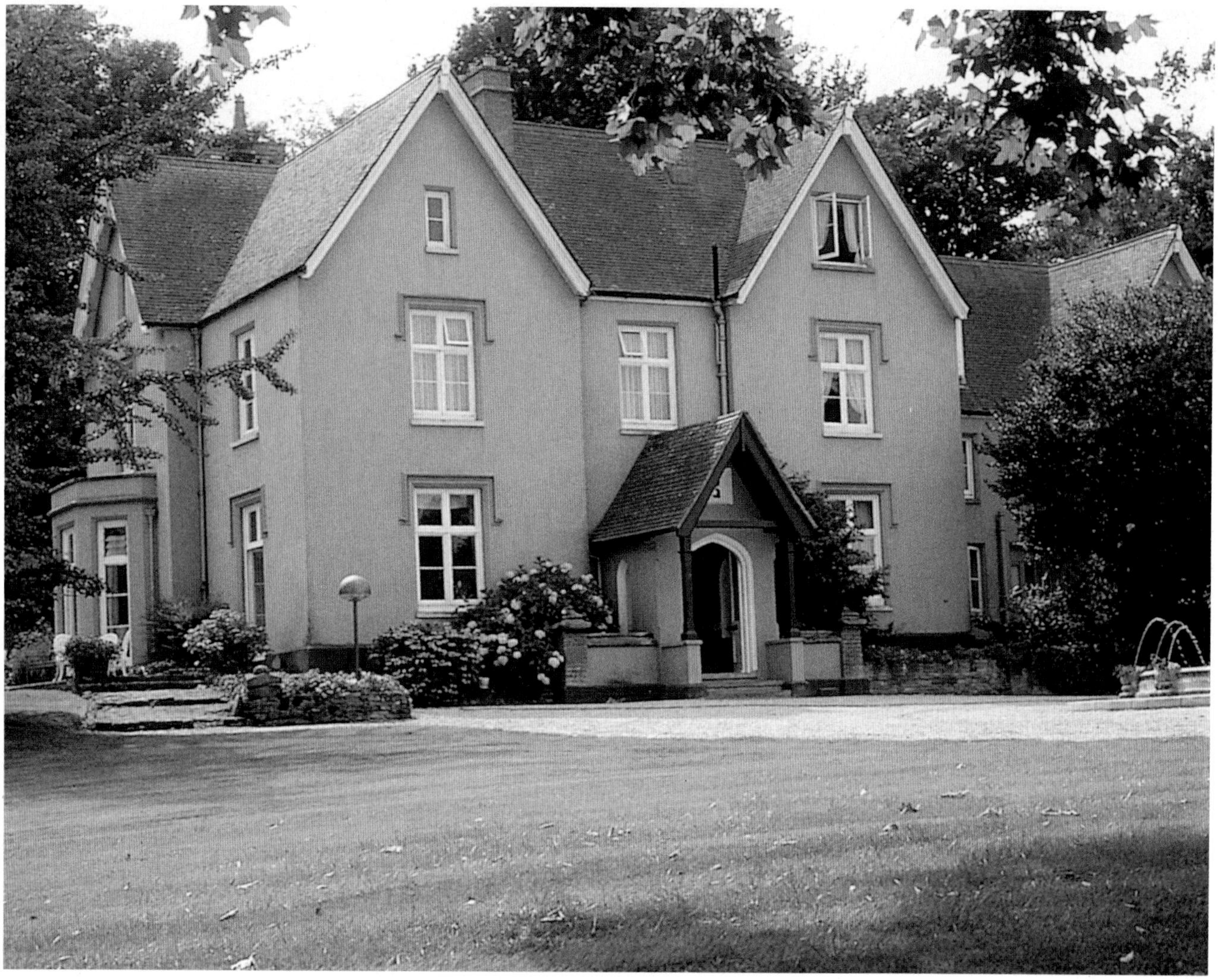

MAISON TALBOOTH

STRATFORD ROAD, DEDHAM, COLCHESTER, ESSEX CO7 6HN
TEL: 01206 322367 FAX: 01206 322752 E-MAIL: maison@talbooth.co.uk

In the north-east corner of Essex, where the River Stour borders with Suffolk, is the Vale of Dedham, an idyllic riverside setting immortalised in the early 19th century by the paintings of John Constable. One summer's day in 1952, the young Gerald Milsom enjoyed a 'cuppa' in the Talbooth tearoom and soon afterwards took the helm at what would develop into Le Talbooth Restaurant. Business was soon booming and the restaurant built itself a reputation as one of the best in the country. In 1969 Maison Talbooth was created in a nearby Victorian rectory, to become, as it still is, a standard bearer for Britain's premier country house hotels. Indeed, in 1982 Gerald Milsom became the founder of the Pride of Britain group. With its atmosphere of opulence, Maison Talbooth has ten spacious guest suites which all have an air of quiet luxury. Every comfort has been provided. Breakfast is served in the suites. The original Le Talbooth Restaurant is about half a mile upstream on a riverside terrace reached by leisurely foot or courtesy car. The hotel arranges special Constable tours. **Directions:** Dedham is about a mile from the A12 between Colchester and Ipswich. Price Guide: Single £120–£150; double/twin £155–£210. Telephone for details of special short breaks. Exclusive use available.

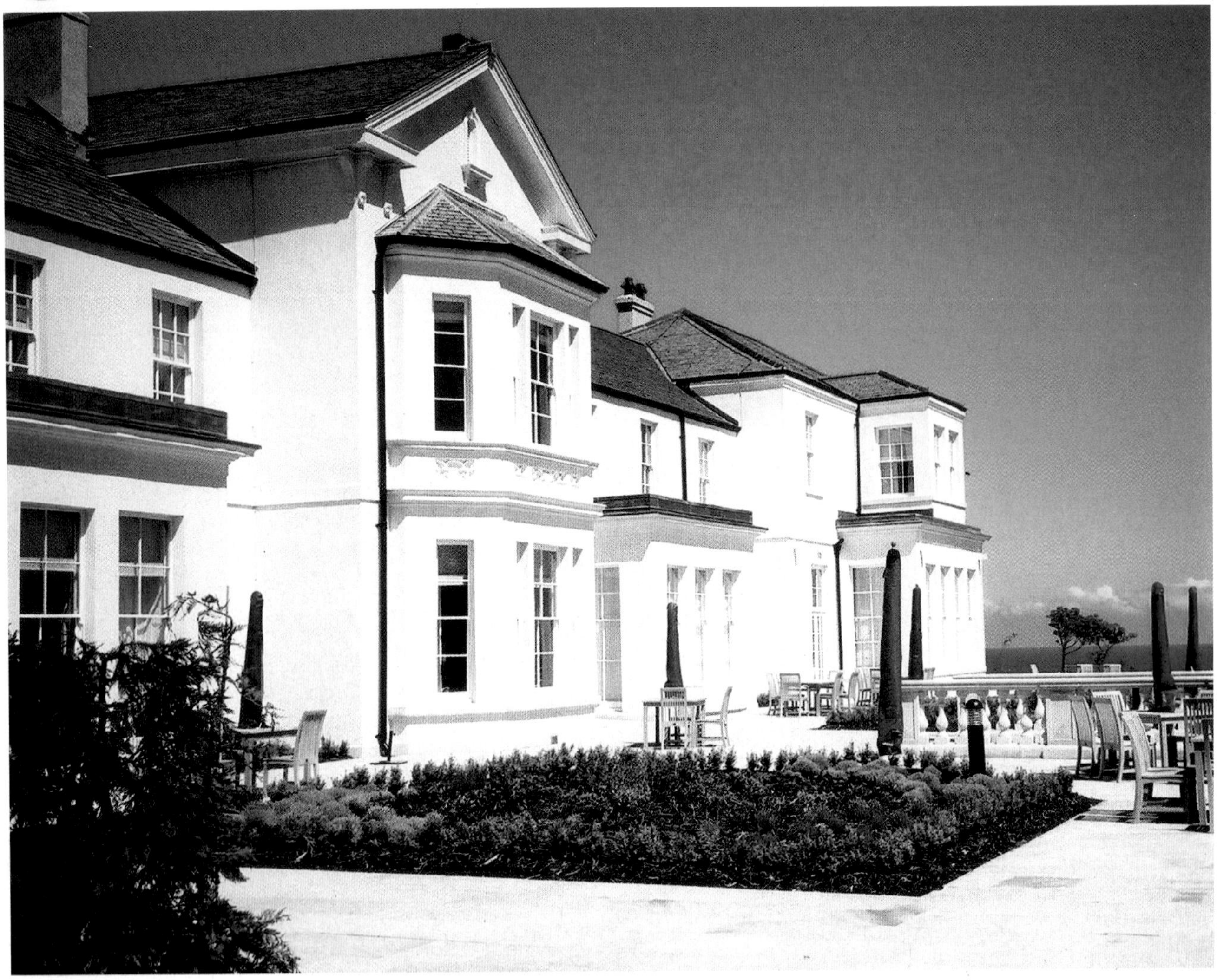

Seaham Hall Hotel & Oriental Spa

LORD BYRON'S WALK, SEAHAM, CO DURHAM SH7 7AG
TEL: 0191 516 1400 FAX: 0191 516 1410 E-MAIL: reservations@seaham–hall.com

This grand hall with views of the North Sea, the Cheviots and the Yorkshire Dales has had a chequered history. The poet Byron married daughter of the house Annabella Millbanke here is 1815 and the Londonderry family of mining magnates held regal court within its solid stone walls. It was bought in 1997 to be developed into this superb private hotel with its mix of 21st-century design and standards of quality from an earlier era. Standing in the heart of 30 acres of landscaped cliff top grounds and gardens, it offers privacy and relaxation. No expense has been spared by owner Tom Maxfield in the renovation of the building. A magnificent ballroom with a south-facing terrace accommodates 120 guests. The 19 en suite guest rooms, including a penthouse suite, are individually designed and have every facility from air conditioning to mood lighting, limestone fireplace and original contemporary art. Head Chef Simon Haigh and his team produce superb French cuisine reflecting the grandeur of the elegant restaurant. Excellent Thai food can be enjoyed in an eaterie in the Oriental Spa. **Directions:** From A1 (north) take exit A19 for Tyne Tunnel. From A1 (south) take exit at Jct62 for A690, then travel north through Houghton le Spring. Take exit for A19 southbound. Come off A19 at exit marked B1404 Seaham. Price Guide: Single £185–£315; double/twin £195–£325; suites £385–£600.

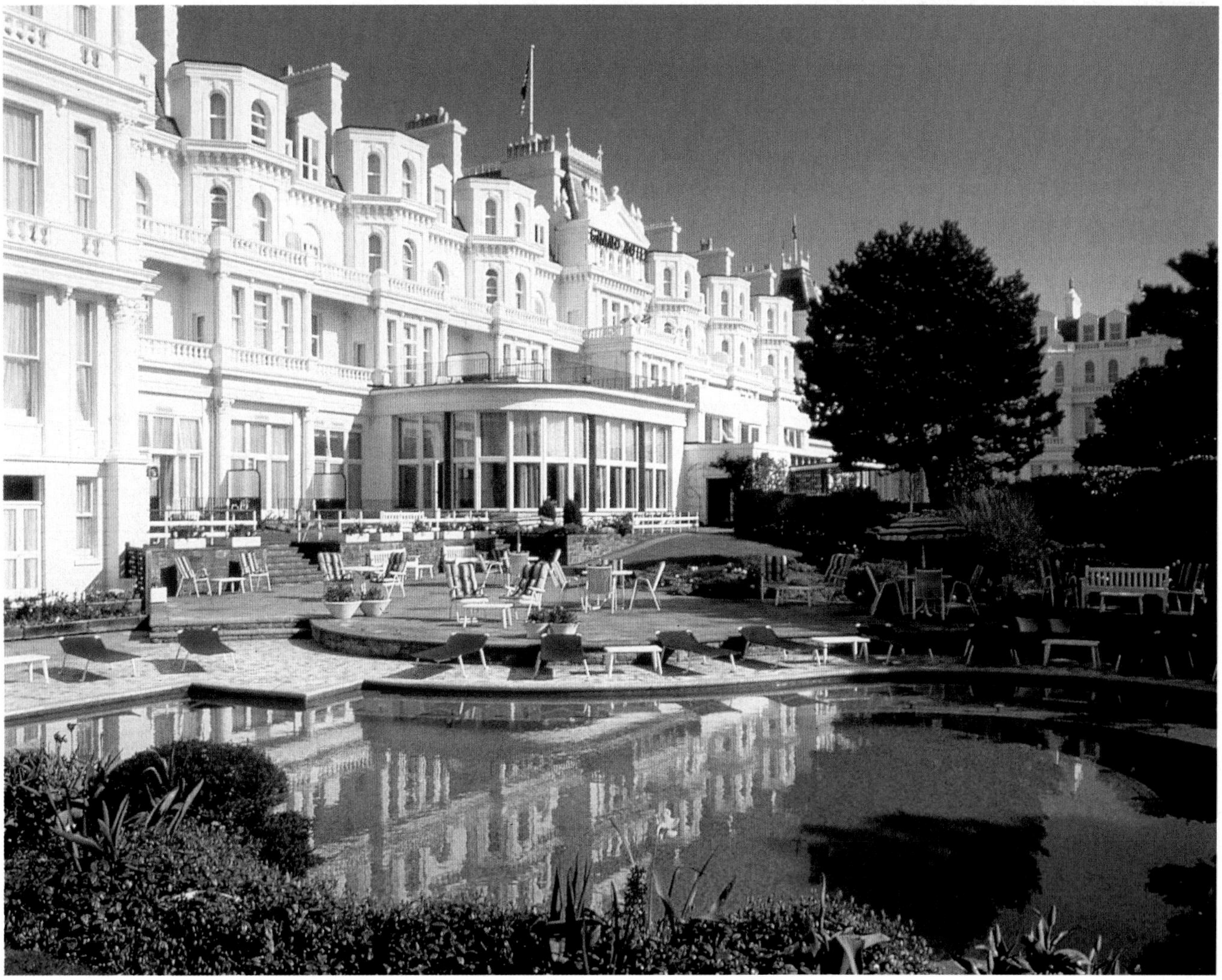

THE GRAND HOTEL

KING EDWARD'S PARADE, EASTBOURNE, EAST SUSSEX BN21 4EQ
TEL: 01323 412345 FAX: 01323 412233 E-MAIL: reservations@grandeastbourne.com

The Grand Hotel is a fine property, steeped in history, which evokes the charm and splendour of the Victorian era. The majestic facade complements the elegant interior whilst the reception rooms are beautifully appointed with rich fabrics and ornaments. Many of the 152 bedrooms are of vast proportions: all being refurbished to include every comfort with attractive bathrooms. The hotel has numerous areas in which to relax and a good choice of restaurants and bars. 'The Mirabelle' in particular achieves exceptional standards of fine dining. The array of new leisure facilities includes both indoor and outdoor pools, gymnasium, sauna, solarium, spa bath, steam room, snooker tables and a hair salon and 8 beauty rooms. Guests may enjoy membership of nearby racquet and golf clubs. For the meeting organiser, the hotel offers an impressive range of rooms which can cater for a number of business purposes from a board meeting for 12 to a larger conference for up to 300 delegates. Those seeking a peaceful retreat will be pleased with the tranquil atmosphere of Eastbourne. Pastimes include walks along the Downs, sea fishing and trips to the two nearby theatres. **Directions:** A22 from London. A259 from East or West. Hotel is at the western end of the seafront. Price Guide: Single £125–£385; double/twin £159–£210; suite £210–£410.

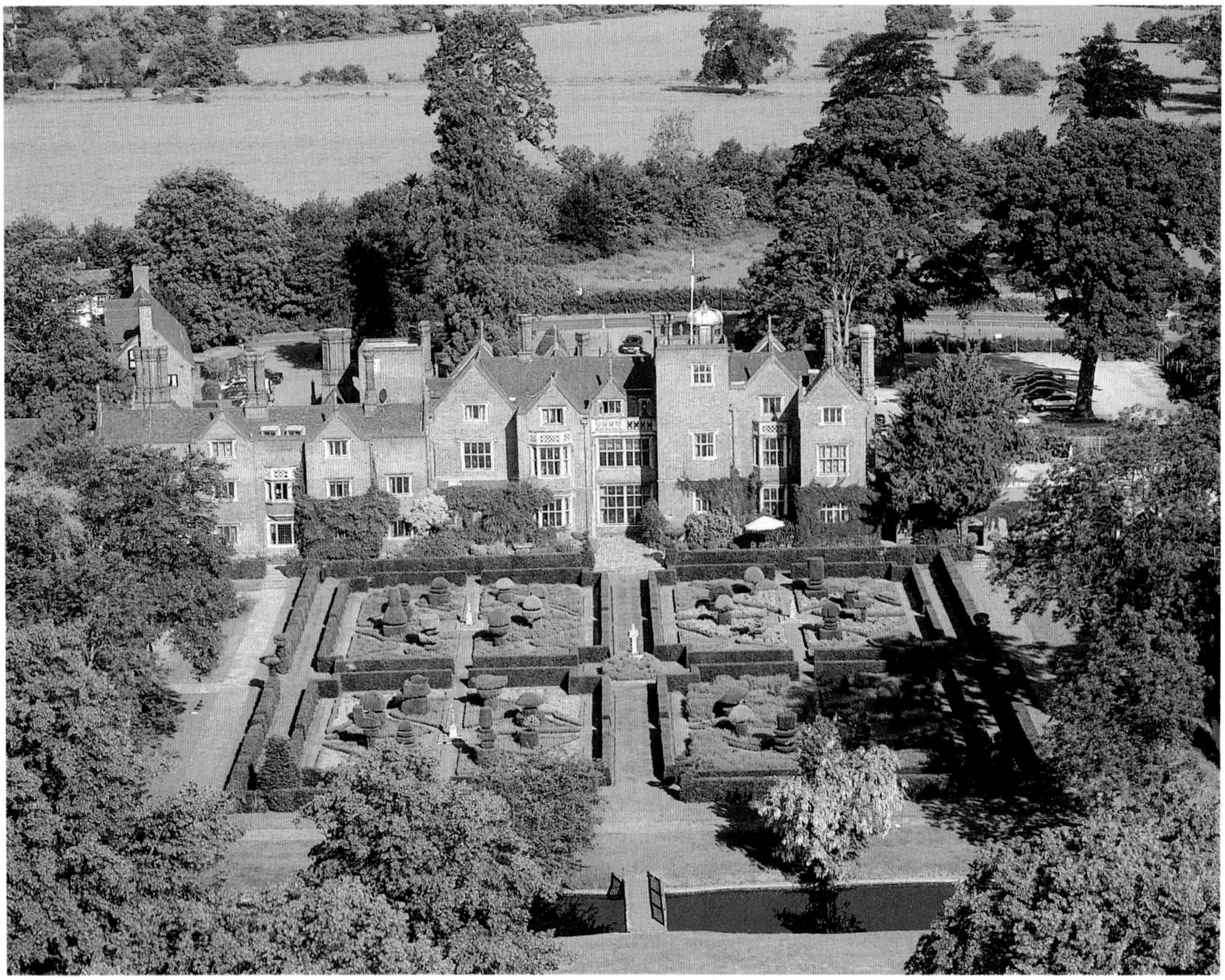

Great Fosters

STROUDE ROAD, EGHAM, SURREY TW20 9UR

TEL: 01784 433822 FAX: 01784 472455 E-MAIL: enquiries@greatfosters.co.uk

Probably built as a Royal Hunting lodge in Windsor Forest, very much a stately home since the 16th century, today Great Fosters is a prestigious hotel within half an hour of both Heathrow Airport and central London. Its past is evident in the mullioned windows, tall chimneys and brick finials, while the Saxon moat – crossed by a Japanese bridge – surrounds three sides of the formal gardens, complete with topiary, statuary and a charming rose garden. Within are fine oak beams and panelling, Jacobean chimney pieces, superb tapestries and a rare oakwell staircase leading to the Tower. Some of the guest rooms are particularly magnificent – one Italian styled with gilt furnishings and damask walls, others with moulded ceilings, beautiful antiques and Persian rugs. Guests relax in the bar, then enjoy good English and French cooking and carefully selected wines, either in the Tudor Dining Room or the Tithe Barn with its vaulted roof. Celebrations, meetings and weddings take place in the elegant Orangery and impressive Painted Hall, the ceiling a riot of exotic birds and animals. Great Fosters is close to polo in Windsor Great Park, racing at Ascot, golf at Wentworth, boating in Henley and pageantry at Windsor Castle, Runneymede and Hampton Court. **Directions:** M25/J13, head for Egham and watch for brown 'Historic Buildings' signs Price Guide: Single from £115; double/twin from £155; suite from £270.

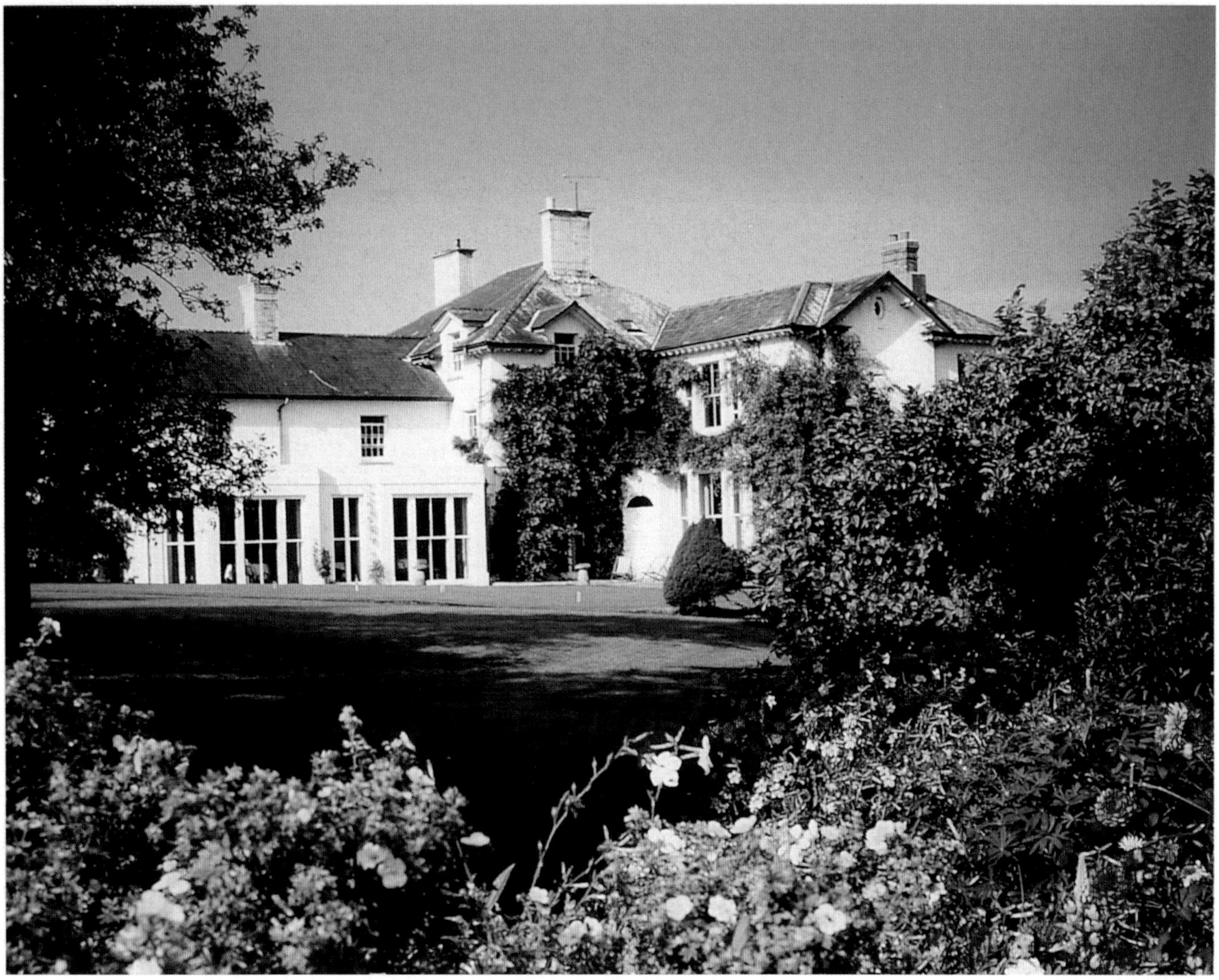

SUMMER LODGE

SUMMER LANE, EVERSHOT, DORSET DT2 0JR
TEL: 01935 83424 FAX: 01935 83005 E-MAIL: reception@summerlodgehotel.com

A charming Georgian building, idyllically located in Hardy country, Summer Lodge was formerly the dower house of the Earls of Ilchester. Now it is a luxurious hotel where owners Nigel and Margaret Corbett offer their guests a genuinely friendly welcome, encouraging them to relax as if in their own home. Summer Lodge was Johansens Country Hotel of the year in 1999. The bedrooms have views over the 4-acre sheltered gardens or overlook the village rooftops across the meadowland. In the dining room, with its French windows that open on to the garden, the cuisine is highly regarded. Fresh local produce is combined with the culinary expertise to create a distinctive brand of English cooking. The unspoiled Dorset countryside and its coastline, 12 miles south, make for limitless exploration and bring to life the setting of Tess of the d'Urbervilles, The Mayor of Casterbridge, Far from the Madding Crowd and the other Hardy novels. Many National Trust properties and gardens in the locality are open to the public. There are stables, golf courses and trout lakes nearby. **Directions:** The turning to Evershot leaves the A37 halfway between Dorchester and Yeovil. Once in the village, turn left into Summer Lane and the hotel entrance is 150 yards on the right. Price Guide: Single from £95; double/twin £135–£295.

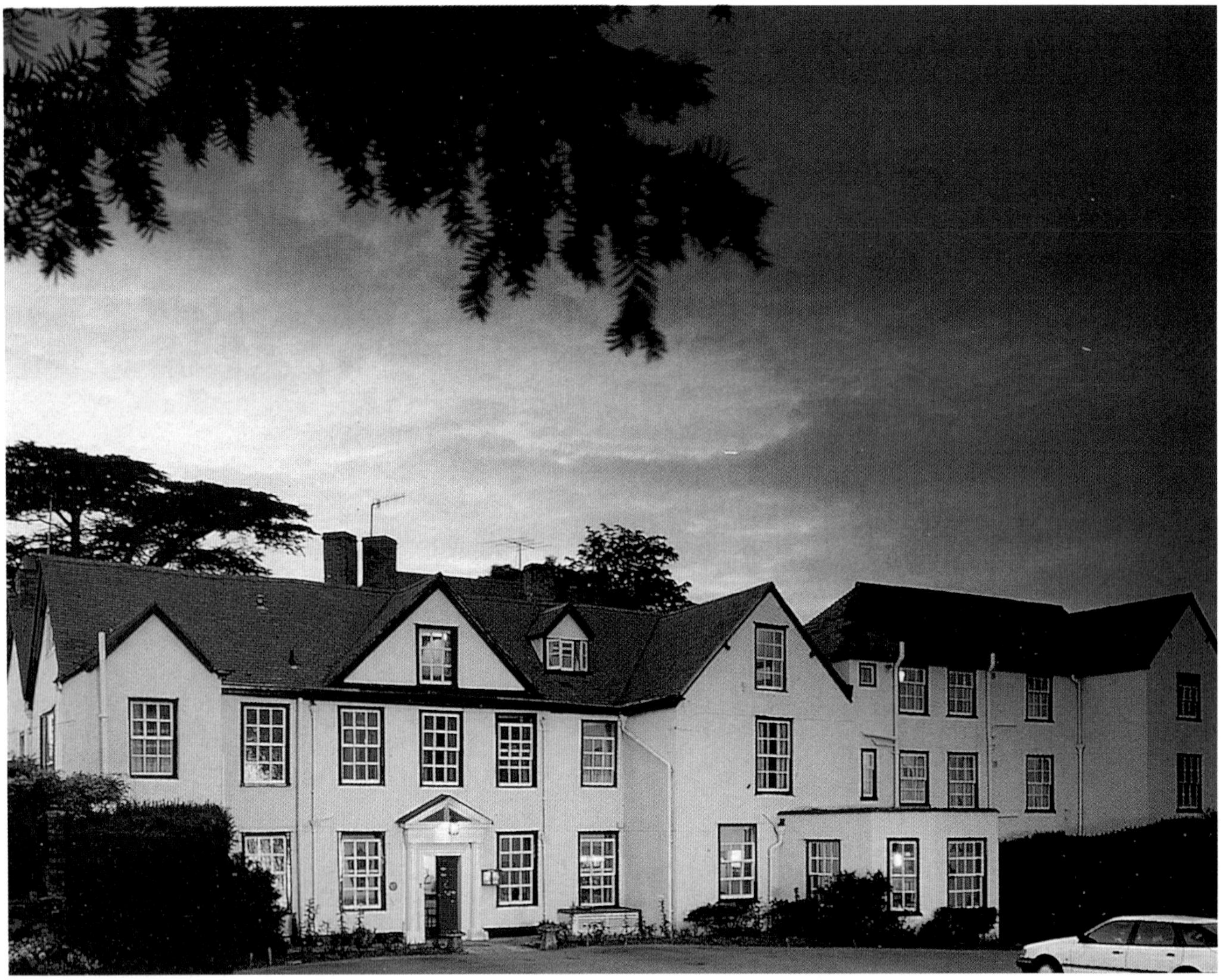

THE EVESHAM HOTEL

COOPERS LANE, OFF WATERSIDE, EVESHAM, WORCESTERSHIRE WR11 6DA
TEL: 01386 765566 RESERVATIONS: 0800 716969 FAX: 01386 765443 E-MAIL: reception@eveshamhotel.com

It is the somewhat unconventional atmosphere at the Evesham Hotel that stays in the memory. Originally a Tudor farmhouse, the hotel was extended and converted into a Georgian mansion house in 1809. Unusually, it combines an award-winning welcome for families with the relaxed but efficient style required by business users. For the past quarter of a century it has been successfully run by the Jenkinson family. Each of the 40 en suite bedrooms is furnished complete with a teddy bear and a toy duck for the bath. The restaurant offers delicious cuisine from a very imaginative and versatile menu, accompanied by a somewhat unique "Euro-sceptic" wine list (everything but French and German!). The drinks selection is an amazing myriad. The indoor swimming pool has a seaside theme. The peace of the 2½ acre garden belies the hotel's proximity to the town – a 5 minute walk away. In the gardens are six 300 year-old mulberry trees and a magnificent cedar of Lebanon, planted in 1809. The hotel is a good base from which to explore the Cotswolds, Stratford-upon-Avon and the Severn Valley. Closed at Christmas. **Directions:** Coopers Lane lies just off Waterside (the River Avon). Price Guide: Single £68–£79; double/twin £108; family £160.

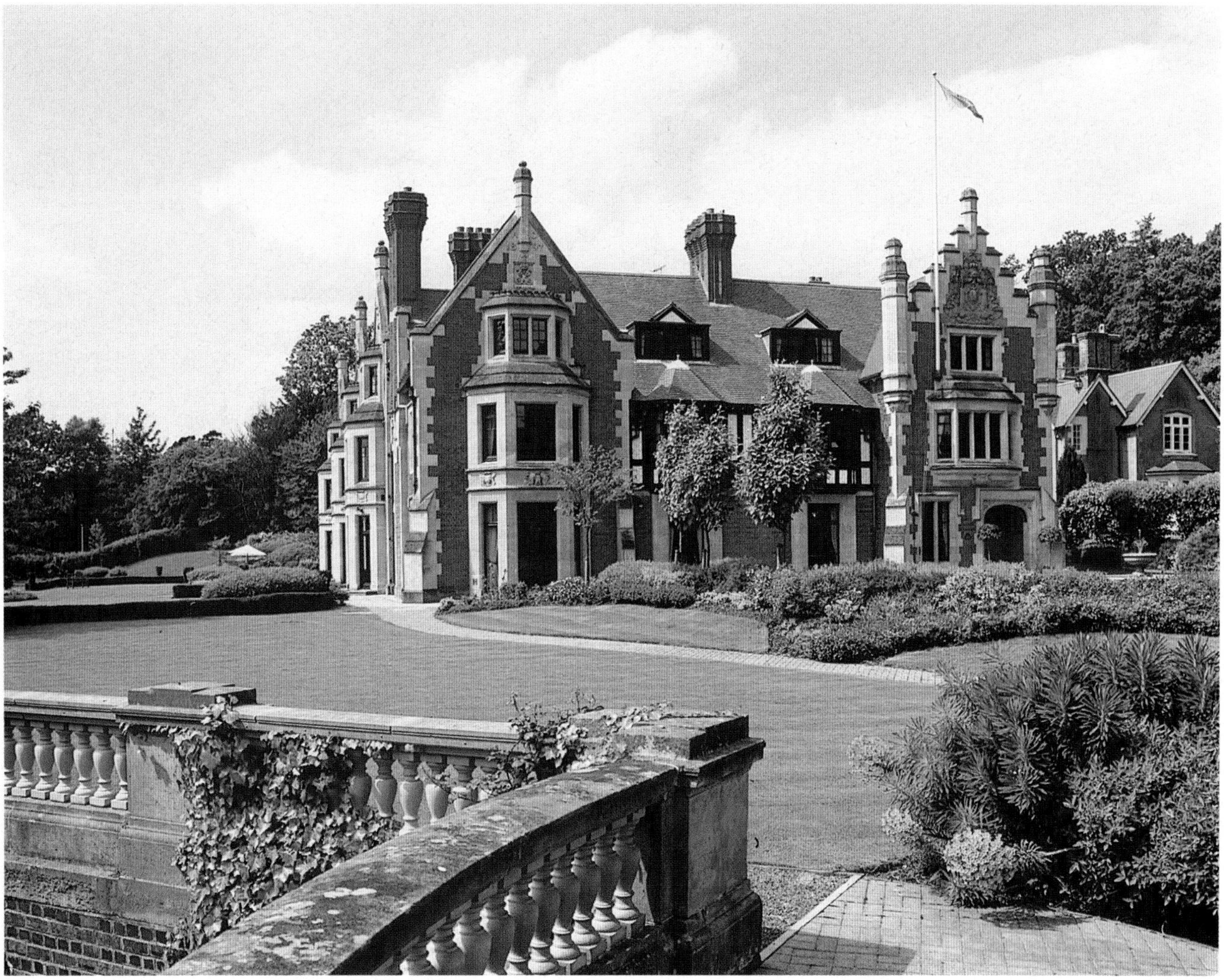

WOOD NORTON HALL

WOOD NORTON, EVESHAM, WORCESTERSHIRE WR11 4YB
TEL: 01386 420007 FAX: 01386 420190 E-MAIL: Woodnorton.hall@bbc.co.uk

Wood Norton Hall is a glorious Grade II listed Victorian country house standing in 170 acres of beautiful Worcestershire countryside. A short drive from the historic market town of Evesham, eight miles from Broadway and the Cotswolds with Stratford-upon-Avon only 15 miles away. French connections date back to 1872 culminated in the wedding of Princess Louise of Orléans and Prince Charles of Bourbon in 1907. Original fleur-de-lys carved oak panelling lines the walls; grand fireplaces, elegant furniture and beautiful tapestries add comfort and colour. The en suite rooms are furnished to the highest standards. The ground floor public rooms reflect the grandeur of the Victorian era with voluptuous window drapes framing views to the Vale of Evesham and the River Avon. The award-winning Le Duc's Restaurant provides the perfect ambience to savour a fine culinary tradition, and a small, intimate bar offers pre and post dining relaxation. The hall has eight rooms suitable for conferences, private banquets and is an ideal venue for incentive programmes. Extensive leisure facilities include a billiard room, fitness suite and golf at a nearby international course. Directions: The hotel stands on the A4538 Worcester Road 3 m north of the town centre. Price Guide: Single £85-135; double/twin £130-£200; suite £145-£220. Weekend breaks and themed weekends throughout the year; details available on request.

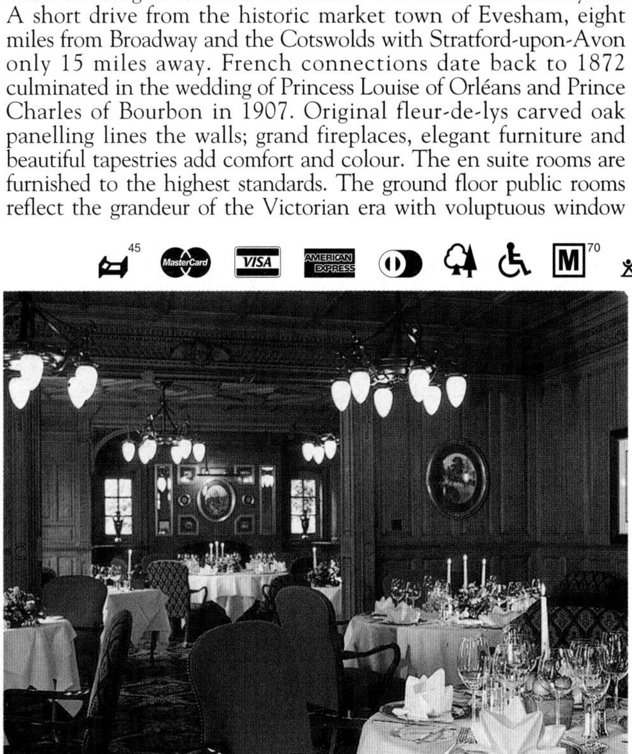

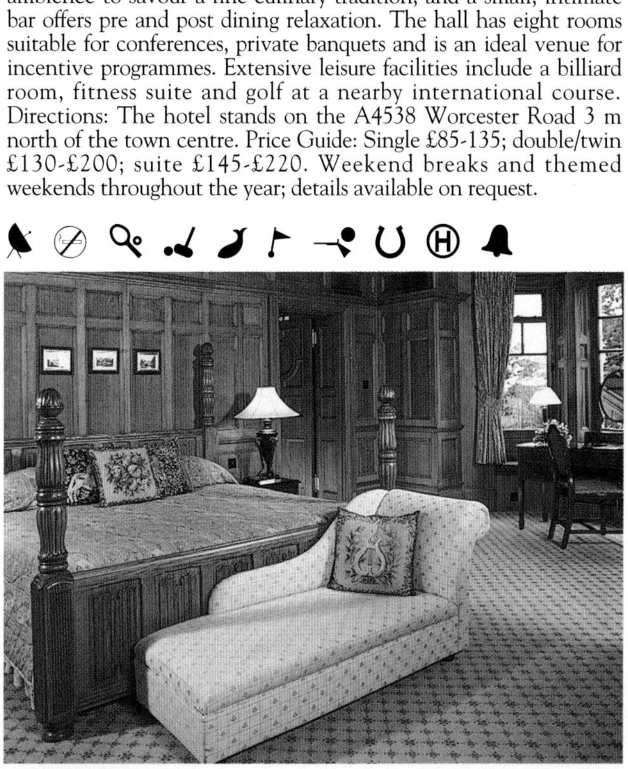

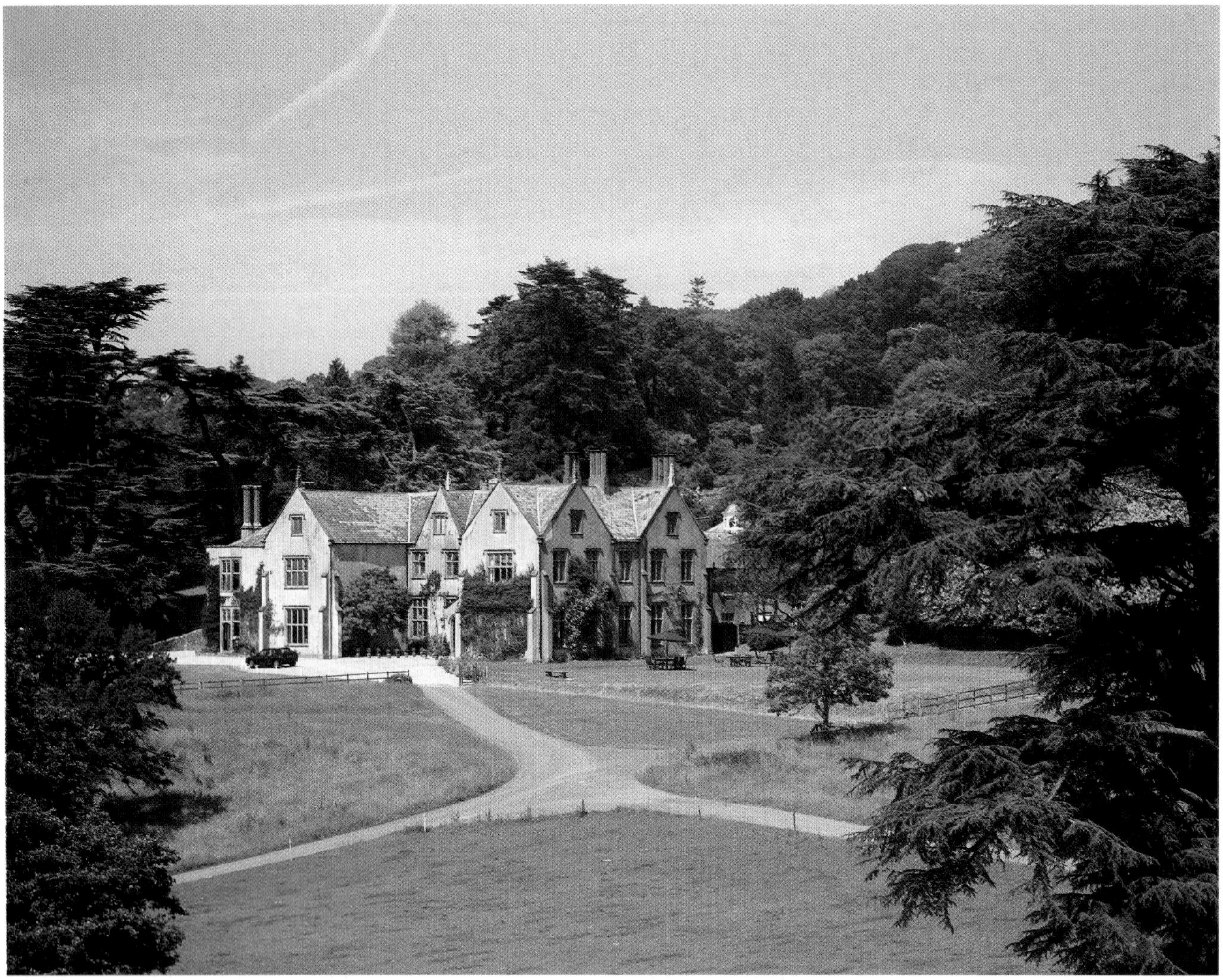

Combe House At Gittisham

HONITON, NR EXETER, DEVON EX14 3AD
TEL: 01404 540400 FAX: 01404 46004 E-MAIL: stay@thishotel.com

Set on one of Devon's finest estates at the head of a hidden valley lies Combe House, a wildly romantic Elizabethan manor. Enjoy total peace and tranquillity, great food, fine wines and generous hospitality. Proprietors Ken and Ruth Hunt have combined country house charm with elegance and style, providing a warm, welcoming atmosphere. You will find treasured antiques, ancestral family portraits, huge log fires and amazing garden flower displays. The fifteen luxury en suite bedrooms have been sensitively refurbished with handcrafted quilts and collectors' items. Many have stunning views across the valley, where magnificent Arabian horses and pheasants roam freely. Master Chef of Great Britain, Philip Leach, is earning the restaurant numerous awards, making Combe a popular choice for relaxing gourmet breaks and special occasions. Exclusive use is also available for weddings, executive meetings and corporate hospitality. Gittisham, once described by HRH Prince Charles as 'the ideal English Village', lies at the end of the mile-long drive. Nearby is the World Heritage coastline Sidmouth to Lyme Regis, Honiton antique shops and numerous historic houses and gardens. **Directions:** From M5 take exit 28 to Honiton and Sidmouth, or exit 29 to Honiton. Follow signs to Fenny Bridges and Gittisham. Price Guide: Single £99–£165; double/twin £130–£190; suites £245.

Hotel Barcelona

MAGDALEN ROAD, EXETER, DEVON EX2 4HY
TEL: 01392 281000 FAX: 01392 281001 E-MAIL: info@hotelbarcelona-uk.com

This glamorous new hotel is simply unique. Situated at the heart of one of the most historic cities of Britain, it is surrounded by ancient buildings and bustling shopping streets. Designed to appeal to both leisure and business visitors, it blends sophistication, comfort and enjoyment with excellent food and attentive service. A lively, vibrant Mediterranean atmosphere is evident throughout, extending into every one of the 46 bedrooms, which feature teak and ebony designer furniture, aqua blue en suite bathrooms and all modern facilities. The Café Paradiso can cater for everything from light lunches to private dinner parties, and offers a great selection of dishes from a plate of antipasti to a freshly baked pizza or fresh fish dinner. There is also a private nightclub where guests can enjoy cocktails, dancing and the performing arts. Guests can explore the historic buildings of Exeter, including the Norman cathedral, and many National Trust gardens like Killerton, Exmouth, and Dartmoor National Park. **Directions:** Exit M5 at junction 30 and take A379 towards Exeter city centre. Follow Topsham Road for approximately two miles and turn right into Magdalen Road. The hotel is on the right. Price Guide: Single from £70; double/twin £80–£90; suite from £110.

WOODBURY PARK HOTEL, GOLF & COUNTRY CLUB

WOODBURY CASTLE, WOODBURY, EXETER, DEVON EX5 1JJ
TEL: 01395 233382 FAX: 01395 234701 E-MAIL: woodbury–park@eclipse.co.uk

A warm welcome awaits visitors at this idyllic hotel, golf and country club. Set in 500 acres of magnificent Devonshire countryside, it is the perfect venue in which to relax or enjoy championship standard golf and comprehensive leisure facilities. The excellently appointed spacious en suite bedrooms and five chalets have been designed for ultimate comfort. An elegant dining room with vast glass roof and marbled floor serves superb cuisine, supported by an extensive wine list. Golfing enthusiasts have the choice of two courses. The 6,870-yards, par 72 Oaks championship course is set in stunning parkland with rolling fairways, European standard greens, lakes and mature trees. Less testing is the contoured Acorns course. Both are complemented by a club where you can relax in the bar, enjoy a light meal in the Conservatory, or an à la carte meal in the restaurant. A large heated swimming pool is the centrepiece of the leisure centre where trained staff are available to help you enjoy a range of facilities including tennis, aerobics and a gym. There is also a spa, sauna and a range of beauty therapies. Woodbury has excellent conference, meetings and corporate banqueting facilities complete with state-of-the-art equipment. Directions: Exit M5 at Jct30. Follow A376 and then A3052 towards Sidmouth before joining B3180 where the hotel is signed. Price Guide: Single £98; double £128; suites from £185.

www.johansens.com/woodburyparkexeter

Budock Vean - The Hotel On The River

NEAR HELFORD PASSAGE, MAWNAN SMITH, FALMOUTH, CORNWALL TR11 5LG
TEL: RESERVATIONS: 01326 252100 FAX: 01326 250892 E-MAIL: relax@budockvean.co.uk

This friendly 4 star hotel is nestled in 65 acres of award-winning gardens and parkland with a private foreshore on the tranquil Helford River. Set in a designated area of breathtaking natural beauty, the hotel is a destination in itself with outstanding leisure facilities and space to relax and be pampered. The two AA rosette restaurant offers excellent cuisine using the finest local produce to create exciting and imaginative five-course dinners, with fresh seafood being a speciality. On site are a golf course, large indoor swimming pool, tennis courts, a billiard room, boating, fishing, and the Natural Health Spa. The local ferry will take guests from the hotel's jetty to waterside pubs, to Frenchman's Creek or to hire a boat. The hotel also takes out guests on its own 32 foot 'Sunseeker'. A myriad of magnificent country and coastal walks from the wild grandeur of Kynance and the Lizard to the peace and tranquillity of the Helford itself, as well as several of the Great Gardens of Cornwall, are in the close vicinity. **Directions:** From the A39 Truro to Falmouth road, follow the brown tourist signs for Trebah Garden. Budock Vean appears ½ mile after passing Trebah on the left-hand side. Price Guide: Single £53–£92; double/twin £106–£184; suites £191–£249 (Add £10 per person per night for 5-course dinner in the 2 AA Rosette restaurant).

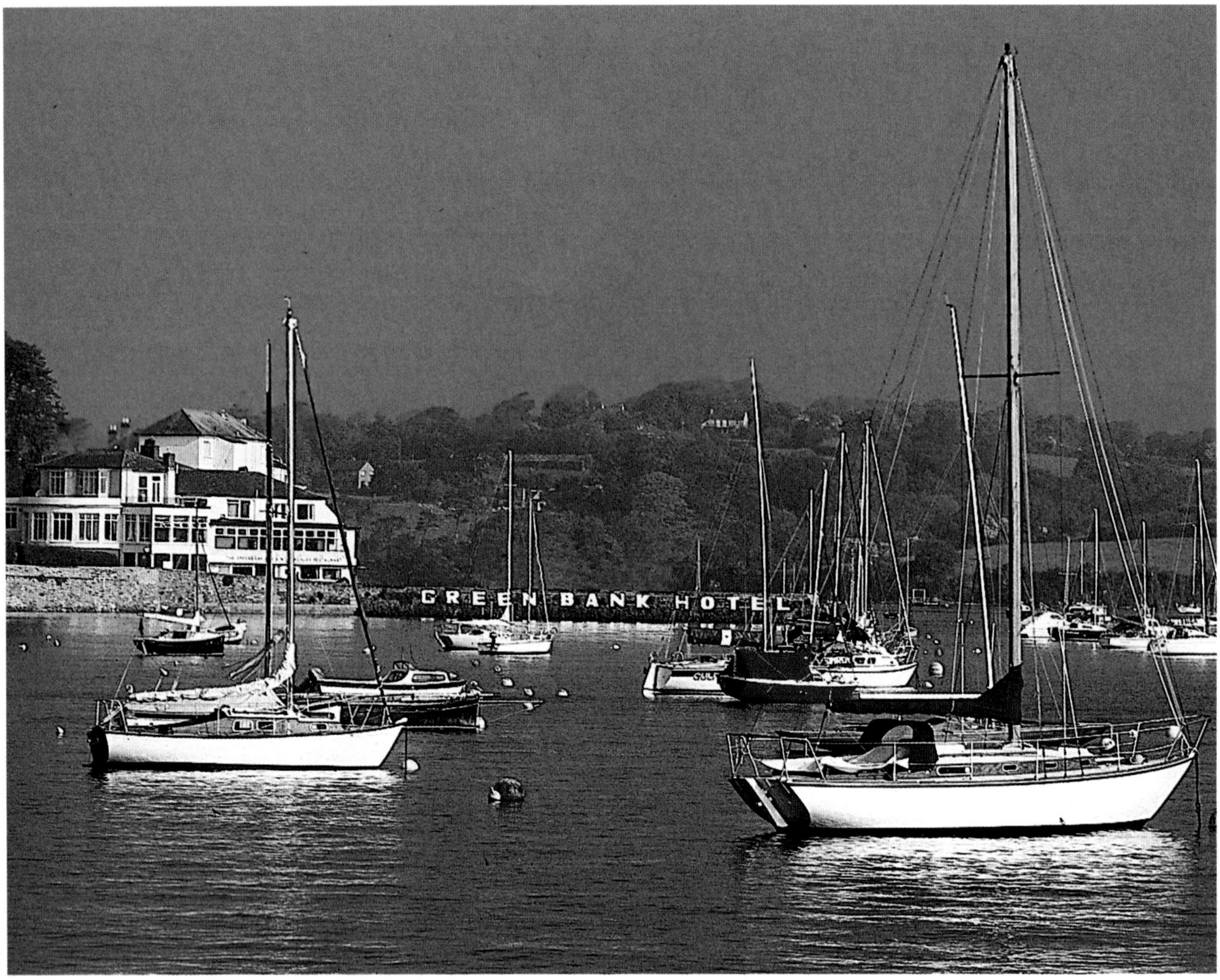

The Greenbank Hotel

HARBOURSIDE, FALMOUTH, CORNWALL TR11 2SR
TEL: 01326 312440 FAX: 01326 211362 E-MAIL: sales@greenbank-hotel.com

Surrounded by the vibrant atmosphere of Falmouth, the Greenbank is the only hotel on the banks of one of the world's largest and deepest natural harbours. Because of its position as a ferry point to Flushing its history stretches back to the18th century, and visitors have included Florence Nightingale and Kenneth Grahame, whose letters from the hotel to his son formed the basis for his book 'The Wind in the Willows'. Seaward views from the hotel are stunning, and reaching out from each side are lovely clifftop paths leading to secluded coves where walkers can relax while enjoying a paddle in clear blue waters and breathing in fresh, clean sea air. Most of the charming, delightfully furnished and well equipped en suite bedrooms enjoy panoramic views across the harbour to Flushing and St Mawes. Keen appetites will be well satisfied by the variety of dishes offered in the Harbourside Restaurant with seafood and local lamb specialities on the menu. There are opportunities locally for golf, sailing, riding and fishing. Interesting places nearby include Cornwall's National Maritime Museum, several heritage sites and many National Trust properties and gardens. **Directions:** Take the A39 from Truro and on approaching Falmouth join the Old Road going through Penryn. Turn left at the second roundabout where the hotel is signposted. Price Guide: Single £60–£75; double/twin £90–£145; suite £200.

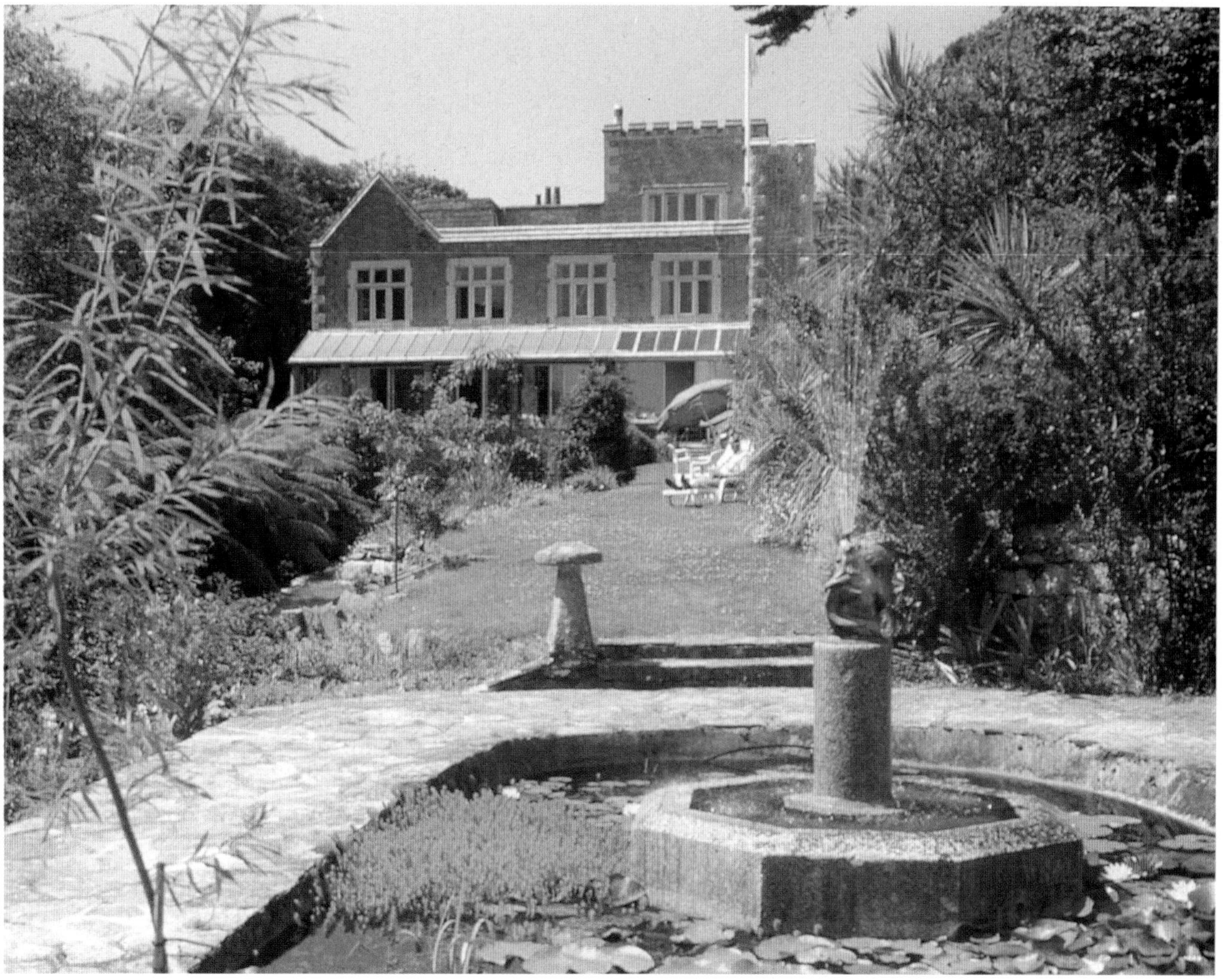

MEUDON HOTEL

MAWNAN SMITH, NR FALMOUTH, CORNWALL TR11 5HT
TEL: 01326 250541 FAX: 01326 250543 E-MAIL: wecare@meudon.co.uk

Set against a delightfully romantic backdrop of densely wooded countryside between the Fal and Helford Rivers, Meudon Hotel is a unique, superior retreat: a luxury, family-run establishment which has its origins in two humble 17th century coastguards' cottages. The French name comes from a nearby farmhouse built by Napoleonic prisoners of war and called after their eponymous home village in the environs of Paris. Set in nearly nine acres of subtropical gardens coaxed annually into early bloom by the mild Cornish climate – Meudon is safely surrounded by 200 acres of beautiful National Trust land and the sea. All bedrooms in a modern wing are en suite and enjoy spectacular views over subtropical gardens. Many a guest is enticed by the cuisine to return: in the restaurant (or the gardens during warm weather); fresh seafood and kitchen garden produce are served with wines from a judiciously compiled list. There are opportunities locally for fishing, sailing and walking. A 34-foot yacht is available for skippered charter – explore the Fal and Helford Rivers while enjoying native oysters and sipping Chablis! Golf is free at nearby Falmouth Golf Club and five others in Cornwall. **Directions:** From Truro A39 to Hillhead roundabout turn off and the hotel is four miles on the left. Price Guide: (including dinner): Single £105; double/twin £210; suite £270.

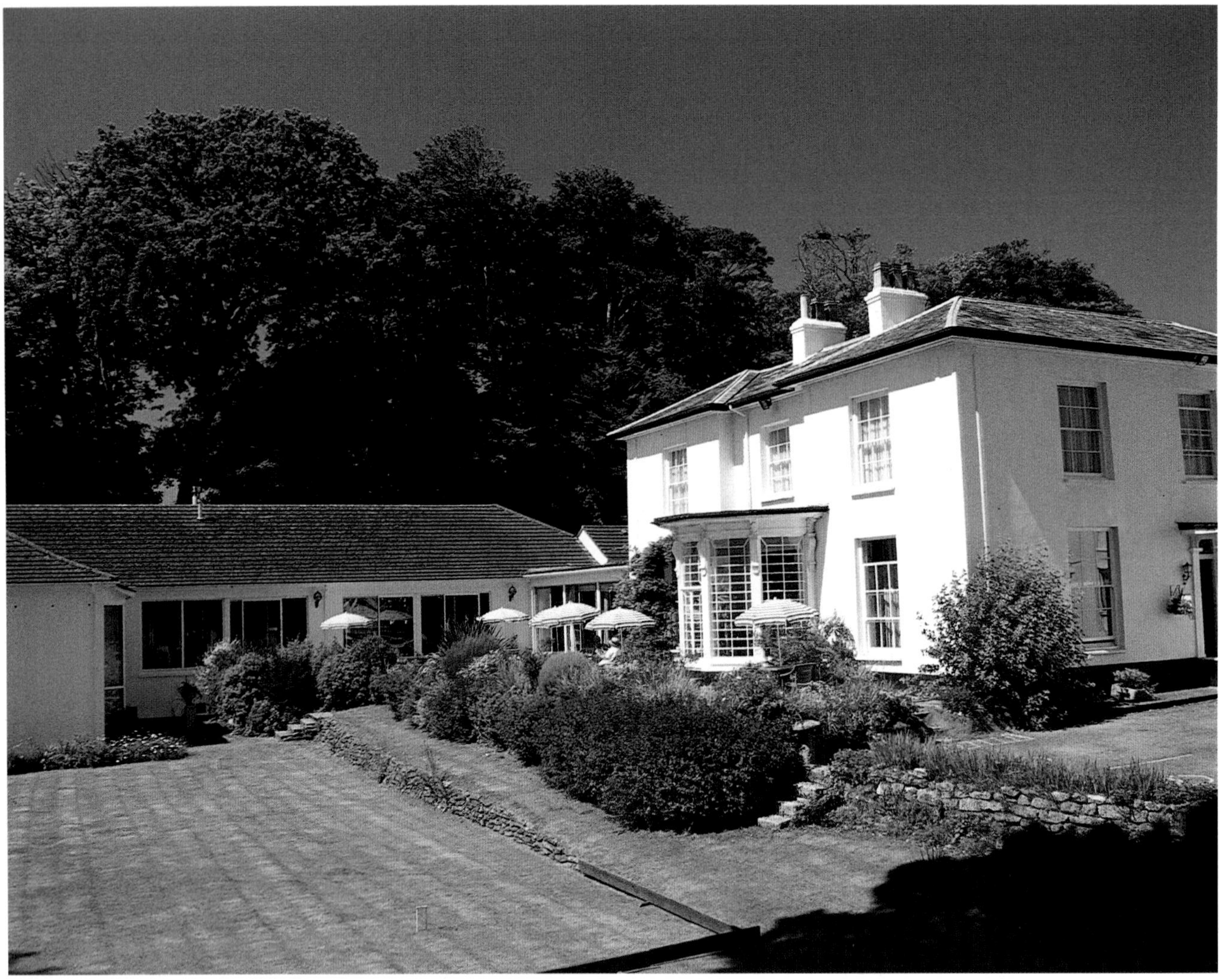

PENMERE MANOR

MONGLEATH ROAD, FALMOUTH, CORNWALL TR11 4PN

TEL: 01326 211411 FAX: 01326 317588 E-MAIL: reservations@penmere.co.uk

Set in five acres of subtropical gardens and woodlands, this elegant Georgian country house is an oasis of gracious living and fine food. From arrival to departure the Manor's attentive staff ensure that guests have everything they need to enjoy their stay. Bedrooms offer every comfort and are furnished to maintain the country house ambience. The spacious Garden rooms (as illustrated) are delightful. Each is named after a famous Cornish garden and has either king or queen size beds and a lounge area. The restaurant serves excellent international cuisine that includes an extensive lobster speciality menu which must be ordered 24 hours in advance. Light snacks and substantial lunchtime dishes are also provided in the bar which overlooks the garden and terrace. There is a heated outdoor swimming pool in the old walled garden and a splendid indoor pool, together with Jacuzzi spa, sauna, solarium and gym. Golfers can benefit from reduced green fees at Falmouth Golf Course. Cornish gardens, National Trust and English Heritage properties are within reach. Flambards Theme Park, Poldark Mine and Gweek Seal Sanctuary are less than ten miles away. **Directions:** From Truro follow the A39 towards Falmouth. Turn right at Hillhead roundabout and after 1 mile turn left into Mongleath Road. Price Guide: Single £56–£97; double/twin £86–£126.

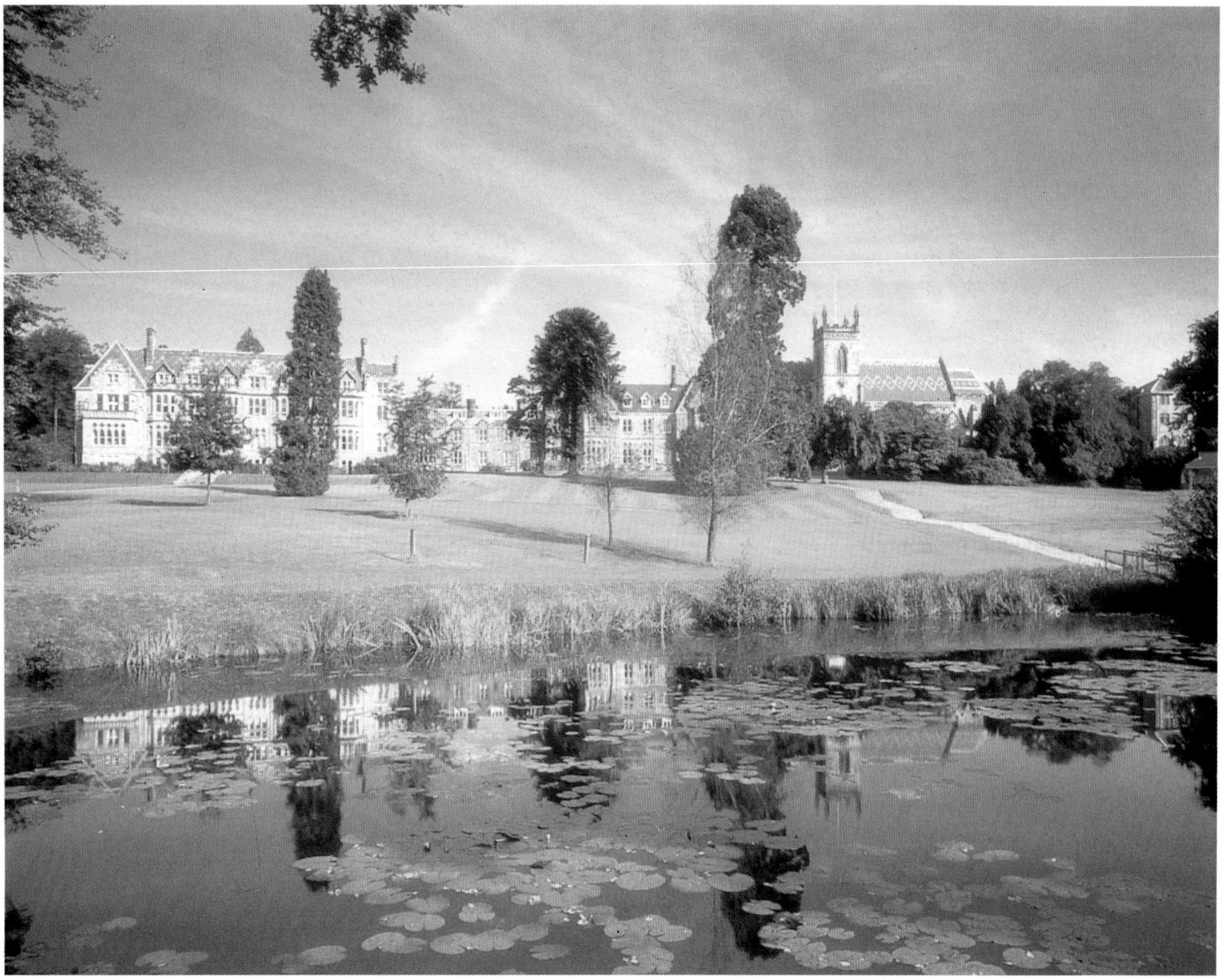

Ashdown Park Hotel And Country Club

WYCH CROSS, FOREST ROW, EAST SUSSEX RH18 5JR
TEL: 01342 824988 FAX: 01342 826206 E-MAIL: reservations@ashdownpark.com

Ashdown Park is a grand, rambling 19th century mansion overlooking almost 200 acres of landscaped gardens to the forest beyond. Built in 1867, the hotel is situated within easy reach of Gatwick Airport, London and the South Coast and provides the perfect backdrop for every occasion, from a weekend getaway to a honeymoon or business convention. The hotel is subtly furnished throughout to satisfy the needs of escapees from urban stress. The 107 en suite bedrooms are beautifully decorated – several with elegant four-poster beds, all with up-to-date amenities. The Anderida restaurant offers a thoughtfully compiled menu and wine list, complemented by discreetly attentive service in soigné surroundings. Guests seeking relaxation can retire to the indoor pool and sauna, pamper themselves with a massage, before using the solarium, or visiting the beauty salon. Alternatively, guests may prefer to amble through the gardens and nearby woodland paths; the more energetic can indulge in tennis, croquet or use the Fitness Studio and Beauty Therapy. There is also an indoor driving range, a lounge/bar and an 18-hole par 3 golf course with an outdoor driving range. **Directions:** East of A22 at Wych Cross traffic lights on road signposted to Hartfield. Price Guide: Single £125–£315; double/twin £159–£310; suite £340.

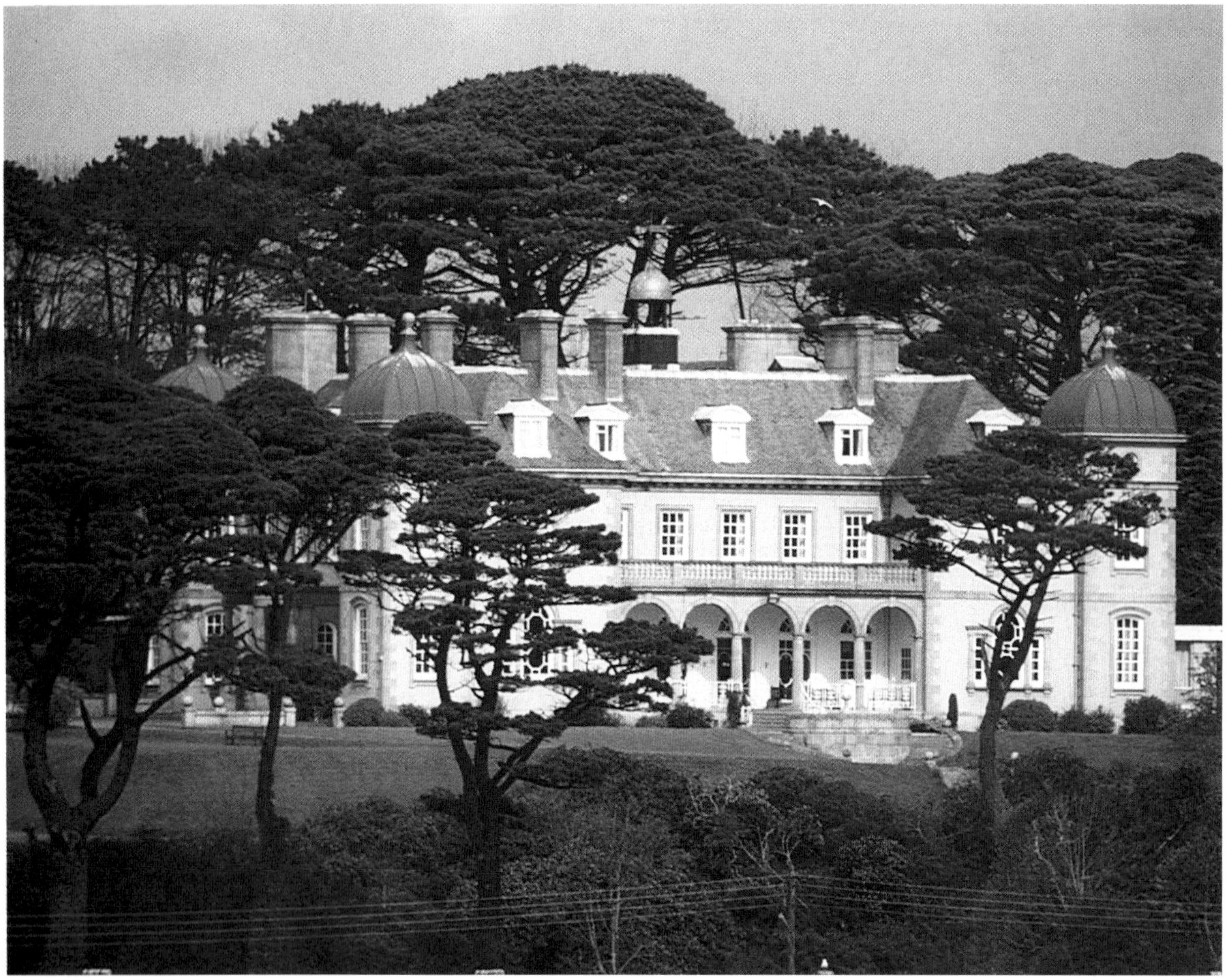

FOWEY HALL HOTEL & RESTAURANT

HANSON DRIVE, FOWEY, CORNWALL PL23 1ET
TEL: 01726 833866 FAX: 01726 834100 E-MAIL: info@foweyhall.com

Situated in five acres of beautiful grounds overlooking the Estuary, Fowey Hall Hotel is a magnificent Victorian mansion renowned for its excellent service and comfortable accommodation. The fine panelling and superb plasterwork ceilings add character to the spacious public rooms. Located in either the main house or the Court, the 25 bedrooms include suites and interconnecting rooms. All are well-proportioned with a full range of modern comforts. The panelled dining rooms provide an intimate atmosphere where guests may savour the local delicacies. Using the best of regional produce, the menu comprises tempting seafood and fish specialities. The hotel offers a full crèche service. Guests may swim in the indoor swimming pool or play croquet in the gardens. Older children have not been forgotten and the cellars of the mansion are well-equipped with table tennis, table football and many other games. Outdoor pursuits include sea fishing, boat trips and a variety of water sports such as sailing, scuba-diving and windsurfing. There are several coastal walks for those who wish to explore Cornwall and its beautiful landscape. **Directions:** On reaching Fowey, go straight over the mini roundabout and turn right into Hanson Drive. Fowey Hall Drive is on the right. Price Guide: Double/twin from £125; superior double from £166; suite from £180.

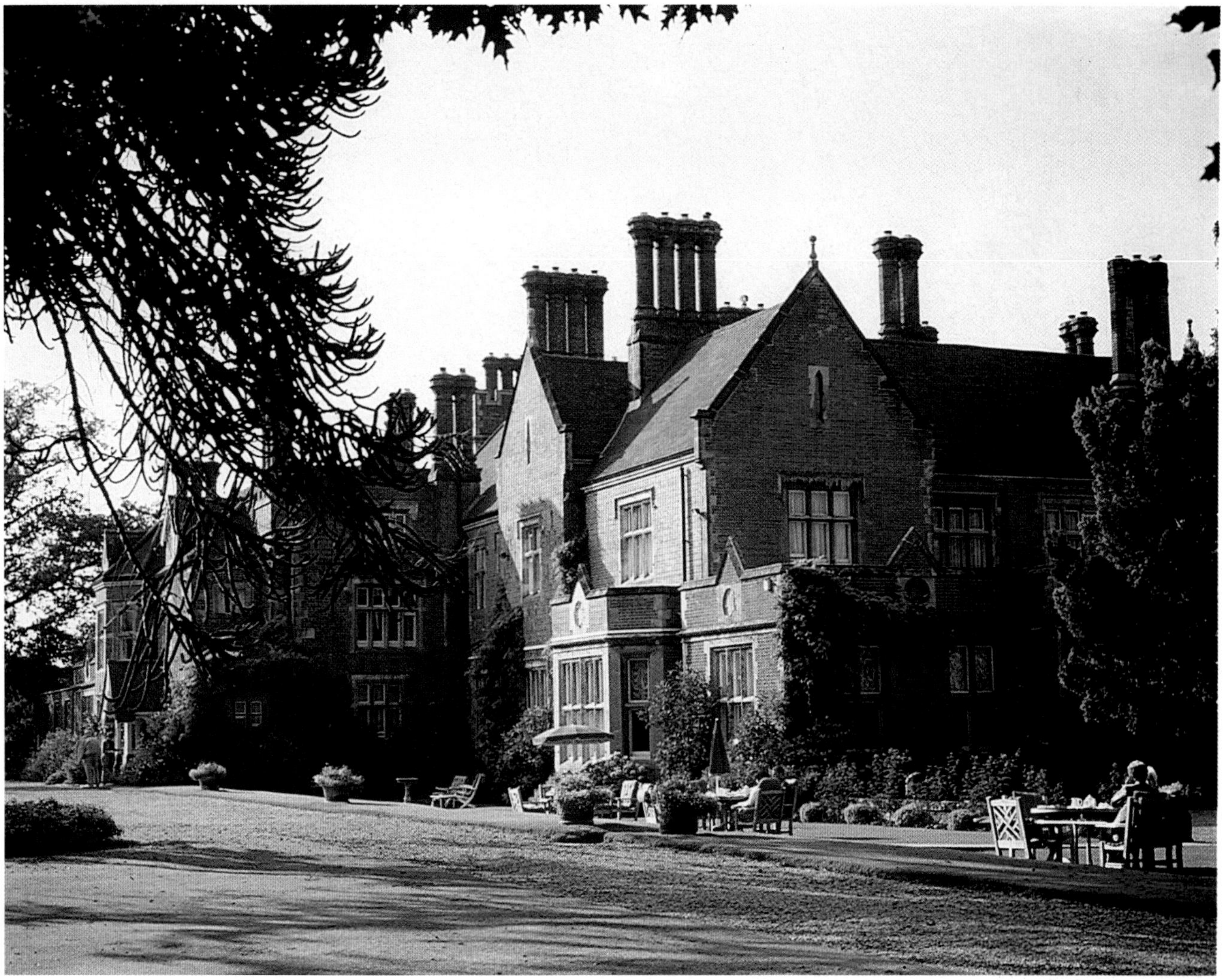

ALEXANDER HOUSE HOTEL

EAST STREET, TURNER'S HILL, WEST SUSSEX RH10 4QD

TEL: 01342 714914 FAX: 01342 717328 E-MAIL: info@alexanderhouse.co.uk

A previous winner of Johansens Most Excellent Service award, Alexander House is a magnificent mansion with its own secluded 135 acres of parkland, including a gently sloping valley which forms the head of the River Medway. Records trace the estate from 1332 when a certain John Atte Fen made it his home. Alexander House is now a modern paragon of good taste and excellence. Spacious rooms throughout this luxurious hotel are splendidly decorated to emphasise their many original features and the bedrooms are lavishly furnished to the highest standards of comfort. The House is renowned for its delicious classic English and French cuisine, rare wines and vintage liqueurs. Music recitals and garden parties feature among a full programme of special summer events and the open fires and cosy atmosphere make this the ideal place to pamper yourself in winter. The many facilities include a resident beautician. Courtesy transport can take guests to Gatwick Airport in under 15 minutes. Antique shops, National Trust properties, museums and the Royal Pavilion in Brighton are nearby. Gardens close by include Wakehurst Place, Nymans and Leonardslee. **Directions:** Alexander House lies on the B2110 road between Turner's Hill and East Grinstead, six miles from junction 10 of the M23 motorway Price Guide: Single £135; double £165; twin/junior suite £235; four-poster suite £310.

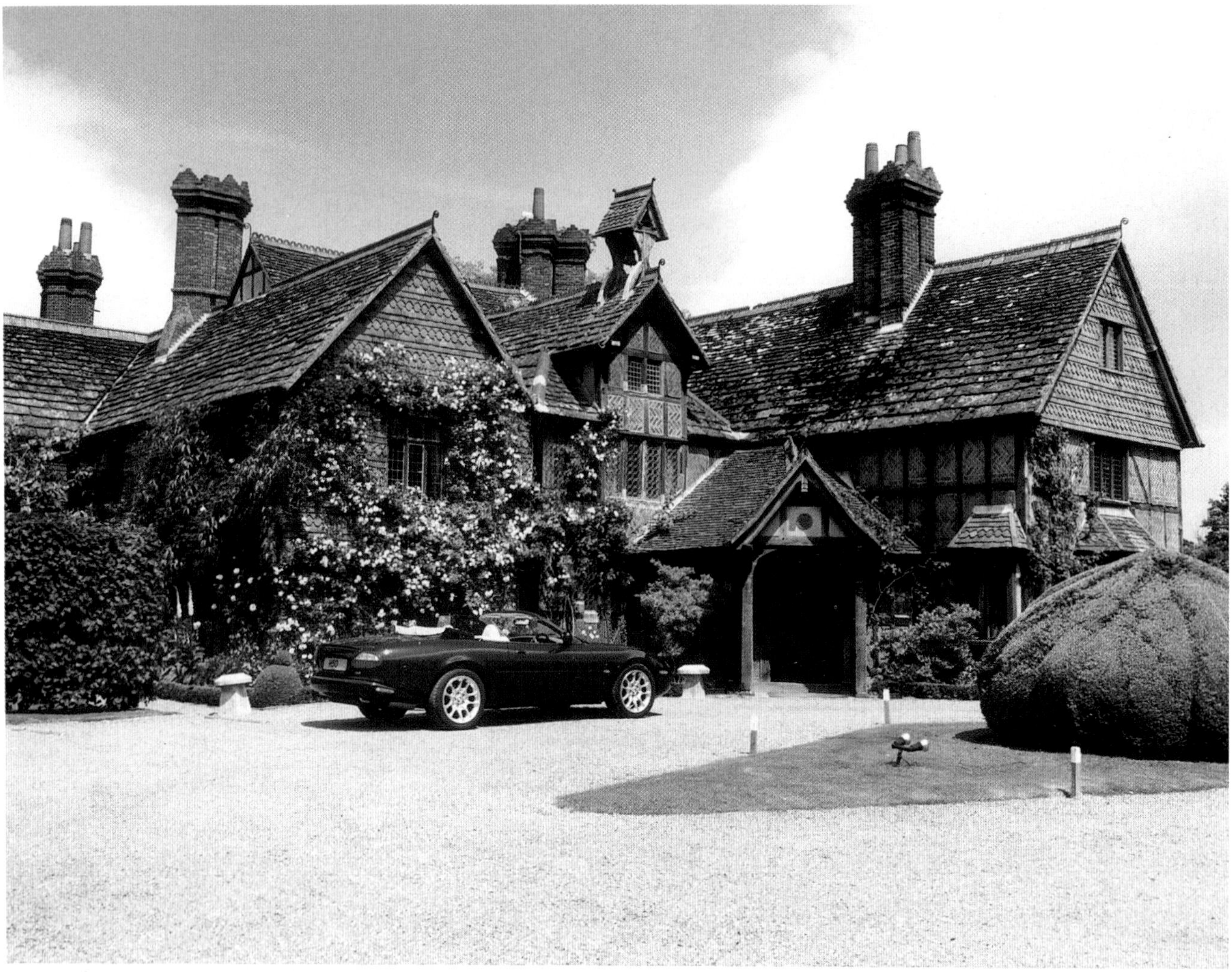

LANGSHOTT MANOR

LANGSHOTT, HORLEY, SURREY RH6 9LN
TEL: 01293 786680 **FAX:** 01293 783905 **E-MAIL:** admin@langshottmanor.com

The peace and seclusion of this beautiful Manor House belies its close proximity to London's Gatwick Airport, 8 minutes away by car. Retaining the essential feel of a fine Elizabethan home, Langshott offers stylish bedrooms and an intimate dining room with every provision for your comfort. The Manor becomes the perfect beginning or end to your holiday in Britain. Free car parking is offered locally for one week and a complimentary car is made available to guests travelling to Gatwick. Although Langshott Manor is situated near to the airport, the house is tucked away down a quiet country lane amidst 3 acres of beautiful gardens and enchanting ponds. A peaceful ambience pervades the manor, ensuring complete relaxation for all its guests. For a longer stay, the area is also a haven for sport enthusiasts with racing at Epsom and Goodwood and polo at Cowdray and Gaurds. Many National Trust gardens and properties are clustered around Langshott Manor such as Hever Castle, Chartwell and Knole Park. Central London is 30 minutes away via the Gatwick/Victoria Express. **Directions:** From A23 in Horley take Ladbroke Road (Chequers Hotel roundabout) to Langshott. The Manor is three quarters of a mile (one kilometre) on the right. Price Guide: Single from £155; double/twin £175–£250; suite £275.

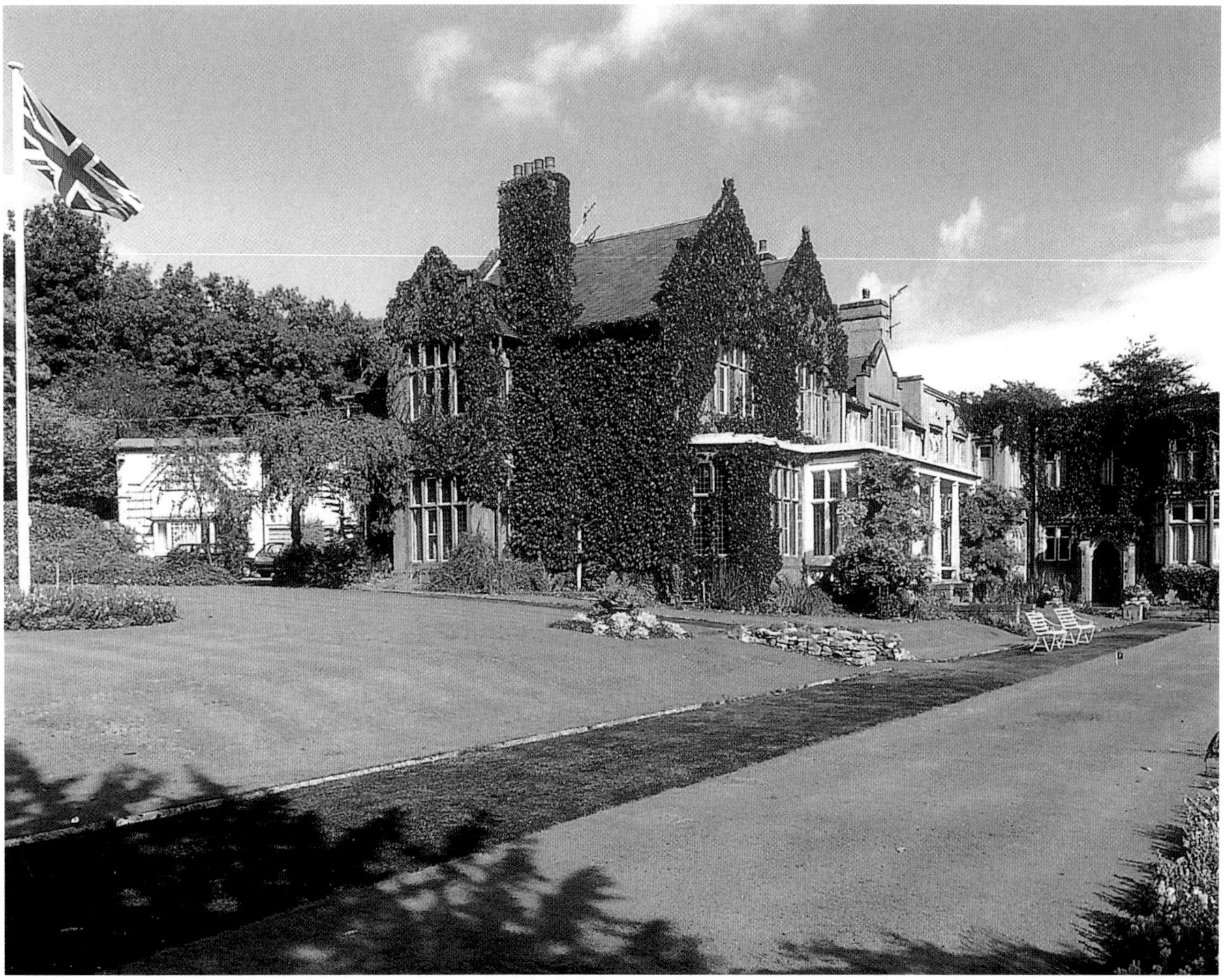

GRAYTHWAITE MANOR

FERNHILL ROAD, GRANGE-OVER-SANDS, CUMBRIA LA11 7JE

TEL: 015395 32001 FAX: 015395 35549 E-MAIL: sales@graythwaitemanor.co.uk

This beautifully furnished, traditionally run country house has been run by the Blakemore family since 1937 and extends a warm welcome to its guests. It enjoys a superb setting in eight acres of private landscaped gardens and woodland on the hillside overlooking Morecambe Bay. Each bedroom is decorated and furnished in the best of taste and many offer superb views across the gardens and bay to the Pennines beyond. Elegant, spacious lounges with fresh flowers and antiques provide an exclusive setting and log fires are lit to add extra cheer on cooler nights. The Manor enjoys an excellent reputation for its cuisine and guests can look forward to a six-course dinner comprising carefully prepared dishes complemented by the right wine from the extensive cellar. A few miles inland from Grange-over-Sands are Lake Windermere and Coniston Water and some of the most majestic scenery in the country. Nearby are the village of Cartmel, Holker Hall, Levens Hall and Sizergh Castle. The area abounds with historic buildings, gardens and museums **Directions:** Take M6 to junction 36 and then the A590 towards Kendal, followed by the A590 towards Barrow. At roundabout take B5277 to Grange-over-Sands and go through town turning right opposite the fire station into Fernhill Road. The hotel is on the left. Price Guide: Single £55–£75; double/twin £99–£120.

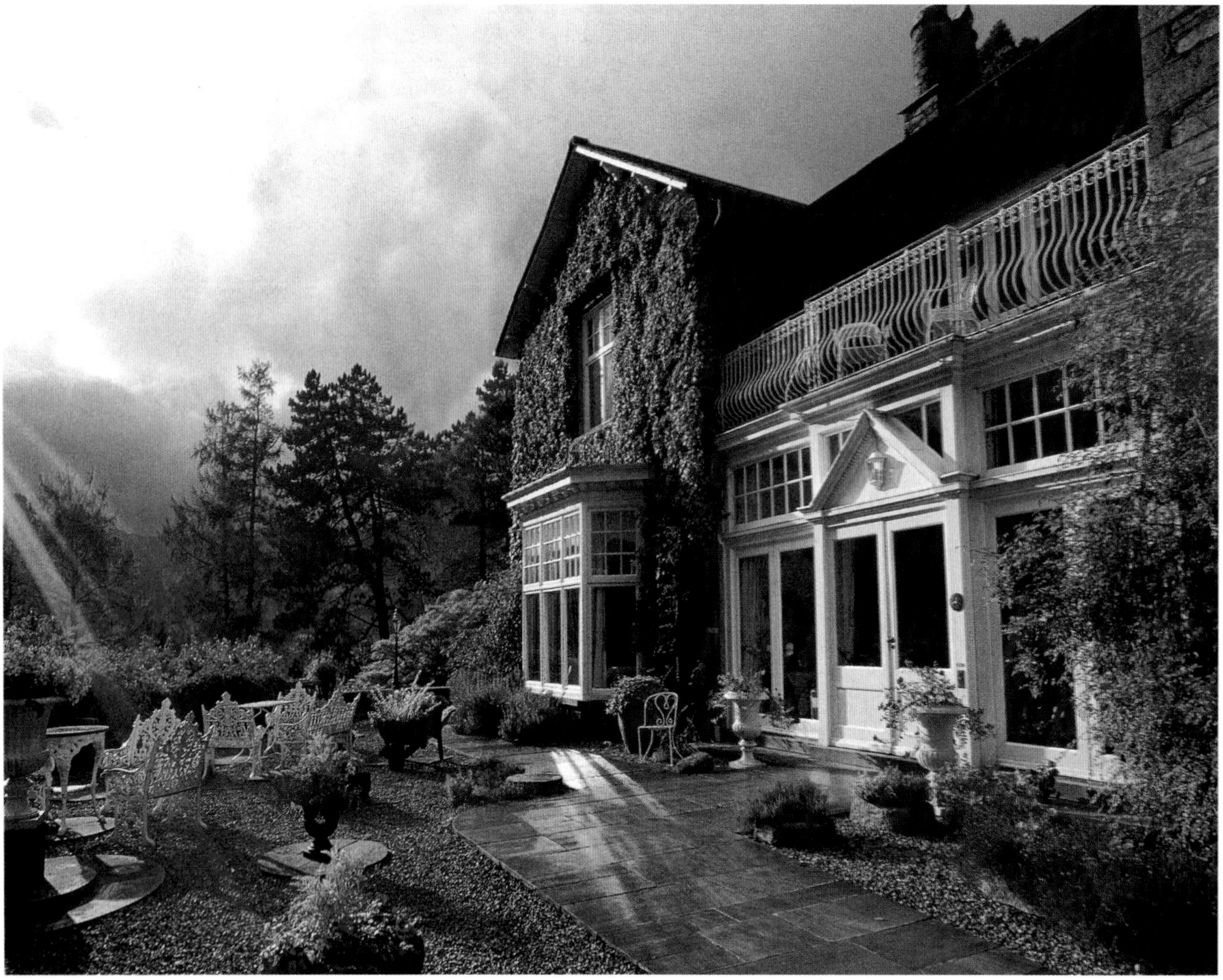

MICHAELS NOOK

GRASMERE, CUMBRIA LA22 9RP
TEL: 015394 35496 FAX: 015394 35645 E-MAIL: michaelsnook@btinternet.com

Built in 1859 and named after Michael the eponymous shepherd of Wordsworth's poem, Michael's Nook has long been established as one of Britain's leading country house hotels. Opened as a hotel in 1969 by Reg and Elizabeth Gifford, it overlooks Grasmere Valley and is surrounded by gardens and trees. The hotel's interior reflects Reg's appreciation of antique English furniture, rugs, prints and porcelain. There are two suites and twelve individually designed bedrooms. Reg's hobby of showing Great Danes has brought him many awards, including Best of Breed at Crufts. In the acclaimed restaurant, polished tables are set with fine Stuart crystal and Wedgwood china. The best ingredients are used to create dishes memorable for their delicate flavours and artistic presentation. An extensive and high quality wine list compliments the food. The panelled Oak Room, with its stone fireplace and gilt furnishings, can be booked for private parties and executive meetings. Leisure facilities at the nearby Wordsworth Hotel are available to guests, as is free golf Mon–Fri at Keswick Golf Club. Michael's Nook is, first and foremost, a home where comfort is the watchword. It is rated the best restaurant in the North of England with a Michelin Star and 4 AA rosettes.

Directions: Michaels Nook is on the hillside behind the Swan Hotel – East of A591. Price Guide: (including 5 course dinner): Single from £140; double/twin £180–£290; suite £220–£370.

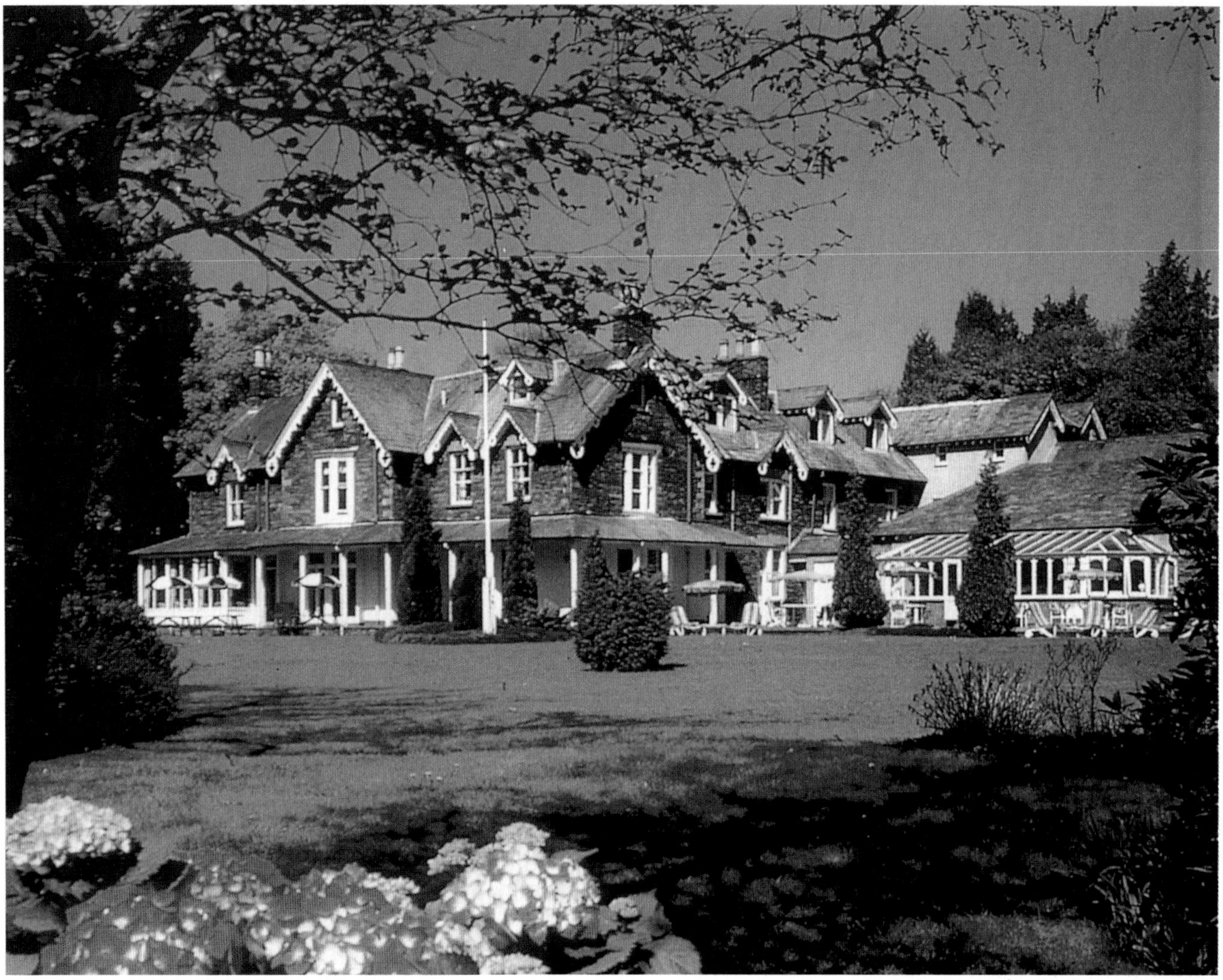

THE WORDSWORTH HOTEL

GRASMERE, CUMBRIA LA22 9SW
TEL: 015394 35592 FAX: 015394 35765 E-MAIL: enquiry@wordsworth–grasmere.co.uk

In the very heart of the English Lakeland, The Wordsworth Hotel combines AA 4 Star standards with the magnificence of the surrounding fells. Set in its own grounds in the village of Grasmere, the hotel provides first-class, year-round facilities for both business and leisure travellers. It has a reputation for the high quality of its food, accommodation and hospitality. The comfortable bedrooms have well-equipped bathrooms and there are two suites with whirlpool baths. 24-hour room service is available for drinks and light refreshments. Peaceful lounges overlook landscaped gardens and the heated indoor pool opens on to a sun-trap terrace. There is a Jacuzzi, mini-gym, sauna and solarium. As well as a Cocktail Bar, the hotel has its own pub, "The Dove and Olive Branch", which has received many accolades. In "The Prelude Restaurant", which has 2 AA Rosettes, menus offer a good choice of dishes, prepared with skill and imagination from the freshest produce. The Wordsworth Hotel is a perfect venue for conferences, incentive weekends and corporate entertaining. Three function rooms are available with highly professional back-up. Lakeland's principal places of interest are all within easy reach. **Directions:** The hotel is located next to Grasmere village church. Price guide: Price Guide: Single £80–£135; double/twin £130–£190; suite £220–£270.

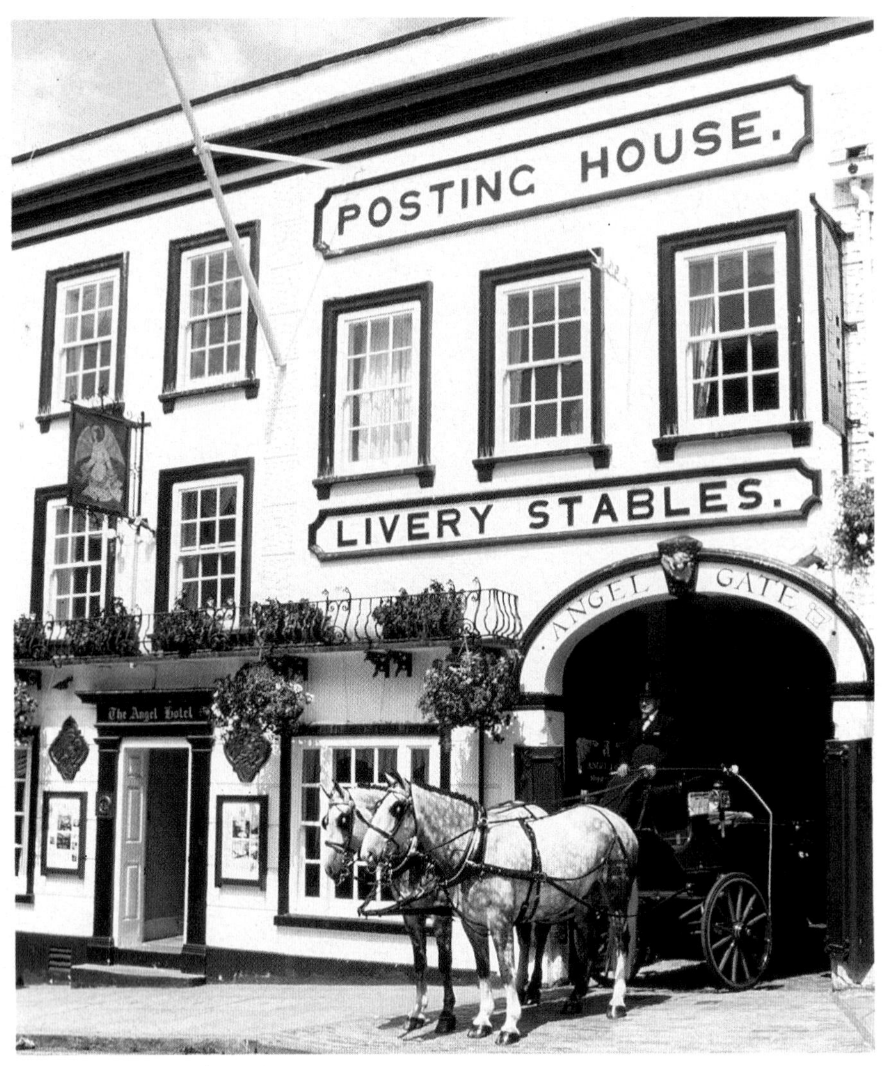

THE ANGEL POSTING HOUSE AND LIVERY

91 THE HIGH STREET, GUILDFORD, SURREY GU1 3DP

TEL: 01483 564555 FAX: 01483 533770 E-MAIL: angelhotel@hotmail.com

The Angel, a delightful historic coaching inn on the old Portsmouth road, now a luxurious small hotel, has stood on the cobbled High Street in the centre of Guildford since the 16th century. This timber-framed building has welcomed many famous visitors, including Lord Nelson, Sir Francis Drake, Jane Austen and Charles Dickens. Today, with easy access to Gatwick, Heathrow, the M4, M3 and M25, it is ideally placed for both business and leisure weekends. Relax with afternoon tea in the galleried lounge with its oak-beamed Jacobean fireplace and 17th-century parliament clock; a welcome retreat from the bustle of the nearby shops. The No. 1 Angel Gate Restaurant, with its vaulted ceiling and intimate atmosphere, serves a wide choice of superb English and continental cuisine together with fine wines and impeccable service. The charming bedrooms and suites are all unique and named after a famous visitor. Excellent communications, presentation facilities and 24-hour service make this a good choice for business meetings. Guests can enjoy complimentary use of modern leisure club facilities just a short drive away.. **Directions:** From M3 jct3 take A322; or from M25 jct10 take A3. The Angel is in the centre of Guildford, within the pedestrian priority area – guests should enquire about vehicle access and parking when booking. Price Guide: (room only): Double/twin £140–£165; suite £185–£205.

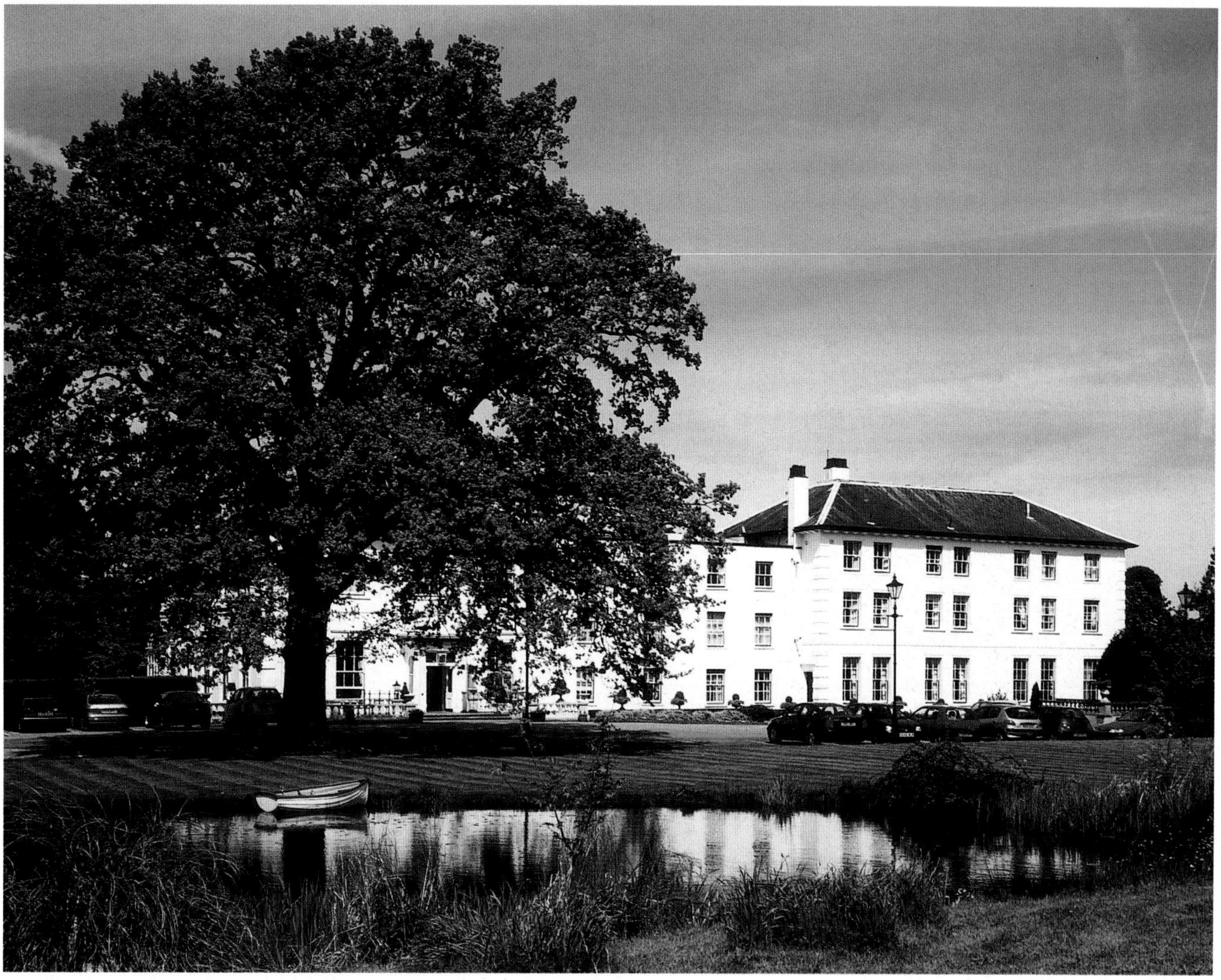

West Lodge Park Country House Hotel

COCKFOSTERS ROAD, HADLEY WOOD, BARNET, HERTFORDSHIRE EN4 0PY
TEL: 020 8216 3900 **FAX:** 020 8216 3937 **E-MAIL:** info@westlodgepark.com

West Lodge Park is a country house hotel which stands in 34 acres of Green Belt parklands and gardens. These include a lake and an arboretum with hundreds of mature trees. Despite the advantages of this idyllic setting, the hotel is only 1 mile from the M25 and within easy reach of London. Run by the Beale family for over 50 years, West Lodge Park was originally a gentleman's country seat, rebuilt in 1838 on the site of an earlier keeper's lodge. In the public rooms, antiques, original paintings and period furnishings create a restful atmosphere. All the bright and individually furnished bedrooms, many of which enjoy country views, have a full range of modern amenities. Well presented cuisine is available in the elegant restaurant. Residents enjoy free membership and a free taxi to the nearby leisure centre, which has excellent facilities. Hatfield House and St Albans Abbey are 15 minutes drive. The hotel is credited with AA 4 stars and 2 Rosettes, RAC 4 stars plus 3 merit awards. **Directions:** The hotel is on A111 one mile north of Cockfosters underground station and one mile south of junction 24 on M25. Price Guide: Single £75–£140; double/twin from £95–£180.

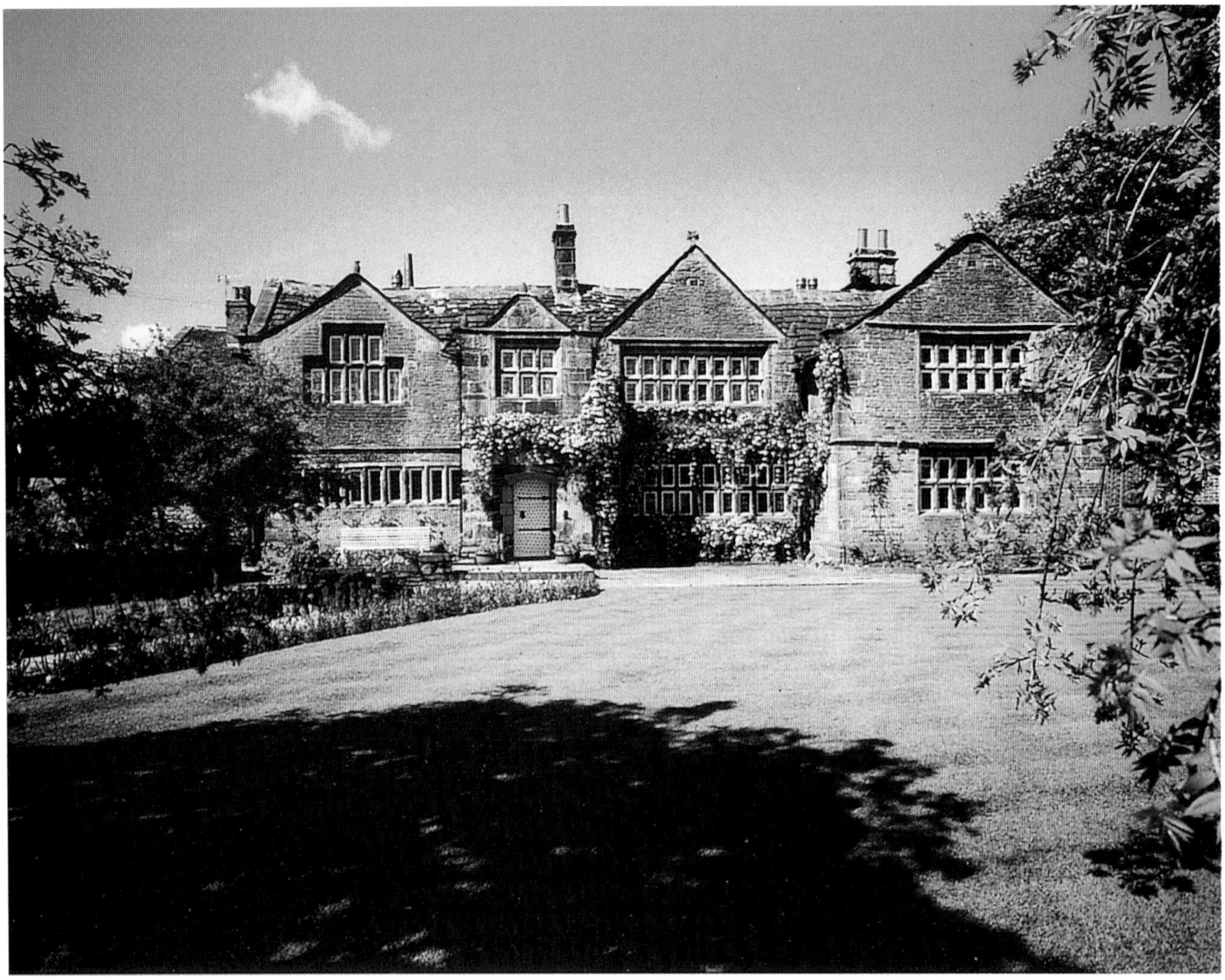

HOLDSWORTH HOUSE

HOLDSWORTH ROAD, HOLMFIELD, HALIFAX, WEST YORKSHIRE HX2 9TG
TEL: 01422 240024 FAX: 01422 245174 E-MAIL: info@holdsworthhouse.co.uk

Holdsworth House is a retreat of quality and charm standing three miles north of Halifax in the heart of Yorkshire's West Riding. Built in 1633, it was acquired by the Pearson family over 35 years ago. With care, skill and professionalism they have created a hotel and restaurant of considerable repute. The interior, with its polished panelling and open fireplaces, has been carefully preserved and embellished with fine antique furniture and ornaments. The comfortable lounge opens onto a pretty courtyard and overlooks the herb garden and gazebo. The restaurant comprises three beautifully furnished rooms, ideal for private dinner parties. Exciting modern English and Continental cuisine is meticulously prepared and presented, complemented by a thoughtfully compiled wine list. The restaurant has two AA Rosettes and Head Chef, Neal Birtwell and his talented team are constantly striving to attain a third. Each cosy bedroom has its own style, from the four split-level suites to the two single rooms designed for wheelchair access. This is the perfect base from which to explore the Pennines, the Yorkshire Dales and Haworth, home of the Brontë family. Closed at Christmas. **Directions:** From M1 Jct42 take M62 west to Jct26. Follow A58 to Halifax (ignore signs to town centre). At Burdock Way roundabout take A629 to Keighley; after 1½ miles go right into Shay Lane; hotel is 1 mile on right Price Guide: Single £87–£125; double/twin £107 –£132; suite £140. Weekend breaks are available.

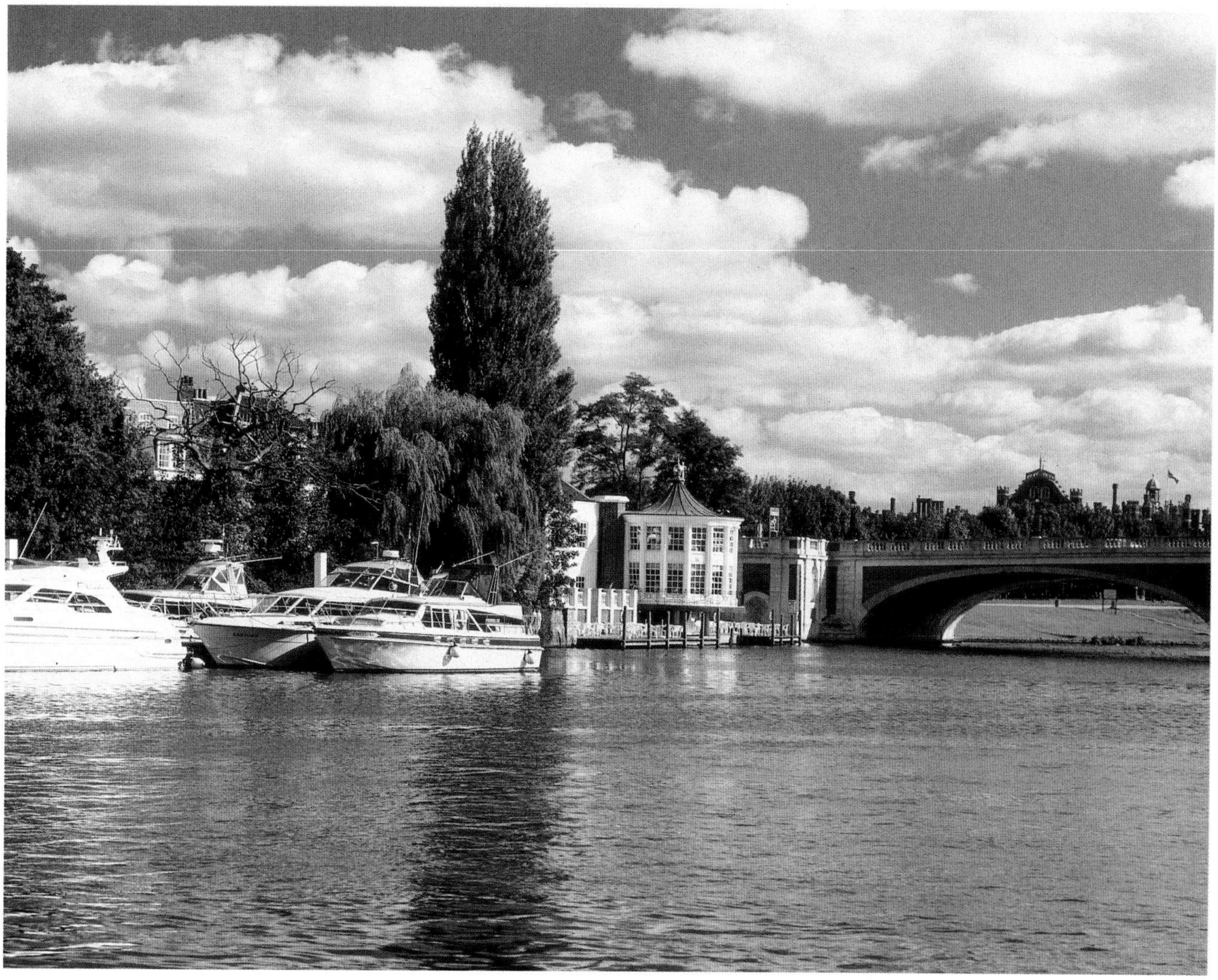

THE CARLTON MITRE HOTEL

HAMPTON COURT ROAD, HAMPTON COURT, SURREY KT8 9BN
TEL: 020 8979 9988 FAX: 020 8979 9777 E-MAIL: gmmitre@carltonhotels.co.uk

Set on the banks of the River Thames, this impressive hotel enjoys glorious views over Hampton Court Palace, the Thames and the courtyard. Built in 1665 at the request of Charles II, The Carlton Mitre Hotel maintains a fine equilibrium between tradition and modernity. The elegant en suite bedrooms are individually furnished and include all the latest amenities such as satellite television and tea and coffee facilities. Guests must savour the chef's creations in the superb River's Edge Restaurant, with its panoramic views of the bustling Thames scene. The recently refurbished Bar, renowned for its fine Jazz, BBQ's on Sundays, serves light snacks and imaginative Mediterranean cuisine. During the summer months, cocktails and other refreshments are served by the riverside as the boats pass by. The hotel's private terrace and jetty are perfect for guests wishing to relax and unwind. An excellent standard of service is offered throughout the hotel. Nearby attractions include the neighbouring Hampton Court Palace, the beautiful Kew Gardens and the racecourses of Kempton Park, Sandown Park and Epsom Downs. Golf enthusiasts will be pleased with the number of excellent courses close by. **Directions:** Leave M3 at jct1 and take A308 following signs for Hampton Court. The hotel is beside Hampton Court bridge opposite the Palace. Price Guide: Double/twin £170–£205; suite £250–£295.

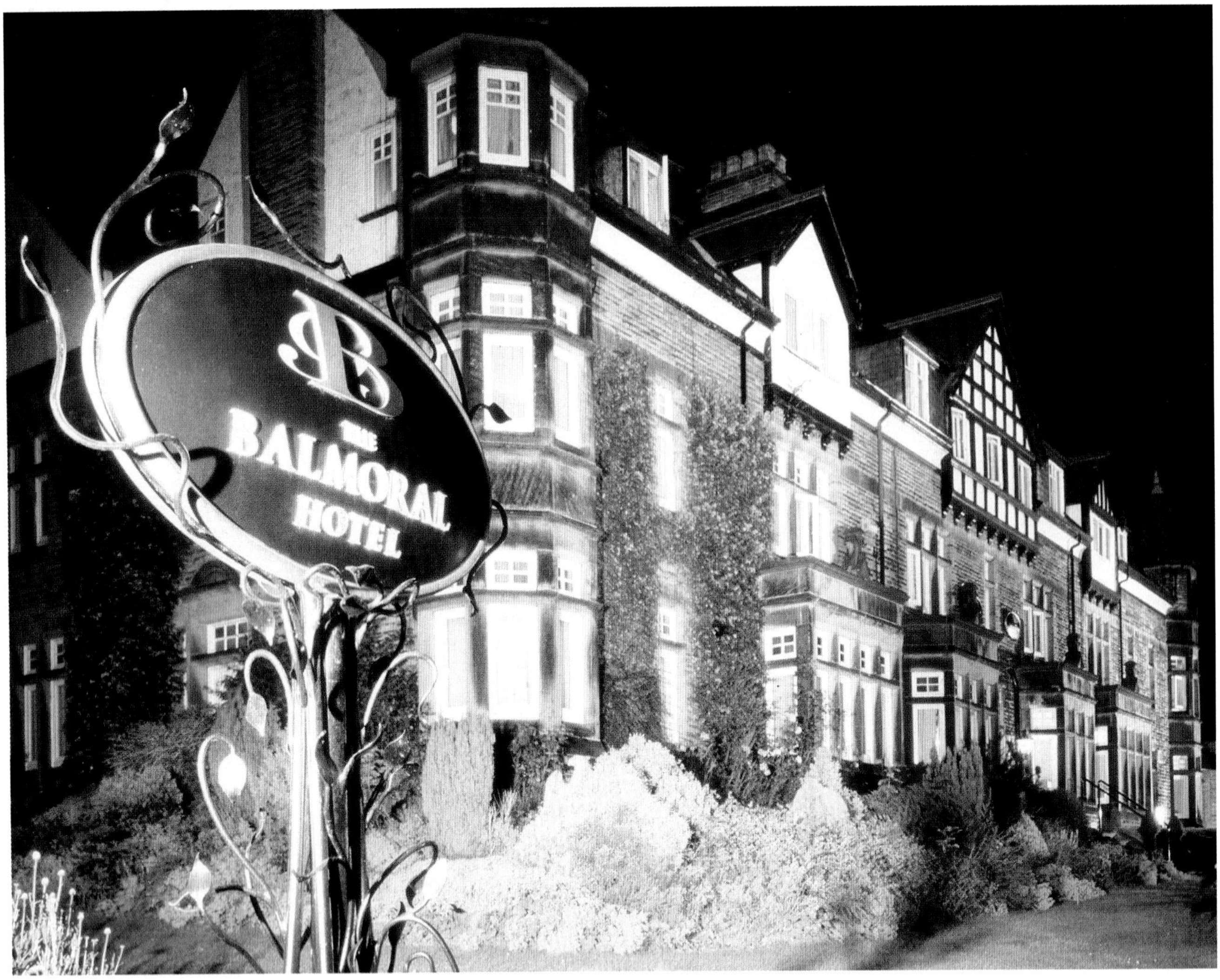

THE BALMORAL HOTEL

FRANKLIN MOUNT, HARROGATE, NORTH YORKSHIRE HG1 5EJ
TEL: 01423 508208 FAX: 01423 530652 E-MAIL: info@balmoralhotel.co.uk

The Balmoral is a delightful privately owned individual hotel with an award-winning garden, near the heart of the elegant spa town of Harrogate. All the bedrooms are luxurious with individual decoration and furnishings offering the highest standards of comfort. Ten rooms have four-posters, each in a different style. For ultimate luxury, The Windsor Suite even boasts its own whirlpool. Guests enjoy the fascinating memorabilia on various themes throughout the Hotel and they can relax in the exquisite Harry's Bar or enjoy a quiet drink in the cosy Snug before taking dinner in Villu Toots. The extensive modern Mediterranean menu embraces both the traditional and unexpected, popular with non-residents. The wine list is equally diverse with fine vintages rubbing shoulders with more youthful newcomers. Guests can enjoy the use of the Academy – one of the finest Health & Fitness Centres in the North, five minutes from the Hotel. Special Spa Breaks throughout the year. Harrogate is famed for its antique and fashion shops, art galleries and Herriot country and the many historic homes and castles in the area. **Directions:** From Harrogate Conference Centre, follow the Kings Road up and the hotel is 1/2 mile on the right. Price Guide: Single £90–£100; double/twin £114–£130; suites £137–£185. Special Breaks available.

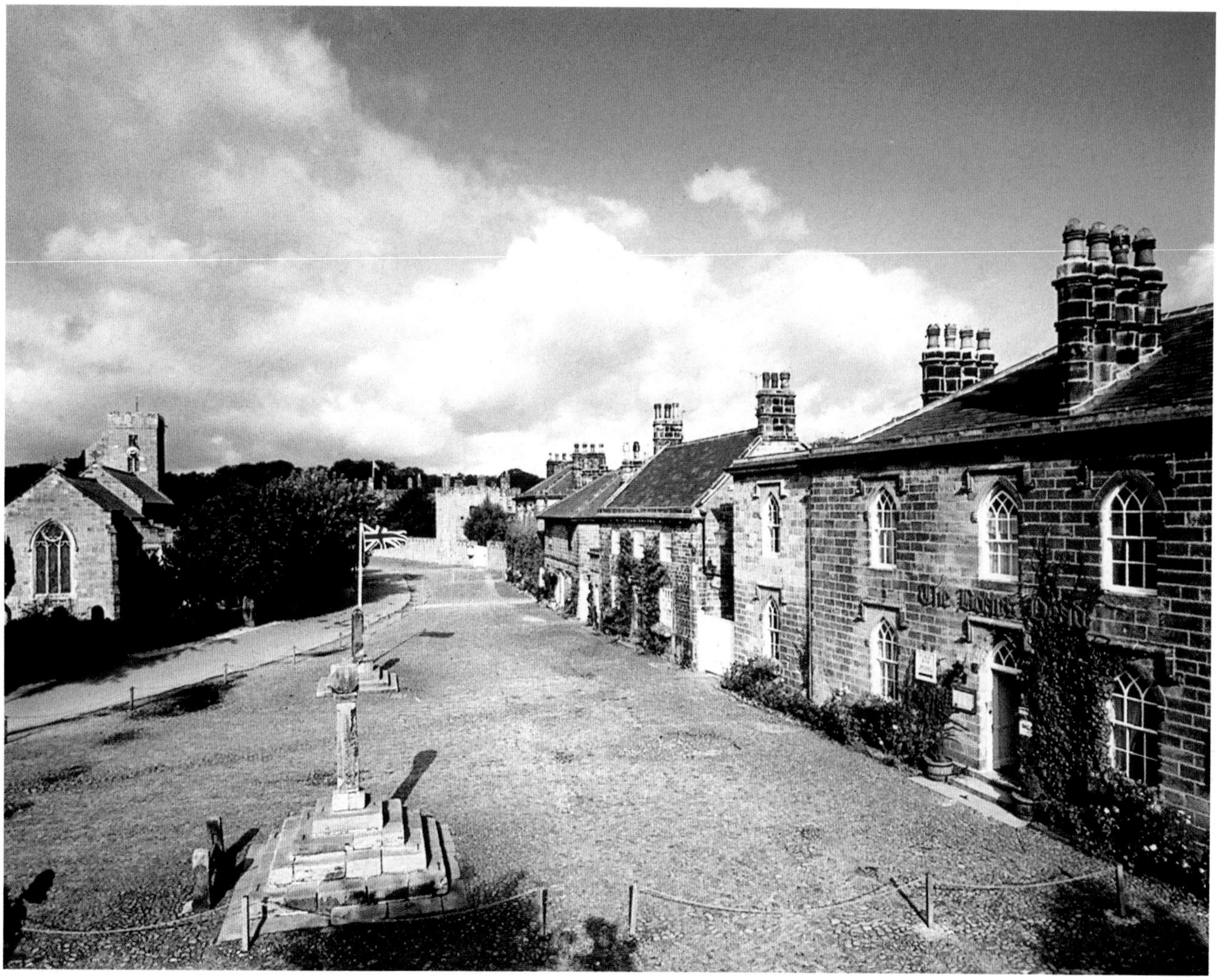

The Boar's Head Hotel

THE RIPLEY CASTLE ESTATE, HARROGATE, NORTH YORKSHIRE HG3 3AY
TEL: 01423 771888 FAX: 01423 771509 E-MAIL: reservations@boarsheadripley.co.uk

Imagine relaxing in a luxury hotel at the centre of a historic private country Estate in England's incredibly beautiful North Country. The Ingilby family who have lived in Ripley Castle for 28 generations invite you to enjoy their hospitality at The Boar's Head Hotel. There are 25 luxury bedrooms, individually decorated and furnished, most with king-size beds. The Restaurant menu is outstanding, presented by a creative and imaginative kitchen brigade and complemented by a wide selection of reasonably priced, good quality wines. There is a welcoming bar serving traditional ales straight from the wood and popular bar meal selections. When staying at The Boar's Head, guests can enjoy complimentary access to the delightful walled gardens and grounds of Ripley Castle, which include the lakes and a deer park. A conference at Ripley is a different experience – using the idyllic meeting facilities available in the castle, organisers and delegates alike will appreciate the peace and tranquillity of the location which also offers opportunities for all types of leisure activity in the Deer Park. **Directions:** Ripley is very accessible, just 10 minutes from the conference town of Harrogate, 20 minutes from the motorway network, and Leeds/Bradford Airport, and 40 minutes from the City of York. Price Guide: Single £99–£125; double £120–£145.

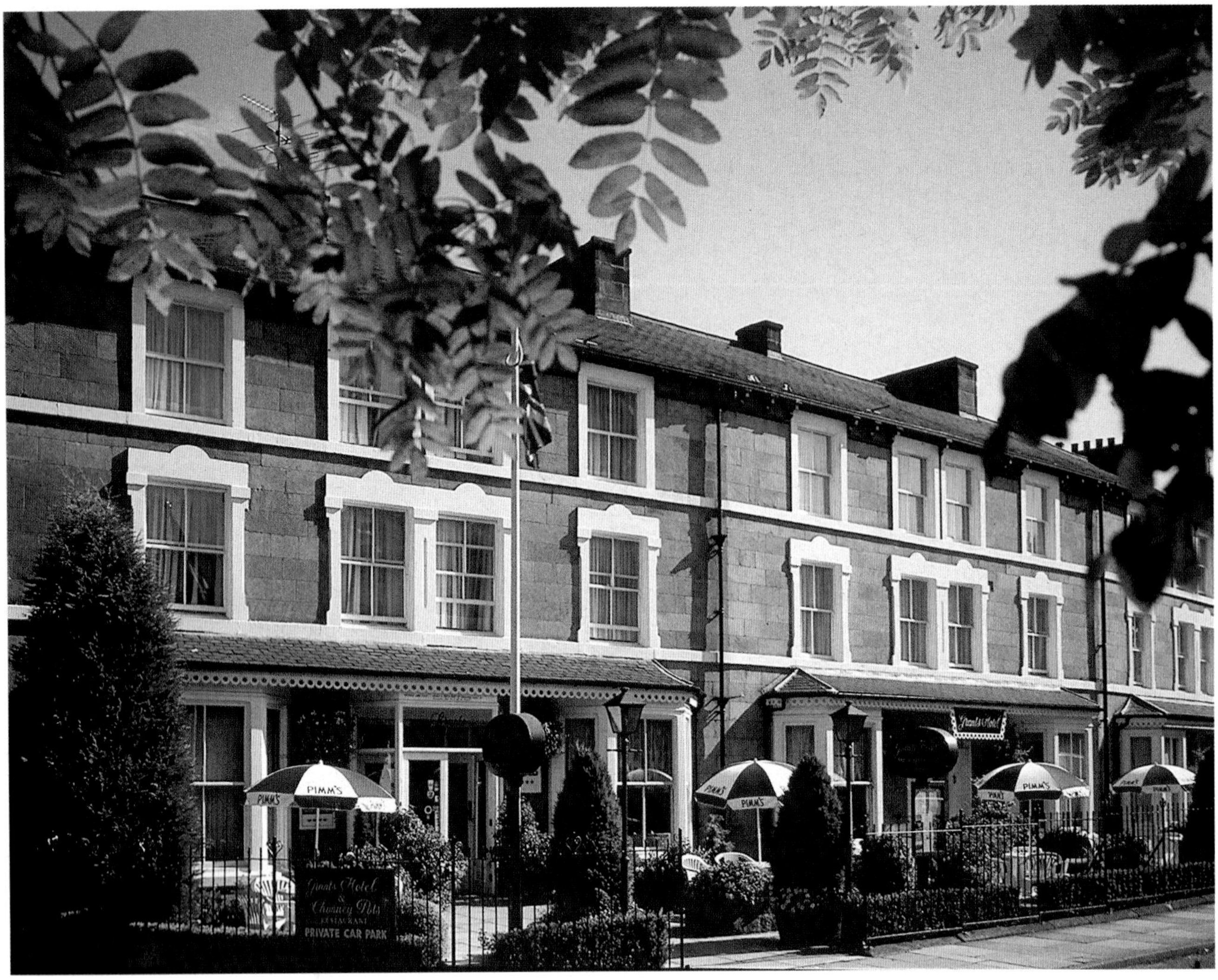

Grants Hotel

SWAN ROAD, HARROGATE, NORTH YORKSHIRE HG1 2SS

TEL: 01423 560666 FAX: 01423 502550 E-MAIL: enquiries@grantshotel–harrogate.com

Towards the end of the last century, Harrogate became fashionable among the gentry, who came to 'take the waters' of the famous spa. Today's visitors have one advantage over their Victorian counterparts – they can enjoy the hospitality of Grants Hotel, the creation of Pam and Peter Grant. Their friendly welcome, coupled with high standards of service, ensures a pleasurable stay. All the bedrooms are attractively decorated and have en suite bathrooms. Downstairs, guests can relax in the comfortable lounge or take refreshments out to the terrace gardens. Drinks and light meals are available at all times from Harry Grant's Bar and dinner is served in the French café-style Chimney Pots Bistro, complete with brightly coloured check blinds and cloths and lots of humorous 'Beryl Cook' pictures. Cuisine is basically traditional rustic with a smattering of Oriental influence complemented by the mouth-watering home-made puddings. Located less than five minutes' walk from Harrogate's Conference and Exhibition Centre, Grants offers its own luxury meeting and syndicate rooms, the Herriot Suite. The Royal Pump Room Museum and the Royal Baths Assembly Rooms are nearby. Guests have free use of 'The Academy Health and Leisure Club'. **Directions:** Swan Road is in the centre of Harrogate, off the A61 to Ripon. Price Guide: Single £99–£118; double/twin £114–£165; suites £170. Super value breaks available.

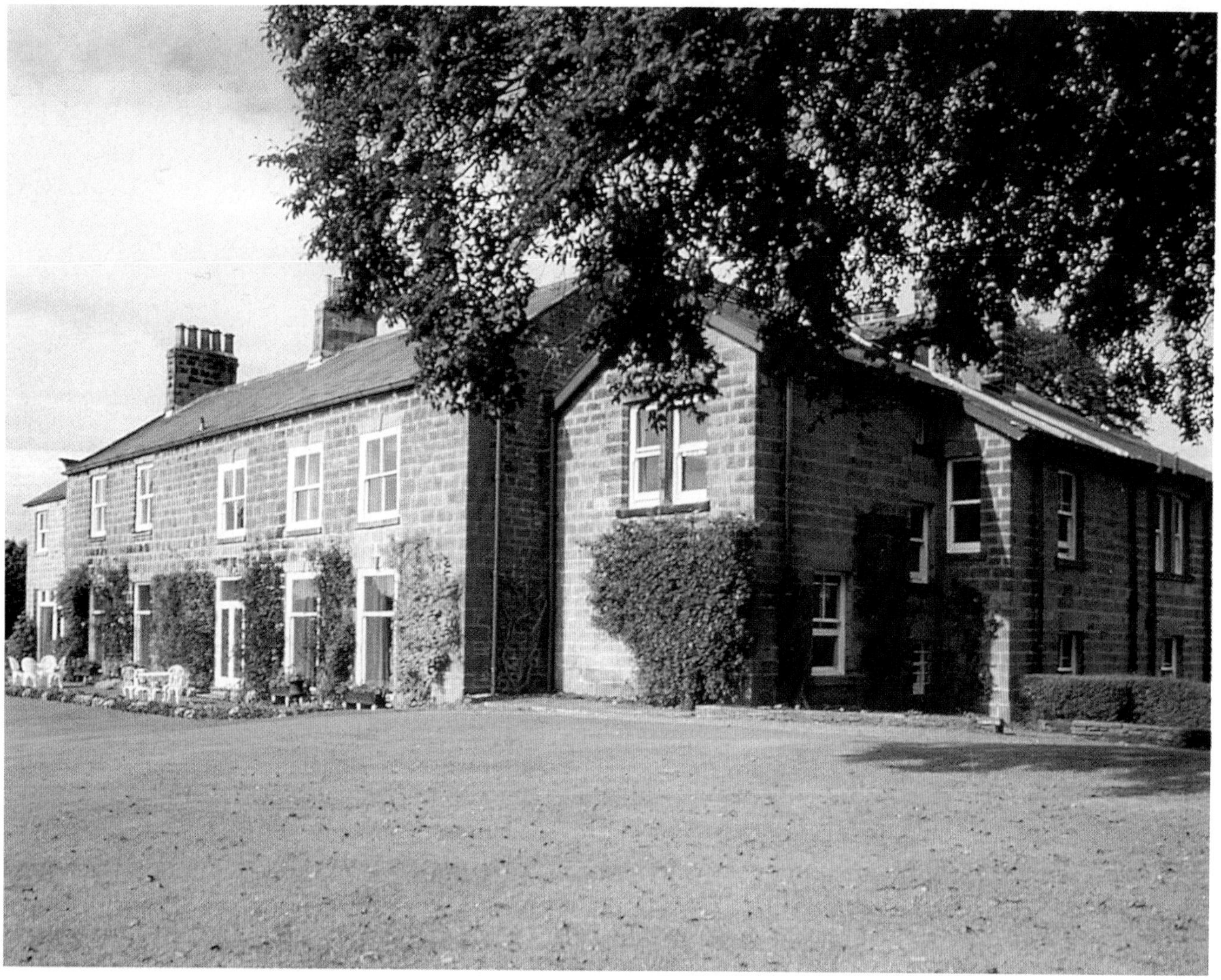

Hob Green Hotel And Restaurant

MARKINGTON, HARROGATE, NORTH YORKSHIRE HG3 3PJ
TEL: 01423 770031 FAX: 01423 771589 E-MAIL: info@hobgreen.com

Set in 870 acres of farm and woodland this charming 'country house' hotel is only a short drive from the spa town Harrogate and the ancient city of Ripon. The restaurant has an excellent reputation locally with only the finest fresh local produce being used, much of which is grown in the hotel's own garden. The interesting menus are complemented by an excellent choice of sensibly priced wines. All twelve bedrooms have been individually furnished and tastefully equipped to suit the most discerning guest. The drawing room and hall, warmed with log fires in cool weather, are comfortably furnished with the added attraction of fine antique furniture, porcelain and pictures. Situated in the heart of some of Yorkshire's most dramatic scenery, the hotel offers magnificent views of the valley beyond from all the main rooms. York is only 23 miles away. There is a wealth of cultural and historical interest nearby with Fountains Abbey and Studley Royal water garden and deer park a few minutes' drive. The Yorkshire Riding Centre is in Markington Village. Simply relax in this tranquil place where your every comfort is catered for. **Directions:** Turn left signposted Markington off the A61 Harrogate to Ripon road, the hotel is one mile after the village on the left Price Guide: Single £90; double/twin £95–£120; suite £130.

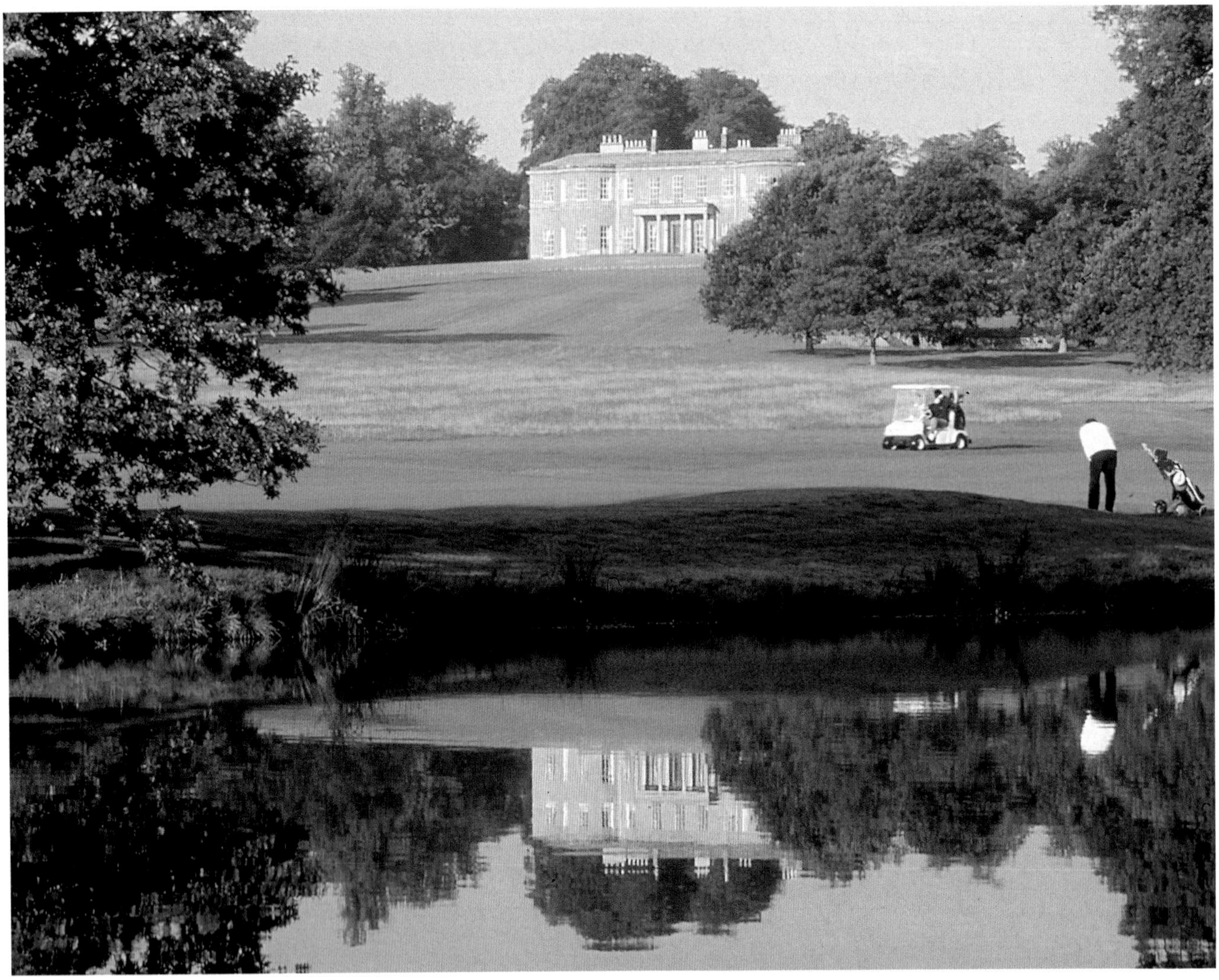

Rudding Park Hotel & Golf

RUDDING PARK, FOLLIFOOT, HARROGATE, NORTH YORKSHIRE HG3 1JH
TEL: 01423 871350 FAX: 01423 872286 E-MAIL: sales@ruddingpark.com

Rudding Park's award winning hotel is just 2 miles from Harrogate town centre. The house, built in the early 19th century, is a fine conference and banqueting centre. The adjoining hotel has been brilliantly designed and built to harmonise with the original mansion. Its setting is superb, surrounded by 230 acres of parkland. The hotel has an elegant façade and entrance, approached by a sweeping driveway. A warm welcome awaits guests in the pleasant foyer, with its big fireplace and easy chairs. The bedrooms are spacious, with contemporary cherry wood furniture, relaxing colour schemes, many modern accessories and lovely views over the estate. Guests can relax in the Mackaness Drawing Room. The stylish two AA Rosetted Clocktower Restaurant and Bar are inviting and on sunny days they extend onto the terrace. The food is delicious and the wine list extensive. Leisure facilities are excellent – there is an 18-hole par 72 parkland golf course which has played host to the PGA Mastercard tour series. The golf academy and driving range are ideal for lessons and practice. Croquet, fishing and riding are available close by. **Directions:** Rudding Park is accessible from the A1 north or south, via A661, being just off A658. Price Guide: Single £120–£140; double/twin £150–£170; suite from £280.

The Pier At Harwich

THE QUAY, HARWICH, ESSEX CO12 3HH
TEL: 01255 241212 **FAX:** 01255 551922 **E-MAIL:** Info@pieratharwich.co.uk

Housed in two historic, listed buildings, The Pier Hotel stands on the quayside of old Harwich, overlooking the bustling east coast harbour where the rivers Orwell and Stour meet. The main blue and white building is topped by a stubby tower and was built in the 1850s to serve travellers bound for the continent. Inside are two celebrated seafood restaurants, the blue and white nautically themed Ha'Penny Bistro on the ground floor opposite the bar and the first floor Harbourside with its splendid views. Chef patron Chris Oakley provides frequently changing menus to take maximum advantage of the fresh fish and shellfish. The hotel's salt-water tanks make lobster the house speciality and ensure they are always in prime condition. Most of the comfortably furnished second floor en suite bedrooms overlook the estuary which is alive with a preponderance of bobbing boats, high-speed craft and cruise liners heading for sunny climes. The next door building, a former public house dating from the 18th century, was acquired last year. It has been handsomely refurbished and converted into seven further guestrooms, including the Mayflower Suite with panoramic sea views. The building's sitting room is simply delightful. This is Constable country, and there are many charming old towns and villages to visit. **Directions:** From the A12 at Colchester, take the A120 directly to The Quay Price Guide: Single £62.50–£75; double/twin £80–£100; suite £150.

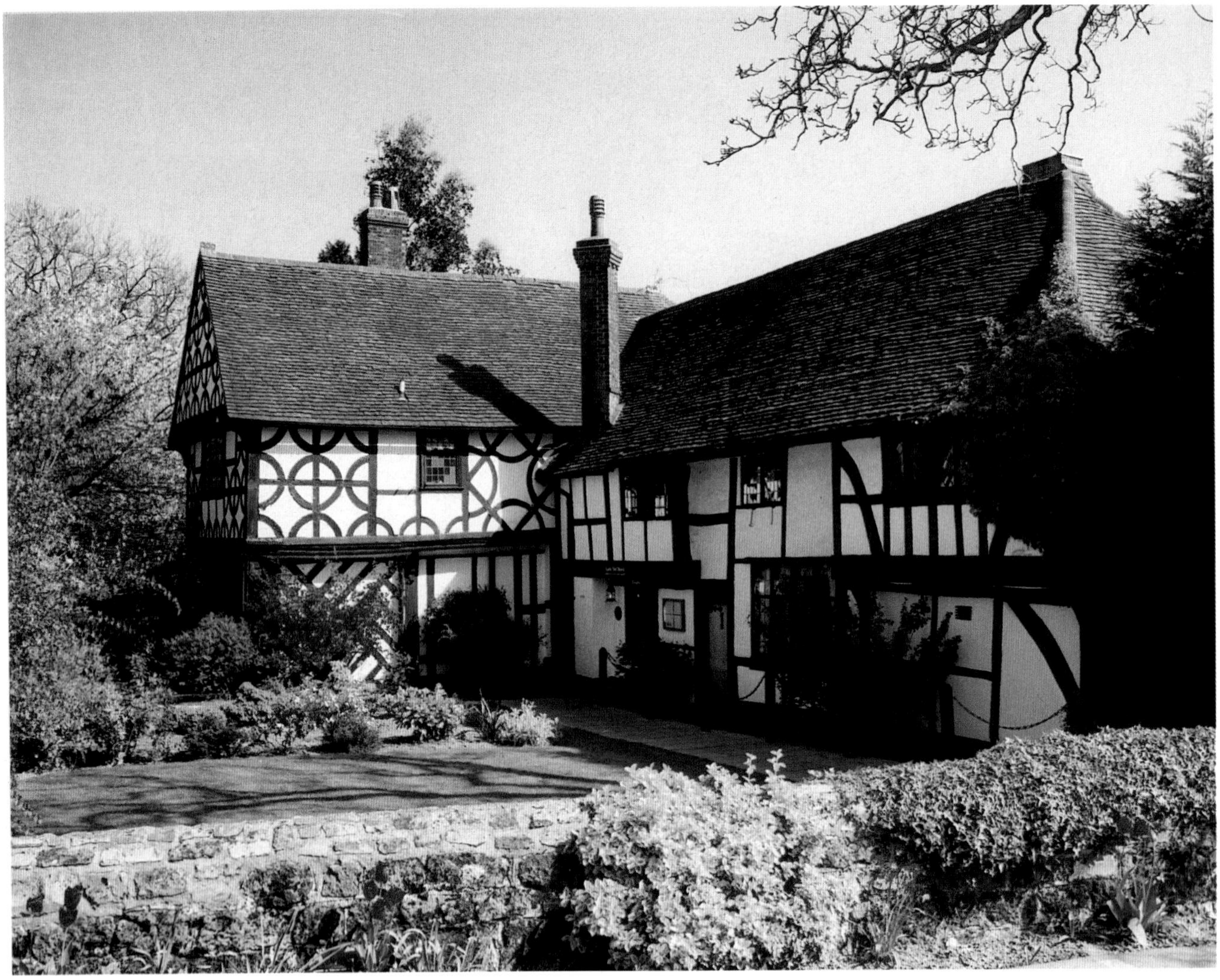

LYTHE HILL HOTEL

PETWORTH ROAD, HASLEMERE, SURREY GU27 3BQ
TEL: 01428 651251 FAX: 01428 644131 E-MAIL: lythe@lythehill.co.uk

Cradled by the Surrey foothills in a tranquil setting is the enchanting Lythe Hill Hotel. It is an unusual cluster of ancient buildings – parts of which date from the 14th century. While most of the beautifully appointed accommodation is in the more recently converted part of the hotel, there are five charming bedrooms in the Tudor House, including the Henry VIII room with a four-poster bed dated 1614! There are two delightful restaurants, the Auberge de France offers classic French cuisine in the oak-panelled room which overlooks the lake and parklands, and the 'Dining Room' has the choice of imaginative English fare. An exceptional wine list offers over 200 wines from more than a dozen countries. New for 2002, a splendid Egyptian featured leisure facility which will include a pool, steam room and sauna, gym, hairdressing, treatment rooms and a nail bar. National Trust hillside adjoining the hotel grounds provides interesting walking and views over the surrounding countryside. The area is steeped in history, with the country houses of Petworth, Clandon and Uppark to visit as well as racing at Goodwood and polo at Cowdray Park. Brighton and the south coast are only a short drive away. **Directions:** Lythe Hill lies about 1½ miles from the centre of Haslemere, east on the B2131. Price Guide: (excluding breakfast): Single from £98; double/twin from £135; suite from £160.

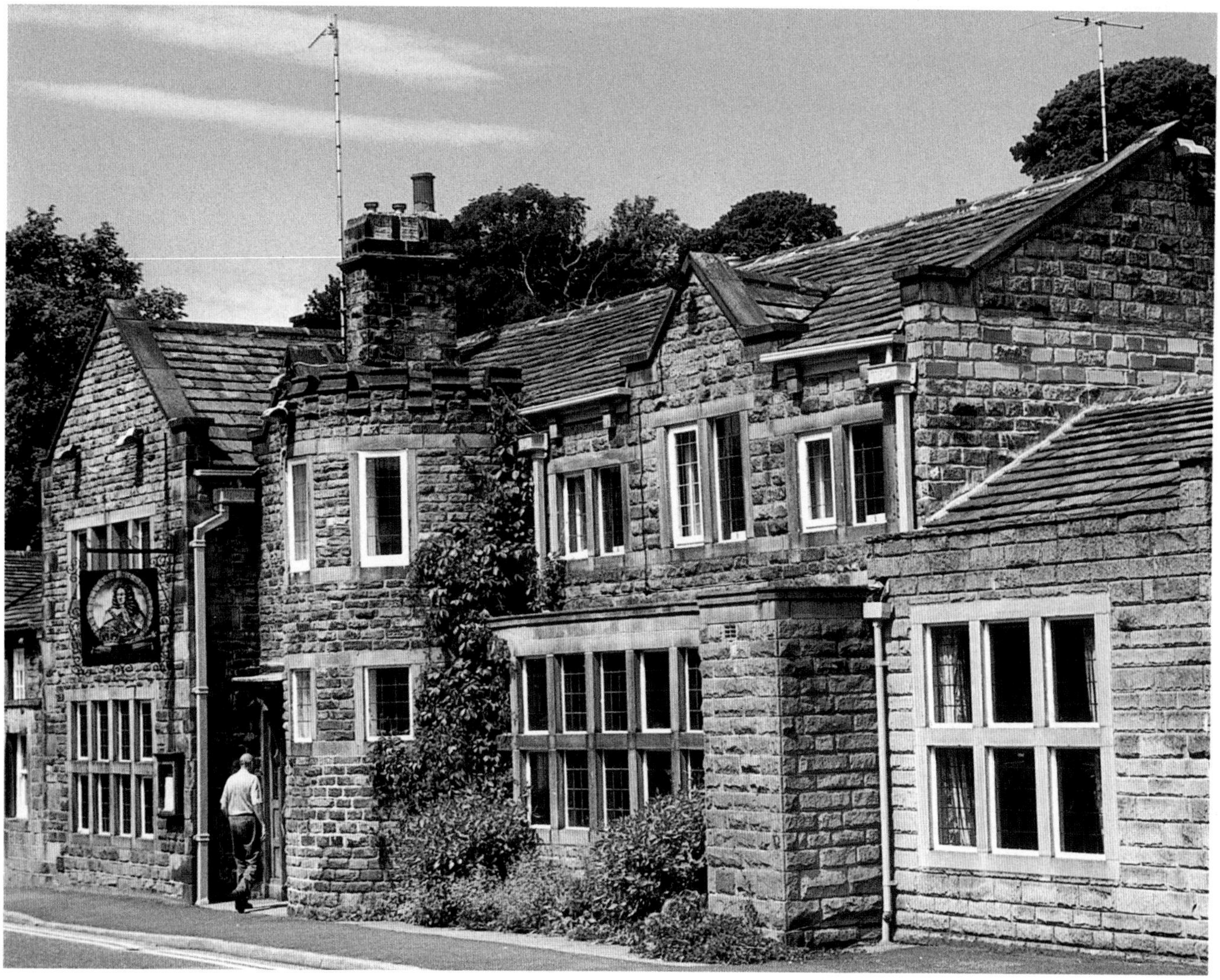

The George At Hathersage

MAIN ROAD, HATHERSAGE, DERBYSHIRE S32 1BB
TEL: 01433 650436 FAX: 01433 650099 E-MAIL: info@george-hotel.net

The George dates back to the end of the Middle Ages when it was an alehouse serving the packhorse road. Later it was well-known to Charlotte Brontë and it features anonymously in Jane Eyre. The present owner, an experienced hotelier, is ably backed by a team of professional senior personnel who guarantee guests a warm welcome and excellent personal service. In its latest hands the building has undergone extensive renovation. However, great care has been taken to preserve the character of the old inn and the stone walls, oak beams, open fires and antique furniture all remain as reminders of a distant age. The simple and pleasant bedrooms offer every modern amenity, including power showers and luxuriously enveloping bath sheets. There is a well-equipped bar in which to relax and enjoy a drink before moving on to the brasserie-style restaurant with its regularly changed menu. Places of interest nearby include Chatsworth and Haddon Halls, Buxton and Bakewell. The area provides some of the most picturesque countryside for walking including renowned Stanage Ridge (with stunning views overlooking the Derwent Reservoirs) and Hope Valley. "Great for the energetic, relaxing for the not-so-energetic". **Directions:** From the M1 Jct29 take the A617 to Baslow, then the A623 and B6001 to Hathersage. The George is in the main street of the village. Price Guide: Single £65–£75; double/twin £95–£125.

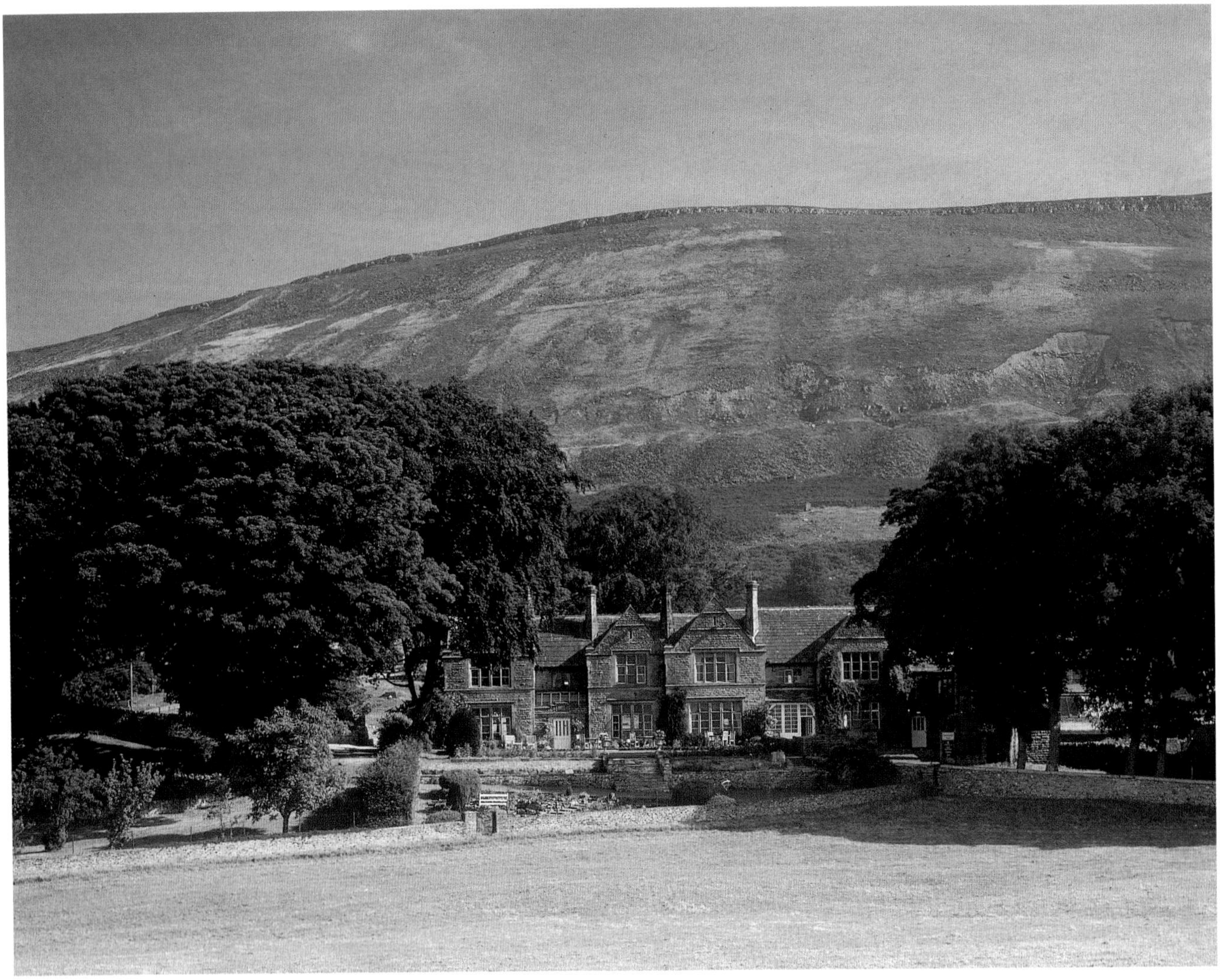

SIMONSTONE HALL

HAWES, NORTH YORKSHIRE DL8 3LY

TEL: 01969 667255 FAX: 01969 667741 E-MAIL: email@simonstone.demon.co.uk

Fine cuisine, comfort, peace and tranquillity combine with breathtaking scenery to make any stay at Simonstone Hall totally memorable. This former 18th century hunting lodge has been lovingly restored and furnished with antiques to create an idyllic retreat for its guests.The Hall stands in 5 acres of beautiful landscaped gardens with an adjacent 14,000 acres of grouse moors and upland grazing. Many period features have been retained such as the panelled dining room, mahogany staircase with ancestral stained glass windows and a lounge with ornamental fireplace and ceilings. The bedrooms are of the highest standards and offer every modern comfort including four-poster and sleigh beds. In the restaurant, guests savour the freshest local produce presented with flair and imagination, whilst enjoying stunning views across Upper Wensleydale. An excellent wine list is available to complement any dish. Informal meals are served in the Game Tavern which provides a particularly warm and local atmosphere. Simonstone Hall, with its fine views, is the perfect base for enjoying and exploring the hidden Yorkshire Dales. The area abounds with ancient castles, churches and museums. Hardraw Force, England's highest single drop waterfall which can be heard from the gardens, is only a walk away **Directions:** Hawes is on A684. Turn north on Buttertubs Pass towards Muker. Simonstone Hall is ½m on the left Price Guide: Single £55–£85; double/twin £110–£170.

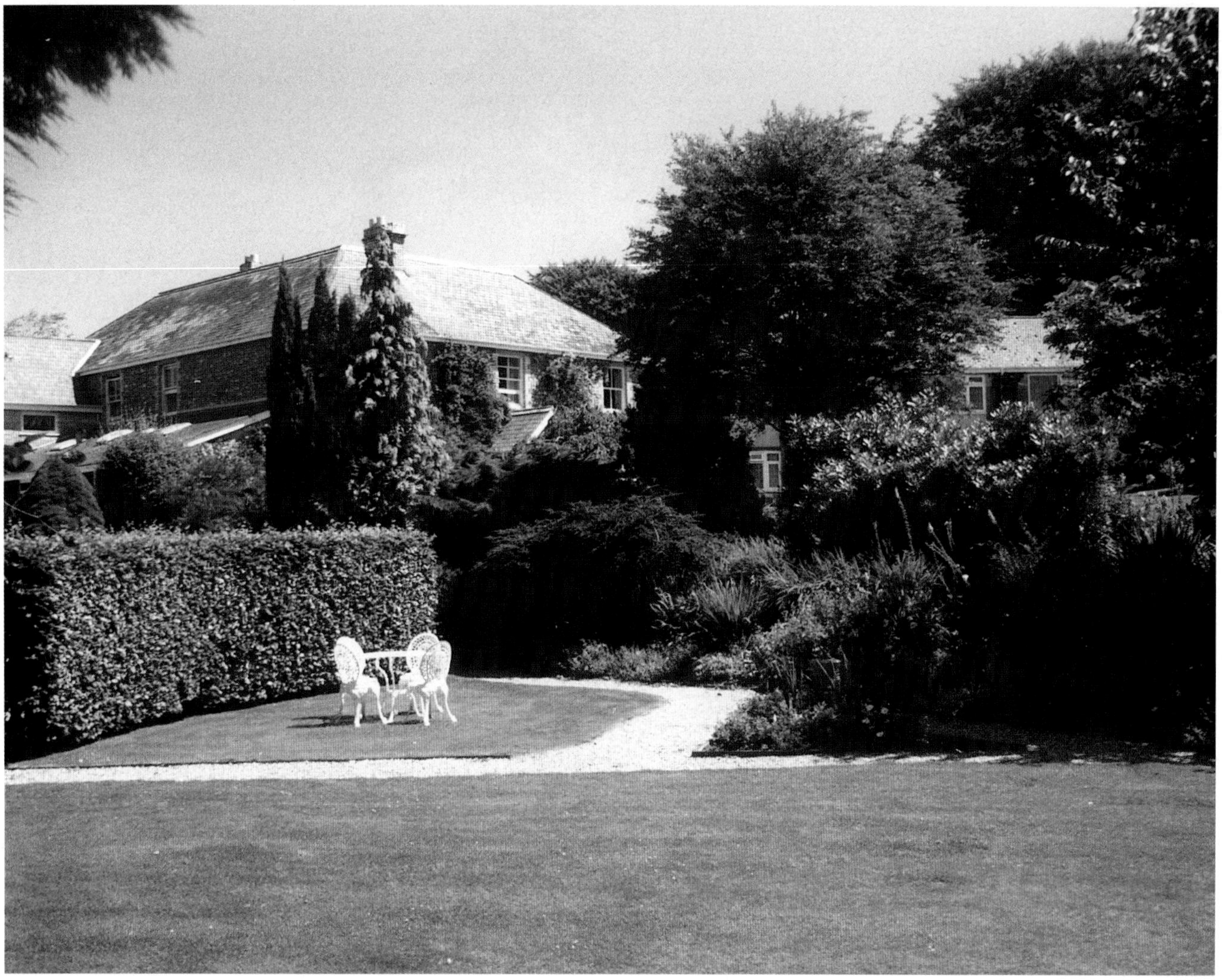

FAIRWATER HEAD COUNTRY HOUSE HOTEL

HAWKCHURCH, AXMINSTER, DEVON EX13 5TX
TEL: 01297 678349 FAX: 01297 678459 E-MAIL: jclowe@btinternet.com

In an idyllic setting on the Devon, Dorset and Somerset borders, Fairwater Head – also the name of the stream's source – not only has its own magnificent landscaped gardens but is situated at the highest point of the land and boasts the most spectacular views over the Axe valley. Built from local stone and with a rich local history, this is a perfect retreat for guests seeking peace and tranquillity from which to explore the Devon and Dorset environs. The bedrooms are charming, both in the main house and the "garden rooms", and most overlook the beautiful grounds and open countryside. The spacious dining room is light and airy, and again has wonderful views, and it is here that a superb menu of traditional and contemporary cuisine is served – recently awarded 1 AA Rosette and 2 RAC dining awards. This is an area rich in countryside walks and historic houses and gardens, and there is also Forde Abbey, picturesque Lyme Regis, and a donkey sanctuary nearby. AA rosette. Escorted tours and special breaks are available. **Directions:** Exit M5 at junction 25 onto A358. Then left onto A35 towards Bridport; left onto B3165 to Lyme Regis, Crewkerne road. Follow signs for Hawkchurch and hotel on left. Price Guide: Single £87–£92; double/twin £151–£161.

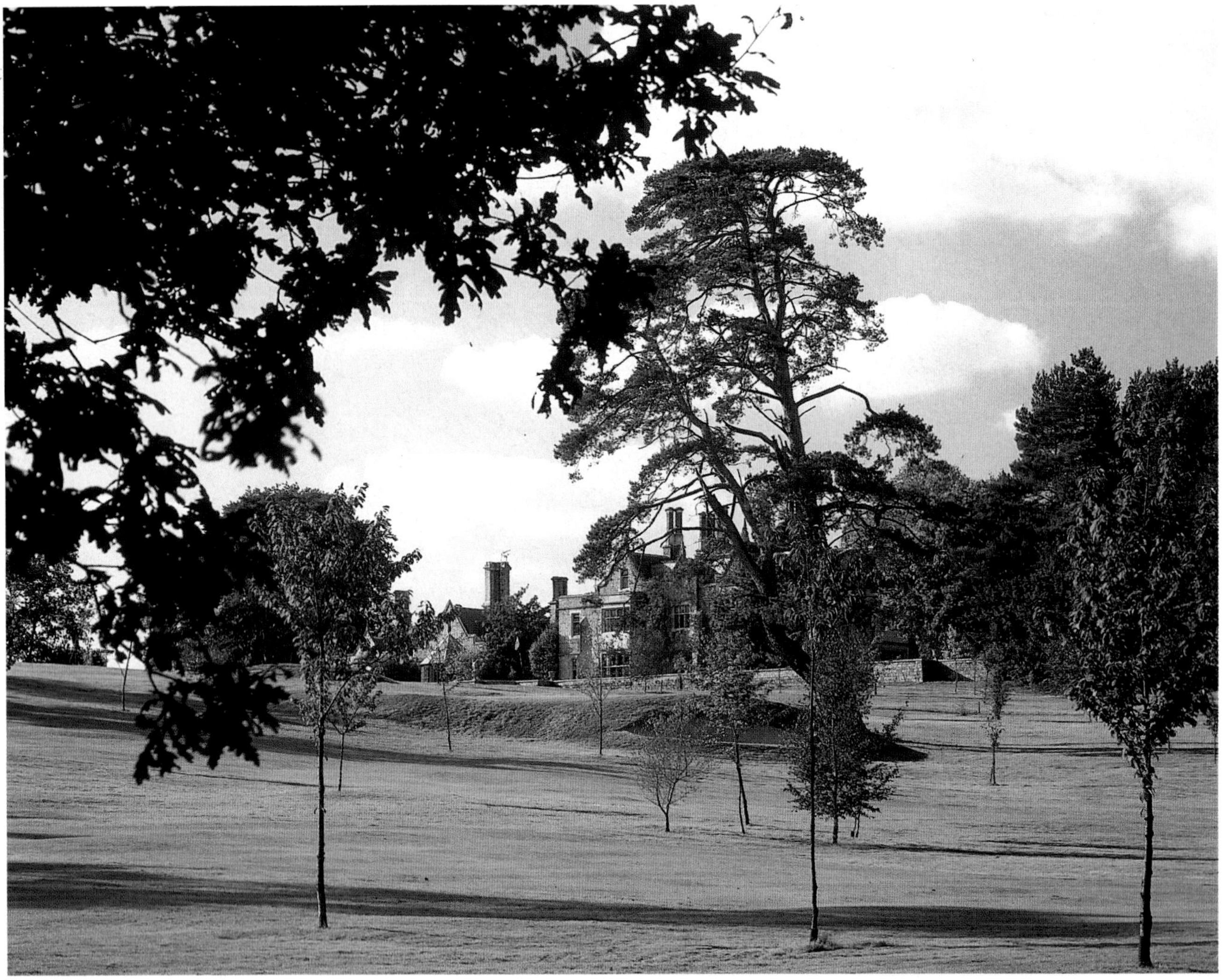

FOXHILLS

STONEHILL ROAD, OTTERSHAW, SURREY KT16 0EL
TEL: 01932 704500 FAX: 01932 874762 E-MAIL: reservations@foxhills.co.uk

This magnificent 400 acre estate is a delightful environment for any discerning traveller, whatever their interests may be. Named after the 18th century foreign secretary, Charles James Fox, Foxhills comprises of a large Manor House, elegant suites, three golf courses, numerous tennis courts, indoor and outdoor swimming pools, three restaurants and a host of health and fitness facilities including a gymnasium and a spa or beauty salon. The 38 bedrooms, located in a superb courtyard setting, are the essence of comfort; elegantly furnished and offering all the latest amenities, they are designed in a number of styles; some have gardens whilst others are on two floors. The two restaurants pride themselves in their culinary excellence. Inside the Manor itself, the award-winning restaurant serves fine cuisine and is renowned for the Sunday buffet – a gourmet's delight! The sport and health facilities at Foxhills are particularly impressive and with 20 qualified instructors on hand, guests may wish to acquire a new skill such as racquetball or T'ai Chi. Those wishing to be pampered will enjoy the sauna, steamroom and the fine beauty salon. Awarded 4 stars by the AA. **Directions:** From M25 Jct 11, follow signs to Woking. After a dual carriageway, turn left into Guildford Road. 3rd exit at roundabout and immediately right into Foxhills Road. Turn left at the end of the road, Foxhills is on the right. Price Guide: (room only): Double/twin from £150; suite from £225.

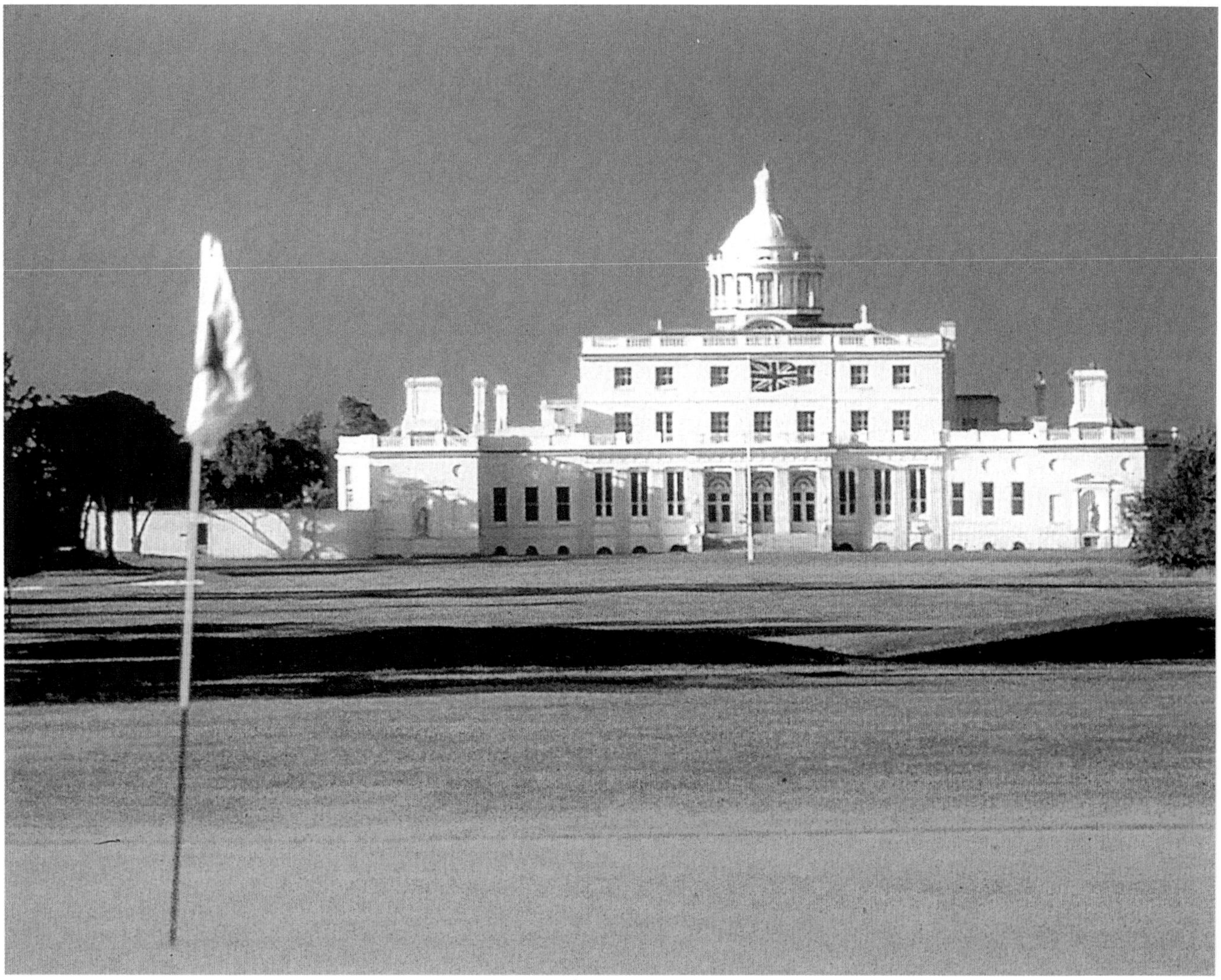

Stoke Park Club

PARK ROAD, STOKE POGES, BUCKINGHAMSHIRE SL2 4PG
TEL: 01753 717171 FAX: 01753 717181 E-MAIL: info@stokeparkclub.com

This impressive Palladian mansion was built in 1791 and Capability Brown was responsible for the magnificent landscaped grounds. The Estate, featured in the Domesday Book, can truly boast that Queen Elizabeth I and King Charles I slept here. It is the clubhouse of Stoke Park Club and also a splendid hotel, 8 miles from Heathrow and only 30 minutes from London, wonderfully secluded and surrounded by extensive parkland and the 27-hole championship golf course. The interior is palatial, with tall ceilings, fine antiques and art with original etchings. The bedrooms are lavishly decorated with exquisite fabrics and elegant period furniture and have luxurious bathrooms. The Club shares its spacious drawing rooms and traditional President's Bar with residents. The Brasserie is art deco and the menu lists great British modern cuisine. Stoke Park Club has many well equipped meeting rooms, including the Ballroom, quickly transformed into attractive venues for celebrations. Croquet, snooker and fishing are house sports, with shooting nearby. Windsor, Ascot and Henley are in easy reach. April 2002 sees the opening of a £9m Spa, Health and Racquets facility, completing the Club's mission of becoming 'The Great British Club'. **Directions:** From M4/Jct6 or M40/Jct2 take A344; at double roundabout at Farnham Royal take B416. The entrance is just over a mile on the right. Price Guide: Single £270; suite £390.

THE FEVERSHAM ARMS

HIGH STREET, HELMSLEY, NORTH YORKSHIRE YO6 5AG
TEL: 01439 770766 FAX: 01439 770346 E-MAIL: fevershamarms@hotmail.com

This historic coaching inn dates back to 1855 and has long been a favourite North Yorkshire retreat. Completely redeveloped by Studford Inns, it offers the highest standards of hospitality and comfort in a relaxing, casual ambience. The accommodation comprises 17 individually decorated en suite bedrooms, seven of which are suites. Guests can dine in front of the fires in either of the re-designed lounges, or in the traditional Dining Room or the more contemporary Brasserie at the Fev, both of which are also available for private dining, small meetings and wedding receptions. In fine weather, the poolside terrace and the corner garden are popular venues to enjoy the exceptional cuisine, accompanied by ales, beers and wines from around the world. During the summer months seafood is a speciality. Sports enthusiasts will be delighted with the Feversham Health & Fitness Club, which includes a state-of-the-art fitness suite, an outdoor pool and a tennis court. Helmsley is the gateway to the North York Moors, whilst York and the Yorkshire Dales are just 40 minutes away. Other places of interest nearby include Helmsley Castle, Castle Howard and Nunnington Hall.. **Directions:** From A1 take A64, then take the York north bypass (A1237) and then B1363. Alternatively, from A1 take A168 signposted Thirsk, then A170. Price Guide: Single £70–£90; double/twin £90–£110; suite £110–£140.

THE PHEASANT

HAROME, HELMSLEY, NORTH YORKSHIRE YO62 5JG
Tel: 01439 771241 Fax: 01439 771744

The Pheasant, rich in oak beams and open log fires, offers two types of accommodation, some in the hotel and some in a charming, 16th-century thatched cottage. The Binks family, who built the hotel and now own and manage it, have created a friendly atmosphere which is part of the warm Yorkshire welcome that awaits all guests. The bedrooms and suites are brightly decorated in an attractive, cottage style, and are all complete with en suite facilities. Traditional English cooking is the speciality of the restaurant; many of the dishes are prepared using fresh fruit and vegetables from the hotel's garden. During the summer, guests may relax on the terrace overlooking the pond. A new indoor heated swimming pool is an added attraction. Other sporting activities available locally include swimming, riding, golf and fishing. Yoerk is a short drive away, as are a host of historic landmarks including Byland and Rievaulx Abbeys and Castle Howard of Brideshead Revisited fame. Also nearby is the magnificent North York Moors National Park. Dogs by arrangement. Closed Christmas, January and February. **Directions:** From Helmsley, take the A170 towards Scarborough; after ¼ mile turn right for Harome. The hotel is near the church in the village. Price Guide: Single £65.50–£72; double/twin £131–£142 (including five-course dinner).

Phyllis Court Club

MARLOW ROAD, HENLEY-ON-THAMES, OXFORDSHIRE RG9 2HT
TEL: 01491 570500 FAX: 01491 570528 E-MAIL: sue.gill@phylliscourt.co.uk

Founded in 1906 by the owner of the house and a group of friends and London businessmen, the Club has an intriguing history spanning six centuries and involving royal patronage. Phyllis Court occupies an unrivalled position on the banks of the Thames and overlooking the Henley Royal Regatta course. Phyllis Court prides itself on retaining the traditions of its illustrious past while guests today who now stay in this fine historic residence can, in modern times, enjoy the highest standards of up to date hospitality. Oliver Cromwell slept here and he built the embankment wall; and it was here that William II held his first Royal Court. Years later, when the name Henley became synonymous with rowing, there came as patrons of the Royal Regatta Prince Albert, King George V and Edward, Prince of Wales. The character of the place remains unaltered in its hallowed setting, but the comfortable bedrooms, the restaurant, the "cellar" and the entire complement of amenities are of the latest high quality. What is more, they are available for all. Likely to be fully booked far ahead during the season. Ideal for meetings, functions and wedding parties. **Directions:** M40 junction 4 to Marlow or M4 junction 8/9 then follow signposts to Henley-on-Thames. Price Guide: Single £106; twin/double £124.

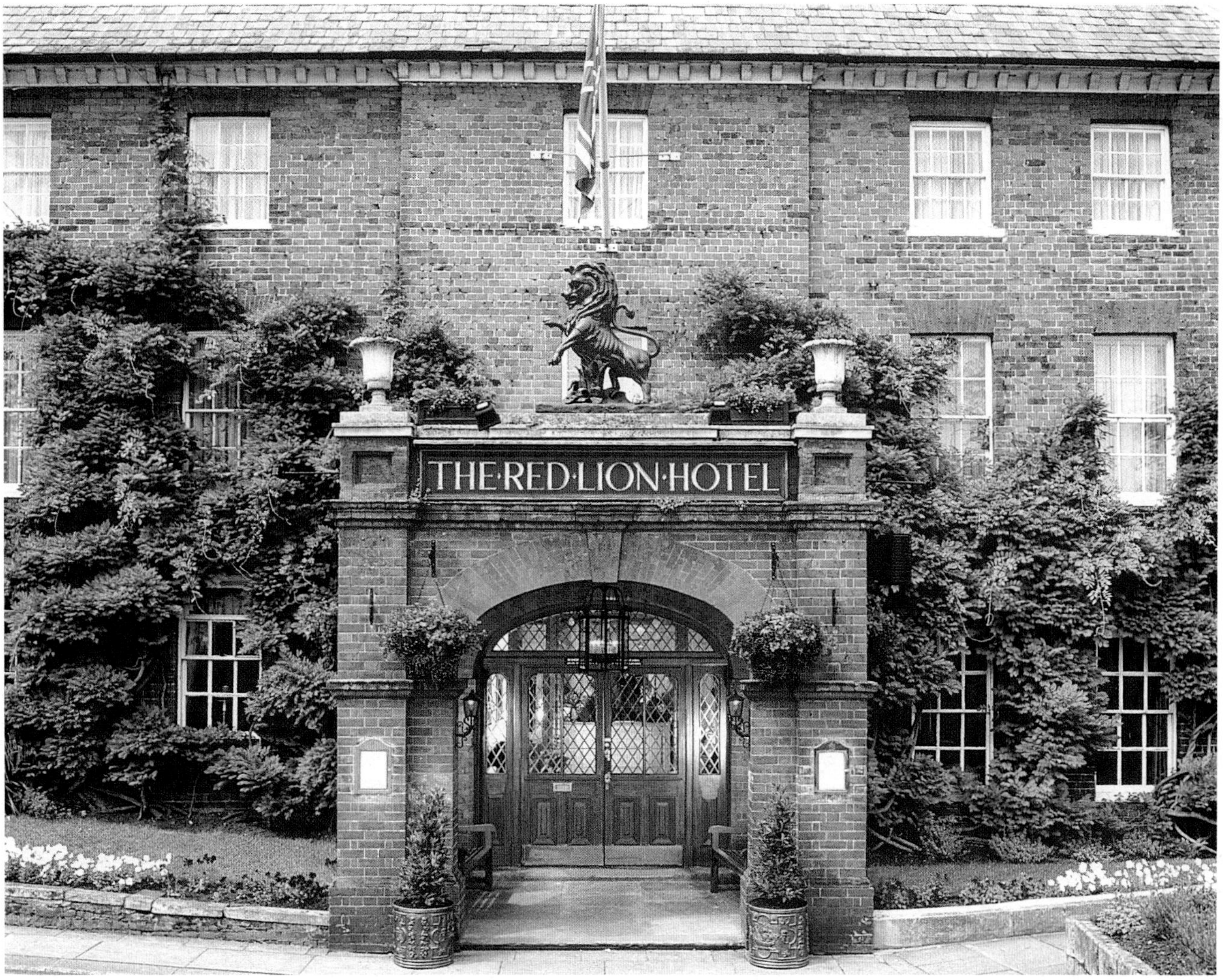

THE RED LION HOTEL

HENLEY-ON-THAMES, OXFORDSHIRE RG9 2AR
TEL: 01491 572161 FAX: 01491 410039 E-MAIL: reservations@redlionhenley.co.uk

This uniquely situated hotel has been playing host to travellers since the 15th century, and is today privately owned by the Miller family. Overlooking the Royal Regatta Course on the River Thames, its elegant and comprehensive facilities can accommodate leisure guests, business meetings and weddings. Under the watchful eye of chef, Stephen Fowler, The Red Lion Restaurant has an outstanding reputation for serving modern and traditional dishes alongside excellent wines. Lunch and dinner are both available in the restaurant, and advisers are happy to offer assistance in creating menus for private events. Visitors are also warmly welcomed in the Snug Bar with its open fire, fine wines and spirits and locally brewed beers. Although the hotel has been recently restored, each of its 26 en suite bedrooms is individually decorated to reflect its age and character, and many benefit from river views. The many antiques and paintings throughout include a portrait of Charles I, just one of three English kings to have stayed at the Hotel. History and beauty are very much on offer here, as The Red Lion provides a perfect base from which to explore Henley, the Thames Valley, Oxford and the countryside of the Cotswolds. **Directions:** From the M40 take junction 4 towards Henley-on-Thames. Price Guide: Single £99–£125; double £140–£155; suites £170

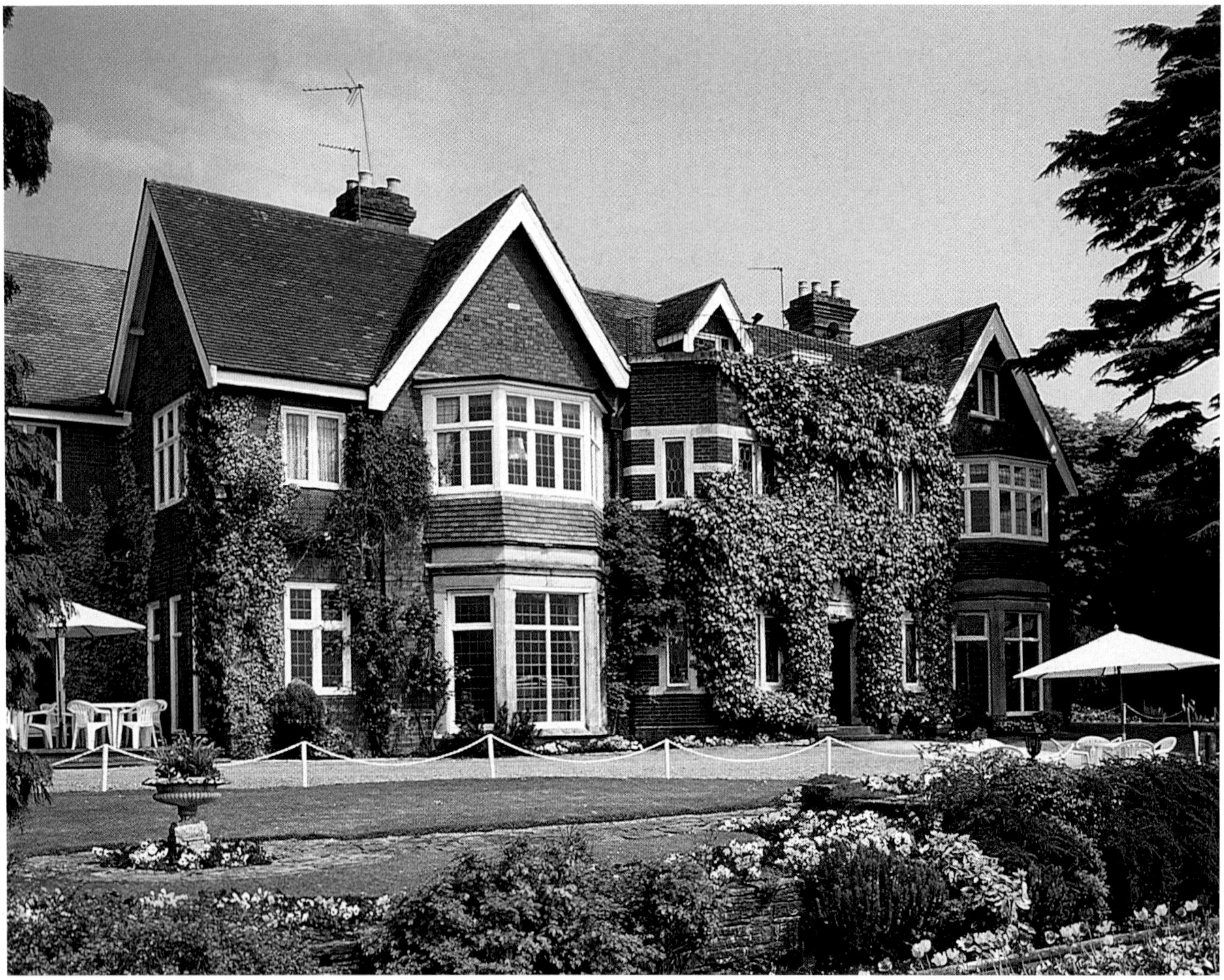

NUTHURST GRANGE

HOCKLEY HEATH, WARWICKSHIRE B94 5NL

TEL: 01564 783972 FAX: 01564 783919 E-MAIL: info@nuthurst-grange.com

The most memorable feature of this friendly country house hotel is its outstanding restaurant. Chef-patron David Randolph and his team have won many accolades for their imaginative menus, described as 'English, cooked in the light French style'. Diners can enjoy their superb cuisine in one of the three adjoining rooms which comprise the restaurant and form the heart of Nuthurst Grange. The rest of the house is no less charming – the spacious bedrooms have a country house atmosphere and are appointed with extra luxuries such as an exhilarating air-spa bath, a trouser press, hairdryer and a safe for valuables. For special occasions there is a room furnished with a four-poster bed and a marble bathroom. There are fine views across the 7½ acres of landscaped gardens. Executive meetings can be accommodated at Nuthurst Grange – within a 12 mile radius of the hotel lie central Birmingham, the NEC, Stratford-upon-Avon, Coventry and Birmingham International Airport. Sporting activities available nearby include golf, canal boating and tennis. **Directions:** From M42 exit 4 take A3400 signposted Hockley Heath (2 miles, south). Entrance to Nuthurst Grange Lane is ¼ mile south of village. Also, M40 (exit 16 – southbound only), take first left, entrance 300 yards. Price Guide: Single £135; double/twin £155–£170; suite £185.

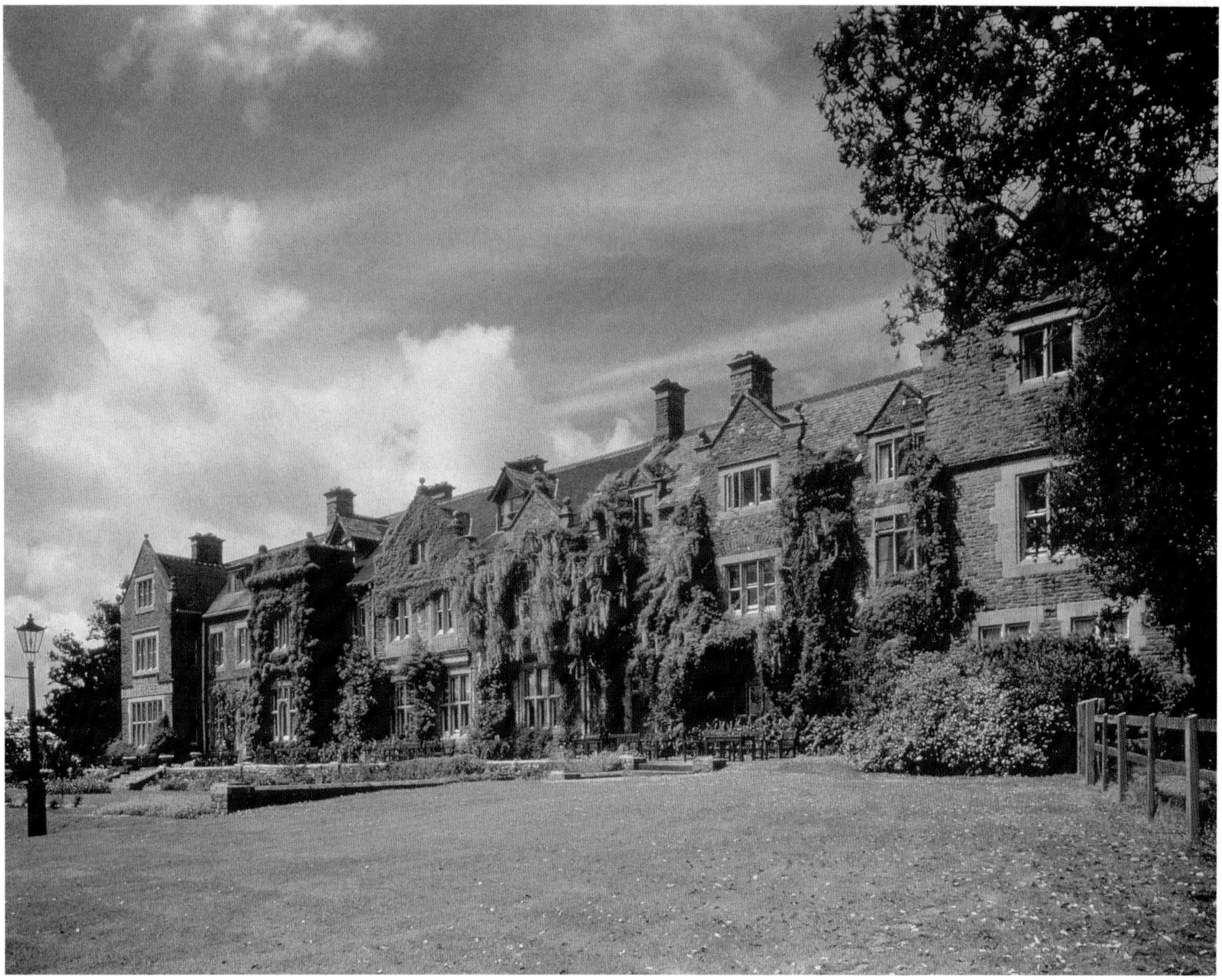

South Lodge Hotel

LOWER BEEDING, NR HORSHAM, WEST SUSSEX RH13 6PS
TEL: 01403 891711 FAX: 01403 891766 E-MAIL: enquiries@southlodgehotel.co.uk

South Lodge is a magnificent country house hotel, which has successfully captured the essence of Victorian elegance. With one of the most beautiful settings in rural Sussex, unrivalled views may be enjoyed over the South Downs from the hotel's elevated position. The mansion was originally built by Frederick Ducane Godman, a 19th-century botanist and explorer, and the hotel's wonderful 90 acre grounds are evidence of his dedication. Many original features have been preserved, wood panelling throughout the hotel and open fires in the reception rooms. The 41 individually designed bedrooms are luxuriously equipped with every modern requirement. There is also a beautiful cottage within the grounds – The Bothy, with two double and two single rooms, kitchen, bathrooms, lounge, conservatory and dining room. It is set in its own garden and can be used for leisure and conference purposes. The Camellia Restaurant has seasonally changing menus complemented by an international wine list. A variety of leisure facilities include a fitness centre, snooker room, croquet, tennis and clay pigeon shooting (shooting and archery by prior arrangement), as well as golf at South Lodge's two 18-hole championship courses. **Directions:** On A281 at Lower Beeding, south of Horsham. Gatwick airport 12 miles. Nearest motorway M23 Jct11. Price Guide: (Room only) Single from £150; double/twin £175–£215; suite/premier rooms £295–£350.

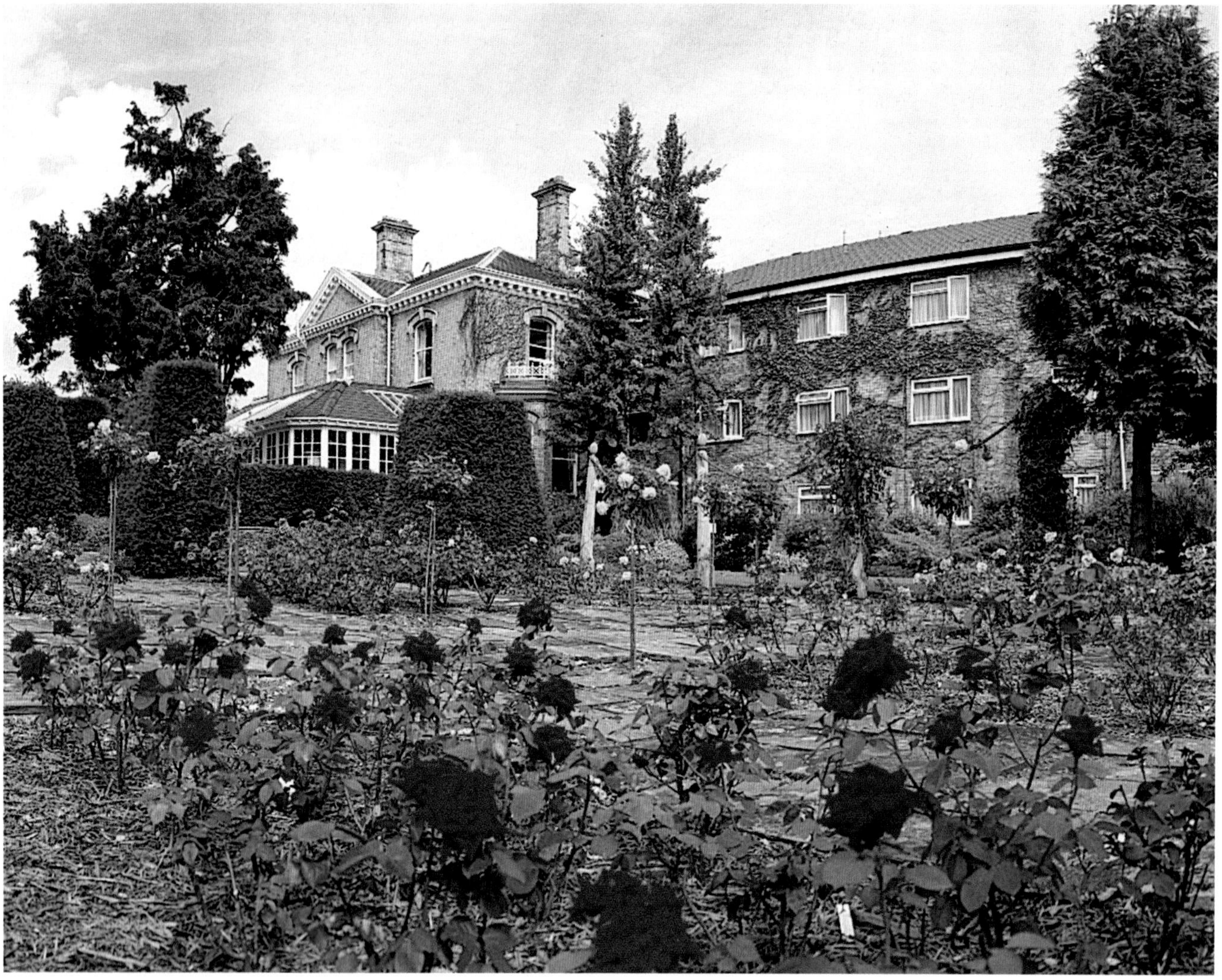

Willerby Manor Hotel

WELL LANE, WILLERBY, HULL, EAST YORKSHIRE HU10 6ER
TEL: 01482 652616 FAX: 01482 653901 E-MAIL: info@willerbymanor.co.uk

Originally the home of the Edwardian shipping merchant, Sir Henry Salmon, Willerby Manor was bought in the early 1970s by John Townend, a Wine Merchant from Hull. The elegance of the hotel, as its stands today, is testament to the careful work of the Townend family over the years. Furnished in a stylish manner, the public rooms are the essence of comfort. The 51 bedrooms are beautifully decorated with colour co-ordinated fabrics and soft furnishings. Every modern amenity is provided as well as an array of thoughtful extras such as fresh floral arrangements. The Restaurant serves modern English food and is complemented by an extensive well-chosen wine list from the House of Townend. A more informal ambience pervades the Everglades Brasserie where guests may savour bistro-style meals and beverages. Fitness enthusiasts will be delighted with the well-equipped Health Club which includes a spacious gymnasium, whirlpool spa bath, an exercise studio with daily classes and a beauty treatment room. The hotel is in a convenient location for those wishing to explore the cities of Hull and York. **Directions:** Take the M62 towards Hull which runs into the A63, turn off onto the A164 in the direction of Beverley. Follow the signs to Willerby and then Willerby Manor. Price Guide: Single £44–£86; double/twin £70–£130.

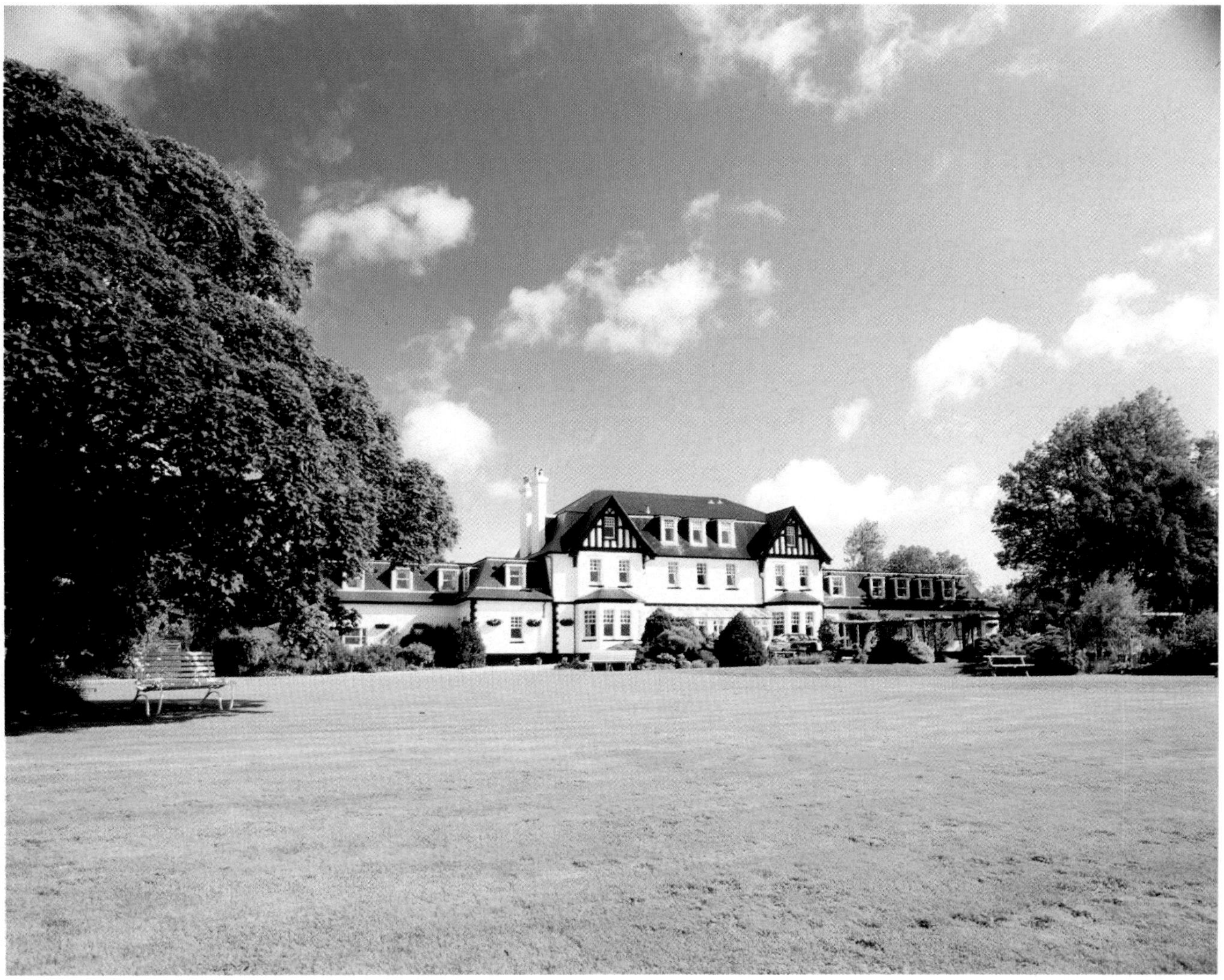

ILSINGTON COUNTRY HOUSE HOTEL

ILSINGTON VILLAGE, NEAR NEWTON ABBOT, DEVON TQ13 9RR
TEL: 01364 661452 FAX: 01364 661307 E-MAIL: hotel@ilsington.co.uk

The Ilsington Country House Hotel stands in ten acres of beautiful private grounds within the Dartmoor National Park. Run by friendly proprietors, Tim and Maura Hassell, the delightful furnishings and ambience offer a most comfortable environment in which to relax. Stylish bedrooms all boast outstanding views across the rolling pastoral countryside and every comfort and convenience to make guests feel at home, including English toiletries. The distinctive candle-lit dining room is perfect for savouring the superb cuisine, awarded an AA Rosette, created by talented chefs from fresh local produce. The library is ideal for an intimate dining party or celebration whilst the conservatory or lounge is the place for morning coffee or a Devon cream tea. There is a fully equipped purpose built gymnasium, heated indoor pool, sauna, steam room and spa. Some of England's most idyllic and unspoilt scenery surrounds Ilsington, with the picturesque villages of Lustleigh and Widecombe-in-the-Moor close by. Footpaths lead from the hotel on to Dartmoor. Riding, fishing and many other country pursuits can be arranged. **Directions:** From M5 join A38 at Exeter following Plymouth signs. After approximately 12 miles exit for Moretonhampstead and Newton Abbot. At roundabout follow signs for Ilsington. Price Guide: (including dinner): Single from £71; double/twin from £110.

Belstead Brook Hotel

BELSTEAD ROAD, IPSWICH, SUFFOLK IP2 9HB
TEL: 01473 684241 FAX: 01473 681249 E-MAIL: sales@belsteadbrook.co.uk

An oasis on the edge of Ipswich, Belstead Brook Hotel is surrounded by nine acres of landscaped gardens and woodlands. It combines the charm and tranquillity of the original 16th century country house with every modern day comfort. Bedrooms are pleasantly furnished and many overlook the garden where resident peacocks stroll. Guests may use the luxurious swimming pool with sauna, steam room, large Jacuzzi, separate pool for children and a well-equipped gymnasium. There are new executive garden rooms with allocated parking. The award-winning restaurant offers a choice of menus, complemented by a comprehensive cellar. For weddings, conferences or banquets, the hotel offers private dining rooms and a choice of purpose-built meeting and syndicate rooms to accommodate up to 130 guests or delegates. The hotel is an ideal base from which to explore the delights of Suffolk. These include Southwold, Aldeburgh, Woodbridge, the estuaries of the Deben and the Orwell, the wool towns of Lavenham and Long Melford and the countryside of the Stour Valley, made famous by John Constable. **Directions:** From A12/A14 junction take A1214 to Ipswich West. At first roundabout turn right to Belstead and follow the brown signs to the hotel. Price Guide: Double/twin £99–£110; suites £150.

88 MasterCard VISA AMERICAN EXPRESS M 130

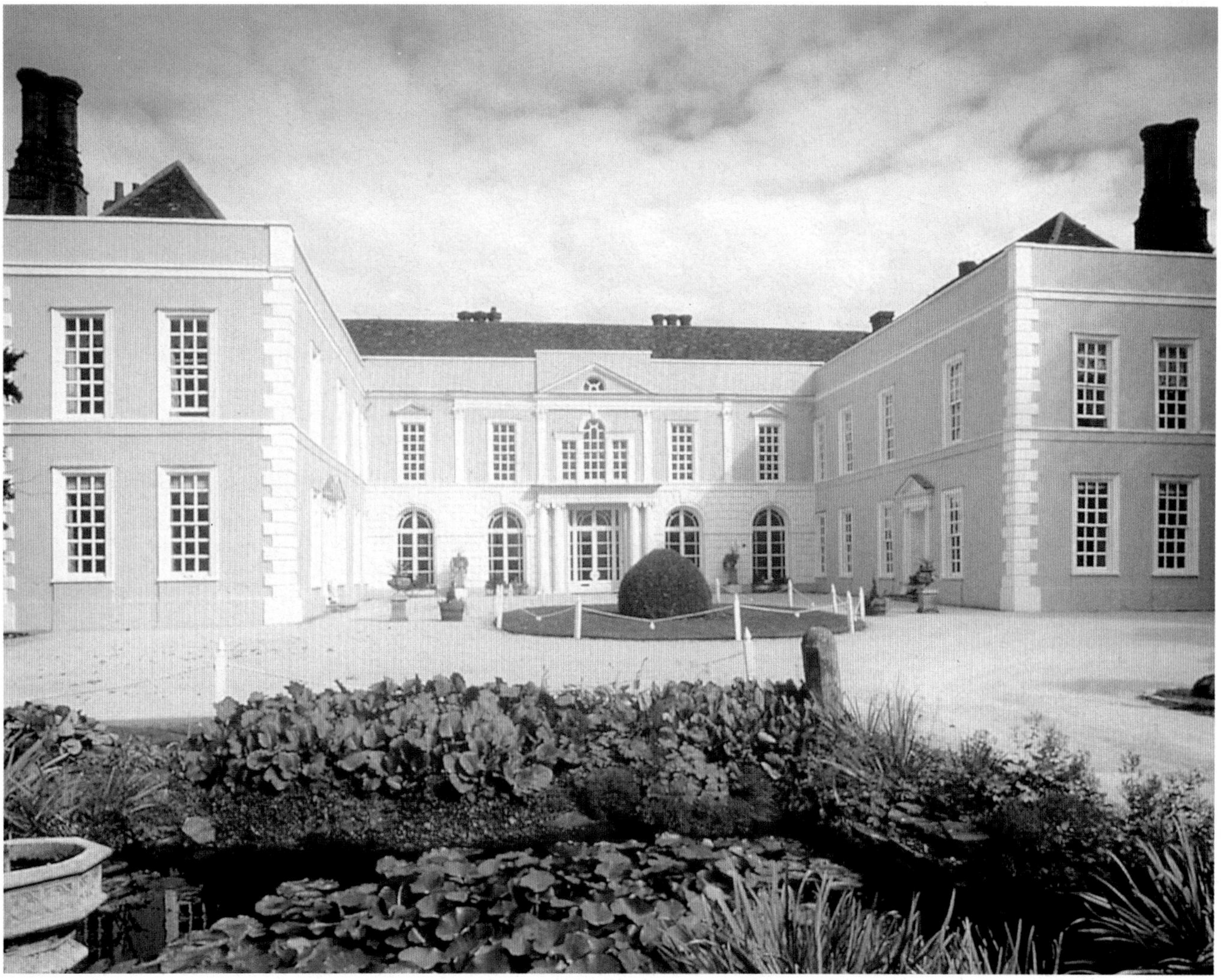

HINTLESHAM HALL

HINTLESHAM, IPSWICH, SUFFOLK IP8 3NS
TEL: 01473 652268 FAX: 01473 652463 E-MAIL: reservations@hintlesham–hall.co.uk

The epitome of grandeur, Hintlesham Hall is a house of evolving styles: its splendid Georgian façade belies its 16th-century origins, to which the red-brick Tudor rear of the hall is a testament. The Stuart period also left its mark, in the form of a magnificent carved-oak staircase leading to the north wing of the hall. The combination of styles works extremely well, with the lofty proportions of the Georgian reception rooms contrasting with the timbered Tudor rooms. The décor throughout is superb – all rooms are individually appointed in a discriminating fashion. Iced mineral water, toiletries and towelling robes are to be found in each of the comfortable bedrooms. The herb garden supplies many of the flavours for the well-balanced menu which will appeal to the gourmet and the health-conscious alike, complemented by a 300-bin wine list. Bounded by 175 acres of rolling countryside, leisure facilities include the Hall's own 18-hole championship golf course, new state of the art gymnasium, sauna, steam room, spa bath, tennis, croquet, snooker and a health and beauty suite with a full range of E'Spa products available at weekends and by arrangement during the week. Guests can also explore Suffolk's 16th-century wool merchants' villages, its pretty coast, 'Constable country' and Newmarket. **Directions:** Hintlesham Hall is 4 miles west of Ipswich on the A1071 Sudbury road. Price Guide: Single £98–£120; double/twin £120–£230; suite £250–£375.

THE MARLBOROUGH HOTEL

HENLEY ROAD, IPSWICH, SUFFOLK IP1 3SP

TEL: 01473 257677 FAX: 01473 226927 E-MAIL: sales@themarlborough.co.uk

Set in a stunning residential area in the environs of Ipswich, the Marlborough is a renovated Victorian hotel whose owners, the Gough family, guarantee a friendly and hospitable ambience. The interior is a model of modern stylishness, with rich coloured décor complementing the comfortable furnishings, freshly picked flowers and breathtaking pictures. Chef Shaun Thurlow serves Rosette-winning fare, emphasising the freshness of the local produce, in an elegant and beautifully-decorated room which overlooks the magnificent garden. Some of the hotel's individually-designed bedrooms have delightful balconies with views of the garden, while all are spacious and have modern bathrooms. Visitors can take advantage of windsurfing and walking at Alton, with nearby Woodbridge a haven for sailing. Christchurch Park and its Tudor mansion, formerly the home of Thomas Wolsey, are practically next door. Within easy driving distance are the rugged Suffolk coastline, historic Aldeburgh and the world-famous Snape Maltings. The Marlborough Hotel is also on the edge of beautiful Constable Country. **Directions:** At Junction of A12/A14 take Tesco exit, continue to A1214, turn left into A1214 (direction Woodbridge) over double mini roundabout to lights, then turn right into Henley Road. Price Guide: Single from £69; double/twin from £84; suite £112.

22 MasterCard VISA AMERICAN EXPRESS M 60

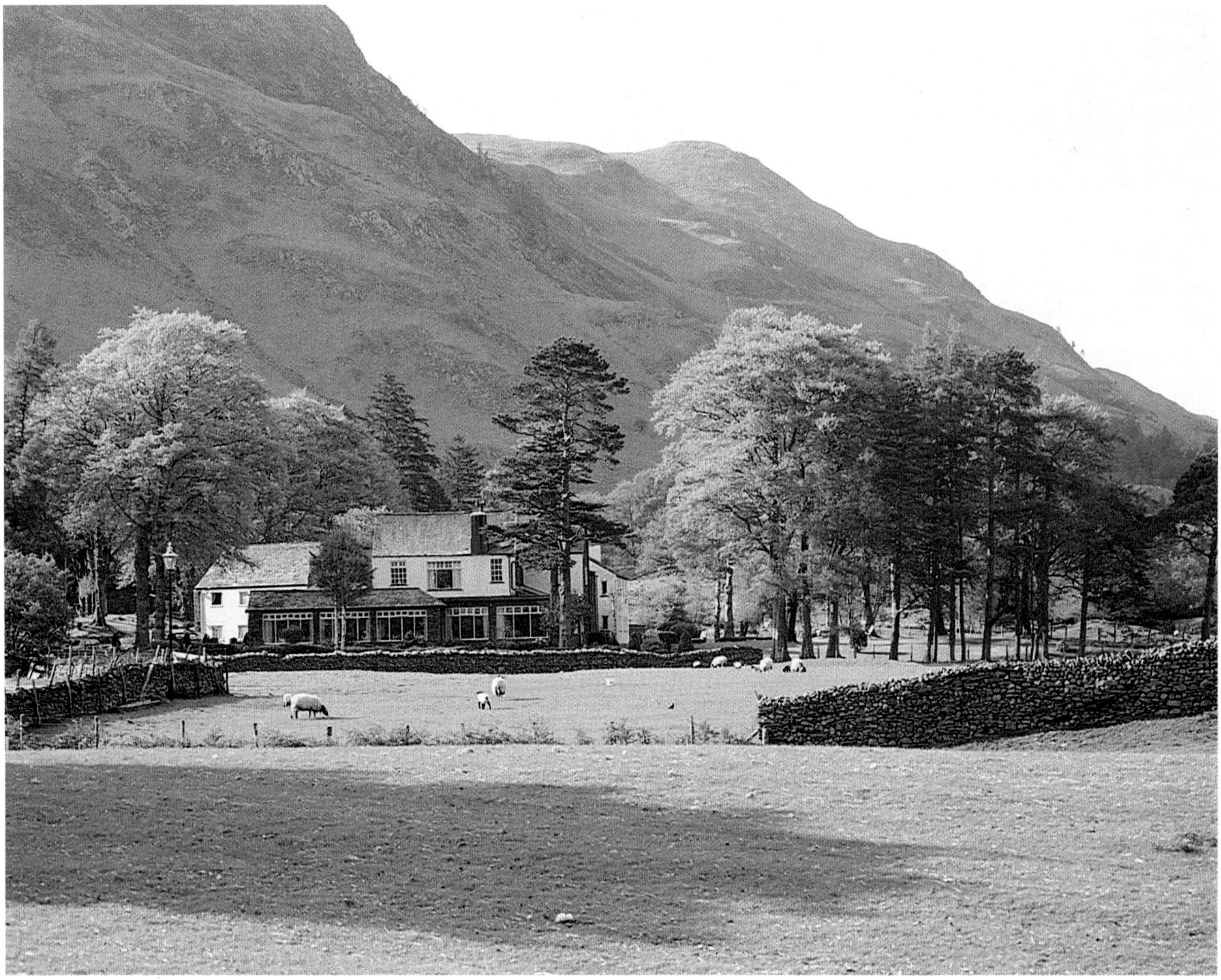

The Borrowdale Gates Country House Hotel

GRANGE-IN-BORROWDALE, KESWICK, CUMBRIA CA12 5UQ
TEL: 017687 77204 FAX: 017687 77254 E-MAIL: hotel@borrowdale-gates.com

Built in 1860, Borrowdale Gates is surrounded on all sides by the rugged charm of the Lake District National Park. It affords a panoramic vista of the Borrowdale Valley and glorious fells and nestles in two acres of wooded gardens on the edge of the ancient hamlet of Grange, close to the shores of Derwentwater. Tastefully decorated bedrooms offer every modern comfort and most command picturesque views of the surrounding scenery. The comfortable lounges and bar, decorated with fine antiques and warmed by glowing log fires in cooler months, create the perfect setting in which to enjoy a drink and forget the bustle of everyday life. Fine food is served in the restaurant, with menus offering a wide and imaginative selection of dishes. The cuisine is complemented by a thoughtfully chosen wine list and excellent service. This Lakeland home is a haven of peace and tranquillity and is ideally located for walking, climbing and touring. There are also many places of literary and historical interest within easy reach, for example Wordsworth's birthplace in Cockermouth. The hotel is closed throughout January. **Directions:** M6 junction 40 A66 into Keswick. B5289 to Borrowdale. After four miles right into Grange over double hump back bridge. Price Guide: Single £60–£87; double/twin £115–£175 (Including dinner). Special breaks available.

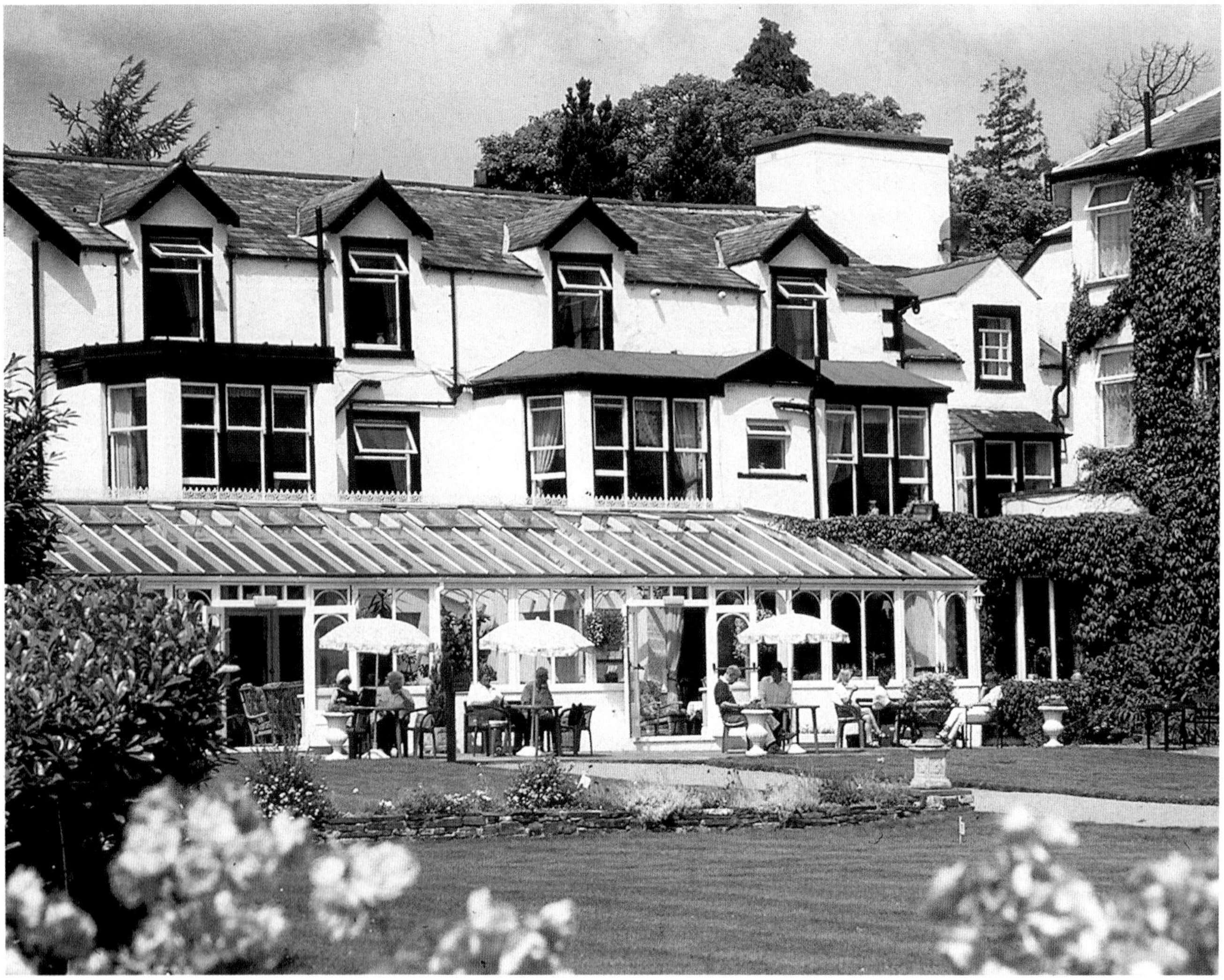

THE DERWENTWATER HOTEL

PORTINSCALE, KESWICK, CUMBRIA CA12 5RE
TEL: 017687 72538 FAX: 017687 71002 E-MAIL: info@derwentwater–hotel.co.uk

Built as a doctor's summer residence in 1837, this handsome lakeside hotel lies amidst 16 acres of gardens and watermeadow, dedicated to the preservation of local wildlife. For a number of years the Hotel's owners have worked alongside English Nature to create a safe and natural haven for hundreds of creatures. Guests can sit in the comfortable conservatory and watch red squirrels, mallards, hedgehogs and pheasants, while a wander down to the lake may reveal sightings of water fowl, frogs, and even a family of timid roe deer. The Derwentwater has a unique style, each bedroom is individually furnished, and most enjoy views over the lake or the mountains beyond. Local produce is used in the wide variety of dishes served in The Deer's Leap restaurant. The Hotel is immensely proud of its excellent reputation for quality of staff and high standards of hospitality. The surrounding area lends itself to numerous activities, from walking and cycling, to fishing, trips on the lake and golf. Adult guests have complimentary use of nearby health spa. **Directions:** Take the M6, exit at junction 40. Take the A66 westwards, bypass Keswick, after about a mile turn left into Portinscale, then follow signs to hotel. Price Guide: Single £79–£120; double/twin £130–£180; suite £190.

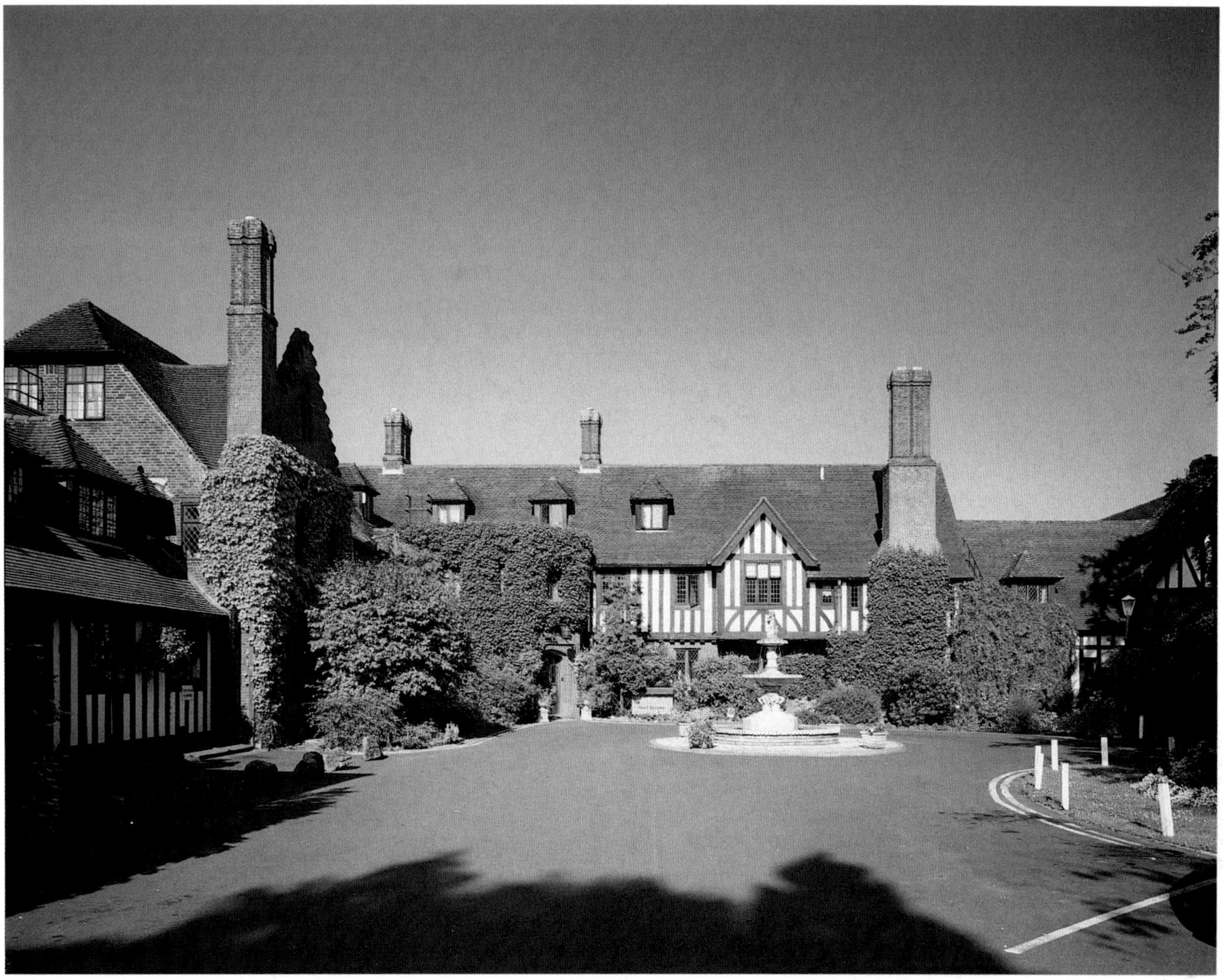

Stone Manor Hotel

STONE, KIDDERMINSTER, WORCESTERSHIRE DY10 4PJ

TEL: 01562 777555 FAX: 01562 777834 E-MAIL: enquiries@stonemanorhotel.co.uk

Built as a private home in the mid 1920s, this sprawling black and white timber-framed house opened as a hotel nearly forty years later. The warmth and character of bygone times have been retained and blend harmoniously with the modern facilities. Upon entering the hotel, guests will be pleased by the traditional furnishings and layout. The public rooms are decorated with soft fabrics whilst the 57 bedrooms are individually styled and offer every modern amenity. The heart of Stone Manor is Fields Restaurant, where memorable dishes are served and the speciality is flambé cuisine. The à la carte menu makes fine use of the seasonal produce and is complemented by the wine list, comprising both New World and European vintages. Three banqueting suites, catering for between 50 and 199 guests, have full self-contained facilities, including dance floors and bars, making Stone Manor Hotel an ideal venue for weddings, conferences and other private functions. Birmingham Indoor Arena and the NEC are renowned for their extensive programmes of entertainment and Worcester Cathedral is also within easy reach. **Directions:** Stone Manor Hotel is situated in the village of Stone, on the A448 Kidderminster to Bromsgrove road, approximately two miles from Kidderminster town centre. Price Guide: All rooms from £90–£135.

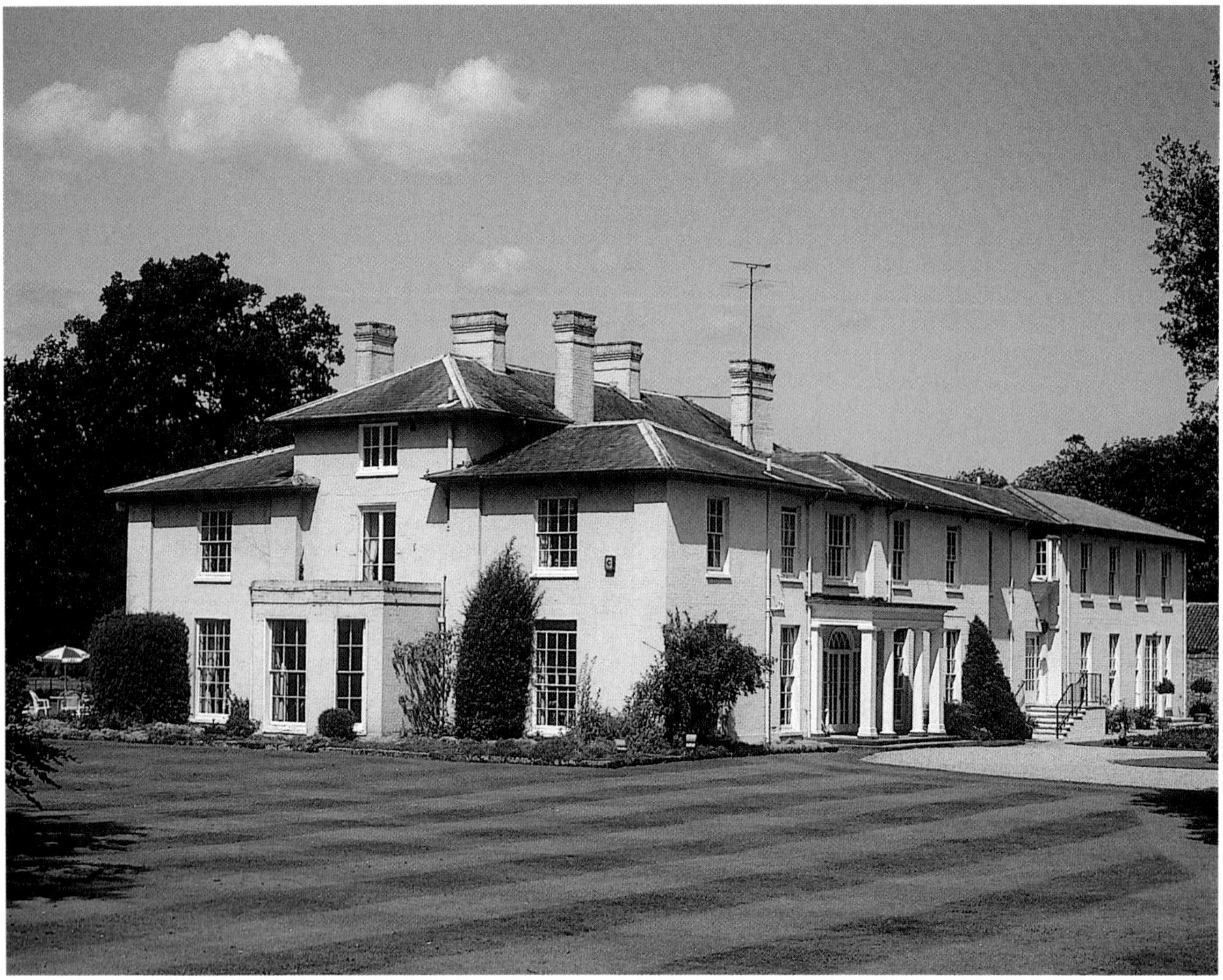

CONGHAM HALL

GRIMSTON, KING'S LYNN, NORFOLK PE32 1AH
TEL: 01485 600250 FAX: 01485 601191 E-MAIL: reception@conghamhallhotel.co.uk

Dating from the mid-18th century, this stately manor house is set in 30 acres of paddocks, orchards and gardens. The conversion from country house to luxury hotel in 1982 was executed with care to enhance the elegance of the classic interiors. There is a renowned herb garden and flower displays enliven the décor throughout, while the delicate fragrance of home-made pot-pourri perfumes the air. Winners of the Johansens Hotel Award for Excellence 1993. Light lunches available in the bar, lounge, restaurant and terrace. In the Orangery restaurant, guests can relish modern English cooking. The origin of many of the flavours is explained by the herb garden, with over 100 varieties for the chef's use. Even the most discerning palate will be delighted by the choice of wines. Congham Hall is an ideal base for touring the countryside of West Norfolk, as well as Sandringham, Fakenham races and the coastal nature reserves. **Directions:** Go to the A149/A148 interchange northeast of King's Lynn. Follow the A148 towards Sandringham/Fakenham/Cromer for 100 yards. Turn right to Grimston. The hotel is then 2½ miles on the left. Price Guide: Single £85–£150; double/twin £130–£240; suites from £205–£240.

BUCKLAND-TOUT-SAINTS

GOVETON, KINGSBRIDGE, DEVON TQ7 2DS
TEL: 01548 853055 FAX: 01548 856261 E-MAIL: buckland@tout–saints.co.uk

Buckland-Tout-Saints is an impressive Grade II listed manor house, built in 1690 during the reign of William and Mary. Recently refurbished to a superb standard, the wonderful hospitality and cuisine that guests enjoy at this hotel today would certainly have impressed its royal visitors of the past. Idyllic amongst its own woodlands and beautiful gardens, it is invitingly close to the spectacular beaches and dramatic cliffs of the Devonshire coastline. A warm and welcoming atmosphere prevails throughout, from the leather-clad couches of the convivial bar to the family of bears – Teddy Tout-Saints – whose individual members welcome guests to their deluxe rooms and suites. Many of these delightful period style rooms enjoy stunning views across the beautiful South Hams area with its moorland and river estuaries. The food served in the Queen Anne restaurant is delectable and deserving of the many accolades it has won. The combination of fresh local produce and exotic foreign cuisine is selected and prepared by a renowned chef and is accompanied by an equally tantalising selection of fine wines and vintage ports. Conferences, weddings and seminars are effortlessly accommodated in the Kestrel Rooms, where helpful staff and elegant surroundings ensure a successful occasion. Several well-known golf courses and sailing centres are nearby.

Directions: Signed from A381 between Totnes and Kingsbridge.

Price Guide: Single from £95; double/twin from £190; suite from £240

MERE COURT HOTEL

WARRINGTON ROAD, MERE, KNUTSFORD, CHESHIRE WA16 0RW
TEL: 01565 831000 FAX: 01565 831001 E-MAIL: sales@merecourt.co.uk

This attractive Edwardian house stands in seven acres of mature gardens and parkland in one of the loveliest parts of Cheshire. Maintained as a family home since being built in 1903, Mere Court has been skilfully restored into a fine country house hotel offering visitors a peaceful ambience in luxury surroundings. Comforts and conveniences of the present mix excellently with the ambience and many original features of the past. The bedrooms have views over the grounds and ornamental lake. All are individually designed and a number of them have a four-poster beds, Jacuzzi spa bath, mini bar and separate lounge. Facilities include safes, personalised voice mail telephones and modem points. Heavy ceiling beams, polished oak panelling and restful waterside views are features of the elegant Aboreum Restaurant which serves the best of traditional English and Mediterranean cuisine. Lighter meals can be enjoyed in the Lounge Bar. The original coach house has been converted into a designated conference centre with state of the art conference suites and syndicate rooms accommodating up to 120 delegates. Warrington, Chester, Manchester Airport and many National Trust properties are within easy reach. **Directions:** From M6, exit at junction 19. Take A556 towards Manchester. After 1 mile turn left at cross-roads onto A50 towards Warrington. Mere Court is on the right. Price Guide: Single £75–£140; double/twin £80–£185.

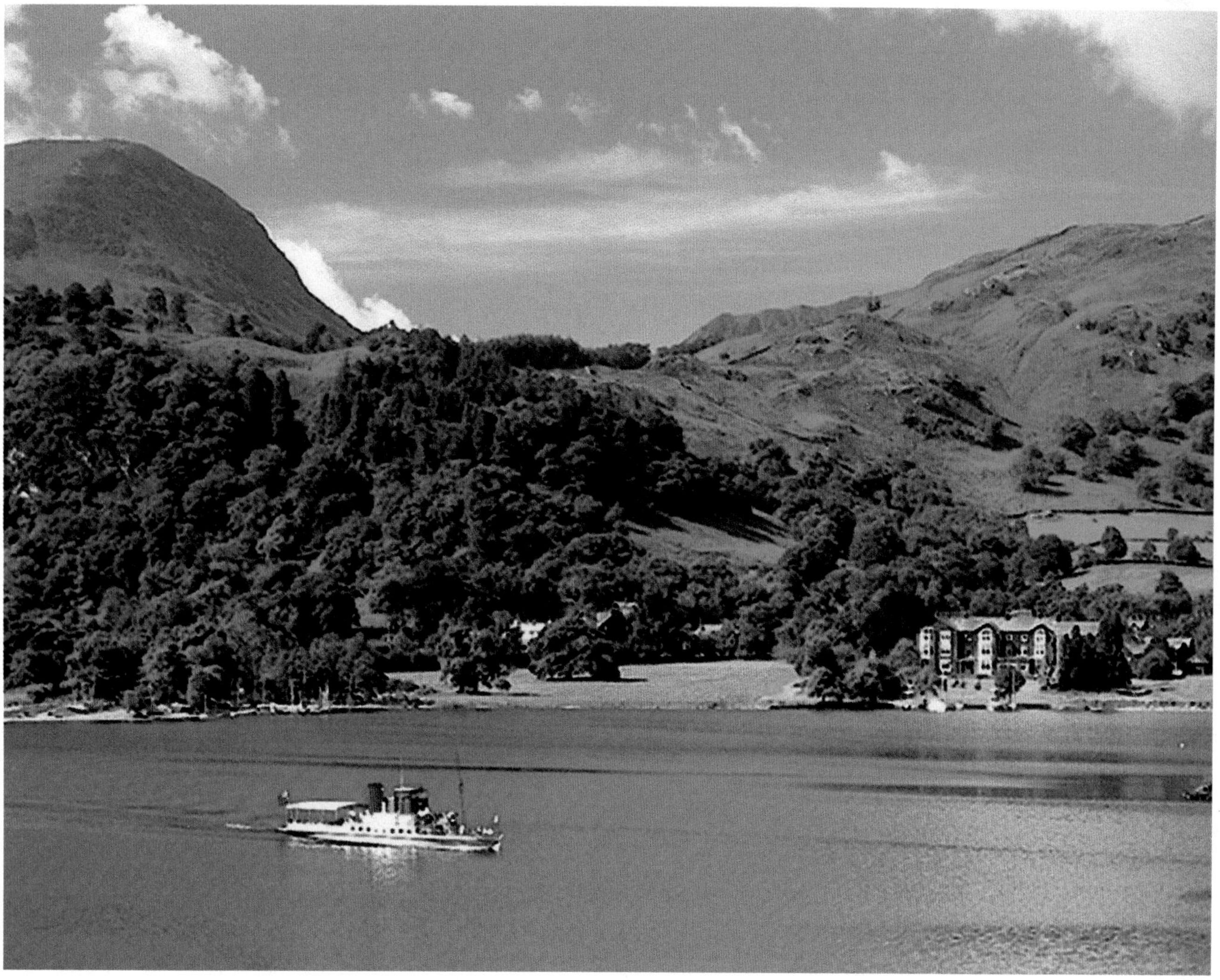

THE INN ON THE LAKE

LAKE ULLSWATER, GLENRIDDING, CUMBRIA CA11 0PE

TEL: 017684 82444 FAX: 017684 82303 E-MAIL: info@innonthelakeullswater.co.uk

With its 15 acres of grounds and lawns sweeping down to the shore of Lake Ullswater, the Inn on the Lake truly boasts one of the most spectacular settings in the Lake District. Recently bought and refurbished by the Graves family, it now offers a wide range of excellent facilities as well as stunning views of the surrounding scenery. Downstairs, comfortable lounges provide a calm environment in which to relax with a drink, whilst dinner can be enjoyed in the Lake View restaurant. Most of the 46 en suite bedrooms look across to the lake or the fells, and five lake view four-poster rooms add an extra touch of luxury. The Hotel welcomes wedding ceremonies and receptions, and is happy to provide a full private function service as well as conference facilities for up to 120 business delegates. The list of nearby leisure activities for children and adults alike is endless, and includes rock climbing, pony trekking, canoeing, windsurfing, sailing and fishing. Trips around the lake can be taken aboard the Ullswater steamers, and many of the most stunning Lake District walks begin in this area. **Directions:** Leave M6 at Jct40, then take A66 west and at first roundabout, by Rheged Discovery Centre, head towards Pooley Bridge, then follow the shoreline of Lake Ullswater to Glenridding. Price Guide: Single £51–£100; double/twin £82–£135.

RAMPSBECK COUNTRY HOUSE HOTEL

WATERMILLOCK, LAKE ULLSWATER, NR PENRITH, CUMBRIA CA11 0LP
TEL: 017684 86442 FAX: 017684 86688 E-MAIL: enquiries@rampbeck.fsnet.co.uk

A beautifully situated hotel, Rampsbeck Country House stands in 18 acres of landscaped gardens and meadows leading to the shores of Lake Ullswater. Built in 1714, it first became a hotel in 1947, before the present owners acquired it in 1983. Thomas and Marion Gibb, with the help of Marion's mother, Marguerite MacDowall, completely refurbished Rampsbeck with the aim of maintaining its character and adding only to its comfort. Most of the well-appointed bedrooms have lake and garden views. Three have a private balcony and the suite overlooks the lake. In the elegant drawing room, a log fire burns and French windows lead to the garden. Guests and non-residents are welcome to dine in the intimate candle-lit restaurant. Imaginative menus offer a choice of delicious dishes, carefully prepared by head chef Andrew McGeorge and his team. A good bar lunch menu offers light snacks as well as hot food. Guests can stroll through the gardens, play croquet or fish from the lake shore, around which there are designated walks. Lake steamer trips, riding, golf, sailing, wind-surfing and fell-walking are available nearby. Closed from end of January to mid-February. Dogs by arrangement only

Directions: Leave M6 at junction 40, take A592 to Ullswater. At T-junction at lake turn right; hotel is 1½ miles on left. Price Guide: Single £60–£110; double/twin £100–£190; suite £190.

SHARROW BAY COUNTRY HOUSE HOTEL

HOWTOWN, LAKE ULLSWATER, PENRITH, CUMBRIA CA10 2LZ
TEL: 017684 86301/86483 FAX: 017684 86349 E-MAIL: enquiries@sharrow–bay.com

Now in its 54th year, Sharrow Bay is known to discerning travellers the world over, who return again and again to this magnificent lakeside hotel. It wasn't always so. The late Francis Coulson arrived in 1948. He was joined by Brian Sack in 1952 and the partnership flourished, to make Sharrow Bay what it is today. They were joined by the Managing Director, Nigel Lightburn, who is carrying on the tradition with Brian. All the bedrooms are elegantly furnished and guests are guaranteed the utmost comfort. In addition to the main hotel, there are four cottages nearby which offer similarly luxurious accommodation. All the reception rooms are delightfully decorated. Sharrow Bay is universally renowned for its wonderful cuisine. The team of chefs led by Johnnie Martin and Colin Akrigg ensure that each meal is a special occasion, a mouth-watering adventure! With its private jetty and 12 acres of lakeside gardens Sharrow Bay offers guests boating, swimming and fishing. Fell-walking is a challenge for the upwardly mobile. Sharrow Bay is the oldest British member of Relais et Châteaux. Closed in December, January and February. **Directions:** M6 junction 40, A592 to Lake Ullswater, into Pooley Bridge, then take Howtown road for 2 miles. Price Guide: (including 7-course dinner and full English breakfast) Single £130–£250; double/twin £300–£400; suites from £400.

Mallory Court

HARBURY LANE, BISHOPS TACHBROOK, LEAMINGTON SPA, WARWICKSHIRE CV33 9QB
TEL: 01926 330214 FAX: 01926 451714 E-MAIL: reception@mallory.co.uk

Surrounded by ten acres of attractive gardens, Mallory Court affords a stunning vista across the beautiful Warwickshire countryside. Offering every home comfort, arriving guests are enveloped by the welcoming ambience and peace and quiet of a private house rather than a hotel. The public rooms are bedecked with floral arrangements and during the winter season, afternoon tea may be enjoyed in the comfortable lounges beside the burning log fires. The luxurious bedrooms are enhanced by soft fabrics, thick carpets and en suite facilities. The sun lounge is at its most inviting throughout the summer months when it opens onto the terrace. Guests may enjoy a chilled drink whilst listening to the soft tones of the piano before rambling through the gardens which feature a rose garden, herbaceous border and an ornamental stream. The dishes served in the elegant restaurant are a fusion of classical and modern British flavours. Diners may begin with chicken liver and foie gras parfait with truffle dressing, followed by pan-fried monkfish with mussels and a saffron sauce and ending with a baked custard tart with plum compôte. The hotel is set in a particularly historic area: stately homes, castles and gardens abound. **Directions:** 2 miles south of Leamington Spa on Harbury Lane, just off B4087 Bishops Tachbrook-Leamington Spa road, Harbury Lane runs from B4087 towards Fosse Way. M40 Jct13 from London/Jct14 from Birmingham. Price Guide: Double single occupancy from £175; double from £195; suite from £320.

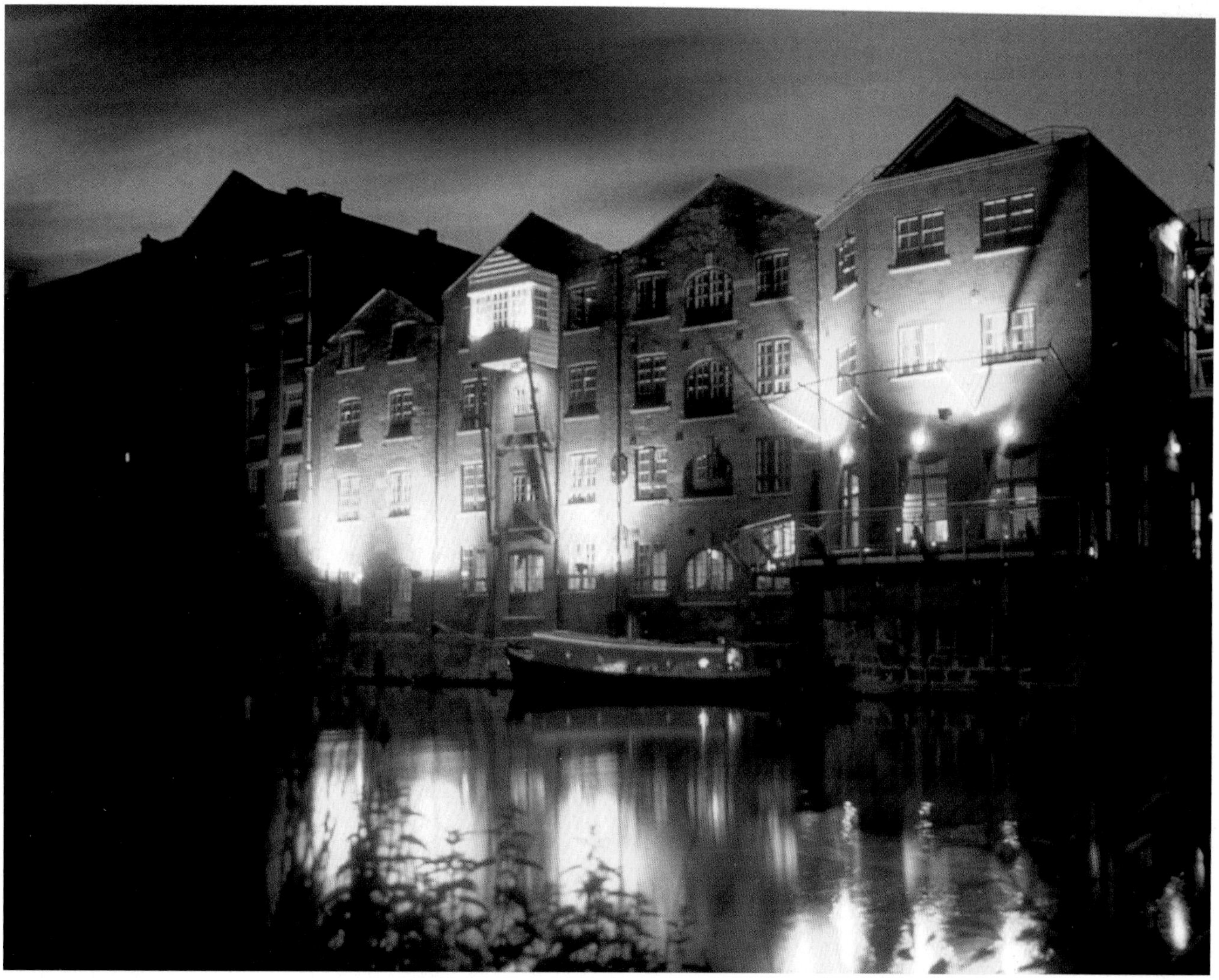

42 The Calls

42 THE CALLS, LEEDS, WEST YORKSHIRE LS2 7EW
TEL: 0113 244 0099 FAX: 0113 234 4100 E-MAIL: hotel@42thecalls.co.uk

This remarkable hotel is absolutely unique. Converted from an old riverside corn mill, it is run as a very personal and luxurious hotel by The Scotsman Hotel Group with General Manager Belinda Dawson and a dedicated team of staff in a peaceful location in the centre of Leeds. Shops, offices and theatres are within a few minutes' walk. The bedrooms have been individually decorated and furnished, taking full advantage of the many original features from small grain shutes to massive beams, girders and old machinery. Each room has 12 channel TV, a fresh filter coffee machine, complimentary sweets and cordials, luxury toiletries, trouser press and hair dryer. Stereo CD players are fitted in all the bedrooms and a library of disks is available to guests. Every comfort has been provided with full-size desks, handmade beds and armchairs, a liberal scattering of eastern rugs and beautiful bathrooms. Valet car parking and 24-hour room service are offered. Next door to the hotel is the simple but stylish Brasserie 44 and the superb Michelin Starred Pool Court at 42. **Directions:** M621 junction 3. Follow city centre and West Yorkshire Playhouse signs, turn left after Tetley's Brewery, then turn left onto City Centre Loop, following City signs. Take junction 15 off loop, 42 The Calls is immediately in front of you Price Guide: Single £117–£175; double/twin £164–£195; suite £220–£300. Special weekend breaks apply.

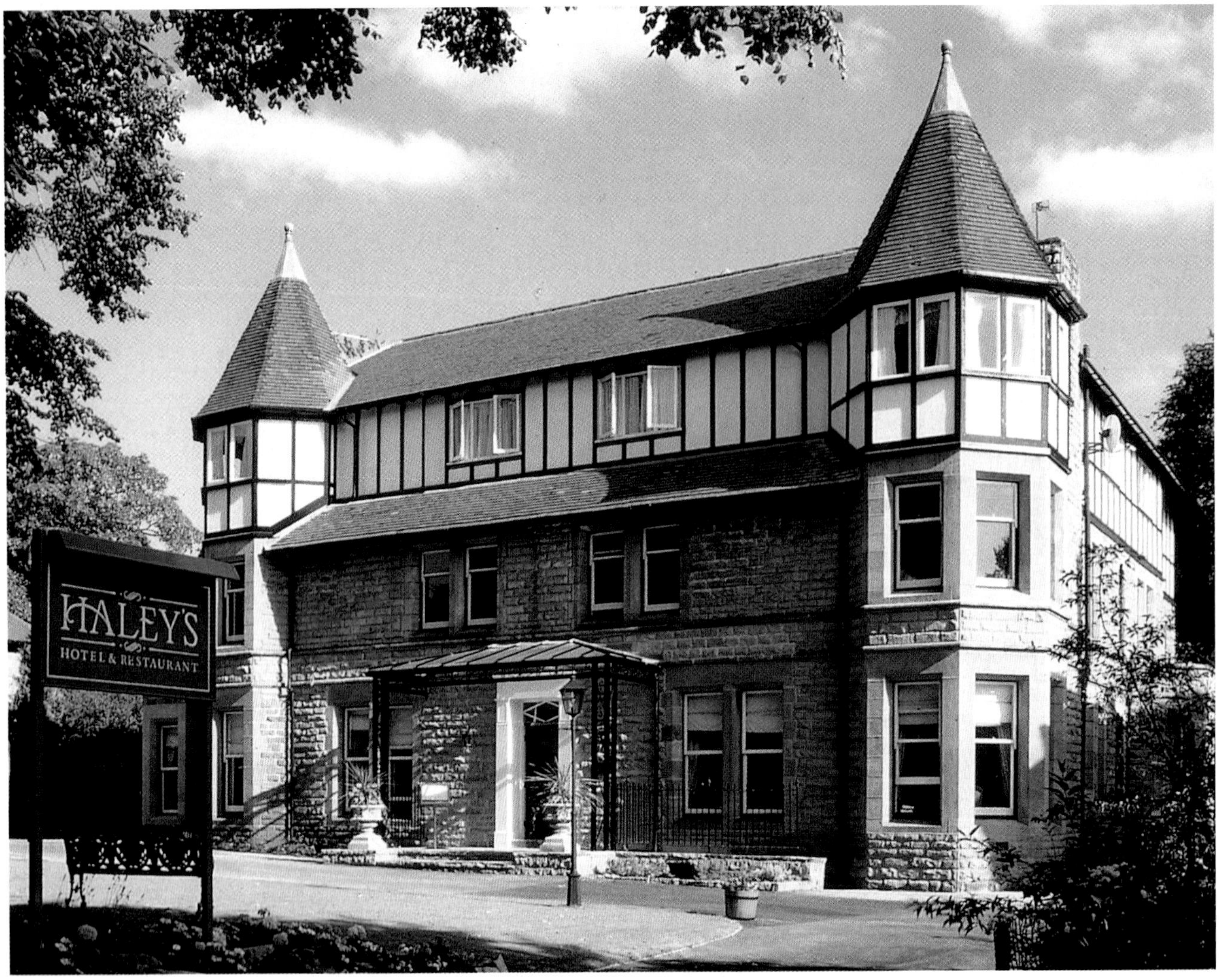

Haley's Hotel & Restaurant

SHIRE OAK ROAD, HEADINGLEY, LEEDS, WEST YORKSHIRE LS6 2DE
TEL: 0113 278 4446 FAX: 0113 275 3342 E-MAIL: info@haleys.co.uk

Just two miles from Leeds City Centre, yet set in a quiet leafy lane in the Headingley conservation area close to the cricket ground and the university, Haley's is truly the Country House Hotel in the City. Each of the 29 guest rooms offers the highest levels of comfort and is as individual as the fine antiques and rich furnishings which grace the hotel. A new addition to the existing accommodation is Bedford House, the elegant Victorian Grade II listed building next door which contains seven outstandingly furnished and beautifully equipped modern bedrooms, including two suites, one with its own private entrance. The Bramley Room and Library are popular venues for private meetings, lunch or dinner parties. Haley's Restaurant has an enviable reputation, holding two AA Rosettes. An imaginative menu of modern English cuisine is accompanied by a fine wine list. Leeds offers superb shopping (including Harvey Nichols) and the Victorian Arcades. Opera North and the theatres combine with Haley's superb accommodation and food to provide entertaining weekends. **Directions:** Two miles north of Leeds City Centre off the main A660 Otley Road – the main route to Leeds/Bradford Airport, Ilkley and Wharfedale. Price Guide: Single £95–£120; double/twin £125–£185; suite from £230. Special weekend and Sunday rates are available.

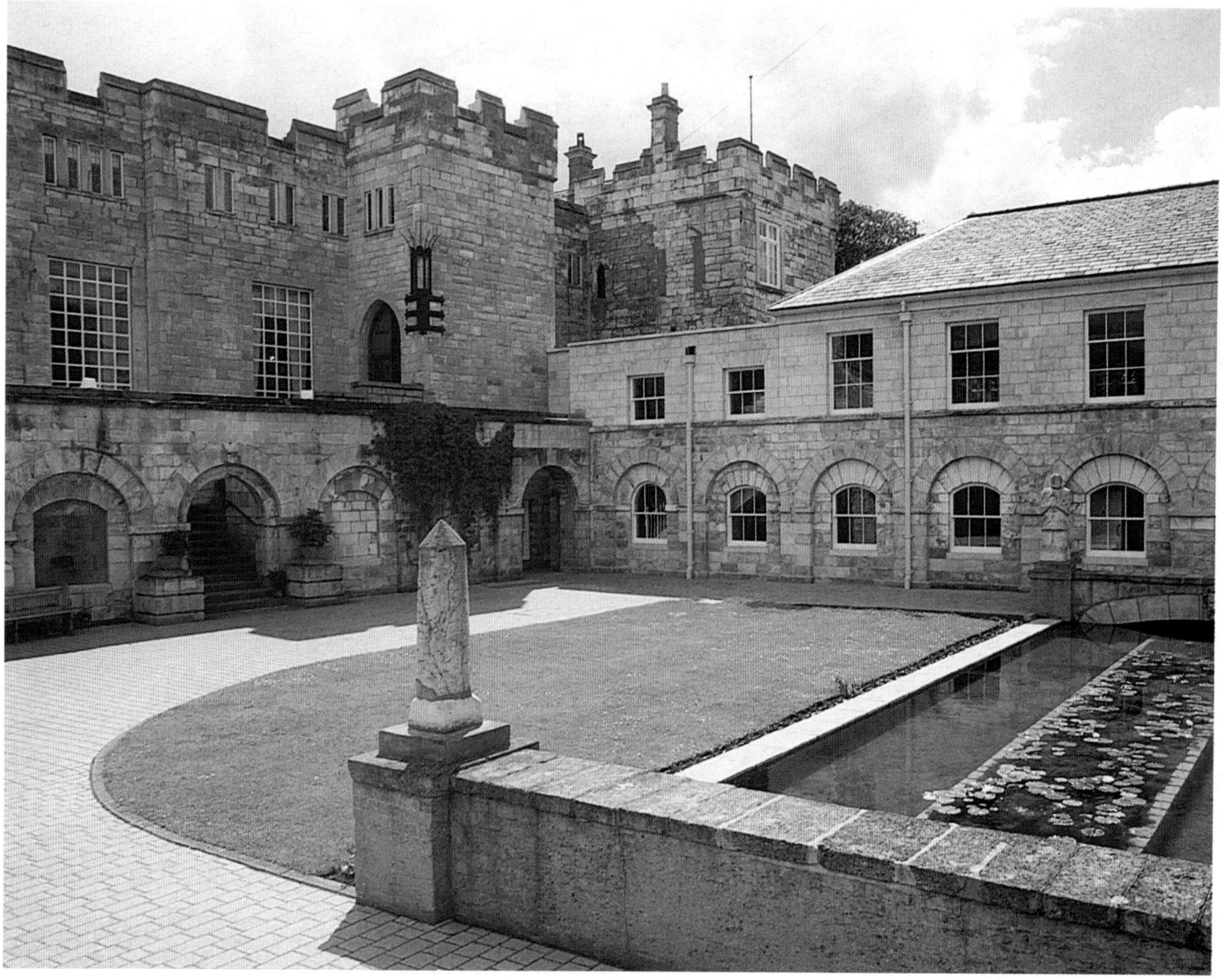

Hazlewood Castle Hotel

PARADISE LANE, HAZLEWOOD, TADCASTER, NR LEEDS & YORK, NORTH YORKSHIRE LS24 9NJ
TEL: 01937 535353 FAX: 01937 530630 E-MAIL: info@hazlewood-castle.co.uk

Behind the restored 13th-century façade of this fascinating castle lies a vibrant and professional hotel, where outstanding cuisine and flawless hospitality are offered in magnificent surroundings. Famed for its gourmet food, the hotel houses its own cookery school, where John Benson-Smith, formerly a Masterchef Judge, gives lively demonstrations. The hotel has two excellent restaurants, the informal Prickly Pear and the chic Restaurant 1086, as well as a range of facilities for private dining. A distinct panache is lent to the atmosphere of a banquet set in the Old Dining Room and State Drawing Rooms, and Restaurant 1086, the signature restaurant of John Benson-Smith, can be hired to add charismatic zest to a dinner party. Hazlewood Castle is well designed to accommodate corporate or private events, whilst providing a sense of privilege and individuality for its guests. Its fortified buildings include the impressive Great Hall and the Chapel of St Leonards, ideal for musical occasions, amongst its many convivial reception rooms. The beautifully decorated bedrooms reflect the perfect balance of tradition and design that is evident throughout the hotel. Numerous activities include golf and clay pigeon shooting. **Directions:** Off the A64 east of the A1 Leeds/York intersection. Price Guide: Single from £110; double/twin £175–£275; suites £195–£300.

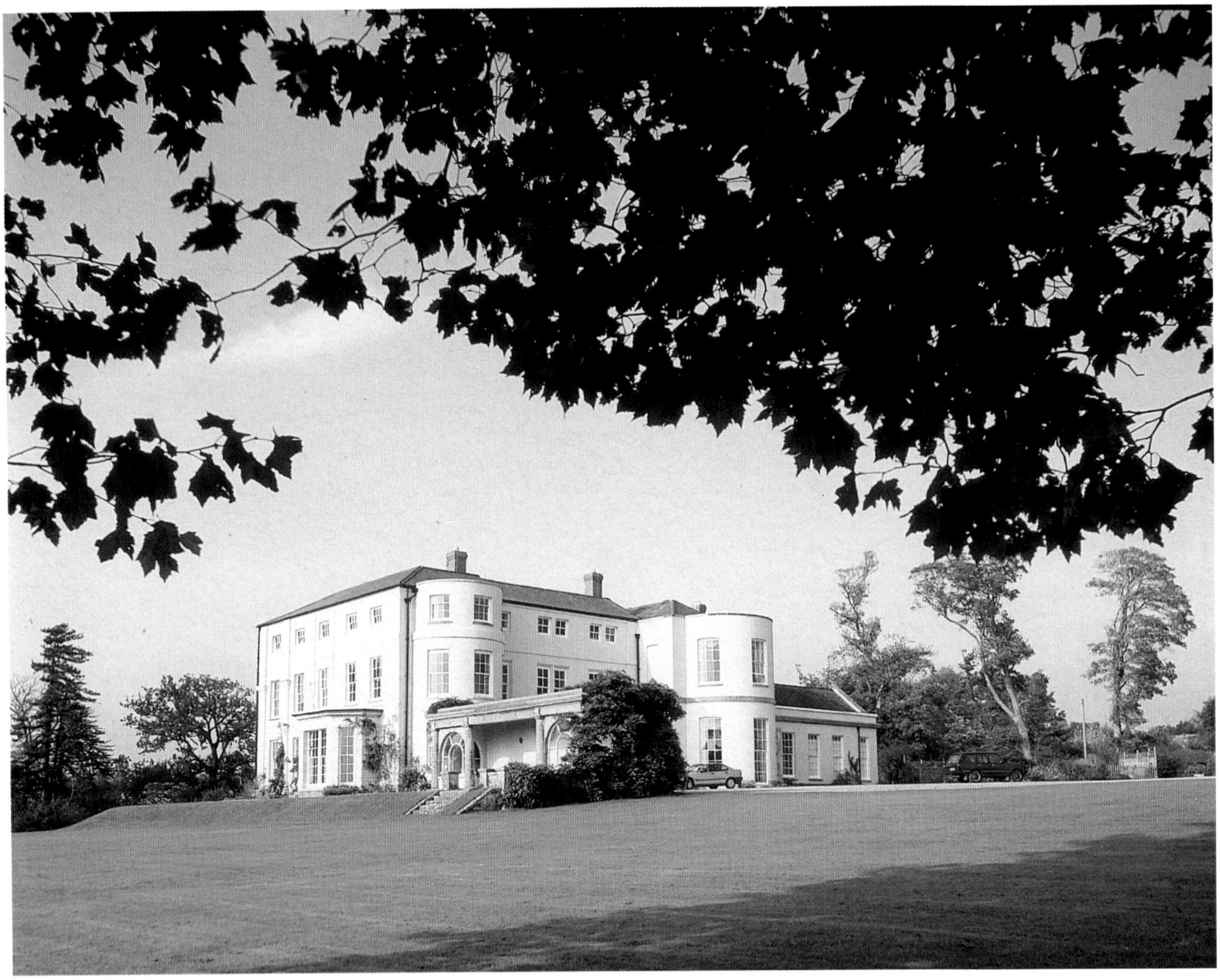

Newick Park

NEWICK, NEAR LEWES, EAST SUSSEX BN8 4SB

TEL: 01825 723633 FAX: 01825 723969 E-MAIL: bookings@newickpark.co.uk

This magnificent Grade II listed Georgian country house, set in over 200 acres of breath-taking parkland and landscaped gardens, overlooks the Longford River and lake and the South Downs. Whilst situated in a convenient location near to the main road and rail routes and only 30 minutes away from Gatwick Airport, Newick Park maintains an atmosphere of complete tranquillity and privacy. The en suite bedrooms are decorated in a classic style and contain elegant antique furnishings. The exquisite dining room offers a wide choice of culinary delights, carefully devised by the Head Chef, Billy Butcher. The convivial bar complements the restaurant with its delicate style and understated elegance. The friendly staff ensure that guests receive a warm welcome and an outstanding level of comfort. The house and grounds are ideal for weddings or conferences and may be hired for exclusive use by larger groups. The Dell gardens, planted primarily in Victorian times, include a rare collection of Royal Ferns. Vibrant and diverse colours saturate the lawns during the changing seasons, courtesy of the various flowers and shrubs encompassing the gardens. The activities on the estate itself include fishing, shooting and tennis, whilst nearby distractions include the East Sussex Golf Club and racing at Goodwood. **Directions:** The nearest motorway is the M23, jct 11. Price Guide: Single £95–£120; double/twin £165–235.

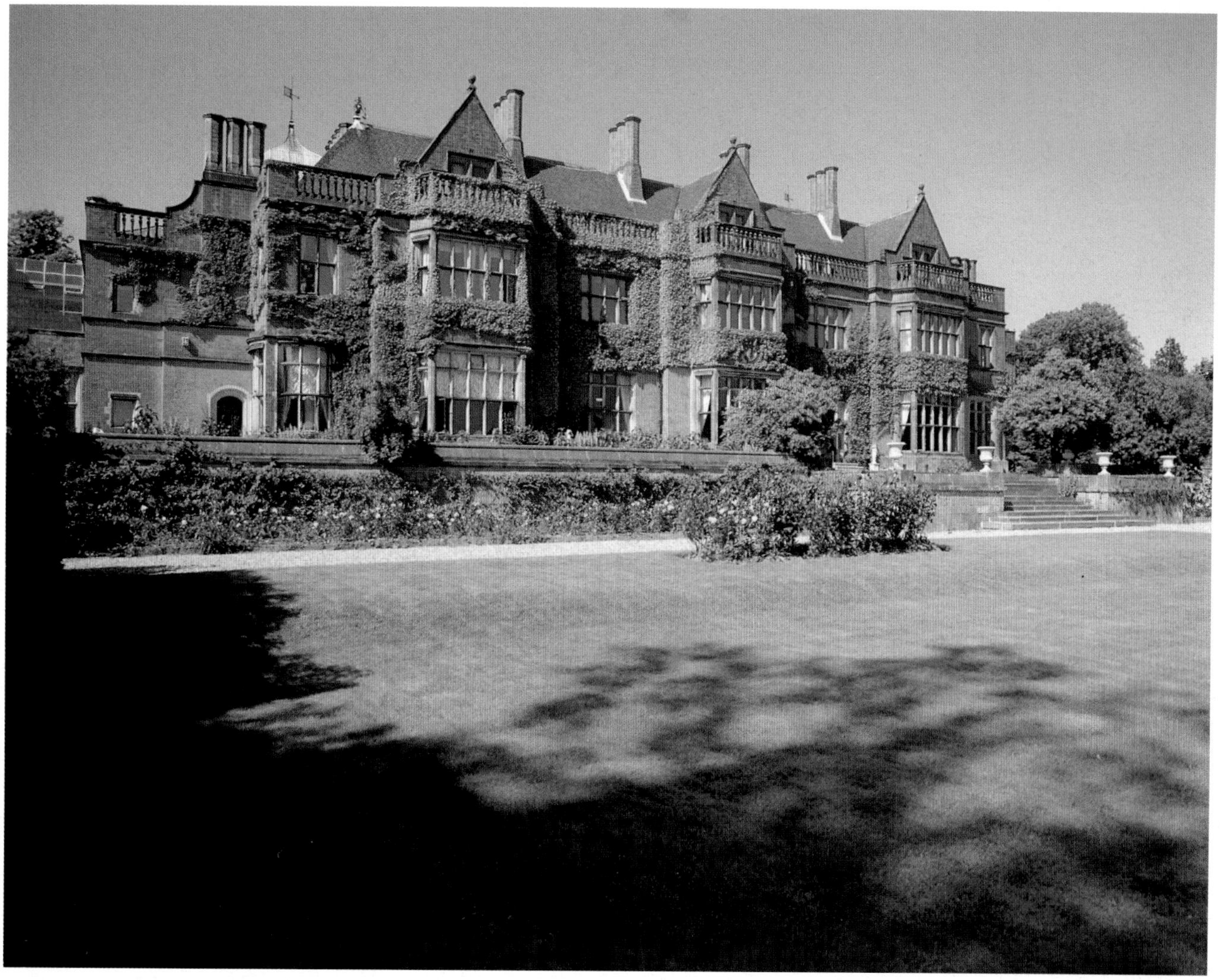

HOAR CROSS HALL HEALTH SPA RESORT

HOAR CROSS, NR YOXALL, STAFFORDSHIRE DE13 8QS
TEL: 01283 575671 FAX: 01283 575652 E-MAIL: info@hoarcross.co.uk

Hoar Cross Hall is a health spa resort in a stately home, hidden in the Staffordshire countryside with all the facilities of a four star hotel. Built in the 1860s, it is a graceful listed residence. Today's guests expect more than just to languish in beautiful surroundings; they also wish to rejuvenate their minds and bodies. Water-based treatments are behind the Spa's successful philosophy; from hydro-therapy baths and blitz jet douches, floatation therapy, saunarium, sauna and steam rooms, to the superb hydrotherapy swimming pool and water grotto, with over 80 therapists to pamper you with your choice of over 80 treatments. Peripheral activities are extensive. Partake of a full fitness assessment, a new hairstyle or venture into the 100 acres of woodlands and formal gardens. Play tennis, croquet and boules, or bicycle through the countryside. A Golf Academy with a PGA professional will teach you to play or improve your golf. Delight in the à la carte dining room where mouthwatering dishes are served. Enjoy a day of relaxed luxury or a week of professional pampering (minimum guest age is sixteen years). The price includes accommodation, breakfast, lunch, dinner, as well as unlimited use of facilities and treatments according to length of stay. **Directions:** From Lichfield turn off A51 onto A515 towards Ashbourne. Go through Yoxall and turn left to Hoar Cross. Price Guide: (fully inclusive, see above): Single £149; double/twin £273.

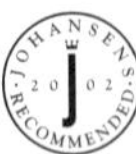

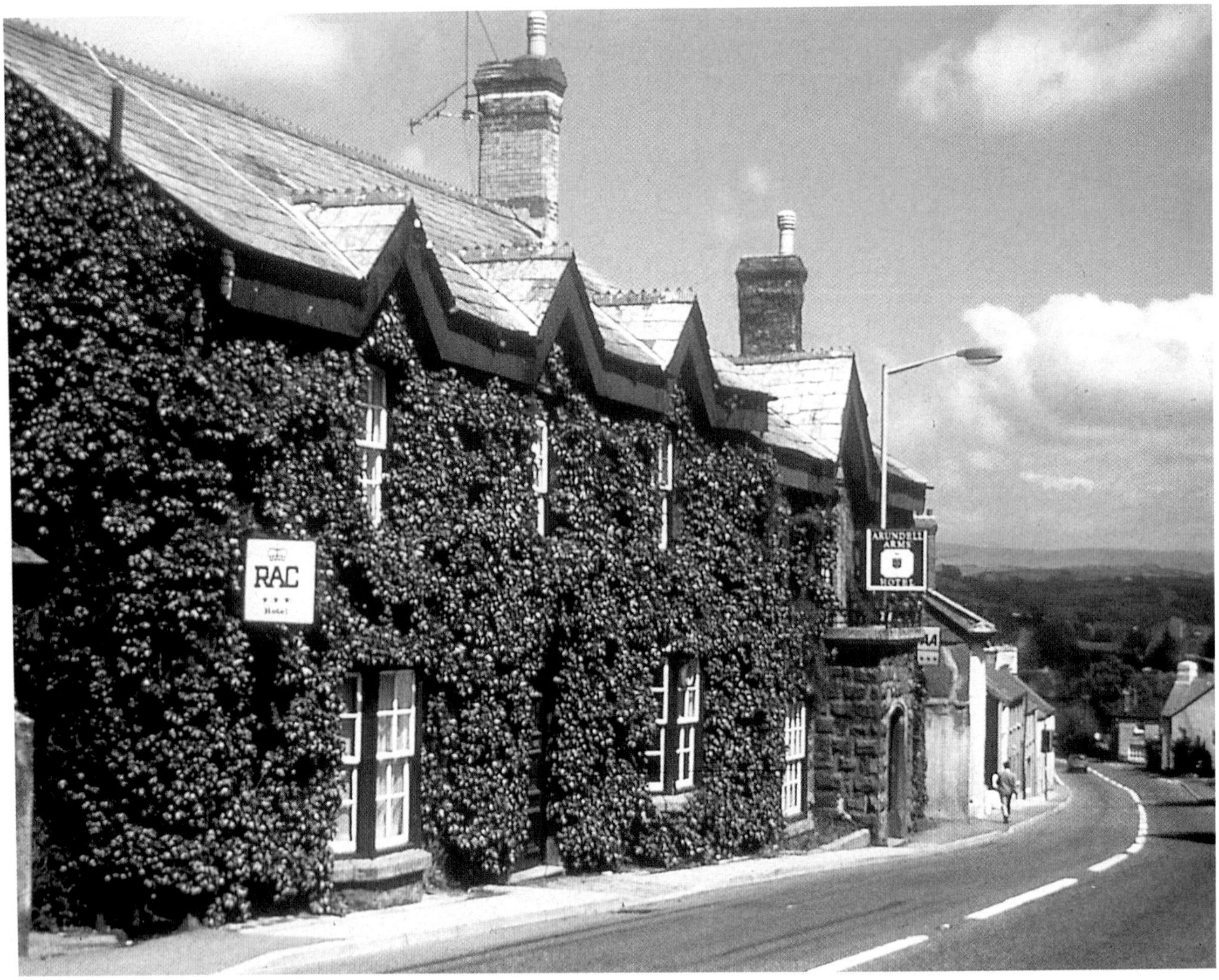

THE ARUNDELL ARMS

LIFTON, DEVON PL16 0AA
TEL: 01566 784666 FAX: 01566 784494 E-MAIL: reservations@arundellarms.com

In a lovely valley close to the uplands of Dartmoor, the Arundell Arms is a former coaching inn which dates back to Saxon times. Its flagstone floors, cosy fires, paintings and antiques combine to create a haven of warmth and comfort in an atmosphere of old world charm. One of England's best-known sporting hotels for more than half a century, it boasts 20 miles of exclusive salmon and trout fishing on the Tamar and five of its tributaries and a famous school of Fly Fishing. Guests also enjoy a host of other country activities, including hill walking, shooting, riding and golf. The hotel takes great pride in its elegant 3 AA Rosette restaurant, presided over by Master Chef Philip Burgess. His gourmet cuisine has won the restaurant an international reputation. A splendid base from which to enjoy the wonderful surfing beaches nearby, the Arundell Arms is also well placed for visits to Tintagel and the historic houses and gardens of Devon and Cornwall and the Eden Project. Only 45 minutes from Exeter and Plymouth, it is also ideal for the business executive, reached by fast roads from all directions. A spacious conference suite is available. **Directions:** Lifton is approximately ¼ mile off A30 2 miles east of Launceston and the Cornish Border. Price Guide: Single £76.50; double/twin £117; suite £150.

23 MasterCard VISA AMERICAN EXPRESS M 100

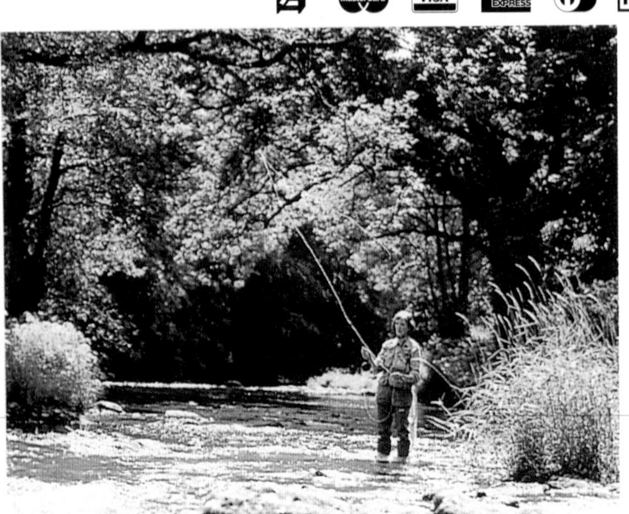

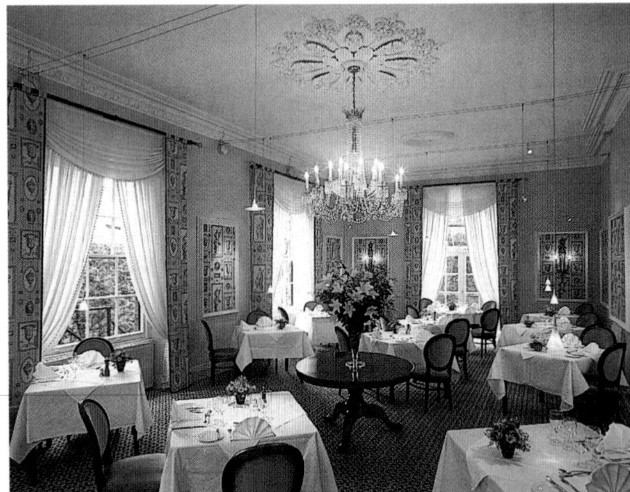

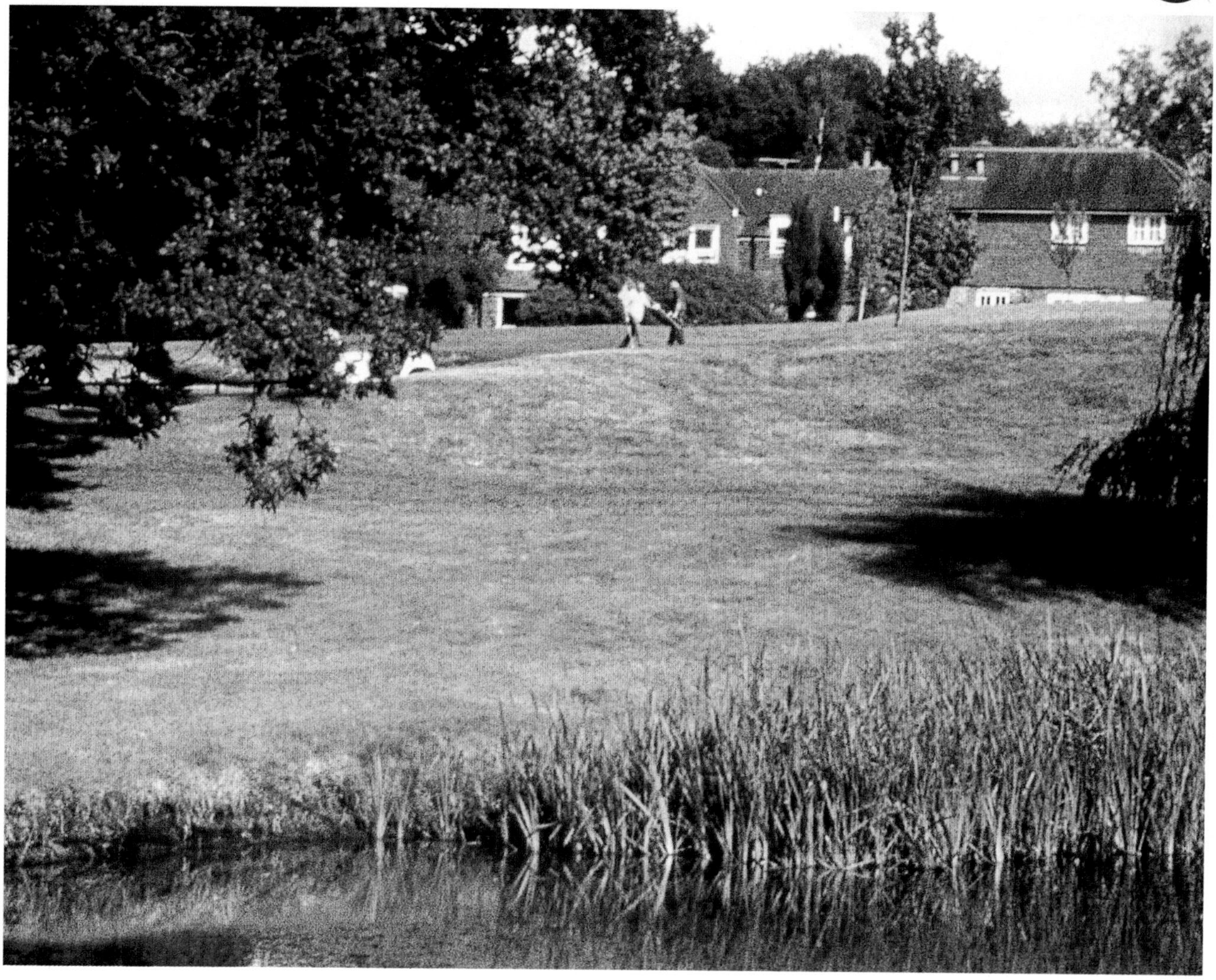

Old Thorns Hotel, Golf & Country Club

LONGMOOR ROAD, GRIGGS GREEN, LIPHOOK, HAMPSHIRE GU30 7PE
TEL: 01428 724555 FAX: 01428 725036 E-MAIL: info@oldthorns.com

Originally a 17th-century farmhouse, Old Thorns is situated within 400 acres of some of the finest Hampshire countryside. The stunning 18-hole championship golf course was designed by well-known golf course architect, Commander John Harris and completed by Peter Alliss and Dave Thomas. The elevated positions of many of the holes offer spectacular views and the rolling fairways bring the numerous natural springs, lakes and trees into play. The design of the course ensures a challenge for the top player, whilst affording satisfaction for the amateur. There are 33 four-star deluxe en suite bedrooms, and the Country Club offers an indoor pool, sauna, steam room, fitness centre, outdoor tennis courts as well as a range of facials, wraps and spa treatments. Three restaurants offer a variety of cuisine from the Nippon Kan Japanese restaurant where the Teppan Yaki is a speciality, to the informal Sands brasserie and the more traditional Garden Room. Old Thorns is also a popular conference venue, easily accessible from London and the M25. The Executive Boardroom has its own balcony overlooking the 1st tee and 18th green of the golf course. Places of interest include Jane Austen's house, the Gilbert White Museum and the Hollycombe Steam Collection. **Directions:** From M25 Jct10 turn south on A3 and take Griggs Green exit. The hotel is signed after ½ mile. Price Guide: Single from £125; double/twin from £145; suite from £195.

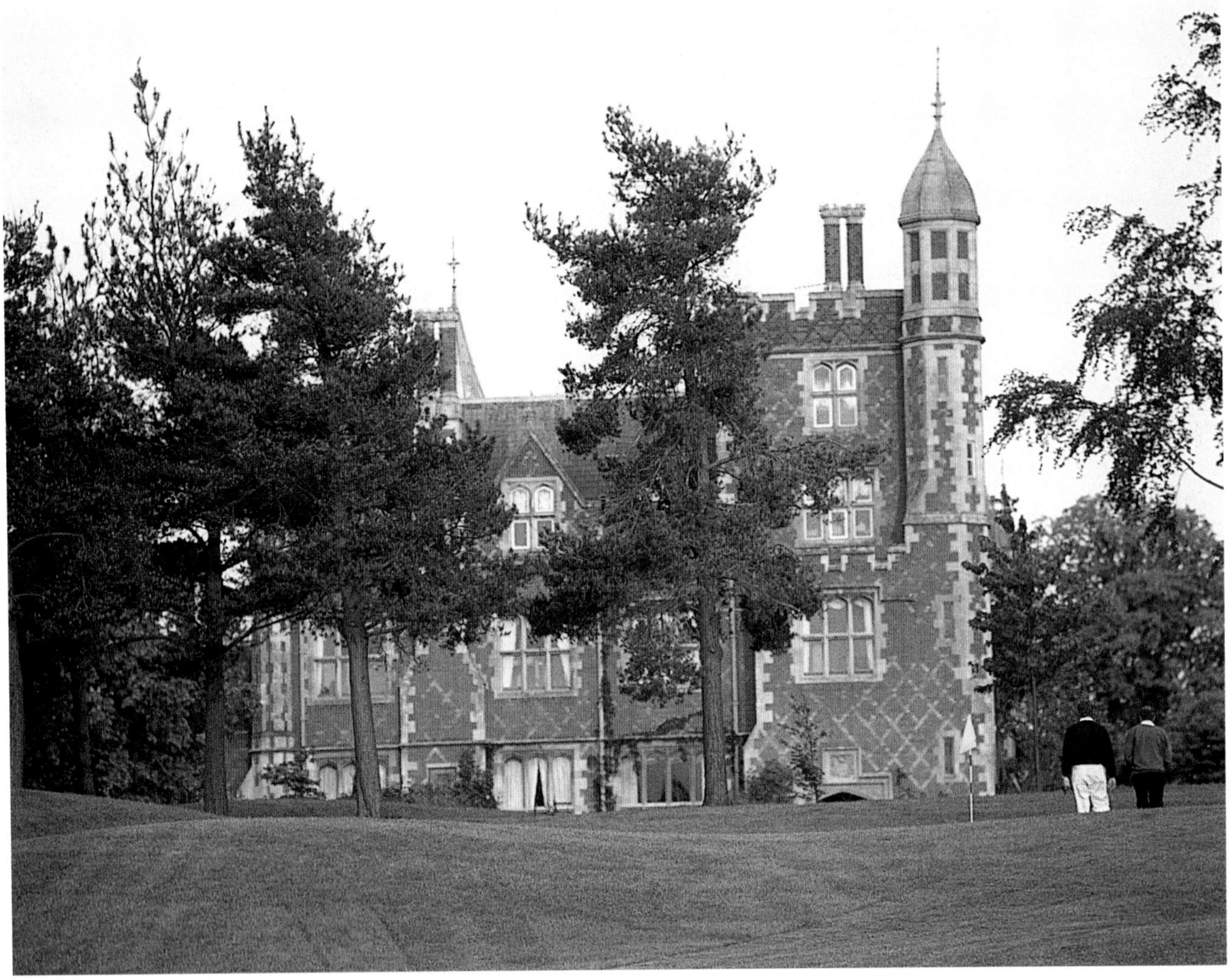

HORSTED PLACE SPORTING ESTATE & HOTEL

LITTLE HORSTED, EAST SUSSEX TN22 5TS
Tel: 01825 750581 Fax: 01825 750459 E-Mail: hotel@horstedplace.co.uk

Horsted Place enjoys a splendid location amid the peace of the Sussex Downs. This magnificent Victorian Gothic Mansion, which was built in 1851, overlooks the East Sussex National golf course and boasts an interior predominantly styled by the celebrated Victorian architect, Augustus Pugin. In former years the Queen and Prince Philip were frequent visitors. Guests today are invited to enjoy the excellent service offered by a committed staff. Since the turn of 2001, and under new management, the bedrooms have been refurbished to provide luxurious décor and every modern comfort, whilst all public areas have been refurbished and upholstered. Dining at Horsted is guaranteed to be a memorable experience. Chef Allan Garth offers a daily fixed price menu as well as the seasonal à la carte menu. The Horsted Management Centre is a suite of air-conditioned rooms which have been specially designed to accommodate theatre-style presentations and training seminars or top level board meetings. Places of interest nearby include Royal Tunbridge Wells, Lewes and Glyndebourne. For golfing enthusiasts there is the added attraction of the East Sussex National Golf Club, one of the finest golf complexes in the world. **Directions:** The hotel entrance is on the A26 just short of the junction with the A22, two miles south of Uckfield and signposted towards Lewes. Price Guide: Double/twin from £125; suite from £205.

20 MasterCard VISA AMERICAN EXPRESS M 80 7 VCR H

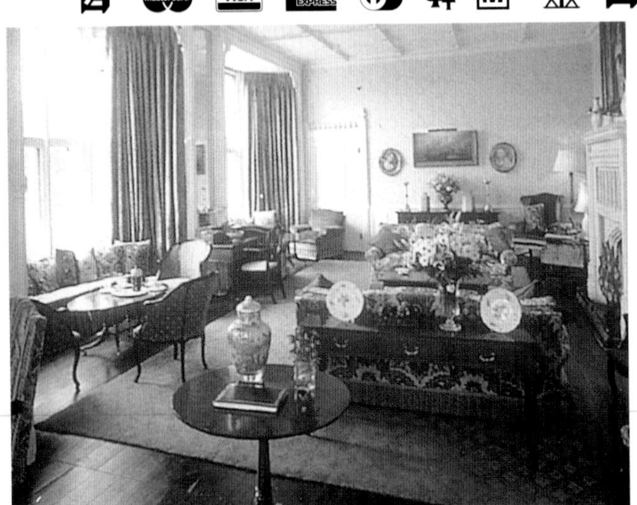

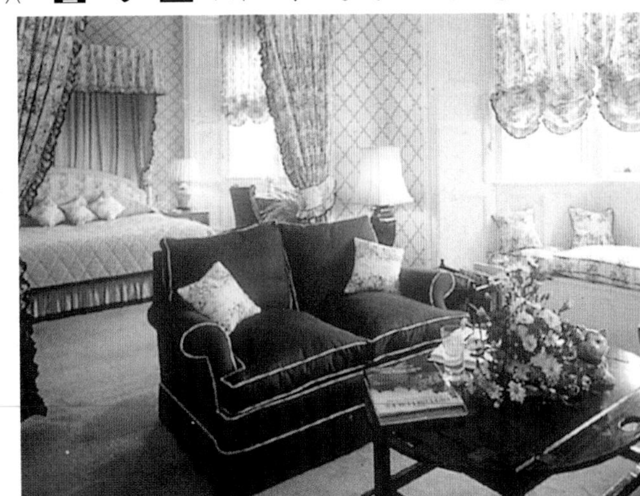

BLACK LION

CHURCH WALK, THE GREEN, LONG MELFORD, SUFFOLK CO10 9DN
TEL: 01787 312356 FAX: 01787 374557 E-MAIL: enquiries@blacklionhotel.net

One of Long Melford's oldest Inns, The Black Lion glories in its superb position overlooking the Green, and the Village with its elegant broad street and imposing church. Having been in existence for over 300 years, the Hotel recently entered a fresh era in its illustrious history. Under new owner Craig Jarvis a transformation has taken place, with rich colours, comfortable antique furniture and welcoming open fires all creating a charming country house ambience. Flanked by the Kentwell and Melford Hall Estates, good sized bedrooms offer picturesque views. The menu, based on traditional dishes with a modern approach, may be sampled casually in the Lounge Bar or more formally in the Restaurant each providing superb presentation and excellent food. A prolifery of antique emporiums, interesting shops, picturesque country walks and stately homes are within walking distance of the Inn, and many other places of interest are just a short drive away. From Constable country to Cambridge, historic Bury St Edmunds and Gainsborough's birthplace, there is much to appreciate. Racegoers will find The Black Lion a perfect base from which to attend Newmarket, while those simply longing to get away from it all could not wish for a more peaceful and inviting country retreat. **Directions:** From A14 take A134 in direction of Sudbury. Hotel overlooks Long Melford village green. Price Guide: Single from £71; double/twin from £93; suite from £118.50.

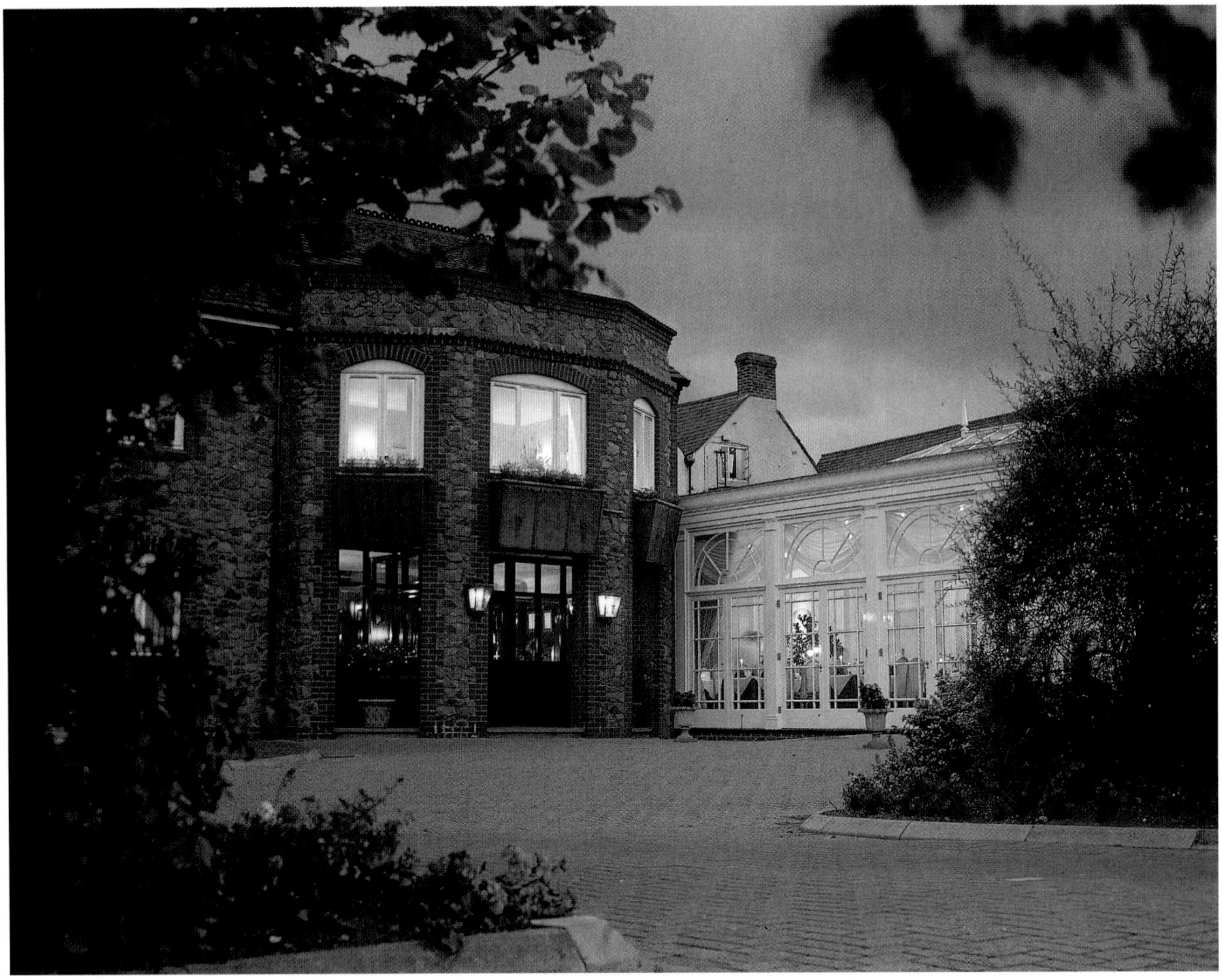

QUORN COUNTRY HOTEL

66 LEICESTER ROAD, QUORN, LEICESTERSHIRE LE12 8BB
TEL: 01509 415050 FAX: 01509 415557

Originally Leicestershire's most exclusive private club, created around the original 17th century listed building, this award winning 4 star hotel is set in 4 acres of landscaped gardens. For the tenth consecutive year the hotel has received all 3 RAC merit awards for excellence in cuisine, hospitality and comfort and was also a recipient of a second AA Rosette Award in 1997. The bedrooms are equipped to the very highest standard with attention given to every detail. Suitable for both the business traveller or for weekend guests seeking those extra 'touches' which help create the ideal peaceful retreat. Ladies travelling alone can feel reassured that their special needs are met and indeed exceeded. Particular emphasis is given to the enjoyment of food with a declared policy of using, whenever possible, the freshest local produce. Guests' stay will be enhanced by the choice of two different dining experiences. They can choose between the Shires Restaurant with its classical cuisine with a modern style or the Orangery Brasserie with its changing selection of contemporary dishes. **Directions:** Situated just off the A6 Leicester to Derby main road, in the bypassed village of Quorn (Quorndon), five miles from junction 23 of the M1 from North, junction 21A from South, East and West. Price Guide: Single £102; double/twin £115; suite £140.

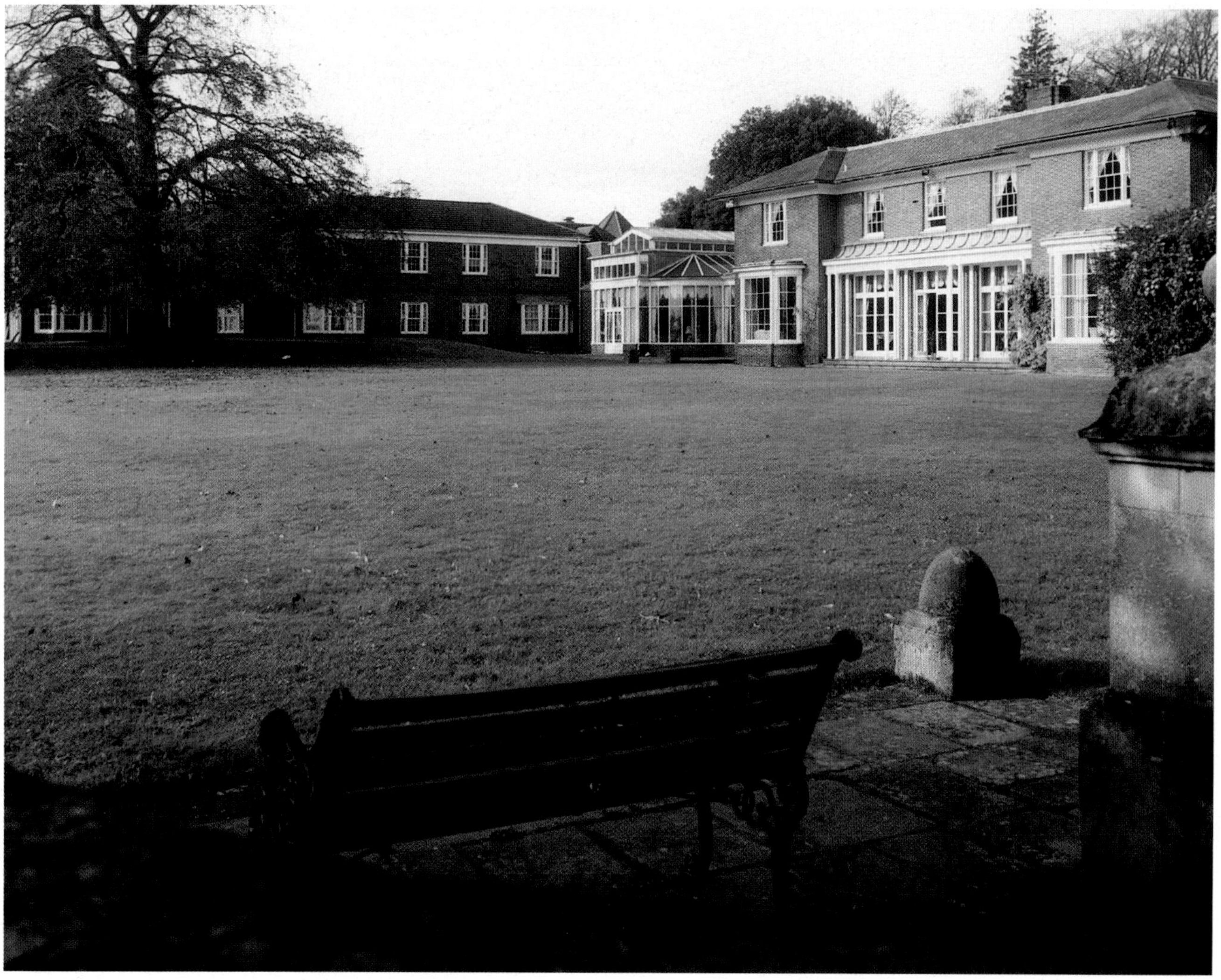

KENWICK PARK HOTEL & LEISURE CLUB

KENWICK PARK, LOUTH, LINCOLNSHIRE LN11 8NR
TEL: 01507 608806 FAX: 01507 608027 E-MAIL: kenwick–park.co.uk

Kenwick Park stands in magnificent, extensive parkland with sweeping views over the rolling hills, deep valleys, quiet streams and hanging birchwoods of the beautiful Lincolnshire Wolds. It is a three-star luxury hotel with spacious rooms furnished and serviced in grand, Georgian country house style. Peace, tranquillity and comfort combine with the finest facilities for both the leisure and business guest. Each of the 34 en suite bedrooms is furnished and decorated in the best of taste and many offer superb views over the gardens to the estate's acclaimed international standard golf course beyond. Guests have access to the Par 72 course on a green fee basis. The hotel is justifiably proud of its two AA Rosettes for its fine dining and gourmet menus. Chef Mark Vines produces excellent, imaginative à la carte cuisine to suit the most discerning palate in the elegant Fairway Restaurant and delicious meals are served in the Keepers Bar. Kenwick Park has facilities for the corporate visitor, including three meeting rooms. The leisure club features a 20-metre swimming pool, gymnasium, sauna and steam rooms. There are also squash and tennis courts and nearby there is horse racing at Market Rasen and motor racing at Cadwell Park. **Directions:** From the Louth Bypass (A16) follow the signs to Manby. Kenwick Park is one mile from Louth. Price Guide: Single £79.50; double/twin £98–£120; suite £130.

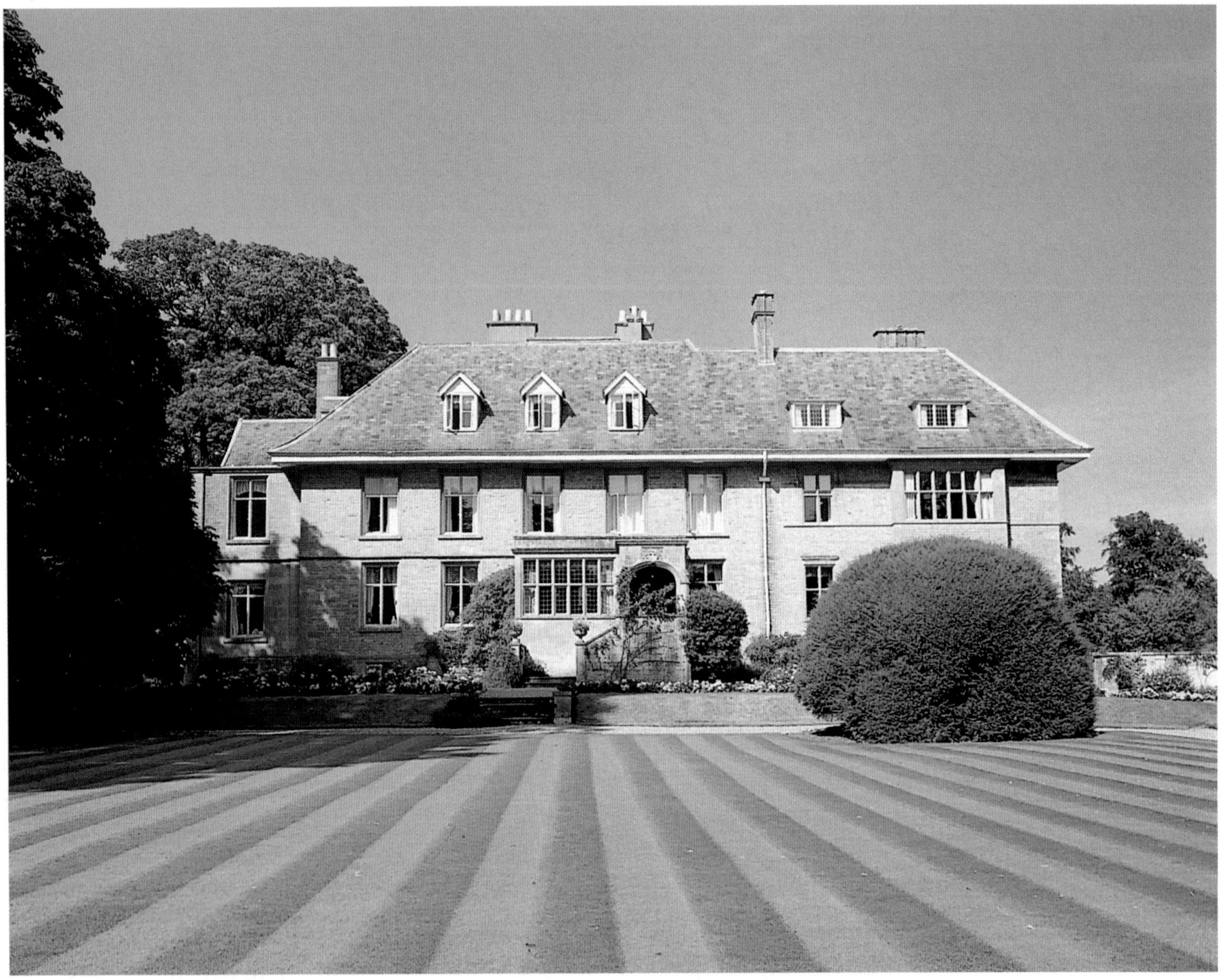

Lower Slaughter Manor

LOWER SLAUGHTER, GLOUCESTERSHIRE GL54 2HP
TEL: 01451 820456 FAX: 01451 822150 E-MAIL:lowsmanor@aol.com

With a history that spans nearly a thousand years, this Grade II listed Manor stands in complete tranquillity within private grounds on the edge of one of the Cotswold's prettiest villages. Lower Slaughter Manor is now owned by Daphne and Roy Vaughan, who have lovingly overseen its transformation. Visitors are warmly welcomed by a team of dedicated staff, and enjoy elegant, spacious surroundings. All rooms are beautifully furnished, with carefully chosen antiques, fine china and original paintings. The Manor has a stunning indoor heated swimming pool, while outside the wonderful grounds reveal a croquet lawn and tennis court, and, within the delightful walled garden, a unique two-storey dovecote dating back to the 15th century when the Manor was a convent. The award-winning cuisine is prepared using the best local and continental ingredients, and an outstanding wine list offers a range of 800 specially selected wines from the Old and New Worlds. An excellent setting for business meetings, The Sir George Whitmore Suite accommodates up to 25 people, and offers phone line, full secretarial services and audio visual equipment. For more leisurely pursuits, visitors can explore the Cotswolds, Cheltenham, Stratford, and Warwick and Sudeley Castles. Lower Slaughter Manor is a member of The Leading Hotels of the World. **Directions:** The Manor is on the right as you enter Lower Slaughter from A429. Price Guide: Single £175–£375; double/twin £200–£400; suite £350–£400.

16 MasterCard VISA AMERICAN EXPRESS M 30 10

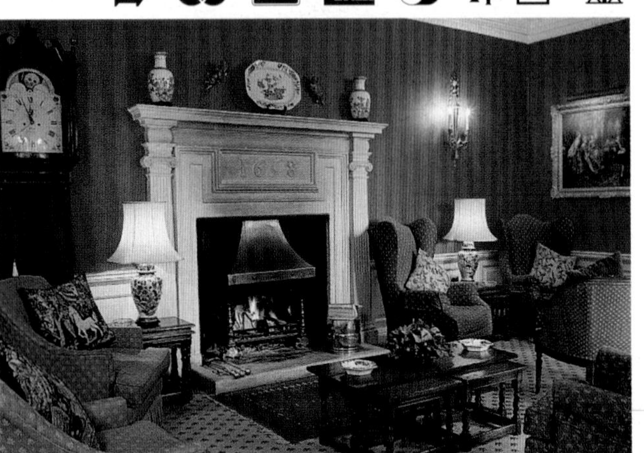

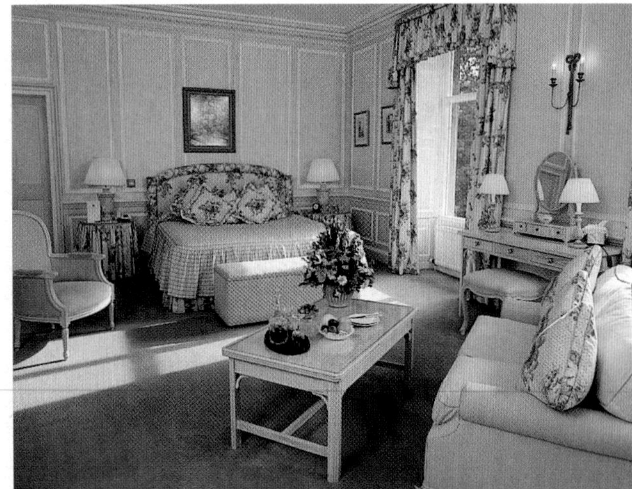

WASHBOURNE COURT HOTEL

LOWER SLAUGHTER, GLOUCESTERSHIRE GL54 2HS
TEL: 01451 822143 FAX: 01451 821045

Under the private ownership of Roy and Daphne Vaughan, Washbourne Court Hotel is in the heart of the tranquil and beautiful Cotswold village of Lower Slaughter, set on the bank of the River Eye. The four acres of private gardens have been lovingly re-landscaped with lawns and many delightful features. With just twenty eight bedrooms, it has parts dating back to the 17th century. The recent additions to the hotel, a spacious new dining room and a further six guest rooms with comfortable and elegant furnishings, blend in perfectly with the original building. Always full of freshly picked flowers and planted bowls, the hotel has the feel of a private house with the many personal touches. The modern English cuisine offers an abundance of fresh local produce, concentrating on good textures and intense flavours combined with outstanding presentation. Head Chef Sean Ballington now oversees the running of the kitchen. Drinks, light lunches and traditional afternoon tea are also served on the garden terrace during the summer months. **Directions:** The hotel is situated ½ a mile from the main A429 Fosseway between Stow-on-the-Wold and Bourton-on-the-Water (signed To the Slaughters). Price Guide (including dinner): Single from £155; double/twin £210–£270.

DINHAM HALL

LUDLOW, SHROPSHIRE SY8 1EJ

TEL: 01584 876464 FAX: 01584 876019 E-MAIL: info@dinhamhall.co.uk

Built in 1792 Dinham Hall is situated in the historic town of Ludlow. It lies only 40 metres from the Castle which, having played an important part in England's history, today hosts the Shakespearian productions forming the major part of the annual Ludlow Festival. Dinham's enviable location provides a combination of ready access to the town and picturesque views over the open Shropshire countryside. There is a magnificent fireplace in the sitting room, with log fires in the winter. The elegant and sumptuous restaurant serves succulent dishes prepared by rising star Olivier Bossut, who specialises in creative modern French cooking. The Merchant Suite, with its 14th century timbers, is an ideal setting for private dinners and meetings. During the summer afternoon teas are served on the terrace overlooking the walled garden. The décor of the bedrooms is a harmony of modern facilities and period design, a number of rooms having four-poster beds. The restaurant and many bedrooms command views over the gardens and Teme Valley to wooded hills. Guests may also enjoy a visit to Ludlow races or spend a few hours browsing in the town's antique shops. South Shropshire is one of the most beautiful parts of the country with Ludlow itself being one of the finest market towns **Directions:** In the centre of Ludlow overlooking the castle. Price Guide: Single £70–£99; double/twin £120–£170.

14 MasterCard VISA AMERICAN EXPRESS M 20

PASSFORD HOUSE HOTEL

MOUNT PLEASANT LANE, LYMINGTON, HAMPSHIRE SO41 8LS
TEL: 01590 682398 FAX: 01590 683494 E-MAIL: sales@passfordhousehotel.co.uk

Set in nine acres of picturesque gardens and rolling parkland, the Passford House Hotel lies midway between the charming New Forest village of Sway and the Georgian splendour of Lymington. Once the home of Lord Arthur Cecil, it is steeped in history and the traditions of leisurely country life. Pleasantly decorated bedrooms include a number of superior rooms, while comfort is the keynote in the four public lounges. The hotel prides itself on the standard and variety of cuisine served in its delightful restaurant and the extensive menu aims to give pleasure to the most discerning of palates. Meals are complemented by a speciality wine list. The hotel boasts a compact leisure centre, catering for all ages and activities. In addition to two heated swimming pools, there is a multi-gym, sauna, pool table, croquet lawn, pétanque and tennis court. Just a short drive away are Beaulieu, the cathedral cities of Winchester and Salisbury and ferry ports to the Isle of Wight and France. The New Forest has numerous golf courses, riding and trekking centres, cycling paths, beautiful walks, and of course sailing on the Solent. Milford-on-Sea, four miles away, is the nearest beach. **Directions:** At Lymington leave the A337 at the Tollhouse Inn, then take the first turning right and the hotel is on the right. Price Guide: Single from £80; double/twin from £125.

Stanwell House

HIGH STREET, LYMINGTON, NEW FOREST, HAMPSHIRE SO41 9AA
TEL: 01590 677123 FAX: 01590 677756 E-MAIL: sales@stanwellhousehotel.co.uk

Stanwell House Hotel combines a highly individual style with informal and unobtrusive personal service. This Georgian town house is set on Lymington's fine wide high street, which still hosts a bustling Saturday market, serving the local community and antiques hunters alike. The owner's vibrant personality and theatrical background are reflected in her choice of colours and furnishings which set the mood for some surprises in the 23 bedrooms and five fantasy suites. The restaurant has been awarded two rosettes, and there is an intimate bar and bistro. A delightful conservatory leads onto a flower-filled patio and charming walled garden. Adjacent to the hotel, in a quiet courtyard off the high street, is Elgars Cottage. This pretty period cottage is furnished to a very high standard and offers a full range of amenities. The house yacht Alpha is available for corporate or private charter, overnight stays or cruising. Lymington is a charming Regency town, close to the New Forest and the magnificent Solent with all its yacht facilities. There are opportunities for walking, riding and golf and river or sea fishing. Crossings by car ferry from Lymington to Yarmouth bring the Isle of Wight within a 30 minute journey. **Directions:** From the M27 junction 1 through Lyndhurst and Brockenhurst. Price Guide: Single £85; double/twin £110–£130; suites £150–£160; Stanwell Cottage £825 per week for two people.

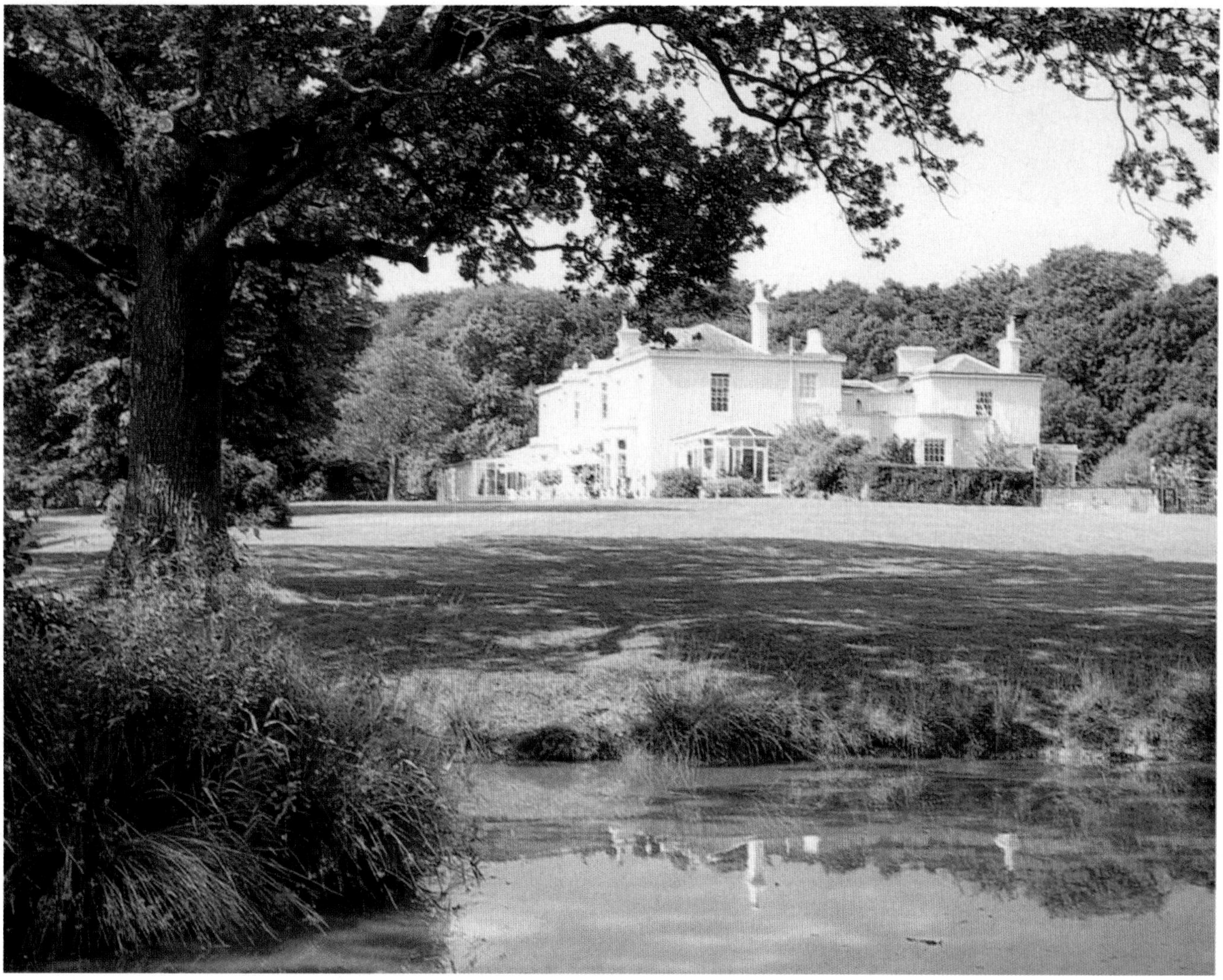

LE POUSSIN AT PARKHILL

BEAULIEU ROAD, LYNDHURST, NEW FOREST, HAMPSHIRE SO43 7FZ
TEL: 023 8028 2944 FAX: 023 8028 3268 E-MAIL: sales@lepoussinatparkhill.co.uk

A winding drive through glorious parkland and lawned grounds leads to this gracious 18th century country house which is now a renowned and popular restaurant with accommodation. Built on the site of a 13th century hunting lodge, Le Poussin stands in an elevated position with superb views across its 13-acre surrounds and open forest. It offers remoteness and period comfort coupled with an outstanding excellence of standards, service and cuisine. Dining in the elegant restaurant is a delight to be sampled leisurely while viewing deer grazing just a few steps away. Internationally acclaimed Chef patron Alex Aiken holds a Michelin Star and three AA Rosettes. His innovative, imaginative cuisine is a joy not to be missed. The bedrooms are being refurbished to high standards compatible with the delightful restaurant and public rooms. There is also a small cottage with its own walled garden for those wishing to bring a dog. It is ideal for visiting the many places of interest, all within easy driving distance. These include Exbury Gardens, home to one of the world's finest collections of rhododendrons and azaleas, Broadlands, the old home of Lord Mountbatten, and the cathedral cities of Salisbury and Winchester. **Directions:** From Lyndhurst take B3056 towards Beaulieu. Parkhill is approximately 1 m from Lyndhurst on the right. Price Guide: Single from £70; double/twin from £80; suites from £140.

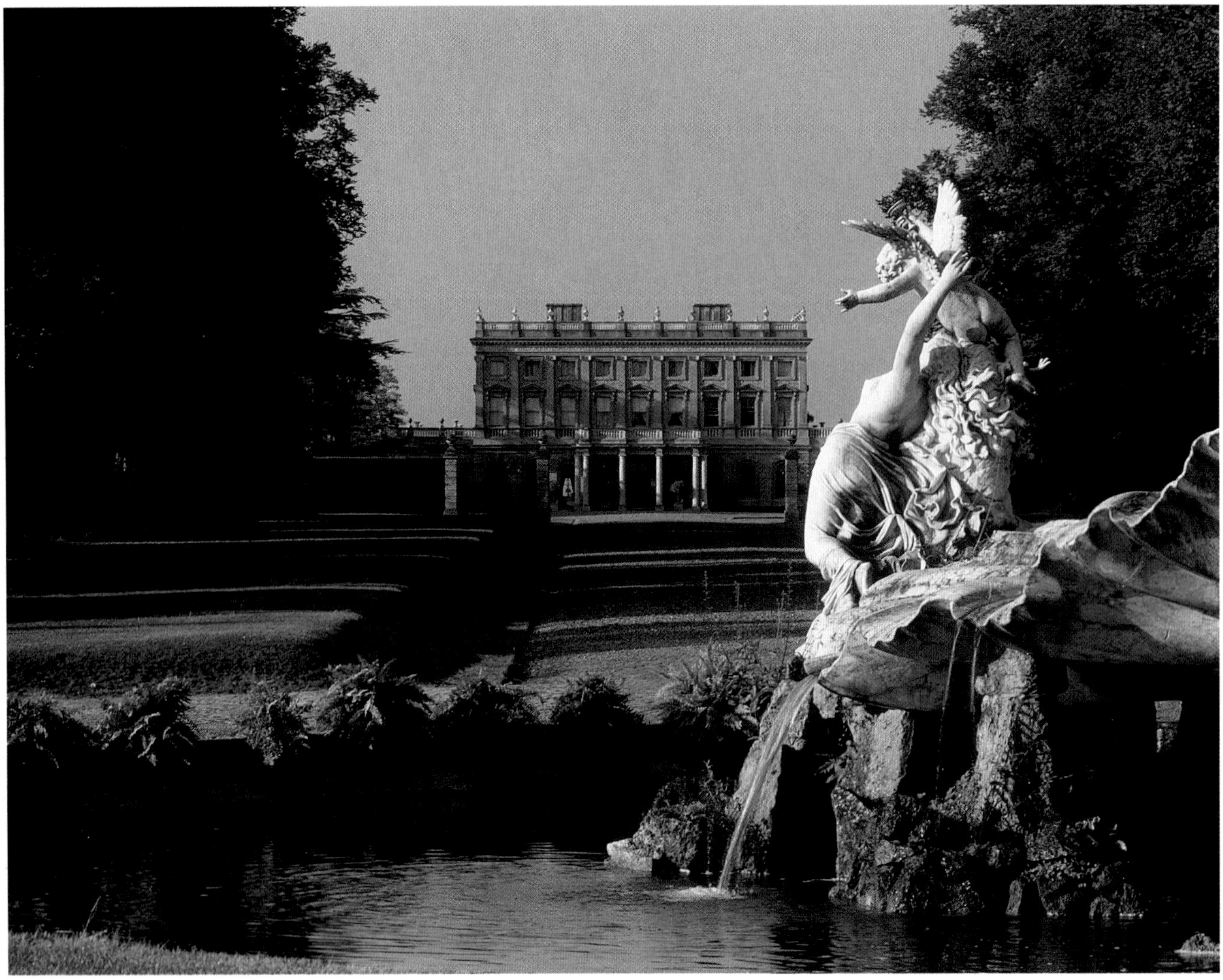

CLIVEDEN

TAPLOW, BERKSHIRE SL6 0JF

TEL: 01628 668561 FAX: 01628 661837 E-MAIL: Reservations@clivedenhouse.co.uk

Cliveden, Britain's only 5 Red AA star hotel that is also a stately home, is set in 376 acres of gardens and parkland, overlooking the Thames. As the former home of Frederick, Prince of Wales, three Dukes and the Astor family, Cliveden has been at the centre of Britain's social and political life for over 300 years. It is exquisitely furnished in a classical English style; oil paintings, antiques and objets d'art abound. The spacious guest rooms and suites are appointed to the most luxurious standards. The choice of dining rooms and the scope of the menus are superb. The French Dining Room, with its original Madame de Pompadour rococo decoration, is the finest 18th-century boiserie outside France. Relish the award-winning cuisine of Waldo's Restaurant. Spring Cottage, secluded in its own gardens on the edge of the Cliveden Reach of the River Thames, is truly a cottage for a Queen, boasting a 20-feet domed Gothic ceiling within the drawing room. The pavilion offers a full range of health and fitness facilities and beauty therapies. Guests can enjoy walking on the estate or a river cruise on an Edwardian launch. Well-equipped, the two secure private boardrooms provide self-contained business meeting facilities. Exclusive use of the House can be arranged. Cliveden's style may also be enjoyed at the Cliveden Town House in London and the Royal Crescent Hotel in Bath. **Directions:** Situated on B476, 2 miles north of Taplow. Price Guide: (room only excluding VAT) Double/twin from £320; suites from £485.

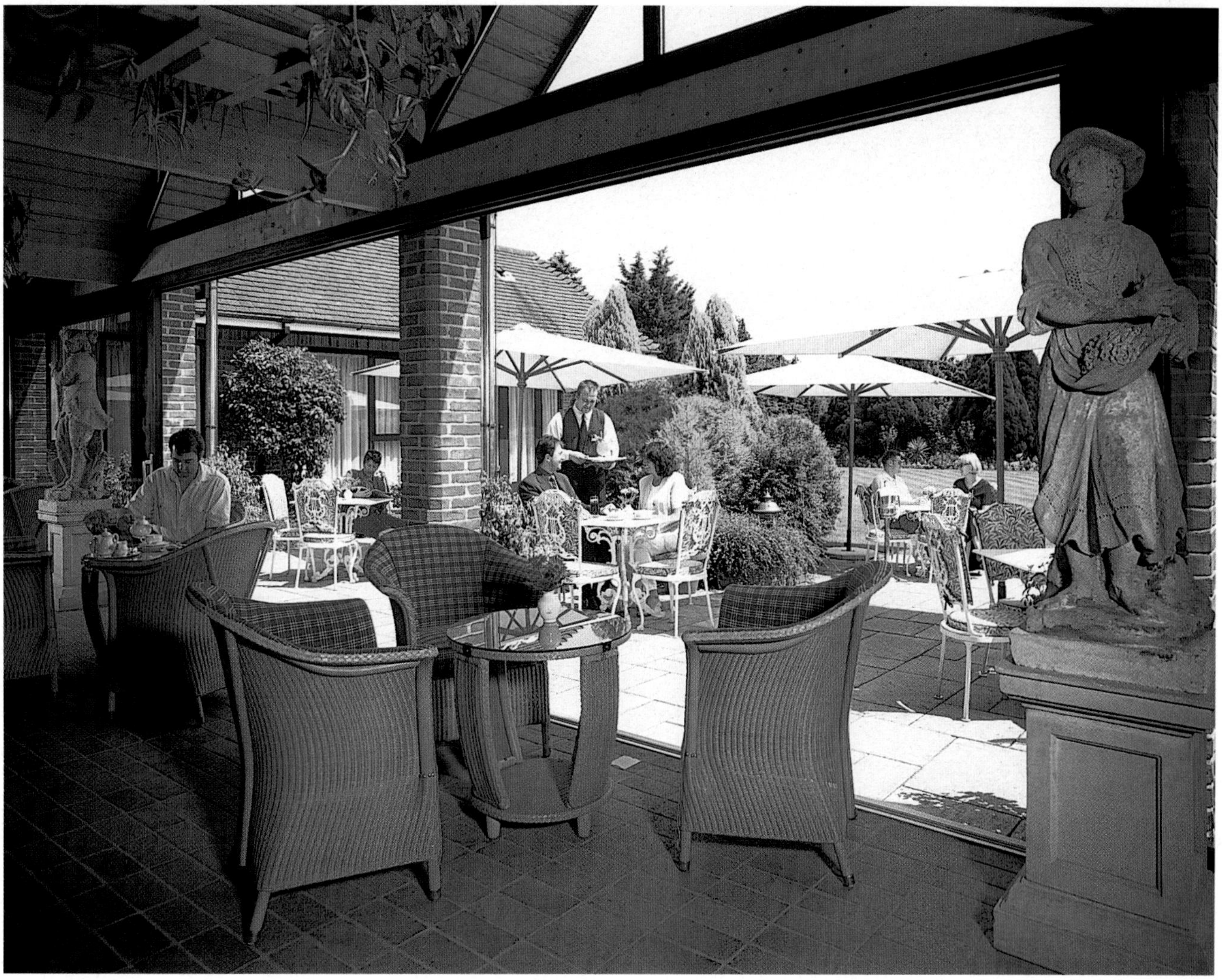

FREDRICK'S HOTEL & RESTAURANT

SHOPPENHANGERS ROAD, MAIDENHEAD, BERKSHIRE SL6 2PZ
TEL: 01628 581000 FAX: 01628 771054 E-MAIL: reservations@fredricks–hotel.co.uk

'Putting people first' is the guiding philosophy behind the running of this sumptuously equipped hotel and indeed, is indicative of the uncompromising service guests can expect to receive. Set in two acres of grounds, Fredrick's overlooks the fairways and greens of Maidenhead Golf Club beyond. The immaculate reception rooms are distinctively styled to create something out of the ordinary. Minute attention to detail is evident in the 37 bedrooms, all immaculate with gleaming, marble-tiled bathrooms, while the suites have their own patio garden or balcony. A quiet drink can be enjoyed in the light, airy Wintergarden lounge, or in warmer weather on the patio, before entering the air-conditioned restaurant. Amid the elegant décor of crystal chandeliers and crisp white linen, fine gourmet cuisine is served which has received recognition from leading guides for many years. Particularly suited to conferences, four private function rooms with full secretarial facilities are available. Helicopter landing can be arranged. Easily accessible from Windsor, Henley, Ascot, Heathrow and London. Closed 24 Dec to 3 Jan. **Directions:** Leave M4 at exit 8/9, take A404(M) and leave at first turning signed Cox Green/White Waltham. Turn into Shoppenhangers Road; Fredrick's is on the right. Price Guide: Single £195; double/twin £240; suite £370.

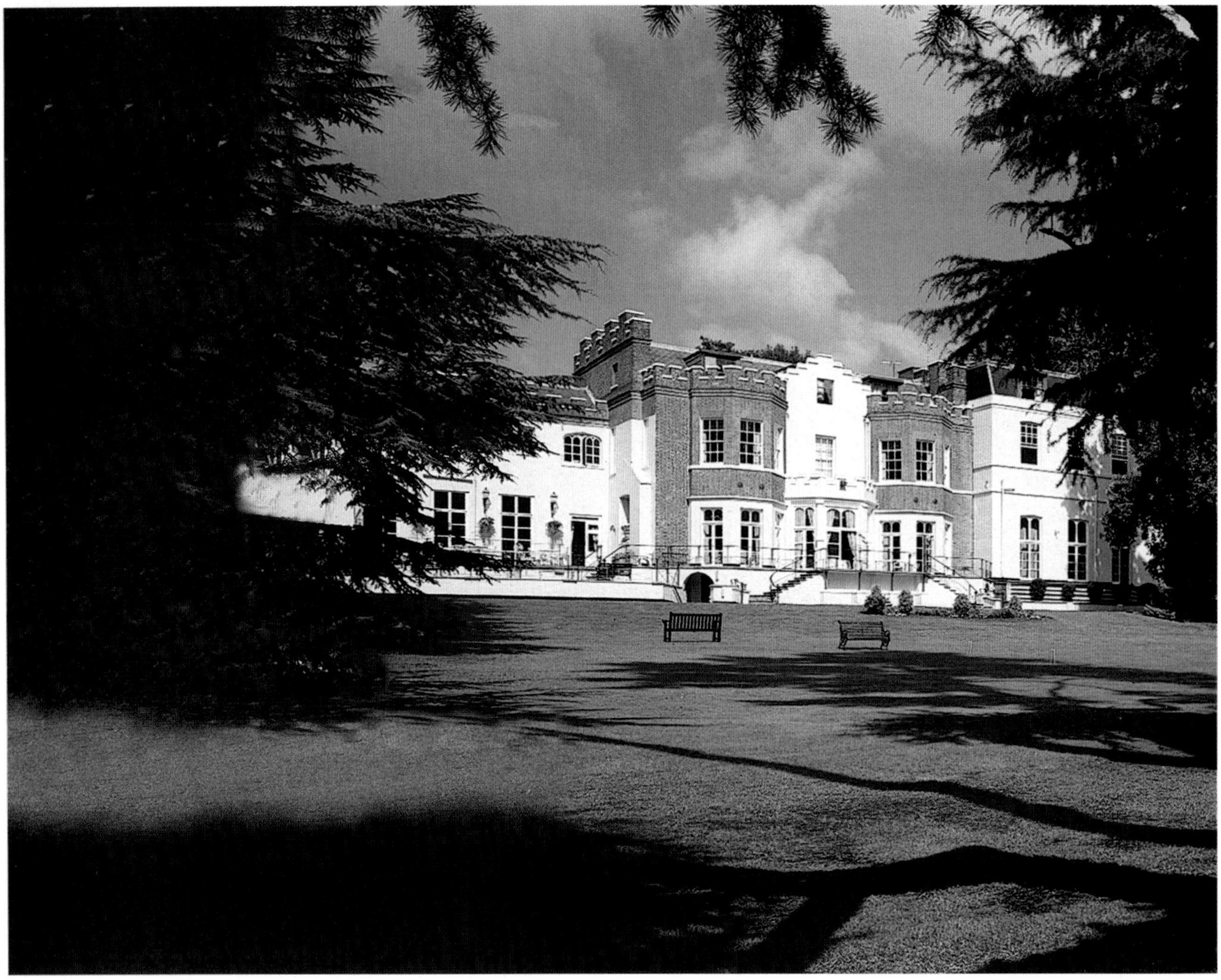

TAPLOW HOUSE HOTEL

BERRY HILL, TAPLOW, NR MAIDENHEAD, BERKSHIRE SL6 0DA
TEL: 01628 670056 FAX: 1628 773625 E-MAIL: taplow@wrensgroup.com

Elegance and splendour are the hallmarks of this majestic hotel which stands in six acres of land adorned by a historic and protected landscape. Taplow House dates back to 1598 and was given by James I to the first Governor of Virginia in 1628. Most of the house was destroyed by fire in the early 1700s but was rebuilt and purchased by the Grenfell family, famed for their equestrian activities, who commissioned the renowned gardener, Springhall, to landscape the grounds. The results can be seen today in the great trees, one of which is reputed to have been planted by Queen Elizabeth I. When the Marquess of Thomond took over the house in 1838 he had architect George Basevi redesign it to introduce the magnificent Doric columns to the reception hall and the elaborate chiselled brass banisters to the staircase which greet today's guests. It was last a private residence in 1958. Taplow House is splendid inside and out. It has recently had a £1.5 million refurbishment which has further enhanced its traditional charm and luxurious comfort. All 34 en suite bedrooms have every comfort. Chef Amanda Pay produces creative cuisine to please every palate. Her outstanding menus are complemented by an excellent and extensive wine list. Windsor, Henley, Ascot and Cliveden are close by **Directions:** From the M40, exit at junction 4. Price Guide: (room only) Single £145; double/twin £160–£190; suite £230–£300.

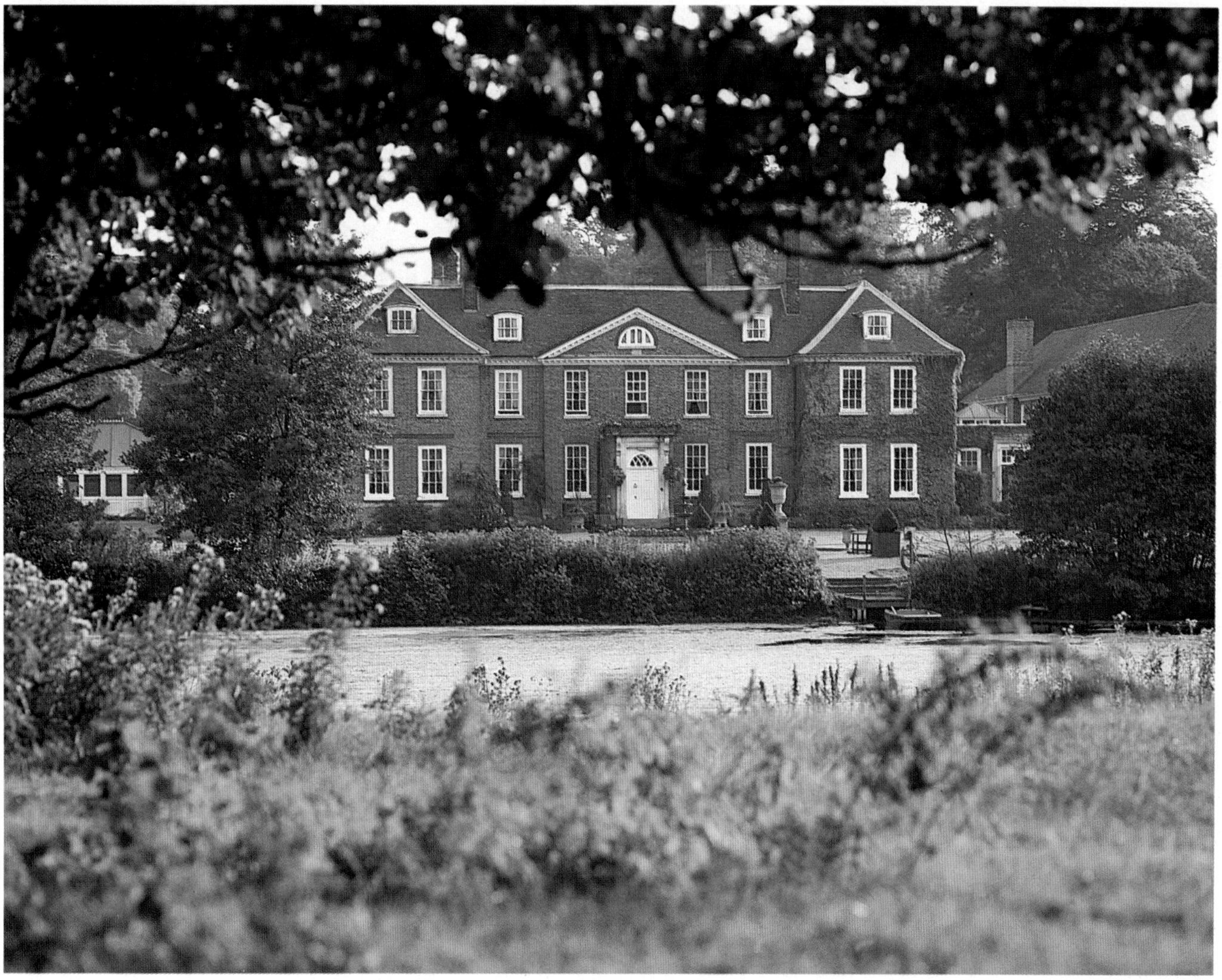

CHILSTON PARK

SANDWAY, LENHAM, NR MAIDSTONE, KENT ME17 2BE
TEL: 01622 859803 FAX: 01622 858588 E-MAIL: chilstonpark@arcadianhotels.co.uk

This magnificent Grade I listed mansion, one of England's most richly decorated hotels, was built in the 13th century and remodelled in the 18th century. Now sensitively refurbished, the hotel's ambience is enhanced by the lighting, at dusk each day, of over 200 candles. The drawing room and reading room offer guests an opportunity to relax and to admire the outstanding collection of antiques. The entire hotel is a treasure trove full of many interesting objets d'art. The opulently furnished bedrooms are fitted to a high standard and many have four-poster beds. Good, fresh English cooking features on outstanding menus supported by an excellent wine list. Several intimate and delightful rooms afford wonderful opportunities for private dining parties. In keeping with the traditions of a country house, a wide variety of sporting activities are available, golf and riding nearby, fishing in the natural spring lake and punting. **Directions:** Take junction 8 off the M20, then A20 to Lenham Station. Turn left into Boughton Road. Go over the crossroads and M20; Chilston Park is on the left. Price Guide: Single from £105; double/twin from £105; suite from £250.

THE OLD BELL

ABBEY ROW, MALMESBURY, WILTSHIRE SN16 0AG
TEL: 01666 822344 FAX: 01666 825145 E-MAIL: info@oldbellhotel.com

The Old Bell was established by the Abbot of Malmesbury during the reign of King John as a place to refresh guests who came to consult the Abbey's library. Situated at the edge of the Cotswolds, this Grade I listed building may well be England's most ancient hotel, including features such as a mediaeval stone fireplace in the Great Hall. A classsic and imaginative menu exemplifies the best in English cooking, with meals ranging from four course dinners complemented by fine wines served in the Edwardian dining room, to innovative snacks in the Great Hall. In the main house rooms are decorated and furnished with an individual style and character. The Coach House features bedrooms styled on an oriental theme and many of these are suitable for families as interconnecting pairs of suites. Families are particularly welcomed at The Old Bell; there is no charge for children sharing parents' rooms and children's menus are available. The 'Den' is equipped with a multitude of toys and open every day. Malmesbury is only 30 minutes from Bath and is close to a number of other beautiful villages such as Castle Combe, Bourton-on-the-Water and Lacock. Other places of interest include the mysterious stone circle at Avebury and the Westonbirt Arboretum. **Directions:** Near the market cross in the centre of Malmesbury. Price Guide: Single from £75; double/twin £100–£160; suites £175–£190.

THE OLD RECTORY

CRUDWELL, NR MALMESBURY, WILTSHIRE SN16 9EP
TEL: 01666 577194 FAX: 01666 577853 E-MAIL: office@oldrectorycrudwell.co.uk

Surrounded by a large garden and with a grand entrance, Victorian pond and Cotswold stone walls, this picturesque hotel was originally a 14th-century house and has a welcoming atmosphere complemented by friendly, professional staff. Flagstone floors, open fireplaces, fresh flowers and lush décor all contribute to the plush and cosy rooms, which are enhanced by the exceptional combination of modern conveniences with antique grandeur and all the comforts of home. All the newly refurbished en suite bedrooms are individually and luxuriously furnished, some with window seats overlooking the beautifully landscaped gardens. The larger bedrooms benefit from stunning four-poster beds and luxurious spa baths. The superb British cuisine using fresh, mostly organic ingredients is lovingly created by the hotel's brigade of chefs who have recently been awarded 3 AA rosettes. There is a choice between two dining locations: the formal, oak-panelled restaurant with beams and period detail or the airy and light conservatory, which is perfect for private lunch or dinner parties. Apéritifs and coffee are served outside around the pond when the weather is sunny and warm. Leisure pursuits such as horse riding and golf are a short distance away, and guests can explore Bath, the surrounding Cotswold towns and countryside. **Directions:** From M4 Jct17 take A429 to Cirencester; the hotel is opposite The Plough next to the church. Price Guide: Single £75; double/twin from £98.

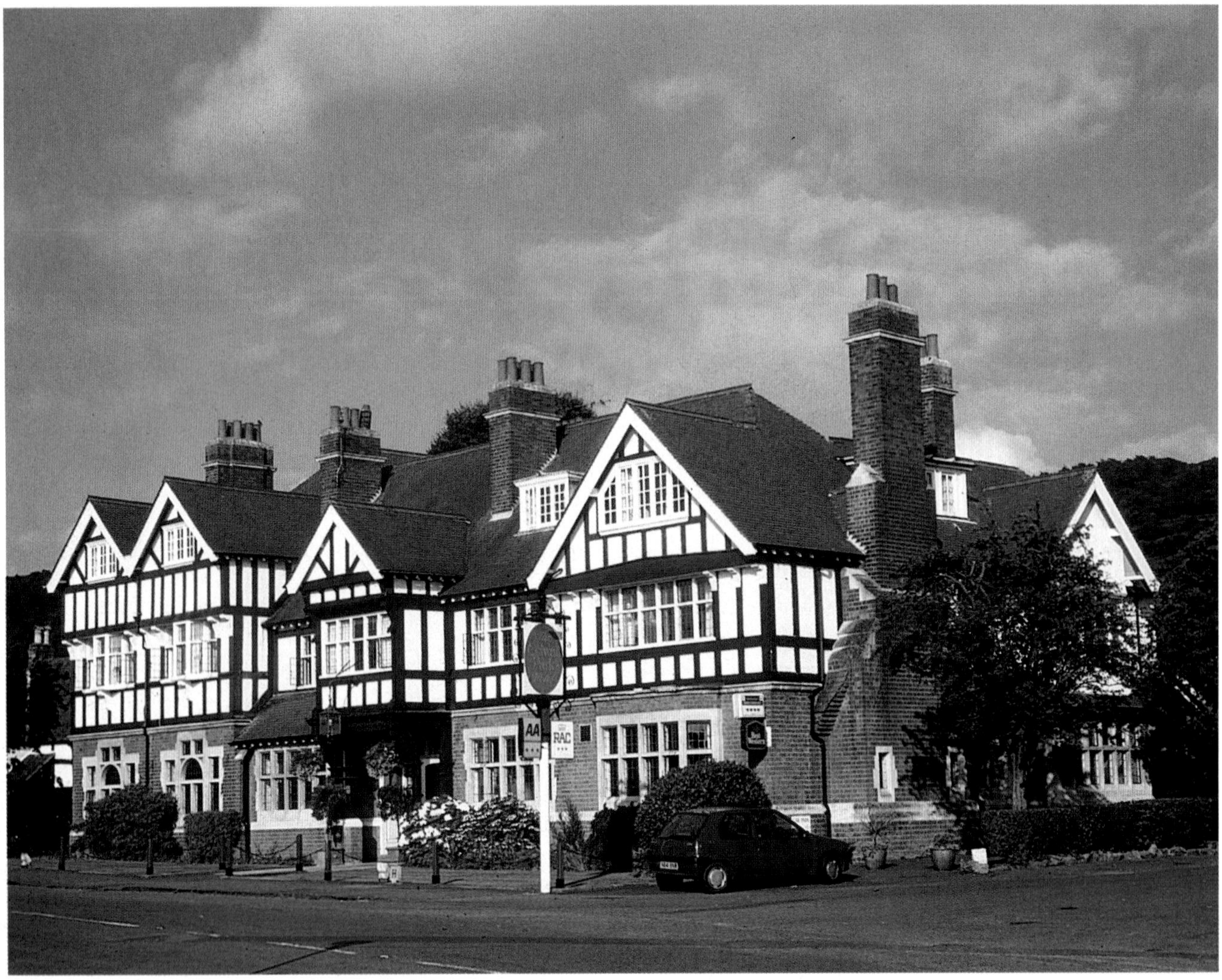

COLWALL PARK

COLWALL, NEAR MALVERN, WORCESTERSHIRE WR13 6QG
TEL: 01684 540000 FAX: 01684 540847 E-MAIL: hotel@colwall.com

This delightful hotel is in the centre of the village and set against a background of the Malvern Hills – to which it has direct access from its mature gardens. It also has the privilege of almost a private railway station, (just over 2 hours from Paddington). The hotel is thriving under new management who have undertaken a thorough renovation of the hotel without spoiling its character. The bedrooms are pristine and comfortable and suites have been introduced – including one for families with an amusing children's bedroom. A bottle of the local Hereford water is always at hand. Residents enjoy the library (which can accommodate private dinners for 8 people), the first floor 'video' snug and the inviting panelled Lantern bar where light meals are ordered from attentive bar staff. The Seasons Restaurant has table settings of delicate china and fine crystal. A pianist plays during Sunday lunches. The kitchen is in the hands of a creative chef, offering à la carte and full vegetarian menus to 2 AA Rosette standard. Interesting international wines are listed. The ballroom, ideal for corporate events, leads onto the garden where wedding groups pose by the beautiful lime tree. Special breaks feature Cheltenham Races and Malvern Theatre weekends. Hotel sports are boules and croquet. **Directions:** M5/J7, A442 then A449. Colwall village is on B4218 between Malvern and Ledbury. Price Guide: Single £65-£80; double/twin £110–£150; suite £150.

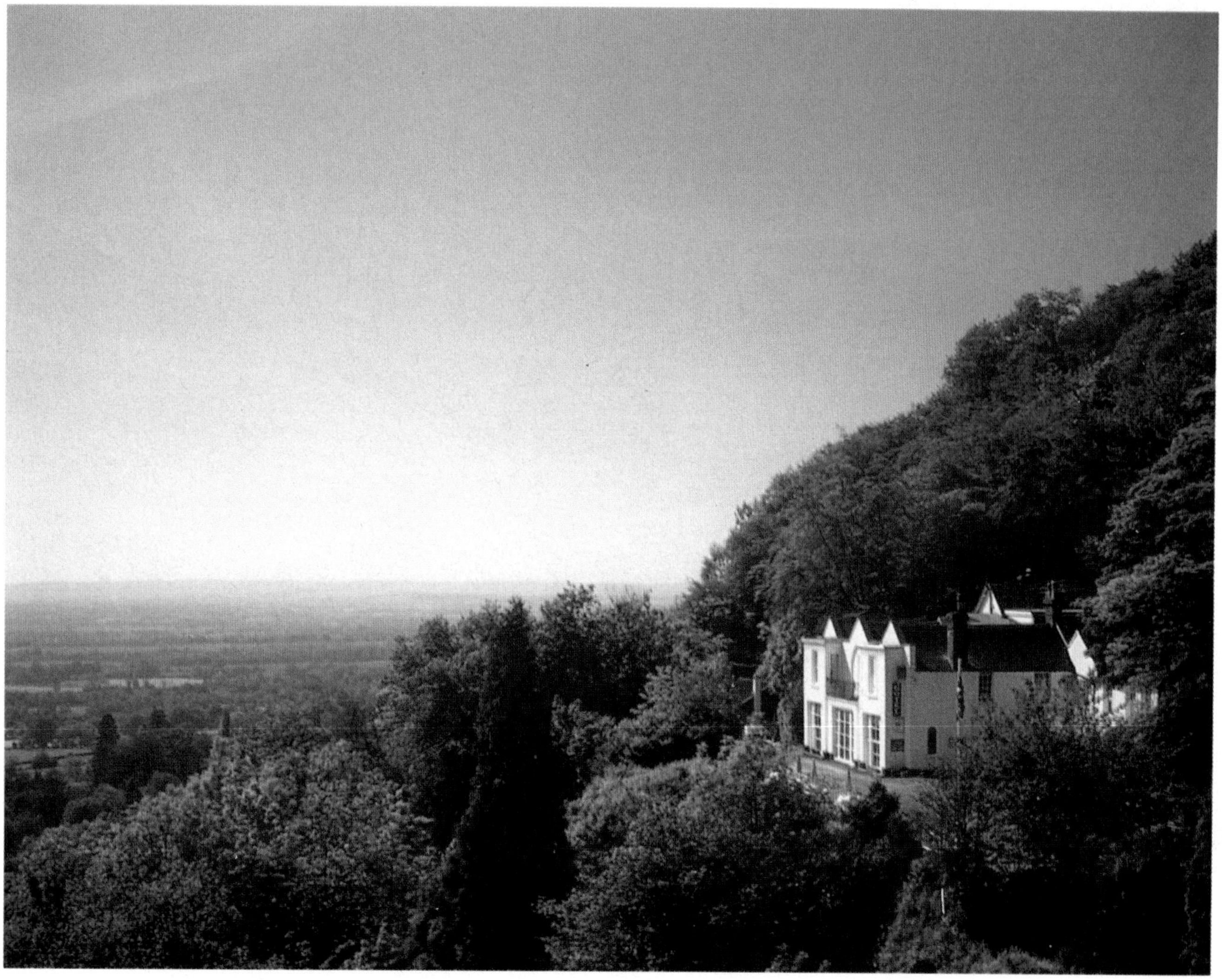

The Cottage In The Wood

HOLYWELL ROAD, MALVERN WELLS, WORCESTERSHIRE WR14 4LG
TEL: 01684 575859 FAX: 01684 560662 E-MAIL: proprietor@cottageinthewood.co.uk

The Malvern Hills once the home and inspiration for England's most celebrated composer Sir Edward Elgar, are the setting for The Cottage in the Wood. With its spectacular outlook across the Severn Valley plain, this unique hotel won acclaim from the Daily Mail for the best view in England. The main house was originally the Dower House to the Blackmore Park estate and accommodation is offered here and in Beech Cottage, an old scrumpy house – and the Coach House. The cottage-style furnishings give an intimate and cosy impression and the smaller Coach House rooms have suntrap balconies and patios. Owned and run by the Pattin family for over 14 years, the atmosphere is genuinely warm and relaxing. A regularly changing modern English menu is complemented by an almost obsessional wine list of 600 bins. If this causes any over-indulgence, guests can walk to the tops of the Malvern Hills direct from the hotel grounds. Nearby are the Victorian spa town of Great Malvern, the Three Counties Showground and the Cathedral cities of Worcester, Gloucester and Hereford. **Directions:** Three miles south of Great Malvern on A449, turn into Holywell Road by post box and hotel sign. Hotel is 250 yards on right. Price Guide: Single £77–£87; double/twin £95–£150. Bargain short breaks available all days throughout the year.

ETROP GRANGE

THORLEY LANE, MANCHESTER AIRPORT, GREATER MANCHESTER M90 4EG
TEL: 0161 499 0500 FAX: 0161 499 0790 E-MAIL: etropgrange@corushotels.com

Hidden away near Manchester Airport lies Etrop Grange, a beautiful country house hotel and restaurant. The original house was built in 1780 and more than 200 years on has been lovingly restored. Today, the hotel enjoys a fine reputation for its accommodation, where the luxury, character and sheer elegance of the Georgian era are evident in every feature. The magnificent award winning restaurant offers a well balanced mix of traditional and modern English cuisine, complemented by an extensive selection of fine wines. Attention to detail ensures personal and individual service. In addition to the obvious advantage of having an airport within walking distance, the location of Etrop Grange is ideal in many other ways. With a comprehensive motorway network and InterCity stations minutes away, it is accessible from all parts of the UK. Entertainment for visitors ranges from the shopping, sport and excellent nightlife offered by the city of Manchester to golf, riding, clay pigeon shooting, water sports and outdoor pursuits in the immediate countryside. Cheshire also boasts an abundance of stately homes, museums and historical attractions. **Directions:** Leave M56 at junction 5 towards Manchester Airport. Follow signs for Terminal 2. Go up the slip road. At roundabout take first exit, take immediate left and hotel is 400yds on the right. Price Guide: Single £121-£130; double/twin £142–£170; suites £162–£180.

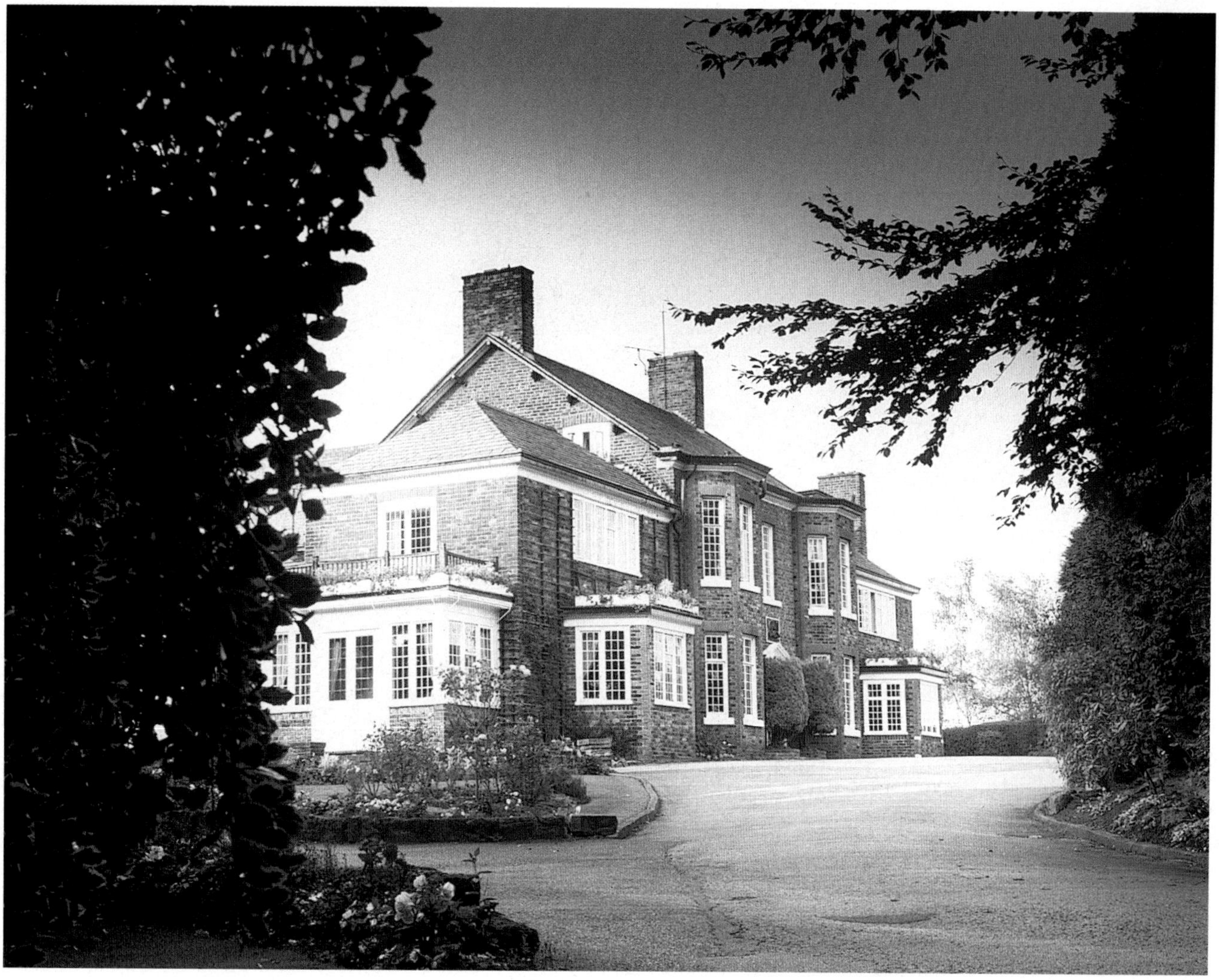

THE STANNEYLANDS HOTEL

STANNEYLANDS ROAD, WILMSLOW, CHESHIRE SK9 4EY
TEL: 01625 525225 FAX: 01625 537282 E-MAIL: reservations@stanneylandshotel.co.uk

Owned and managed by a dedicated family, Stanneylands is a handsome country house set in several acres of impressive, tranquil gardens with a collection of unusual trees and shrubs. Guests experience a truly warm welcome in a unique and special atmosphere, where luxurious comfort provides the perfect setting for business or pleasure. Some of the bedrooms offer lovely views over the gardens whilst others overlook the undulating Cheshire countryside. A sense of quiet luxury prevails in the reception rooms, where classical décor and comfortable furnishings create a relaxing ambience. In the award-winning restaurant guests can choose from an enticing blend of innovative and traditional English and international cuisine. Stanneylands is an excellent venue for both private and business events. The Oak Room accommodates up to 60 people, whilst the Stanley Suite is available for conferences and larger celebrations. The hotel is conveniently located for tours of the Cheshire plain or the more rugged Peak District, as well as the bustling market towns and industrial heritage of the area. Special corporate and weekend rates are available. **Directions:** Three miles from Manchester International Airport. Come off at Junction 5 on the M56 (airport turn off). Follow signs to Wilmslow, turn left into station road, bear right onto Stanneylands Road. Price Guide: Single £70–£135; double/twin £123–£145; suite £145.

The Compleat Angler

MARLOW BRIDGE, MARLOW, BUCKS SL7 1RG

TEL: 0870 400 8100 FAX: 01628 486388 E-MAIL: heritagehotels_marlow.compleat_angler@forte-hotels.com

In a truly idyllic setting with lush lawns sweeping down to the banks of the Thames, this pretty hotel evokes a feeling of English heritage at its best. Ideally placed for Henley Regatta, Ascot Races and the Marlow Regatta in June, The Compleat Angler is the place to relax and enjoy strawberries and cream and freshly baked scones, whilst watching life on the water beneath shady garden parasols. In winter, warm log fires and snug bars keep out the winter chill, and the original bar, dating back some 350 years, is the ultimate "den". All of the 64 bedrooms are decorated in an elegant style with classical striped wallpapers and rich drapes, and there are five four-poster bedrooms. The Riverside Restaurant and Waltons Brasserie offer an exciting choice of cuisine and there is a 24 hour room service facility. Besides the delights of the English Riverbank with fishing and boat trips on offer, Marlow itself has some fine clothes and china shops, and croquet is played on the hotel lawns. **Directions:** The A404 dual carriageway links the M4 and M40 motorways. At the first roundabout follow signs for Bisham – the hotel is on the right immediately before Marlow Bridge. Price Guide: Single £215–£235, double/twin £235–£270, suite £395–£495.

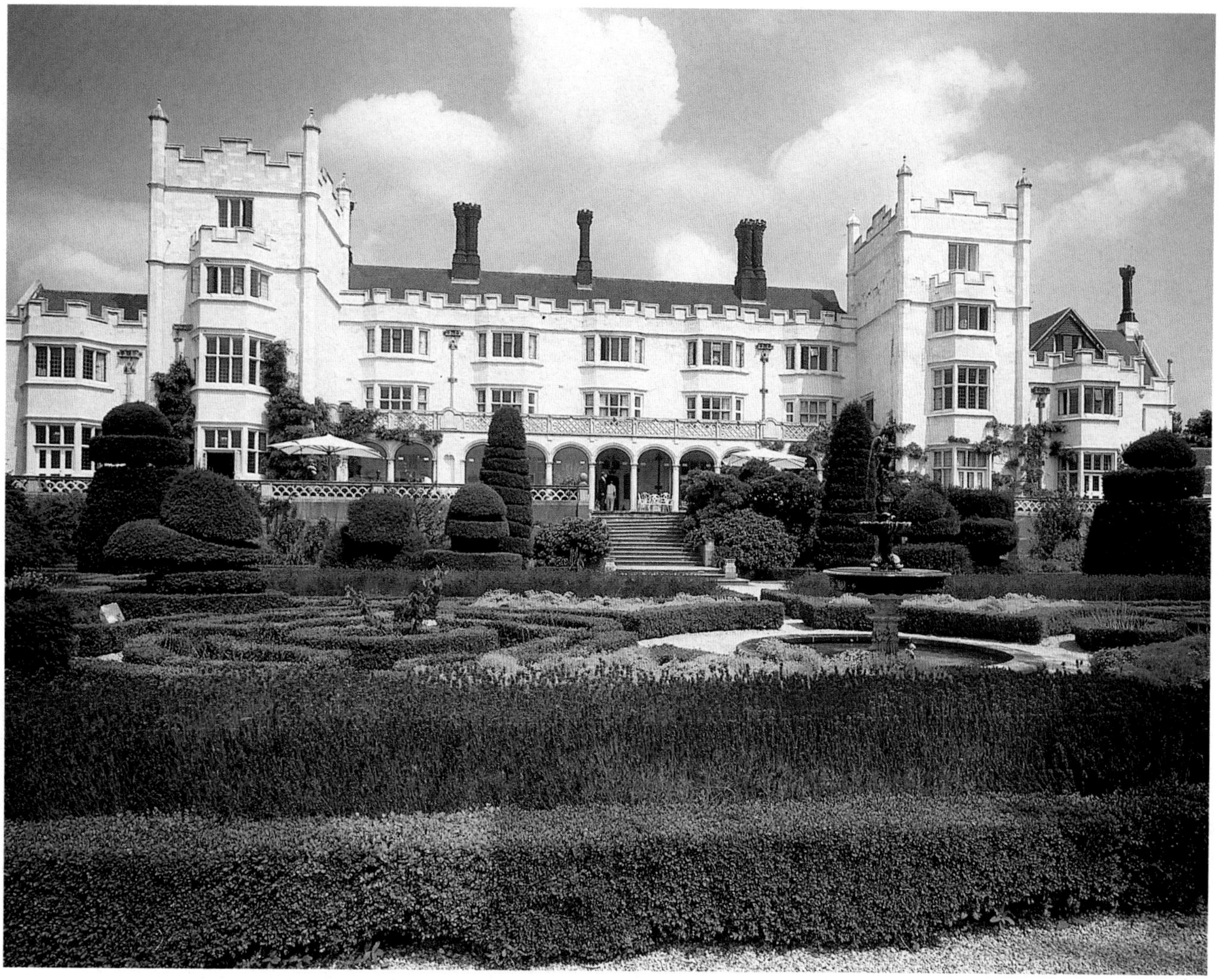

DANESFIELD HOUSE HOTEL & SPA

HENLEY ROAD, MARLOW-ON-THAMES, BUCKINGHAMSHIRE SL7 2EY
TEL: 01628 891010 FAX: 01628 890408 E-MAIL: sales@danesfieldhouse.co.uk

Danesfield House is set within 65 acres of gardens and parkland overlooking the River Thames and offering panoramic views across the Chiltern Hills. It is the third house since 1664 to occupy this lovely setting and it was designed and built in sumptuous style at the end of the 19th century. After years of neglect the house has been fully restored, combining its Victorian splendour with the very best modern hotel facilities. Among the many attractions of its luxury bedrooms, all beautifully decorated and furnished, are the extensive facilities they offer. These include two telephone lines (one may be used for personal fax), satellite TV, in-room movies, mini bar, trouser press, hair dryers, bath robes and toiletries. Guests can relax in the magnificent drawing room with its galleried library or in the sunlit atrium. There is a choice of two restaurants the Oak Room and Orangery Brasserie both of which offer a choice of international cuisine. The hotel also has six private banqueting and conference rooms. Leisure facilities include luxurious Spa with 20-metre pool, fitness studio and treatment rooms. Windsor Castle, Disraeli's home at Hughenden Manor, Milton's cottage and the caves of West Wycombe are nearby. **Directions:** Between M4 and M40 on A4155 between Marlow and Henley-on-Thames. Price Guide: £185; double/twin £225; suites £265.

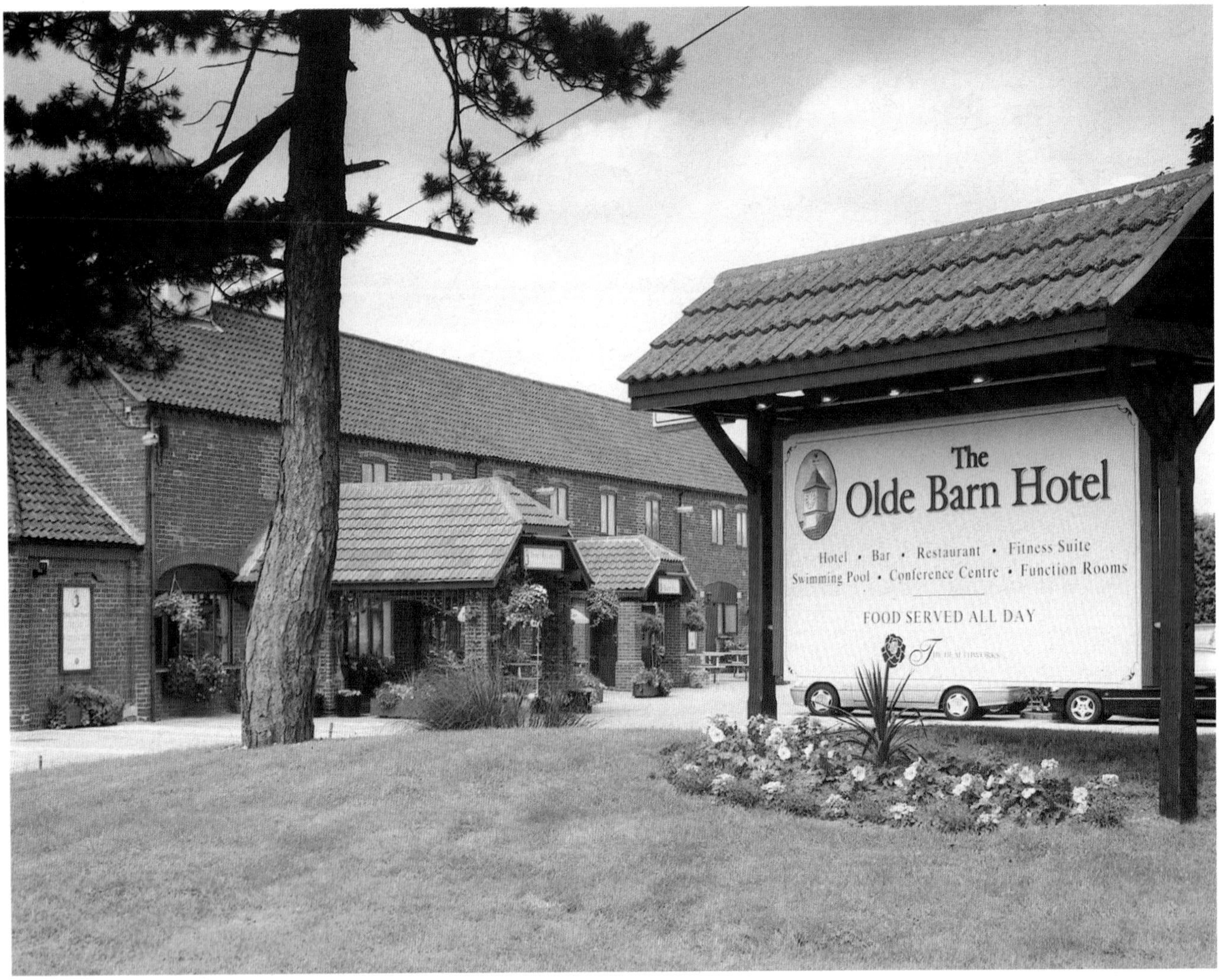

THE OLDE BARN HOTEL

TOLL BAR ROAD, MARSTON, LINCOLNSHIRE NG32 2HT
Tel: 01400 250909 **Fax:** 01400 250130 **E-Mail:** sales@olde-barn-hotel.co.uk

Once a farmstead, this recently refurbished hotel is set in peaceful and picturesque countryside and provides every modern facility whilst retaining its rustic charm. The Olde Barn Hotel is a stylish hideaway ideal for exploring the area's cultural sites, which are steeped in history. Each of the 60 bedrooms are spacious, well equipped and tastefully decorated for a comfortable stay. There are also specially designed disabled rooms on the ground floor. Three luxurious suites are available for families, long-term guests or for an extra-special stay. Visitors can enjoy the romantic ambience of the newly refurbished Barn Restaurant which serves delicious traditional English and continental cuisine, complemented by an extensive list of fine wines. Less formal meals may be taken in the welcoming atmosphere of the hotel's traditional country bar. A state-of-the-art fitness centre and heated indoor swimming pool are available as well as spa, steam and sauna facilities, and eight golf courses are nearby. Excellent business services for conferences and meetings are provided, and wedding ceremonies and receptions for up to 120 guests can be arranged. The charming market town of Newark is nearby, and visitors can explore its bustling antiques and agricultural fairs. Directions: 4 miles north of Grantham off the southbound carriageway. The Hotel is signposted from Marston. Price Guide: Single £65-£100; double/twin £75-£120.

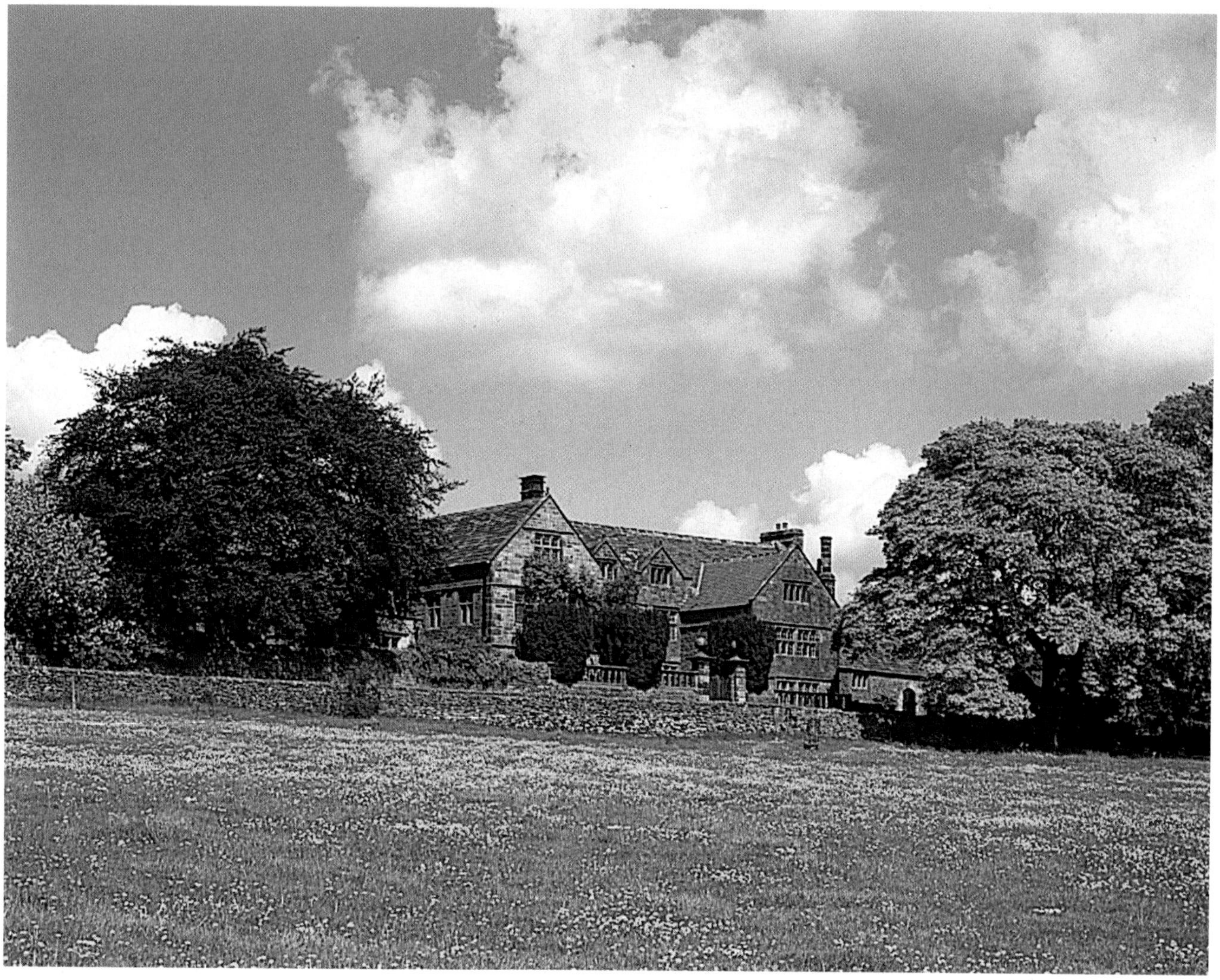

Riber Hall

MATLOCK, DERBYSHIRE DE4 5JU

TEL: 01629 582795 FAX: 01629 580475 E-MAIL: info@riber-hall.co.uk

Relax in this tranquil and historic Derbyshire country house, which dates from the 1400s and has been privately owned and proprietor-run for thirty years. Set in picturesque countryside, Riber Hall is recommended by all major hotel and restaurant guides and has been nominated as "One of the most romantic hotels in Britain". Many original features have been preserved – magnificent oak beams, exposed stone work and period fireplaces. The restaurant, awarded 2 AA Rosettes and RAC 2 Blue Ribbons, serves excellent cuisine, such as game when in season, on bone china in elegant dining rooms. Superb wines, especially New World, are enjoyed in fine crystal glasses. Quietly located around an attractive courtyard and in the Old Hall, the bedrooms are appointed to a high standard with antiques throughout, including four-poster beds and many thoughtful extras. The peaceful setting can be appreciated in the secluded old wall garden and orchard which is full of bird life, whilst energetic guests can pit their skills against the tennis trainer ball machine on the all-weather court. Conferences, weddings, wedding receptions and small dinner parties are catered for to the highest standard. Nearby are Chatsworth House, Haddon Hall, Hardwick Hall and Calke Abbey; and the Peak National Park. **Directions:** 20 minutes from Jct28 of M1, off A615 at Tansley; 1 mile further to Riber. Price Guide: Single £95–£105; double/twin £123–£165.

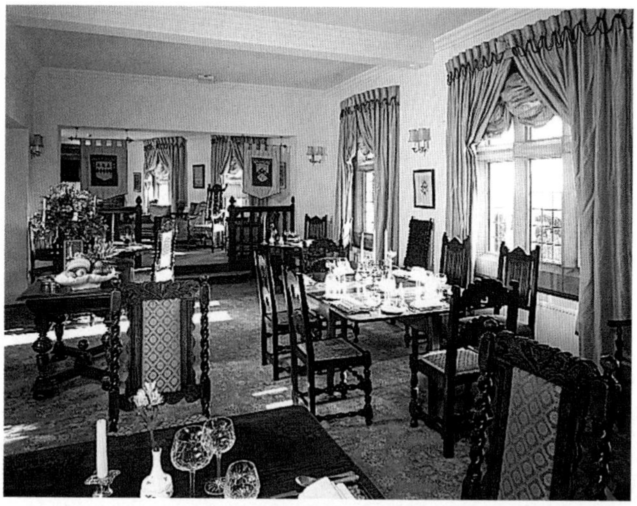

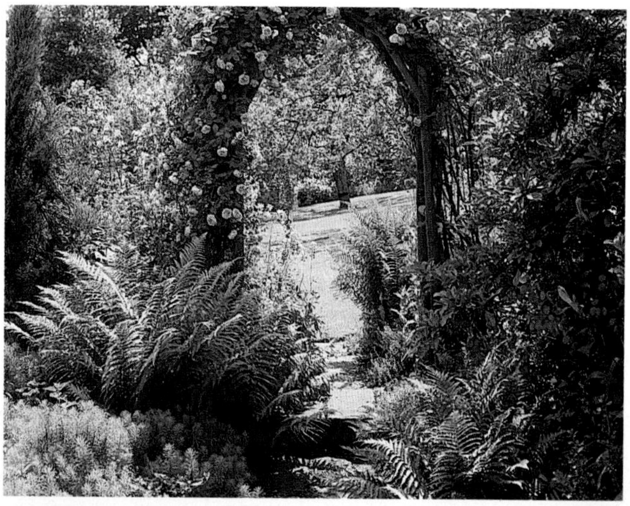

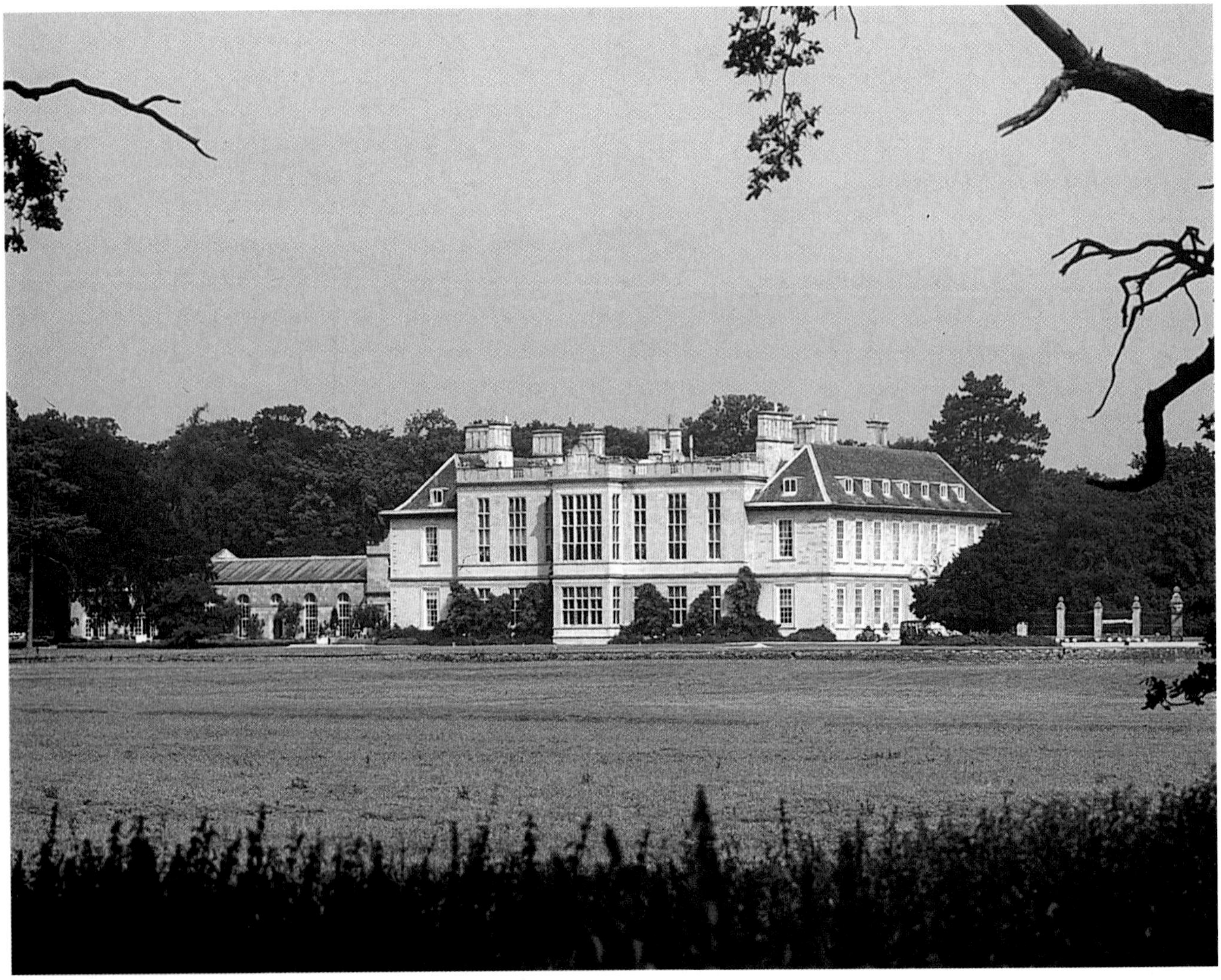

STAPLEFORD PARK HOTEL, SPA, GOLF & SPORTING ESTATE

NR MELTON MOWBRAY, LEICESTERSHIRE LE14 2EF
TEL: 01572 787 522 FAX: 01572 787 651 E-MAIL: reservations@stapleford.co.uk

A stately home and sporting estate where casual luxury is the byword. This 16th-century house was once coveted by Edward, Prince of Wales, but his mother Queen Victoria forbade him to buy it for fear that his morals would be corrupted by the Leicestershire hunting society! Today, Stapleford Park offers guests and club members a "lifestyle experience" to transcend all others in supreme surroundings with views over 500 acres of parkland. Stapleford was voted 'Top UK Hotel for Leisure Facilities' Conde Nast Traveller, Johansens' most 'Excellent Business Meeting Venue 2000' and holds innumerable awards for its style and hospitality. Individually designed bedrooms and a four-bedroom cottage have been created by famous names such as Mulberry, Wedgwood, Liberty and Crabtree & Evelyn. English cuisine with regional specialities is carefully prepared to the highest standards and complemented by an adventurous wine list. Sports include fishing, shooting, falconry, riding, tennis and an 18-hole championship golf course designed by Donald Steel. The luxurious Carnegie Clarins Spa with indoor pool, Jacuzzi, sauna and fitness room offers an array of health therapies. 11 elegant function and dining rooms are suited to private dinners, special occasions and corporate hospitality. **Directions:** By train Kings Cross/Grantham in 1 hour. A1 north to Colsterworth then B676 via Saxby. Price Guide: Double/twin £205–£345; suites from £425.

51 MasterCard VISA AMERICAN EXPRESS M 300

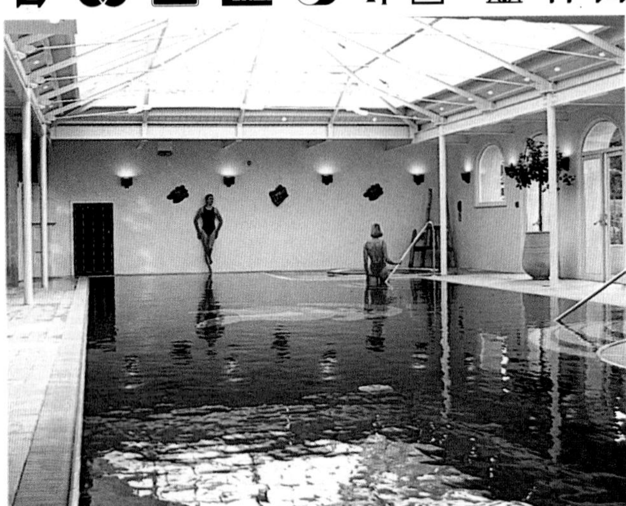

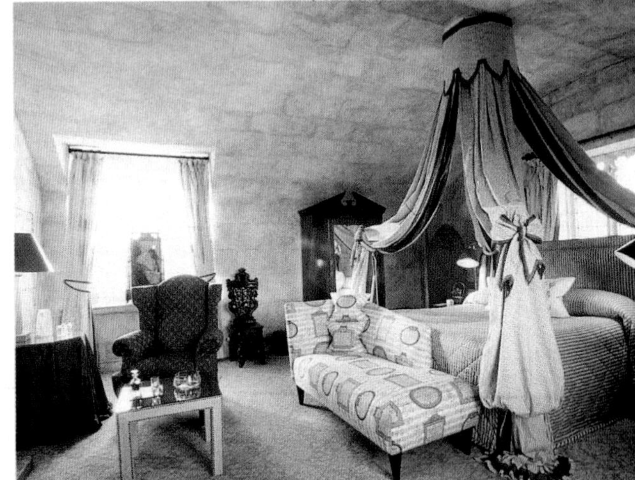

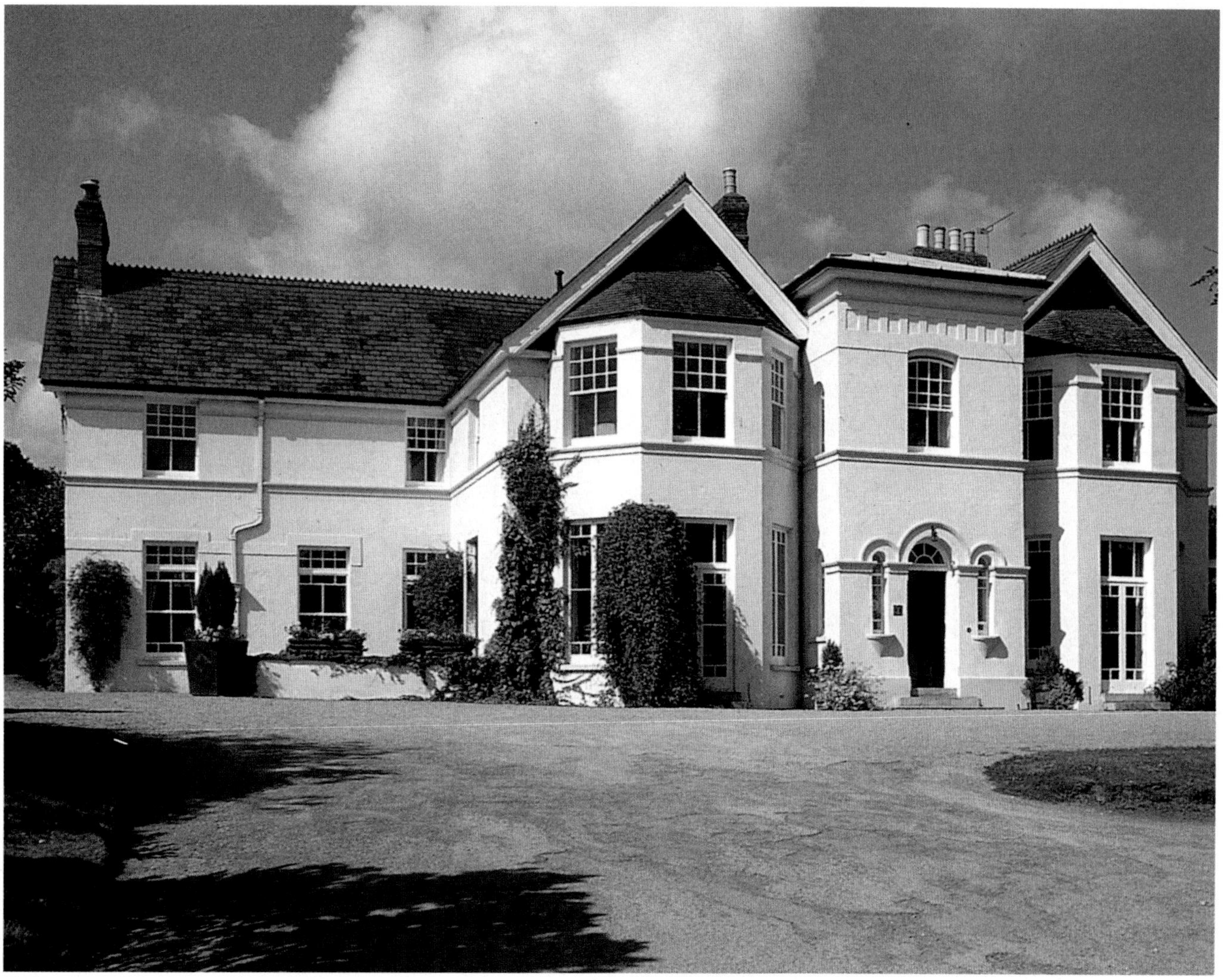

PERITON PARK HOTEL

MIDDLECOMBE, NR MINEHEAD, SOMERSET TA24 8SN
TEL: 01643 706885 FAX: 01643 706885 E-MAIL: peritonpark@ukgateway.net

Some of the joys of staying in a small independent hotel are the individuality of the rooms, the interesting and varied food and the personal care and attention given to guests by its owners. Periton Park is just such a hotel which Richard and Angela Hunt run in an efficient, yet friendly way. Unusually perhaps today, the large bedrooms are very spacious and well-appointed, with warm colours creating a restful atmosphere. From its secluded and quiet position guests may enjoy wonderful views of the Exmoor National Park in all directions and the early riser may well be rewarded by the sight of a herd of red deer grazing on the surrounding countryside. The wood panelled restaurant, with its double aspect views, is the perfect place to enjoy some of the best food on Exmoor. Fresh fish, local game, delicately cooked vegetables, local cheeses and Somerset wine have all helped the restaurant to achieve an AA Red Rosette. Exmoor is very much for country lovers with miles of varied, unspoilt and breathtaking landscape. Riding is available from stables next to the hotel. Shooting is available in season. **Directions:** Periton Park is situated off the A39 on the left just after Minehead, in the direction of Lynmouth and Porlock Price Guide: Single £62; double/twin £104.

The Angel Hotel

NORTH STREET, MIDHURST, WEST SUSSEX GU29 9DN

TEL: 01730 812421 FAX: 01730 815928 E-MAIL: angel@hshotels.co.uk

The Angel Hotel is a stylishly restored 16th century coaching inn which has earned widespread praise from its guests, the national press and guidebooks. Sympathetically renovated to combine contemporary comfort with original character, The Angel bridges the gap between town house bustle and country house calm. To the front, a handsome Georgian façade overlooks the High Street, while at the rear, quiet rose gardens lead to the parkland and ruins of historic Cowdray Castle. There are 28 bedrooms, all offering private bathrooms and modern amenities. Individually furnished with antiques, many rooms feature original Tudor beams. The Brasserie restaurant offers an excellent value contemporary menu. For corporate guests the hotel offers two attractive meeting rooms, a business suite, presentation aids and secretarial services. Racegoers will find it very convenient for Goodwood and theatregoers for the internationally acclaimed Chichester Festival Theatre. The historic market town of Midhurst is well placed for visits to Petworth House, Arundel Castle and the South Downs. Directions: From the A272, the hotel is on the left as the town centre is approached from the east. Price Guide: Single £80–£115; double/twin £110–£150.

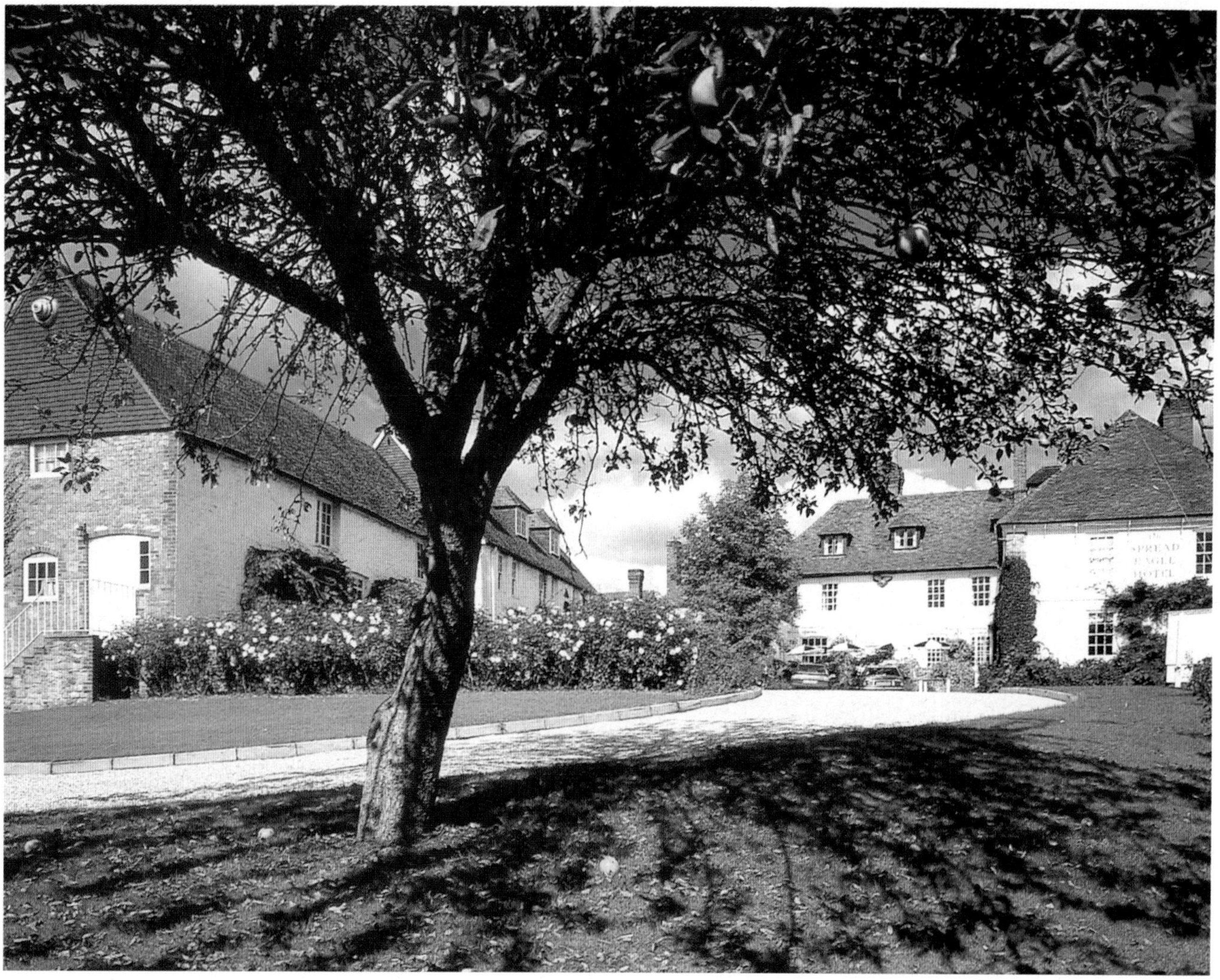

The Spread Eagle Hotel & Health Spa

SOUTH STREET, MIDHURST, WEST SUSSEX GU29 9NH
TEL: 01730 816911 FAX: 01730 815668 E-MAIL: spreadeagle@hshotels.co.uk

Dating from 1430, when guests were first welcomed here, The Spread Eagle Hotel is one of England's oldest hotels and is steeped in history. Following a recent refurbishment, the hotel is the essence of opulence and those wishing to be pampered will enjoy the superb fitness facilities and excellent standard of service. Located in either the main building or the market house, the 39 en suite bedrooms, some with four-poster beds, are well-appointed with soft furnishings and fine ornaments. A roaring log fire attracts guests into the historic lounge bar, ideal for relaxing in the afternoons or enjoying an apéritif. Sumptuous modern British cuisine may be savoured in the candlelit restaurant, complemented by an extensive wine list. Weddings, banquets and meetings are held in the Jacobean Hall and Polo Room. The Aquila Health Spa is an outstanding facility featuring a blue tiled swimming pool as its centrepiece. A Scandinavian sauna, Turkish steam room, hot tub, fitness centre and a range of beauty treatments, aromatherapy and massage are also offered. The stately homes at Petworth, Uppark and Goodwood are all within a short drive, with Chichester Cathedral, the Downland Museum and Fishbourne Roman Palace among the many local attractions. Cowdray Park Polo Club is only 1 mile away. **Directions:** Midhurst is on the A286 between Chichester and Milford. Price Guide: Single £80–£180; double/twin £110–£210.

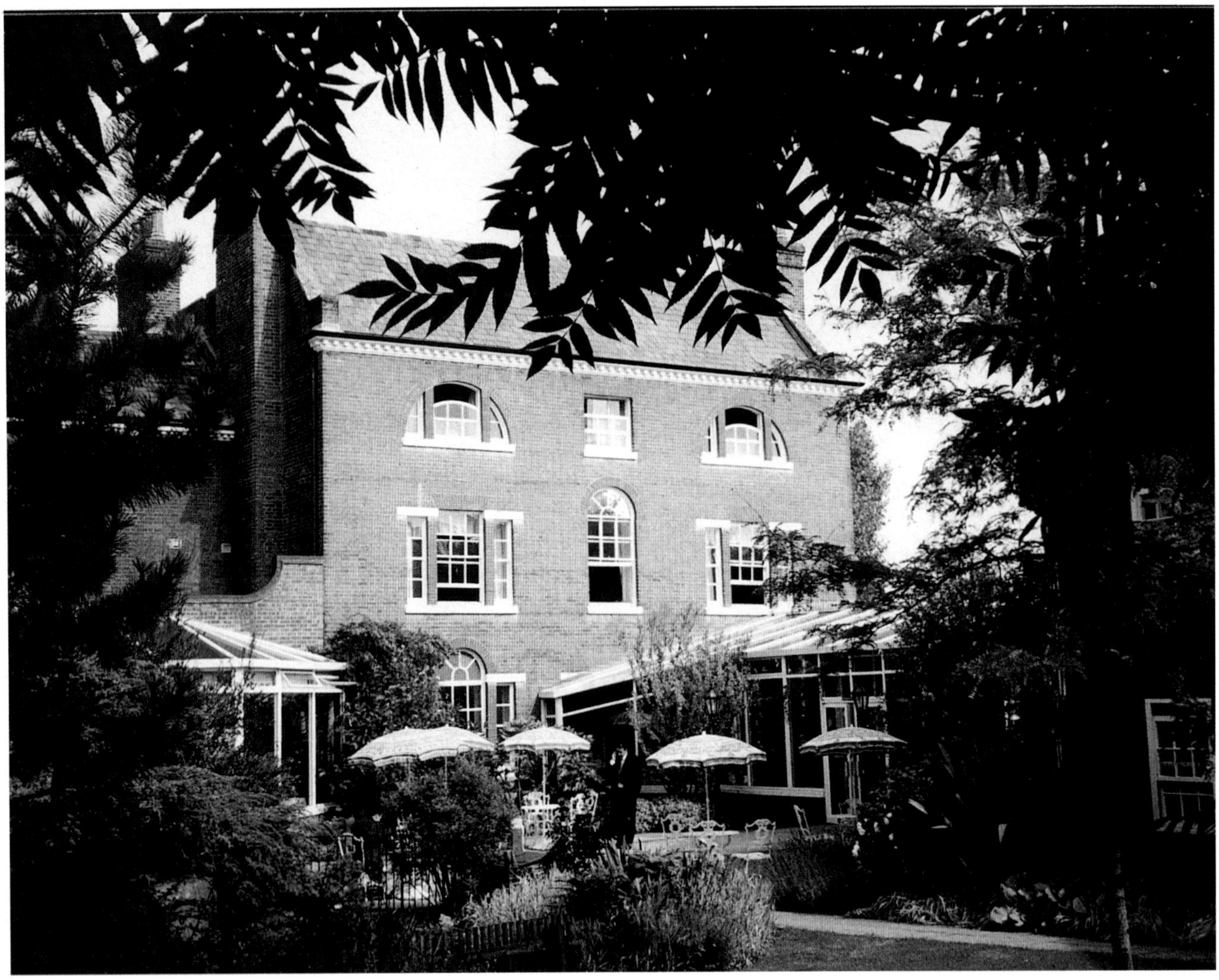

MOORE PLACE HOTEL

THE SQUARE, ASPLEY GUISE, MILTON KEYNES, BEDFORDSHIRE MK17 8DW
TEL: 01908 282000 FAX: 01908 281888 E-MAIL: info@mooreplace.co.uk

This elegant Georgian mansion was built by Francis Moore in the peaceful Bedfordshire village of Aspley Guise in 1786. The original house, which is set on the village square, has been sympathetically extended to create extra rooms. The additional wing has been built around an attractive courtyard with a rock garden, lily pool and waterfall. The pretty Victorian-style award winning conservatory restaurant, serves food that rates among the best in the area. Vegetarian options and special diets can always be found on the menus, which offer dishes prepared in the modern English style and balanced with a selection of fine wines. The 52 bedrooms are well-appointed with many amenities, including a trouser press, hairdryer, welcome drinks and large towelling bathrobes. Banquets, conferences and dinner parties can be accommodated in five private function rooms: all are decorated in traditional style and can be equipped with the latest audiovisual facilities. The hotel is close to Woburn Abbey, Safari Park, Bletchely Park, Station X, Silverstone, Whipsnade Zoo, Milton Keynes. The convenient location and accessibility to the motorway network makes Moore Place Hotel an attractive choice, whether travelling for business or pleasure. **Directions:** Only two minutes' drive from the M1 junction 13. Price Guide: Single from £100; double/twin £110–£130; suite £150–£200.

The Manor House Hotel

MORETON-IN-MARSH, GLOUCESTERSHIRE GL56 0LJ
TEL: 01608 650501 FAX: 01608 651481 E-MAIL: bookings@cotswold–inns–hotels.co.uk

This former 16th century manor house and coaching inn is set in beautiful gardens in the Cotswold village of Moreton-in-Marsh. The Manor House Hotel has been tastefully extended and restored, yet retains many of its historic features, among them a priest's hole and secret passages. The 38 well-appointed bedrooms have been individually decorated and furnished. The restaurant offers imaginative and traditional English dishes using only the freshest ingredients, accompanied by an expertly selected wine list. For the guest seeking relaxation, leisure facilities include an indoor heated swimming pool and spa bath. Sports enthusiasts will also find that tennis, golf, riding and squash can be arranged locally. Spacious modern business facilities, combined with the peaceful location, make this an excellent venue for executive meetings. It is also an ideal base for touring, with many attractions nearby, including Stratford-upon-Avon, Warwick and the fashionable centres of Cheltenham, Oxford and Bath. **Directions:** The Manor House Hotel is on the A429 Fosse Way near the junction of the A44 and A429 north of Stow, on the Broadway side of the intersection. Price Guide: Single £99; double/twin £115–£160.

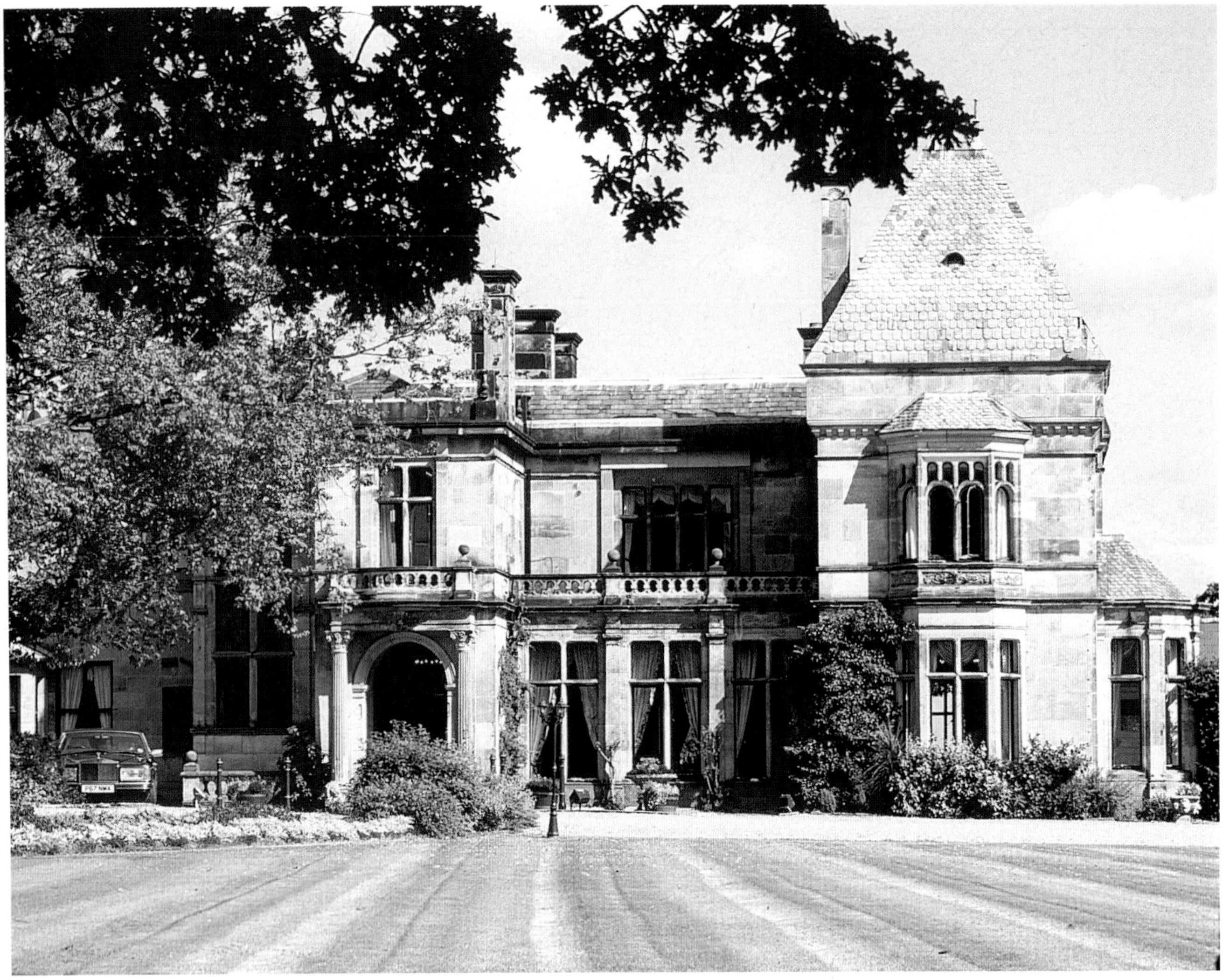

ROOKERY HALL

WORLESTON, NANTWICH, NR CHESTER, CHESHIRE CW5 6DQ
TEL: 01270 610016 FAX: 01270 626027 E-MAIL: rookery@arcadianhotels.co.uk

Rookery Hall enjoys a peaceful setting where guests can relax, yet is convenient for road, rail and air networks. Within the original house are elegant reception rooms and the mahogany and walnut panelled restaurant, which is renowned for its cuisine. Dine by candlelight in the intimate dining room overlooking the lawns. Over 300 wines are in the cellar. Private dining facilities are available for meetings and weddings – summer lunches can be taken alfresco on the terrace. Companies can hire the hotel as their own "Country House", with leisure pursuits such as archery, clay pigeon shooting and off road driving available within the grounds. Tennis or croquet, fishing, golf and riding can be arranged. All of the bedrooms are individually designed and luxuriously furnished with spacious marbled bathrooms. Many afford views over fields and woodlands. Suites are available including the self-contained stable block. Special breaks and celebrations packages are offered with gourmet evenings in the restaurant. The hotel is perfectly situated for historic Chester and North Wales and is an ideal location for weddings and conferences. **Directions:** From M6 junction 16 take A500 to Nantwich, then B5074 to Worleston. Price Guide: Single £95–£150; double/twin £95–£175; suite £185.

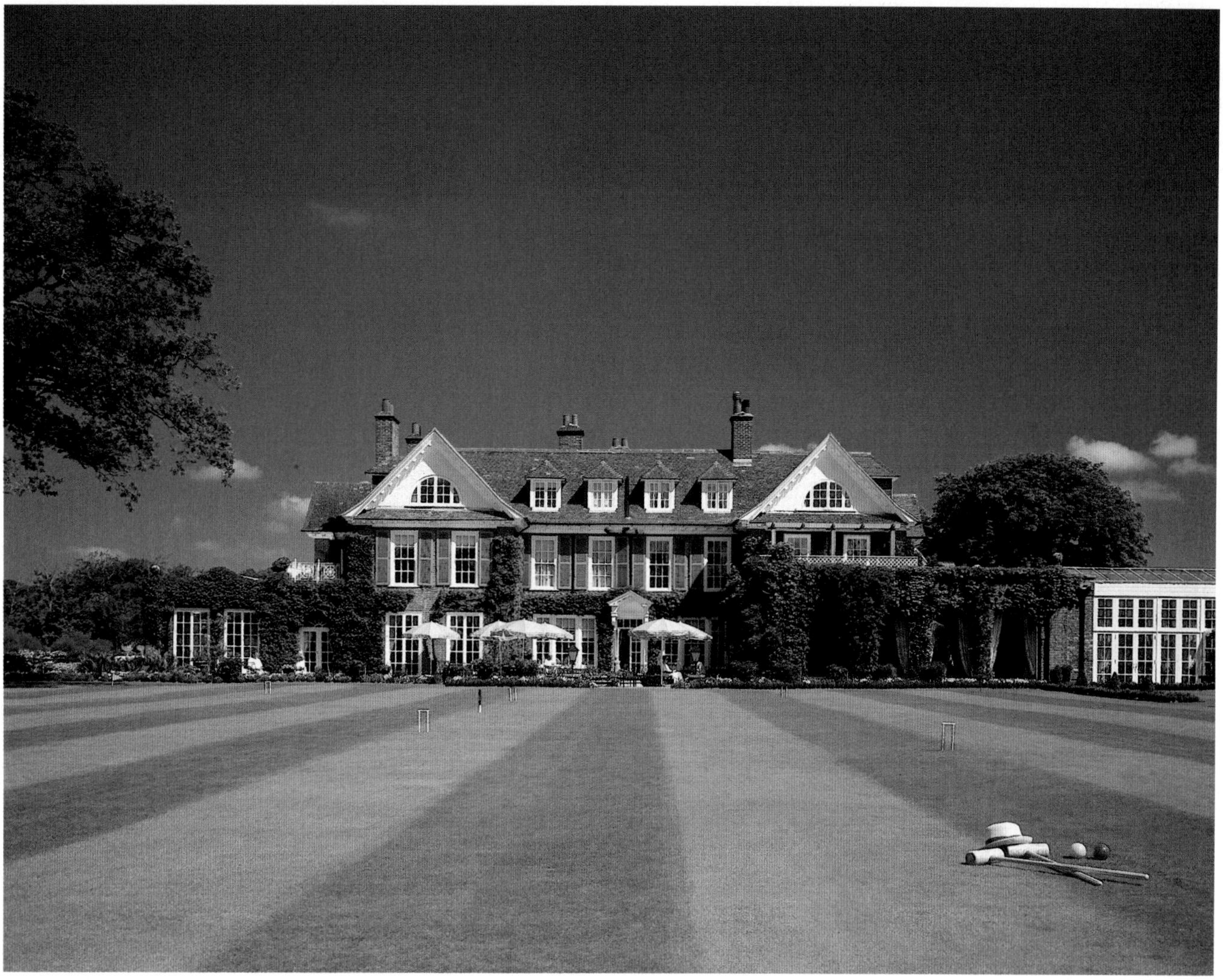

CHEWTON GLEN

NEW MILTON, HAMPSHIRE BH25 6QS

TEL: 01425 275341 FAX: 01425 272310 E-MAIL: reservations@chewtonglen.com

Voted 'Best Country House Hotel in the World' by Gourmet magazine and the only privately owned hotel in the UK to hold five AA Red Stars, Chewton Glen is set in 130 acres of gardens, woodland and parkland on the edge of the New Forest, close to the sea. Owners Martin and Brigitte Skan have created a haven of tranquillity, luxury and comfort. The wonderful setting of the Michelin Star restaurant, which overlooks the landscaped gardens, adds to the sublime culinary experience created by Head Chef Pierre Chevillard, who uses fresh local produce to create surprising and delicious dishes, complemented by an impressive wine list. The 62 sumptuous bedrooms, all individually designed with carefully chosen fabrics, are the ultimate in luxury with fantastic marble bathrooms, cosy bathrobes, crystal sherry decanters and views over the surrounding parkland. A large, crystal-clear swimming pool, whirlpool, steam room and saunas as well as a range of relaxing beauty treatments and massage are available in the award-winning Health Club. For the more energetic there are indoor and outdoor tennis courts, croquet and a 9-hole par 3 golf course and an outdoor swimming pool. Fishing, shooting and riding can be arranged locally. **Directions:** Take A35 from Lyndhurst towards Bournemouth. Turn left at Walkford, then left before roundabout. The hotel is on the right. Price Guide: (Room only) Double £250–£405; suites £480–£720.

Donnington Valley Hotel & Golf Club

OLD OXFORD ROAD, DONNINGTON, NEWBURY, BERKSHIRE RG14 3AG
TEL: 01635 551199 FAX: 01635 551123 E-MAIL: general@donningtonvalley.co.uk

Uncompromising quality is the hallmark of this hotel built in contrasting styles in 1991 with its own golf course. The grandeur of the Edwardian era has been captured by the interior of the hotel's reception area with its splendid wood-panelled ceilings and impressive overhanging gallery. Each individually designed bedroom has been thoughtfully equipped to guarantee comfort and peace of mind. In addition to the standard guest rooms Donnington Valley offers a number of non-smoking rooms, family rooms, superior executive rooms and luxury suites. With its open log fire and elegant surroundings, the Piano Bar is an ideal place to meet friends or enjoy the relaxed ambience. Guests lunch and dine in the The Wine Press Restaurant which offers fine international cuisine is complemented by an extensive choice of wines and liqueurs. The 18-hole, par 71, golf course is a stern test for golfers of all abilities, through a magnificent parkland setting. Special corporate golfing packages are offered and tournaments can be arranged. Seven purpose-built function suites provide the flexibility to meet the demands of corporate and special events. Donnington Castle, despite a siege during the Civil War, still survives for sight-seeing. **Directions:** Leave the M4 at junction 13, go south towards Newbury on A34, then follow signs for Donnington Castle Price Guide: Single from £135; double/twin £135–£160; suite from £215.

58 MasterCard VISA AMERICAN EXPRESS M 100

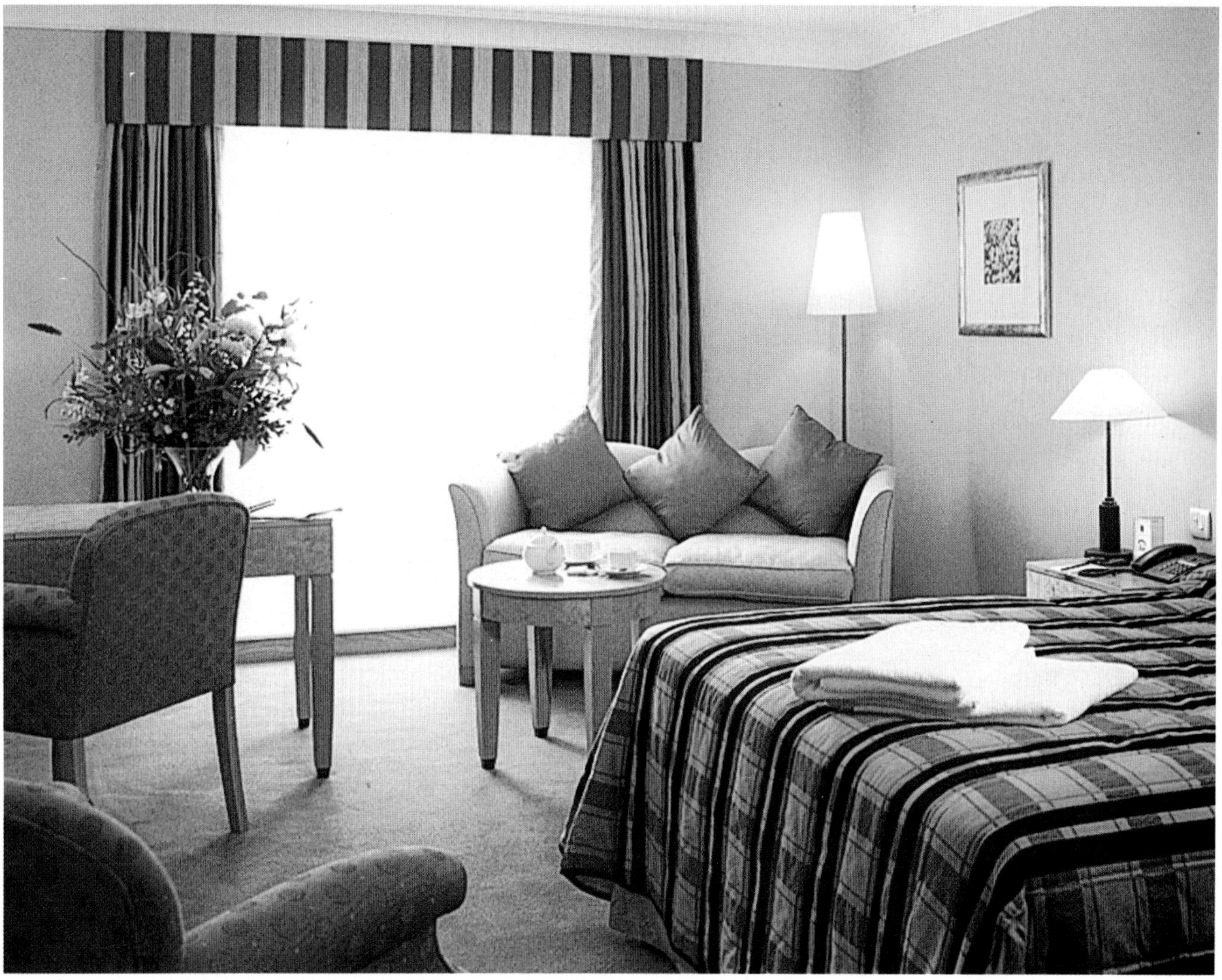

THE REGENCY PARK HOTEL

BOWLING GREEN ROAD, THATCHAM, BERKSHIRE RG18 3RP
TEL: 01635 871555 FAX: 01635 871571 E-MAIL: info@regencyparkhotel.co.uk

Ideally situated for access to both London and the South West, the Regency Park is a modern hotel that takes great pride in providing not only the most sophisticated facilities but combining them with the most attentive service and care. The style is neat and crisp with an understated elegance throughout, from the airy and spacious bedrooms to the array of meeting venues housed in the Business Centre. The Parkland Suite is a beautiful setting for any occasion, and with its own entrance and facilities for up to 200 guests it is the ideal place for wedding receptions and parties, as well as conferences and launches. "Escape" is the name of the leisure complex, and true to its name it really is a place where state-of-the-art technology and sheer luxury meet to form a special retreat. The serenity of the 17m swimming pool and the large health and beauty salon create an instantly relaxing atmosphere where fully qualified staff offer holistic health and beauty treatments. The Watermark Restaurant again has a contemporary elegance and stunning views over the Waterfall gardens, that is reflected in its excellent menu of modern flavours and fusions. There is even a children's menu to ensure all guests are catered for. **Directions:** Between Newbury and Reading. Leave M4 at Jct12 or 13; the hotel is signposted on A4, on the western outskirts of Thatcham. Price Guide: Single £65–£170; double/twin £79–£190; suite £180–£360.

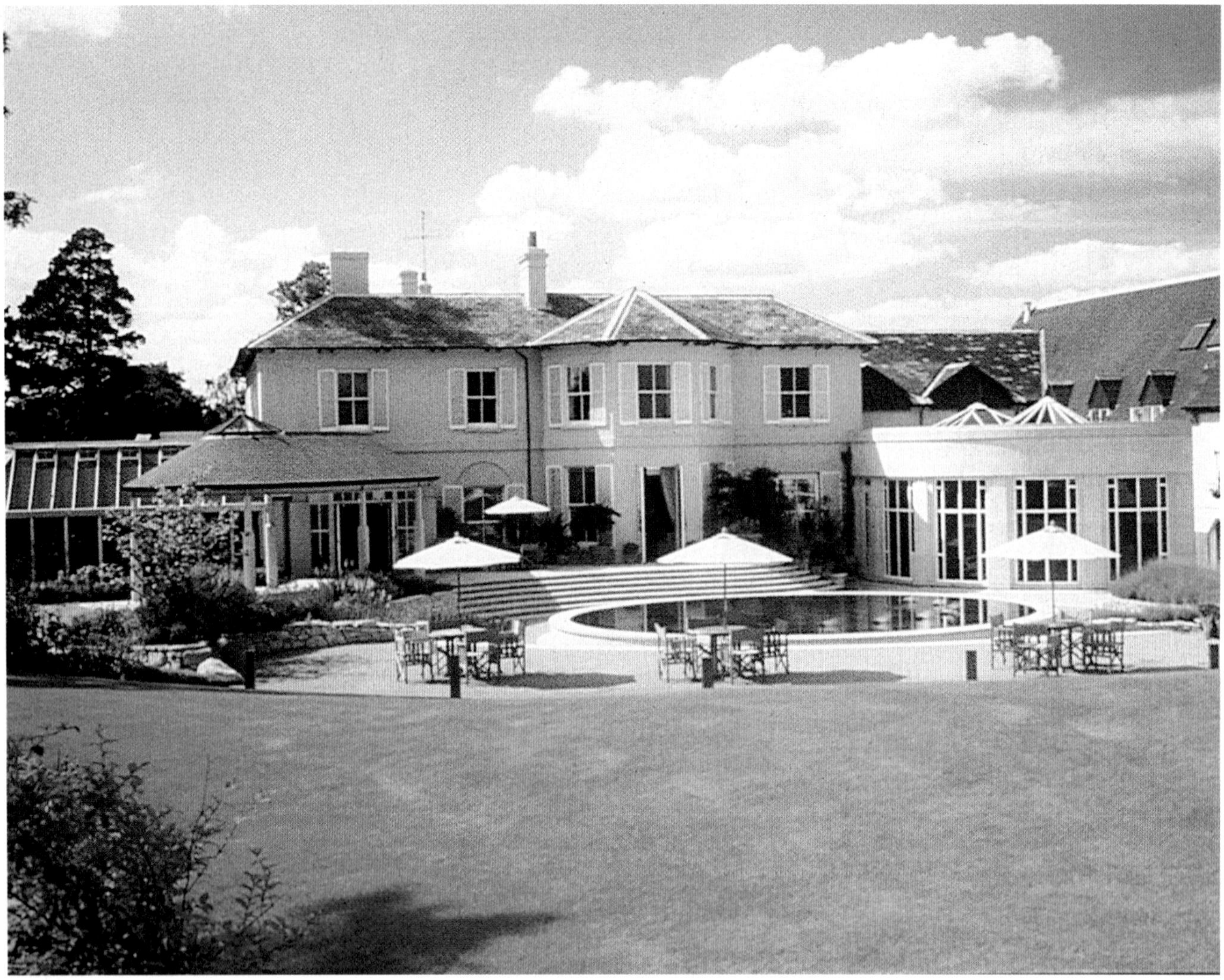

THE VINEYARD AT STOCKCROSS

NEWBURY, BERKSHIRE RG20 8JU

TEL: 01635 528770 FAX: 01635 528398 E-MAIL: general@the-vineyard.co.uk

The Vineyard at Stockcross, Sir Peter Michael's 'restaurant-with-suites' is a European showcase for the finest Californian wines including those from the Peter Michael Winery. Head Sommelier, Edoardo Amadi, has selected the best from the most highly-prized, family owned Californian wineries, creating one of the widest, most innovative, international wine lists. Awarded 4 Red Stars and 3 Rosettes by the AA, the classical French cuisine with a modern British twist matches the calibre of the wines. Pure flavours, fresh ingredients and subtle design blend harmoniously with the fine wines. A stimulating collection of paintings and sculpture includes the keynote piece, Fire and Water by William Pye FRBS and 'Deconstructing the Grape', a sculpture commissioned for the The Vineyard Spa. A vine-inspired, steel balustrade elegantly dominates the restaurant and the luxurious interior is complemented by subtle attention to detail throughout with stunning china and glass designs. The 31 well-appointed bedrooms include 13 suites offering stylish comfort with distinctive character. The Vineyard Spa features an indoor pool, spa bath, sauna, steam room, gym and treatment rooms. **Directions:** From M4, exit Jct13, A34 towards Newbury, then Hungerford exit. 1st roundabout Hungerford exit, 2nd roundabout Stockcross exit. Hotel on right. Price Guide: Single/double/twin £170–£255; suite £255–£455.

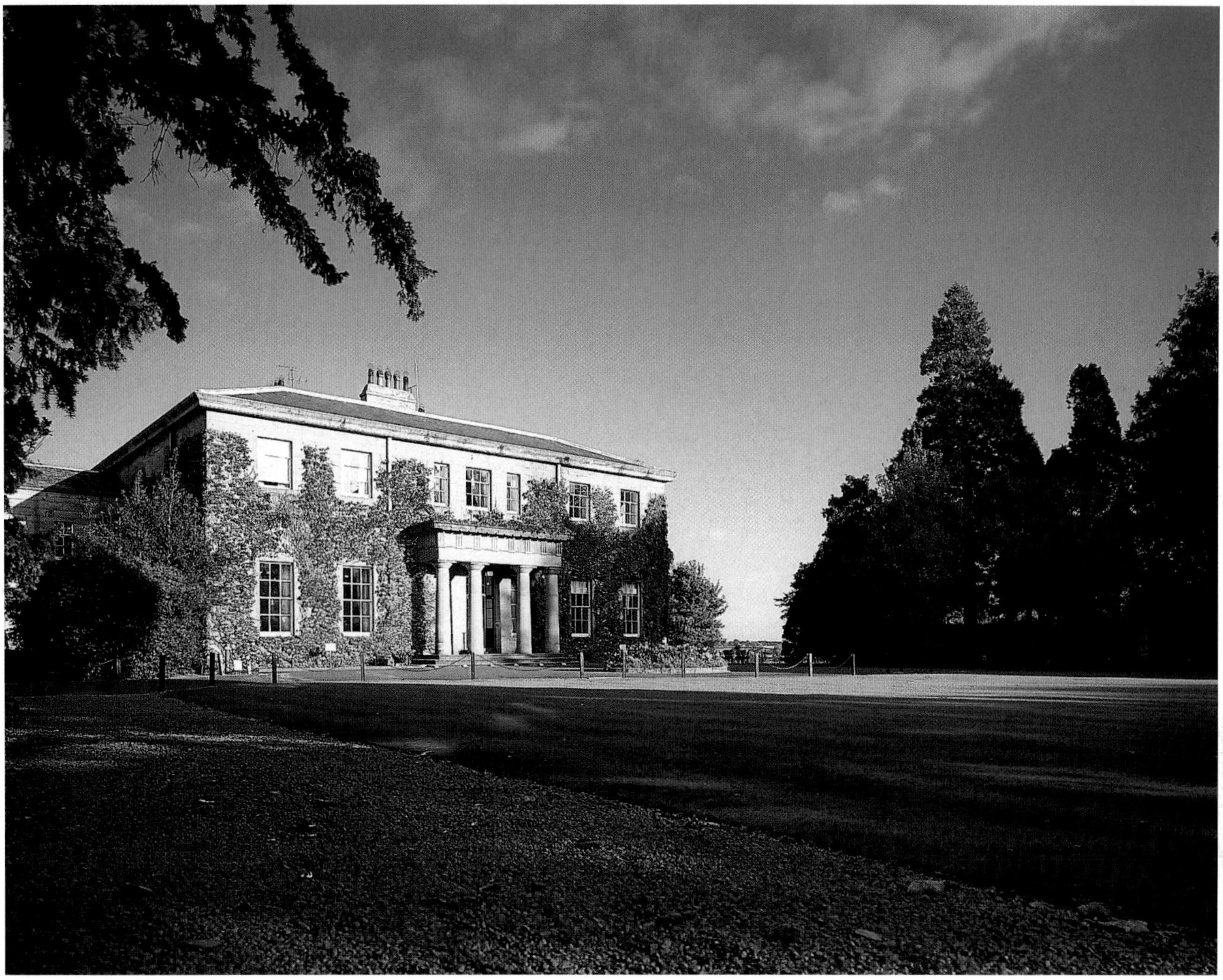

LINDEN HALL

LONGHORSLEY, MORPETH, NORTHUMBERLAND NE65 8XF
TEL: 01670 50 00 00 FAX: 01670 50 00 01 E-MAIL: stay@lindenhall.co.uk

Ivy-clad, hidden away among 450 acres of fine park and woodland in mid-Northumberland, Linden Hall is a superb Georgian country house within easy reach of Newcastle-upon-Tyne. An impressive mile-long drive sweeps up to its main door where, upon entering, the visitor will discover a relaxed, dignified atmosphere enhanced by gracious marble hearths, antiques and period pieces. Those wishing to escape the urban stress will be delighted to find every fitness and relaxation requirement catered for on the 18-hole golf course or at the health and beauty spa. Beauty therapy treatments, fitness and steam room, swimming pool, sun terrace and solarium are all available on the premises. The 50 bedrooms are individually and elegantly furnished. Some rooms have four-poster beds; each has its own private bathroom, supplied with thoughtful extras. The Linden Tree serves informal drinks and bar meals and the Dobson Restaurant, with panoramic views of the Northumberland coastline, serves delicious food, imaginatively prepared. Wedding ceremonies & receptions, banquets, dinner parties and business conferences can be held in comfort in any one of Linden Hall's conference and banqueting suites. **Directions:** From Newcastle take A1 north for 15 miles, then A697 toward Coldstream and Wooler. The hotel is 1 mile north of Longhorsley. Price Guide: Single £73–£110; double/twin £104–£180; suite: £180.

Matfen Hall Hotel & Golf Course

MATFEN, NORTHUMBERLAND, NE20 0RH
TEL: 01661 886500 FAX: 01661 886055 E-MAIL: info@matfenhall.com

Originally built in 1830 by Sir Edward Blackett, Matfen Hall opened as a hotel in 1999. Carefully restored by Sir Edward's descendants, Sir Hugh and Lady Blackett, this magnificent family seat lies in the heart of some of Northumberland's most beautiful countryside and offers splendid facilities for conferences, weddings and leisure breaks. The Great Hall is awe-inspiring with its stained glass windows, massive pillars and stone floors, while each of the 31 bedrooms have their own individual character, combining modern features with traditional opulence. A huge open fireplace adds charm to the elegantly furnished Drawing Room and the unique, book-lined Library restaurant serves English and International cuisine, under the guidence of Terence Laybourne. Matfen Hall enjoys stunning views over its own 18-hole golf course, laid out on a classic parkland landscape with manicured greens and fairways flanked by majestic trees. Rated as one of the finest in the North East, it provides a pleasurable test for players of all abilities. There is also a 9 hole par 3 golf course. Pampering treatments are available and the area offers plenty to explore. Scenic coastal, rural and ancient sites are within comfortable driving distance. Newcastle-upon-Tyne is only 20 minutes away. **Directions:** From A1 take A69 towards Hexham. At Heddon on the Wall take B6318 towards Chollerford, travel 7 miles and turn right to Matfen. Price Guide: Single £95–£135; double £120–£205. Special breaks available

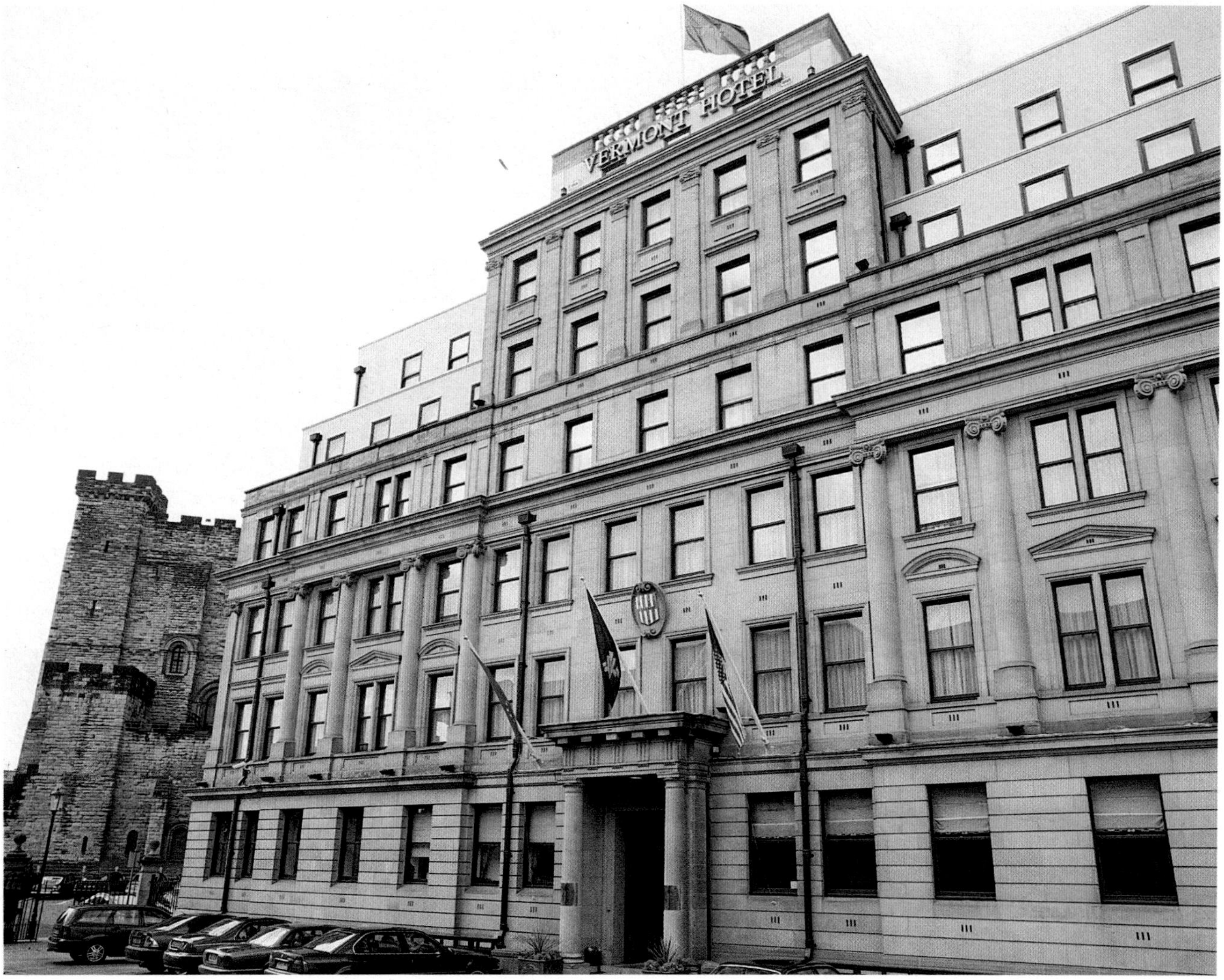

The Vermont Hotel

CASTLE GARTH, NEWCASTLE-UPON-TYNE, TYNE & WEAR NE1 1RQ
Tel: 0191 233 1010 Fax: 0191 233 1234 E-Mail: info@vermont-hotel.co.uk

Situated next to the historic Castle and overlooking the famous Tyne Bridge, The Vermont boasts an unrivalled position and impressive façade. Winner of the RAC Blue Ribbon and the AA Courtesy & Care Award, it was converted from the County Hall into a 12-storey hotel in 1993, and today its charm lies in an attentive service which makes guests feel welcome and pampered. With classical décor and stylish design throughout, all bedrooms offer maximum comfort, whilst pleasant public areas provide ample space for further relaxation. Morning coffee or afternoon tea is served in the Lounge, and the traditional Redwood Bar with its fireplace and sofas is the ideal venue to meet for a drink. For food, The Bridge Restaurant is informal with great views, while the Blue Room has won awards for its service and modern classical cuisine. All menus are complemented by a carefully chosen wine list. For those wishing to sample the atmosphere of the Quayside, Martha's Bar and Courtyard on the ground floor is the entrance to the bars, restaurants and bustling nightlife. Located in the heart of the city, The Vermont is the ideal base from which to explore Newcastle's excellent shops as well as the surrounding areas of Northumberland, Durham and The Borders. **Directions:** Close to the A1(M), and 7 miles from Newcastle International Airport. Price Guide: Single £145-£190; double £165-£190; suites £275-£450.

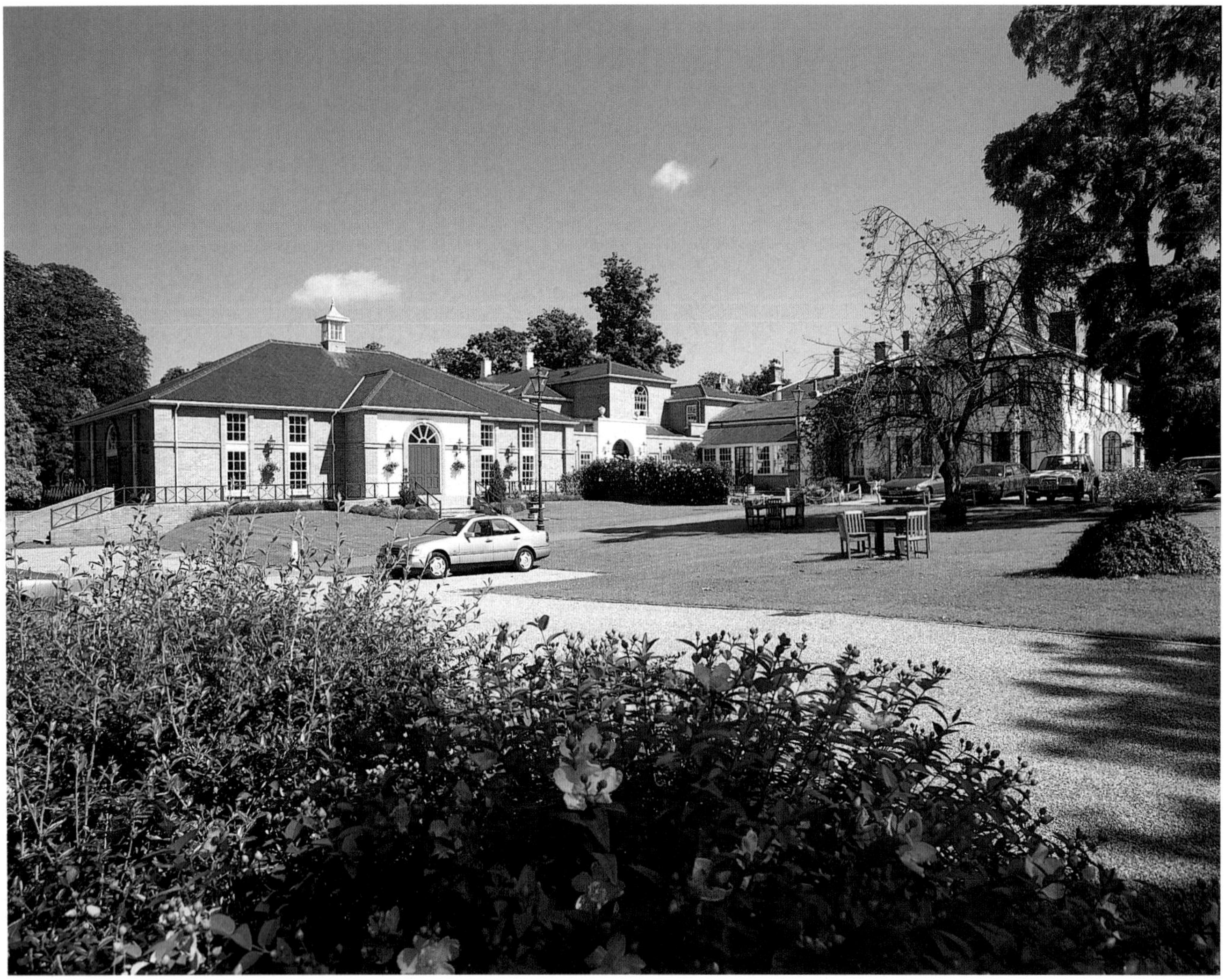

BEDFORD LODGE HOTEL

BURY ROAD, NEWMARKET, CB8 7BX
TEL: 01638 663175 FAX: 01638 667391 E-MAIL: info@bedfordlodgehotel.co.uk

This elegant hotel stands in three acres of glorious secluded gardens, adjacent to paddocks and training stables and just a short walk from Newmarket town centre. Formerly a Georgian hunting lodge built for the Duke of Bedford in the late 18th century, it offers a striking combination of both classic and modern styles. The atmosphere is relaxing and the service impeccable. This is horse racing country and the sport of kings is reflected throughout the hotel. A picture of Roxanna, the most famous mare of 18th-century England, hangs in the attractive hallway beyond the bar that bears her name. The newly refurbished bedrooms are carefully designed and offer a range of modern facilities. Contemporary dining in an elegant and charming ambience is offered in the award-winning Orangery restaurant with magnificent trompe-l'oeil fruit trees. Guests can relax in the hotel's superb leisure complex, which includes an indoor swimming pool, sauna, spa pool, solarium and fully equipped air-conditioned gym. Beauty treatments by prior arrangement. The University City of Cambridge, Suffolk and South Norfolk are all within easy reach. **Directions:** From M11 exit at Junction 9 onto A11. Follow signs to Newmarket. From the Clock Tower in centre of Town go straight across two mini roundabouts onto the Bury Road. The hotel is ¼ mile on the left Price Guide: (incl. breakfast and VAT) Single from £105; double/twin from £140; suites £130–£205. Weekend package from £75 per person per night (incl. dinner, bed and breakfast and VAT).

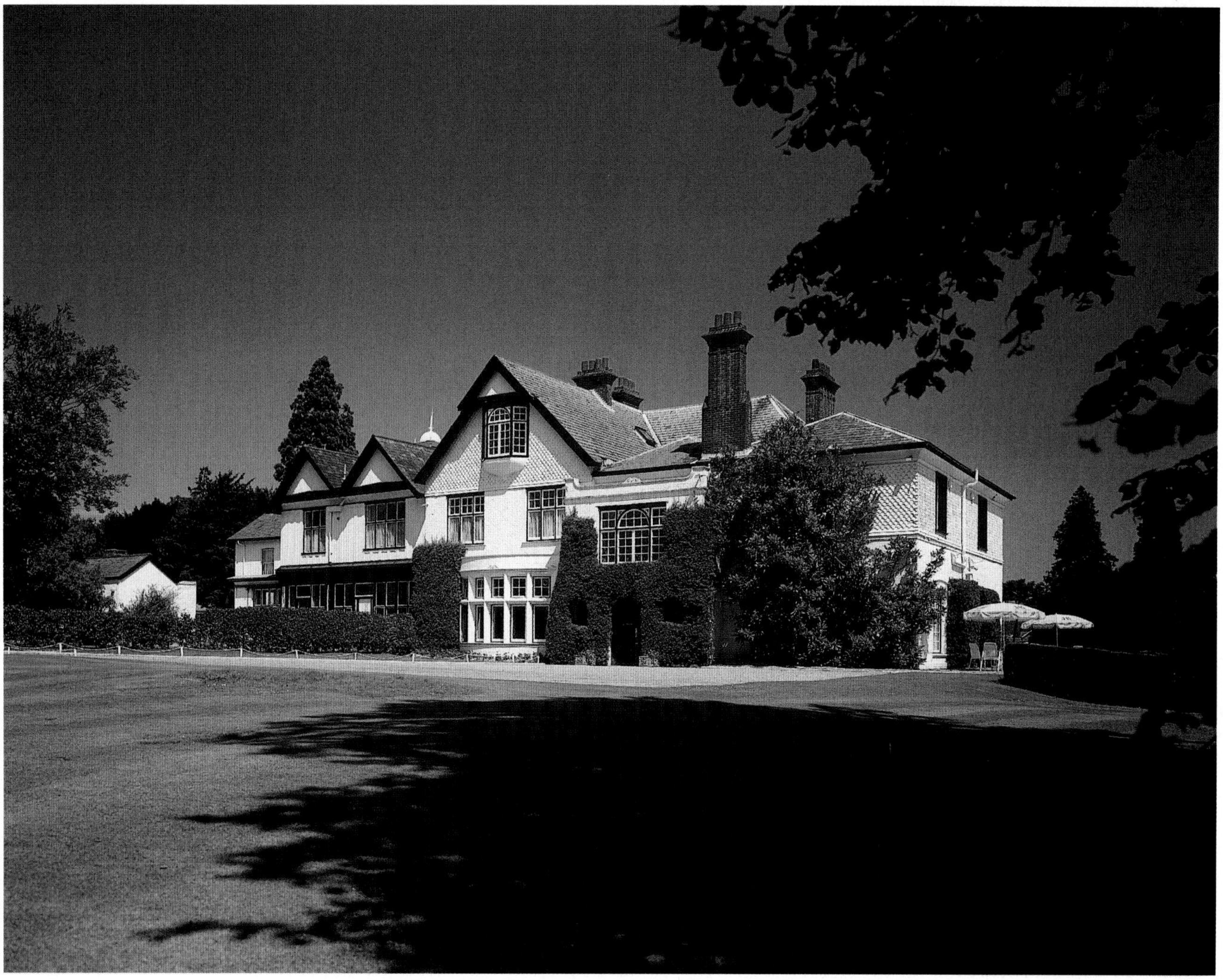

SWYNFORD PADDOCKS HOTEL AND RESTAURANT

SIX MILE BOTTOM, NR NEWMARKET, SUFFOLK CB8 0UE
TEL: 01638 570234 FAX: 01638 570283 E-MAIL: info@swynfordpaddocks.com

This classical white mansion standing in glorious gardens and idyllic countryside with racehorses grazing its pastures has a romantic history. In 1813 it was the scene of a passionate love affair between Lord Byron and the wife of the owner, Colonel George Leigh. Swynford was converted into a hotel 20 years ago. It has a country house atmosphere with antique furniture, open fires and attention to detail of times gone by. Each individually decorated, en suite bedroom has colour television, clock radio alarm, telephone, mini-bar and many other amenities. The lounge bar overlooks the gardens and the dining room offers an imaginative menu, changed regularly to incorporate the season's fresh produce. The award-winning restaurant has been awarded two RAC Dining Awards and two AA Rosettes. Conference facilities are available and a luxury marquee for private and special functions. Tennis, putting and croquet are within the grounds and guided tours of Newmarket with a look at the horseracing world can be arranged. Heliquisine: For a special occasion guests are chauffeur driven in a limousine to Cambridge airport for a helicopter ariel view of the surrounding towns, then land for a superb lunch at the hotel. **Directions:** From M11, exit at jct 9 and take A11 towards Newmarket. After 10 miles join A1304 signed Newmarket. Hotel is on left after 3/4 of a mile. Price Guide: Single £110; double/twin £135–£155; suite £175.

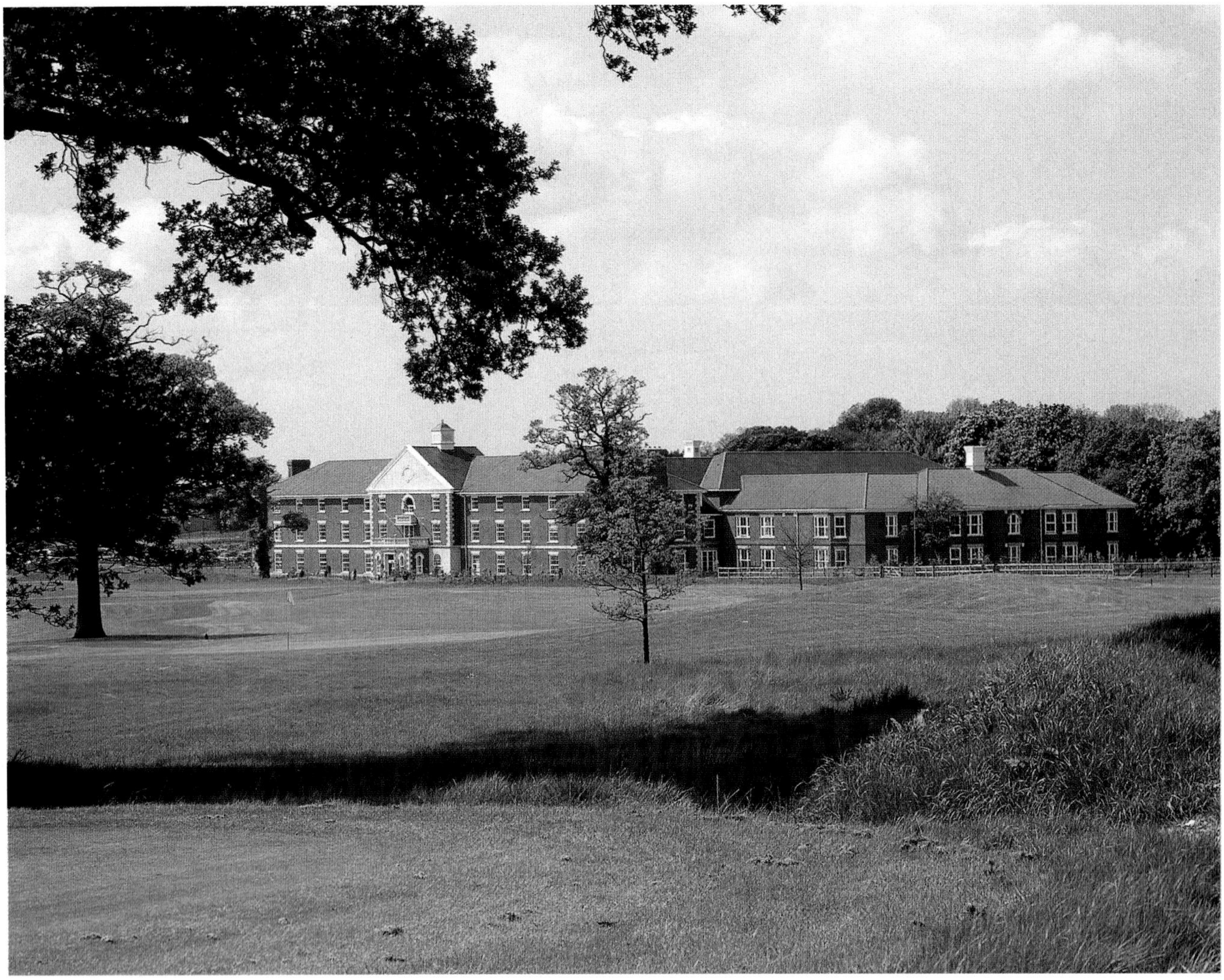

WHITTLEBURY HALL

WHITTLEBURY, NR TOWCESTER, NORTHAMPTONSHIRE NN12 8QH

TEL: 01327 857857 FAX: 01327 857867 E-MAIL: sales@whittleburyhall.co.uk

Whittlebury Hall is a modern building where the elegance of classic Georgian architecture has been complemented by contemporary furnishings and fabrics to create a truly fabulous hotel. The spacious bedrooms have all been elegantly decorated with a host of modern touches and thoughtful extras, whilst three superbly appointed, individually styled suites have a whirlpool spa bath and shower. The Silverstone Bar is aptly named with a host of motor racing memorabilia adorning the walls. Astons Restaurant offers a relaxed atmosphere with menus blending classic and contemporary cuisine with a dash of continental inspiration, complemented by fine wines from around the globe. The management training centre offers 12 suites and 24 dedicated syndicate rooms, all equipped with state-of-the-art audio visual equipment. Guests can relax and unwind at the Spa, where over 50 treatments are available in the health and beauty treatment suite. There is a 19-metre swimming pool, whirlpool spa, Turkish steam room, sauna and a 42-station StairMaster® gym, whilst the adjacent Whittlebury golf course offers preferred rates for guests. Motor racing enthusiasts can enjoy racing action at nearby Silverstone. Warwick Castle, Towcester racecourse and Oxford are all within a easy drive. **Directions:** 11 miles from M1 Jct15A. Luton and Birmingham airports are within easy reach. Price Guide: Single £120; double/twin £150; suite £250.

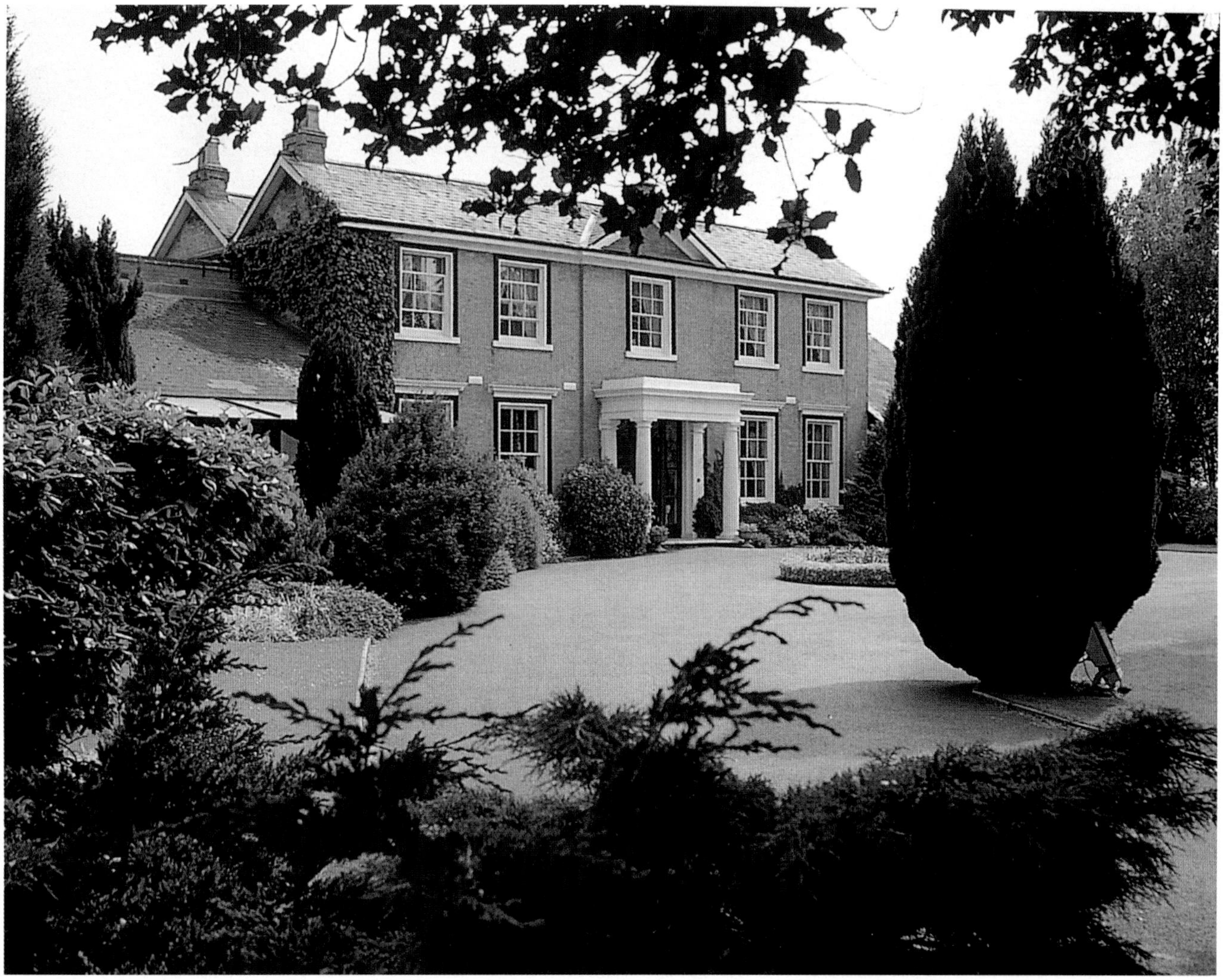

PARK FARM COUNTRY HOTEL & LEISURE

HETHERSETT, NORWICH, NORFOLK NR9 3DL
TEL: 01603 810264 FAX: 01603 812104 E-MAIL: enq@parkfarm–hotel.co.uk

Park Farm Hotel occupies a secluded location in beautifully landscaped grounds south of Norwich, once the second greatest city in England. There are executive rooms for additional comforts, with four poster beds and Jacuzzi baths. Additional bedrooms have been sympathetically converted from traditional and new buildings to reflect the style of the six rooms available in the main house. A superb leisure complex to suit all ages has been carefully incorporated alongside the original Georgian house to include heated swimming pool, sauna, steam room, solarium, spa bath, gymnasium, aerobics studio and a new beauty therapy area. The delightful Georgian restaurant is renowned for high standards of cuisine and service, with a wide selection of dishes and fine choice of wines. Conference facilities cater for up to 120 candidates, (24 hour and daily delegate rates available). Ideal location for wedding receptions. The Norfolk broads, the coast, Norwich open market, Castle museum and Cathedral are nearby. **Directions:** By road, just off A11 on B1172, Norwich Airport eight miles, Norwich rail station six miles and Norwich bus station five miles. Price Guide: Single £80–£110; double/twin £110–£145.

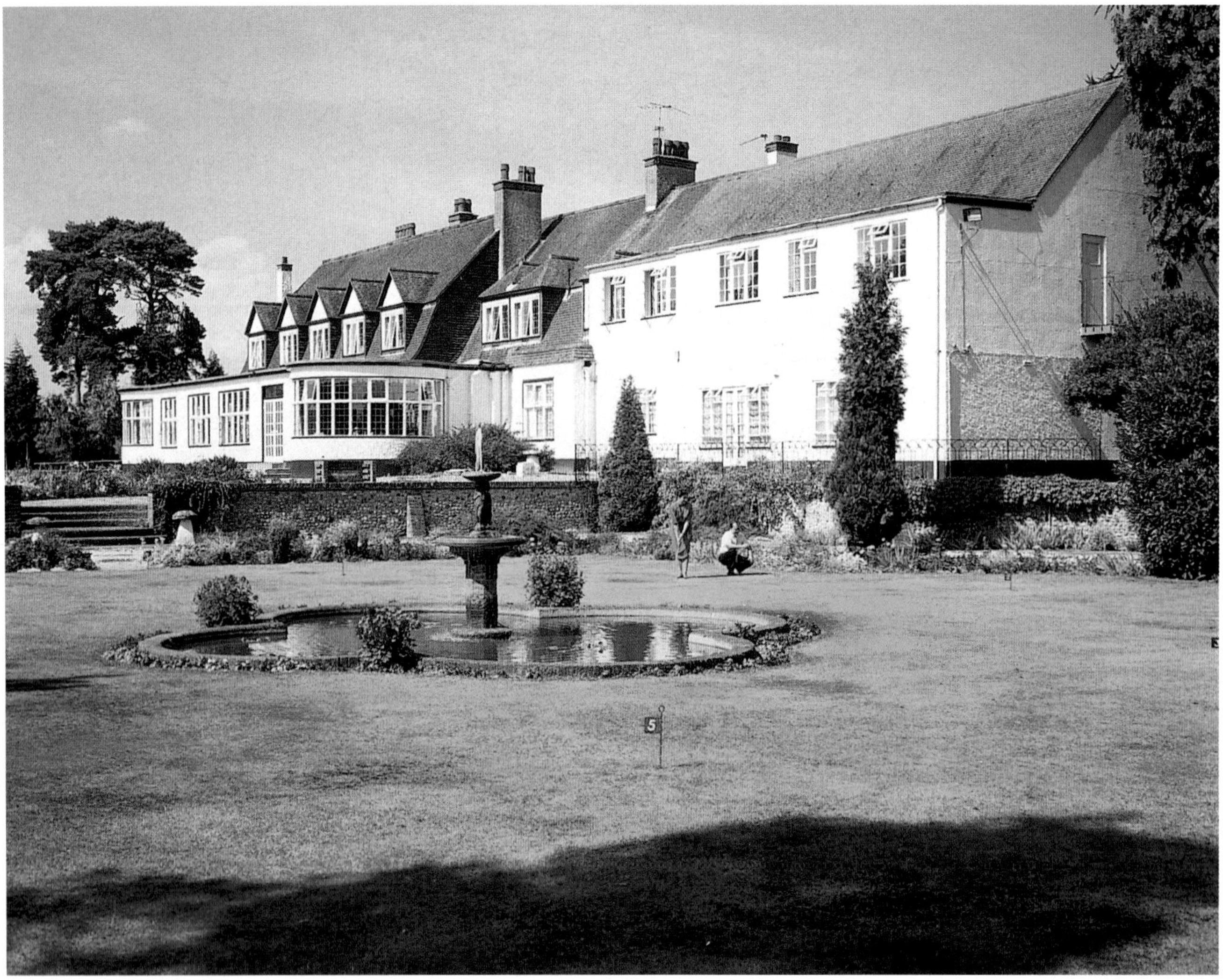

PETERSFIELD HOUSE HOTEL

LOWER STREET, HORNING, NR NORWICH, NORFOLK NR12 8PF
TEL: 01692 630741 FAX: 01692 630745 E-MAIL: reception@petersfieldhotel.co.uk

Petersfield House Hotel is set back from one of the most attractive reaches of the River Bure in the area known as the Norfolk Broads. The original property was built in the twenties on a prime site as a large private residence in two acres of gardens with its own moorings on a grassy bank of the river. Today it is a secluded family run hotel whose reputation is based on traditional comfort and hospitality. Guests can be sure of receiving personal attention at all times. The bedrooms are bright and welcoming – most rooms overlook the well-kept landscaped gardens which feature an ornamental pond, a putting green and a flintstone moon gate. Varied fixed-price and extensive à la carte menus are served in the restaurant where a list of over 60 wines provides an ideal accompaniment. Regular Saturday night dinner-dances are held with the hotel occupying one of the choicest positions on the Norfolk Broads. Sailing is the popular local pastime and open regattas are held during the summer. Golf is within easy driving distance. Other local attractions include Norwich with its famous art gallery and "Ten Ancient Monuments" and Blickling Hall with its interesting furniture and gardens. **Directions:** From Norwich ring road, take A1151 to Wroxham. Cross bridge, turn right at Hoveton on A1062 to Horning; hotel is beyond centre of the village Price Guide: Single from £60; double from £80.

18 MasterCard VISA AMERICAN EXPRESS M 100

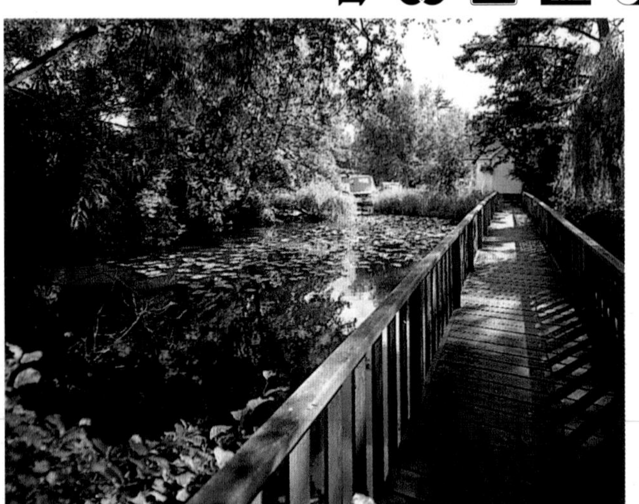

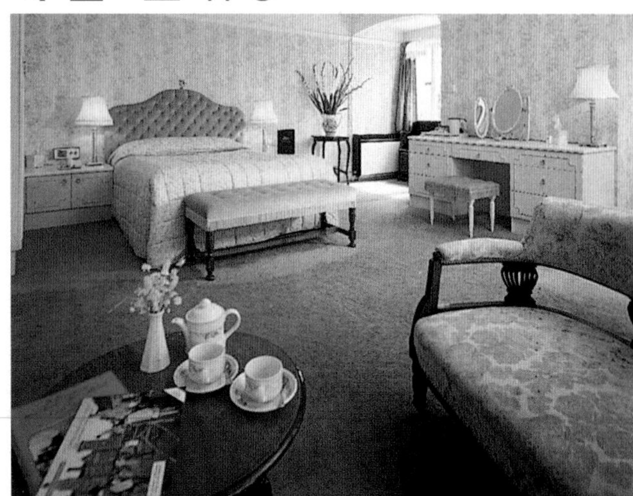

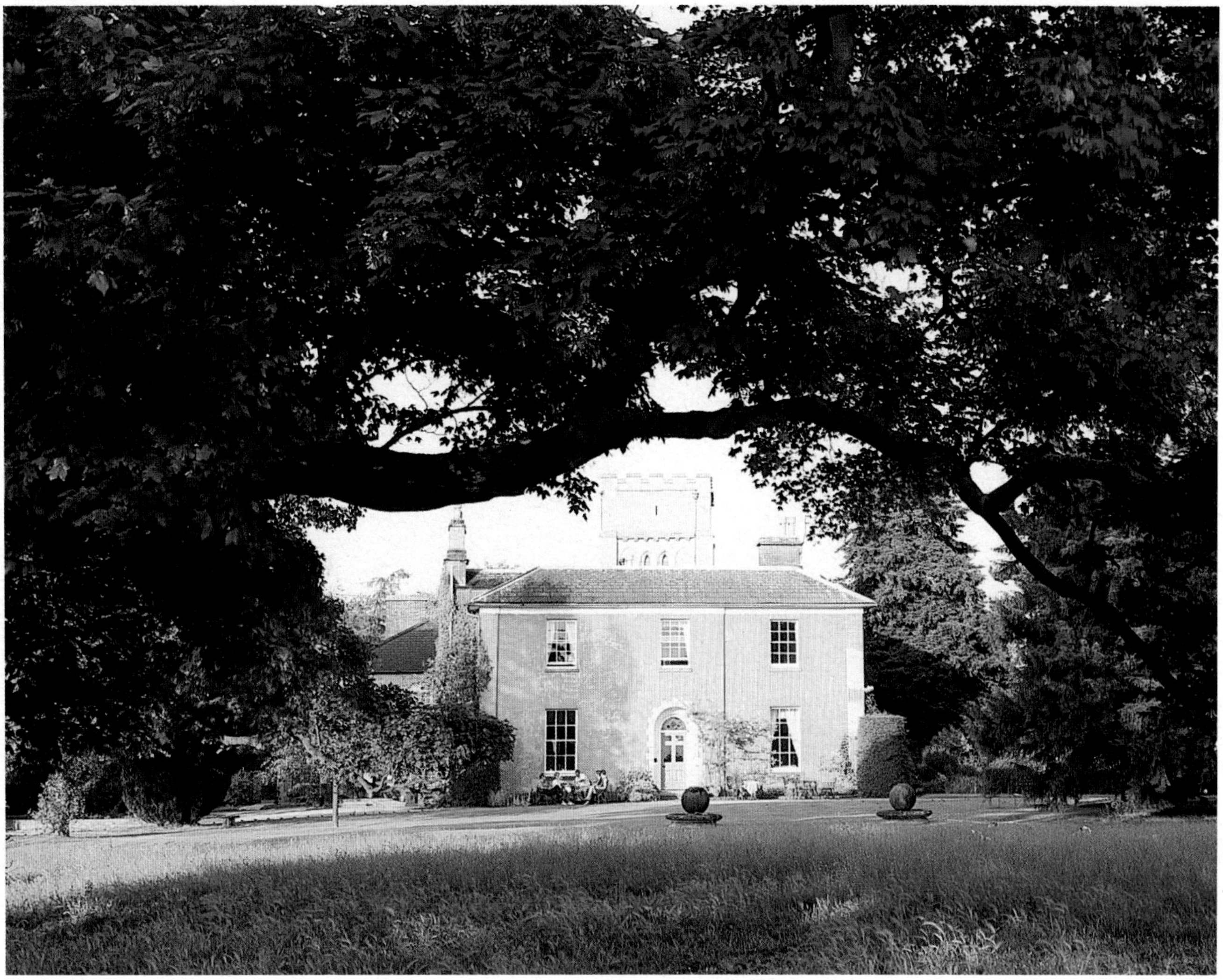

LANGAR HALL

LANGAR, NOTTINGHAMSHIRE NG13 9HG
TEL: 01949 860559 FAX: 01949 861045 E-MAIL: langarhall–hotel@ndirect.co.uk

Set in the Vale of Belvoir, mid-way between Nottingham and Grantham, Langar Hall is the family home of Imogen Skirving. It was built in 1837 on the site of a great historic house, the home of Admiral Lord Howe. It stands in quiet seclusion overlooking gardens, where sheep graze among the ancient trees in the park. Below the croquet lawn lies a romantic network of medieval fishponds stocked with carp. Epitomising "excellence and diversity", Langar Hall combines the standards of good hotel-keeping with the hospitality and style of country house living. Having received a warm welcome, guests can enjoy the atmosphere of a private home that is much loved and cared for. The en suite bedrooms are individually designed and comfortably appointed. The public rooms feature fine furnishings and most rooms afford beautiful views of the garden, park and moat. Langar Hall is an ideal venue for small boardroom meetings. It is also an ideal base from which to visit Belvoir Castle, to see cricket at Trent Bridge, to visit students at Nottingham University and to see Robin Hood's Sherwood Forest. Dogs can be accommodated by arrangement. **Directions:** Langar is accessible via Bingham on the A52, or via Cropwell Bishop from the A46 (both signposted). The house adjoins the church and is hidden behind it. Price Guide: Single £65–£97.50; double/twin £130–£150; suite £175.

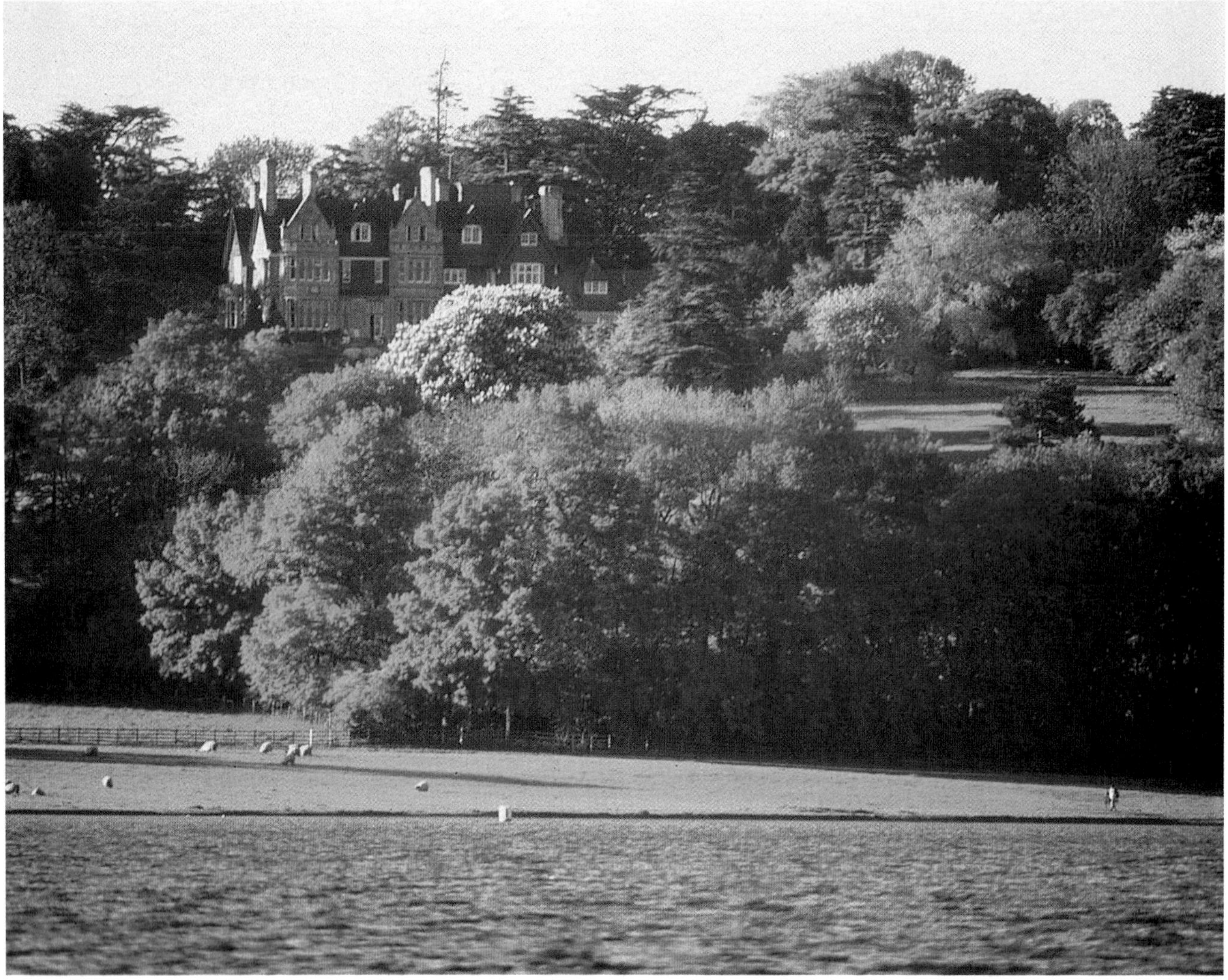

Hambleton Hall

HAMBLETON, OAKHAM, RUTLAND LE15 8TH
TEL: 01572 756991 FAX: 01572 724721 E-MAIL: hotel@hambletonhall.com

Winner of Johansens Most Excellent Country Hotel Award 1996, Hambleton Hall, originally a Victorian mansion, became a hotel in 1979. Since then its renown has continually grown. It enjoys a spectacular lakeside setting in a charming and unspoilt area of Rutland. The hotel's tasteful interiors have been designed to create elegance and comfort, retaining individuality by avoiding a catalogue approach to furnishing. Delightful displays of flowers, an artful blend of ingredients from local hedgerows and the London flower markets colour the bedrooms. In the restaurant, chef Aaron Patterson and his enthusiastic team offer a menu which is strongly seasonal. Grouse, Scottish ceps and chanterelles, partridge and woodcock are all available at just the right time of year, accompanied by the best vegetables, herbs and salads from the Hall's garden. The Croquet Pavilion, a two bedroom suite with living room and breakfast room is a luxurious addition to the accommodation options. For the energetic there are lovely walks around the lake and opportunities for tennis and swimming, golf, riding, bicycling, trout fishing, and sailing. Burghley House and Belton are nearby, as are the antique shops of Oakham, Uppingham and Stamford. Hambleton Hall is a Relais & Châteaux member. **Directions:** In the village of Hambleton, signposted from the A606, 1 mile east of Oakham. Price Guide: Single £150; double/twin £175–£335; suite £500.

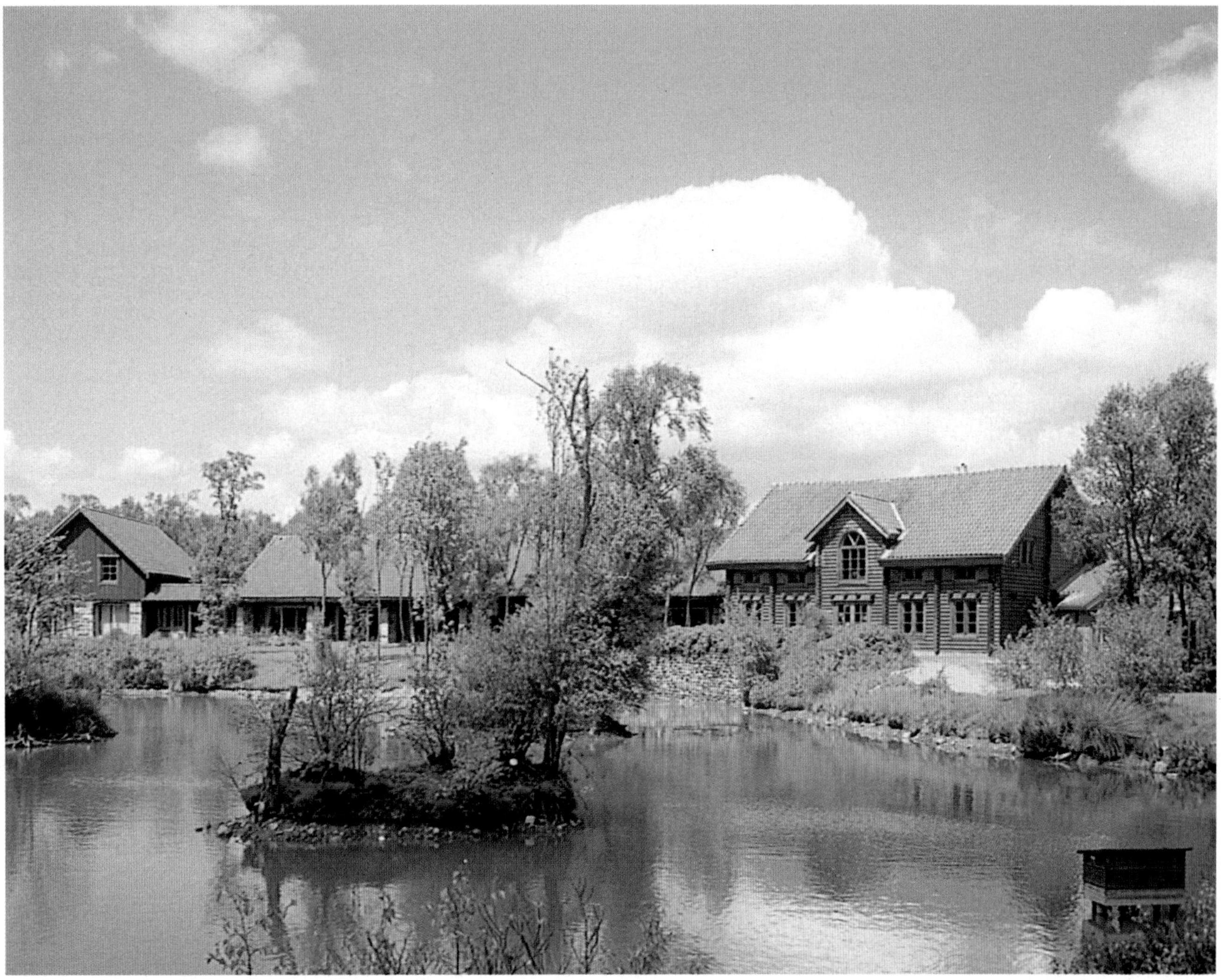

Chevin Lodge Country Park Hotel

YORKGATE, OTLEY, WEST YORKSHIRE LS21 3NU

TEL: 01943 467818 FAX: 01943 850335 E-MAIL: reception@chevinlodge.co.uk

A quite unique hotel – you would probably need to travel to Scandinavia to discover a similar hotel to Chevin Lodge. Built entirely of Finnish logs and surrounded by birch trees, it is set in 50 acres of lake and woodland in the beauty spot of Chevin Forest Park. The spacious, carefully designed bedrooms are tastefully furnished with pine and some have patio doors leading to the lakeside gardens. In addition, there are several luxury lodges tucked away in the woods, providing alternative accommodation to the hotel bedrooms. Imaginative and appetising meals are served in the beautiful balconied restaurant, which overlooks the lake. Chevin Lodge offers conference facilities in the Woodlands Suite which is fully- equipped for all business requirements. The Leisure Club has a 11 x 7 metres swimming pool, spa bath, sauna, solarium and gym. There is also a games room, all weather tennis court and jogging and cycling trails that wind through the woods. Leeds, Bradford and Harrogate are within 20 minutes' drive. Special weekend breaks are available. **Directions:** From A658 between Bradford and Harrogate, take the Chevin Forest Park road, then left into Yorkgate for Chevin Lodge. Price Guide: Single £95–£130; double/twin £110–£140. Special breaks available.

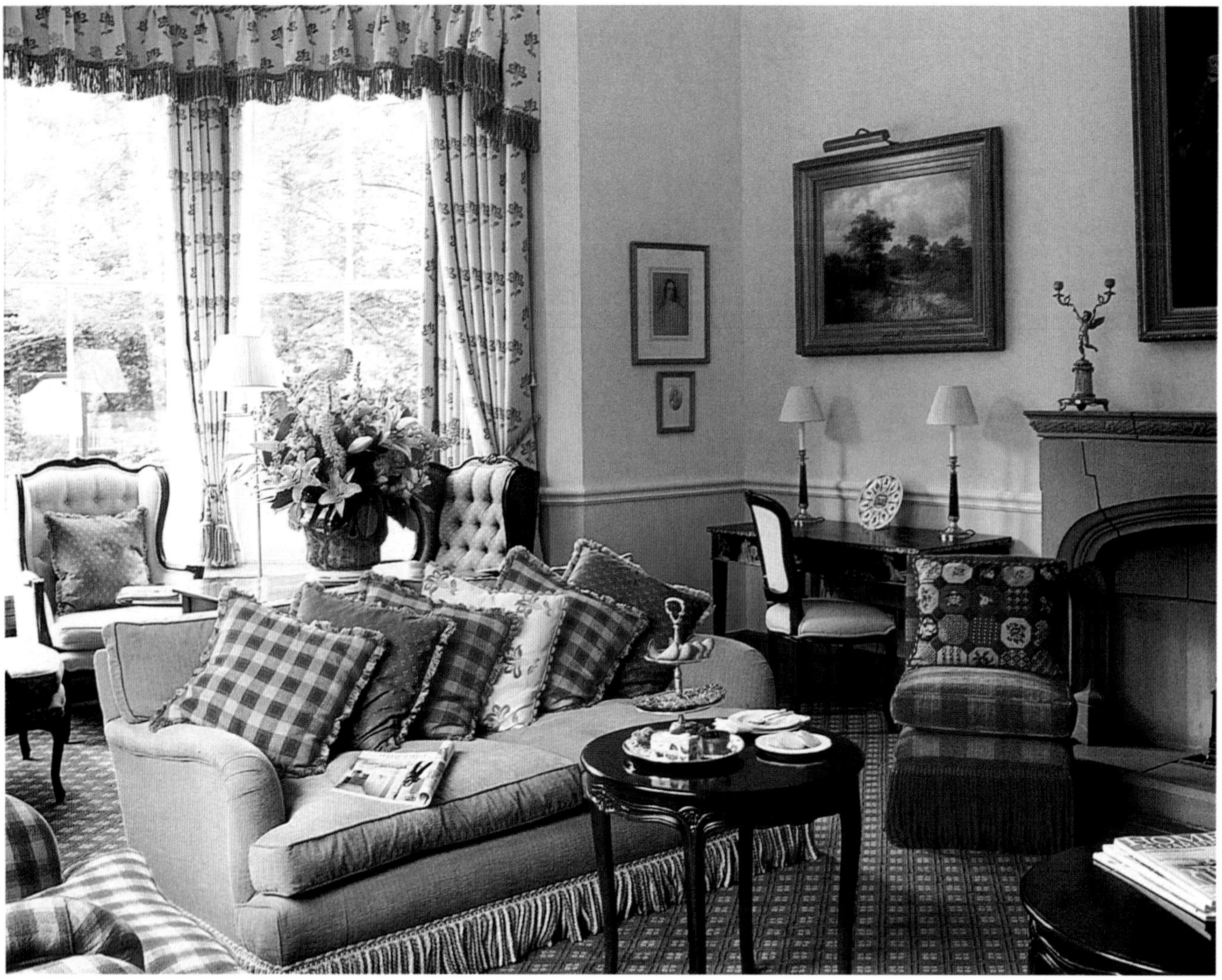

THE COTSWOLD LODGE HOTEL

66A BANBURY ROAD, OXFORD OX2 6JP
TEL: 01865 512121 FAX: 01865 512490

Situated in a quiet conservation area just 1/2 mile away from Oxford is this picturesque Victorian building which has been restored in the style of a stately manor house. An ideal location for tourists and those on business, the Hotel offers a comfortable and relaxed environment. The Scholars bar is ideal for a light lunch or pre-dinner drink, and during winter, log fires enhance the cosy ambience. The elegant Fellows restaurant serves outstanding seasonal menus, with high quality ingredients a priority. Fresh fish and lobster come from Cornwall, sausages are made specially for the hotel, wild salmon is delivered from Scotland, and local lamb and game are used extensively. An impressive wine list ensures that there is something to suit all tastes and complement every meal. The tastefully furnished en suite bedrooms differ in size and style. The Cotswold Lodge happily caters for conferences on a daily or residential basis, and over the years has become renowned for its superb reputation in hosting wedding receptions. Staff are on hand to provide their expertise and tailor arrangements to suit individual requirements. The Banquet room accommodates up to 100 people and has access to a patio with fountain and walled garden. **Directions:** From M40 junction 8, take A40 for Oxford; or junction 9, take A34; or from M4, junction 13, take A34 for Oxford. Price Guide: Single £125; double/twin £175; suite from £295.

49 MasterCard VISA AMERICAN EXPRESS M 100 VCR

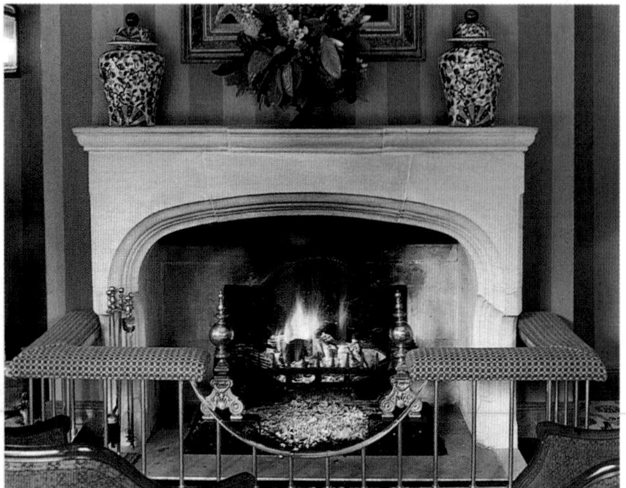

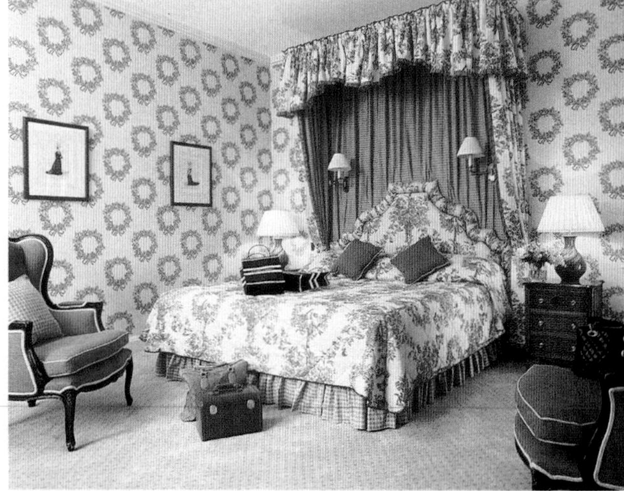

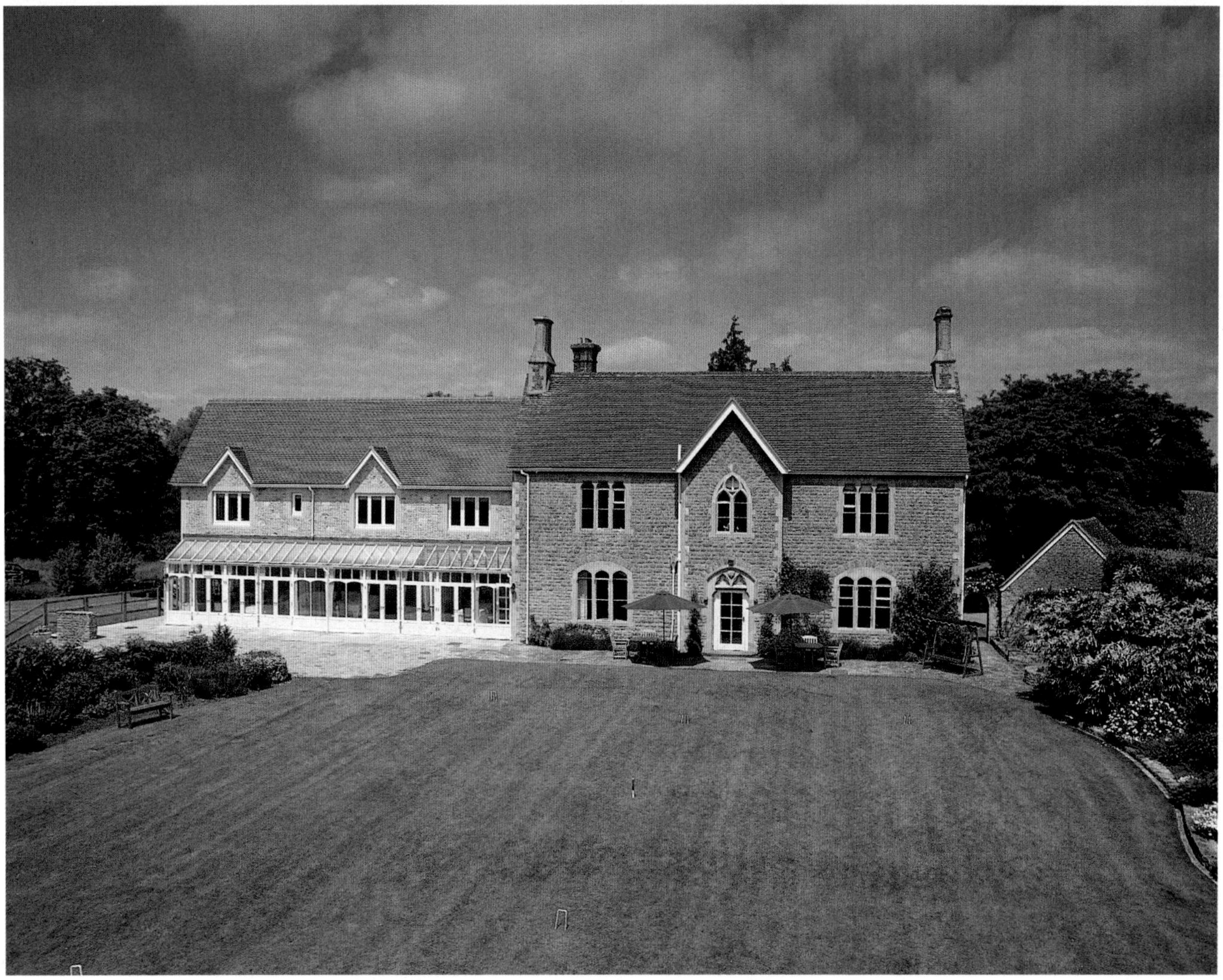

FALLOWFIELDS

KINGSTON BAGPUIZE WITH SOUTHMOOR, OXON OX13 5BH
TEL: 0001865 820416 FAX: 01865 821275 E-MAIL: stay@fallowfields.com

Fallowfields, once the home of Begum Aga Khan, dates back more than 300 years. It has been updated and extended over past decades and today boasts a lovely early Victorian Gothic southern aspect. The house is set in two acres of gardens, surrounded by ten acres of grassland. The guests' bedrooms, which offer a choice of four poster or coroneted beds, are large and well appointed and offer every modern amenity to ensure maximum comfort and convenience. The house is centrally heated throughout and during the winter months, there are welcoming log fires in the elegant main reception rooms. The cuisine is mainly British, imaginative in style and presentation and there is a good choice of menus available The walled kitchen garden provides most of the vegetables and salads for the table and locally grown organic produce is otherwise used wherever possible. Fallowfields is close to Stratford, the Cotswolds, Stonehenge, Bath and Bristol to the west, Oxford, Henley on Thames, the Chilterns and Windsor to the east. Heathrow airport is under an hour away. **Directions:** Take the Kingston Bagpuize exit on the A420 Oxford to Swindon. Fallowfields is at the west end of Southmoor and just after the Longworth sign Price Guide: £105–120; double/twin £122–£155.

THE RANDOLPH

BEAMONT STREET, OXFORD OX1 2LN

TEL: 0870 400 8200 FAX: 01865 792133 E-MAIL: heritagehotels_oxford.randolph@forte–hotels.com

This is luxury, comfort and style in the old-fashioned way, combined with all the modern facilities expected by today's guests. The Randolph stands majestically in the heart of the city. It is Oxford's premier hotel and over the years has been visited by royalty, statesmen and celebrities. The newly named Morse Bar, a favourite haunt of Inspector Morse and his creator, Colin Dexter, sits alongside the refurbished restaurant, where excellent cuisine can be enjoyed in an atmosphere of comfort and soft lighting. For more casual dining, the new Oyster Bar offers champagnes, fine wines, seafood and delicious cold dishes in a fresh, young atmosphere. Equally grand are the hotel's 114 en suite bedrooms and suites, most of which have been totally refurbished during 2001. Each is beautifully decorated and furnished and provides every facility from satellite television and CD players to hairdryers and 24-hour service. For sheer luxury, why not choose one of the hotel's deluxe suites, each with their own private spacious sitting area, decorated with crystal hanging chandeliers and sumptuous furnishings. Car parking is available at the adjacent car park at a reduced rate of £10 per 24 hours (must be pre-booked on 01865 248689). **Directions:** From M40/A40 follow signs to Oxford city centre and St Giles. The hotel is on the corner to your right Price Guide: Single £160; double/twin £170–£210; suites £350–£700.

114 MasterCard VISA AMERICAN EXPRESS M 200

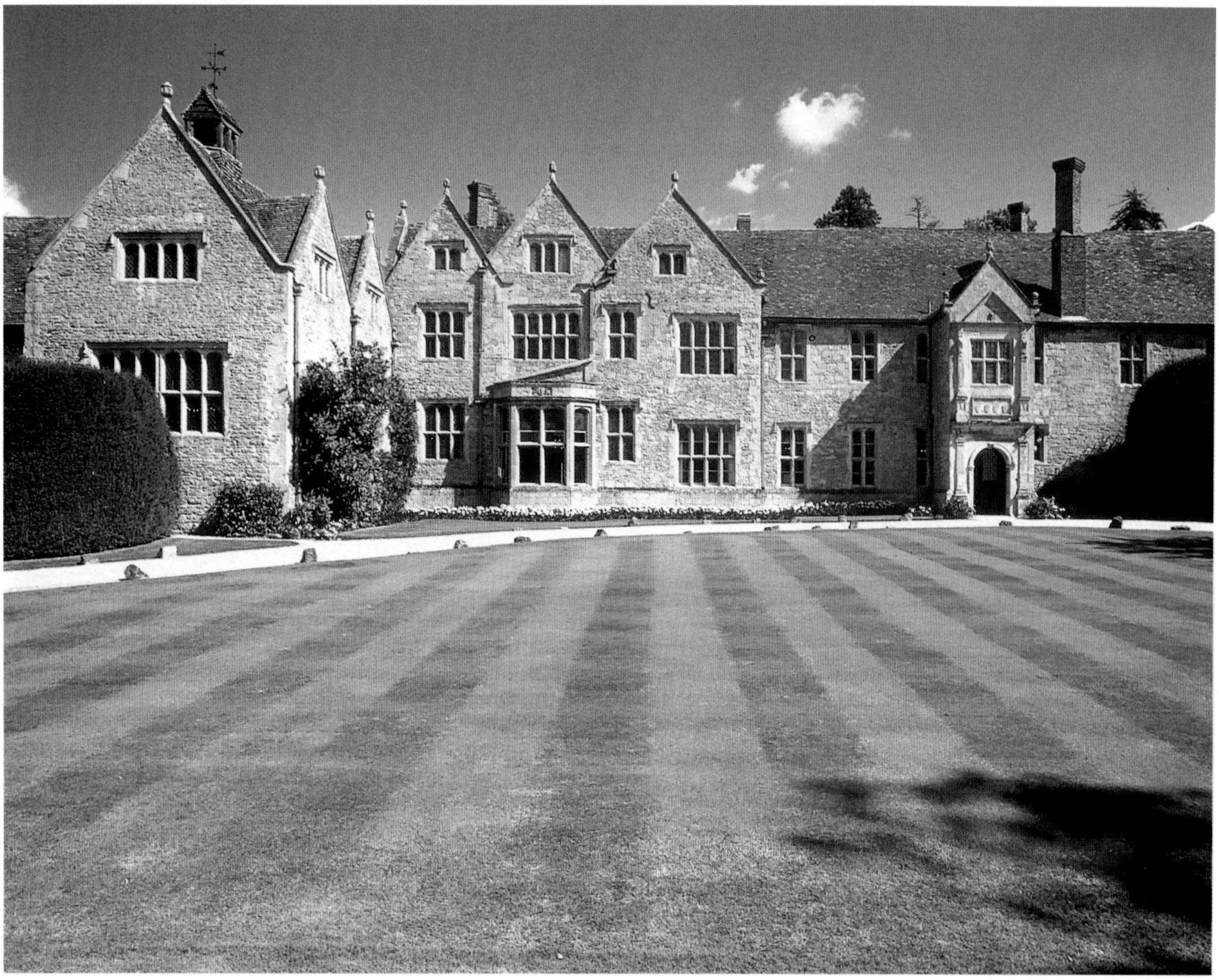

Studley Priory

HORTON HILL, HORTON-CUM-STUDLEY, OXFORD, OXFORDSHIRE OX33 1AZ
TEL: 01865 351203 FAX: 01865 351613 E-MAIL: res@studley-priory.co.uk

Set a few miles from the famous University City of Oxford, close to the beautiful villages and countryside of the Cotswolds and convenient for motorway connections via the nearby M40, Studley Priory is ideally suited for business and pleasure. The hotel exudes a sense of timelessness, its exterior little altered since Elizabethan times. The interior has been sympathetically updated to offer 18 lovely en suite bedrooms, each complemented by fine furnishings and luxurious bathrooms. The Elizabethan Suite offers a half tester bed dating from 1700, and many fine antiques remain in this historic property. The Croke Restaurant, which has received 3 AA Rosettes for its excellent cuisine, offers a seasonally changing menu of contemporary dishes created using only the finest local produce, complemented by an extensive wine list. Conference facilities are available for up to 50 people, and larger events, such as weddings, can be accommodated in an attached marquee. Nearby attractions include 2 fine golf courses, Blenheim Palace, the Manors of Waddesdon and Milton, The Cotswolds and Oxford, horse-racing at Cheltenham and Ascot, motor racing at Silverstone. Member of Small Luxury Hotels of the World. **Directions:** From London leave M40 at Jct8. Follow A40 toward Oxford. Turn right for Horton-cum-Studley. Hotel is at the top of the hill. Price Guide: Single £105–£175; double/twin £140–£250; suite £275–£300.

WESTON MANOR

WESTON-ON-THE-GREEN, OXFORDSHIRE OX25 3QL
TEL: 01869 350621 FAX: 01869 350901 E-MAIL: reception@westonmanor.co.uk

Imposing wrought-iron gates flanked by sculptured busts surmounting tall grey stone pillars lead into the impressive entrance to this delightful old manor house, the showpiece of the lovely village of Weston-on-the Green since the 11th century. The ancestral home of the Earls of Abingdon and Berkshire, and once the property of Henry VIII, Weston Manor stands regally in 13 acres of colourful gardens restored as a unique country house hotel of character. A peaceful retreat for visitors wishing to discover the delights of the surrounding Cotswold countryside and of Oxford, Woodstock, Blenheim Palace and Broughton Castle. Many of the Manor's 34 charming bedrooms, including four in a cottage and 14 in the old coach-house, retain antique furniture and all have garden views, private bathrooms and elegant surroundings. There is a squash court, croquet lawn and a secluded, heated outdoor swimming pool. Golf and riding are nearby. At the heart of the Manor is the restaurant, a magnificent vaulted and oak panelled Baronial Hall where delectable cuisine is served. Dining in such historic splendour is very much the focus of a memorable stay. **Directions:** From the M40, exit at junction 9 onto the A34. Leave A34 on 1st exit, towards Oxford. After approximately one mile turn right onto the B340. Weston Manor is on the left. Price Guide: Single £115; double/twin £154; suite £225.

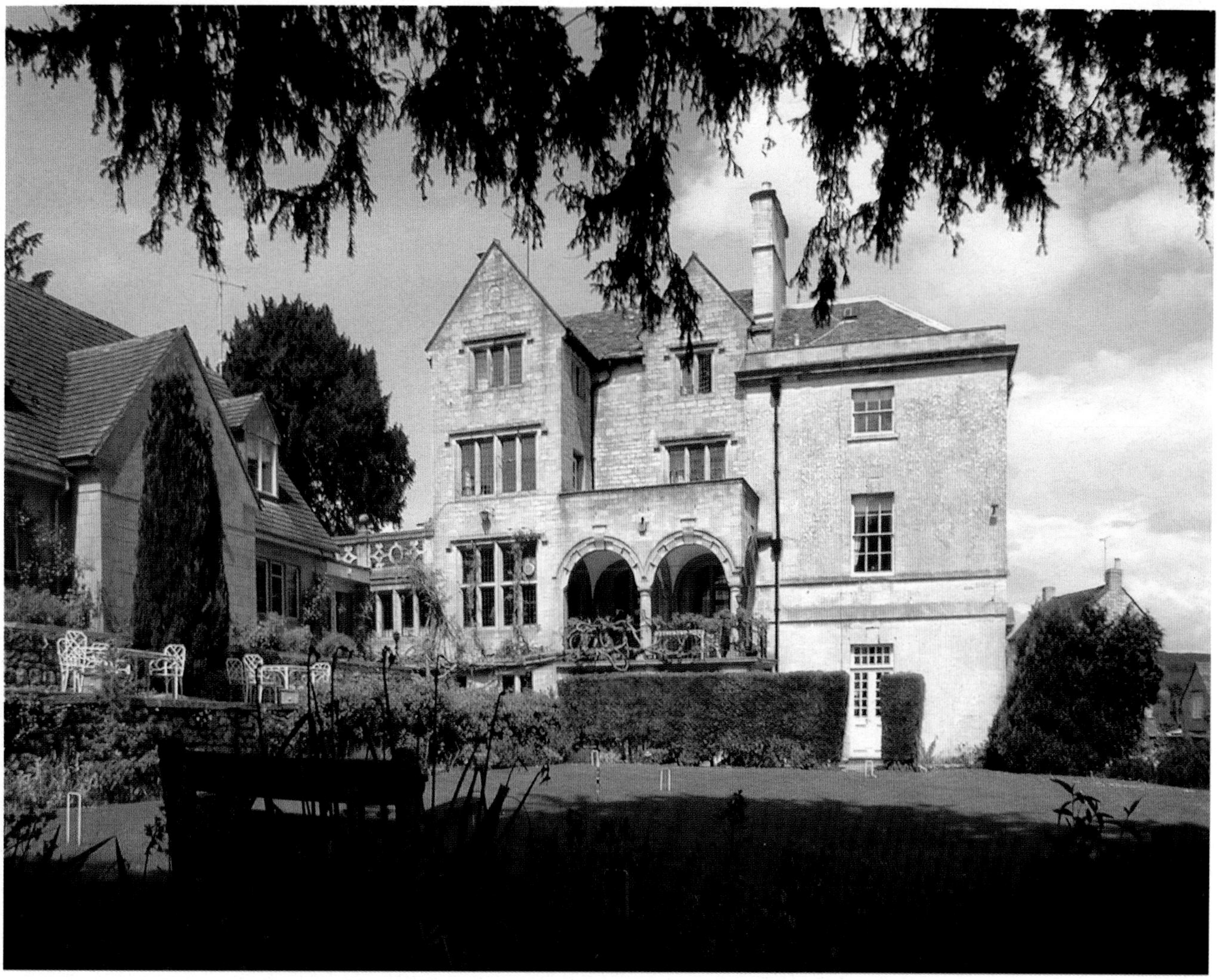

THE PAINSWICK HOTEL

KEMPS LANE, PAINSWICK, GLOUCESTERSHIRE GL6 6YB
TEL: 01452 812160 FAX: 01452 814059 E-MAIL: Reservations@Painswickhotel.com

The village of Painswick stands high on a hill overlooking the beautiful rolling valleys of the Cotswolds. Dating back to the 14th century, the village was an old wool community, medieval cottages mingle gracefully with elegant Georgian merchants' houses. A feature of the village is the church, with its ancient churchyard graced by 99 Yew trees planted in 1792 and 17th century table tombs in memory of the wealthy clothiers. Situated majestically within these architectural gems is the Palladian-style Painswick Hotel, built in 1790 and formerly the home of affluent village rectors. Each of the luxury en suite bedrooms have modern amenities, beautiful fabrics, antique furniture and objets d'art; creating a restful atmosphere and the impression of staying in a comfortable private house. The stylish restaurant, with its pine panelling, offers delicious cuisine with an emphasis upon regional produce such as locally reared Cotswold meat, game, wild Severn salmon and Gloucestershire cheeses. The private Dining Room accommodates quiet dinner parties, wedding occasions and business meetings. **Directions:** M5 Jct13. Painswick is on A46 between Stroud and Cheltenham, turn into road by the church and continue round the corner, taking the first right. The hotel is at the bottom of the road on the right hand side. Price Guide: Single from £90; double/twin from £120–£195.

THE HAYCOCK

WANSFORD, PETERBOROUGH, CAMBRIDGESHIRE PE8 6JA
TEL: 01780 782223 FAX: 01780 783031 E-MAIL: haycock@arcadianhotels.co.uk

The Haycock is a handsome old coaching inn of great charm, character and historic interest. It was host to Mary Queen of Scots in 1586 and Princess Alexandra Victoria, later Queen Victoria, in 1835. Overlooking the historic bridge that spans the River Nene, the hotel is set in a delightful village of unspoilt cottages. All bedrooms are individually designed and equipped to the highest standards with beautiful soft furnishings. The Restaurant is renowned for the quality of its contemporary style menu complemented by a selection of interesting and fine wines with dishes utilising the freshest possible ingredients. It is also famed for its outstanding wine list. A purpose-built ballroom, with lovely oak beams and its own private garden, is a popular venue for a wide range of events, including Balls, Wedding receptions and Christmas parties. The Business Centre has also made its mark; it is well equipped with every facility required and offers the flexibility to cater for meetings, product launches, seminars and conferences. Places of interest nearby include Burghley House, Nene Valley Railway, Elton Hall, Rutland Water and Peterborough Cathedral. **Directions:** Clearly signposted on A1 a few miles south of Stamford, on A1/A47 intersection west of Peterborough. Price Guide: Single from £75; double/twin room from £90; Four posters from £115.

50 MasterCard VISA AMERICAN EXPRESS M 250

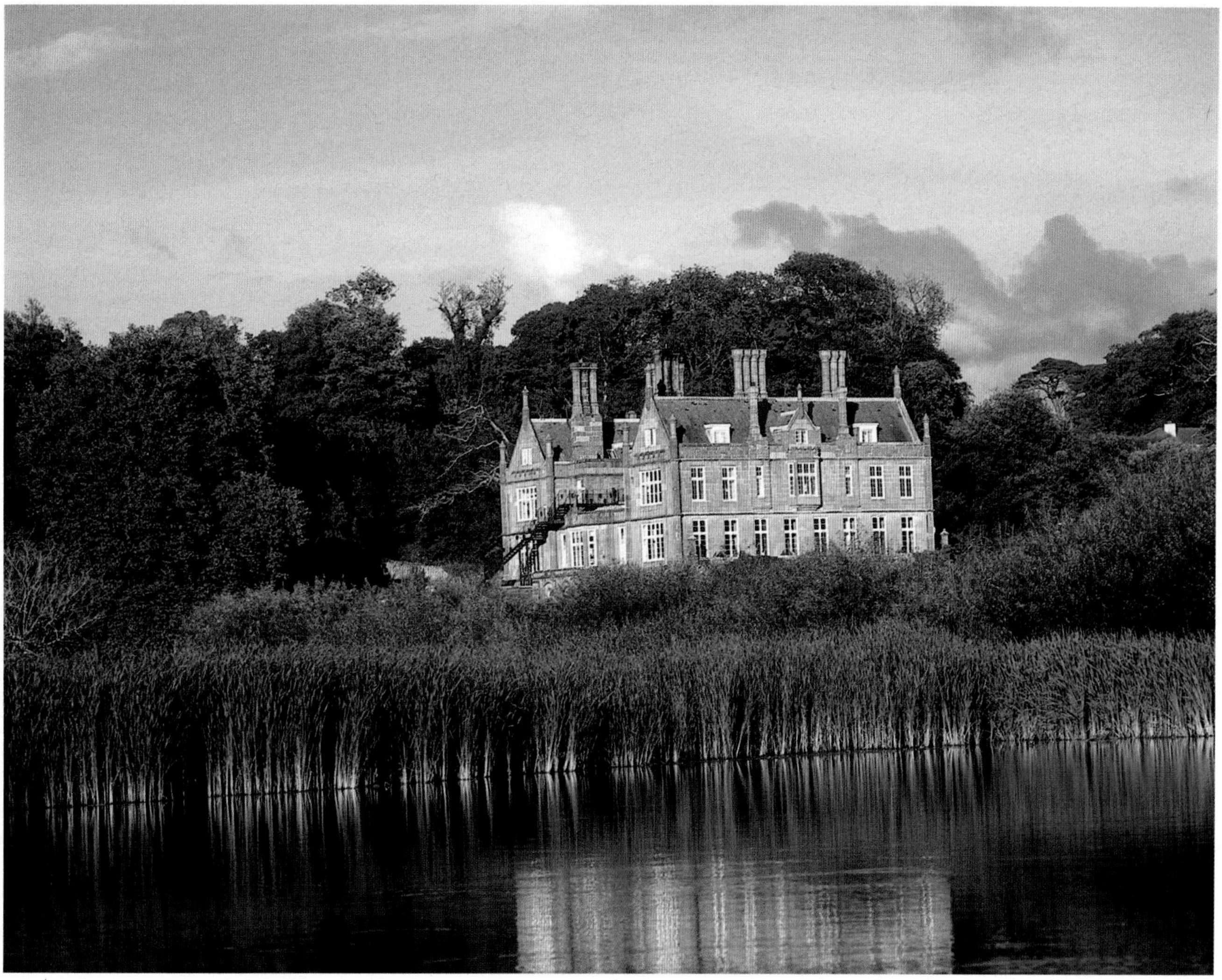

KITLEY HOUSE HOTEL & RESTAURANT

THE KITLEY ESTATE, YEALMPTON, PLYMOUTH, DEVON PL8 2NW
TEL: 01752 881555 FAX: 01752 881667 E-MAIL: sales@kitleyhousehotel.com

This imposing Grade I listed country house hotel, built of silver grey Devonshire "marble", is situated in 300 acres of richly timbered parkland at the head of one of Yealm estuary's wooded creeks, only ten minutes from the city of Plymouth. It is one of the earliest Tudor revival houses in England and has been splendidly restored to its former glory. Approached by a mile long drive through a magnificent private estate, Kitley is an oasis of quiet luxury, providing the highest standards in comfort, cuisine and personal service. A sweeping staircase leads to 20 spacious bedrooms and suites. Each has panoramic views over the estate and is richly appointed with furnishings designed to reflect the traditional elegance of the house whilst incorporating all modern facilities. The lounge area, with its huge open fireplace, and bar are stylish and relaxing. The restaurant is sumptuously decorated in burgundy and gold and provides the perfect atmosphere in which to enjoy the finest of cuisine – whatever the occasion. Guests can enjoy fishing in the private lake and golf, shooting and riding are nearby. **Directions:** A38 towards Plymouth, exit at the sign for the National Shire Horse Centre (A3121). Then turn right onto the A379. The hotel entrance is on the left after Yealmpton village. Price Guide: Single £95–£115; double/twin £110–£130; suite from £160.

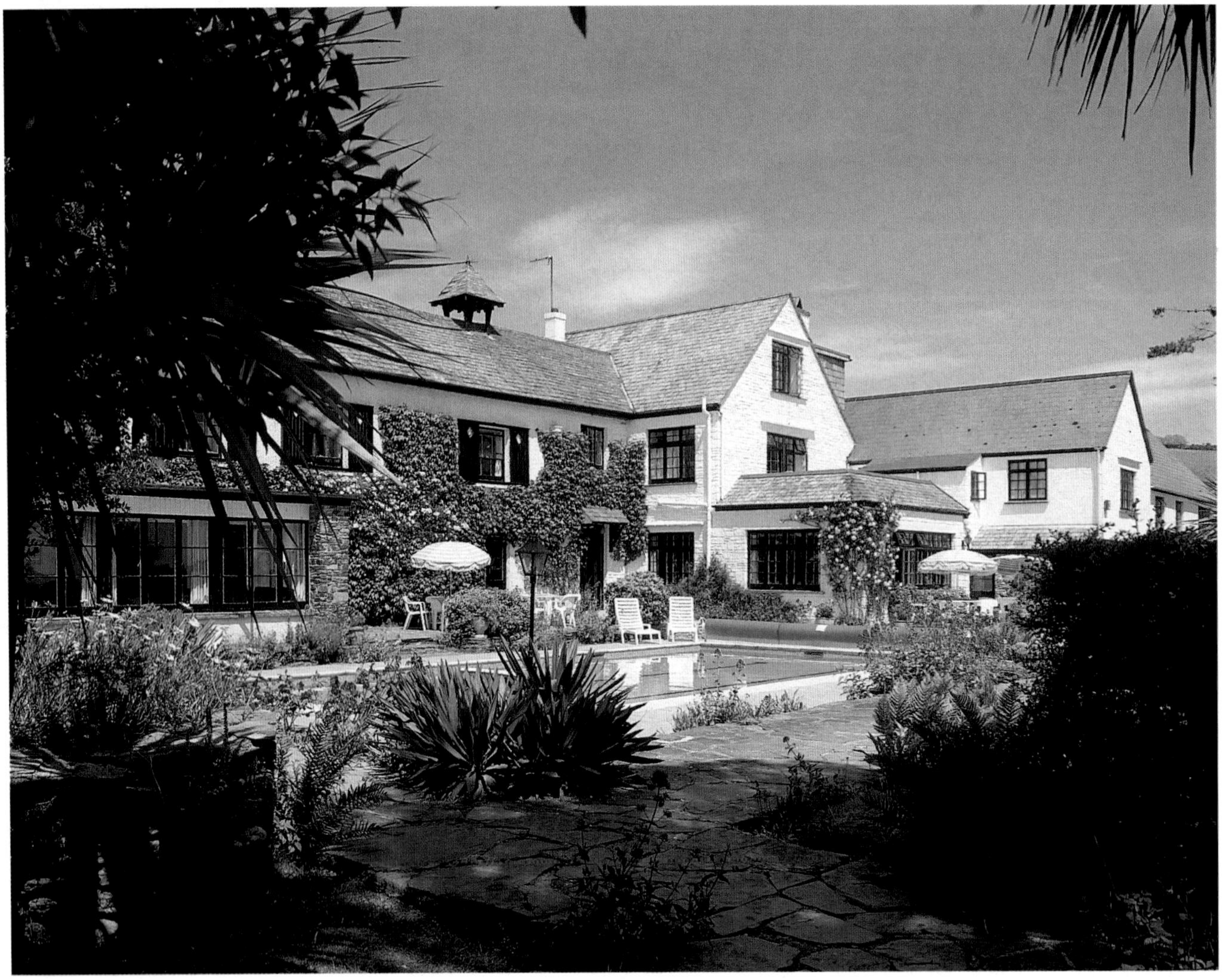

Talland Bay Hotel

TALLAND-BY-LOOE, CORNWALL PL13 2JB

TEL: 01503 272667 FAX: 01503 272940 E-MAIL: tallandbay@aol.com

This lovely old Cornish manor house, parts of which date back to the 16th century, enjoys a completely rural and unspoilt setting. Surrounded by over two acres of beautiful gardens, it offers glorious views over the dramatic headlands of Talland Bay itself. Bedrooms are individually furnished to a high standard, some having lovely sea views. Sitting rooms open to the south-facing terrace by a heated outdoor swimming pool. In keeping with the period of the house, the newly refurbished restaurant, bar and lounges are tastefully decorated. Dinner menus are imaginative and incorporate seafood from Looe, Cornish lamb and West Country cheeses. A choice of à la carte supplementary dishes changes with the seasons. Meals are complemented by a list of about 100 carefully selected wines. Leisure pursuits at the hotel include putting, croquet, table tennis, sauna, painting courses and other special interest holidays. Talland Bay is a magically peaceful spot from which to explore this part of Cornwall: there are breathtaking coastal walks at the hotel's doorstep and many National Trust houses and gardens to visit locally. This hotel provides old-fashioned comfort in beautiful surroundings at exceptionally moderate prices. Resident owners: Barry and Annie Rosier. Closed Jan–late Feb. **Directions:** The hotel is signposted from the A387 Looe–Polperro road. Price Guide: (including dinner) Single £67–£99; double/twin £134–£198.

THE LUGGER HOTEL

PORTLOE, NR TRURO, CORNWALL TR2 5RD
TEL: 01872 501322 FAX: 01872 501691 E-MAIL: office@luggerhotel.com

Set on the water's edge and sheltered on three sides by green rolling hills tumbling into the sea, this lovely little former inn is as picturesque as any you will come across. Reputedly the haunt of 17th-century smugglers The Lugger Hotel overlooks a tiny working harbour in the scenic village of Portloe on the unspoilt Roseland Peninsula. It is a conservation area of outstanding beauty and an idyllic location in which to escape the stresses of today's hectic world. Seaward views from the hotel are stunning and reaching out from each side are lovely coastal paths leading to secluded coves. Welcoming owners Sheryl and Richard Young have created an atmosphere of total comfort and relaxation whilst retaining a historic ambience. The 23 bedrooms have every amenity; each is en suite, tastefully decorated and furnished, whilst some are situated across an attractive courtyard. A great variety of dishes and innovative dinner menus are offered in the restaurant overlooking the harbour. Local seafood is a specialty with crab and lobster being particular favourites. For beach lovers, the sandy stretches of Pendower and Carne are within easy reach, as are many National Trust properties and gardens, including the Lost Gardens of Heligan and the Eden project. **Directions:** Turn off A390 St Austell to Truro onto B3287 Tregony. Then take A3048 signed St Mawes, after 2 miles take left fork following signs for Portloe. Price Guide: (including dinner) Single £185; double/twin £250.

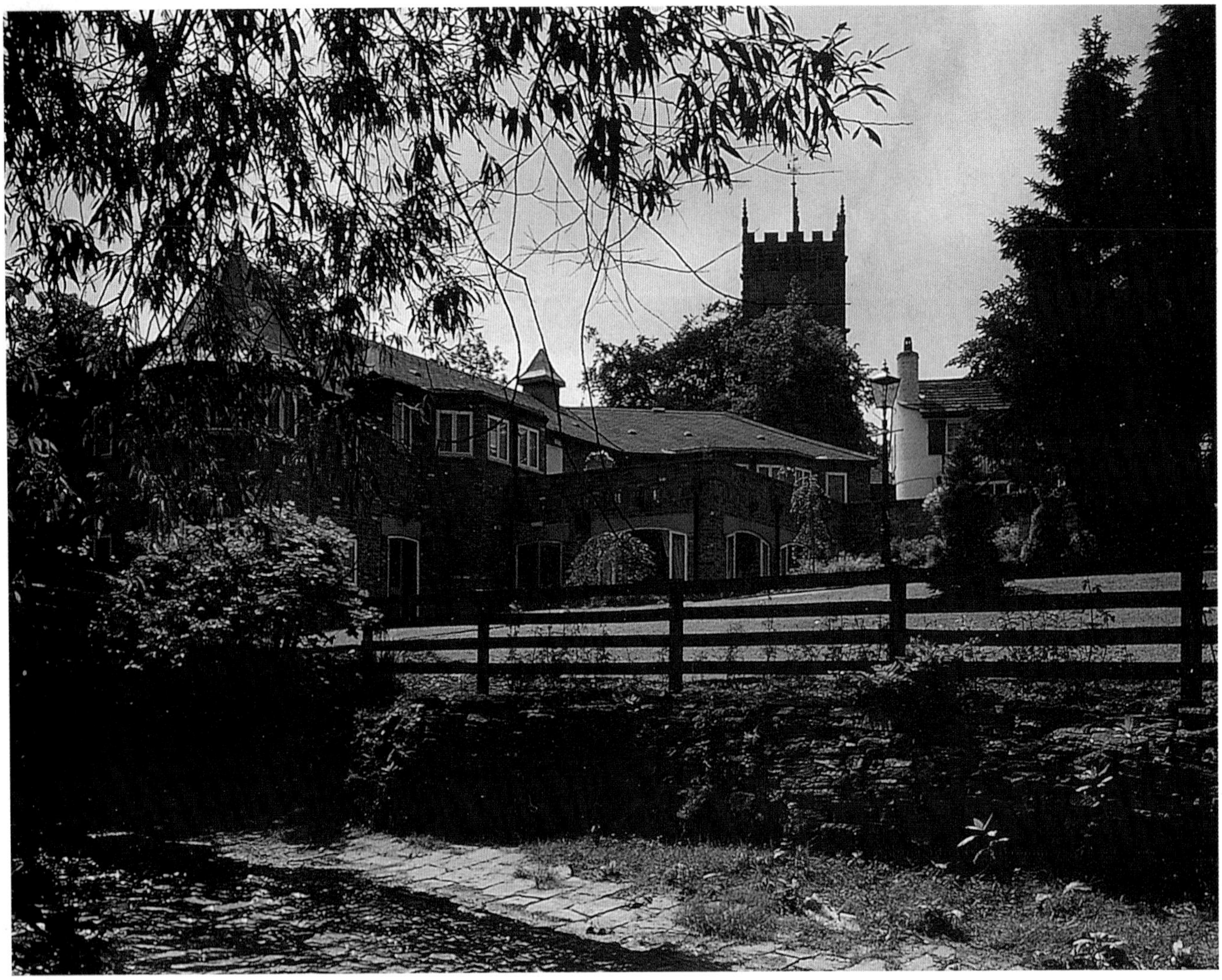

THE BRIDGE HOTEL

PRESTBURY, MACCLESFIELD, CHESHIRE SK10 4DQ
TEL: 01625 829326 FAX: 01625 827557 E-MAIL: reception@bridge–hotel.co.uk

The Bridge Hotel is situated in the centre of the village of Prestbury, one of the prettiest villages in the North West of England. Originally dating from 1626, The Bridge today combines the old world charm of an ancient and historic building with the comfort and facilities of a modern hotel, yet within easy reach of Manchester Airport and major motorways. The public rooms have retained much of the former inn's original character, with oak panelling and beams in the bar and reception area. The bedrooms, many of which overlook the River Bollin, are decorated to a high standard, five of which are in the original building. In the attractive galleried dining room, table d'hôte and à la carte menus offer traditional English cuisine. There is an extensive selection of wines to accompany your meal. It is also the perfect place for business with three conference suites. While enjoying a quiet location, the hotel is convenient for Manchester, just 30 minutes away and Manchester Airport only 15 minutes away. The Peak District National Park and Cheshire are nearby with Stately Homes including Chatsworth, Tatton Park and Capesthorne. **Directions:** In the centre of the village next to the church. Prestbury is on the A538 from Wilmslow to Macclesfield. Price Guide: Single £94–£100; double/twin £112–£125; suite £130. Special weekend rates available.

23 MasterCard VISA AMERICAN EXPRESS M 100

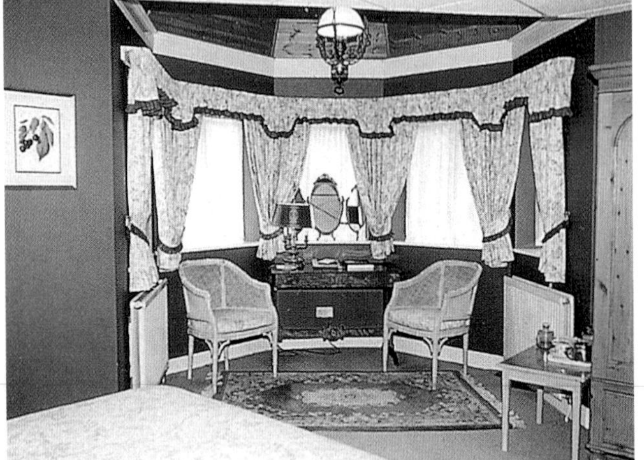

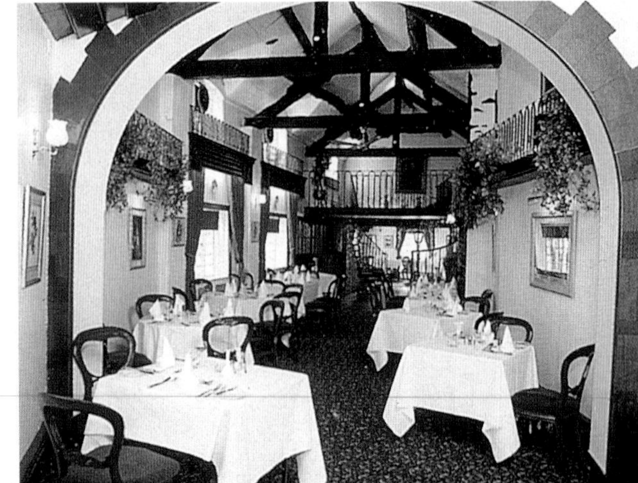

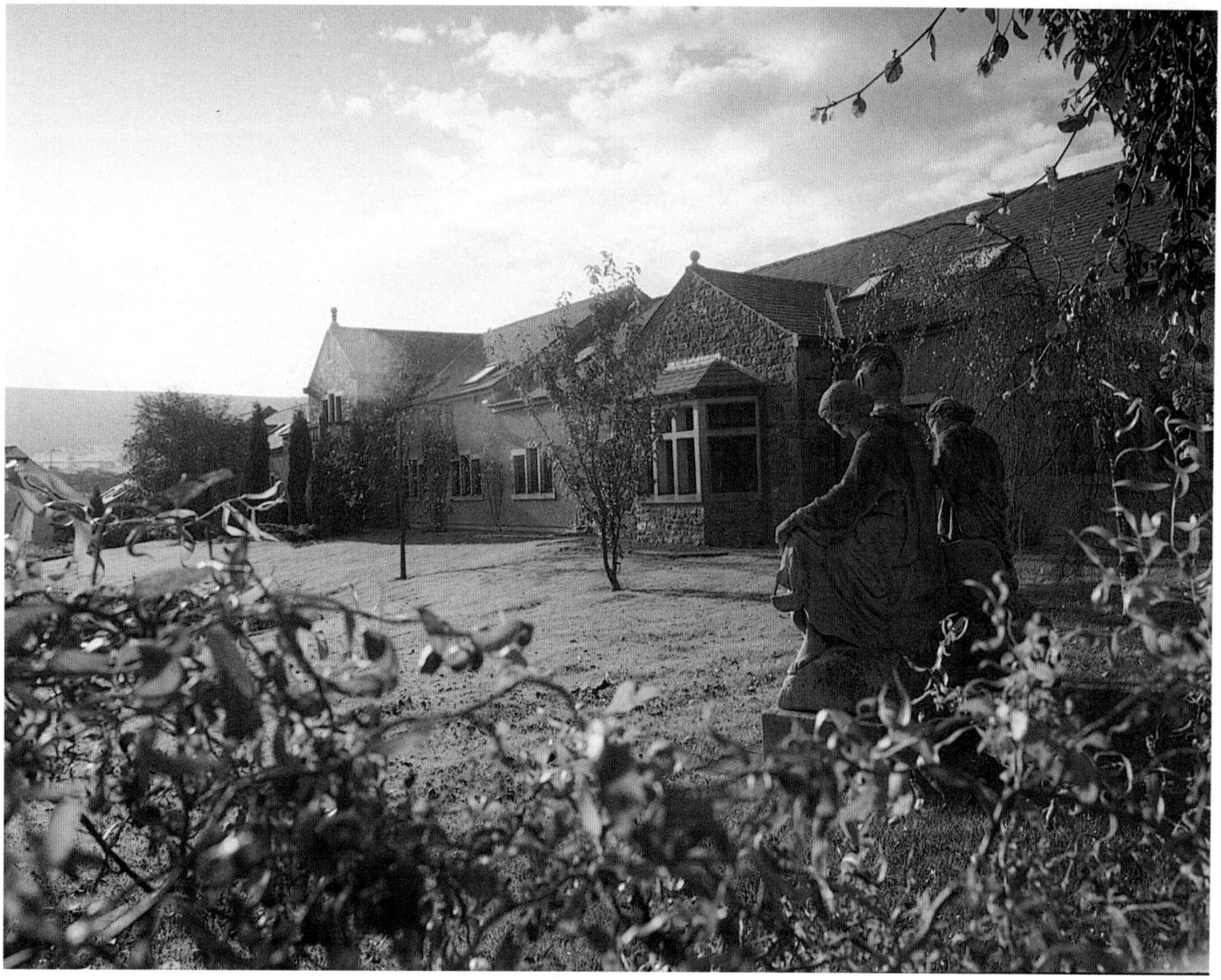

THE GIBBON BRIDGE HOTEL

NR CHIPPING, FOREST OF BOWLAND, LANCASHIRE PR3 2TQ

TEL: 01995 61456 FAX: 01995 61277 E-MAIL: reception@gibbon–bridge.co.uk

This award-winning hotel in the heart of Lancashire in the Forest of Bowland is a welcoming and peaceful retreat. The area, a favourite of the Queen, is now officially recognised as the centre of the Kingdom! Created in 1982 by resident proprietor Janet Simpson and her late Mother Margaret, the buildings combine traditional architecture with interesting Gothic masonry. Individually designed and equipped to the highest standard, the seven bedrooms and 22 suites include four-posters, half-testers, Gothic brass beds and whirlpool baths. The restaurant overlooks the garden and is renowned for traditional and imaginative dishes incorporating home-grown vegetables and herbs. The garden bandstand is perfect for musical repertoires or civil wedding ceremonies. Elegant rooms and lounges are available for private dinner parties and wedding receptions. For executive meetings and conference facilities the hotel will offer that 'something a bit different'. Leisure facilities include beauty salon, gymnasium, solarium, steam room, all-weather tennis court and outdoor activities. **Directions:** From the south: M6 Exit 31A, follow signs for Longridge. From the north: M6 Exit 32, follow A6 to Broughton and B5269 to Longridge; follow signs for Chipping. In the village turn right at T-junction; hotel is 3⁄4 miles on the right. Price Guide: Single £70–£110; double/twin £100–£160; suites £130–£275.

NUTFIELD PRIORY

NUTFIELD, REDHILL, SURREY RH1 4EN
TEL: 01737 824400 FAX: 01737 823321 E-MAIL: nutfield@arcadianhotels.co.uk

Built in 1872 by the millionaire MP, Joshua Fielden, Nutfield Priory is an extravagant folly embellished with towers, elaborate carvings, intricate stonework, cloisters and stained glass, all superbly restored to create an unusual country house hotel. Set high on Nutfield Ridge, the priory has far-reaching views over the Surrey and Sussex countryside, while being within easy reach of London and also Gatwick Airport. The elegant lounges and library have ornately carved ceilings and antique furnishings. Unusually spacious bedrooms – some with beams – enjoy views over the surrounding countryside. Fresh fruit is a thoughtful extra. The Cloisters Restaurant provides a unique environment in which to enjoy the high standard of cuisine, complemented by an extensive wine list. Conferences and private functions can be accommodated in the splendid setting of one of the hotel's 10 conference rooms. The Priory Health and Leisure Club, adjacent to the hotel, provides all the facilities for exercise and relaxation that one could wish for, including a swimming pool, sauna, spa, solarium, gym, steam room, beauty & hairdressing. **Directions:** Nutfield is on the A25 between Redhill and Godstone and can be reached easily from junctions 6 and 8 of the M25. From Godstone, the Priory is on the left just after the village. Price Guide: Single from £105; double/twin £135–£165; suite £195–£255.

60 MasterCard VISA AMERICAN EXPRESS M 100

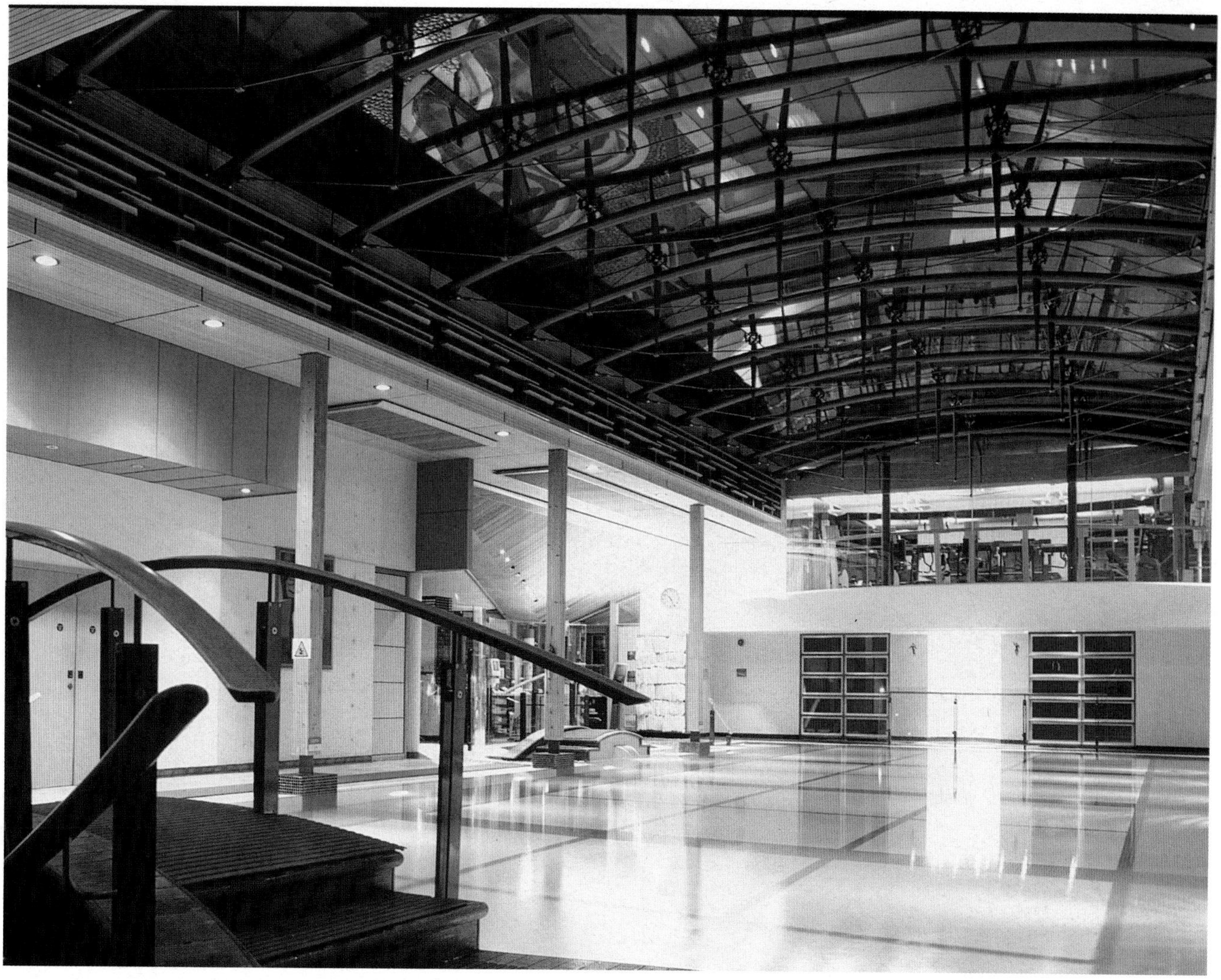

THE RICHMOND GATE HOTEL AND RESTAURANT

RICHMOND HILL, RICHMOND-UPON-THAMES, SURREY TW10 6RP
TEL: 020 8940 0061 FAX: 020 8332 0354 E-MAIL: richmondgate@corushotels.com

This former Georgian country house stands on the crest of Richmond Hill close to the Royal Park and Richmond Terrace with its commanding views over the River Thames. The 68 stylishly furnished en suite bedrooms combine every comfort of the present with the elegance of the past and include several luxury four-poster rooms and suites. Exceptional and imaginative cuisine, complemented by an extensive wine list offering over 100 wines from around the world is served in the sophisticated surroundings of 'Gates On The Park Restaurant'. Weddings, business meetings and private dining events can be arranged in a variety of rooms. The beautiful victorian walled garden provides for summer relaxation. Cedars Health and Leisure Club is accessed through the hotel and includes a 20 metre pool, 6 metre spa, sauna, steam room, aerobics studio, cardiovascular and resistance gymnasia and a health and beauty suite. Richmond is close to London and the West End yet in a country setting. The Borough offers a wealth of visitor attractions, including Hampton Court Palace, Syon House and Park and the Royal Botanic Gardens at Kew. **Directions:** Opposite the Star & Garter Home at the top of Richmond Hill. Price Guide: Single from £120; double/twin from £150; suite from £225.

SWINTON PARK

MASHAM, NR RIPON, NORTH YORKSHIRE HG4 4JH
TEL: 01765 680900 FAX: 01765 680901

Swinton Park with its battlement-topped turrets and a round tower coloured green with climbing ivy, is a Grade II* listed 'castle' dating from the late 1600s. The heart of the building is essentially Regency style, but heavily disguised by the Victorians with the addition of turrets and castellations. Sold by the Earl of Swinton in 1980, but recently bought back by the family and extensively refurbished, it is a luxurious hotel with every comfort and up-to-date facility. Rising picturesquely against the skyline, it is set in 200 acres of deer-stocked parkland and formal gardens surrounded by a 2,000-acre family estate ½ mile from the market town of Masham. The ground floor rooms enjoy sweeping views over the parkland, lake and gatehouse and are all furnished with antiques and family portraits. The guest rooms sharing the first and second floors are individually designed on the theme of a Yorkshire town, dale, castle, abbey or garden. Three are suites and the turret room is on two floors with a wonderful free standing rain bath. Superb British cuisine is served in an elegant dining room which features a gold leaf ceiling and sumptuous décor. Guests can enjoy country pursuits and golf, mountain biking, off roading and model boat racing. There is a spa in the hotel's conservatory. **Directions:** Masham is off A6108 between Leyburn and Ripon. Price Guide: Single £95–£250; double/twin £95–£250; suites £300–£350.

20 MasterCard VISA AMERICAN EXPRESS M 120

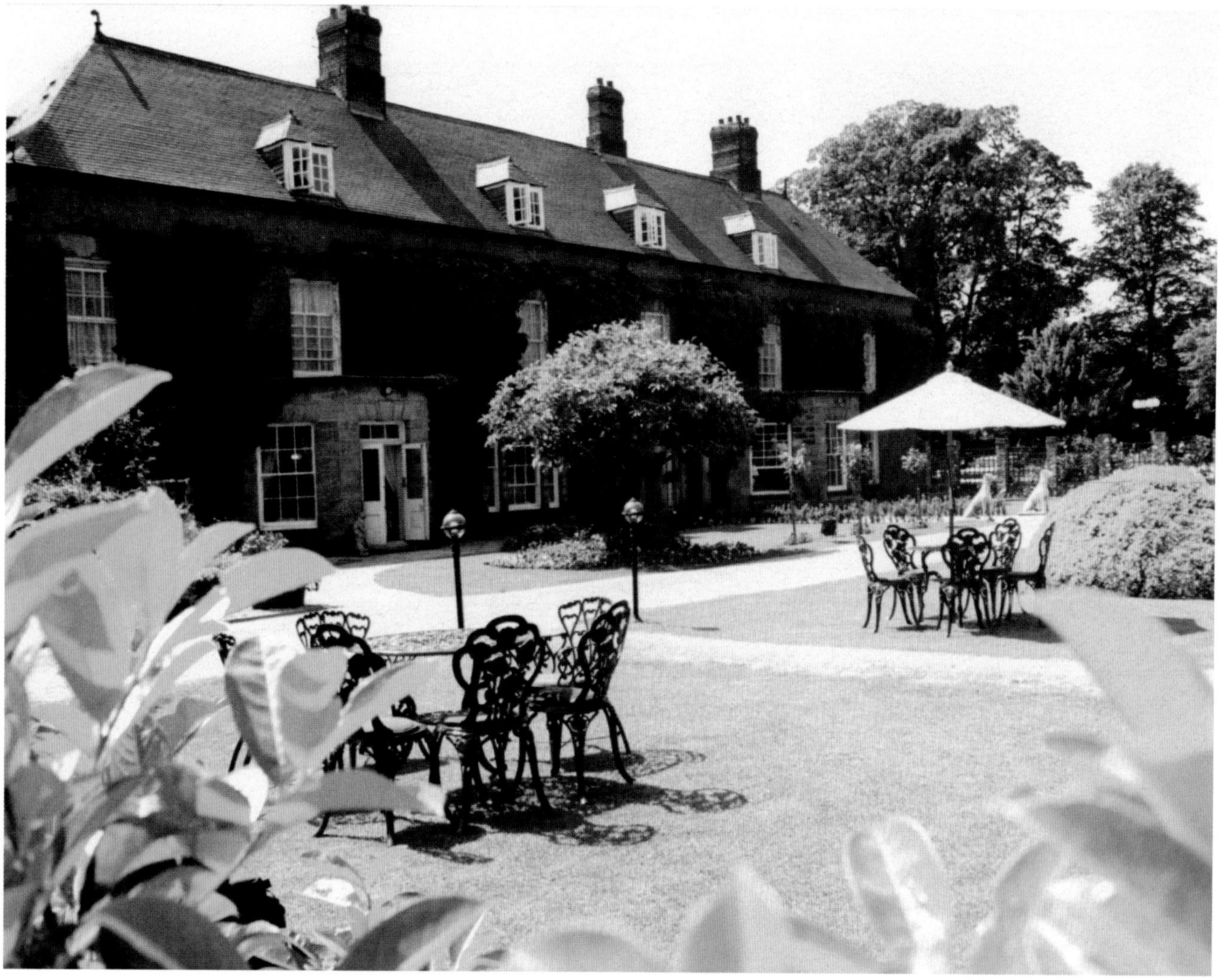

RISLEY HALL COUNTRY HOUSE HOTEL

DERBY ROAD, RISLEY, DERBYSHIRE DE72 3SS
TEL: 0115 939 9000 FAX: 0115 939 7766 E-MAIL: johansens@risleyhallhotel.co.uk

The former glory of Risley Hall is evident once more as this country house hotel has recently undergone a careful and extensive restoration. A grade II listed building, Risley Hall Country House Hotel is an ideal retreat for those seeking a peaceful atmosphere. The beautiful gardens were laid out in Elizabethan times and are quite spectacular with colourful floral arrangements and an old moat. Inside, the décor is rather charming with comfortable furnishings, oak beams and ornate fireplaces. The bedrooms, individually designed and all tastefully decorated in period style, offer every modern amenity including a television, hairdryer and tea/coffee making facilities. Guests recline in the cosy Drawing Room with their afternoon tea or enjoy an after dinner coffee, whilst the Cocktail Lounge serves lunchtime drinks or pre-dinner apéritifs. Within close proximity of junction 25 of the M1 midway between Nottingham and Derby, Risley Hall has the perfect surroundings for corporate meetings or any special occasions. The area is surrounded by historic buildings such as Chatsworth House, Nottingham Castle and Kedleston Hall and is also known for its literary connections with Lord Byron and DH Lawrence. **Directions:** The nearest motorway is the M1. Exit at junction 25 towards Sandiacre. Price Guide: Single £85–£105; double/twin £105–£125.

The Chase Hotel

GLOUCESTER ROAD, ROSS-ON-WYE, HEREFORDSHIRE HR9 5LH
TEL: 01989 763161 FAX: 01989 768330 E-MAIL: info@chasehotel.co.uk

The Chase Hotel, just a few minutes' walk from the historic market town of Ross-on-Wye, is a handsome Georgian Country House Hotel situated in 11 acres of beautiful grounds and landscape gardens. The 36 en suite bedrooms contain all the latest amenities, including satellite television. The bedrooms and lounge areas, preserve the original Georgian style of the Hotel. Guests wishing to relax will enjoy the convivial ambience and comfortable décor in the Chase Lounge and Bar. Overlooking Chase Hill, the tall elegant windows of the Lounge expose the splendour of the surrounding landscape. The delightful Chase Restaurant, with its delicate peach furnishings, is renowned for its superb traditional cuisine and excellent service and has won several accolades and awards including an AA Rosette. The hotel is an ideal venue for conferences, exhibitions, training activities, weddings including civil ceremonies and events for up to 300 guests. Activities within the locality include water sports, theatre, countryside rambles, fascinating antique centres or perusing the shops in either the historic city of Hereford or Regency Cheltenham. **Directions:** From the M50 (Jct4) turn left for Ross-on-Wye, take A40 Gloucester at the second roundabout and turn right for town centre at third roundabout. The Hotel is ½ mile on the left. Price Guide: Single £65–£105; double/twin £80–£120; suite £140.

36 MasterCard VISA AMERICAN EXPRESS M 300

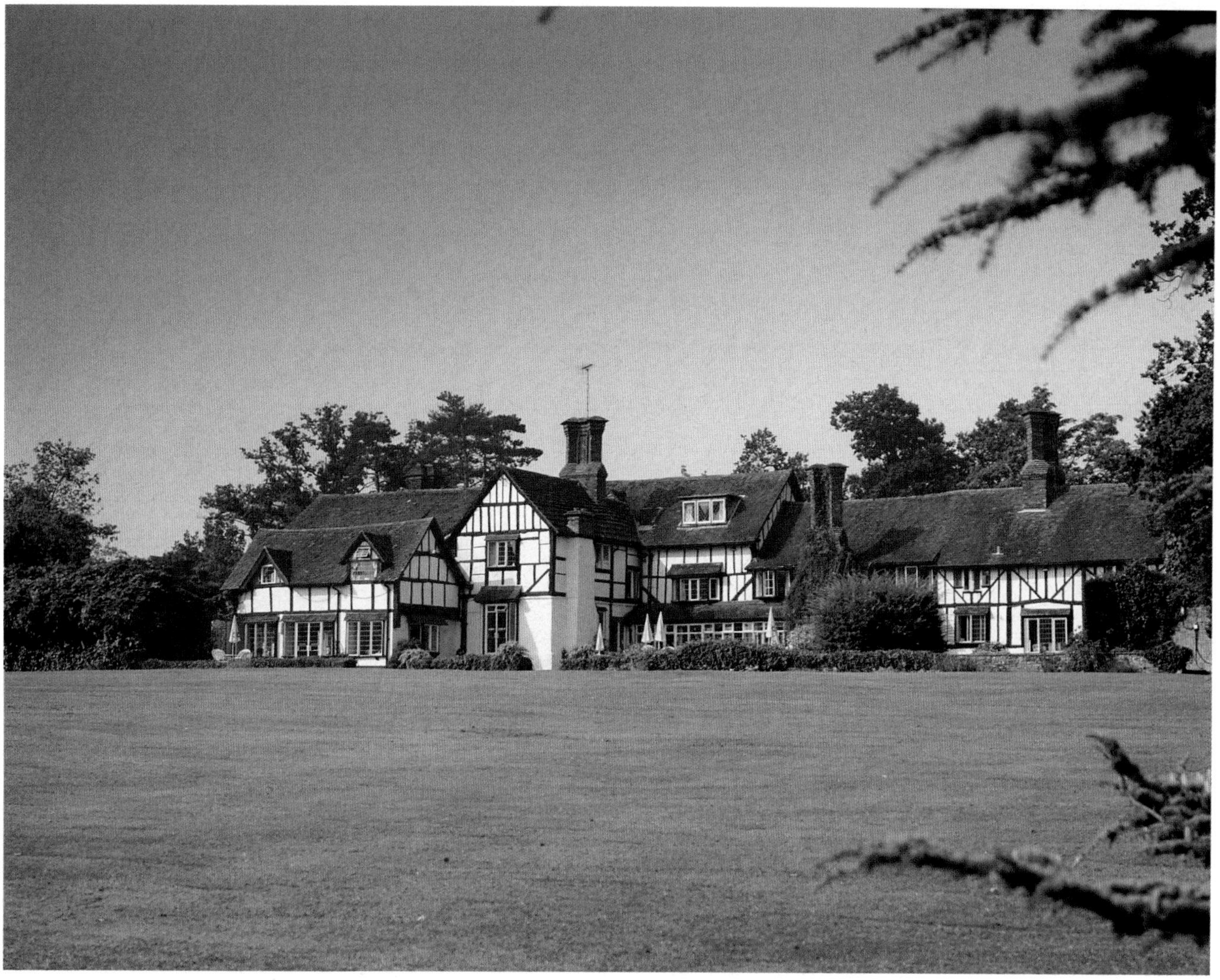

Ghyll Manor Country Hotel

HIGH STREET, RUSPER, NEAR HORSHAM, WEST SUSSEX RH12 4PX
TEL: 01293 871571 FAX: 01293 871419 E-MAIL: patbarksby@csma.uk.com

Ghyll Manor Country Hotel dates back to the 17th century and was once the family home of Sir Geoffrey and Lady Kitchen. The manor house and stable mews were converted in the early 1980's and still retain many of the original features such as beamed ceilings and charming log fires. Over the recent years the hotel has undergone an extensive restoration, resulting in a splendid hotel with excellent facilities. Guests have the choice of staying in the house itself, the Stable Mews complex or in seven delightful self-contained cottages. Attractive covered walkways connect the cottages and the complex to the main house. All the 29 bedrooms have been individually furnished and have en suite facilities. A relaxing atmosphere may be found in the library lounge and orangery, whilst those wishing to relax outdoors will enjoy the open terraces overlooking the beautiful grounds and lakes. The award-winning Benedictine Restaurant serves fine cuisine and is renowned for its excellent Sunday lunches. The tennis court and croquet lawn are on site whilst golf and riding can be arranged nearby. Ghyll Manor is an ideal location for those wishing to discover Sussex and Surrey and is in an area surrounded by National Trust houses and famous gardens such as Nymans **Directions:** Leave M23 at junction 11 and follow A264 to Horsham. Turn off at roundabout signed Faygate and Rusper Price Guide: Single £117; double/twin £139–£166.

Barnsdale Lodge

THE AVENUE, RUTLAND WATER, NR OAKHAM, RUTLAND, LEICESTERSHIRE LE15 8AH
TEL: 01572 724678 FAX: 01572 724961 E-MAIL: barnsdale.lodge@btconnect.com

Situated in the ancient county of Rutland, amid unspoiled countryside, Barnsdale Lodge overlooks the rippling expanse of Rutland Water. After nine years, the expansion is finally complete and guests are invited to enjoy the hospitality offered by hosts The Hon. Thomas Noel and Robert Reid. A restored 17th century farmhouse, the atmosphere and style are distinctively Edwardian. This theme pervades throughout, from the courteous service to the furnishings, including chaises-longues and plush, upholstered chairs. The 45 en suite bedrooms, mostly on the ground floor, including two superb rooms specifically designed for disabled guests, evoke a mood of relaxing comfort. Traditional English cooking and fine wines are served. The chef makes all the pastries and cakes as well as preserves. Elevenses, buttery lunches, afternoon teas and suppers are enjoyed in the garden, conservatory, courtyard and à la carte dining rooms. There are 5 conference rooms and facilities for wedding receptions and parties. Interconnecting bedrooms, a baby-listening service and safe play area are provided for children. Robert Reid has strived to maintain the friendly intimacy of the lodge and is often on hand, offering advice and suggestions. Belvoir and Rockingham Castles are nearby. Rutland Water, a haven for nature lovers, offers several water sports. **Directions:** The Lodge is on A606 Oakham–Stamford road. Price Guide: Single £69; double/twin £89; junior suite £109.50.

Rose-In-Vale Country House Hotel

MITHIAN, ST AGNES, CORNWALL TR5 0QD
TEL: 01872 552202 FAX: 01872 552700 E-MAIL: reception@rose–in–vale–hotel.co.uk

This 18th-century Cornish manor house, hiding in 11 acres of glorious gardens, woodland and pasture in a wooded valley of great natural beauty, successfully blends the old with the new. There is a sense of timelessness: a world apart from the bustle of modern living. Tasteful floral décor contrasts with dark mahogany throughout the elegant public rooms and pretty bedrooms, many of which have outstanding views across the valley gardens. Three ground floor rooms have level access. The Rose Suite and Master Rooms feature four-poster/half-tester beds. Chef Phillip Sims serves imaginative, international cuisine and speciality Cornish Crab/Lobster dishes in the "Opie's Room" where sweeping, softly-draped bay windows overlook lawns and flower-beds. The gardens feature ponds with a collection of waterfowl, a secluded, heated swimming pool, croquet, badminton, dovecote and summer house. There is a solarium, sauna and games room, and massage, aromatherapy and reflexology can be arranged. National Trust properties abound and special walks are available. Six golf courses, The Eden Project, The Glorious Gardens of Cornwall, riding, fishing, gliding, swimming and water sports are all close by. Extensive refurbishment has been carried out this year; now some rooms have coronet king-sized beds. **Directions:** A30 through Cornwall. Two miles beyond Zelah turn right onto B3284. Cross A3075 and take third left turn signposted Rose-in-Vale. Price Guide: Single £50–£66; double/twin £110–£132; suite £155.

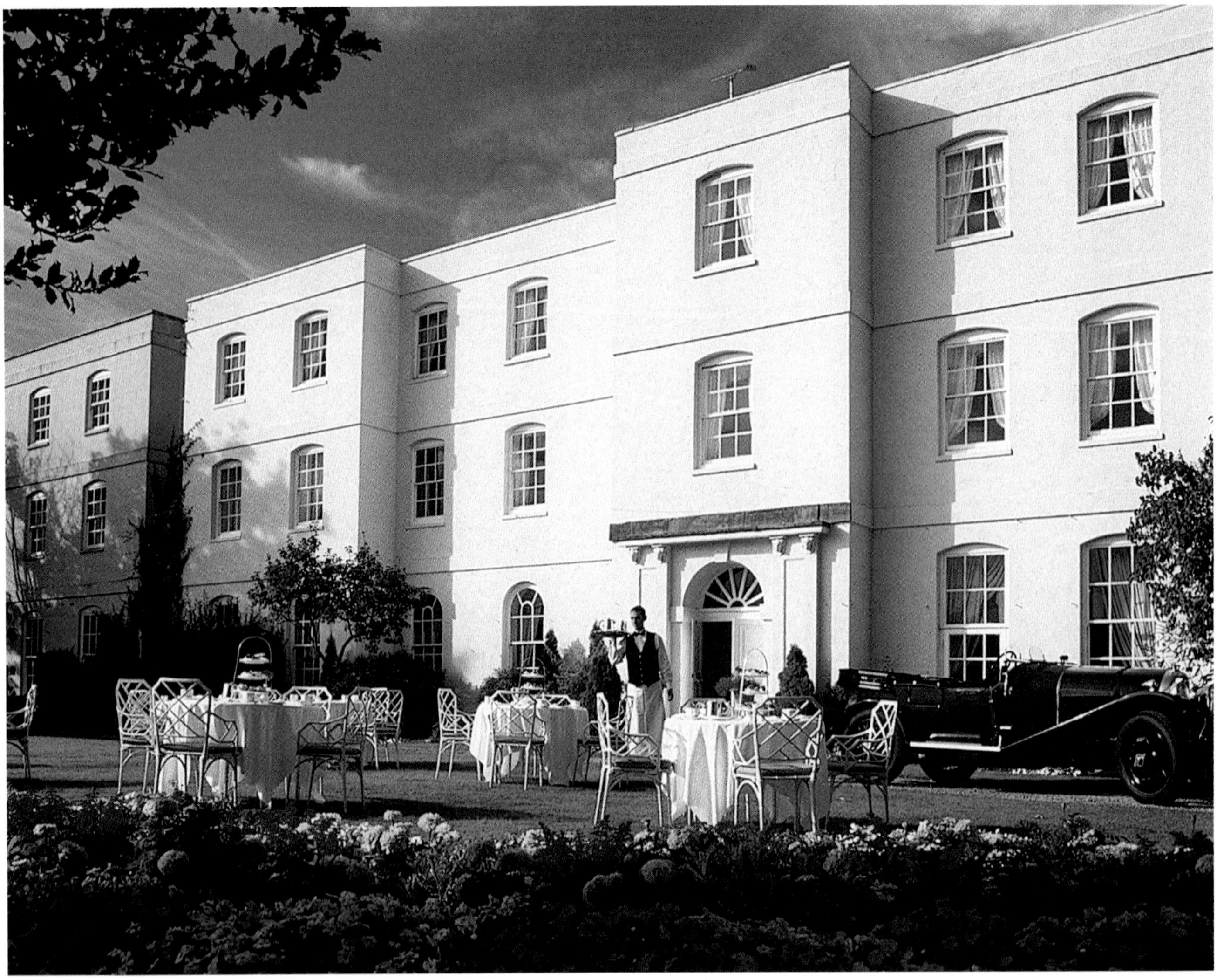

SOPWELL HOUSE HOTEL, COUNTRY CLUB & SPA

COTTONMILL LANE, SOPWELL, ST ALBANS, HERTFORDSHIRE AL1 2HQ
TEL: 01727 864477 FAX: 01727 844741/845636 E-MAIL: equiries@sopwellhouse.co.uk

Once the country home of Lord Mountbatten, surrounded by a peaceful and verdant 12-acre estate, Sopwell House is an oasis just minutes away from the motorways. The classical reception rooms reflect its illustrious past and the grand panelled ballroom opens out onto the terraces and gardens. The bedrooms, many with four-posters, are spacious and well-equipped. Superb English cuisine and fine wines are served in the enchanting Magnolia Restaurant amidst the trees after which it is named, whilst Bejerano's Brasserie offers an informal ambience. Beautifully designed Mews Suites are ideal for long-stay executives and bridal parties. These are complemented by the conference and banqueting suites, overlooking the splendid gardens and terrace, which are popular venues for weddings and special events. The Business Centre provides guests with facilities such as photocopier, fax and e-mail. The Country Club & Spa, dedicated to health and relaxation, has a full range of fitness facilities and highly qualified beauty therapists. **Directions:** Close to M25, M1, M10, M11 & A1(M). 22m from Heathrow. From A414 take A1081 to St Albans. Turn left at Grillbar. Cross mini-roundabout. Hotel is ¼m on left. Price Guide: Single £85–£125; double/twin £120–£165; suites from £175. Breakfast: Full English £12.50, continental £10.50.

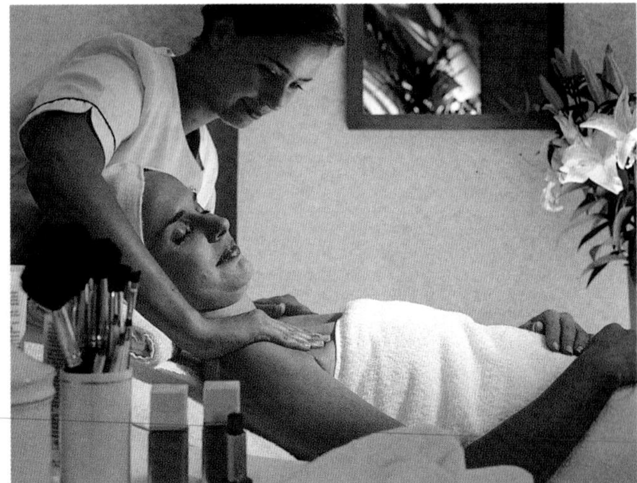

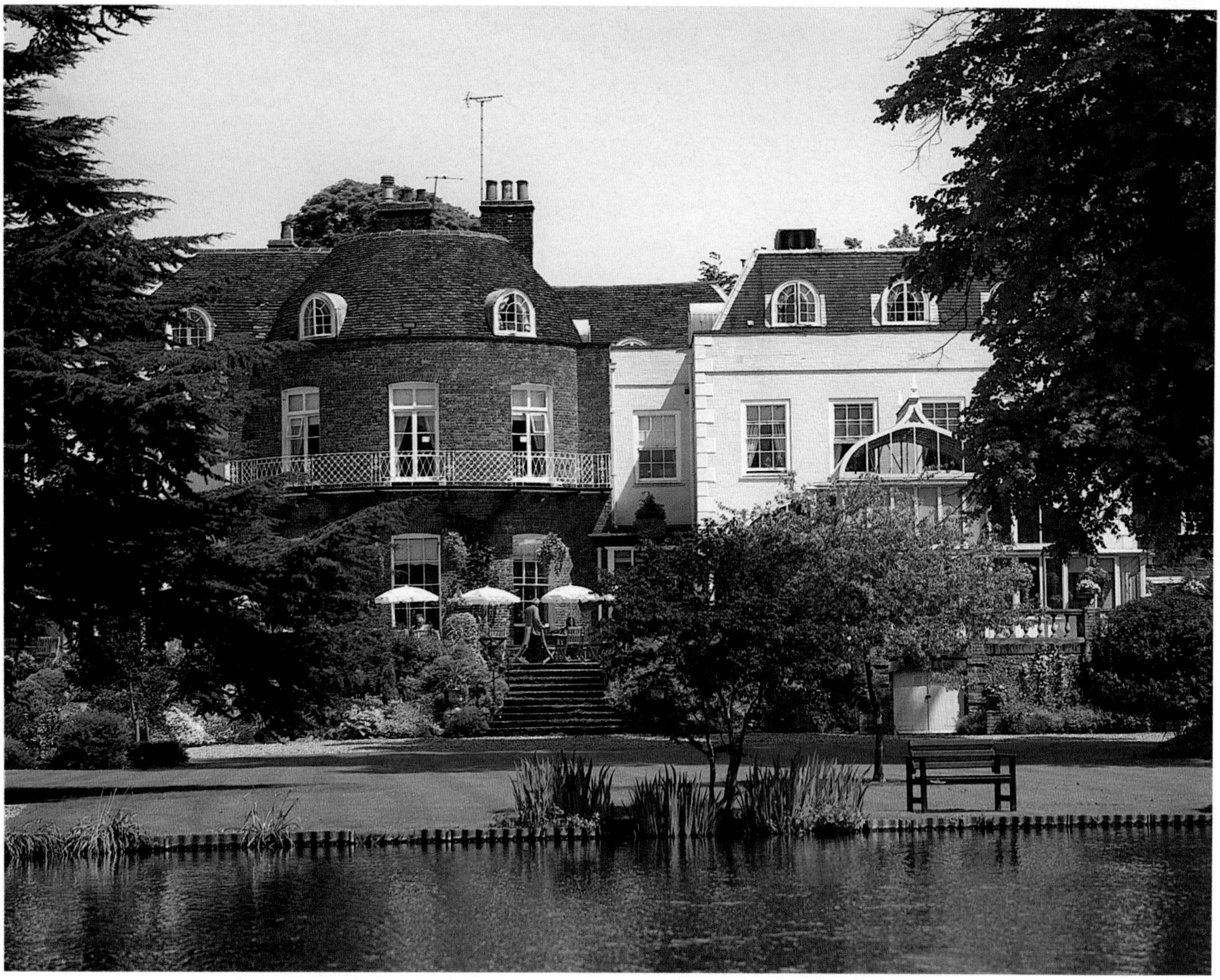

St Michael's Manor

ST MICHAEL'S VILLAGE, FISHPOOL STREET, ST ALBANS, HERTFORDSHIRE AL3 4RY
TEL: 01727 864444 FAX: 01727 848909 E-MAIL: smmanor@globalnet.co.uk

Owned and run by the Newling Ward family for the past thirty-five years, St Michael's Manor is a rare gem – peaceful, intimate, and set in delightful landscaped grounds. It is also within the historic village of St Michael's and a stone's throw from the magnificent St Albans Abbey. Each of the 23 bedrooms has been individually designed – some have four-poster beds and some are sitting-room suites – and all have an elegance and charm. Many of the bedrooms overlook the award-winning grounds, set in five acres, with wide sweeping lawns and a beautiful lake that hosts a variety of wildlife. The Georgian lounge and the award-winning conservatory dining room also overlook the gardens and make a wonderful setting for a tantalising dinner. There is also an excellent variety of vegetarian dishes. Coffee may be served in the Oak Lounge, which dates from 1586, with its fine panelled walls and original Elizabethan ceiling. Hatfield House and the Roman remains of Verulamium are within easy reach, as is London, which is only twenty minutes away by train **Directions:** Easy access to M1 Junction 6/7, M25 Junction 21a 10 minutes, M4/M40 25 minutes, Luton airport 20 minutes. Price Guide: Single £125–£195; double/twin £160–£260; suites £245–£320.

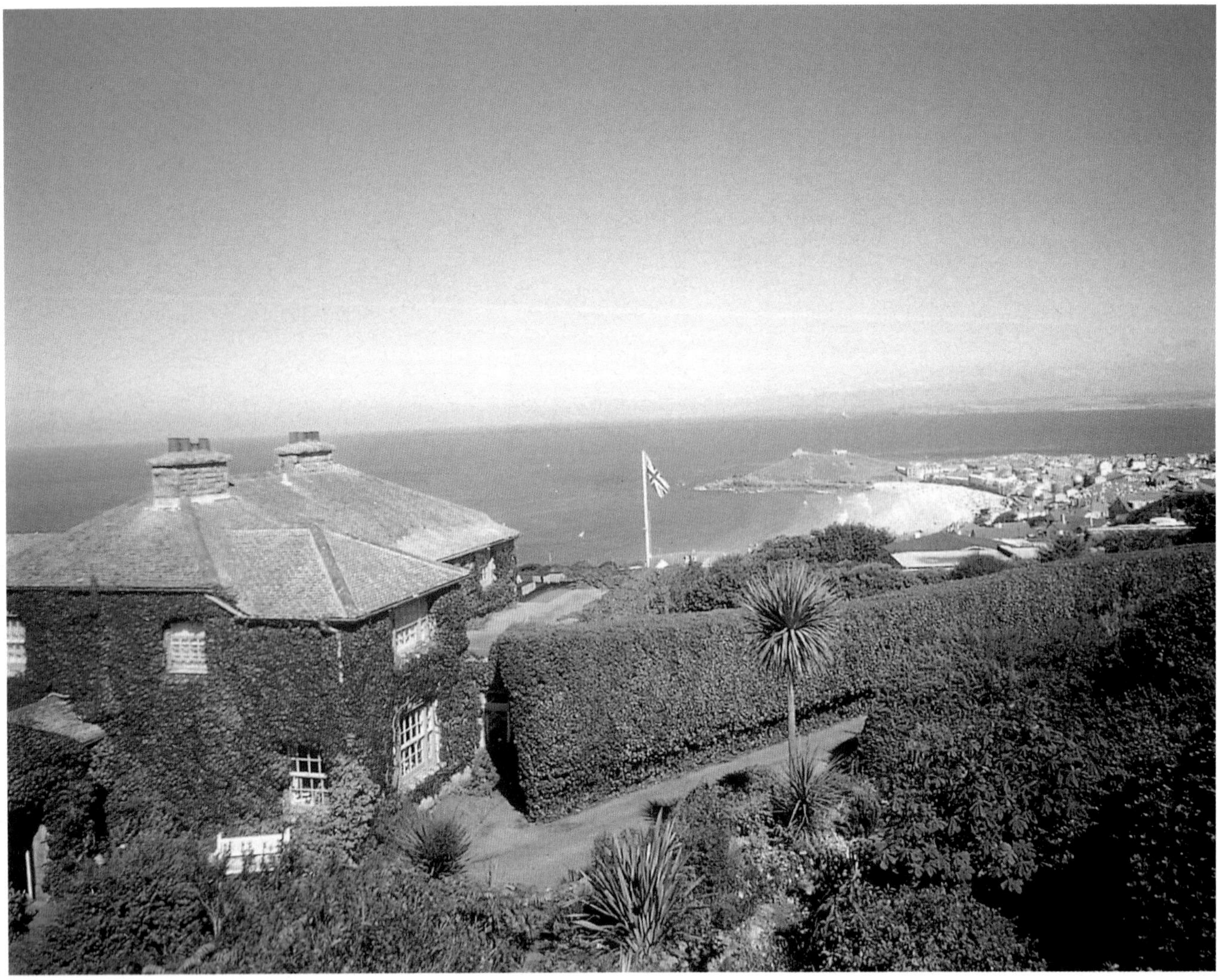

THE GARRACK HOTEL & RESTAURANT

BURTHALLAN LANE, ST IVES, CORNWALL TR26 3AA

TEL: 01736 796199 FAX: 01736 798955 FREEPHONE: 08000 197 393 E-MAIL: garrack@accuk.co.uk

This family-run hotel, secluded and full of character, ideal for a family holiday, is set in two acres of gardens with fabulous sea views over Porthmeor Beach, the St Ives Tate Gallery and the old town of St Ives. The bedrooms in the original house are in keeping with the style of the building. The additional rooms are modern in design. All rooms have private bathrooms and baby-listening facilities. Superior rooms have either four-poster beds or whirlpool baths. A ground-floor room has been fitted for guests with disabilities. Visitors return year after year to enjoy informal yet professional service, good food and hospitality. The restaurant specialises in seafood especially fresh lobsters. The wine list includes over 70 labels from ten regions. The lounges have books, magazines and board games for all and open fires. The small attractive leisure centre contains a small swimming pool with integral spa, sauna, solarium and fitness area. The hotel has its own car park. Porthmeor Beach, just below the hotel, is renowned for surfing. Riding, golf, bowls, sea-fishing and other activities can be enjoyed locally. St Ives, with its harbour, is famous for artists and for the new St Ives Tate Gallery. Dogs by prior arrangement. Directions: A30–A3074–B3311–B3306. Go ½ mile, turn left at mini-roundabout, hotel signs are on the left as the road starts down hill. Price Guide: Single £64–£67; double/twin £108–£168.

THE WELL HOUSE

ST KEYNE, LISKEARD, CORNWALL PL14 4RN
TEL: 01579 342001 FAX: 01579 343891 E-MAIL: enquiries@wellhouse.co.uk

The West Country is one corner of England where hospitality and friendliness are at their most spontaneous and nowhere more so than at The Well House, just beyond the River Tamar. New arrivals are entranced by their first view of this lovely Victorian country manor. Its façade wrapped in rambling wisteria and jasmine trailers is just one of a continuous series of delights including top-quality service, modern luxury and impeccable standards of comfort and cooking. The hotel is professionally managed by proprietor Nick Wainford and General Manager Denise Manning, whose attention to every smallest detail has earned his hotel numerous awards, among them the AA 2 Red Stars. From the tastefully appointed bedrooms there are fine rural views and each private bathroom offers luxurious bath linen, soaps and gels by Neutrogena. Continental breakfast is served in bed – or a traditional English breakfast may be taken in the dining room. Chef Matthew Corner selects fresh, seasonal produce to create his superbly balanced and presented cuisine. Tennis and swimming are on site and the Cornish coastline offers matchless scenery for walks.The Eden Project is a short drive away. **Directions:** Leave A38 at Liskeard, take A390 to town centre, then take B3254 south to St Keyne Well and hotel Price Guide: Single from £75; double/twin £110–£165; family suite from £180.

The Rosevine Hotel

PORTHCURNICK BEACH, PORTSCATHO, ST MAWES, TRURO, CORNWALL TR2 5EW
TEL: 01872 580206 FAX: 01872 580230 E-MAIL: info@rosevine.co.uk

At the heart of Cornwall's breathtaking Roseland Peninsula, the Rosevine is an elegant and gracious late Georgian hotel that offers visitors complete comfort and peace. The Rosevine stands in its own landscaped grounds overlooking Portscatho Harbour, a traditional Cornish fishing village. The superbly equipped bedrooms are delightfully designed, with some benefiting from direct access into the gardens and from their own private patio. This is the only hotel in Cornwall to hold the awards of 3 AA Red Stars and the RAC Blue Ribbon and Triple Dining Rosettes. The restaurant serves exceptional food, utilising the freshest seafood and locally grown produce. After dining, guests can relax in any of the three tasteful and comfortably presented lounges, bathe in the spacious heated swimming pool, or read in the hotel's well stocked library. Drinks are served in the convivial bar which offers a dizzy array of top quality wines and spirits. Visitors to the region do not forget the walks to the charming villages dotted along the Roseland Peninsula, and the golden sand of the National Trust maintained beach. Visitors can also take river trips on small ferries, once the only means of travel around the peninsula. The region is awash with National Trust gardens and the beautiful town of Truro is easily reached. **Directions:** From Exeter take A30 towards Truro. Take the St. Mawes turn and the hotel is on the left. Price Guide: Single £68–£120; double/twin £135–£200; suite from £210.

17 MasterCard VISA AMERICAN EXPRESS

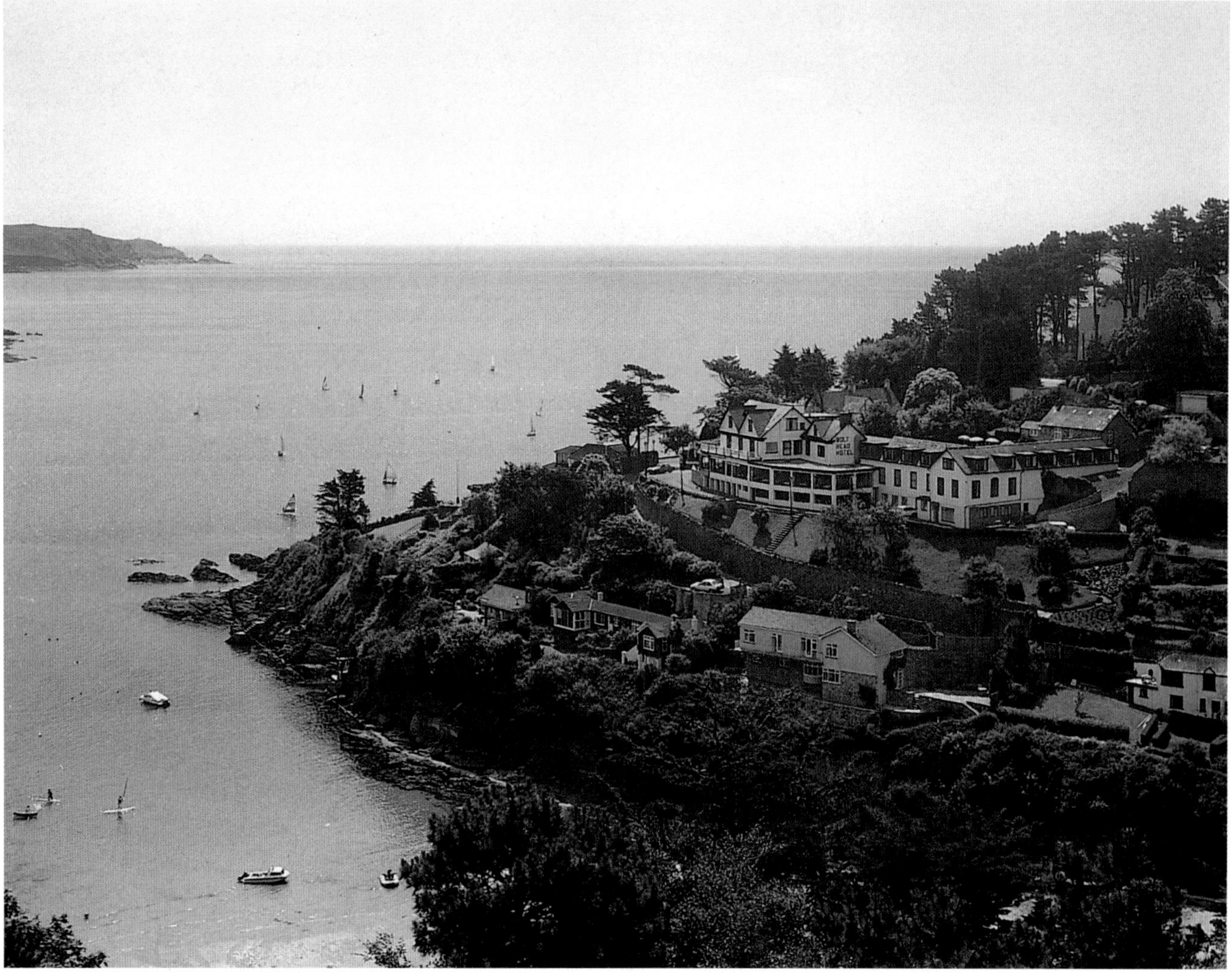

Bolt Head Hotel

SOUTH SANDS, SALCOMBE, SOUTH DEVON TQ8 8LL
TEL: 01548 843751 FAX: 01548 843061 E-MAIL: info@boltheadhotel.com

Bolt Head Hotel occupies a spectacular position overlooking Salcombe Estuary, where the mild climate ensures a lengthy holiday season. The bedrooms are comfortable, most with sea views, all with en suite bathrooms and there is a family suite available, complete with a baby-listening service. The light and sunny lounge, refurbished in unique Roman style, is ideal for relaxation, or guests may sit on the adjoining sun terrace with sweeping views of the sea. In the air-conditioned restaurant special care is taken to cater for all tastes. Both English and French cuisine are prepared, with freshly caught fish, lobster and crab delivered daily, as well as wholesome farm produce and local cheeses. Palm trees surround the heated outdoor swimming pool and Time share apartments within a sunny terrace. There is a good golf course within a few miles. Riding, sailing and windsurfing can be arranged. Sea fishing trips can be organised and private moorings are available. The hotel is adjacent to miles of magnificent National Trust cliff land at Bolt Head, including Overbecks, an unusual house and garden with rare plants. Dogs by arrangement. Closed mid-November to mid-March. **Directions:** Contact the hotel for directions. Price Guide: (including dinner): Single £72–£95; double/twin £144–£190; superior rooms available, as illustrated.

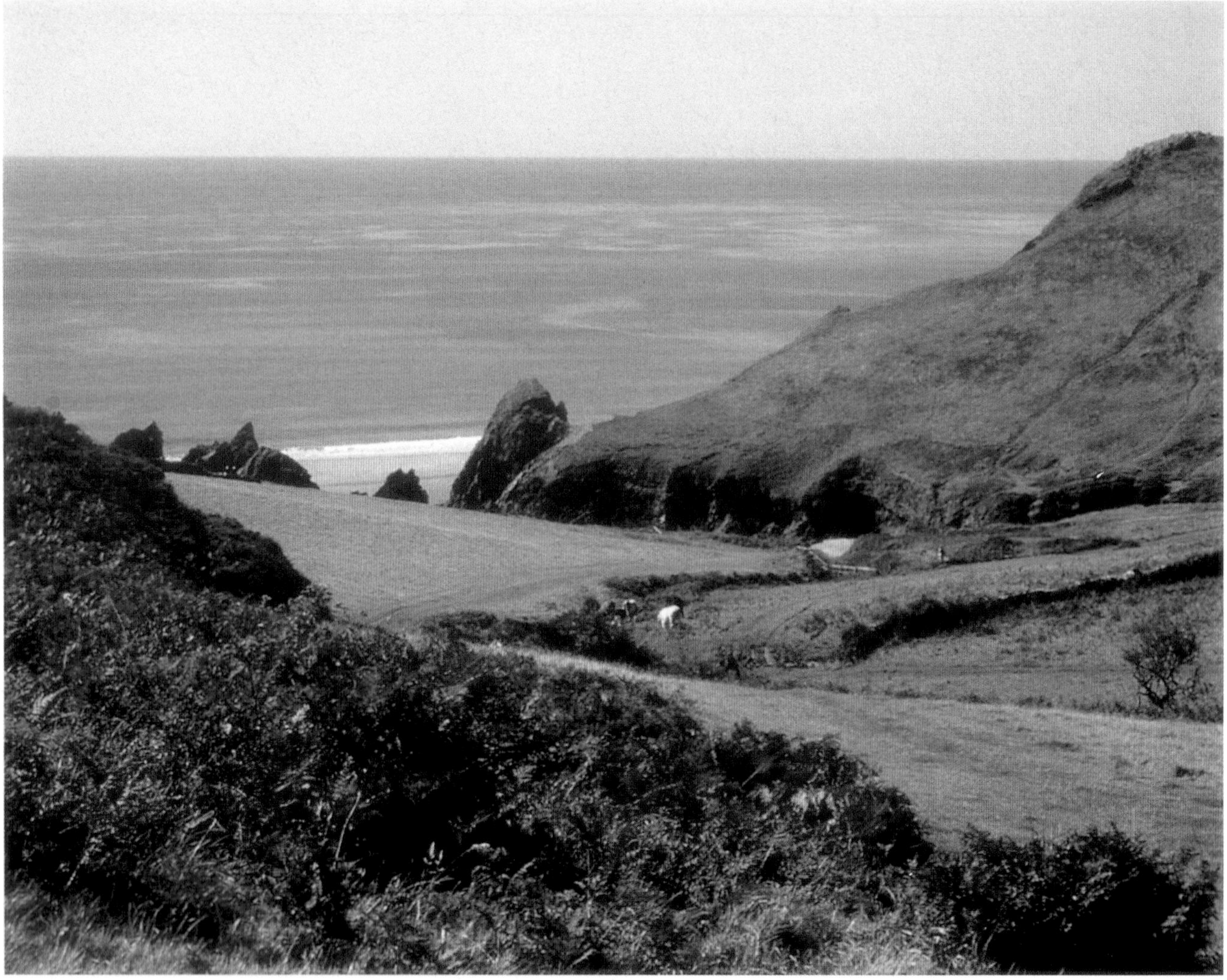

Soar Mill Cove Hotel

SOAR MILL COVE, SALCOMBE, SOUTH DEVON TQ7 3DS
TEL: 01548 561566 FAX: 01548 561223 E-MAIL: info@makepeacehotels.co.uk

Owned and loved by the Makepeace family who, for over 21 years, have provided a special blend of friendly yet professional service. The hotel's spectacular setting is a flower-filled combe, facing its own sheltered sandy bay and entirely surrounded by 2000 acres of dramatic National Trust coastline. While it is perhaps one of the last truly unspoiled corners of South Devon, Soar Mill Cove is only 15 miles from the motorway system (A38). The hotel has been awarded the prestigious RAC Blue Ribbon and 3 AA Red Stars. All the bedrooms are at ground level, each with a private patio opening onto the gardens, which in spring or summer provides wonderful alfresco opportunities. In winter, crackling log fires and efficient double glazing keeps cooler weather at bay. A strict "no conference policy" guarantees that the peace of guests shall not be compromised. Both the indoor and outdoor pools are spring-water fed, the former being maintained all year at a constant 88°F. Here is Keith Stephen Makepeace's award winning cuisine, imaginative and innovative, reflecting the very best of the West of England; fresh crabs and lobster caught in the bay are a speciality. Soar Mill Cove is situated midway between the old ports of Plymouth and Dartmouth. **Directions:** A384 to Totnes, then A381 to Soar Mill Cove. Price Guide: Single £72–£130; double/twin £144–£180; suite from £216.

THE TIDES REACH HOTEL

SOUTH SANDS, SALCOMBE, DEVON TQ8 8LJ
TEL: 01548 843466 FAX: 01548 843954 E-MAIL: enquire@tidesreach.com

This luxuriously appointed hotel is situated in an ideal position for those wishing to enjoy a relaxing or fun-filled break. Facing south in a tree-fringed sandy cove just inside the mouth of the Salcombe Estuary it has an extensive garden on one side, the sea and a safe bathing sandy beach a few steps opposite and, to the rear, a sheltering hill topped by the subtropical gardens of Overbecks. The Tides Reach has been under the supervision of owners, Mr and Mrs Roy Edwards, for more than 30 years and they have built up a reputation for hospitality and courteous service. The atmosphere is warm and friendly, the décor and furnishings tasteful and comfortable. All 35 spacious bedrooms are en suite, well equipped and decorated with flair and originality. The lawned garden centres around an ornamental lake with waterfall and fountain which is surrounded by landscaped tiers of colourful plants, shrubs and palms. Overlooking it is the restaurant where chef Finn Ibsen's excellent gourmet cuisine has earned two AA Rosettes. A superb indoor heated swimming pool is the nucleus of the hotel's leisure complex which includes a sauna, solarium, spa bath, gymnasium, squash court and snooker room. The hotel has facilities for windsurfing, water skiing, sailing and canoeing. **Directions:** From the M5, exit at junction 30 and join the A38 towards Plymouth. Exit for Totnes and then take the A381. Price Guide: (incl. dinner): Single £75–£110; double/twin £130–£250. Special breaks available.

35 MasterCard VISA AMERICAN EXPRESS 8

Howard's House

TEFFONT EVIAS, SALISBURY, WILTSHIRE SP3 5RJ
TEL: 01722 716392 FAX: 0722 716820 E-MAIL: enquiries@howardshousehotel.com

Tucked away in the depths of rural Wiltshire and surrounded by two acres of glorious gardens, stone-built Howard's House is a haven of tranquillity for those seeking to escape the noise and stress of the modern world. An inscribed date in the East Gable shows that the house was built in 1623. In 1837 it was extended and roofed in Swiss style for a member of the Mayne family, who have owned the village of Teffont Evias since 1692. After extensive renovations, present owner and chef Paul Firmin opened the house as a hotel in 1990 and has built a reputation for hospitality and attentive service. His restaurant, decorated in cool greens and whites, is the height of elegance and serves modern British cuisine. Dishes are cooked with flair and imagination, using the best local ingredients supplemented with herbs and vegetables from the hotel's garden. The 9 bedrooms are luxuriously equipped and their pastel shades enhance the feeling of informality and relaxation. The sitting room with its contemporary fabrics in warm yellows and reds, ceiling beams and open log fire is also wonderfully comfortable. Howard's House is ideally situated for visiting Stonehenge, Old Sarum, Salisbury Cathedral, Wilton House and Stourhead Gardens. **Directions:** From London, turn left off A303 2 miles after the Wylye intersection. Follow signs to Teffont and on entering the village join B3089. Howard's House is signposted

Price Guide: Single £75; double/twin £125–£145.

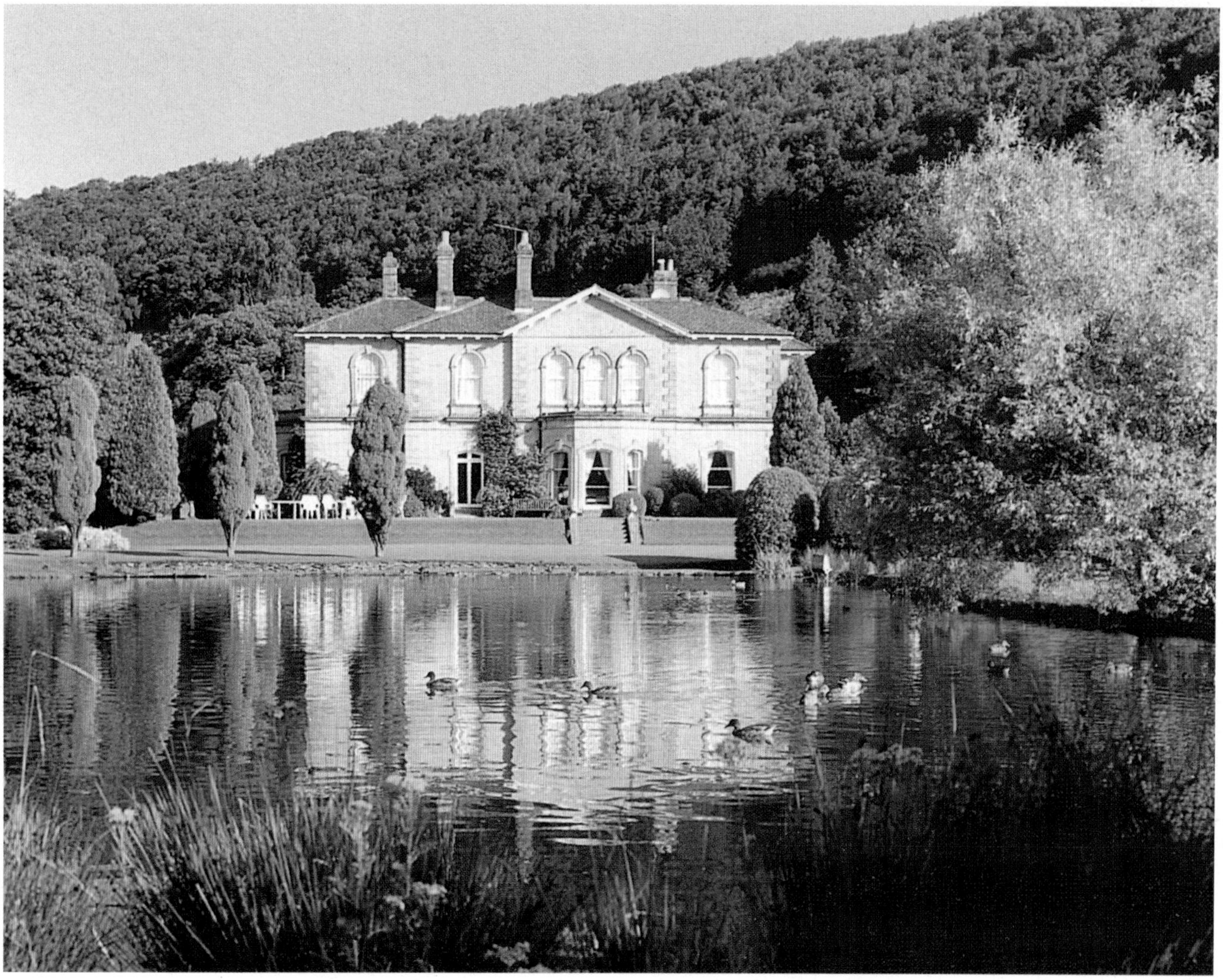

HACKNESS GRANGE

NORTH YORK MOORS NATIONAL PARK, SCARBOROUGH, NORTH YORKSHIRE YO13 0JW
TEL: 01723 882345 FAX: 01723 882391 E-MAIL: hacknessgrange@englishrosehotels.co.uk

The attractive Georgian Hackness Grange country house lies at the heart of the dramatic North York Moors National Park – miles of glorious countryside with rolling moorland and forests. Set in acres of private grounds, overlooking a tranquil lake, home to many species of wildlife, Hackness Grange is a haven of peace and quiet for guests. There are charming bedrooms in the gardens and courtyard together with de luxe rooms in the main house. For leisure activities, guests can enjoy 9-hole pitch 'n' putt golf, tennis and an indoor heated swimming pool with Jacuzzi. Hackness Grange is an ideal meeting location for companies wishing to have exclusive use of the hotel for VIP gatherings.

The attractive Derwent Restaurant with its quality décor, paintings and Rosette, is the setting for lunch and dinner. Here you will enjoy creatively prepared delicious cuisine, which is partnered by a wide choice of international wines. When you choose to stay at Hackness Grange you will find you have chosen well – a peaceful and relaxing location with so much to see and do: for example, visit Great Ayton, birthplace of Captain Cook

Directions: Take A64 York road until left turn to Seamer on to B1261, through to East Ayton and Hackness. Price Guide: Single £60–£90; double/twin £90–£150; suite £190.

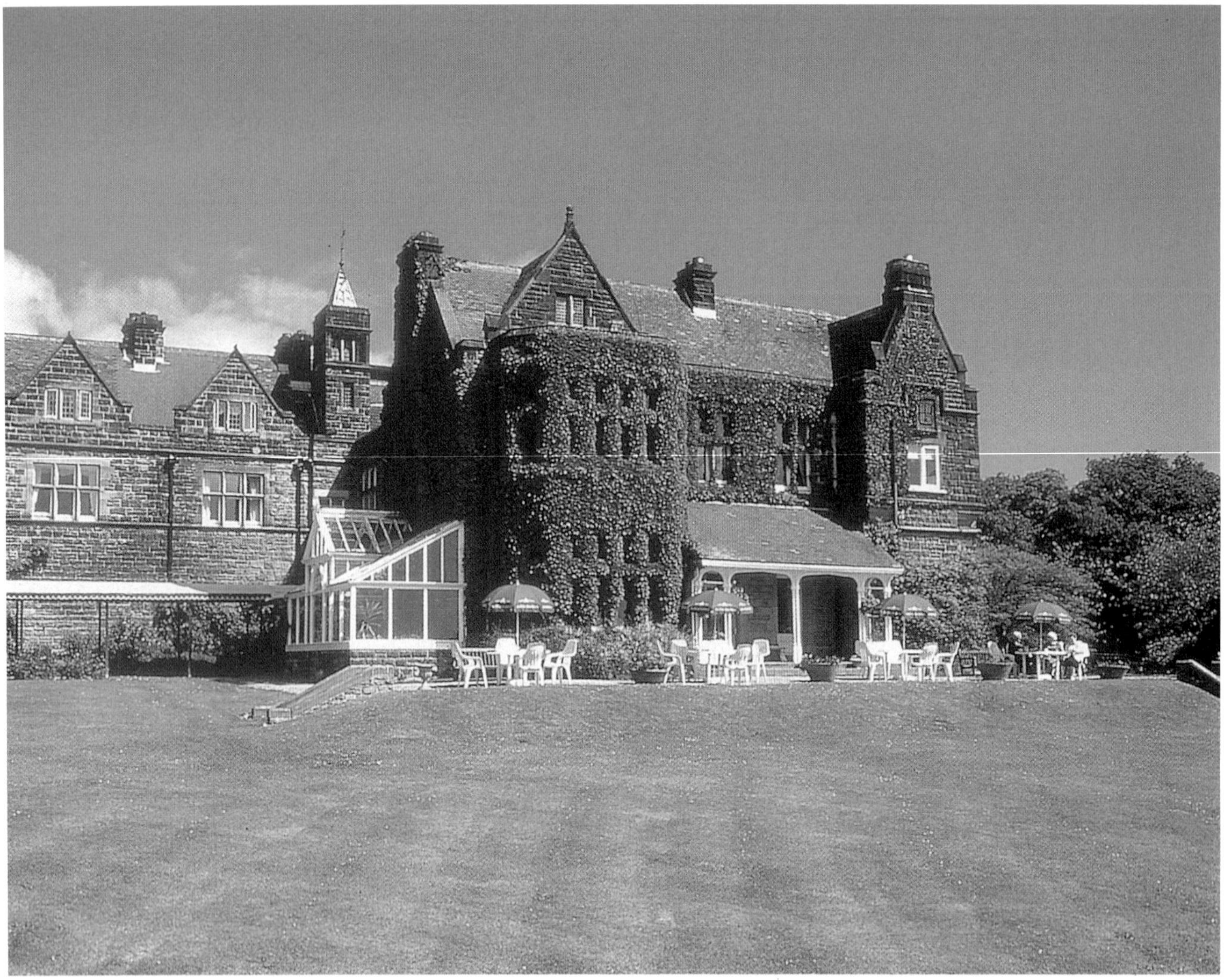

WREA HEAD COUNTRY HOTEL

SCALBY, NR SCARBOROUGH, NORTH YORKSHIRE YO13 0PB
TEL: 01723 378211 FAX: 01723 355936 E-MAIL: wreahead@englishrosehotels.co.uk

Wrea Head Country Hotel is an elegant, beautifully refurbished Victorian country house built in 1881 and situated in 14 acres of wooded and landscaped grounds on the edge of the North York Moors National Park, just three miles from Scarborough. The house is furnished with antiques and paintings and the oak-panelled front hall with its inglenook fireplace with blazing log fires in the winter, is very welcoming. All the bedrooms are individually decorated to the highest standards, with most having delightful views of the gardens. The elegant Four Seasons Restaurant is renowned for serving the best traditional English fare using fresh local produce and has a reputation for outstanding cuisine. There are attractive meeting rooms, each with natural daylight, ideal for private board meetings and training courses requiring privacy and seclusion. Scarborough is renowned for its cricket, music and theatre. Wrea Head is a perfect location from which to explore the glorious North Yorkshire coast and country and you can take advantage of special English Rose breaks throughout the year. Directions: Follow the A171 north from Scarborough, past the Scalby Village, until the hotel is signposted. Follow the road past the duck pond and then turn left up the drive. Price Guide: Single from £75; double/twin £120–£190; suite £190.

THE PRIORY BAY HOTEL

PRIORY DRIVE, SEAVIEW, ISLE OF WIGHT PO34 5BU
TEL: 01983 613146 FAX: 01983 616539 E-MAIL: reception@priorybay.co.uk

From decades gone by this beautiful site has been built upon by Medieval monks, Tudor farmers and Georgian gentry. Now its medley of buildings has been sympathetically restored and brought to life as a splendid hotel. Situated in gorgeous open countryside to the south of Seaview, the Priory Bay overlooks its own private beach. Everything about it is stylish and elegant, from the massive arched stone entrance with magnificent carved figures to the delightful, flower-filled gardens with their shady corners and thatched roofed tithe barns. The public rooms are a delight, exquisitely and comfortably furnished, with tall windows framed by rich curtains and liberally filled with vases of flowers. Log fires blaze in open fireplaces during colder months. Each of the 18 comfortable bedrooms is individually decorated and has picturesque views over the gardens. The dining room is establishing a reputation for first-class gastronomy, complemented by a fine wine list. Guests can relax under shady umbrellas in the garden or on the surrounding terraces. For the more energetic guest, there is an outdoor pool and the hotel's adjoining 9-hole golf course. Butterfly World, a tiger sanctuary, Carisbrook Castle and Osborne House are all nearby. Directions: Ferry from Portsmouth, Lymington or Southampton to Fishbourne, Yarmouth. Ryde, East or West Cowes. The hotel is on the B3330. Price Guide: Single from £65; double/twin from £130.

18 MasterCard VISA AMERICAN EXPRESS M 70 H

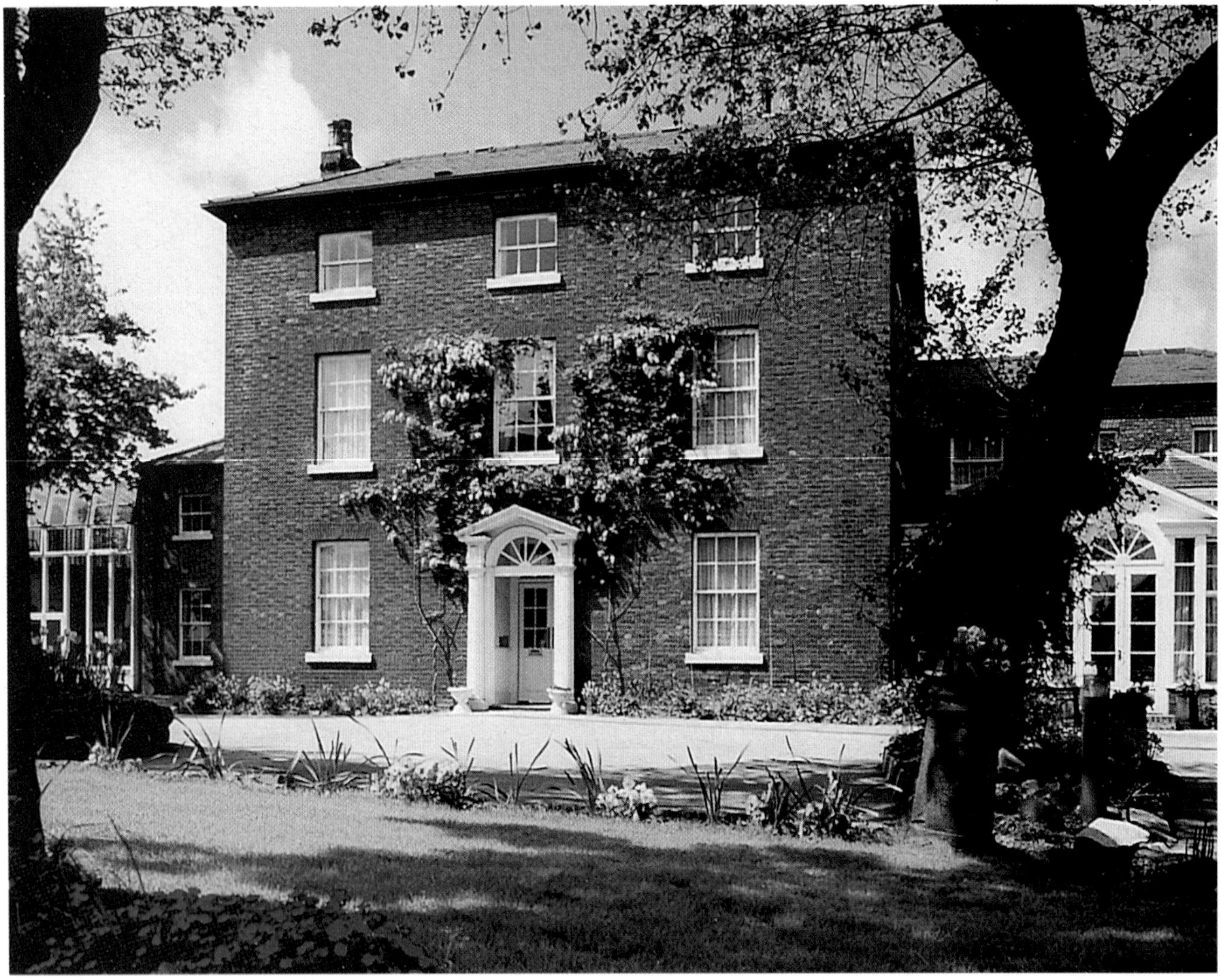

CHARNWOOD HOTEL

10 SHARROW LANE, SHEFFIELD, SOUTH YORKSHIRE S11 8AA
TEL: 0114 258 9411 FAX: 0114 255 5107 E-MAIL: king@charnwood.force9.co.uk

The Charnwood Hotel is a listed Georgian mansion dating from 1780. Originally owned by John Henfrey, a Sheffield Master Cutler, it was later acquired by William Wilson of the Sharrow Snuff Mill. Restored in 1985, this elegant 'country house in town' is tastefully furnished, with colourful flower arrangements set against attractive décor. The no smoking bedrooms are all individually decorated and the Woodford suite is designed specifically to meet the requirements of a family. Brasserie Leo has a relaxed atmosphere serving traditional English and French cuisine. The Library and Henfrey's are ideal for private dining or small meetings and larger functions are catered for in the Georgian Room and Coach House. Also there are 19 self catering apartments nearby. While approximately a mile from Sheffield city centre, with its concert hall, theatre and hectic night-life, Charnwood Hotel is also convenient for the Peak District National Park. Meadowhall shopping centre and Sheffield Arena are a short ride away. **Directions:** Sharrow Lane is near the junction of London Road and Abbeydale Road, 1½ miles from city centre. Junction 33 from the M1. Price Guide: Single £58–£92; double/twin £73–£110.

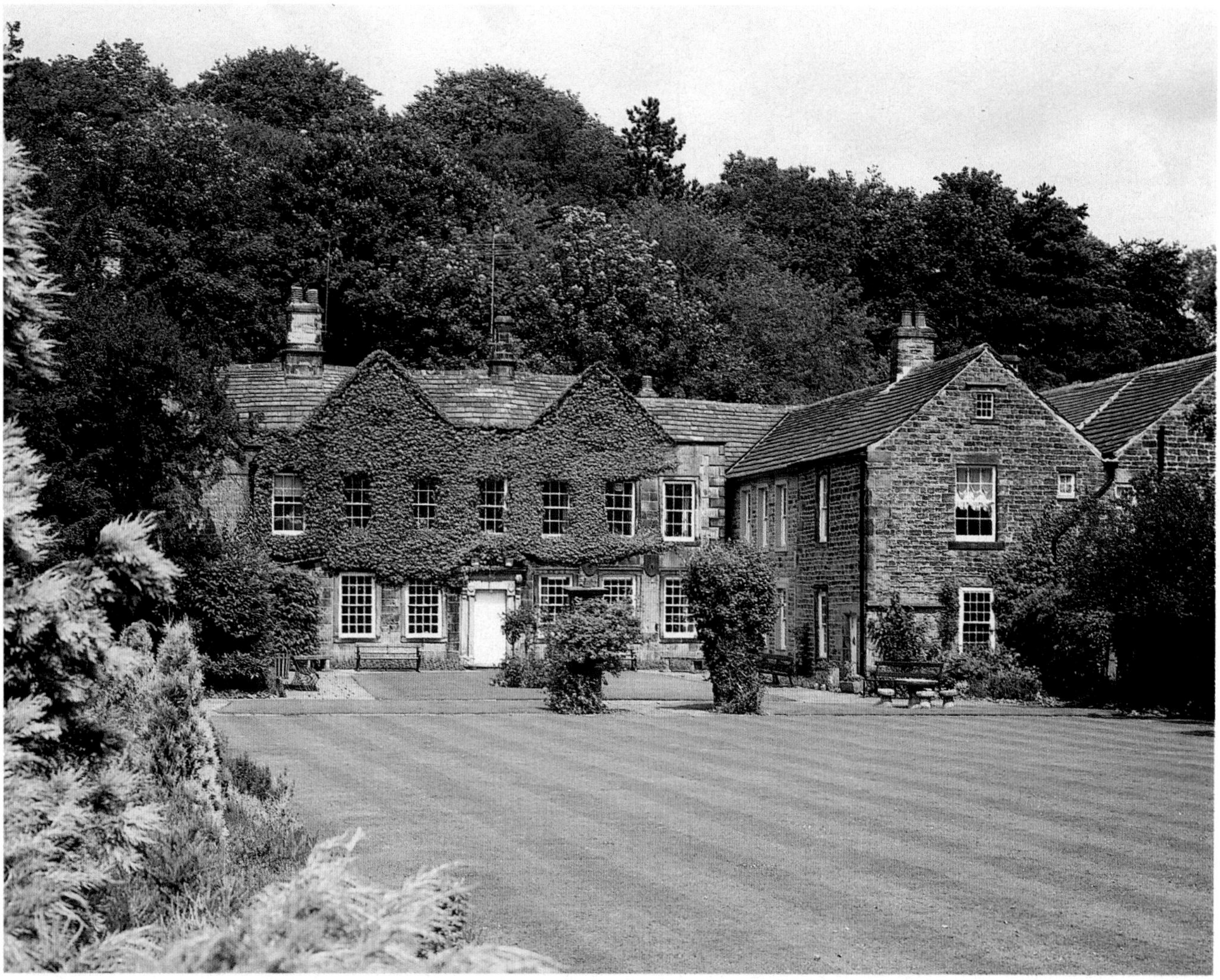

WHITLEY HALL HOTEL

ELLIOTT LANE, GRENOSIDE, SHEFFIELD, SOUTH YORKSHIRE S35 8NR
TEL: 0114 245 4444 FAX: 0114 245 5414 E-MAIL: reservations@whitleyhall.com

Carved into the keystone above one of the doors is the date 1584, denoting the start of Whitley Hall's lengthy country house tradition. In the bar is a priest hole, which may explain the local belief that a tunnel links the house with the nearby 11th century church. In the 18th century, the house was a prestigious boarding school, with Gothic pointed arches and ornamentation added later by the Victorians. Attractively refurbished, Whitley Hall is now a fine hotel with all the amenities required by today's visitors. Stone walls and oak panelling combine with richly carpeted floors and handsome decoration. A sweeping split staircase leads to the bedrooms, all of which have en suite bathrooms. Varied yet unpretentious cooking is served in generous portions and complemented by a wide choice from the wine cellar, including many clarets and ports. Peacocks strut around the 30 acre grounds, which encompass rolling lawns, mature woodland and two ornamental lakes. Banquets and private functions can be held in the conference suite. **Directions:** Leave M1 at junction 35, following signs for Chapeltown (A629), go down hill and turn left into Nether Lane. Go right at traffic lights, then left opposite Arundel pub, into Whitley Lane. At fork turn right into Elliott Lane; hotel is on left. Price Guide: Single £75–£90; double/twin £95–£115.

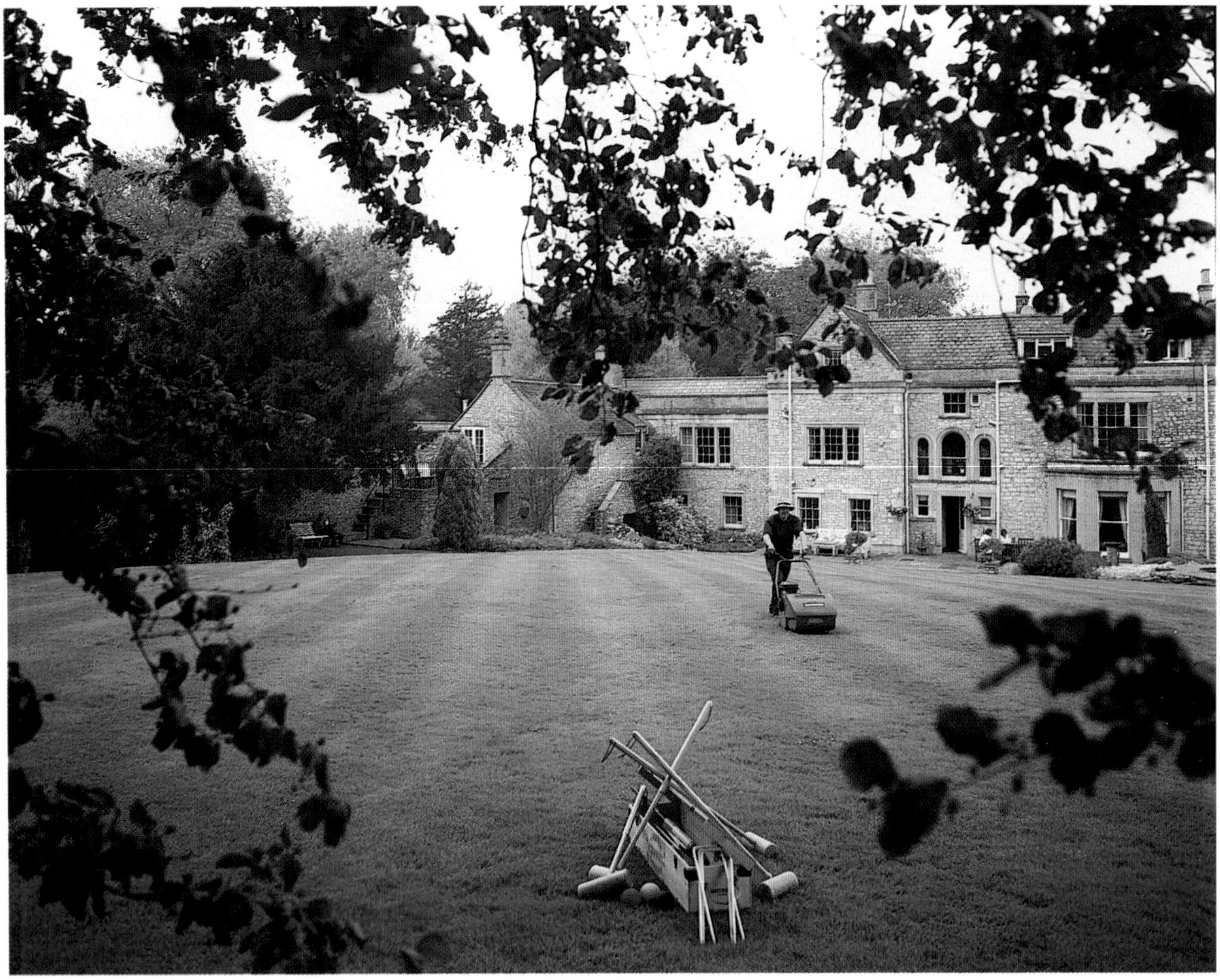

Charlton House And The Mulberry Restaurant

CHARLTON ROAD, SHEPTON MALLET, NEAR BATH, SOMERSET BA4 4PR
TEL: 01749 342008 FAX: 01749 346362 E-MAIL: enquiry@charltonhouse.com

This grand 17th century country manor, is now owned by Roger and Monty Saul, founders of the Mulberry Design Co. They have lovingly and skilfully created an exquisite hotel of the highest international standards without detracting from Charlton's own history and architecture. The reception rooms have wonderful proportions and are not overwhelmed by the sumptuous furnishings, fine antiques, brilliant rugs on polished floors, witty memorabilia and exciting paintings adorning their walls – veritable Aladdin's Caves! The bedrooms, some in the adjacent Coach House, are equally magical, totally luxurious and yet restful, with opulent bathrooms. Professional yet friendly staff play an important part both in the drawing room, with its marvellous intimate atmosphere and in the dramatic dining room presided over by award-winning chef, Adam Fellows. Fantastic cooking and sublime wines make every meal a sybaritic experience. The hotel prides itself on catering for "special occasions". Charlton House recreations include shove-halfpenny(!), croquet, a trout lake, tennis, a sauna and pool and strolling in the landscaped gardens. Nearby are Bath, Wincanton Races, sailing, golf, the Mendip Hills – and the Mulberry factory shop. **Directions:** A303, then A37 to Shepton Mallet. Take A361 towards Frome and find hotel drive on the right. Price Guide: Single £112.50–£155; double/twin £155–£225; suite £250–£355.

16 MasterCard VISA AMERICAN EXPRESS M 55

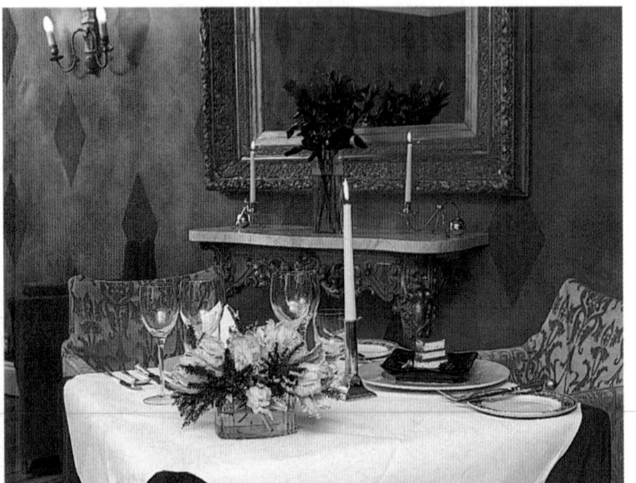

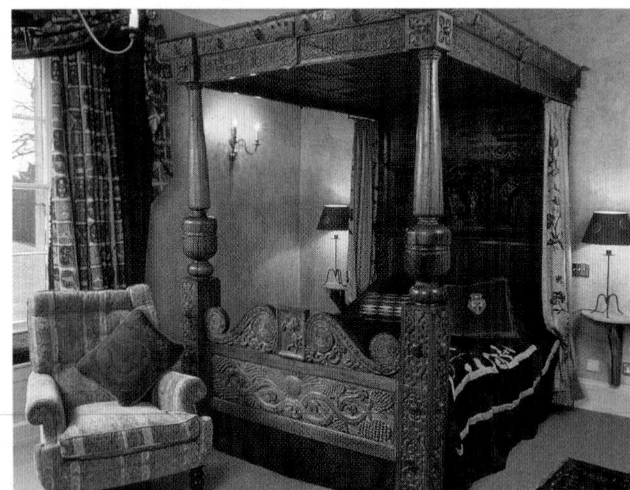

PRINCE RUPERT HOTEL

BUTCHER ROW, SHREWSBURY, SHROPSHIRE SY1 1UQ

TEL: 01743 499955 FAX: 01743 357306 E-MAIL: post@prince-rupert-hotel.co.uk

Ornamented by a pink sandstone castle and narrow cobbled streets lined with black-and-white Tudor buildings, Shrewsbury is an historic county town on the banks of the River Severn. The Prince Rupert Hotel is at its medieval heart. Once the 12th century home of Prince Rupert, grandson of King James I, it combines old world charm with the comfort, service and facilities expected in a premier hotel. Although spread over various old buildings with linking corridors, the overall feeling is that the hotel is intimate and small. The 70 tastefully refurbished en suite bedrooms, some with king-size four-poster beds, include 12th century beamed suites, have every home-from-home comfort and are surprisingly quiet for a town centre location. The elegant Royalist Restaurant with its oak-panelled walls, fireplaces and suits of armour is known for Head Chef Graeme Williams' cuisine. A brasserie, Chambers, is in the oldest part of the hotel, and light lunches and afternoon teas are served in the main lounge. The Health and Beauty Spa includes a Jacuzzi, steam shower, weights room and beauty salon. Attingham Park, Ironbridge Gorge, and Powys castles are within easy reach. **Directions:** After leaving M54 follow signs to Shrewsbury town centre. Cross English Bridge and bear right up the Wyle Cop. After 70m turn sharp right into the cobblestoned Fish Street. The Prince Rupert is 150m ahead. Price Guide: Single £60–£75; double/twin £95; suite £130–£160.

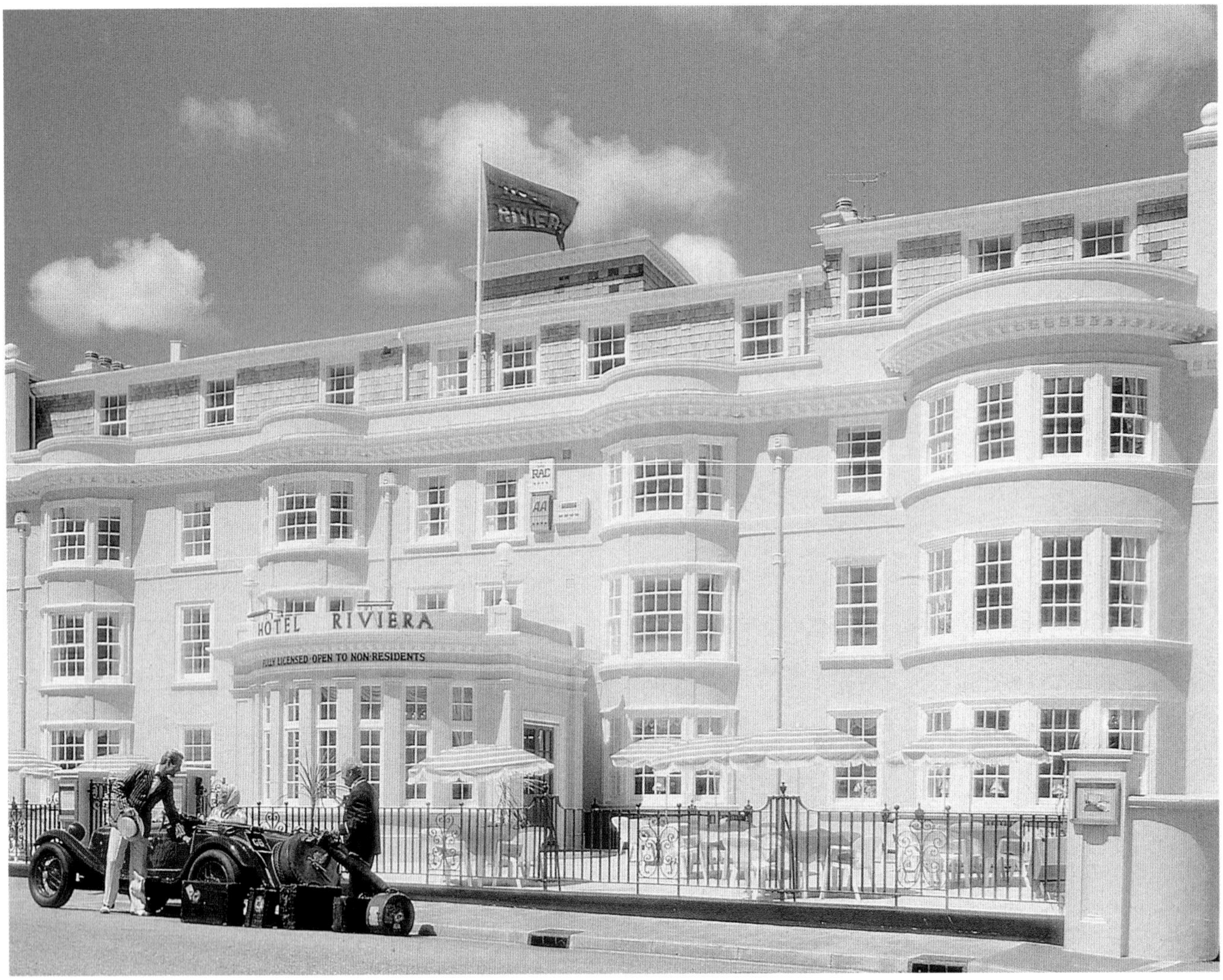

HOTEL RIVIERA

THE ESPLANADE, SIDMOUTH, DEVON EX10 8AY

TEL: 01395 515201 FAX: 01395 577775 E-MAIL: enquiries@hotelriviera.co.uk

A warm welcome awaits guests arriving at this prestigious award-winning hotel. With accolades such as the AA Courtesy and Care Award and more recently, the Which? Hotel Guide's Hotel of the Year 1999, it comes as no surprise that Peter Wharton's Hotel Riviera is arguably one of the most comfortable and most hospitable in the region. The exterior, with its fine Regency façade and bow fronted windows complements the elegance of the interior comprising handsome public rooms and beautifully appointed bedrooms, many with sea views. Perfectly located at the centre of Sidmouth's historic Georgian esplanade and awarded four stars by both the AA and the RAC, the Riviera is committed to providing the very highest standard of excellence which makes each stay at the property a totally pleasurable experience. Guests may dine in the attractive salon, which affords glorious views across Lyme Bay, and indulge in the superb cuisine, prepared by Swiss and French trained chefs. The exceptional cellar will please the most discerning wine connoisseur. Activities include coastal walks, golf, bowling, croquet, putting, tennis, fishing, sailing, riding and exploring the breathtaking surroundings with its gardens, lush countryside and stunning coastline. **Directions:** The hotel is situated at the centre of the esplanade. Price Guide: (including seven-course dinner): Single £90–£118; double/twin £160–£216; suite £216–£236.

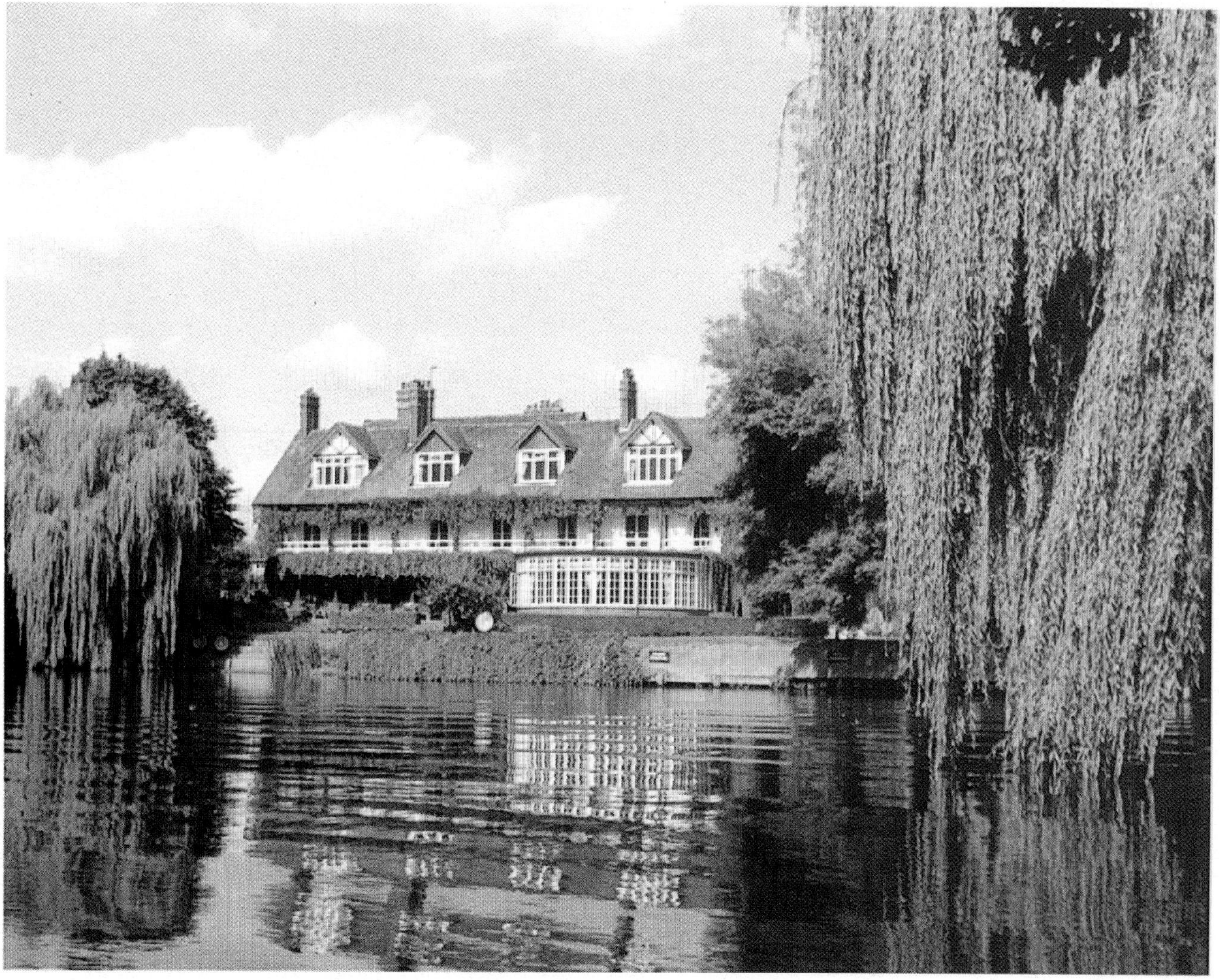

THE FRENCH HORN

SONNING-ON-THAMES, BERKSHIRE RG4 OTN
TEL: 01189 692204 FAX: 01189 442210 E-MAIL: TheFrenchHorn@Compuserve.com

For over 150 years The French Horn has provided a charming riverside retreat from the busy outside world. Today, although busier on this stretch of the river, it continues that fine tradition of comfortable accommodation and outstanding cuisine in a beautiful setting. The hotel nestles beside the Thames near the historic village of Sonning. The well-appointed bedrooms and suites are fully-equipped with modern amenities and many have river views. The old panelled bar provides an intimate scene for pre-dinner drinks and the restaurant speciality, locally reared duck, is spit roasted here over an open fire. By day the sunny restaurant is a lovely setting for lunch, while by night diners can enjoy the floodlit view of the graceful weeping willows which fringe the river. Dinner is served by candlelight and the cuisine is a mixture of French and English cooking using the freshest ingredients. The French Horn's wine list is reputed to be amongst the finest in Europe. Places of interest include Henley, Stratfield Saye, Oxford, Blenheim Palace and Mapledurham. There are numerous golf courses and equestrian centres in the area. **Directions:** Leave the M4 at J8/9. Follow A404/M then at Thickets Roundabout turn left on A4 towards Reading for 8 miles. Turn right for Sonning. Cross Thames on B478. Hotel is on right. Price Guide: Single £110–£155; double/twin £130–£185.

THE SWAN HOTEL

MARKET PLACE, SOUTHWOLD, SUFFOLK IP18 6EG

TEL: 01502 722186 FAX: 01502 724800 E-MAIL: swan.hotel@adnams.co.uk

Rebuilt in 1659, following the disastrous fire which destroyed most of the town, The Swan was remodelled in the 1820s, with further additions in 1938. The hotel provides all modern services while retaining its classical dignity and elegance. Many of the antique-furnished bedrooms in the main hotel offer a glimpse of the sea, while the garden rooms – decorated in a more contemporary style – are clustered around the old bowling green. The Drawing Room has the traditional character of an English country house and the Reading Room upstairs is perfect for quiet relaxation or as the venue for a private party. The daily menu offers dishes ranging from simple, traditional fare through the English classics to the chef's personal specialities as well as a full a la carte menu. An exciting selection of wines is offered. Almost an island, Southwold is bounded on three sides by creeks, marshes and the River Blyth – making it a paradise for birdwatchers and nature lovers. Hardly changed for a century, the town, built around a series of greens, has a fine church, lighthouse and golf course. Music lovers flock to nearby Snape Maltings for the Aldeburgh Festival. **Directions:** Southwold is off the A12 Ipswich–Lowestoft road. The Swan Hotel is in the town centre. Price Guide: Single £70; double/twin £110; suite £185.

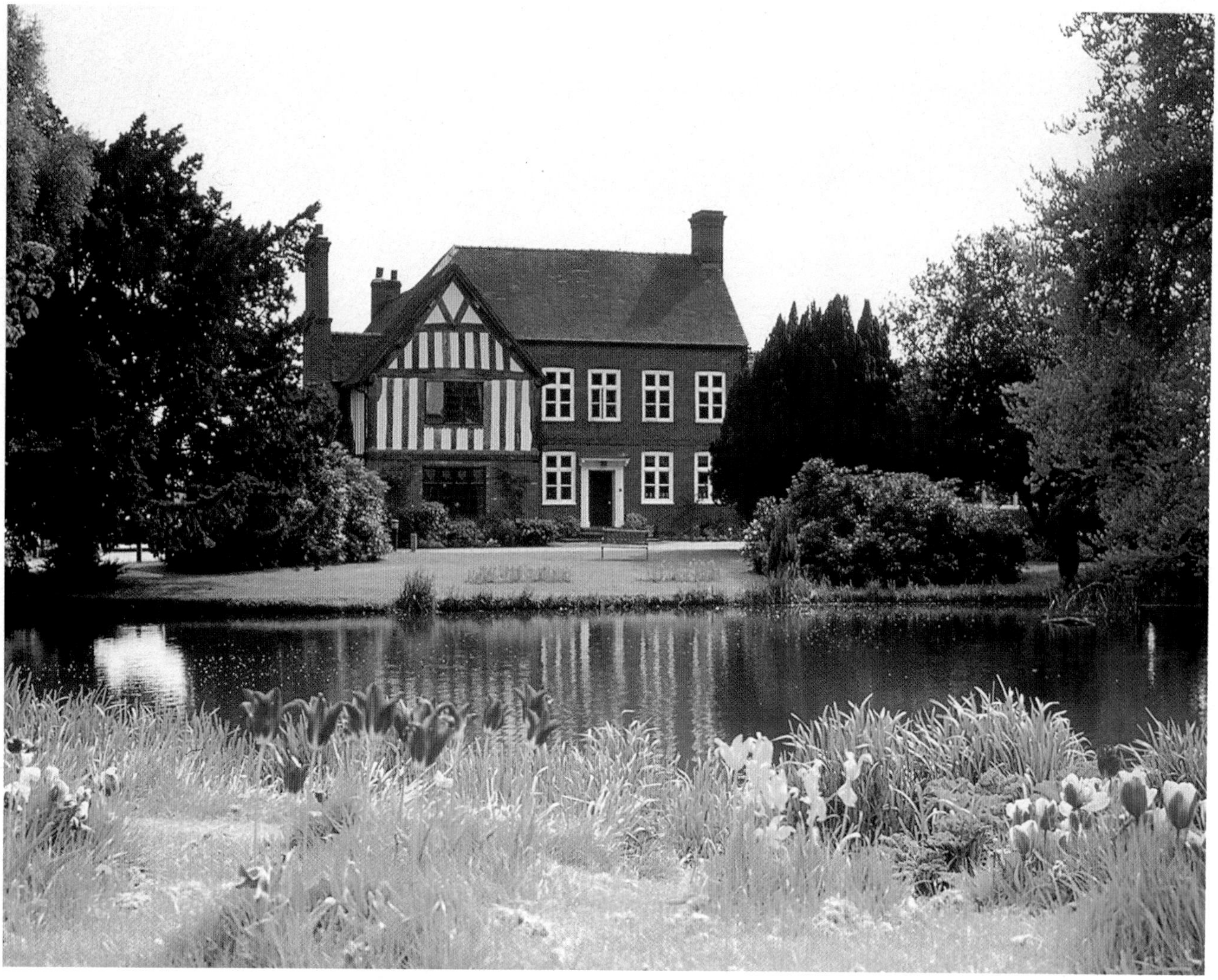

THE MOAT HOUSE

ACTON TRUSSELL, STAFFORD, STAFFORDSHIRE ST17 0RJ

TEL: 01785 712217 FAX: 01785 715344 E-MAIL: info@moathouse.co.uk

This impressive, oak-beamed and moated manor house was nominated 'Hotel of the Year 2000' for the Heart of England region. History, luxurious comfort, superb food, ultra modern amenities and a spectacular canal side setting combine in a picturesque village in the heart of rural Staffordshire. Built in the 15th century, the Moat House is the perfect retreat for those seeking tranquillity and leisurely enjoyment. There are 32 luxury en suite bedrooms, including four suites, with every facility; most are air-conditioned. The bar retains the character and charm of the hotel's past with exposed beams and a magnificent inglenook fireplace. Dining is an experience, with chef Matthew Davies producing sophisticated and imaginative dishes in the elegant, 2 AA Rosette restaurant. The Moat House is also a first-class business venue, offering seven meeting rooms including a suite. Local attractions include Alton Towers, The Potteries, Weston Park, Shugborough Hall, and Cannock Chase Country Park. The hotel's corporate event field is ideal for clay pigeon shooting, archery and off road driving. Uttoxeter racecourse is within easy reach. **Directions:** From M6, exit at junction 13 and take A449 towards Stafford. At first island turn right, signposted Acton Trussell. The Moat House is at the far end of the village. Price Guide: Single £75–£140; double/twin £100–£140; suite £156–£199.

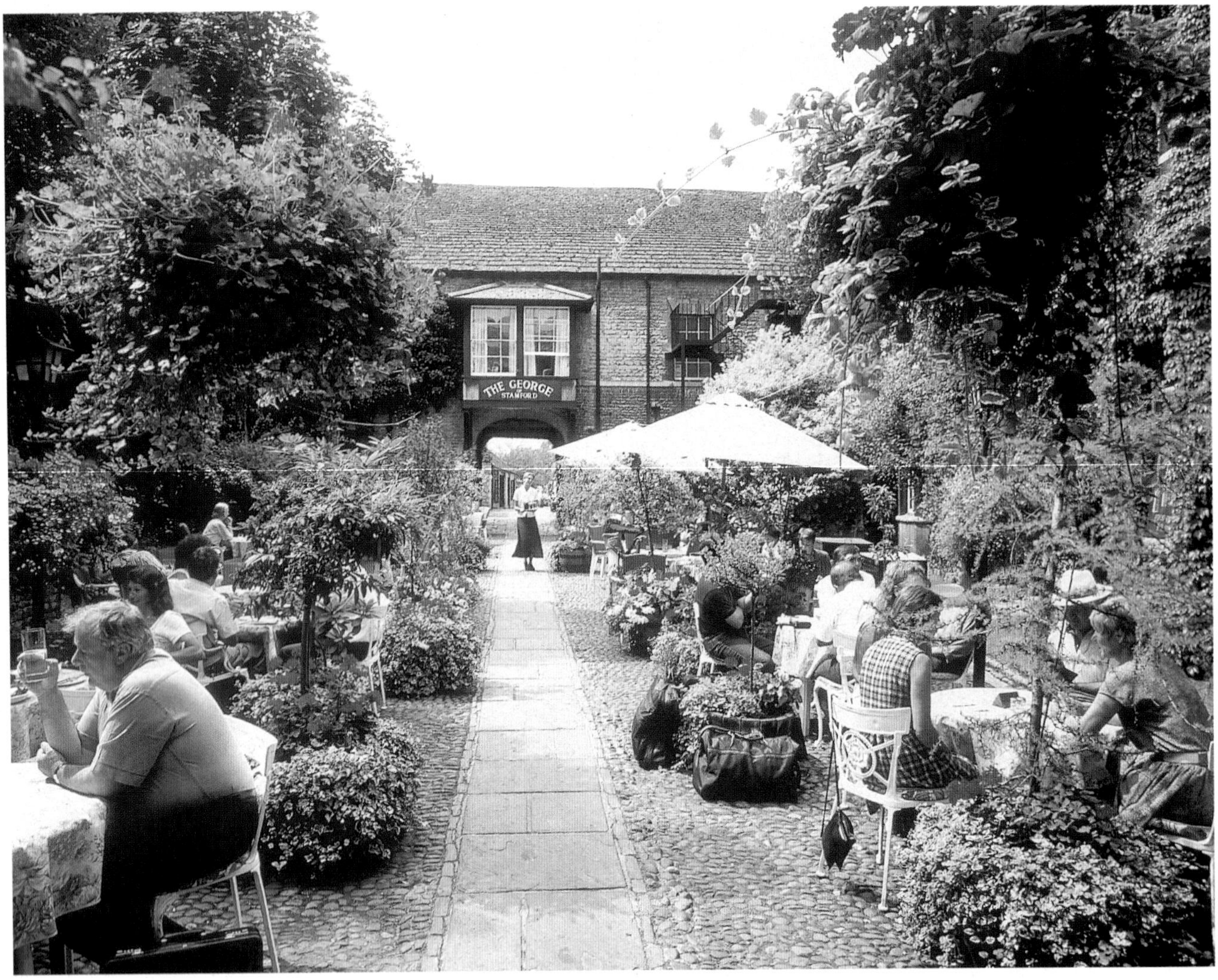

The George Of Stamford

ST MARTINS, STAMFORD, LINCOLNSHIRE PE9 2LB

TEL: 01780 750750 RESERVATIONS: 01780 750700 FAX: 01780 750701 E-MAIL: reservations@georgehotelofstamford.com

The George, a beautiful, 16th century coaching inn, retains the charm of its long history, as guests will sense on entering the reception hall with its oak travelling chests and famous oil portrait of Daniel Lambert. Over the years, The George has welcomed a diverse clientèle, ranging from highwaymen to kings – Charles I and William III were both visitors. At the heart of the hotel is the lounge, its natural stone walls, deep easy chairs and softly lit alcoves imparting a cosy, relaxed atmosphere, while the blazing log fire is sometimes used to toast muffins for tea! The flair of Julia Vannocci's interior design is evident in all the expertly styled, fully appointed bedrooms. Exotic plants, orchids, orange trees and coconut palms feature in the Garden Lounge, where a choice of hot dishes and an extensive cold buffet are offered. Guests may also dine alfresco in the courtyard garden. The more formal, oak-panelled restaurant serves imaginative but traditional English dishes and an award-winning list of wines. Superb facilities are incorporated in the Business Centre, converted from the former livery stables. Special weekend breaks available. **Directions:** Stamford is 1 mile from the A1 on the B1081. The George is in the town centre opposite the gallows sign. Car parking is behind the hotel. Price Guide: Single from £80–£110; double/twin from £105–£145; suite £145–£220.

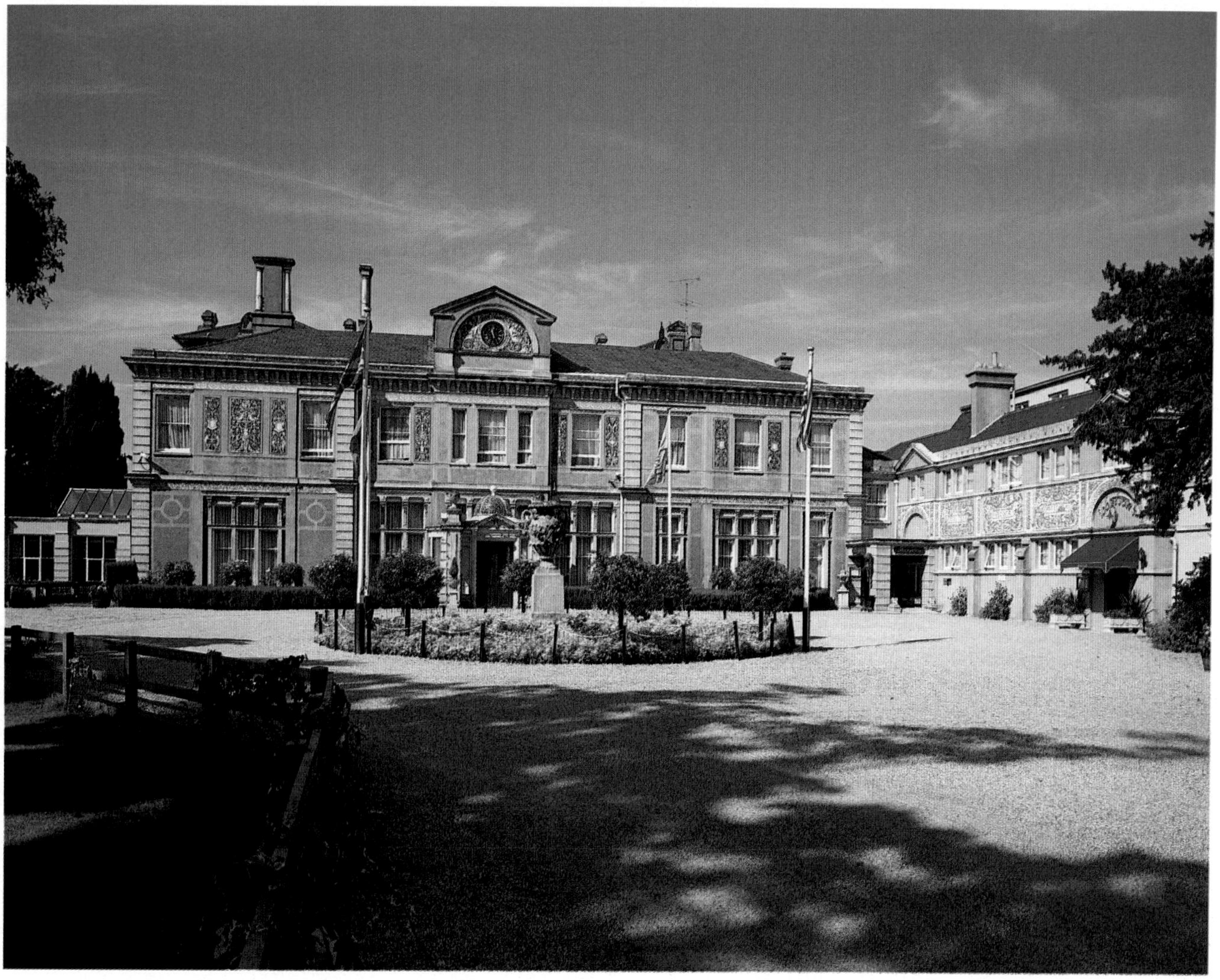

DOWN HALL COUNTRY HOUSE HOTEL

HATFIELD HEATH, NR BISHOP'S STORTFORD, HERTFORDSHIRE CM22 7AS
TEL: 01279 731441 FAX: 01279 730416 E-MAIL: reservations@downhall.co.uk

Set in 110 acres of parkland, this Italianate mansion is the perfect choice for those wishing to escape the pressures of everyday life. A peaceful ambience pervades this recently restored country house hotel. The well-appointed bedrooms all feature period furnishings and in-room safes and afford picturesque views across the grounds. This is an ideal venue for board meetings, conferences and corporate hospitality as it offers elegant, airy meeting rooms, a range of good facilities and a secluded environment. The rooms accommodate 10 delegates boardroom-style and up to 180 theatre-style with back projection. Gastronomes will be pleased with the excellent cuisine served in the Downham and the new Ibbetsons 2-Rosette restaurant. Here, English and French dishes are prepared with only the finest fresh ingredients. The superb on site sporting facilities include two all-weather tennis courts, a putting green, croquet lawn, swimming pool, sauna and whirlpool. Clay pigeon shooting, horse-riding, canoeing and golf can be arranged nearby. Day excursions include visits to Cambridge, horse racing at Newmarket, Constable Country and the old timbered village of Thaxted. **Directions:** The hotel is 14 miles from the M25, 7 miles from the M11 and Bishop's Stortford Station. Heathrow airport is 60 miles away; Stansted is within 11 miles. There is ample free parking. Price Guide: Single £120–£155; double/twin £175–£245; suite £235–£275.

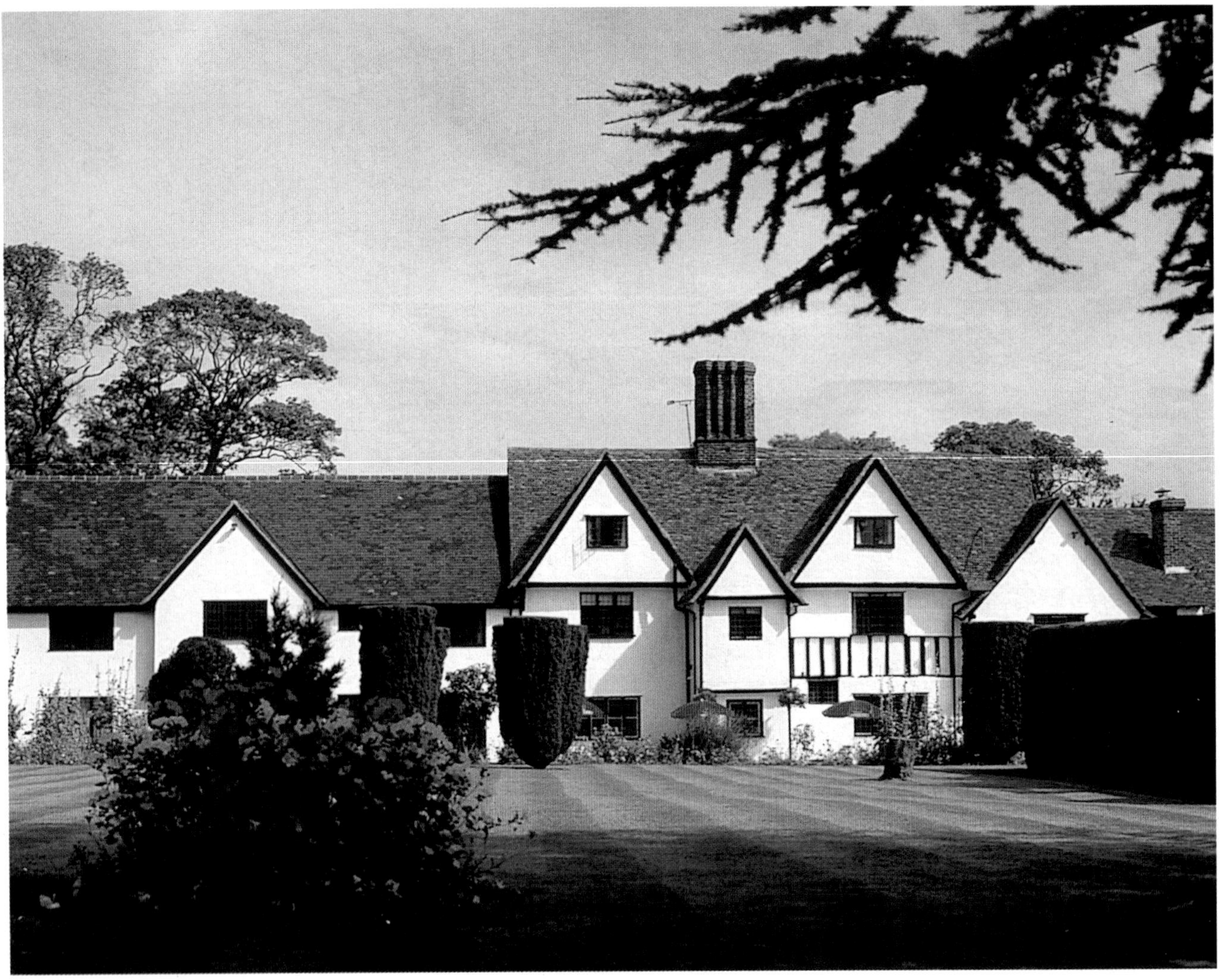

WHITEHALL

CHURCH END, BROXTED, ESSEX CM6 2BZ

TEL: 01279 850603 FAX: 01279 850385 E-MAIL: sales@whitehall.com

Set on a hillside overlooking the delightful rolling countryside of north-west Essex is Whitehall, one of East Anglia's leading country hotels. While its origins can be traced back to 1151, the manor house is ostensibly Elizabethan in style, with recent additions tastefully incorporated. Traditional features such as beams, wide fireplaces and log fires blend well with the contemporary, fresh pastel shades and subtle-hued fabrics. A spectacular vaulted ceiling makes the dining room an impressive setting for dinner, with an à la carte or six-course set menu offering many a delicious bonne-bouche. For large private functions, the timbered Barn House is an ideal venue, where guests can enjoy the same high standards of cuisine found in the restaurant. Overlooked by the old village church is the attractive Elizabethan walled garden. Whitehall is only a short drive from London's most modern international airport at Stansted, opened in 1989 and easily accessible from the M11 motorway, while Cambridge and Newmarket are only 30 minutes' drive away. Directions: Take junction 8 from the M11, follow Stansted Airport signs to new terminal building and then signs for Broxted. Price Guide: (Room only): Single £98; double/twin £125–£220.

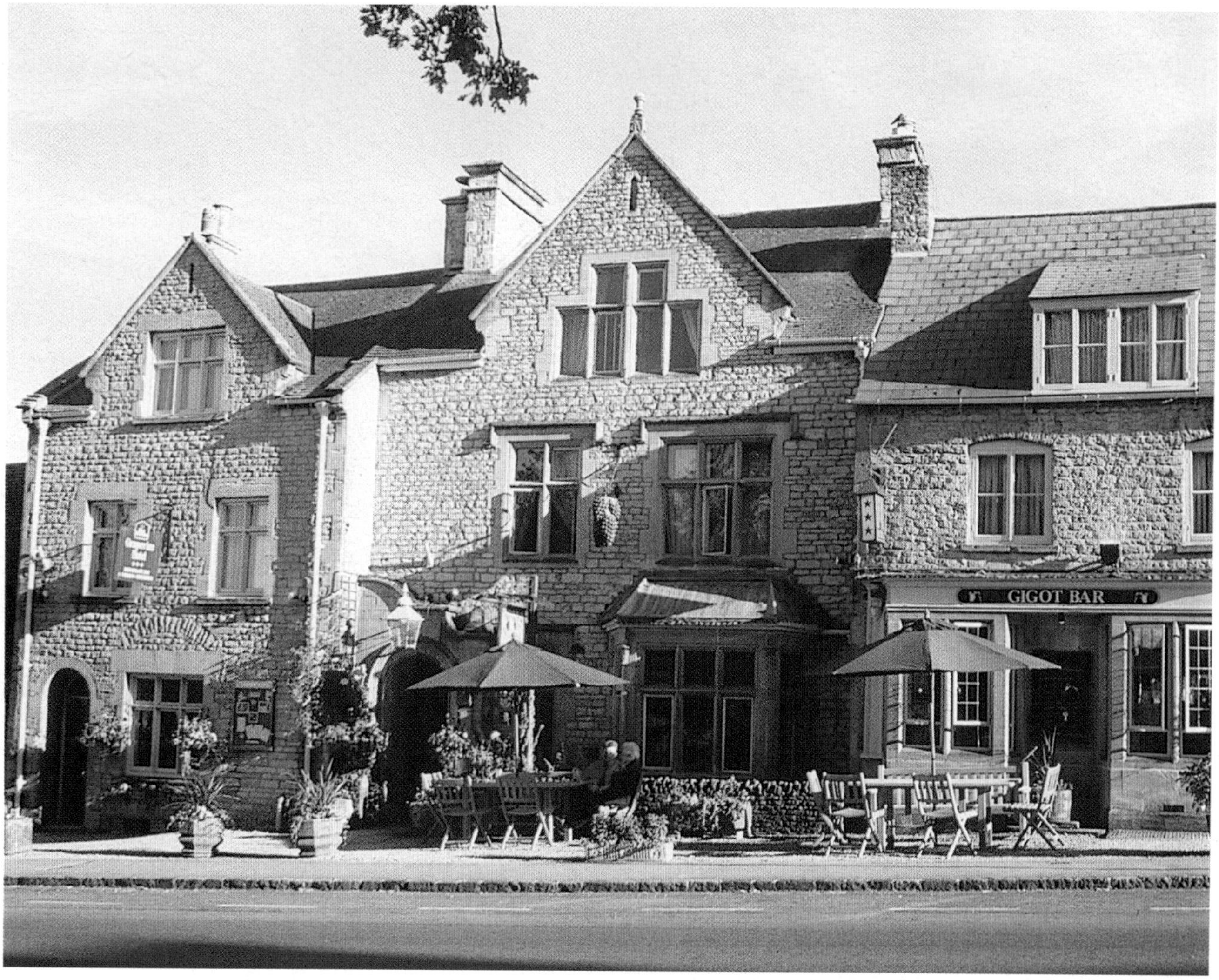

THE GRAPEVINE HOTEL

SHEEP STREET, STOW-ON-THE-WOLD, GLOUCESTERSHIRE GL54 1AU
TEL: 01451 830344 FAX: 01451 832278 E-MAIL: johansens@vines.co.uk

Set in the pretty town of Stow-on-the-Wold, regarded by many as the jewel of the Cotswolds, The Grapevine Hotel has an atmosphere which makes visitors feel welcome and at ease. The outstanding personal service provided by a loyal team of staff is perhaps the secret of the hotel's success. This, along with the exceptionally high standard of overall comfort and hospitality, earned The Grapevine the 1991 Johansens Hotel Award for Excellence – a well-deserved accolade. Beautifully furnished bedrooms, including six superb garden rooms across the courtyard, offer every facility. Visitors can linger over imaginative cuisine in the relaxed and informal atmosphere of the conservatory restaurant. Awarded one AA Rosettes for food. The restaurant, like all of the bedrooms, is non-smoking. The hotel has its own tennis court, 1.5 miles away. Whether travelling on business or pleasure, guests will wish to return to The Grapevine again and again. The local landscape offers unlimited scope for exploration, whether to the numerous picturesque villages in the Cotswolds or to the towns of Oxford, Cirencester and Stratford-upon-Avon. Nature enthusiasts must visit the beautiful gardens of Hidcote, Kifsgate and Barnsley House nearby. Open over Christmas. **Directions:** Sheep Street is part of A436 in the centre of Stow-on-the-Wold. Price Guide: Single from £85; double/twin from £129

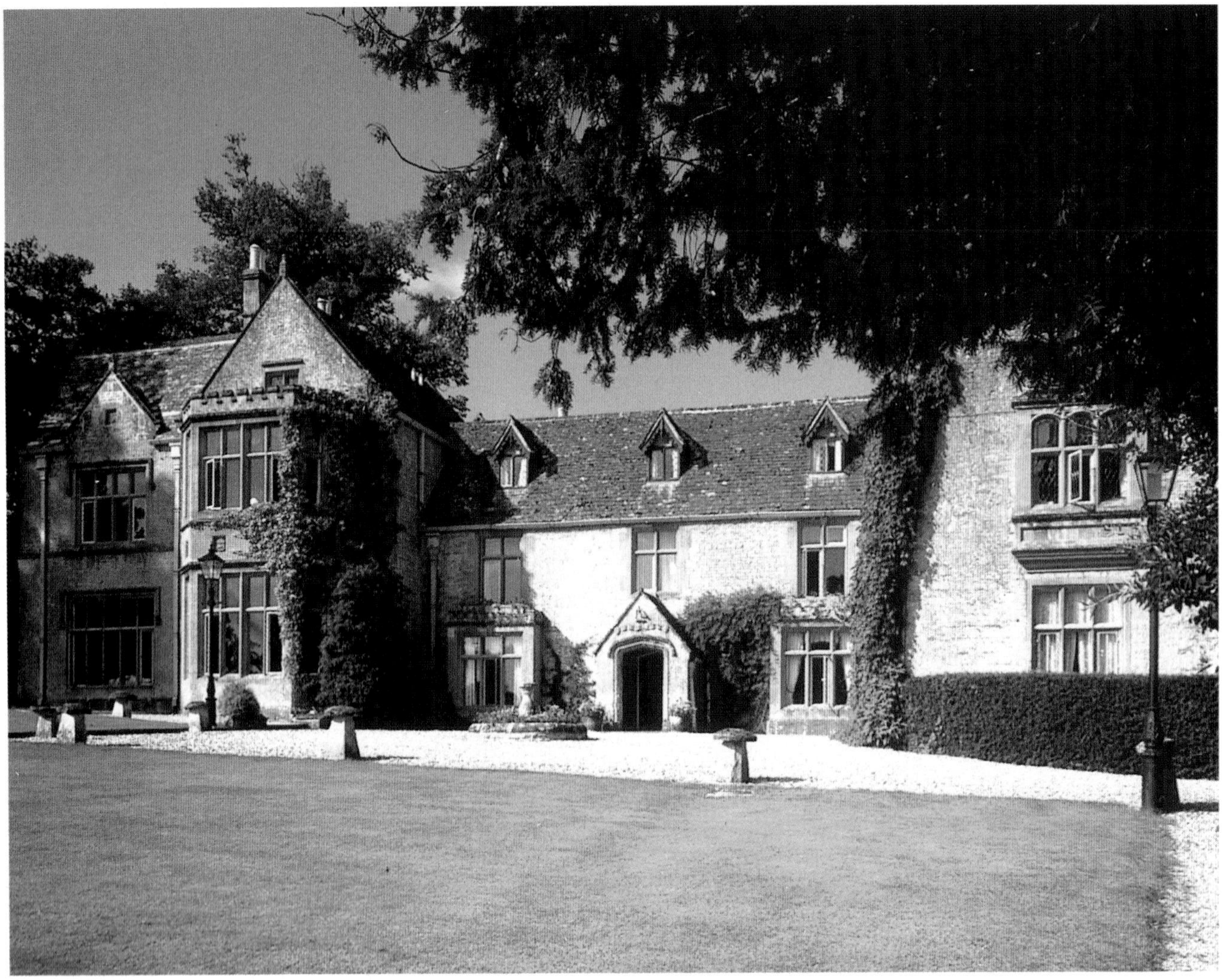

Lords Of The Manor Hotel

UPPER SLAUGHTER, NR BOURTON-ON-THE-WATER, GLOUCESTERSHIRE GL54 2JD
TEL: 01451 820243 FAX: 01451 820696 E-MAIL: lordsofthemanor@btinternet.com

Situated in the heart of the Cotswolds, on the outskirts of one of England's most unspoiled and picturesque villages, stands the Lords of the Manor Hotel. Built in the 17th century of honeyed Cotswold stone, the house enjoys splendid views over the surrounding meadows, stream and parkland. For generations the house was the home of the Witts family, who historically had been rectors of the parish. It is from these origins that the hotel derives its distinctive name. Charming, walled gardens provide a secluded retreat at the rear of the house. Each bedroom bears the maiden name of one of the ladies who married into the Witts family; each room is individually and imaginatively decorated with period furniture. The reception rooms are magnificently furnished with fine antiques, paintings, traditional fabrics and masses of fresh flowers. Log fires blaze in cold weather. The heart of this English country house is its dining room, where truly memorable dishes are created from the best local ingredients. Nearby are Blenheim Palace, Warwick Castle, the Roman antiquities at Bath and Shakespeare country. **Directions:** Upper Slaughter is two miles west of the A429 between Stow-on-the-Wold and Bourton-on-the-Water. Price Guide: Single from £99; double/twin £149–£299.

THE UNICORN HOTEL

SHEEP STREET, STOW-ON-THE-WOLD, GLOUCESTERSHIRE GL54 1HQ
TEL: 01451 830257 FAX: 01451 831090 E-MAIL: bookings@cotswold–inns–hotels.co.uk

Low oak-beamed ceilings and large stone fireplaces pay tribute to The Unicorn's lengthy past. Over the last 300 years, the inn has changed its standards of accommodation, incorporating the latest modern facilities, yet many vestiges of the former centuries remain. The recently refurbished interior is decorated in a stylish manner featuring Jacobean furniture and antique artefacts whilst log fires abound. Enhanced by floral quilts and comfortable armchairs, the 20 en suite bedrooms are simple yet charming. Fine paintings adorn the walls of the public rooms and the cosy bar offers hand-carved wooden chairs and rich carpets. Modern British cooking is served in the elegant surroundings of the Georgian restaurant from an imaginative à la carte menu. The hotel is well-frequented on Sundays by guests wishing to indulge in the delicious lunchtime roast. Local leisure facilities include horse-riding and the golf course. Shooting and fishing are popular outdoor pursuits. Many historic buildings and castles are within easy reach including the magnificent Blenheim Palace and Warwick Castle. Nature enthusiasts will be delighted with the splendid gardens at Sudeley Castle. **Directions:** The nearest motorway is the M40 junction 10. Then take the A44 or the A436 in the direction of Stow-on-the-Wold. Price Guide: Single £60–£70; double/twin £105–£120.

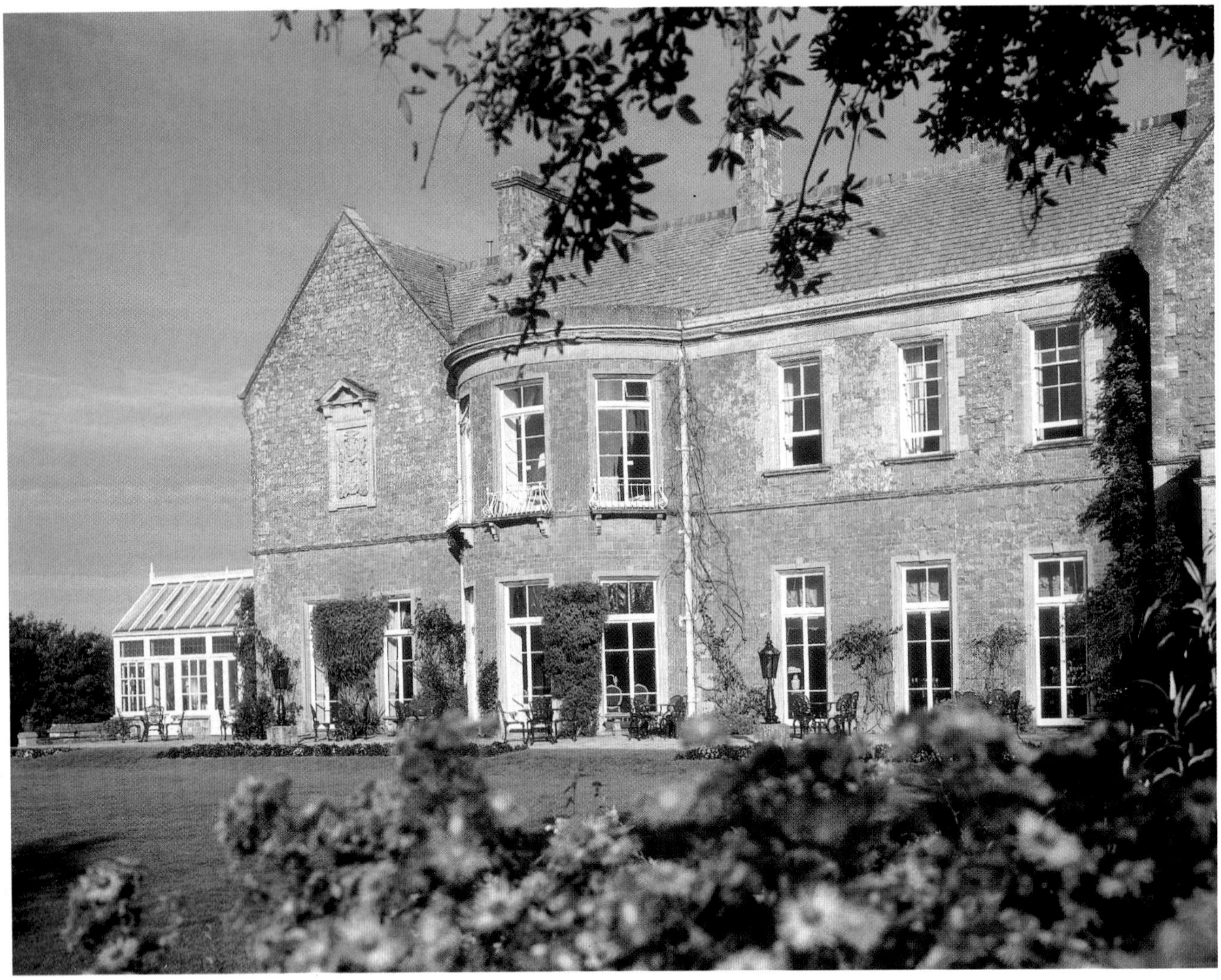

WYCK HILL HOUSE

WYCK HILL, STOW-ON-THE WOLD, GLOUCESTERSHIRE GL54 1HY
TEL: 01451 831936 FAX: 01451 832243 E-MAIL: wyckhill@wrensgroup.com

Wyck Hill House is a magnificent Cotswold mansion built in the early 1700s, reputedly on the site of an early Roman settlement. It is set in 100 acres of wooded and landscaped gardens, overlooking the beautiful Windrush Valley. The hotel has been elegantly restored and the bedrooms, some of which are located in the Coach House and Orangery, are individually furnished to combine superb antiques with modern comforts. There is a suite with a large, antique four-poster bed, which is perfect for a honeymoon or for other special occasions. The cedar-panelled library is an ideal room in which to read, if you wish, and to relax with morning coffee or afternoon tea. The award-winning restaurant provides the highest standards of modern British cuisine from the freshest seasonally available local produce. The menus are complemented by a superb wine list. Wyck Hill House hosts several special events, including opera, travel talks, cultural weekends and a variety of theme activities. The hotel is an ideal base from which to tour the university city of Oxford and the Georgian city of Bath. Cheltenham, Blenheim Palace and Stratford-upon-Avon are just a short drive away. Special price 2-night breaks are available. **Directions:** 1½ miles south of Stow-on-the-Wold on A424 Stow–Burford road. Price Guide: Single £110; double/twin £160; suite £260.

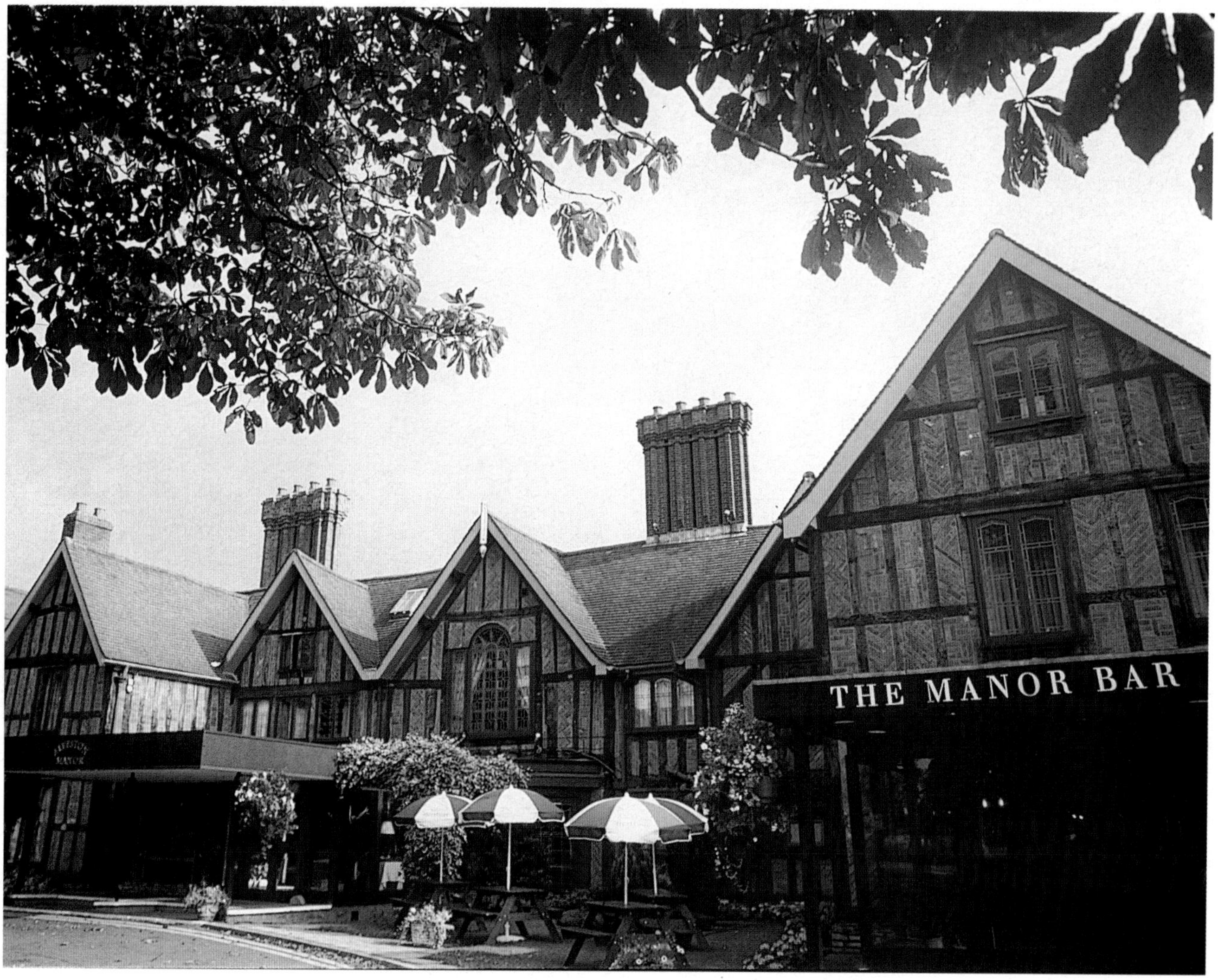

ALVESTON MANOR

CLOPTON BRIDGE, STRATFORD-UPON-AVON, WARWICKSHIRE
TEL: 0870 400 8181 FAX: 01789 414095 E-MAIL: alvestonmanor@heritage–hotels.co.uk

Legend has it that the first performance of Shakespeare's A Midsummer's Night Dream was given under the ancient cedar tree standing in the grounds of this historic and charming hotel. Alveston Manor is conveniently situated on the south side of the River Avon a short walk from the town centre. With its wood-framed façade, leaded windows, pointed roof peaks and tall, ornate chimneys it is an imposing sight to visitors and passing travellers. The interior is enhanced by tasteful décor, rich furnishings, antiques, fine pictures and striking floral displays. There is also a delightful, delicate aroma created by years of polish on original oak panelling and an Elizabethan staircase. Guests can relax in total peace and enjoy an appealing period charm that sympathetically encompasses every modern day comfort. The en suite bedrooms are fitted to a high standard, with many of the bedrooms being situated in the adjoining modern Warwick and Charlecote Wings. A selection of suites and feature rooms are located in the original Manor House. Pre-dinner apéritifs can be sipped in an intimate cocktail bar before the enjoyment of a superbly prepared dinner **Directions:** Exit M40 at junction 15 and take A46 and A439 towards Stratford. Join the one-way system towards Banbury and Oxford. Alveston Manor is at the junction of A422/A3400. Price Guide: Single from £70; double/twin from £140; suite from £160.

Billesley Manor

BILLESLEY, ALCESTER, NR STRATFORD-UPON-AVON, WARWICKSHIRE B49 6NF
TEL: 01789 279955 FAX: 01789 764145 E-MAIL: bookings@billesleymanor.co.uk

This magnificent 16th-century Manor House is set in 11 acres of its own private parkland and has a unique topiary garden and sun terrace. Centuries of history and tradition welcome guests to this beautiful hotel. An impressive indoor heated swimming pool, tennis courts, six-hole pitch and putt course, croquet lawn and rough ground are available. The organisation of corporate events such as clay pigeon shooting, archery and quad biking are also on offer. The hotel has 61 beautiful bedrooms, including four-poster rooms and suites, all of which are en suite and many with stunning gardens views. A selection of rooms for private dining are available for family, friends or business guests. Cuisine of the highest standards is served in the Stuart restaurant, awarded 2 AA Rosettes. The recently completed 'Cedar Barns' offer a new dimension in conference facilities incorporating state-of-the-art equipment in unique and impressive surroundings. Weekend breaks are available – ideal for visiting the Royal Shakespeare Theatre, Warwick Castle, Ragley Hall and the Cotswolds. Situated in the heart of England, minutes away from Shakespeare's Stratford-upon-Avon and only 23 miles from Birmingham International Airport, the hotel can be easily accessed by air, rail and road. Directions: Leave M40 at exit 15, follow A46 towards Evesham and Alcester. 3 miles beyond Stratford-upon-Avon turn right to Billesley. Price Guide: Single £115; double/twin £170; suite £220.

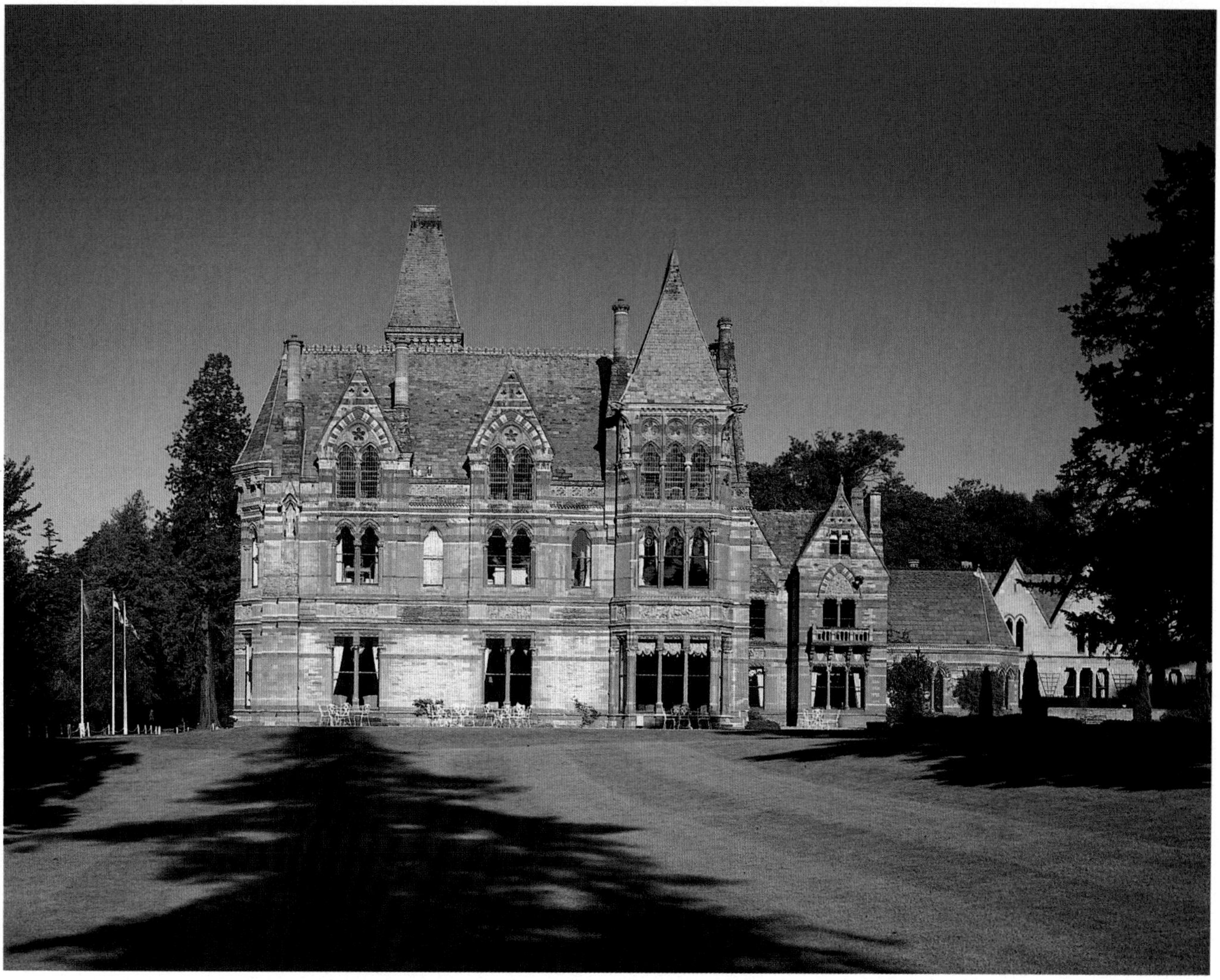

ETTINGTON PARK

ALDERMINSTER, STRATFORD-UPON-AVON, WARWICKSHIRE CV37 8BU
TEL: 01789 450123 FAX: 01789 450472 E-MAIL: ettington@arcadianhotels.co.uk

The foundations of Ettington Park date back at least 1000 years. Mentioned in the Domesday Book, Ettington Park rises majestically over 40 acres of Warwickshire parkland, surrounded by terraced gardens and carefully tended lawns, where guests can wander at their leisure to admire the pastoral views. The interiors are beautiful, their striking opulence enhanced by flowers, beautiful antiques and original paintings. Amid these elegant surroundings guests can relax totally, pampered with every luxury. On an appropriately grand scale, the 48 bedrooms and superb leisure complex, comprising an indoor heated swimming pool, spa bath, solarium and sauna, make this a perfect choice for the sybarite. The menu reflects the best of English and French cuisine, served with panache in the dining room, with its elegant 18th century rococo ceiling and 19th century carved family crests. The bon viveur will relish the fine wine list. Splendid conference facilities are available: the panelled Long Gallery and 14th century chapel are both unique venues. Riding is a speciality, while clay pigeon shooting, archery and fishing can also be arranged on the premises. **Directions:** From M40 junction 15 (Warwick) take A46, A439 signposted Stratford, then left-hand turn onto A3400. Ettington Park is five miles south of Stratford-upon-Avon off the A3400. Price Guide: Single £105; double/twin from £185; suites from £265.

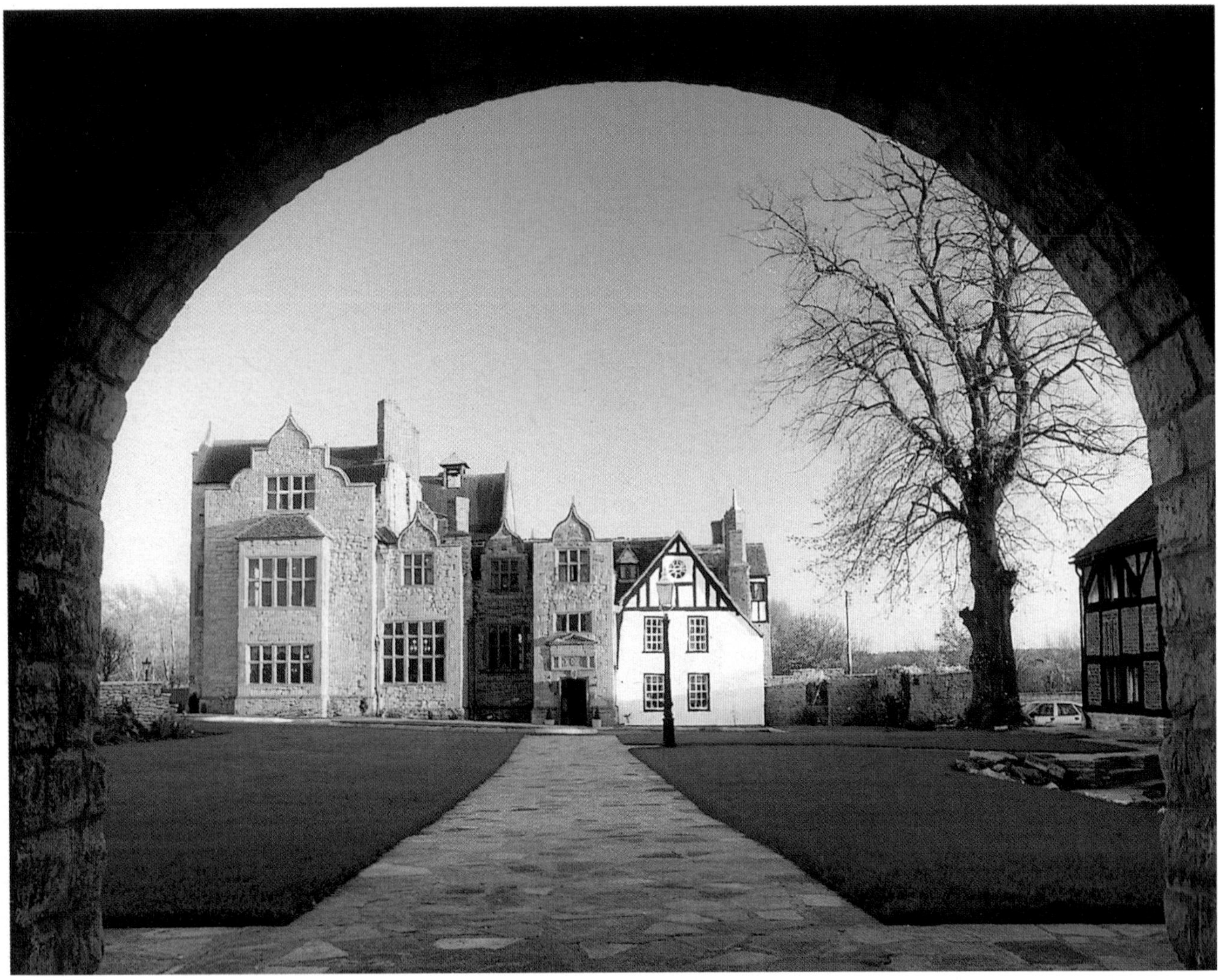

SALFORD HALL HOTEL

ABBOTS SALFORD, NR EVESHAM, WORCESTERSHIRE WR11 5UT
TEL: 01386 871300 FAX: 01386 871301 E-MAIL: reception@salfordhall.co.uk

Between Shakespeare's Stratford-upon-Avon, the rolling Cotswolds and the Vale of Evesham is the Roman village of Abbot's Salford. Steeped in history, Salford Hall is a romantic Grade I listed manor house. It was built in the late 15th century as a retreat for the monks of Evesham Abbey and the imposing stone wing was added in the 17th century. Essentially unchanged, stained glass, a priest hole, exposed beams, oak panelling and original decorative murals are examples of the well-preserved features of the interior. The period charm is doubly appealing when combined with modern comforts, gracious furnishings, delicious food and an extensive selection of fine wines. Reflecting the past associations of the hall, the bedrooms are named after historical figures and all are individually appointed with oak furniture and luxury fittings. Guests may relax in the conservatory lounge or on the sunny terrace within the walled flower garden. The Hawkesbury room was formerly a medieval kitchen. Facilities include snooker, a sauna and a solarium. Special weekends are arranged for hot-air ballooning, horse-racing, touring the Cotswolds, discovering Shakespeare and murder mysteries. Closed for Christmas. **Directions:** Abbot's Salford is 8 miles west of Stratford-upon-Avon on B439 towards The Vale of Evesham. Price Guide: Single £85–118; double/twin £118–£140.

33 MasterCard VISA AMERICAN EXPRESS VCR M 50

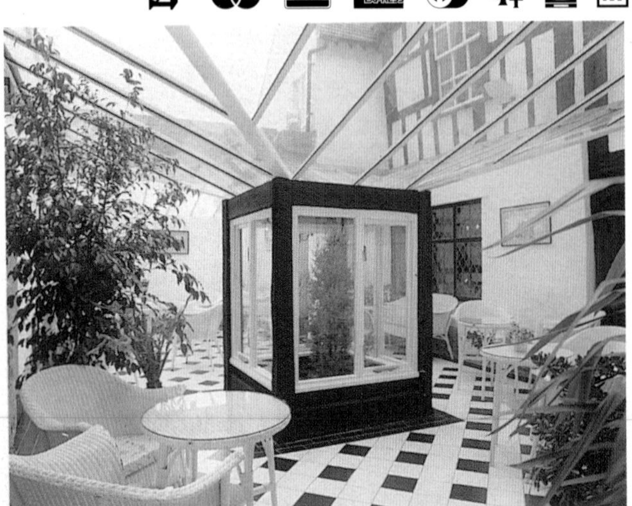

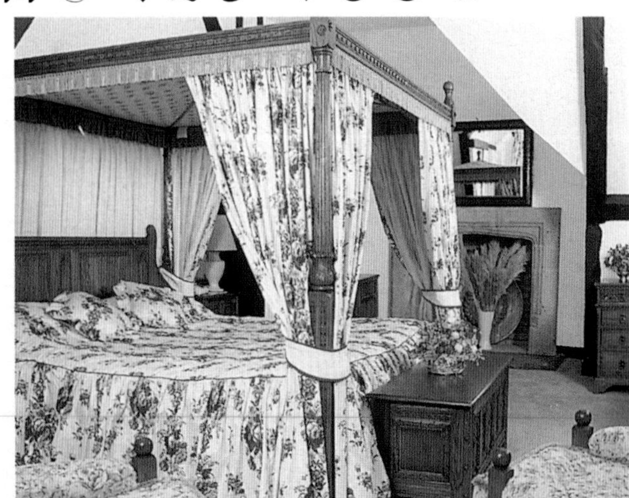

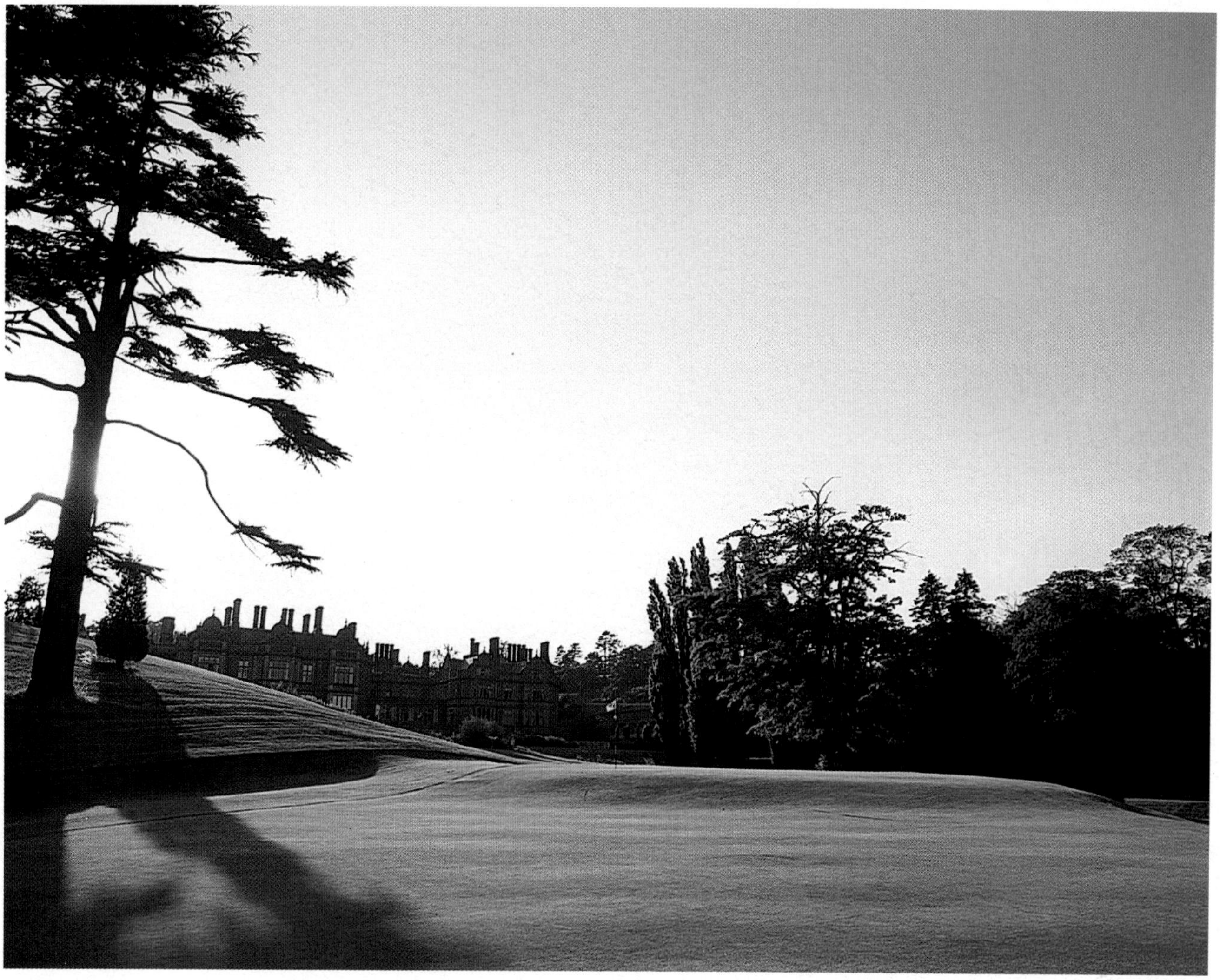

WELCOMBE HOTEL AND GOLF COURSE

WARWICK ROAD, STRATFORD-UPON-AVON, WARWICKSHIRE CV37 0NR
TEL: 01789 295252 FAX: 01789 414666 E-MAIL: sales@welcombe.co.uk

Only minutes from the motorway network, yet peacefully set amid its own 157-acre parkland estate, the Welcombe Hotel & Golf Course is the leading hotel in the heart of England. Continuous refurbishment of the 1869 mansion has resulted in a stunning hotel and championship 18-hole golf course. The public areas include an oak-panelled lounge, immaculate cocktail bar and light and airy 2 AA Rosette restaurant, where finest contemporary cuisine is matched by a well-balanced wine list. The setting is extremely elegant, with breathtaking views over the gardens to the parkland beyond. Accommodation includes suites, gallery rooms and bedrooms, all beautifully decorated and appointed to the highest standards. Superb private rooms are available for conferences, board meetings and product launches. All enjoy natural daylight and three feature French doors onto a terrace overlooking the gardens. Corporate golf events can be arranged on the hotel's own course, with brand new clubhouse facilities including private function rooms, bistro style restaurant, changing rooms and professional golf shop. Floodlit tennis courts are on site. Stratford-upon-Avon, Royal Shakespeare Theatres, The Cotswolds and Warwick Castle are nearby. **Directions:** 5m from exit 15 off M40, on A439. 1m from Stratford-upon-Avon. Price Guide: Single £120–£160; double/twin £160–£310; suite £275–£750.

THE SWAN DIPLOMAT HOTEL

STREATLEY-ON-THAMES, BERKSHIRE RG8 9HR
TEL: 01491 878800 FAX: 01491 872554 E-MAIL: sales@swan–diplomat.co.uk

In a beautiful setting on the banks of the River Thames, this hotel offers visitors comfortable accommodation. All of the 46 bedrooms, many of which have balconies overlooking the river, are appointed to high standards with individual décor and furnishings. The hotel's innovative cooking ensures it maintains its two AA Rosettes. Guests can dine in the The Racing Swan restaurant, which, with the Cygnet Bar and outdoor terrace, offers superb riverside views. Business guests are well catered for with six conference suites – all with natural daylight. Moored alongside the hotel is the Magdalen College Barge – a unique venue for small meetings and cocktail parties. Special themed programmes can be arranged such as Bridge weekends. Reflexions leisure club is equipped with a heated 'fitness' pool, sauna, sunbeds, spa bath, steam room and a wide range of exercise equipment. Cruising on the river may be arranged by the hotel and golf, horse riding, and clay pigeon shooting are available locally. Events in the locality include Henley Regatta, Ascot and Newbury Races, while Windsor Castle, Blenheim Palace, Oxford and London's airports are easily accessible. **Directions:** The hotel lies just off the A329 in Streatley village. Price Guide: Single £75.50–£137.50; double/twin £105–£174; suites £224.

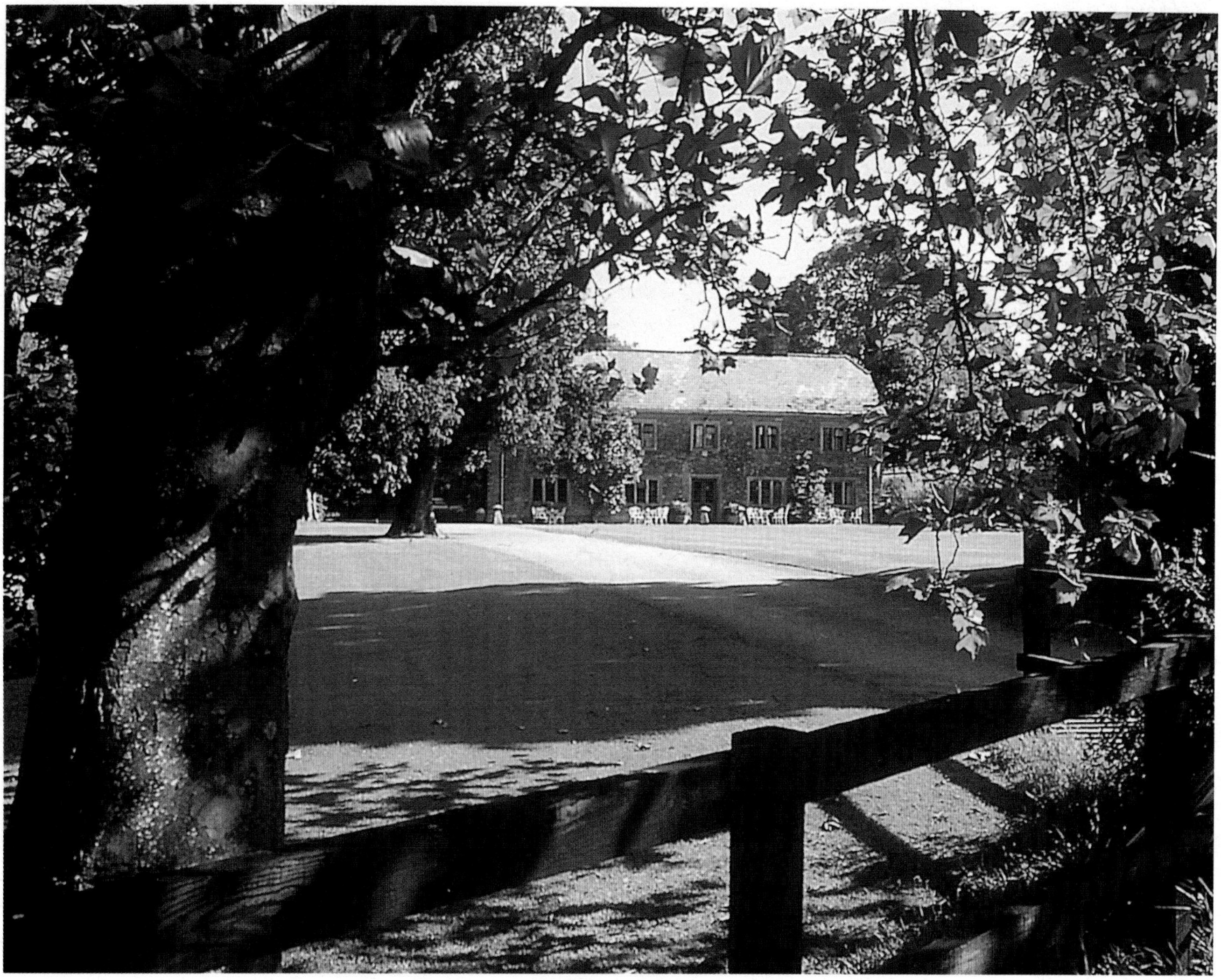

Plumber Manor

STURMINSTER NEWTON, DORSET DT10 2AF

TEL: 01258 472507 FAX: 01258 473370 E-MAIL: book@plumbermanor.com

An imposing Jacobean building of local stone, occupying extensive gardens in the heart of Hardy's Dorset, Plumber Manor has been the home of the Prideaux-Brune family since the early 17th century. Leading off a charming gallery, hung with family portraits, are six very comfortable bedrooms. The conversion of a natural stone barn lying within the grounds, as well as the courtyard building, has added a further ten spacious bedrooms, some of which have window seats overlooking the garden and the Develish stream. Three interconnecting dining rooms comprise the restaurant, where a good choice of imaginative, well-prepared dishes is presented, supported by a wide-ranging wine list. Chef Brian Prideaux-Brune's culinary prowess has been recognised by all the major food guides. Open for dinner every evening and Sunday lunch. The Dorset landscape, with its picture-postcard villages such as Milton Abbas and Cerne Abbas, is close at hand, while Corfe Castle, Lulworth Cove, Kingston Lacy and Poole Harbour are not far away. Riding can be arranged locally: however, if guests wish to bring their own horse to hack or hunt with local packs, the hotel provides free stabling on a do-it-yourself basis. Closed during February. **Directions:** Plumber Manor is two miles south west of Sturminster Newton on the Hazelbury Bryan road, off the A357. Price Guide: Single from £85; double/twin from £100.

THE PEAR TREE AT PURTON

CHURCH END, PURTON, SWINDON, WILTSHIRE SN5 4ED
TEL: 01793 772100 FAX: 01793 772369 E-MAIL: relax@peartreepurton.co.uk

Dedication to service is the hallmark of this excellent honey-coloured stone hotel nestling in the Vale of the White Horse between the Cotswolds and Marlborough Downs. Owners Francis and Anne Young are justly proud of its recognition by the award of the RAC's Blue Ribbon for excellence. Surrounded by rolling Wiltshire farmland, The Pear Tree sits majestically in 7½ acres of tranquil grounds on the fringe of the Saxon village of Purton, famed for its unique twin towered Parish Church and the ancient hill fort of Ringsbury Camp. Each of the 18 individually and tastefully decorated bedrooms and suites is named after a character associated with the village, such as Anne Hyde, mother of Queen Mary II and Queen Anne. All are fitted to a high standard and have satellite television, hairdryer, trouser press, a safe and a host of other luxuries. The award-winning conservatory restaurant overlooks colourful gardens and is the perfect setting in which to enjoy good English cuisine prepared with style and flair. Cirencester, Bath, Oxford, Avebury, Blenheim Palace, Sudeley Castle and the Cotswolds are all within easy reach. **Directions:** From M4 exit 16 follow signs to Purton and go through the village until reaching a triangle with Spar Grocers opposite. Turn right up the hill and the Pear Tree is on the left after the Tithe Barn. Price Guide: Single £110; double/twin £110–£130; suites £130.

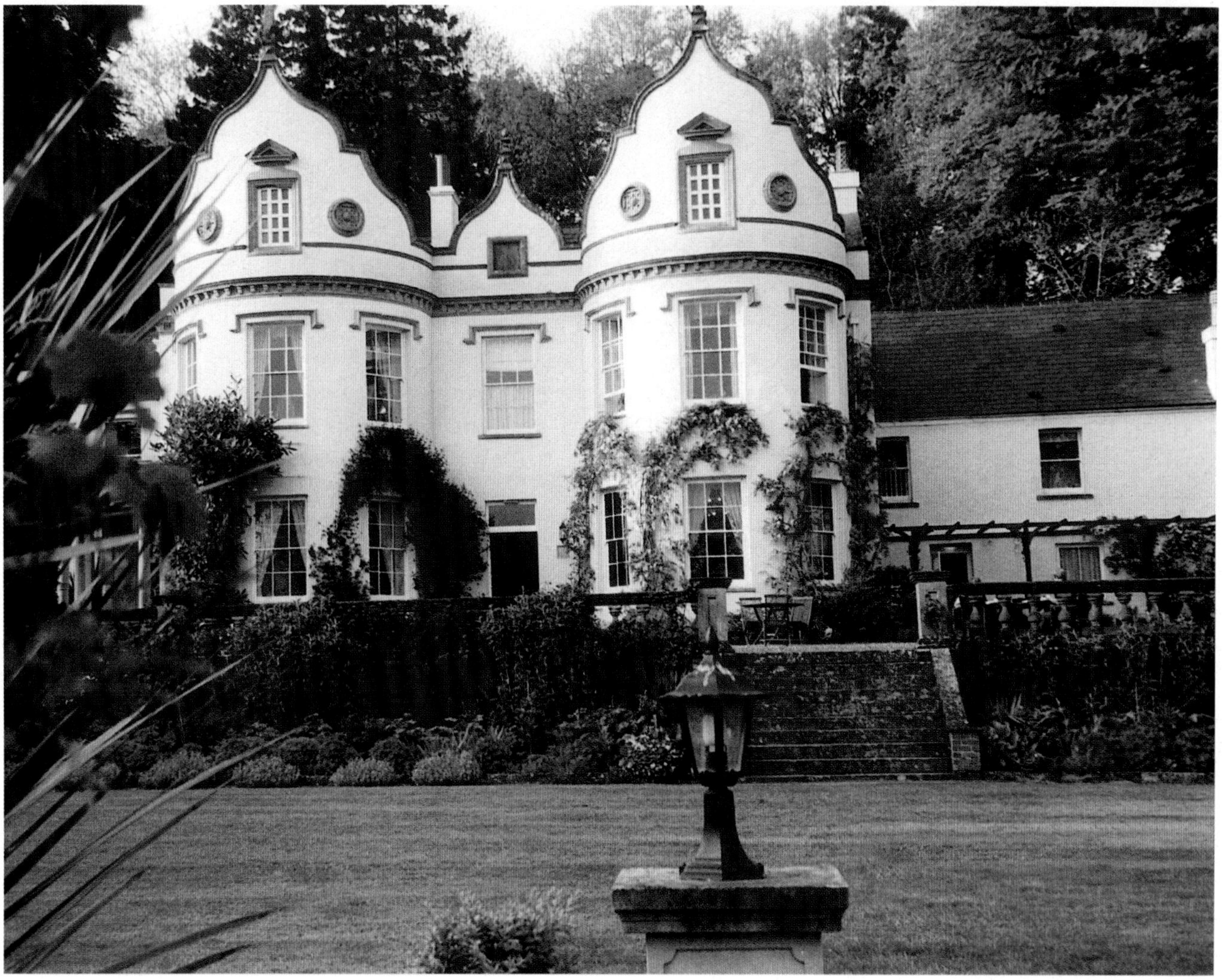

Bindon Country House Hotel

LANGFORD BUDVILLE, WELLINGTON, SOMERSET TA21 0RU
TEL: 01823 400070 FAX: 01823 400071 E-MAIL: BindonHouse@msn.com

This splendid baroque country house has a motto over the west wing door which, although put there in the 1860s, is appropriate today. 'Je trouve bien' is the perfect sentiment for this hotel, albeit in an old setting. Mark and Lynn Jaffa have meticulously restored Bindon. It is tranquil and private, surrounded by seven acres of gardens and woodland. New arrivals immediately have a feeling of well-being, as they respond to greetings from their hosts and drop into sofas in the charming lounge. There are just twelve beautifully proportioned, luxurious bedrooms, all extremely comfortable with many 'extras' including robes in the well-designed bathrooms. The handsome panelled Jacobean bar is convivial and it is advisable to reserve a table in the Wellesley Restaurant, as its reputation is far flung. The graceful setting and excellent wines accompanying the exquisitely presented gourmet dishes make dining a memorable occasion. Country pursuits – fishing, riding, shooting and golf are nearby and Bindon has its own pool, tennis court and croquet lawn. Wells Cathedral and stately homes are there to visit. **Directions:** 15 minutes from M5/J26, drive to Wellington take B3187 to Langford Budville, through village, right towards Wiveliscombe, then right at junction. Pass Bindon Farm and after 450 yards turn right. Price Guide: Single £85; double/twin £105–£205; suite from £135. Short break £75–£110 per person dinner, bed and breakfast.

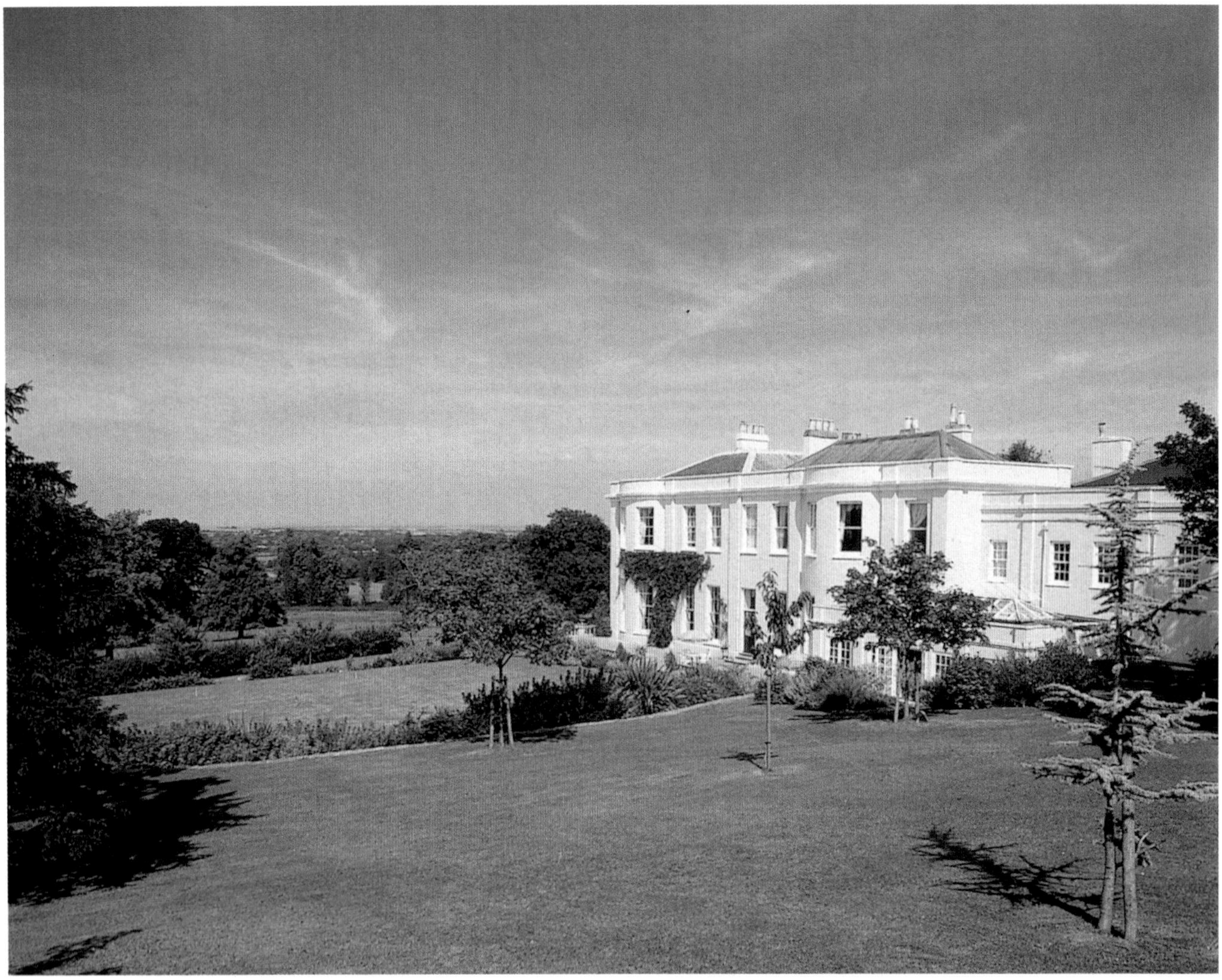

Mount Somerset Country House Hotel

HENLADE, TAUNTON, SOMERSET TA3 5NB
TEL: 01823 442500 FAX: 01823 442900 E-MAIL: info@mountsomersethotel.co.uk

This elegant Regency residence, awarded a Rosette and 3 Stars, stands high on the slopes of the Blackdown Hills, overlooking miles of lovely countryside. The hotel is rich in intricate craftsmanship and displays fine original features. Its owners have committed themselves to creating an atmosphere in which guests can relax, confident that all needs will be catered for. The bedrooms are sumptuously furnished and many offer excellent views over the Quantock Hills. Most of the luxurious en suite bathrooms have spa baths. Tea, coffee and home-made cakes can be enjoyed in the beautifully furnished drawing room, while in the evening the finest food and wines are served in the dining room. A team of chefs work together to create dishes to meet the expectations of the most discerning gourmet. The President's Health Club is close by and its pool and equipment can be used by hotel guests by arrangement. Somerset is a centre for traditional crafts and exhibitions of basket making, sculpture, wood turning and pottery abound. Places of interest nearby include Glastonbury Abbey and Wells Cathedral. **Directions:** At M5 exit at junction 25 and join A358 towards Ilminster. Just past Henlade turn right at sign for Stoke St Mary. At T-junction turn left, the hotel drive is 150 yards on the right. Price Guide: Single from £95–£125; double/twin from £110–£135; suites £155–£170; 3-Course Luncheon from £19.95 and 3-Course Dinner from £24.95.

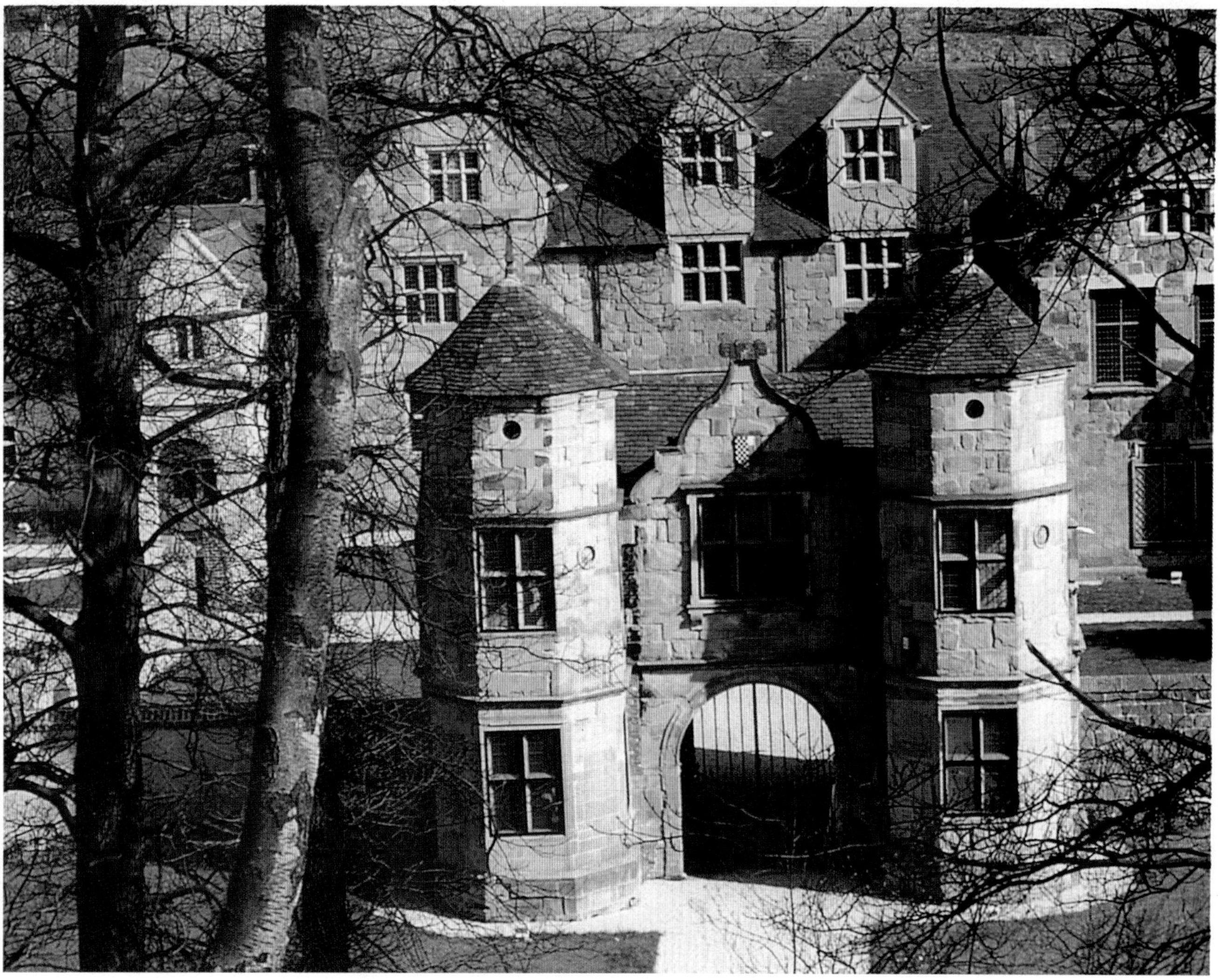

MADELEY COURT

TELFORD, SHROPSHIRE TF7 5DW
TEL: 01952 680068 FAX: 01952 684275

This veritable gem of a residence was European Hotel of the Year 2000. Its characteristic manor house façade stands virtually unaltered since the 16th century, while its interior has been recently expertly rejuvenated – with respect for its history – to provide accommodation suitable for both pleasure or business. Furnishings have been judiciously selected to enrich Madeley's period appeal: scatterings of fine fabrics, handsome antique pieces and elaborate fittings all accentuate the historic atmosphere and ensure that every guest leaves with an indelible impression. The bedrooms, whether located in the old part of the Court or in the newer wing, are quiet and full of character; all are en suite and offer interactive television; some have whirlpool baths and views over the lake. At the heart of Madeley is the original 13th-century hall where the restaurant is now located, serving inventive food, awarded 2 RAC Ribbons, with a wine list to match. Another dining option is the Cellar, which offers a more informal setting. Business meetings and private functions are happily catered for in the three rooms available. Places of interest nearby include Ironbridge Gorge, Shrewsbury, Powys Castle and Weston Park. Directions: Four miles from junction 4 off M54; follow A442 then B4373. Signposted Dawley then Madeley. Price Guide: (room only): Single from £105; double/twin £120–£145; historic £137.

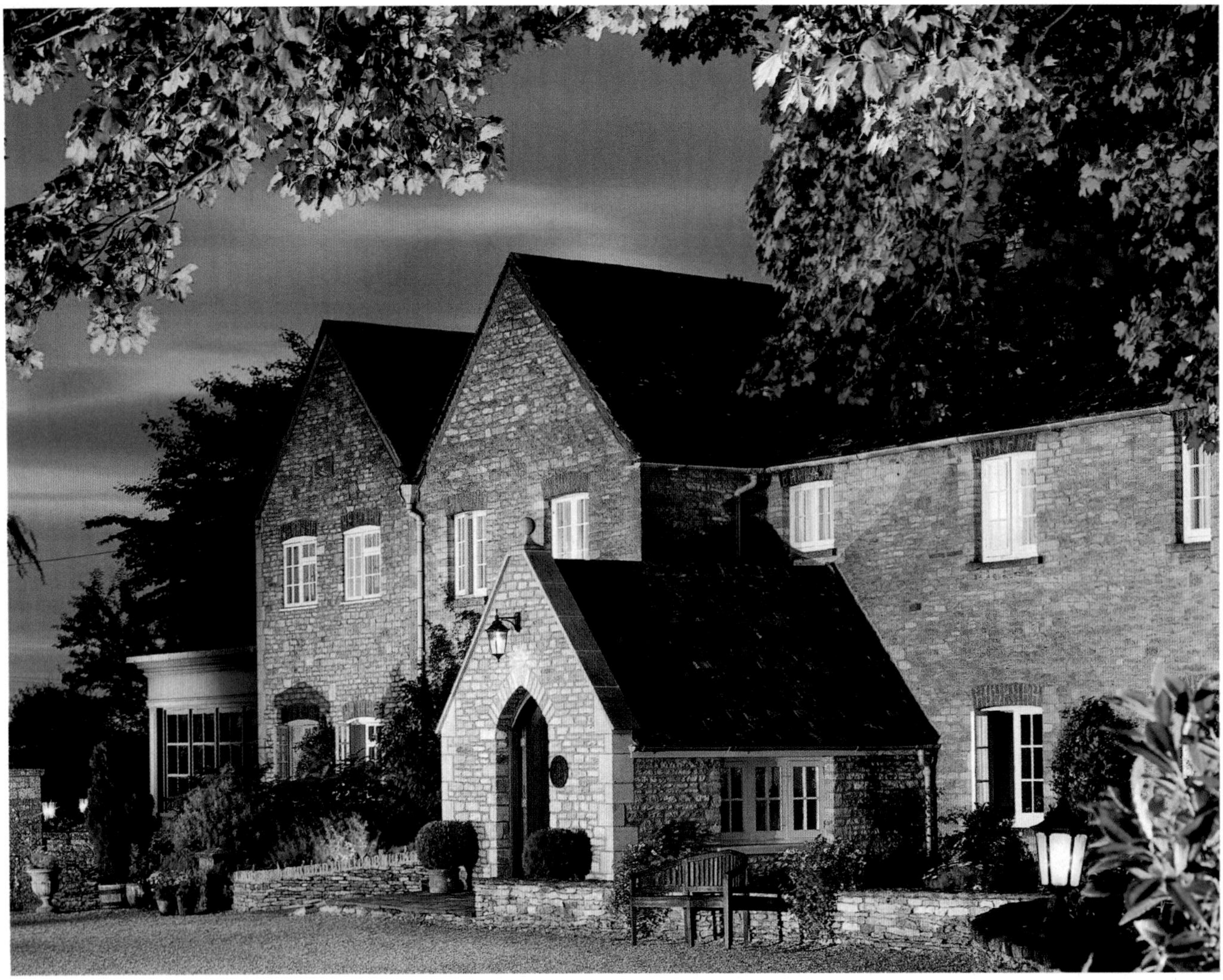

CALCOT MANOR

NR TETBURY, GLOUCESTERSHIRE GL8 8YJ

TEL: 01666 890391 FAX: 01666 890394 E-MAIL: reception@calcotmanor.co.uk

This delightful old manor house, built of Cotswold stone, offers guests tranquillity amidst acres of rolling countryside. Calcot Manor is situated in the southern Cotswolds close to the historic town of Tetbury. The building dates back to the 15th century and was a farmhouse until 1983. Its beautiful stone barns and stables include one of the oldest tithe barns in England, built in 1300 by the Cistercian monks from Kingswood Abbey. These buildings form a quadrangle and the stone glistening in the dawn or glowing in the dusk is quite a spectacle. Calcot achieves the rare combination of professional service and cheerful hospitality without any hint of over formality. The atmosphere is one of peaceful relaxation. All the cottage style rooms are beautifully appointed as are the public rooms. Calcot also has a discreet conference facility and charming cottage providing four family suites, with the sitting areas convertible into children's bedrooms and six family rooms. At the heart of Calcot Manor is its elegant conservatory restaurant where dinner is very much the focus of a memorable stay. There is also the congenial Gumstool Bistro and bar offering a range of simpler traditional food and local ales. **Directions:** From Tetbury, take the A4135 signposted Dursley; Calcot is on the right after 3½ miles Price Guide: Double/twin £135–£180; family rooms £180; family suites £190.

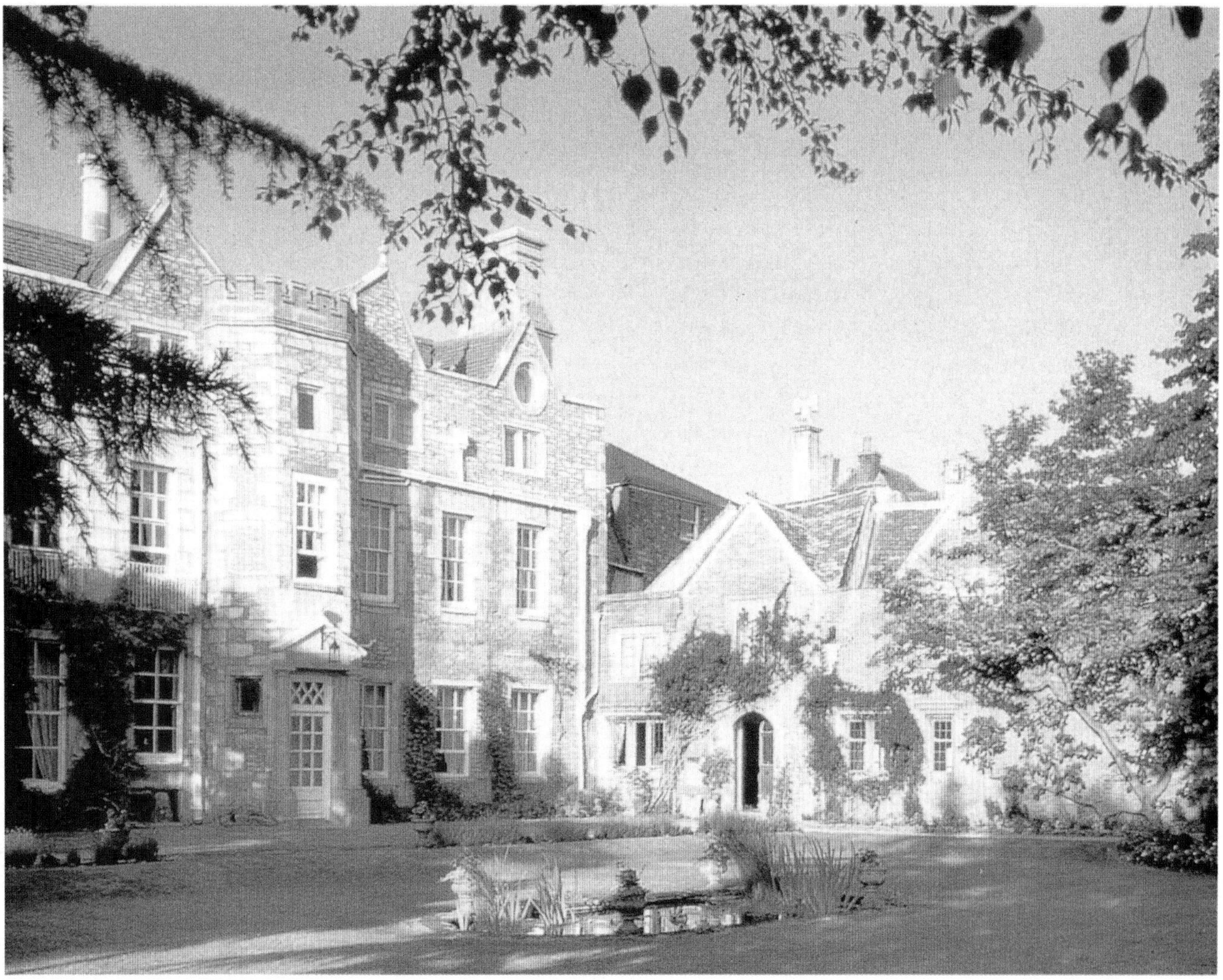

THE CLOSE HOTEL

LONG STREET, TETBURY, GLOUCESTERSHIRE GL8 8AQ
TEL: 01666 502272 FAX: 01666 504401 E-MAIL: reception@theclosehotel.co.uk

Built in 1585, the Close Hotel and Restaurant is an idyllic Elizabethan manor house with 15 charming, individually styled bedrooms, set in the heart of the delightful market town of Tetbury. Since becoming a hotel in 1974, its reputation has developed, and today it holds the prestigious accolade of 3 AA rosettes for food over three consecutive years. The dinner menu offers a delightful composition of modern and contemporary tastes, each enhanced by thoughtful companions such as star anise ice cream or balsamic jelly and pear chutney, whilst the Tastings menu offers guests a gastronomic journey through 7 courses of the chef's latest creations. An appetite for such a culinary experience can easily be worked up by scouring the many antique shops within walking distance of the hotel, as this area really is a collector's paradise. The historic towns of Cirencester, Cheltenham and Bath are all within easy access, as are the Royal Estates of Highgrove and Gatcombe. Horticulturalists will love the arboretum at Westonbirt, and sporting enthusiasts can enjoy Cheltenham races and motor racing at Castle Combe. The Close is an ideal venue for weddings and small conferences, offering a range of beautifully styled meeting rooms and private use. (N.B. min. age in the restaurant: 12 years). **Directions:** The Close is on Long Street, the main street of Tetbury which can be found on the A433, minutes from the M4 and M5. Private parking is at the rear of the hotel in Close Gardens.. Price Guide: (incl. dinner) Single £90; double/twin £160.

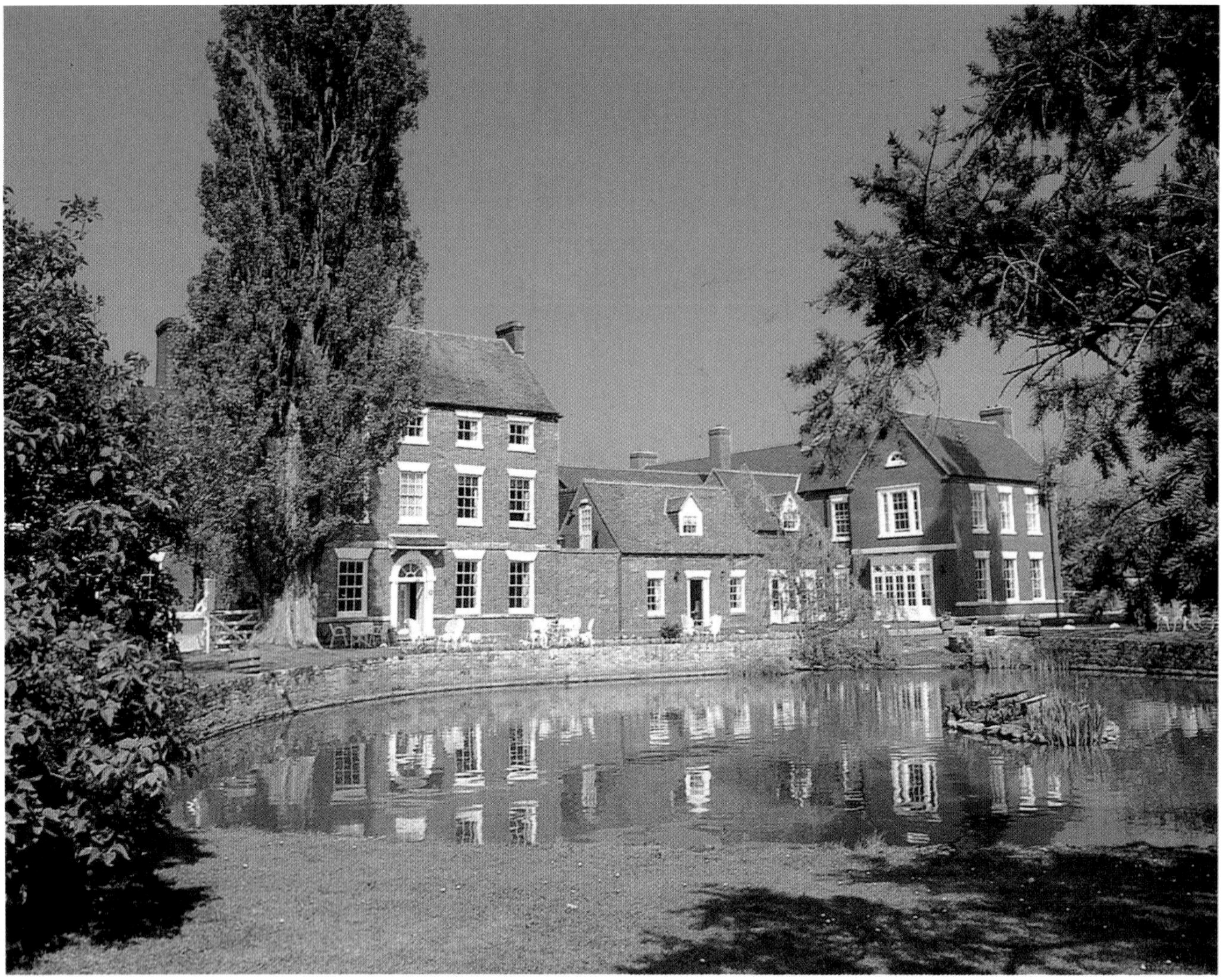

Corse Lawn House Hotel

CORSE LAWN, NR TEWKESBURY, GLOUCESTERSHIRE GL19 4LZ
TEL: 01452 780479/771 FAX: 01452 780840 E-MAIL: hotel@corselawnhouse.u–net.com

Although only 6 miles from the M5 and M50, Corse Lawn is a completely unspoiled, typically English hamlet in a peaceful Gloucestershire backwater. The hotel, an elegant Queen Anne listed building set back from the village green, stands in 12 acres of gardens and grounds and still displays the charm of its historic pedigree. Visitors can be assured of the highest standards of service and cooking: Baba Hine is famous for the dishes she produces, while Denis Hine, of the Hine Cognac family, is in charge of the wine cellar. The service here, now in the hands of son Giles, is faultlessly efficient, friendly and personal. As well as the renowned restaurant, there are three comfortable drawing rooms, a large lounge bar, a private dining-cum-conference room for up to 45 persons and a similar, smaller room for up to 20. A tennis court, heated indoor swimming pool and croquet lawn adjoin the hotel and most sports and leisure activities can be arranged. Corse Lawn is ideal for exploring the Cotswolds, Malverns and Forest of Dean. **Directions:** Corse Lawn House is situated on the B4211 between the A417 (Gloucester–Ledbury road) and the A438 (Tewkesbury–Ledbury road). Price Guide: Single £80; double/twin £125; four-poster £145; suites £160. Good reductions for short breaks.

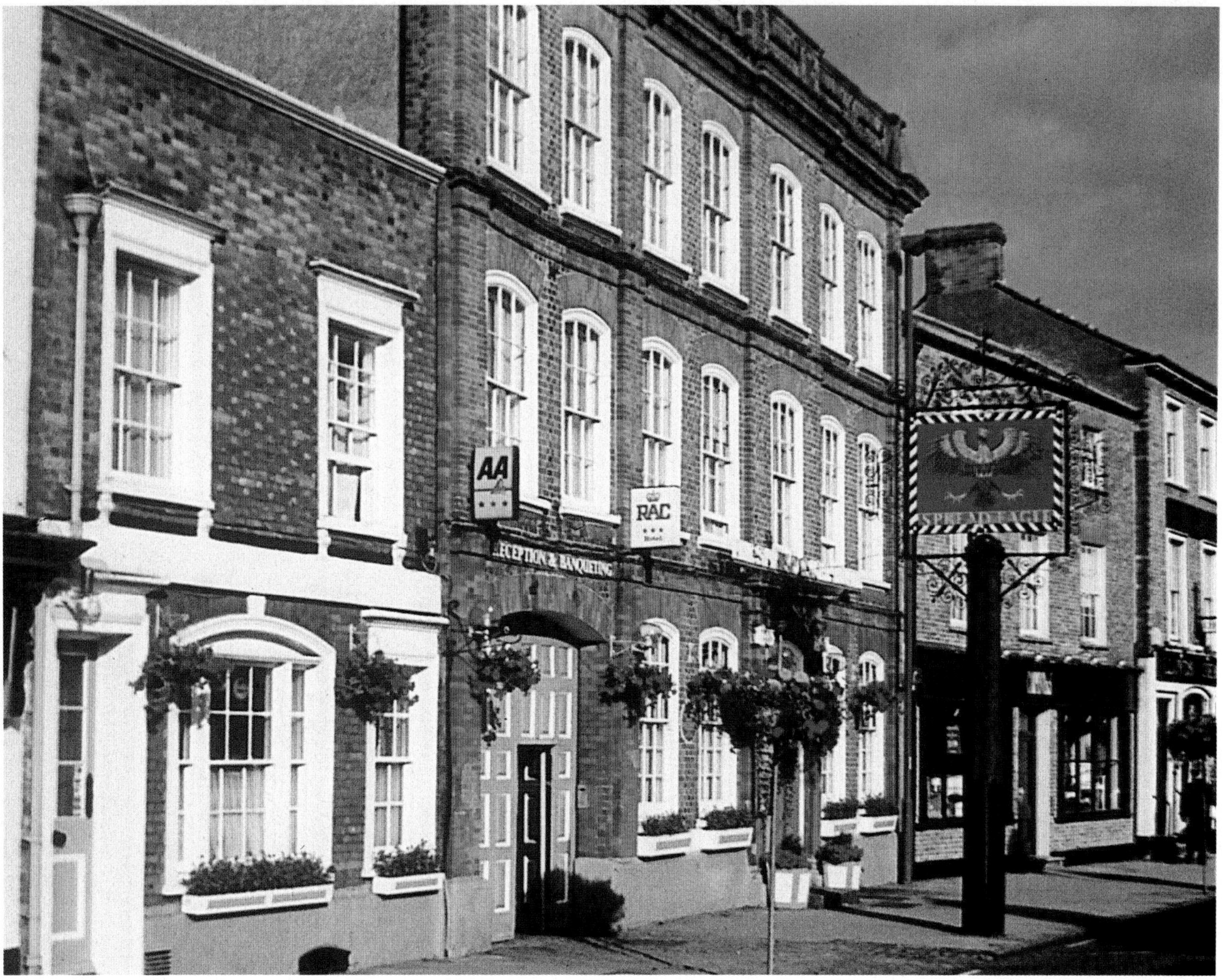

THE SPREAD EAGLE HOTEL

CORNMARKET, THAME, OXFORDSHIRE OX9 2BW
TEL: 01844 213661 FAX: 01844 261380 E-MAIL: enquiries@spreadeaglethame.co.uk

The historic market town of Thame with its mile long main street is a delightful town just six miles from the M40 and surrounded by beautiful countryside speckled with tiny, charming villages, many of them with cosy thatched cottages. The Spread Eagle has stood tall, square and imposingly in the heart of Thame since the 16th century and over the years has played host to Charles II, French prisoners from the Napoleonic wars, famous politicians and writers such as Evelyn Waugh. The former proprietor John Fothergill introduced haute cuisine to the provinces and chronicled his experiences in the best seller, 'An Innkeeper's Diary'. The book is still available at The Spread Eagle and the restaurant is named after him. It serves excellent English and French cuisine made with the freshest local produce. Seasonal changing menus are complemented by a well balanced wine list which includes some superb half-bottles of unusual vintages. Guests have 33 bedrooms to choose from, comprising two suites, 23 doubles, three twins and five singles. All are en suite, well equipped and tastefully decorated. Good conference facilities are available. The Spread Eagle is ideally situated for visits to many fascinating historic places such as Blenheim Palace and Waddesdon Manor. **Directions:** Exit M40 at junction 6. Take B4009 to Chinnor and then B4445 to Thame. The hotel is on the left after the roundabout at the west end of Upper High Street. Price Guide: Single £95; double/twin from £110.

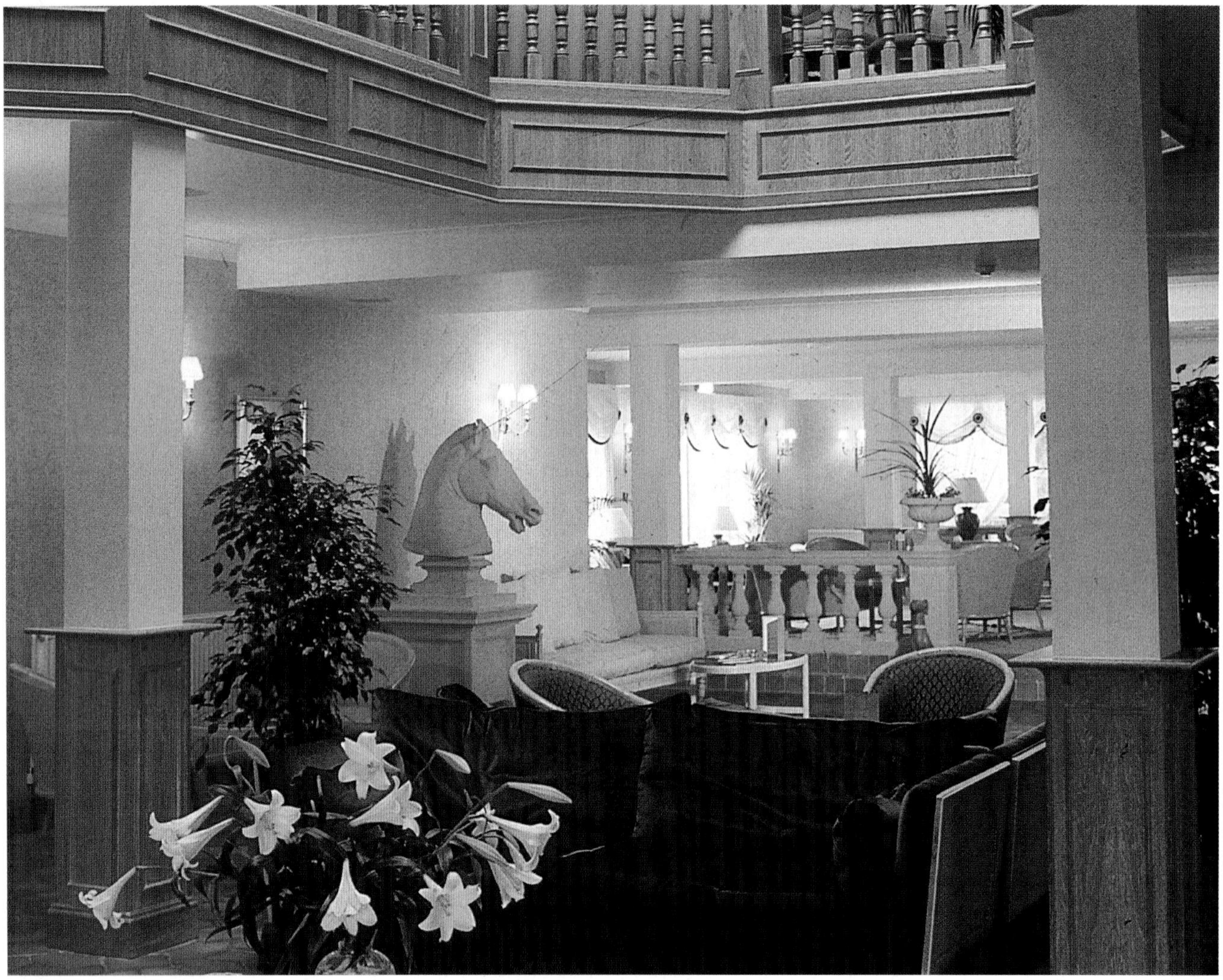

DALE HILL

TICEHURST, NR WADHURST, EAST SUSSEX TN5 7DQ
TEL: 01580 200112 FAX: 01580 201249 E-MAIL: info@dalehill.co.uk

Situated in over 300 acres of fine grounds, high on the Kentish Weald, Dale Hill is a modern hotel which combines the best in golfing facilities with the style and refinement desired by discerning guests. The décor is enhanced by soft coloured fabrics and carpets, creating a summery impression throughout the year. The eight new luxury self contained apartments added in 2001 are ideal for families and set new standards of both comfort and convenience. Golfers have the choice of two 18-hole courses, a gently undulating, 6,093 yards par 70 and a new, challenging championship-standard course designed by former U.S. Masters champion Ian Woosnam. Tuition is available from a PGA professional. Diners enjoy glorious views in a choice of restaurants where traditional award winning cuisine is complemented by a fine wine list and service. The fully equipped health club features a heated swimming pool and a range of health, beauty and fitness facilities. Dale Hill is only a short drive from Tunbridge Wells and its renowned Pantiles shopping walk. Also nearby are medieval Scotney Castle, which dates back to 1380, Sissinghurst, a moated Tudor castle with gardens and Bewl Water, renowned for fly-fishing and water sports **Directions:** From the M25, junction 5, follow the A21 to Flimwell. Then turn right onto the B2087. Dale Hill is on the left Price Guide: Single from £70; double/twin £80–£140.; Suites: £90-£160

ORESTONE MANOR HOTEL & RESTAURANT

ROCKHOUSE LANE, MAIDENCOMBE, TORQUAY, DEVON TQ1 4SX
TEL: 01803 328098 FAX: 01803 328336 E-MAIL: enquiries@orestone.co.uk

This delightful Georgian manor house has recently been the subject of a complete and loving restoration programme by its new owners, and now offers guests the epitome of elegance and luxury in this delightful location on the rural fringe of Torbay. Standing in two acres of its own grounds, the hotel has beautiful views out to the sea beyond and has a refreshing sense of peace and calm. This serenity is continued inside the hotel, where elegant high ceilings and an abundance of space lead guests from the stylish new drawing room into the fresh leafy conservatory and out to the pretty sun terrace with its lovely gardens and views. The 12 bedrooms are delightfully presented and many have their own terrace or balcony; attention to detail is obvious with fresh orange juice, flowers and fluffy bathrobes. The restaurant is stunning with a tempting range of dishes – choose from Chargrilled Scallops with garden leaves and sun-dried tomato dressing, or Red Mullet on a bed of cracked wheat with a Herb Veloute. A wide range of watersports is available, and there are a number of coastal walks from the hotel, while Dartmoor itself is nearby as are many National Trust properties and a Food & Wine Trail. **Directions:** About 3 miles north of Torquay on the A379 (Formerly B3199). Take the coast road towards Teignmouth. Price Guide: Single £50–£120; double/twin £100–£160.

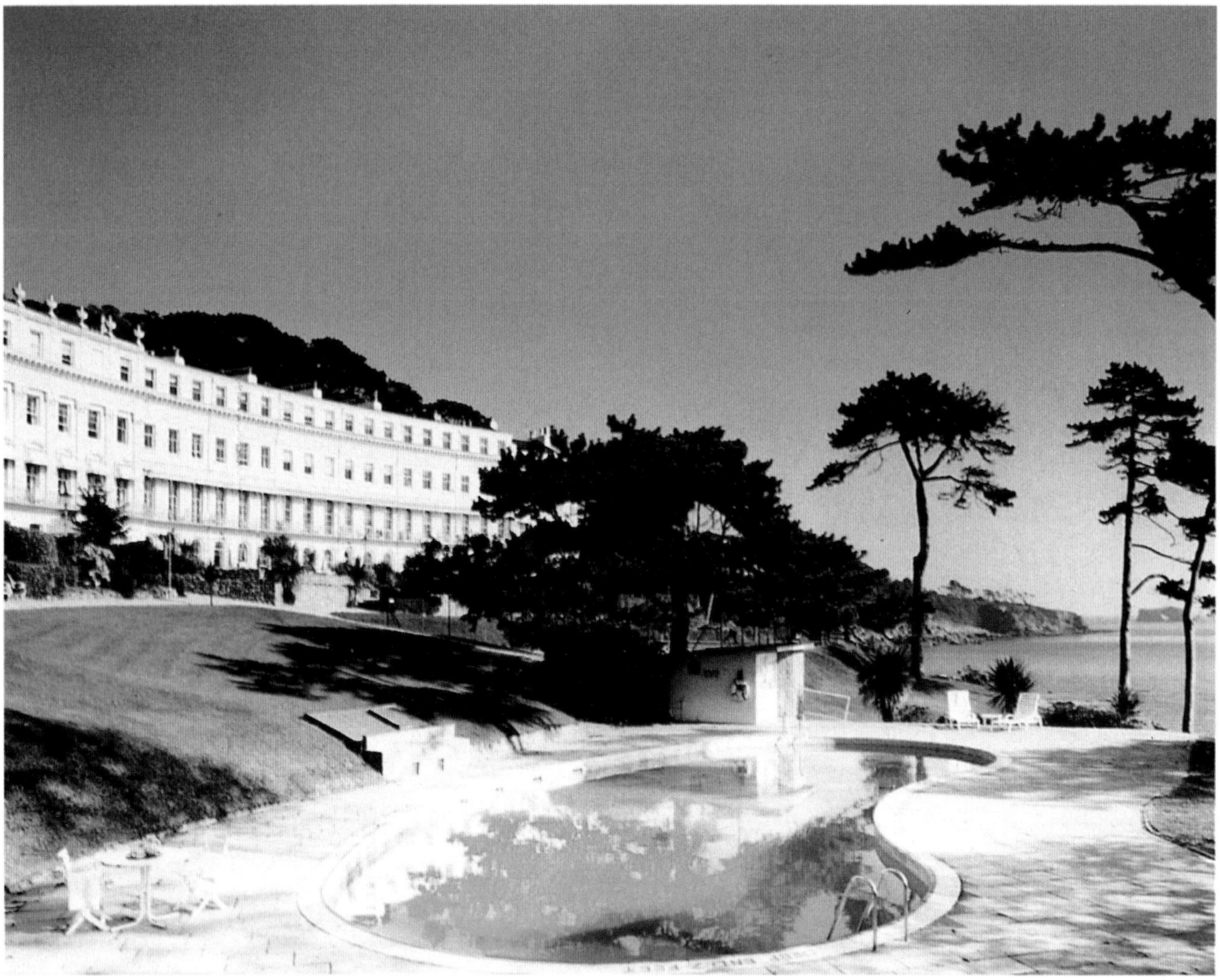

THE OSBORNE HOTEL & LANGTRY'S RESTAURANT

MEADFOOT BEACH, TORQUAY, DEVON TQ1 2LL
TEL: 01803 213311 **FAX:** 01803 296788 **E-MAIL:** enq@osborne-torquay.co.uk

The combination of Mediterranean chic and the much-loved Devon landscape has a special appeal which is reflected at The Osborne. The hotel is the centrepiece of an elegant recently refurbished Regency crescent in Meadfoot, a quiet location within easy reach of the centre of Torquay. Known as a 'country house by the sea', the hotel offers the friendly ambience of a country home complemented by the superior standards of service and comfort expected of a hotel on the English Riviera. Most of the 29 bedrooms have magnificent views and are decorated in pastel shades. Overlooking the sea, Langtry's acclaimed award-winning restaurant provides fine English cooking and tempting regional specialities, while the Brasserie has a menu available throughout the day. Guests may relax in the attractive 5-acre gardens and make use of indoor and outdoor swimming pools, gymnasium, sauna, solarium, tennis court and putting green – all without leaving the grounds. Sailing, archery, clay pigeon shooting and golf can be arranged. Devon is a county of infinite variety, with its fine coastline, bustling harbours, tranquil lanes, sleepy villages and the wilds of Dartmoor. The Osborne is ideally placed to enjoy all these attractions. **Directions:** The hotel is in Meadfoot, to the east of Torquay. Price Guide: Single £45–£80; double/twin £90–£150; suite £120–£200.

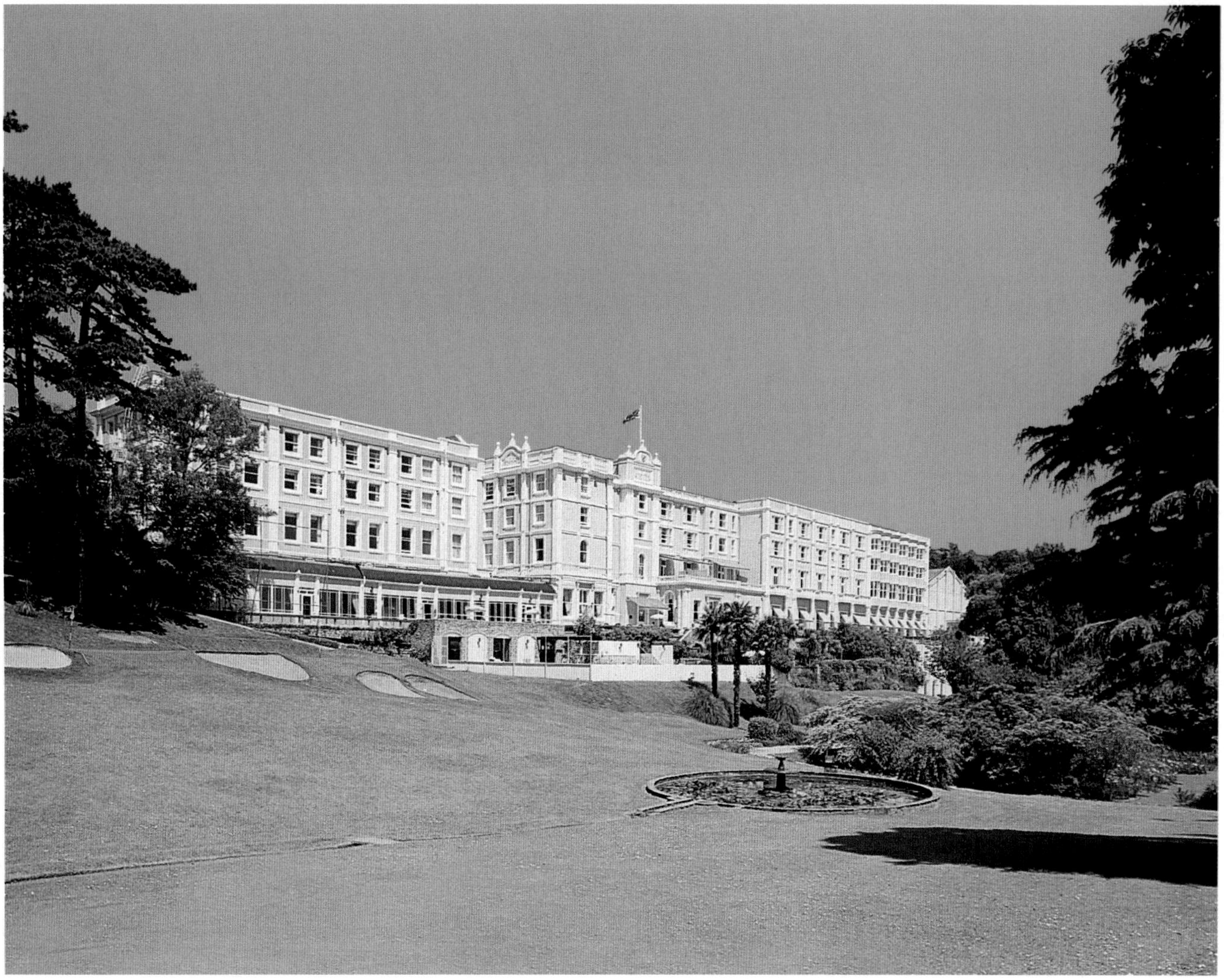

THE PALACE HOTEL

BABBACOMBE ROAD, TORQUAY, DEVON TQ1 3TG
TEL: 01803 200200 FAX: 01803 299899 E-MAIL: info@palacetorquay.co.uk

Once the residence of the Bishop of Exeter, the privately owned Palace Hotel is a gracious Victorian building set in 25 acres of beautifully landscaped gardens and woodlands. The comfortable bedrooms are equipped with every modern amenity and there are also elegant, spacious suites available. Most rooms overlook the hotel's magnificent grounds. The main restaurant provides a high standard of traditional English cooking, making full use of fresh, local produce, as well as offering a good variety of international dishes. The cuisine is complemented by a wide selection of popular and fine wines. Light meals are also available from the lounge and during the summer months, a mediterranean style menu is served on the terrace. A host of sporting facilities has made this hotel famous. These include a short par 3 9-hole championship golf course, indoor and outdoor swimming pools, two indoor and four outdoor tennis courts, two squash courts, saunas, snooker room and a well equipped fitness suite. Places of interest nearby include Dartmoor, South Hams and Exeter. Paignton Zoo, Bygone's Museum and Kent's Cavern are among the local attractions **Directions:** From seafront follow signs for Babbacombe. Hotel entrance is on the right. Price Guide: Single £71–£81; double/twin £142–£162; executive £196; suites £236–£280. Leisure breaks and special weekly rates on request.

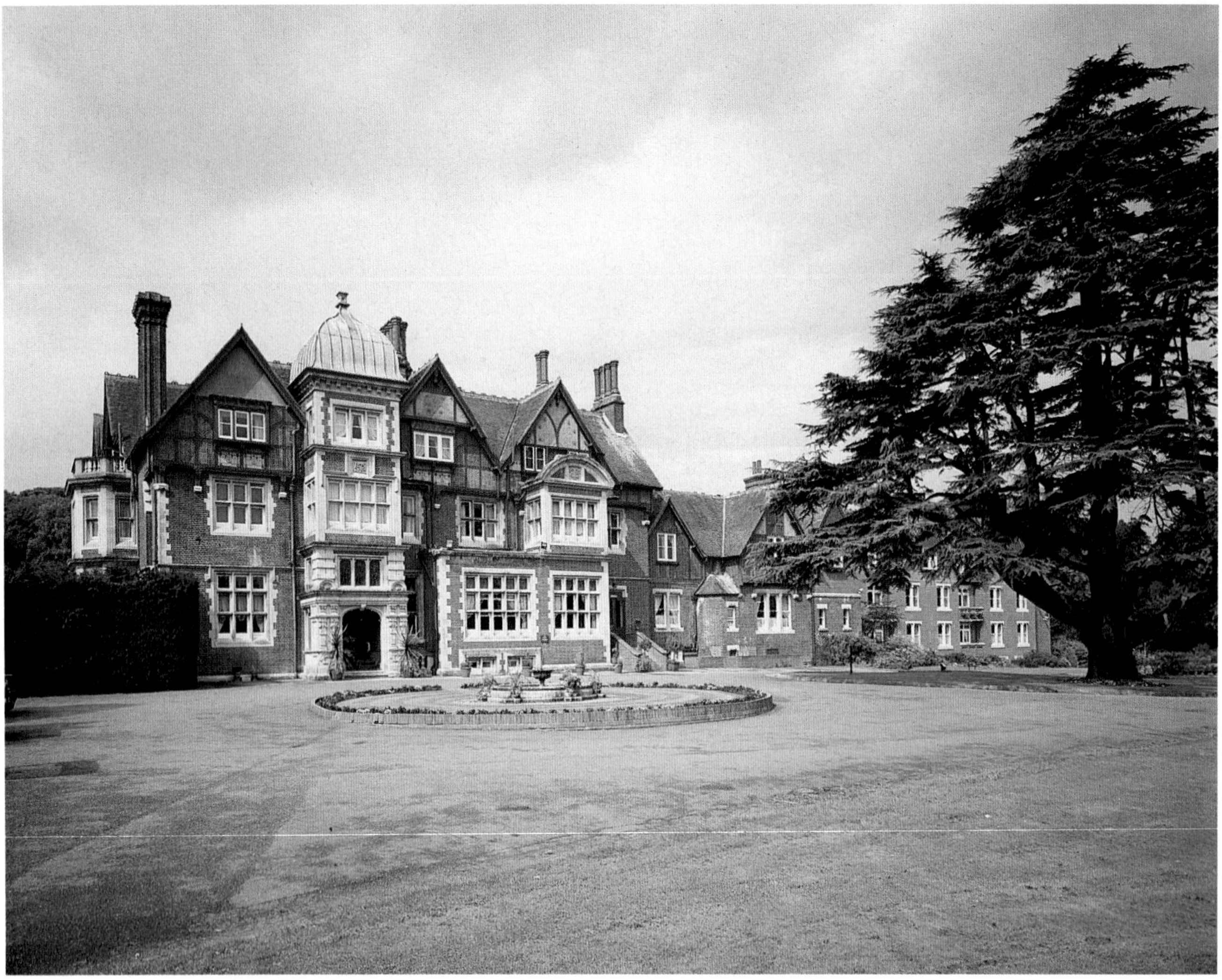

PENDLEY MANOR HOTEL & CONFERENCE CENTRE

COW LANE, TRING, HERTFORDSHIRE HP23 5QY
TEL: 01442 891891 FAX: 01442 890687 E-MAIL: sales@pendley–manor.co.uk

The Pendley Manor was commissioned by Joseph Grout Williams in 1872. His instructions to architect John Lion were to build it in the Tudor style, reflecting the owner's interest in flora and fauna on the carved woodwork and stained glass panels. It stayed in the Williams family for three generations, but in 1987 the Manor was purchased by an independent hotel company, Craydawn Ltd. A refurbishment programme transformed it to its former glory and today's guests can once again enjoy the elegance and beauty of the Victorian era. The bedrooms are attractively furnished and well-equipped, while the cuisine is appealing and well presented. Pendley Manor offers flexible conference facilities for up to 250 people. On the estate, which lies at the foot of the Chiltern Hills, sporting facilities include tennis courts, gymnasium, a snooker room with full-size table, games rooms, buggy riding, laser shooting, archery and hot-air balloon rides. The hotel's newest addition is the impressive 'Lido', which provides health and leisure facilities including an indoor heated swimming pool, Jacuzzi, sauna and solarium. Places of interest nearby include Woburn, Winslow Hall, Chenies Manor, Tring Zoological Museum and Dunstable Downs. **Directions:** Leave the M25 at Jct20 and take the new A41; take exit marked 'Tring'. At the roundabout, take the A4251, then the first right turn into Cow Lane. Price Guide: Single £110; double/twin £130–£150; suites £160.

Hotel Du Vin & Bistro

CRESCENT ROAD, ROYAL TUNBRIDGE WELLS, KENT TN1 2LY
TEL: 01892 526455 FAX: 01892 512044 E-MAIL: reception@tunbridgewells.hotelduvin.com

Set in the historic town of Tunbridge Wells, this Grade II sandstone mansion dates back to 1762 and although in the centre, it enjoys spectacular views over Calverley Park. An inviting ambience is present throughout the property, from the convivial bar to the sunny terrace. The 32 en suite bedrooms have been individually decorated and are enhanced by the superb Egyptian linen, CD players and satellite television. The spacious bathrooms feature power showers, large baths and fluffy robes and towels. The hotel takes great pride in its excellent bistro cuisine and the outstanding wine list. The imaginative dishes are prepared using the freshest local ingredients and are exceptionally good value. Fine wine dinners are often held at the hotel, whilst private tastings may be organised given prior notice. There are many castles, gardens and stately homes within the vicinity, such as Chartwell, Groombridge Place and Hever Castle. Guests can work up their appetites by rambling through the orchards and hop fields, perusing the shops and boutiques in the Pantiles or playing golf nearby. **Directions:** From M25 take A21 south in the direction of Hastings. to Tunbridge Wells. The hotel has excellent parking facilities. Price Guide: (room only): Double/twin £80–£140.

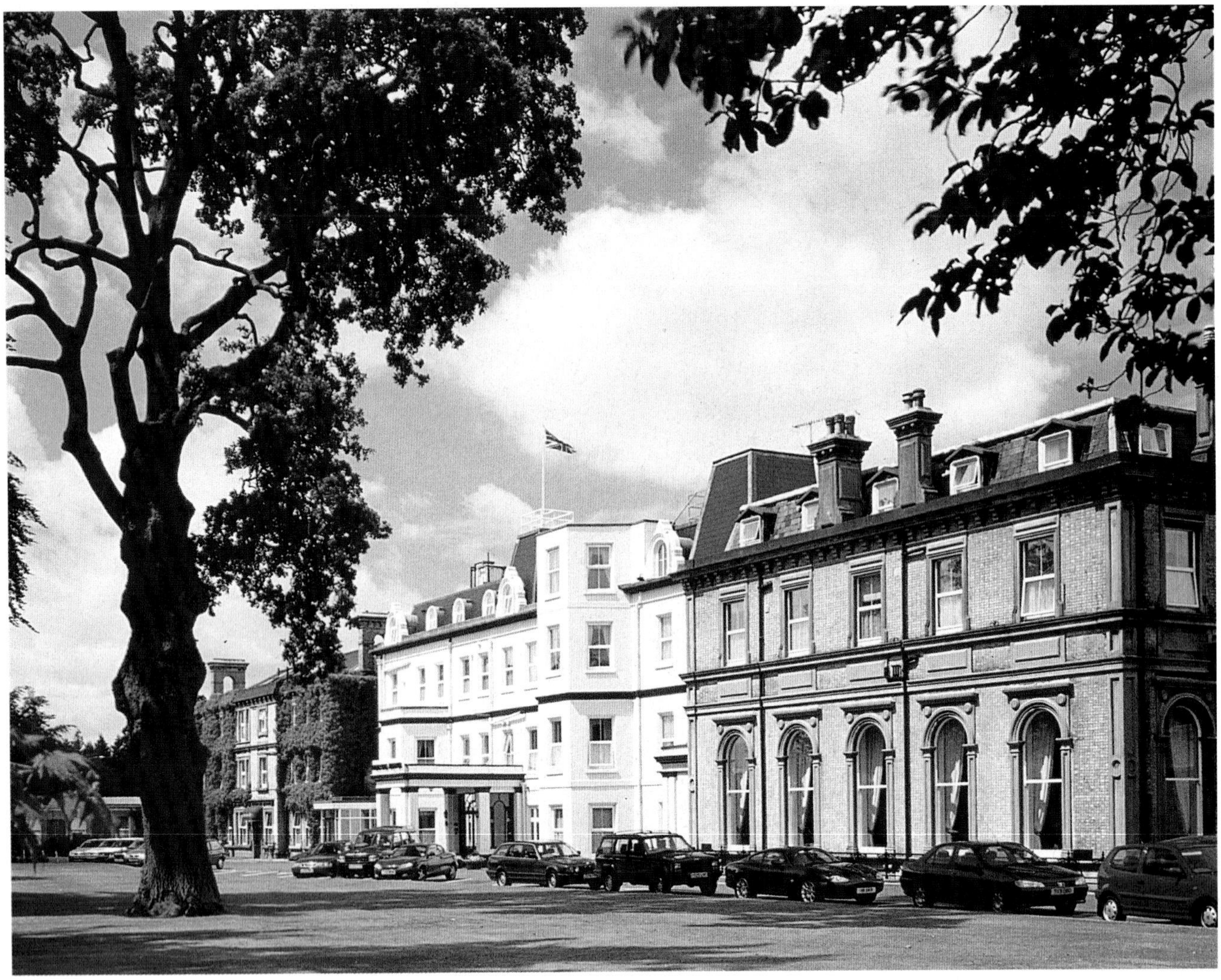

THE SPA HOTEL

MOUNT EPHRAIM, ROYAL TUNBRIDGE WELLS, KENT TN4 8XJ
TEL: 01892 520331 FAX: 01892 510575 E-MAIL: info@spahotel.co.uk

The Spa was originally built in 1766 as a country mansion with its own landscaped gardens and three beautiful lakes. A hotel for over a century now, it retains standards of service reminiscent of life in Georgian and Regency England. All the bedrooms are individually furnished and many offer spectacular views. Above all else, The Spa Hotel prides itself on the excellence of its cuisine. The grand, award winning Chandelier restaurant features the freshest produce from Kentish farms and London markets, complemented by a carefully selected wine list. Within the hotel is Sparkling Health, a magnificent health and leisure centre which is equipped to the highest standards. Leisure facilities include an indoor heated swimming pool, a fully equipped state-of-the-art gymnasium, cardiovascular gymnasium, steam room, sauna, beauty clinic, hairdressing salon, flood-lit hard tennis court and ½ mile jogging track. The newly established stables include gentle trails and safe paddocks for children to enjoy pony riding under expert guidance. Special weekend breaks are offered, with rates from £82 per person per night – full details available on request. **Directions:** Facing the common on the A264 in Tunbridge Wells. Price Guide: (room only): Single £85–£95; double/twin £105–£165.

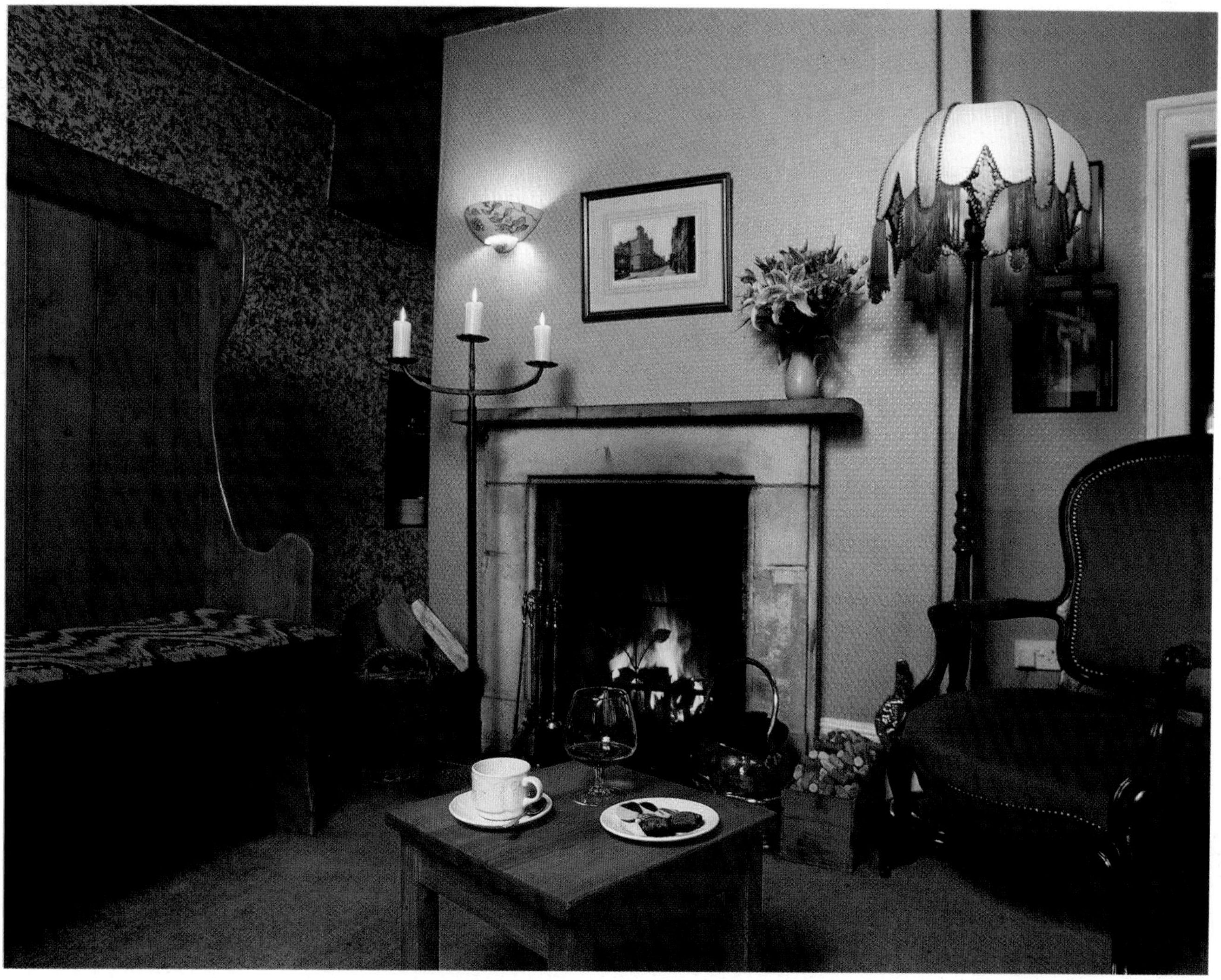

THE LAKE ISLE

16 HIGH STREET EAST, UPPINGHAM, RUTLAND LE15 9PZ

TEL: 01572 822951 FAX: 01572 822951 E-MAIL: Info@LakeIsleHotel.com

This small personally run restaurant and town house hotel is situated in the pretty market town of Uppingham, dominated by the famous Uppingham School and close to Rutland Water. The entrance to the building, which dates back to the 18th century, is via a quiet courtyard where a wonderful display of flowering tubs and hanging baskets greets you. In winter, sit in the bar where a log fire burns or relax in the upstairs lounge which overlooks the High Street. In the bedrooms, each named after a wine growing region in France and all of which are en suite, guests will find fresh fruit, home-made biscuits and a decanter of sherry. Those in the courtyard are cottage-style suites. Under the personal direction of chef Gary Thomas, the restaurant offers small weekly changing menus using fresh ingredients from far afield. There is an extensive wine list of more than 300 wines ranging from regional labels to old clarets. Special 'Wine Dinners' are held throughout the year, enabling guests to appreciate this unique cellar. Burghley House, Rockingham and Belvoir Castles are within a short drive. **Directions:** Uppingham is near the intersection of A47 and A6003. The hotel is on the High Street and is reached on foot via Reeves Yard and by car via Queen Street. Price Guide: Single £45–£62; double/twin £65–£74; suite £80–£84.

PERCY'S COUNTRY HOTEL & RESTAURANT

COOMBESHEAD ESTATE, VIRGINSTOW, DEVON EX21 5EA
TEL: 01409 211236 FAX: 01409 211275 E-MAIL: info@percys.co.uk

Offering tranquillity and seclusion, the 130-acre Coombeshead Estate is the perfect venue for those wishing to relax in a smoke and child free environment, with stunning views across Bodmin Moor and Dartmoor. This charming, tastefully restored 16th-century Devon Longhouse with its intelligent architectural design blends old and new; the older part of the building retains low ceilings, an original cloam oven and oak beams, whilst the modern extension houses two lounges and a zinc bar which opens onto a decked patio. The hotel & restaurant has won numerous awards and has attracted praise from both the Sunday Observer and Saturday Telegraph. Devons's top female chef, Tina Bricknell-Webb, creates contemporary country cuisine using fresh herbs, salad leaves, vegetables, eggs, game, trout and lamb supplied by the organically managed estate. Beef and cheeses are sourced locally, whilst fish is bought at Looe harbour market. Outdoor pursuits include water sports and fishing at nearby Roadford Lake and equestrian workshops for horse owners. Percy's is situated between the Eden Project to the west and Rosemoor Gardens to the north. Among the nearby National Trust properties are the Garden House, Cothele, Castle Drogo and Killerton House. **Directions:** From Okehampton take A3079 to Metherell Cross. After 8.3 miles turn left. The hotel is 6.5 miles on the left. Price Guide: Single £99.50–£125; double £125.50–£165..

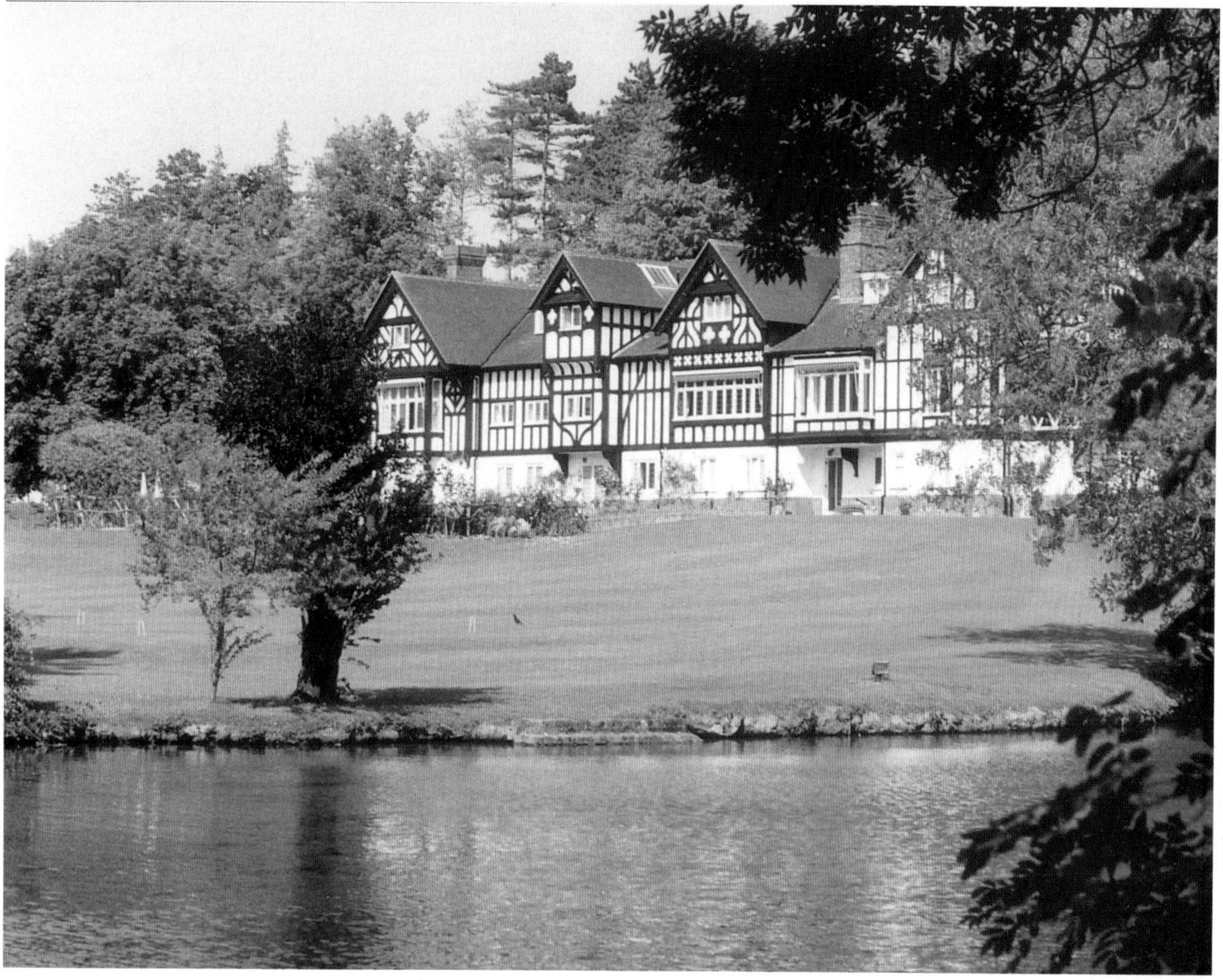

THE SPRINGS HOTEL & GOLF CLUB

NORTH STOKE, WALLINGFORD, OXFORDSHIRE OX10 6BE
TEL: 01491 836687 FAX: 01491 836877 E-MAIL: info@thespringshotel.co.uk

The Springs is a grand old country house which dates from 1874 and is set deep in the heart of the beautiful Thames valley. One of the first houses in England to be built in the Mock Tudor style, it stands in six acres of grounds. The hotel's large south windows overlook a spring fed lake, from which it takes its name. Many of the luxurious bedrooms and suites offer beautiful views over the lake and lawns, while others overlook the quiet woodland that surrounds the hotel. Private balconies provide patios for summer relaxation. The Lakeside restaurant has an intimate atmosphere inspired by its gentle décor and the lovely view of the lake. The award-winning restaurant's menu takes advantage of fresh local produce and a well stocked cellar of international wines provides the perfect accompaniment to a splendid meal. Leisure facilities include a new 18-hole par 72 golf course, Clubhouse and putting green, a swimming pool, sauna and touring bicycles. Oxford, Blenheim Palace and Windsor are nearby, and the hotel is conveniently located for racing at Newbury and Ascot and the Royal Henley Regatta. **Directions:** From M40 take exit 6 onto B4009, through Watlington to Benson; turn left onto A4074 towards Reading. After ½ mile go right onto B4004. The hotel is ½ mile further on the right. Price Guide: Single from £90; double/twin from £100; suite from £165.

Hanbury Manor

WARE, HERTFORDSHIRE SG12 0SD
TEL: 01920 487722 FAX: 01920 487692

An outstanding 5-star hotel, Marriott Hanbury Manor, London's favourite Hotel and Country Club and English Tourism Council Hotel of the year combines palatial grandeur with the most up-to-date amenities. Designed in 1890 in a Jacobean style, the many impressive features include elaborately moulded ceilings, carved wood panelling, leaded windows, chandeliers, portraits and huge tapestries. These create an elegant and comfortable environment. The two dining rooms vary in style from the formal Zodiac Restaurant to the informal Oakes Grill. All the cuisine is under the inspired guidance of Executive Chef Glen Watson. The health club includes a 17m indoor swimming pool, spa bath, resistance gymnasium, cardiovascular suite, dance studio, crèche, sauna and steam rooms. Professional treatments include herbal wraps, aromatherapy, mineral baths and massage, while specialists can advise on a personal fitness programme. There is an 18-hole golf course par excellence designed by Jack Nicklaus II, previous host to the PGA European Tour English Open. Outdoor pursuits include shooting, archery, horse-riding and hot-air ballooning. Ideal for conferences, twelve rooms offer versatile business meetings facilities, with fax, photocopying, secretarial services and full professional support available. Stansted Airport is 16 miles away. **Directions:** On the A10 25 miles north of London and 32 miles south of Cambridge Price Guide: Single/double/twin from £149; suites £249–£349.

THE PRIORY HOTEL

CHURCH GREEN, WAREHAM, DORSET BH20 4ND
TEL: 01929 551666 FAX: 01929 554519 E-MAIL: reception@theprioryhotel.co.uk

Dating from the early 16th century, the one-time Lady St Mary Priory has, for hundreds of years, offered sanctuary to travellers. In Hardy's Dorset, 'far from the madding crowd', it placidly stands on the bank of the River Frome in four acres of immaculate gardens. Steeped in history, The Priory has undergone a sympathetic conversion to a hotel which is charming yet unpretentious. Each bedroom is distinctively styled, with family antiques lending character and many rooms have views of the Purbeck Hills. A 16th century clay barn has been transformed into the Boathouse, consisting of four spacious luxury suites at the river's edge. Tastefully furnished, the drawing room, residents' lounge and intimate bar together create a convivial atmosphere. The Garden Room Restaurant is open for breakfast and lunch, while splendid dinners are served in the vaulted stone cellars. There are moorings for guests arriving by boat. Dating back to the 9th century, the market town of Wareham has more than 200 listed buildings. Corfe Castle, Lulworth Cove, Poole and Swanage are all close by with superb walks and beaches **Directions:** Wareham is on the A351 to the west of Bournemouth and Poole. The hotel is beside the River Frome at the southern end of the town near the parish church. Price Guide: Single £85–£140; double/twin £110–£230; suite £265.

19 MasterCard VISA AMERICAN EXPRESS M 20 8

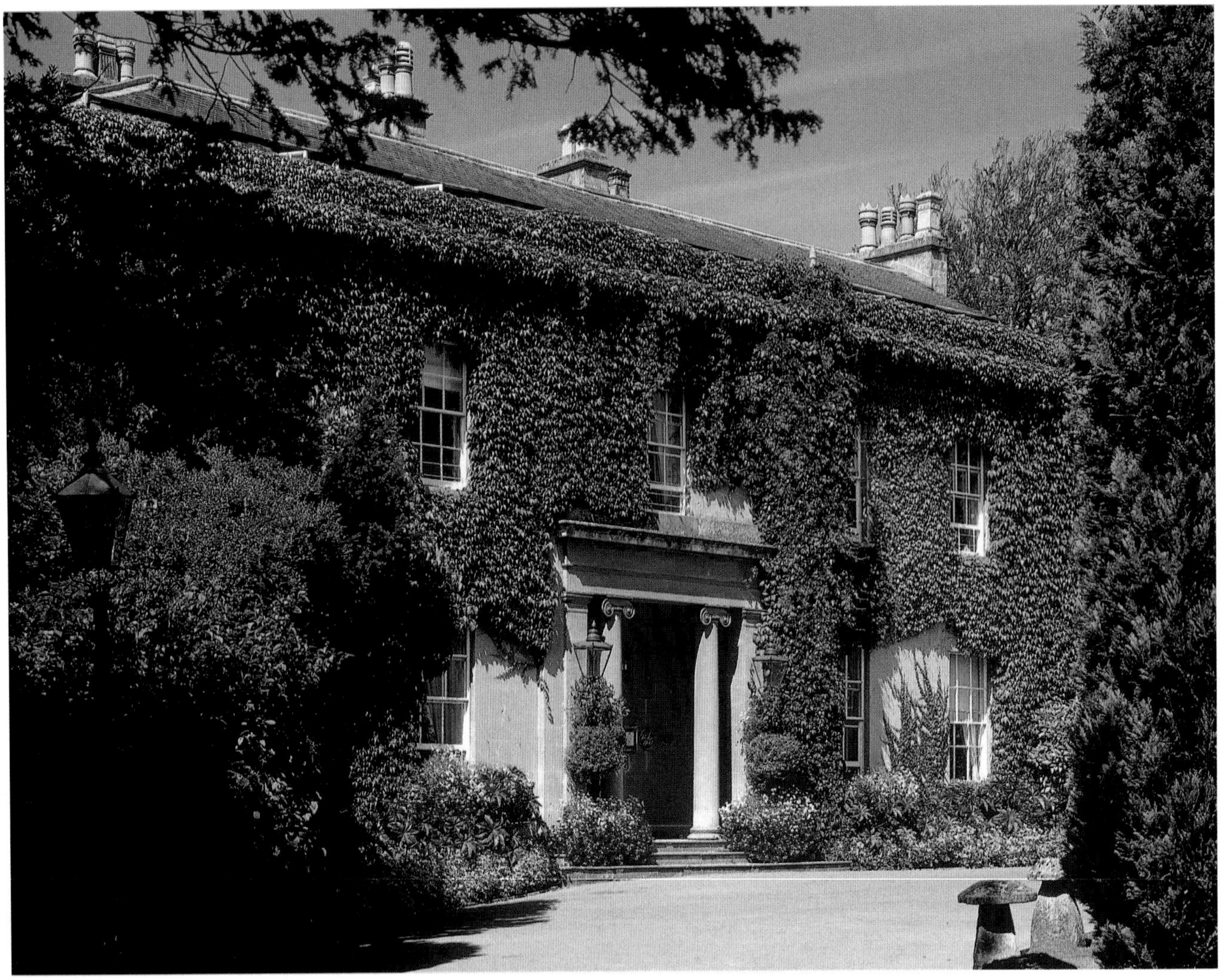

Bishopstrow House

WARMINSTER, WILTSHIRE BA12 9HH
TEL: 01985 212312 FAX: 01985 216769 E-MAIL: enquiries@bishopstrow.co.uk

Bishopstrow House is the quintessential Georgian mansion. It combines the intimacy of a grand country hotel retreat with all the benefits of modern facilities and the luxury of the new Ragdale spa, offering a superb range of beauty, fitness and relaxation therapies in addition to Michaeljohn's world class hair styling. A Grade II listed building, Bishopstrow House was built in 1817 and has been sympathetically extended to include indoor and outdoor heated swimming pools, a high-tech gymnasium and a sauna. The attention to detail is uppermost in the Library, Drawing Room and Conservatory with their beautiful antiques and Victorian oil paintings. The bedrooms are grandly furnished; some have opulent marble bathrooms and whirlpool baths. Skilfully prepared modern British food is served in the Mulberry Restaurant, with lighter meals available in the Mulberry Bar and the Conservatory which overlooks 27 acres of gardens. There is fly–fishing on the hotel's private stretch of the River Wylye, golf at five nearby courses, riding, game and clay-pigeon shooting. Longleat House, Wilton House, Stourhead, Stonehenge, Bath, Salisbury and Warminster are within easy reach. **Directions:** Bishopstrow House is southeast of Warminster on the B3414 from London via the M3. **Price Guide:** Single £99; double/twin £190–£245; suite from £305.

32 MasterCard VISA AMERICAN EXPRESS M 60

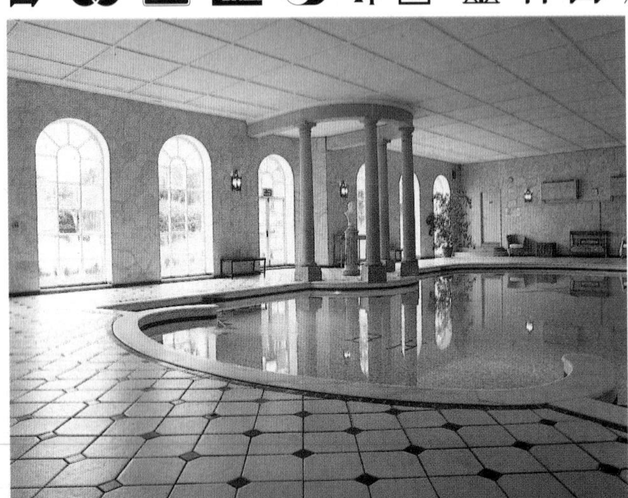

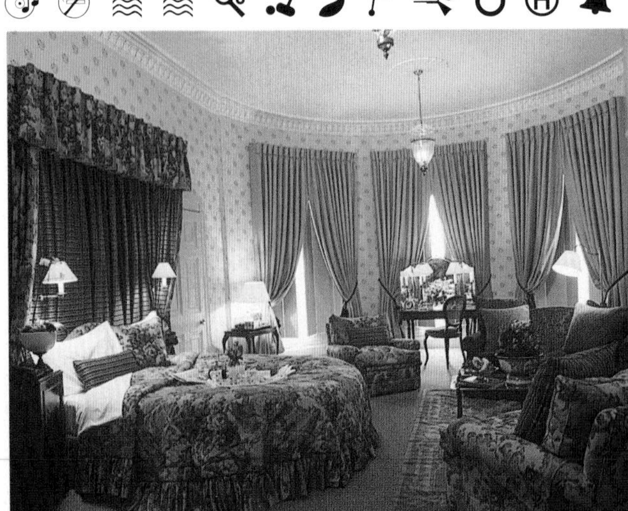

ARDENCOTE MANOR HOTEL AND COUNTRY CLUB

LYE GREEN ROAD, CLAVERDON, WARWICKSHIRE CV35 8LS
TEL: 01926 843111 FAX: 01926 842646 E-MAIL: hotel@ardencote.com

Under private ownership, this former Gentlemen's residence, which was built around 1860, has been sympathetically refurbished and substantially extended to provide a luxury hotel with all modern amenities and comforts, whilst retaining its traditional elegance and appealing intimacy. Set in 42 acres of landscaped grounds in the heart of Shakespeare country, it offers beautifully appointed en suite accommodation – many rooms have glorious views of the lake and gardens – fine cuisine and extensive sports and leisure facilities, including indoor pool and spa, sauna and steamrooms, squash and tennis courts, two fully equipped gymnasia and a 9-hole golf course. The Hair and Beauty Salon is also at the disposal of guests, offering an extensive range of beauty, stress relief and holistic treatments. Two superb restaurants provide a choice of venues – from imaginative à la carte dining in the intimate Oak Room, to the lakeside Lodge with its varied and exciting cuisine in a more informal ambience. Places of interest nearby include the NEC, Warwick Castle (discounted tickets available through hotel), Stratford-upon-Avon and the Cotswolds. **Directions:** From M40 follow signs to Henley-in-Arden. Lye Green Road is off A4189 Henley-in-Arden/Warwick Road at Claverdon Village Green. Price Guide: Single £95; double £145 (Weekend breaks available).

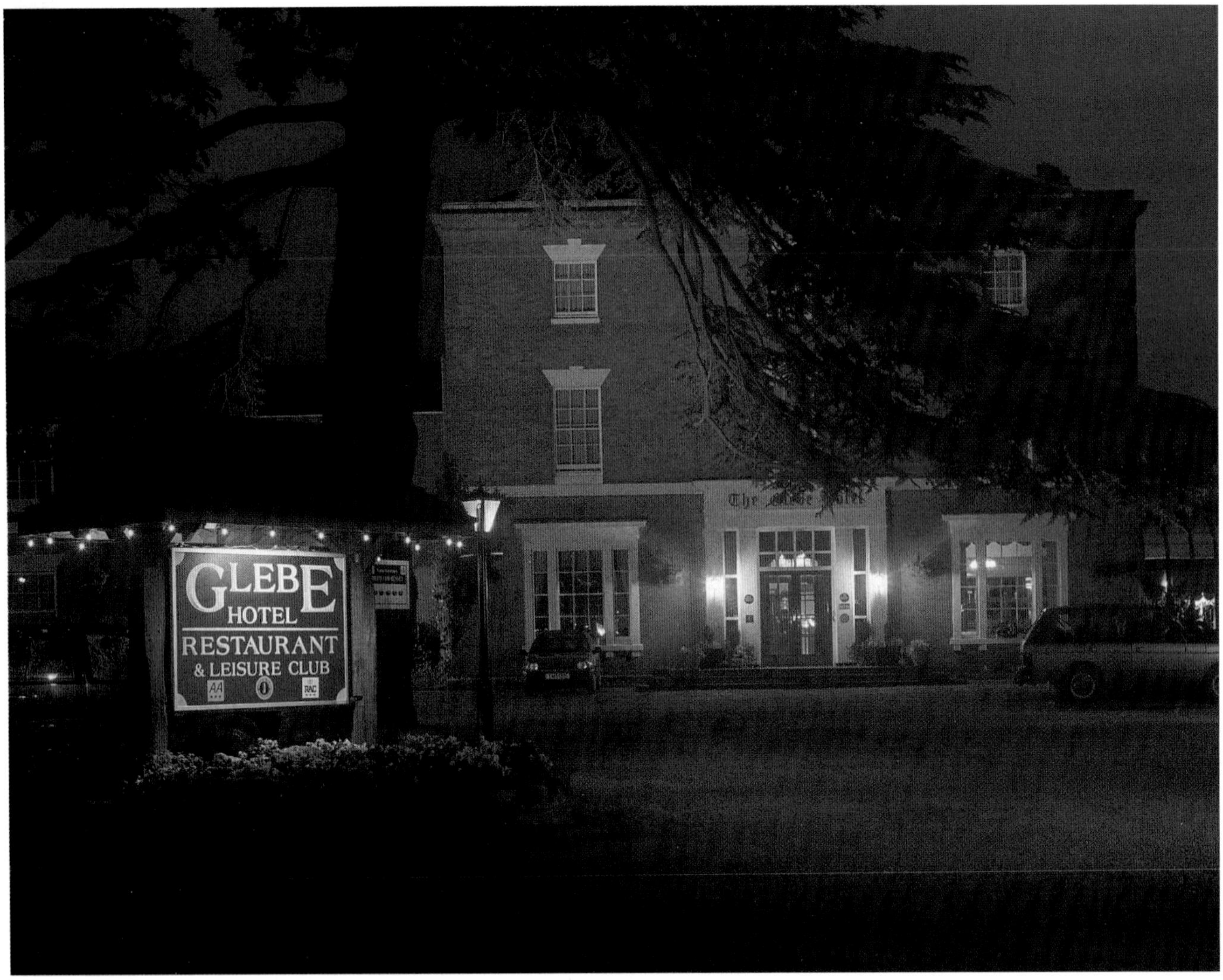

The Glebe At Barford

CHURCH STREET, BARFORD, WARWICKSHIRE CV35 8BS
TEL: 01926 624218 FAX: 01926 624625 E-MAIL: sales@glebe.co.uk

"Glebe" means belonging to the Church, which explains why this beautiful Georgian country house is in a unique and quiet position next to the church in Barford, one of the most attractive villages in Warwickshire. It is a Grade II listed building, dating back to 1820, with an unusual central atrium and surrounded by landscaped gardens. The bedrooms are spacious, comfortable and peaceful. They have all the accessories expected by today's travellers. The restaurant is in an elegant, conservatory, green plants adding cool colour. There are excellent table d'hôte and à la carte menus and the wine list has been carefully selected to complement the dishes. The Glebe is an ideal venue for private celebrations and corporate events as it has several well-equipped conference rooms – the Bentley Suite seats 120 people for a banquet and the Directors Suite, with leather armchairs, is ideal for a discreet strategy meeting. Those wishing to be pampered will be pleased with the new beauty and sunbed room. Guests appreciate the Glebe Leisure Club with a pool, gymnasium, sauna, steam room and spa facilities. They can play tennis and golf nearby. Ideally situated for Warwick and Stratford races. **Directions:** M40 exit Junction 15 A429 signed Barford & Wellesbourne. Turning left at mini-roundabout, the hotel is on the right just past the church. Price Guide: Single £98; double/twin £118; suite £150.

Wood Hall

TRIP LANE, LINTON, NR WETHERBY, WEST YORKSHIRE LS22 4JA
TEL: 01937 587271 FAX: 01937 584353 E-MAIL: woodhall@arcadianhotels.co.uk

Off the A1/M1 link about 15 miles due west of York, built of stone from the estate, Wood Hall is an elegant Georgian country house overlooking the River Wharfe. Its grounds, over 100 acres in all, are approached along a private drive that winds through a sweep of parkland. The sumptuously furnished drawing room and the oak-panelled bar, with its gentlemen's club atmosphere, lead off the grand entrance hall. Superb floral displays, gleaming chandeliers and immaculately designed interiors hint at the careful attention that has been lavished on Wood Hall. Gastronomes will relish the excellent à la carte menu, which combines contemporary Anglo-French style with attractive presentation. The mile-long private stretch of the Wharfe offers up trout and barbel to the keen angler, while miles of walks and jogging paths encompass the estate. There is a leisure club including a swimming pool, spa bath, steam room, gymnasium, solarium and treatment salon. Near to the National Hunt racecourse at Wetherby, York, Harrogate, Leeds, the Dales and Harewood House are only a short distance away. **Directions:** From Wetherby, take the A661 towards Harrogate. Take turning for Sicklinghall and Linton, then left for Linton and Wood Hall. Turn right opposite the Windmill public house; hotel is 1½ miles further on. Price Guide (incl. breakfast): Single from £98; double/twin from £110.

OATLANDS PARK HOTEL

146 OATLANDS DRIVE, WEYBRIDGE, SURREY KT13 9HB
TEL: 01932 847242 FAX: 01932 842252 E-MAIL: info@oatlandsparkhotel.com

Records of the Oatlands estate show that Elizabeth I and the Stuart kings spent time in residence in the original buildings. The present mansion dates from the late-18th century and became a hotel in 1856: famous guests included Émile Zola, Anthony Trollope and Edward Lear. The hotel stands in acres of parkland overlooking Broadwater Lake, with easy access to Heathrow, Gatwick and central London. Although it caters for the modern traveller, the hotel's historic character is evident throughout. The accommodation ranges from superior rooms to large de luxe rooms and suites. The elegant, high-ceilinged Broadwater Restaurant is the setting for creative à la carte menus with dishes to suit all tastes. A traditional roast is served every Sunday lunchtime. The six air-conditioned meeting rooms and up-to-date facilities include video conferencing and are complemented by the professional conference team. Theme evenings, such as Henry VIII banquets, are a speciality. Many sporting and leisure activities are offered including a new 9 hole, par 27, golf course. **Directions:** From M25 junction 11, follow signs to Weybridge. Follow A317 through High Street into Monument Hill to mini-roundabout. Turn left into Oatlands Drive; hotel is 50 yards on left. Price Guide: (room only) Single £120–£155; double/twin £165–£185; suite from £200. Special Break rate: Single £60; double/twin £90.

137 MasterCard VISA AMERICAN EXPRESS M 300

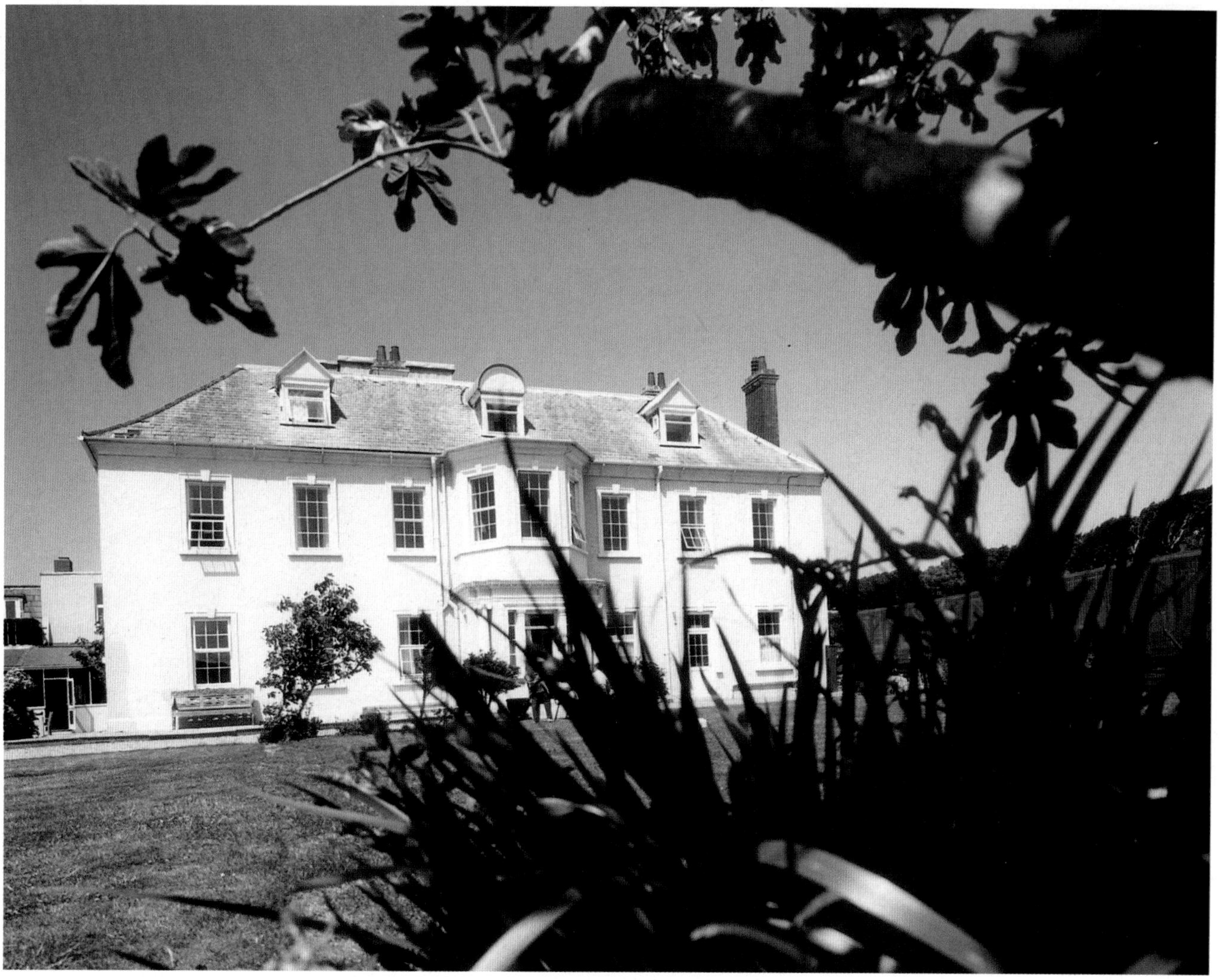

MOONFLEET MANOR

FLEET, WEYMOUTH, DORSET DT3 4ED
TEL: 01305 786948 FAX: 01305 774395 E-MAIL: info@moonfleetmanor.com

Overlooking Chesil Beach, a unique feature of the Dorset coast, Moonfleet Manor is both a luxury hotel and a family resort. The owners have applied the same flair for design evident in their other family friendly properties, Woolley Grange and Fowey Hall in Cornwall. The use of a variety of unusual antiques and objects from around the world lends a refreshing and individual style to this comfortable and attractive hotel. Refurbished bedrooms are beautifully decorated and furnished and a range of amenities ensures that guests enjoy standards of maximum comfort and convenience. An enthusiastic and attentive staff works hard to ensure that guests feel at home, whatever their age. Moonfleet's dining room, whose décor and style would do credit to a fashionable London restaurant, offers an excellent and varied menu based on fresh local produce but bringing culinary styles from around the world. Facilities at the hotel include an indoor swimming pool with squash and tennis courts for the more energetic. Key places of interest nearby include Abbotsbury, Dorchester, Corfe Castle and Lulworth Cove, while in Weymouth itself the Sea Life Park, The Deep Sea Adventure and The Titanic Story are worth a visit. **Directions:** Take B3157 Weymouth to Bridport Road, then turn off towards the sea at sign for Fleet. Price Guide: Single from £75; double/twin £95–£170; suite £200–£285.

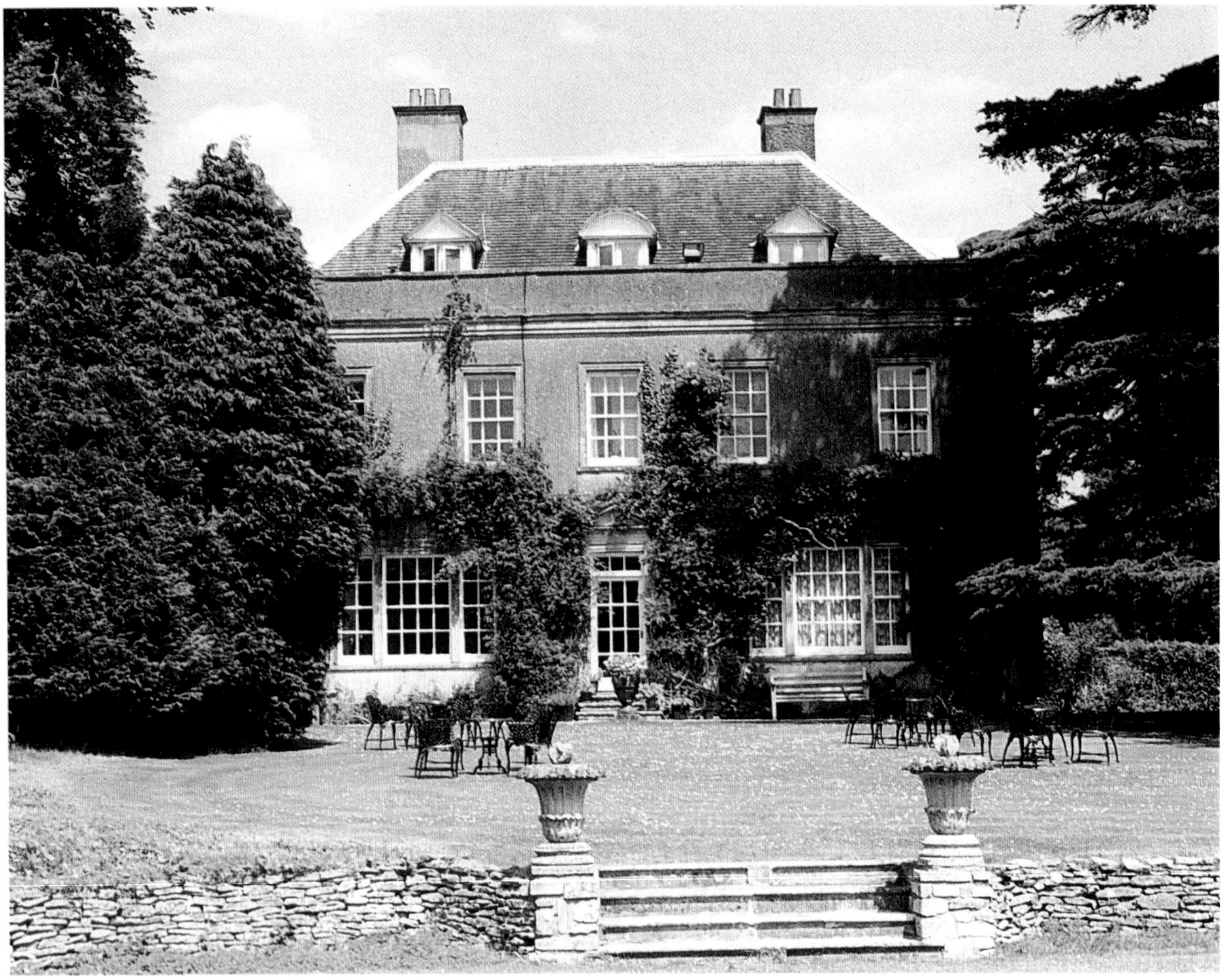

HOLBROOK HOUSE HOTEL & SPA

WINCANTON, SOMERSET BA9 8BS
TEL: 01963 32377 FAX: 01963 32681 E-MAIL: reservations@holbrookhouse.co.uk

The history of Holbrook dates back to Saxon times, with the earliest records of a property on the site having been drawn up during the reign of Edward III. The house, which is easily accessed from Bath, Bristol and London, has undergone a major refurbishment and lies in a most peaceful country location with glorious views across the Blackmore Vale. The 20 bedrooms are spacious and are superbly equipped. Each room affords pleasant views of the attractive surrounds. The recently refurbished public rooms are most inviting and include the comfortable lounge and convivial bar. Holder of two AA Rosettes, The Holbrook Restaurant serves fresh meat from traditionally reared animals with venison and game selected from shoots on estates and fresh fish delivered daily. Sports on offer include swimming, tennis, and croquet whilst the newly opened Health Spa will delight those wishing to be pampered. With state-of-the-art equipment, the beauty rooms offer an array of treatments. Seating 200 people, the new function and conference suite provides the latest business facilities and is perfect for wedding receptions, private banqueting and corporate meetings. **Directions:** Leave A303 at Wincanton slip Road and join A371 towards Castle Cary at the first roundabout. Over three more roundabouts and the hotel driveway is on the right immediately after the third. Price Guide: Single from £95; double/twin from £135; suite from £170.

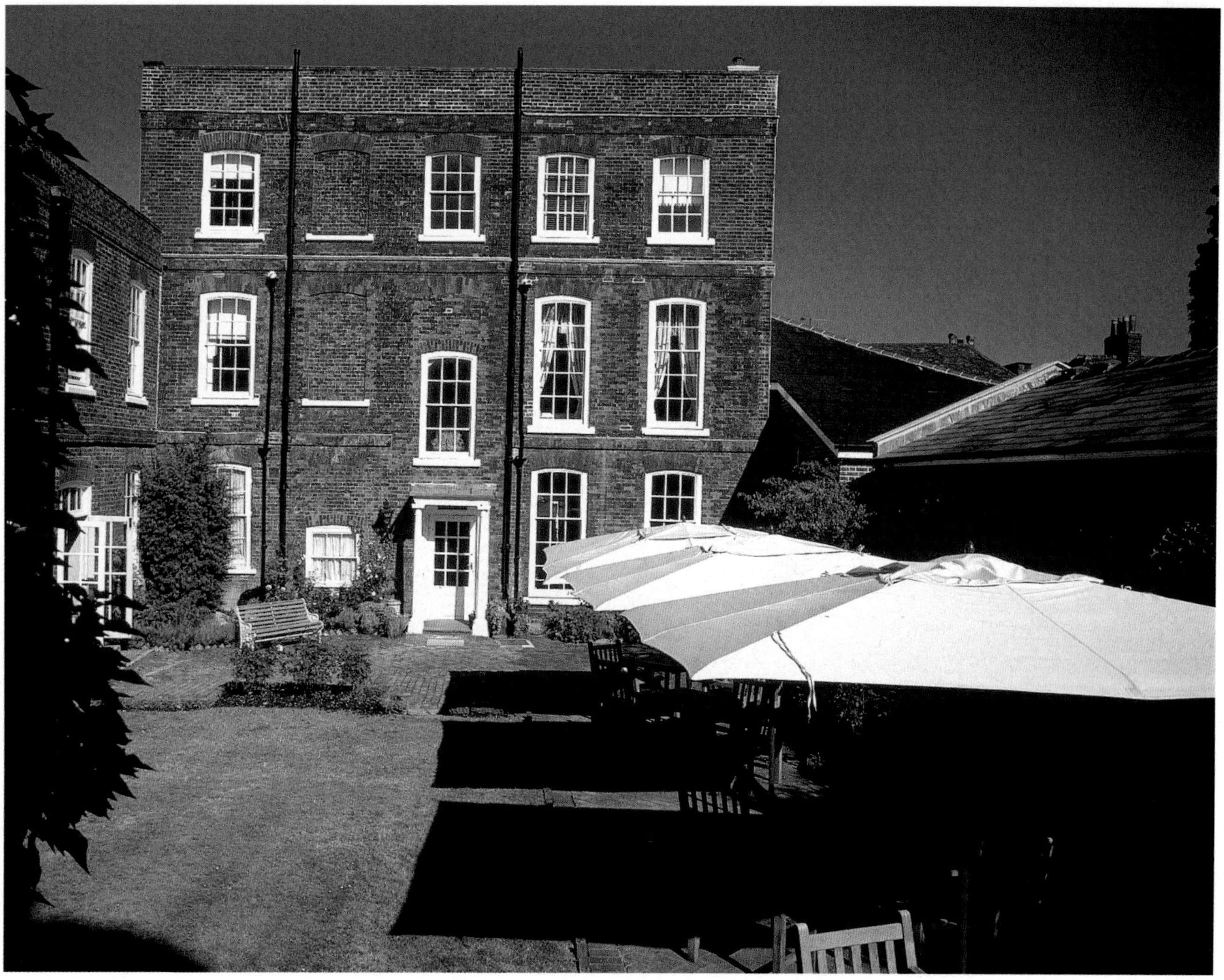

Hotel Du Vin & Bistro

SOUTHGATE STREET, WINCHESTER, HAMPSHIRE SO23 9EF
TEL: 01962 841414 FAX: 01962 842458 E-MAIL: info@winchester.hotelduvin.com

Relaxed, charming and unpretentious are words which aptly describe the stylish and intimate Hotel du Vin & Bistro. This elegant hotel is housed in one of Winchester's most important Georgian buildings, dating back to 1715. The hotel is owned and managed by Hotel Du Vin Ltd. The 23 individually decorated bedrooms feature superb beds made up with crisp, Egyptian cotton and offer every modern amenity, including trouser press, mini bar and CD players. Each bedroom is sponsored by a wine house whose vineyard features in its decorations. Bathrooms boasting power showers, oversized baths and fluffy towels and robes add to guests' sense of luxury and comfort. Quality food cooked simply with fresh ingredients is the philosophy behind the Bistro, where an excellent and reasonably priced wine list is available. There are also 2 function rooms available for special occasions. A welcoming and enthusiastic staff cater for every need. The hotel is a perfect base for exploring England's ancient capital, famous for its cathedral, its school and antique shops. The New Forest is a short drive away. **Directions:** M3 to Winchester. Southgate Street leads from the City centre to St. Cross. Price Guide: Single/double/twin £95–£135; suite £185.

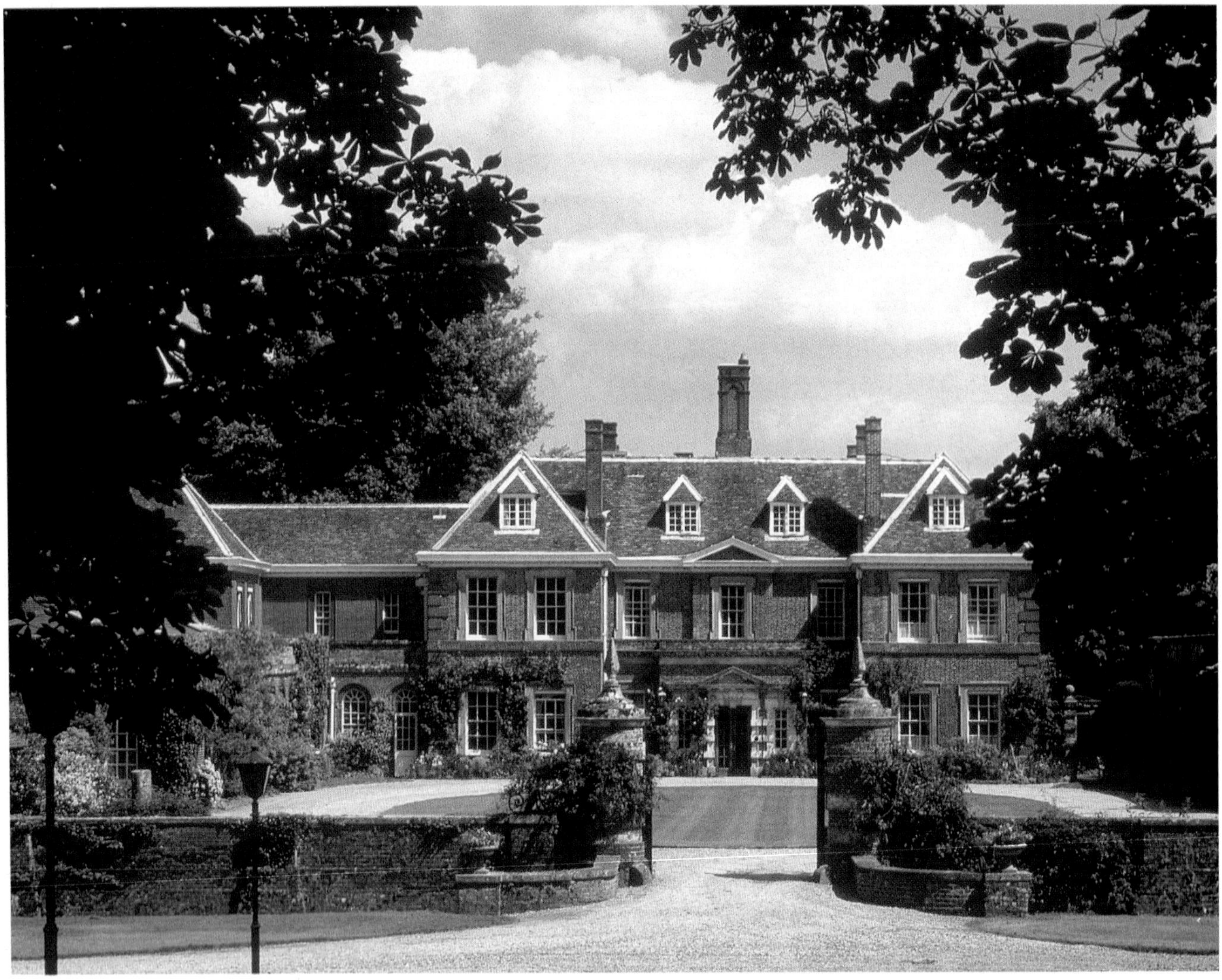

LAINSTON HOUSE HOTEL

SPARSHOLT, WINCHESTER, HAMPSHIRE SO21 2LT
TEL: 01962 863588 FAX: 01962 776672 E-MAIL: enquiries@lainstonhouse.com

The fascinating history of Lainston House is well documented, some of its land having been recorded in the Domesday Book of 1087. Set in 63 acres of superb downland countryside, this graceful William and Mary country house has been sympathetically restored to create a beautiful hotel with a stately home atmosphere. From the individually designed bedrooms to the main reception rooms, elegant and comfortable furnishings are the hallmark of Lainston House. Freshly prepared food, attentive service and views over the lawn make the restaurant one of the most popular in Hampshire. Facilities are available for small meetings in the Mountbatten Room or larger functions in the 17th century Dawley Barn. Latest facillities include a fully equipped gymnasium. The charming grounds hold many surprises – an ancient chapel, reputedly haunted by the legendary Elizabeth Chudleigh, an 18th century herb garden and a dovecote. Historic Winchester is only 2½miles south, while Romsey Abbey, Salisbury and the New Forest are a short drive away. Other local activities include riding, country walking and good trout fishing on the River Test at nearby Stockbridge. Directions: Lainston House is well signposted off the B3049 Winchester–Stockbridge road, at Sparsholt 2½ miles from Winchester. Price Guide: Single from £100; double/twin from £150; suite from £285.

50 MasterCard VISA AMERICAN EXPRESS M 80

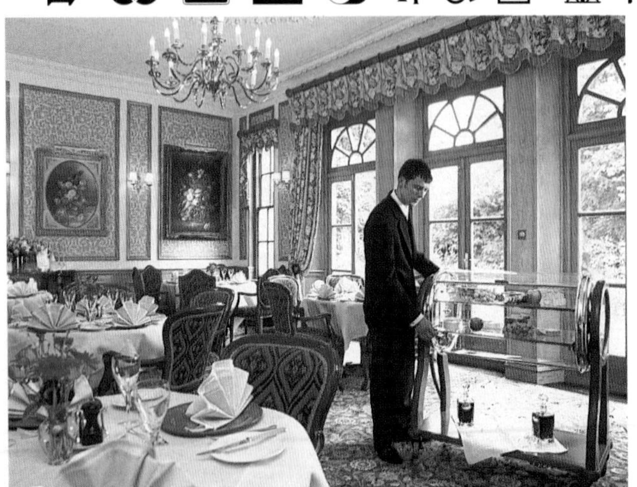

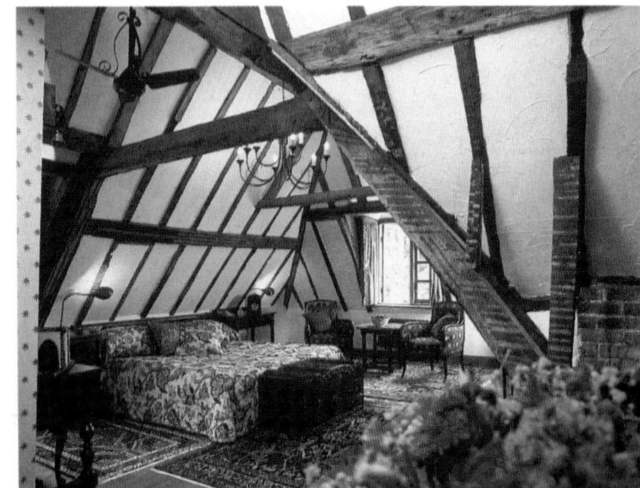

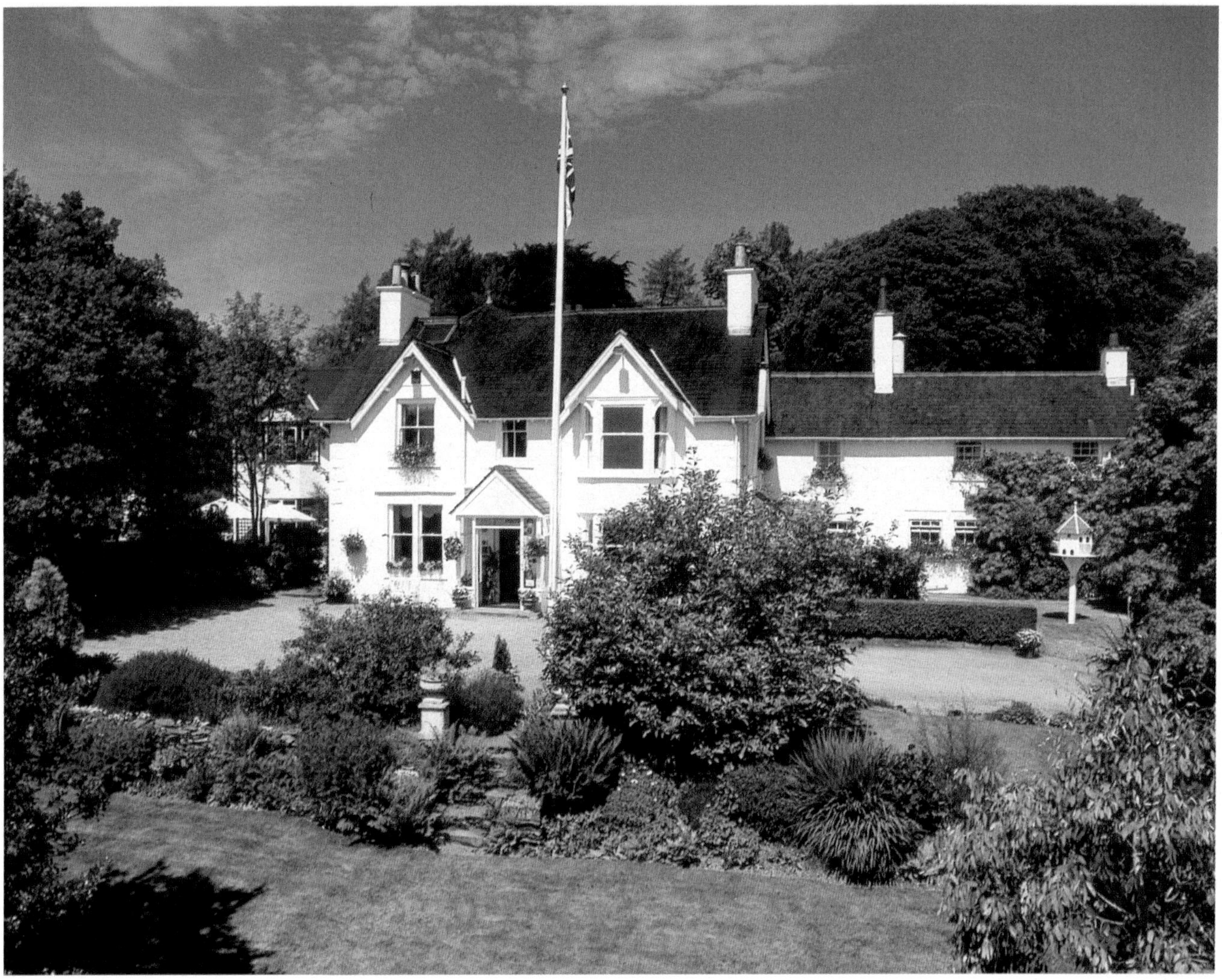

Gilpin Lodge

CROOK ROAD, NEAR WINDERMERE, CUMBRIA LA23 3NE
TEL: 015394 88818 FAX: 015394 88058 E-MAIL: hotel@gilpin-lodge.co.uk

Gilpin Lodge is a friendly, elegant, relaxing country house hotel set in 20 acres of woodlands, moors and country gardens 2 miles from Lake Windermere, yet just 12 miles from the M6. The original building, tastefully extended and modernised, dates from 1901. A profusion of flower arrangements, picture-lined walls, antique furniture and log fires in winter are all part of John and Christine Cunliffe's perception of hospitality. The 14 sumptuous bedrooms all have en suite bathrooms and every comfort. Some have four-poster beds, split levels and whirlpool baths. The exquisite food, created by a team of 7 chefs, earns 3 rosettes from the AA. The award winning wine list contains 175 labels from 13 different countries. The beautiful gardens are the perfect place in which to muse while savouring the lovely lake-land scenery. Windermere golf course is ½ a mile away. There is almost every kind of outdoor activity imaginable. Guests have free use of a nearby private leisure club. This is Wordsworth and Beatrix Potter country and nearby there are several stately homes, gardens and castles. England for Excellence Silver award 1997 Hotel of the year, English Tourist Board Gold award, AA 3 Red Stars and RAC Gold Ribbon award. A Pride of Britain Hotel. **Directions:** M6 exit 36. A591 Kendal bypass then B5284 to Crook. Price Guide: (including dinner): Single £105–£125; double/twin £130–£250. Year-round short-break rates and golf packages available.

Lakeside Hotel On Lake Windermere

LAKESIDE, NEWBY BRIDGE, CUMBRIA LA12 8AT
TEL: 08701 541586 FAX: 015395 31699 E-MAIL: sales@lakesidehotel.co.uk

Lakeside Hotel offers you a unique location on the water's edge of Lake Windermere. It is a classic, traditional Lakeland hotel offering four star facilities and service. All the bedrooms are en suite and enjoy individually designed fabrics and colours, many of the rooms offer breathtaking views of the lake. Guests may dine in either the award-winning Lakeview Restaurant or Ruskin's Brasserie, where extensive menus offer a wide selection of dishes including Cumbrian specialities. The Lakeside Conservatory serves drinks and light meals throughout the day – once there you are sure to fall under the spell of this peaceful location. Berthed next to the hotel there are cruisers which will enable you to explore the lake from the water. To enhance your stay, there is a leisure club including a 17m indoor pool, gymnasium, sauna, steam room and health & beauty suites. The hotel offers a fully equipped conference centre and many syndicate suites allowing plenty of scope and flexibility. Most of all you are assured of a stay in an unrivalled setting of genuine character. The original panelling and beams of the old coaching inn create an excellent ambience, whilst you are certain to enjoy the quality and friendly service. **Directions:** From M6 junction 36 join A590 to Newby Bridge, turn right over bridge towards Hawkshead; hotel is one mile on right. Price Guide: Single from £100; double/twin £145–£210; suites from £210. Special breaks available.

75 MasterCard VISA AMERICAN EXPRESS M 100

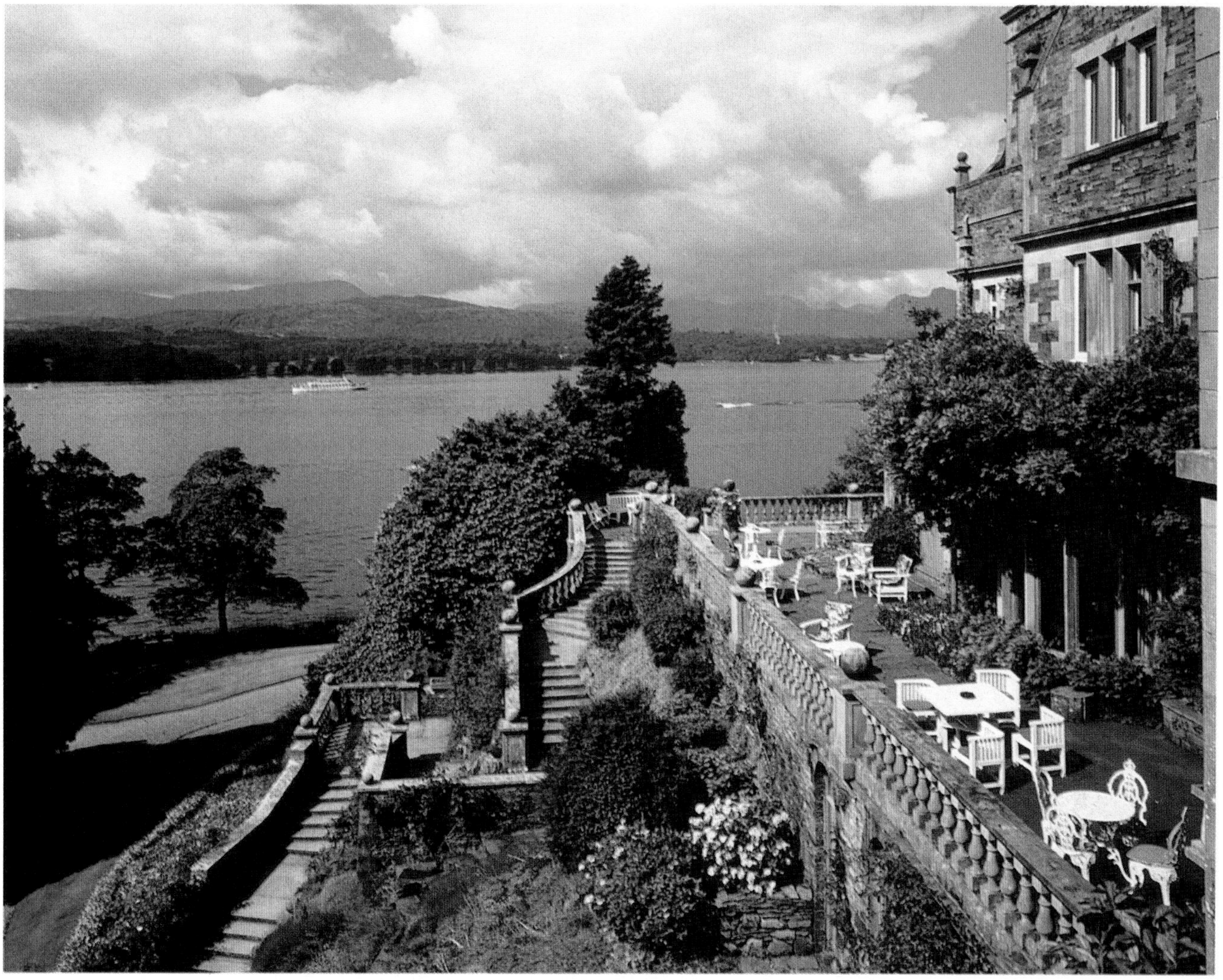

LANGDALE CHASE

WINDERMERE, CUMBRIA LA23 1LW

TEL: 015394 32201 FAX: 015394 32604 E-MAIL: sales@langdalechase.co.uk

Langdale Chase stands in five acres of landscaped gardens on the shores of Lake Windermere, with panoramic views over England's largest lake to the Langdale Pikes beyond. Visitors will receive warm-hearted hospitality in this well-run country home, which is splendidly decorated with oak panelling, fine oil paintings and ornate, carved fireplaces. A magnificent staircase leads to the well-appointed bedrooms, many overlooking the lake. One unique bedroom is sited over the lakeside boathouse, where the traveller may be lulled to sleep by the gently lapping waters below. The facilities also include a private boat mooring which is available on request. For the energetic, there is a choice of water-skiing, swimming or sailing from the hotel jetty. Guests can stroll through the gardens along the lake shore, in May the gardens are spectacular when the rhododendrons and azaleas are in bloom. Being pampered by attentive staff will be one of the many highlights of your stay at Langdale Chase. The variety of food and wine is sure to delight the most discerning diner. Combine this with a panoramic tableau across England's largest and loveliest of lakes and you have a truly unforgettable dining experience. **Directions:** Situated on the A591, three miles north of Windermere, two miles south of Ambleside. Price Guide: Single £80–£140; double/twin £100–£165; suite £195.

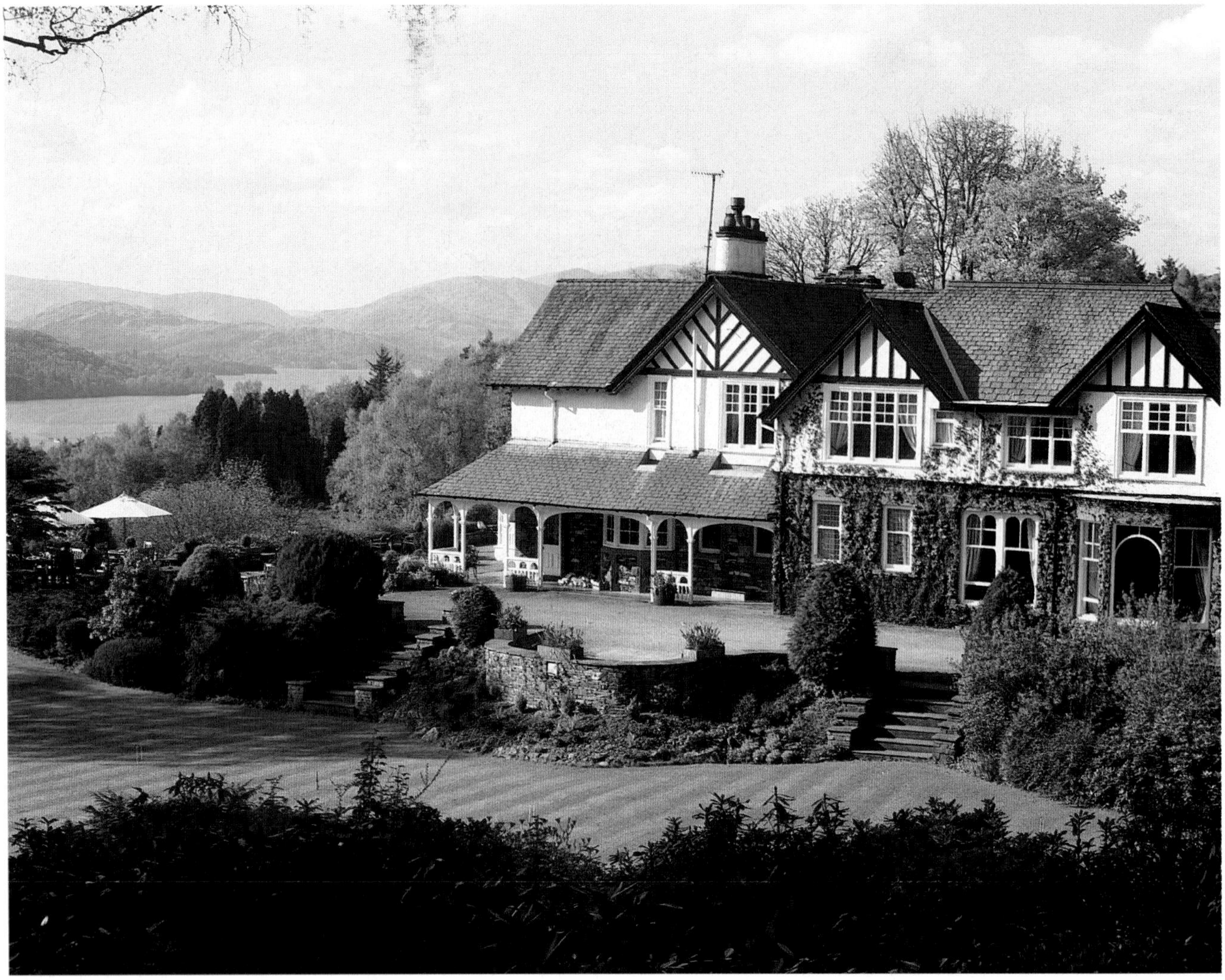

LINTHWAITE HOUSE HOTEL

CROOK ROAD, BOWNESS-ON-WINDERMERE, CUMBRIA LA23 3JA
TEL: 015394 88600 FAX: 015394 88601 E-MAIL: admin@linthwaite.com

Situated in 14 acres of gardens and woods in the heart of the Lake District, Linthwaite House overlooks Lake Windermere and Belle Isle, with Claife Heights and Coniston Old Man beyond. Here, guests will find themselves amid spectacular scenery, yet only a short drive from the motorway network. The hotel combines stylish originality with the best of traditional English hospitality. Superbly decorated en suite bedrooms, most of which have lake or garden views. The comfortable lounge is the perfect place to unwind and there is a fire on winter evenings. In the restaurant, excellent cuisine features the best of fresh, local produce, accompanied by a fine selection of wines. Within the hotel grounds, there is a 9-hole putting green and a par 3 practice hole. Fly fishermen can fish for brown trout in the hotel tarn. Guests have complimentary use of a private swimming pool and leisure club nearby, while fell walks begin at the hotel's front door. The area around Linthwaite abounds with places of interest: this is Beatrix Potter and Wordsworth country, and there is much to interest the visitor. **Directions:** From the M6 junction 36 follow Kendal by-pass (A590) for 8 miles. Take B5284 Crook Road for 6 miles. 1 mile beyond Windermere Golf Club, Linthwaite House is signposted on left. Price Guide: Single £95–£120; double/twin £95–£220; suite £240–£270.

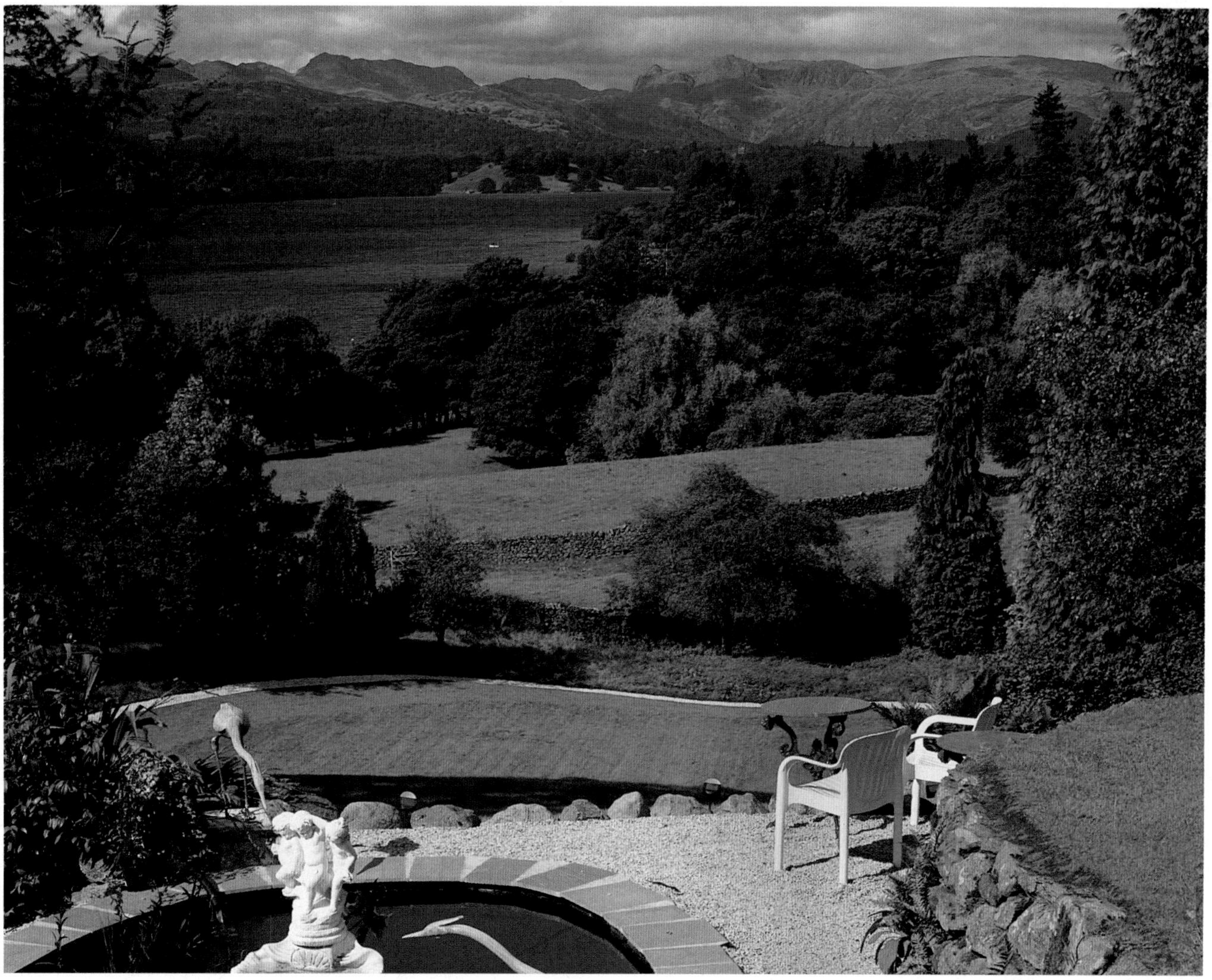

MILLER HOWE

RAYRIGG ROAD, WINDERMERE, CUMBRIA LA23 1EY
TEL: 015394 42536 FAX: 015394 45664 E-MAIL: lakeview@millerhowe.com

One of the finest views in the entire Lake District is from the restaurant, conservatory and terrace of this lovely hotel which stands high on the shores of Lake Windermere. Lawned gardens bedded with mature shrubs, trees and borders of colour sweep down to the water's edge. It is a spectacular scene. Visitors receive warm hospitality from this well-run and splendidly decorated hotel now owned by Charles Garside, the former Editor-in-Chief of the international newspaper 'The European'. Previous owner John Tovey, the celebrated chef and author, remains as a consultant. All the bedrooms are furnished in a luxurious style, the majority of which have views over the lake to the mountains beyond. There are 3 luxury cottage suites They feature every modern amenity amongst the antiques. Chef Susan Elliott's imaginative menus will delight the most discerning guest, while the panoramic tableau across England's largest lake as the sun sets, presents an unforgettable dining experience. Guests can enjoy a range of water sports or boat trips on Lake Windermere and there are many interesting fell walks close by. **Directions:** From the M6 junction 36 follow the A591 through Windermere, then turn left onto the A592 towards Bowness. Miller Howe is ½ mile on the right. Price Guide: (including 5-course dinner): Single £95–£175; double/twin £140–£300.; cottage suites £240–£350

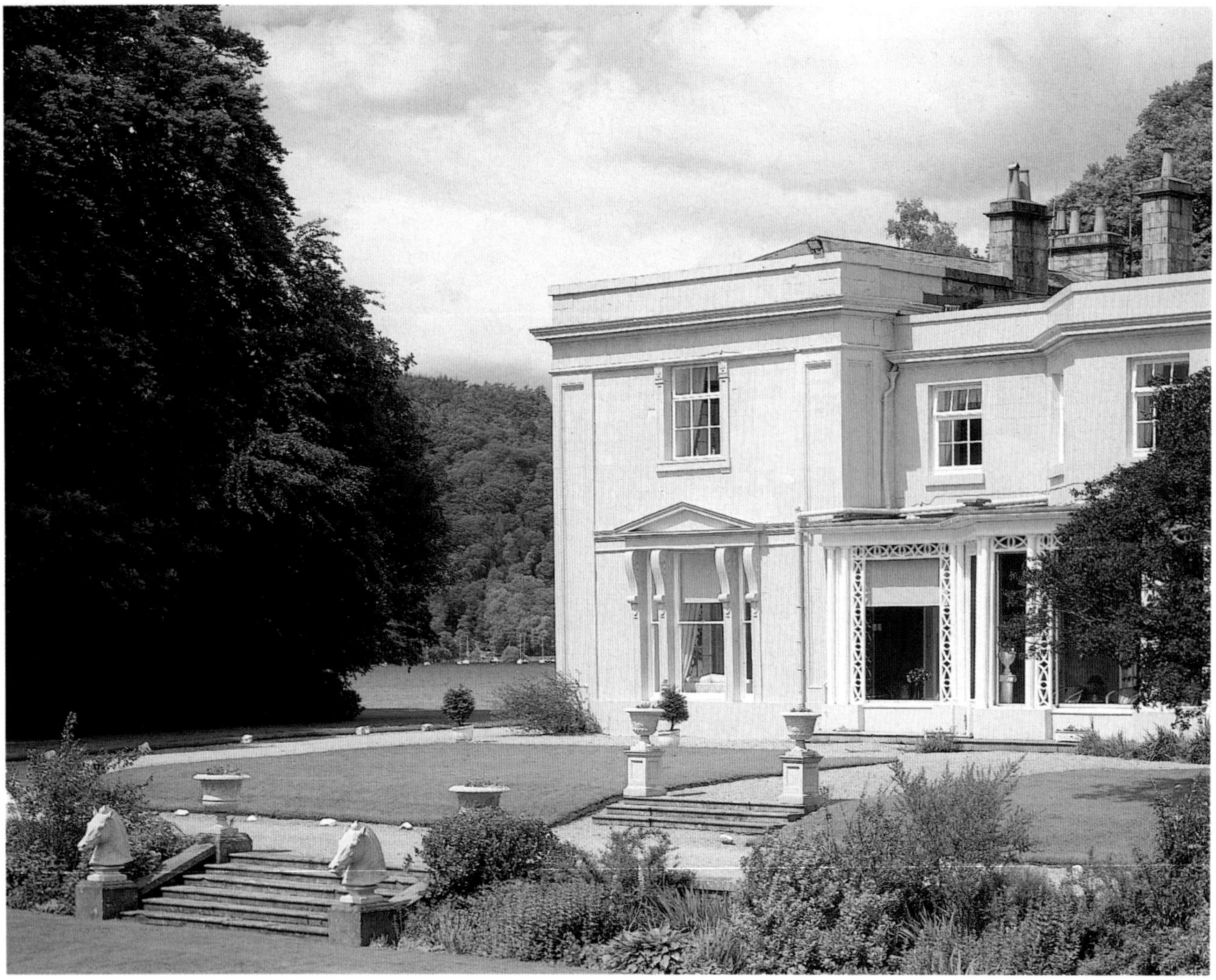

STORRS HALL

WINDERMERE, CUMBRIA LA23 3LG
TEL: 015394 47111 FAX: 015394 47555 E-MAIL: reception@storrshall.co.uk

From this magnificent listed Georgian manor house not another building can be seen. Just a spectacular, seemingly endless view over beautiful Lake Windermere. Built in the 18th century for a Lancashire shipping magnate, Storrs Hall stands majestically in an unrivalled peninsular position surrounded by 17 acres of landscaped, wooded grounds which slope down to half a mile of lakeside frontage. Apart from Wordsworth, who first recited 'Daffodils' in the Drawing Room at Storrs, the hotel was frequented by all the great Lakeland poets and Beatrix Potter. It is owned by Mr Les Hindle, a property developer and Richard Livock, a fine art and antiques dealer, who rescued the manor from decay and restored it to its former glory, furnishing the rooms with antiques and objets d'art including a private collection of ship models, reflecting the maritime fortunes which built the hall. Opened as a hotel in 1998, the Hall has 25 beautifully furnished bedrooms, each en suite, spacious and with every comfort. Most have views over the lake, which was once the property of the Hall. Equally splendid views are enjoyed from an exquisite lounge, library, writing room and cosy bar. The Terrace Restaurant is renowned for the superb cuisine prepared by Head Chef Michael Dodd. **Directions:** On A592 2 m S of Bowness and 5 m N of Newby Bridge. Price Guide: Single £130; double/twin £160–£305.

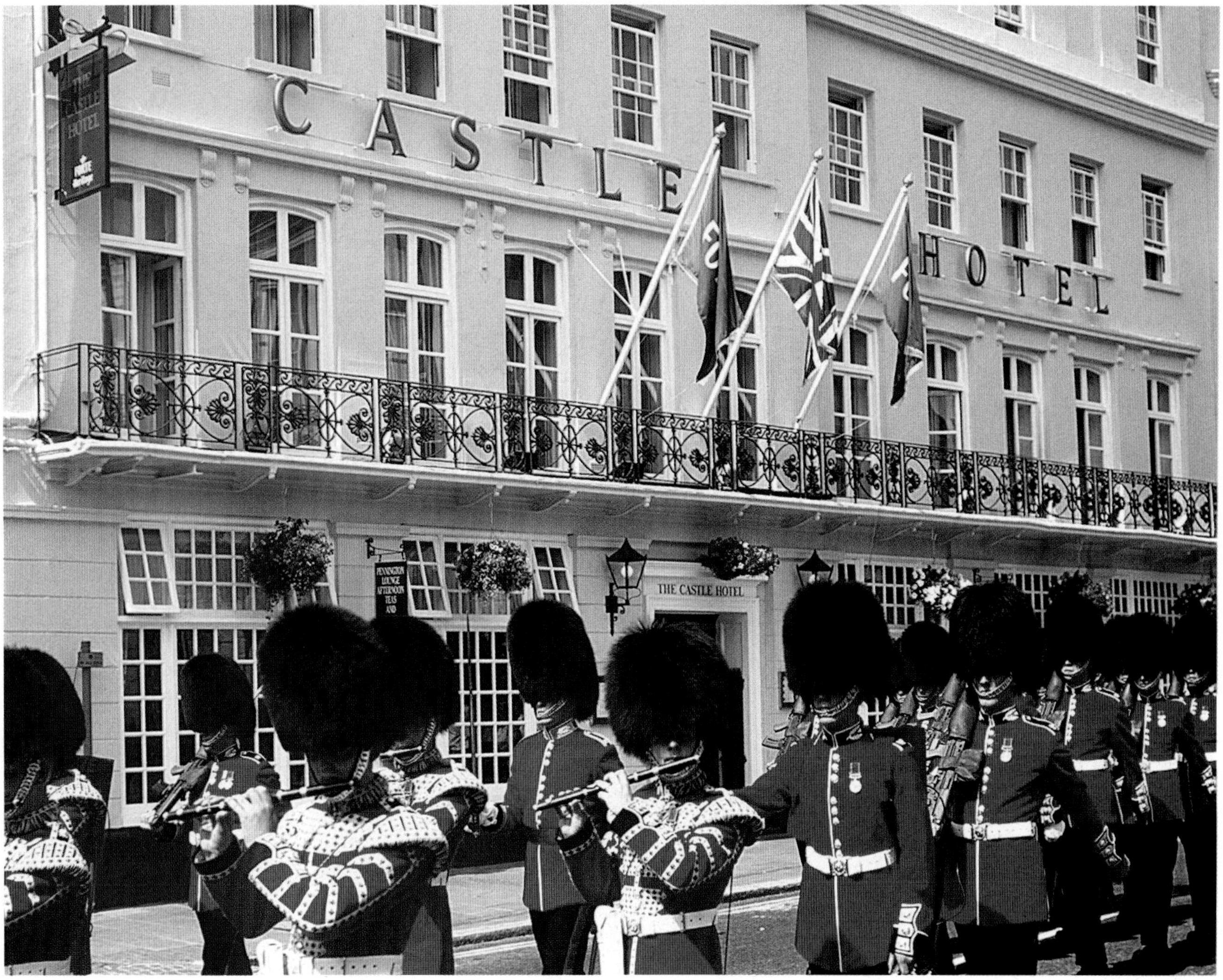

THE CASTLE HOTEL

HIGH STREET, WINDSOR, BERKSHIRE SL4 1LJ

TEL: 0870 400 8300 FAX: 01753 830244 E-MAIL: heritagehotels_windsor.castle@forte–hotels.com

Steeped in history, this splendid Georgian hotel stands in the High Street beneath the solid rampards and towers of Windsor's magnificent Norman castle. With a quiet charm and dignity, the hotel combines fine furnishings from the past with every comfort associated with life today. The stylish interior décor of the hotel creates a prestigious venue for visitors, who receive a bonus when discovering it provides one of the finest views of the Changing of the Guard procession. The ancient ceremony can be enjoyed by guests while taking morning coffee with teacakes in the elegant lounge at 11am. Sympathetic additions and refurbishment over the years have enhanced the appeal of this attractive town hotel which now offers 111 opulent bedrooms and superb suites, each providing the highest standards of facilities and amenities. The grand and beautifully decorated Castle Restaurant provides award-winning British and International cuisine, whilst the Fresh Fields Restaurant, Pennington Lounge and Windsor Bar offer a superb choice for relaxed informal dining. As well as the Castle and Windsor Great Park, among the many attractions within easy reach are Eton College, Ascot, Henley, Maidenhead, Thorpe Park and Legoland. **Directions:** Exit M4 at junction 6, follow signs for Windsor Castle. Price Guide: Single £165; double/twin £185; suite £265.

Sir Christopher Wren's House

THAMES STREET, WINDSOR, BERKSHIRE SL4 1PX
TEL: 01753 861354 FAX: 01753 860172

A friendly and homely atmosphere makes Sir Christopher Wren's House a perfect location for guests seeking a break from the hectic pace of modern life. Built by the famous architect in 1676, it nestles beneath the ramparts and towers of Windsor Castle, beside the River Thames and Eton Bridge.With a quiet charm and dignity of its own, the hotel combines fine furnishings from the past with every comfort and convenience associated with life today. Additions to the original house have been made at different times over the centuries and there are now 80 bedrooms available for guests. These have all recently been refurbished to the highest standards and while some feature a balcony and river views, others overlook the famous castle. All offer a full range of amenities, including direct dial telephone, cable TV, trouser press, tea and coffee-making facilities, mineral water and an air cooling system. Stroks Riverside Restaurant offers a good selection of beautifully cooked and well-presented meals by master chef Philip Wild. The Windsor area has a great deal to offer, for those with time to explore. Among the many attractions within easy reach are Windsor Castle, Eton College, Royal Ascot, Thorpe park, Henley, Saville Gardens and Legoland. **Directions:** Windsor is just 2 miles from junction 6 of the M4. Price Guide: Single from £170, double/twin from £225, suite from £325.

84 MasterCard VISA AMERICAN EXPRESS M 90

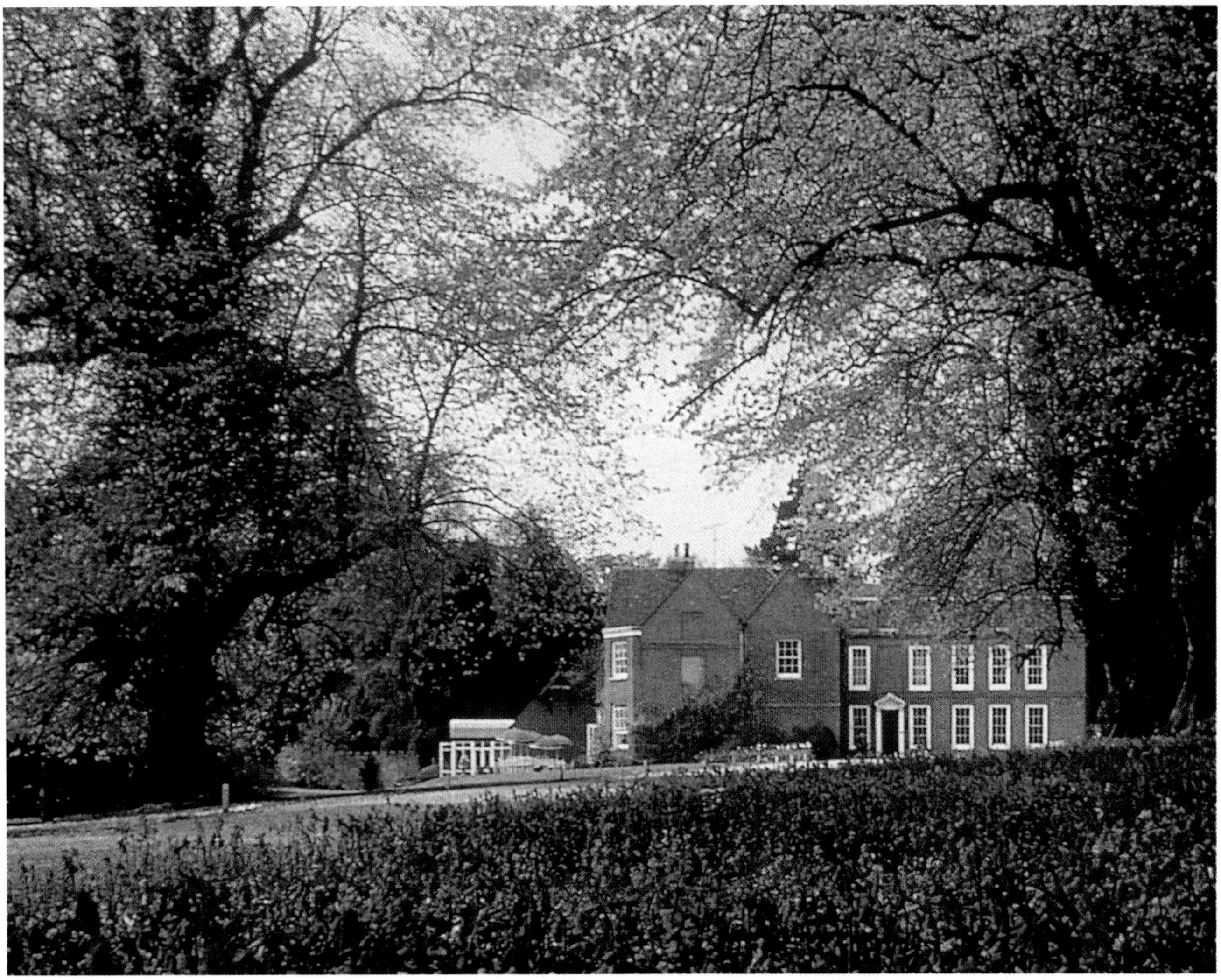

FLITWICK MANOR

CHURCH ROAD, FLITWICK, BEDFORDSHIRE MK45 1AE
TEL: 01525 712242 FAX: 01525 718753 E-MAIL: flitwick@menzies–hotels.co.uk

Flitwick Manor is a Georgian gem, classical in style, elegant in décor, comfortable in appointment, a country house hotel that remains true to the traditions of country house hospitality. Nestling in acres of glorious rolling parkland complete with lake, grotto and church, the manor has the intimacy and warmth that make it the ideal retreat for both pleasure and business. The seventeen bedrooms, with their distinctive characters and idiosyncrasies, add to the charm of the reception rooms: a soothing drawing room, a cosy library and pine panelled morning room, the latter two doubling up as both meeting and private dining rooms. Fine antiques and period pieces, easy chairs and inviting sofas, winter fires and summer flowers, they all blend effortlessly together to make a perfect combination. The restaurant is highly acclaimed by all the major food guides and indeed the AA, with its bestowal of two Rosettes, rated Flitwick Manor as the county's best. Outside pleasures are afforded by the all-weather tennis court, croquet lawns and putting green as well as a range of local attractions such as Woburn Abbey and Safari Park. **Directions:** Flitwick is on the A5120 just north of the M1 junction 12. Price Guide (room only): Single from £120; double/twin/suite £145–£275. Special weekend rates available.

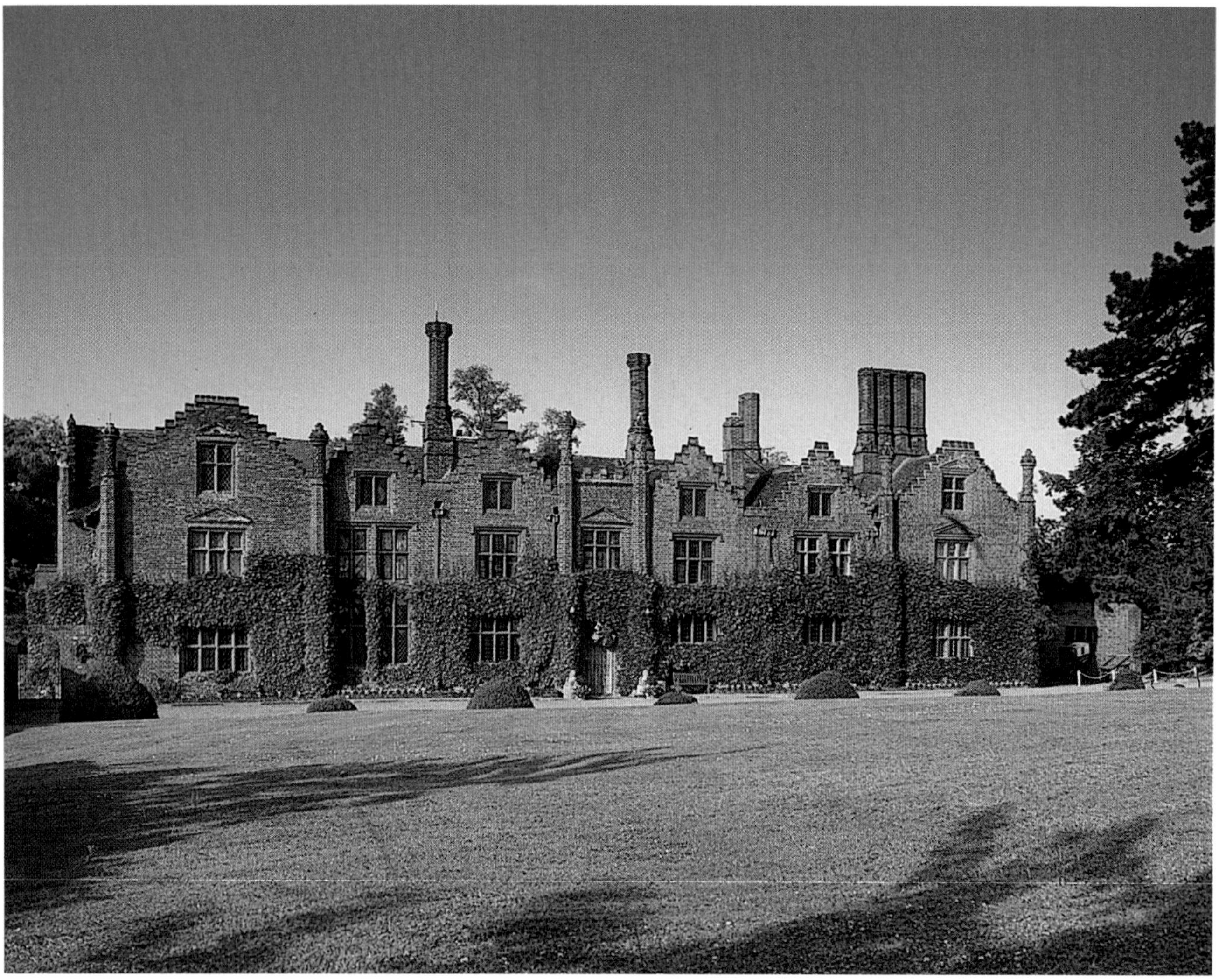

SECKFORD HALL

WOODBRIDGE, SUFFOLK IP13 6NU

TEL: 01394 385678 FAX: 01394 380610 E-MAIL: reception@seckford.co.uk

Seckford Hall dates from 1530 and it is said that Elizabeth I once held court there. The hall has lost none of its Tudor grandeur. Furnished as a private house with many fine period pieces, the panelled rooms, beamed ceilings, carved doors and great stone fireplaces are displayed against the splendour of English oak. Local delicacies such as the house speciality, lobster, feature on the à la carte menu. The original minstrels gallery can be viewed in the banqueting hall, which is now a conference and function suite designed in keeping with the general style. The Courtyard area was converted from a giant Tudor tithe barn, dairy and coach house. It now incorporates ten charming cottage-style suites and a modern leisure complex, which includes a heated swimming pool, exercise machines, spa bath and beauty salon. The hotel is set in 34 acres of tranquil parkland with sweeping lawns and a willow-fringed lake and guests may stroll about the grounds or simply relax in the attractive terrace garden. There is a 18-hole golf course, where equipment can be hired, and a gentle walk along the riverside to picturesque Woodbridge, with its tide mill, antique shops and yacht harbours. Visit the site of the Sutton Hoo buriel ship site and new museum. Constable country and the Suffolk coast are nearby. **Directions:** Remain on the A12 Woodbridge bypass until the blue-and-white hotel sign. Price Guide: Single £79–£125; double/twin £120–£170; suite £150–£170.

The Feathers Hotel

MARKET STREET, WOODSTOCK, OXFORDSHIRE OX20 1SX
TEL: 01993 812291 FAX: 01993 813158 E-MAIL: enquiries@feathers.co.uk

The Feathers is a privately owned and run town house hotel, situated in the centre of Woodstock, a few miles from Oxford. Woodstock is one of England's most attractive country towns, constructed mostly from Cotswold stone and with some buildings dating from the 12th century. The hotel, built in the 17th century, was originally four separate houses. Antiques, log fires and traditional English furnishings lend character and charm. There are 20 bedrooms, all of which have private bathrooms and showers. Public rooms, including the drawing room and study, are intimate and comfortable. The small garden is a delightful setting for a light lunch or afternoon tea and guests can enjoy a drink in the cosy courtyard bar, which has an open fire in winter. The antique-panelled restaurant is internationally renowned for its fine cuisine, complemented by a high standard of service and 3 AA Rosettes. The menu changes frequently and offers a wide variety of dishes, using the finest local ingredients. Blenheim Palace, seat of the Duke of Marlborough and birthplace of Sir Winston Churchill, is just around the corner. The Cotswolds and the dreaming spires of Oxford are a short distance away. **Directions:** From London leave the M40 at junction 8; from Birmingham leave at jct 9. Take A44 and follow the signs to Woodstock. The hotel is on the left. Price Guide: Single £95; double/twin £130–£185; suite £235–£295.

WATERSMEET HOTEL

MORTEHOE, WOOLACOMBE, DEVON EX34 7EB

TEL: 01271 870333 FAX: 01271 870890 RESERVATIONS: 0800 731 7493 E-MAIL: info @watermeethotel.co.uk

Watersmeet personifies the comfortable luxury of a country house hotel. Majestically situated on the rugged North Atlantic coastline, the hotel commands dramatic views across the waters of Woolacombe Bay past Hartland Point to Lundy Island. The gardens reach down to the sea and nearby steps lead directly to the beach. Attractive décor, combined with striking coloured fabrics, creates a warm impression all year round. All the bedrooms look out to sea and guests can drift off to sleep to the sound of lapping waves or rolling surf. Morning coffee, lunch and afternoon tea can be served in the relaxing comfort of the lounge, on the terrace or by the heated outdoor pool. The new indoor pool and spa is a favourite with everyone. English and international dishes are served in the award-winning Watersmeet Restaurant where each evening candles flicker as diners absorb a view of the sun slipping below the horizon. The hotel has been awarded an AA Rosette for cuisine, the AA Courtesy and Care Award and a Silver Award by the English Tourism Council. There is a grass tennis court and local surfing, riding, clay pigeon shooting and bracing walks along coastal paths. Open February to January. **Directions:** From M5, Jct27, follow A361 towards Ilfracombe, turn left at roundabout and follow signs to Mortehoe. Price Guide: (including dinner): Single £91–£134; double/twin £152–£238.

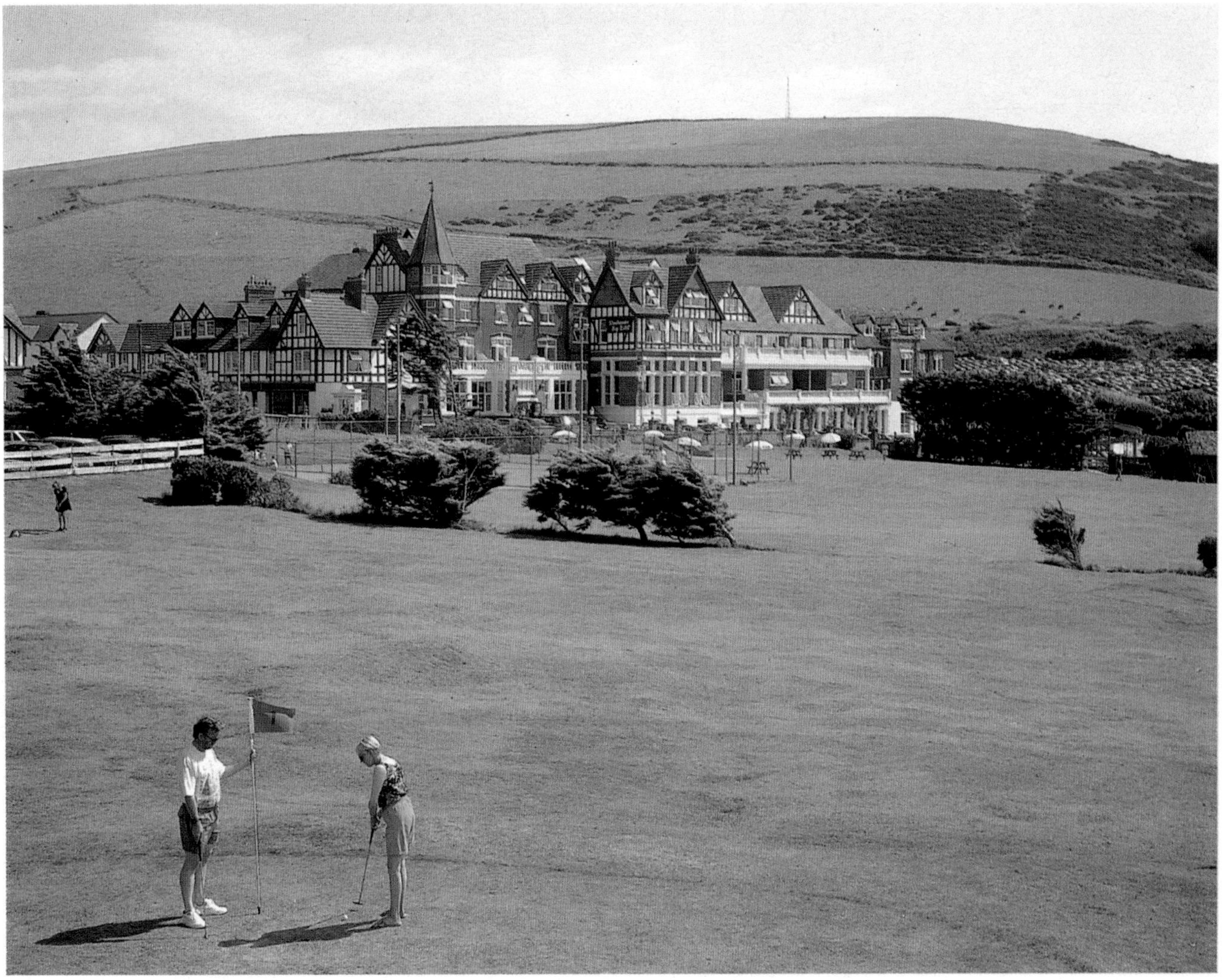

Woolacombe Bay Hotel

SOUTH STREET, WOOLACOMBE, DEVON EX34 7BN
TEL: 01271 870388 FAX: 01271 870613 E-MAIL: woolacombe.bayhotel@btinternet.com

Woolacombe Bay Hotel stands in 6 acres of grounds, leading to three miles of golden sand. Built by the Victorians, the hotel has an air of luxury, style and comfort. All rooms are en suite with satellite TV, baby listening, ironing centre, some with a balcony. Traditional English and French dishes are offered in the dining room. Superb recreational amenities on site include unlimited free access to tennis, squash, indoor and outdoor pools, billiards, bowls, croquet, dancing and films, a health suite with steam room, sauna, spa bath with high impulse shower. Power-boating, fishing, shooting and riding can be arranged and preferential rates are offered for golf at the Saunton Golf Club. The "Hot House" aerobics studio, beauty salon, cardio vascular weights room, solariums, masseur and beautician. However, being energetic is not a requirement for enjoying the qualities of Woolacombe Bay. Many of its regulars choose simply to relax in the grand public rooms and in the grounds, which extend to the rolling surf of the magnificent bay. A drive along the coastal route in either direction will guarantee splendid views. Exmoor's beautiful Doone Valley is an hour away by car. Closed January. **Directions:** At the centre of the village, off main Barnstaple–Ilfracombe road. Price Guide: (including dinner): Single £50–£110; double/twin £160–£220.

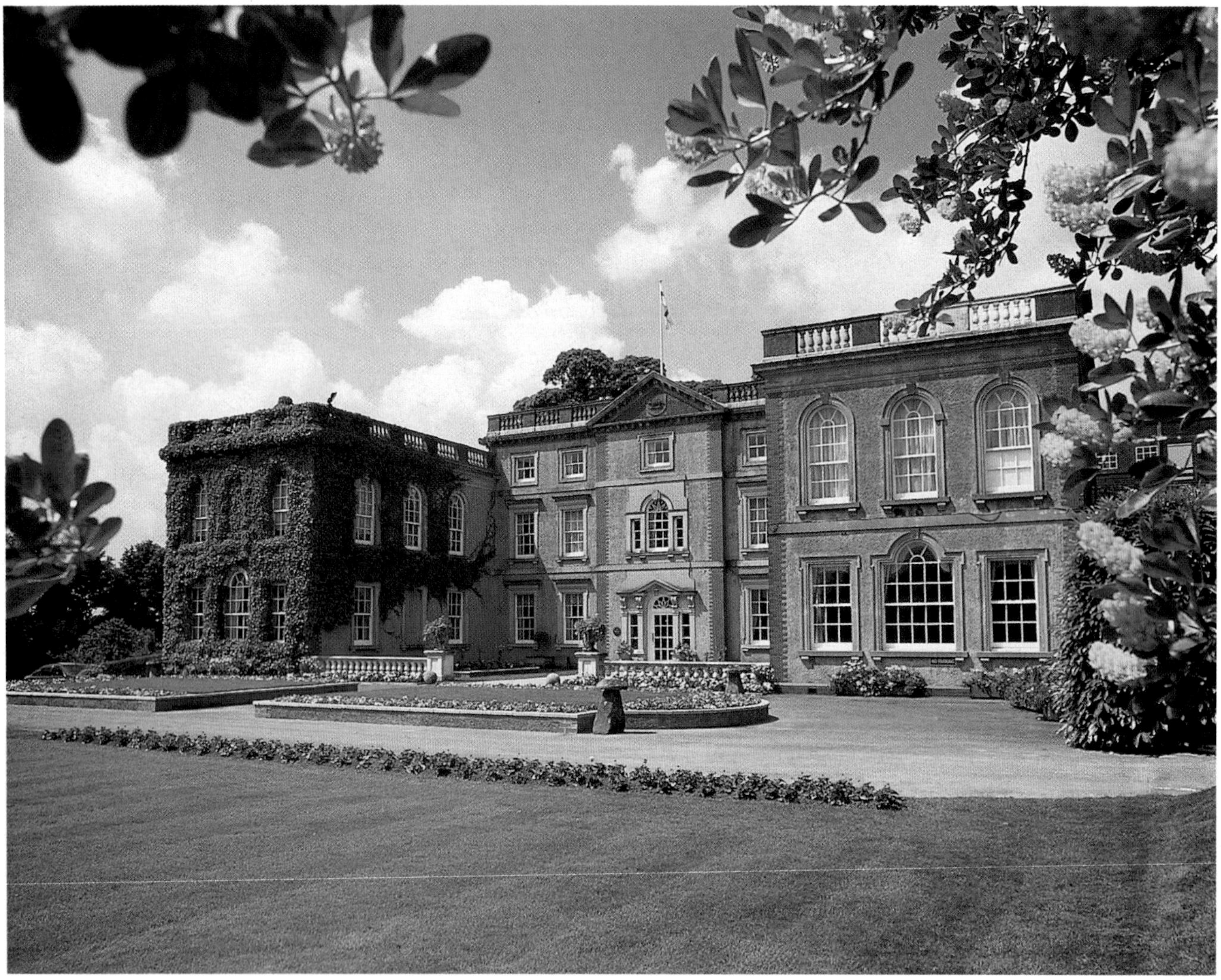

THE ELMS

ABBERLEY, WORCESTERSHIRE WR6 6AT

TEL: 01299 896666 FAX: 01299 896804 E-MAIL: elmshotel@ukonline.co.uk

Built in 1710 by a pupil of Sir Christopher Wren, and converted into a country house hotel in 1946, The Elms has achieved an international reputation for excellence spanning the past half century. Standing impressively between Worcester and Tenbury Wells, this fine Queen Anne mansion is surrounded by beautiful meadows, woodland, hop fields and orchards of cider apples and cherries of the Teme Valley, whose river runs crimson when in flood from bank-side soil tinged with red sandstone. Each of the hotel's 21 bedrooms has its own character, is furnished with period antiques and has splendid views across the landscaped gardens and beyond to the valley. There is a panelled bar and elegant restaurant offering fine and imaginative cuisine to award-winning standards. The surrounding countryside is ideal for walking, fishing, shooting, golf and horse-racing. Within easy reach are the attractions of the market town of Tenbury Wells, Hereford with meppa murdi (oldest map in the world), Witley Court, Bewdley and the ancient city of Worcester with its cathedral, county cricket ground and porcelain factory. A member of Small Luxury Hotels. **Directions:** From M5, exit at jct 5 (Droitwich) or jct 6 (Worcester) then take A443 towards Tenbury Wells. The Elms is 2 m after Great Witley. Do not take turning into Abberley village. Price Guide: Single £110–£130; double/twin £175–£250; coach house £70–£90.

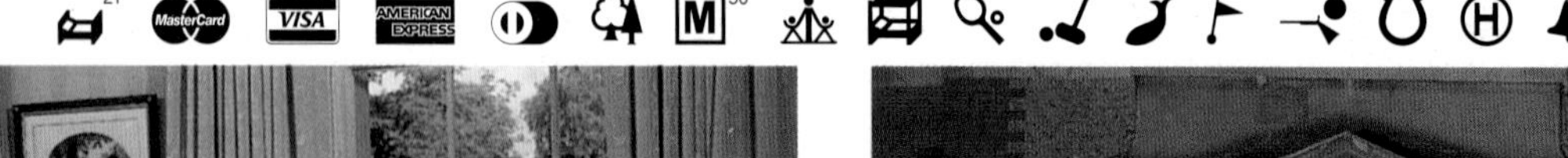

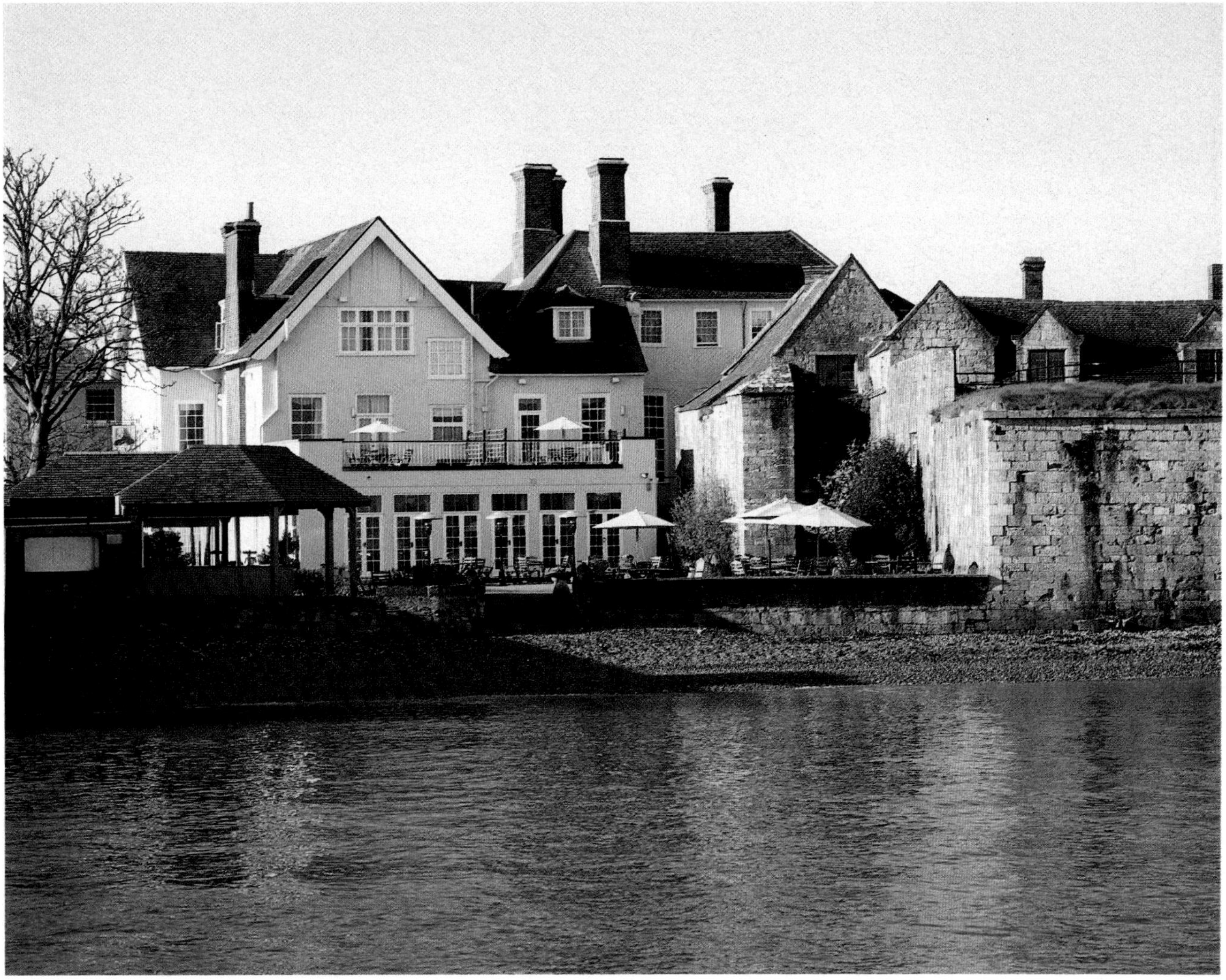

THE GEORGE HOTEL

QUAY STREET, YARMOUTH, ISLE OF WIGHT PO41 0PE
TEL: 01983 760331 FAX: 01983 760425 E-MAIL: res@thegeorge.co.uk

This historic 17th century town house is superbly located just a few paces from Yarmouth's ancient harbour. Built for Admiral Sir Robert Holmes, a former governor of the island, it once welcomed Charles II through its doors. With the cosy ambience of a well-loved home, The George is the perfect place for self-indulgence. Beautifully furnished and well-equipped bedrooms complement the luxurious surroundings. Enjoy either the 3 AA Rosette cuisine in the elegant restaurant or opt for a more informal à la carte meal in the lively brasserie with its lovely sea views. The excellent cellar contains particularly good claret. The hotel has its own private beach and there is no shortage of leisure opportunities in the near vicinity, including world class sailing on the Solent. Yarmouth remains the gateway to the downs and villages of the West Wight and there are countless opportunities to make the most of this area of outstanding natural beauty by walking, hiking or enjoying a host of other country pursuits, golf too. Historic places of interest include Carisbrook Castle and Osborne House. **Directions:** From the M3/M27, exit at junction 1 and take the A377 to Lymington and then the ferry to Yarmouth. Alternatively, ferry services run regularly to the island from Southampton and Portsmouth. The A3054 leads direct to Yarmouth. Price Guide: Single from £105; double/twin from £155.

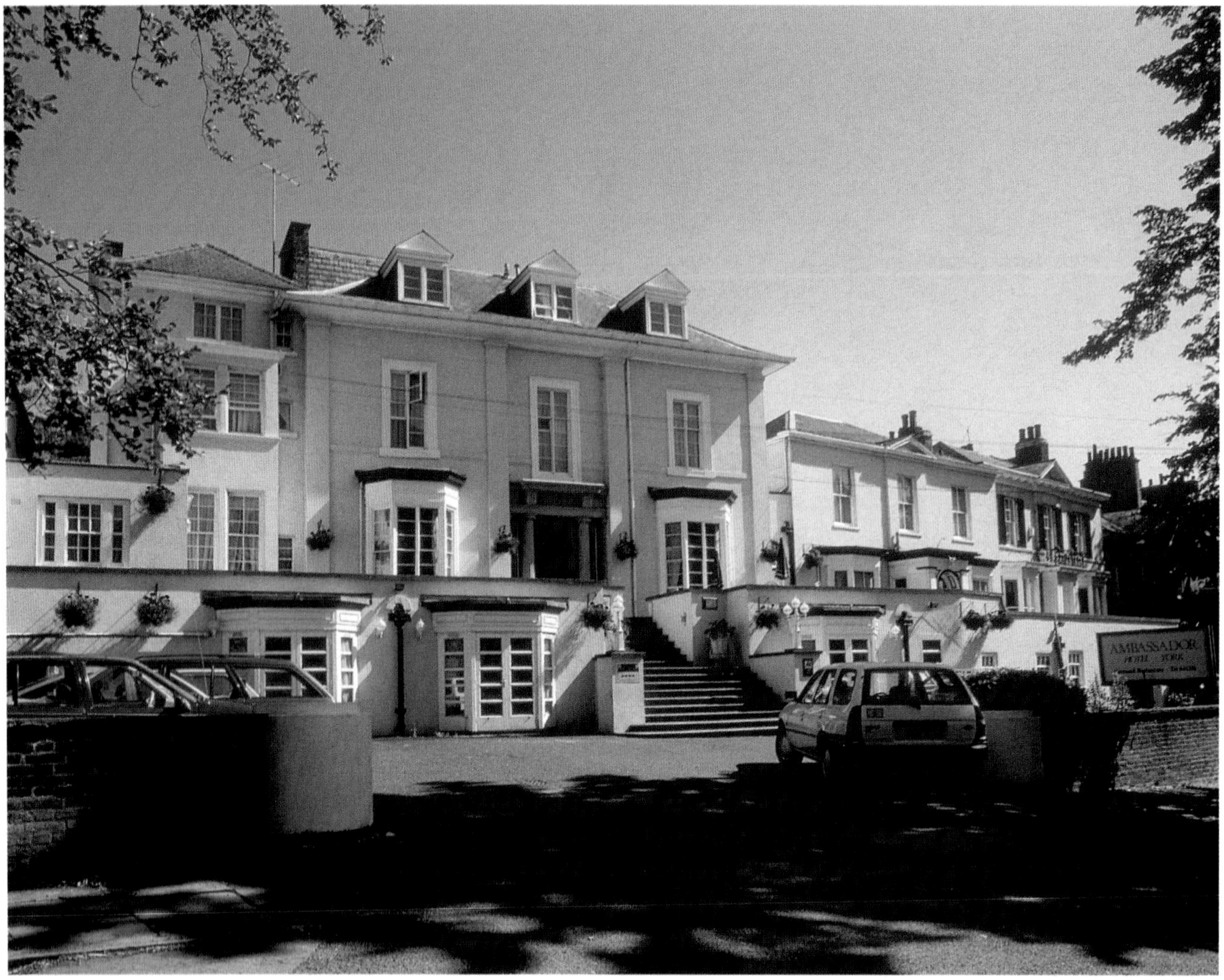

Ambassador Hotel

123–125 THE MOUNT, YORK, NORTH YORKSHIRE YO24 1DU
TEL: 01904 641316 FAX: 01904 640259 E-MAIL: stay@ambassadorhotel.co.uk

Built in 1826 for a wealthy York merchant, this elegant Georgian haven has been attractively refurbished by Sallie Gray, retaining the style and elegance of that glorious era. Each of the 25 beautiful bedrooms have been individually style and decorated, all of them have private bath or shower rooms, direct dial telephones, data points, television, trouser press, courtesy trays, radios, hairdryers and big fluffy towels. The classically decorated Grays Restaurant has been awarded numerous accolades and awards for its excellent cuisine, for which only the finest of local foods is being used. The extensive gardens at the rear of The Ambassador are a wonderful place to relax and unwind. York City centre is a short stroll away as is York's magnificent racecourse. For residents, there is ample parking available at the front and rear of the hotel. The Ambassador is a perfect conference and meeting venue, recognising that a successful meeting reflects a professional image. The conference rooms are a superb range of unique character and, with high ceilings and natural daylight, create a serene but businesslike atmosphere. **Directions:** From the A64 turn onto the A1036 signposted York. Go past the racecourse; The Ambassador is on the right before the traffic lights. Price Guide: Single £98–£105; double/twin £118–£135.

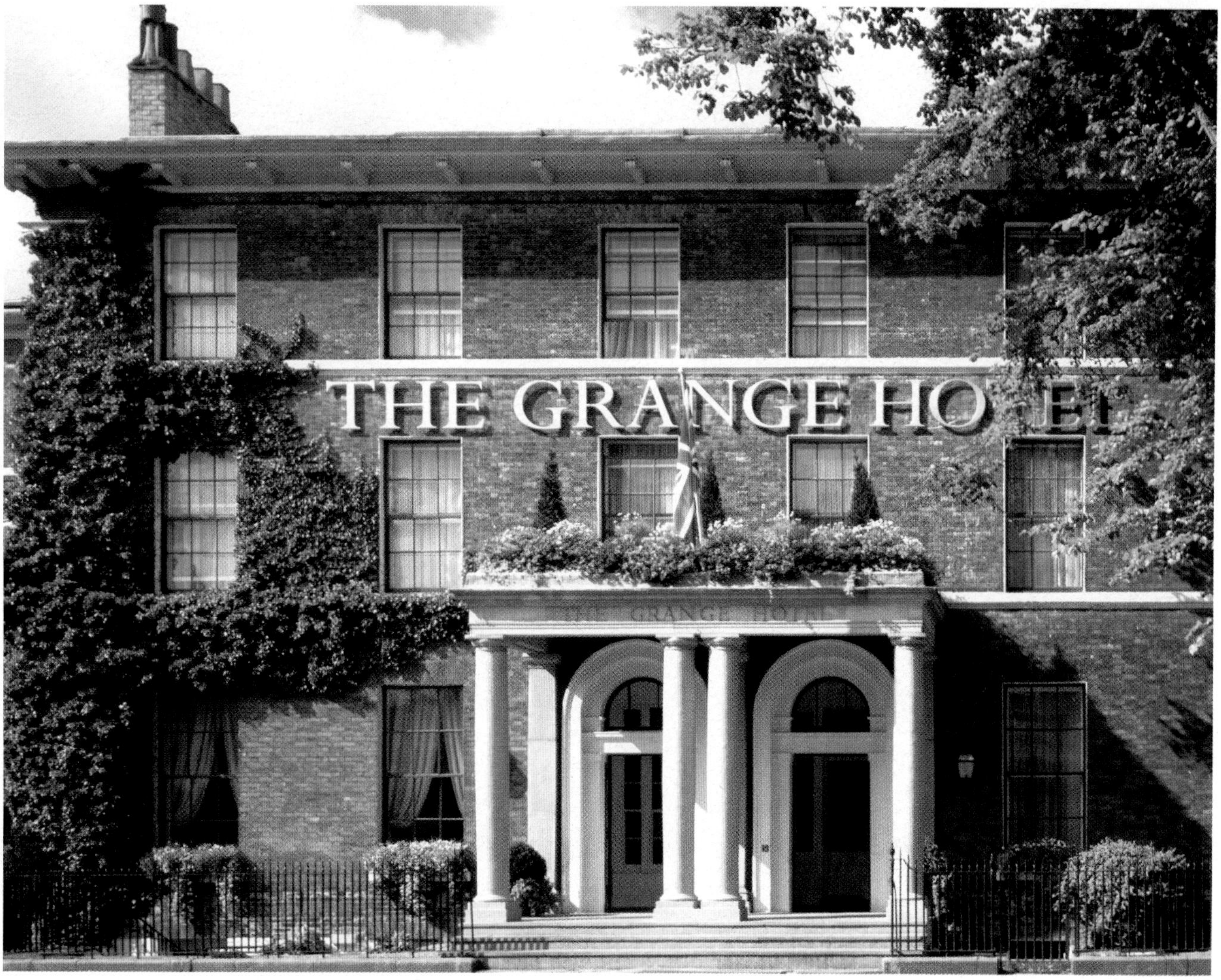

THE GRANGE HOTEL

1 CLIFTON, YORK, NORTH YORKSHIRE YO30 6AA
TEL: 01904 644744 FAX: 01904 612453 E-MAIL: info@grangehotel.co.uk

Set near the ancient city walls, just a short walk from the world famous Minster, this sophisticated Regency town house has been carefully restored and its spacious rooms richly decorated. Beautiful stone-flagged floors lead to the classically styled reception rooms. The flower-filled Morning Room is welcoming, with its deep sofas and blazing fire in the winter months. Double doors between the panelled library and drawing room can be opened up to create a dignified venue for parties, wedding receptions or business entertaining. Prints, antiques and English chintz in the bedrooms reflect the proprietor's careful attention to detail. The Ivy Restaurant has an established reputation for first-class gastronomy, incorporating the best in modern British and French cuisine. The Seafood bar has two murals depicting racing scenes. The Brasserie is open for lunch Monday to Saturday and dinner every night until after the theatre closes most evenings. For conferences, a computer and fax are available as well as secretarial services. Brimming with history, York's list of attractions includes the National Railway Museum, the Jorvik Viking Centre and the medieval Shambles. **Directions:** The Grange Hotel is on the A19 York–Thirsk road, 400 yards from the city centre. Price Guide: Single £100–£160; double/twin £128–£195; suites £220.

MIDDLETHORPE HALL

BISHOPTHORPE ROAD, YORK, NORTH YORKSHIRE YO23 2GB
TEL: 01904 641241 FAX: 01904 620176 E-MAIL: info@middlethorpe.com

Middlethorpe Hall is a delightful William III house, built in 1699 for Thomas Barlow, a wealthy merchant and was for a time the home of Lady Mary Wortley Montagu, the 18th century writer of letters. The house has been immaculately restored by Historic House Hotels who have decorated and furnished it in its original style and elegance. There are beautifully designed bedrooms and suites in the main house and the adjacent 18th century courtyard. The restaurant, which has been awarded 3 Rosettes from the AA, offers the best in contemporary English cooking. A health and beauty Spa with an indoor swimming pool opened in 1999. Middlethorpe Hall, which is a member of Relais & Chateaux Hotels, stands in 20 acres of parkland and overlooks York Racecourse yet is only 1½ miles from the medieval city of York with its fascinating museums, restored streets and world-famous Minster. From Middlethorpe you can visit Yorkshire's famous country houses, like Castle Howard, Beningbrough and Harewood, the ruined Abbeys of Fountains and Rievaulx and explore the magnificent Yorkshire Moors. Helmsley, Whitby and Scarborough are nearby. **Directions:** Take A64 (T) off A1 (T) near Tadcaster, follow signs to York West, then smaller signs to Bishopthorpe. Price Guide: Single £124–£160; double/twin £190–£290; suite from £250–£360.

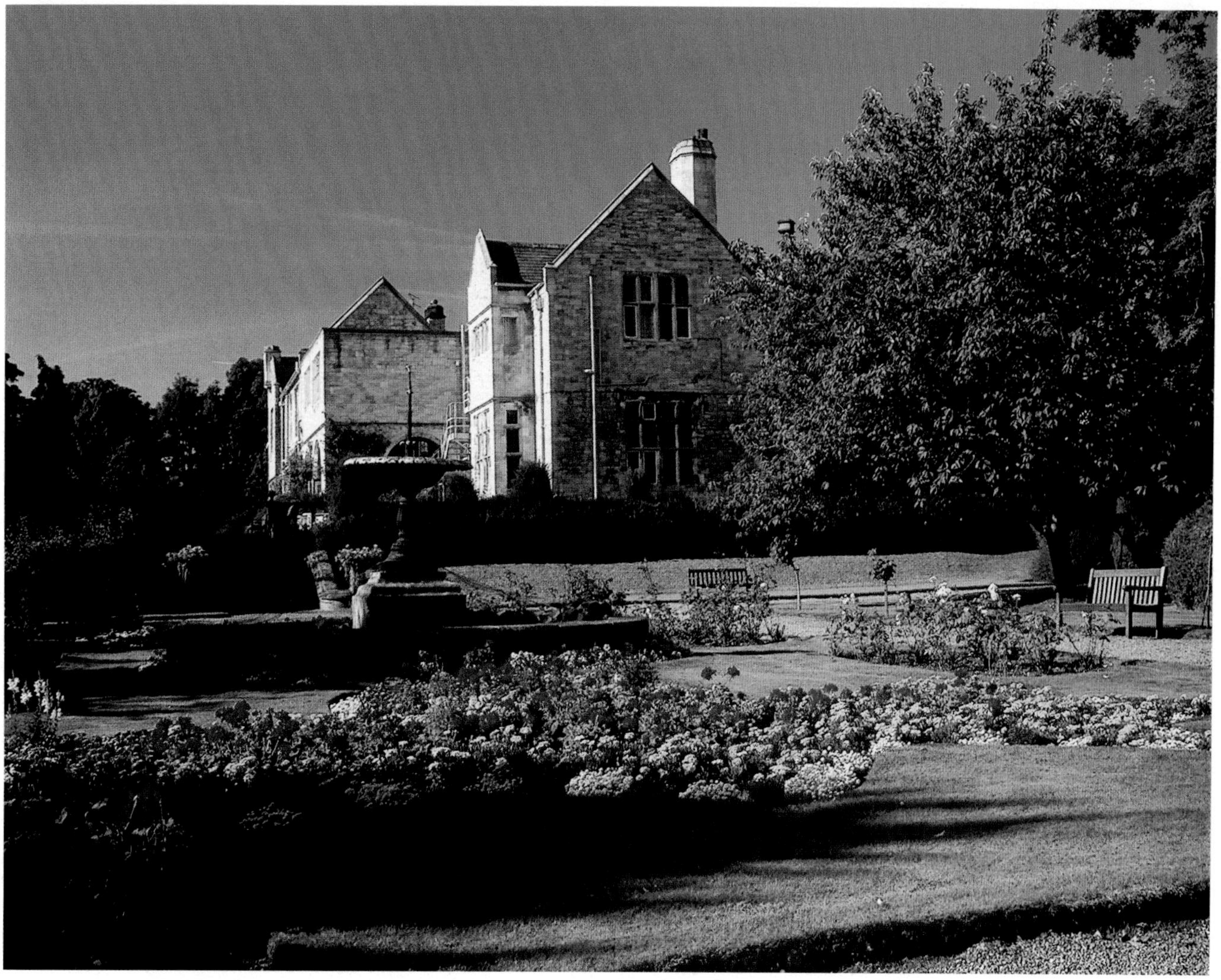

Monk Fryston Hall Hotel

MONK FRYSTON, NORTH YORKSHIRE LS25 5DU
TEL: 01977 682369 FAX: 01977 683544 E-MAIL: reception@monkfryston-hotel.com

A short distance from the A1 and almost equidistant from Leeds and York, this mellow old manor house hotel, built in 1109, is ideal for tourists, business people and those looking for an invitingly secluded spot for a weekend break. The mullioned and transom windows and the family coat of arms above the doorway are reminiscent of Monk Fryston's fascinating past. In 1954 the Hall was acquired by the late Duke of Rutland, who has created an elegant contemporary hotel, while successfully preserving the strong sense of heritage and tradition. The bedrooms, ranging from cosy to spacious, have private en suite bathrooms and are appointed to a high standard. A generous menu offers a wide choice of traditional English dishes with something to suit all tastes. From the Hall, the terrace leads down to an ornamental Italian garden which overlooks a lake and is a delight to see at any time of year. Wedding receptions are held in the oak-panelled Haddon Room with its splendid Inglenook fireplace. The Rutland Room provides a convenient venue for meetings and private parties. York is 17 miles, Leeds 13 miles and Harrogate 18 miles away. **Directions:** The Hall is three miles off the A1, on the A63 towards Selby in the centre of Monk Fryston.
Price Guide: Single £85–£135; double/twin £105–£165.

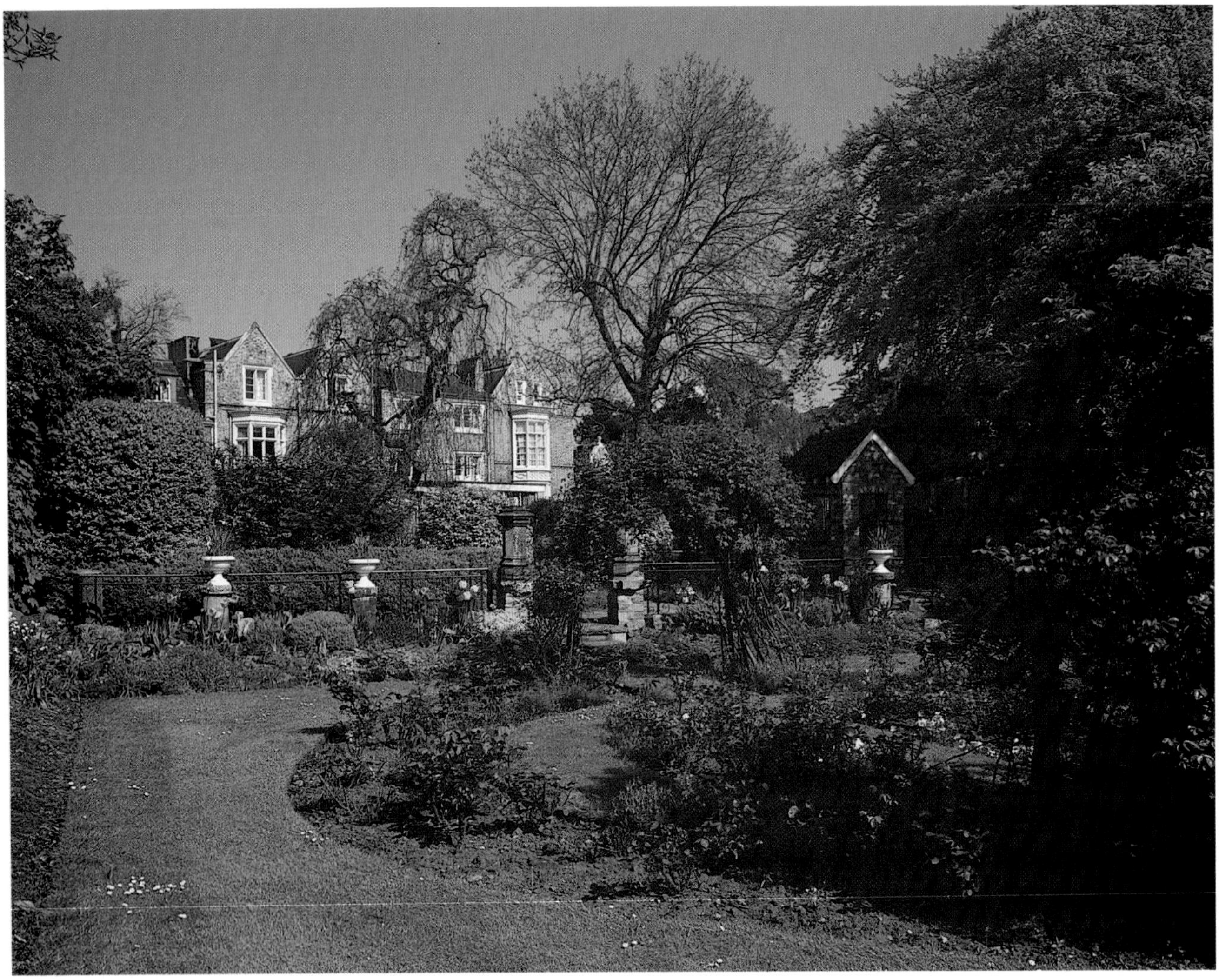

Mount Royale Hotel

THE MOUNT, YORK, NORTH YORKSHIRE YO24 1GU
TEL: 01904 628856 FAX: 01904 611171 E-MAIL: reservations@mountroyale.co.uk

Two elegant William IV houses have been restored to their former glory to create the Mount Royale Hotel, which is personally run by the Oxtoby family. Comfortable bedrooms are furnished with imagination, all in an individual style. Each of the garden rooms opens onto the garden and has its own verandah. Downstairs, the public rooms are filled with interesting items of antique furniture, objets d'art and gilt-framed paintings. To the rear of the building, overlooking the gardens, is the restaurant, where guests can enjoy the best of traditional English cooking and French cuisine. Amenities include a snooker room with a full-sized table, steam room, sauna, solarium and health and beauty treatment centre. With a delightful English garden and heated outdoor pool, the one acre grounds are a peaceful haven just minutes from York's centre. York is a historic and well-preserved city, famous for its Minster and medieval streets. Also within walking distance is York racecourse, where the flat-racing season runs from May to October. Lovers of the great outdoors will find the Yorkshire Dales and North York Moors a 45 minute drive away. Only small dogs by arrangement. **Directions:** From A64, turn onto the A1036 signposted York. Go past racecourse; hotel is on right before traffic lights. Price Guide: Single £95–£109; double/twin £105–£155; suites £155.

The Worsley Arms Hotel

HOVINGHAM, NEAR YORK, NORTH YORKSHIRE YO62 4LA

TEL: 01653 628234 FAX: 01653 628130 E-MAIL: worsleyarms@aol.com

The Worsley Arms is an attractive stone-built Georgian spa hotel in the heart of Hovingham, a pleasant and unspoiled Yorkshire village with a history stretching back to Roman times. The hotel, which overlooks the village green and is set amid delightful gardens, was built in 1841 by the baronet Sir William Worsley is now owned and personally run by Anthony and Sally Finn. Hovingham Hall, the Worsley family and childhood home of the Duchess of Kent, is nearby. Elegant furnishings and open fires create a welcoming atmosphere. The spacious sitting rooms are an ideal place to relax over morning coffee or afternoon tea. The award-winning Restaurant offers creatively prepared dishes, including game from the estate, cooked and presented with flair. Guests can visit the wine cellar to browse or choose their wine for dinner. The Cricketers bar provides a more informal setting to enjoy modern cooking at its best. The en suite bedrooms range in size and have recently all been redecorated. There is plenty to do nearby, including tennis, squash, jogging, golf and scenic walks along nature trails. Guests can explore the beautiful Dales, the North Yorkshire Moors and the spectacular coastline or discover the abbeys, stately homes and castles nearby. **Directions:** Hovingham is on the B1257, eight miles from Malton and Helmsley. 20 minutes North of York. Price guide Price Guide: Single £60–£80; double/twin £90–£135. Special breaks available.

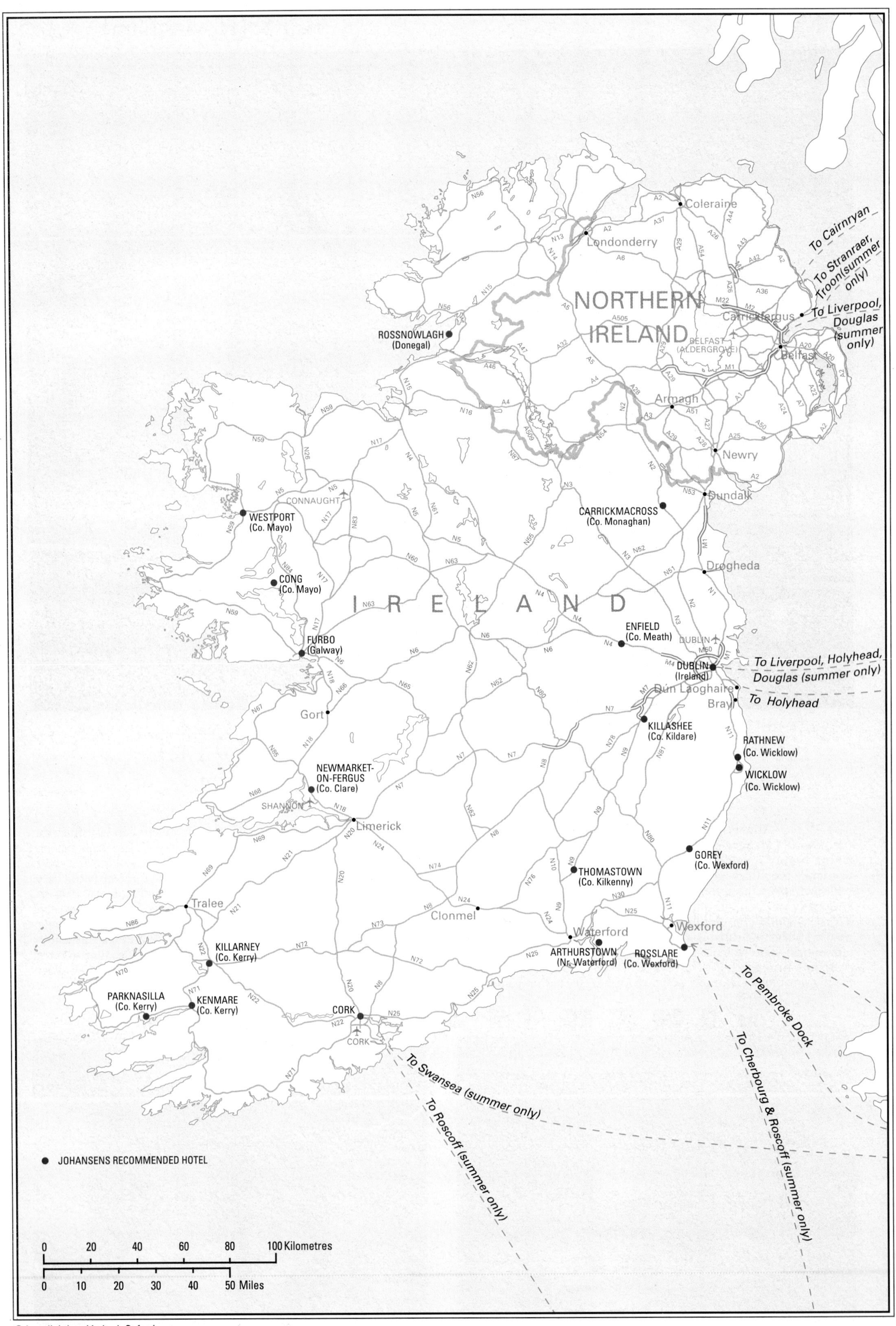

NORTHERN IRELAND
IRELAND
Coleraine
Londonderry
Carrickfergus
BELFAST (ALDERGROVE)
Belfast
Armagh
Newry
Dundalk
Drogheda
DUBLIN
Dún Laoghaire
Bray
Wexford
Waterford
Clonmel
Limerick
Tralee
Gort
CONNAUGHT
SHANNON
CORK
To Cairnryan
To Stranraer, Troon(summer only)
To Liverpool, Douglas (summer only)
To Liverpool, Holyhead, Douglas (summer only)
To Holyhead
To Pembroke Dock
To Cherbourg & Roscoff (summer only)
To Swansea (summer only)
To Roscoff (summer only)
ROSSNOWLAGH (Donegal)
WESTPORT (Co. Mayo)
CONG (Co. Mayo)
FURBO (Galway)
CARRICKMACROSS (Co. Monaghan)
ENFIELD (Co. Meath)
DUBLIN (Ireland)
KILLASHEE (Co. Kildare)
RATHNEW (Co. Wicklow)
WICKLOW (Co. Wicklow)
NEWMARKET-ON-FERGUS (Co. Clare)
GOREY (Co. Wexford)
THOMASTOWN (Co. Kilkenny)
ARTHURSTOWN (Nr. Waterford)
ROSSLARE (Co. Wexford)
KILLARNEY (Co. Kerry)
PARKNASILLA (Co. Kerry)
KENMARE (Co. Kerry)
CORK
● JOHANSENS RECOMMENDED HOTEL
0 20 40 60 80 100 Kilometres
0 10 20 30 40 50 Miles

Johansens Recommended Hotels

Ireland - Eire

Sheen Falls Lodge, Co Kerry

Ireland consists of an amazing blend of verdant countryside, vast costlines and rich cultural traditions, celtic legends and fine foods, and provides the warmest of welcomes to its visitors. It is a breathtakingly beautiful and friendly country, where the sleepy pace of life in rural communities is evidence of the inhabitants' relaxed outlook.

From the craggy cliffs on the west coast of Galway to the gentle flow of the River Liffey in Dublin, Ireland's scenery is dramatic and serene in equal measure. The rugged coast and the barren lands of Connemara seeem a world away from the ordered beauty of the landscaped gardens at Powerscourt or the lush landscape of Killarney National Park, and the incredible geometric rock formations at the Giant's Causeway on the Antrim Coast in Northern Ireland, which consists of 37,000 black basalt columns deposited 60 million years ago, reinforce the country's claim to having some of the most varied scenery in Europe.

While mountains dominate the coast, the midlands area is characterised by flat landscape. The Shannon, the longest river in Britain or Ireland, creates a natural division between east and west, running from Cavan to the Shannon Estuary in Limerick.

Irish hospitality can be enjoyed all over the world, but devotees of Guinness should note that the best is kept within these borders. The pubs of Dublin are the perfect place to sample a pint or two, and the city is enjoying a boom in tourism.

Ireland's festivals are also worth a visit. Galway Arts Festival, held annually in July, brings together international artists and home-grown talent in a fascinating blend of circus art, physical theatre, music, mime and storytelling. Traditional music lovers will enjoy County Kerry's Fleadh Cheoil Na hEireann, where more than 10,000 international and Irish musicians and dancers compete for the All-Ireland Ceili Band title. Fine food is celebrated at the Clarenbridge Oyster Festival in County Galway. For almost 50 years, the village of Clarenbridgehas celebrated the finest oysters in the world with good food, good stout and entertainment.

For further information on Ireland and Northern Ireland, please contact:

The Irish Tourist Board
St Andrews Church
Suffolk Street
Dublin 2
Tel: +353 (0)1 602 4000
Internet: www.ireland.travel.ie

Northern Ireland Tourist Board
St Anne's Court
59 North Street
Belfast BT1 1NB
Tel: +44 (0)28 9024 6609
Internet: www.nitb.com

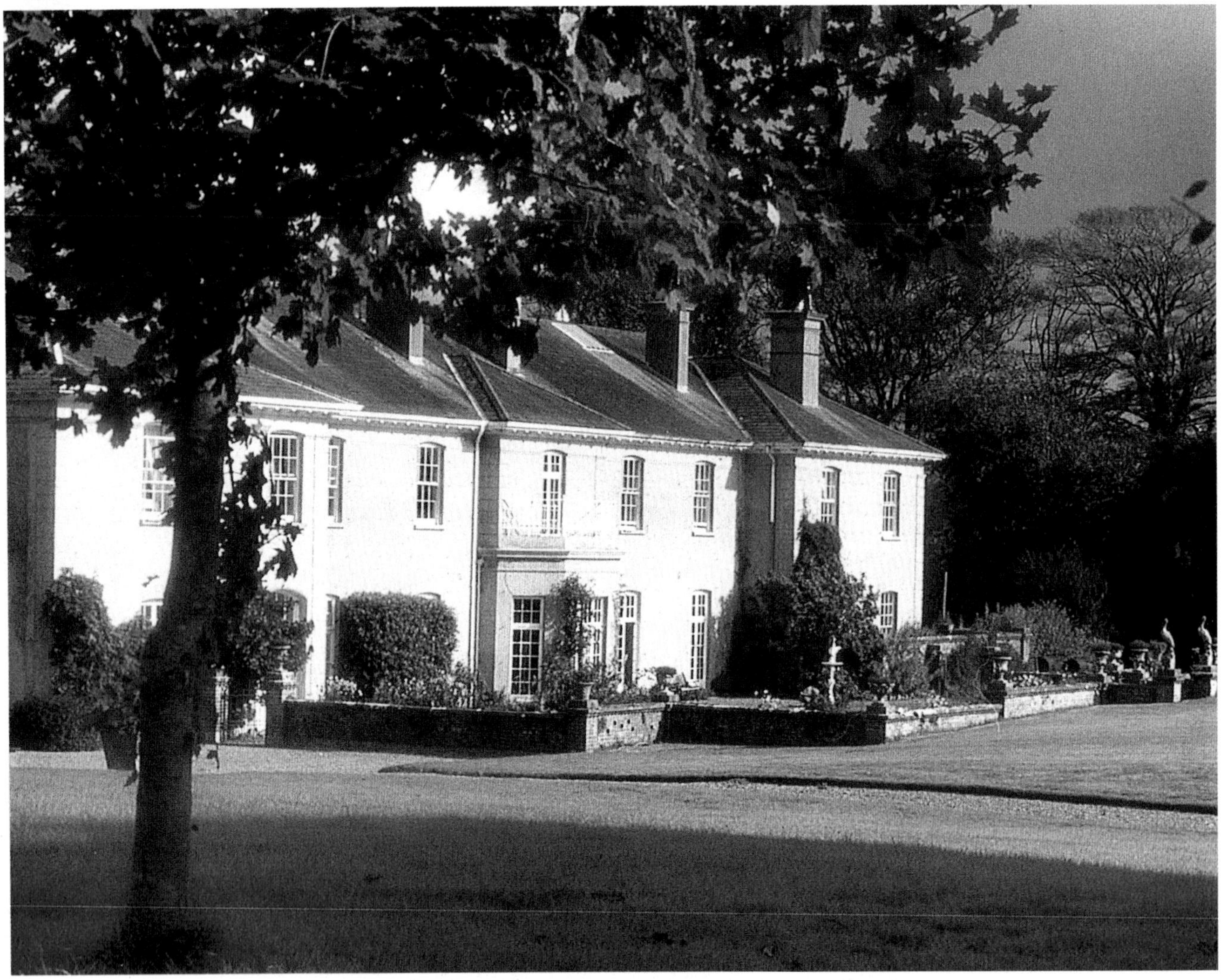

DUNBRODY COUNTRY HOUSE & RESTAURANT

ARTHURSTOWN, NEW ROSS, CO WEXFORD, IRELAND
TEL: 00 353 51 389 600 FAX: 00 353 51 389 601 E-MAIL: dunbrody@indigo.ie

Once home to the Marquess of Donegal, this beautiful Georgian country house hotel stands in the heart of 20 acres of woodland and gardens on the dramatic hook peninsula of Ireland's sunny south-east coast. The charming interior is adorned with comfortable furniture, furnishings and paintings, fresh flowers, potted plants and crackling log fires in period fireplaces during cooler months. Owners Kevin and Catherine Dundon have perfected the art of relaxed elegance. Public rooms are large and comfortable with views over to distant parkland. Bedrooms and suites are understated opulence: spacious, delightfully decorated, superbly appointed and with a high standard of facilities including luxurious bathrooms. Kevin acquired star-status as Master Chef in Canada and creates gastronomic delights for a discerning clientele in an elegant dining room overlooking the lawned garden. He creates imaginative dishes for which he uses plenty of local fresh fish. Also highly acclaimed is the late breakfast which is served daily until noon. Waterford and Wexford are close, as are Tintern Abbey, Dunbody Abbey and a multitude of sandy coves. Croquet and clay pigeon shooting is on site, golf, riding and fishing nearby. Directions: From Wexford take R733 to Duncannon and Arthurstown. Dunbrody is on the left coming into Arthurstown village. Price Guide: Single €100–€200; double/twin €190–€260; suite €280–€360.

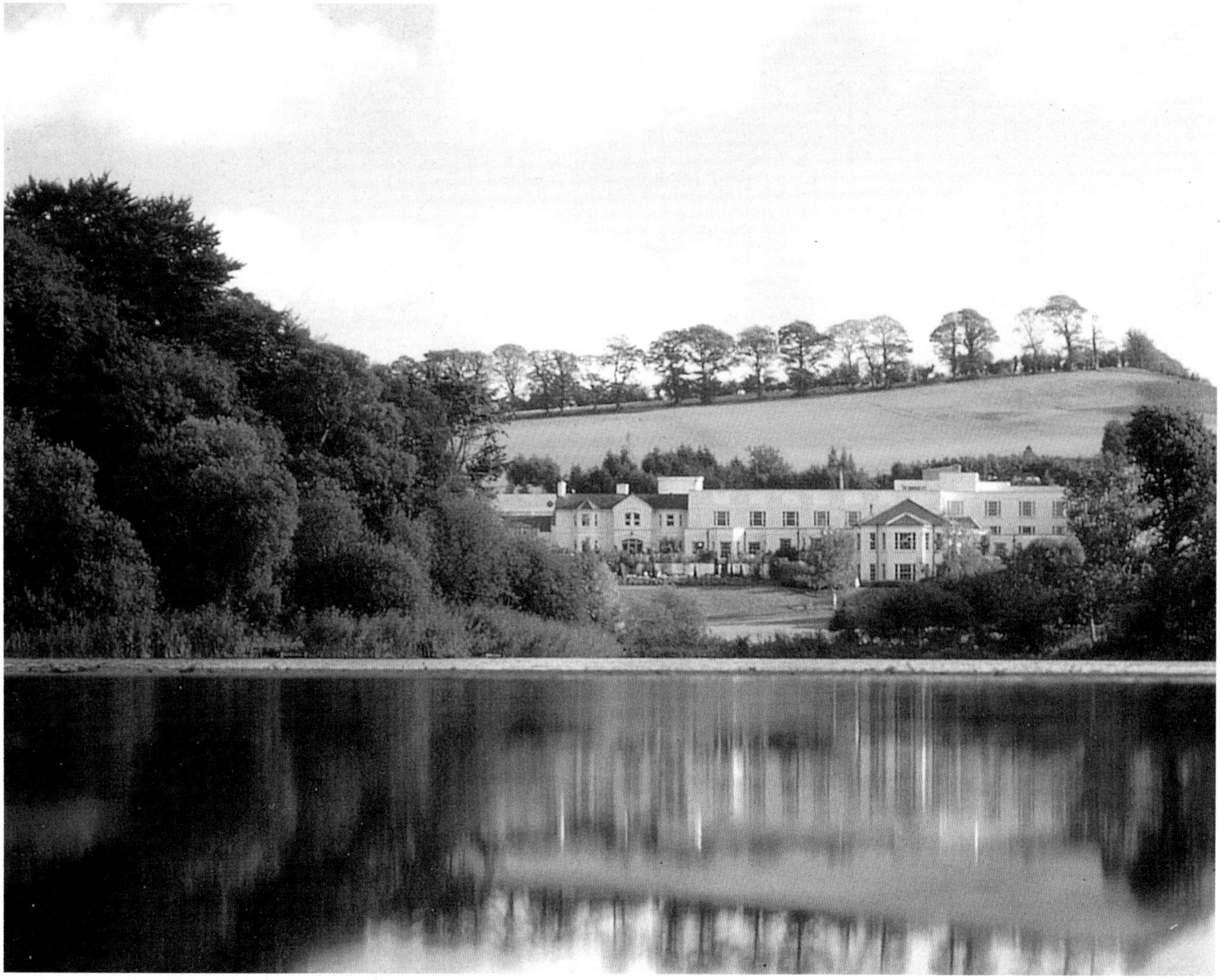

NUREMORE HOTEL AND COUNTRY CLUB

CARRICKMACROSS, CO MONAGHAN, IRELAND

TEL: 00 353 42 9661438 FAX: 00 353 42 9661853 E-MAIL: nuremore@eircom.net

Set in 200 acres of glorious countryside on the fringe of Carrickmacross, the Nuremore Hotel offers guests all-round enjoyment, a vast array of activities and facilities and all that is best in a first-class country hotel. The bedrooms are well-appointed and attractively designed to create a generous sense of personal space. Lunch and dinner menus, served in an elegant dining room, emphasise classic European cooking with French and Irish dishes featured alongside. For sport, fitness and relaxation, guests are spoiled for choice. A major feature is the championship-length, par 71, 18-hole golf course designed by Eddie Hackett to present an exciting challenge to beginners and experts alike. Maurice Cassidy has been appointed as resident professional and is on hand to give tuition. Riding nearby in Carrickmacross. The leisure club has a superb indoor pool, modern gymnasium, squash and tennis courts, sauna, steam room and whirlpool bath. Meetings and seminars held here are guaranteed a professional support service. Recent additions include a private dining room, 13 executive rooms and three purpose built syndicate rooms with air-conditioning and blackout facilities. Dublin is 75 minutes' drive away, while Drogheda and Dundalk are nearby for shopping. **Directions:** The hotel is on main N2 road between Dublin and Monaghan. Price Guide: Single €120–€160; double/twin €200–€250; suite €280.

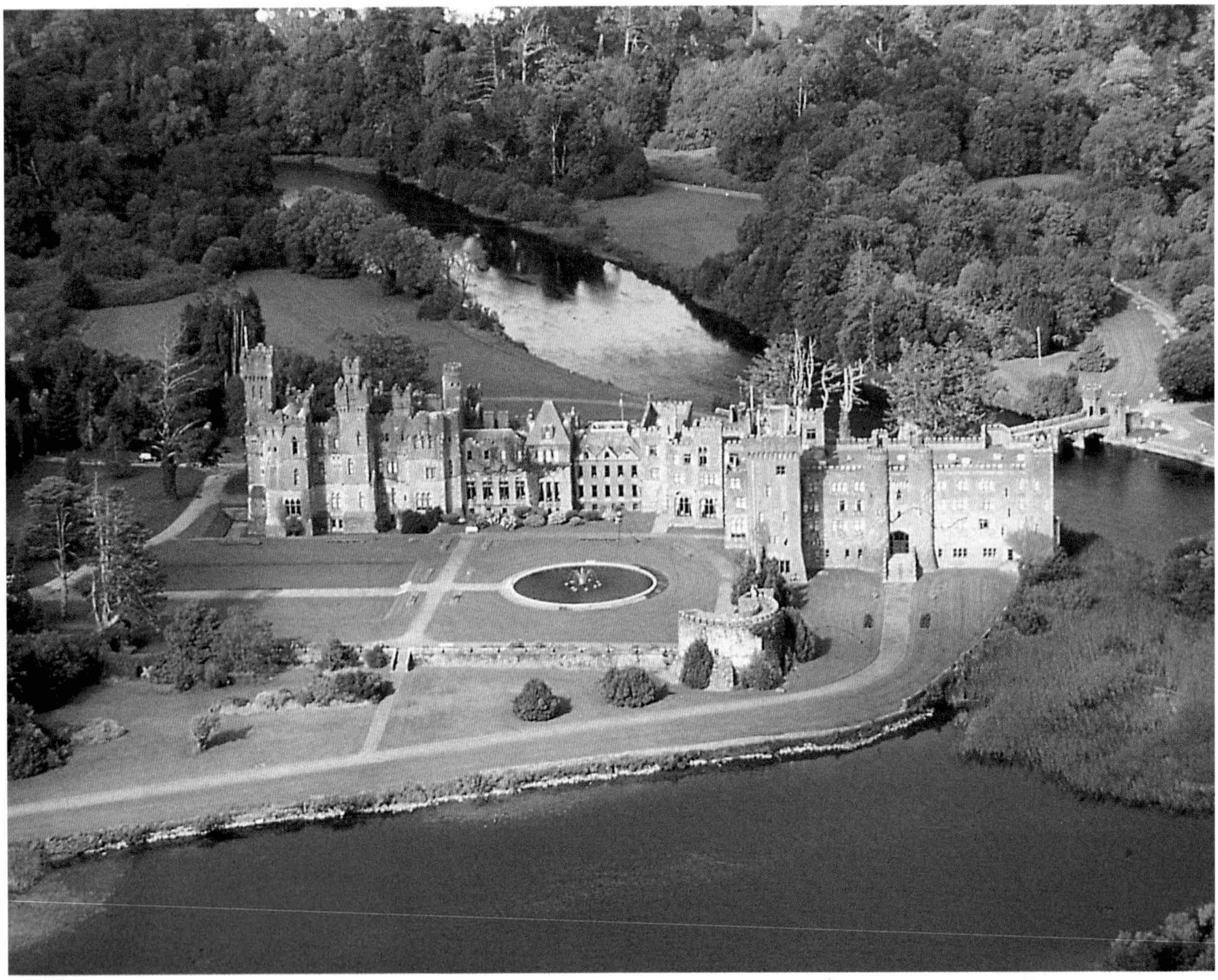

ASHFORD CASTLE

CONG, CO MAYO

TEL: 00 353 92 46003 FAX: 00 353 92 46260 E-MAIL: ashford@ashford.ie

Ashford Castle is set on the northern shores of Lough Corrib amidst acres of beautiful gardens and forests. Once the country estate of Lord Ardilaun and the Guinness family, it was transformed into a luxury hotel in 1939. The castle's Great Hall is lavishly decorated with rich panelling, fine period pieces, objets d'art and masterpiece paintings. Guest rooms are of the highest standards and many feature high ceilings, enormous bathrooms and delightful lake views. The main dining room offers superb continental and traditional menus, while the gourmet restaurant, The Connaught Room, specialises in excellent French cuisine. Before and after dinner in the Dungeon Bar guests are entertained by a harpist or pianist. Ashford Castle offers a full range of country sports, including fishing on Lough Corrib, clay pigeon shooting, riding, an exclusive 9-hole golf course and Ireland's only school of falconry. The hotel has a modern health centre comprising a whirlpool, sauna, steam room, fully equipped gymnasium and conservatory. Ashford is an ideal base for touring the historic West of Ireland, places like Kylemore Abbey, Westport House and the mediaeval town of Galway. **Directions:** 30 minutes from Galway on the shore of Lough Corrib, on the left when entering the village of Cong. Price Guide: Single/twin/double €194–€466; suite €517–€902.

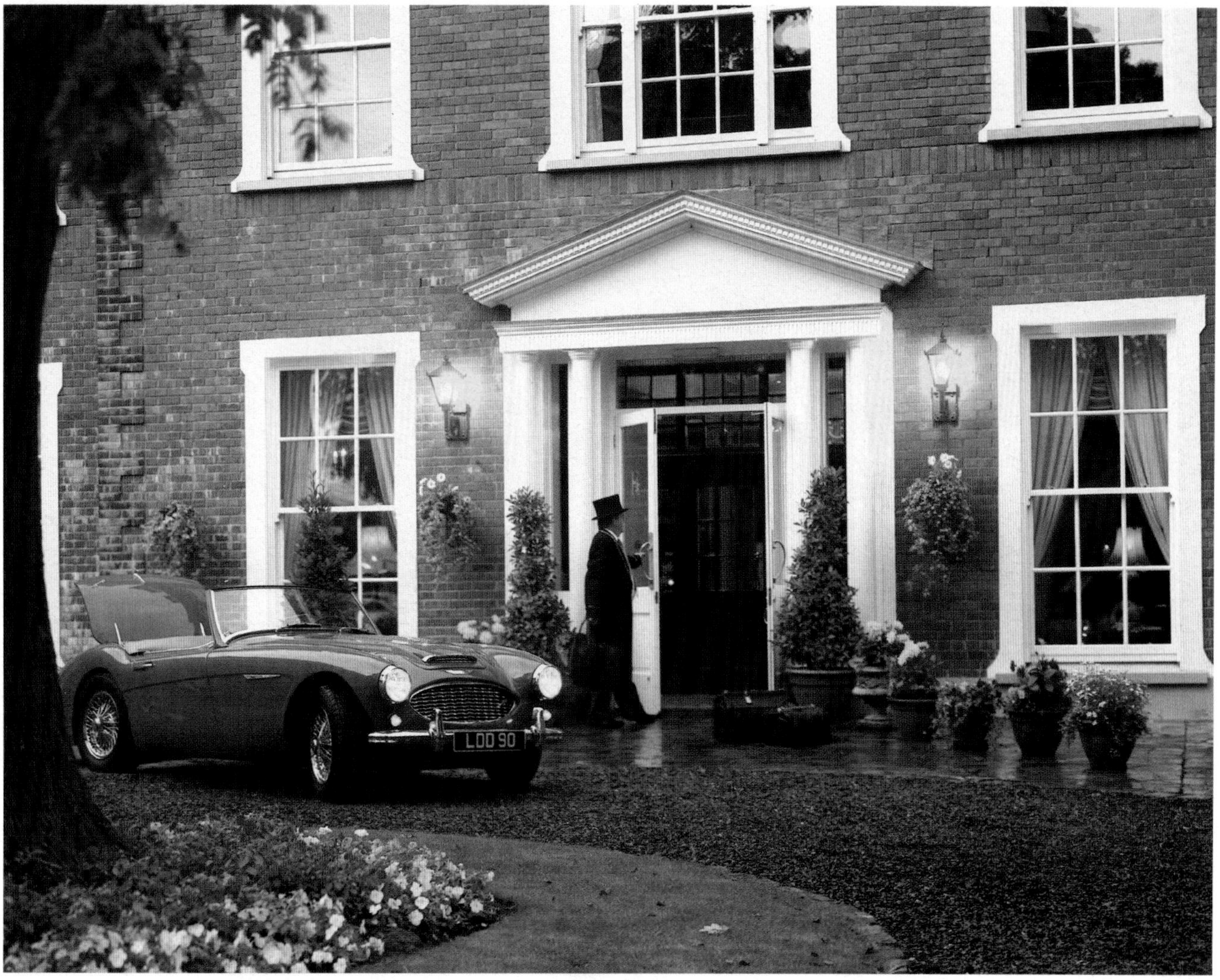

Hayfield Manor Hotel

PERROTT AVENUE, COLLEGE ROAD, CORK, IRELAND
TEL: 00 353 21 4845900 FAX: 00 353 21 4316839 E-MAIL: enquiries@hayfieldmanor.ie

From the tall, pillared entrance and richly curtained sash windows to the two acres of mature gardens, this hotel is the essence of style. Hayfield Manor Hotel, is a veritable country manor estate within a comfortable walk of the heart of Ireland's second largest city. Situated adjacent to University College Cork, the hotel provides seclusion and privacy and maintains the atmosphere of unhurried tranquillity that has been established since its Georgian days. The magnificently furnished lounge, with its soft sofas and chairs, ornate open fire and vases of fragrant fresh flowers, is particularly restful. Every modern comfort is to hand and none more so than in the 87 spacious and elegant guest rooms. Furnishings and décor are excellent, matched by marble bathrooms with fluffy robes and baskets brimming with toiletries. Directly linked to the bedrooms is a health club exclusive to hotel residents only where even the palm-surrounded pool has views across the garden. Before or after a swim you can work out in the gym, enjoy the steam room or relax in the outdoor Jacuzzi. Gourmet cuisine is served in the intimate Manor Room restaurant with its wonderful ambience and high standard of service. Hayfield Manor is the sister property of Joe and Margaret Scally's charming town centre hotel in Killarney,The Killarney Royal. Golf, riding and fishing are nearby as are Blarney Castle, Kinsale and Cobh Heritage Centre **Directions:** 1 mile from city centre Price Guide: Double/twin €320–€345; suite €380–€550.

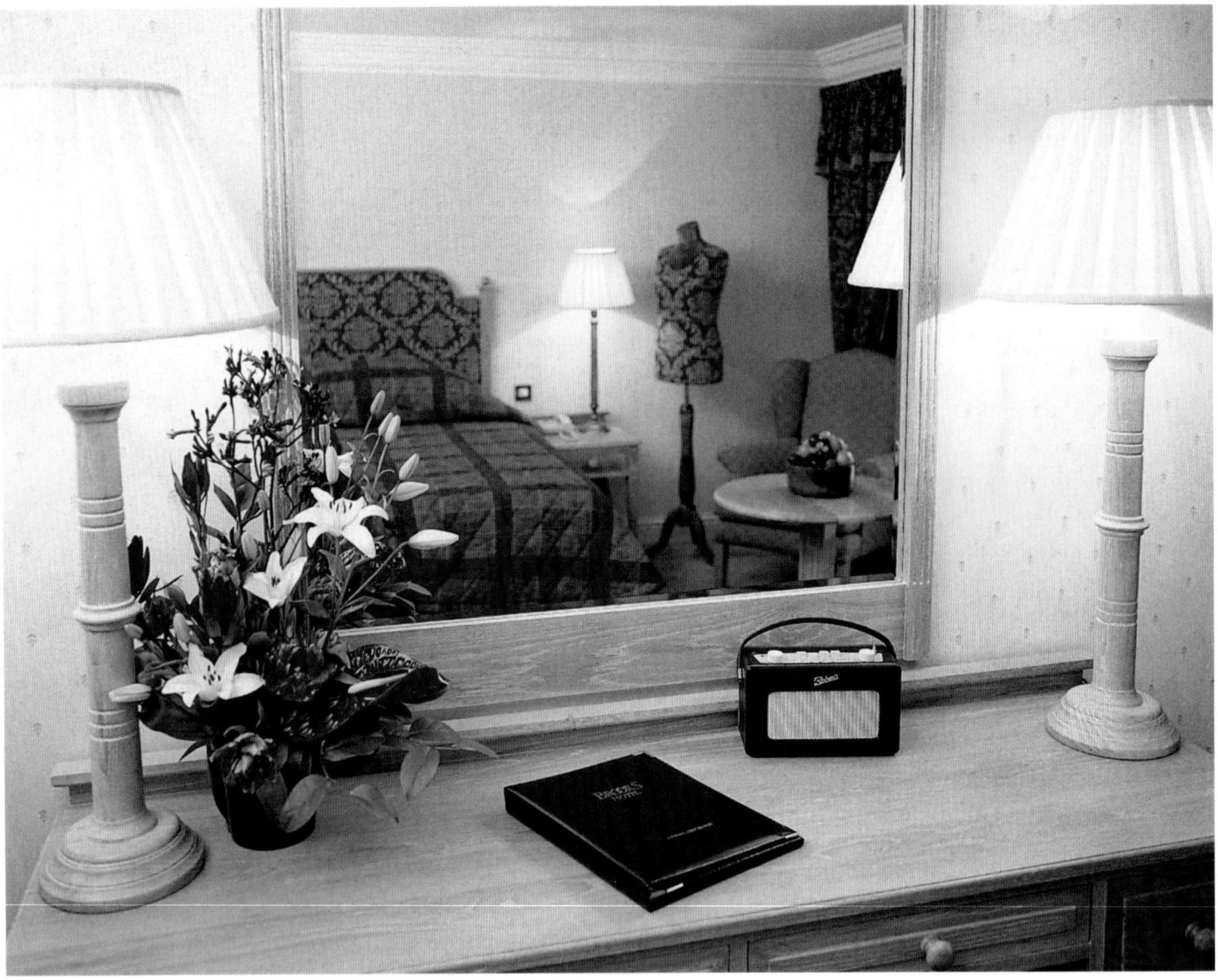

Brooks Hotel

59–62 DRURY STREET, DUBLIN 2
TEL: 00 353 1 670 4000 FAX: 00 353 1 670 4455 E-MAIL: reservations@brookshotel.ie

Brooks Hotel, sister hotel to the Connemara Coast Hotel in Galway, offers a delightful fusion of fine décor, excellent service and comfortable accommodation. Located on a quiet street in the heart of Dublin, the hotel is distinctly avant-garde with a spacious interior and beautifully appointed public rooms. The Drawing Room is dominated by an impressive fireplace creating a warm and intimate atmosphere, perfect for reclining with a good book or enjoying a postprandial drink. The 75 bedrooms are the essence of opulence featuring elegant furnishings and every modern comfort. Well-equipped with air conditioning, personal safes and computer points with ISDN telephone connections, these rooms are ideal for both the leisure and business traveller. Guests may converse in the attractive Piano Bar before dining in the stylish restaurant, where the menu comprises modern Irish dishes and specialities include fresh fish. Those seeking a more informal ambience may relax and converse in the welcoming bar. Business meetings and seminars can be held in the fully-equipped meeting room which can accommodate up to 70 delegates. Childcare facilities are available **Directions:** Brooks is located within easy reach of Grafton Street, Stephen Green and Trinity College. Price Guide: (room only): Single †172-†197; double †210-†248; executive rooms †280. Weekend rates also available, please

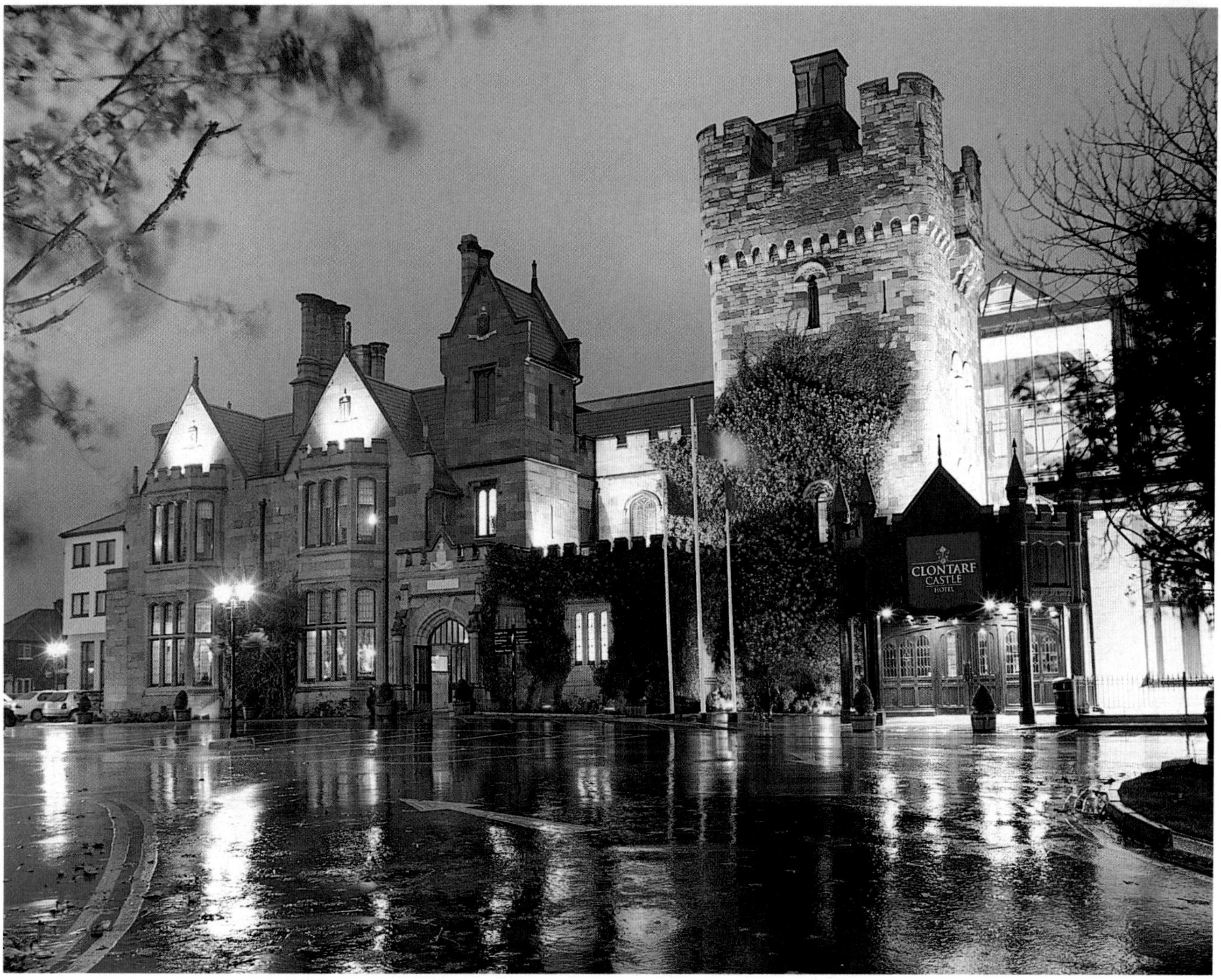

Clontarf Castle Hotel

CASTLE AVENUE, CLONTARF, DUBLIN 3, IRELAND
TEL: 00 353 1 833 2321 FAX: 00 353 1 833 0418 E-MAIL: info@clontarfcastle.ie

Clontarf Castle is a rare find for anyone wishing to visit Dublin. Just two miles from the city centre and only five miles from the airport, it is the combination of a luxuriously tranquil country retreat, and skilful piece of historical restoration. The castle was built in 1172, and was later given to a loyal servant of Cromwell's army, whose family owned it for another 300 years. Today, the castle is a fine and stately hotel, with state-of-the-art conference and leisure facilities; yet no stone has been left unturned to retain the atmosphere of its mediaeval and chivalric origins. The magnificent entrance hall is adorned with tapestries and fires roar in the grates, whilst Templars Bistro, the Knights bar and The Drawbridge pub offer a variety of drinking and dining locations that are evocative of a bygone era. There are 111 guest suites offering a refreshing amount of space and comfort, enhanced by a rich décor of castellated pelmets and drapes and carved four-poster beds. Clontarf lies within a short drive of some of the world's most famous racetracks, Fairyhouse, Leopardstown and the Curragh, and there is a choice of 18-hole championship courses within an equally short drive. Furthermore, All-Ireland club rugby is played within walking distance, and Dublin City centre is only a stone's throw away. Directions: 2 miles from city centre. Dublin airport 5 miles. Price Guide: Single €171 – €239 ; double/twin €229 – €286 ; suite €330 – €489 .

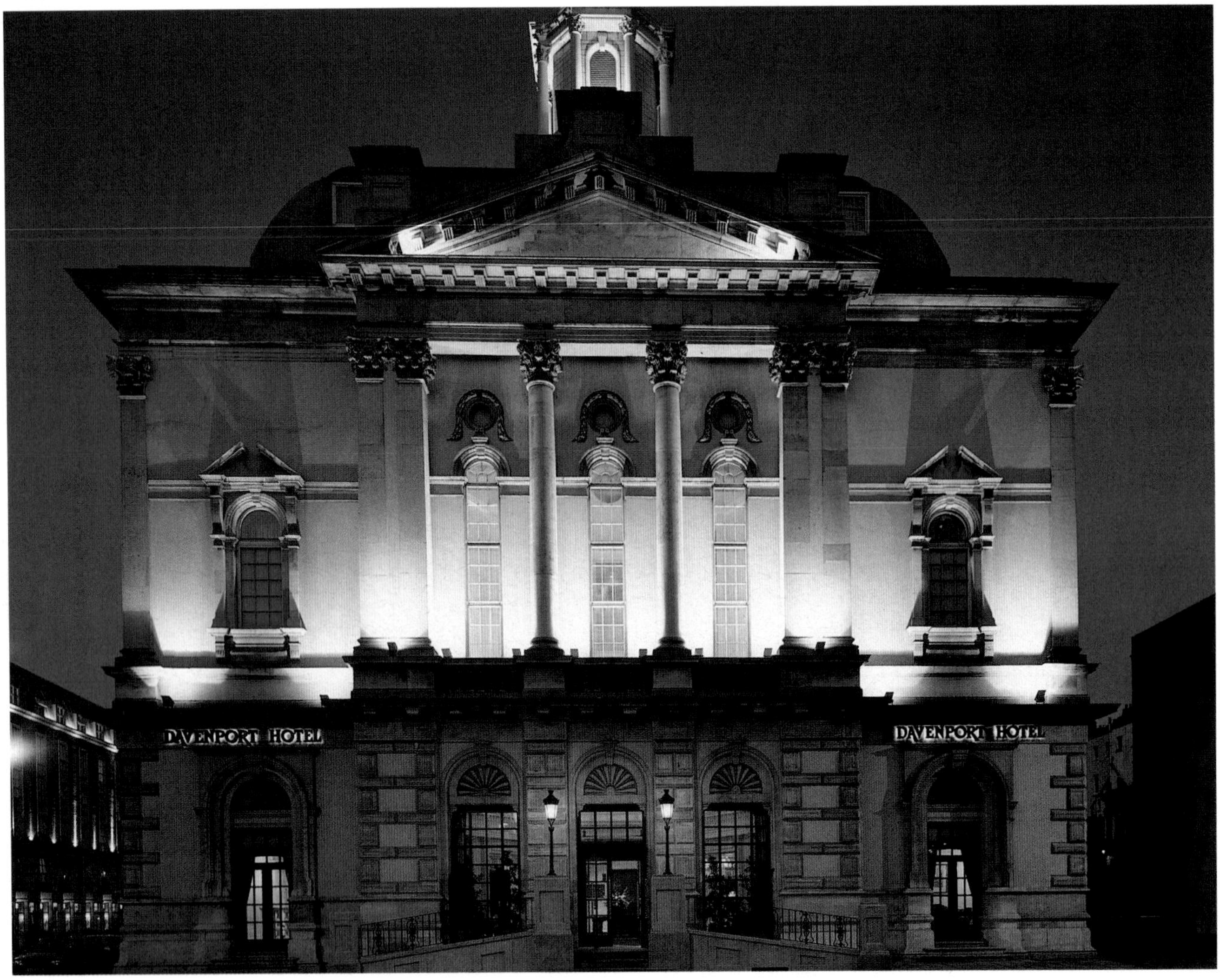

THE DAVENPORT HOTEL

MERRION SQUARE, DUBLIN 2, IRELAND
TEL: 00 353 1 607 3500 FAX: 00 353 1 661 5663 E-MAIL: davenportres@ocallaghanhotels.ie

Built in 1863 as a Gospel Hall, The Davenport still boasts the dramatic façade that graced the original building, and is now an elegant boutique-style hotel. Conveniently located in the heart of Georgian Dublin, it is surrounded by tall, graceful architecture and wide, surburban streets. Designed with both the tourist and business traveller in mind, The Davenport is modern and stylish – the bedrooms are cool and spacious with every modern amenity, whilst the junior suites contain an additional executive desk with direct line fax machine and laser printer. Large conferences or small meetings can both be catered for here, with The Gandon Suite accommodating up to 400, whilst the Boardroom with its natural daylight and air conditioning is ideally suited to smaller high level discussions. Lanyons Restaurant offers the finest cuisine amidst a stunning Georgian interior, whilst the Presidents Bar is a warm and comfortable retreat in which to relax and contemplate the various presidents and associations of bygone days. Merrion Square really is central to all that Dublin has to offer – The National Gallery, The Natural History Museum, Irish Parliament and Trinity College, or the fine shopping district of Grafton Street and St Stephen's Green. **Directions:** Located at Merrion Square in the heart of Dublin. Price Guide: Double/twin €290; suite €360.

MERRION HALL

54-56 MERRION ROAD, BALLSBRIDGE, DUBLIN 4

TEL: 00 353 1 668 1426 FAX: 00 353 1 668 4280 E-MAIL: merrionhall@iol.ie

This exclusive Edwardian property is located close to the RDS Convention centre just minutes from downtown Dublin. Merrion Hall shares its neighbourhood with the world's embassies in the fashionable Ballsbridge area of Dublin City. Executive bedrooms, some with four-poster suites, offer air conditioning, whirlpool spas and all the modern comforts expected by the discerning traveller. The hotel's library stocks a fine selection of Irish and international literature, whilst afternoon teas and fine wines are served in the main drawing room. A feature of this Edwardian town house is a very special breakfast, which can be enjoyed overlooking mature secluded gardens. There are also numerous restaurants within a short stroll of the hotel, leaving guests utterly spoilt for choice. There is a direct luxury coach link to and from Dublin airport. Residents have complimentary parking on the grounds. The hotel can arrange golfing packages and scenic tours. **Directions:** From the city centre take Merrion Road; the hotel is on the left hand side overlooking the RDS Convention Centre, near Lansdowne Road, and is linked to major tourist sites and the business district by the DART electric train. Price Guide: Single €99–€129; double/twin €124–€189; suite €159–€239.

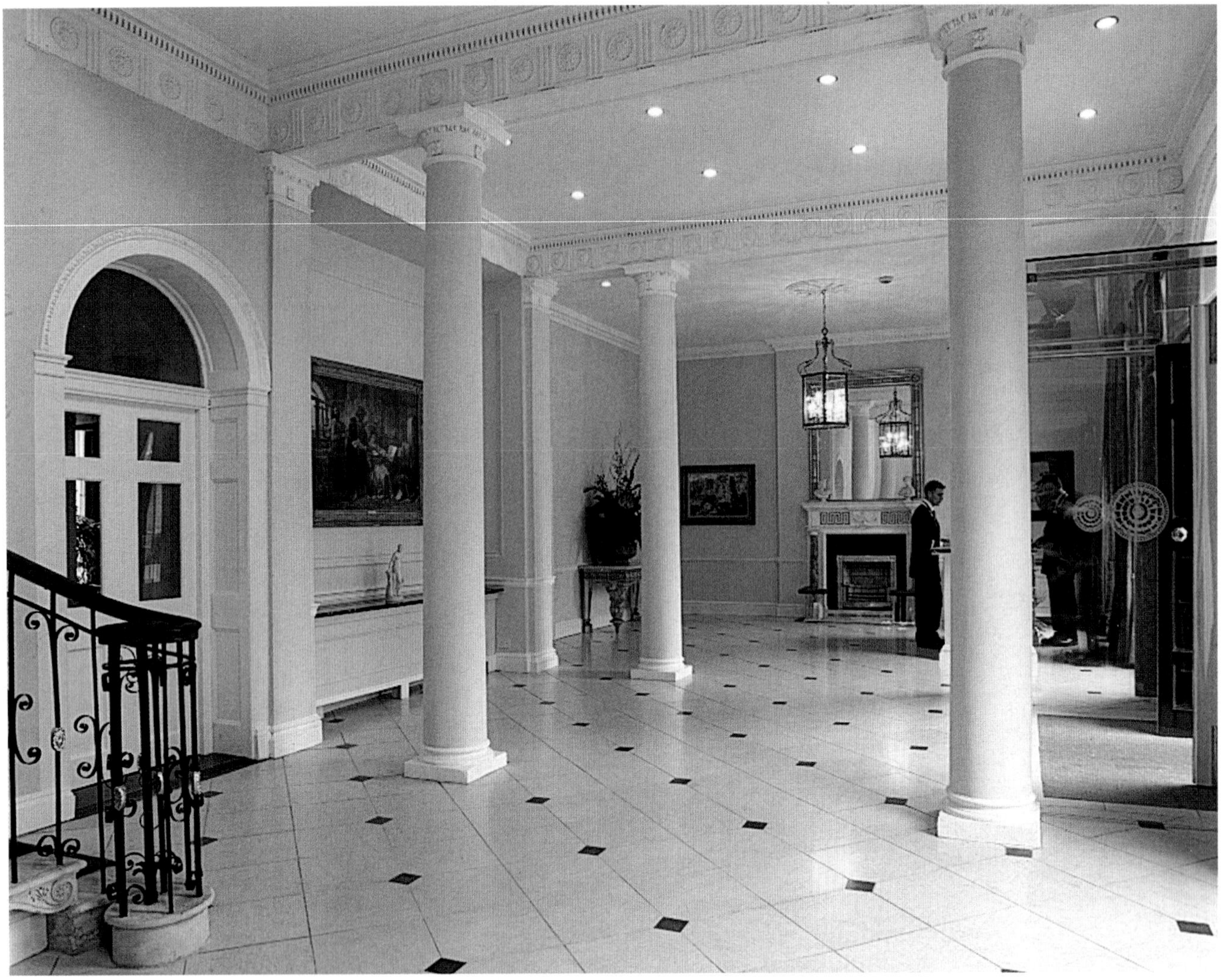

The Merrion Hotel

UPPER MERRION STREET, DUBLIN 2, IRELAND
TEL: 00 353 1 603 0600 FAX: 00 353 1 603 0700 E-MAIL: info@merrionhotel.com

The Merrion is Dublin's most luxurious hotel and a historic landmark. It has been imaginatively and brilliantly conceived, four superb Grade I Georgian terrace houses meticulously restored. There is also an elegant Garden Wing. The interior decorations are impressive, authentically reflecting the Georgian era by the choice of wall colours, specially commissioned fabrics and well researched antiques. By contrast, a private collection of 20th-century art is displayed throughout the hotel, and the neo-classic stairwell has a series of contemporary murals. Every guest room is luxurious, some situated in the Garden Wing, with views over the two gardens – delightful with box hedges, statuary and fountains, approached from the drawing rooms in summer. The Merrion offers a choice of two handsome bars, the larger a fascinating 18th century cellar, the other more intimate and two restaurants, the legendary Restaurant Patrick Guilbaud in a dramatic setting and 'Morningtons', offering traditional dishes with an Irish influence. The Merrion has a state-of-the-art meeting and private dining facility, perfect for hosting banquets. Guests relax in The Tethra Spa, which has an 18m pool, gymnasium and salons for pampering. Directions: City Centre. The hotel has valet parking. Price Guide: Single €279.34–€355.53; double/twin €304.74–€393.62; suite €571.34–€1015.80.

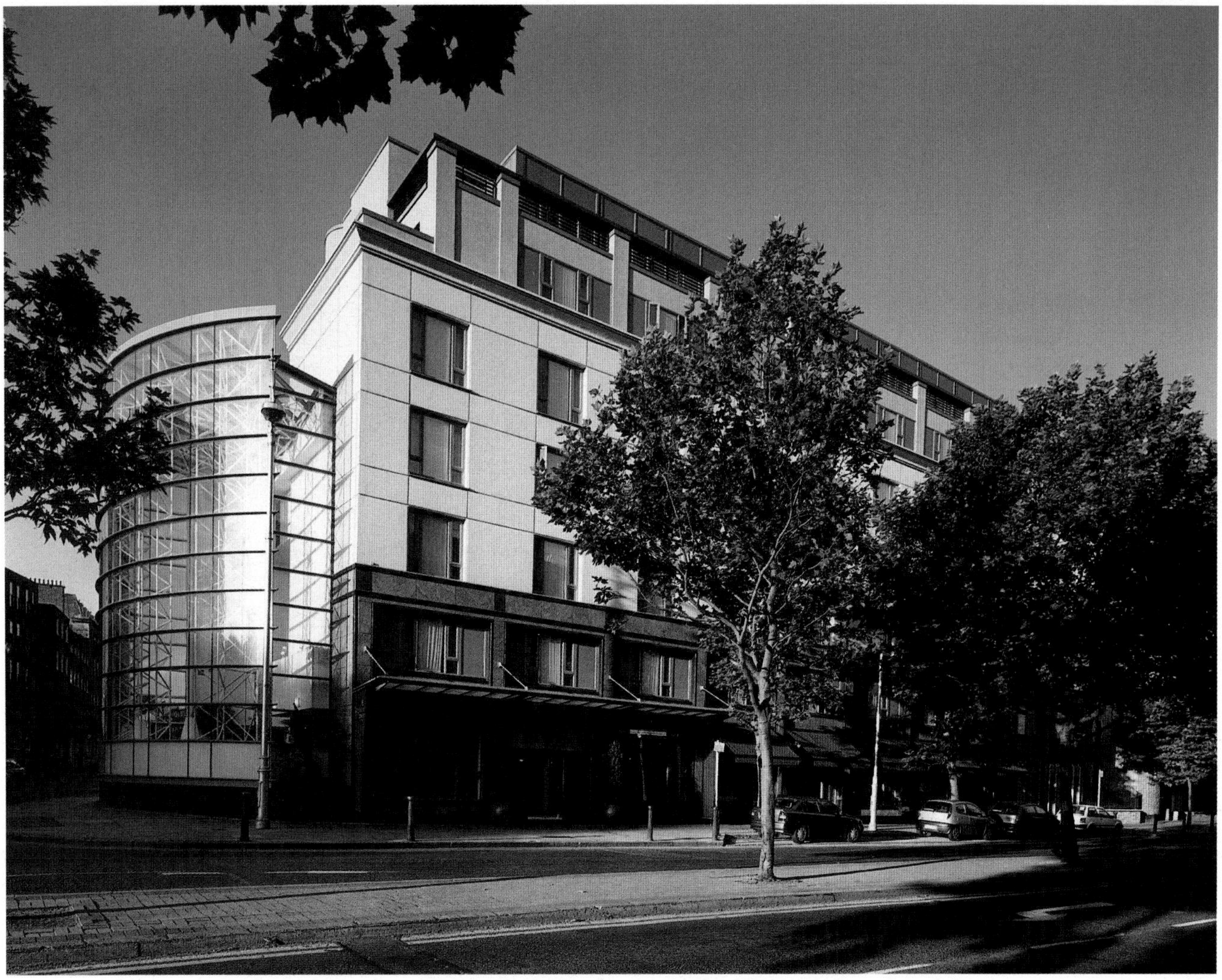

STEPHEN'S GREEN HOTEL

ST STEPHEN'S GREEN, DUBLIN 2, IRELAND

TEL: 00 353 1 607 3600 FAX: 00 353 1 661 5663 E-MAIL: stephensgreenres@ocallaghanhotels.ie

Once a collection of Georgian buildings, the Stephen's Green Hotel is a stunning mix of classical architecture and clean, modern style. Stuccoed ceilings and elegant dado rails combine with bold stripes and strong colours to create an atmosphere that is reflective of the cosmopolitan city that Dublin has become, yet still offers a tranquil and dignified escape from life outside. The "Magic Glasses" bar and "Pie Dish" restaurant both take their names from the lesser-known writings of George Fitzmaurice, the Irish playwright, and again reflect the ethos of the hotel incorporating classical style within a contemporary setting. Bistro style cuisine of the 21st century is also cleverly combined with traditional Irish fayre in the "Pie Dish", which is a warm and inviting place to dine after a day in the city. Dublin has rapidly become one of the world's most popular cities, and its diversity is key to its attraction. From bustling street markets to splendid Georgian buildings, cultural museums to horseracing tracks there really is something for everyone, and all within easy access of the hotel. **Directions:** The hotel lies alongside St Stephen's Green, between St Stephen's Green Shopping Centre and the National Concert Hall. Price Guide: Double/twin €310; suite €420–€890.

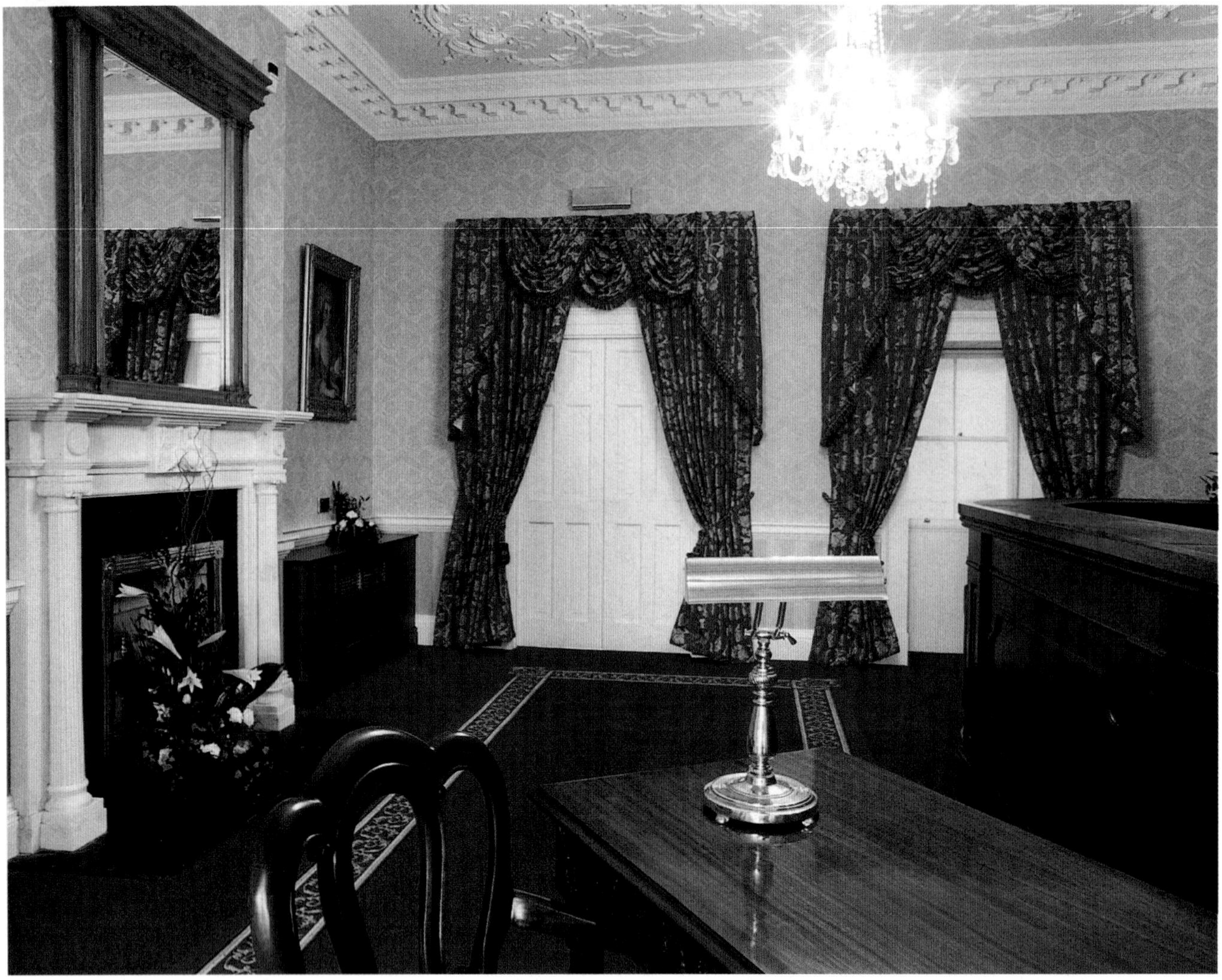

JOHNSTOWN HOUSE HOTEL & SPA

ENFIELD, CO MEATH, IRELAND
TEL: 00 353 405 40000 FAX: 00 353 405 40001 E-MAIL: info@johnstownhouse.com

Set in the heart of Meath and built around a grand 17th-century Georgian Mansion, this purpose built spa development is the first of its kind in Ireland. Restored walled gardens within 80 acres of private wooded parkland, with an elegant tree lined avenue and a relaxing riverside walk create an intimate and peaceful oasis in which to unwind. A warm welcome given by the friendly staff combined with comfortable surroundings provides a homely atmosphere. Attention to detail, superb linen and colour co-ordinated décor are evident in the luxurious bedrooms, which have en suite facilities and all modern conveniences. After unwinding in the cosy bar and spacious lounge with its open fireplace, guests can enjoy fine dining or take advantage of the more informal restaurant. A holistic approach is taken in the ESPA Spa with aromatherapy, massage, hydrotherapy, preventative healthcare and lifestyle management as well as beauty therapy and a hair salon for those who wish to be pampered. There is also an indoor pool and outdoor hydro therapy pool, gymnasium, dance studio and tennis courts for the more energetic. Other local outdoor activities include horse riding, golf, fishing and clay pigeon shooting. Johnstown House is ideal for all business events and also caters for weddings and other special occasions. Directions: In Enfield on N4, just after the end of the M4, approx. 30 minutes from Dublin. Price Guide: Single €230 ; double/twin €250 ; suite €280 .

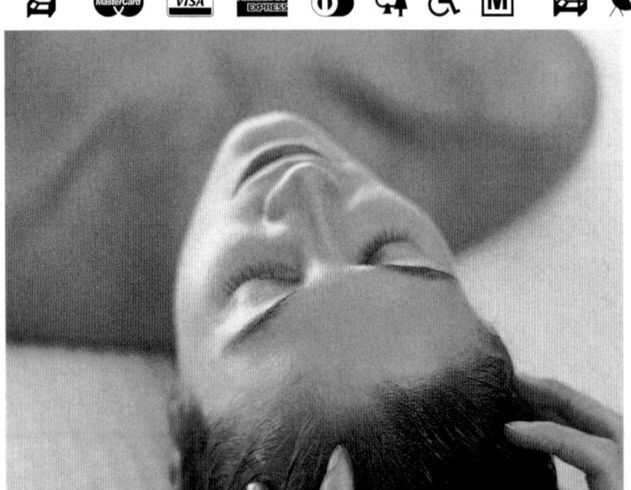

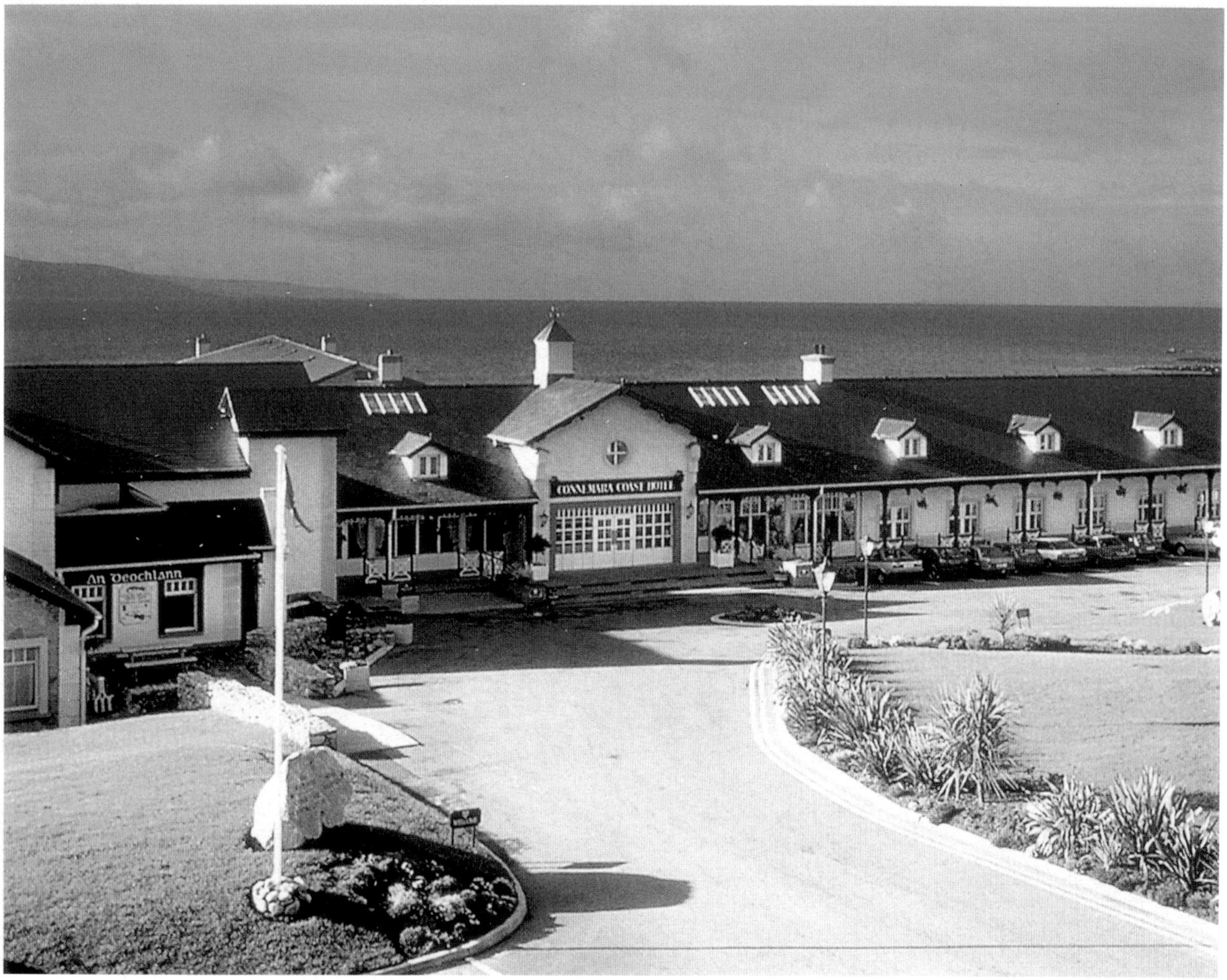

CONNEMARA COAST HOTEL

FURBO, GALWAY

TEL: 00 353 91 592108 FAX: 00 353 91 592065 E-MAIL: sinnott@iol.ie

This modern resort hotel, sister hotel of Brooks in Dublin, is located just 6 miles from Galway city centre on the shores of Galway Bay. With magnificent views, The Connemara Coast Hotel combines a friendly and welcoming atmosphere with elegant décor and a picturesque landscape. The stylish interior is bedecked with fresh floral arrangements whilst the reception rooms are spacious with plush furnishings, comfortable armchairs and rich fabrics. The 112 bedrooms, many with views across the Bay, are well-appointed with attractive colour schemes and a range of thoughtful extras including tea/coffee making facilities. Guests indulge in a preprandial drink in the typically Irish Bar, which exudes character and charm, before dining in the fine restaurant. The imaginative menu uses the best of regional produce and is complemented by an excellent wine list. There are well-equipped conference rooms and the hotel provides additional services including fax, typing and photocopying services. The Leisure Centre features an indoor pool, fitness facilities including a gymnasium and outdoor hot tub. This is an ideal base for exploring Galway City and Connemara. Attractions include the Spanish Arch, Pearse's Cottage, Kylemore Abbey and Coole Park. Fishing enthusiasts must visit Lough Corrib with its plentiful supply of salmon, trout and pike **Directions:** The hotel is 10 minutes out of Galway on R336. Price Guide: Single €85–€165; double/twin €190–€250.

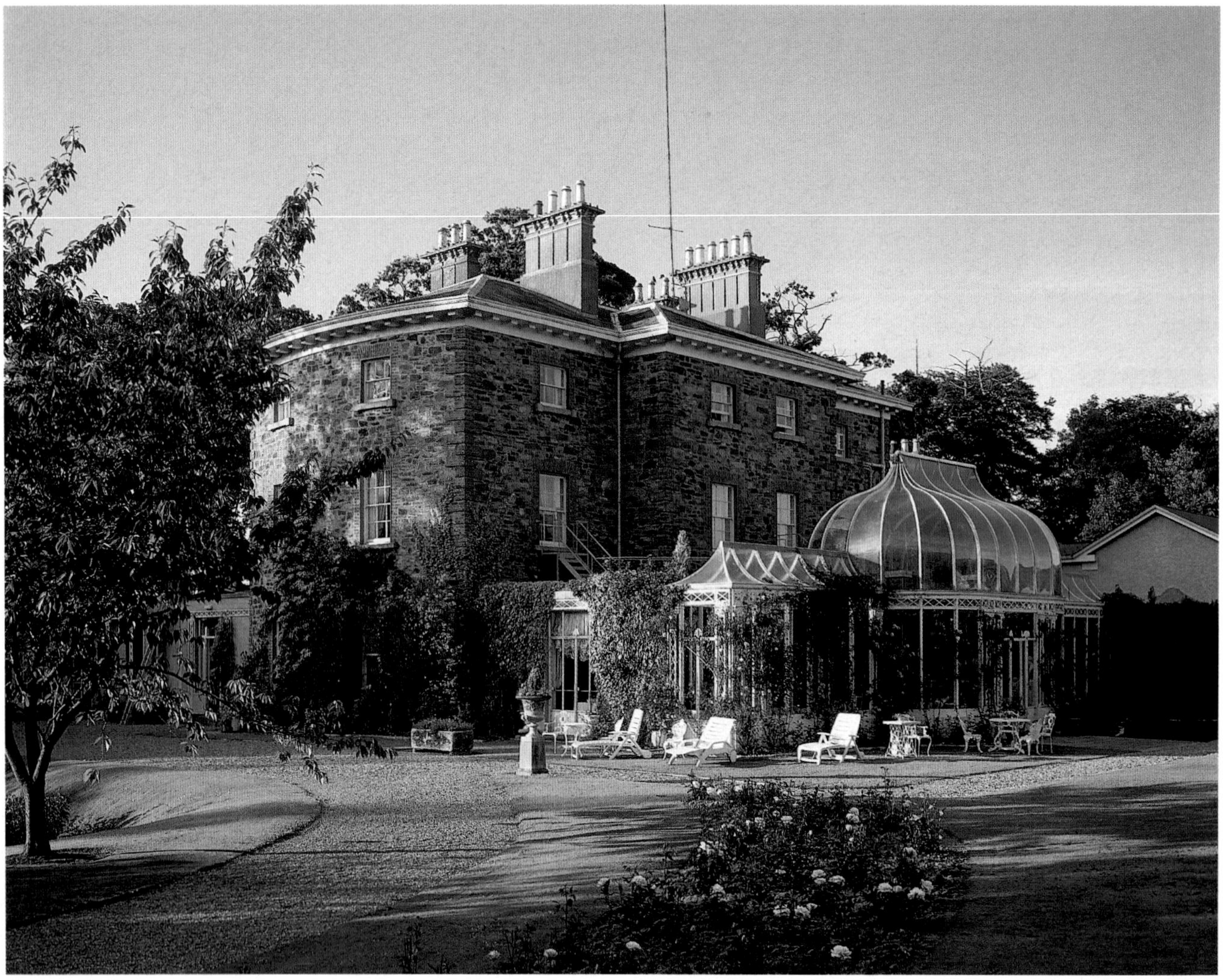

MARLFIELD HOUSE

GOREY, CO WEXFORD

TEL: 00 353 55 21124 FAX: 00 353 55 21572 E-MAIL: info@marlfieldhouse.ie

Staying at Johansens award-winning Marlfield House is a memorable experience. Set in 34 acres of woodland and gardens, this former residence of the Earl of Courtown preserves the Regency lifestyle in all its graciousness. Built in 1820 and situated just 55 miles south of Dublin, it is recognised as one of the finest country houses in Ireland and is supervised by its welcoming hosts and proprietors, Raymond and Mary Bowe and their daughter Margaret. The State Rooms have been built in a very grand style and have period fireplaces where open fires burn even in the cooler weather. All of the furniture is antique and the roomy beds are draped with sumptuous fabrics. The bathrooms are made of highly polished marble and some have large freestanding bathtubs. There is an imposing entrance hall, luxurious drawing room and an impressive curved Richard Turner conservatory. The kitchen's gastronomic delights have earned it numerous awards. Located two miles from fine beaches and Courtown golf club, the house is central to many touring high points: Glendalough, Waterford Crystal and Powerscourt Gardens and the medieval city of Kilkenny. Closed mid-December to the end of January. **Directions:** On the Gorey–Courtown road, just over a mile east of Gorey. Price Guide: Single from €120; double/twin €222–€240; state rooms from €400–€695.

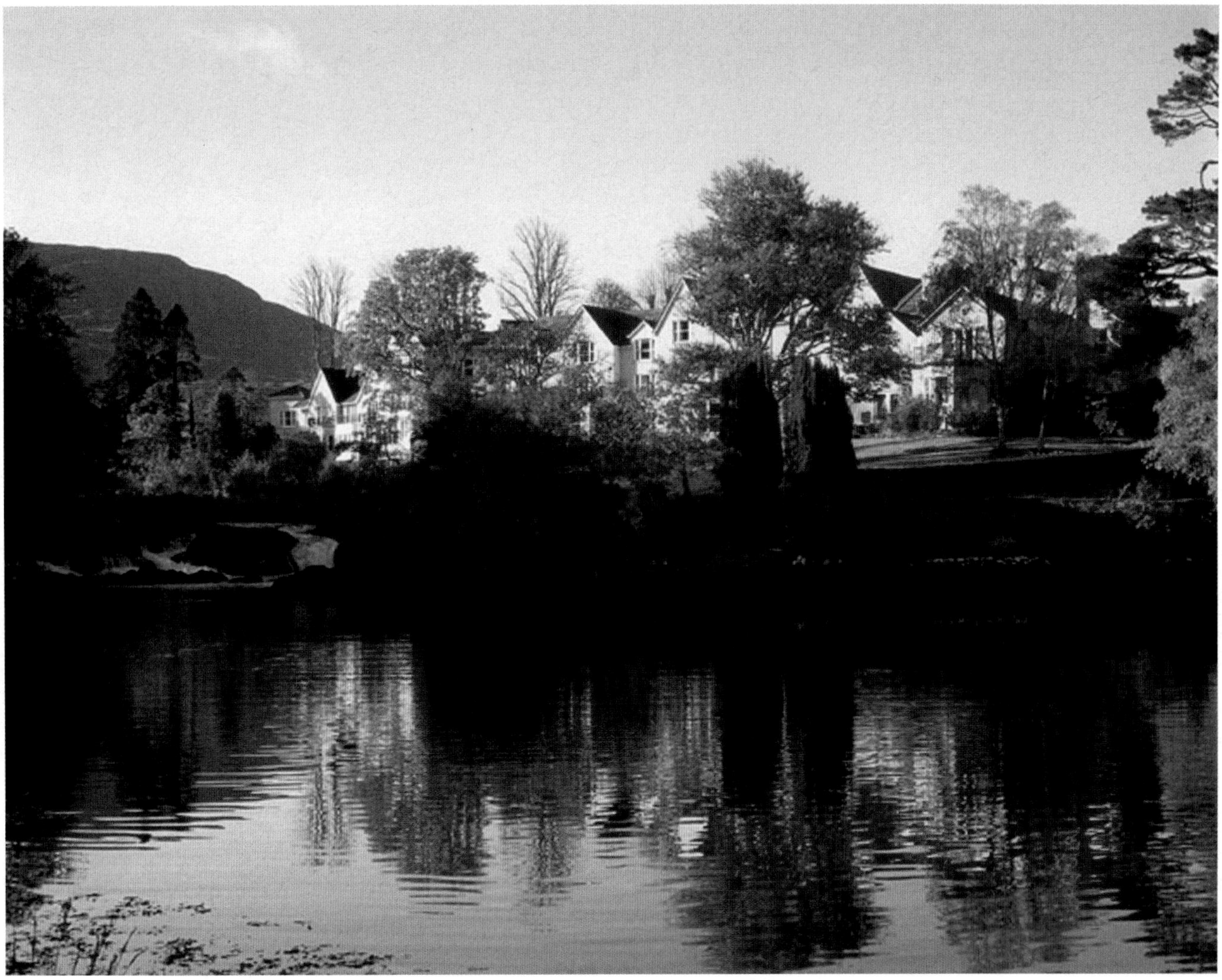

SHEEN FALLS LODGE

KENMARE, CO. KERRY, IRELAND
TEL: 00 353 64 41600 FAX: 00 353 64 41386 E-MAIL: info@sheenfallslodge.ie

You could be forgiven for expecting a magic carpet instead of a plane to land you at Sheen Falls Lodge – one of the Emerald Isle's most romantic and luxurious hotels. Standing amidst a vast estate of green countryside and well-kept gardens, with the sparkling Sheen River tumbling down the falls. The Lodge is a magnificent mansion, and the interior, with its country house ambience, is evocative of the past. The Library, with traditional leather furniture, holds many fine books and the spacious lounges have warm colour schemes, log fires and generous sofas. Flowers, lovely antiques and memorabilia enhance the atmosphere. The guest rooms are exquisite, luxuriously appointed and decorated in soft restful shades. They have opulent bathrooms. Dining here starts with the privilege of touring the extensive wine cellar with the sommelier to select a great vintage to accompany a magnificent meal – local salmon, lobster or duck perhaps. Riding, tennis, croquet, fishing, shooting and billiards are 'house' sports. The Lodge also has a superb Health Spa and fitness centre, with indoor heated swimming pool. Nearby are several excellent golf courses, marvellous walking, bikes to hire and deep sea fishing can be arranged. **Directions:** The hotel is signed from the junction of N70 and N71 at Kenmare. Helipad. Price Guide: Deluxe Room €240–€380; suite €413–€585.

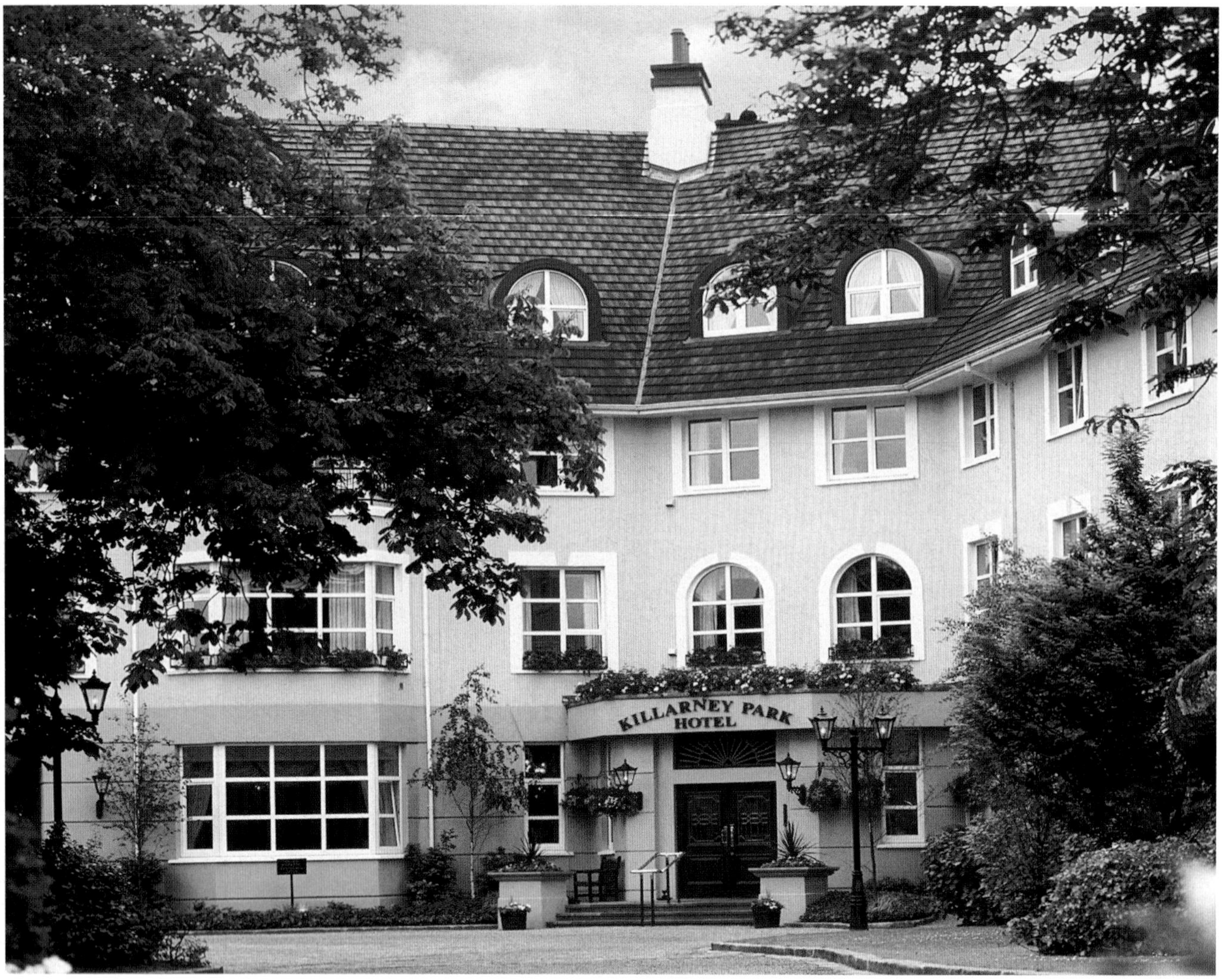

KILLARNEY PARK HOTEL

KENMARE PLACE, KILLARNEY, CO KERRY, IRELAND

TEL: 00 353 64 35555 FAX: 00 353 64 35266 E-MAIL: info@killarneyparkhotel.ie

Warm, soothing décor, plush sofas by log fires, subdued lighting, flower displays and discreet, efficient service make visitors believe they have wandered into a Victorian country home. This particular home is located near the town centre, a stone's throw from almost everything Killarney has to offer yet with the hospitality associated with bygone times. Killarney Park is a premier hotel of character, luxury and style where a sense of opulence abounds. Fine antique furniture, thoughtful colour schemes and lavish soft furnishings create an atmosphere of comfort in the individually designed guestrooms and the suites with splendid sitting areas and open fires. A private entrance hall enhances the sense of exclusivity and privacy. Large chandeliers hang from the ornate ceiling in the Park Restaurant, which echoes a time of courteous dining. The cuisine is award-winning, the service excellent. A pianist plays softly in the background. Drinks can be savoured around a magnificent marble fireplace in the richly curtained Drawing Room, and quiet moments can be enjoyed in the well-stocked library. There is also a panelled billiards room and a Health Spa featuring a Grecian-style pool and a range of leisure, fitness and beauty facilities. Golf, fishing, riding and shooting can be arranged nearby. **Directions:** In the centre of Killarney. Price Guide: Single €220–€335; double/twin €220–€335; suites €320–€650.

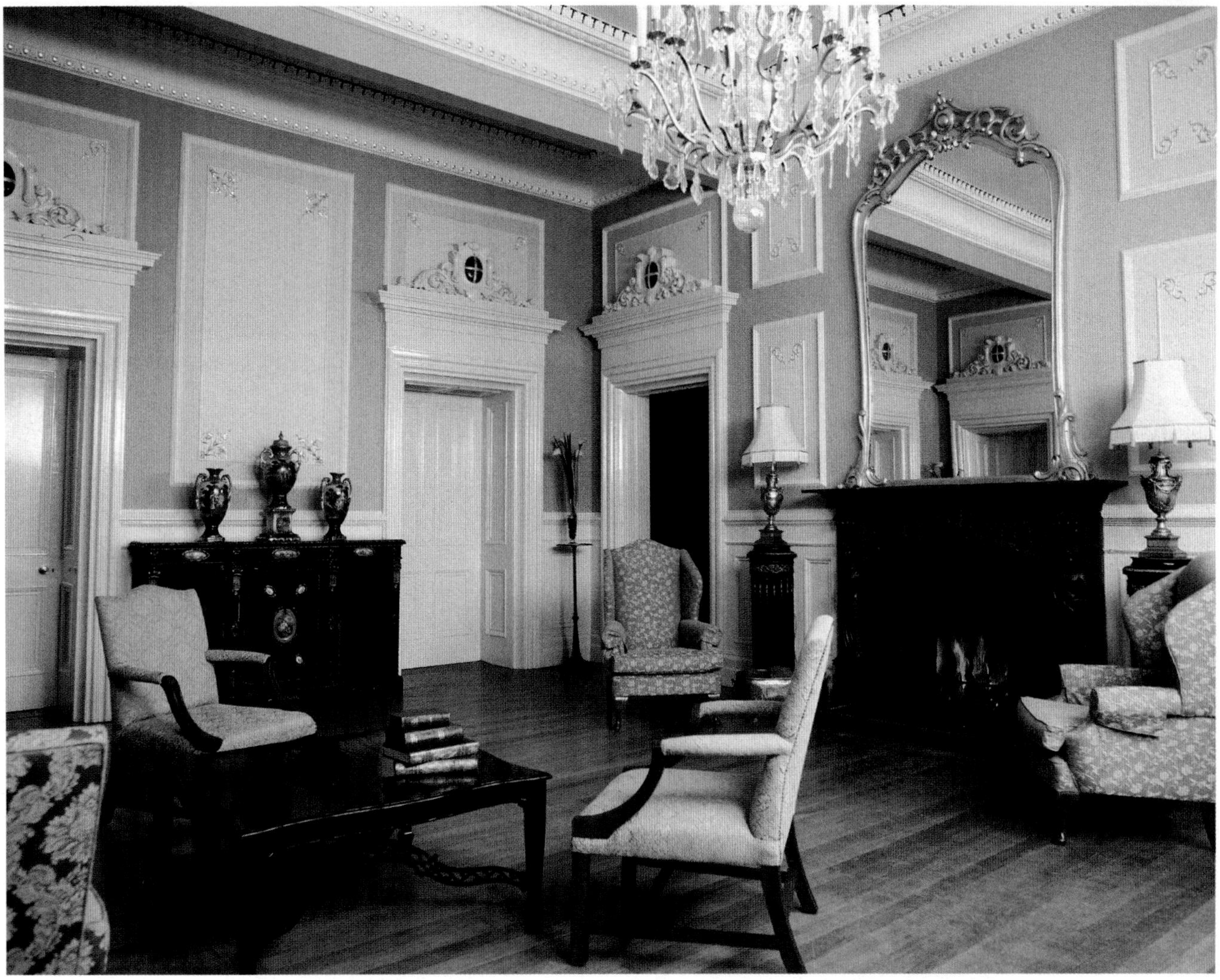

KILLASHEE HOUSE HOTEL

KILLASHEE, NAAS, CO KILDARE, IRELAND

TEL: 00 353 45 879277 FAX: 00 353 45 879266 E-MAIL: reservations@killasheehouse.com

Originally a Victorian hunting lodge in 1861, Killashee House still bears the coats of arms of its founders, the Moore family. It has since changed hands many times, been the victim of fire, and housed a preparatory school for boys, before being sold to its current owners in 1998. Today it is a glorious hotel situated within 27 acres of gardens and woodland, just 30 minutes from Dublin. There are 84 luxurious and comfortable guest rooms including 12 suites and 6 Presidential rooms, many with four-poster beds and stunning views of the gardens and, sometimes, the Wicklow Mountains. Every bedroom has multi-line telephone, data port and voicemail. The conference facilities are at the forefront of modern technology with sophisticated audio-visual equipment as well as video conferencing and fibre optic data ports. A state-of-the-art Leisure Centre and Spa opens in late 2001, the National Stud and the racecourses of Curragh, Punchestown and Naas are all within easy reach, whilst there is an exceptional selection of championship golf courses nearby, including the K Club and the Curragh. There is car racing at Mondello Park, and the Japanese and St Fiachra's Gardens provide a tranquil setting for horticultural enthusiasts. **Directions:** 30 minutes from Dublin on N7/M7 to Naas, then 1 mile along R448 Kilcullen Road. Price Guide: (p.p. sharing) Single €140–€150; double/twin €95–€105; suite €105–€419.

DROMOLAND CASTLE

NEWMARKET-ON-FERGUS, SHANNON AREA, CO CLARE
TEL: 00 353 61 368144 FAX: 00 353 61 363355 E-MAIL: sales@dromoland.ie

Dromoland Castle, just 8 miles from Shannon Airport, is one of the most famous baronial castles in Ireland, dating from the 16th century. Dromoland was the ancestral seat of the O'Briens, direct descendants of Irish King Brian Boru. Priceless reminders of its past are everywhere: in the splendid wood and stone carvings, magnificent panelling, oil paintings and romantic gardens. The 100 en suite guest rooms and suites are all beautifully furnished. Stately halls and an elegant dining room are all part of the Dromoland experience. The new Dromoland International Centre is one of Europe's most comprehensive conference venues, hosting groups of up to 450. Classical cuisine is prepared by award-winning chef David McCann. Fishing, 18 hole golf, clay pigeon shooting and Full Health and Beauty Centre are all available on the estate, whilst activities nearby include horse riding and golf on some of Ireland's other foremost courses. The castle is an ideal base from which to explore this breathtakingly beautiful area. Dromoland Castle is a member of Preferred Hotels & Resorts World Wide. **Directions:** Take the N18 to Newmarket-on-Fergus, go two miles beyond the village and the hotel entrance is on the right-hand side. Price Guide: Double/twin €194–€469; suite €412–€1130.

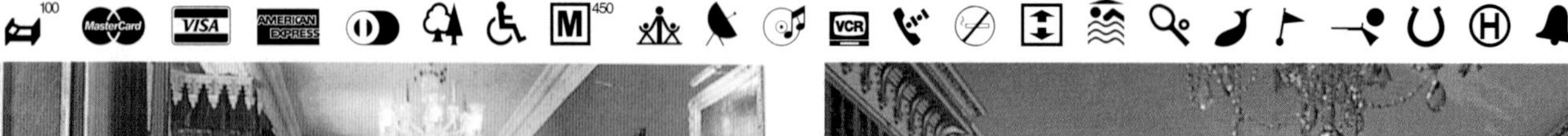

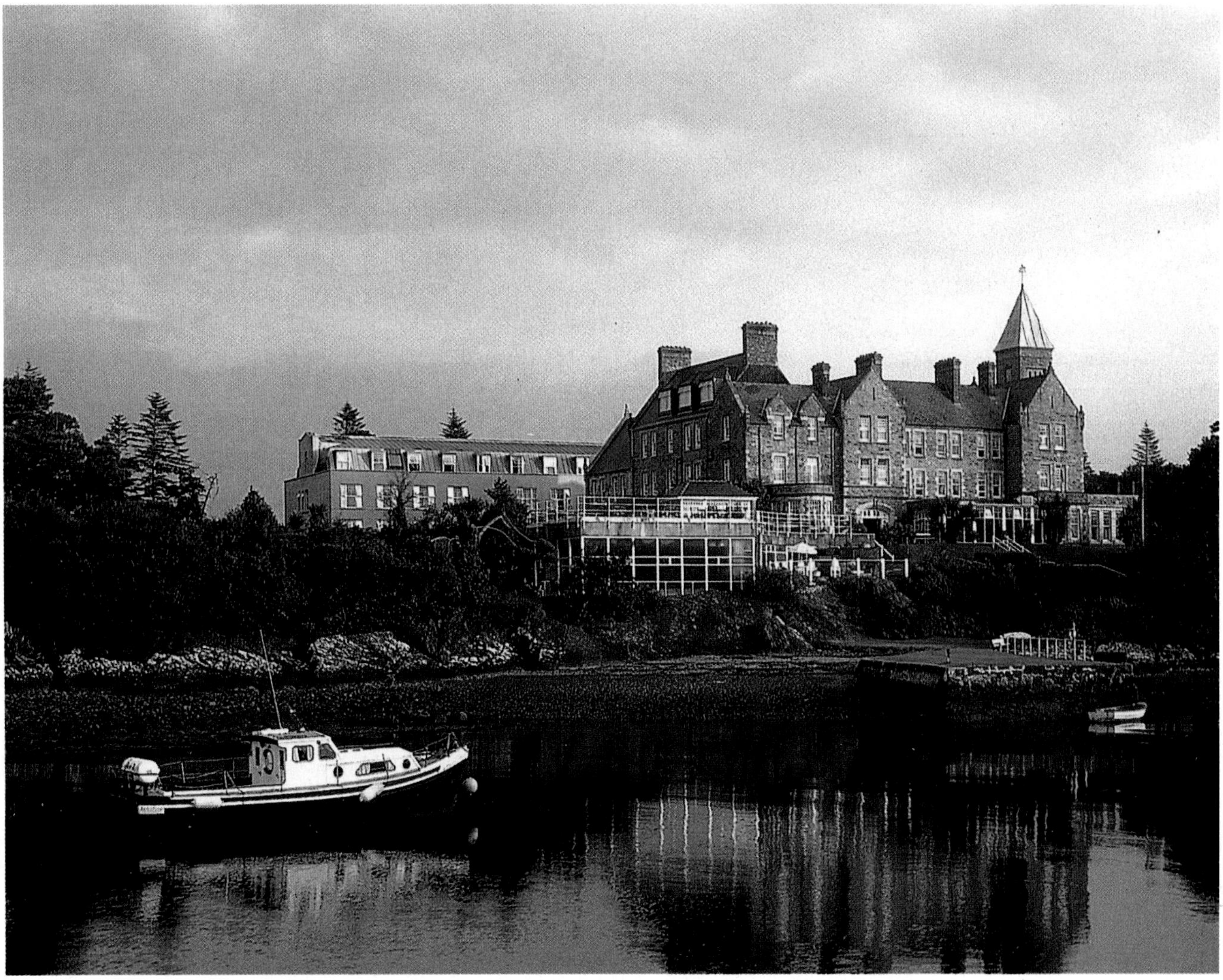

PARKNASILLA HOTEL

GREAT SOUTHERN HOTEL, PARKNASILLA, CO. KERRY, IRELAND
TEL: 00 353 64 45122 FAX: 00 353 64 45323 E-MAIL: res@parknasilla.gsh.ie

County Kerry has an equitable climate from the warm Gulf Stream. Parknasilla is a splendid Victorian mansion surrounded by extensive parkland and subtropical gardens leading down to the seashore. New arrivals appreciate the graceful reception rooms which, like the luxurious bedrooms, look out on the mountains, across the verdant countryside or down to Kenmare Bay. Wonderful damask and chintz harmonize with the period furniture and thoughtful 'extras' have been provided. The bathrooms are lavishly appointed. George Bernard Shaw's many visits are reflected in the names of the inviting Doolittle Bar and the elegant Pygmalion Restaurant. The sophisticated menus always include fish fresh from the sea and the international wine list will please the most discerning guests. Corporate activities and private celebrations are hosted in the traditional Shaw Library or handsome Derryquin Suite. Leisure facilities abound: a private 9-hole golf course with challenging championship courses close by, riding, water sports, sailing, clay pigeon shooting and archery. Parknasilla has 7 recommended walks through the estate and its own motor yacht for cruises round the coast. Indoors there is a superb pool, sauna, steam room, Jacuzzi, hot tub, hydrotherapy seaweed baths, aromatherapy and massage **Directions:** The hotel is south west of Killarney off N70. Price Guide: Single €133–€152; double/twin €213–€249; suite (room only) €380.

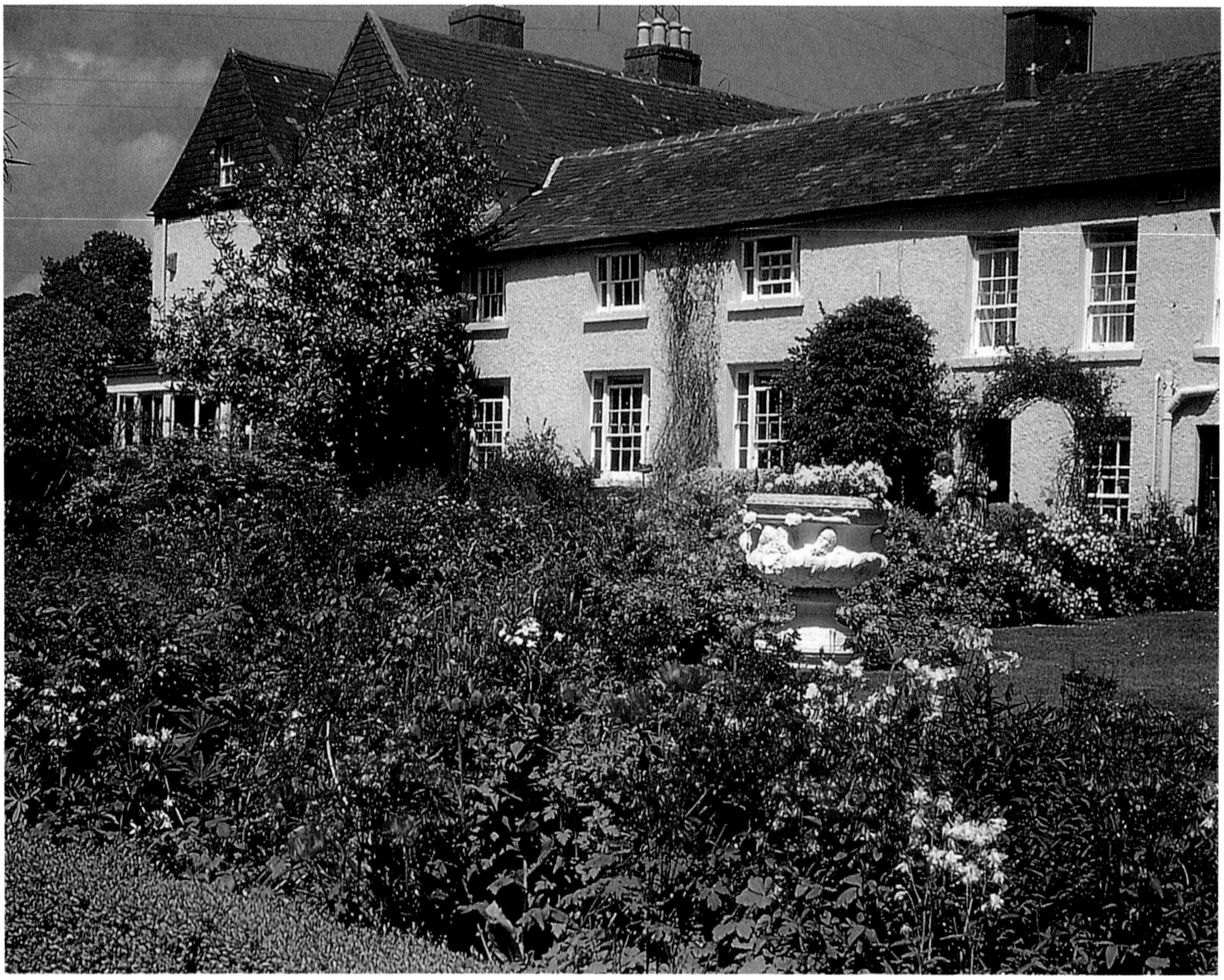

HUNTER'S HOTEL

NEWRATH BRIDGE, RATHNEW, CO WICKLOW

TEL: 00 353 404 40106 FAX: 00 353 404 40338 E-MAIL: reception@hunters.ie

Hunter's Hotel, one of Ireland's oldest coaching inns, has been established since the days of post horses and carriages. Run by the Gelletlie family for five generations, the hotel has a long-standing reputation for hospitality, friendliness and excellent food. The restaurant is known for its roast joints, its locally caught fish and its home-grown vegetables. The hotel gardens above the river Vartry are a delightful scene for enjoying afternoon tea, lunch or dinner. All the reception rooms retain the character of bygone days with antique furniture, open fires, fresh flowers and polished brass. Most of the 16 attractive en suite bedrooms overlook the award-winning gardens. Business meetings and seminars for up to 25 delegates are held in the new Garden Room. Hunter's is an ideal base from which to visit Mount Usher gardens, Powerscourt Gardens, Russborough House, Glendalough, Killruddery House, Avondale House and the other attractions of Co. Wicklow, "The Garden of Ireland", where a Garden Festival is held each year in May/June. Local amenities include twenty 18-hole golf courses within half an hour's drive, most notably Druid's Glen and the highly regarded European. Horse riding and hill walking are other pursuits which can be arranged. **Directions:** Take N11 to Rathnew; turn left just before village on Dublin side. Price Guide: Single€88.90–€108; double/twin €177.80–€215.90.

KELLY'S RESORT HOTEL

ROSSLARE, CO WEXFORD, IRELAND
TEL: 00 353 53 32114 FAX: 00 353 53 32222 E-MAIL: kellyhot@iol.ie

Situated beside the long, sandy beach at Rosslare, Kelly's is very much a family hotel, now managed by the fourth generation of Kellys. With a firm reputation as one of Ireland's finest hotels, based on a consistently high standard of service, Kelly's extends a warm welcome to its guests, many of whom return year after year. The public rooms are tastefully decorated and feature a collection of carefully selected paintings. All bedrooms have been refurbished and extended in the last three years and have en suite facilities. The hotel restaurant is highly regarded for its superb cuisine and great attention to detail. An extensive wine list includes individual estate wines imported from France. To complement Chef Aherne's fine cuisine Kelly's have now opened a new French Bar/Bistro "La Marine", which is an inspired assemblage of design and offers the ideal venue for pre-dinner drinks. Ireland's numerous endevour awards for tourism. For exercise and relaxation, guests have the use of the hotel's Aqua Club, with two swimming pools and a range of water and health facilities with extensive range of treatments, 'swimming lounge', plunge pool and canadian hot tub, also a beauty salon. Golfers have courses at Rosslare, St Helens' Bay and Wexford, which has an excellent shopping centre. Places of interest nearby include the Irish National Heritage Park at Ferrycarrig. **Directions:** Follow signs to Rosslare. Price Guide: Single €84–€90; double/twin €148–€187.

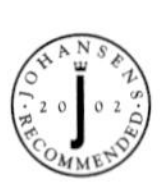

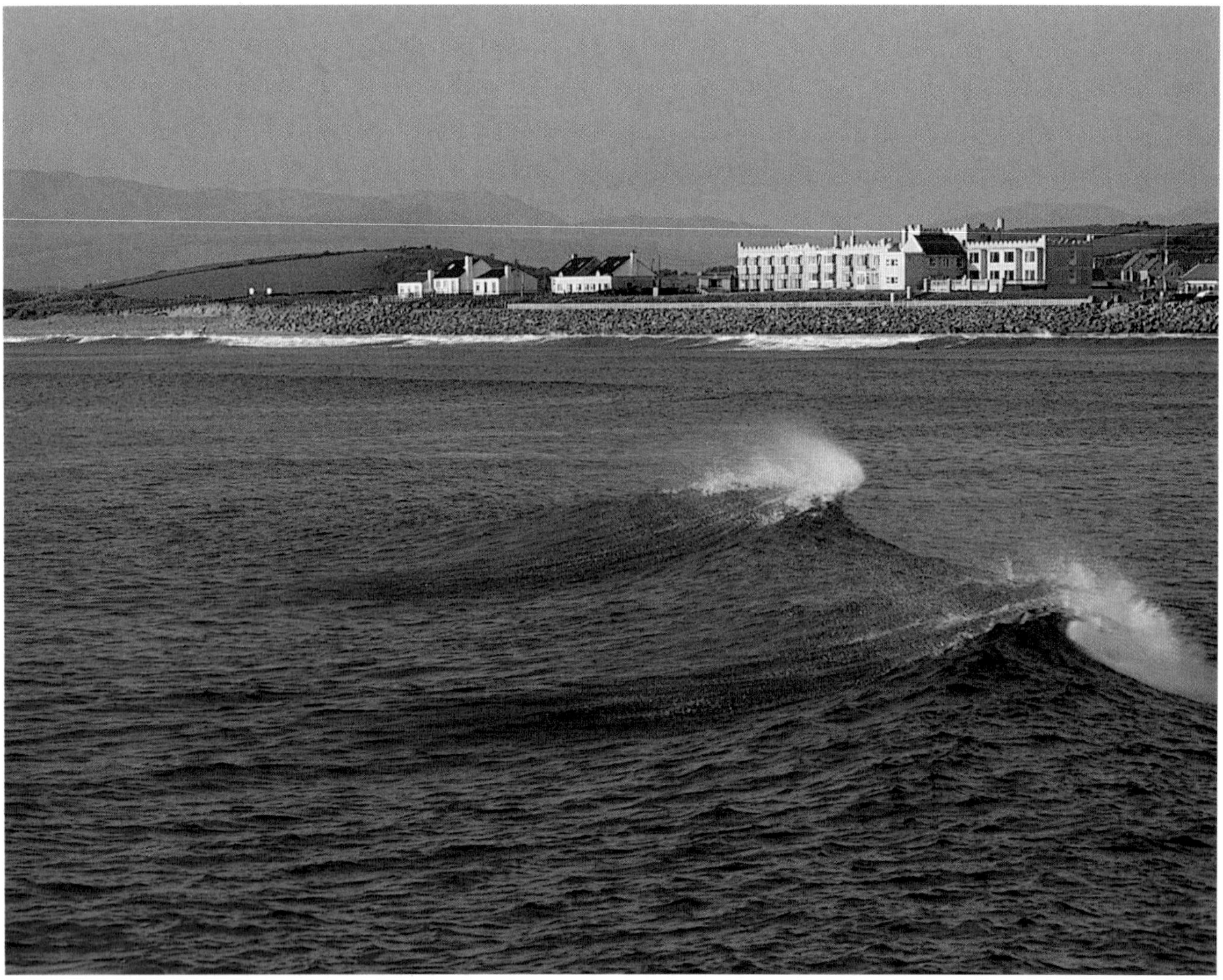

THE SAND HOUSE HOTEL

ROSSNOWLAGH, DONEGAL BAY, IRELAND
TEL: 00 353 72 51777 FAX: 00 353 72 52100 E-MAIL: Reserv@SandHouse–Hotel.ie

The Sand House has been delightfully converted from a 19th century fishing lodge into a gracious hotel which combines high standards of accommodation, service and cuisine with the charm, luxury and leisurely ambience of bygone days. It is excellent in every way and has been described as one of Ireland's west coast treasures. Situated between Ballyshannon and historic Donegal Town, The Sand House overlooks the blue waters of the Atlantic and a superb three miles crescent of golden sand. Rossnowlagh is regarded as the most scenic and dramatic beach in the North West. Each of the 45 en suite bedrooms are individually styled and offer all home comforts. The elegant restaurant has been awarded two AA Red Rosettes for excellent cuisine which is enhanced by a carefully chosen wine list. Seafood specialities include Donegal Bay salmon, trout, scallops, crab, mussels and fresh oysters. Fishing, horseriding and three championship golf courses are nearby. Being half-way between the wild beauty of Connemara and the North Donegal Highlands, The Sand House provides an ideal base for touring. Places of interest nearby include Glenveagh National Park, Yeats country and Lough Gill. **Directions:** From Dublin follow the N3 via Cavan or the N4 via Sligo. From Galway take the N17 via Sligo, and from Belfast take the M1 and A4 via Enniskillen Price Guide: Single from €75; double/twin from €90; suite from €110 per person.

45 MasterCard VISA AMERICAN EXPRESS M 75

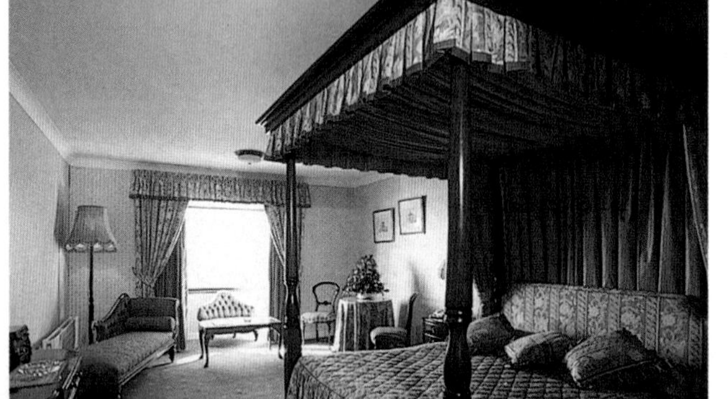

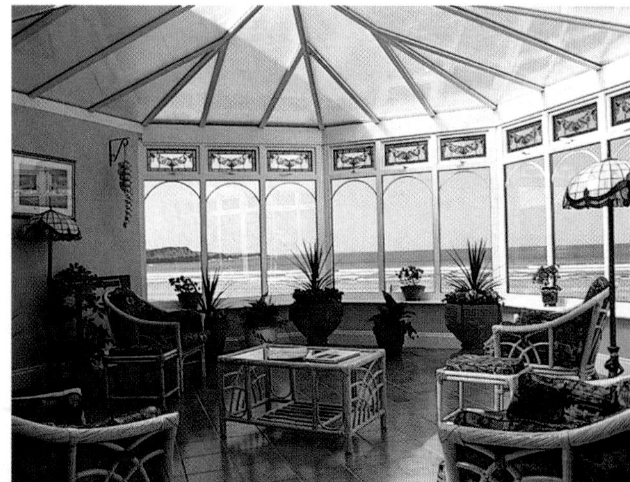

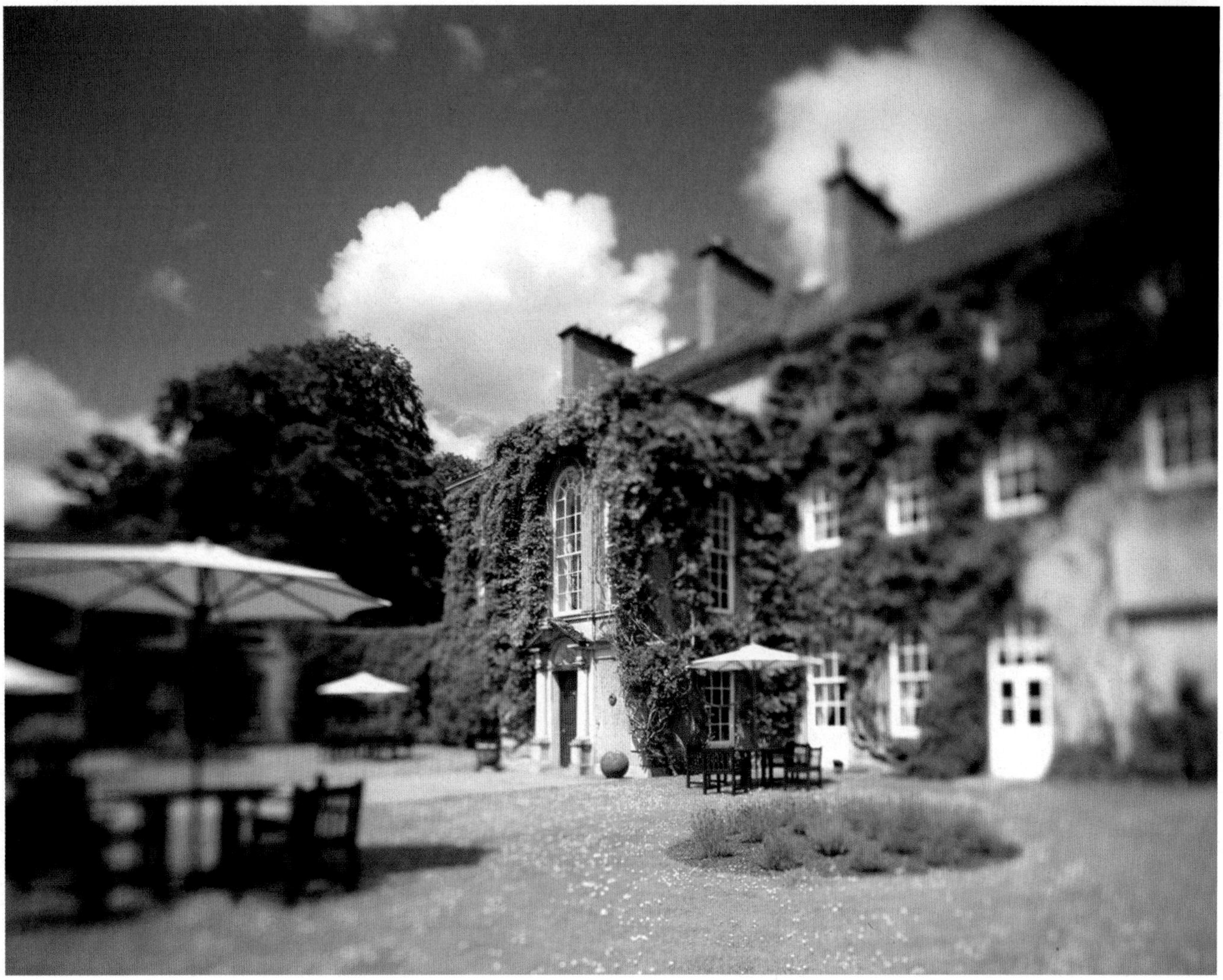

MOUNT JULIET

THOMASTOWN, CO. KILKENNY, IRELAND
TEL: 00 353 56 73000 FAX: 00 353 56 73019 E-MAIL: info@mountjuliet.ie

Mount Juliet is an architectural gem, a magnificent 18th-century Georgian mansion standing proudly on the banks of the River Nore in the heart of a lush 1,500-acre estate that teems with natural activity. The entrance doorway leads into an impressive hall featuring elaborate stucco work with bas-reliefs on walls and ceilings. A feeling of opulence pervades all reception rooms, the bars recall a glorious equestrian past whilst the homeliness of the library and drawing rooms provide comfortable venues for relaxation. Afternoon tea or a pre-dinner glass of champagne can be enjoyed in the elegant Majors Room. Jewel in the crown, however, is the exquisite Lady Helen Dining Room, famed for its original stucco plasterwork, pastoral views and superb cuisine. Chef Peter Brennan produces gourmet delights that have earned a RAC Gold Ribbon and two AA Rosettes. The hotel's 32 en suite guest rooms are individually designed, light and airy, comfortable and full of the character and charm that reflects quiet good taste and refinement. Centre of activity for guests is Hunters Yard, which is situated on the edge of a championship golf course. It envelopes all of the estate's sporting and leisure life, together with stylish dining and 16 en suite 'Club' style guest rooms offering total privacy and access to the sybaritic new spa. **Directions:** 16 miles from Kilkenny on the N9 via N10. Price Guide: Single €290; double/twin €470; suite €560.

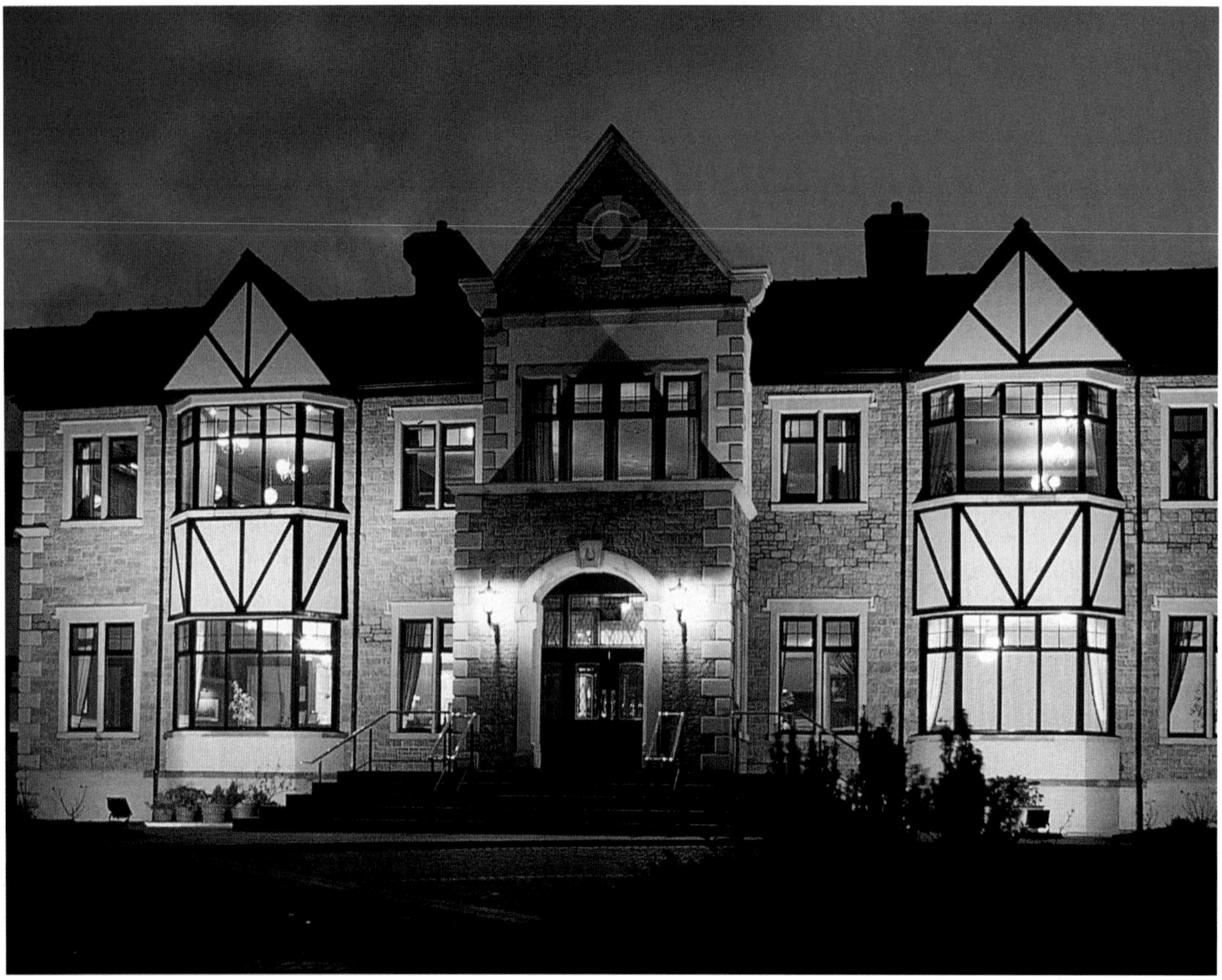

KNOCKRANNY HOUSE HOTEL

KNOCKRANNY, WESTPORT, CO MAYO, IRELAND

TEL: 00 353 982 8600 FAX: 00 353 982 8611 E-MAIL: info@khh.ie

Situated on secluded grounds overlooking the picturesque Heritage town of Westport, Knockranny House Hotel enjoys unrivalled views of Croagh Patrick, Clew Bay and the Atlantic Ocean. This Victorian style hotel is privately owned and managed by Adrian and Geraldine Noonan, who guarantee the best in Irish hospitality. The 54 charming bedrooms and suites are tastefully furnished and offer luxury, comfort and every up-to-date convenience. The Executive Suites have four-poster beds, spa baths, a sunken lounge area with panoramic views and all the trimmings of pure luxury. Fresh flowers in spring to roaring open log fires in winter create a relaxing ambience with every possible comfort. The restaurant La Fougère offers excellent cuisine with an emphasis on fresh seafood and the finest local ingredients complemented by a selection of fine wines. Activities such as golf, fishing, sailing, horse riding and much more can be enjoyed in the dramatic surrounding countryside, whilst a climb to the top of Croagh Patrick makes an exhilarating day's journey. The ideal location to combine business with pleasure, Knockranny offers extensive conference and banqueting facilities for up to 400. The Conference Suites are fully air-conditioned with state-of-the-art communication and audiovisual equipment. **Directions**: Left off the N60 before entering Westport town. Price Guide: Single €175; double/twin €230; suite €294.

Tinakilly House Hotel

RATHNEW, WICKLOW, CO WICKLOW

TEL: 00 353 404 69274 FAX: 00 353 404 67806 E-MAIL: reservations@tinakilly.ie

Less than an hour's drive from Dublin, romantic secret hideaway Tinakilly House, stands on seven acres of beautifully landscaped gardens overlooking the Irish Sea. Tinakilly was built for Captain Halpin, who as Commander of the Great Eastern, laid the transatlantic telegraph cables in the 1860's. Owners Josephine and Raymond Power look forward to welcoming you to their luxury Country House and Restaurant. A perfect blend of Victorian splendour and modern comfort, the bedrooms include 5 Captain Suites and 23 junior suites, most with sea view. The superb modern Irish cuisine featuring local produce is augmented by an excellent wine cellar. Open all year round, Tinakilly offers many special short breaks including Romantic Rendezvous and Dickensian Christmas and New Year Programme. The county of Wicklow is renowned for its wonderful gardens such as Powerscourt and Mount Usher. The breathtaking Wicklow Mountains, Glendalough and of course, Ballykissangel also attract many visitors. Top class golf courses include the European Club and Druid's Glen, venue for 1996 to 1999 Irish Open. Tinakilly is an AA Red Star, ITB 4 Star, RAC Gold Ribbon hotel **Directions:** Take N11 from Dublin to Rathnew village. Hotel is 500 metres along the R750 to Wicklow Town. Dublin 29 miles. Dun Laoghaire ferry port 20 miles. Rosslare 60 miles. Price Guide: Single €163–€180; double/twin €252–€304; suite €340–€600.

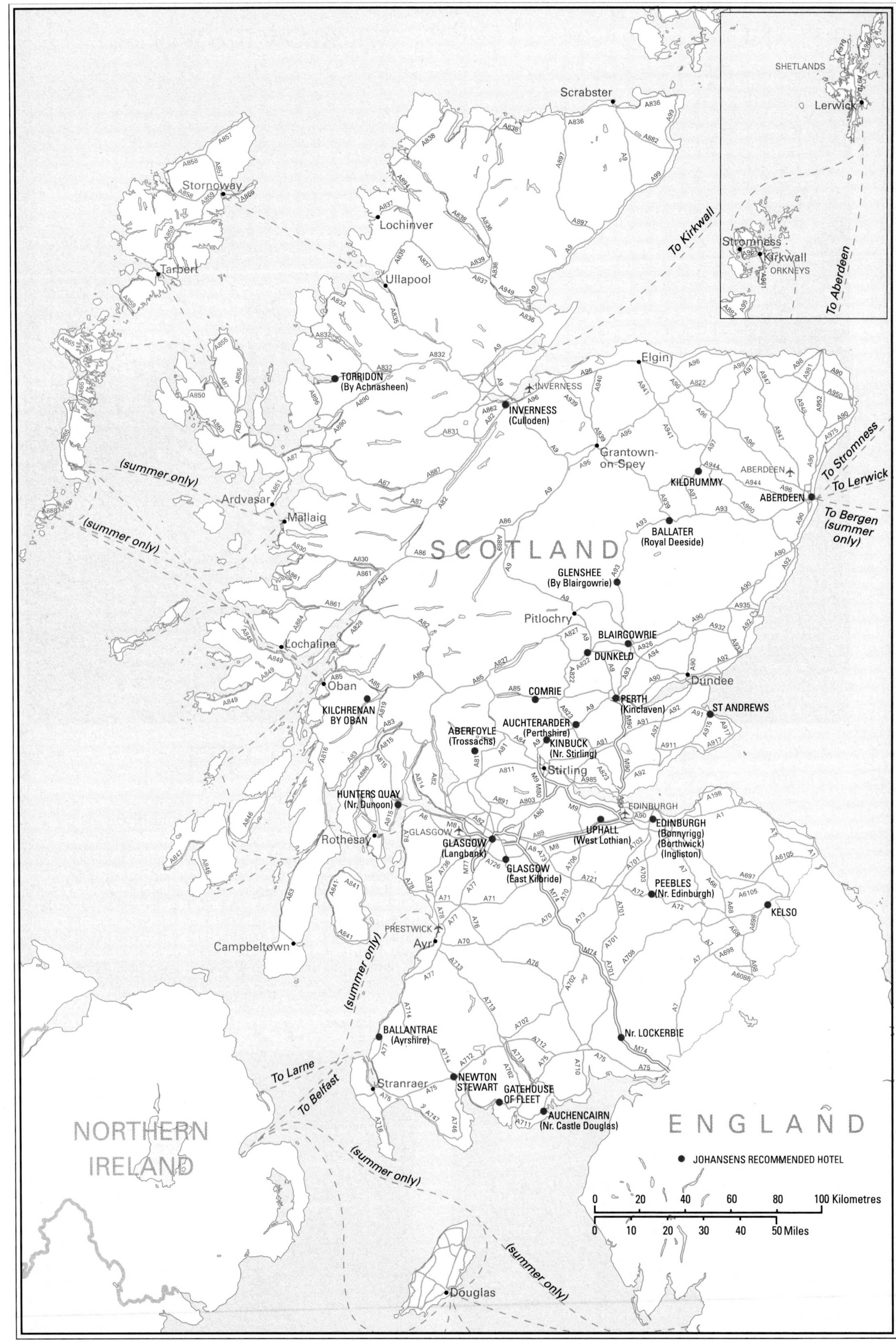
SHETLANDS
Lerwick
Stromness
Kirkwall
ORKNEYS
To Kirkwall
To Aberdeen
Scrabster
Stornoway
Lochinver
Tarbert
Ullapool
TORRIDON
(By Achnasheen)
INVERNESS
INVERNESS
(Culloden)
Elgin
Grantown-on-Spey
(summer only)
Ardvasar
Mallaig
(summer only)
KILDRUMMY
ABERDEEN
ABERDEEN
To Stromness
To Lerwick
To Bergen
(summer only)
SCOTLAND
BALLATER
(Royal Deeside)
GLENSHEE
(By Blairgowrie)
Pitlochry
BLAIRGOWRIE
DUNKELD
Lochaline
Oban
KILCHRENAN
BY OBAN
COMRIE
PERTH
(Kinclaven)
Dundee
ST ANDREWS
AUCHTERARDER
(Perthshire)
ABERFOYLE
(Trossachs)
KINBUCK
(Nr. Stirling)
Stirling
HUNTERS QUAY
(Nr. Dunoon)
EDINBURGH
EDINBURGH
(Bonnyrigg)
(Borthwick)
(Ingliston)
UPHALL
(West Lothian)
GLASGOW
GLASGOW
(Langbank)
GLASGOW
(East Kilbride)
Rothesay
PEEBLES
(Nr. Edinburgh)
KELSO
Campbeltown
PRESTWICK
Ayr
(summer only)
BALLANTRAE
(Ayrshire)
Nr. LOCKERBIE
NEWTON
STEWART
GATEHOUSE
OF FLEET
AUCHENCAIRN
(Nr. Castle Douglas)
Stranraer
To Larne
To Belfast
NORTHERN
IRELAND
ENGLAND
JOHANSENS RECOMMENDED HOTEL
0 20 40 60 80 100 Kilometres
0 10 20 30 40 50 Miles
(summer only)
(summer only)
Douglas

Johansens Recommended Hotels

Scotland

Ardanaiseig, Argyll

This land of contrast conjures up images of dramaric mountains, deep, glassy lochs, tartan, whisky and a fiercely proud nation. From the wild coast of the Highlands to the elegant streets of Edinburgh, from the staggeringly beautiful lochs of Stirling to the majestic heights of Glen Coe, Scotland will put a never-ending spell on you.

The border counties, running from the Cheviot Hills in the south to the outskirts of Edinburgh in the north, contain some of the country's most beautiful scenery. Verdant landscape shelters castles, abbeys, stately homes, woollen mills and a host of pretty villages, and the quiet country roads are ideal for cycling.

Tucked away in the South West corner of Scotland, between the border with England and the Irish Sea, Dumfries and Galloway is a very special place. The Gulf Stream sweeps across the west and makes the climate milder, allowing visitors to enjoy the outdoors to the full. It also accounts for a profusion of glorious gardens and nurseries, filled with tropical plants and ablaze with colour all year round. This is outstanding golfing country, and the coast is attractive for its abundance of water sports. Rich in Scotland's bloody and romantic history, this region has numerous castles, and ancient traditions like the Riding of the Marches are still upheld.

The Highlands remain largely untouched by man, and are perhaps the most consistently beautiful part of the British Isles. From the deep lochs in the east to the rugged coastline of the north, the natural features here seem to represent the very essence of all things Scottish. The wildlife is plentiful and varied. Any visit to the Highlands should include a trip to the Grampian Mountains, the lush island of Skye, and, of course, the mysterious Loch Ness.

No trip to Scotland would be complete without a visit to its major cities. Glasgow, Scotland's largest city, is one of the liveliest and most cosmopolitan destinations in Europe, and, combined with its spectacular rural surroundings, is 'Scotland in miniature'. Edinburgh remains one of the world's greatest cities. It stands with one foot in the past and one in the future, proud of a long history rich in tradition yet always at the cutting edge of culture. The world famous Edinburgh Festival – the most renowned and largest arts festival in the world – is held each year, offering theatre, dance, music and comedy shows in over 200 venues.

For further information on Scotland, please contact:

The Scottish Tourist Board
23 Ravelston Terrace
Edinburgh EH4 3TP
Tel: +44 (0)131 332 2433
Internet: www.visitscotland.com

Ardoe House Hotel And Restaurant

SOUTH DEESIDE ROAD, BLAIRS, ABERDEEN AB12 5YP
TEL: 01224 860600 FAX: 01224 861283 E-MAIL: info@ardoe.macdonald-hotels.co.uk

Built in 1878 by a local manufacturer for his wife, the majestic, turreted Ardoe House is designed in the Scottish Baronial style favoured by Queen Victoria for Balmoral Castle. Situated within its own beautifully landscaped grounds with magnificent views over the River Dee and open countryside, Ardoe House has the style of an elegant country mansion with all modern comforts. Rich oak panelling, ornate ceilings and stained glass windows abound. The Great Hall reception area is truly spectacular, the richly furnished public rooms are relaxing and there are various small secluded areas where guests can privately enjoy a glass of malt whisky. Every bedroom has a pleasant and comfortable atmosphere and whatever your taste in cuisine, the fare available in the hotel's 2 AA Rosettes award-winning restaurant will more than match expectations. Ardoe House is only 10 minutes from Aberdeen City Centre yet is a fine gateway to tour Royal Deeside. Guests will enjoy complimentary use of a fully equipped leisure centre, which comprises an 18m x 8m swimming pool, sauna, steam room, state-of-the-art gymnasium, aerobics studio, blitz room and four health and beauty treatment rooms. **Directions:** Leave Aberdeen on A92 south and join B9077 south Deeside Road at the Bridge of Dee Price Guide: Single £70–£160; double/twin £90–£170; suite £130–£170. Short break rates to include dinner and breakfast on request.

Forest Hills Hotel

KINLOCHARD BY ABERFOYLE, THE TROSSACHS FK8 3TL
TEL: 01877 387277 FAX: 01877 387307

The majestic Forest Hills hotel is idyllically situated in 25 acres of mature wooded landscaped gardens overlooking beautiful Loch Ard in the foothills of the Trossachs, scattered with tumbling burns, rocky waterfalls, winding pathways and meandering forest trails. It is a stunning, history-steeped scenic location where guests can completely unwind and enjoy sumptuous comfort, warming log fires in winter and watching the summer sun illuminating Ben Lomond across the waters whilst sipping a cooling drink on the terrace. Forest Hills is excellent in every way, particularly so in its service, friendliness and hospitality. Each of the 55 elegantly furnished en suite bedrooms has every facility that visitors could wish for. The lounges are a joy and the restaurant is renowned for its sumptuous cuisine prepared by award-winning chefs. Grills, pastas and salads are offered in the New Rafters Bar and Bistro, which stages a weekly Ceilidh with Scottish music and dancing. The Hotel's leisure centre has a heated swimming pool, sauna, steam room, gym, billiards and a curling rink which converts into an extensive children's play area with go-karts. The more adventurous guests can try canoeing, windsurfing and sailing on the Loch, or mountain biking, archery, fly fishing and guided and ghost walks. Beauty treatments can also be arranged. **Directions:** From M9, exit at Jct10. Take A873 to Aberfoyle and then join B892 to Kinlochard. Price Guide: Single £60–90; double/twin £80–£140; suite 110–190.

55 MasterCard VISA AMERICAN EXPRESS M 150

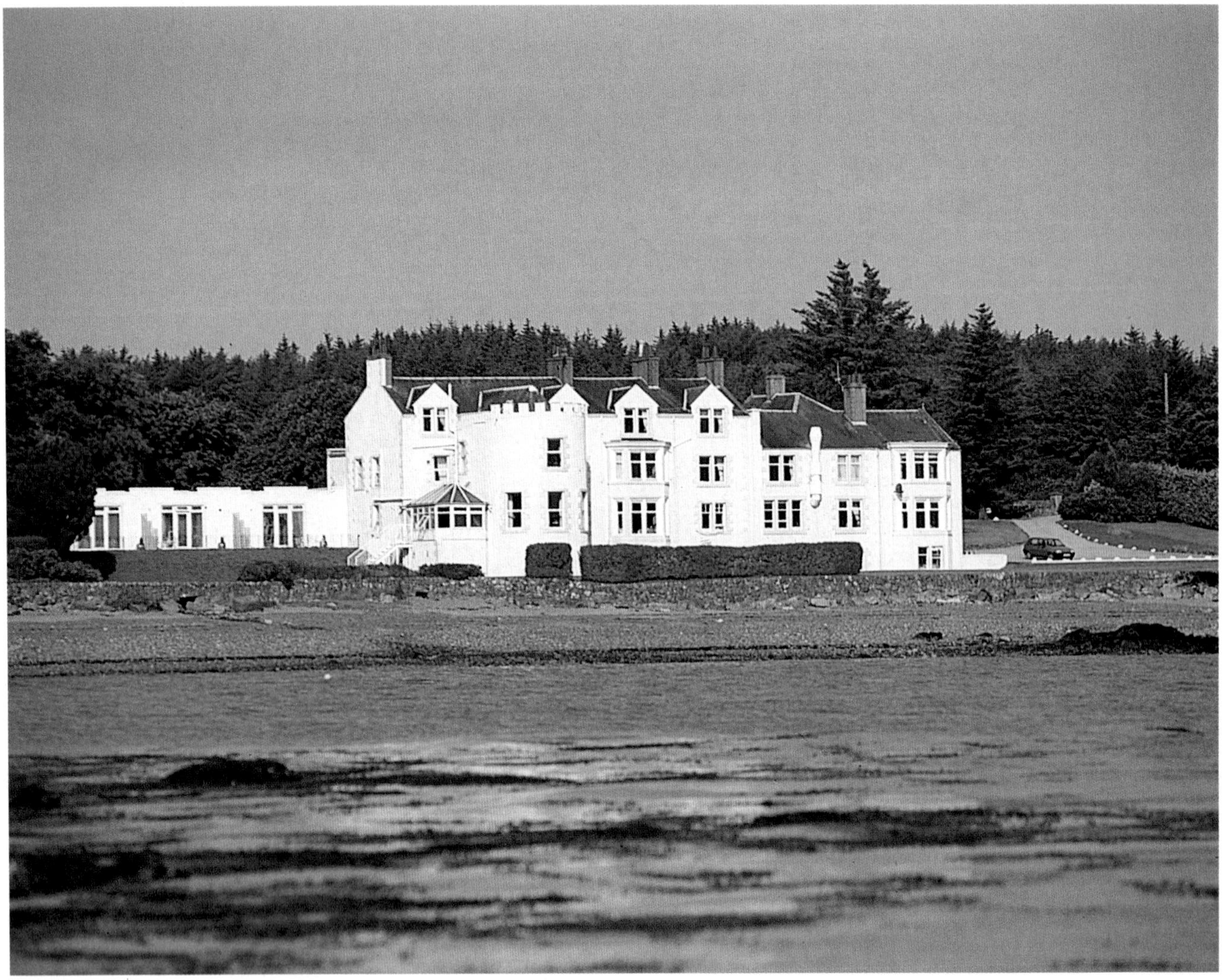

Balcary Bay Hotel

AUCHENCAIRN, NR CASTLE DOUGLAS, DUMFRIES & GALLOWAY DG7 1QZ
TEL: 01556 640217/640311 FAX: 01556 640272 E-MAIL: reservations@balcary-bay-hotel.co.uk

Enjoying a very warm climate due to its proximity to the Gulf Stream, Balcary Bay is one of Scotland's more romantic and secluded hideaways, yet only ½ hour from the bustling market town of Dumfries. As you sit in the lounge overlooking Balcary Bay, the dong of birds and the gently lapping waves compete for your attention. Guests will be greeted by genuine Scottish hospitality, which includes the provision of modern facilities with a traditional atmosphere, imaginatively prepared local delicacies such as lobsters, prawns and salmon, plus the reassuring intimacy of a family-run hotel. This hotel is a true haven for those wishing to get away from their hectic lives, and an ideal break for a romantic weekend. This exciting corner of Scotland offers numerous great coastal and woodland walks, whilst nearby are several 9 and 18-hole golf courses at Colvend, Kirkcudbright, Castle Douglas, Southerness and Dumfries. There are also salmon rivers and trout lochs, sailing, shooting, riding and bird watching facilities. The area abounds with National Trust historic properties and gardens. **Directions:** Located off the A711 Dumfries–Kirkcudbright road, two miles out of Auchencairn on the Shore Road. Price Guide: Single £61; double/twin £108–£122. Seasonal short breaks and reduced inclusive rates for 3 and 7 nights.

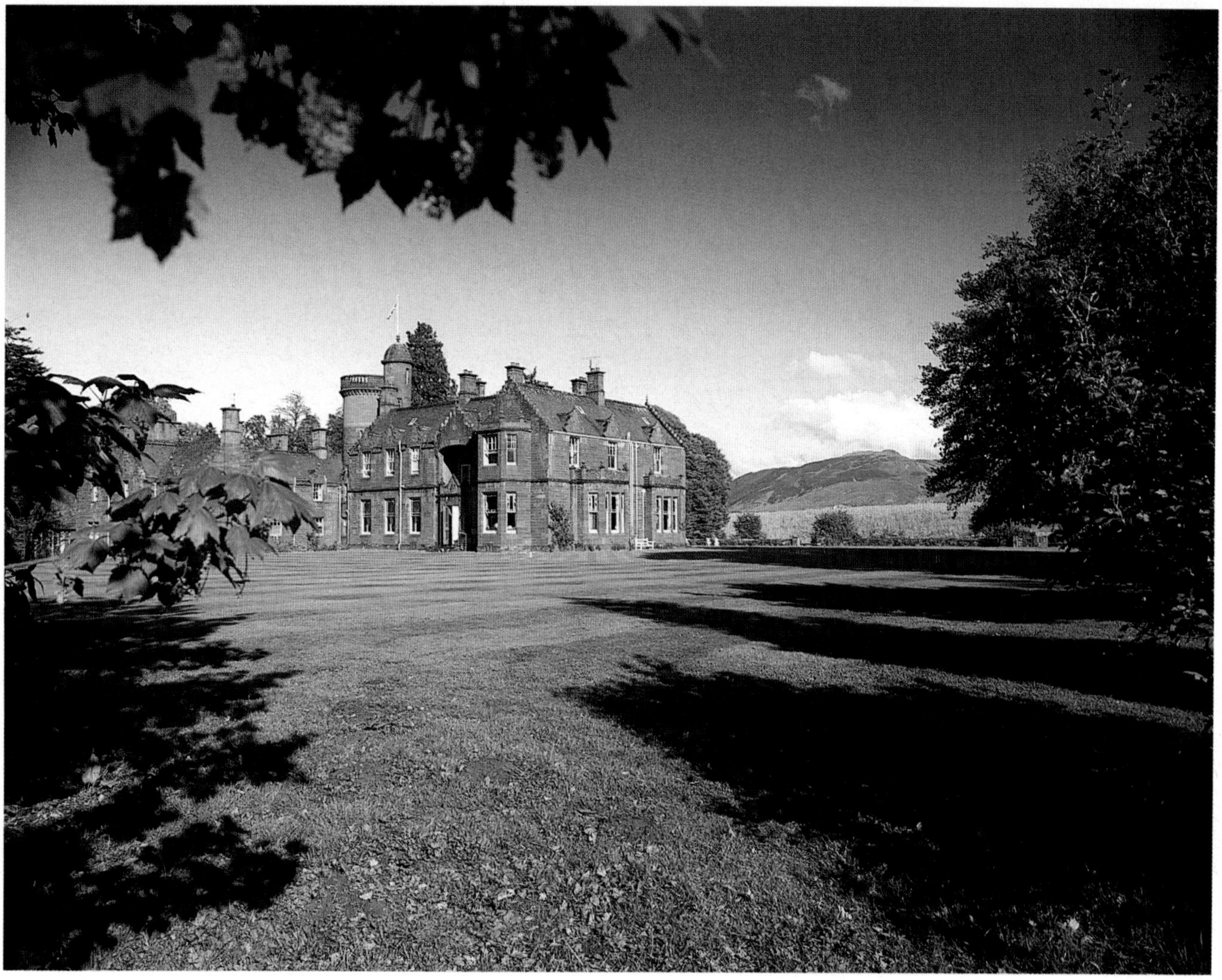

AUCHTERARDER HOUSE

AUCHTERARDER, PERTHSHIRE PH3 1DZ
TEL: 01764 663646 FAX: 01764 662939 E-MAIL: auchterarder@wrensgroup.com

This splendid mansion, set amidst the rolling hills and glens of Perthshire, is a 19th century Scottish Baronial style house. Built over 150 years ago as a family home, the mansion retains its elegance whilst providing all the modern facilities. The opulent bedrooms are beautifully appointed, overlooking either the surrounding countryside or the grounds. All are double rooms and offer colour satellite television, radio, telephone and en suite facilities. The fine public rooms are enhanced by warming log fires and crystal chandeliers and the oak-panelled walls are adorned with paintings. This beautiful house has a warm, informal ambience that is omnipresent. In the traditional dining room, guests indulge in the sumptuous cuisine, a fusion of Scottish recipes and exquisite French presentation. The original cellars boast an extensive selection of both New World and European wines, but specialising in vintage Bordeaux. The 17½ acre grounds will delight nature lovers, with brilliant colour emanating from the various species of azaleas and rhododendrons. Traditional country pursuits such as fishing and shooting are readily available whilst croquet and golf may be played on site, or at the Gleneagles courses. **Directions:** From the A9, junction 8, drive into Auchterarder. Take the B8062 signposted Crieff for 1½ miles, the hotel is on the right. Price Guide: Single from £135-£225; double/twin from £170-£295; suite from £195.

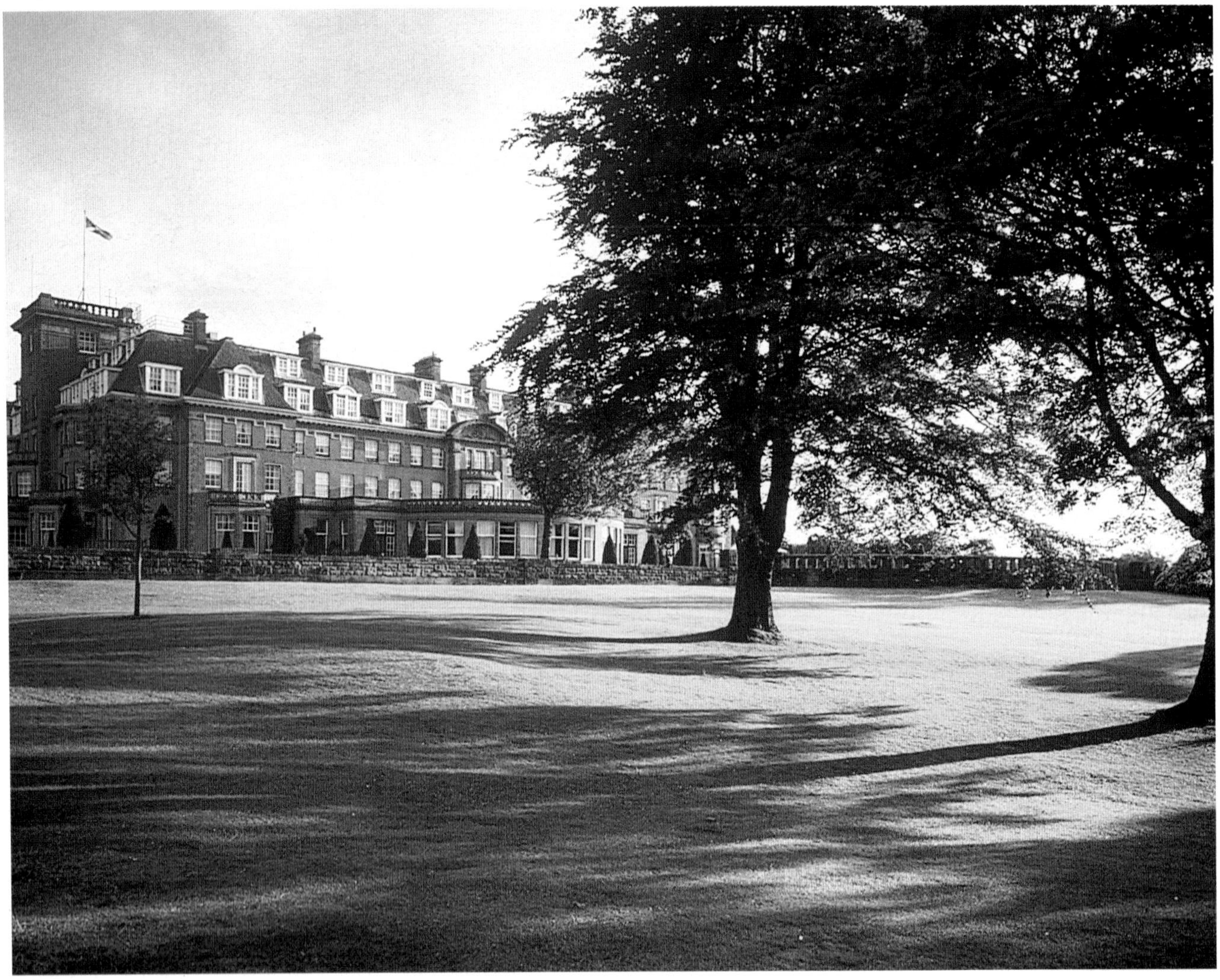

GLENEAGLES

AUCHTERARDER, PERTHSHIRE PH3 1NF
TEL: 01764 662231 FAX: 01764 662134 E-MAIL: resort.sales@gleneagles.com

Known as the 'great palace in the glen' this luxurious hotel nestles in the heart of the Ochil Hills on the edge of the Highlands in the White Muir of Auchterarder. From its Georgian-style windows and lush green grounds guests can marvel at views of Ben Lomond and the Grampians. Gleneagles is enveloped by clean, crisp air and an artistic landscape capped by an ever-changing sky of blue, violet and autumnal gold. It is a haven of comfort and impeccable service. The interior has been redesigned and refurbished with 21st-century amenities, whilst offering the charm and atmosphere of a Scottish country house. The elegant public rooms are enhanced by superb antique furniture. The 203 bedrooms and 13 suites have every home-from-home comfort and stunning views across Gleneagles' lawns, estate and golf courses; some have hand-woven carpets, crystal chandeliers, tasseled silk hangings and four-poster beds. Guest may dine in the sophisticated Andrew Fairlie and Strathearn restaurants, whilst a cosy bar serves light lunches and afternoon teas. Championship golf facilities and a variety of country sports and pursuits can be enjoyed. Superb leisure facilities. Less than 50 miles from Edinburgh and Glasgow airports. **Directions:** From the north, leave A9 at the exit for A823 and follow sign for Gleneagles Hotel. From the south, turn off M9/A9 at junction with A823 signed Crieff and Gleneagles. Price Guide: Single £200; double/twin £410.

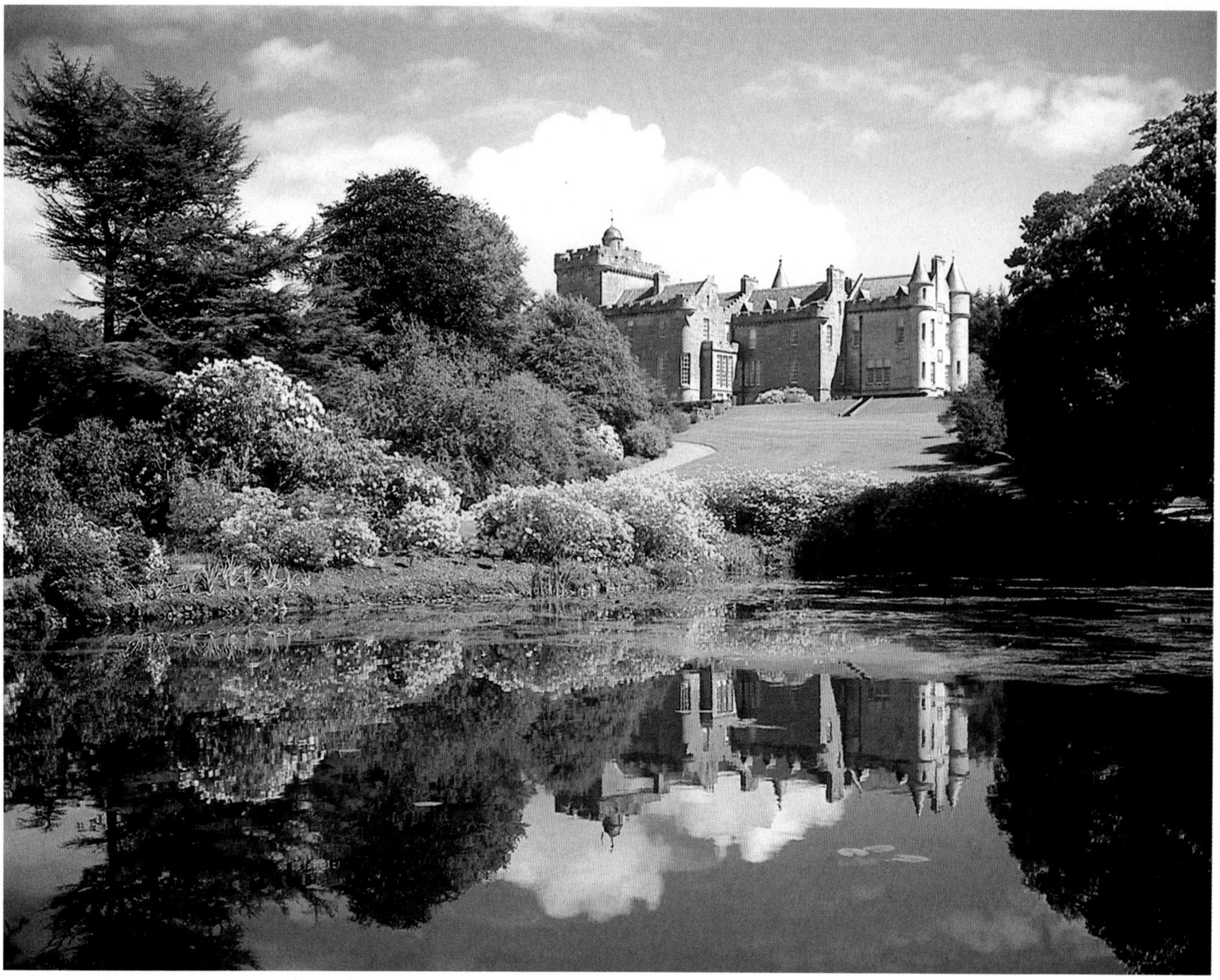

GLENAPP CASTLE

BALLANTRAE, SCOTLAND KA26 0NZ

TEL: 01465 831212 FAX: 01465 831000 E-MAIL: enquiries@glenappcastle.com

Glenapp is more of an experience rather than 'just another hotel'. As you turn through the castle gates, Glenapp stands proudly in front of you; imposing, exciting and inviting. The owners, Fay and Graham Cowan, offer a truly Scottish welcome to their glorious Ayrshire home. They bought Glenapp in a state of neglect and spent six years refurbishing it to combine the requirements of the discerning guest with the classic style of the house. No expense has been spared, from the stone fireplaces carved with the family crest to the Castle's own monogrammed china. Head Chef Laurent Gueguen will prepare exciting, innovative 6-course dinners, complemented by specially selected fine wines. The castle retains many original features as well as personally selected oil paintings and antique furnishings throughout bedrooms, lounges and oak panelled hallways. The 17 en suite bedrooms are spacious, individually decorated, and furnished to the highest standard, all offering either views of the garden or coastline. The 30-acre gardens contain many rare trees and shrubs and an impressive Victorian glasshouse and walled garden. Tennis and croquet are available in the grounds. Guests may play golf on the many local courses including championship courses, and shoot or fish on local estates. **Directions:** Glenapp Castle is approximately 15 miles north of Stranraer or 35 miles south of Ayr on A77. Price Guide: (All inclusive) Luxury double/twin £410; suite £450; master room £500.

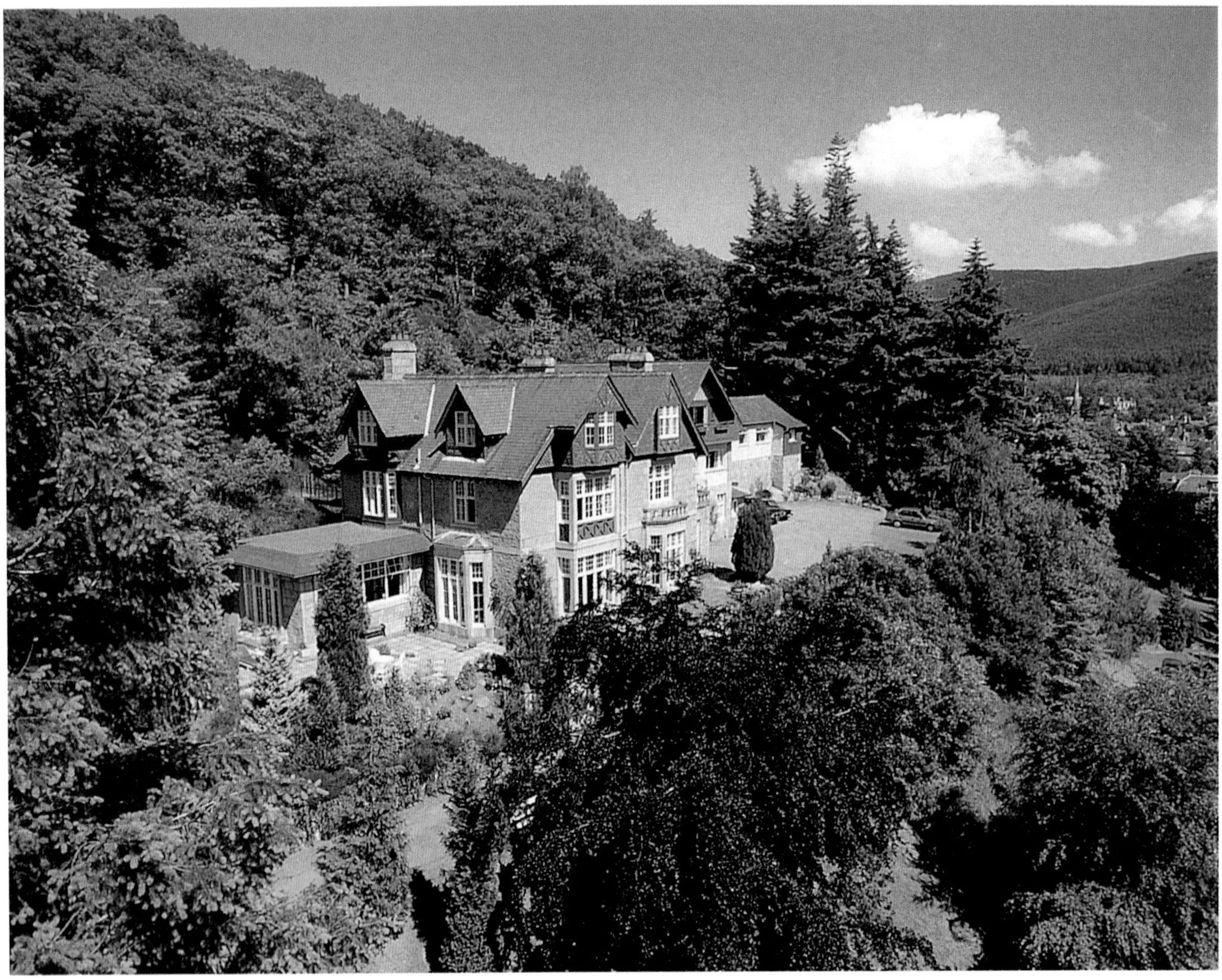

DARROCH LEARG HOTEL

BRAEMAR ROAD, BALLATER, ABERDEENSHIRE AB35 5UX
TEL: 013397 55443 FAX: 013397 55252 E-MAIL: nigel@darrochlearg.co.uk

Four acres of leafy grounds surround Darroch Learg, sited on the side of the rocky hill which dominates Ballater. The hotel, which was built in 1888 as a fashionable country residence, offers panoramic views over the golf course, River Dee and Balmoral Estate to the fine peaks of the Grampian Mountains. Oakhall, an adjacent mansion built in Scottish baronial style and adorned with turrets, contains five of the 18 bedrooms ideal for private groups. All bedrooms are individually furnished and decorated, providing modern amenities. The reception rooms in Darroch Learg are similarly elegant and welcoming, a comfortable venue in which to enjoy a relaxing drink. Log fires create a particularly cosy atmosphere on chilly nights. The beautifully presented food has been awarded 3AA Rosettes. A wide choice of wines, AA "Wine List of the Year for Scotland", complements the cuisine, which is best described as modern and Scottish in style. To perfect the setting, there is a wonderful outlook south towards the hills of Glen Muick. The wealth of outdoor activities on offer include walking, riding, mountain-biking, loch and river fishing, gliding and skiing. The surrounding areas are interesting with an old ruined Kirk and ancient Celtic stones. A few miles away stands Balmoral Castle, the Highland residence of the British sovereign. **Directions:** At the western edge of Ballater on the A93. Price Guide: Single £62–£77; double/twin £124–£154.

Kinloch House Hotel

BY BLAIRGOWRIE, PERTHSHIRE PH10 6SG

TEL: 01250 884237 FAX: 01250 884333 E-MAIL: reception@kinlochhouse.com

Winner of the 1994 Johansens Country Hotel Award, Kinloch House is an elegant example of a Scottish country home built in 1840. Set in 25 acres, including a magnificent walled garden and wooded parkland grazed by Highland cattle, it offers panoramic views to the south over Marlee Loch to the Sidlaw Hills beyond. It has a grand galleried hall with an ornate glass ceiling and fine paintings and antiques in the reception rooms. Chef Bill McNicoll and his team have established Kinloch House as one of the top dining venues in Scotland and his daily changing menus are complemented by the very extensive wine list. The cocktail bar, which stocks over 155 malt whiskies, is adjacent to the conservatory and is a focal point of the hotel. In August 1997 a fully equipped Health and Fitness Centre was opened for the exclusive use of guests. The Shentall Family offer a warm personal welcome to all their guests, whether they come simply to enjoy the beauty of the area, or to take advantage of the local pursuits of golf, hill walking, fishing and shooting. For the sightseer, Glamis Castle, Scone Palace and Blair Castle are among the area's attractions. 3 AA Rosettes and 3 AA Red Stars. Closed at Christmas. **Directions:** The hotel is 3 miles west of Blairgowrie, off the A923 Dunkeld road. Price Guide: : Single £105; double/twin £175–£215; suite to £260.

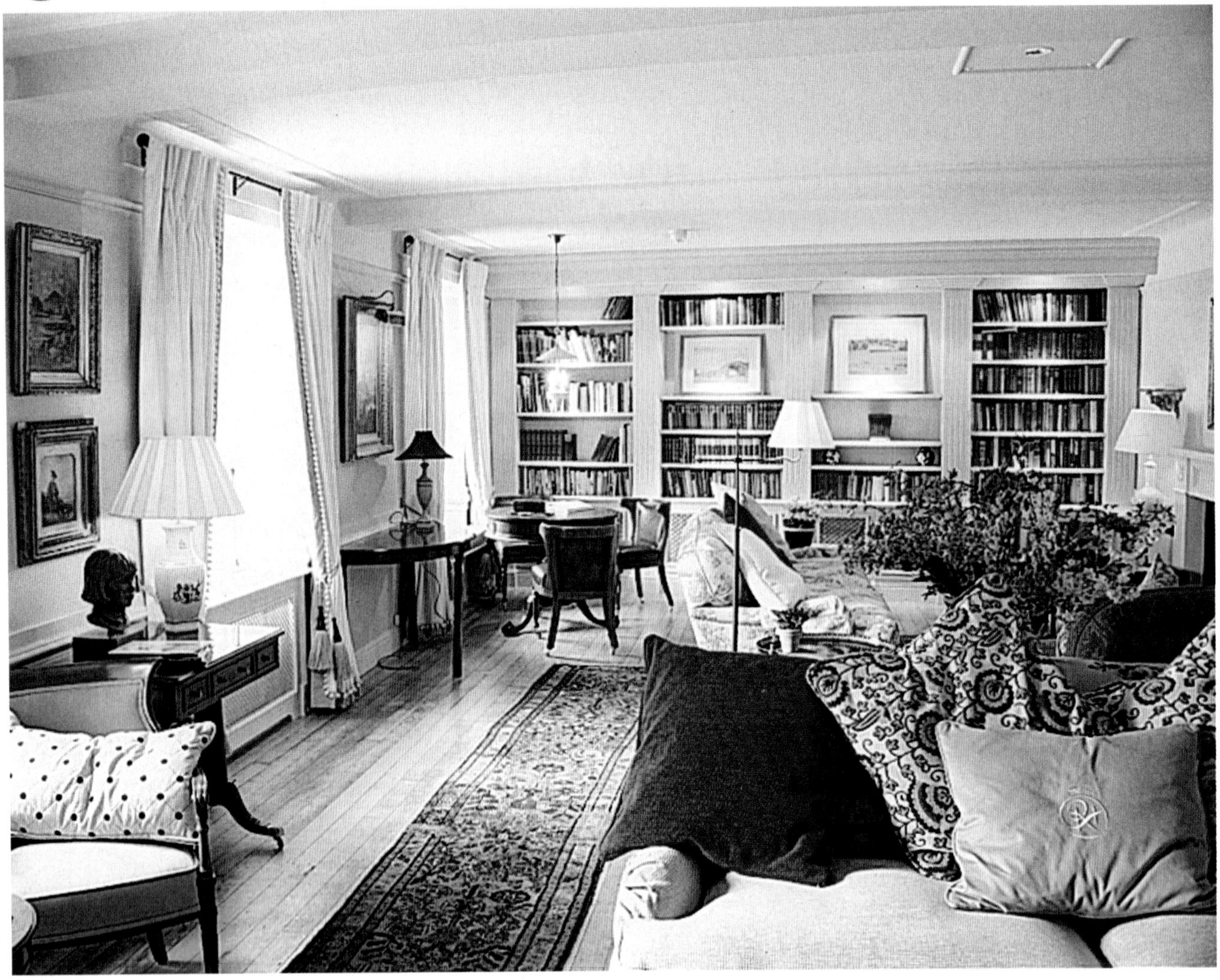

The Royal Hotel

MELVILLE SQUARE, COMRIE, PERTHSHIRE PH6 2DN
TEL: 01764 679200 FAX: 01764 679219 E-MAIL: reception@royalhotel.co.uk

Set in an area of outstanding natural beauty, this former inn was once frequented by personalities such as Rob Roy McGregor and Queen Victoria, whose stay bestowed the name of The Royal Hotel on Comrie's major inn. Its homely yet luxurious and elegant atmosphere is enhanced by open log fires, period furnishings and genuine Highland hospitality provided by the cheerful staff and the Milsom family, who also own the Tufton Arms Hotel, Appleby. Each of the 11 bedrooms has been individually designed and shows exceptional attention to detail. An ideal place to unwind, the comfortable Lounge Bar is popular for pre-dinner drinks which include a choice of over 130 whiskies. Guests may enjoy Scottish cuisine and fine wines in the conservatory-style Brasserie or the more intimate Royal Restaurant, where Chef David Milsom and his team, awarded an AA Rosette, create delicious dishes based on fresh local produce. The hotel is located amidst superb walking country; guests can go for gentle walks in the nearby Glens and across the hills and moorlands. The hotel has its own stretch of the river Earn for fishing, and horse riding and fowl or clay pigeon shooting can be arranged. Comrie is surrounded by excellent golf courses, which range from scenic Highland layouts to idyllic parkland settings, such as the famous Gleneagles. Directions: Located in the centre of the village. Price Guide: Single £70; double £110; suite £150.

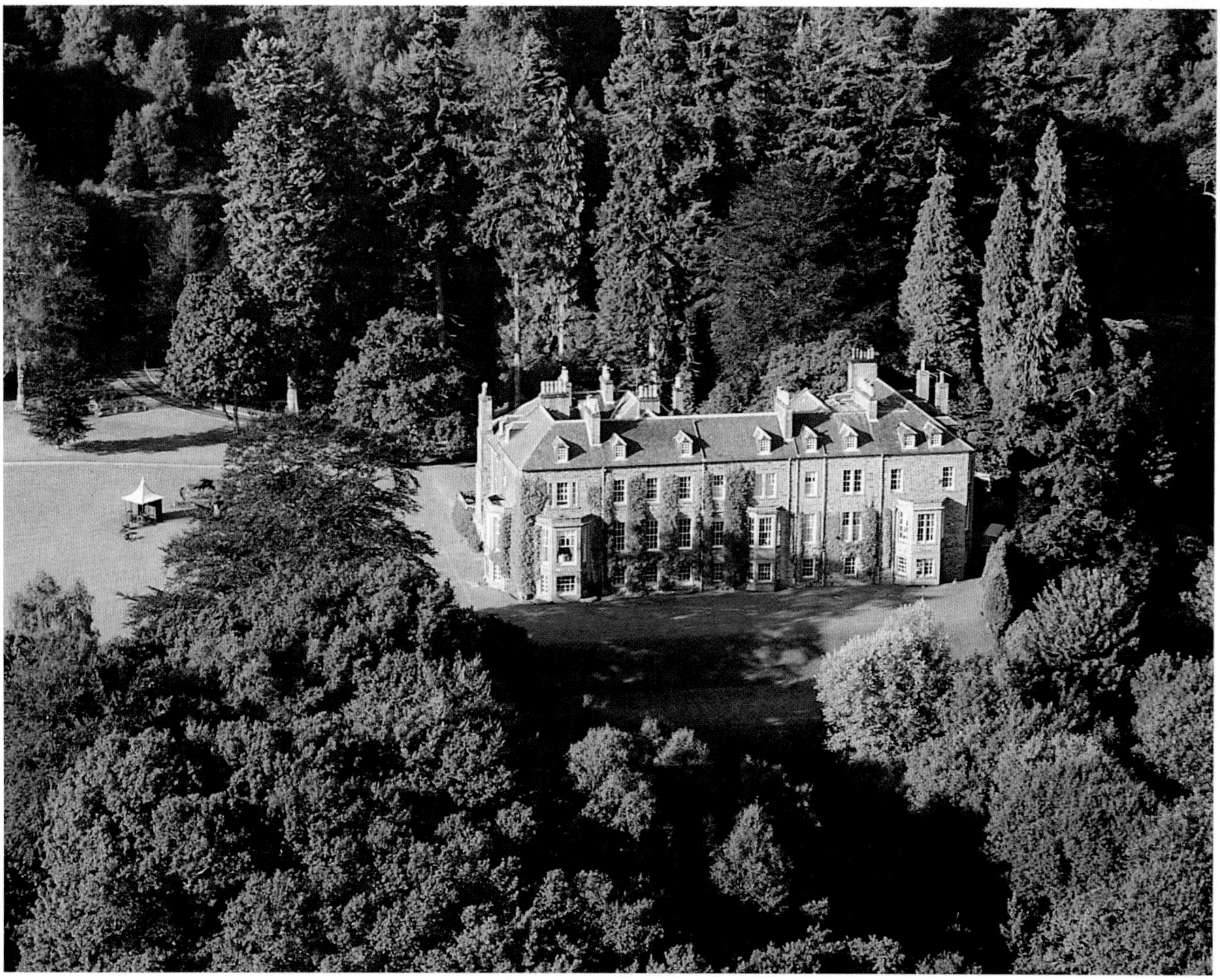

KINNAIRD

KINNAIRD ESTATE, BY DUNKELD, PERTHSHIRE PH8 0LB
TEL: 01796 482440 FAX: 01796 482289 E-MAIL: enquiry@kinnairdestate.com

Offering a panoramic vista across the moors and the Tay valley, Kinnaird is surrounded by a beautiful estate of 9000 acres and is ideally located for those seeking a relaxing break or enthusiasts of outdoor pursuits. Built in 1770, the house has been privately owned by the Ward family since 1927 and was completely renovated by Mrs Constance Ward in 1990. The nine bedrooms are individually decorated with exquisite fabrics, gas log fires and opulent bathrooms. Throughout the house, rare pieces of antique furniture, china and fine paintings abound. The panelled Cedar Room is the essence of comfort, where guests may relax before enjoying gourmet cuisine in the restaurant, enhanced by hand-painted Italian frescoes. The private dining room is furnished in a stylish manner and affords magnificent views of the surrounding Perthshire countryside. The original wine cellars are stocked with an extensive range of wines, liqueurs and malt whiskies. Sporting facilities include salmon and trout fishing, bird-watching and shooting of pheasant, grouse, duck and partridge. The estate also features an all-weather tennis court and croquet lawns. During the months of January and February, the hotel will be closed on Monday, Tuesday and Wednesday. **Directions:** Two miles north of Dunkeld on A9, take B898 for 4½ mile. Price Guide: Double/twin £365–£475. Winter rates £275 or £225 for 2 or more nights.

The Bonham

35 DRUMSHEUGH GARDENS, EDINBURGH EH3 7RN

TEL: RESERVATIONS: 0131 623 6060 **TEL:** 0131 226 6050 **FAX:** 0131 226 6080 **E-MAIL:** **reserve@thebonham.com**

The award-winning boutique style hotel The Bonham is situated just a few minutes walk from the West End of Edinburgh and is equally suitable for a restful weekend or a high-intensity business trip. Whilst many of the original Victorian features of the three converted town houses have been maintained, the interior has been designed to create a contemporary feel of the highest quality. Each room has been elegantly and dramatically created with contemporary furniture and modern art, using rich, bold colours to produce tasteful oversized abundance throughout. The Bonham promises to offer a traditional feel with a modern twist, coupled with impeccable standards and individuality. Purely for pleasure, each of the 48 bedrooms offers 55 channel cable TV, a mini-bar and e-TV, which provides a complete PC capability, Internet and e-mail access as well as DVD video and CD player. The Events Room is a perfect setting for a range of select meetings and private dining, while the Restaurant at The Bonham offers a relaxing ambience and surroundings in which excellent food and drink can be enjoyed. Along with its famous castle and numerous shops, Edinburgh houses Scotland's national galleries and some splendid museums. **Directions:** The hotel is situated in the city's West End. Price Guide: Single: £135–£155; double/twin £165–£235; suites £295.

48 MasterCard VISA AMERICAN EXPRESS M 50

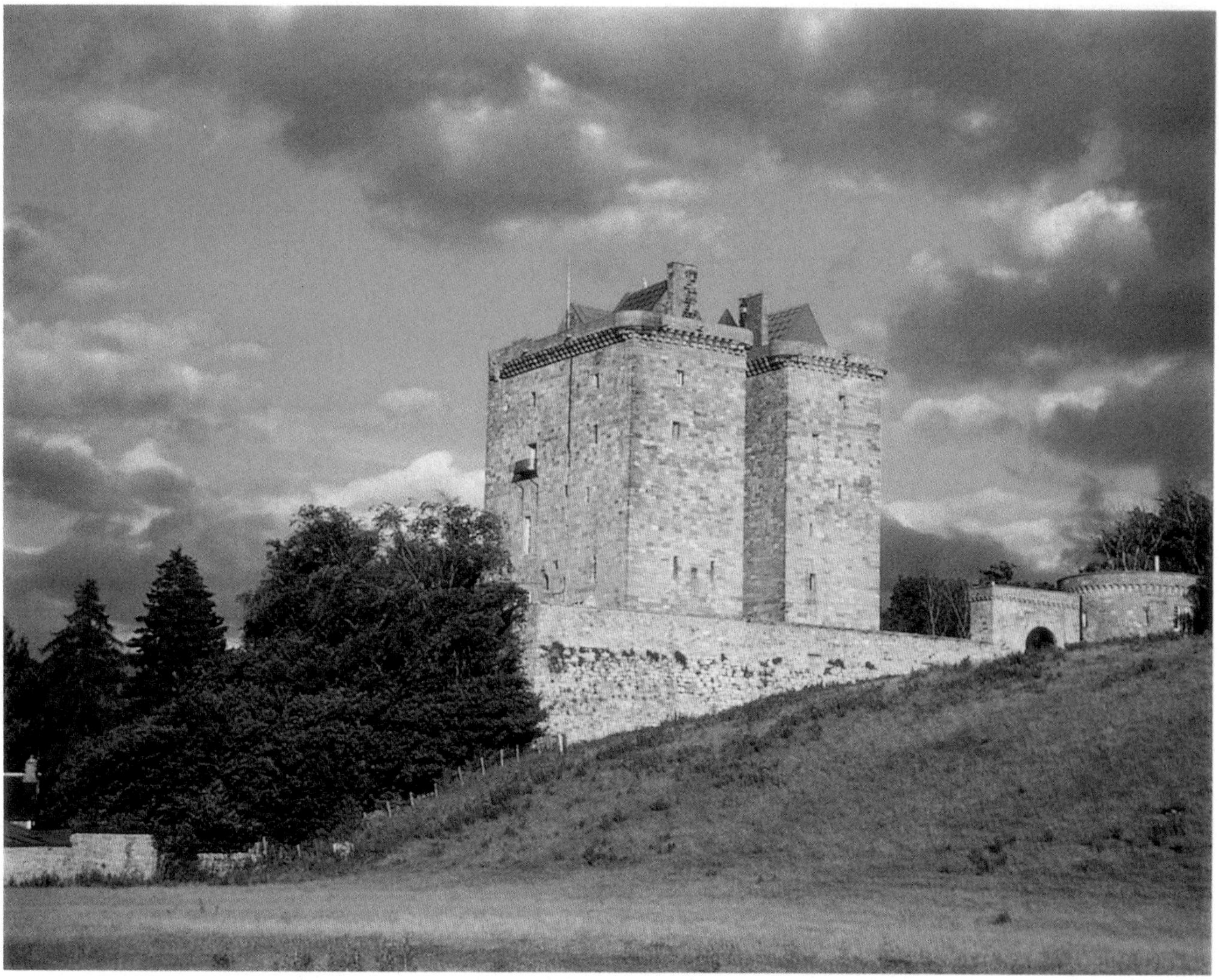

Borthwick Castle

BORTHWICK, NORTH MIDDLETON, MIDLOTHIAN EH23 4QY
TEL: 01875 820514 FAX: 01875 821702

To the south of Edinburgh, off the A7, stands historic Borthwick Castle Hotel, a twenty minute drive from Scotland's capital. Built in 1430 by the Borthwick family, this ancient stronghold has witnessed many of the great events of Scotland's history at first hand. Notably, the safe keeping of Mary Queen of Scots following her wedding to the Earl of Bothwell and a forceful visitation by Oliver Cromwell in 1650. At Borthwick Castle there are 10 bedchambers, each with en suite facilities and six with four-poster beds. In the evening, guests dine in the magnificent setting of the candle-lit Great Hall where a four-course set menu is prepared by the chef. The cooking is traditional Scottish, serving fresh local produce. A comprehensive wine list is complemented by a fine selection of malt whiskies. While the castle caters for banquets of up to 65 guests, it especially welcomes those in search of that intimate dinner for two. In either case, the experience is unforgettable. Open from March to January 3rd. **Directions:** 12 miles south of Edinburgh on the A7. At North Middleton, follow signs for Borthwick. A private road then leads to the castle. Price Guide: Single £80–£100; double/twin £135–£195.

CHANNINGS

SOUTH LEARMONTH GARDENS, EDINBURGH EH4 1EZ

RESERVATIONS: 0131 332 3232 **TEL:** 0131 315 2226 **FAX:** 0131 332 9631 **E-MAIL:** reserve@channings.co.uk

Channings is located on a quiet cobbled street only 10 minutes walk from the centre of Edinburgh, with easy access to the shops on Princes Street and the timeless grandeur of Edinburgh Castle. Formerly 5 Edwardian town houses, the original features have been restored with flair and consideration and the atmosphere is like that of an exclusive country club. Guests can relax in one of the lounges with coffee or afternoon tea. For those who like to browse, the hotel has an interesting collection of antique prints, furniture, objets d'art, periodicals and books. The atmosphere is perfect for discreet company meetings, small conferences and private or corporate events. These may be held in the oak-panelled Library, Kingsleigh or the Conservatory. The warm and richly coloured Restaurant with its Edwardian features is in direct contrast to the contemporary, simple Wine Bar and Conservatory. This award-winning restaurant has the reputation for consistently great cooking, offering a distinctive and contemporary French menu. Channings underwent major renovation at the beginning of 2000 to further raise its level of excellence. Closed for Christmas. **Directions:** Go north-west from Queensferry Street, over Dean Bridge on to Queensferry Road. Take 3rd turning on right down South Learmonth Avenue, turn right at end into South Learmonth Gardens Price Guide: Single £125–£155; double/twin £155–£195; four poster £185–£205; suites £235–£240.

46 MasterCard VISA AMERICAN EXPRESS M 63

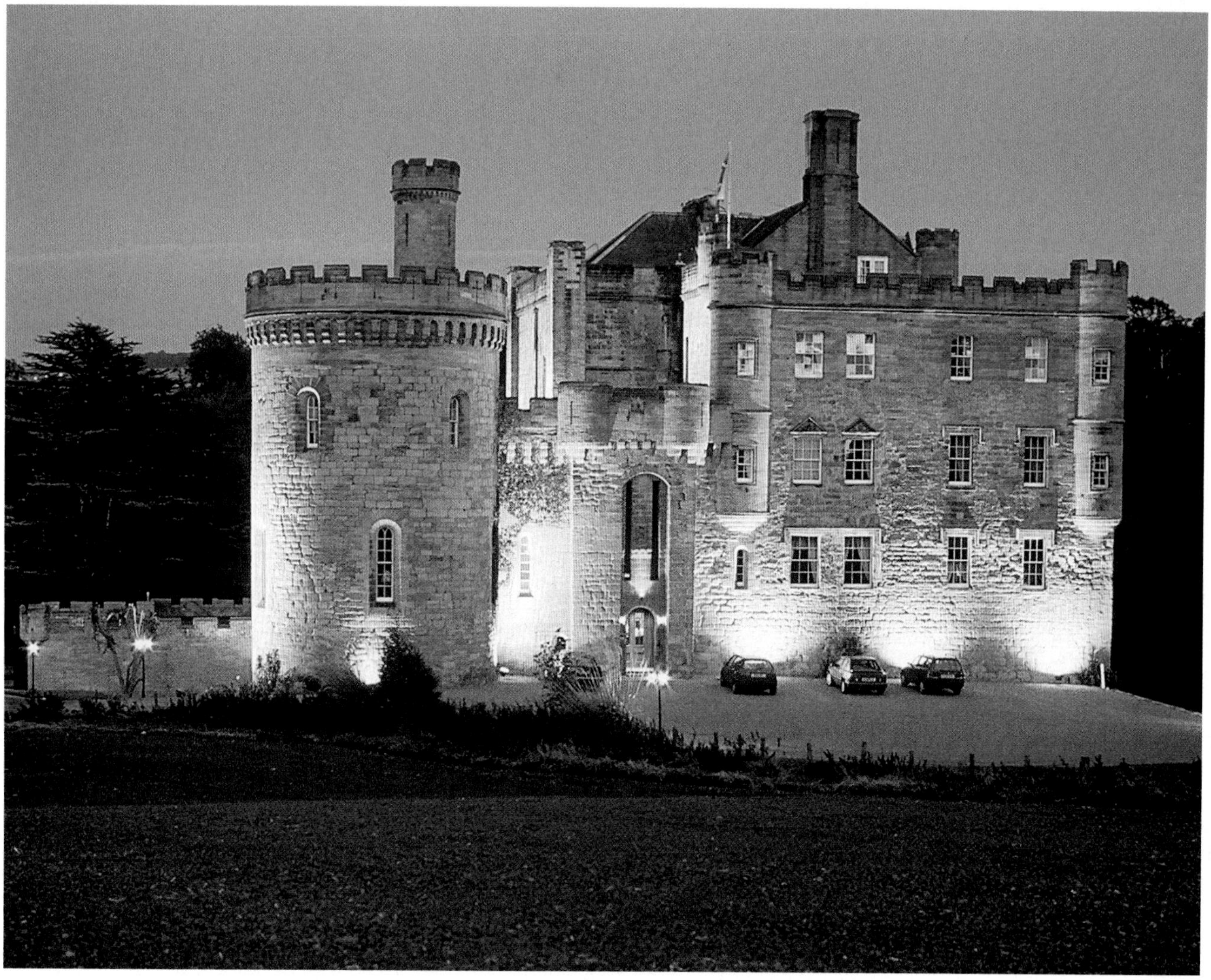

DALHOUSIE CASTLE AND SPA

NR EDINBURGH, BONNYRIGG EH19 3JB

TEL: 01875 820153 **FAX:** 01875 821936 **CONFERENCE FAX:** 01875 823365 **E-MAIL:** enquiries@dalhousiecastle.co.uk

For over 700 years Dalhousie Castle has nestled in beautiful parkland, providing warm Scottish hospitality. There are fascinating reminders of a rich and turbulent history, such as the AA Rosette Vaulted Dungeon Restaurant; a delightful setting in which to enjoy classical French and traditional Scottish 'Castle Cuisine'. 12 of the 28 bedrooms are historically themed and include the James VI, Robert the Bruce and William Wallace (The "de Ramseia" suite houses the 500 year old "Well"). and are complemented by the 5 en suite bedrooms in the 100 year old Lodge. Five carefully renovated function rooms provide a unique setting for conferences, banquets and weddings for up to 120 delegates or guests. Extensive parking and a helipad are on site. Only 7 miles from Edinburgh City Centre and just 14 miles from the International Airport. The Castle is a Scottish Tourist Board 4 Stars classification and Taste of Scotland approved. The new Aqueous Spa includes a hydro pool, Laconium, Ottoman and treatment rooms. The Orangery Restaurant offers contemporary Scottish/European dining. Activities including falconry and clay pigeon shooting can be arranged given prior notice as well as golf at nearby courses. **Directions:** From Edinburgh A7 south, through Newtongrange. Right at Jct onto B704, hotel is ¾ mile. Price Guide: Single from £90; double £115–£275.

THE HOWARD

34 GREAT KING STREET, EDINBURGH BA2 7TB
TEL: RESERVATIONS: 0131 315 2220 TEL: 0131 557 3500 FAX: 0131 557 6515 E-MAIL: res@howardpark.com

Since its conversion from private residence to hotel, The Howard has been sumptuously appointed throughout and offers a service to match the surroundings. The original character of this Georgian town house still prevails. The eighteen bedrooms are individually decorated and include two junior suites and three terrace suites, which benefit from their own private terrace and entrance to Great King Street. All are beautifully furnished with antiques, whilst the Drawing Room centres on an elaborate crystal chandelier. Visitors to The Howard are received as guests in a private home, where the ambience of the welcoming entrance hall and Drawing Room reflects its residential atmosphere. The Howard is an integral part of the largest classified historical monument in Britain: Edinburgh's New Town. Having a private car park to the rear, The Howard is superb city centre base from which to explore Edinburgh's cultural heritage, being in close proximity to such monuments as Edinburgh Castle, the Palace of Holyrood and the Royal Mile. Equally it is just minutes from much of the city's business community. **Directions:** From Queen Street turn north into Dundas Street, then 2nd right into Great King Street. The hotel is on the left. Price Guide: Single £155–£175; double £225–£280; junior suite £295–£325; terrace suite £335–£385.

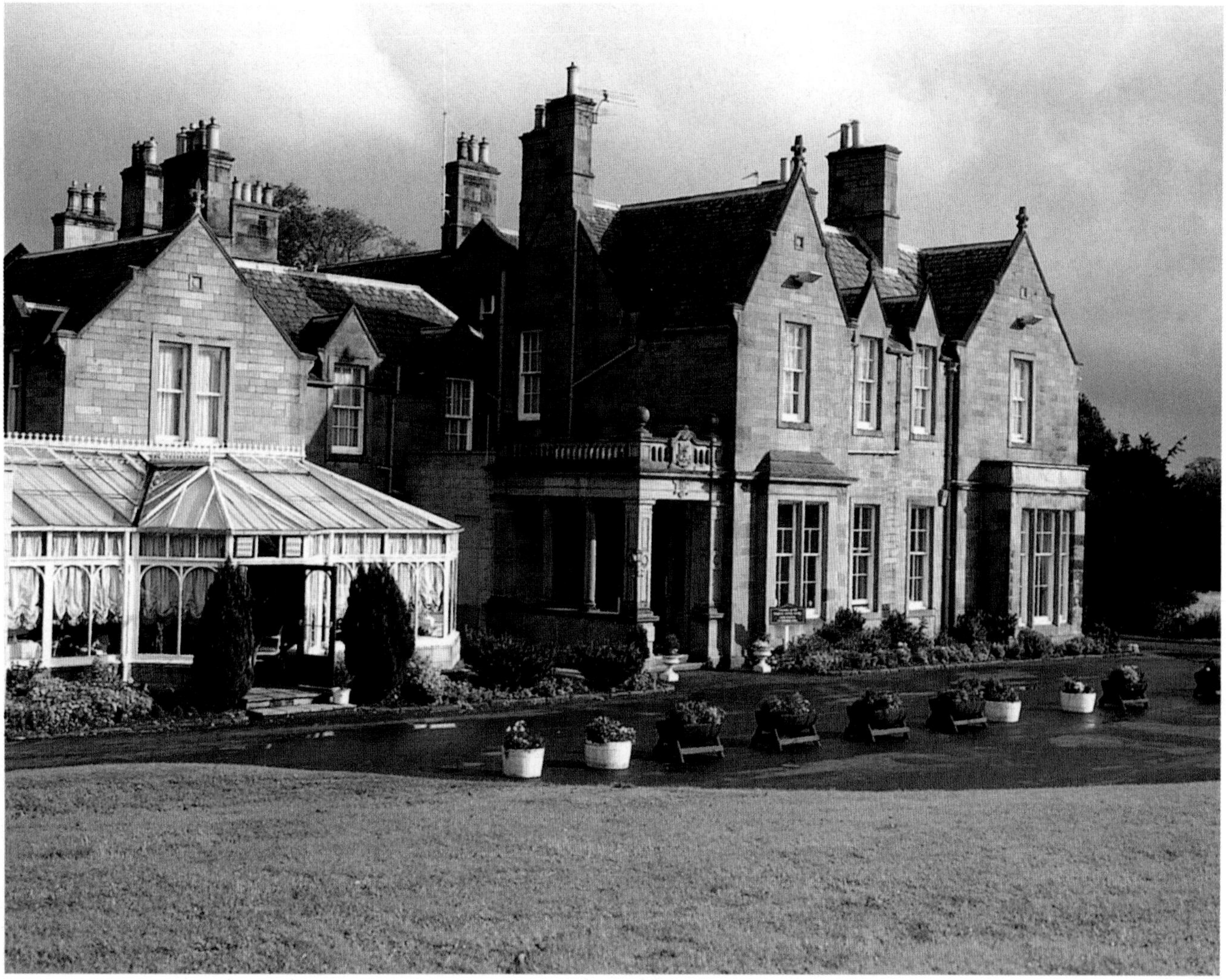

THE NORTON HOUSE HOTEL

INGLISTON, EDINBURGH EH28 8LX

TEL: 0131 333 1275 **FAX:** 0131 333 5305 **E-MAIL:** **events.nhh@arcadianhotels.co.uk**

This Victorian mansion, dating back to 1840, is a part of the Arcadian Hotel Group. Situated in 55 acres of mature parkland, Norton House combines modern comforts with elegance. The 47 en suite bedrooms are bright and spacious, with many facilities, including a video channel and satellite TV. Influenced by the best Scottish and French traditions, the menu offers a balanced choice. Moments away, through leafy woodlands, a former stable block has been converted into The Gathering Bistro and Bar, where drinks and snacks are available to family and friends. Set in a walled garden, it is an ideal venue for the barbecues which are a regular feature in the summer months. The Patio, Veranda and Boardroom lend a sense of occasion to small gatherings, while the Linlithgow Suite can cater for large-scale events such as banquets, weddings and conferences. Norton House is conveniently 1 mile from Edinburgh Airport and 6 miles from the city centre, it is also a base from which to explore the Trossachs, Borders and Lothians **Directions:** From Edinburgh take A8 past airport and hotel is Price Guide: Single £115–£150; double/twin £140–£165; suites £165–£200.

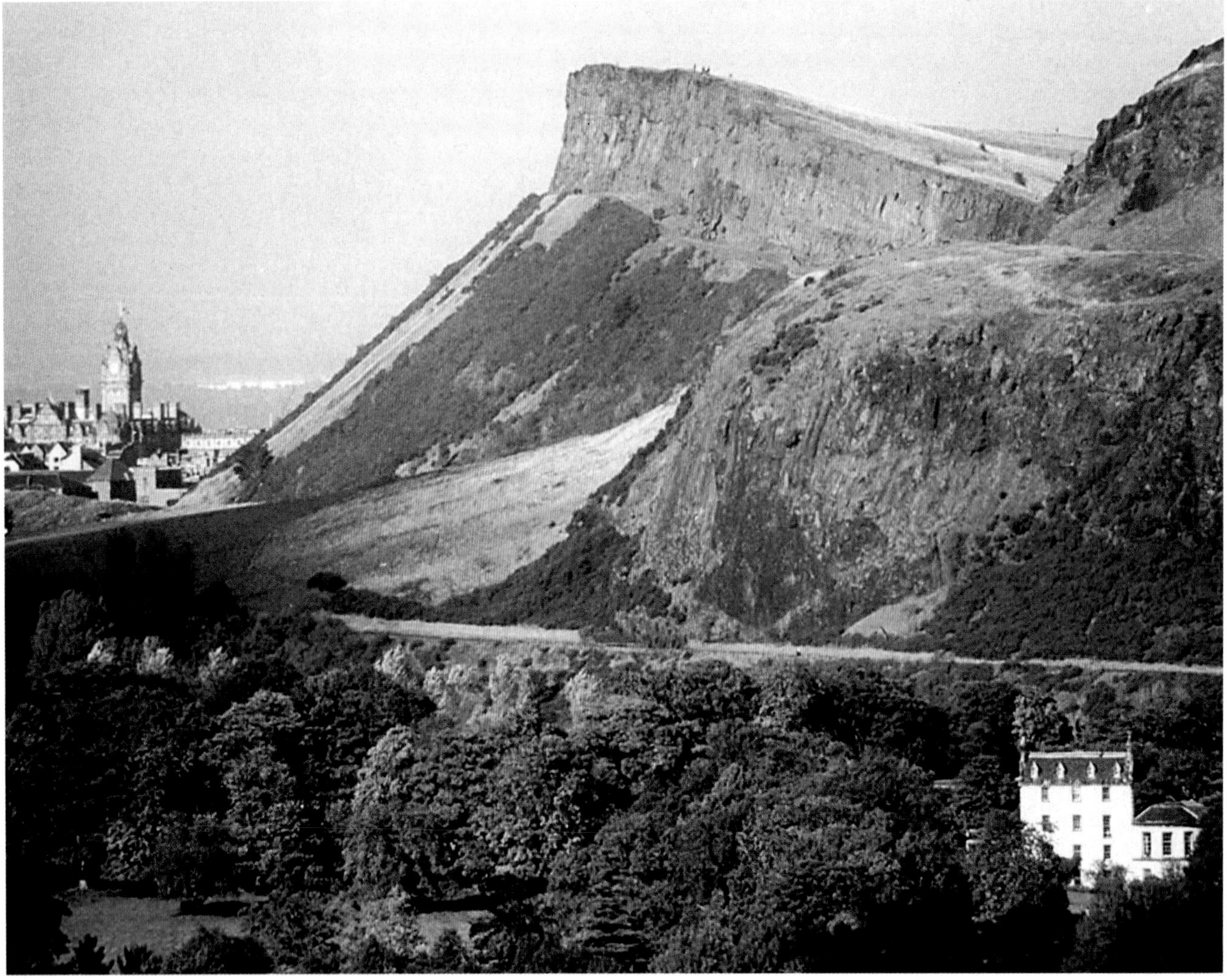

PRESTONFIELD HOUSE

PRIESTFIELD ROAD, EDINBURGH EH16 5UT
TEL: 0131 668 3346 FAX: 0131 668 3976 E-MAIL: info@prestonfieldhouse.com

13 acres of landscaped gardens and a challenging golf course encompass the grounds and parklands of this fine estate. Built in 1687 for the Lord Provost of Edinburgh, Prestonfield House is one of Scotland's finest historic mansions and part of its great architectural heritage. The interior has retained many of its original 17th and 18th century features and houses the family's collection of paintings and antique furniture. An ornate ceiling forms the centrepiece in the Tapestry Room whilst the next door room is entirely panelled in 17th century Spanish leather. The spacious bedrooms are beautifully appointed and are located in either the original house or in the new extension. Every room enjoys spectacular views across the surrounding landscape and gardens which makes it hard to believe that Prestonfield is a city centre hotel, only five minutes by taxi from the centre of Edinburgh. The Old Dining Room serves a mouth-watering à la carte menu comprising traditional cuisine such as grilled turbot steak and fillet of guinea fowl. Five private rooms, varying in size, may be hired for parties, meetings or special occasions. **Directions:** Approaching Edinburgh from the south, follow the City bypass to the Sheriffhall roundabout and take the A7. At Cameron Toll roundabout go straight across and turn right at third set of traffic lights onto Priestfield Road. Price Guide: Single £145–£245 double/twin £145–£245; suite £325.

31 MasterCard VISA AMERICAN EXPRESS M 500

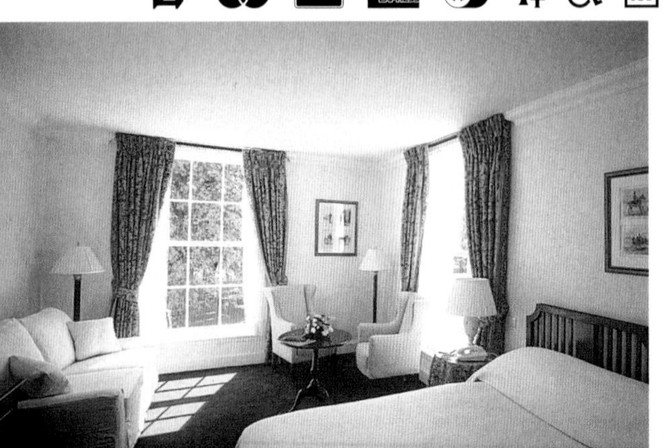

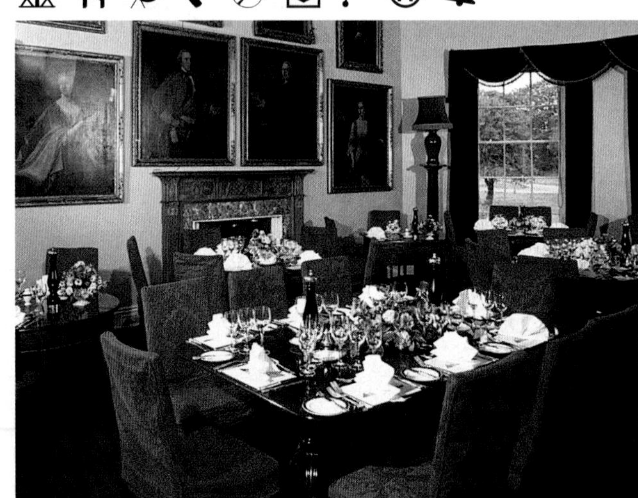

The Roxburghe

38 CHARLOTTE SQUARE, EDINBURGH EH2 4HG
TEL: 0131 240 5500 FAX: 0131 240 5555 E-MAIL: info@roxburghe.macdonald-hotels.co.uk

Offering some of the finest Georgian architecture in Scotland, this hotel provides an ideal base from which to explore the city of Edinburgh. Having undergone an extensive period of renovation in 1999, The Roxburghe has added a distinctly modern wing, carefully designed to complement the Georgian architecture of Adam's original terraced houses. Overlooking Charlotte Square, the classic rooms retain fine period detailing. The rooms in the modern wing are held in contemporary design, with an open aspect across the handsome George Street. The south-facing rooms on the top floor have stunning views across the rooftops to Edinburgh Castle. The Roxburghe's Rosette awarded restaurant is situated in a beautiful Georgian drawing room overlooking Charlotte Square. The cuisine is a blend of classical British style with the best flavours of the world beyond, complemented by a selection of wines from both the old and new worlds. The fitness facilities include a pool, fitness centre, sauna, steam room and solarium. Many rooms are suitable for conference and meeting purposes. Special packages include two to five day beauty breaks with massages and facial treatments. George Street, Prince's Street and Edinburgh Castle are all within easy walking distance. **Directions:** The hotel is 5 minutes from Waverley Station and 20 minutes from Edinburgh Airport. Price Guide: Single £85; double/twin £120; suite £240.

CALLY PALACE HOTEL

GATEHOUSE OF FLEET, DUMFRIES & GALLOWAY DG7 2DL

TEL: 01557 814341 FAX: 01557 814522 E-MAIL: info@callypalace.co.uk

Set in over 100 acres of forest and parkland, on the edge of Robert Burns country, this 18th century country house has been restored to its former glory by the McMillan family, the proprietors since 1981. On entering the hotel, guests will initially be impressed by the grand scale of the interior. Two huge marble pillars support the original moulded ceiling of the entrance hall. All the public rooms have ornate ceilings, original marble fireplaces and fine reproduction furniture. Combine these with grand, traditional Scottish cooking and you have a hotel par excellence. The 56 en suite bedrooms have been individually decorated. Some are suites with a separate sitting room; others are large enough to accommodate a sitting area. An indoor leisure complex, completed in the style of the marble entrance hall, includes heated swimming pool, Jacuzzi, saunas and solarium. The hotel has an all-weather tennis court, a putting green, croquet and a lake. Also, for exclusive use of hotel guests is an 18-hole golf course, par 70, length 5,802 yards set around the lake in the 150 acre grounds. Special weekend and over-60s breaks are available out of season. Closed January. **Directions:** Sixty miles west of Carlisle, 1–1½ miles from Gatehouse of Fleet junction on the main A75 road. : Price Guide: (including dinner)Single £71–£89; double/twin £128–£178 per night (min 2 nights).

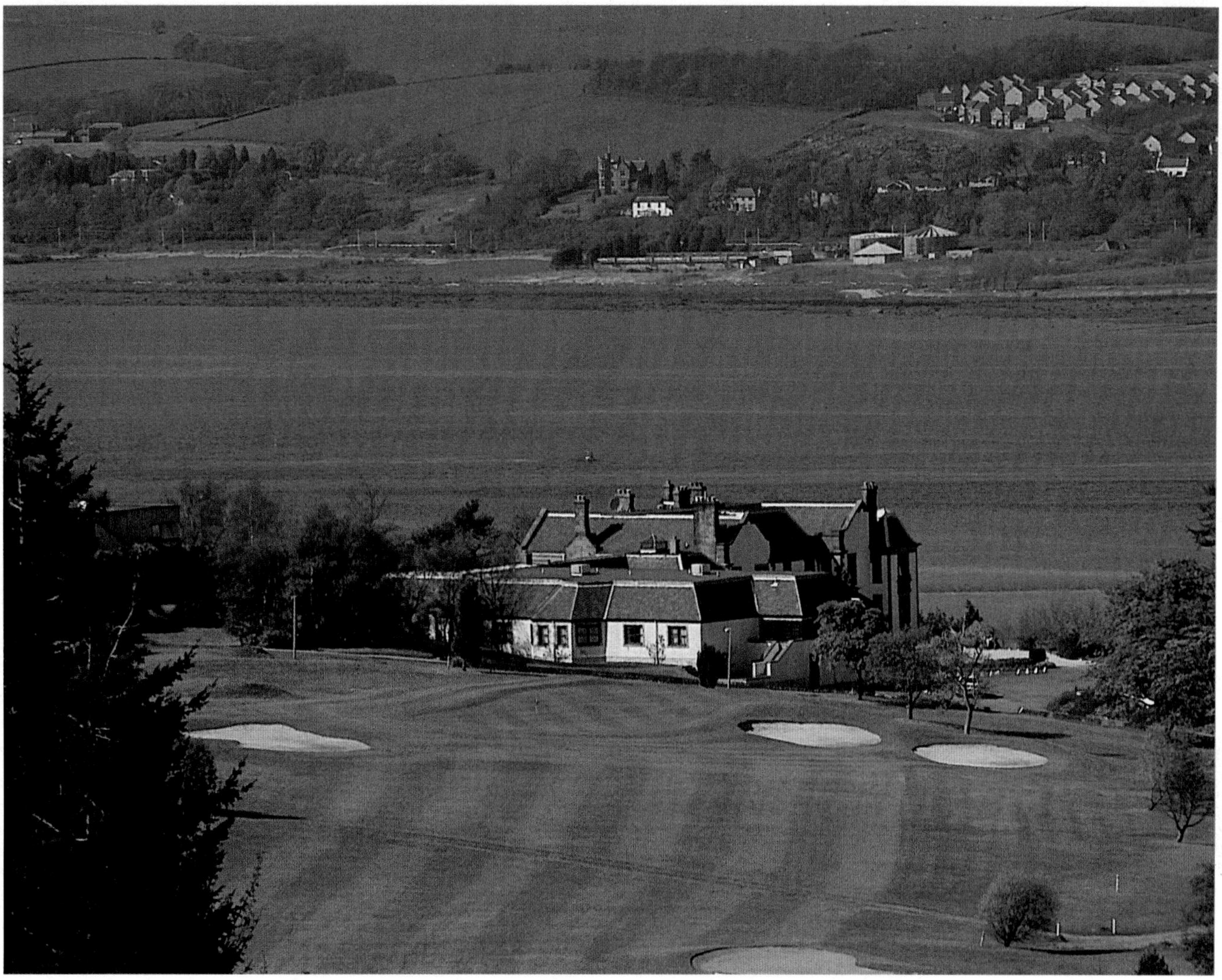

Gleddoch House

LANGBANK, RENFREWSHIRE PA14 6YE
TEL: 01475 540711 FAX: 01475 540201

Once the home of a Glasgow shipping baron, Gleddoch House stands in 360 acres, with dramatic views across the River Clyde to Ben Lomond and the hills beyond. The individually appointed bedrooms all have en suite facilities and some have four-poster beds. Executive rooms and suites and family rooms are also available. There are also self-catering lodges on the estate. Other amenities include a range of meeting rooms to cater for up to 120 delegates theatre style. The Restaurant is renowned for its award-winning modern Scottish cuisine and is complemented by a comprehensive wine list. On the estate a series of activities are available such as golf, clay pigeon shooting, archery and off-road driving, making Gleddoch an ideal venue to host corporate events. Additionally the equestrian centre caters for all levels, from trekking to pony rides and individual tuition. Gleddoch's location offers an experience of a bygone era yet amid the sophistication that today's traveller requires. A range of short breaks, golfing packages and gourmet events are available throughout the year. Glasgow Airport is only 10 minutes drive away and the City Centre, 20 minutes. **Directions:** M8 towards Greenock; take B789 Langbank/ Houston exit. Follow signs to left and then right after 1/2 mile; hotel is on left Price Guide: Single £99; double/twin £150; suite £185.

MACDONALD CRUTHERLAND HOUSE HOTEL

STRATHAVEN ROAD, EAST KILBRIDE G75 0QZ
TEL: 01355 577000 FAX: 01355 220855 E-MAIL: crutherland@macdonald–hotels.co.uk

Standing in 37 acres of garden and woodland just outside the market town of Strathaven, which became prosperous in the middle ages because of the silk industry, the Crutherland is a fine example of a great Scottish house restored in superb style. It is extravagantly decorated and boasts every luxury whilst evoking an age of elegance. The Crutherland House was built in 1705 as a dower house for the Lady Dowager from Torrance Castle, which was situated in what is now Calderglen Country Park. After being home to many families it was converted into a hotel in 1964 and recently had a £6million refurbishment which has enhanced and added to every facility. Each of the 76 spacious bedrooms has views over the grounds and all comforts from satellite television to hospitality tray and 24-hour service. The best of Scottish and international cuisine is served in the attractive restaurant and less formal meals can be enjoyed in the lively Peligrino's Cafe Bar. A new leisure club features an 18-metre swimming pool, high-tech gymnasium, sauna and four beauty treatment rooms. The hotel also offers extensive business meeting facilities including 11 conference suites. Glasgow is within easy reach and Caldergren Country Park and Strathclyde Park are worth relaxing visits. **Directions:** From M74, exit at Jct5. Take A726 to East Kilbride and follow signs for Strathaven. Price Guide: Single £89–£105; double/twin £90–£130; suites £150–£200.

www.johansens.com/macdonaldcrutherlandhouse

Dalmunzie House

SPITTAL O'GLENSHEE, BLAIRGOWRIE, PERTHSHIRE PH10 7QG
TEL: 01250 885224 FAX: 01250 885225 E-MAIL: dalmunzie@aol.com

Dalmunzie House is beautifully tucked away high in the Scottish Highlands, 18 miles north of Blairgowrie and 15 miles south of Braemar. Standing in its own mountainous 6,000-acre sporting estate, it is run by Simon and Alexandra Winton. Guests come to enjoy the relaxed family atmosphere which, together with unobtrusive service and attention, ensures a comfortable stay. The bedrooms are individual in character, some with antiques, others romantically set in the turrets of the house, all tastefully decorated. Delicately cooked traditional Scottish fare is created from local ingredients fresh from the hills and lochs. The menu changes daily and meals are served in the dining room, accompanied by wines from the well-stocked cellar. Among the sporting activities available on site are golf (the 9-hole course is one of the highest in Britain) and shooting for grouse, ptarmigan and black game. Other country pursuits include river and loch fishing, clay pigeon shooting, mountain biking, stalking for red deer and pony-trekking. Glenshee Ski Centre is 6 miles away: it offers cross-country and downhill skiing. Closer to home, the hotel games room provides more sedate pastimes for all the family. Closed late November to 28 December. Special winter/skiing rates. **Directions:** Dalmunzie is on the A93 at the Spittal O'Glenshee, south of Braemar. Price Guide: Single £41–£63; double/twin £62–£114.

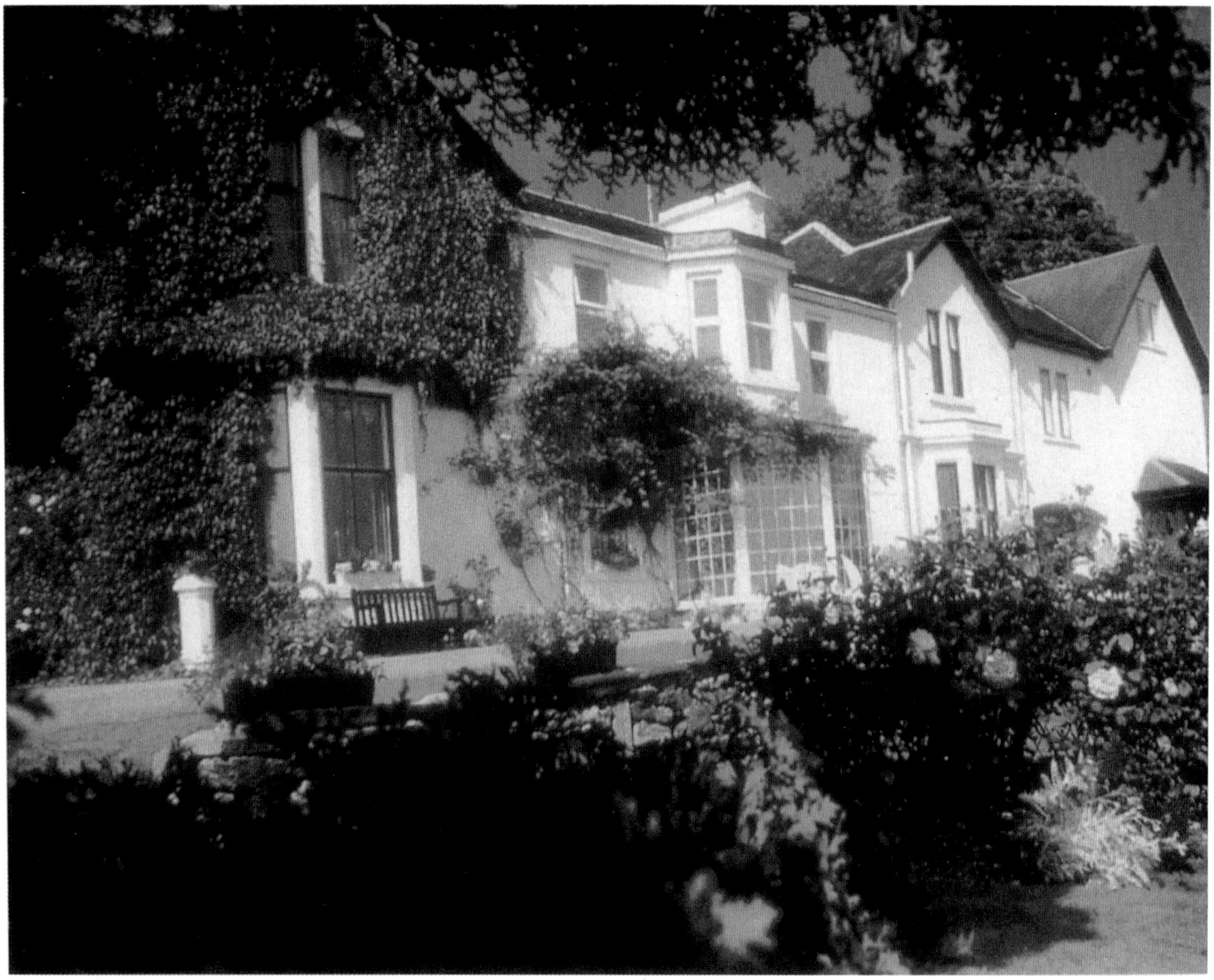

ENMORE HOTEL

MARINE PARADE, KIRN, DUNOON, ARGYLL PA23 8HH
TEL: 01369 702230 FAX: 01369 702148 E-MAIL: enmorehotel@btinternet.com

Known as the jewel on the Clyde, the waterfront town of Dunoon on the Cowal peninsula is often regarded as the gateway to the Western Highlands yet only ¾ hour from Glasgow airport. Enmore Hotel is an attractive house, built in 1785 as a summer retreat for a wealthy cotton merchant. It has since been fully restored by owners David and Angela Wilson. Pretty country wallpaper and bright fabrics characterise the bedrooms, with fluffy towelling robes and flowers among the extras. One of the bedrooms has a double whirlpool bath complete with underwater lighting and another has a four-poster bed with a Jacuzzi. In the restaurant, the emphasis is on the use of fresh, local produce to create traditional Scottish dishes. Typical choices may include Arbroath smokies, haggis soup, kippers or the best fillet steaks available in Scotland. Chef-patron David Wilson offers a five-course table d'hôte along with an á la carte menu each evening. Two international-standard squash courts are available. Dunoon is well equipped with recreational amenities, including bowling, tennis, sailing and a championship golf course. **Directions:** Kirn is on the A815, north-west of Dunoon (A885). A continuous car-ferry crosses to and from Gourock across the Firth of Clyde Price Guide: Single £49–£79; double/twin £78–£158.

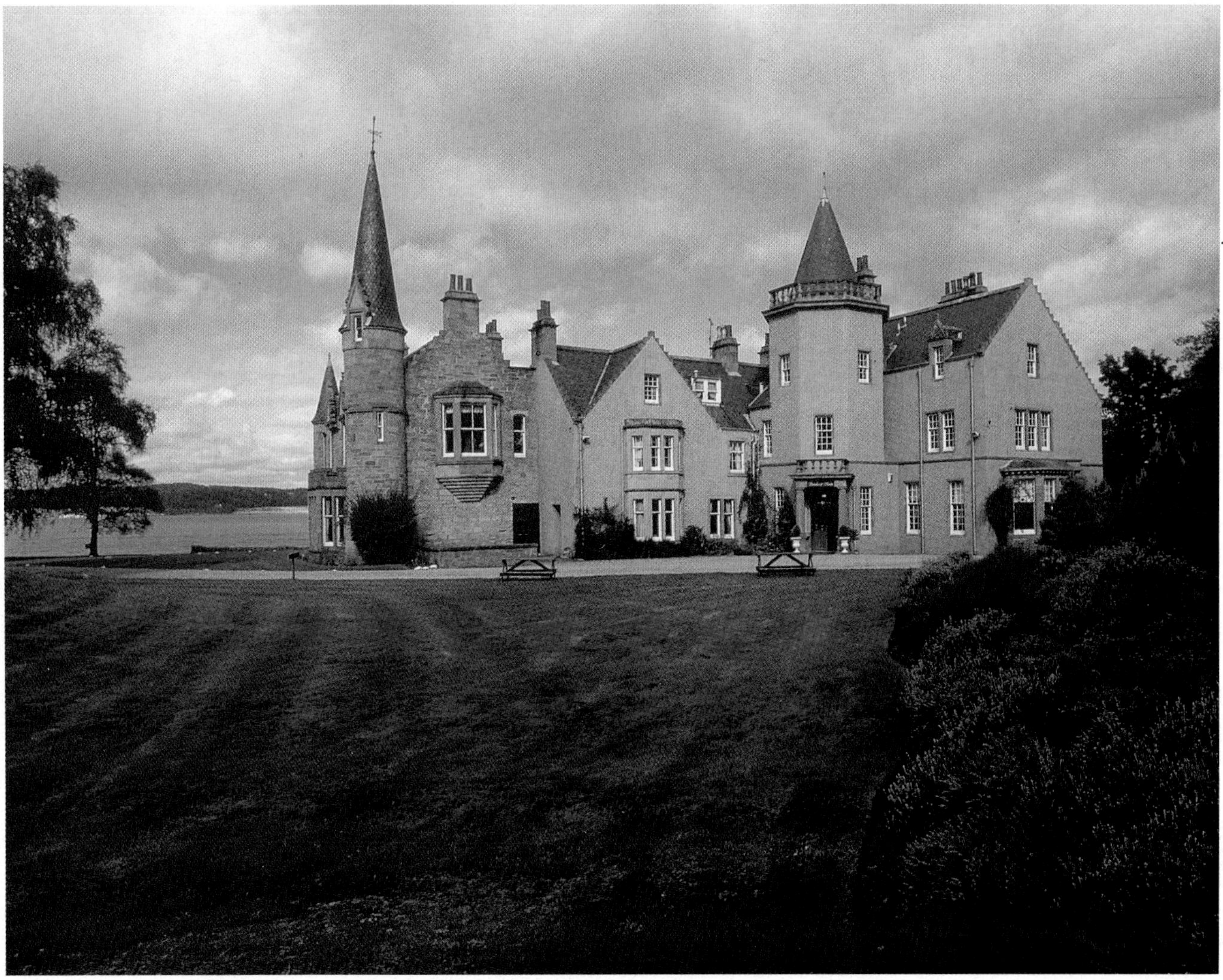

BUNCHREW HOUSE HOTEL

INVERNESS, SCOTLAND IV3 8TA

TEL: 01463 234917 FAX: 01463 710620 E-MAIL: welcome@bunchrew–inverness.co.uk

This splendid 17th century Scottish mansion, owned by Graham and Janet Cross, is set amidst 20 acres of landscaped gardens and woodlands on the shores of the Beauly Firth. Guests can enjoy breathtaking views of Ben Wyvis and the Black Isle, while just yards from the house the sea laps at the garden walls. Bunchrew has been carefully restored to preserve its heritage, while still giving its guests the highest standards of comfort and convenience. A continual schedule of refurbishment is on-going. The luxury suites are beautifully furnished and decorated to enhance their natural features. The elegant panelled drawing room is the ideal place to relax at any time, while during the winter log fires lend it an added appeal which has given the hotel 4 Star status. In the candle-lit restaurant the traditional cuisine includes prime Scottish beef, fresh lobster and langoustines, locally caught game and venison and freshly grown vegetables which has been rewarded with two AA Rosettes. A carefully chosen wine list complements the menu. Local places of interest include Cawdor Castle, Loch Ness, Castle Urquhart and a number of beautiful glens. For those who enjoy sport there is skiing at nearby Aviemore, sailing, cruising and golf. **Directions:** From Inverness follow signs to Beauly, Dingwall on the A862. One mile from the outskirts of Inverness the entrance to Bunchrew House is on the right Price Guide: Single £80–£130; double/twin £110–£200.

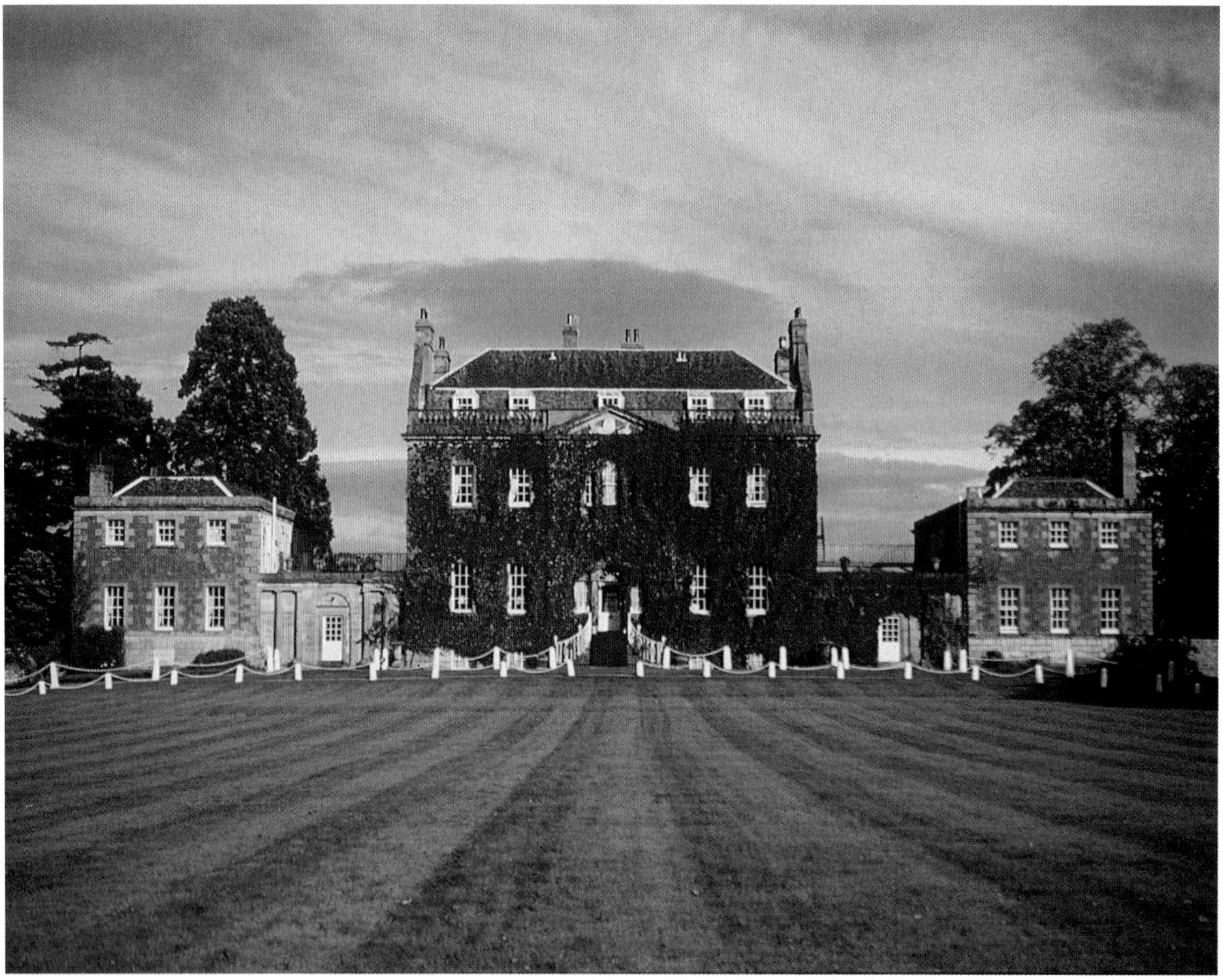

Culloden House Hotel

INVERNESS, INVERNESS-SHIRE IV2 7BZ
TEL: 01463 790461 FAX: 01463 792181 E-MAIL: info@cullodenhouse.co.uk

A majestic circular drive leads to the splendour of this handsome Georgian mansion, battle headquarters of Bonnie Prince Charlie 253 years ago. Three miles from Inverness this handsome Palladian country house stands in 40 acres of beautiful gardens and peaceful parkland roamed by roe deer. Princes past and present and guests from throughout the world have enjoyed the hotel's ambience and hospitality. Rich furnishings, sparkling chandeliers, impressive Adam fireplaces and ornate plaster reliefs add to the grandness of the hotel's luxurious, high-ceilinged rooms. The bedrooms are appointed to the highest standard many having four-poster beds and Jacuzzis. Four non-smoking suites are in the Pavilion Annex which overlooks a three-acre walled garden and two in the newly renovated West Pavilion. In the Dining Room guests can savour superb cuisine prepared by chef Michael Simpson, who trained at the Gleneagles Hotel and the Hamburg Conference Centre. There is an outdoor tennis court and indoor sauna. Shooting, fishing and pony-trekking can be arranged, while nearby are Cawdor Castle, the Clava Cairns Bronze Age burial ground and Culloden battlefield. AA 4 stars and 2 Rosettes, Scottish Tourist Board 4 stars. From USA Toll Free Fax/Phone 0800 980 4561 **Directions:** Take the A96 going east from Inverness and turn right to Culloden. Price Guide: Single £85–£150; double/twin £130–£235; suite: £235–£275.

Ednam House Hotel

BRIDGE STREET, KELSO, ROXBURGHSHIRE TD5 7HT
TEL: 01573 224168 FAX: 01573 226319

Overlooking the River Tweed, in 3 acres of gardens, Ednam House is one of the region's finest examples of Georgian architecture. This undulating, pastoral countryside was immortalised by Sir Walter Scott. Ednam House has been owned and managed by the Brooks family for over 70 years, spanning four generations. Although the grandiose splendour may seem formal, the warm, easy-going atmosphere is all-pervasive. The lounges and bars are comfortably furnished and command scenic views of the river and grounds. All 32 bedrooms are en suite, individually decorated and well equipped. In the elegant dining room which overlooks the river, a blend of traditional and creative Scottish cuisine, using fresh local produce, is served. The wine list is very interesting and reasonably priced. Ednam House is extremely popular with fishermen, the Borders being renowned for its salmon and trout. Other field sports such as stalking, hunting and shooting can be arranged as can riding, golfing and cycling. Local landmarks include the abbeys of Kelso, Melrose, Jedburgh and Dryburgh. Closed Christmas and New Year. **Directions:** From the south, reach Kelso via A698; from the north, via A68. Hotel is just off market square by the river. Price Guide: Single from £58; double/twin £76–£107.

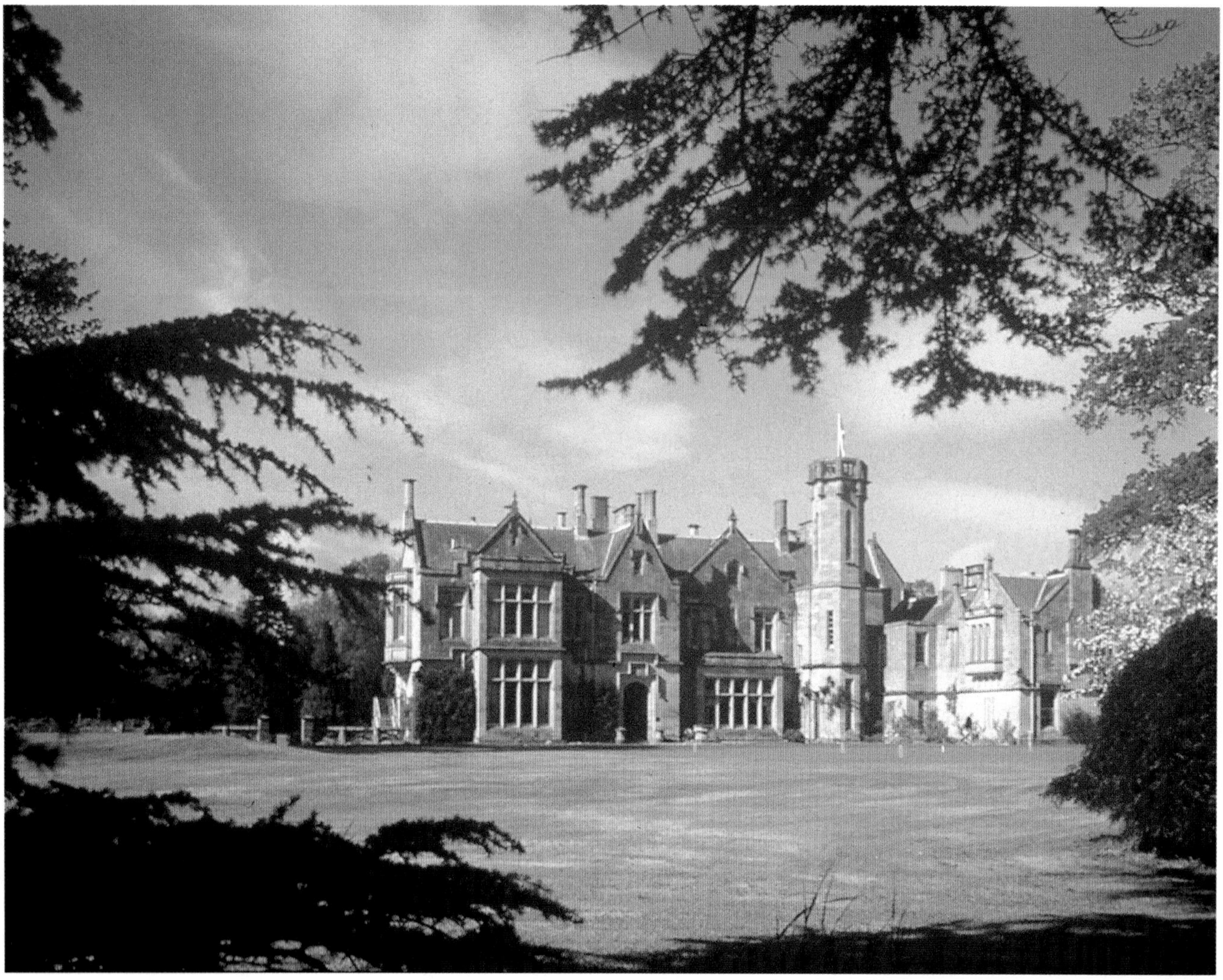

THE ROXBURGHE HOTEL & GOLF COURSE

KELSO, ROXBURGHSHIRE TD5 8JZ
TEL: 01573 450331 FAX: 01573 450611 E-MAIL: hotel@roxburghe.net

Converted by its owners, the Duke and Duchess of Roxburghe, into a luxury hotel of character and charm, The Roxburghe is situated in over 200 acres of rolling grounds on the bank of the River Teviot. There are 22 bedrooms, including four poster rooms and suites, and like the spacious reception rooms, they are furnished with care and elegance. The menu, which is changed daily, reflects the hotel's position at the source of some of Britain's finest fish, meat and game – salmon and trout from the waters of the Tweed, or grouse, pheasant and venison from the Roxburghe estate – complemented with wines from the Duke's own cellar. Fine whiskies are served in the Library Bar, with its log fire and leather-bound tomes. The Beauty Clinic Elixir brings to guests the régimes of Decleor, Paris. Surrounding the hotel is the magnificent Roxburghe Golf Course, designed by Dave Thomas. This parkland course is the only championship standard golf course in the Scottish Borders. A full sporting programme can be arranged, including fly and coarse fishing, and falconry. The shooting school offers tuition in game and clay shooting. Seven great country houses are within easy reach including Floors Castle, the home of the Duke and Duchess of Roxburghe. **Directions:** The hotel is at Heiton, just off the A698 Kelso–Jedburgh road Price Guide: Single £120; double/twin £165; 4-poster £205; suite £255.

ARDANAISEIG

KILCHRENAN BY TAYNUILT, ARGYLL PA35 1HE
TEL: 01866 833333 FAX: 01866 833222 E-MAIL: ardanaiseig@clara.net

This romantic small luxury hotel, built in 1834, stands alone in a setting of almost surreal natural beauty at the foot of Ben Cruachan. Directly overlooking Loch Awe and surrounded by wild wooded gardens, Ardanaiseig is evocative of the romance and history of the Highlands. Skilful restoration has ensured that this lovely old mansion has changed little since it was built. The elegant drawing room has log fires, bowls of fresh flowers, superb antiques, handsome paintings and marvellous views of the islands in the Loch and of faraway mountains. The traditional library, sharing this outlook, is ideal for postprandial digestifs. The charming bedrooms are peaceful, appropriate to the era of the house, yet equipped thoughtfully with all comforts. True Scottish hospitality is the philosophy of the Ardanaiseig Restaurant, renowned for its inspired use of fresh produce from the Western Highlands. The wine list is magnificent. Artistic guests enjoy the famous 100 acre Ardanaiseig gardens and nature reserve, filled with exotic shrubs and trees brought back from the Himalayas over the years. Brilliant rhododendrons and azaleas add a riot of colour. The estate also offers fishing, boating, tennis and croquet (snooker in the evenings) and exhilarating hill or lochside walks.

Directions: Reaching Taynuilt on A85, take B845 to Kilchrenan

Price Guide: Single £80–£119; double/twin £108–£230.

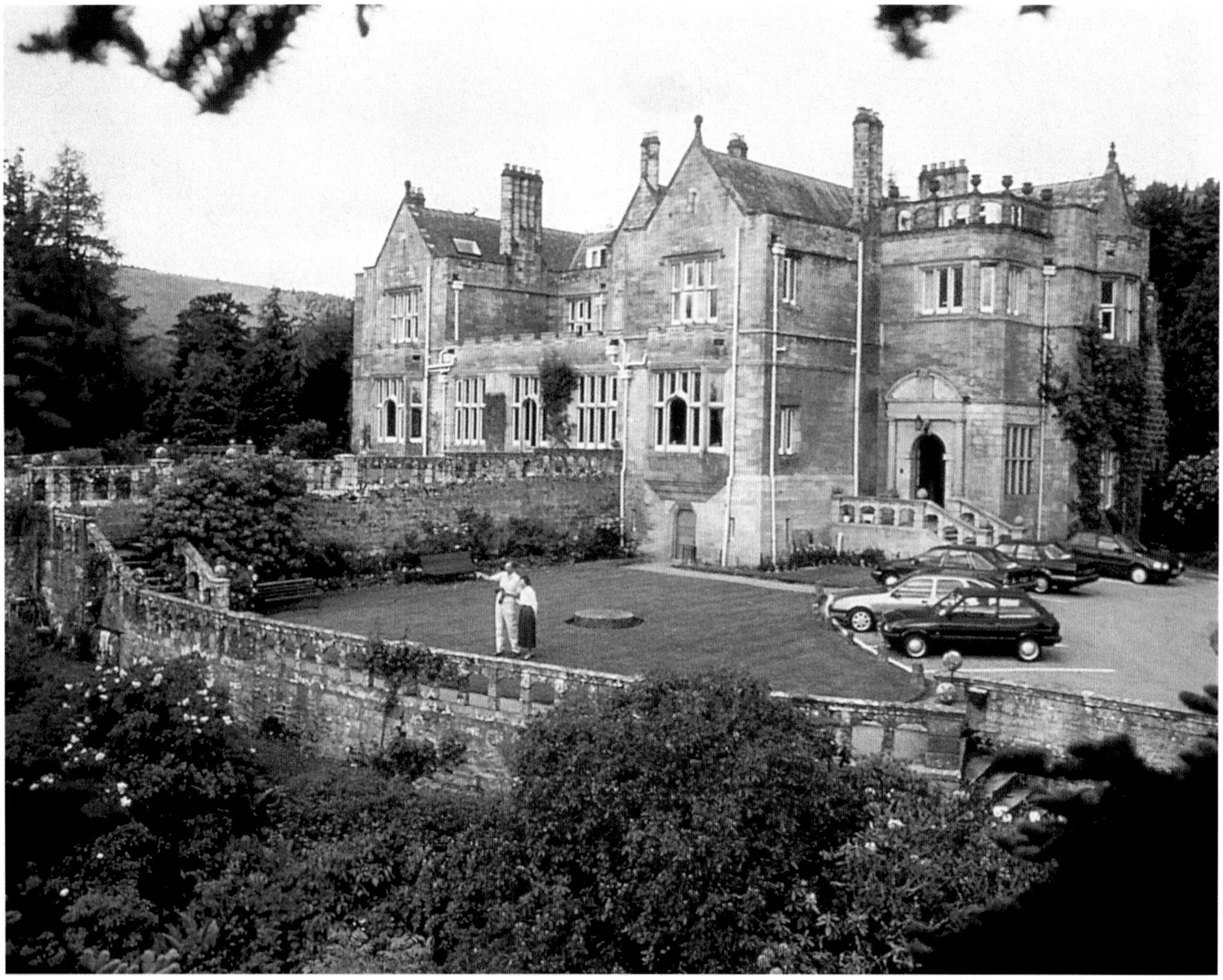

KILDRUMMY CASTLE HOTEL

KILDRUMMY, BY ALFORD, ABERDEENSHIRE AB33 8RA
TEL: 019755 71288 FAX: 019755 71345 E-MAIL: bookings@kildrummycastlehotel.co.uk

In the heart of Donside near to the renowned Kildrummy Castle Gardens and overlooking the ruins of the original 13th century castle from which it takes its name, Kildrummy Castle Hotel offers a rare opportunity to enjoy the style and elegance of a bygone era combined with all the modern comforts of a first-class hotel. Recent improvements have not detracted from the turn-of-the century interior, featuring the original wall tapestries and oak-panelled walls and high ceilings. The bedrooms, some with four-poster beds, all have en suite bathrooms. All have been refurbished recently to a high standard. The hotel restaurant was runner-up for Johansens 1996 Restaurant Award. Chef Kenneth White prepares excellent menus using regional produce that includes local game and both fish and shellfish from the Moray Firth. Kildrummy Castle is ideally located for touring Royal Deeside and Balmoral, the Spey Valley, Aberdeen and Inverness, while the surrounding Grampian region has more castles than any other part of Scotland – 8 of the National Trust for Scotland's finest properties are within an hour's drive of the hotel. Also within an hour's drive are more than 20 golf courses. Visitors can discover the 'Scotch Whisky Trail' and enjoy a tour of some of Scotland's most famous distilleries. **Directions:** Off the A97 Ballater/Huntly road, 35 miles west of Aberdeen. Price Guide: Single £90; double/twin £145–£180.

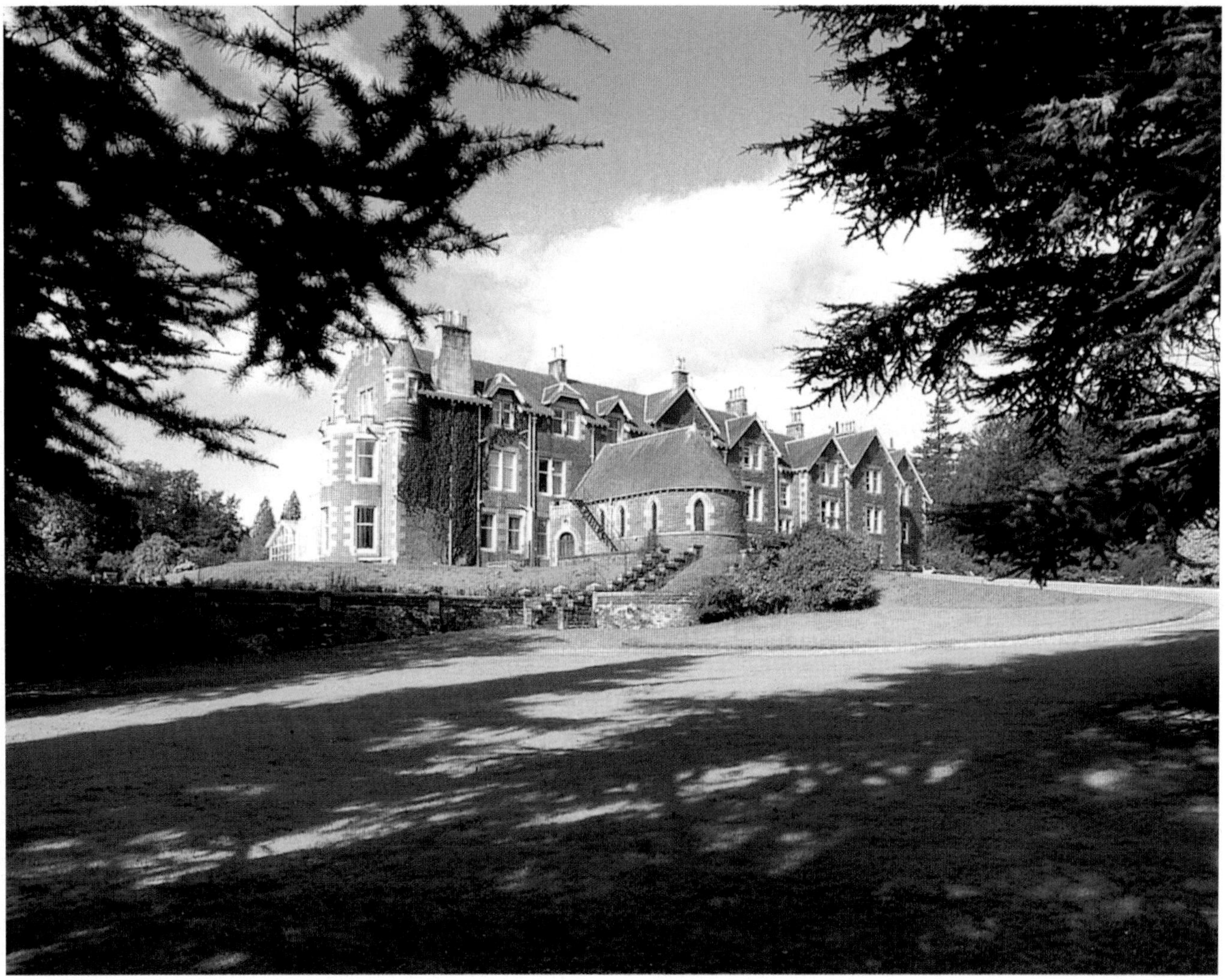

CROMLIX HOUSE

KINBUCK, BY DUNBLANE, PERTHSHIRE FK15 9JT

TEL: 01786 822125 FAX: 01786 825450 E-MAIL: reservations@cromlixhouse.com

Set in a 2,000 acre estate in the heart of Perthshire, just off the A9, the STB 5 Star Cromlix House is a rare and relaxing retreat. Built as a family home in 1874, much of the house remains unchanged including many fine antiques acquired over the generations. Proprietors David and Ailsa Assenti are proud of their tradition of country house hospitality. The individually designed bedrooms and spacious suites have been redecorated with period fabrics to enhance the character and fine furniture whilst retaining the essential feeling of a much loved home. Unpretentious, restful and most welcoming, the large public rooms have open fires. In the restaurant, the finest local produce is used. Cromlix is an ideal venue for small exclusive conferences and business meetings. The private Chapel is a unique feature and perfect for weddings. The hotel won the Andrew Harpers European Hideaway 2000 Award. Extensive sporting and leisure facilities include trout and salmon fishing and game shooting in season. There are several challenging golf courses within easy reach including Gleneagles, Rosemount, Carnoustie and St Andrews. The location is ideal for touring the Southern Highlands, with Edinburgh and Glasgow only an hour away. **Directions:** Cromlix House lies four miles north of Dunblane, north of Kinbuck on B8033 and four miles south of Braco. Price Guide: Single £115–£190; double/twin £195–£245; suite with private sitting room £235–£345.

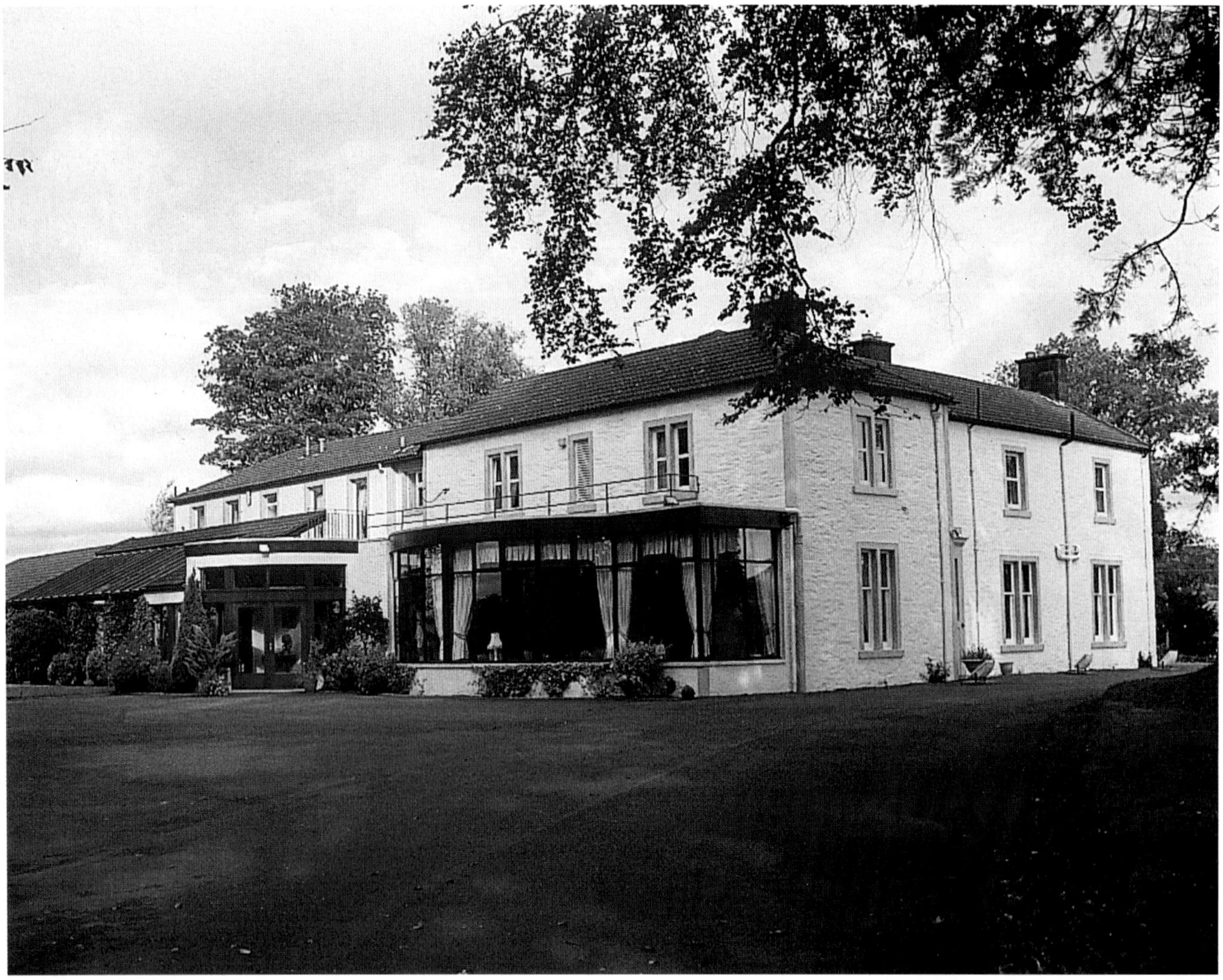

THE DRYFESDALE HOTEL

LOCKERBIE, DUMFRIESSHIRE DG11 2SF
TEL: 01576 202427 FAX: 01576 204187 E-MAIL: reception@dryfesdalehotel.co.uk

Built in 1782, this former manse was converted into a country house hotel in the early 1950s. Situated in one of the most beautiful and peaceful settings in the area of Annandale, yet only a few minutes from the M74, this family-run hotel has greatly enhanced its standards. There is very much a happy ambience throughout. The lounges and bar are comfortably relaxing, while the individually decorated bedrooms are of a luxury standard. The AA Rosette restaurant serves the best regional produce, and has been rewarded with several awards. Amongst the many attractions in the surrounding area are Samye Ling Tibetan centre and Temple at Eskdalemuir, Drumlanrigg Castle near Thornhill and the beautiful Galloway coastline passing Shambellie House museum at New Abbey, Gem Rock museum at Cree Town and Threave gardens near Castle Douglas. Dumfries is situated 20 minutes to the west of Lockerbie, the home of Robbie Burns monument and museum, historic buildings and shopping centre. A 20-minute drive to the south of Lockerbie takes you to the historic city of Carlisle, with cathedral and the Lanes shopping centre. The beautiful Cumbrian lakes and mountains are within driving distance as are the cities of Glasgow and Edinburgh. The Dryfesdale Hotel is a Member of Taste of Scotland. **Directions:** Dryfesdale Hotel is situated on junction 17 of the M74, approximately 27 miles north of Carlisle. Price Guide: Single £65–£85; double/twin £90–£120; suites £120.

15 MasterCard VISA AMERICAN EXPRESS M 50

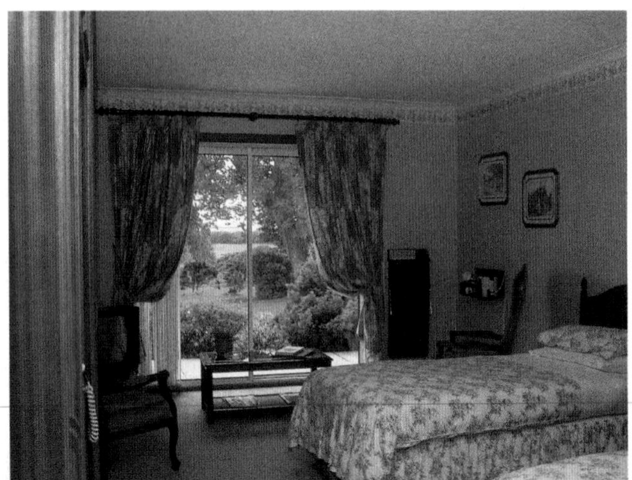

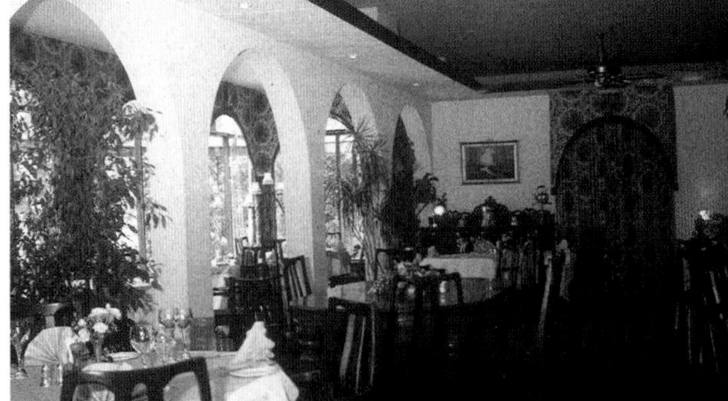

KIRROUGHTREE HOUSE

NEWTON STEWART, WIGTOWNSHIRE DG8 6AN

TEL: 01671 402141 FAX: 01671 402425 E-MAIL: info@kirroughtreehouse.co.uk

Winner of the Johansens Most Excellent Service Award 1996, Kirroughtree House is situated in the foothills of the Cairnsmore of Fleet, on the edge of Galloway Forest Park. The hotel stands in eight acres of landscaped gardens, where guests can relax and linger over the spectacular views. This striking mansion was built by the Heron family in 1719 and the oak-panelled lounge with open fireplace reflects the style of that period. From the lounge rises the original staircase, from which Robert Burns often recited his poems. Each bedroom is well furnished – guests may choose to spend the night in one of the hotel's spacious de luxe bedrooms with spectacular views over the surrounding countryside. Many guests are attracted by Kirroughtree's culinary reputation – only the finest produce is used to create meals of originality and finesse. This is a good venue for small conferences. Pitch-and-putt, lawn tennis and croquet can be enjoyed in the grounds. Residents can play golf on the many local courses and also have use of our sister hotel's exclusive 18-hole course at Gatehouse of Fleet. Trout and salmon fishing can be arranged nearby, as can rough shooting and deer stalking during the season. Closed 3 January to mid February. **Directions:** The hotel is signposted one mile outside Newton Stewart on the A75. Price Guide: Spingle £70–£95; double/twin £130–£140; suite £160.

CASTLE VENLAW

EDINBURGH ROAD, PEEBLES, EH45 8QG

TEL: 01721 720384 FAX: 01721 724066 E-MAIL: enquiries@evenlaw.co.uk

Just half an hour from the city of Edinburgh, yet within the peaceful Borders countryside, the Castle with its distinctive tower sits majestically on the slopes of Venlaw Hill overlooking the Royal and ancient town of Peebles. Originally built as a private house in 1782, it was bought by John and Shirley Sloggie in 1997 and has undergone major refurbishment. Now recognised as one of the leading hotels in the area, Castle Venlaw keeps the country house tradition alive and offers an air of elegance and relaxed informality. From the welcoming Library Bar and Lounge with its oak panelling and log fire to the 12 bedrooms – all named after Scotland's finest malt whiskies – great care has been taken to preserve the Castle's charm and character. Guests can choose from a range of suites, and at the top of the tower a family suite comes complete with children's den. The spacious and airy restaurant provides the perfect ambience in which to enjoy award-winning menus where delicious local produce such as Borders salmon, lamb and game are given an international flavour. Outside, acres of beautiful woodland grounds can be explored as well as nearby Edinburgh, Stirling and Glasgow. **Directions:** From Edinburgh, follow the A703 to Peebles. After 30mph sign, the hotel drive is signposted on the left. Price Guide: Single £60–£85; double/twin £120–£160. Short breaks available.

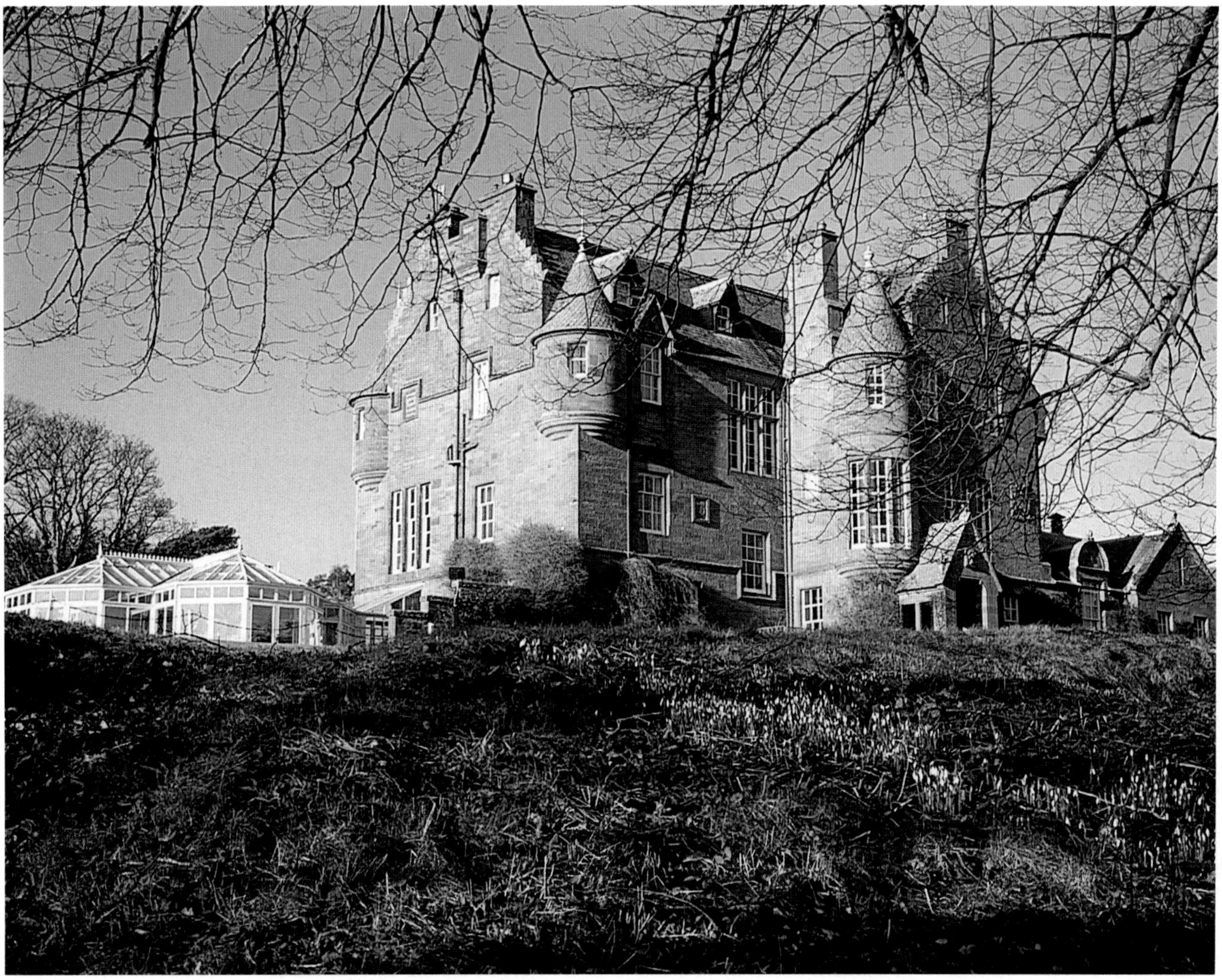

CRINGLETIE HOUSE HOTEL

PEEBLES EH45 8PL

TEL: 01721 730233 FAX: 01721 730244 E-MAIL: enquiries@cringletie.com

This distinguished mansion, turreted in the Scottish baronial style, stands in 28 acres of beautiful gardens and woodland. Designed by Scottish architect David Bryce, Cringletie was built in 1861 for the Wolfe Murray family, whose ancestor, Colonel Alexander Murray, accepted the surrender of Quebec after General Wolfe was killed. All of the bedrooms have fine views and many have been redesigned with attractively co-ordinated curtains and furnishings. The splendid panelled lounge has an impressive carved oak and marble fireplace, a painted ceiling and many oil portraits. The imaginative cooking, prepared with flair, attracts consistently good reports and the range and quality of fruit and vegetables grown make this the only Scottish garden recommended in Geraldene Holt's The Gourmet Garden. Cringletie House Hotel has recently won a game cookery award for excellence in game and game fish cooking and presentation, sponsored by the Balvenie range of Single Malt Whiskies. On-site facilities include a tennis court, croquet lawn and putting green. Golf can be played at Peebles; fishing is available by permit on the River Tweed. Cringletie is a good base from which to discover the rich historic and cultural heritage of the Borders and is convenient for visiting Edinburgh. **Directions:** The hotel is on the A703 Peebles–Edinburgh road, 2½ miles from Peebles. Price Guide: Single £75; double/twin £150–£180.

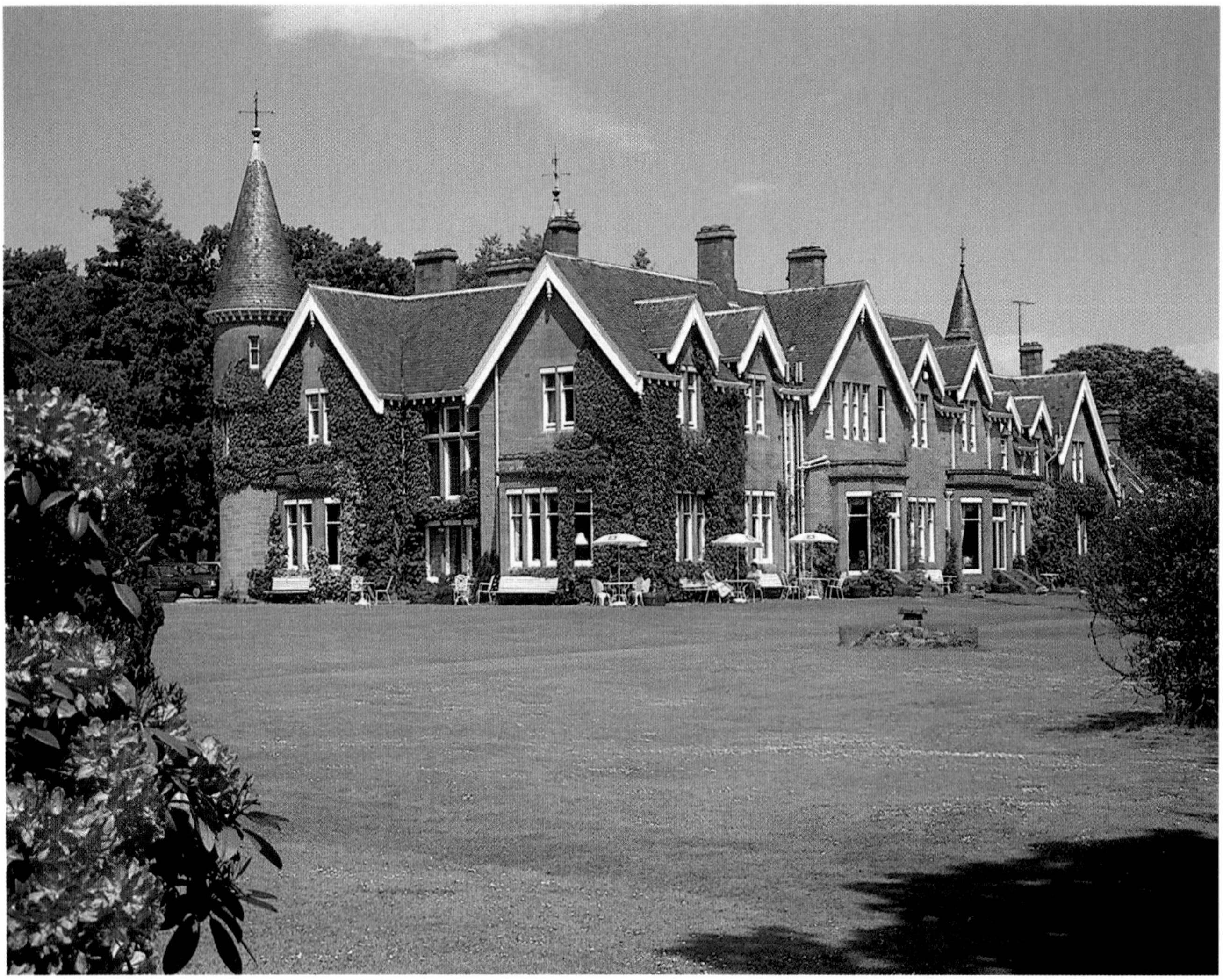

BALLATHIE HOUSE HOTEL

KINCLAVEN, STANLEY, PERTHSHIRE PH1 4QN

TEL: 01250 883268 FAX: 01250 883396 E-MAIL: email@ballathiehousehotel.com

Set in an estate overlooking the River Tay near Perth, Ballathie House Hotel offers Scottish hospitality in a house of character and distinction. Dating from 1850, this mansion has a French baronial façade and handsome interiors. Overlooking lawns which slope down to the riverside, the drawing room is an ideal place to relax with coffee and the papers, or to enjoy a malt whisky after dinner. The premier bedrooms are large and elegant, while the standard rooms are designed in a cosy, cottage style. On the ground floor there are several bedrooms suitable for guests with disabilities. Local ingredients such as Tay salmon, Scottish beef, seafood and piquant soft fruits are used by chef Kevin MacGillivray winner of the title Scottish "Chef of the Year" 1999–2000, to create menus catering for all tastes. The hotel has two rosettes for fine Scottish cuisine. Activities available on the estate include salmon fishing, river walks, croquet and putting. The new Riverside Rooms are ideal for both house guests or sportsmen. The area has many good golf courses. Perth, Blairgowrie and Edinburgh are within an hour's drive. STB 4 star. Dogs in certain rooms only **Directions:** From the A93 at Beech Hedges, signposted for Kinclaven and Ballathie, or off the A9, 2 miles north of Perth, take the Stanley Road. The hotel is 8 miles north of Perth. Price Guide: Single £75–£95; double/twin £150–£200; suite £220–£240. 2 day breaks from £88 incl. dinner.

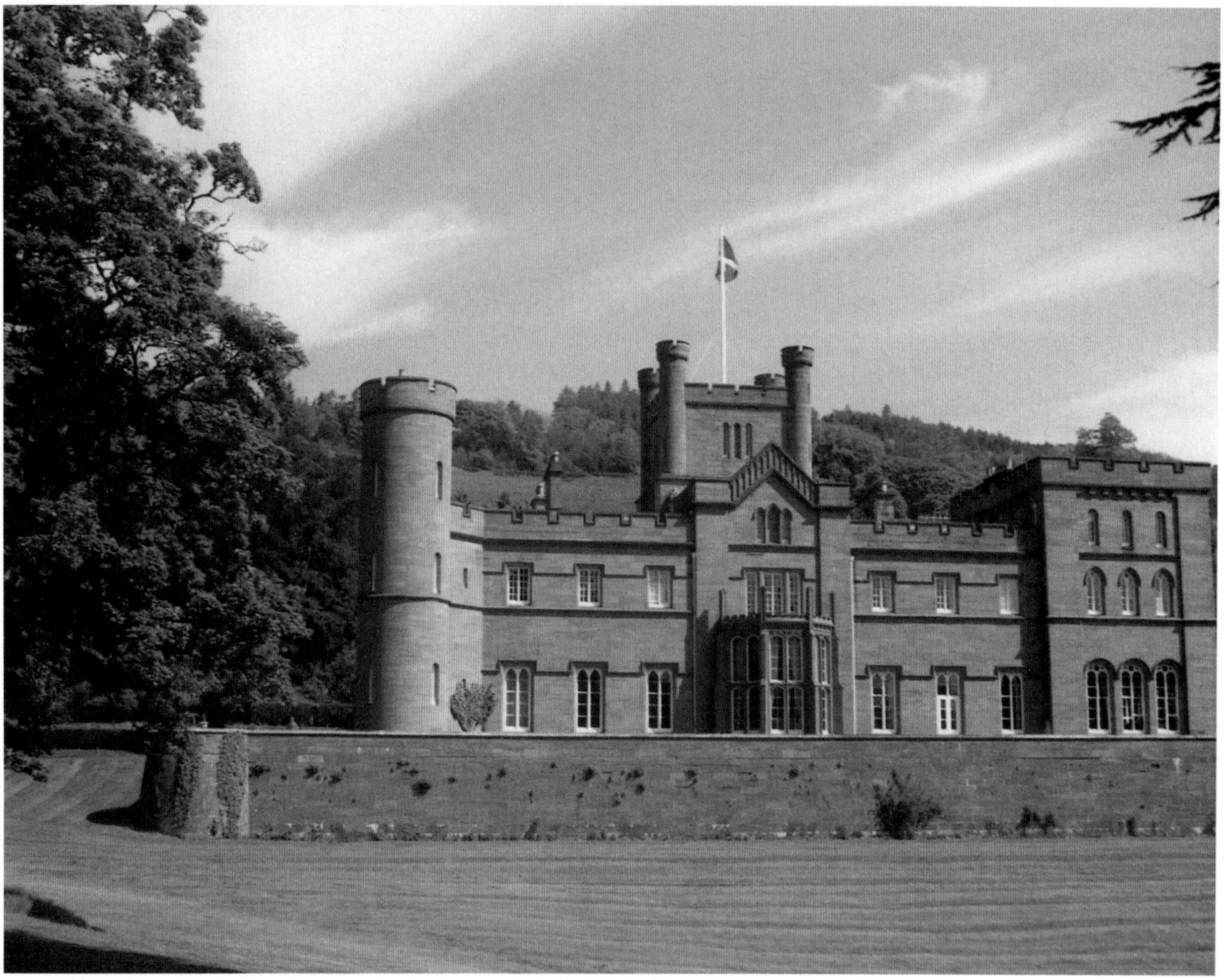

KINFAUNS CASTLE

NR PERTH, PERTHSHIRE PH2 7JZ

TEL: 01738 620777 FAX: 01738 620778 E-MAIL: email@kinfaunscastle.co.uk

Set within 26 acres of parkland and landscaped gardens, Kinfauns Castle stands on a promontory overlooking the River Tay. The castle, built by Lord Gray in the 1820s is located immediately off the A90 Dundee Road, just two miles from Perth. The new Directors, Mr and Mrs James A. Smith, made a commitment to the restoration of the wonderful building, the historical seat of Lord Gray. James Smith was until recently Vice-President of Central Asia for Hilton International. The 16 suites and rooms are individually decorated and reflect the quality, comfort and ambience one expects of a luxury country house. The public rooms feature the rich Victorian décor which has survived the Castle's 70 years as a hikers' hotel. One particular lounge sports a William Morris hunting scene paper whilst another contains a Dragon Boat Bar, brought back from Taipai by the present owner. Chef Jeremy Brazelle leads an award-winning brigade serving an exquisite fusion of modern Scottish and classical French cuisine produced from the finest locally-sourced ingredients. The area abounds with castles and sites of historic interest: Scone Palace and Glamis Castle are only a few miles away. Salmon fishing on the River Tay, golf, shooting and riding are easily available. **Directions:** The hotel is two miles from Perth on the A90 Dundee Road. Price Guide: Single £100–£180; double £180–£260; suite £260–£300.

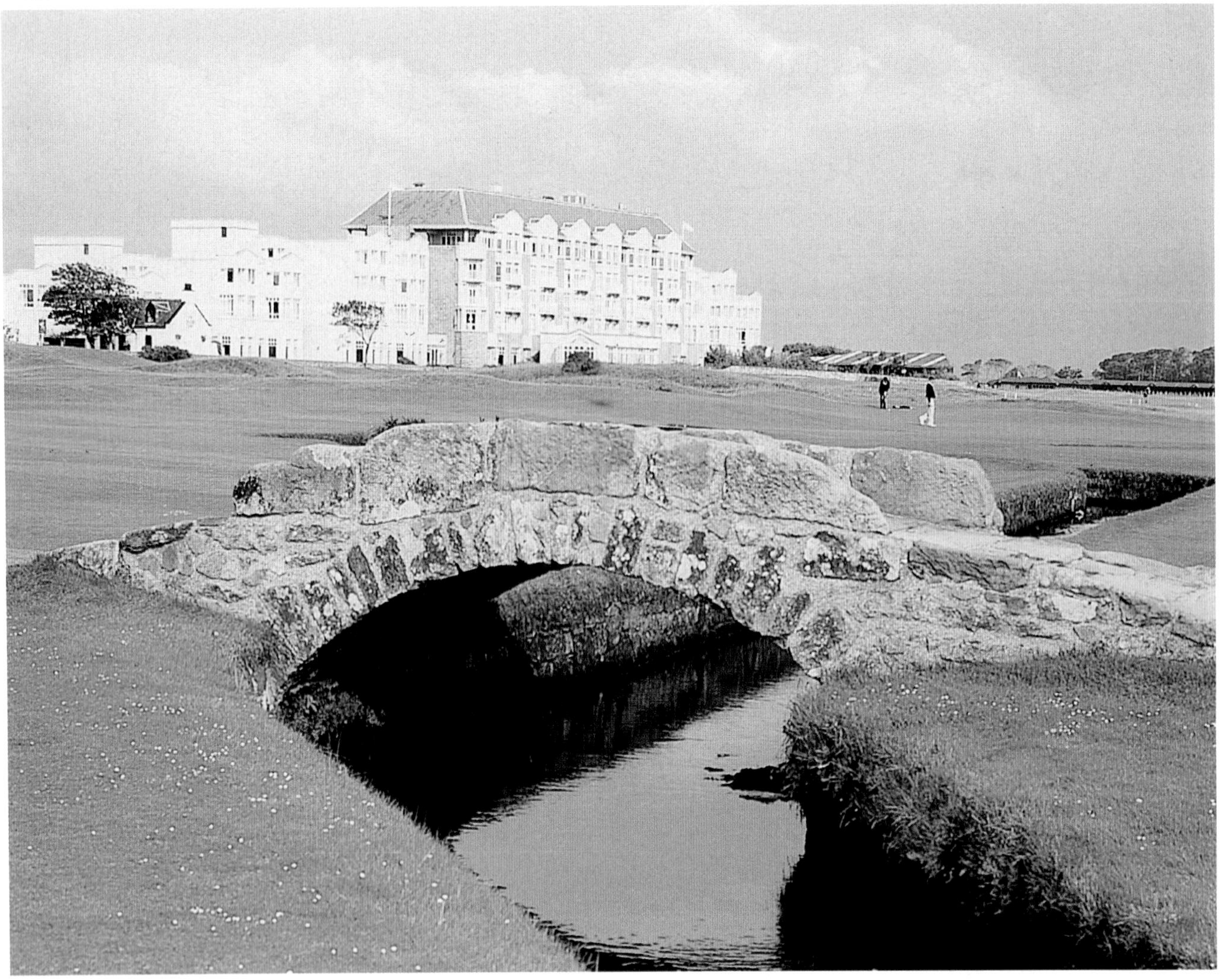

Old Course Hotel Golf Resort & Spa

ST ANDREWS, FIFE, SCOTLAND KY16 9SP
TEL: 01334 474371 FAX: 01334 477668 E-MAIL: reservations@oldcoursehotel.co.uk

Situated alongside the most famous golf course in the world, and amidst the largest golf complex in Europe, the Old Course Hotel is a stunning luxury hotel, which has much to offer the golfer and non-golfer alike. The surrounding countryside is magnificent and resembles a Scotland in miniature, whilst just a short stroll away are the antiques shops, galleries and traditional ice-cream parlours of the ancient university town of St Andrews. The Duke's Course is the hotel's own championship course offering the perfect complement to the links courses of St Andrews. A host of experts and stewards are all on hand to ensure a stay here can definitely enhance one's game. The Spa offers a complete retreat from the hallowed turf outdoors, with a stunning pool, whirlpool, steam and sauna rooms, fitness and weights rooms and a veritable army of aromatherapists, reflexologists, beauty therapists and masseuses. Traditional and contemporary are carefully blended in the spacious guest rooms, where elegant fabrics and clean styling lend a relaxing ambience. The 32 suites all have balconies overlooking the old course and the sand dunes beyond. For dinner, guests can choose the informality of Sands, the legendary Road Hole Bar and Grill, or the romantic intimacy of dining in the privacy of their own suite.
Directions: Just off A91, adjacent to St Andrews. Price Guide: Single £205–£339; double/twin £225–£369; suite £275–£520.

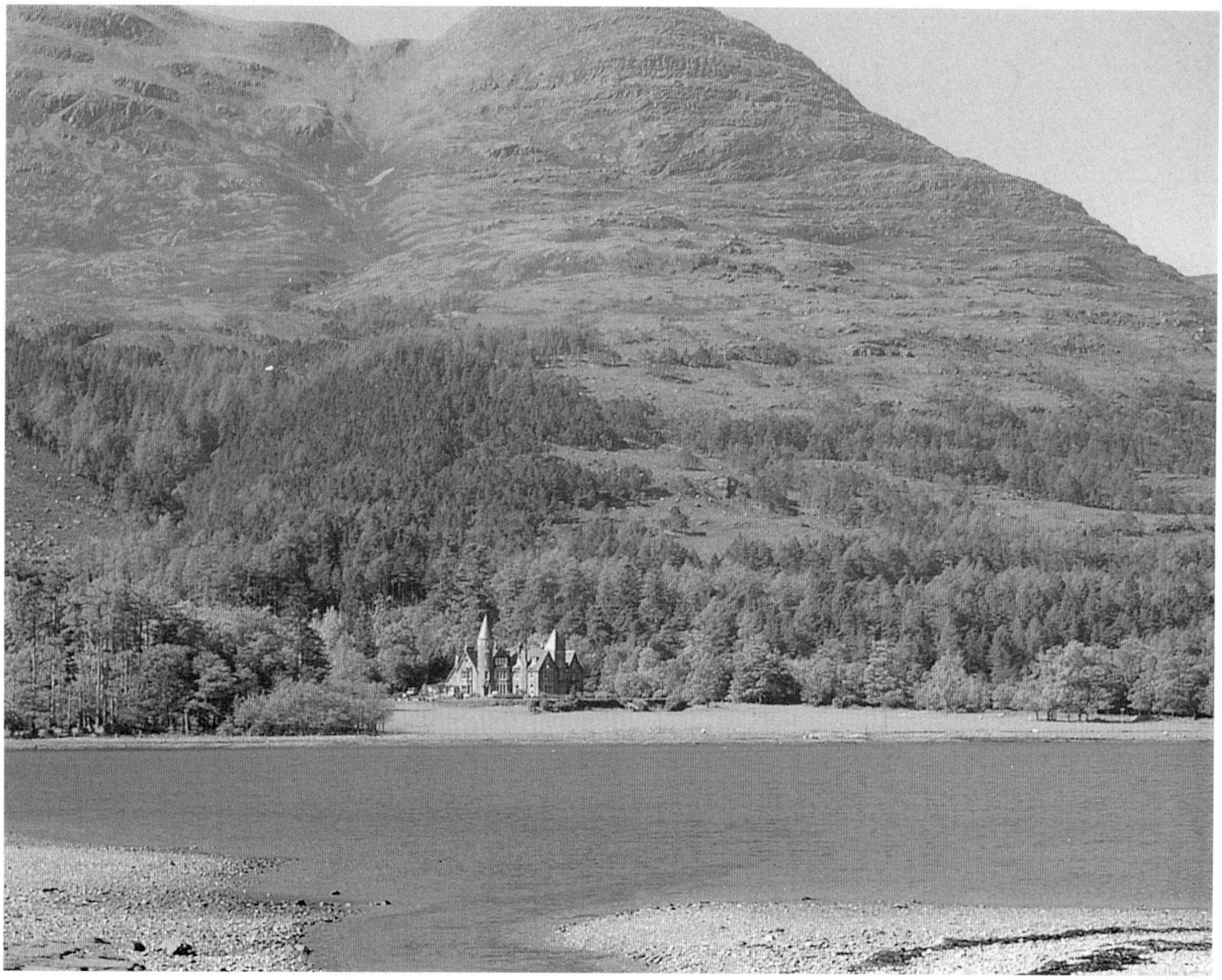

Loch Torridon Country House Hotel

TORRIDON, BY ACHNASHEEN, WESTER-ROSS IV22 2EY
TEL: 01445 791242 FAX: 01445 791296 E-MAIL: enquiries@lochtorridonhotel.com

The Loch Torridon Hotel is gloriously situated at the foot of wooded mountains on the shores of the loch from which it derives its name. The hotel was built as a shooting lodge for the first Earl of Lovelace in 1887 in a 58 acre estate containing formal gardens, mature trees and resident Highland cattle. David and Geraldine Gregory acquired the hotel in March 1992 and have since brought in their daughter Rohaise and son-in-law Dan Rose-Bristow to take over management of the hotel. Winner of the AA Scottish 'Hotel of the Year' award in 1998, Loch Torridon has 20 bedrooms, all of which are furnished in a stylish manner. During the summer months the hotel is bedecked with flowers from the attractive garden. The Victorian kitchen garden provides the chef, Neil Dowson, with fresh herbs, salad, potatoes, broad beans, apples and many other fruits and vegetables. Dinner is served between 7.15pm and 8.30pm and guests may begin with a salad of Kenmore Bay Langoustines with Gazpacho dressing and lemon confit followed by pan fried John Dory with olive oil crushed potatoes, confit tomatoes and a tomato sauce. Outdoor pursuits include archery, clay pigeon shooting, walking in the mountains, boating, fishing and the opportunity to watch otters, seals and whales. **Directions:** Ten miles from Kinlochewe on A896. Do not turn off to Torridon village. Price Guide: Single £50–£90; double/twin £80–£260.

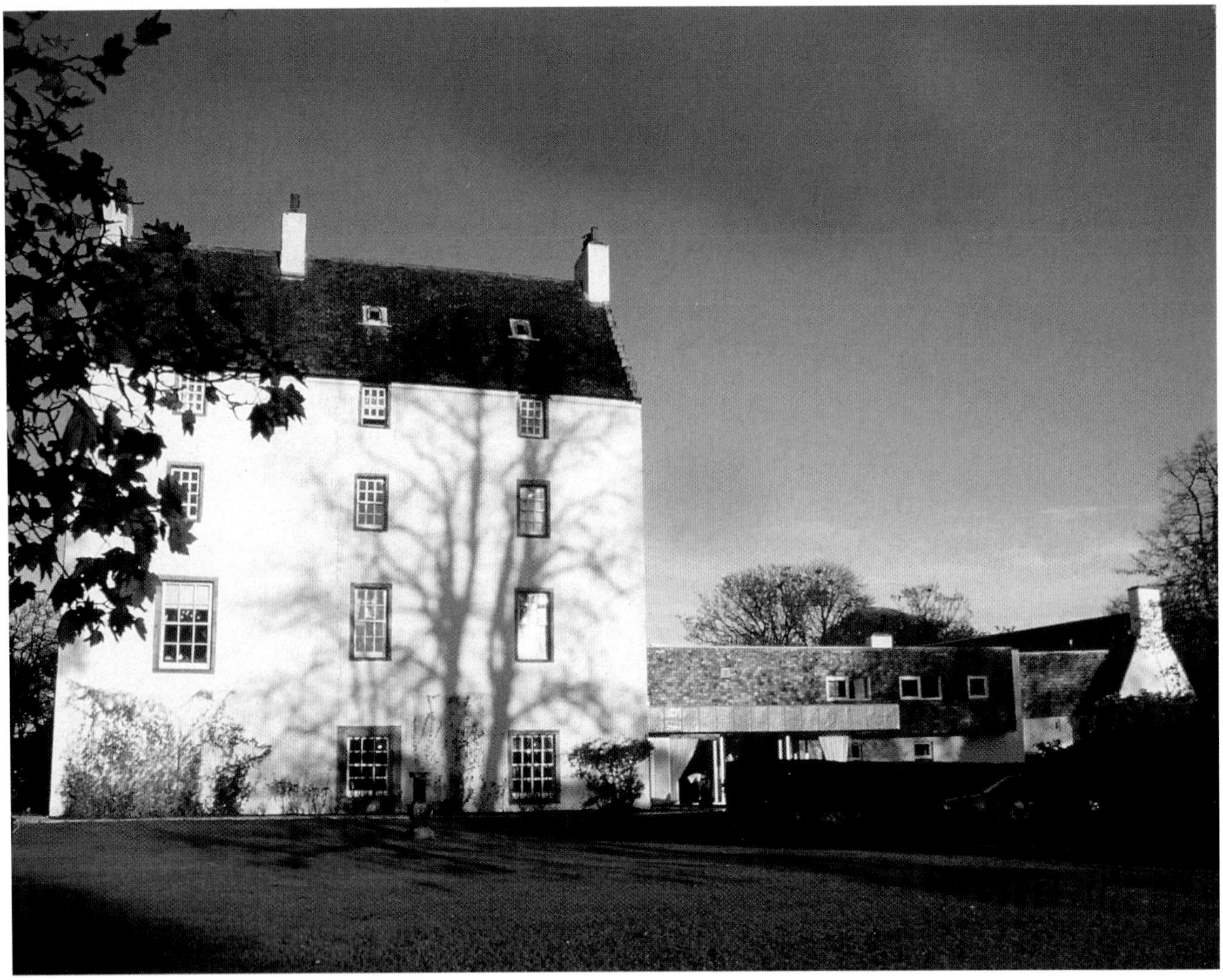

Houstoun House

UPHALL, NR EDINBURGH, SCOTLAND EH52 6JS

TEL: 01506 853831 FAX: 01506 854220 E-MAIL: events.houstoun@macdonald-hotels.co.uk

Houstoun House is a beautiful, unspoilt example of a 16th-century Scottish laird's house, which has been complemented by a number of sympathetically designed new buildings. The gardens include a great cedar tree, grown from seed brought from the Lebanon by one of the early lairds, and the 20 acres of grounds and woodland are adjacent to Uphall Golf Course where guests can play by arrangement. The house is divided into three buildings – the Tower, containing the dining rooms and vaulted bar, the Woman House, joined to the Tower by a stone-flagged courtyard, and the Steading, formerly the estate factor's house. Guest rooms range from standard, to family, to four-poster rooms and suites, and some are specifically adapted for the disabled. All are elegantly furnished and well equipped, and have views of the gardens or the Ecclesmachan Hills. The wood-panelled dining rooms enjoy an excellent reputation for cuisine, while the Leisure Club offers a relaxed and informal Italian Bistro. Health and fitness facilities include a hi-tech gymnasium, 18-metre pool, beauty salon and all-weather tennis court. The city of Edinburgh and its airport are close by, as are access routes to Glasgow and Perth. **Directions:** From M8 Jct 3 (Livingston), turn right at first roundabout, follow signs for Broxburn – A89 left at traffic lights on A899 to Uphall. Price Guide (exclusive of Breakfast): Single £90–£140 double/twin £120–£180; suites £140–£180.

PREFERRED PARTNERS

Preferred partners are those organisations specifically chosen and exclusively recommended by Johansens for the quality and excellence of their products and services for the mutual benefit of Johansens recommendations, readers and independent travellers. For further details, please contact Fiona Patrick at Johansens on +44 (0)20 7566 9700.

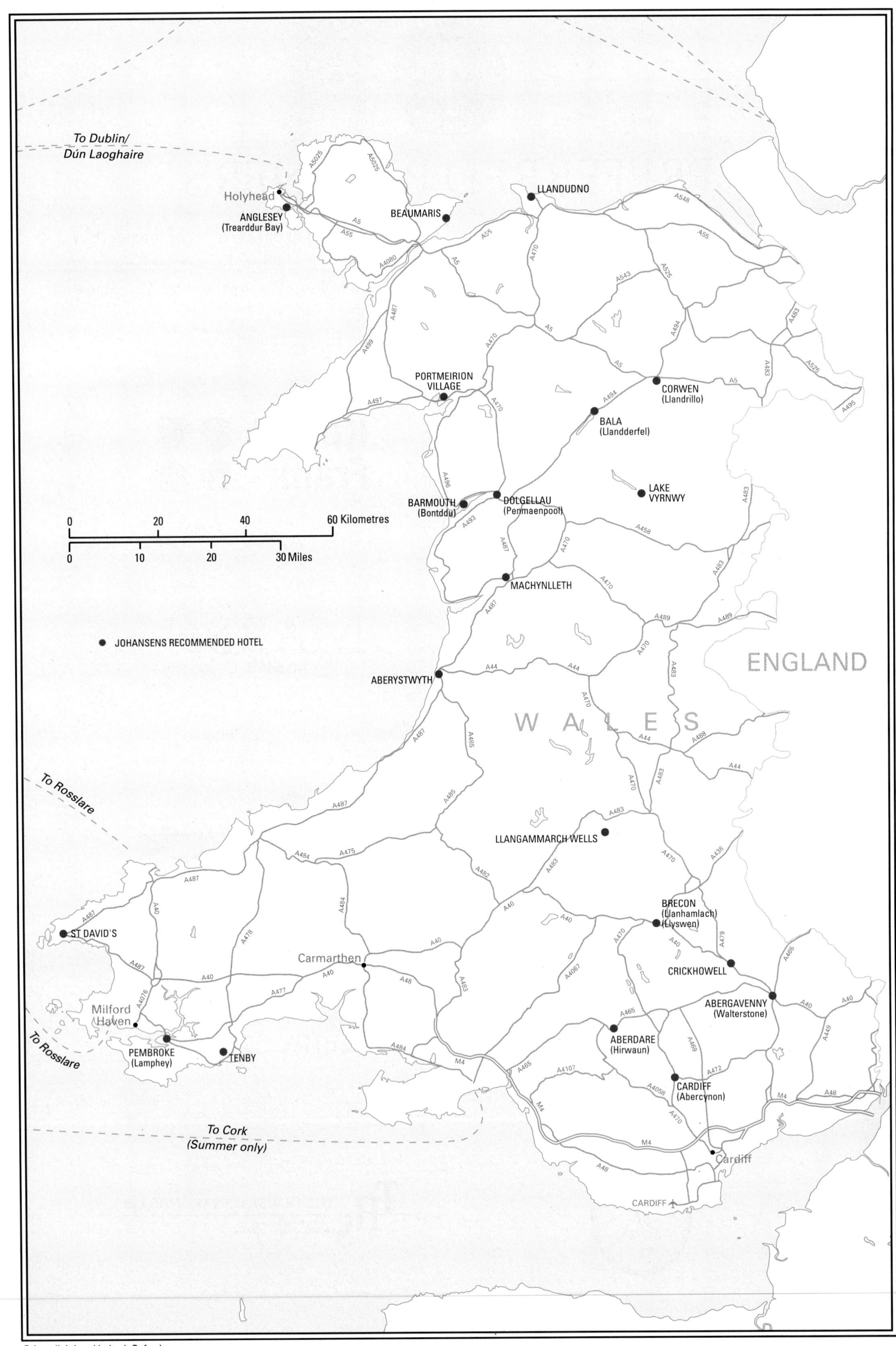

© Lovell Johns Limited, Oxford

Johansens Recommended Hotels

Wales - Cymru

Llyn Nantlle (©Wales Tourist Board Photo Library)

With its rugged natural beauty, Wales continues to inspire inhabitants and visitors alike, and although the country is becoming an ever more popular tourist destination, it is still easy to find oneself entirely alone in unspoilt countryside. Wales has three national parks and possesses more castles and churches per square mile than anywhere else in Europe. It is an enchanting place where the visitor will be captivated by romantic and magic stories such as the tale of King Arthur, his Queen Guinevere and the magician Merlin.

The northern coastline is understandably popular: crystal-clear waters lap the dramatic rocky shores, along which are numerous pretty fishing villages. The mighty castle at Caernarfon bears witness to a tempestuous past, which has now given way to an air of tranquillity in the quiet towns of Criccieth and Porthmadog. Further inland, the mountains of Snowdonia reward energetic walkers with breathtaking views over the mist-shrouded valleys, whilst the Llyn Peninsula has some of the most idyllic scenery in the country. Further south, the moors are studded with limpid mountain lakes, and rocky streams tumble through the wooded valleys.

Probably the least exploited part of the country is rural Mid Wales. Visitors can hike through rolling hills, gaze at rare red kites circling in the sky above or just wander through the streets of old market towns. To the west, in Ceredigion, is Britain's first Marine Heritage Coast at Cardigan Bay.

The flat southern planes of Wales are more heavily populated, but they offer some of the most beautiful coastlines in Europe with long golden beaches in Pembrokeshire and the Gower Peninsula, tiny coves and impressive cliffs.

The towns, cities and villages of Wales are all highly individual in character. Whether you visit cosmopolitan Cardiff, bustling Swansea, historic Caernarfon or sleepy Machynlleth – they are all part of the unique Welsh experience.

For further information on Wales, please contact:
Wales Tourist Board
Brunel House, 2 Fitzalan Road, Cardiff CF24 0UY
Tel: +44 (0)29 2049 9909
Internet: www.visitwales.com

North Wales Tourism
Tel: +44 (0)1492 531731
Internet: www.nwt.co.uk

Mid Wales Tourism
Tel: (Freephone) 0800 273747
Internet: www.mid-wales-tourism.org.uk

Tourism South & West Wales
Tel: +44 (0)1792 781212
Internet: www.tsww.org.uk

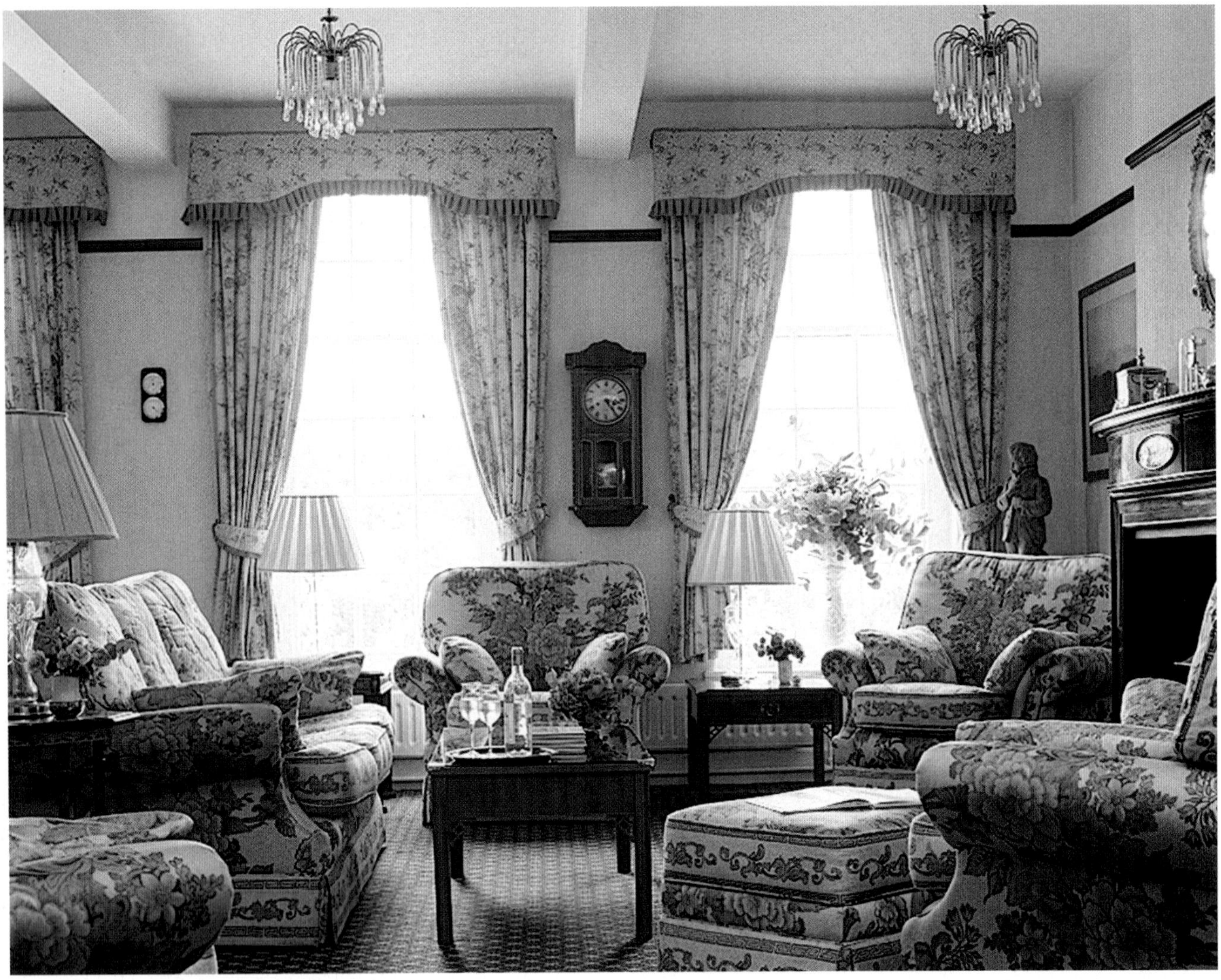

Ty Newydd Country Hotel

PENDERYN ROAD, HIRWAUN, MID-GLAMORGAN CF44 9SX
TEL: 01685 813433 FAX: 01685 813139

Surrounded by undisturbed woodland and beautiful, mature gardens this attractive hotel stands serenely midway between Cardiff and Swansea on the southern edge of the magnificent 520 square miles of the Brecon Beacons National Park. The original house was built by a coal baron, William Llewellyn, uncle of Sir Harry Llewellyn who rode Foxhunter to a gold medal in the 1956 Olympic Games. Peace, comfort and a warm welcome are the hallmarks of Ty Newydd, which offers guests all modern facilities whilst retaining the character and ambience of a fine Georgian country house. The lounges with their open fires are particularly comfortable while the individually styled bedrooms are a delight. Each is en suite and tastefully furnished with a mixture of antique and locally made traditional pieces. There are connecting rooms for families and cots, high chairs and baby listening service are available. For lovers of good food, the spacious restaurant with an adjoining conservatory overlooking the landscaped gardens serves superb traditional favourites alongside varied and seasonal international cuisine. The hotel is an excellent base for exploring the many historic properties nearby, including the 13th century castle at Caerphilly, the largest in Wales. **Directions:** Leave M4 at Jct32. and take A470 and A465 to Hirwaun. Then follow A4059 Brecon road towards Penderyn. Price Guide: Single £52–£70; double/twin £67.50–£95.

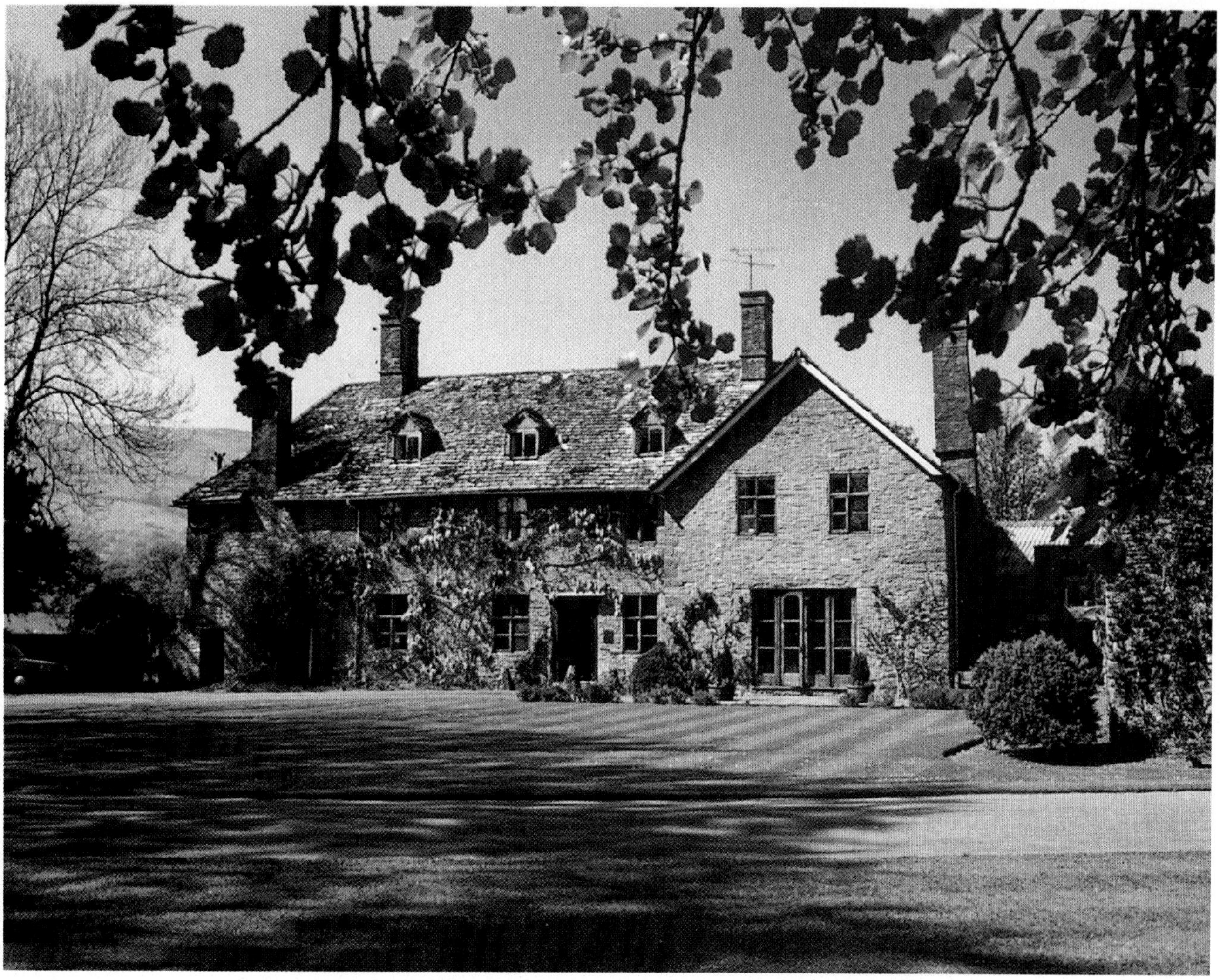

ALLT-YR-YNYS HOTEL

WALTERSTONE, NR ABERGAVENNY HEREFORDSHIRE HR2 0DU
TEL: 01873 890307 FAX: 01873 890539 E-MAIL: allthotel@compuserve.com

Nestling in the foothills of the Black Mountains, on the fringes of the Brecon Beacons National park, Allt-yr-Ynys is an impressive Grade II 16th century manor house hotel. The Manor was the home of the Cecil family whose ancestry dates back to Rhodri Mawr, King of Wales in the 8th century. A more recent Cecil was Lord Burleigh, Chief Minister to Queen Elizabeth I, portrayed by Sir Richard Attenborough in the recent film, 'Elizabeth'. Features of this interesting past still remain and include moulded ceilings, oak panelling and beams and a 16th century four-poster bed in the Jacobean suite. However, whilst the charm and the character of the period remains, the house has been sympathetically adapted to provide all the comforts expected of a modern hotel. The former outbuildings have been transformed into spacious and well-appointed guest bedrooms. Fine dining is offered in the award-winning restaurant and the conference/function suite accommodates up to 200 guests. Facilities include a heated pool, Jacuzzi, clay pigeon shooting range and private river fishing. Pastimes include exploring the scenery, historic properties and plethora of tourist attractions. **Directions:** 5 miles north of Abergavenny on A465 Abergavenny/ Hereford trunk road, turn west at Old Pandy Inn in Pandy. After 400 metres turn right down lane at grey/green barn. The hotel is on the right after 400 metres. Price Guide: Single from £65; double/twin from £95; suite £130.

LLANSANTFFRAED COURT HOTEL

LLANVIHANGEL GOBION, ABERGAVENNY, MONMOUTHSHIRE NP7 9BA
TEL: 01873 840678 FAX: 01873 840674 E-MAIL: reception@llch.co.uk

Llansantffraed Court is a perfect retreat from the fast pace of modern life. This elegant Georgian-style country house hotel, part of which dates back to the 14th century, is set in spacious grounds on the edge of the Brecon Beacons and the Wye Valley. Guests are provided with the highest level of personal, yet unobtrusive service. Most of the tastefully decorated and luxuriously furnished bedrooms offer views over the hotel's garden, and ornamental trout lake. While one has a four poster bed, others feature oak beams and dormer windows. An excellent reputation is enjoyed by the 2 AA Rosette restaurant; the menus reflect the changing seasons and the availability of fresh local produce. Exquisite cuisine is complemented by fine wines. Afternoon tea can be taken in the lounge, where guests enjoy a blazing log fire during the cooler months and savour the views of the South Wales countryside. A range of excellent facilities is available for functions, celebrations and meetings. Llansantffraed Court is an ideal base for exploring the diverse history and beauty of this area and there are plenty of opportunities to take advantage of energetic or relaxing pursuits, including, golf, trekking, walking, and salmon and trout fishing. **Directions:** From M4 J24 (Via A449) off B4598 (formerly A40 old road) Leave A40 D/C at Abergavenny or Raglan. Price Guide: Single from £72; double/twin from £90; suites £157.

21 MasterCard VISA AMERICAN EXPRESS M 400

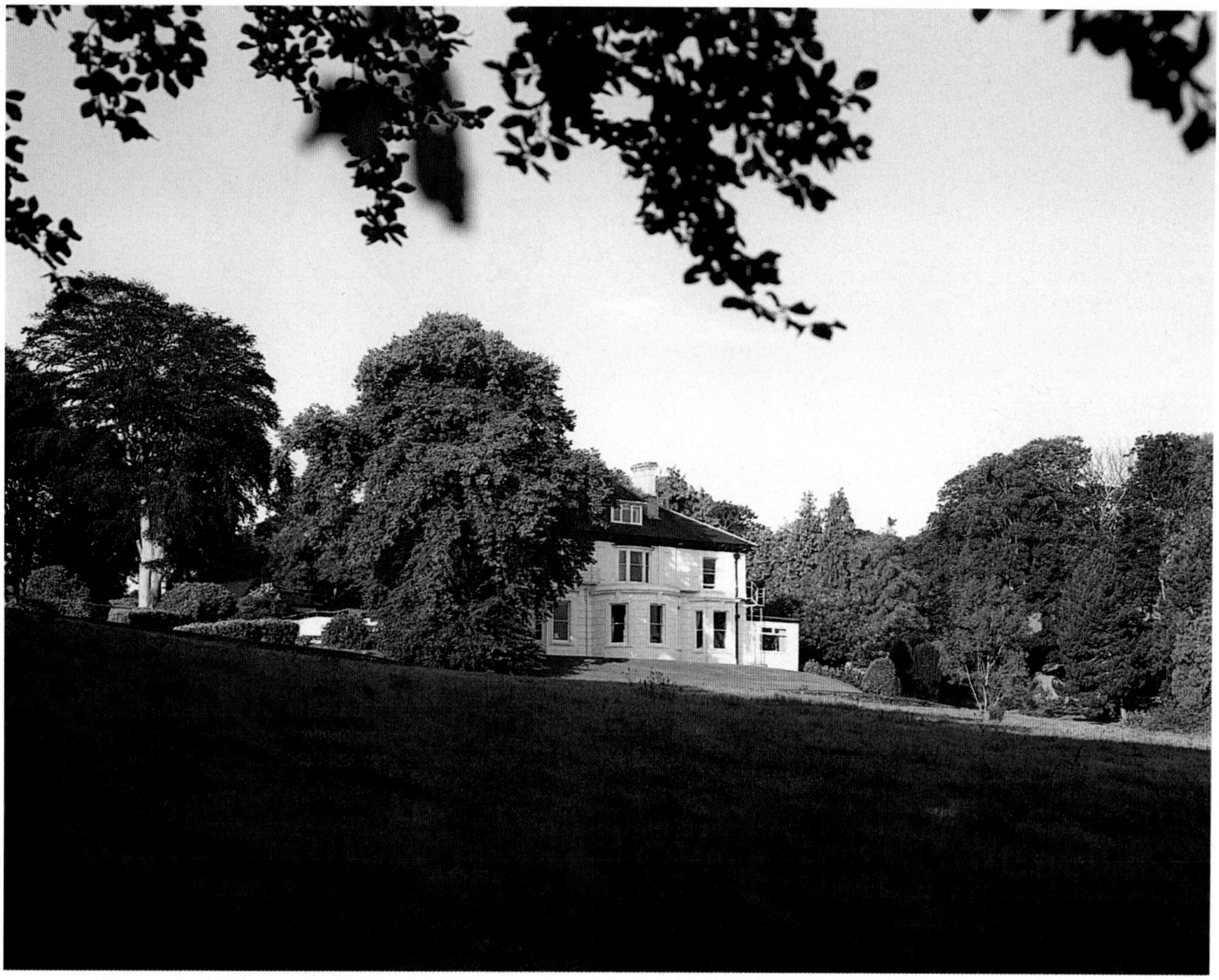

Conrah Country House Hotel

RHYDGALED, CHANCERY, ABERYSTWYTH, CEREDIGION SY23 4DF
TEL: 01970 617941 FAX: 01970 624546 E-MAIL: enquiries@conrah.co.uk

One of Wales' much loved country house hotels, the Conrah is tucked away at the end of a rhododendron-lined drive, only minutes from the spectacular rocky cliffs and sandy bays of the Cambrian coast. Set in 22 acres of rolling grounds, the Conrah's magnificent position gives views as far north as the Cader Idris mountain range. Afternoon tea and Welsh cakes or pre-dinner drinks can be taken at leisure in the quiet writing room or one of the comfortable lounges, where antiques and fresh flowers add to the relaxed country style. The acclaimed restaurant uses fresh local produce, together with herbs and vegetables from the Conrah kitchen garden, to provide the best of both classical and modern dishes. The hotel is owned and run by the Heading family who extend a warm invitation to guests to come for a real 'taste of Wales', combined with old-fashioned, high standards of service. For recreation, guests may enjoy a game of table-tennis in the summer house, croquet on the lawn or a walk around the landscaped gardens. The heated swimming pool and sauna are open all year round. Golf, pony-trekking and sea fishing are all available locally, while the university town of Aberystwyth is only 3 miles away. Closed Christmas. **Directions:** The Conrah lies 3 miles south of Aberystwyth on the A487. Price Guide: Single £70–£90; double/twin £100–£140.

TREARDDUR BAY HOTEL

LON ISALLT, TREARDDUR BAY, NR HOLYHEAD, ANGLESEY LL65 2UN
TEL: 01407 860301 FAX: 01407 861181 E-MAIL: enquiries@trearddurbayhotel.co.uk

This seaside hotel enjoys a magnificent location on the Anglesey coast, overlooking Trearddur Bay and close to a medieval chapel dedicated to the nun St Brigid. An extensive refurbishment programme in recent years has given the hotel a completely new look. Many of the spacious bedrooms, all of which are en suite, have panoramic views over the bay. All are furnished to a high standard. There are also fifteen studio suites, including one with a four-poster bed. The comfortable lounge is the perfect place to relax and read the papers over morning coffee or afternoon tea. Before dinner, enjoy an apéritif in one of the hotel bars. Superb views apart, the hotel restaurant enjoys a reputation for excellent food – including locally caught fish and seafood – complemented by fine wines. An extensive table d'hôte menu offers a good choice of dishes. For those who find the Irish Sea too bracing, the hotel has an indoor pool. The beach is just a short walk away and there is an 18-hole golf course nearby. Anglesey is a haven for water sports enthusiasts and bird-watchers. Places of interest include Beaumaris Castle and the Celtic burial mound at Bryn Celli Ddu. Snowdonia is a little further afield. **Directions:** From Bangor, leave A55 at Valley turnoff take A5 to Valley crossroads. Turn left onto B4545 for 3 miles, then turn left at garage. Hotel is 350 yards on right Price Guide: Single £82–£105; double/twin £120–£150; executive suite £140.

PALÉ HALL

PALÉ ESTATE, LLANDDERFEL, BALA, GWYNEDD LL23 7PS
TEL: 01678 530285 FAX: 01678 530220 E-MAIL: palehall@fsbdial.co.uk

One of the ten best-kept private residences throughout Wales and renowned for its shooting and fishing facilities, Palé Hall stands in 150 acres of mature woodland on the fringe of the Snowdonia National Park above the Vale of Edeinion. The Hall's stunning interiors include a magnificent entrance hall, a 32-foot-high galleried staircase and ornate hand-painted ceilings in the Boudoir. Built in 1870 at no spared expense for Henry Robertson, a Scottish gentleman responsible for construction of the local railways, the Hall's notable guests have included Queen Victoria, who described the house as enchanting, and Winston Churchill. The comfortable lounges (including 2 non-smoking lounges) enable quiet relaxation. Each of the 17 suites is individually decorated and contains en suite bathroom, television, hospitality tray and luxury toiletries. All have magnificent views of the surrounding scenery. The restaurant offers seasonal table d'hôte menus (AA 2 Rosettes) and is complemented by an extensive cellar. Outdoor pursuits include walking, riding, golf and white-water rafting. Guests can go fishing at no extra charge on the River Dee, just a 3-minute walk away. The hotel has its own clay shooting and can organise shooting parties. Exclusive use is available for executive conferences and weddings. **Directions:** Situated off B4401 Corwen to Bala road, four miles from Llandrillo. Price Guide: Single £79–£120; double/twin £95–£155.

17 MasterCard VISA M 40

Bontddu Hall

BONTDDU, NR BARMOUTH, GWYNEDD LL40 2UF
TEL: 01341 430661 FAX: 01341 430284 E-MAIL: reservations@bontdduhall.co.uk

Solid and grey-stoned, with a rampart-topped tower and slim, arched windows, Bontddu Hall looks in every way like a small fairytale castle. Situated in the beautiful Southern Snowdonia National Park, the hotel stands majestically in 14 acres of gardens and woodlands overlooking the picturesque magnificence of the Mawddach Estuary. It is a superb example of Gothic architecture, reflected inside by the grandeur, elegance and tradition of high, beamed ceilings, huge fireplaces, handsome portraits and rich furnishings. Peace, privacy and relaxation are guaranteed with owners Mr & Mrs Tong ensuring that guests receive the very best service and hospitality. Period furniture and Victorian style wallpapers add to the country-house ambience of the bedrooms, each named after a past visiting Prime Minister. Each bedroom is en suite, delightfully decorated and has all modern facilities. Four rooms in the Lodge have balconies from which occupants can enjoy mountain views. There are two comfortable lounges and a Victorian-style bar where local artists regularly exhibit their work. Lunch and tea are served in the brasserie or on the sun-catching garden terrace. The devoted team of chefs produce traditional cuisine using fresh, local produce in the Mawddach Restaurant. **Directions:** Bontddu Hall is on A496 between Dolgellau and Barmouth. Price Guide: Single £65–£75; double/twin £110–£130; suite £160.

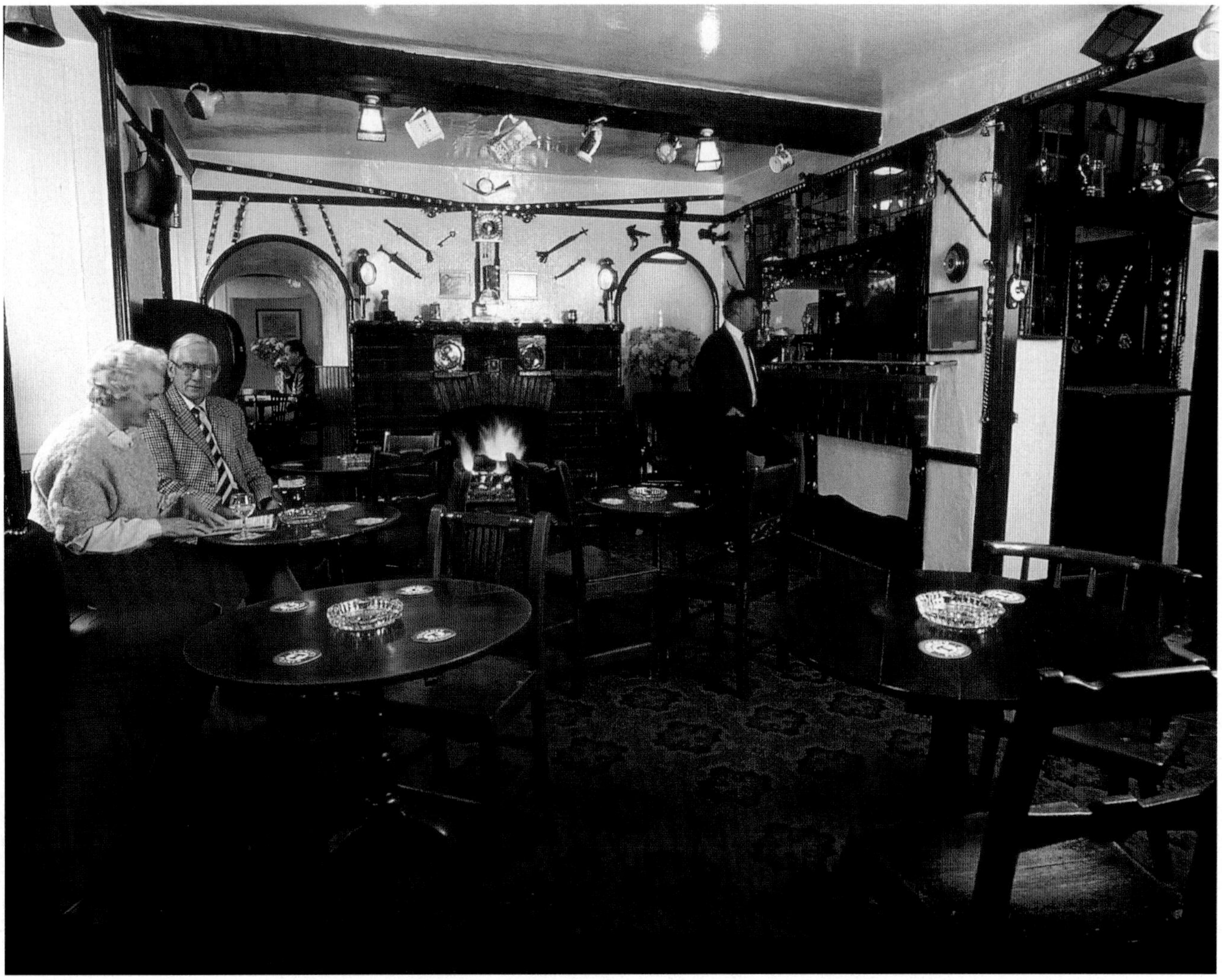

Ye Olde Bull's Head

CASTLE STREET, BEAUMARIS, ISLE OF ANGLESEY LL58 8AP
TEL: 01248 810329 FAX: 01248 811294 E-MAIL: info@bullsheadinn.co.uk

Situated in the centre of Beaumaris, Ye Olde Bull's Head is a Grade II listed building and is the original posting house of the borough. Many vestiges of the hotel's 17th-century past are evident; the single hinged gate which closes the courtyard of the inn is listed as the largest in Britain. Despite a history dating back to 1472, the Bull retains a more Dickensian feel with bedrooms named after the author's characters. All have been built or refurbished in the last five years and offer comfortable furnishings, en suite facilities and modern amenities. Guests relax in the intimate lounge with its chintz furnishings and roaring open fire and may choose to dine in the new restaurant or equally stylish but less formal brasserie. Chef proprietor Keith Rothwell ensures that highest quality standards are maintained. Creative modern British dishes incorporate the finest local produce and are complemented by a carefully selected wine list. Guests and townsfolk alike enjoy the ambience of the historic bar with a glass of real ale by the open fire. Nearby facilities include sailing, climbing in Snowdonia and fishing in The Menai Straits and Conwy Coast. Beaumaris Castle is 100 yards away whilst Plas Newydd and Anglesey Sea Zoo are worth a visit. **Directions:** From Britannia Road Bridge (A5), follow A545 for approx 5m to Beaumaris. Price Guide: Single £60; double/twin £87; four-poster £100.

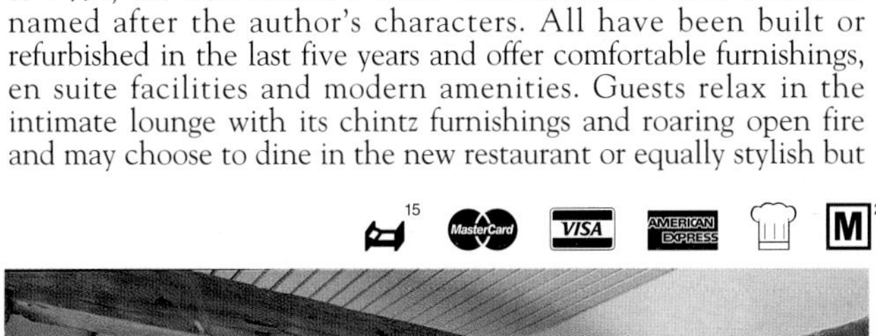

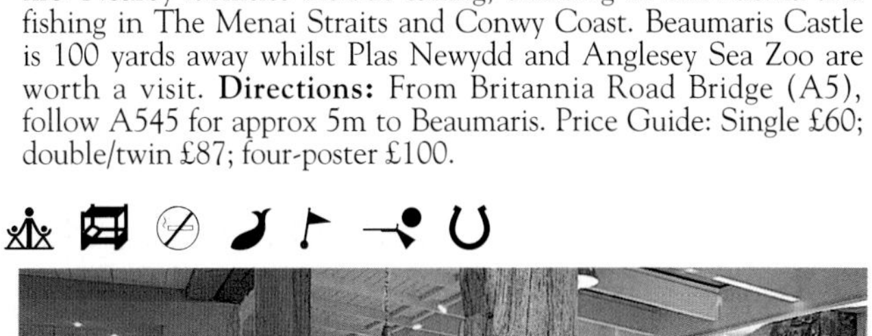

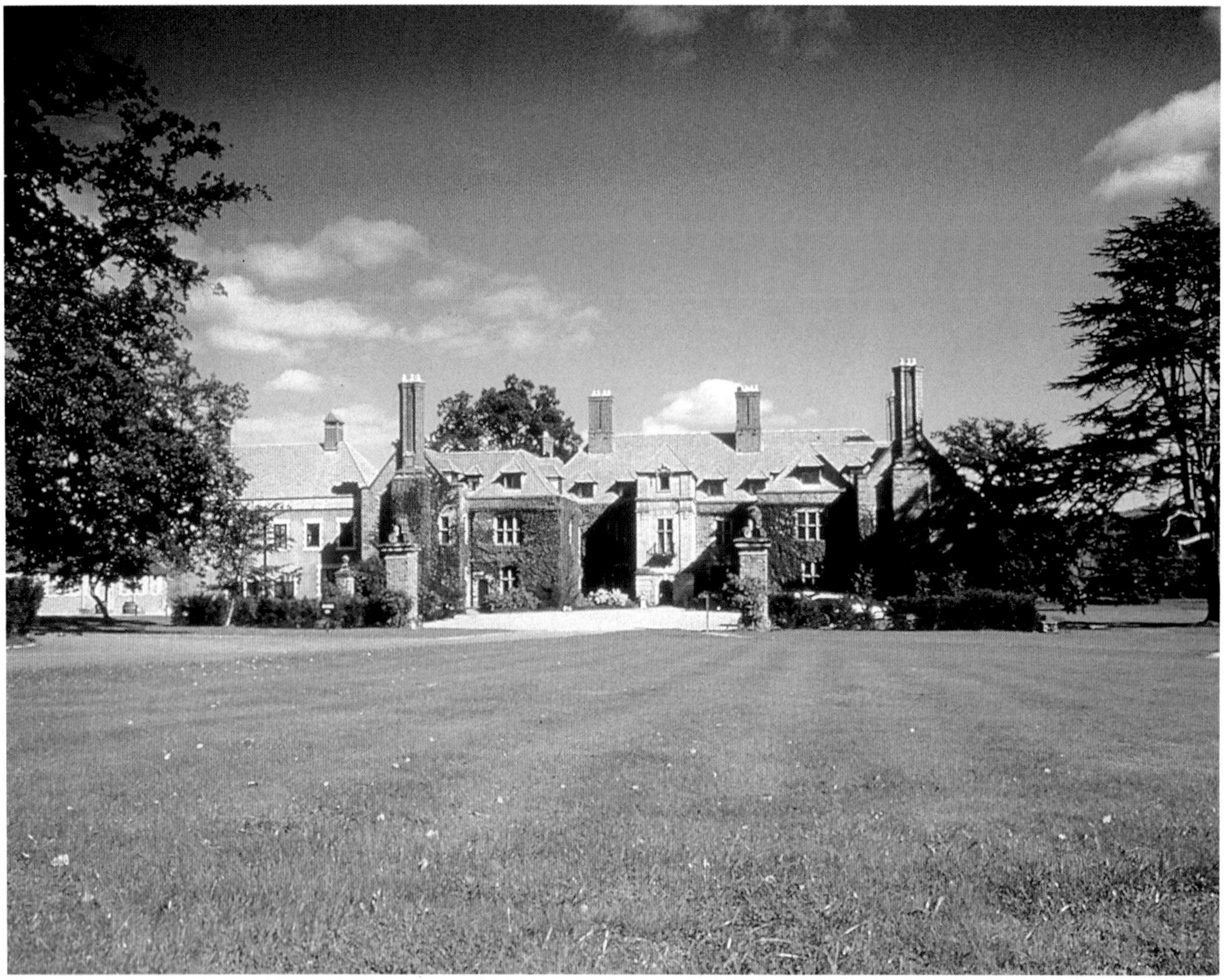

LLANGOED HALL

LLYSWEN, BRECON, POWYS, WALES LD3 0YP

TEL: 01874 754525 FAX: 01874 754545 E-MAIL: Llangoed_Hall_Co_Wales_UK@compuserve.com

The history of Llangoed Hall dates back to 560 AD when it is thought to have been the site of the first Welsh Parliament. Inspired by this legend, the architect Sir Clough Williams-Ellis, transformed the Jacobean mansion he found here in 1914 into an Edwardian country house. Situated deep in a valley of the River Wye, surrounded by a walled garden, the hotel commands magnificent views of the Black Mountains and Brecon Beacons beyond. The rooms are warm and welcoming, furnished with antiques and oriental rugs and on the walls, an outstanding collection of paintings acquired by the owner, Sir Bernard Ashley. The luxurious and spacious bedrooms enjoy fine views of the Wye Valley. Llangoed's restaurant is one of the principal reasons for going there. Classic but light, the Michelin starred menus represent the very best of modern cuisine, complemented by a cellar of more than 300 wines. Exclusive use of the entire hotel can be made available for board meetings. Outdoor pursuits include golf, riding, shooting and some of the best mountain walking and gliding in Britain. For expeditions, there are Hay-on-Wye and its bookshops, the border castles, Hereford and Leominster. Children over 8 are welcome. There are 3 heated kennels for dogs. The hotel is a member of Welsh Rarebits. **Directions:** 9 miles west of Hay, 11 miles north of Brecon on A470 Price Guide: Single from £110; double/twin from £145; suite from £295.

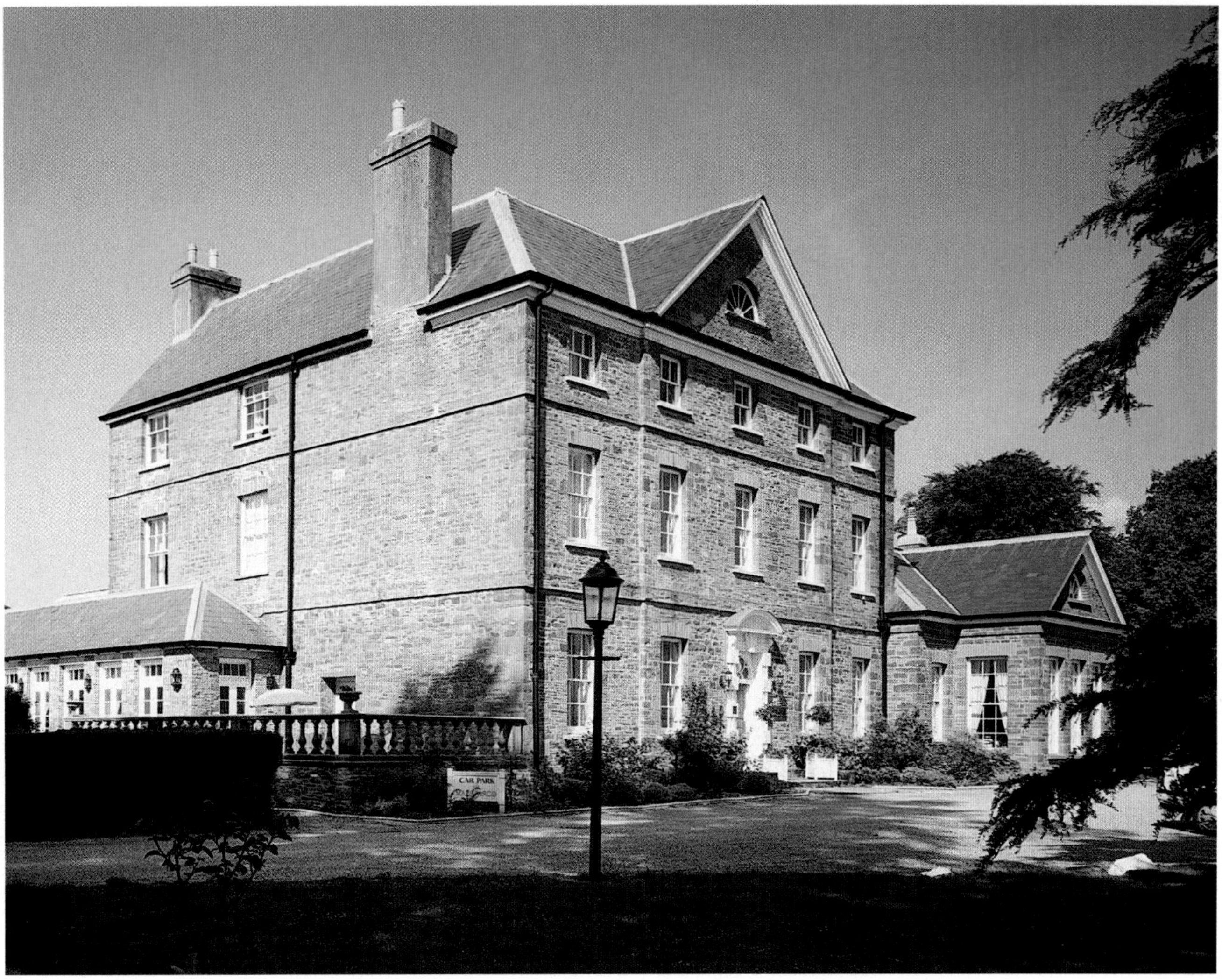

PETERSTONE COURT

LLANHAMLACH, BRECON, POWYS LD3 7YB
TEL: 01874 665387 FAX: 01874 665376

Set in a tiny village on the eastern edge of the mysterious Brecon Beacons National Park, Peterstone is a carefully restored Georgian manor, swathed in history which can be traced back to the time of William the Conqueror. It was voted the best new hotel in Wales by the AA in 1992 and, amongst a string of awards, the hotel has collected merits from the RAC and the Welsh Tourist Board. There are just 12 guest bedrooms at the court, eight beautifully proportioned period style rooms in the main house, and four split level rooms in the former stable that have all the things you expect to find and many you don't, such as tape players and video players. Intimate parties and special occasions can be accommodated in one of the two private rooms. The surrounding countryside has an abundance of walks, one of which starts at the end of the hotel drive and goes along the river and the canal back into Brecon. Alternatively, or perhaps even after all the walking, there is in the hotel basement a fully equipped health club, with gymnasium, sauna, solarium and Jacuzzi. In the grounds are an outdoor heated pool, croquet and putting. **Directions:** Peterstone Court is located in the village of Llanhamlach, on the A40, three miles east of Brecon. Price Guide: Single £85; double/twin £95–£115. Short breaks available all year round.

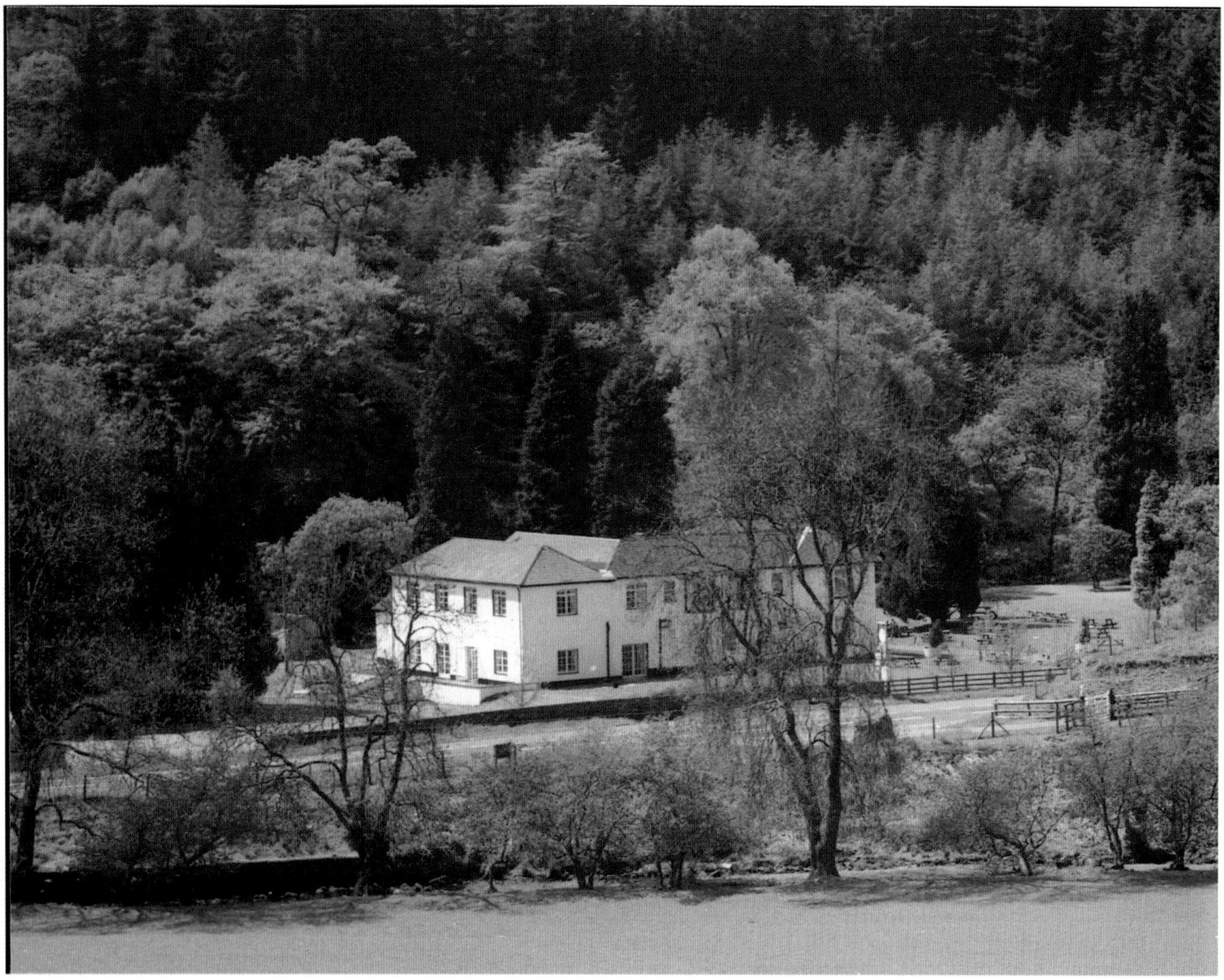

NANT DDU LODGE HOTEL

CWM TAF, BRECON BEACONS NR BRECON, POWYS, WALES CF48 2HY
TEL: 01685 379111 FAX: 01685 377088 E-MAIL: enquiries@nant–ddu–lodge.co.uk

This award-winning country hotel and inn offers excellent value for money in the lovely unspoilt heart of the Brecon Beacons National Park. Its proprietors, the Ronson family, extend a warm welcome and the bustling, informal atmosphere has proved to be popular since they began running the Nant Ddu in 1992. The hotel's history dates back to before the 19th century, and the name refers to the stream that still runs in the grounds. Nowadays, the Nant Ddu is renowned for its exceptional contemporary décor and superb cuisine. Each individually designed bedroom displays inventiveness and style, and the very best are the new river rooms which come complete with queen size or four poster beds, sofas and video players. An atmospheric bar provides an intimate environment for drinking and eating, as food can be served here or in the Bistro style restaurant. The chalkboard menu offers a surprising array of traditional and creative dishes, and changes daily according to the availability of top quality ingredients. Views from the hotel are spectacular, and it boasts its own well kept lawns which broaden out into the green hills of the surrounding area. Country walks are a must, but there is also much to explore in Wales' many castles and cathedrals. For shopping, Cardiff city centre is just 35 minutes away **Directions:** On A470, 12 miles south of Brecon, six miles north of Merthyr Tydfil. Price Guide: Single £55–£68; double/twin £70–£90.

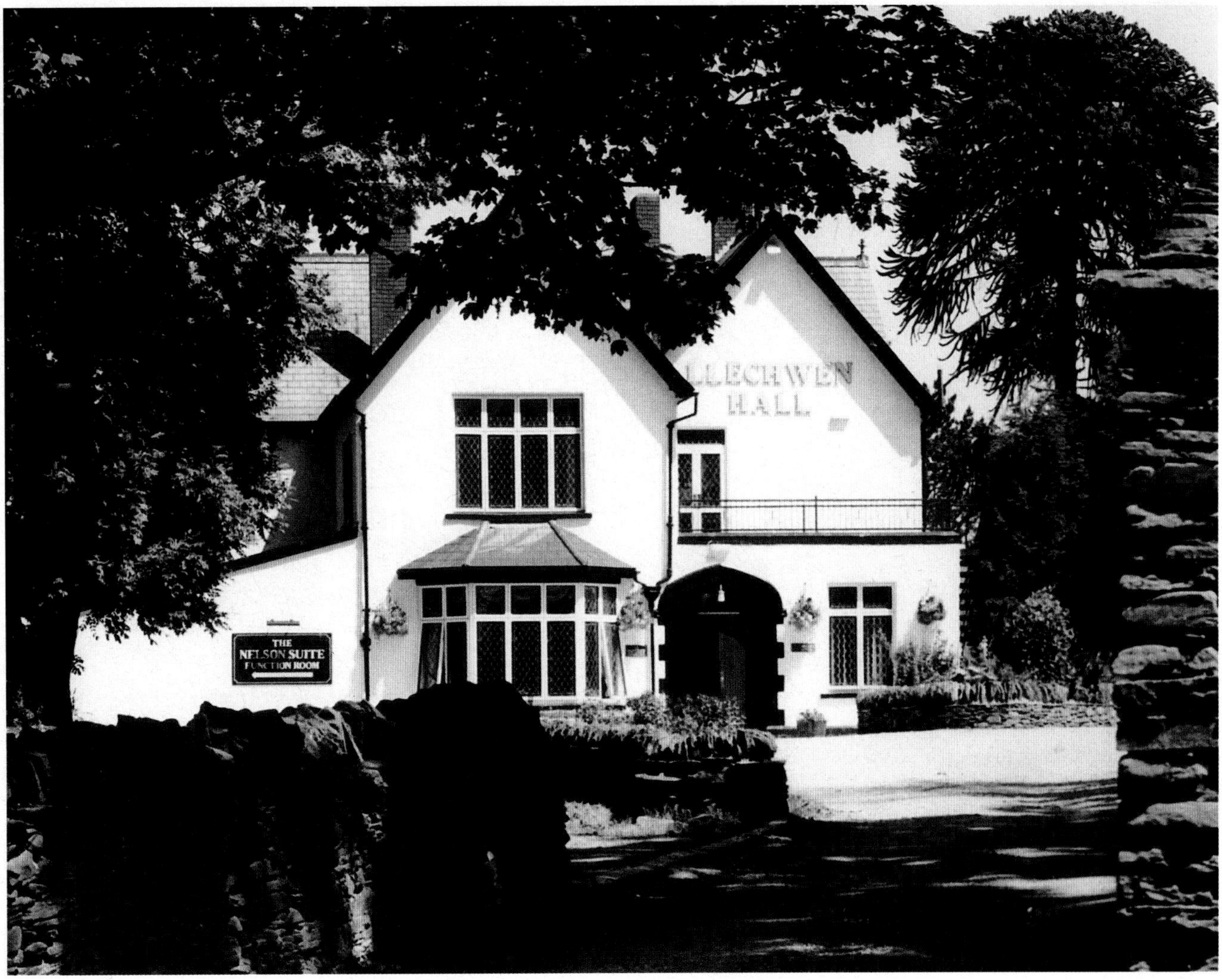

LLECHWEN HALL

ABERCYNON, NR LLANFABON, CARDIFF, MID GLAMORGAN CF37 4HP
TEL: 01443 742050 FAX: 01443 742189 E-MAIL: llechwen@aol.com

Visitors step back in time when they enter this lovely 17th-century Welsh Long House with its Victorian frontage standing in six acres of mature gardens on the hillside overlooking the Aberdare and Merthyr valleys. There are four -foot thick walls with narrow embrasures, low ceilings, stout-blackened oak beams, huge fireplaces and stone-roofed outbuildings. Careful restoration and sympathetic refurbishment over the years since being purchased as a near derelict building in 1988 has created a 3-star country house hotel with an award-winning restaurant. The 20 superbly appointed bedrooms are individually decorated and furnished to provide a truly comfortable environment. Guests have a choice of restaurants for memorable dining. The intimate St Cynons Restaurant in the original Welsh Long House provides excellent French cuisine, whilst the equally charming, Victorian-style Llanfabon Dining Room serves traditional lunches and dinners. Pre and after dinner drinks can be enjoyed in an elegant cocktail lounge. The hotel is just a 20-minute drive from Cardiff and 15 minutes from the foothills of the Brecon Beacons. **Directions:** Exit M4 at junction 32 and follow A470 towards Merthyr Tydfil for approximately 11 miles. Join A472 towards Nelson and then A4054 towards Cilfynydd. The hotel is on the left after ½ mile. Price Guide: Single £54.50–£65.50; double/twin £75–£106.

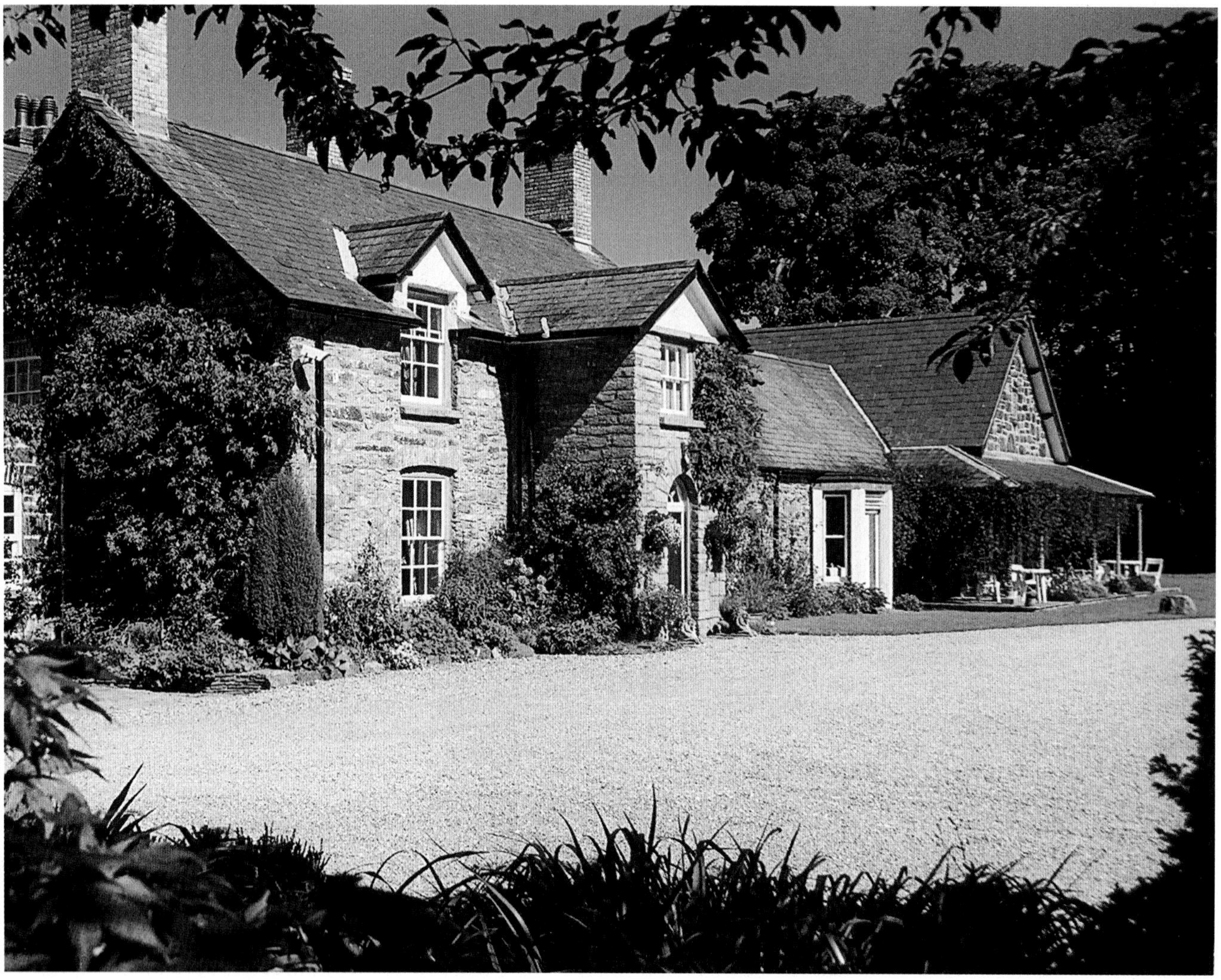

Tyddyn Llan Country House Hotel

LLANDRILLO, NR CORWEN, DENBIGHSHIRE LL21 0ST
TEL: 01490 440264 FAX: 01490 440414 E-MAIL: tyddynllanhotel@compuserve.com

Set in beautifully tended gardens amid some of mid-Wales' finest scenery, Tyddyn Llan is a Georgian country house built in Welsh stone and slate that was once used by the Dukes of Westminster as a shooting lodge. It is the home today of Peter and Bridget Kindred who have brought to its modernised interior just the right degree of comfortable elegance, enhanced by Peter's skill in interior design and enriched by his own paintings that adorn the hall and lounges. Individually decorated, the bedrooms are filled with fine antiques and period furniture and enjoy fine views of the garden and surrounding hills. Dining has always been a highlight at Tyddyn Llan and the nightly dinner menus are complemented by a carefully selected wine list. Quality local ingredients, from salmon caught on the Dee to lamb, beef and dairy products, make for memorable dishes to partner the fresh vegetables and herbs from the kitchen garden. Three AA Rosettes constitute well-earned recognition of Tyddyn Llan's unique attention to detail. The hotel has rights to four miles of fly-fishing on the River Dee. Keen walkers can trace the ancient Roman road, Ffordd Gam Elin, which traverses the Berwyn Mountains. Here naturalists will find many species of birds and wild flowers. **Directions:** Llandrillo is midway between Corwen and Bala on B4401, 4 miles from A5 at Corwen. Price Guide: (bed and breakfast): Single £67.50–£85; double/twin £105–£140.

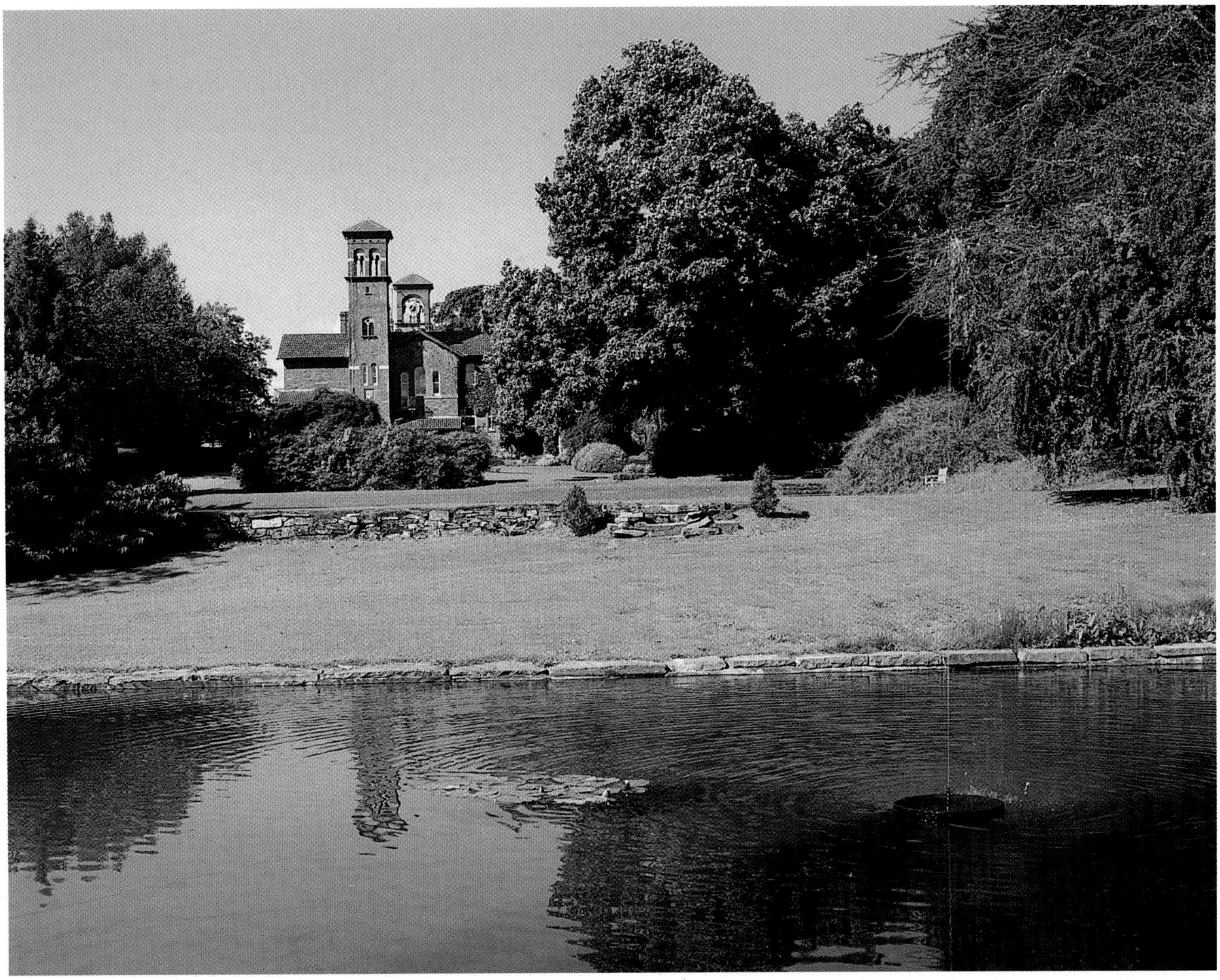

GLIFFAES COUNTRY HOUSE HOTEL

CRICKHOWELL, POWYS NP8 1RH

TEL: 01874 730371 FAX: 01874 730463 FREEPHONE: 0800 146719 E-MAIL: calls@gliffaeshotel.com

Visitors may be surprised to discover a hotel featuring distinctive Italianate architecture midway between the Brecon Beacons and the Black Mountains. Gliffaes Country House Hotel is poised 150 feet above the River Usk and commands glorious views of the surrounding hills and valley. The elegantly furnished, Regency style drawing room is an ideal place to relax and leads to a large sun room and on to the terrace, from which guests may enjoy the magnificent scenery. In addition to a panelled sitting room, there is a billiard room with a full-size table. In the dining room a wide choice from an imaginative menu covers the best of National dishes and Mediterranean specialities. The Gliffaes fishery includes every type of water, from slow-flowing flats to fast-running rapids, on 2½ miles of the River Usk renowned for its wild brown trout and salmon fishing. The 33 acre hotel grounds have rare trees and shrubs as well as lawns for putting and croquet. There are two Golf courses within easy reach. Riding can be arranged nearby. Open throughout the year. There are now conference facilities available in the grounds. **Directions:** Gliffaes is signposted from the A40, 2½ miles west of Crickhowell. Price Guide: Single from £55–£77; double/twin £115–£145.

PENMAENUCHAF HALL

PENMAENPOOL, DOLGELLAU, GWYNEDD LL40 1YB
TEL: 01341 422129 FAX: 01341 422787 E-MAIL: relax@penhall.co.uk

The splendour of Cader Idris and the Mawddach Estuary forms the backdrop for this handsome Victorian mansion which is an exceptional retreat. Set within the Snowdonia National Park, the 21-acre grounds encompass lawns, a formal sunken rose garden, a water garden and woodland. The beautiful interiors feature oak and mahogany panelling, stained-glass windows, log fires in winter, polished Welsh slate floors and freshly cut flowers. There are 12 luxurious bedrooms, some with four-poster and half-tester beds and all with interesting views. In the Gothic-style conservatory restaurant, guests can choose from an imaginative menu prepared with the best seasonal produce and complemented by an extensive list of wines. An elegant panelled dining room can be used for private dinners or meetings. Penmaenuchaf Hall is perfect for a totally relaxed holiday. For recreation, guests can fish for trout and salmon along ten miles of the Mawddach River or take part in a range of water sports. They can also enjoy scenic walks, visit sandy beaches and historic castles and take trips on narrow-gauge railways. **Directions:** The hotel is off the A493 Dolgellau–Tywyn road, about two miles from Dolgellau. Price Guide: Single £70–£110; double/twin £110–£170.

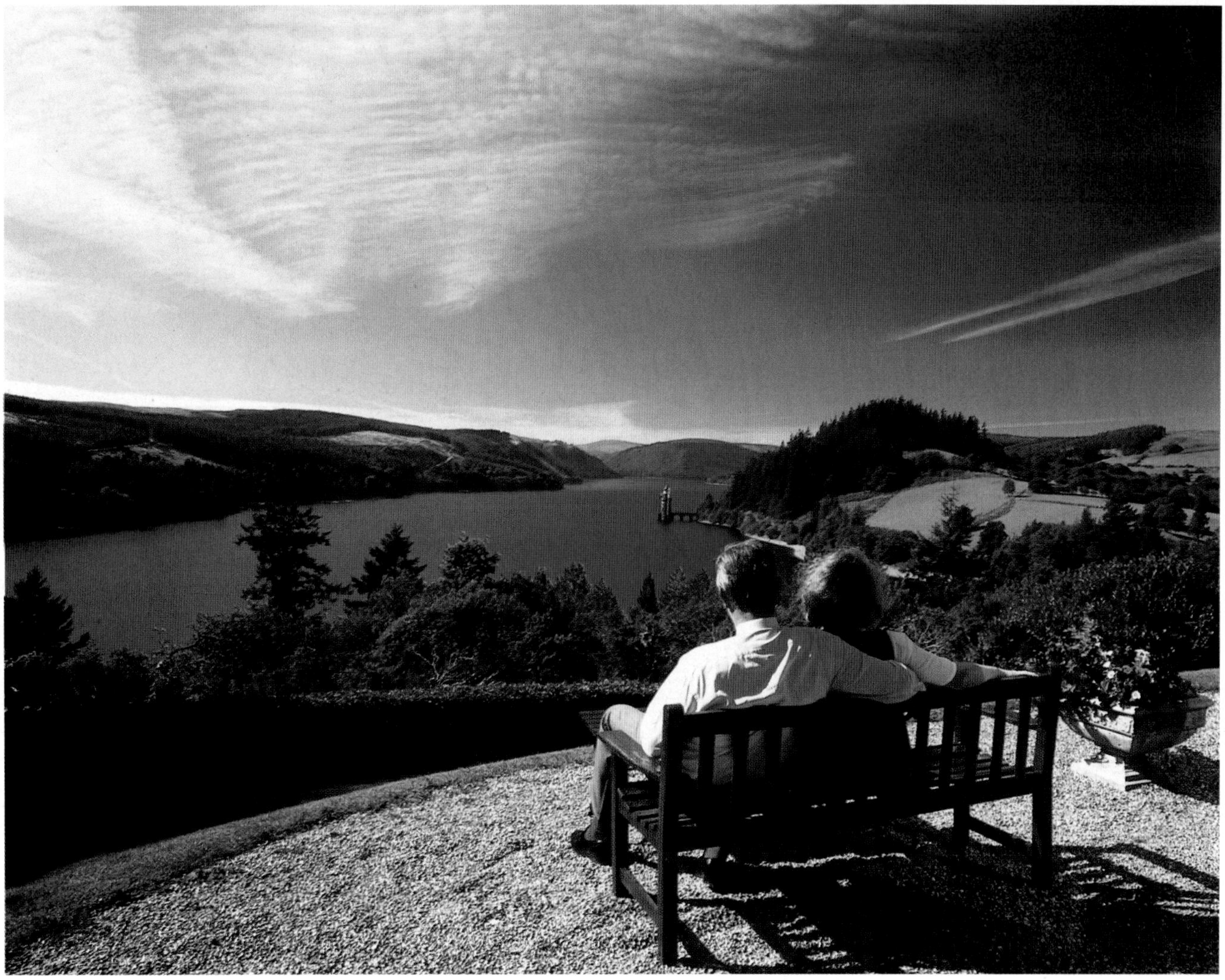

LAKE VYRNWY HOTEL

LAKE VYRNWY, LLANWDDYN, MONTGOMERYSHIRE SY10 0LY
TEL: 01691 870 692 FAX: 01691 870 259 E-MAIL: res@lakevyrnwy.com

Situated high on the hillside within the 24,000-acre Vyrnwy Estate the hotel commands breathtaking views of mountains, lakes and moorland. Also an RSPB sanctuary, the estate provides a wealth of wildlife and represents true peace and tranquillity, surrounded by lawns, an abundance of rhododendrons, woods and meadowlands. Built in 1860, its heritage has been maintained for well over a hundred years as a retreat for all lovers of nature and fine dining. There are 35 bedrooms, all individually furnished and decorated, many with antiques and some with special features such as Jacuzzis, balconies, four-posters or suites. There are also dedicated meeting and private dining facilities. The award-winning candlelit restaurant has a seasonally changing menu. Everything from the marmalade to the petits fours at dinner are created in the Vyrnwy kitchens. The hotel owns some of Wales' best fishing together with some 24,000 acres of sporting rights. Other pursuits include sailing, cycling, tennis, quad trekking, clay shooting, archery and some beautiful walking trails. Riders can bring their own horses, which can be accommodated in the livery. Kennels for dogs are also available. **Directions:** From Shrewsbury take the A458 to Welshpool, then turn right onto B4393 just after Ford (signposted to Lake Vyrnwy 28 miles). Price Guide: Single £85–£150; double/twin £115–£185; suite £185–£215.

BODYSGALLEN HALL

LLANDUDNO LL30 1RS

TEL: 01492 584466 FAX: 01492 582519 E-MAIL: info@bodysgallen.com

Bodysgallen Hall, owned and restored by Historic House Hotels, lies at the end of a winding drive in 200 acres of wooded parkland and beautiful formal gardens. Magnificent views encompass the sweep of the Snowdonia range of mountains and the hotel looks down on the imposing medieval castle at Conwy. This Grade I listed house was built mainly in the 17th century, but the earliest feature is a 13th century tower, reached by a narrow winding staircase, once used as a lookout for soldiers serving the English kings of Conwy and now a safe place from which to admire the fabulous views. The hotel has 19 spacious bedrooms in the house and 16 delightful cottage suites in the grounds. Two of the finest rooms in the house are the large oak-panelled entrance hall and the first floor drawing room, both with splendid fireplaces and mullioned windows. The restaurant has been awarded 3 Rosettes by the AA and menus feature delicious dishes using fresh local ingredients. The Bodysgallen Spa comprises a spacious swimming pool, steam room, sauna, solaria, gym, beauty salons and a club room. The hotel is ideally placed for visiting the many historic castles and stately homes in North Wales. Famous golf courses adorn the coastline. Bodysgallen Hall is a member of Relais & Chateaux Hotels **Directions:** On A470 1 mile from the intersection with the A55. Llandudno is a mile further on the A470. Price Guide: Single £110–£160; double/twin £195–£240; suite £185–£250.

OSBORNE HOUSE

17 NORTH PARADE, LLANDUDNO, CONWY LL30 2LP
TEL: 01492 860555 FAX: 01492 860791 E-MAIL: Sales@OSBORNEHOUSE.COM

Built in 1851 and restored after a major fire in 1992, Osborne House is simply unique. This all-suite luxury hotel offers a very special experience to those seeking traditional comfort, service and originality. Standing on the promenade opposite Llandudno's Victorian Pier its magnificent views encompass the sweep of the bay towards craggy Little Ormes Head and, to the rear, the slopes of 679-feet high Great Ormes Head. The elegantly furnished hotel offers a warm welcome from owners Len and Elizabeth Maddocks and their family who purchased the property in 1990. Although modernised, Osborne House retains many original features, including ornate cornices and a magnificent black and white marble entrance floor. A superb collection of antiques, period pieces and original artworks complement the attractive interior décor. The comfortable suites have been individually designed with many thoughtful extras; all have sea views, a Victorian fireplace and well appointed bathrooms, whilst five have antique king-size beds. Complimentary drinks are served in the library between 5pm and 7pm. The hotel is ideally situated for visiting Snowdonia National Park, the castles of Conwy and Caernarfon, Bodnant Gardens and the Italianate village of Portmeirion. Golf, riding, swimming and dry-slope skiing are available locally. **Directions:** Exit A55 at A470 intersection for Llandudno. Price Guide: Suites from £150.

6 MasterCard VISA AMERICAN EXPRESS VCR

ST TUDNO HOTEL

PROMENADE, LLANDUDNO LL30 2LP

TEL: 01492 874411 FAX: 01492 860407 E-MAIL: sttudnohotel@btinternet.com

Without doubt one of the most delightful small hotels to be found on the coast of Britain, St Tudno Hotel, a former winner of the Johansens Hotel of the Year Award for Excellence, certainly offers a very special experience. The hotel, which has been elegantly and lovingly furnished with meticulous attention to detail, offers a particularly warm welcome from owners, Martin and Janette Bland and their caring and friendly staff. Each beautifully co-ordinated bedroom has been individually designed with many thoughtful extras provided to ensure guests' comfort. The bar lounge and sitting room, which overlook the sea, have an air of Victorian charm. Regarded as one of Wales' leading restaurants, the air-conditioned Garden Room has won three AA Rosettes for its excellent cuisine. This AA Red Star hotel has won a host of other awards, including Best Seaside Resort Hotel in Great Britain, Welsh Hotel of the Year, national winner of the AA's Warmest Welcome Award and the British Tea Council 'Tea places award of excellence 1996–1998'. St Tudno is ideally situated for visits to Snowdonia, Conwy and Caernarfon Castles, Bodnant Gardens and Anglesey. Golf, riding, swimming and dry-slope skiing and tobogganing can be enjoyed locally. **Directions:** On the promenade opposite the pier entrance and gardens. Price Guide: Single from £78; double/twin £95–£190; suite £270.

19 MasterCard VISA AMERICAN EXPRESS M 30

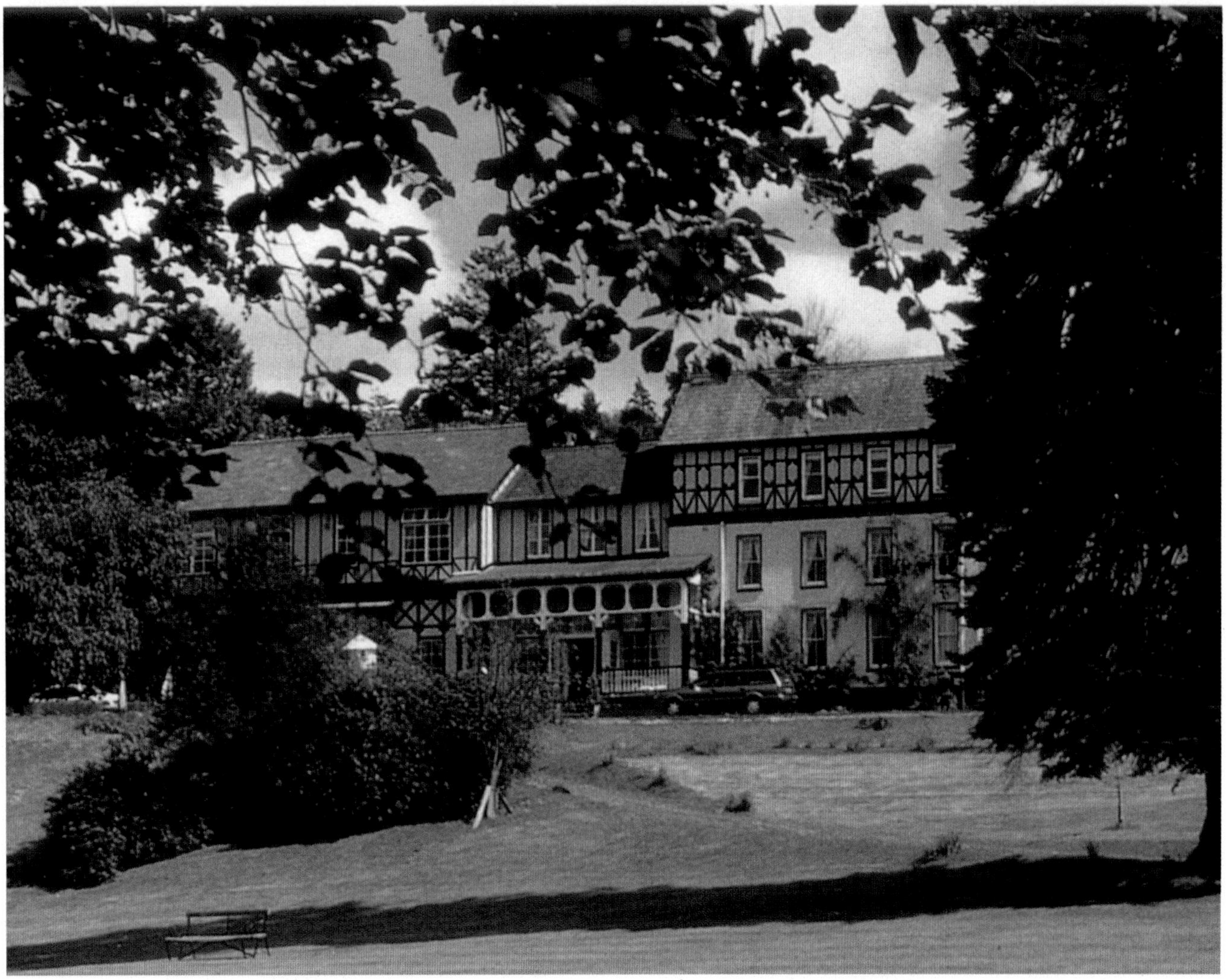

THE LAKE COUNTRY HOUSE

LLANGAMMARCH WELLS, POWYS LD4 4BS
TEL: 01591 620202 FAX: 01591 620457 E-MAIL: info@lakecountryhouse.co.uk

A welcoming Welsh Country house set in its own 50 acres with rhododendron lined pathways, riverside walks and a large well stocked trout lake. Within the hotel, airy rooms filled with fine antiques, paintings and fresh flowers make this the perfect place to relax. Delicious home-made teas are served everyday beside log fires. From the windows, ducks and geese can be glimpsed wandering in the gardens which cascade down to the river. In the award winning restaurant, fresh produce and herbs from the gardens are used for seasonal Country House menus, complemented by one of the finest wine lists in Wales. Each of the supremely comfortable bedrooms or suites with beautifully appointed sitting rooms are furnished with the thoughtful attention to details seen throughout the hotel. Guests can fish for trout or salmon on the four miles of river which runs through the grounds and the 3 acre lake regularly yields trout of five pounds and over. The grounds are a haven for wildlife: herons, dippers and kingfishers skim over the river, there are badgers in the woods and swans and waterfowl abound. There is a large billiard room in the hotel and a 9 hole par three golf course, tennis court, croquet lawn and putting green. Awarded an AA 3 Red star and RAC Blue Ribbon. **Directions:** From the A483, follow signs to Llangammarch Wells and then to the hotel. Price Guide: Single/double/twin £135–£160; suite £185–£215.

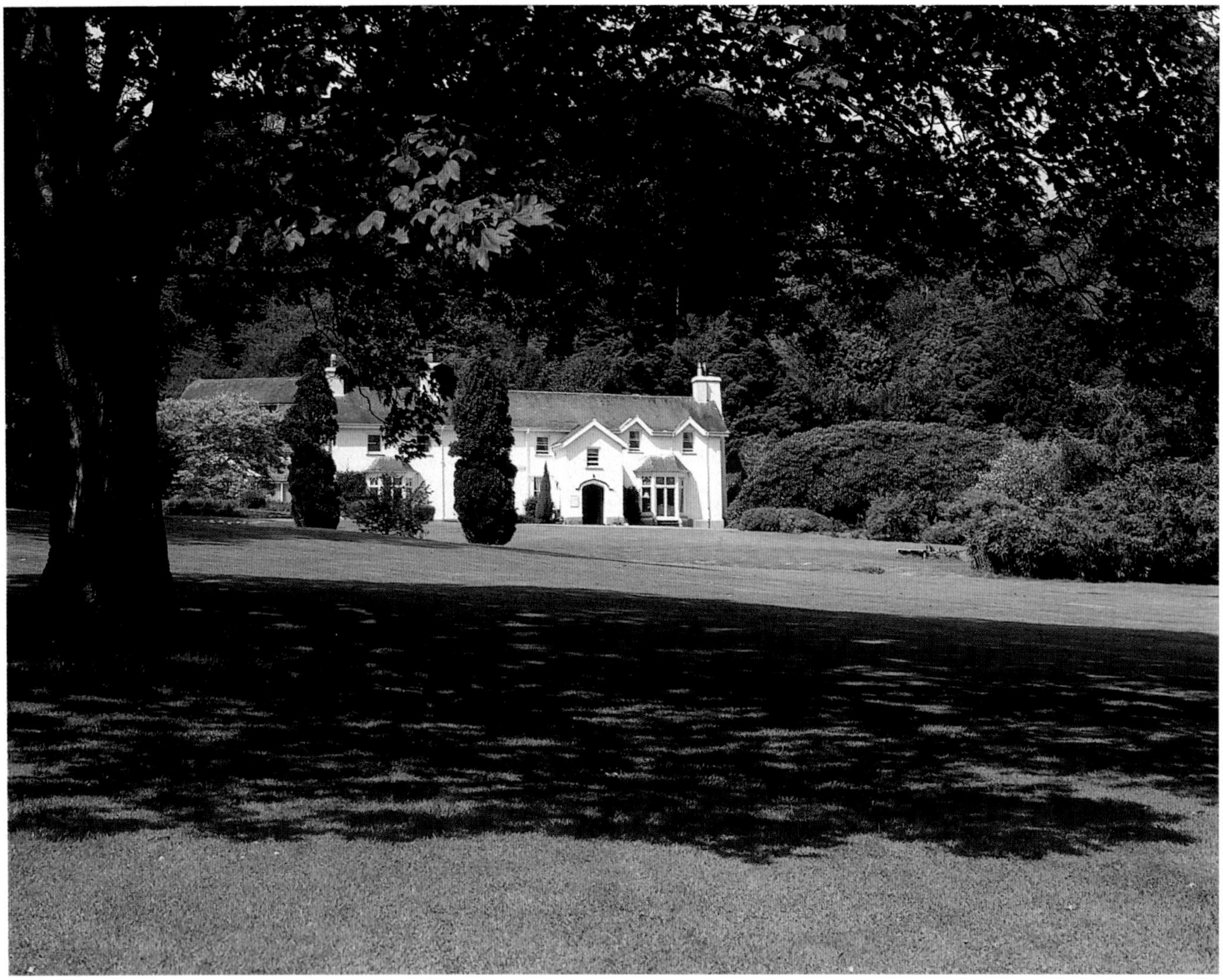

YNYSHIR HALL

EGLWYSFACH, MACHYNLLETH, CEREDIGION SY20 8TA
TEL: 01654 781209 FAX: 01654 781366 E-MAIL: info@ynyshir–hall.co.uk

Once owned by Queen Victoria, Ynyshir Hall is a captivating Georgian manor house that perfectly blends modern comfort and old-world elegance. Its 12 acres of landscaped gardens are set alongside the Dovey Estuary, one of Wales' most outstanding areas of natural beauty. The hotel is surrounded by the Ynyshir Bird Reserve. Hosts Rob and Joan Reen offer guests a warm welcome and ensure a personal service, the hallmark of a good family-run hotel. Period furniture and opulent fabrics enhance the ten charming bedrooms. The suites, including a four-poster room and ground floor room, are particularly luxurious. The interiors are exquisitely furnished throughout with sofas, antiques, contemporary colour schemes, oriental rugs and original paintings. These works of art are the creation of Rob, an acclaimed artist. The artistry continues in the kitchen where local seafood, game and vegetables from the garden are used to create superb modern interpretations of classic French cuisine. The imaginative dishes prepared by Les Rennie, comprise a wonderful balance of colours, textures and flavours. Awarded 2001 Welsh Hotel of the Year by the AA . Winner of Johansens 'Most Excellent Restaurant Award 1999'. Landmarks include Cader Idris, Wales' 2nd highest mountain. Closed in Jan. **Directions:** Off main road between Aberystwyth and Machynlleth. Price Guide: Single £110–£135; double/twin £125–£180; suite £210.

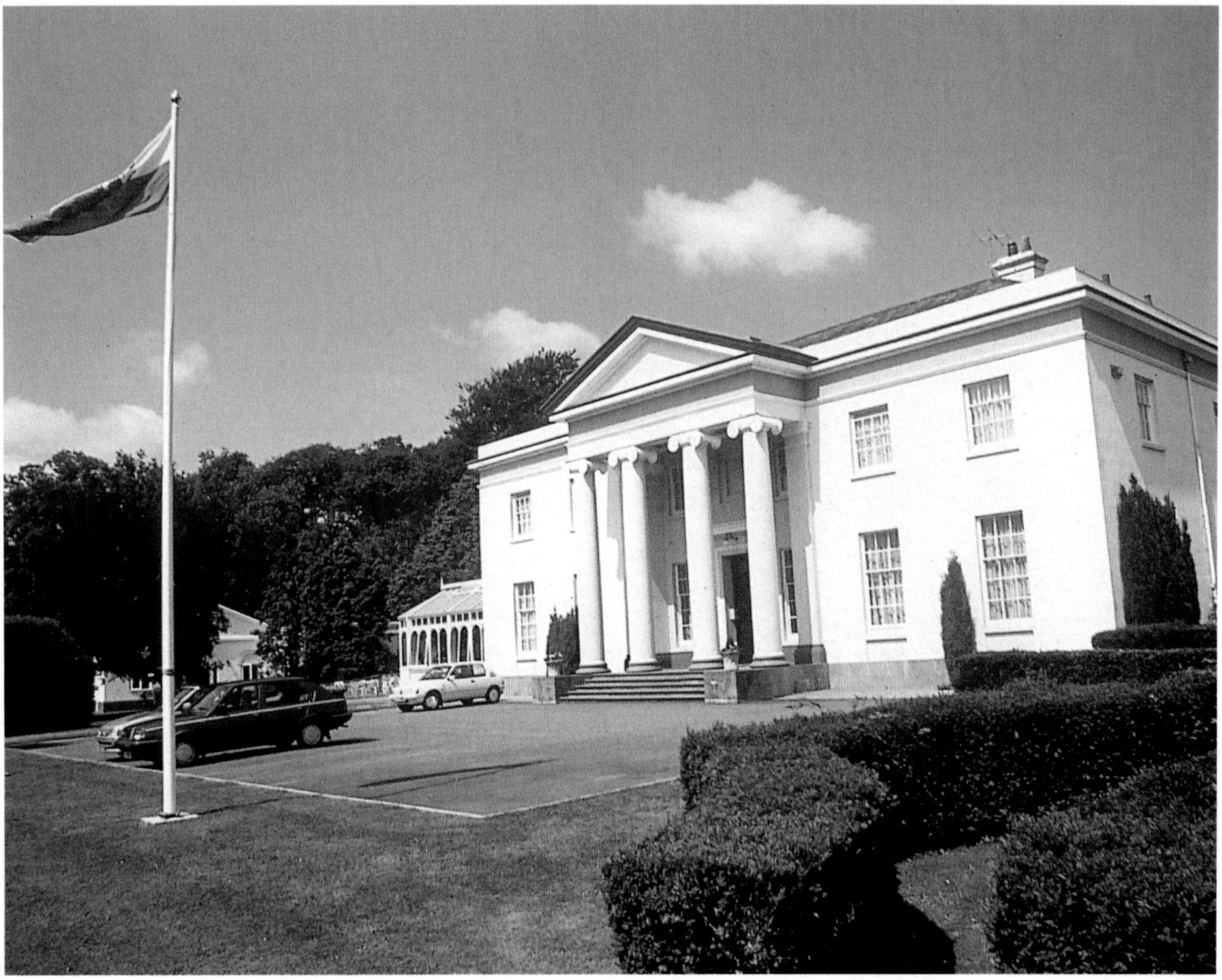

LAMPHEY COURT HOTEL AND RESTAURANT

LAMPHEY, NR TENBY, PEMBROKESHIRE SA71 5NT

TEL: 01646 672273 FAX: 01646 672480 E-MAIL: info@lampheycourt.co.uk

This magnificent Georgian mansion, is idyllically situated in acres of grounds bordered by the beautiful Pembrokeshire National Park and just one mile from some of Britain's finest coastal scenery and beaches. Warm, friendly and efficient service is enriched by comfortable furnishings and decor. There are deluxe and superior bedrooms within the hotel and purpose built Coach House studios provide the extra space required by families. The restaurant serves traditional flavours and local produce including such pleasures as Teifi salmon and Freshwater Bay lobster. Lighter meals and snacks can be taken in the elegant conservatory. The wide range of facilities in the superb leisure centre include an indoor heated swimming pool, Jacuzzi, sauna and a gymnasium. There are aerobics classes, massage fitness programmes and a beautician by appointment. Golf, sailing, fishing and yacht charter are all nearby. Well worth a visit is picturesque Tenby, the cliffside chapel of St Govan's, the Bishops Palace at Lamphey and Pembroke's impressive castle. **Directions:** From M4, exit at Junction 49 onto the A48 to Carmarthen. Then follow the A477 and turn left at Milton Village for Lamphey. Price Guide: Single £72–£82; double/twin £90–£135. Special breaks from £47–£75per person per night, dinner, bed and breakfast, all year.

PORTMEIRION AND CASTELL DEUDRAETH

PORTMEIRION, GWYNEDD LL48 6ET
TEL: 01766 770000 FAX: 01766 771331 E-MAIL: hotel@portmeirion–village.com

Portmeirion is a private village created by Welsh architect Sir Clough Williams-Ellis from 1926 to 1976. His aim was to show how a naturally beautiful place could be developed without spoiling its original charm. Portmeirion attracted a celebrated clientèle from the start – writers such as George Bernard Shaw, H G Wells, Bertrand Russell and Noel Coward were habitués. The village contains several interesting shops and a beauty salon and is surrounded by acres of sub-tropical woodlands and miles of sandy beaches. The hotel is based upon the Victorian mansion facing the estuary which houses the main restaurant, bar and several lounges. The village accommodation also contains several oak-panelled conference rooms, which are also licensed for civil weddings. During 2000, the hotel gained the Wales Tourist Board's top five star grading. Of Portmeirion's 51 rooms, 14 are located in the hotel's main building, 26 in the village and 11 in Castell Deudraeth,(pictured below). Castell Deudraeth, located mid-way along Portmeirion's drive, also has a brasserie-style restaurant and bar together with exhibition facilities and a Victorian garden. **Directions:** Portmeirion is signposted off the A487 mid-way between Penrhyndeudraeth and Porthmadog. Price Guide: (room only): Single £100–£140; double/twin £120–£180; suite £150–£230.

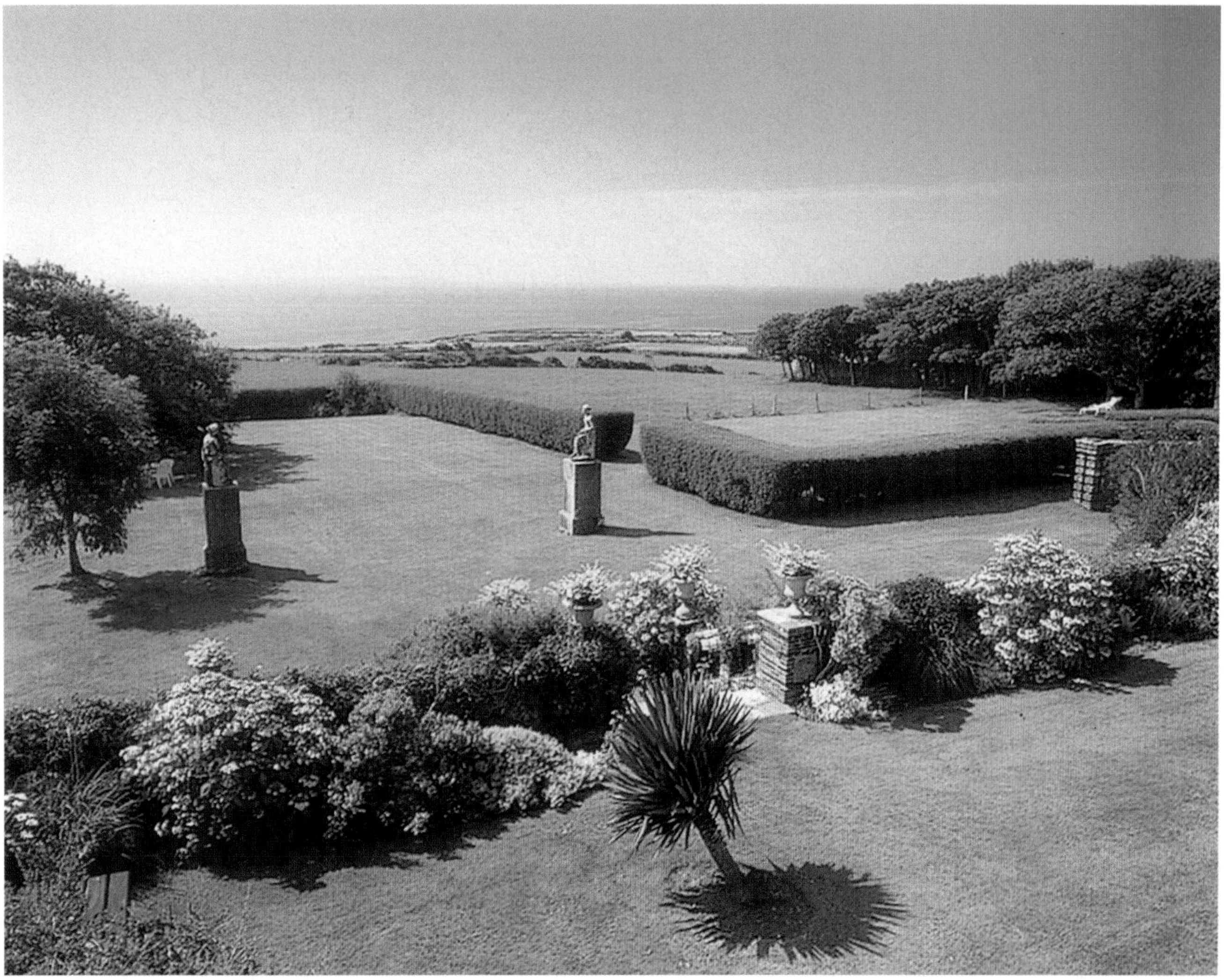

WARPOOL COURT HOTEL

ST DAVID'S, PEMBROKESHIRE SA62 6BN
TEL: 01437 720300 **FAX:** 01437 720676 **E-MAIL:** warpool@enterprise.net

Originally built as St David's Cathedral Choir School in the 1860s, Warpool Court enjoys spectacular scenery at the heart of the Pembrokeshire National Park, with views over the coast and St Bride's Bay to the islands beyond. First converted to a hotel over 40 years ago, continuous refurbishment has ensured all its up-to-date comforts are fit for the new century. All 25 bedrooms have immaculate en suite bathrooms and most enjoy sea views. The hotel restaurant enjoys a splendid reputation. Imaginative menus, including vegetarian, offer a wide selection of modern and traditional dishes. Local produce, including Welsh lamb and beef, is used whenever possible, with crab, lobster, sewin and sea bass caught just off the coast. Salmon and mackerel are smoked on the premises. The hotel gardens are ideal for a peaceful stroll or an after-dinner drink in the summer. There is a covered heated swimming pool (open April to end of October) and all-weather tennis court in the grounds. A path from the hotel leads straight on to the Pembrokeshire Coastal Path, with its rich variety of wildlife and spectacular scenery. Boating and water sports are available locally. St David's Peninsula offers a wealth of history and natural beauty and has inspired many famous artists. closed in January. **Directions:** The hotel is signposted from St David's town centre. Price Guide: Single from £75; double/twin from £132.

PENALLY ABBEY

PENALLY, TENBY, PEMBROKESHIRE SA70 7PY

TEL: 01834 843033 FAX: 01834 844714 E-MAIL: penally.abbey@btinternet.com

Penally Abbey, a beautiful listed Pemrokeshire country house, offers comfort and hospitality in a secluded setting by the sea. Standing in five acres of gardens and woodland on the edge of Pembrokeshire National Park, the hotel overlooks Carmarthen Bay and Caldey Island. The bedrooms in the main building and in the adjoining coach house are well furnished, many with four-poster beds. The emphasis is on relaxation – enjoy a late breakfast and dine at leisure. Fresh seasonal delicacies are offered in the candlelit restaurant, with its chandeliers and colonnades. Guests can enjoy a game in the snooker room or relax in the elegant sunlit lounge, overlooking the terrace and gardens. In the grounds there is a wishing well and a ruined chapel – the last surviving link with the hotel's monastic past. Water-skiing, surfing, sailing, riding and parascending are available nearby. Sandy bays and rugged cliffs are features of the Pembrokeshire coastal park. As the rates include the cost of dinner, this friendly hotel offers splendid value for money. **Directions:** Penally Abbey is situated adjacent to the church on Penally village green Price Guide: (including dinner): Single £128; double/twin £164; suite £188.

MINI LISTINGS

Here in brief are the entries that appear in full in

Johansens Recommended Country Houses, Small Hotels & Traditional Inns Great Britain & Ireland 2002

To order Johansens guides turn to the order forms at the back of this book.

CHANNEL ISLANDS

Guernsey – La Favorita Hotel, Fermain Bay, Guernsey, Channel Islands GY4 6SD. Tel: 01481 235666

Guernsey – Les Rocquettes Hotel, Les Gravees, St Peter Port, Guernsey, Channel Islands GY1 1RN. Tel: 01481 722146

Herm Island – The White House, Herm Island, Guernsey, Channel Islands GY1 3HR. Tel: 01481 722159

Sark – La Sablonnerie, Little Sark, Sark, Channel Islands GY9 0SD. Tel: 01481 832061 Channel Isle GY9 0SD. Tel: 01481 832061

ENGLAND

Ambleside – Grey Friar Lodge, Clappersgate, Ambleside, Cumbria LA22 9NE. Tel: 015394 33158

Ambleside – Nanny Brow Country House Hotel & Restaurant, Clappersgate, Ambleside, Cumbria LA22 9NF. Tel: 015394 32036

Appleton-Le-Moors – Appleton Hall, Appleton-Le-Moors, North Yorkshire YO62 6TF. Tel: 01751 417227

Arundel – Burpham Country House Hotel, Old Down, Burpham, Nr Arundel, West Sussex BN18 9RJ. Tel: 01903 882160

Ashbourne – Red Lion Inn, Main Street, Hognaston, Ashbourne, Derbyshire DE6 1PR. Tel: 01335 370396

Ashington – The Mill House Hotel, Mill Lane, Ashington, West Sussex RH20 3BX. Tel: 01903 892426

Badby – The Windmill At Badby, Main Street, Badby, Daventry, Northamptonshire NN11 6AN. Tel: 01327 702363

Bakewell – The Peacock Hotel at Rowsley, Rowsley, Nr Matlock, Derbyshire DE4 2EB. Tel: 01629 733518

Bamburgh – Waren House Hotel, Waren Mill, Bamburgh, Northumberland NE70 7EE. Tel: 01668 214581

Barnstaple – Downrew House Hotel, Bishops Tawton, Barnstaple, Devon EX32 0DY. Tel: 01271 342497

Basingstoke – New Mill Restaurant, New Mill Road, Eversley, Hampshire RG27 0RA. Tel: 0118 973 2277

Bath – Apsley House, 141 Newbridge Hill, Somerset BA1 3PT. Tel: 01225 336966

Bath – Bath Lodge Hotel, Norton St Philip, Bath, Somerset BA2 7NH. Tel: 01225 723040

Bath – The County Hotel, 18/19 Pulteney Road, Bath, Somerset BA2 4EZ. Tel: 01225 425003

Bath – The Old Priory Hotel, Church Square, Midsomer Norton, Bath, Somerset BA3 2HX. Tel: 01761 416784/410846

Bath – Oldfields, 102 Wells Road, Bath, Somerset BA2 3AL. Tel: 01225 317984

Bath – Villa Magdala, Henrietta Road, Bath, Somerset BA2 6LX. Tel: 01225 466329

Bath – Widbrook Grange, Trowbridge Road, Bradford-On-Avon, Wiltshire BA15 1UH. Tel: 01225 864750/863173

Belford – The Blue Bell Hotel, Market Place, Belford, Northumberland NE70 7NE. Tel: 01668 213543

Belper – Dannah Farm Country House, Bowman's Lane, Shottle, Nr Belper, Derbyshire DE56 2DR. Tel: 01773 550273/550630

Bibury – Bibury Court, Bibury Court, Bibury, Gloucestershire GL7 5NT. Tel: 01285 740337

Bideford – Yeoldon House Hotel, Durrant Lane, Northam, Nr Bideford EX39 2RL. Tel: 01237 474400

Biggin-By-Hartington – Biggin Hall, Biggin-By-Hartington, Buxton, Derbyshire SK17 0DH. Tel: 01298 84451

Billericay-Great Burstead – The Pump House Apartment, 132 Church Street, Great Burstead, Essex CM11 2TR. Tel: 01277 656579

Blockley – Lower Brook House, Blockley, Nr Moreton-In-Marsh, Gloucestershire GL56 9DS. Tel: 01386 700286

Bourton-On-The-Water – Dial House, The Chestnuts, High Street, Bourton-On-The-Water, Gloucestershire GL54 2AN. Tel: 01451 822244

Bovey Tracey – The Edgemoor, Haytor Road, Bovey Tracey, South Devon TQ13 9LE. Tel: 01626 832466

Brancaster Staithe – The White Horse, Brancaster Staithe, Norfolk PE31 8BW. Tel: 01485 210262

Bridport – The Manor Hotel, West Bexington, Dorchester, Dorset DT2 9DF. Tel: 01308 897616

Brighton – The Granville, 124 Kings Road, Brighton BN1 2FA. Tel: 01273 326302

Brighton – The Old Tollgate Restaurant And Hotel, The Street, Bramber, Steyning, West Sussex BN44 3WE. Tel: 01903 879494

Brockenhurst – Thatched Cottage Hotel & Restaurant, 16 Brookley Road, Brockenhurst, Hampshire SO42 7RR. Tel: 01590 623090

Brockenhurst – Whitley Ridge Country House Hotel, Beaulieu Road, Brockenhurst, New Forest, Hampshire SO42 7QL. Tel: 01590 622354

Broughton-In-Furness – Underwood, The Hill, Millom, Cumbria LA18 5EZ. Tel: 01229 771116

Burford – The Lamb Inn, Sheep Street, Burford, Oxfordshire OX18 4LR. Tel: 01993 823155

Burnham Market – The Hoste Arms Hotel, The Green, Burnham Market, Norfolk PE31 8HD. Tel: 01328 738777

Burnley – FENCE GATE INN, Wheatley Lane Road, Fence, Nr Burnley, Lancashire BB12 9EE. Tel: 01282 618101

Burnsall – The Devonshire Fell Hotel & Restaurant, Burnsall, Skipton, North Yorkshire BD23 6BT. Tel: 01756 729000

Burton Upon Trent – Boar's Head Hotel, Lichfield Road, Sudbury, Derbyshire DE6 5GX. Tel: 01283 820344

Burton Upon Trent – Ye Olde Dog & Partridge, High Street, Tutbury, Burton-On-Trent, Staffordshire DE13 9LS. Tel: 01283 813030

Calstone-Wellington – Manor House, Manor Farm, Calstone-Wellington, Nr Calne, Wiltshire SN11 8PY. Tel: 01249 816804

Cambridge – Melbourn Bury, Melbourn, Cambridgeshire, Nr Royston SG8 6DE. Tel: 01763 261151

Cambridge – The White Horse Inn, Hollow Hill, Withersfield, Haverhill, Suffolk CB9 7SH. Tel: 01440 706081

Canterbury – The Abbot's Fireside Hotel, High Street, Elham, Near Canterbury, Kent CT4 6TD. Tel: 01303 840265

Canterbury – Howfield Manor, Chartham Hatch, Nr Canterbury, Kent CT4 7HQ. Tel: 01227 738294

Carlisle – Crosby Lodge Country House Hotel, High Crosby, Crosby-On-Eden, Carlisle, Cumbria CA6 4QZ. Tel: 01228 573618

Carlisle – The Tarn End House Hotel, Talkin Tarn, Brampton, Cumbria CA8 1LS. Tel: 016977 2340

Castle Ashby – The Falcon Hotel, Castle Ashby, Northamptonshire NN7 1LF. Tel: 01604 696200

Cheltenham – The Green Dragon Inn, Cockleford, Nr Cowley, Cheltenham, Gloucester GL53 9NW. Tel: 01242 870271

Chester – Broxton Hall Country House Hotel, Whitchurch Road, Broxton, Chester, Cheshire CH3 9JS. Tel: 01829 782321

Chichester – Crouchers Bottom Country Hotel, Birdham Road, Apuldram, Near Chichester, West Sussex PO20 7EH. Tel: 01243 784995

Chichester – Forge Hotel, Chilgrove, Chichester, West Sussex PO18 9HX. Tel: 01243 535333

Chippenham – Stanton Manor, Stanton Saint Quintin, Nr Chippenham, Wiltshire SN14 6DQ. Tel: 01666 837552

Chipping Campden – The Malt House, Broad Campden, Gloucestershire GL55 6UU. Tel: 01386 840295

Church Stretton – Stretton Hall Hotel, All Stretton, Church Stretton, Shropshire SY6 6HG. Tel: 01694 723224

Cirencester – The New Inn at Coln, Coln St-Aldwyns, Nr Cirencester, Gloucestershire GL7 5AN. Tel: 01285 750651

Clare – The Plough Inn, Brockley Green, Nr Hundon, Sudbury, Suffolk CO10 8DT. Tel: 01440 786789

Coalville – Abbots Oak, Warren Hills Road, Near Coalville, Leicestershire LE67 4UY. Tel: 01530 832 328

Colchester – The Stoke By Nayland Club, Keeper's Lane, Leavenheath, Colchester, Essex CO6 4PZ. Tel: 01206 262836

Coleford – The New Inn, Coleford, Crediton, Devon EX17 5BZ. Tel: 01363 84242

Coningsby – The Lea Gate Inn, Leagate Road, Coningsby, Lincolnshire LN4 4RS. Tel: 01526 342370

Corfe Castle – Mortons House Hotel, East Street, Corfe Castle, Dorset BH20 5EE. Tel: 01929 480988

Cranbrook – The George Hotel, Stone Street, Cranbrook, Kent TN17 3HE. Tel: 01580 713348

Dartmoor – Bel Alp House, Haytor, Nr Bovey Tracey, South Devon TQ13 9XX. Tel: 01364 661217

Dartmoor – Easton Court Hotel - Quills Restaurant, Easton Cross, Chagford, Devon TQ13 8JL. Tel: 01647 433469

Derby – Littleover Lodge Hotel, 222 Rykneld Road, Littleover, Derby, Derbyshire DE23 7AN. Tel: 01332 510161

Diss – Chippenhall Hall, Fressingfield, Eye, Suffolk IP21 5TD. Tel: 01379 588180

Diss – Gissing Hall, Gissing, Diss, Norfolk IP22 5UN. Tel: 01379 677291

Dorchester – Yalbury Cottage Hotel, Lower Bockhampton, Dorchester, Dorset DT2 8PZ. Tel: 01305 262382

Dorchester-On-Thames – The George Hotel, High Street, Dorchester-On-Thames, Oxford OX10 7HH. Tel: 01865 340404

Dover – Wallett's Court, West Cliffe, St Margaret's-At-Cliffe, Dover, Kent CT15 6EW. Tel: 01304 852424

Dulverton – Ashwick Country House Hotel, Dulverton, Somerset TA22 9QD. Tel: 01398 323868

East Witton – The Blue Lion, East Witton, Nr Leyburn, North Yorkshire DL8 4SN. Tel: 01969 624273

Enfield – Oak Lodge Hotel, 80 Village Road, Bush Hill Park, Enfield, Middlesex EN1 2EU. Tel: 020 8360 7082

Eton – The Christopher Hotel, High Street, Eton, Windsor, Berkshire SL4 6AN. Tel: 01753 811677 / 852359

Evershot – Acorn Inn, Evershot, Dorset DT2 0JW. Tel: 01935 83228

Evesham – The Mill at Harvington, Anchor Lane, Harvington, Evesham, Worcestershire WR11 5NR. Tel: 01386 870688

Evesham – Riverside Restaurant And Hotel, The Parks, Offenham Road, Nr Evesham, Worcestershire WR11 5JP. Tel: 01386 446200

Exeter – The Lord Haldon Country Hotel, Dunchideock, Nr Exeter, Devon EX6 7YF. Tel: 01392 832483

Exford – The Crown Hotel, Exford, Exmoor National Park, Somerset TA24 7PP. Tel: 01643 831554

Fakenham – The Manor House, Barsham Road, Great Snoring, Norfolk NR21 OHP. Tel: 01328 820597

Fakenham – Vere Lodge, South Raynham, Fakenham, Norfolk NR21 7HE. Tel: 01328 838261

Falmouth – Trelawne Hotel – The Hutches Restaurant, Mawnan Smith, Nr Falmouth, Cornwall TR11 5HS. Tel: 01326 250226

Folkestone – Sandgate Hotel Et Restaurant La Terrasse, Wellington Terrace, The Esplanade, Sandgate, Folkestone, Kent CT20 3DY. Tel: 01303 220444

Fowey – Cormorant On The River, Hotel & Riverside Restaurant, Golant By Fowey, Cornwall PL23 1LL. Tel: 01726 833426

Gatwick – Stanhill Court Hotel, Stan Hill Road, Charlwood, Nr Horley, Surrey RH6 0EP. Tel: 01293 862166

Glossop – The Wind In The Willows, Derbyshire Level, Glossop, Derbyshire SK13 7PT. Tel: 01457 868001

Goring-On-Thames – The Leatherne Bottel Riverside Inn & Restaurant, The Bridleway, Goring-On-Thames, Berkshire RG8 0HS. Tel: 01491 872667

Grasmere – White Moss House, Rydal Water, Grasmere, Cumbria LA22 9SE. Tel: 015394 35295

Great Chesterford – The Crown House, Great Chesterford, Saffron Walden, Essex CB10 1NY. Tel: 01799 530515 / 530257

Great Yarmouth – Caldecott Hall, Fritton, Great Yarmouth, Norfolk NR31 9EY. Tel: 01493 488488

Grimsthorpe – The Black Horse Inn, Grimsthorpe, Bourne, Lincolnshire PE10 0LY. Tel: 01778 591247

Grindleford – The Maynard Arms, Main Road, Grindleford, Derbyshire S32 2HE. Tel: 01433 630321

Hadleigh – Edge Hall Hotel, 2 High Street, Hadleigh, Ipswich, Suffolk IP7 5AP. Tel: 01473 822458

Halifax – The Shibden Mill Inn, Shibden Mill Fold, Shibden, Halifax, West Yorkshire HX3 7UL. Tel: 01422 365840

Halifax/Huddersfield – The Rock Inn Hotel, Holywell Green, Halifax, West Yorkshire HX4 9BS. Tel: 01422 379721

Hampton Court – Chase Lodge, 10 Park Road, Hampton Wick, Kingston-Upon-Thames, Surrey KT1 4AS. Tel: 020 8943 1862

Hamsterley Forest – Grove House, Hamsterley Forest, Nr Bishop Auckland, Co Durham DL13 3NL. Tel: 01388 488203

Handcross – The Chequers At Slaugham, Slaugham, Nr Handcross, West Sussex RH17 6AQ. Tel: 01444 400239/400996

Harrogate – The Boar's Head Hotel, The Ripley Castle Estate, Harrogate, North Yorkshire HG3 3AY. Tel: 01423 771888

Hathersage – The Plough Inn, Leadmill Bridge, Hathersage, Derbyshire S30 1BA. Tel: 01433 650319

Hawes – Rookhurst Country House Hotel, West End, Gayle, Hawes, North Yorkshire DL8 3RT. Tel: 01969 667454

Hawkshead – The Queen's Head Hotel, Main Street, Hawkshead, Cumbria LA22 0NS. Tel: 015394 36271

Hawkshead – Sawrey House Country Hotel, Nr Sawrey, Hawkshead, Ambleside, Cumbria LA22 0LF. Tel: 015394 36387

Helmsley – Ryedale Country Lodge, Nunnington, Near Helmsley, North Yorkshire YO62 5XB. Tel: 01439 748246

Hereford – The Steppes, Ullingswick, Nr Hereford, Herefordshire HR1 3JG. Tel: 01432 820424

Higham – Santo's Higham Farm, Main Road, Higham, Derbyshire DE55 6EH. Tel: 01773 833812/3/4

Holkham – The Victoria At Holkham, Park Road, Holkham, Wells-Next-The-Sea, Norfolk NR23 1RG. Tel: 01328 711008

Holt – Felbrigg Lodge, Aylmerton, North Norfolk NR11 8RA. Tel: 01263 837588

Holt – The Roman Camp Inn, Holt Road, Aylmerton, Norwich, Norfolk NR11 8QD. Tel: 01263 838291

Honiton – Home Farm Hotel, Wilmington, Nr Honiton, Devon EX14 9JR. Tel: 01404 831278

Huddersfield – The Weavers Shed Restaurant With Rooms, Knowl Road, Golcar, Huddersfield, West Yorkshire HD7 4AN. Tel: 01484 654284

Ilsington – Ilsington Country House Hotel, Ilsington Village, Near Newton Abbot, Devon TQ13 9RR. Tel: 01364 661452

Isle Of Wight – Rylstone Manor, Rylstone Gardens, Shanklin, Isle Of Wight PO37 6RE. Tel: 01983 862806

Kenilworth – Clarendon House , Old High Street, Kenilworth, Warwickshire CV8 1LZ. Tel: 01926 857668

Keswick – Dale Head Hall Lakeside Hotel, Thirlmere, Keswick, Cumbria CA12 4TN. Tel: 017687 72478

Keswick – The Leathes Head, Borrowdale, Keswick, Cumbria CA12 5UY. Tel: 017687 77247

Keswick – Swinside Lodge Hotel, Grange Road, Newlands, Keswick, Cumbria CA12 5UE. Tel: 017687 72948

Kingsbridge – The White House, Chillington, Kingsbridge, Devon TQ7 2JX. Tel: 01548 580580

Kirkby Lonsdale – Hipping Hall, Cowan Bridge, Kirkby Lonsdale, Cumbria LA6 2JJ. Tel: 015242 71187

Launceston – Penhallow Manor Country House Hotel, Altarnun, Launceston, Cornwall PL15 7SJ. Tel: 01566 86206

Leominster – Lower Bache House, Kimbolton, Nr Leominster, Herefordshire HR6 OER. Tel: 01568 750304

Lichfield / Tamwoth – Oak Tree Farm, Hints Road, Hopwas, Nr Tamworth, Staffordshire B78 3AA. Tel: 01827 56807

Lincoln – Washingborough Hall, Church Hill, Washingborough, Lincoln LN4 1BE. Tel: 01522 790340

Looe – Trehaven Manor Hotel, Station Road, Looe, Cornwall PL13 1HN. Tel: 01503 262028

Loughborough – The Old Manor Hotel, 11-14 Sparrow Hill, Loughborough, Leicestershire LE11 1BT. Tel: 01509 211228

Ludlow – Overton Grange Hotel, Overton, Ludlow, Shropshire SY8 4AD. Tel: 01584 873500

Luton – Little Offley, Hitchin, Hertfordshire SG5 3BU. Tel: 01462 768243

Lydford – Moor View House, Vale Down, Lydford, Devon EX20 4BB. Tel: 01822 820220

Lymington – Gordleton Mill Inn, Silver Street, Hordle, Nr Lymington, New Forest, Hampshire SO41 6DJ. Tel: 01590 682219

Lymington – The Nurse's Cottage, Station Road, Sway, Lymington, Hampshire SO41 6BA. Tel: 01590 683402

Lymington – Westover Hall, Park Lane, Milford-On-Sea, Lymington, Hampshire SO41 0PT. Tel: 01590 643044

Lynmouth – The Rising Sun, Harbourside, Lynmouth, Devon EX35 6EQ. Tel: 01598 753223

Maidstone – Ringlestone Inn and Farmhouse Hotel, Twixt Harrietsham And Wormshill, Nr Maidstone, Kent ME17 1NX. Tel: 01622 859900

Malmesbury – The Horse And Groom Inn, Charlton, Near Malmesbury, Wiltshire SN16 9DL. Tel: 01666 823904

Manchester – Eleven Didsbury Park, Didsbury Village, Manchester M20 5LH. Tel: 0161 448 7711

Mells – The Talbot 15th Century Coaching Inn, Selwood Street, Mells, Nr Bath, Somerset BA11 3PN. Tel: 01373 812254

Middlecombe – Periton Park Hotel, Middlecombe, Nr Minehead, Somerset TA24 8SN. Tel: 01643 706885

Mildenhall – The Bell Hotel, High Street, Mildenhall, Suffolk IP28 7EA. Tel: 01638 717272

Mullion – Mullion Cove Hotel, Mullion Cove, Mullion, Cornwall TR12 7EP. Tel: 01326 240328

New Romney – Romney Bay House, Coast Road, Littlestone, New Romney, Kent TN28 8QY. Tel: 01797 364747

Newbury – The Royal Oak Hotel, Yattendon, Newbury RG16 0UF. Tel: 01635 201325

Newent – Three Choirs Vineyards Estate, Newent, Gloucestershire GL18 1LS. Tel: 01531 890223

Newlyn – Higher Faugan Country House Hotel, Chywoone Hill, Newlyn, Cornwall TR18 5NS. Tel: 01736 362076

Newmarket – Newmarket Apartments, Cambridge Apartments Ltd, 69 Rustat Road, Cambridge CB1 3QR. Tel: 01223 500675

North Norfolk Coast – The Great Escape Holiday Company, Docking, Kings Lynn, Norfolk PE31 8LY. Tel: 01485 518717

North Walsham – Beechwood Hotel, Cromer Road, North Walsham, Norfolk NR28 0HD. Tel: 01692 403231

North Walsham – Elderton Lodge, Gunton Park, Thorpe Market, Nr North Walsham,Norfolk NR11 8TZ. Tel: 01263 833547

Norwich – The Beeches Hotel And Victorian Gardens, 2–6 Earlham Road, Norwich, Norfolk NR2 3DB. Tel: 01603 621167

Norwich – Catton Old Hall, Lodge Lane, Catton, Norwich, Norfolk NR6 7HG. Tel: 01603 419379

Norwich – The Norfolk Mead Hotel, Coltishall, Norwich, Norfolk NR12 7DN. Tel: 01603 737531

Norwich – The Old Rectory, 103 Yarmouth Road, Norwich, Norfolk NR7 0HF. Tel: 01603 700772

Norwich – The Stower Grange, School Road, Drayton, Norfolk NR8 6EF. Tel: 01603 860210

Nottingham – Cockliffe Country House Hotel, Burnt Stump Country Park, Burnt Stump Hill, Nottinghamshire NG5 8PQ. Tel: 01159 680179

Nottingham – The Cottage Country House Hotel, Easthorpe Street, Ruddington, Nottingham NG11 6LA. Tel: 01159 846882

Nottingham – Hotel Des Clos, Old Lenton Lane, Nottingham, Nottinghamshire NG7 2SA. Tel: 01159 866566

Nottingham – Langar Hall, Langar, Nottinghamshire NG13 9HG. Tel: 01949 860559

Nottingham – Sutton Bonington Hall, Main Street, Sutton Bonington, Loughborough, Leicestershire LE12 5PF. Tel: 01509 672355

Onneley – Wheatsheaf Inn, Onneley, Staffordshire CW3 9QF. Tel: 01782 751581

Oswestry – Pen-Y-Dyffryn Hall Hotel, Rhydycroesau, Nr Oswestry, Shropshire SY10 7JD. Tel: 01691 653700

Otterburn – The Otterburn Tower, Otterburn, Northumberland NE19 1NS. Tel: 01584 873500

Oxford – Fallowfields, Kingston Bagpuize With Southmoor, Oxon OX13 5BH. Tel: 01865 820416

Oxford – Holcombe Hotel, High Street, Deddington, Nr Woodstock, Oxfordshire OX15 0SL. Tel: 01869 338274

Oxford – The Jersey Arms, Middleton Stoney, Oxfordshire OX6 8SE. Tel: 01869 343234

Oxford – Westwood Country Hotel , Hinksey Hill, Nr. Boars Hill, Oxford OX1 5BG. Tel: 01865 735 408

Pelynt – Jubilee Inn, Pelynt, Nr Looe, Cornwall PL13 2JZ. Tel: 01503 220312

Penrith – Temple Sowerby House Hotel, Temple Sowerby, Penrith, Cumbria CA10 1RZ. Tel: 017683 61578

Petersfield – Langrish House, Langrish, Nr Petersfield, Hampshire GU32 1RN. Tel: 01730 266941

Pickering – The White Swan, The Market Place, Pickering, North Yorkshire YO18 7AA. Tel: 01751 472288

Porlock Weir – Andrew's On The Weir, Porlock Weir, Porlock, Somerset TA24 8PB. Tel: 01643 863300

Porlock Weir – Porlock Vale House, Porlock Weir, Somerset TA24 8NY. Tel: 01643 862338

Port Gaverne – The Port Gaverne Inn, Nr. Port Isaac, North Cornwall PL29 3SQ. Tel: 01208 880244

Preston – Ye Horn's Inn, Horn's Lane, Goosnargh, Nr Preston, Lancashire PR3 2FJ. Tel: 01772 865230

Pulborough – Chequers Hotel, Old Rectory Lane, Pulborough, West Sussex RH20 1AD. Tel: 01798 872486

Ringwood – Moortown Lodge, 244 Christchurch Road, Ringwood, Hampshire BH24 3AS. Tel: 01425 471404

Ross-On-Wye – Glewstone Court, Nr Ross-On-Wye, Herefordshire HR9 6AW. Tel: 01989 770367

Ross-On-Wye – Wilton Court Hotel, Wilton, Ross-On-Wye, Herefordshire HR9 6AQ. Tel: 01989 562569

Rutland Water – Barnsdale Lodge, The Avenue, Rutland Water, Nr Oakham, Rutland, Leicestershire LE15 8AH. Tel: 01572 724678

Rye – White Vine House, High Street, Rye, East Sussex TN31 7JF. Tel: 01797 224748

Saddleworth – The Old Bell Inn Hotel, Huddersfield Road, Delph, Saddleworth, Nr Oldham, Greater Manchester OL3 5EG. Tel: 01457 870130

St Ives – The Countryman At Trink Hotel, Old Coach Road, St Ives, Cornwall TR26 3JQ. Tel: 01736 797571

St Mawes – The Hundred House Hotel, Ruan Highlanes, Nr Truro, Cornwall TR2 5JR. Tel: 01872 501336

Salisbury – The Museum Inn, Farnham, Near Blandford Forum, Dorset DT11 8DE. Tel: 01725 516261

Saunton – Preston House & Little's Restaurant, Saunton, Braunton, North Devon EX33 1LG. Tel: 01271 890472

Sharnbrook – Mill House Hotel & Restaurant, Mill House, Mill Road, Sharnbrook, Bedfordshire MK44 1NP. Tel: 01234 781678

Sherborne – The Eastbury Hotel, Long Street, Sherborne, Dorset DT9 3BY. Tel: 01935 813131

Sherborne – The Grange Hotel And Restaurant, Oborne, Nr Sherborne, Dorset DT9 4LA. Tel: 01935 813463

Shipton Under Wychwood – The Shaven Crown Hotel, High Street, Shipton Under Wychwood, Oxfordshire OX7 6BA. Tel: 01993 830330

Southport – Tree Tops Country House Restaurant & Hotel, Southport Old Road, Formby, Nr Southport, Lancashire L37 0AB. Tel: 01704 572430

Stamford – Black Bull Inn, Lobthorpe, Nr Grantham, Lincolnshire NG33 5LL. Tel: 01476 860086

Stamford – The Crown Hotel, All Saints Place, Stamford, Lincolnshire PE9 2AG. Tel: 01780 763136

Stanhope – Horsley Hall, Eastgate, Nr Stanhope, Bishop Auckland, Co. Durham DL13 2LJ. Tel: 01388 517239

Stanton Wick – The Carpenters Arms, Stanton Wick, Nr Pensford, Somerset BS39 4BX. Tel: 01761 490202

Staverton – Kingston House, Staverton, Totnes, Devon TQ9 6AR. Tel: 01803 762 235

Stevenage – Redcoats Farmhouse Hotel And Restaurant, Redcoats Green, Near Hitchin, Herts SG4 7JR. Tel: 01438 729500

Stow-On-The-Wold – The Kings Head Inn & Restaurant, The Green, Bledington, Nr Kingham, Oxfordshire OX7 6XQ. Tel: 01608 658365

Stratford-Upon-Avon – Glebe Farm House, Loxley, Warwickshire CV35 9JW. Tel: 01789 842501

Stratford-Upon-Avon – The Old Windmill, Withybed Lane, Inkberrow, Worcester WR7 4JL. Tel: 01386 792801

Tarporley – Willington Hall Hotel, Willington, Nr Tarporley, Cheshire CW6 0NB. Tel: 01829 752321

Taunton – Farthings Hotel & Restaurant, Hatch Beauchamp, Somerset TA3 6SG. Tel: 01823 480664

Telford – The Hundred House Hotel, Bridgnorth Road, Norton, Nr Shifnal, Telford, Shropshire TF11 9EE. Tel: 01952 730353

Thetford – Broom Hall Country Hotel, Richmond Road, Saham Toney, Thetford, Norfolk IP25 7EX. Tel: 01953 882125

Tintagel – The Port William, Trebarwith Strand, Nr Tintagel, Cornwall PL34 0HB. Tel: 01840 770230

Tintagel – Trebrea Lodge, Trenale, Tintagel, Cornwall PL34 0HR. Tel: 01840 770410

Totnes – The Sea Trout Inn, Staverton, Nr Totnes, Devon TQ9 6PA. Tel: 01803 762274

Uckfield – Hooke Hall, High Street, Uckfield, East Sussex TN22 1EN. Tel: 01825 761578

Upton-Upon-Severn – The White Lion Hotel, High Street, Upton-Upon-Severn, Nr Malvern, Worcestershire WR8 0HJ. Tel: 01684 592551

Wadebridge – Tredethy House, Helland Bridge, Bodmin, Cornwall PL30 4QS. Tel: 01208 841262

Wadebridge – Trehellas House & Memories Of Malaya Restaurant, Washaway, Bodmin, Cornwall PL30 3AD. Tel: 01208 72700

Wareham – Kemps Country House Hotel & Restaurant, East Stoke, Wareham, Dorset BH20 6AL. Tel: 01929 462563

Warminster – The George Inn, Longbridge Deverill, Warminster, Wiltshire BA12 7DG. Tel: 01985 840396

Wells – Beryl, Wells, Somerset BA5 3JP. Tel: 01749 678738

Wells – Glencot House, Glencot Lane, Wookey Hole, Nr Wells, Somerset BA5 1BH. Tel: 01749 677160

Wem – Soulton Hall, Nr Wem, Shropshire SY4 5RS. Tel: 01939 232786

West Auckland – The Manor House Hotel & Country Club, The Green, West Auckland, County Durham DL14 9HW. Tel: 01388 834834

Whitby – Dunsley Hall, Dunsley, Whitby, North Yorkshire YO21 3TL. Tel: 01947 893437

Whitewell – The Inn At Whitewell, Forest Of Bowland, Clitheroe, Lancashire BB7 3AT. Tel: 01200 448222

Wimborne Minster – Beechleas, 17 Poole Road, Wimborne Minster, Dorset BH21 1QA. Tel: 01202 841684

Windermere – Broadoaks Country House, Bridge Lane, Troutbeck, Windermere, Cumbria LA23 1LA. Tel: 01539 445566

Windermere – Fayrer Garden House Hotel, Lyth Valley Road, Bowness-On-Windermere, Cumbria LA23 3JP. Tel: 015394 88195

Windermere – Lakeshore House, Ecclerigg, Windermere, Cumbria LA23 1LJ. Tel: 015394 33202

Wisbech – Crown Lodge Hotel, Downham Road, Outwell, Wisbech, Cambridgeshire PE14 8SE. Tel: 01945 773391

Witherslack – The Old Vicarage Country House Hotel, Church Road, Witherslack, Nr Grange-Over- Sands, Cumbria LA11 6RS. Tel: 015395 52381

Woolavington – Chestnut House, Hectors Stone, Lower Road, Woolavington, Bridgwater, Somerset TA7 8EQ. Tel: 01278 683658

York – The Parsonage Country House Hotel, Escrick, York, North Yorkshire YO19 6LF. Tel: 01904 728111

IRELAND

Caragh Lake – Caragh Lodge, Caragh Lake, Co Kerry. Tel: 00 353 66 9769115

Cashel – Cashel Palace Hotel, Main Street, Cashel, Co Tipperary. Tel: 00 353 62 62707

Connemara – Ross Lake House Hotel, Rosscahill, Oughterard, Co Galway, Ireland. Tel: 00 353 91 550109

Craughwell – St Clerans, Craughwell, Co Galway, Ireland . Tel: 00 353 91 846555

Dingle – Emlagh House, Dingle, Co.Kerry. Tel: 00 353 66 915 2345

Dingle Peninsula – Gorman's Clifftop House & Restaurant, Glaise Bheag, Ballydavid, Dingle Peninsula - Tralee Co. Kerry. Tel: 00 353 66 9155162

Donegal – Castle Murray House, Hotel & Restaurant, St. John's Point, Dunkineely, Co. Donegal, Ireland. Tel: 00 353 73 37022

Donegal Town – The Mill Park Hotel, Killybegs Road, Donegal Town, Co Donegal, Ireland. Tel: 00 353 73 22880

Dublin – Blakes Townhouse, 50 Merrion Road, Ballsbridge, Dublin 4. Tel: 00 353 1 6688324

Killarney – Earls Court House, Woodlawn Junction, Muckross Road, Killarney, Co Kerry. Tel: 00 353 64 34009

Killarney – Killarney Royal Hotel, College Street, Killarney, Co Kerry, Ireland. Tel: 00 353 64 31853

Kilmokea – Kilmokea Country Manor & Gardens, Kilmokea - Gt. Island, Campile Co. Wexford. Tel: 00 353 51 388109

Letterkenny – Castle Grove Country House Hotel, Ramelton Road, Letterkenny, Co Donegal. Tel: 00 353 74 51118

Riverstown – Coopershill House, Riverstown, Co Sligo. Tel: 00 353 71 65108

Sligo – Markree Castle, Collooney, County Sligo, Ireland. Tel: 00 353 71 67800

SCOTLAND

Arisaig – The Old Library Lodge & Restaurant, Arisaig, Inverness-Shire PH39 4NH. Tel: 01687 450651

Ayr – Culzean Castle – The Eisenhower Apartment, Maybole, Ayrshire KA19 8LE. Tel: 01655 884455

Ballachulish – Ballachulish House, Ballachulish, Argyll PH49 4JX. Tel: 01855 811266

Ballater – Balgonie Country House, Braemar Place, Ballater, Royal Deeside, Aberdeenshire AB35 5NQ. Tel: 013397 55482

Banchory – Banchory Lodge Hotel, Banchory, Royal Deeside, Aberdeenshire AB31 5HS. Tel: 01330 822625

By Pitlochry – The Killiecrankie Hotel, Killiecrankie, By Pitlochry, Perthshire PH16 5LG. Tel: 01796 473220

Cornhill – Castle Of Park, Cornhill, Nr Huntly, Aberdeenshire AB45 2AX. Tel: 01466 751111/751667

Dunkeld – The Pend, 5 Brae Street, Dunkeld, Perthshire PH8 0BA. Tel: 01350 727586

Edinburgh – Garvock House Hotel, St John's Drive, Transy, Dunfermline, Fife KY12 7TU. Tel: 01383 621067

Fintry – Culcreuch Castle Hotel & Country Park, Fintry, Loch Lomond, Stirling & Trossachs, Stirlingshire G63 0LW. Tel: 01360 860555

Forfar – Castleton House Hotel, Glamis, By Forfar, Angus DD8 1SY. Tel: 01307 840340

Fort William – Corriegour Lodge Hotel, Loch Lochy, By Spean Bridge, Inverness-Shire PH34 4EB. Tel: 01397 712685

Glendevon – Tormaukin Hotel, Glendevon, By Dollar, Perthshire FK14 7JY. Tel: 01259 781252

Inverness – Culduthel Lodge, 14 Culduthel Road, Inverness, Inverness-Shire IV2 4AG. Tel: 01463 240089

Isle Of Skye – Hotel Eilean Iarmain, Sleat, Isle Of Skye IV43 8QR. Tel: 01471 833332

Kentallen Of Appin – Ardsheal House, Kentallen Of Appin, Argyll PA38 4BX. Tel: 01631 740227

Killin – Ardeonaig, South Loch Tay Side, By Killin, Perthshire FK21 8SU. Tel: 01567 820400

Loch Earn – The Four Seasons Hotel, St Fillans, Perthshire PH6 2NF. Tel: 01764 685333

Old Meldrum – The Redgarth, Kirk Brae, Oldmeldrum, Aberdeenshire AB51 0DJ. Tel: 01651 872 353

Pitlochry – Knockendarroch House, Higher Oakfield, Pitlochry, Perthshire PH16 5HT. Tel: 01796 473473

Port Of Menteith – The Lake Hotel, Port Of Menteith, Perthshire FK8 3RA. Tel: 01877 385258

St Andrews – The Inn at Lathones, By Largoward, St Andrews, Fife, Scotland KY9 1JE. Tel: 01334 840494

Tighnabruaich – Royal Hotel, Tighnabruaich, Argyll, Scotland PA21 2BE. Tel: 01700 811239

Wick – Portland Arms Hotel, Lybster, Caithness KW3 6BS. Tel: 01593 721721

WALES

Aberdovey – Plas Penhelig Country House Hotel And Restaurant, Aberdovey, Gwynedd LL35 ONA. Tel: 01654 767676

Abersoch – Porth Tocyn Country House Hotel, Abersoch, Pwllheli, Gwynedd LL53 7BU. Tel: 01758 713303

Barmouth – Bae Abermaw, Panorama Hill, Barmouth, Gwynedd LL42 1DQ. Tel: 01341 280550

Betws-Y-Coed – Tan-Y-Foel, Capel Garmon, Nr Betws-Y-Coed, Conwy LL26 0RE. Tel: 01690 710507

Bridgend – The Great House, High Street, Laleston, Bridgend, Wales CF32 0HP. Tel: 01656 657644

Caernarfon – Ty'n Rhos Country Hotel, Seion Llanddeiniolen, Caernarfon, Gwynedd LL55 3AE. Tel: 01248 670489

Conwy – The Castle Hotel, High Street, Conwy LL32 8DB. Tel: 01492 582 800

Conwy – The Old Rectory Country House, Llanrwst Road, Llansanffraid Glan Conwy, Conwy LL28 5LF. Tel: 01492 580611

Dolgellau – Plas Dolmelynllyn, Ganllwyd, Dolgellau, Gwynedd LL40 2HP. Tel: 01341 440273

Llanarmon Dyffryn Ceiriog – The West Arms Hotel, Llanarmon D C, Ceriog Valley, Nr Llangollen, Denbighshire LL20 7LD. Tel: 01691 600665

Llandegla – Bodidris Hall, Llandegla, Wrexham, Denbighshire LL11 3AL. Tel: 01978 790434

Llandeilo – The Cawdor Arms Hotel, Rhosmaen Street, Llandeilo, Carmarthenshire SA19 6EN. Tel: 01558 823500

Swansea – Norton House Hotel And Restaurant, Norton Road, Mumbles, Swansea SA3 5TQ. Tel: 01792 404891

Swansea – Stembridge Mill, Stembridge, Reynoldston, Swansea, Gower SA3 1BT. Tel: 01792 391640

Tenby – Waterwynch House Hotel, Waterwynch Bay, Tenby, Pembrokeshire SA70 8JT. Tel: 01834 842464

Tintern – Parva Farmhouse And Restaurant, Tintern, Chepstow, Monmouthshire NP16 6SQ. Tel: 01291 689411

MINI LISTINGS

Here in brief are the entries that appear in full in

Johansens Recommended Hotels, Europe & The Mediterranean 2002

To order Johansens guides turn to the order forms at the back of this book.

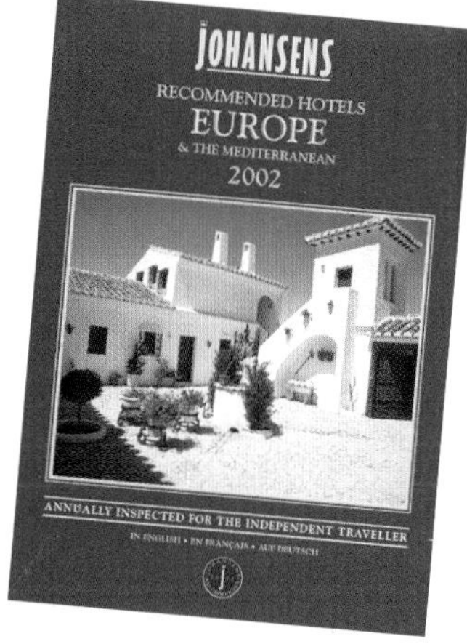

ANDORRA

Pas de la Casa – Hotel Font d'Argent, C/ Bearn 20, 22, 24, Pas De La Casa, Andorra. Tel: +376 739 739

AUSTRIA

Carinthia (Klagenfurt) – Hotel Palais Porcia, Neuer Platz 13, 9020 Klagenfurt, Austria. Tel: +43 463 51 15 90

Carinthia (Velden) – Seeschlössl Velden, Klagenfurter Strasse 34, 9220 Velden, Austria. Tel: +43 4274 2824

Lower Austria (Dürnstein) – Hotel Schloss Dürnstein, 3601 Dürnstein, Austria. Tel: +43 2711 212

Salzburg (Bad Gastein) – Hotel & Spa Haus Hirt, Kaiserhofstrasse 14, 5640 Bad Gastein, Austria. Tel: +43 64 34 27 97

Salzburg (Bad Hofgastein) – Das Moser, Kaiser-Franz-Platz 2, 5630 Bad Hofgastein, Austria. Tel: + 43 6432 6209

Salzburg (Bad Hofgastein) – Grand Park Hotel Bad Hofgastein, Kurgartenstrasse 26, 5630 Bad Hofgastein, Austria. Tel: +43 6432 63560

Salzburg (Salzburg) – Hotel Schloss Mönchstein, Mönchsberg Park 26, 5020 Salzburg, Austria. Tel: +43 662 84 85 55 0

Tyrol (Alpbach) – Romantik Hotel Böglerhof, 6236 Alpbach, Austria. Tel: +43 5336 5227

Tyrol (Igls) – Schlosshotel Igls, Viller Steig 2, 6080 Igls, Tyrol, Austria. Tel: +43 512 37 72 17

Tyrol (Igls) – Sporthotel Igls, Hilberstrasse 17, 6080 Igls, Tyrol, Austria. Tel: +43 512 37 72 41

Tyrol (Kitzbühel) – Romantik Hotel Tennerhof, Griesenauweg 26, 6370 Kitzbühel, Austria. Tel: +43 5356 6 3181

Upper Austria (Grünau im Almtal) – Romantik Hotel Almtalhof, 4645 Grünau im Almtal, Austria. Tel: +43 7616 82040

Upper Austria (St. Wolfgang am See) – Romantik Hotel Im Weissen Rössl, 5360 St. Wolfgang am See, Salzkammergut, Austria. Tel: +43 6138 23060

Vienna (Vienna) – Ana Grand Hotel Wien, Kärntner Ring 9, 1010 Vienna, Austria. Tel: +43 1 515 800

Vienna (Vienna) – Hotel im Palais Schwarzenberg, Schwarzenbergplatz 9, 1030 Vienna, Austria. Tel: +43 1 798 4515

Vorarlberg (Bezau im Bregenzerwald) – Hotel Gasthof Gams, 6870 Bezau, Austria. Tel: +43 5514 2220

Vorarlberg (Lech) – Sporthotel Kristiania, Omesberg 331, 6764 Lech am Arlberg, Austria. Tel: +43 5583 25 610

Vorarlberg (Zürs) – Thurnhers Alpenhof, 6763 Zürs - Arlberg, Austria. Tel: +43 5583 2191

BELGIUM

Antwerp – Firean Hotel, Karel Oomsstraat 6, 2018 Antwerp, Belgium. Tel: +32 3 237 02 60

Bruges – Hotel Acacia, Korte Zilverstraat 3a, 8000 Bruges, Belgium. Tel: +32 50 34 44 11

Bruges – Hotel Montanus, Nieuwe Gentweg 78, 8000 Bruges, Belgium. Tel: +32 50 33 11 76

Bruges – Hotel Prinsenhof, Ontvangersstraat 9, 8000 Bruges, Belgium. Tel: +32 50 34 26 90

De Haan – Romantik Manoir Carpe Diem, Prins Karellaan 12, 8420 De Haan, Belgium. Tel: +32 59 23 32 20

Florenville – Hostellerie Le Prieuré de Conques, Rue de Conques 2, 6820 Florenville, Belgium. Tel: +32 61 41 14 17

Knokke-Heist – Romantik Hotel Manoir du Dragon, Albertlaan 73, 8300 Knokke-Heist, Belgium. Tel: +32 50 63 05 80

Malmédy – Hostellerie Trôs Marets, Route des Trôs Marets, 4960 Malmédy, Belgium. Tel: +32 80 33 79 17

Marche-en-Famenne – Château d'Hassonville, Route d'Hassonville 105, 6900 Marche-en-Famenne, Belgium. Tel: +32 84 31 10 25

CYPRUS

Girne – Hotel Bellapais Gardens, Crusader Road, Bellapais, Girne, Cyprus. Tel: +90 392 815 60 66

Limassol – The Four Seasons Hotel, PO Box 57222, 3313 Limassol, Cyprus. Tel: +357 5 858 000

Limassol – Le Meridien Limassol Spa & Resort, PO Box 56560, 3308 Limassol, Cyprus. Tel: +357 5 862 000

CZECH REPUBLIC

Breznice – Starosedlsky Hrádek, 26272 Breznice, Czech Republic. Tel: +420 306 683851-5

Prague – Hotel Hoffmeister, Pod Bruskou 7, Klárov, 11800 Prague 1, Czech Republic. Tel: +420 2 51017 111

Prague – Hotel U Páva, U Luzického Semináre 32, Malá Strana, 11800 Prague 1, Czech Republic. Tel: +420 2 5753 3573

Prague – Sieber Hotel & Apartments, Slezská 55, 130 00 Prague 3, Czech Republic. Tel: +420 2 24 25 00 25

Prague (Jíloviste) – Cinema Palace Hotel, Vsenorská 45, 25202 Jíloviste, Czech Republic. Tel: +420 2 9913285/3349

DENMARK

Langå – Fru Larsen - Hotel & Gourmet Restaurant, Østergade 1, Laurbjerg, 8570 Langå, Denmark. Tel: +45 86 46 83 88

Nyborg – Hotel Hesselet, Christianslundsvej 119, 5800 Nyborg, Denmark. Tel: +45 65 31 30 29

ESTONIA

Pärnu – Villa Ammende, Mere Pst. 7, 80012 Pärnu, Estonia. Tel: +372 44 73888

Tallinn – Park Consul Schlössle, Pühavaimu 13-15, 10123 Tallinn, Estonia. Tel: +372 699 7700

FRANCE

Alps (Courchevel) – Hôtel Annapurna, 73120 Courchevel (1850), France. Tel: +33 4 79 08 04 60

Alps (Divonne-les-Bains) – Le Domaine de Divonne, Avenue des Thermes, 01220 Divonne-les-Bains, France. Tel: +33 4 50 40 34 34

Alps (Les Gêts) – Chalet Hôtel La Marmotte, 74260 Les Gêts, France. Tel: + 33 4 50 75 80 33

Alps (Sciez-sur-Léman) – Château de Coudrée, Domaine de Coudrée, Bonnatrait, 74140 Sciez-sur-Léman, France. Tel: +33 4 50 72 62 33

Alps (Serre-Chevalier) – L'Auberge du Choucas, 05220 Monetier-Les-Bains, Serre-Chevalier, Hautes-Alpes, France. Tel: +33 4 92 24 42 73

Alsace – Lorraine (Colmar) – Hostellerie Le Maréchal, 4 Place Six Montagnes Noires, Petite Venise, 68000 Colmar, France. Tel: +33 3 89 41 60 32

Alsace – Lorraine (Colmar) – Hôtel Les Têtes, 19 Rue de Têtes, 68000 Colmar, France. Tel: +33 3 89 24 43 43

Alsace – Lorraine (Gérardmer – Vosges) – Hostellerie Les Bas Rupts, 88400 Gérardmer, Vosges, France. Tel: +33 3 29 63 09 25

Alsace – Lorraine (Murbach – Buhl) – Hostellerie St Barnabé, 68530 Murbach – Buhl, France. Tel: +33 3 89 62 14 14

Alsace – Lorraine (Thann) – Hôtel du Parc, 23 Rue Kleber, 68800 Thann, France. Tel: +33 3 89 37 37 47

Auvergne (Saint-Flour) – Hostellerie Château de Varillettes, 15100 Saint-Georges par Saint-Flour, France. Tel: +33 4 71 60 45 05

Brittany (Billiers) – Domaine de Rochevilaine, Pointe de Pen Lan, 56190 Billiers, France. Tel: +33 2 97 41 61 61

Brittany (La Gouesnière – Saint Malo) – Château de Bonaban, 35350 La Gouesnière, France. Tel: +33 2 99 58 24 50

Brittany (Moëlan-sur-Mer) – Manoir de Kertalg, Route de Riec-sur-Belon, 29350 Moelan-sur-Mer, France. Tel: +33 2 98 39 77 77

Brittany (Ploerdüt) – Château du Launay, 56160 Ploerdüt, France. Tel: +33 2 97 39 46 32

Brittany (Rennes) – LeCoq-Gadby, 156 Rue d'Antrain, 35700 Rennes, France. Tel: +33 2 99 38 05 55

Brittany (Saint Malo – Pleven) – Manoir du Vaumadeuc, 22130 Pleven, France. Tel: +33 2 96 84 46 17

Brittany (Saint Malo – Saint Brieuc) – Manoir de la Hazaie, 22400 Planguenoual, France. Tel: +33 2 9632 7371

Burgundy – La Belle Epoque, European Waterways Ltd, 35 Wharf Road, Wraysbury, Staines, Middlesex TW19 5JQ England. Tel: +44 1784 482439

Burgundy (Avallon) – Château de Vault de Lugny, 11 Rue du Château, 89200 Avallon, France. Tel: +33 3 86 34 07 86

Burgundy (Avallon) – Hostellerie de la Poste, 13 Place Vauban, 89200 Avallon, France. Tel: +33 3 86 34 16 16

Burgundy (Beaune) – Ermitage de Corton, R.N. 74, 21200 Chorey-les-Beaune, France. Tel: +33 3 80 22 05 28

Burgundy – Franche-Comté (Poligny – Jura) – Hostellerie des Monts de Vaux, Les Monts de Vaux, 39800 Poligny, France. Tel: +33 3 84 37 12 50

Burgundy (Villefargeau – Auxerre) – Le Petit Manoir des Bruyères, 5 Allée de Charbuy-Les-Bruyères, 89240 Villefargeau, France. Tel: +33 3 86 41 32 82

Champagne (Épernay) – Hostellerie La Briqueterie, 4 Route de Sézanne, 51530 Vinay – Épernay, France. Tel: +33 3 26 59 99 99

Champagne (Fère-en-Tardenois) – Château de Fère, 02130 Fère-en-Tardenois, France. Tel: + 33 3 23 82 21 13

Champagne (Tinqueux – Reims) – L'Assiette Champenoise, 40 Avenue Paul Vaillant Couturier, 51430 Tinqueux, France. Tel: +33 3 26 84 64 64

Loire Valley (Amboise) – Château de Pray, Route de Chargé, 37400 Amboise, France. Tel: +33 2 47 57 23 67

Loire Valley (Amboise) – Le Manoir Les Minimes, 34 Quai Charles Guinot, 37400 Amboise, France. Tel: +33 2 47 30 40 40

Loire Valley (Beaugency) – Les Bordes, 41220 Saint-Laurent-Nouan, France. Tel: +33 2 54 87 72 13

Loire Valley (Chissay-en-Tourraine) – Hostellerie Château de Chissay, 41400 Chissay-en-Touraine, France. Tel: +33 2 54 32 32 01

Loire Valley (Langeais) – Château de Rochecotte, Saint-Patrice, 37130 Langeais, France. Tel: 33 2 47 96 16 16

Loire Valley (Tours – Noyant de Touraine) – Château de Brou, 37800 Noyant de Touraine, France. Tel: +33 2 47 65 80 80

Loire West (Champigné) – Château des Briottières, 49330 Champigné, France. Tel: +33 2 41 42 00 02

Loire West (Missillac) – Domaine de la Bretesche, 44780 Missillac, France. Tel: +33 2 51 76 86 96

Loire West (Nantes – Les Sorinières) – Hostellerie Abbaye de Villeneuve, 4480 Nantes – Les Sorinières, France. Tel: +33 2 40 04 40 25

Loire West (Noiremoutier) – Hostellerie du Général d'Elbée, Place du Château, 85330 Noirmoutier-en-l'Isle, France. Tel: +33 2 51 39 10 29

Normandy (Breuil-en-Bessin) – Château de Goville, 14330 Breuil-en-Bessin, France. Tel: +33 2 31 22 19 28

Normandy (Etretat) – Le Donjon, Chemin de Saint Clair, 76790 Etretat, France. Tel: +33 2 35 27 08 23

Normandy (Pacy-sur-Eure) – Hostellerie Château de Brécourt, Douains, 27120 Pacy-sur-Eure, France. Tel: +33 2 32 52 40 50

North – Picardy (Elincourt-Sainte-Marguerite) – Château de Bellinglise, 60157 Elincourt-Sainte-Marguerite, France. Tel: +33 3 44 96 00 33

North – Picardy (Lille) – Carlton Hotel, Rue de Paris, 59000 Lille, France. Tel: +33 3 20 13 33 13

North – Picardy (Vervins) – La Tour du Roy, 02140 Vervins, France. Tel: +33 3 23 98 00 11

Paris (Champs-Elysées) – Hôtel Plaza Athénée, 25 Avenue Montaigne, 75008 Paris, France. Tel: +33 1 53 67 66 65

Paris (Champs-Elysées) – Hôtel San Regis, 12 Rue Jean Goujon, 75008 Paris, France. Tel: +33 1 44 95 16 16

Paris (Champs-Elysées) – Résidence Alma Marceau, 5 Rue Jean Giraudoux, 75016 Paris, France. Tel: +33 1 53 57 67 89

Paris (Étoile – Porte Maillot) – L'Hôtel Pergolèse, 3 Rue Pergolèse, 75116 Paris, France. Tel: +33 1 53 64 04 04

Paris (Étoile – Porte Maillot) – La Villa Maillot, 143 Avenue de Malakoff, 75116 Paris, France. Tel: +33 1 53 64 52 52

Paris (Invalides) – Hôtel Le Tourville, 16 Avenue de Tourville, 75007 Paris, France. Tel: +33 1 47 05 62 62

Paris (Jardin du Luxembourg) – Le Sainte-Beuve, 9 Rue Sainte-Beuve, 75006 Paris, France. Tel: +33 1 45 48 20 07

Paris (Madeleine) – Hôtel de L'Arcade, 9 Rue de l'Arcade, 75008 Paris, France. Tel: +33 1 53 30 60 00

Paris (Madeleine) – Hôtel Le Lavoisier, 21 Rue Lavoisier, 75008 Paris, France. Tel: +33 1 53 30 06 06

Paris Outskirts (Cernay-La-Ville) – Hostellerie Abbaye des Vaux de Cernay, 78720 Cernay-La-Ville, France. Tel: +33 1 34 85 23 00

Paris Outskirts (Ermenonville) – Hostellerie Château d'Ermenonville, 60950 Ermenonville, France. Tel: +33 3 44 54 00 26

Paris – Outskirts (Gressy-en-France – Chantilly) – Le Manoir de Gressy, 77410 Gressy-en-France, Roissy Cdg, Nr Paris, France. Tel: +33 1 60 26 68 00

Paris Outskirts (Yerres – Orly) – Château du Maréchal de Saxe, Domaine de la Grange, 91330 Yerres, France. Tel: +33 1 69 48 78 53

Paris (Panthéon) – Hôtel du Panthéon, 19 Place du Panthéon, 75005 Paris, France. Tel: +33 1 43 54 32 95

Paris (Saint-Germain) – Hôtel Le Saint-Grégoire, 43 Rue de l'Abbé Grégoire, 75006 Paris, France. Tel: 33 1 45 48 23 23

Paris (Saint-Germain) – Hôtel Pont Royal, 7 Rue de Montalembert, 75007 Paris, France. Tel: +33 1 42 84 70 00

Paris (Saint-Germain) – Hôtel Buci Latin, 34 Rue de Buci, 75006 Paris, France. Tel: +33 1 43 29 07 20

Poitou – Charentes (Crazannes – Saintes) – Château de Crazannes, 17350 Crazannes, France. Tel: +33 6 80 65 40 96

Poitou – Charentes (Poitiers – Mignaloux) – Manoir de Beauvoir Golf & Hôtel, 635 Route de Beauvoir, 86550 Mignaloux - Beauvoir, France. Tel: +33 5 49 55 47 47

Poitou – Charentes (Poitiers – Saint-Maixent-L'Ecole) – Logis Saint-Martin, Chemin de Pissot, 79400 Saint-Maixent-l'Ecole, France. Tel: +33 5 49 05 58 68

Provence – Côte d'Azur (Beaulieu-sur-Mer) – La Réserve de Beaulieu, 5 Boulevard Général Leclerc, 06310 Beaulieu-sur-Mer, France. Tel: +33 4 93 01 00 01

Provence – Côte d'Azur (Cannes) – Le Cavendish, 11 Boulevard Carnot, 06400 Cannes, France. Tel: +33 4 97 06 26 00

Provence – Côte d'Azur (Èze Village) – Château Eza, Rue de la Pise, O6360 Eze Village, France. Tel: +33 4 93 41 12 24

Provence – Côte d'Azur (Les-Baux-de-Provence) – Mas de l'Oulivie, 13520 Les-Baux-de-Provence, France. Tel: +33 4 90 54 35 78

Provence – Côte d'Azur (Mandelieu – Cannes) – Ermitage du Riou, Avenue Henri Clews, 06210 Mandelieu-La-Napoule, France. Tel: + 33 4 93 49 95 56

Provence – Côte d'Azur (Mougins – Cannes) – Le Mas Candille, Boulevard Clement Rebuffel, 06250 Mougins, France. Tel: +33 4 92 28 43 43

Provence – Côte d'Azur (Ramatuelle – Nr Saint-Tropez) – La Ferme d'Augustin, Plage de Tahiti, 83350 Ramatuelle, Nr Saint-Tropez, France. Tel: +33 4 94 55 97 00

Provence – Côte d'Azur (Saint-Paul-de-Vence) – La Grande Bastide, Route de la Colle, 06570 Saint-Paul-de-Vence, France. Tel: +33 4 93 32 50 30

Provence – Côte d'Azur (Saint-Rémy-de-Provence) – Château des Alpilles, Route Départementale 31, Ancienne Route du Grès, 13210 Saint-Rémy-de-Provence, France. Tel: +33 4 90 92 03 33

Provence – Côte d'Azur (Saint-Tropez) – Hôtel Sube, 15 Quai Suffren, 83990 Saint-Tropez, France. Tel: +33 4 94 97 30 04

Provence – Côte d'Azur (Saint-Tropez) – Résidence de la Pinède, Plage de la Bouillabaisse, 83990 Saint-Tropez, France. Tel: +33 4 94 55 91 00

Provence – Côte d'Azur (Uzès) – Château d'Arpaillargues, Hôtel Marie d'Agoult, 30700 Uzès, France. Tel: +33 4 66 22 14 48

Provence – Côte d'Azur (Vence) – Relais Cantemerle, 258 Chemin Cantemerle, 06140 Vence, France. Tel: +33 4 93 58 08 18

Rhône Valley (Grignan) – Manoir de la Roseraie, Route de Valréas, 26230 Grignan, France. Tel: +33 4 75 46 58 15

Rhône Valley (Lyon) – La Tour Rose, 22 Rue du Boeuf, 69005 Lyon, France. Tel: +33 4 78 92 69 10

South-West – Basque Country (Biarritz) – Hôtel du Palais, Avenue de l'Impératrice, 64200 Biarritz, France. Tel: +33 5 59 41 64 00

South-West – Basque Country (Saint-Jean-de-Luz) – Grand Hôtel, 43 Boulevard Thiers, 64500 Saint-Jean-de-Luz, France. Tel: +33 5 59 26 35 36

South-West – Basque Country (Saint-Jean-de-Luz) – Hotel Lehen Tokia, Chemin Achotarreta, 64500 Ciboure – Saint-Jean-de-Luz, France. Tel: +33 5 59 47 18 16

South-West – Dordogne (Le Buisson-de-Cadouin) – Le Manoir de Bellerive, Route de Siorac, 24480 Le-Buisson-de-Cadouin, France. Tel: +33 5 53 22 16 16

South-West – Midi-Pyrénées (Aiguefonde) – Château d'Aiguefonde, 81200 Aiguefonde, France. Tel: +33 5 63 98 13 70

South-West – Midi-Pyrénées (Mazamet) – Château de Montlédier, 81660 Pont-de-l'Arn, Mazamet, France. Tel: +33 5 63 61 20 54

South-West (Sainte-Radegonde) – Château de Sanse, 33350 Sainte-Radegonde, France. Tel: +33 5 57 56 41 10

GERMANY

Düsseldorf – Wassenberg – Hotel Burg Wassenberg, Kirchstrasse 17, 41849 Wassenberg, Germany. Tel: +49 2432 9490

Oberwesel – Rhein – Burghotel auf Schönburg, 55430 Oberwesel - Rhein, Germany. Tel: +49 67 44 93 930

Rothenburg ob der Tauber – Hotel Eisenhut, Herrngasse 3-7, 91541 Rothenburg ob der Tauber, Germany. Tel: +49 9861 7050

Sylt – Christian VIII, Heleeker 1, 25980 Archsum, Sylt, Germany. Tel: +49 4651 97070

Sylt – Hotel-Restaurant Jörg Müller, Süderstrasse 8, 25980 Westerland, Sylt, Germany. Tel: +49 4651 27788

GREAT BRITAIN & IRELAND

England

Amberley – Amberley Castle, Amberley, Nr Arundel, West Sussex BN18 9ND, England. Tel: +44 1798 831 992

Bamburgh – Waren House Hotel, Waren Mill, Bamburgh, Northumberland NE70 7EE, England. Tel: +44 1668 214581

Lichfield – Hoar Cross – Hoar Cross Hall Health Spa Resort, Hoar Cross, Nr Yoxall, Staffordshire DE13 8QS, England. Tel: +44 1283 575671

London – The Academy, The Bloomsbury Town House, 21 Gower Street, London WC1E 6HG, England. Tel: +44 20 7631 4115

London – The Beaufort, 33 Beaufort Gardens, Knightsbridge, London SW3 1PP, England. Tel: +44 20 7584 5252

London – Beaufort House, 45 Beaufort Gardens, Knightsbridge, London SW3 1PN, England. Tel: +44 20 7584 2600

London – Cannizaro House, West Side, Wimbledon Common, London SW19 4UE, England. Tel: +44 20 8879 1464

London – The Colonnade, The Little Venice Town House, 2 Warrington Crescent, London W9 1ER, England. Tel: +44 20 7286 1052

London – The Cranley, 10-12 Bina Gardens, South Kensington, London SW5 0lA, England. Tel: +44 20 7373 0123

London – The Dorchester, Park Lane, Mayfair, London W1A 2HJ, England. Tel: +44 20 7629 8888

London – Draycott House Apartments, 10 Draycott Avenue, Chelsea, London SW3 3AA, England. Tel: +44 20 7584 4659

London – The Gallery, 8-10 Queensberry Place, South Kensington, London, SW7 2EA, England. Tel: +44 20 7915 0000

London – Great Eastern Hotel, 40 Liverpool Street, London EC2M 7QN, England. Tel: +44 7618 5000

London – Grim's Dyke Hotel, Old Redding, Harrow Weald, Middlesex HA3 6SH, England. Tel: +44 20 8385 3100

London – The Halcyon, 81 Holland Park, London W11 3RZ. Tel: +44 20 7727 7288

London – The Halkin, 5 Halkin Street, Belgravia, London SW1X 7DJ, England. Tel: +44 20 7333 1000

London – The Leonard, 15 Seymour Street, London W1H 7JW, England. Tel: +44 20 7935 2010

London – The Milestone Hotel and Apartments, 1 Kensington Court, London W8 5DL, England. Tel: +44 20 7917 1000

London – Number Sixteen, 16 Sumner Place, London SW7 3EG, England. Tel: +44 20 7589 5232 US TOLL FREE: 1 800 553 6674

London – Pembridge Court Hotel, 34 Pembridge Gardens, London W2 4DX, England. Tel: +44 20 7229 9977

London – The Rookery, Peter's Lane, Cowcross Street, London EC1M 6DS, England. Tel: +44 20 7336 0931

London – Threadneedles, 5 Threadneedle Street, London EC2R 8BD, England. Tel: +44 20 7432 8451

London – Twenty Nevern Square, 20 Nevern Square, London SW5 9PD, England. Tel: +44 20 7565 9555

London – Westbury Hotel, Bond Street, Mayfair, London W1S 2YF, England. Tel: +44 20 7629 7755

Melton Mowbray – Stapleford Park Hotel, Spa, Golf & Sporting Estate, Nr Melton Mowbray, Leicestershire LE14 2EF, England. Tel: +44 1572 787 522

Windermere – Miller Howe, Rayrigg Road, Windermere, Cumbria LA23 1EY. Tel: +44 15394 42536

Ireland

Ireland (Caragh Lake) – Carrig House & Restaurant, Caragh Lake, Killorgin, Co Kerry, Ireland. Tel: +353 66 976 91 00

Ireland (Dublin) – Aberdeen Lodge, 53 Park Avenue, Ballsbridge, Dublin 4, Ireland. Tel: +353 1 283 8155

Wales

Llandudno – Osborne House, 17 North Parade, Llandudno, LL30 2LP Wales. Tel: +44 1492 860555

GREECE

Athens – Hotel Pentelikon, 66 Diligianni Street, 14562 Athens, Greece. Tel: +30 1 62 30 650-6

Crete – St Nicolas Bay Hotel, 72100 Agios Nikolaos, Crete, Greece. Tel: +30 841 25041/2/3

Paros – Astir of Paros, Kolymbithres, Naoussa, 84401 Paros, Greece. Tel: +30 284 51976

HUNGARY

Kossuth – Kastélyhotel Sasvár, Parádsasvár, 3242 Kossuth U. 1., Hungary. Tel: +36 36 444 444

ITALY

Campania (Positano) – Romantik Hotel Poseidon, Via Pasitea 148, 84017 Positano (Salerno), Italy. Tel: +39 089 811111

Campania (Sorrento) – Grand Hotel Cocumella, Via Cocumella 7, 80065 Sant'Agnello, Sorrento, Italy. Tel: +39 081 878 2933

Campania (Sorrento) – Grand Hotel Excelsior Vittoria, Piazza Tasso 34, 80067 Sorrento (Naples), Italy. Tel: +39 081 807 1044

Emilia Romagna (Bagno di Romagna Terme) – Hotel Tosco Romagnolo, Piazza Dante Alighieri 2, 47021 Bagno di Romagna Terme, Italy. Tel: +39 0543 911260

Emilia Romagna (Brisighella) – Relais Torre Pratesi, Via Cavina 11, 48013 Brisighella, Italy. Tel: +39 0546 84545

Emilia Romagna (Ferrara) – Albergo Annunziata, Piazza Repubblica 5, 44100 Ferrara, Italy. Tel: +39 0532 201111

Emilia Romagna (Ferrara) – Ripagrande Hotel, Via Ripagrande 21, 44100 Ferrara, Italy. Tel: +39 0532 765250

Emilia Romagna (Riccione) – Hotel des Nations, Lungomare Costituzione 2, 47838 Riccione (RN), Italy. Tel: +39 0541 647878

Lazio (Rome) – Hotel Farnese, Via Alessandro Farnese 30 (Angolo Viale Giulio Cesare), 00192 Rome, Italy. Tel: +39 06 321 25 53/4

Lazio (Rome) – Hotel Giulio Cesare, Via Degli Scipioni 287, 00192 Rome, Italy. Tel: +39 06 321 0751

Lazio (Rome) – Ripa All Suites Hotel, Via degli Orti di Trastevere 1, 00153 Rome, Italy. Tel: +39 06 58611

Liguria (Finale Ligure) – Hotel Punta Est, Via Aurelia 1, 17024 Finale Ligure, Italy. Tel: +39 019 600611/2

Lombardy (Erbusco) – L'Albereta, Via Vittorio Emanuele 11, 25030 Erbusco (BS), Italy. Tel: +39 030 7760 550

Lombardy (Mantova) – Albergo San Lorenzo, Piazza Concordia 14, 46100 Mantova, Italy. Tel: +39 0376 220500

Piedmont (Stresa – Lake Maggiore) – Hotel Villa Aminta, Via Sempione Nord 123, 28838 Stresa (VB), Italy. Tel: +39 0323 933818

Piedmont (Torino) – Hotel Victoria, Via Nino Costa 4, 10123 Torino, Italy. Tel: +39 011 5611909

Sicily (Etna) – Hotel Villa Paradiso dell'Etna, Via Per Viagrande 37, 95037 San Giovanni La Punta, Italy. Tel: +39 095 7512409

Sicily (Giardini Naxos) – Hellenia Yachting Hotel, Via Jannuzzo 41, 98035 Giardini Naxos (ME), Italy. Tel: +39 0942 51737

Sicily (Taormina Riviera – Marina d'Agro) – Hotel Baia Taormina, Statale Dello Ionio 39, 98030 Marina d'Agro (ME), Italy. Tel: +39 0942 756292

South Tyrol (Marling – Meran) – Romantik Hotel Oberwirt, St Felixweg 2, 39020 Marling – Meran, Italy. Tel: +39 0473 44 71 11

South Tyrol (Mauls – Vipiteno) – Romantik Hotel Stafler, Mauls 10, Freienfeld, 39040 Mauls (BZ), Italy. Tel: +39 0472 771136

South Tyrol (Meran) – Park Hotel Mignon, Via Grabmayr 5, 39012 Meran, Italy. Tel: +39 0473 230353

South Tyrol (Nova Levante) – Posthotel Weisses Rössl, Via Carezza 30, 39056 Nova Levante (BZ), Dolomites, Italy. Tel: +39 0471 613113

Trentino (Madonna di Campiglio) – Hotel Lorenzetti, Via Dolomiti di Brenta 119, 38084 Madonna di Campiglio (TN) Italy. Tel: +39 0465 44 14 04

Tuscany (Florence) – Hotel J and J, Via Mezzo 20, 50121 Florence, Italy. Tel: +39 055 263121

Tuscany (Florence) – Hotel Montebello Splendid, Via Montebello 60, 50123 Florence, Italy. Tel: +39 055 2398051

Tuscany (Florence) – Villa Montartino, Via Gherardo Silvani 151, 50125 Florence, Italy. Tel: +39 055 223520

Tuscany (Lido di Camaiore) – Hotel Villa Ariston, Viale C. Colombo 355, 55043 Lido di Camaiore – Lucca, Italy. Tel: +39 0584 610633

Tuscany (Monteriggioni – Siena) – Hotel Monteriggioni, Via 1 Maggio 4, 53035 Monteriggioni, Italy. Tel: +39 0577 305009

Tuscany (Monteriggioni – Strove) – Castel Pietraio, Strada di Strove 33, 53035 Monteriggioni, Italy. Tel: +39 0577 300020

Tuscany (Pievescola) – Hotel Relais La Suvera, 53030 Pievescola – Siena, Italy. Tel: +39 0577 960300

Tuscany (Porto Ercole) – Il Pellicano, 58018 Porto Ercole (GR), Tuscany, Italy. Tel: +39 0564 858111

Tuscany (Porto Santo Stefano – Argentario) – Hotel Torre di Cala Piccola, Porto Santo Stefano, 58019 Argentario, Italy. Tel: +39 0564 825111

Umbria (Assisi) – Romantik Hotel Le Silve di Armenzano, 06081 Loc. Armenzano, Assisi (PG), Italy. Tel: +39 075 801 9000

Umbria (Scritto di Gubbio) – Castello di Petroia, Località di Petroia, 06020 Scrito di Gubbio (PG), Italy. Tel: +39 075 92 02 87

Umbria (Spoleto) – Villa Milani Residenza d'Epoca, Loc. Colle Attivoli 4, 06049 Spoleto, Italy. Tel: +39 0743 225056

Venetia (Negrar) – Relais La Magioca, Via Moron 3, 37024 Negrar (Verona), Italy. Tel: +39 045 6000167

Venetia (Sarcedo) – Casa Belmonte Relais, Via Belmonte 2, 36030 Sarcedo, Italy. Tel: +39 0445 884833

Venetia (Venice) – Hotel Giorgione, SS. Apostoli 4587, 30131 Venice, Italy. Tel: +39 041 5225810

Venetia (Verona) – Hotel Gabbia d'Oro, Corso Porta Borsari 4a, 37121 Verona, Italy. Tel: +39 045 8003060

LATVIA

Riga – Hotel de Rome, Kalku Str. 28, Riga, LV 1050, Latvia. Tel: +371 7087600

Riga – Hotel Grand Palace, Pils Iela 12, Riga, LV 1050, Latvia. Tel: +371 704 4000

Riga – Hotel Konventa Seta, Kaleju Str. 9/11, Riga, LV 1050, Latvia. Tel: +371 708 7501

LUXEMBOURG

Remich – Hotel Saint Nicolas, 31 Esplanade, 5533 Remich, Luxembourg. Tel: +352 2666 3

MONACO

Monte-Carlo – Hôtel Hermitage, Square Beaumarchais, 98000 Principauté de Monaco. Tel: +377 92 16 25 25

Monte-Carlo – Monte-Carlo Beach Hotel, Avenue Princesse Grace, 06190 Roquebrune – Cap-Martin, France. Tel: +377 92 16 25 25

THE NETHERLANDS

Amsterdam – Ambassade Hotel, Herengracht 341, 1016 Az Amsterdam, The Netherlands. Tel: +31 20 5550222

Amsterdam – The Canal House Hotel, Keizersgracht 148, 1015 Cx Amsterdam, The Netherlands. Tel: +31 20 622 5182

Amsterdam – Hotel Toren, Keizersgracht 164, 1015 Amsterdam, The Netherlands. Tel: +31 20 622 63 52

Amsterdam – Seven One Seven, Prinsengracht 717, 1017 Jw Amsterdam, The Netherlands. Tel: +31 20 42 70 717

De Lutte – Landhuishotel & Restaurant De Bloemenbeek, Beuningerstraat 6, 7587 De Lutte, The Netherlands. Tel: +31 541 551224

Ootmarsum – Hotel De Wiemsel, Winhofflaan 2, 7631 Hx Ootmarsum, Netherlands. Tel: +31 541 292 155

Molenhoek – Jachtslot De Mookerheide, Heumensebaan 2, 6584 Cl Molenhoek, The Netherlands. Tel: +31 24 358 30 35

NORWAY

Moss – Hotel Refsnes Gods, PO Box 236, 1501 Moss, Norway. Tel: +47 69 27 83 00

Oppdal – Kongsvold Fjeldstue, 7340 Oppdal, Norway. Tel: +47 72 40 43 40

Oslo – Hotel Bastion, Skippergaten 7, 0152 Oslo, Norway. Tel: +47 22 47 77 00

Sandane – Gloppen Hotel, 6823 Sandane, Norway. Tel: +47 57 86 53 33

Solvorn – Walaker Hotell, 6879 Solvorn, Sogn, Norway. Tel: +47 576 82080

Voss – Fleischers Hotel, 5700 Voss, Norway. Tel: +47 56 52 05 00

PORTUGAL

Algarve (Lagos) – Romantik Hotel Vivenda Miranda, Porto de Mós, 8600 Lagos, Portugal. Tel: +351 282 763222

Algarve (Moncarapacho) – Adolfo da Quinta, Monte Dos Calicos, 8700-069 Moncarapacho, Portugal. Tel: +351 289 790790

Alto Alentejo (Évora) – Solar de Monfalim, Largo da Misericórdia 1, 7000-646 Évora, Portugal. Tel: +351 266 750000

Alto Alentejo (Redondo) – Convento de São Paulo, Aldeia da Serra, 7170-120 Redondo, Portugal. Tel: +351 266 989160

Alto Alentejo (Reguengos de Monsaraz) – Hotel Rural Horta da Moura, Monsaraz, Apt. 64, 7200-999 Reguengos de Monsaraz, Portugal. Tel: +351 266 550100

Madeira (Câmara de Lobos) – Quinta do Estreito, Rua José Joaquim da Costa, 9325-034 Estreito de Câmara de Lobos, Madeira, Portugal. Tel: +351 291 910530

Madeira (Eira do Serrado) – Estalagem Eira do Serrado, Eira do Serrado – Curral Das Freiras, 9000-421 Funchal, Madeira, Portugal. Tel: +351 291 710060

Madeira (Funchal) – Quinta da Bela Vista, Caminho do Avista Navios 4, 9000 Funchal, Madeira, Portugal. Tel: +351 291 706400

Madeira (Funchal) – Quinta Perestrello, Rua do Dr. Pita 3, 9000-089 Funchal, Madeira, Portugal. Tel: +351 291 763720

SPAIN

Andalucia (Almuñecar) – Hotel Suites Albayzin del Mar, Avenida Costa del Sol 23, 18690 Almuñécar (Granada), Spain. Tel: +34 958 63 21 61

Andalucia (Arcos de La Frontera) – Hacienda El Santiscal, Avda. El Santiscal 129 (Lago de Arcos), 11630 Arcos de la Frontera, Spain. Tel: +34 956 70 83 13

Andalucia (Benahavis – Marbella) – Amanhavis Hotel, Calle del Pilar 3, 29679 Benahavis, Málaga, Spain. Tel: +34 952 85 60 26

Andalucia (Doñana National Park) – El Cortijo de los Mimbrales, Ctra del Rocio, A-483, Km 30, 21750 Almonte (Huelva), Spain. Tel: +34 959 44 22 37

Andalucia (Granada) – Hotel La Bobadilla, Finca La Bobadilla, Apto. 144, 18300 Loja, Granada, Spain. Tel: +34 958 32 18 61

Andalucia (Málaga) – La Posada del Torcal, 29230 Villanueva de la Concepción, Málaga, Spain. Tel: +34 952 03 11 77

Andalucia (Málaga) – Molino de Santillán, Ctra. de Macharaviaya, Km 3, Apdo de Correos 101, 29730 Rincón de la Victoria, Málaga, Spain. Tel: +34 952 40 09 49

Andalucia (Marbella – Estepona) – Las Dunas Suites, La Boladilla Baja, Crta. de Cádiz Km 163.5, 29689 Marbella – Estepona (Málaga), Spain. Tel: +34 952 79 43 45

Andalucia (Mijas-Costa) – Hotel Byblos Andaluz, Mijas Golf Apt. 138, 29640 Fuengirola (Málaga), Spain. Tel: +34 952 47 30 50

Andalucia (Seville) – Cortijo Águila Real, Crta. Guilleña-Burguillos Km 4, 41210 Guilleña, Seville, Spain. Tel: +34 955 78 50 06

Andalucia (Seville) – Hacienda Benazuza, 41800 Sanlúcar La Mayor, Seville, Spain. Tel: +34 955 70 33 44

Andalucia (Sotogrande) – Almenara Golf Hotel - Spa, Avenida Almenara, 11310 Sotogrande, Spain. Tel: + 34 956 58 20 00

Aragón (Teruel) – La Parada del Compte, Antigua Estación del Ferrocarril, 44597 Torre del Compte, Teruel, Spain. Tel: +34 978 76 90 72

Aragón (Zaragoza) – Hotel Palafox, C/ Casa Jiménez S/N, 50004 Zaragoza, Spain. Tel: +34 976 23 77 00

Asturias (Llanes) – La Posada de Babel, La Pereda S/N, 33509 Llanes, Asturias, Spain. Tel: +34 985 40 25 25

Asturias (Oviedo) – Hotel Palacio de la Viñona, C/ Julián Claveria 14, Colloto, Oviedo, Asturias, Spain. Tel: +34 985 79 33 99

Asturias (Villamayor) – Palacio de Cutre, La Goleta S/N Villamayor, 33583 Infiesto, Asturias, Spain. Tel: +34 985 70 80 72

Balearic Islands (Mallorca) – Ca's Xorc, Carretera de Deía, Km 56,1 07100 Sóller, Mallorca, Balearic Islands, Spain. Tel: +34 971 63 82 80

Balearic Islands (Mallorca) – Hotel Monnaber Nou, Possessió Monnaber Nou, 07310 Campanet, Mallorca, Balearic Islands, Spain. Tel: +34 971 87 71 76

Balearic Islands (Mallorca) – Hotel Vistamar de Valldemossa, Ctra Valldemossa, Andratx Km. 2, 07170 Valldemossa, Mallorca, Balearic Islands, Spain. Tel: +34 971 61 23 00

Balearic Islands (Mallorca) – Read's, Ca'n Moragues, 07320 Santa María, Mallorca, Balearic Islands, Spain. Tel: +34 971 14 02 62

Balearic Islands (Mallorca) – SA Pedrissa, Carretera Valldemossa - Deía, 07179 Deía, Mallorca, Balearic Islands, Spain. Tel: +34 971 63 91 11

Balearic Islands (Mallorca) – Sa Posada d'Aumallia, Camino Son Prohens 1027, 07200 Felanitx, Mallorca, Balearic Islands, Spain. Tel: +34 971 58 26 57

Balearic Islands (Mallorca) – Scott's, Plaza de la Iglesia 12, 07350 Binissalem, Mallorca, Balearic Islands, Spain. Tel: +34 971 87 01 00

Canary Islands (Tenerife) – Gran Hotel Bahía del Duque, 38660 Adeje, Costa Adeje, Tenerife South, Canary Islands. Tel: +34 922 74 69 00

Canary Islands (Tenerife) – Hotel Botánico, Avda. Richard J. Yeoward, Urb. Botánico, 38400 Puerto de la Cruz, Tenerife, Canary Islands. Tel: +34 922 38 14 00

Canary Islands (Tenerife) – Hotel Jardín Tropical, Calle Gran Bretaña, 38670 Costa Adeje, Tenerife, Canary Islands. Tel: +34 922 74 60 00

Castille (Salamanca) – Hotel Rector, Rector Esperabé 10-Apartado 399, 37008 Salamanca, Spain. Tel: +34 923 21 84 82

Catalonia (Barcelona) – The Gallery, Rossellón 249, 08008 Barcelona, Spain. Tel: +34 934 15 99 11

Catalonia (Barcelona) – Hotel Claris, Pau Claris 150, 08009 Barcelona, Spain. Tel: +34 934 87 62 62

Catalonia (Barcelona) – Hotel Colón, Avenida de la Catedral 7, 08002 Barcelona, Spain. Tel: +34 933 01 14 04

Catalonia (Costa Brava) – Hotel Rigat Park, Playa de Fenals, 17310 Lloret de Mar, Costa Brava, Spain. Tel: +34 972 36 52 00

Catalonia (Sitges) – Hotel Estela Barcelona, Avda. Port d'Aiguadolç S/N, 08870 Sitges (Barcelona), Spain. Tel: +34 938 11 45 45

Catalonia (Tarragona) – Hotel Termes Montbrió Resort, Spa & Park, Carrer Nou 38, 43340 Montbrió del Camp (Tarragona), Spain. Tel: +34 977 81 40 00

Catalonia (Viladrau) – Xalet La Coromina, Carretera de Vic S/N, 17406 Viladrau, Spain. Tel: +34 938 84 92 64

Madrid (Madrid) – Villa Real, Plaza de las Cortes 10, Madrid 28014, Spain. Tel: +34 914 20 37 67

Navarra (Jauntsarats) – Hotel Peruskenea, Beruete, 31866 Jauntsarats (Basaburua Mayor), Spain. Tel: +34 948 50 33 70

SWEDEN

Borgholm – Halltorps Gästgiveri, 38792 Borgholm, Sweden. Tel: +46 485 85000

Göteborg – Mölndal – Stensjöhill Herrgård, Höjdgatan 22, 43136 Mölndal, Sweden. Tel: +46 31 70688 75

Lagan – Romantik Hotel Toftaholm Herrgård, Toftaholm Pa, 34014 Lagan, Sweden. Tel: +46 370 44055

Söderköping – Romantik Hotel Söderköpings Brunn, Skönbergagatan 35, Box 44, 61421 Söderköping, Sweden. Tel: +46 121 10900

Tällberg – Romantik Hotel Åkerblads, 79370 Tällberg, Sweden. Tel: +46 247 50800

SWITZERLAND

Burgdorf-Bern – Hotel Stadthaus, Kirchbühl 2, 3402 Burgdorf-Bern, Switzerland. Tel: +41 34 428 8000

Château D'Oex – Hostellerie Bon Accueil, 1837 Château d'Oex, Switzerland. Tel: +41 26 924 6320

Gstaad – Grand Hotel Park, Wispilestrasse, 3780 Gstaad, Switzerland. Tel: +41 33 748 98 00

Gstaad – Le Grand Chalet, Neueretstrasse, 3780 Gstaad, Switzerland. Tel: +41 33 748 7676

Kandersteg – Royal Park ***** Hotel, 3718 Kandersteg, Switzerland. Tel: +41 33 675 88 88

Zuoz – Posthotel Engiadina, Via Maistra, 7524 Zuoz, Switzerland. Tel: +41 0818 541 021

TURKEY

Antalya – Marina Residence & Restaurant, Mermerli Sokak No. 15, Kaleici, 07100 Antalya, Turkey. Tel: +90 242 247 5490

Antalya – Talya Hotel, Fevzi Çakmak Caddesi No. 30, 07100 Antalya, Turkey. Tel: +90 242 248 6800

Bodrum – Divan Palmira Hotel, Kelesharim Cad 6, 48483 Türkbükü - Bodrum, Turkey. Tel: +90 252 377 5601

Bodrum – Hotel Adahan, Merkez Mahallesi, Çökertme Mevkii, Yalikavak, Bodrum, Turkey. Tel: +90 252 385 4759

Göreme – Cappadocia – Cappadocia Caves & Suites, Gafelli Mahallesi, Cevizler Sokak, 05180 Göreme - Nevsehir, Turkey. Tel: +90 384 271 2800

Kalkan – Hotel Villa Mahal, P.K. 4 Kalkan, 07960 Antalya, Turkey. Tel: +90 242 844 32 68

MINI LISTINGS

Here in brief are the entries that appear in full in

Johansens Recommended Hotels Inns & Resorts North America, Bermuda, Caribbean, Pacific 2002

To order Johansens guides turn to the order forms at the back of this book.

BERMUDA (HAMILTON)

Rosedon Hotel

Po Box Hm 290, Hamilton HMAX, Bermuda
Tel: 1 441 295 1640
Fax: 1 441 295 5904

BERMUDA (PAGET)

Fourways Inn

Po Box PG 294, Paget, Bermuda
Tel: 1 441 236 6517
Fax: 1 441 236 5528

BERMUDA (PAGET)

Harmony Club All Inclusive

South Shore Road, Paget, Bermuda
Tel: 1 441 236 3500
Fax: 1 441 236 2624

BERMUDA (PAGET)

Newstead Hotel

27 Harbour Road, Paget PG02, Bermuda
Tel: 1 441 236 6060
Fax: 1 441 236 7454

BERMUDA (WARWICK)

Surf Side Beach Club

90 South Shore Road, Warwick, Bermuda
Tel: 1 441 236 7100
Fax: 1 441 236 9765

CARIBBEAN (ANGUILLA)

Frangipani Beach Club

Po Box 1378, Meads Bay, Anguilla, West Indies
Tel: 1 264 497 6442/6444
Fax: 1 264 497 6440

CARIBBEAN (ANTIGUA)

Blue Waters

Po Box 256, St Johns, Antigua, West Indies
Tel: 1 268 462 0290
Fax: 1 268 462 0293

CARIBBEAN (ANTIGUA)

Cocobay

Valley Church, Po Box 431, St Johns, Antigua, West Indies
Tel: 1 268 562 2400
Fax: 1 268 562 2424

CARIBBEAN (ANTIGUA)

Curtain Bluff

Po Box 288, Antigua, West Indies
Tel: 1 268 462 8400
Fax: 1 268 462 8409

CARIBBEAN (ANTIGUA)

Galley Bay

Five Islands, Po Box 305, St John's, Antigua, West Indies
Tel: 1 268 462 0302
Fax: 1 268 462 4551

CARIBBEAN (ANTIGUA)

The Inn At English Harbour

Po Box 187, St Johns, Antigua, West Indies
Tel: 1 268 462 0302
Fax: 1 268 460 1603

CARIBBEAN (ANTIGUA)

Jumby Bay Resort

Jumby Bay Island, Po Box 243, St Johns, Antigua, West Indies
Tel: 1 268 462 6000
Fax: 1 268 462 6020

CARIBBEAN (CURAÇAO)

Avila Beach Hotel

Penstraat 130, Willemstad, Curaçao, Netherlands Antilles, West Indies
Tel: 599 9 461 4377
Fax: 599 9 461 1493

CARIBBEAN (JAMAICA)

Goldeneye

Oracabessa, St Mary, Jamaica West Indies
Tel: 1 876 975 3354
Fax: 1 876 975 3620

CARIBBEAN (JAMAICA)

Half Moon Golf, Tennis & Beach Club

Montego Bay, Jamaica, West Indies
Tel: 1 876 953 2211
Fax: 1 876 953 2731

CARIBBEAN (JAMAICA)

Mocking Bird Hill

Po Box 254, Port Antonio, Jamaica
Tel: 1 876 993 7134
Fax: 1 876 993 7133

CARIBBEAN (MARTINIQUE)

Hôtel Fregate Bleue

Quartier Fregate, Vauclin Road 97240, Le Francois, Martinique, French West Indies
Tel: 00 596 54 54 66
Fax: 0 596 54 78 48

CARIBBEAN (NEVIS)

The Hermitage

Nevis, West Indies
Tel: 1 869 469 3477
Fax: 1 869 469 2481

CARIBBEAN (NEVIS)

The Old Manor Hotel

Po Box 70, Charlestown, Nevis
Tel: 1 869 469 3445
Fax: 1 869 469 3388

CARIBBEAN (ST KITTS)

The Golden Lemon

Dieppe Bay, St Kitts, West Indies
Tel: 1 869 465 7260
Fax: 1 869 465 4019

CARIBBEAN (ST KITTS)

Ottley's Plantation Inn

Po Box 345, Basseterre, St Kitts, West Indies
Tel: 1 869 465 7234
Fax: 1 869 465 4760

CARIBBEAN (ST KITTS)

Rawlins Plantation Inn

Po Box 340, St Kitts, West Indies
Tel: 1 869 465 6221
Fax: 1 869 465 4954

CARIBBEAN (ST LUCIA)

Mago Estate Hotel

Po Box 247, Soufrière, St Lucia, West Indies
Tel: 1 758 459 5880
Fax: 1 758 459 7352

CARIBBEAN (ST. VINCENT)

Camelot Inn - A Boutique Hotel

Po Box 787, Kingstown, The Grenadines, St Vincent, West Indies
Tel: 1 784 456 2100
Fax: 1 784 456 2233

CARIBBEAN (ST. VINCENT)

Grand View Beach Hotel

Villa Point, Box 173, St Vincent, West Indies
Tel: 1 784 458 4811
Fax: 1 784 457 4174

CARIBBEAN (ST VINCENT & THE GRENADINES)

Palm Island

St Vincent & The Grenadines, West Indies
Tel: 1 954 481 8787
Fax: 1 954 481 1661

CARIBBEAN (TOBAGO)

Mount Irvine Bay Hotel

Box 222, Mount Irvine Bay, Tobago, West Indies
Tel: 1 868 639 8871
Fax: 1 868 639 8800

CARIBBEAN (TURKS & CAICOS ISLANDS)

Point Grace

Po Box 700, Grace Bay, Turks And Caicos Islands, West Indies
Tel: 1 649 946 5096
Fax: 1 649 946 5097

CARIBBEAN (TURKS & CAICOS)

The Sands At Grace Bay

Po Box 681, Providenciales, Turks & Caicos, West Indies
Tel: 1 649 946 5199
Fax: 1 649 946 5198

FIJI ISLANDS (LAUTOKA)

Blue Lagoon Cruises

183 Vitogo Parade, Lautoka, Fiji Islands
Tel: 679 661 622
Fax: 679 664 098

FIJI ISLANDS (MAMANUCA)

Tokoriki Island Resort

Po Box 10547, Nadi, Fiji Islands
Tel: 679 725 474
Fax: 679 725 928

FIJI ISLANDS (VOMO ISLANDS)

Vomo Island

Po Box 5650, Lautoka, Fiji Islands
Tel: 679 667 955
Fax: 679 667 997

FIJI ISLANDS (YASAWA ISLANDS)

Turtle Island

Yasawa Islands, Po Box 9371, Nadi Airport, Nadi, Fiji Islands
Tel: 61 3 9618 1100
Fax: 61 3 9618 1199

MEXICO (ZIHUATANEJO)

Hotel Villa Del Sol

Playa La Ropa S/N, Po Box 84, Zihuatanejo 40880, Mexico
Tel: 52 755 4 2239/3239
Fax: 52 7554 2758/4066

ARIZONA (GREER)

Red Setter Inn And Cottages

8 Main Street, Po Box 133, Greer, Arizona 85927
Tel: 1 888 994 7337
Fax: 1 520 735 7425

ARIZONA (SEDONA)

Canyon Villa Inn

125 Canyon Circle Drive, Sedona, Arizona 86351
Tel: 1 520 284 1226
Fax: 1 520 284 2114

ARIZONA (TUCSON)

Tanque Verde Ranch

14301 East Speedway, Tuscon, Arizona, 85748
Tel: 1 520 296 6275
Fax: 1 520 721 9426

ARIZONA (TUCSON)

White Stallion Ranch

9251 West Twin Peaks Road, Tucson, Arizona 85743
Tel: 1 520 297 0252
Fax: 1 520 744 2786

CALIFORNIA (AVALON)

Snug Harbor Inn

108 Summer Avenue, Po Box 2470, Avalon, California 90704
Tel: 1 310 510 8400
Fax: 1 310 510 8418

CALIFORNIA (AVALON)

Vista Del Mar

417 Crescent Avenue, Po Box 1979, Avalon, Catalina Island, California 90704
Tel: 1 310 510 8400
Fax: 1 310 510 2917

CALIFORNIA (EUREKA)

Carter House

301 L Street, Eureka, California 95501
Tel: 1 707 444 8062
Fax: 1 707 444 8067

CALIFORNIA (FERNDALE)

Gingerbread Mansion Inn

P.O.Box 40; 400 Berding Street, Ferndale, California 95536
Tel: 1 707 786 4000
Fax: 1 707 786 4381

CALIFORNIA (LA JOLLA)

The Bed & Breakfast Inn At La Jolla

7753 Draper Avenue, La Jolla, California 92037
Tel: 1 858 456 2066
Fax: 1 858 456 1510

CALIFORNIA (MILL VALLEY)

Mill Valley Inn

165 Throckmorton Avenue, Mill Valley, California 94941
Tel: 1 415 389 6608
Fax: 1 415 389 5051

CALIFORNIA (PALM DESERT)

Shadow Mountain Resort

45750 San Luis Rey, Palm Desert, California 92260
Tel: 1 760 346 6123
Fax: 1 760 346 6518

CALIFORNIA (PALM SPRINGS)

Caliente Tropics Resort

411 East Palm Canyon Drive, Palm Springs, California, 92264
Tel: 1 760 327 1391
Fax: 1 760 318 1883

CALIFORNIA (PALM SPRINGS)

L'horizon

1050 East Palm Canyon Drive, Palm Springs, California 92264
Tel: 1 760 323 1858
Fax: 1 760 327 2933

CALIFORNIA (PALM SPRINGS)

The Willows

412 West Tahquitz Canyon Way, Palm Springs, California 92262
Tel: 1 760 320 0771
Fax: 1 760 320 0780

CALIFORNIA (SAN FRANCISCO)

Nob Hill Lambourne

725 Pine Street, San Francisco, California 94108
Tel: 1 415 433 2287
Fax: 1 415 433 0975

CALIFORNIA (SAN FRANCISCO BAY AREA)

Gerstle Park Inn

34 Grove Street, San Rafael, California, 94901
Tel: 1 415 721 7611
Fax: 1 415 721 7600

CALIFORNIA (SAN LUIS OBISPO)

Sycamore Mineral Springs Resort

1215 Avila Beach Drive, San Luis Obispo, California, 93405
Tel: 1 805 595 7302
Fax: 1 805 781 2510

CALIFORNIA (SANTA ANA)

Woolley's Petite Suites

2721 Hotel Terrace Road, Santa Ana, California 92705
Tel: 1 714 540 1111
Fax: 1 714 662 1643

CALIFORNIA (SANTA BARBARA)

Upham Hotel

1404 De La Vina Street, Santa Barbara, California 93101
Tel: 1 805 962 0058
Fax: 1 805 963 2825

CALIFORNIA (TIBURON)

Waters Edge Hotel

25 Main Street, Tiburon, California 94920
Tel: 1 415 789 5999
Fax: 1 415 789 5888

COLORADO (BEAVER CREEK)

The Inn At Beaver Creek

10 Elk Track, Beaver Creek, Colorado, 81620
Tel: 1 970 845 5787
Fax: 1 970 845 6204

COLORADO (DENVER)

Castle Marne

1572 Race Street, Denver, Colorado 80206
Tel: 1 303 331 0621
Fax: 1 303 331 0623

COLORADO (DENVER)

The Holiday Chalet

1820 East Colfax Avenue, Denver, Colorado 80218
Tel: 1 303 321 9975
Fax: 1 303 377 6556

COLORADO (STEAMBOAT SPRINGS)

Vista Verde Guest Ranch

POBox 770465, Steamboat Springs, Colorado 80477
Tel: 1 970 879 3858
Fax: 1 970 879 1413

DELAWARE (REHOBOTH BEACH)

Boardwalk Plaza Hotel

Olive Avenue & The Boardwalk, Rehoboth Beach, Delaware 19971
Tel: 1 302 227 0441
Fax: 1 302 227 0561

GEORGIA (PERRY)

Henderson Village

125 South Langston Circle, Perry, Georgia 31069
Tel: 1 912 988 8696
Fax: 1 912 988 9009

GEORGIA (SAVANNAH)

The Eliza Thompson House

5 West Jones Street, Savannah, Georgia 31401
Tel: 1 912 236 3620
Fax: 1 912 238 1920

GEORGIA (SAVANNAH)

Granite Steps

126 East Gaston Street, Savannah, Georgia 31401
Tel: 1 912 233 5380
Fax: 1 912 236 3116

GEORGIA (SAVANNAH)

Magnolia Place Inn

503 Whittaker Street, Savannah, Georgia 31401
Tel: 1 912 236 7674
Fax: 1 912 236 1145

GEORGIA (SAVANNAH)

The President's Quarters

225 East President Street, Savannah, Georgia 31401
Tel: 1 912 233 1600
Fax: 1 912 238 0849

FLORIDA (KEY WEST)

Simonton Court Historic Inn & Cottages

320 Simonton Street, Key West, Florida 33040
Tel: 1 305 294 6386
Fax: 1 305 293 8446

FLORIDA (MIAMI BEACH)

The Hotel

801 Collins Avenue, Miami Beach, Florida 33139
Tel: 1 305 531 2222
Fax: 1 305 531 3222

FLORIDA (NAPLES)

Hotel Escalante

290 Fifth Avenue South, Naples, Florida 34102
Tel: 1 941 659 3466
Fax: 1 941 262 8748

FLORIDA (PALM BEACH)

The Chesterfield Hotel

363 Cocoanut Row, Palm Beach, Florida 33480
Tel: 1 561 659 5800
Fax: 1 561 659 6707

ILLINOIS (CHICAGO)

The Sutton Place Hotel

21 East Bellevue Place, Chicago, Illinois 60611
Tel: 1 312 266 2100
Fax: 1 312 266 2103

MARYLAND (TANEYTOWN)

Antrim 1844

30 Trevanion Rd, Taneytown, Maryland 21787
Tel: 1 410 756 6812
Fax: 1 410 756 2744

MISSISSIPPI (BILOXI)

Father Ryan House Inn

1196 Beach Boulevard, Biloxi, Mississippi 39530
Tel: 1 228 435 1189
Fax: 1 228 436 3063

MISSISSIPPI (JACKSON)

Fairview Inn

734 Fairview Street, Jackson, Mississippi 39202
Tel: 1 601 948 3429
Fax: 1 601 948 1203

MISSISSIPPI (NATCHEZ)

Monmouth Plantation

36 Melrose Avenue At, John A Quitman Parkway, Natchez, Mississippi, 39120
Tel: 1 601 442 5852
Fax: 1 601 446 7762

MISSISSIPPI (NATCHEZ)

Shields Town House

701 North Union Street, Natchez, Mississippi 39120
Tel: 1 601 442 7680
Fax: 1 601 445 0843

MISSISSIPPI (VICKSBURG)

The Duff Green Mansion

1114 First East Street, Vicksburg, Mississippi 39180
Tel: 1 601 636 6968
Fax: 1 601 661 0079

NEW ENGLAND / CONNECTICUT (GREENWICH)

Homestead Inn

420 Fieldpoint Road, Greenwich, Connecticut 06830
Tel: 1 203 869 7500
Fax: 1 203 869 7502

NEW ENGLAND / CONNECTICUT (OLD MYSTIC)

The Old Mystic Inn

52 Main Street, Old Mystic, Connecticut 06372-0733
Tel: 1 860 572 9422
Fax: 1 860 572 9954

NEW ENGLAND / MAINE (CAMDEN)

Hartstone Inn

41 Elm Street, Camden, Maine, 04843
Tel: 1 207 236 4259
Fax: 1 207 236 9575

NEW ENGLAND / MAINE (GREENVILLE)

The Lodge At Moosehead Lake

Upon Lily Bay Road, Box 1167, Greenville, Maine 04441
Tel: 1 207 695 4400
Fax: 1 207 695 2281

NEW ENGLAND / MAINE (MOOSEHEAD LAKE)

Greenville Inn

Po Box 1194, Norris Street, Greenville, Maine 04441
Tel: 1 207 695 2206
Fax: 1 207 695 0335

NEW ENGLAND / MASSACHUSETTS (BOSTON)

The Charles Street Inn

94 Charles Street, Boston, Massachusetts 02114-4643
Tel: 1 617 314 8900
Fax: 1 617 371 0009

NEW ENGLAND / MASSACHUSETTS (BOSTON)

The Lenox Hotel

710 Boylston Street, Boston, Massachusetts, 02116-2699
Tel: 1 617 536 5300
Fax: 1 617 236 0351

NEW ENGLAND / MASSACHUSETTS (CAMBRIDGE)

A Cambridge House

2218 Massachusetts Avenue, Cambridge, Massacgusetts 02140-1836
Tel: 1 617 491 6300
Fax: 1 617 868 2848

NEW ENGLAND / MASSACHUSETTS (CAPE COD)

Wedgewood Inn

83 Main Street, Route 6a, Yarmouthport, Massachusetts 02675
Tel: 1 508 362 5157
Fax: 1 508 362 5851

NEW ENGLAND / MASSACHUSETTS (CAPE COD)

The Whalewalk Inn

220 Bridge Road, Eastham (Cape Cod), Massachusetts 02642
Tel: 1 508 255 0617
Fax: 1 508 240 0017

NEW ENGLAND / MASSACHUSETTS (LENOX)

Wheatleigh

Hawthorne Road, Lenox, Massachusetts 01240
Tel: 1 413 637 0610
Fax: 1 413 637 4507

NEW ENGLAND / MASSACHUSETTS (MARTHA'S VINEYARD)

The Victorian Inn

24 South Water Street, Edgartown, Massachusetts 02539
Tel: 1 508 627 4784
Fax:

NEW ENGLAND / MASSACHUSETTS (ROCKPORT)

Seacrest Manor

99 Marmion Way, Rockport, Massachusetts 01966
Tel: 1 978 546 2211
Fax:

NEW ENGLAND / RHODE ISLAND (BLOCK ISLAND)

The Atlantic Inn

Po Box 1788, Block Island, Rhode Island, 02807
Tel: 1 401 466 5883
Fax: 1 401 466 5678

NEW ENGLAND / VERMONT (CHITTENDEN)

Fox Creek Inn

49 Dam Road, Chittenden, Vermont 05737
Tel: 1 802 483 6213
Fax: 1 802 483 2623

NEW ENGLAND / VERMONT (MANCHESTER VILLAGE)

1811 House

Po Box 39, Route 7a, Manchester Village, Vermont 05254
Tel: 1 802 362 1811
Fax: 1 802 362 2443

NEW ENGLAND / VERMONT (NEWFANE)

Four Columns Inn

Po Box 278, Newfane, Vermont 05345
Tel: 1 802 365 7713
Fax: 1 802 365 0022

NEW ENGLAND / VERMONT (STOWE)

The Mountain Road Resort At Stowe

Po Box 8, 1007 Mountain Road, Stowe, Vermont 05672
Tel: 1 802 253 4566
Fax: 1 802 253 7397

NEW ENGLAND / VERMONT (WESTON)

The Inn At Weston

Scenic Route 100, Weston, Vermont 05161
Tel: 1 802 824 6789
Fax: 1 802 824 3073

NEW YORK (CAZENOVIA)

The Brewster Inn

6 Ledyard Avenue, Cazenovia, New York 13035
Tel: 1 315 655 9232
Fax: 1 315 655 2130

NEW YORK (EAST AURORA)

Roycroft Inn

40 South Grove Street, East Aurora, New York 14052
Tel: 1 877 652 5552
Fax: 1 716 655 5345

NEW YORK (GENEVA)

Geneva On The Lake

1001 Lochland Road (Route 14 South), Geneva, New York 14456
Tel: 1 315 789 7190
Fax: 1 315 789 0322

NEW YORK (ITHACA)

William Henry Miller Inn

303 North Aurora Street, Ithaca, New York 14850
Tel: 1 607 256 4553
Fax: 1 607 256 0092

NEW YORK (NEW YORK CITY)

The Kitano New York

66 Park Avenue New York, New York 10016
Tel: 1 212 885 7000
Fax: 1 212 885 7100

NEW YORK (NORTHERN CATSKILL MOUNTAINS)

Albergo Allegria

Route 296, Windham, New York 12496
Tel: 1 518 734 5560
Fax: 1 518 734 5570

NEW YORK (SARATOGA)

Saratoga Arms

495-497 Broadway, Saratoga, New York 12866
Tel: 1 518 584 1775
Fax: 1 518 581 4064

NORTH CAROLINA (BALSAM)

Balsam Mountain Inn

Po Box 40, Balsam, North Carolina 28707
Tel: 1 828 456 9498
Fax: 1 828 456 9298

NORTH CAROLINA (EDENTON)

The Lords Proprietors' Inn

300 North Broad Street, Edenton, North Carolina 27932
Tel: 1 252 482 3641
Fax: 1 252 482 2432

NORTH CAROLINA (ROBBINSVILLE)

Snowbird Mountain Lodge

275 Santeetlah Road, Robbinsville, North Carolina 28771
Tel: 1 828 479 3433
Fax: 1 828 479 3473

NORTH CAROLINA (TRYON)

Pine Crest Inn

85 Pine Crest Lane, Tryon, North Carolina 28782
Tel: 1 828 859 9135
Fax: 1 828 859 9135

NORTH CAROLINA (WAYNESVILLE)

The Swag Country Inn

2300 Swag Road, Waynesville, North Carolina 28785
Tel: 1 828 926 0430
Fax: 1 828 926 2036

NORTH CAROLINA (WILMINGTON)

The Verandas

202 Nun Street, Wilmington, North Carolina 28401-5020
Tel: 1 910 251 2212
Fax: 1 910 251 8932

OREGON (GRANTS PASS)

Weasku Inn

5560 Rogue River Highway, Grants Pass, Oregon 97527
Tel: 1 541 471 8000
Fax: 1 541 471 7038

PENNSYLVANIA (PHILADELPHIA)

Rittenhouse Square Bed & Breakfast

1715 Rittenhouse Square, Philadelphia, Pennsylvania 19103
Tel: 1 215 546 6500
Fax: 1 215 564 8787

SOUTH CAROLINA (CHARLESTON)

Vendue Inn

19 Vendue Range, Charleston, South Carolina, 29401
Tel: 1 843 577 7970
Fax: 1 843 577 2913

SOUTH CAROLINA (PAWLEYS ISLAND)

Litchfield Plantation

Kings River Road, Box 290, Pawleys Island, South Carolina 29585
Tel: 1 843 237 9121
Fax: 1 843 237 1041

SOUTH CAROLINA (TRAVELERS REST)

La Bastide

10 Road Of Vines, Travelers Rest, South Carolina, 29690
Tel: 1 864 836 8463
Fax: 1 864 836 4820

TENNESSEE (KINGSTON)

Whitestone Country Inn

1200 Paint Rock Road, Kingston, Tennessee 37763
Tel: 1 865 376 0113
Fax: 1 865 376 4454

VIRGINIA (CHARLOTTESVILLE)

Prospect Hill Plantation Inn

2887 Poindexter Road, Trevilians, Virginia, 23093
Tel: 1 540 967 0844
Fax: 1 540 967 0102

VIRGINIA (MIDDLEBURG)

The Goodstone Inn & Estate

36205 Snake Hill Road, Middleburg, Virginia 20117
Tel: 1 540 687 4645
Fax: 1 540 687 6115

WYOMING (CHEYENNE)

Nagle Warren Mansion

222 East 17th Street, Cheyenne, Wyoming 82001
Tel: 1 307 637 3333
Fax: 1 307 638 6879

PREFERRED PARTNERS

Preferred partners are those organisations specifically chosen and exclusively recommended by Johansens for the quality and excellence of their products and services for the mutual benefit of Johansens recommendations, readers and independent travellers. For further details, please contact Fiona Patrick at Johansens on +44 (0)20 7566 9700.

HILDON, PART OF YOUR LIFE.
BY ANDREAS HEUMANN

ENGLAND

BEDFORDSHIRE

Cecil Higgins Art Gallery & Museum – Castle Lane, Bedford, Bedfordshire MK40 4AF. Tel: 01234 211222

John Bunyan Museum – Bunyan Meeting Free Church, Mill Street, Bedford, Bedfordshire MK40 3EU. Tel: 01234 213722

Woburn Abbey – Woburn, Bedfordshire MK17 9WA. Tel: 01525 290666

BERKSHIRE

Basildon Park – Lower Basildon, Reading, Berkshire RG8 9NR. Tel: 0118 984 3040

Dorney Court – Dorney, Nr Windsor, Berkshire SL4 6QP. Tel: 01628 604638

Mapledurham House and Watermill – Mapledurham, Nr Reading, Berkshire RG4 7TR. Tel: 0118 972 3350

Stratfield Saye House – Stratfield Saye Park, Berkshire RG7 2BZ. Tel: 01256 882882

Taplow Court – Taplow, Nr Maidenhead, Berkshire SL6 0ER. Tel: 01628 773163

Windsor Castle – Windsor, Berkshire SL4 1NJ. Tel: 01753 869 898 or 83118

BUCKINGHAMSHIRE

Claydon House – Middle Claydon, Buckingham, Buckinghamshire MK18 2EY. Tel: 01296 730349

Stowe Gardens – Stowe, Buckingham, Buckinghamshire MK18 5EH. Tel: 01280 822850

Stowe House – Stowe School, Stowe, Buckinghamshire MK18 5EH. Tel: 01280 818232

Waddesdon Manor – Nr Aylesbury, Buckinghamshire HP18 0JH. Tel: 01296 653211

CAMBRIDGESHIRE

Island Hall – Post Street, Godmanchester, Cambridgeshire PE29 2BA. Tel: 020 7491 3724

Kettles Yard – Castle Street, Cambridge, Cambridgeshire CB3 0AQ. Tel: 01223 352124

Kimbolton Castle – Kimbolton, Cambridgeshire PE28 0AE. Tel: 01480 860505

King's College – Cambridge, Cambridgeshire CB2 1ST. Tel: 01223 331212

St Peter's Church – Off Castle Street, Cambridge, Cambridgeshire. Tel: 01223 352124

The Manor of Green Knowe – Hemingford Grey, Cambridgeshire PE28 9BN. Tel: 01480 463134

CHESHIRE

Adlington Hall – Nr Macclesfield, Cheshire SK10 4LF. Tel: 01625 820201

Arley Hall & Gardens – Arley, Northwich, Cheshire CW9 6NA. Tel: 01565 777353

Cholmondeley Castle Gardens – Malpas, Cheshire SY14 8AH. Tel: 01829 720383

Christ Church – Catherine St, Macclesfield, Cheshire. Tel: 01625 423894

Dorfold Hall – Nantwich, Cheshire CW5 8LD. Tel: 01270 625245

Macclesfield Museum – The Heritage Centre, Roe Street, Macclesfield, Cheshire SK11 6UT. Tel: 01625 613210

Ness Botanic Gardens – Ness, Neston, South Wirral, Cheshire CH64 4AY. Tel: 0151 353 0123

Norton Priory Museum – Tudor Road, Manor Park, Runcorn, Cheshire WA7 1SX. Tel: 01928 569895

Tabley House Stately Home – Tabley House, Knutsford, Cheshire WA16 0HB. Tel: 01565 750151

COUNTY DURHAM

Raby Castle – Staindrop, Darlington, County Durham DL2 3AH. Tel: 01833 660207

The Bowes Museum – Barnard Castle, County Durham DL12 8NP. Tel: 01833 690606

CUMBRIA

Holker Hall and Gardens – Cark-in-Cartmel, Nr Grange-over-Sands, Cumbria LA11 7PL. Tel: 01539 558328

Hutton-in-the-Forest – Penrith, Cumbria CA11 9TH. Tel: 01768 484449

Levens Hall – Kendal, Cumbria LA8 0PB. Tel: 01539 560321

Mirehouse – Keswick, Cumbria CA12 4QE. Tel: 01768 772287

Muncaster Castle – Ravenglass, Cumbria CA18 1RQ. Tel: 01229 717614

DERBYSHIRE

Buxton Museum & Art Gallery – Terrace Road, Buxton, Derbyshire SK17 6DA. Tel: 01298 24658

Haddon Hall – Bakewell, Derbyshire DE45 1LA. Tel: 01629 812855

Hardwick Hall – Doe Lea, Chesterfield, Derbyshire S44 5QJ. Tel: 01246 850430

Melbourne Hall and Gardens – Melbourne, Derbyshire DE73 1EN. Tel: 01332 862502

DEVON

Cadhay – Ottery St Mary, Devon EX11 1QT. Tel: 01404 812432

Hartland Abbey & Gardens – Hartland, Nr Bideford, North Devon EX39 6DT. Tel: 01237 441264/234

Museum of Dartmoor Life – 3 West Street, Okehampton, Devon EX20 1HQ. Tel: 01837 52295

The Royal Horticultural Society, Garden Rosemoor – Great Torrington, North Devon EX38 8PH. Tel: 01805 624067

Ugbrooke Park – Ugbrooke, Chudleigh, Devon TQ13 0AD. Tel: 01626 852179

DORSET

Chiffchaffs – Chaffeymoor, Bourton, Gillingham, Dorset SP8 5BY. Tel: 01747 840841

Cranborne Manor Garden – Cranborne, Wimborne, Dorset BH21 5PP. Tel: 01725 517248

Deans Court Garden – Deans Court, Wimborne, Dorset BH21 1EE. Tel: 01202 882456

Mapperton Gardens – Mapperton, Beaminster, Dorset DT8 3NR. Tel: 01308 862645

Minterne Gardens – Minterne Magna, Dorchester, Dorset DT2 7AU. Tel: 01300 341370

Sherborne Castle – New Road, Sherborne, Dorset DT9 5NR. Tel: 01935 813182

St Mary the Virgin's Church – (3 miles SE of Blandford off A350), Tarrant, Crawford, Dorset. Tel: 020 7936 2285

Tolpuddle Museum – Tolpuddle Cottages, Tolpuddle, Dorset DT2 7EH. Tel: 01305 848237

EAST SUSSEX

Anne of Cleves House – 52 Southover High Street, Lewes, East Sussex BN7 1JA. Tel: 01273 474610

Charleston – Firle, Nr Lewes, East Sussex BN8 6LL. Tel: 01323 811265

Firle Place – Nr Lewes, East Sussex BN8 6LP. Tel: 01273 858307

Garden and Grounds of Herstmonceux Castle – Herstmonceux Castle, Hailsham, East Sussex BN27 1RN. Tel: 01323 833816

Glynde Place – Glynde, Lewes, East Sussex BN7 2HX. Tel: 01273 858224

Great Dixter House & Gardens – Great Dixter, Northiam, Rye, East Sussex TN31 6PH. Tel: 01797 252878

Lewes Castle and Barbican House Museum – Barbican House, 169 High Street, Lewes, East Sussex BN7 1YE. Tel: 01273 486290

Merriments Gardens – Hurst Green, East Sussex TN19 7RA. Tel: 01580 860666

Michelham Priory – Upper Dicker, Hailsham, East Sussex BN27 3QS. Tel: 01323 844 224

Pashley Manor Gardens – Ticehurst, Wadhurst, East Sussex TN5 7HE. Tel: 01580 200888

The Priest House – North Lane, West Hoathly, (Nr East Grinstead), East Sussex RH19 4PP. Tel: 01342 810479

Wilmington Priory – Wilmington, Nr Eastbourne, East Sussex BN26 5SW. Tel: 01628 825925

EAST YORKSHIRE

Burton Agnes Hall – Burton Agnes, Driffield, Nr Bridlington, East Yorkshire YO25 0ND. Tel: 01262 490324

ESSEX

Hedingham Castle – Castle Hedingham, Nr Halstead, Essex CO9 3DJ. Tel: 01787 460261

The Gardens of Easton Lodge – Warwick House, Easton Lodge, Great Dunmow, Essex CM6 2BB. Tel: 01371 876 979

The Royal Horticultural Society, Garden Hyde Hall – Rettendon, Chelmsford, Essex CM3 8ET. Tel: 01245 400256

The Sir Alfred Munnings Art Museum – Castle House, Dedham, Essex CO7 6AZ. Tel: 01206 322127

GLOUCESTERSHIRE

Berkeley Castle – Berkeley, Gloucestershire GL13 9BQ. Tel: 01453 810332

Chavenage House – Tetbury, Gloucestershire GL8 8XP. Tel: 01666 502329

Chedworth Roman Villa – Yanworth, Cheltenham, Gloucestershire GL54 3LJ. Tel: 01242 890256

Cheltenham Art Gallery & Museum – Clarence Street, Cheltenham, Gloucestershire GL50 3JT. Tel: 01242 237431

Frampton Court – Frampton-on-Severn, Gloucestershire GL2 7EU. Tel: 01452 740698

Hardwicke Court – Nr Gloucester, Gloucestershire GL2 4RS. Tel: 01452 720212

Kelmscott Manor – Kelmscott, Nr Lechlade, Gloucestershire GL7 3HJ. Tel: 01367 252486

Rodmarton Manor Garden – Cirencester, Gloucestershire GL7 6PF. Tel: 01285 841253

Sezincote – Moreton-in-Marsh, Gloucestershire GL56 9AW. Tel: Appointment Only - Please Write

Snowshill Manor – Snowshill, Broadway, Gloucestershire WR12 7JU. Tel: 01386 852410

GREATER MANCHESTER

Heaton Hall – Heaton Park, Prestwich, Manchester, Greater Manchester M25 2SW. Tel: 0161 773 1231/ 0161 235 8888

Salford Museums & Art Gallery – Peel Park, Salford, Greater Manchester M5 4WU. Tel: 0161 736 2649

HAMPSHIRE

Avington Park – Winchester, Hampshire SO21 1DB. Tel: 01962 779260

Beaulieu – Montagu Ventures Ltd, John Montagu Building, Beaulieu, Hampshire SO42 7ZN. Tel: 01590 612345

Beaulieu Vineyard and Gardens – Beaulieu Estate, John Montagu Building, Beaulieu, Hampshire SO42 7ZN. Tel: 01590 612345

Breamore House & Museum – Breamore, Nr Fordingbridge, Hampshire SP6 2DF. Tel: 01725 512468

Broadlands – Romsey, Hampshire SO51 9ZD. Tel: 01794 505010

Family Trees – Sandy Lane, Shedfield, Hampshire SO32 2HQ. Tel: 01329 834812

Gilbert White's House and The Oates Museum – Selborne, Hampshire GU34 3JH. Tel: 01420 511275

Hall Farm – Bentworth, Alton, Hampshire GU34 5JU. Tel: 01420 564010

Houghton Lodge Gardens – Houghton, Stockbridge, Hampshire SO20 6LQ. Tel: 01264 810912

Langley Boxwood Nursery – Rake, Liss, Hampshire GU33 7JL. Tel: 01730 894467

Mottisfont Abbey & Gardens – Mottisfont, Nr Romsey, Hampshire SO51 0LP. Tel: 01794 340757

Pylewell – South Baddesley, Hampshire SO41 55N. Tel: 01329 833130

The Sir Harold Hillier Gardens and Arboretum – Jermyns Lane, Ampfield, Romsey, Hampshire SO51 0QA. Tel: 01794 368787

The Vyne - The National Trust – Sherborne St John, Basingstoke, Hampshire RG24 9HL. Tel: 01256 881337

HEREFORDSHIRE

Eastnor Castle – Nr Ledbury, Hereford, Herefordshire HR8 1RL. Tel: 01531 633160

Hergest Croft Gardens – Kington, Herefordshire HR5 3EG. Tel: 01544 230160

Kentchurch Court – Kentchurch, Nr Pontrilas, Hereford, Herefordshire HR2 0DB. Tel: 01981 240228

Moccas Court – Moccas, Herefordshire HR2 9LH. Tel: 01981 500381

HERTFORDSHIRE

Ashridge – Ringshall, Berkhamsted, Hertfordshire HP4 1NS. Tel: 01442 843491

Cromer Windmill – Ardley, Stevenage, Hertfordshire SG2 7AT. Tel: 01279 843301

First Garden City Heritage Museum – 296 Norton Way South, Letchworth, Hertfordshire SG6 1SU. Tel: 01462 482710

Gorhambury – St Albans, Hertfordshire AL3 6AH. Tel: 01727 855000

Hatfield House, Park and Gardens – Hatfield, Hertfordshire AL9 5NQ. Tel: 01707 287010

Scott's Grotto – Scott's Road, Ware, Hertfordshire SG12 9SQ. Tel: 01920 464131

The Gardens of the Rose – St Albans, Hertfordshire AL2 3NR. Tel: 01727 850461

ISLE OF WIGHT

Deacons Nursery (H.H.) – Moor View, Godshill, Isle of Wight PO38 3HW. Tel: 01983 840750

Dinosaur Isle – Culver Parade, Sandown, Isle of Wight PO36 8QA. Tel: 01983 404344

Newport Roman Villa – Cypress Road, Newport, Isle of Wight PO30 1HE. Tel: 01983 529720

KENT

Belmont – Throwley, Nr Faversham, Kent ME13 0HH. Tel: 01795 890202

Bromley Museum – The Priory, Church Hill, Orpington, Kent BR6 0HH. Tel: 01689 873826

Cobham Hall – Cobham, Kent DA12 3BL. Tel: 01474 823371
Crofton Roman Villa – Crofton Road, Orpington, Kent BR6 8AD. Tel: 01689 873826
Dickens House Museum – 2 Victoria Parade, Broadstairs, Kent CT10 1QS. Tel: 01843 861232
Doddington Place Gardens – Doddington, Sittingbourne, Kent ME9 0BB. Tel: 01795 886101
Finchcocks – Goudhurst, Kent TN17 1HH. Tel: 01580 211702
Graham Clarke Up the Garden Studio – Green Lane, Boughton Monchelsea, Maidstone, Kent ME17 4LF. Tel: 01622 743938
Hever Castle & Gardens – Edenbridge, Kent TN8 7NG. Tel: 01732 865224
Leeds Castle – Maidstone, Kent ME17 1PL. Tel: 01622 765400
Maidstone Museum & Bentlif Art Gallery – St Faith's Street, Maidstone, Kent ME14 1LH. Tel: 01622 754497
Mount Ephraim Gardens – Hernhill, Nr Faversham, Kent ME13 9TX. Tel: 01227 751496
Museum of Kent Life – Loch Lane, Sandling, Maidstone, Kent ME14 3AU. Tel: 01622 763936
Penshurst Place & Gardens – Penshurst, Nr Tonbridge, Kent TN11 8DG. Tel: 01892 870307
Riverhill House Gardens – Riverhill, Sevenoaks, Kent TN15 0RR. Tel: 01732 458802 / 452557
Scotney Castle Garden – Lamberhurst, Royal Tunbridge Wells, Kent TN3 8JN. Tel: 01892 891081
Smallhythe Place – Tenterden, Kent TN30 7NG. Tel: 01580 762334
The New College of Cobham – Cobhamburt Road, Cobham, Kent DA12 3BG. Tel: 01474 812503 / 01474 814280
Tunbridge Wells Museum & Art Gallery – Civic Centre, Mount Pleasant, Royal Tunbridge Wells, Kent TN1 1JN. Tel: 01892 554171
Tyrwhitt-Drake Museum of Carriages – Mill Street, Maidstone, Kent ME15 6YE. Tel: 01622 754497

LANCASHIRE

Astley Hall Museum & Art Gallery – Astley Park, Chorley, Lancashire PR7 1NP. Tel: 01257 515555
Browsholme Hall – Nr Clitheroe, Lancashire BB7 3DE. Tel: 01254 826719
Stonyhurst College Delvco Ltd – Stonyhurst College, Stonyhurst, Clitheroe, Lancashire BB7 9PZ. Tel: 01254 826345
Towneley Hall Art Gallery & Museums – Towneley Park, Burnley, Lancashire BB11 3RQ. Tel: 01282 424213

LEICESTERSHIRE

Belvoir Castle – Grantham, Leicestershire NG32 1PD. Tel: 01476 870262
Kayes Garden Nursery – 1700 Melton Rd, Rearsby, Leicester, Leicestershire LE7 4YR. Tel: 01664 424578
St Mary Magdalene's Church – Stapleford Park, Nr Melton Mowbray off B676, Leicestershire. Tel: 020 7936 2285
Stanford Hall – Stanford Park, Lutterworth, Leicestershire LE17 6DH. Tel: 01788 860250

LINCOLNSHIRE

Burghley House – Stamford, Lincolnshire PE9 3JY. Tel: 01780 752451
Normanby Hall Country Park – Normanby, Scunthorpe, Lincolnshire DN15 9HU. Tel: 01724 720588

LONDON

Apsley House – Hyde Park Corner, London W1J 7NT. Tel: 020 7499 5676
Banqueting House – Whitehall Palace, London SW1A 2ER. Tel: 020 7930 4179
Buckingham Palace – London SW1A 1AA. Tel: 020 7321 2233
Burgh House – New End Square, Hampstead, London NW3 1LT. Tel: 020 7431 0144
Chelsea Physic Garden – 66 Royal Hospital Road, Chelsea, London SW3 4HS. Tel: 020 7352 5646
Design Museum – Butler's Wharf, 28 Shad Thames, London SE1 2YD. Tel: 020 7940 8790
Dulwich Picture Gallery – Gallery Road, London SE21 7AD. Tel: 020 8693 5254
Fenton House – Windmill Hill, Hampstead, London NW3 6RT. Tel: 020 7435 3471
Guildhall Art Gallery – Guildhall Yard, London EC2P 2EJ. Tel: 020 7332 3700
Handel House Museum – 25 Brook Street, London W1K 4HB. Tel: 020 7495 1685
HM Tower of London – Tower Hill, London EC3N 4AB. Tel: 020 7709 0765
Leighton House Museum – 12 Holland Park Road, London W14 8LZ. Tel: 020 7602 3316
Merton Heritage Centre – The Cânons, Madeira, Mitcham, London CR4 4HD. Tel: 020 8640 9387
Museum of Garden History – Lambeth Palace Road, Lambeth, London SE1 7LB. Tel: 020 7401 8865
National Portrait Gallery – St Martin's Place, London WC2H 0HE. Tel: 020 7306 0055
Pitshanger Manor & Gallery – 5 Walpole Park, Mattock Lane, Ealing, London W5 5EQ. Tel: 020 8567 1227
Royal Institution Michael Faraday Museum – 21 Albemarle Street, W1S 4BS. Tel: 020 7409 2992
Sir John Soane's Museum – 13 Lincoln's Inn Fields, London WC2A 3BP. Tel: 020 7405 2107
Somerset House with Courtauld Institute Gallery, Gilbert Collection & Heritage Rooms – Strand, London WC2R 1LA. Tel: 020 7845 4600
St. John's Gate – St John's Lane, Clerkenwell, London EC1M 4DA. Tel: 020 7324 4000
Strawberry Hill House – St Mary's University College, Strawberry Hill, Waldegrave Road, Twickenham, TW1 4SX. Tel: 020 8240 4044
Syon Park – London Road, Brentford, TW8 8JF. Tel: 020 8560 0882
The Fan Museum – 12 Crooms Hill, Greenwich, London SE10 8ER. Tel: 020 8305 1441
The Jewish Museum – 129-131 Albert Street, Camden Town, London NW1 7NB. Tel: 020 7284 1997
The Traveller's Club – 106 Pall Mall, London SW1Y 5EP. Tel: 020 7930 8688
Victoria & Albert Museum – Cromwell Road, South Kensington, London SW7 2RL. Tel: 020 7942 2000
Westminster Abbey Museum – Broad Sanctuary, London SW1P 3PA. Tel: 020 7222 5152

MERSEYSIDE

Christ Church Old Church – Waterloo, Jct of Alexandra, Victoria & Waterloo Rd, off Crosby Rd South, Liverpool, Merseyside. Tel: 020 7936 2285

NORFOLK

Fairhaven Woodland and Water Garden – School Road, South Walsham, Norwich, Norfolk NR13 6EA. Tel: 01603 270449
Holkham Hall – Holkham Estate Office, Wells-next-the-Sea, Norfolk NR23 1AB. Tel: 01328 710227
Hoveton Hall – Hoveton, Norwich, Norfolk NR12 8RJ. Tel: 01603 782798
Mannington Hall – Saxthorpe, Norwich, Norfolk NR11 7BB. Tel: 01263 584175
Raveningham Gardens – Raveningham, Norwich, Norfolk NR14 6NS. Tel: 01508 548222
Walsingham Abbey Grounds – Little Walsingham, Norfolk NR22 6BP. Tel: 01328 820259

NORTH YORKSHIRE

Brockfield Hall – Warthill, York, North Yorkshire YO19 5XJ. Tel: 01904 489298
Christ the Consoler's Church – (4 miles SE of Ripon off B6265), Newby Hall Grounds, Skelton-cum-Newby, North Yorkshire. Tel: 020 7936 2285
Constable Burton Hall – Leyburn, North Yorkshire DL8 5LJ. Tel: 01677 450428
Dales Countryside Museum – Station Yard, Hawes, North Yorkshire DL8 3NT. Tel: 01969 667450
Duncombe Park – Helmsley, York, North Yorkshire YO62 5EB. Tel: 01439 770213
Kiplin Hall – Nr Scorton, Richmond, North Yorkshire. Tel: 01748 818178
National Railway Museum – Leeman Road, York, North Yorkshire YO26 4XJ. Tel: 01904 621261
Newburgh Priory – Coxwold, North Yorkshire YO61 4AS. Tel: 01347 868435
Ripley Castle – Ripley, North Yorkshire HG3 3AY. Tel: 01423 770152
Scarborough Museums & Art Gallery – c/o Londesborough Lodge, The Crescent, Scarborough, North Yorkshire YO11 2PW. Tel: 01723 374839 / 367326 / 374753
Sion Hill Hall – Kirby Wiske, Thirsk, North Yorkshire YO7 4EU. Tel: 01845 587206
Swaledale Folk Museum – The Green, Reeth, Nr Richmond, North Yorkshire DL11 6QT. Tel: 01748 884373
The Forbidden Corner – The Tupgill Park Estate, Coverham, Middleham, Leyburn, North Yorkshire DL8 4TJ. Tel: 01969 640638
Thorp Perrow Arboretum & The Falcons of Thorp Perrow – Bedale, North Yorkshire DL8 2PR. Tel: 01677 425323
Yorkshire Garden World – Main Road, West Haddlesey, Nr Selby, North Yorkshire YO8 8QA. Tel: 01757 228279

NORTHAMPTONSHIRE

Althorp – Northampton, Northamptonshire NN7 4HQ. Tel: 01604 770107
Boughton House – Kettering, Northamptonshire NN14 1BJ. Tel: 01536 515731
Cottesbrooke Hall and Gardens – Cottesbrooke, Nr Northampton, Northamptonshire NN6 8PF. Tel: 01604 505808
Haddonstone Show Garden – The Forge House, Church Lane, East Haddon, Northamptonshire NN6 8DB. Tel: 01604 770711
Kelmarsh Hall – Kelmarsh, Northampton, Northamptonshire NN6 9LY. Tel: 01604 686543
Southwick Hall – Nr Oundle, Peterborough, Northamptonshire PE8 5BL. Tel: 01832 274064

NORTHUMBERLAND

Alnwick Castle – Estate Office, Alnwick, Northumberland NE66 1NQ. Tel: 01665 510777 / 511100
Chillingham Castle – Chillingham, Alnwick, Northumberland NE66 5NJ. Tel: 01668 215359
Chipchase Castle and Gardens – Chipchase, Wark on Tyne, Hexham, Northumberland NE48 3NT. Tel: 01434 230203
Paxton House & Country Park – Berwick-upon-Tweed, Northumberland TD15 1SZ. Tel: 01289 386291
Seaton Delaval Hall – Seaton Sluice, Nr Whitley Bay, Northumberland NE26 4QR. Tel: 0191 237 1493 / 0786

NOTTINGHAMSHIRE

Papplewick Hall – Papplewick, Nottingham, Nottinghamshire NG15 8FE. Tel: 0115 963 3491

OXFORDSHIRE

Ardington House – Wantage, Oxfordshire OX12 8QA. Tel: 01235 821566
Blenheim Palace – Woodstock, Oxfordshire OX20 1PX. Tel: 01993 811325
Buscot Park – Buscot, Faringdon, Oxfordshire SN7 8BU. Tel: 01367 240786 / 0845 345338
Christ Church Picture Gallery – Christ Church, Oxford, Oxfordshire OX1 1DP. Tel: 01865 276172
Ditchley Park – Ditchley Foundation, Enstone, Oxfordshire OX7 4ER. Tel: 01608 677346
Kingston Bagpuize House – Kingston Bagpuize, Abingdon, Oxfordshire OX13 5AX. Tel: 01865 820259
Museum of Modern Art – 30 Pembroke Street, Oxford, Oxfordshire OX1 1BP. Tel: 01865 722733
River & Rowing Museum – Mill Meadows, Henley-on-Thames, Oxfordshire RG9 1BF. Tel: 01491 415600
Rousham House – Rousham, Bichester, Oxfordshire OX25 4QX. Tel: 01869 347110
Stonor Park – Stonor, Nr Henley-on-Thames, Oxfordshire RG9 6HF. Tel: 01491 638587
Sulgrave Manor – Manor Road, Sulgrave, Banbury, Oxfordshire OX17 2SD. Tel: 01295 760205
University of Oxford Botanic Garden – Rose Lane, Oxford, Oxfordshire OX1 4AZ. Tel: 01865 286690
Wallingford Castle Gardens – Castle Street, Wallingford, Oxfordshire. Tel: 01491 835373

SHROPSHIRE

Hawkstone Park – Weston-under-Redcastle, Shrewsbury, Shropshire SY4 5UY. Tel: 01939 200611
Hodnet Hall Gardens – Hodnet, Market Drayton, Shropshire TF9 3NN. Tel: 01630 685202
Hopton Court – Hopton Wafers, Kidderminster, Shropshire DY14 0EF. Tel: 01299 270734
Shipton Hall – Much Wenlock, Shropshire TF13 6JZ. Tel: 01746 785225
Shrewsbury Castle & Shropshire Regimental Museum – Castle Street, Shrewsbury, Shropshire SY1 2AT. Tel: 01743 358516
The Dorothy Clive Garden – Willoughbridge, Nr Market Drayton, Shropshire TF9 4EU. Tel: 01630 647237
The Ironbridge Gorge Museum Trust – Ironbridge, Telford, Shropshire TF8 7AW. Tel: 01952 433522
The Royal Airforce Museum – Cosford, Shifnal, Shropshire TF11 8UP. Tel: 01902 376200
Weston Park – Weston-under-Lizard, Nr Shifnal, Shropshire TF11 8LE. Tel: 01952 852100

SOMERSET

Barford Park – Enmore, Nr Bridgwater, Somerset TA5 1AG. Tel: 01278 671269
Crowe Hall – Widcombe Hill, Bath, Somerset BA2 6AR. Tel: 01225 310322
Forde Abbey and Gardens – Chard, Somerset TA20 4LU. Tel: 01460 220231
Great House Farm – Theale, Wedmore, Somerset BS28 4SJ. Tel: 01934 713133
Maunsel House – North Newton, Nr North Petherton, Bridgwater, Somerset TA7 0BU. Tel: 01278 661076
Milton Lodge Gardens – Milton Lodge, Wells, Somerset BA5 3AQ. Tel: 01749 672168
Museum of Costume & Assembly Rooms – Bennett Street, Bath, Somerset BA1 2QH. Tel: 01225 477789
Orchard Wyndham – Williton, Taunton, Somerset TA4 4HH. Tel: 01984 632309
Pepperpot Castle – Exmoor National Park, Somerset. Tel: 01398 341615
Roman Baths & Pump Room – Abbey Church Yard, Bath, Somerset BA1 1LZ. Tel: 01225 477791
The American Museum in Britain – Claverton Manor, Bath, North Somerset BA2 7BD. Tel: 01225 460503
The Bishop's Palace – Wells, Somerset BA5 2PD. Tel: 01749 678691

STAFFORDSHIRE

Dunwood Hall – Longsdon, Nr Leek, Staffordshire ST9 9AR. Tel: 01538 385071
Ford Green Hall – Ford Green Road, Smallthorne, Stoke-on-Trent, Staffordshire ST6 1NG. Tel: 01782 233195
The Bass Museum – PO Box 220, Horninglow Street, Burton-upon-Trent, Staffordshire DE14 1YQ. Tel: 01283 511000
Whitmore Hall – Whitmore, Newcastle-under-Lyme, Staffordshire ST5 5HW. Tel: 01782 680478

SUFFOLK

Ancient House – Clare, Suffolk CO10 8NY. Tel: 01628 825925
Christchurch Mansion – Christchurch Park, Ipswich, Suffolk 1P4 2BE. Tel: 01473 433554
Hengrave Hall Centre – Hengrave Hall, Bury St Edmunds, Suffolk IP28 6LZ. Tel: 01284 701561
Ipswich Museum – Ipswich, Suffolk IP1 3QH. Tel: 01473 433550
Kentwell Hall – Long Melford, Suffolk CO10 7JS. Tel: 01787 310207
Otley Hall – Hall Lane, Otley, Nr Ipswich, Suffolk IP6 9PA. Tel: 01473 890264
Shrubland Park Gardens – Coddenham, Ipswich, Suffolk IP6 9QQ. Tel: 01473 830221

SURREY

Addington Palace – Gravel Hill, Addington Village, Croydon, Surrey CR0 5BB. Tel: 020 8662 5000
Farnham Castle – Farnham, Surrey GU4 0AG. Tel: 01252 721194
Goddards – Abinger Common, Dorking, Surrey RH5 6TH. Tel: 01628 825925
Great Fosters Hotel – Stroude Road, Egham, Surrey TW20 9UR. Tel: 01784 433822
Guildford House Gallery – 155, High Street, Guildford, Surrey GU1 3AJ. Tel: 01483 444740
Hampton Court Palace – East Molesey, Surrey KT8 9AU. Tel: 020 8781 9500

Loseley Park – Estate Office, Guildford, Surrey GU3 1HS. Tel: 01483 304440
Painshill Landscape Garden – Portsmouth Road, Cobham, Surrey KT11 1JE. Tel: 01932 868113
Rural Life Centre – Reeds Road, Tilford, Farnham, Surrey GU10 2DL. Tel: 01252 795571
The Royal Horticultural Society, Wisley Garden – Nr Woking, Surrey GU23 6QB. Tel: 01483 224234

WARWICKSHIRE
Arbury Hall – Nuneaton, Warwickshire CV10 7PT. Tel: 024 7638 2804
Bosworth Battlefield Visitor Centre & Country Park – Sutton Cheney, Nr Nuneaton, Warwickshire CV13 0AD. Tel: 01455 290429
Honington Hall – Shipston-on-Stour, Warwickshire CV36 5AA. Tel: 01608 661434
Ragley Hall – Alcester, Warwickshire B49 5NJ. Tel: 01789 762090
Stoneleigh Abbey – Kenilworth, Warwickshire CV8 2LF. Tel: 01926 858585
The Shakespeare Houses – The Shakespeare Centre, Henley Street, Stratford-upon-Avon, Warwickshire CV37 6QW. Tel: 01789 204016

WEST MIDLANDS
Barber Institute of Fine Arts – The University of Birmingham, Edgbaston, Birmingham, West Midlands B15 2TS. Tel: 0121 414 7333
Birmingham Botanical Gardens and Glasshouses – Westbourne Road, Edgbaston, Birmingham, West Midlands B15 3TR. Tel: 0121 454 1860

WEST SUSSEX
Arundel Castle – Arundel, West Sussex BN18 9AB. Tel: 01903 883136
Denmans Garden – Clock House, Denmans, Fontwell, Arundel, West Sussex BN18 0SU. Tel: 01243 542808
Fishbourne Roman Palace – Salthill Road, Fishbourne, Chichester, West Sussex PO19 3QR. Tel: 01243 785859
Goodwood House – Goodwood, Chichester, West Sussex PO18 0PX. Tel: 01243 755000
High Beeches Gardens – High Beeches, Handcross, West Sussex RH17 6HQ. Tel: 01444 400589
Leonardslee Gardens – Lower Beeding, Horsham, West Sussex RH13 6PP. Tel: 01403 891212
Marlipins Museum – High Street, Shoreham-by-Sea, West Sussex BN43 5DA. Tel: 01273 462994
North Stoke Church – 5 miles North of Arundel, off B2139, West Sussex. Tel: 020 7936 2285
Pallant House Gallery – 9 North Pallant, Chichester, West Sussex PO19 1TJ. Tel: 01243 774557
Parham House and Gardens – Parham Park, Nr Pulborough, West Sussex RH20 4HS. Tel: 01903 742021
St John's Chapel – St John's Street, Chichester, West Sussex. Tel: 01243 787674
The Weald and Downland Open Air Museum – Singleton, West Sussex PO18 0EU. Tel: 01243 811363
West Dean Gardens – West Dean, Chichester, West Sussex PO18 0QZ. Tel: 01243 818210
Worthing Museum & Art Gallery – Chapel Road, Worthing, West Sussex BN11 1HP. Tel: 01903 239999

WEST YORKSHIRE
Bramham Park – Wetherby, West Yorkshire LS23 6ND. Tel: 01937 846002
Harewood House – The Harewood Estate, Leeds, West Yorkshire LS17 9LQ. Tel: 0113 218 1010
Shibden Hall – Listers Road, Halifax, West Yorkshire HX3 6XG. Tel: 01422 352246
St John the Evangelist's Church – New Briggate, Leeds, West Yorkshire. Tel: 0113 244 1689

WILTSHIRE
Charlton Park House – Charlton Park House Management Ltd, Malmesbury, Wiltshire SN16 9DG. Tel: 01666 824389
Hamptworth Lodge – Landford, Salisbury, Wiltshire SP5 2EA. Tel: 01794 390215
Longleat – The Estate Office, Warminster, Wiltshire BA12 7NW. Tel: 01985 844400
Salisbury Cathedral – Visitor Services, 33 The Close, Salisbury, Wiltshire SP1 2EJ. Tel: 01722 555120
St Nicholas' Church – (1m NW Salisbury, off A36, 1m N of Wylye), Fisherton Delamere, Wiltshire. Tel: 020 7936 2285
The Peto Garden At Iford Manor – Bradford-on-Avon, Wiltshire BA15 2BA. Tel: 01225 863146

WORCESTERSHIRE
Hartlebury Castle – Nr Kidderminster, Worcestershire DY11 7XX. Tel: 01299 250410 (state rooms sec) / (museum) 01299 250416
Little Malvern Court & Gardens – Nr Malvern, Worcestershire WR14 4JN. Tel: 01684 892988
The Commandery – Sidbury, Worcester, Worcestershire WR1 2HU. Tel: 01905 361821

SCOTLAND

ABERDEENSHIRE
Craigston Castle – Turriff, Aberdeenshire AB53 5PX. Tel: 01888 551228

ANGUS
Glamis Castle – Glamis, by Forfar, Angus DD8 1RJ. Tel: 01307 840393

ARGYLL & BUTE
Torosay Castle and Gardens – Craignure, Isle of Mull, PA72 6AY. Tel: 01680 812421

AYRSHIRE
Auchinleck House – Ochiltree, Ayrshire. Tel: 01628 825920
Blairquhan Castle and Gardens – Straiton, Maybole, Ayrshire KA19 7LZ. Tel: 01655 770239
Kelburn Castle and Country Centre – Kelburn, Fairlie, Ayrshire KA29 0BE. Tel: 01475 568685
Maybole Castle – Maybole, Ayrshire KA19 7BX. Tel: 01655 883765
Sorn Castle – Sorn Estate, Sorn, Mauchline, Ayrshire KA5 6HR. Tel: 01505 612124

DUMFRIES & GALLOWAY
Ardwell Gardens – Ardwell House, Stranraer, Wigtownshire DG9 9LY. Tel: 01776 860227
Drumlanrig Castle Gardens and Country Park – Nr Thornhill, Dumfries & Galloway DG3 4AQ. Tel: 01848 330248
Dumfries & Galloway Tourist Board – 64 Whitesands, Dumfries DG1 2RS. Tel: 01387 253862
Galloway Country Style – High Street, Gatehouse of Fleet, Galloway DG7 2HP. Tel: 01557 814001
Rammerscales House – Lockerbie, Dumfries DG11 1LD. Tel: 01387 810229

EDINBURGH & LOTHIAN
Dalmeny House – The Estate Office, South Queensferry, Edinburgh EH30 9TQ. Tel: 0131 331 1888
Hopetoun House – South Queensferry, Nr Edinburgh, West Lothian EH30 9SL. Tel: 0131 331 2451
The Palace of Holyroodhouse – Edinburgh, EH8 8DX. Tel: 0131 556 7371 / 5661096

FIFE
Callendar House – Callendar Park, Falkirk, Fife FK1 1YR. Tel: 01324 503770

GLASGOW
Glasgow Museums – Glasgow City Council, Art Gallery & Museum, Kelvingrove, Glasgow G3 8AG. Tel: 0141 287 2758

HIGHLANDS
Dunrobin Castle – Golspie, Sutherland, Highlands KW10 6SF. Tel: 01408 633177

LANARKSHIRE
New Lanark World Heritage Village – New Lanark Mills, Lanark, South Lanarkshire ML11 9DB. Tel: 01555 661345
The Tower of Hallbar – Braidwood Rd, Braidwood, Lanarkshire ML8 5RD. Tel: 020 7930 8030

PERTHSHIRE
Scone Palace – Scone, Perth, Perthshire PH2 6BD. Tel: 01738 552300
Stobhall – Guildtown, Perthshire PH2 6DR. Tel: 01821 640332

SCOTTISH BORDERS
Bowhill House & Country Park – Bowhill, Selkirk, Scottish Borders TD7 5ET. Tel: 01750 22204
Floors Castle – Kelso, Borders TD5 7SF. Tel: 01573 223333
Manderston – Duns, Berwickshire, Scottish Borders TD11 3PP. Tel: 01361 882636
Traquair House – Innerleithen, Peeblesshire EH44 6PW. Tel: 01896 830323

WALES

CARDIFF
Museum Of Welsh Life – St Fagans, Cardiff CF5 6XB. Tel: 029 2057 3500
The National Museum & Gallery – Cathays Park, Cardiff CF10 3NP. Tel: 029 2039 7951

CARMARTHENSHIRE
Aberglasney Gardens – East Bailiff's Lodge, Llangathen, Carmarthenshire SA32 8QH. Tel: 01558 668998
Museum of the Welsh Woollen Industry – Dre-fach Felindre, Llandysul, Carmarthenshire SA44 5UP. Tel: 01559 370929

CEREDIGION
The School of Art Gallery and Museum – University of Wales, Buarth Mawr, Aberystwyth, Ceredigion SY23 1NG. Tel: 01970 622460

GWYNEDD
Bodnant Garden – Tal-y-Cafn, Nr Colwyn Bay, Gwynedd LL28 5RE. Tel: 01492 650460
Gwydir Castle – Llanrwst, Gwynedd LL26 0PN. Tel: 01492 641687
Oriel Plas Glyn-y-Weddw Art Gallery – Llanbedrog, Pwllheli, Gwynedd LL53 7TT. Tel: 01758 740763
Plas Brondanw Gardens – Menna Angharad, Plas Brondanw, Llanfrothen, Gwynedd LL48 6SW. Tel: 01766 770484
Welsh Slate Museum – Padarn Country Park, Llanberis, Gwynedd LL55 4TY. Tel: 01286 870630

MONMOUTHSHIRE
Llanvihangel Court – Abergavenny, Monmouthshire NP7 8DH. Tel: 01873 890217
Penhow Castle – Penhow, Nr Newport, Monmouthshire NP26 3AD. Tel: 01633 400800

NEWPORT
Big Pit National Mining Museum – Big Pit, Blaenafon, Torfaen, NP4 9XP. Tel: 01495 790311
Fourteen Locks Canal Centre – Cwm Lane, Rogerstone, Newport NP10 9GN. Tel: 01633 894802
Newport Museum and Art Gallery – John Frost Square, Newport NP20 1PA. Tel: 01633 840064
Newport Transporter Bridge Visitor Centre – Usk Way, Newport NP20 2JT. Tel: 01633 257302
Roman Legionary Museum – High Street, Caerleon, NP18 1AE. Tel: 01633 423134
Tredegar House – Newport NP10 8YW. Tel: 01633 815880

PEMBROKESHIRE
Carew Castle & Tidal Mill – Carew, Nr.Tenby, Pembrokeshire SA70 8SL. Tel: 01646 651782
St Davids Cathedral – The Deanery, The Close, St David's, Pembrokeshire SA62 6RH. Tel: 01437 720199

POWYS
The Judge's Lodging – Broad Street, Presteigne, Powys LD8 2AD. Tel: 01544 260650

IRELAND

CO ANTRIM
Benvarden Gardens – Benvarden, Ballybogey, Ballymoney, Co Antrim BT53 6NN. Tel: 028 2074 1331

CO CORK
Bantry House & Gardens – Bantry, Co Cork. Tel: + 353 2 750 047

CO DOWN
North Down Heritage Centre – Town Hall, Bangor Castle, Bangor, Co Down BT20 4BT. Tel: 028 9127 1200
Seaforde Gardens – Seaforde, Downpatrick, Co Down BT30 8PG. Tel: 028 4481 1225

CO DUBLIN
Ardgillan Victorian Gardens – Ardgillan Castle, Balbriggan, Co Dublin. Tel: +353 1 849 2212
Dublin Writer's Museum – 18 Parnell Square, Dublin 1. Tel: +353 1 872 2077
Malahide Castle – Malahide, Co Dublin. Tel: +353 1 846 2184
Newbridge House – Donabate, Co Dublin. Tel: +353 1 843 6534
Newman House – 85/86 St Stephen's Green, Dublin 2. Tel: +353 706 7422
Talbot Botanic Gardens – Malahide Castle Demesne, Malahide, Co Dublin. Tel: +353 1 816 9914

CO GALWAY
Kylemore Abbey & Gardens – Kylemore, Connemara, Co Galway. Tel: +353 95 41146

CO KERRY
Dunloe Castle Hotel Gardens – Gap of Dunloe, Beaufort, Killarney, Co Kerry. Tel: +353 64 44111
Muckross House and Gardens & Traditional Farms – National Park, Killarney, Co Kerry. Tel: + 353 64 31440

CO KILDARE
The Irish National Stud – Tully, Kildare Town, Co Kildare. Tel: +353 45 521617

CO OFFALY
Birr Castle Demesne & Ireland's Historic Science Centre – Birr, Co Offaly. Tel: + 353 509 20336

CO WICKLOW
Powerscourt Gardens & Waterfall – Powerscourt Estate, Enniskerry, Co Wicklow. Tel: +353 1 204 6000

FRANCE

Château and Floral Park of Martinvast – Domaine de Beaurepaire, 50690 Martinvast, Basse Normandie. Tel: +33 2 33 87 20 80
Château de Chenonceau – 37150 Chenonceau, Indre et Loire. Tel: +33 2 47 23 90 07
Château de Vaux-le-Vicomte – 77950 Maincy, Ile de France. Tel: +33 1 64 14 41 90
Jardins du Château de Villiers – Villiers, 18800 Chassy. Tel: +33 2 48 77 53 20

HOLLAND

Palace Het Loo National Museum – Koninklijk Park 1, 7315 JA Apeldoorn. Tel: +31 55 577 2400

Johansens Recommended Hotels listed by region

To enable you to use your Johansens Recommended Hotels Guide more effectively the following pages of indexes contain a wealth of useful information about the hotels featured in the guide. As well as listing the hotels alphabetically by region and by county, the indexes also show at a glance which hotels offer certain specialised facilities.

The indexes are as follows:

- By region
- By location
- With a heated indoor swimming pool
- With a golf course on site
- With shooting on site
- With fishing on site
- With health/fitness facilities
- With conference facilities for 250 delegates or more
- With childcare facilities
- Pride of Britain members
- Relais & Châteaux members
- Small Luxury Hotels of the World members
- Grand Heritage members
- Johansens Preferred Partners

LONDON

ENGLAND

Johansens Recommended Hotels by region continued

WALES

SCOTLAND

Johansens Recommended Hotels by region continued

IRELAND

CHANNEL ISLANDS

ENGLAND

Bath/Avon: Please refer to the Somerset listing

London

Johansens Recommended Hotels by county

Bedfordshire

Berkshire

Bristol

Buckinghamshire

Cambridgeshire

Cheshire

Co Durham

Cornwall

Cumbria

Derbyshire

Devon

Dorset

Johansens Recommended Hotels by county (continued)

Johansens Recommended Hotels by county (continued)

Johansens Recommended Hotels by location

ENGLAND

Johansens Recommended Hotels by location (continued)

Johansens Recommended Hotels by location (continued)

WALES

SCOTLAND

IRELAND

CHANNEL ISLANDS

Hotels with a heated indoor swimming pool

Swimming pools at these hotels are open all year round

ENGLAND

SCOTLAND

WALES

IRELAND

CHANNEL ISLANDS

Hotels with golf

Hotels with golf on site

ENGLAND

SCOTLAND

IRELAND

CHANNEL ISLANDS

Hotels with fishing

Guests may obtain rights to fishing within the hotel grounds

ENGLAND

SCOTLAND

WALES

IRELAND

Hotels with shooting

Shooting on site, to which guests have access, can be arranged

ENGLAND

SCOTLAND

WALES

IRELAND

Hotels with childcare facilities

Comprehensive childcare facilities are available, namely crèche, babysitting & organised activities for children.

ENGLAND

Hotels with childcare facilities (continued)

SCOTLAND

WALES

IRELAND

CHANNEL ISLANDS

Hotels with health/fitness facilities

At the following hotels there are health/fitness facilities available

ENGLAND

SCOTLAND

WALES

IRELAND

CHANNEL ISLANDS

Hotels with conference facilities

These hotels can accommodate theatre-style conferences for 250 delegates or more.

ENGLAND

SCOTLAND

WALES

IRELAND

Pride of Britain members

Relais & Châteaux members

Small Luxury Hotels of the World members

Grand Heritage members

Johansens Preferred Partners

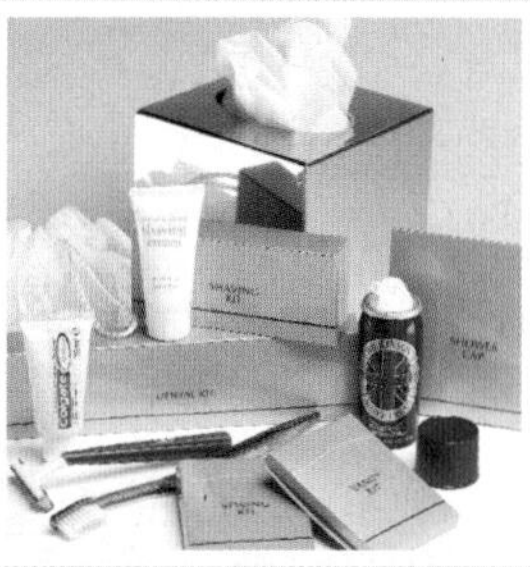

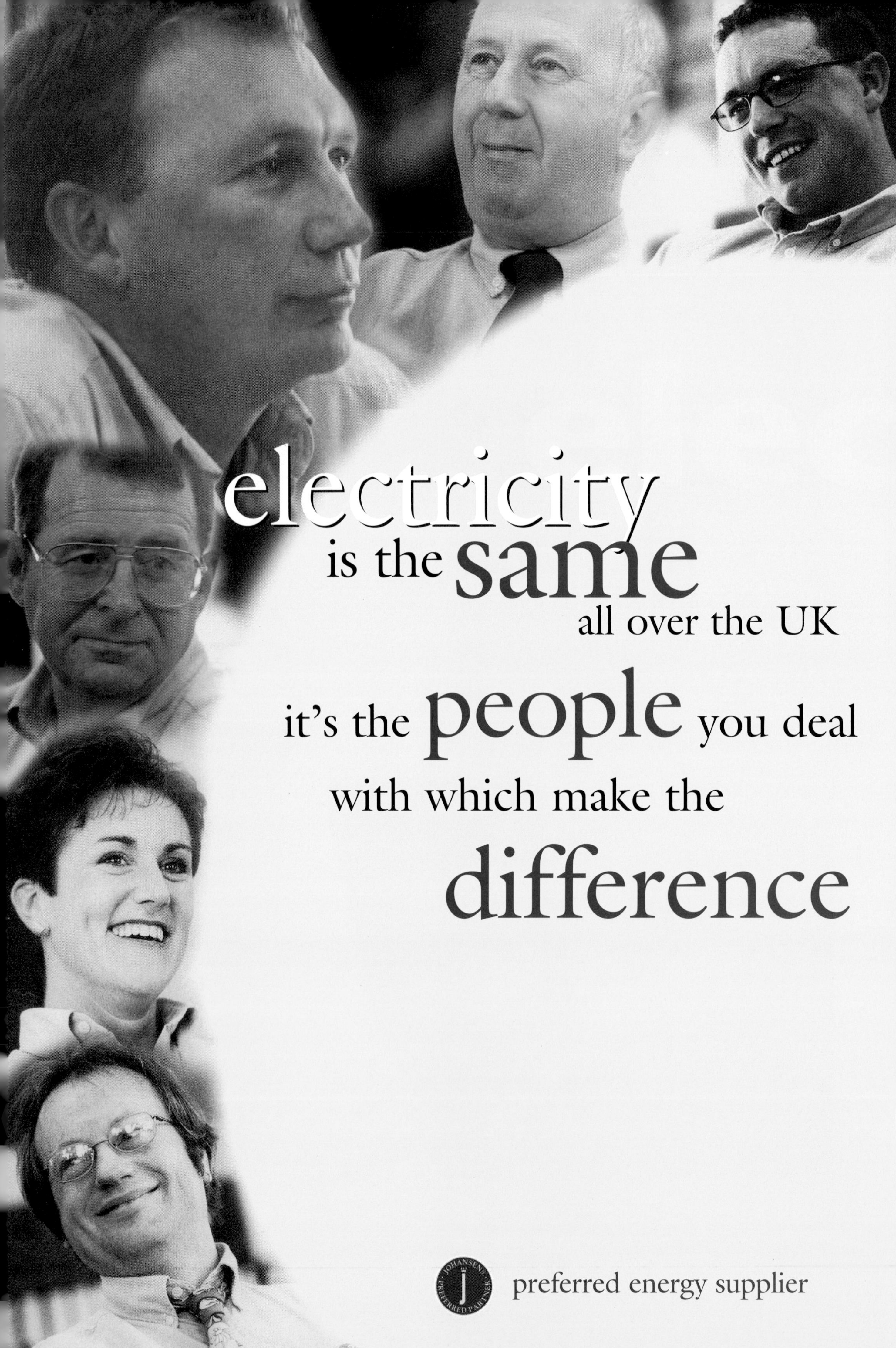
electricity
is the same
all over the UK
it's the people you deal
with which make the
difference
JOHANSENS PREFERRED PARTNER
j
preferred energy supplier

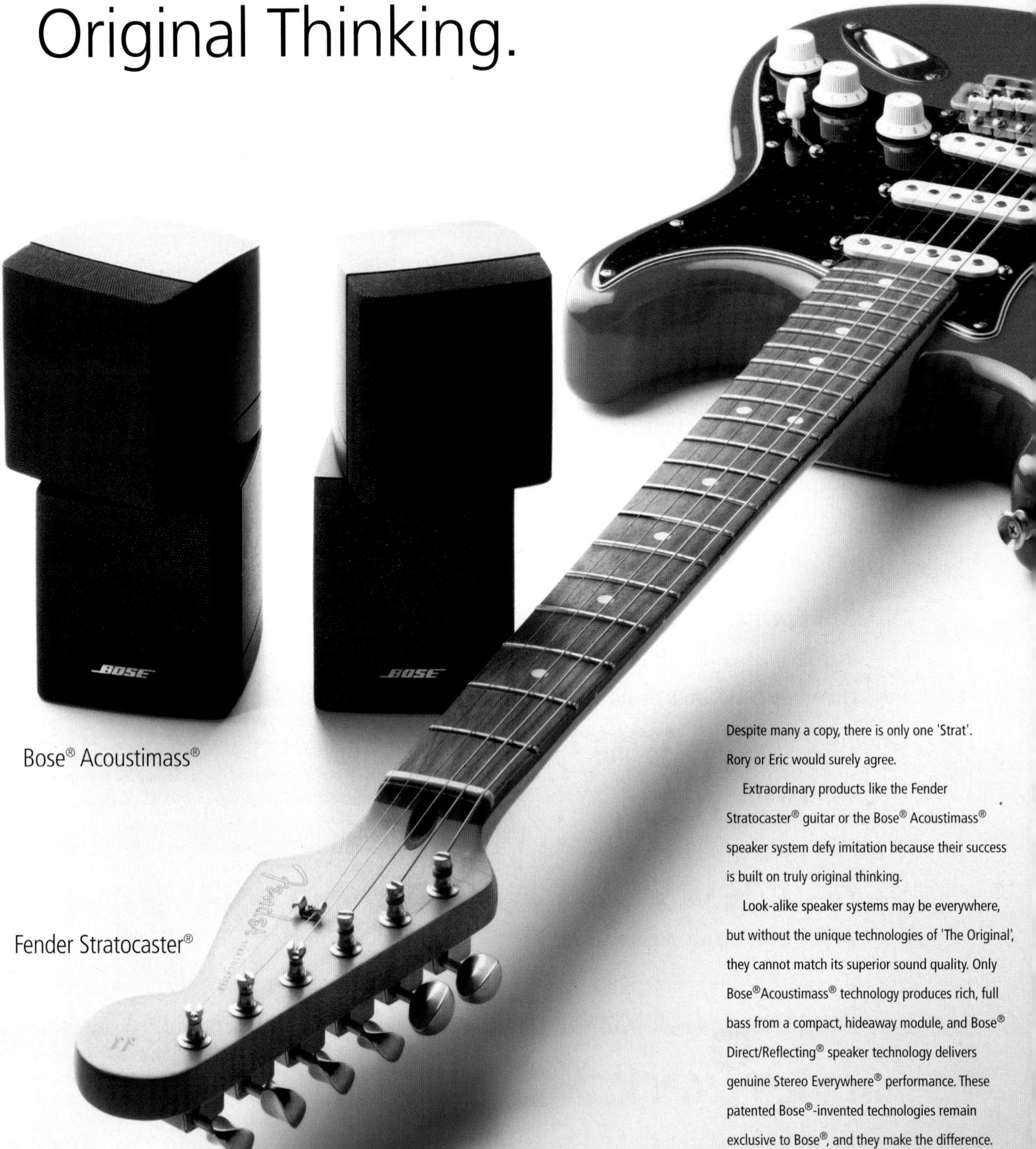

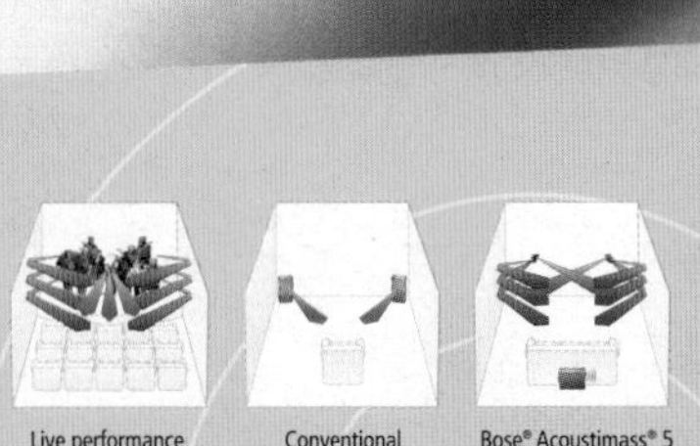

JOHANSENS

ORDER FORM

order 2 guides get £5 off • order 3 guides get £10 off • order 4 guides get £20 off
or order the Chairman's Collection worth £100 for just £75

Simply complete the form below, total the cost and then deduct the appropriate discount. State your preferred method of payment and mail to Johansens Ltd, FREEPOST 1045, Sandwich, Kent CT13 9BR (no stamp required). Fax orders welcome on 01304 617 727

ALTERNATIVELY YOU CAN ORDER IMMEDIATELY ON FREEPHONE 0800 269 397, please quote ref C007

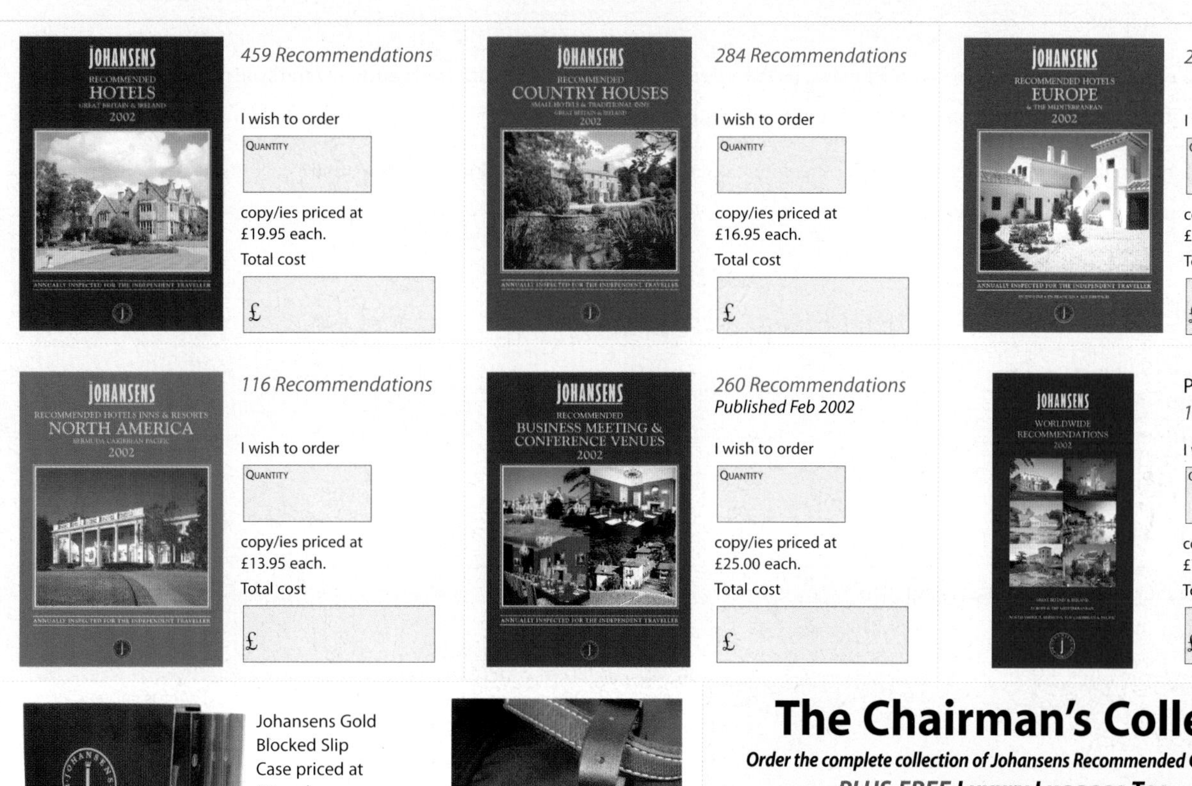

459 Recommendations

I wish to order

QUANTITY

copy/ies priced at £19.95 each.

Total cost

£

284 Recommendations

I wish to order

QUANTITY

copy/ies priced at £16.95 each.

Total cost

£

285 Recommendations

I wish to order

QUANTITY

copy/ies priced at £16.95 each.

Total cost

£

116 Recommendations

I wish to order

QUANTITY

copy/ies priced at £13.95 each.

Total cost

£

260 Recommendations
Published Feb 2002

I wish to order

QUANTITY

copy/ies priced at £25.00 each.

Total cost

£

Pocket Guide
1150 Recommendations

I wish to order

QUANTITY

copy/ies priced at £7.95 each.

Total cost

£

Johansens Gold Blocked Slip Case priced at £5 each

Johansens Luxury Luggage Tag priced at £15 each

To order these items please fill in the appropriate section below

The Chairman's Collection

Order the complete collection of Johansens Recommended Guides for only £75

PLUS FREE Luxury Luggage Tag worth £15

PLUS FREE Slip Case worth £5

The Chairman's Collection contains the following titles:

Johansens Recommended Business Meeting & Conference Venues (available for dispatch on publication in Feb 2002) • Johansens Recommended Hotels - GB & Ireland • Johansens Recommended Country Houses, Small Hotels & Traditional Inns - GB & Ireland • Johansens Recommended Hotels, Inns & Resorts - North America, Bermuda, Caribbean, Pacific • Johansens Recommended Hotels - Europe & The Mediterranean • Johansens Worldwide Recommendations (Pocket Guide)

Now please complete your order and payment details

I have ordered 2 titles - £5 off		–£5
I have ordered 3 titles - £10 off		–£10
I have ordered 4 titles - £20 off		–£20
Total cost of books ordered minus discount (excluding the Chairman's Collection)	£	
Luxury Luggage Tag at £15 Quantity and total cost:		£
Johansens Gold Blocked SLIP CASE at £5 Quantity and total cost:		£
I wish to order the Chairman's Collection at £75 Quantity and total cost:		£
PACKING & DELIVERY (UK) add £4.90 / (Outside UK) add £6.00 per guide or Chairman's Collection add £25.00	☐ ☐ ☐	£
GRAND TOTAL	£	

I have chosen my Johansens Guides and (please tick)

I enclose a cheque payable to Johansens ☐

Please debit my credit/charge card account ☐

☐ **MasterCard** ☐ **Amex** ☐ **Visa** ☐ **Switch** (Issue Number)

Card Holders Name (Mr/Mrs/Miss)

Address

Postcode

Telephone

E-mail

Card No.

Exp Date

Signature

NOW simply detach the order form and send it to

Johansens Ltd, FREEPOST 1045, Sandwich, Kent CT13 9BR (no stamp required)

Fax orders welcome on 01304 617 727

The details provided may be used to keep you informed of future products and special offers provided by Johansens and other carefully selected third parties. If you do not wish to recieve such information please tick this box ☐.
(Your phone number will only be used to ensure the fast and safe delivery of your order)

JOHANSENS

GUEST SURVEY REPORT

Dear Guest,

Following your stay in a Johansens Recommendation, please spare a moment to complete this Guest Survey Report. This is an important source of information for Johansens, to maintain the highest standards for our Recommendations and to support the work of our team of inspectors.

It is also the prime source of nominations for Johansens Awards for Excellence, which are made annually to those properties worldwide that represent the finest standards and best value for money in luxury, independent travel.

Thank you for your time and I hope that when choosing future accommodation in Great Britain, Ireland, Europe, North America, Bermuda, the Caribbean and the Pacific, Johansens will be your guide.

Yours faithfully,

Tim Sinclair
Sales & Marketing Director, Johansens

p.s. Guest Survey Reports may also be completed online at www.johansens.com

Name of hotel: ....

Location: .... Date of visit: ....

Your name: ....

Your address: ....

.... Postcode: ....

Telephone: .... E-mail: ....

The details provided may be used to keep you informed of future products and special offers provided by Johansens and other carefully selected third parties. If you do not wish to recieve such information please tick this box ☐.

Please tick one box in each category below: (as applicable)	Excellent	Good	Disappointing	Poor
Bedrooms				
Public Rooms				
Food/Restaurant				
Service				
Welcome/Friendliness				
Value For Money				

Comments:

If you wish to make additional comments, please write separately to the Publisher, Johansens Ltd, Freepost CB264, Therese House, Glasshouse Yard, London EC1B 1HP

Please return completed form to **Johansens, FREEPOST (CB264), LONDON SE27 0BR** (no stamp required).
Alternatively send by fax to 020 8766 6096

JOHANSENS
ORDER FORM

order 2 guides get £5 off • order 3 guides get £10 off • order 4 guides get £20 off
or order the Chairman's Collection worth £100 for just £75

Simply complete the form below, total the cost and then deduct the appropriate discount. State your preferred method of payment and mail to Johansens Ltd, FREEPOST 1045, Sandwich, Kent CT13 9BR (no stamp required). Fax orders welcome on 01304 617 727

ALTERNATIVELY YOU CAN ORDER IMMEDIATELY ON FREEPHONE 0800 269 397, please quote ref C007

459 Recommendations

I wish to order

QUANTITY

copy/ies priced at £19.95 each.

Total cost

£

284 Recommendations

I wish to order

QUANTITY

copy/ies priced at £16.95 each.

Total cost

£

285 Recommendations

I wish to order

QUANTITY

copy/ies priced at £16.95 each.

Total cost

£

116 Recommendations

I wish to order

QUANTITY

copy/ies priced at £13.95 each.

Total cost

£

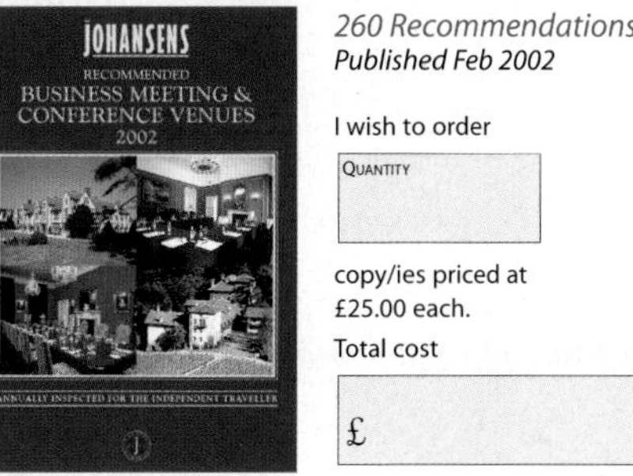

260 Recommendations
Published Feb 2002

I wish to order

QUANTITY

copy/ies priced at £25.00 each.

Total cost

£

Pocket Guide
1150 Recommendations

I wish to order

QUANTITY

copy/ies priced at £7.95 each.

Total cost

£

Johansens Gold Blocked Slip Case priced at £5 each

Johansens Luxury Luggage Tag priced at £15 each

To order these items please fill in the appropriate section below

The Chairman's Collection

Order the complete collection of Johansens Recommended Guides for only £75

PLUS FREE Luxury Luggage Tag worth £15

PLUS FREE Slip Case worth £5

The Chairman's Collection contains the following titles:

Johansens Recommended Business Meeting & Conference Venues (available for dispatch on publication in Feb 2002) • Johansens Recommended Hotels - GB & Ireland • Johansens Recommended Country Houses, Small Hotels & Traditional Inns - GB & Ireland • Johansens Recommended Hotels, Inns & Resorts - North America, Bermuda, Caribbean, Pacific • Johansens Recommended Hotels - Europe & The Mediterranean • Johansens Worldwide Recommendations (Pocket Guide)

Now please complete your order and payment details

I have ordered 2 titles - £5 off		–£5
I have ordered 3 titles - £10 off		–£10
I have ordered 4 titles - £20 off		–£20
Total cost of books ordered minus discount (excluding the Chairman's Collection)	£	
Luxury Luggage Tag at £15 Quantity and total cost:		£
Johansens Gold Blocked SLIP CASE at £5 Quantity and total cost:		£
I wish to order the Chairman's Collection at £75 Quantity and total cost:		£

PACKING & DELIVERY

(UK) add £4.90 ☐

(Outside UK) add £6.00 per guide ☐

or Chairman's Collection add £25.00 ☐ £

GRAND TOTAL £

I have chosen my Johansens Guides and (please tick)

I enclose a cheque payable to Johansens ☐

Please debit my credit/charge card account ☐

☐ **MasterCard** ☐ **Amex** ☐ **Visa** ☐ **Switch** (Issue Number)

Card Holders Name **(Mr/Mrs/Miss)**

Address

Postcode

Telephone

E-mail

Card No.

Exp Date

Signature

NOW simply detach the order form and send it to

Johansens Ltd, FREEPOST 1045, Sandwich, Kent CT13 9BR (no stamp required)

Fax orders welcome on 01304 617 727

The details provided may be used to keep you informed of future products and special offers provided by Johansens and other carefully selected third parties. If you do not wish to recieve such information please tick this box ☐.
(Your phone number will only be used to ensure the fast and safe delivery of your order)

JOHANSENS

GUEST SURVEY REPORT

Dear Guest,

Following your stay in a Johansens Recommendation, please spare a moment to complete this Guest Survey Report. This is an important source of information for Johansens, to maintain the highest standards for our Recommendations and to support the work of our team of inspectors.

It is also the prime source of nominations for Johansens Awards for Excellence, which are made annually to those properties worldwide that represent the finest standards and best value for money in luxury, independent travel.

Thank you for your time and I hope that when choosing future accommodation in Great Britain, Ireland, Europe, North America, Bermuda, the Caribbean and the Pacific, Johansens will be your guide.

Yours faithfully,

T. Sinclair

Tim Sinclair
Sales & Marketing Director, Johansens

p.s. Guest Survey Reports may also be completed online at www.johansens.com

Name of hotel: ....

Location: .... Date of visit: ....

Your name: ....

Your address: ....

.... Postcode: ....

Telephone: .... E-mail: ....

The details provided may be used to keep you informed of future products and special offers provided by Johansens and other carefully selected third parties. If you do not wish to recieve such information please tick this box ☐.

Please tick one box in each category below: (as applicable)	Excellent	Good	Disappointing	Poor
Bedrooms				
Public Rooms				
Food/Restaurant				
Service				
Welcome/Friendliness				
Value For Money				

Comments:

If you wish to make additional comments, please write separately to the Publisher, Johansens Ltd, Freepost CB264, Therese House, Glasshouse Yard, London EC1B 1HP

Please return completed form to **Johansens, FREEPOST (CB264), LONDON SE27 0BR** (no stamp required).
Alternatively send by fax to 020 8766 6096

JOHANSENS

HOTEL BROCHURE REQUEST

The Johansens Hotel Brochure Request Service has been established to give guests the opportunity to obtain more information about a Recommendation, additional to that contained within the Johansens guide.

Johansens will pass your request to the Recommendation specified who will directly send you a brochure.

Hotel name(s) and location(s) (BLOCK CAPITALS) .... Page in guide

1 ....

2 ....

3 ....

4 ....

5 ....

The Recommendation(s) you have chosen will send their brochures directly to the address below

Your name: ....

Your address: ....

.... Postcode: ....

Telephone: .... E-mail: ....

The details provided may be used to keep you informed of future products and special offers provided by Johansens and other carefully selected third parties. If you do not wish to recieve such information please tick this box ☐.

Please return completed form to **Johansens, FREEPOST (CB264), LONDON SE27 0BR** (no stamp required).

Alternatively send by fax to 020 8766 6096

JOHANSENS

HOTEL BROCHURE REQUEST

The Johansens Hotel Brochure Request Service has been established to give guests the opportunity to obtain more information about a Recommendation, additional to that contained within the Johansens guide.

Johansens will pass your request to the Recommendation specified who will directly send you a brochure.

Hotel name(s) and location(s) (BLOCK CAPITALS) .... Page in guide

1 ....

2 ....

3 ....

4 ....

5 ....

The Recommendation(s) you have chosen will send their brochures directly to the address below

Your name: ....

Your address: ....

.... Postcode: ....

Telephone: .... E-mail: ....

The details provided may be used to keep you informed of future products and special offers provided by Johansens and other carefully selected third parties. If you do not wish to recieve such information please tick this box ☐.

Please return completed form to **Johansens, FREEPOST (CB264), LONDON SE27 0BR** (no stamp required).

Alternatively send by fax to 020 8766 6096

NO STAMP REQUIRED

JOHANSENS
FREEPOST CB264
LONDON
SE27 0BR
Great Britain

NO STAMP REQUIRED

JOHANSENS
FREEPOST CB264
LONDON
SE27 0BR
Great Britain